BACKCOUNTRY ADVENTURES

ARIZONA

Printed in Korea

Fifth printing, 2004

Publisher's Cataloging-in-Publication
(Provided by Quality Books, Inc.)

Massey, Peter, 1951-
Backcountry adventures Arizona : the ultimate guide to the Arizona backcountry for anyone with a sport utility vehicle / Peter Massey and Jeanne Wilson. — 1st ed.
p. cm.
Includes bibliographical references and index.
ISBN: 0-9665675-0-1

1. Automobile travel—Arizona—Guidebooks. 2. Trails—Arizona—Guidebooks 3. Four-wheel drive vehicles. 4. Arizona—Guidebooks. I. Wilson, Jeanne, 1960- II. Title.

GV1024.M37 2001 917.9104'54
QB100-941

BACKCOUNTRY ADVENTURES

ARIZONA

THE ULTIMATE GUIDE TO THE
ARIZONA BACKCOUNTRY FOR ANYONE
WITH A SPORT UTILITY VEHICLE

PETER MASSEY AND JEANNE WILSON

SWAGMAN
PUBLISHING

Acknowledgments

Many people and organizations have made significant contributions to the research and production of this book. We owe them all special thanks for their assistance.

The production of the book has been a team effort, and we would especially like to thank the following people who have played the major roles in its production.

Project Editor:	**Timothy Duggan**
Senior Field Researchers:	**Donald McGann, Maggie Pinder**
Researchers:	**Scott Bloemendaal, Julie Jackson, Evan Gist, Chris Munden**
Copy Editing and Proofreading:	**Alice Levine, Jody Berman**
Graphic Design and Maps:	**Deborah Rust**
Finance:	**Douglas Adams**
Office Administration:	**Peg Anderson**

We received a great deal of assistance from many other people and organizations. We would like to thank Alfredo L. Casillas, public information officer at the United States Border Patrol, Yuma, for guidelines on encounters with undocumented aliens; Joanne Scruggs, Interagency Office in Phoenix, for assistance with trails and attractions on BLM land; Susanna Henry, assistant refuge manager at the KOFA NWR office, for information on the Hovatter homestead site and reviewing the trails within the KOFA NWR; Teresa Duggan for locating historic reference materials; Dan Weed for trail research on the Edwards Park Trail; Paul O'Donoghue for assistance with historical research; Shaun Whitaker for reviewing the geological history on Sunset Crater; Kee Long and the staff at the Navajo Film Office; the Navajo Tourist Office; John Largo, Largo Navajoland Tours, Window Rock, Arizona; Carol Ann Ciallella, library director of the Miami Memorial Library in Miami, Arizona, for information about the silver mining history of Globe; Doug Von Gausig of Naturesongs, for consulting on the flora and fauna section and for reviewing our final photographs; the staff of Wide World of Maps in Phoenix; and Matt Hannen, Bob Sharp, and other members of the Arizona Land Rover Owners Club. Staff at many offices of the National Forest Service also provided us with valuable assistance. Special thanks also to Meredith Wilson for his support of this project.

The book includes more than five hundred photos, and we are most thankful to the following organizations and people who have helped to research photographs or allowed us to publish the wonderful photographs they have taken: Earle Robinson; Paul Berquist; James Cokendolpher; Don Baccus; Doug Von Gausig, www.naturesongs.com; Lauren Livo and Steve Wilcox; "Bayou" Bob Popplewell at Brazos River Rattlesnake Ranch, www.wf.net/~snake; Kim Buck, Arizona–Sonora Desert Museum in Tucson; Magdalene Hagedorn, librarian, Tucson Botanical Gardens; Laurie Devine, photo archivist of the Arizona State Capitol History and Archives Division in Phoenix; Lori Swingle, archivist of the Denver Public Library, Western History Department, Denver; Kim Kliewer and the staff at Northern Arizona University's Cline Library in Flagstaff; Michael Wurtz, archivist at the Sharlot Hall Museum in Prescott; Susan Sheehan, Arizona Historical Society in Tucson; and the Bushducks—Maggie Pinder and Donald McGann. We also thank Mark Dreher at Werner's Mile High Camera in Denver for developing and transferring to Kodak PhotoDisc the thousands of photos we took while researching this book.

For maintaining our vehicles, we would like to thank Land Rover in Las Vegas, Nevada, and Scottsdale, Arizona, and Dave's European, Denver, Colorado.

We would like to draw our readers' attention to the website (www.bushducks.com) of our senior researchers, the Bushducks—Donald McGann and Maggie Pinder. It provides information on current 4WD trail conditions and offers their valuable assistance to anyone who is planning a backcountry itinerary.

Publisher's Note: Every effort has been taken to ensure that the information in this book is accurate at press time. Please visit our website to advise us of any changes or corrections you find. We also welcome recommendations for new 4WD trails or other suggestions to improve the information in this book.

SWAGMAN PUBLISHING

Swagman Publishing, Inc.
PO Box 519, Castle Rock, CO 80104
Phone: (303) 660-3307
Toll-free: (800) 660-5107
Fax: (303) 688-4388
www.4wdbooks.com

Contents

Introduction

The rugged landscape of Arizona, still very much untouched, stretches from the vast Sonoran Desert of the south, through towering red canyons, to the stunning mountain country in the north. Although primarily known for its arid, saguaro-strewn deserts, Arizona is also home to rich forest regions in the higher elevations as well as open range and canyon country. This wide variety of terrain hides beneath its surface an equally diverse collection of mineral resources. Mining, in one form or another, has taken place in Arizona since the time when Spain still claimed the land as part of its empire. As Americans began to move farther west, the promise of vast gold and silver deposits attracted many to the region. Others came into the area to escape the confines of city life in favor of Arizona's vast wilderness. However, the sheer beauty of the landscape, highlighted by such landforms as the Grand Canyon and Sunset Crater, has been responsible for attracting both settlers and tourists to Arizona throughout the years. Today, Arizona continues to thrive, and tourism ranks as one of the state's leading industries.

Arizona's rich Indian heritage persists to this day in such places as the Navajo Nation and the Hopi Indian Reservation. Although many Native Americans live on reservations today, the homes of their ancestors can be seen scattered throughout the state in such places as Tuzigoot National Monument, Tonto National Monument, and Canyon de Chelly. The state's Spanish influence can be seen in the remains of old missions and in the current names of many roads and towns. Deep within the backcountry, legends still whisper through the cracked woodwork of abandoned cabins. The remains of many abandoned mining camps, military forts, and stagecoach way stations, each with its own story, stand quietly in the wilderness as they slowly crumble into the landscape. Although Arizona is still a young state, its varied cultural traditions have created a rich and colorful history. Did you know that Francisco Vásquez de Coronado once searched for the fabled Seven Cities of Gold in what is now Arizona? Or that Edward F. Beale imported camels from Africa to help blaze a trail through the region? These and many other tales of daring, bizarre, and otherwise unbelievable events make up the state's eclectic history.

Driving through the backcountry of Arizona, you will notice countless natural wonders and traces of the past. We have selected 157 of our favorite unpaved drives and 4WD trails to take you off the paved roads and into the wild backcountry where much of the state's history has taken place. Our trails often follow the routes of ancient Indian trails, old wagon roads, abandoned train lines, early emigrant paths, and disused mining roads. You will literally follow in the path of Arizona's pioneers and founders as you drive through the backcountry visiting ancient Indian ruins, old mining remains, and deteriorating ghost towns.

For those with little or no off-highway driving experience, we have included a number of unpaved scenic drives. These trails present only easily negotiable obstacles. However, for those accustomed to off-highway touring, we have also provided a range of more difficult trails that guarantee an exciting day's drive. All our trails are within the range of most stock SUVs. The same car you take to work or to the grocery store can now take you to the remote wilds of Arizona.

We hope that as you head off the highways for a slow drive through the scenic Southwest, you too will enjoy the rewards of backcountry touring. Get ready to see the natural beauty and history of Arizona as you visit the state's most remote, spectacular, and treasured sites.

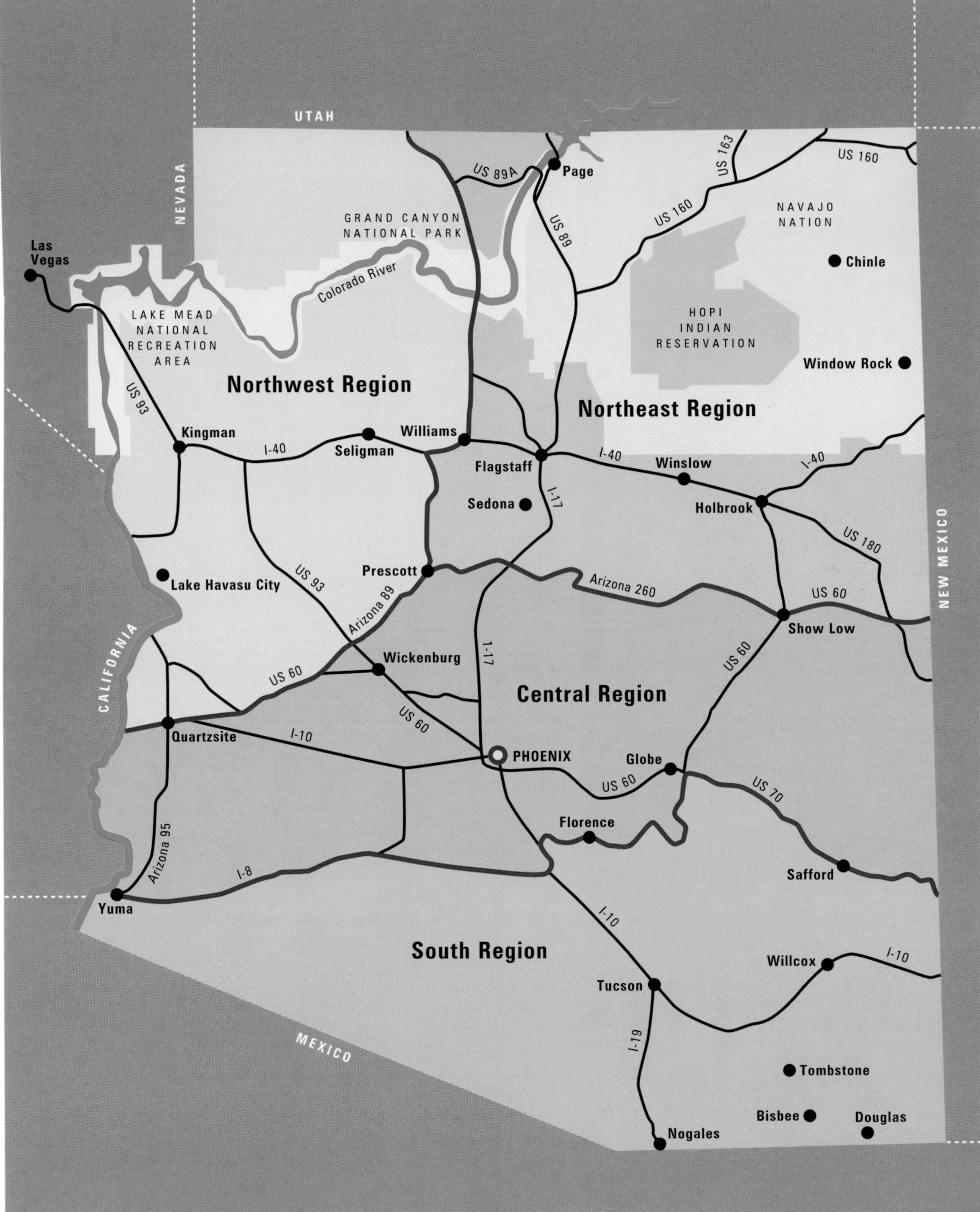
UTAH
NEVADA
Las Vegas
GRAND CANYON NATIONAL PARK
Colorado River
LAKE MEAD NATIONAL RECREATION AREA
US 89A
Page
US 89
US 163
US 160
NAVAJO NATION
Chinle
HOPI INDIAN RESERVATION
Window Rock
Northwest Region
Northeast Region
US 93
Kingman
I-40
Seligman
Williams
Flagstaff
Winslow
Holbrook
Sedona
I-17
US 180
NEW MEXICO
Prescott
Lake Havasu City
Arizona 260
US 60
Show Low
Arizona 89
CALIFORNIA
Wickenburg
Central Region
Quartzsite
I-10
PHOENIX
Globe
US 70
Florence
Arizona 95
I-8
Safford
Yuma
South Region
Willcox
Tucson
I-19
MEXICO
Tombstone
Bisbee
Douglas
Nogales

Before You Go

Why a 4WD Does It Better

The design and engineering of 4WD vehicles provide them with many advantages over normal cars when you head off the paved road:

■ improved distribution of power to all four wheels;

■ a transmission transfer case, which provides low-range gear selection for greater pulling power and for crawling over difficult terrain;

■ high ground clearance;

■ less overhang of the vehicle's body past the wheels, which provides better front- and rear-clearance when crossing gullies and ridges;

■ large-lug, wide-tread tires;

■ rugged construction (including underbody skid plates on many models).

If you plan to do off-highway touring, all of these considerations are important whether you are evaluating the capabilities of your current 4WD or are looking to buy one; each is considered in detail in this chapter.

To explore the most difficult trails described in this book, you will need a 4WD vehicle that is well rated in each of the above features. If you own a 2WD sport utility vehicle, a lighter car-type SUV, or a pickup truck, your ability to explore the more difficult trails will depend on conditions and your level of experience.

A word of caution: Whatever type of 4WD vehicle you drive, understand that it is not invincible or indestructible. Nor can it go everywhere. A 4WD has a much higher center of gravity and weighs more than a car, and so has its own consequent limitations.

Experience is the only way to learn what your vehicle can and cannot do. Therefore, if you are inexperienced, we strongly recommend that you start with trails that have lower difficulty ratings. As you develop an understanding of your vehicle and of your own taste for adventure, you can safely tackle the more challenging trails.

One way to beef up your knowledge quickly, while avoiding the costly and sometimes dangerous lessons learned from on-the-road mistakes, is to undertake a 4WD course taught by a professional. Look in the Yellow Pages for courses in your area.

Using This Book

Route Planning

Regional maps at the beginning of each section provide a convenient overview of the trails in that portion of the state. Each 4WD trail is highlighted in color, and major highways and towns are indicated, to help you plan various routes by connecting a series of 4WD trails and paved roads.

As you plan your overall route, you will probably want to utilize as many 4WD trails as possible. However, check the difficulty rating and time required for each trail before finalizing your plans. You don't want to be stuck 50 miles from the highway—at sunset and without camping gear, since your trip was supposed to be over hours ago—when you discover that your vehicle can't handle a certain difficult passage.

You can calculate the distances between Arizona towns by turning to the Arizona Distance Chart at the end of this chapter.

Difficulty Ratings

We utilize a point system to rate the difficulty of each trail. Any such system is subjective, and your experience of the trails will vary depending on your skill and the road conditions at the time. Indeed, any amount of rain may make the trails much more difficult, if not completely impassable.

We have rated the 4WD trails on a scale of 1 to 10—1 being passable for a normal passenger vehicle in good conditions and 10 requiring a heavily modified vehicle and an experienced driver who expects to encounter vehicle damage. Because this book is designed for owners of unmodified 4WD vehicles—who we assume do not want to damage their vehicles—most of the trails are rated 5 or lower. A few trails are included that rate as high as 7, while those rated 8 to 10 are beyond the scope of this book.

This is not to say that the moderate-rated trails are easy. We strongly recommend that inexperienced drivers not tackle trails rated at 4 or higher until they have undertaken a number of the lower-rated ones, so that they can gauge their skill level and prepare for the difficulty of the higher-rated trails.

In assessing the trails, we have always assumed good road conditions (dry road surface, good visibility, and so on). The factors influencing our ratings are as follows:

■ obstacles such as rocks, mud, ruts, sand, slickrock, and stream crossings;

■ the stability of the road surface;

■ the width of the road and the vehicle clearance between trees or rocks;

■ the steepness of the road;

■ the margin for driver error (for example, a very high, open shelf road would be rated more difficult even if it was not very steep and had a stable surface).

The following is a guide to the ratings.

Rating 1: The trail is graded dirt but suitable for a normal passenger vehicle. It usually has gentle grades, is fairly wide, and has very shallow water crossings (if any).

Rating 2: High-clearance vehicles are preferred but not

necessary. These trails are dirt roads, but they may have rocks, grades, water crossings, or ruts that make clearance a concern in a normal passenger vehicle. The trails are fairly wide, making passing possible at almost any point along the trail. Mud is not a concern under normal weather conditions.

Rating 3: High-clearance 4WDs are preferred, but any high-clearance vehicle is acceptable. Expect a rough road surface; mud and sand are possible but will be easily passable. You may encounter rocks up to 6 inches in diameter, a loose road surface, and shelf roads, though these will be wide enough for passing or will have adequate pull-offs.

Rating 4: High-clearance 4WDs are recommended, though most stock SUVs are acceptable. Expect a rough road surface with rocks larger than 6 inches, but there will be a reasonable driving line available. Patches of mud are possible but can be readily negotiated; sand may be deep and require lower tire pressures. There may be stream crossings up to 12 inches deep, substantial sections of single-lane shelf road, moderate grades, and sections of moderately loose road surface.

Rating 5: High-clearance 4WDs are required. These trails have either a rough, rutted surface, rocks up to 9 inches, mud and deep sand that may be impassable for inexperienced drivers, or stream crossings up to 18 inches deep. Certain sections may be steep enough to cause traction problems, and you may encounter very narrow shelf roads with steep drop-offs and tight clearance between rocks or trees.

Rating 6: These trails are for experienced four-wheel drivers only. They are potentially dangerous, with large rocks, ruts, or terraces that may need to be negotiated. They may also have stream crossings at least 18 inches deep, involve rapid currents, unstable stream bottoms, or difficult access; steep slopes, loose surfaces, and narrow clearances; or very narrow sections of shelf road with steep drop-offs and possibly challenging road surfaces.

Rating 7: Skilled, experienced four-wheel drivers only. These trails include very challenging sections with extremely steep grades, loose surfaces, large rocks, deep ruts, and/or tight clearances. Mud or sand may necessitate winching.

Rating 8 and above: Stock vehicles are likely to be damaged and may find the trail impassable. Highly skilled, experienced four-wheel drivers only.

Scenic Ratings

If rating the degree of difficulty is subjective, rating scenic beauty is guaranteed to lead to arguments. For many, Arizona probably conjures up images of vast saguaro-covered deserts. Although there are certainly vast tracts of desert, the state contains a wide variety of scenery. Despite the subjectivity of attempting a comparative rating of diverse scenery, we have tried to provide a guide to the relative scenic quality of the various trails. The ratings are based on a scale of 1 to 10, with 10 being the most attractive.

Remoteness Ratings

Many trails in Arizona are in remote country; sometimes the trails are seldom traveled, and the likelihood is low that another vehicle will appear within a reasonable time to assist you if you get stuck or break down. We have included a ranking for remoteness of +0 through +2. Extreme summer temperatures can make a breakdown in the more remote areas a life-threatening experience. Prepare carefully before tackling the higher-rated, more remote trails (see "Special Preparations for Remote Travel," page 12). For trails with a high remoteness rating, consider traveling with a second vehicle.

Estimated Driving Times

In calculating driving times, we have not allowed for stops. Your actual driving time may be considerably longer depending on the number and duration of the stops you make. Add more time if you prefer to drive more slowly than good conditions allow.

Current Road Information

All the 4WD trails described in this book may become impassable in poor weather conditions. Storms can alter roads, remove tracks, and create impassable washes. Most of the trails described, even easy 2WD trails, can quickly become impassable even to 4WD vehicles after only a small amount of rain. For each trail, we have provided a phone number for obtaining current information about conditions.

Abbreviations

The route directions for the 4WD trails use a series of abbreviations as follows:

SO	CONTINUE STRAIGHT ON
TL	TURN LEFT
TR	TURN RIGHT
BL	BEAR LEFT
BR	BEAR RIGHT
UT	U-TURN

Using Route Directions

For every trail, we describe and pinpoint (by odometer reading) nearly every significant feature along the route—such as intersections, streams, washes, gates, cattle guards, and so on—and provide directions from these landmarks. Odometer readings will vary from vehicle to vehicle, so you should allow for slight variations. Be aware that trails can quickly change in the desert. A new trail may be cut around a washout, a faint trail can be graded by the county, or a well-used trail may fall into disuse. All these factors will affect the accuracy of the given directions.

If you diverge from the route, zero your trip meter upon your return and continue along the route, making the necessary adjustment to the point-to-point odometer readings. In the directions, we regularly reset the odometer readings—at significant landmarks or popular lookouts and spur trails—so that you won't have to recalculate for too long.

Most of the trails can be started from either end, and the route directions include both directions of travel; reverse directions are printed in blue below the main directions. When traveling in reverse, read from the bottom of the table and work up.

Route directions include cross-references whenever two 4WD trails included in this book connect; these cross-references allow for an easy change of route or destination.

Each trail includes periodic latitude and longitude readings to facilitate using a global positioning system (GPS) receiver. These readings may also assist you in finding your location on the maps. The GPS coordinates were taken using the NAD 1927 datum and are in the format dd°mm.mm'. To save time when loading coordinates into your GPS receiver, you may wish to include only one decimal place, since in Arizona, the first decimal place equals about 165 yards and the second only about 16 yards.

Map References

We recommend that you supplement the information in this book with more-detailed maps. For each trail, we list the sheet maps and road atlases that provide the best detail for the area. Typically, the following references are given:

- Bureau of Land Management Maps
- U.S. Forest Service Maps
- *Arizona Road & Recreation Atlas,* 2nd ed. (Medford, Oregon: Benchmark Maps, 1998)—Scale 1:400,000
- *Arizona Atlas & Gazetteer,* 2nd ed. (Freeport, Maine: DeLorme Mapping, 1996)—Scale 1:250,000
- Maptech-Terrain Navigator Topo Maps—Scale 1:100,000 and 1:24,000
- *Trails Illustrated* Topo Maps; National Geographic Maps —Various scales, but all contain good detail
- Recreational Map of Arizona (Canon City, Colorado: GTR Mapping, 1997)—Scale: 1 inch=12.5 miles

We recommend the *Trails Illustrated* series of maps as the best for navigating these trails. They are reliable, easy to read, and printed on nearly indestructible plastic paper. However, this series covers only a few of the 4WD trails described in this book.

The DeLorme *Arizona Atlas & Gazetteer* is useful and has the advantage of providing you with maps of the entire state at a reasonable price. Although its 4WD trail information doesn't go beyond what we provide, it is useful if you wish to explore the hundreds of side roads.

The *Arizona Road & Recreation Atlas* provides two types of maps for each part of the state. The landscape maps show changes in terrain and elevation while the public lands maps show what organizations control what lands. Aside from the maps, the atlas also provides a good recreation guide with a number of local contacts for different recreation opportunities.

U.S. Forest Service maps lack the topographic detail of the other sheet maps and, in our experience, are occasionally out of date. They have the advantage of covering a broad area and are useful in identifying land use and travel restrictions. These maps are most useful for the longer trails.

In our opinion, the best single option by far is the Terrain Navigator series of maps published on CD-ROM by Maptech. These CD-ROMs contain an amazing level of detail because they include the entire set of 1,941 U.S. Geological Survey topographical maps of Arizona at the 1:24,000 scale and all 71 maps at the 1:100,000 scale. These maps offer many advantages over normal maps:

- GPS coordinates for any location can be found and loaded into your GPS receiver. Conversely, if you have your GPS coordinates, your location on the map can be pinpointed instantly.
- Towns, rivers, passes, mountains, and many other sites are indexed by name so that they can be located quickly.
- 4WD trails can be marked and profiled for elevation changes and distances from point to point.
- Customized maps can be printed out.

Maptech uses eight CD-ROMs to cover the entire state of Arizona; they can be purchased individually or as part of a two-state package at a heavily discounted price. The CD-ROMs can be used with a laptop computer and a GPS receiver in your vehicle to monitor your location on the map and navigate directly from the display.

All these maps should be available through good map stores. The Maptech CD-ROMs are available directly from the company (800-627-7236, or on the internet at www.maptech.com).

Backcountry Driving Rules and Permits

Four-wheel driving involves special driving techniques and road rules. This section is an introduction for 4WD beginners.

4WD Road Rules

To help ensure that these trails remain open and available for all four-wheel drivers to enjoy, it is important to minimize your impact on the environment and not be a safety risk to yourself or anyone else. Remember that the 4WD clubs in Arizona fight a constant battle with the government and various lobby groups to retain the access that currently exists.

The fundamental rule when traversing the 4WD trails described in this book is to use common sense. In addition, special road rules for 4WD trails apply:

- Vehicles traveling uphill have the right of way.
- If you are moving more slowly than the vehicle behind you, pull over to let the other vehicle by.
- Park out of the way in a safe place. Blocking a track may restrict access for emergency vehicles as well as for other recreationalists. Set the parking brake—don't rely on leaving the transmission in park. Manual transmissions should be left in the lowest gear.

Tread Lightly!

Remember the rules of the Tread Lightly!® program:

- Be informed. Obtain maps, regulations, and other

information from the forest service or from other public land agencies. Learn the rules and follow them.

■ Resist the urge to pioneer a new road or trail or to cut across a switchback. Stay on constructed tracks and avoid running over young trees, shrubs, and grasses, damaging or killing them. Don't drive across alpine tundra; this fragile environment can take years to recover.

■ Stay off soft, wet roads and 4WD trails readily torn up by vehicles. Repairing the damage is expensive, and quite often authorities find it easier to close the road rather than repair it.

■ Travel around meadows, steep hillsides, stream banks, and lake shores that are easily scarred by churning wheels.

■ Stay away from wild animals that are rearing young or suffering from a food shortage. Do not camp close to the water sources of domestic or wild animals.

■ Obey gate closures and regulatory signs.

■ Preserve America's heritage by not disturbing old mining camps, ghost towns, or other historical features. Leave historic sites, Native American rock art, ruins, and artifacts in place and untouched.

■ Carry out all your trash, and even that of others.

■ Stay out of designated wilderness areas. They are closed to all vehicles. It is your responsibility to know where the boundaries are.

■ Get permission to cross private land. Leave livestock alone. Respect landowners' rights.

Report violations of these rules to help keep these 4WD trails open and to ensure that others will have the opportunity to visit these backcountry sites. Many groups are actively seeking to close these public lands to vehicles, thereby denying access to those who are unable, or perhaps merely unwilling, to hike long distances. This magnificent countryside is owned by, and should be available to, all Americans.

Special Preparations for Remote Travel

Due to the remoteness of some areas in Arizona and the very high summer temperatures, you should take some special precautions to ensure that you don't end up in a life-threatening situation:

■ When planning a trip into the desert, always inform someone as to where you are going, your route, and when you expect to return. Stick to your plan.

■ Carry and drink at least one gallon of water per person per day of your trip. (Plastic gallon jugs are handy and portable.)

■ Be sure your vehicle is in good condition with a sound battery, good hoses, spare tire, spare fan belts, necessary tools, and reserve gasoline and oil. Other spare parts and extra radiator water are also valuable. If traveling in pairs, share the common spares and carry a greater variety.

■ Keep an eye on the sky. Flash floods can occur in a wash any time you see "thunderheads"—even when it's not raining a drop where you are.

■ If you are caught in a dust storm while driving, get off the road and turn off your lights. Turn on the emergency flashers and back into the wind to reduce windshield pitting by sand particles.

■ Test trails on foot before driving through washes and sandy areas. One minute of walking may save hours of hard work getting your vehicle unstuck.

■ If your vehicle breaks down, stay near it. Your emergency supplies are there. Your car has many other items useful in an emergency. Raise your hood and trunk lid to denote "help needed." Remember, a vehicle can be seen for miles, but a person on foot is very difficult to spot from a distance.

■ When you're not moving, use available shade or erect shade from tarps, blankets, or seat covers—anything to reduce the direct rays of the sun.

■ Do not sit or lie directly on the ground. It may be 30 degrees hotter than the air.

■ Leave a disabled vehicle only if you are positive of the route and the distance to help. Leave a note for rescuers that gives the time you left and the direction you are taking.

■ If you must walk, rest for at least 10 minutes out of each hour. If you are not normally physically active, rest up to 30 minutes out of each hour. Find shade, sit down, and prop up your feet. Adjust your shoes and socks, but do not remove your shoes—you may not be able to get them back on swollen feet.

■ If you have water, drink it. Do not ration it.

■ If water is limited, keep your mouth closed. Do not talk, eat, smoke, drink alcohol, or take salt.

■ Keep your clothing on despite the heat. It helps to keep your body temperature down and reduces your body's dehydration rate. Cover your head. If you don't have a hat, improvise a head covering.

■ If you are stalled or lost, set signal fires. Set smoky fires in the daytime and bright ones at night. Three fires in a triangle denote "help needed."

■ A roadway is a sign of civilization. If you find a road, stay on it.

■ When hiking in the desert, equip each person, especially children, with a police-type whistle. It makes a distinctive noise with little effort. Three blasts denote "help needed."

■ To avoid poisonous creatures, put your hands or feet only where your eyes can see. One insect to be aware of in Arizona is the Africanized honeybee. Though indistinguishable from its European counterpart, these bees are far more aggressive and can be a threat. They have been known to give chase of up to a mile and even wait for people who have escaped into the water to come up for air. The best thing to do if attacked is to cover your face and head with clothing and run to the nearest enclosed shelter. Keep an eye on your pet if you notice a number of bees in the area, as many have been killed by Africanized honeybees.

Special Note on Travel Near the Mexican Border

Arizona's long southern border forms part of the international boundary with Mexico. This location can bring with it its own unique set of potential situations that the intrepid traveler may encounter. Every month, thousands of undocumented aliens attempt to gain unauthorized entry into the United States from Mexico. In recent years, the U.S. Border Patrol, which is responsible for monitoring the international boundary, has stepped up surveillance in Texas and California, resulting in more people attempting the more difficult and dangerous crossings into the United States through Arizona.

Apprehensions from the region around the Organ Pipe Cactus National Monument, to give one typical example, have nearly tripled, from 8,000 in 1998 to more than 21,000 in 1999. Apprehensions reported through Wellton, which covers El Camino del Diablo, increased by 142 percent during the first three months of 2000. Other hotspots report similar figures. It is estimated that approximately 70 percent of all border jumpers will be apprehended and returned to Mexico immediately.

What does this mean for you? Any remote area traveler who spends any time at all in the desert of southern Arizona is highly likely to encounter undocumented aliens. First and foremost, it should be stressed that the vast majority of meetings pose absolutely no threat to the traveler at all. You are most likely to meet people just like you who want little more than food and water before they move on, leaving you alone. However, many people find these meetings worrisome and upsetting, and some even feel threatened.

It is suggested that travelers adopt the following guidelines compiled from advice given by the U.S. Border Patrol:

- If possible, avoid all contact with suspected undocumented alien activity. Do not go out of your way to offer unsolicited assistance.
- If it is impossible to avoid contact—for example, if you are approached and asked for help—then stop. Remain in your vehicle. Most of the time you will be asked for food and water. Give them what you can safely spare without running your own supplies dangerously low and move on as soon as possible. This is not seen by the border patrol as aiding and abetting; it is humanitarian aid and you may be saving another human being's life. Many people die each year trying to cross the desert.
- Do not give anyone a lift in your vehicle unless you can see it is a life-threatening situation.
- As soon as is practical, notify the border patrol or sheriff's department of the location, number, and physical condition of the group so that they can be apprehended as soon as possible. Be as specific as you can; GPS coordinates are extremely useful. Again, by doing this you may be saving someone's life.
- Do not attempt to engage people in conversation and avoid giving exact distances to the nearest town. Many undocumented aliens arrive in the United States by paying a "coyote" to bring them safely across the border. They are often deliberately misled and woefully unprepared for the desert conditions they encounter and the distances they will have to travel to safety. Giving exact distances, especially if it is many miles away, is putting yourself and your vehicle at risk. Carjackings are *extremely rare,* but the possibility should not be discounted.
- Be extremely wary of groups traveling in vehicles, as these are the professionals who smuggle both humans and drugs. However, fewer than 5 percent of encounters are with smugglers; most are with individuals or groups after the "coyotes" have dropped them off.
- If you are traveling exceptionally remote routes in areas of high activity, such as South #3: El Camino del Diablo Trail, consider traveling as part of a large group. Individual vehicles and small groups stand a higher chance of being approached.
- Always lock your vehicle when you leave it, even for a short period of time, and carry as few valuables as possible.
- The distance from the border is not the determining factor in how likely you are to have an encounter.
- Finally, do not let this be a deterrent to exploring the wonderful trails to be found in southern Arizona. Be alert and aware but not paranoid. Many thousands of recreationalists travel these trails every year with very little danger to themselves or their vehicles.

Obtaining Permits

Backcountry permits, which usually cost a fee, are required for certain activities on public lands in Arizona, whether the area is a national park, state park, national monument, Indian reservation, or BLM land.

Restrictions may require a permit for all overnight stays, which can include backpacking and 4WD or bicycle camping. Permits may also be required for day use by vehicles, horses, hikers, or bikes in some areas.

When possible, we include information about fees and permit requirements and where permits may be obtained, but these regulations change constantly. If in doubt, check with the most likely governing agency.

Travel Etiquette on Indian Lands

When traveling on Indian lands, the first and foremost rule is to respect the land and its owners. When driving, obey all road signs. If you leave your vehicle to explore a certain area, first make sure that you are allowed on that land. Be gentle with the land and its artifacts as you walk around, resisting the urge to take a "souvenir;" it is illegal to remove artifacts from federal land.

If you wish to take pictures of Native Americans, make sure to obtain their permission first. The Hopi, for example, will not allow you to photograph or sketch them. If you visit an Indian monument, guides will often allow their pictures to be taken. A small gratuity is customary.

When you approach a village, get permission from the village leader before entering. Remember that hogans (traditional mud-covered dwellings) are someone's home, not a tourist attraction. Do not walk up to the hogan without first being invited.

Firearms and alcoholic beverages are both stricly prohibited in the Navajo Nation.

Finally, if you are lucky enough to see a Hopi or Navajo ceremony, remember to act with the utmost respect. Do not photograph, sketch, record, or take notes of the ceremony. Stand quietly in the back, without applauding, so as to avoid interfering; do not walk around or ask questions while the ceremony is taking place. Finally, make sure that you are dressed appropriately. Men should wear long pants and shirts and women should dress so their bodies are covered; hats are discouraged. If you see a "closed" sign at the entrance to the village, there is most likely a ceremony in progress that cannot be disturbed. Obey the sign and continue on your way.

Assessing Your Vehicle's Off-Road Ability

Many issues come into play when evaluating your 4WD vehicle, although most of the 4WDs on the market are suitable for even the roughest trails described in this book. Engine power will be adequate in even the least-powerful modern vehicle. However, some vehicles are less suited to off-highway driving than others, and some of the newest, carlike sport utility vehicles simply are not designed for off-highway touring. The following information should allow you to identify the good, the bad, and the ugly.

Differing 4WD Systems

All 4WD systems have one thing in common: The engine provides power to all four wheels rather than to only two, as is typical in most standard cars. However, there are a number of differences in the way power is applied to the wheels.

The other feature that distinguishes nearly all 4WDs from normal passenger vehicles is that the gearboxes have high and low ratios that effectively double the number of gears. The high range is comparable to the range on a passenger car. The low range provides lower speed and more power, which is useful when towing heavy loads, driving up steep hills, or crawling over rocks. When driving downhill, the 4WD's low range increases engine braking.

Various makes and models of SUVs offer different drive systems, but these differences center on two issues: the way power is applied to the other wheels if one or more wheels slip, and the ability to select between 2WD and 4WD.

Normal driving requires that all four wheels be able to turn at different speeds; this allows the vehicle to turn without scrubbing its tires. In a 2WD vehicle, the front wheels (or rear wheels in a front-wheel-drive vehicle) are not powered by the engine and thus are free to turn individually at any speed. The rear wheels, powered by the engine, are only able to turn at different speeds because of the differential, which applies power to the faster-turning wheel.

This standard method of applying traction has certain weaknesses. First, when power is applied to only one set of wheels, the other set cannot help the vehicle gain traction. Second, when one powered wheel loses traction, it spins, but the other powered wheel doesn't turn. This happens because the differential applies all the engine power to the faster-turning wheel and no power to the other wheels, which still have traction. All 4WD systems are designed to overcome these two weaknesses. However, different 4WDs address this common objective in different ways.

Full-Time 4WD

For a vehicle to remain in 4WD all the time without scrubbing the tires, all the wheels must be able to rotate at different speeds. A full-time 4WD system allows this to happen by using three differentials. One is located between the rear wheels, as in a normal passenger car, to allow the rear wheels to rotate at different speeds. The second is located between the front wheels in exactly the same way. The third differential is located between the front and rear wheels to allow different rotational speeds between the front and rear sets of wheels. In nearly all vehicles with full-time 4WD, the center differential operates only in high range. In low range, it is completely locked. This is not a disadvantage because when using low range the additional traction is normally desired and the deterioration of steering response will be less noticeable due to the vehicle traveling at a slower speed.

Part-Time 4WD

A part-time 4WD system does not have the center differential located between the front and rear wheels. Consequently, the front and rear drive shafts are both driven at the same speed and with the same power at all times when in 4WD.

This system provides improved traction because when one or both of the front or rear wheels slips, the engine continues to provide power to the other set. However, because such a system doesn't allow a difference in speed between the front and rear sets of wheels, the tires scrub when turning, placing additional strain on the whole drive system. Therefore, such a system can be used only in slippery conditions; otherwise, the ability to steer the vehicle will deteriorate and the tires will quickly wear out.

Some vehicles, such as Jeeps with Selec-trac™ and Mitsubishi Monteros with Active Trac 4WD™, offer both full-time and part-time 4WD in high range.

Manual Systems to Switch Between 2WD and 4WD

There are three manual systems for switching between 2WD and 4WD. The most basic requires stopping and getting out of the vehicle to lock the front hubs manually before selecting 4WD. The second requires you to stop, but you change to 4WD by merely throwing a lever inside the vehicle (the hubs lock automatically). The third allows shifting between 2WD and 4WD high range while the vehicle is moving. Any 4WD that does not offer the option of driving in 2WD must have a full-time 4WD system.

Automated Switching Between 2WD and 4WD

Advances in technology are leading to greater automation in the selection of two- or four-wheel drive. When operating in high range, these high-tech systems use sensors to monitor the rotation of each wheel. When any slippage is detected, the vehicle switches the proportion of power from the wheel(s) that is slipping to the wheels that retain grip. The proportion of power supplied to each wheel is therefore infinitely variable as opposed to the original systems where the vehicle was either in two-wheel drive or four-wheel drive.

In recent years, this process has been spurred on by many of the manufacturers of luxury vehicles entering the SUV market—Mercedes, BMW, Cadillac, Lincoln, and Lexus have joined Range Rover in this segment.

Manufacturers of these higher-priced vehicles have led the way in introducing sophisticated computer-controlled 4WD systems. Although each of the manufacturers has its own approach to this issue, all the systems automatically vary the allocation of power between the wheels within milliseconds of the sensors' detecting wheel slippage.

Limiting Wheel Slippage

All 4WDs employ various systems to limit wheel slippage and transfer power to the wheels that still have traction. These systems may completely lock the differentials or they may allow limited slippage before transferring power back to the wheels that retain traction.

Lockers completely eliminate the operation of one or more differentials. A locker on the center differential switches between full-time and part-time 4WD. Lockers on the front or rear differentials ensure that power remains equally applied to each set of wheels regardless of whether both have traction. Lockers may be controlled manually, by a switch or a lever in the vehicle, or they may be automatic.

The Toyota Land Cruiser offers the option of having manual lockers on all three differentials, while other brands such as the Mitsubishi Montero offer manual lockers on the center and rear differential. Manual lockers are the most controllable and effective devices for ensuring that power is provided to the wheels with traction. However, because they allow absolutely no slippage, they must be used only on slippery surfaces.

An alternative method for getting power to the wheels that have traction is to allow limited wheel slippage. Systems that work this way may be called limited-slip differentials, posi-traction systems, or in the center differential, viscous couplings. The advantage of these systems is that the limited difference they allow in rotational speed between wheels enables such systems to be used when driving on a dry surface. All full-time 4WD systems allow limited slippage in the center differential.

For off-highway use, a manually locking differential is the best of the above systems, but it is the most expensive. Limited-slip differentials are the cheapest but also the least satisfactory, as they require one wheel to be slipping at 2 to 3 mph before power is transferred to the other wheel. For the center differential, the best system combines a locking differential and, to enable full-time use, a viscous coupling.

Tires

The tires that came with your 4WD vehicle may be satisfactory, but many 4WDs are fitted with passenger-car tires. These are unlikely to be the best choice because they are less rugged and more likely to puncture on rocky trails. They are particularly prone to sidewall damage as well. Passenger vehicle tires also have a less aggressive tread pattern than specialized 4WD tires, providing less traction in mud.

For information on purchasing tires better suited to off-highway conditions, see "Special 4WD Equipment" below.

Clearance

Road clearances vary considerably among different 4WD vehicles—from less than 7 inches to more than 10 inches. Special vehicles may have far greater clearance. For instance, the Hummer has a 16-inch ground clearance. High ground clearance is particularly advantageous on the rockier or more rutted 4WD trails in this book.

When evaluating the ground clearance of your vehicle, you need to take into account the clearance of the bodywork between the wheels on each side of the vehicle. This is particularly relevant for crawling over larger rocks. Vehicles with sidesteps have significantly lower clearance than those without.

Another factor affecting clearance is the approach and departure angles of your vehicle—that is, the maximum angle the ground can slope without the front of the vehicle hitting the ridge on approach or the rear of the vehicle hitting on departure. Mounting a winch or tow hitch to your vehicle is likely to reduce your angle of approach or departure.

If you do a lot of driving on rocky trails, you will inevitably hit the bottom of the vehicle sooner or later. When this happens, you will be far less likely to damage vulnerable areas such as the oil pan and gas tank if your vehicle is fitted with skid plates. Most manufacturers offer skid plates as an option. They are worth every penny.

Maneuverability

When you tackle tight switchbacks, you will quickly appreciate that maneuverability is an important criterion when assessing 4WD vehicles. Where a full-size vehicle may be forced to go back and forth a number of times to get around a sharp turn, a small 4WD might go straight around. This is not only easier, it's safer.

If you have a full-size vehicle, all is not lost. We have traveled many of the trails in this book in a Suburban. That is not to say that some of these trails wouldn't have been easier to negotiate in a smaller vehicle! We have noted in the route descriptions if a trail is not suitable for larger vehicles.

In Summary

Using the criteria above, you can evaluate how well your 4WD will handle off-road touring, and if you haven't yet purchased your vehicle, you can use these criteria to help select one. Choosing the best 4WD system is, at least partly, subjective. It is also a matter of your budget. However, for the type of off-highway driving covered in this book, we make the following recommendations:

- Select a 4WD system that offers low range and, at a minimum, has some form of limited slip differential on the rear axle.

■ Use light truck, all-terrain tires as the standard tires on your vehicle. For sand and slickrock, these will be the ideal choice. If conditions are likely to be muddy, or traction will be improved by a tread pattern that will give more bite, consider an additional set of mud tires.

■ For maximum clearance, select a vehicle with 16-inch wheels or at least choose the tallest tires that your vehicle can accommodate. Note that if you install tires with a diameter greater than standard, the odometer will undercalculate the distance you have traveled. Your engine braking and gear ratios will also be affected.

■ If you are going to try the rockier 4WD trails, don't install a sidestep or low-hanging front bar. If you have the option, have underbody skid plates mounted.

■ Remember that many of the obstacles you encounter on backcountry trails are more difficult to navigate in a full-size vehicle than in a compact 4WD.

Four-Wheel Driving Techniques

Safe four-wheel driving requires that you observe certain golden rules:

■ Size up the situation in advance.

■ Be careful and take your time.

■ Maintain smooth, steady power and momentum.

■ Engage 4WD and low-range gears before you get into a tight situation.

■ Steer toward high spots, trying to put the wheel over large rocks.

■ Straddle ruts.

■ Use gears and not just the brakes to hold the vehicle when driving downhill. On very steep slopes, chock the wheels if you park your vehicle.

■ Watch for logging and mining trucks and smaller recreational vehicles, such as all-terrain vehicles (ATVs).

■ Wear your seat belt and secure all luggage, especially heavy items such as tool boxes or coolers. Heavy items should be secured by ratchet tie-down straps rather than elastic-type straps, which are not strong enough to hold heavy items if the vehicle rolls.

Arizona's 4WD trails have a number of common obstacles, and the following provides an introduction to the techniques required to surmount them.

Rocks

Tire selection is important in negotiating rocks. Select a multiple-ply, tough sidewall, light-truck tire with a large-lug tread.

As you approach a rocky stretch, get into 4WD low range to give yourself maximum slow-speed control. Speed is rarely necessary, since traction on a rocky surface is usually good. Plan ahead and select the line you wish to take. If a rock appears to be larger than the clearance of your vehicle, don't try to straddle it. Check to see that it is not higher than the frame of your vehicle once you get a wheel over it. Put a wheel up on the rock and slowly climb it, then gently drop over the other side using the brake to ensure a smooth landing. Bouncing the car over rocks increases the likelihood of damage, as the body's clearance is reduced by the suspension compressing. Running boards also significantly reduce your clearance in this respect. It is often helpful to use a "spotter" outside the vehicle to assist you with the best wheel placement.

Steep Uphill Grades

Consider walking the trail to ensure that the steep hill before you is passable, especially if it is clear that backtracking is going to be a problem.

Select 4WD low range to ensure that you have adequate power to pull up the hill. If the wheels begin to lose traction, turn the steering wheel gently from side to side to give the wheels a chance to regain traction.

If you lose momentum, but the car is not in danger of sliding, use the foot brake, switch off the ignition, leave the vehicle in gear (if manual transmission) or park (if automatic), engage the parking brake, and get out to examine the situation. See if you can remove any obstacles, and figure out the line you need to take. Reversing a couple of yards and starting again may allow you to get better traction and momentum.

If halfway up, you decide a stretch of road is impassably steep, back down the trail. Trying to turn the vehicle around on a steep hill is extremely dangerous; you will very likely cause it to roll over.

Steep Downhill Grades

Again, consider walking the trail to ensure that a steep downhill is passable, especially if it is clear that backtracking uphill is going to be a problem.

Select 4WD low range and use first gear to maximize braking assistance from the engine. If the surface is loose and you are losing traction, change up to second or third gear. Do not use the brakes if you can avoid it, but don't let the vehicle's speed get out of control. Feather (lightly pump) the brakes if you slip under braking. For vehicles fitted with ABS, apply even pressure if you start to slip; the ABS helps keep vehicles on line.

Travel very slowly over rock ledges or ruts. Attempt to tackle these diagonally, letting one wheel down at a time.

If the back of the vehicle begins to slide around, gently apply the throttle and correct the steering. If the rear of the vehicle starts to slide sideways, do not apply the brakes.

Sand

As with most off-highway situations, your tires are the key to your ability to cross sand. It is difficult to tell how well a particular tire will handle in sand just by looking at it, so be guided by the manufacturer and your dealer.

The key to driving in soft sand is floatation, which is achieved by a combination of low tire pressure and momentum. Before crossing a stretch of sand, reduce your tire pressure to between 15 and 20 pounds. If necessary, you can safely go to as low as 12 pounds. As you cross, maintain momentum so that your vehicle rides on the top of the soft sand without digging in or stalling. This may require plenty of engine power. Avoid using the brakes if possible; removing your foot from the accelerator alone is normally enough to slow or stop. Using the brakes digs the vehicle deep in the sand.

Air the tires back up as soon as you are out of the sand to avoid damage to the tires and the rims. Airing back up requires a high-quality air compressor. Even then, it is a slow process.

In the backcountry of Arizona, sandy conditions are commonplace. You will therefore find a good compressor most useful.

Slickrock

When you encounter slickrock, first assess the correct direction of the trail. It is easy to lose sight of the trail on slickrock, as there are seldom any developed edges. Often the way is marked with small rock cairns, which are simply rocks stacked high enough to make a landmark.

All-terrain tires with tighter tread are more suited to slickrock than the more open, luggier type tires. As with rocks, a multiple-ply sidewall is important. In dry conditions, slickrock offers pavement-type grip. In rain or snow, you will soon learn how it got its name. Even the best tires may not get an adequate grip. Walk steep sections first; if you are slipping on foot, chances are your vehicle will slip too.

Slickrock is characterized by ledges and long sections of "pavement." Follow the guidelines for travel over rocks. Refrain from speeding over flat-looking sections, as you may hit an unexpected crevice or water pocket, and vehicles bend easier than slickrock! Turns and ledges can be tight, and vehicles with smaller overhangs and better maneuverability are at a distinct advantage—hence the popularity of the compacts in the slickrock mecca of Moab, Utah.

On the steepest sections, engage low range and pick a straight line up or down the slope. Do not attempt to traverse a steep slope sideways.

Mud

Muddy trails are easily damaged, so they should be avoided if possible. But if you must traverse a section of mud, your success will depend heavily on whether you have open-lugged mud tires or chains. Thick mud fills the tighter tread on normal tires, leaving the tire with no more grip than if it were bald. If the muddy stretch is only a few yards long, the momentum of your vehicle may allow you to get through regardless.

If the muddy track is very steep, uphill or downhill, or off camber, do not attempt it. Your vehicle is likely to skid in such conditions, and you may roll or slip off the edge of the road. Also, check to see that the mud has a reasonably firm base. Tackling deep mud is definitely not recommended unless you have a vehicle-mounted winch—and even then, be cautious, because the winch may not get you out. Finally, check to see that no ruts are too deep for the ground clearance of your vehicle.

When you decide you can get through and have selected the best route, use the following techniques to cross through the mud:

- Avoid making detours off existing tracks to minimize environmental damage.
- Select 4WD low range and a suitable gear; momentum is the key to success, so use a high enough gear to build up sufficient speed.
- Avoid accelerating heavily, so as to minimize wheel spinning and to provide maximum traction.
- Follow existing wheel ruts, unless they are too deep for the clearance of your vehicle.
- To correct slides, turn the steering wheel in the direction that the rear wheels are skidding, but don't be too aggressive or you'll overcorrect and lose control again.
- If the vehicle comes to a stop, don't continue to accelerate, as you will only spin your wheels and dig yourself into a rut. Try backing out and having another go.
- Be prepared to turn back before reaching the point of no return.

Stream Crossings

By crossing a stream that is too deep, drivers risk far more than water flowing in and ruining the interior of their vehicles. Water sucked into the engine's air intake will seriously damage the engine. Likewise, water that seeps into the air vent on the transmission or differential will mix with the lubricant and may lead to serious problems in due course.

Even worse, if the water is deep or fast flowing, it could easily carry your vehicle downstream, endangering the lives of everyone in the vehicle.

Some 4WD manuals tell you what fording depth the vehicle can negotiate safely. If your vehicle's owner's manual does not include this information, your local dealer may be able to assist. If you don't know, then avoid crossing through water that is more than a foot or so deep.

The first rule for crossing a stream is to know what you are getting into. You need to ascertain how deep the water is, whether there are any large rocks or holes, if the bottom is solid enough to avoid bogging down the vehicle, and whether the entry and exit points are negotiable. This may take some time and involve getting wet, but you take a great risk by crossing a stream without first properly assessing the situation.

The secret to water crossings is to keep moving, but not too fast. If you go too fast, you may drown the electrics, causing the vehicle to stall midstream. In shallow water (where the surface of the water is below the bumper), your primary concern is to safely negotiate the bottom of the stream, avoiding any rock damage and maintaining momentum if there is a danger of getting stuck or of slipping on the exit.

In deeper water (between 18 and 30 inches), the objective is to create a small bow wave in front of the moving vehicle. This requires a speed that is approximately walking pace. The bow wave reduces the depth of the water around the engine compartment. If the water's surface reaches your tailpipe, select a gear that will maintain moderate engine revs to avoid water backing up into the exhaust; and do not change gears midstream.

Crossing water deeper than 25 to 30 inches requires more extensive preparation of the vehicle and should be attempted only by experienced drivers.

Snow

The trails in this book that receive heavy snowfall are closed in winter. Therefore, the snow conditions that you are most likely to encounter are an occasional snowdrift that has not yet melted or fresh snow from an unexpected storm. Getting through such conditions depends on the depth of the snow, its consistency, the stability of the underlying surface, and your vehicle.

If the snow is no deeper than about 9 inches and there is solid ground beneath it, crossing the snow should not be a problem. In deeper snow that seems solid enough to support your vehicle, be extremely cautious: If you break through a drift, you are likely to be stuck, and if conditions are bad, you may have a long wait.

The tires you use for off-highway driving, with a wide tread pattern, are probably suitable for these snow conditions. Nonetheless, it is wise to carry chains (preferably for all four wheels), and if you have a vehicle-mounted winch, even better.

Vehicle Recovery Methods

If you do enough four-wheel driving, you are sure to get stuck sooner or later. The following techniques will help you get back on the go. The most suitable method will depend on the equipment available and the situation you are in—whether you are stuck in sand, mud, or snow, or are high-centered or unable to negotiate a hill.

Towing

Use a nylon yank strap of the type discussed in the "Special 4WD Equipment" section below. This type of strap will stretch 15 to 25 percent, and the elasticity will assist in extracting the vehicle.

Attach the strap only to a frame-mounted tow point. Ensure that the driver of the stuck vehicle is ready, take up all but about 6 feet of slack, then move the towing vehicle away at a moderate speed (in most circumstances this means using 4WD low range in second gear) so that the elasticity of the strap is employed in the way it is meant to be. Don't take off like a bat out of hell or you risk breaking the strap or damaging a vehicle.

Never join two yank straps together with a shackle. If one strap breaks, the shackle will become a lethal missile aimed at one of the vehicles (and anyone inside). For the same reason, never attach a yank strap to the tow ball on either vehicle.

Jacking

Jacking the vehicle allows you to pack under the wheel (with rocks, dirt, or logs) or use your shovel to remove an obstacle. However, the standard vehicle jack is unlikely to be of as much assistance as a high-lift jack. We highly recommend purchasing a good high-lift jack as a basic accessory if you decide that you are going to do a lot of serious, off-highway four-wheel driving. Remember a high-lift jack is of limited use if your vehicle does not have an appropriate jacking point. Some brush bars have two built-in forward jacking points.

Tire Chains

Tire chains can be of assistance in both mud and snow. Cable-type chains provide much less grip than link-type chains. There are also dedicated mud chains with larger, heavier links than on normal snow chains. It is best to have chains fitted to all four wheels.

Once you are bogged down is not the best time to try to fit the chains; if at all possible, try to predict their need and have them on the tires before trouble arises. An easy way to affix chains is to place two small cubes of wood under the center of the stretched-out chain. When you drive your tires up on the blocks of wood, it is easier to stretch the chains over the tires because the pressure is off.

Winching

Most recreational four-wheel drivers do not have a winch. But if you get serious about four-wheel driving, this is probably the first major accessory you should consider buying.

Under normal circumstances, a winch would be warranted only for the more difficult 4WD trails in this book. Having a winch is certainly comforting when you see a difficult section of road ahead and have to decide whether to risk it or turn back. Also, major obstacles can appear when you least expect them, even on trails that are otherwise easy.

Owning a winch is not a panacea to all your recovery problems. Winching depends on the availability of a good anchor point, and electric winches may not work if they are submerged in a stream. Despite these constraints, no accessory is more useful than a high-quality, powerful winch when you get into a difficult situation.

If you acquire a winch, learn to use it properly; take the time to study your owner's manual. Incorrect operation can be extremely dangerous and may cause damage to the winch or to your anchor points, which are usually trees.

Navigation by the Global Positioning System (GPS)

Although this book is designed so that each trail can be navigated simply by following the detailed directions provided, nothing makes navigation easier than a GPS receiver.

The global positioning system (GPS) consists of a network of 24 satellites, nearly 13,000 miles in space, in six different orbital paths. The satellites are constantly moving at about 8,500 miles per hour, making two complete orbits around the earth every 24 hours.

Each satellite is constantly transmitting data, including its identification number, its operational health, and the date and time. It also transmits its location and the location of every other satellite in the network.

By comparing the time the signal was transmitted to the time it is received, a GPS receiver calculates how far away each satellite is. With a sufficient number of signals, the receiver can then triangulate its location. With three or more satellites, the receiver can determine latitude and longitude coordinates. With four or more, it can calculate altitude. By constantly making these calculations, it can determine speed and direction. To facilitate these calculations, the time data broadcast by GPS is accurate to within 40 billionths of a second.

The U.S. military uses the system to provide positions accurate to within half an inch. When the system was first established, civilian receivers were deliberately fed slightly erroneous information in order to effectively deny military applications to hostile countries or terrorists—a practice called selective availability (SA). However on May 1, 2000, in response to the growing importance of the system for civilian applications, the U.S. government stopped intentionally downgrading GPS data. The military gave its support to this change once new technology made it possible to selectively degrade the system within any defined geographical area on demand. This new feature of the system has made it safe to have higher-quality signals available for civilian use. Now, instead of the civilian-use signal having a margin of error being between 20 and 70 yards, it is only about one-tenth of that.

A GPS receiver offers the four-wheeler numerous benefits:

■ You can track to any point for which you know the longitude and latitude coordinates with no chance of heading in the wrong direction or getting lost. Most receivers provide an extremely easy-to-understand graphic display to keep you on track.

■ It works in all weather conditions.

■ It automatically records your route for easy backtracking.

■ You can record and name any location, so that you can relocate it with ease. This may include your campsite, a fishing spot, or even a silver mine you discover!

■ It displays your position, allowing you to pinpoint your location on a map.

■ By interfacing the GPS receiver directly to a portable computer, you can monitor and record your location as you travel (using the appropriate map software) or print the route you took.

However, remember that GPS units can fail, batteries can go flat, and tree cover and tight canyons can block the signals. Never rely entirely on GPS for navigation. Always carry a compass for backup.

Special 4WD Equipment

Tires

When 4WD touring, you will likely encounter a wide variety of terrain: rocks, mud, talus, slickrock, sand, gravel, dirt, and bitumen. The immense variety of tires on the market includes many specifically targeted at one or another of these types of terrain, as well as tires designed to adequately handle a range of terrain.

Every four-wheel driver seems to have a preference when it comes to tire selection, but most people undertaking the 4WD trails in this book will need tires that can handle all of the above types of terrain adequately.

The first requirement is to select rugged, light-truck tires rather than passenger-vehicle tires. Check the size data on the sidewall: it should have "LT" rather than "P" before the number. Among light-truck tires, you must choose between tires that are designated "all-terrain" and more-aggressive, wider-tread mud tires. Either type will be adequate, especially on rocks, gravel, talus, or dirt. Although mud tires have an advantage in muddy conditions and soft snow, all-terrain tires perform better on slickrock, in sand, and particularly on ice and paved roads.

When selecting tires, remember that they affect not just traction but also cornering ability, braking distances, fuel consumption, and noise levels. It pays to get good advice before making your decision.

Global Positioning System Receivers

GPS receivers have come down in price considerably in the past few years and are rapidly becoming indispensable navigational tools. Many higher-priced cars now offer integrated GPS receivers, and within the next few years, receivers will become available on most models.

Battery-powered, hand-held units that meet the needs of off-highway driving currently range from less than $100 to a little over $300 and continue to come down in price. Some high-end units feature maps that are incorporated in the display, either from a built-in database or from interchangeable memory cards. Currently, only a few of these maps include 4WD trails.

If you are considering purchasing a GPS unit, keep the following in mind:

■ Price. The very cheapest units are likely outdated and very limited in their display features. Expect to pay from $125 to $300.

■ The display. Compare the graphic display of one unit with another. Some are much easier to decipher or offer more alternative displays.

■ The controls. GPS receivers have many functions, and they need to have good, simple controls.

■ Vehicle mounting. To be useful, the unit needs to be placed where it can be read easily by both the driver and the navigator. Check that the unit can be conveniently located in your vehicle. Different units have different shapes and different mounting systems.

■ Map data. More and more units have map data built in. Some have the ability to download maps from a computer. Such maps are normally sold on a CD-ROM. GPS units have a finite storage capacity and having the ability to download maps covering a narrower geographical region means that the amount of data relating to that specific region can be greater.

■ The number of routes and the number of sites (or "waypoints") per route that can be stored in memory. For off-highway use, it is important to be able to store plenty of waypoints so that you do not have to load coordinates into the machine as frequently. Having plenty of memory also ensures that you can automatically store your present location without fear that the memory is full.

■ Waypoint storage. The better units store up to 500 way

points and 20 reversible routes of up to 30 waypoints each. Also consider the number of characters a GPS receiver allows you to use to name waypoints. When you try to recall a waypoint, you may have difficulty recognizing names restricted to only a few characters.

■ Automatic route storing. Most units automatically store your route as you go along and enable you to display it in reverse to make backtracking easy.

After you have selected a unit, a number of optional extras are also worth considering:

■ A cigarette lighter electrical adapter. Despite GPS units becoming more power efficient, protracted in-vehicle use still makes this accessory a necessity.

■ A vehicle-mounted antenna, which will improve reception under difficult conditions. (The GPS unit can only "see" through the windows of your vehicle; it cannot monitor satellites through a metal roof.) Having a vehicle-mounted antenna also means that you do not have to consider reception when locating the receiver in your vehicle.

■ An in-car mounting system. If you are going to do a lot of touring using the GPS, consider attaching a bracket on the dash rather than relying on a Velcro mount.

■ A computer-link cable and digital maps. Data from your GPS receiver can be downloaded to your PC; maps and waypoints can be downloaded from your PC; or if you have a laptop computer, you can monitor your route as you go along, using one of a number of inexpensive map software products on the market.

Yank Straps

Yank straps are industrial-strength versions of the flimsy tow straps carried by the local discount store. They are 20 to 30 feet long and 2 to 3 inches wide, made of heavy nylon, rated to at least 20,000 pounds, and have looped ends.

Do not use tow straps with metal hooks in the ends (the hooks can become missiles in the event the strap breaks free). Likewise, never join two yank straps together using a shackle.

CB Radios

If you are stuck, injured, or just want to know the conditions up ahead, a citizen's band (CB) radio can be invaluable. CB radios are relatively inexpensive and do not require an FCC license. Their range is limited, especially in very hilly country, as their transmission patterns basically follow lines of sight. Range can be improved using single sideband (SSB) transmission, an option on more expensive units. Range is even better on vehicle-mounted units that have been professionally fitted to ensure that the antenna and cabling are matched appropriately.

Winches

There are three main options when it comes to winches: manual winches, removable electric winches, and vehicle-mounted electric winches.

If you have a full-size 4WD vehicle—which can weigh in excess of 7,000 pounds when loaded—a manual winch is of limited use without a lot of effort and considerable time. However, a manual winch is a very handy and inexpensive accessory if you have a small 4WD. Typically, manual winches are rated to pull about 5,500 pounds.

Electric winches can be mounted to your vehicle's trailer hitch to enable them to be removed, relocated to the front of your vehicle (if you have a hitch installed), or moved to another vehicle. Although this is a very useful feature, a winch is heavy, so relocating one can be a two-person job. Consider that 5,000-pound-rated winches weigh only about 55 pounds, while 12,000-pound-rated models weigh around 140 pounds. Therefore, the larger models are best permanently front-mounted. Unfortunately, this position limits their ability to winch the vehicle backward.

When choosing between electric winches, be aware that they are rated for their maximum capacity on the first wind of the cable around the drum. As layers of cable wind onto the drum, they increase its diameter and thus decrease the maximum load the winch can handle. This decrease is significant: A winch rated to pull 8,000 pounds on a bare drum may only handle 6,500 pounds on the second layer, 5,750 pounds on the third layer, and 5,000 pounds on the fourth. Electric winches also draw a high level of current and may necessitate upgrading the battery in your 4WD or adding a second battery.

There is a wide range of mounting options—from a simple, body-mounted frame that holds the winch to heavy-duty winch bars that replace the original bumper and incorporate brush bars and mounts for auxiliary lights.

If you buy a winch, either electric or manual, you will also need quite a range of additional equipment so that you can operate it correctly:

- at least one choker chain with hooks on each end,
- winch extension straps or cables,
- shackles,
- a receiver shackle,
- a snatch block,
- a tree protector,
- gloves.

Grill/Brush Bars and Winch Bars

Brush bars protect the front of the vehicle from scratches and minor bumps; they also provide a solid mount for auxiliary lights and often high-lift jacking points. The level of protection they provide depends on how solid they are and whether they are securely mounted onto the frame of the vehicle. Lighter models attach in front of the standard bumper, but the more substantial units replace the bumper. Prices range from about $150 to $450.

Winch bars replace the bumper and usually integrate a solid brush bar with a heavy-duty winch mount. Some have the brush bar as an optional extra to the winch bar component. Manufacturers such as Warn, ARB, and TJM offer a wide range of integrated winch bars. These are significantly more expensive, starting at about $650.

Remember that installing heavy equipment on the front of

the vehicle may necessitate increasing the front suspension rating to cope with the additional weight.

Portable Air Compressors

Most portable air compressors on the market are flimsy models that plug into the cigarette lighter and are sold at the local discount store. These are of very limited use for four-wheel driving. They are very slow to inflate the large tires of a 4WD vehicle; for instance, to reinflate from 15 to 35 pounds typically takes about 10 minutes for each tire. They are also unlikely to be rated for continuous use, which means that they will overheat and cut off before completing the job. If you're lucky, they will start up again when they have cooled down, but this means that you are unlikely to reinflate your tires in less than an hour.

The easiest way to identify a useful air compressor is by the price—good ones cost $200 or more. Many of the quality units feature a Thomas-brand pump and are built to last. Another good unit is sold by ARB. All these pumps draw between 15 and 20 amps and thus should not be plugged into the cigarette lighter socket but attached to the vehicle's battery with clips. The ARB unit can be permanently mounted under the hood. Quick-Air makes a range of units including a 10-amp compressor that can be plugged into the cigarette lighter socket and performs well.

Auxiliary Driving Lights

There is a vast array of auxiliary lights on the market today, and selecting the best lights for your purpose can be a confusing process.

Auxiliary lights greatly improve visibility in adverse weather conditions. Driving lights provide a strong, moderately wide beam to supplement headlamp high beams, giving improved lighting in the distance and to the sides of the main beam. Fog lamps throw a wide-dispersion, flat beam; and spots provide a high-power, narrow beam to improve lighting range directly in front of the vehicle. Rear-mounted auxiliary lights provide greatly improved visibility for backing up.

For off-highway use, you will need quality lights with strong mounting brackets. Some high-powered off-highway lights are not approved by the Department of Transportation for use on public roads.

Roof Racks

Roof racks can be excellent for storing gear, as well as providing easy access for certain weatherproof items. However, they raise the center of gravity on the vehicle, which can substantially alter the rollover angle. A roof rack is best used for lightweight objects that are well strapped down. Heavy recovery gear and other bulky items should be packed low in the vehicle's interior to lower the center of gravity and stabilize the vehicle.

A roof rack should allow for safe and secure packing of items and be sturdy enough to withstand knocks.

Packing Checklist

Before embarking on any 4WD adventure, whether a lazy Sunday drive on an easy trail or a challenging climb over rugged terrain, be prepared. The following checklist will help you gather the items you need.

Essential

- ❒ Rain gear
- ❒ Small shovel or multipurpose ax, pick, shovel, and sledgehammer
- ❒ Heavy-duty yank strap
- ❒ Spare tire that matches the other tires on the vehicle
- ❒ Working jack and base plate for soft ground
- ❒ Maps
- ❒ Emergency medical kit, including sun protection and insect repellent
- ❒ Bottled water
- ❒ Blankets or space blankets
- ❒ Parka, gloves, and boots
- ❒ Spare vehicle key
- ❒ Jumper leads
- ❒ Heavy-duty flashlight
- ❒ Multipurpose tool, such as a Leatherman™
- ❒ Emergency food—high-energy bars or similar

Worth Considering

- ❒ Global Positioning System (GPS) receiver
- ❒ Cell phone
- ❒ A set of light-truck, off-highway tires and matching spare
- ❒ High-lift jack
- ❒ Additional tool kit
- ❒ CB radio
- ❒ Portable air compressor
- ❒ Tire gauge
- ❒ Tire-sealing kit
- ❒ Tire chains
- ❒ Handsaw and ax
- ❒ Binoculars
- ❒ Firearms
- ❒ Whistle
- ❒ Flares
- ❒ Vehicle fire extinguisher
- ❒ Gasoline, engine oil, and other vehicle fluids
- ❒ Portable hand winch
- ❒ Electric cooler

If Your Credit Cards Aren't Maxed Out

- ❒ Electric, vehicle-mounted winch and associated recovery straps, shackles, and snatch blocks
- ❒ Auxiliary lights
- ❒ Locking differential(s)

Arizona Distance Chart

	AJO	BENSON	BISBEE	BULLHEAD CITY	CHINLE	COVE	DOUGLAS	DRAKE	FLAGSTAFF	FLORENCE	FORT DEFIANCE	GILA BEND	GRAND CANYON NP	HOLBROOK	HEBER	KINGMAN	LAKE HAVASU CITY	LUKEVILLE	MAMMOTH	NOGALES	ORACLE	PARKER	PHOENIX	PRESCOTT	QUARTZSITE	REDINGTON	RODEO, NM	SAFFORD	SALOME	SAWMILL	SEDONA	SHOW LOW	SIERRA VISTA	ST. JOHNS	SUPERIOR	TOMBSTONE	WELLTON	WILLCOX	WILLIAMS	WICKENBURG	WINS	YUMA
BENSON	175																																									
BISBEE	257	46																																								
BULLHEAD CITY	319	481	527																																							
CHINLE	465	516	562	393																																						
COVE	554	605	652	483	81																																					
DOUGLAS	296	72	26	516	451	528																																				
DRAKE	273	460	390	45	372	462	545																																			
FLAGSTAFF	253	304	350	182	216	306	389	160																																		
FLORENCE	142	123	169	333	419	509	208	363	207																																	
FORT DEFIANCE	445	496	542	373	50	87	419	352	196	398																																
GILA BEND	43	171	217	273	419	509	256	227	207	101	399																															
GRAND CANYON NP	335	358	431	203	204	269	457	182	76	287	277	287																														
HOLBROOK	344	394	337	271	123	213	334	250	94	296	103	297	175																													
HEBER	258	290	337	292	168	258	313	271	115	193	148	211	196	45																												
KINGMAN	268	449	495	34	361	451	534	13	149	351	341	222	171	239	260																											
LAKE HAVASU CITY	252	363	409	70	419	509	448	48	208	274	399	197	229	298	318	60																										
LUKEVILLE	38	192	238	332	500	590	260	314	288	157	480	81	372	381	311	303	278																									
MAMMOTH	178	94	116	355	319	399	152	334	270	64	289	156	350	197	169	323	320	195																								
NOGALES	191	109	80	409	535	625	114	387	323	142	515	189	403	412	311	376	374	192	112																							
ORACLE	169	84	130	345	337	417	156	324	260	55	307	147	340	215	187	313	311	186	17	103																						
PARKER	204	315	361	94	485	575	387	113	273	217	465	157	295	363	297	126	41	241	280	333	270																					
PHOENIX	117	160	206	231	357	447	232	209	145	63	337	69	225	234	143	198	196	154	125	179	115	155																				
PRESCOTT	210	260	306	182	307	397	332	160	96	163	287	163	125	186	142	149	208	248	225	279	216	152	101																			
QUARTZSITE	178	288	335	130	479	568	361	149	267	191	458	130	259	356	270	162	76	215	253	307	244	36	129	134																		
REDDINGTON	179	46	92	382	343	423	128	360	296	85	313	162	376	221	193	349	347	196	28	113	37	307	152	252	280																	
RODEO, NM	298	126	77	513	391	469	50	491	427	245	359	293	507	314	295	480	478	314	169	231	207	437	282	383	411	145																
SAFFORD	256	85	126	396	327	405	124	374	272	132	295	251	353	211	189	363	361	273	128	190	146	320	165	265	294	103	106															
SALOME	146	260	306	150	420	510	332	113	208	162	404	102	221	302	242	126	97	186	225	278	215	56	100	96	38	251	382	265														
SAWMILL	451	385	426	378	37	79	424	357	201	403	13	403	282	108	153	346	404	488	295	519	313	470	342	292	463	319	364	300	408													
SEDONA	226	276	332	206	241	330	348	185	29	178	220	179	110	119	128	174	232	263	241	294	231	265	116	67	238	268	398	244	184	226												
SHOW LOW	286	240	282	326	178	259	279	304	149	142	149	244	229	56	38	293	352	299	142	255	159	330	177	239	304	166	261	155	275	154	173											
SIERRA VISTA	201	32	28	416	440	518	54	395	331	149	408	196	411	420	318	383	381	218	120	55	110	341	186	286	314	78	105	113	286	413	302	268										
ST. JOHNS	402	277	318	330	138	215	316	308	152	190	105	355	223	60	79	297	356	439	189	303	207	421	293	244	414	213	256	192	360	110	177	49	305									
SUPERIOR	175	118	164	295	288	369	200	273	209	31	259	133	288	166	128	262	260	188	52	173	70	219	64	164	193	76	207	101	164	264	180	111	151	158								
TOMBSTONE	199	24	22	414	431	509	48	393	329	147	399	195	409	315	316	382	379	216	94	70	108	339	184	284	312	69	93	104	284	404	300	259	29	296	142							
TUCSON	133	48	94	344	470	560	120	322	258	77	450	124	339	348	246	311	309	150	46	67	37	269	114	214	242	41	171	129	213	455	230	191	74	236	100	72						
WELLINGTON	129	256	302	218	511	600	328	238	299	181	490	88	379	388	302	250	165	233	241	274	232	124	161	222	90	247	378	337	126	496	270	330	282	447	219	280	210					
WILLCOX	212	41	82	427	374	451	72	405	341	160	341	207	421	257	236	394	392	229	80	146	89	352	197	297	325	56	88	47	296	346	313	202	69	238	128	60	83	292				
WILLIAMS	284	334	380	152	246	336	406	131	34	236	226	236	56	124	145	120	179	321	299	352	289	244	175	74	208	325	456	302	170	231	59	178	360	182	238	358	288	328	370			
WICKENBURG	138	227	273	163	366	455	299	142	154	129	350	91	183	248	205	131	150	176	192	245	182	110	67	58	92	218	349	232	54	355	125	302	252	306	130	251	181	182	263	132		
WINSLOW	311	361	407	239	157	247	433	217	62	264	137	264	142	35	54	206	265	348	230	380	248	330	202	153	323	254	347	244	269	142	86	90	387	93	173	385	315	355	290	91	215	
YUMA	158	285	331	212	540	630	357	231	328	210	519	117	408	417	331	243	158	203	271	303	261	118	190	216	83	277	407	366	120	525	299	359	311	476	249	309	239	35	322	358	174	385

Distances are calculated using major highways.

Along the Trail

Towns, Ghost Towns, Forts, and Interesting Places

Agua Caliente

Native Americans first visited the hot springs at Agua Caliente (Spanish for "hot water") because of their belief in the springs' natural healing abilities. Notes from the earliest recorded visit, which was made by Spanish missionary Father Jacobo Sedelmayr in 1744, confirm this speculation. After returning to Mexico to report the findings of his first expedition, Sedelmayr set off into central Arizona again in 1748 and 1750. It was during one of these journeys when he first named the Indian rancheria as Santa Maria del Agua Caliente. King Woolsey (see page 73) later enjoyed the hot waters so much that he established a health resort for travelers along this part of the Southern Overland Trail. He also built a small flour mill at the site and opened the first road from Agua Caliente to Prescott.

The gold rush of the late 1800s created an influx of clients to Agua Caliente, which by the 1870s boasted a well-established ranch in addition to the resort. A local resident named Dolores Conde used to work as a waitress and chambermaid at the hotel for one dollar a day. She recalled seeing the first governor of Arizona, George Hunt, relaxing at the resort in the late 1800s. Nearby farmers utilized the natural water source to irrigate crops on large tracts of land. Woolsey, who was becoming one of the more prominent landowners in the Salt River Valley in the late 1800s, sold his resort business but held on to the water rights and part of the land. The Southern Pacific Railroad, Arizona 85, and eventually Interstate 8 all followed routes that bypassed Agua Caliente, and the resort eventually faded. However, U.S. military officers occupied the resort during World War II and even constructed a large swimming pool for training purposes. Today, the springs have long since dried up. One story attributes the lack of water there to over-irrigation; another states that the springs were lost underground when developers were blasting to expand the resort. Some of the earlier resort ruins, including the remains of a 22-room hotel, can be seen near the crumbling buildings.

The ruins of King Woolsey's adobe home in Agua Caliente, circa 1920

GPS COORDINATES: N32°59.07' W113°19.42'
TRAIL: Central #15: Agua Caliente Road
MAP: Page 377

Ajo

One speculation of the derivation of the name Ajo is that it came from the Papago Indians' use of the copper ores from which they produced their red face paint: *au'auho*. Another possible explanation is that the town was named after a lily that grows in abundance in the Ajo Mountains. The plant's root tastes similar to a spring onion and is commonly referred to as wild garlic, or *ajo,* in Spanish.

In a state known for its extensive mineral resources, Ajo was the first mining camp worked by Americans. Although Mexicans knew of the area's potential early in the 1850s (which prior to the Gadsen Purchase of 1853–54 was located in northern Mexico), they left the resources mostly untouched because the low-grade surface ore was too difficult to process. In 1854 Charles D. Poston and Herman Ehrenberg were exploring the region around the Santa Cruz River valley and found some promising copper ore specimens, which they took with them to San Francisco. However, when the two men returned to the region two years later, they focused their efforts on exploiting the mines around Tubac instead of Ajo.

In 1864 Captain Peter Brady is believed to have been the first to lead mining ventures in the Ajo area after scouting the region in 1853 for a railroad route along the 32nd parallel. He initially found some promising silver ore deposits while exploring the area. But his ventures soon ran dry because it was too costly to process the ore in such a remote location. Others, like A. J. Shotwell, tried their luck in the region as well. However, they also found it too difficult to glean a profit from the area's resources.

Basic farming was the main activity of the few folks who remained in Ajo. The abundant rich ores remained in the ground until the 1910s, when newly developed leaching processes made it possible for the New Cornelia Mine (named by former Rough Rider and businessman Colonel John C. Greenway) to prosper to boom levels. Greenway brought with him a solid understanding of mining and a well-financed organization. After discovering a large underground pool of water, he began an open-pit mining operation. Several thousand people moved to the growing region, and the copper mine grew so large it engulfed the town of Ajo.

Phelps Dodge is the current owner of the mine, which is classed as "active," although very little mining activity occurs. No serious mining has taken place since the price of copper plummeted in the 1980s, resulting in the town's

ghostlike atmosphere. At the turn of the twenty-first century, Ajo is becoming an attractive winter destination for many retirees, although the neighboring military land, Indian reservation, and federal lands restrict its growth.
GPS COORDINATES: N32°22.49' W112°52.02'
TRAIL: South #3: El Camino del Diablo Trail
MAP: Pages 478–9

Alamo Crossing

Little is known about the small mining camp of Alamo Crossing other than local legends. Tom Rodgers founded the town in the late 1890s as a camp for transient mining prospectors. The only two permanent buildings were a store and the post office. According to one story, nearby Indians raided the store, poisoned the owner (who died), and pillaged the goods. Meanwhile, the postmaster, tired of his lonely job, fled with his federal loot. In reality, once the mine's ore diminished, the miners deserted the camp. Despite a short revival during a boom in the manganese industry in the 1950s, Alamo Crossing continued to dwindle. Today, the waters of Alamo Lake cover the old town site.
GPS COORDINATES: N34°15.62' W113°34.85'
TRAIL: Northwest #15: Alamo Lake Road
MAP: Page 172

American Flag

A group of Cornish prospectors who discovered ore in the Hualapai Mountains established the American Flag Mine in 1871. In the late 1870s, Isaac Lorraine settled the town of American Flag on the east flank of the range. Although the veins were small, they were worked steadily from 1875 until the late 1880s.

Around that time, the Richardson Mining Company in New York bought out the mine and continued to employ 40 men. Lorraine left the mining business and developed a nearby ranch (called American Flag Ranch) with his profit. In 1884, the population of American Flag numbered only 14. The mine had played out by the mid-1880s and the small community of American Flag dwindled.

A historical marker is affixed to the major surviving building, the old post office, which is still in use as a private cabin.
GPS COORDINATES: N32°34.85' W110°43.18'
TRAIL: South #27: Oracle Control Road
MAP: Page 544

Aubrey Landing

Located at the confluence of the Bill Williams and Colorado Rivers, Aubrey Landing was established in 1864 as a busy steamboat port for shipping ore. The town was named in honor of trapping pioneer François Xavier Aubrey, a decade after his death. Aubrey, nicknamed Skimmer of the Plains, rode horseback from Santa Fe, New Mexico, to Independence, Missouri, in either three or eight days (the exact number is not clear) to win a $1,000 bet.

Despite its prominent location on the river, Aubrey Landing never quite grew as settlers had hoped. During its prime, the town boasted approximately 150 inhabitants who lived in huts along the river and who worked for the steamboat company. Hard times hit Aubrey Landing in the late 1860s: Mines in the area closed and floods washed away large portions of the town. By 1879, many of the town's original settlers had packed up and moved elsewhere. The post office, hotel, general store, and saloon were all located in one building and only a handful of steamboat employees remained. Colorado Steam Navigation Company employee W. J. Hardy lived in an abandoned ship's cabin. In 1886, all activity ceased when the post office shut down. The town of Aubrey Landing was short-lived and is now submerged under the waters of Lake Havasu.
GPS COORDINATES: N34°18.22' W114°8.21'
NEAREST TRAIL: Northwest #7: Mineral Wash–Bill Williams River Trail

Barkerville

From 1924 to 1933 Barkerville served as a small stage stop with a store and post office. The Barker family, which owned a cattle ranch in the area, ran these facilities. Children from surrounding ranches attended classes in a small schoolhouse in town. In those days, a motor stage ran between Florence and Tucson, and Barkerville was located along the route. Today, children attend school in Winkelman and Superior; there is nothing left of Barkerville.
GPS COORDINATES: N32°49.92' W110°56.60'
TRAIL: South #26: Willow Springs Road
MAP: Pages 540–1

Bisbee

During its peak, Bisbee, often referred to as the queen of copper camps, boasted a population of 35,000 residents. The current population is much smaller, down to about 8,500. But the quaint mining town of Bisbee continues to flourish.

A letter from William A. Greene states that local prospector Jack Dunn was the first to discover the ore that would lead to the establishment of Bisbee. Others believe that George Warren was the first to stake his claim. Another report claims that Dunn, a U.S. Army scout, initially staked the claims but hired Warren as prospector while he completed his duties with the military. At any rate, both Dunn and Warren either sold

Bisbee, circa 1890

or lost their shares of the mines early in Bisbee's history.

Named for the prominent investor from California, Judge DeWitt Bisbee (who unfortunately never even saw the town), Bisbee was a huge success as a mining town by 1878. A year later, mining officials realized more profit could be made from the mines if the copper ore was smelted prior to shipping. The result meant more money for the residents of Bisbee as well as continued growth. However, the smelter polluted the air and continually needed fuel, resulting in the deforesting of surrounding mountains.

In 1881, Phelps Dodge invested heavily in the Copper Queen Mine (previously owned by George Warren). About the same time, architect James Douglas was hired to transform Bisbee into a more attractive destination for settlers. By 1901 a new smelter was constructed 25 miles outside of town, a positive factor for continued growth. Now Bisbee could truly become a "Little San Francisco," a nickname it soon acquired and has since retained.

Brewery Gulch, Bisbee's "seedy" side of town, complete with saloons and brothels, burned to the ground during a fire in 1906. Another fire a year later destroyed more than $500,000 worth of residential and commercial property. These were not the only disasters to plague Bisbee. Flooding has also caused devastating problems for the town and its occupants throughout its history.

When Phelps Dodge purchased his competitor, Warren Company, in 1917 and opened Sacramento Pit, Bisbee's mining life was secured for another 60 years. Despite a few labor problems, like the World War I miners' strike, the Copper Queen Mine remained open until 1975. The hugely successful copper mine produced 8 billion pounds of copper during its nearly 100 years of operation.

Today, Bisbee has not floundered in the wake of its closed mines. Instead, Little San Francisco is drawing numerous people who are searching for a mild climate and a relatively low cost of living. Budding artists, retirees, and small business owners continue to keep the town of Bisbee thriving.

GPS COORDINATES: N31°26.61' W109°55.23'
TRAIL: South #18: Mule Mountains Trail
MAP: Page 517

Bouse

The town of Bouse was initially named Brayton after John Brayton, director of the Brayton Commercial Company, which ran the nearby Harquahala Mine. According to one story, officials mistakenly renamed the town Bouse in 1907 when they misread an application and registered the community as the name of the person lodging the form, Thomas Bouse. Another story indicates that the town's new name was not a mistake at all. Instead, long-time residents who wanted to honor the old-timer Bouse lodged the new name on purpose.

Tom Bouse arrived in the area in 1889. His wife, Katherine, and their daughter followed him out in 1892, after he had built the first two rooms of their home. In 1902, the farmer discovered several outcroppings of ore on his 320-acre property but did little to pursue his claims. When the Arizona & California Railroad Company decided to build near his home, Bouse sold part of his ranch and the claims on it to the railroad.

The Arizona & California Railroad depot in Bouse, 1910

W. J. Dunn, a promoter from California, became partners with Bouse in 1909 and created Bouse Townsite, Land & Improvement Company. The pair harbored high hopes to sell the town as the next great mining establishment. Around the same time, a new railroad called the Arizona & Swansea Railroad connected Bouse to the nearby mining town of Swansea. During the 1910s, Bouse enjoyed a degree of prosperity because of its mines and its location along the two rail lines. However, at its peak, Bouse only supported about 550 residents and a decade after Bouse and Dunn launched their fierce campaign, the mines dwindled and dreams of a successful city faded.

In 1929 Tom Bouse died of a rattlesnake bite; he is buried in Bouse Cemetery. A short distance from Bouse on the Plomosa Road, a historical plaque now marks the old homestead site.

GPS COORDINATES: N33°55.90' W114°00.36'
TRAIL: Northwest #6: Swansea Road
MAP: Page 152

Bradshaw City

William D. Bradshaw founded Bradshaw City in 1863 when prospectors discovered gold in the region and an influx of people bolstered the town on the northwest slope of Mount Wasson. Tiger Mine, found a short distance along the Central #26: Crown King Backroad, served as the main mining site in this area. Bradshaw City began as a loose collection of tents, but before long saloons, dance halls, restaurants, and hotels lined the streets of this small town. During its peak in the summer of 1871, the population grew to around 5,000.

Many of the mine managers and owners from the Bradshaw Mining District built ornate houses 30 miles away in Prescott. Some of the houses, which have been carefully restored, can be viewed along Mt. Vernon Street. Residents and visitors accessed Bradshaw City via wagon train from Prescott, a journey that took two and a half days. An ore packer by the name of Simpson ran a saddle train every week between Prescott and Bradshaw City.

However, by the end of 1871, miners began to move away from Tiger Mine to find work elsewhere. By the 1880s, Bradshaw City had faded from the map. Today, a forest service sign marks the spot where Bradshaw City once stood.

GPS COORDINATES: N34°11.78' W112°21.32'
TRAIL: Central #24: Senator Highway
MAP: Pages 402–3

Bueno

In 1863, prospector Bob Groom discovered gold in the Bradshaw Mountains, and the Bully Bueno Mine was born. With their hopes set on staking claims, others soon flocked to the area, and the mining camp of Bueno emerged.

When the Philadelphia-based Walnut Grove Gold Mining Company purchased Bully Bueno, Indians still inhabited much of the area surrounding the town. Two mine company workers, Bigilo and Campbell, while sleeping in a house adjacent to the mill, were awakened one night by several of them. As Bigilo attempted to put out flames supposedly set by one of the angry Indians, he was hit in the stomach by an arrow. Bigilo's friend and co-worker, Campbell, rescued him and shot the Indian. The arrow was never removed from Bigilo's abdomen, but he recovered nonetheless.

Bueno's population reached its highest in 1880. The streets bustled with 250 residents; there was a general store, a school, a lawyer, and even a justice of the peace. Nothing remains of the mining camp today.

GPS COORDINATES: N34°19.03' W112°22.12'
TRAIL: Central #24: Senator Highway
MAP: Pages 402–3

Bumble Bee

Bumble Bee was originally called Snyder's Station (also spelled Snider) after local rancher W. W. Snyder. There are many stories about the origin of the ghost town's eventual name. One account states that prospectors searching for gold in the hills stumbled across a bumblebee hive and suffered a multitude of stings. Another tale claims that visiting U.S. Cavalry troops remarked that the Indians in the area were "as thick as bumblebees." And yet another says that cavalry troops overheard an Indian powwow and mistook the sound for a swarm of bumblebees. Whichever legend rings true, the name stuck like honey.

Although little gold was found in Bumble Bee, numerous surrounding mining camps kept the town in business. Bumble Bee's success lay in its prominent location along the road, which made it a stage stop for many years. So dependent was the town on the stage, it moved three times in order to follow road survey realignments. However, Bumble Bee finally lost its battle when the Black Canyon Highway was built. The town can now only be accessed by a gravel road.

Abandoned by the new highway, Bumble Bee was sold in 1960 to Charles A. Penn, a magazine publisher from the East. Penn and his wife had dreams of renovating the camp to its original splendor but never quite followed through on the idea. Many of the houses have been restored, and a gift shop is located in the old school building. An "authentic" frontier street awaits visitors who stumble into Bumble Bee.

GPS COORDINATES: N34°12.09' W112°9.10'
NEAREST TRAIL: Central #30: Bloody Basin Road

Calabasas

Calabasas, also spelled Calabazas, has worn many hats throughout its almost 400 years of history. Papago Indians first settled the land that is now Calabasas in the early 1600s, although Apaches dominated the area during much of the 1800s.

Arizona historians note that Calabazas (Spanish for "pumpkins") served as a mission for visiting Jesuit priests around 1763. When the Spanish government ordered all Jesuit priests to leave the New World immediately, the establishment was all but abandoned.

Between 1842 and 1852, Governor Gandra of Sonora purchased the town and built a large estate for himself. Apparently, the Apaches disapproved of their new neighbor and successfully destroyed Gandra's legacy. U.S. military troops even protected the area for a while until the men were needed to fight in the Civil War in 1861.

A few years later, Colonel C. P. Sykes had dreams of transforming Calabasas into the next booming border town. Sykes, owner of the Calabasas Land Grant, launched a nationwide advertising campaign surreptitiously peddling his town as the new metropolis of the West. The businessman took a risk and wagered much of his own wealth on an elaborate hotel, the Santa Rita, which opened with grandeur in 1882. To the disappointment of Sykes and several other entrepreneurs, nearby Nogales developed more quickly as a border town and Calabasas began to dwindle.

Sykes's widow inhabited a room in the old hotel until her death in 1910. After being used for many years as a storage facility for farm equipment, the once spectacular Santa Rita burned to the ground around 1927. Nearly all evidence of Calabasas is gone.

GPS COORDINATES: N31°27.75' W110°58.08'
NEAREST TRAIL: South #12: Mexican Border Road

Camp Crittenden

Colonel Thomas L. Crittenden established his camp (which was never formally titled as a fort) on March 4, 1868. With Major Charles E. Norris serving as commanding officer, soldiers constructed adobe facilities for their compound. General George Stoneman diminished the camp to one infantry unit in 1870, probably because the larger force was not needed. By June 1872, top military officials commanded that Camp Crittenden be evacuated. A number of soldiers continued their posts until the following year in order to protect farmers against Indians. The camp closed on June 1, 1873.

GPS COORDINATES: N31°39.60' W110°41.84'
TRAIL: South #9: Canelo Hills Trail
MAP: Page 494

Camp Lowell (Cavalry Camp)

General C. R. Lowell never viewed the camp that bore his name because he died on May 21, 1862, in Cedar Creek, Virginia, before it was established. California military volunteers, under the leadership of Lieutenant Colonel West, established the post in September 1864.

After the camp was briefly abandoned, the military re-established it in August of 1866. At this time, all single officers boarded in nearby Tucson. Camp Lowell was eventually moved out of Tucson and relocated next to Rillito Creek. Adobe ruins from the camp can be viewed at Memorial Park in Tucson.

GPS COORDINATES: Unknown
TRAIL: None near Camp Lowell

Camp Rucker

The military initially constructed Camp Supply in 1878 to protect the region's early settlers. After the wrongful killing of six of Cochise's tribe members at Fort Bowie in 1861, the post also served as an important stronghold in an effort to subdue the warring Chiricahua Apaches. When the camp gained a post office in 1879, it was named Powers.

On the western side of the Chiricahua Mountains, Rucker Canyon, Long John Canyon, and Bruno Canyon all drain into the flood-prone White Water Canyon. In the late 1870s (the exact year varies according to different sources), White Water Canyon was the scene of a raging flood. Lieutenant John A. (Tony) Rucker, who was then in charge of a company of Indian scouts fighting against Victorio, was caught in the flood. One of the men in his party, Lieutenant Henley, mounted his horse and proceeded across the swelling wash. The fierce current first swept Henley away; Rucker followed and attempted to save his friend. Both men drowned, despite the courageous efforts of fellow travelers and accompanying scouts who also risked their lives trying to save the officers. After this unfortunate incident, the name of Camp Supply was changed to Camp Rucker and the canyon became known as Rucker Canyon. Camp Rucker officially closed in 1880, but it was used by the military every now and then for the next six years until Geronimo finally surrendered in 1886.

Now that the area was once again peaceful, the military left and a justice of the peace from Tombstone, "Colonel" Mike Gray, moved into the old adobe commissary building. He brought his cattle into the area and used the old camp as his ranch headquarters. Camp Rucker developed into a small settlement and the land changed hands a few times in the twentieth century. In 1970, Mrs. Ella Dana, the owner at the time, donated the land to the U.S. Forest Service.

GPS COORDINATES: Camp Rucker: N31°46.14' W109°23.19' (approximately)
Cemetery: N31°44.03' W109°29.29'

TRAIL: South #19: Tex Canyon Trail

MAP: Page 520

Camp Verde

Camp Verde (also called Camp Lincoln and Camp La Paz) is believed to be one of the oldest establishments situated on the Verde River. Captain Charles King immortalized the village (originally founded as Camp Lincoln in January 1864) as Camp Sandy in his novel *The Colonel's Daughter*. The town's title officially changed to Verde on November 23, 1868.

Camp Verde, 1900

GPS COORDINATES: N34°33.81' W111°51.22'

NEAREST TRAILS: Northeast #17: Goat Peak Trail and Northeast #27: Cedar Flat Road

Castle Dome City

Long before the Castle Dome Mines existed, Indians and Spaniards extracted minerals from the area. Ancient, worn trails in the desert record the paths used by these early miners to carry the ore to an old adobe furnace south of the Gila River. Mining activity increased dramatically in the Castle Dome region after 1863, when Conner and Jacob Snively established the Castle Dome Mining District. The company initially mined only silver, discarding the high-quality galena, which contained as much as 70 percent lead. The well-respected mining engineer, William P. Blake, was the first to discover the value of the region's copper-lead ores, and in 1864 he convinced investors from California to develop mines in the area. The result was a minor boom in the Castle Dome region.

To adequately work the mines at Castle Dome, a supply and shipping point was set up on the Colorado River, due west of the mining district. Known first as Castle Dome Landing and later as Castle Dome City, the new town was the first stop for steamboats coming from Yuma. The village had a store, post office, saloon, and hotel, and later workers built a small smelter. Boats transported the ore downriver to Yuma. A 17-mile railroad was surveyed east to the Colorado River, but construction never commenced. Many people traveled north from Yuma to attend celebrations and sports days in Castle Dome Landing. Mexican Independence Day in September was a particularly big occasion. In the 1880s, Castle Dome had a larger population than Yuma and almost won the honor of becoming the county's name. Today, Castle Dome City is immersed under the waters of Martinez Lake.

In the mid-1860s, a gold strike in central Arizona drew miners away to richer pickings around Wickenburg and Prescott. However, in the early 1870s, William B. Hooper and James M. Barney, both from Yuma, began shipping ore to San Francisco Bay smelters to process the lead. Although transportation was difficult and expensive, a fair profit from the rich ore was possible. They later built a small furnace on-site to process the ore themselves. In 1877, a group from San Francisco invested in the mines and began purchasing nearby claims. A few old prospectors realized the buyout was the perfect opportunity to discard their nearly exhausted claims. Several independent miners resisted the Californians' buyout efforts but finally gave in under extreme pressure.

Castle Dome, like most mining towns, was rowdy—the scene of fights and shootings. One incident in May 1881 began when an outlaw calling himself Blanco Flores murdered Rafael Gutierrez. Investigating officers quickly determined Blanco Flores to be the fugitive Florencia Sanchez. They offered a $50 reward for his capture. Sanchez evaded apprehension for a while by working on a ferry on the Colorado River. The guilty outlaw was inevitably recognized and shot to death while attempting to escape arrest.

Although it would never relive the wealth of its initial

boom, the Castle Dome region continued producing until the early twentieth century. In 1943, the Arizona Lead Company reactivated the mine and produced 60,000 tons of lead in three years, most of which created ammunition for World War II. In 1948, the mine changed hands again, and the Joplin Lead Company produced another 30,000 tons of lead by 1953.

Today the mine is privately owned and is the site of the Castle Dome Mines Museum.

GPS COORDINATES: N33°02.28' W114°10.50'

TRAIL: Central #4: McPherson Pass Trail

MAP: Page 349

Chinle

Chinle was a well-known Navajo trading post, but today it is better known for being the gateway to the breathtaking Canyon de Chelly. The name translates from Navajo to mean "the place where it flows from the canyon." Chinle was first established in 1882 when a tent was set up in order to conduct trade. A government school was opened nearby in 1910. The historic meeting between Kit Carson and the Navajo was also held near Chinle. Carson had just starved the Indians out of their defensible canyon during a relentless war of attrition. The two forces met, and the Navajo finally surrendered to Carson. Afterward the Indians were marched to the Pecos River Reservation in New Mexico on the infamous "Long Walk."

GPS COORDINATES: N36°09.25' W109°33.52'

TRAILS: Northeast #44: Fluted Rock Road and Northeast #45: Canyon de Chelly Trail

MAP: Pages 326–7 & 330–1

Chloride

As early as the 1840s men sought valuable minerals in the mountains around Chloride. In 1863, a group of volunteers from California stationed at Fort Mohave organized the Chloride Mining District (also known as the Sacramento District), but there was still no settlement. The captain at the fort would allow the soldiers time to work their own claims. Once the men were discharged, some raised funds from California investors and continued to work the mines in the area. However, the miners soon found the high cost of exporting the ore too cumbersome. That, coupled with the slaughter of four visiting mine owners by angry Hualapai Indians, caused the area to be abandoned in 1867.

Chloride, circa 1900

By 1870, another small prospecting group discovered rich silver veins in the district. Armed with a peace treaty with the Indians, this group began mining in earnest. Gaining its name from the silver chloride most were seeking, the town had its own post office by 1873. Chloride increased in both population and popularity and even battled for the distinction of county seat in 1873. It lost the contest, and the post office closed its doors in 1875. But Chloride was destined to return before long. The post office reopened in 1893 when investor Theodore B. Comstock sank $100,000 into the Elkhart Mine and Mill. This rush was the biggest Arizona had seen since that of Tombstone in 1879–80 and raised Chloride's population from 700 to 2,000.

With the mining business back in full swing, a railway was needed to expedite production. When Miss Mary Krider drove a gilded spike into the ground on August 16, 1899, the tracks of the Arizona & Utah Railway were completed. The Atchison, Topeka & Santa Fe Railroad Company also raced day and night to build a track connecting nearby Kingman to Chloride at the same time. Service continued until 1935. The Tennessee, Diana, Mollie Gibson, Merrimac, and Elkhart Mines shipped not only silver but also gold, lead, copper, turquoise, barium, and zinc to the processing plant. As many as 75 mines were active during the period from 1900 to 1920.

Tales of fortunes won and lost were as common in Chloride as in other mining communities across the country. The *San Francisco Chronicle* recounts one such tale—that of Andy Flynn, a railroad brakeman, cowboy, and prospector for 11 years. Flynn staked his own claim, the Mollie Gibson, after working in the silver mines in nearby White Hills. With a borrowed $50, the hopeful prospector began to inspect his claim. After six weeks, Flynn ran out of both funds and food. After unsuccessful attempts to solicit funds in Chloride, a desperate Flynn walked 25 miles to Kingman. No one was interested in buying his claim for $100. Out of options, Flynn took a job on the railroad until he had enough financial stability to return to his diggings one month later. This time, after some blasting, the miner surprisingly discovered promising-looking ore. Much to Flynn's disbelief the ore was assayed at $600 a ton. Within days, the once desperate prospector was offered $20,000 for his claim. Flynn scoffed at that offer, realizing he had struck it rich. One month later Flynn sold just half of his claim for $75,000 and continued to extract ore at the rate of nearly $3,000 a month.

Chloride served as a distribution center for surrounding mines and ranches as far away as Eldorado Canyon. A number of stores, the weekly *Arizona Arrow,* and more than a dozen saloons all testified to the town's success. The Tennessee Mine successfully carried Chloride through its boom between the late 1800s and early 1900s. By 1948, the Tennessee Mine had produced more than $7.5 million and boasted the deepest mine in Mohave County. When the mines finally closed in the late 1940s, Chloride began to wind down.

Not satisfied with the status of ghost town, Chloride has managed to attract residents who enjoy a relaxed approach to life as well as businesses that promote its colorful past. In 1966, Roy Purcell, a student from the University of Utah, decided to turn on, tune in, and drop out of college. He took a job with the Duval Mine in Mineral Park. Roy was a young hippie searching for answers and he expressed his creativity by painting murals throughout the town. An old miner supplied him with automotive paint, and Roy took to living in a cave during the summer of 1966 when he painted his now-famous scenes. The somewhat odd but provocative murals led to a commission from the Kingman Museum, and Roy Purcell became a full-time artist. Purcell returned to Chloride in 1976 to touch up the murals, which are currently one of the town's biggest attractions.

GPS COORDINATES: N35°24.80' W114°11.91'
TRAIL: Northwest #28: Packsaddle Mountain Loop Trail
MAP: Page 205

Clarkdale

William A. Clark once claimed that he would be the richest man in Montana as well as a U.S. senator. He succeeded in achieving both goals, and in 1912 he also established the town of Clarkdale. Five miles away from and 2,000 feet below the large mining town of Jerome, Clarkdale served as a quintessential company town. Under Clark's ownership, United Verde Copper Company provided a village for its employees who worked in the smelter and nearby mines. Clarkdale residents enjoyed swimming pools, tennis courts, a clubhouse, and a golf course, all under the strict supervision of United Verde. A large Hispanic population and others who did not approve of such strict company surveillance resided in a nearby "patio town."

The company constructed a narrow-gauge railroad that kept the mill constantly supplied. Later, a standard-gauge railway was built for shipping ore, and by 1940, the mines had earned more than $80 million. By the 1970s, Clarkdale was all but a ghost town. However, it has yet to die. Residents who work at a nearby cement factory inhabit the town, and the Verde Canyon Railroad serves as a major tourist attraction for the area.

GPS COORDINATES: N34°46.27' W112°03.44'
TRAIL: Northeast #19: Bill Gray–Buckboard Road
MAP: Page 269

Clarkston

Clarkston's founder, Sam Clark, proved to be a shrewd businessman. He not only named the town after himself, but also owned all the property, which he rented to the settlers. Despite its proximity to both Ajo and New Cornelia, Clarkston was more populated than its rival towns by 1916.

The lack of a sufficient water supply turned out to be a major obstacle for Clarkston and its residents. Neighboring New Cornelia stubbornly refused to sell water to its competitor. Until a deeper shaft was drilled to find a natural water source, water had to be shipped in from various locations. Soft-drink stands and bottled water became hot items in the town.

At its peak, Clarkston could boast of many big city luxuries; it had a movie theater, pool hall, two bathhouses, a weekly paper called *Copper News,* and even a music shop. The town's population soared to an amazing 1,500. In 1918, President Woodrow Wilson's popularity ranked high with the locals. In fact, they asked for the town's name to be changed to either Wilson or Woodrow. When both requests were denied, townspeople compromised on Rowood. The Rowood post office served Clarkston for just over a decade before being moved to the nearby town of Gibson. Clarkston's continued shortage of water plagued the town until the very end. In 1931, a fiery blaze destroyed the town and led to its ghost town status.

GPS COORDINATES: N32°22.14' W112°50.72'
TRAIL: South #3: El Camino del Diablo Trail
MAP: Pages 478–9

Cochran

Cochran served as a mining camp for Copper Butte and Silver Bullet Mining Company workers in the early 1900s. The Santa Fe, Prescott & Phoenix Railroad also stopped at the town that once sat on the south side of the Gila River. Named for its postmaster, John S. Cochran, the small settlement supported a population of about 100, a general merchandise store, a boardinghouse, and several businesses.

Cochran established its post office in January 1905 (though some sources say the post office was established in 1904) but closed it 10 years later. The town of Cochran has long since disappeared from the landscape, but the famous and much photographed row of five charcoal kilns, or coke ovens, still stands on the north side of the river. No one knows exactly when the structures were built. The Pinal Consolidated Mining Company probably constructed the ovens around 1882 in order to turn mesquite into charcoal. This fuel source could then be used to fire the smelters in Cochran. However, according to William Fred Jenkins, who homesteaded on the banks of the Gila River in the early 1900s, the kilns were built in the 1850s by Scottish miners, and they were not kilns at all but rather smelters used to process ore.

The ovens' owner modified them in the 1980s with the idea of using the unique structures as guest cottages. Windows were added in the back, the roofs repaired, and concrete was poured for floors. One of the ovens even had an added mezzanine level. Currently, they are abandoned.

GPS COORDINATES: Town: N33°06.59' W111°08.96'
Coke ovens: N33°06.28' W111°09.86'
TRAILS: Central #44: Battleaxe Trail and Central #43: Cochran Coke Ovens Trail
MAP: Pages 457 & 459

Congress

Two old cemeteries are among the few remaining clues that a thriving town once stood in this area. Dennis May founded Congress (also called Congress City) in 1884 after finding gold and staking a claim. A few years later, an eccentric Mississippi steamboat owner named "Diamond Joe" Reynolds purchased May's mine and the town property, believing in their potential.

Congress grew under the watchful care of Diamond Joe. The town was divided into two separate sections: "Mill town" housed the mine, offices, mill, hospital, and residences; "lower

Congress Mine, 1894

town" served as the commercial district with saloons, restaurants, stores, two churches, and a school. By 1893, the Santa Fe, Prescott & Phoenix Railroad passed within 3 miles of town, making it easy and affordable to ship ore.

In 1891, Diamond Joe died at his lavish home in Congress. Three years later, a group of investors including a Phoenix banker, two Chicago businessmen, and the mine's superintendent purchased Congress Mine. The new ownership came on the heels of the big gold boom, and Congress's future indeed looked golden. Congress Consolidated Railroad, completed in 1899, made the shipment of ore between the mine and Congress Junction considerably faster. The mine employed at least 450 men, and the population continued to grow. As icing on the cake, President William McKinley received a flag-waving greeting when he visited Congress in 1900.

Congress was not entirely immune to tragedy. A severe lack of water led to devastating fires in 1898 and 1900, which destroyed a considerable amount of lower town. To combat the constant drought, families were forced to roll 50-gallon whiskey barrels down a steep hill to Congress's only water faucet. Crime, however, was not as much of a problem. The story of a stagecoach robbery just outside of town was recorded. The inexperienced crooks asked for the six passengers' belongings and quickly made their getaway. If they had bothered to search their victims, the robbers would have left the scene $1,000 richer.

Most mining towns disappeared when the ore ran out. By 1910, miners began to vacate Congress in favor of richer mines. A few stayed on to work in the mine dumps, but by 1938 the post office closed and Congress grew quiet.

GPS COORDINATES: N34°9.71' W112°51.11'
TRAIL: Central #22: Stanton Ghost Town Trail
MAP: Page 397

Constellation

The Monte Cristo Mine and the town of Constellation were essentially one in the same thing. The mine was promoted by Phoenix hardware merchant Ezra W. Thayer for a longer period than it actually operated. He actively pursued investors between 1912 and 1920 but never operated the mine himself. Thayer eventually sold out to an oil promoter. The Monte Cristo went through a number of owners, none of whom proved to be very successful.

Constellation's post office was established on April 29, 1901. Author Frank Crampton lived in the small town prior to 1910 and later wrote of his experiences. However, it wasn't until the mid-1920s that the mine finally began production and a small camp of approximately 250 people formed. The town had a two-story saloon, gambling den, stores, and a dance hall. Besides the Monte Cristo, other mines worked by the townsfolk included the Oro Grande, Black Rock, and the Gold Bar.

GPS COORDINATES: N34°03.90' W112°35.01'
TRAIL: Central #20: Buckhorn Creek Trail
MAP: Pages 390–1

Copper Creek Mining District

In 1863, the Yellow Bird Claim began drawing prospectors to what would become the Copper Creek Mining District. Although miners hoped for an abundance of silver, copper was destined to be the dominant ore. By 1910, the town was at its zenith, with three active mining companies: Copper Creek, Calumet & Arizona, and Minnesota Arizona Mining Company. The town thrived; there were 500 people, 50 buildings, a resident physician, and a post office. The Copper Creek Stage Line transported people to and from the area.

Around 1900, Roy Sibley and his wife, Belle, moved to Copper Creek. Roy managed the Minnesota Arizona Mining Company and Belle eventually became the town's first postmaster in 1907. But the Sibleys' legacy would derive from the 20-room mansion they constructed in 1908. Stone masonry, polished oak floors, picture windows, and full-length mirrors adorned the couple's ornate home. Certainly this home served as the hub of Copper Creek's social activities, as many mining investors were entertained there. The Sibleys did not inhabit their luxurious home for long and left the area in 1910.

Martin E. Tew bought and reorganized the mines to form the Copper State Mining Company. However, by 1917 all the mines in the district were closed. Tew, a nature lover and poet, transformed the property into the Monte Bonito Ranch. He wrote poetry, which he left on the trees for passersby to read.

In 1933, the Arizona Molybdenum Corporation took an interest in Copper Creek. During this time, locals were outraged when the *San Diego Union* reported Copper Creek as a wild and crime-ridden town. The mine closed again in 1942, at which time the post office also suspended service after more than 35 years.

Set beneath the shadows of the Galiuro Mountains, Copper Creek and the surrounding area has its share of history and intrigue. In 1918, a shoot-out took place between a posse and brothers Tom and John Power. After his oldest son Charley was turned down when he tried to enlist in the armed forces during World War I, Jeff Power (Charley, Tom, and John's father) decided that none of his sons would participate in the conflict. Consequently, the two younger Power brothers were charged with evading the draft, and four lawmen were dispatched to bring them in. The posse surrounded the Powers' cabin. In the gunfight that followed, three of the four lawmen perished, and Jeff Power lay dead in the cabin.

One of Arizona's greatest manhunts followed. The U.S. Cavalry captured the two Power brothers and family friend Tom Sisson just south of the Mexican border. Local newspapers had already convicted the Power boys; public opinion was against them and the trial was merely a formality. Given life sentences, the two were sent to state prison in Florence. The brothers always maintained their innocence, stating that members of the posse had shot and killed their father without identifying themselves. The Power brothers said they simply reacted in self-defense.

Despite fervent pleadings from the men's relatives at hearings, parole boards refused to release the three men. Sisson died in prison in 1956. After serving 42 years (the longest sentences in Arizona history at the time), the Power brothers were realeased five years after Sisson's death. The brothers spent most of their remaining years in the Galiuro Mountains area near the town of Klondyke. Years after this tragedy unfolded, many still believe that the entire incident had little to do with draft evasion and more to do with the authorities who did not especially care for the Power family; some even think that the authorities acted so strongly because they were interested in the Powers' mining claims.

GPS COORDINATES: N32°46.06' W110°28.51'
TRAIL: South #29: Copper Creek Mining District Trail
MAP: Page 549

Cordes

The history of Cordes follows a legacy of love, pursuit of the American dream, and a hard-working family of the West. A young German immigrant arrived in New York City in 1869 where he met and fell in love with a fellow German newcomer. Determined to find his fortune in the West, John Henry Cordes set out on a journey that finally led him to Yuma Crossing in 1877. After sending for his love, John Cordes married Elise Schrimpfh in Phoenix in 1880. Three years later, the two, now accompanied by their son, Charles, purchased a stop on the California & Arizona Stage Company for $769.43 and began to put down roots.

John originally petitioned for Antelope Station to be the name of his post office. However, the name was already in use, so Cordes was chosen instead. Although Cordes was not a mining town itself, several nearby mines quickly led to the need for a supply depot and banking center. Cordes also became a regular stop for summer and winter sheep drives, for which John constructed pens, a shearing corral, and dipping troughs to accommodate the herders.

Chas Cordes General Merchandise Store, circa 1915

A larger population warranted an easier means of transportation to and from Cordes. The Bradshaw Mountain Railroad solved this problem when it established Cordes Station in the early 1900s. The train also created happy memories for the town's residents. The Cordes family held Fourth of July picnics during which the train delivered a 100-pound block of ice used to make homemade ice cream.

Time marched on, and in 1908, college graduate Charles Cordes took over the family business. The eldest son went to great lengths to develop the station, renovating the old building and adjacent home. A new store, saloon, and warehouse were added to the property in 1914. Another generation passed, and in 1938, Henry Cordes, Charles's oldest son, inherited the business from his father.

A fire in 1940 nearly meant ruin for the long-running station, but thanks to the quick thinking of local miners, there were no losses for the Cordes family. Although the post office shut its doors in 1944, the town lived on until the 1950s when the Black Canyon Highway bypassed it. The Cordes men, anticipating new opportunities, purchased land on the new road and opened a gas station and restaurant. The gas station ceased operation in 1973, but the buildings, along with an abandoned residence and century-old barn, can still be viewed. The Cordes family, whose enterprises were a true testament to the American dream, continues to live in the area.

GPS COORDINATES: N34°18.19' W112°9.97'
NEAREST TRAIL: Central #30: Bloody Basin Road

Crown King

In 1875, a schoolteacher discovered ore and set up what would later be called Crowned King Mine in the heart of the Bradshaw Mountains. Traded for a saddle to O. F. Place, the mine went through several name changes including Red Rock, Buckeye, and finally Crowned (or Crown) King. By the 1880s, a calm mining settlement existed, mainly because of the mining company's discouragement of heavy drinking.

When the post office was established in June 1888, it officially branded the town as Crown King. By this time, the fairly young town boasted 500 buildings, electricity, a phone, and a new postmaster named George P. Harrington. The Illinois banker joined forces with Place and N. C. Sheckles as partners in the Crown King Mining Company. The gold boom of the 1890s served the town well as a Prescott paper exclaimed the ore "runs $80,000 to the ton," and Crown King was declared the richest strike in the history of Arizona. Although these claims proved to be exaggerated, the mine did prosper and produced an estimated $1.5 to $2 million in its lifetime.

Two obstacles lay in the way of the Crown King Mine's success. Extraction of the ore proved so difficult that large amounts were being discarded. Another difficulty was the expense of shipping ore to Prescott. On pack trains, the enormous cost of each load usually ran about $21.50 per ton. When the Prescott & Eastern Railroad completed its line to Crown King, the transportation dilemma was solved.

Because of an ownership dispute that resulted in a lawsuit,

Crown King Mine closed operations in 1901. Despite this major employment drop, the town did not surrender. Workers moved on to nearby mines, and in 1904, Murphy's Impossible Railroad provided residents and merchants with another form of transportation. As the name suggests, the winding track followed such snakelike curves that many deemed the route unnavigable by rail.

By the 1920s, the Impossible Railroad ran its course and the motor vehicle was the new form of transportation. With the rails removed and wooden planks laid in their stead, Model-T cars carefully treaded the towering, narrow roads to and from Crown King. One wrong negotiation could send travelers plummeting hundreds of feet to their deaths. Dances in town were usually sober affairs, with many attendees driving the treacherous roads home in the wee hours of the night.

The old saloon at Crown King remains a popular watering hole

Pack mules carried an old saloon, piece by piece, to Crown King in 1916; the same saloon still serves thirsty customers today. Miners are long gone from the area, and summer vacationers now make up the majority of the population. But Crown King has managed to survive throughout the years by one means or another. Tourists flock to rental cabins and camping spots, trying to savor the atmosphere of days gone by.

GPS COORDINATES: N34°12.32' W112°20.21'
TRAIL: Central #24: Senator Highway
MAP: Page 402–3

Cyclopic

Three prospectors, Robert Patterson, Sol Rowe, and a man named Glenn, set up the small gold mining settlement of Cyclopic in the early 1890s. In 1896, the trio leased the site to a company from Seattle that continued to work it profitably for many years. Stanley Bagg, an early miner, named the town after the mythological beast Cyclops. A post office was established in 1905, and the town and mine continued until their closures in 1917.

GPS COORDINATES: N35°47.00' W114°14.74'
TRAIL: Northwest #29: White Hills Trail
MAP: Page 209

DeNoon

James DeNoon Reymert established DeNoon in 1889 as the milling spot for his mining town, Reymert, a few miles away. Silver mining was only one of Reymert's business ventures. A native of Norway, he served as a lawyer and newspaper editor of the *Pinal Drill* while in Arizona. His small camp grew quickly and provided a general store and two saloons for its 150 residents. The DeNoon post office opened its doors in March 1890. However, with the falling prices of ore, it closed only a year later. Today, many old foundations and the site of an ancient smelter can be viewed.

GPS COORDINATES: N33°13.28' W111°13.84' (approximately)
TRAIL: Central #41: Box Canyon Trail
MAP: Page 452

Duquesne

The tiny settlement of Washington Camp survived for about 20 years before the establishment of Duquesne in 1889, although it was not until this time that both towns reached their peaks. Pittsburgh mining mogul George Westinghouse developed Duquesne as the headquarters for his mining and reduction company in the area. By 1889, both towns were home to about 1,000 people each and measured only 1 mile apart in distance. If the stories are true, Westinghouse himself inhabited Duquesne for a time, living in an elaborate mansion complete with running water. But the copper boom of the 1880s proved to be short-lived and both towns met their demise by the early 1900s.

GPS COORDINATES: N31°22.24' W110°41.12'
TRAIL: South #12: Mexican Border Road
MAP: Pages 502–3

East Verde Settlement/Mazatzal Wilderness Area

Native Americans have used the Mazatzal Wilderness Area more or less continuously for the past 5,000 years. Since the 1500s the Yavapai Indians utilized the land for hunting, food, and resources. Tonto Apaches inhabited the area from approximately 1700 to the late 1880s, when the American army confined Native Americans to reservations. There are two translations of the name Mazatzal (locally mispronounced "madda-zell" but more correctly pronounced "mah'zat-zall"). Modern Aztecs define the word as "place of deer." Although deer certainly roam the Mazatzal Wilderness Area, there is no record of the Aztecs ever occupying the area. An alternative translation is "empty space between" in the Paiute language.

In the 1870s, settlers ventured to the area, bringing horses, sheep, and cattle. They founded a couple of small mining camps and a Mormon village known as East Verde Settlement, just east of the present-day wilderness boundary. Mormons settled Mazatzal City in 1878 near the present-day location of Doll Baby Ranch. Although they planted orchards and built a sawmill and a dairy, the pioneers abandoned the site in 1882, possibly because of harrassment by Indians. The group moved on to the area near Strawberry and Pine. Early records show a variant spelling of Mazatzal City. Mat-a-zell, as it was called, is thought to be an Apache word for "barren" or "bleak." Others believe the name derived from the Apache word *mazatzark,* meaning "space between."

The forest service established the Mazatzal Primitive Area in May 1938, which was declared a wilderness area in June 1940. Further land was added in 1984, giving the wilderness area its present size.

GPS COORDINATES: East Verde Settlement 34°13.35' W111°29.29'
Mazatzal City: N34°13.34' W111°28.11' (approximately)
TRAIL: Central #34: Mazatzal Wilderness Trail
MAP: Page 432

Flagstaff

Far from a ghost town, Flagstaff (at the base of the San Francisco Mountains) reigns as one of the largest cities in northern Arizona, with a population of 53,000. Flagstaff's elevation, 6,900 feet, pales in comparison to its neighboring dormant volcano of 12,633 feet. With a combination of entrancing scenery, four-season weather, and a bustling economy, Flagstaff remains an ever-expanding community.

There are several versions of the tale that relates the origin of the city's name. City officials endorse the most common. In June 1876, immigrants left Boston and journeyed to the region. The group stopped, stripped a small pine tree of its branches, and erected an American flag at the top. Around this self-made monument, the patriotic assembly celebrated Independence Day. Perhaps because of its glorious beginnings, Flagstaff was destined for prosperity.

In 1882, the Atlantic & Pacific Railroad (which was merged into the Santa Fe Railroad) constructed a camp, the first true settlement, and in 1894 the town was incorporated. Even early inhabitants realized the sacred value of the area's ancient Indian ruins. Local lumber tycoon Michael Riordan began excavating artifacts in the late 1800s and continued for many years. By 1891, other, more destructive relic seekers vandalized the sites with their blasting and digging. Luckily, the San Francisco Mountain Forest Preserve has protected the ruins since 1904.

Today, Flagstaff's economy thrives on several industries, including logging, manufacturing, transportation, and tourism. The science community and related industry also have a strong presence with the Lowell and U.S. Naval Observatories. The planet Pluto was first viewed through a telescope at Flagstaff's Lowell Observatory. Tourists flock to the city during all seasons of the year. Several national monuments—Sunset Crater, Walnut Canyon, and Wupatki Canyon—call Flagstaff home. When it snows, skiing enthusiasts engulf Arizona Snowbowl, the town's largest ski resort.

Flagstaff boasts a stable economic base, a steady tourist draw, and breathtaking scenery. With such appealing attributes, the city should continue to grow for many years to come.

Flagstaff, circa 1900

GPS COORDINATES: N35°11.89' W111°39.05'
NEAREST TRAIL: Northeast #7: Schultz Pass Trail

Fort Apache

General William Sherman suggested the camp originally named Camp Thomas be changed to Camp Apache. This alteration proved appropriate considering the numerous incidents the camp would later have with Native Americans. The settlement housed a collection of buildings including log cabin barracks, officer quarters, and a hospital. On April 5, 1879, Camp Apache earned the title of fort.

Cavalry leaving Fort Apache on patrol in 1896

During the attempted arrest of an Apache medicine man, Apache army scouts revolted and instigated a rebellion against the troops. For the next three years, Geronimo and his followers led attacks on the military camp and killed many men. After a period of brief but false peace, Geronimo once again struck against his white adversaries and battled for another year. However, on September 4, 1886, the Apache leader surrendered to the army, and peace was finally attained.

After Geronimo and his followers were interned in Florida, activity at the fort greatly diminished with a few insignificant exceptions. A brief uproar during the 1903 miners' strike in Morenci required the attention of the troops. The fort closed on May 3, 1922, because it was no longer needed, and the soldiers relocated to Fort Huachuca.

The Indian Service acquired the property in 1923 and many original structures remained until a fire destroyed them in 1992. Today, General Crook's temporary field headquarters serves as a museum for the fort's relics.

GPS COORDINATES: N33°47.44' W109°59.29'
TRAIL: None near Fort Apache

Fort Bowie

In 1858, a frustrated Butterfield Overland Stage president pleaded with the federal government to send troops to Apache Pass. Apache Indian attacks caused the man's anxiety, and he closed operations in the area before soldiers arrived in 1862.

When troops finally arrived, Captain L. E. Mitchell

Fort Bowie, circa 1880

selected the camp's site on the eastern side of Apache Pass mainly because of its proximity to a natural spring. This important source provided much needed water to the region, and local Apache Indians guarded it closely. Until 1866 only volunteer troops inhabited the camp. By 1868, the settlement called Fort Bowie was run by regular soldiers.

Apache unrest plagued those in the military camp. In 1861, during a meeting with Cochise, Lieutenant George Bascom and his troops arrested him and several others for allegedly kidnapping a child and stealing some cattle. Ultimately, Cochise escaped and Bascom killed the others. The Indian sought revenge on the white man for the deaths and killed several Americans. Only one day later, a band of natives attacked a traveling wagon train, murdering 14 unfortunate passengers (see page 74). For the next decade, struggle between U.S. troops and Apache Indians continued until a peace treaty in 1872 temporarily halted the fighting.

Much to the Indians' chagrin, the U.S. government ordered Apache tribes to their new home, the San Carlos Reservation, in 1874. Once again, friction between the two forces increased. Between 1885 and 1886, Geronimo's crusade against the army caused the most activity in the fort's history when it served as a rendezvous point for soldiers. After the Apache leader surrendered in September 1886, action declined significantly, and the camp was closed in October 1894.

In 1911, auctioneers sold the land to local farmers for $1.25 to $2.50 per acre, and ranchers used the timber from the buildings for their homes. The federal government declared Fort Bowie a national historic site in 1964 and the ruins are currently maintained by the National Park Service.

GPS COORDINATES: N32°08.67' W109°26.11'
NEAREST TRAIL: South #21: Hands Pass Trail

Fort Buchanan

The First U.S. Dragoons established Fort Buchanan in 1857 in an attempt to protect local settlers. The camp, between the present towns of Patagonia and Sonoita, rested on the Sonoita River bank. Reportedly, the Indians had repeatedly stolen the camp's sheep and cattle, creating numerous retrieving sessions for the soldiers. The men recovered most of the livestock, though the Indians were not as easy to locate. The fort's inhabitants felt their presence, however. None ventured from their homes after dark without a loaded gun for fear of an Indian attack. Inactivity spurred an order from the Department of New Mexico for Fort Buchanan to be destroyed. On July 21, 1861, the camp was reduced to ashes.

GPS COORDINATES: N31°39.39' W110°42.46'
NEAREST TRAIL: South #9: Canelo Hills Trail

Fort Defiance

As its name reveals, Fort Defiance was given the mission of restraining the local Indians from waging battles against the settlers. Established on September 18, 1851, Fort Defiance functioned as the first permanent military post in the Arizona Territory. Commanding officer Major Electus Backus led his troops through the country's first pacification campaign against the Navajo Indians.

In a true act of defiance, 2,000 Indians attacked the fort on April 30, 1860. One hundred and fifty soldiers retaliated and managed to survive the battle. Afterward, a large number of reinforcements arrived at the camp, hoping to prevent further aggression. Six years later, in 1868, the military closed Fort Defiance and transformed it into the Navajo Indian Agency, a role it still serves today.

Fort Defiance, 1933

GPS COORDINATES: N35°44.58' W109°04.43'
NEAREST TRAIL: Northeast #40: Defiance Plateau Trail

Fort Goodwin

Fort Goodwin, which lay 120 miles northeast of Tucson, was named for the first territorial governor of Arizona, John N. Goodwin. Like many military camps of this era, Fort Goodwin had the primary goal of protecting settlers from the Indians, in this case the Apaches.

The soldiers at Fort Goodwin were not known for their good health. Malaria-infected mosquitoes caused an epidemic that lasted throughout most of the camp's existence. With only about 20 of 250 soldiers in reasonably good health, General George Stoneman ordered Fort Goodwin to close in 1870. Five years later, soldiers at Fort Thomas salvaged the fort's adobe materials in order to construct their own barracks.

GPS COORDINATES: N33°5.29' W110°3.48' (approximately)
NEAREST TRAIL: South #25: Tripp Canyon Road

Fort Grant, circa 1900

Fort Grant

The military established Camp Grant (originally called Fort Breckenridge) in November 1865. By 1866 the property had 24 buildings, but heavy flooding demolished 20 of those later that same year. The unfavorable environmental conditions forced most soldiers to live in makeshift tents. In 1870, a number of Pinal and Aravaipa Apache Indians were relocated to a reservation on the property. Volatile Tucson residents, accompanied by 100 Pima Indians, attacked the peaceful Apaches in 1871. In the end, more than 90 Apache men, women, and children perished—mostly women and children. This tragic incident would come to be known as the Camp Grant Massacre. Extremely poor living conditions warranted the closure of Fort Grant in 1872, and the troops were moved upriver near Mount Graham.

GPS COORDINATES: N32°37.48' W109°56.62'
NEAREST TRAIL: South #24: Swift Trail

Fort Huachuca

What began as a temporary camp survives today as an active military installation. Fort Huachuca, a cavalry post founded in March 1877, played a prominent role in subduing the last significant Indian group living outside reservations in the United States. Led by Geronimo, the Chiricahua Apaches moved into Mexico and were pursued by the cavalry who were stationed at the fort. One of the cavalymen at the fort in the late 1870s was Ed Schieffelin. He set out from Fort Huachuca late in 1877 and by February 1878, had already discovered the silver vein that would lead to the founding of Tombstone.

Fort Huachuca, 1884

The post also served as headquarters for the Buffalo Soldiers, the name given by Native Americans to black soldiers (see page 76). The post was the center of operations for the army's four all-black regiments: the 9th and 10th Cavalry Regiments, and the 24th and 25th Infantry Regiments.

Because of heavy rains, the camp needed more solid, permanent structures for its inhabitants. Officials changed its title from camp to fort in 1882 in order to receive additional building funds. More recently, the fort has been used as a proving ground for newly developed technology from the Signal Corps. However, throughout the camp's history, its goals have been to guard the border of the United States. Although the technology has advanced, the fort's mission remains the same.

GPS COORDINATES: N31°33.30' W110°20.73'
NEAREST TRAIL: South #17: Carr Canyon Trail

Fort Lowell

Originally called the Tucson Supply Depot, the camp that later became Fort Lowell was moved outside of Tucson and established as a cavalry post in 1866. Its chief purposes were to patrol the border and monitor the native Indians. The post started small but grew steadily until its peak in 1886, when it had 18 officers and 239 soldiers. During this time, soldiers renovated the once-plain adobe structures by adding porches and shutters to the buildings.

Occupants at the camp also took time to socialize with the Tucson civilians. Frequent dances, concerts, and baseball games occupied the soldiers' time. However, after the campaign against the Apaches ceased, activity for the camp was scarce and it closed in 1891. A museum branch of the Arizona Historical Society was opened at the site in 1963. In 1978, the Fort Lowell Multiple Resource Area entered into the national register. Fort Lowell State Park stands 7 miles northeast of downtown Tucson.

GPS COORDINATES: N32°15.62' W110°52.39'
TRAIL: None near Fort Lowell

Fort McDowell

Established on the banks of the Verde River in 1865, Fort McDowell was also called Camp Verde or Camp Green. Nestled in the heart of the desert, Fort McDowell proved so hot in the summers that soldiers carried their beds outside to sleep under the stars. Its purpose—like that of many military camps of the day—was to control the local tribes: the Yavapai and Apache Indians. In 1866, the post was specified a camp, but not until 12 years later did it earn the status of fort. With the Indians pacified, Fort McDowell was closed in 1890. Its 25,688 acres were allocated by the Department of the Interior for an Indian school.

GPS COORDINATES: N33°38.29' W111°40.58'
NEAREST TRAIL: Central #36: El Oso Road

Fort Misery

There are several stories about this site, which is not a military fort but a lonely cabin in the woods. One story states that a woman nicknamed Virgin Mary provided board for

Fort Misery, circa 1910

the area's first miners in the cabin. Another claims that a stern judge named Howard held court there and caused grief for his subjects. The last simply states that Al Francis, who hauled ore from the Oro Bella to the railroad in Crown King, built the old cabin. Al jokingly referred to his home as Fort Misery and the name stuck.

GPS COORDINATES: N34°08.40' W112°21.96'
TRAIL: Central #26: Crown King Backroad
MAP: Page 410

Fort Mohave

In the 1850s, Mojave Indians saw their land along the Colorado River slowly being settled by white emigrants. Because of this encroachment on their land, the Mojave took to the offensive and attacked survey parties (such as the Sitgreaves and Whipple expeditions). In 1857, Edward Beale requested that a military post be established along the southern Colorado River to protect incoming white settlers. However, it was not until the Mojave decimated a wagon party in 1858 that the War Department decided to follow through on the fort.

Colonel William Hoffman was sent into the area, and he searched for a location on the Mohave River to set up a camp; but finding only a dried river, he settled on the Colorado River at Beale's Crossing. A rustic camp was established with dirt-floored adobe shacks that didn't even have doors. The post trader, Peter Brady, established a small news sheet called

Fort Mojave, circa 1900

Mohave Dog Star. Although a tiny paper taken up mainly as a diversion from the day-to-day rigor, this publication is thought to be the first in northern Arizona.

Because of the Civil War, troops abandoned the fort in 1861. Fearing that the Confederate Army would take over the forts in Arizona, officials had Fort Mohave burned to the ground. A rumor persists that says before the evacuation, Brady hid 300 books, personal journals, official records, and whiskey within the walls of the camp's buildings. No one has ever proven or disproven the rumor. Although the fort reopened as Camp Mohave in 1863, it permanently ceased operations in 1890 when it was turned over to the Indian Service. The buildings were eventually torn down in 1942.

GPS COORDINATES: N35°02.56' W114°37.23'
NEAREST TRAIL: Northwest #23: Moss Mine Trail

Fort Thomas

After the debacle of Fort Goodwin (in which a number of soldiers became ill from malaria-infected mosquitoes) and its horrendous location, military officials assured themselves a second occurrence of the disaster would not happen. Troops at Camp Thomas were given absolutely no funds to build on the

Fort Thomas, 1881

new site, located only a few miles from the old Fort Goodwin. Even the commanding officer and his family conceded to living in a two-room adobe hut. In 1878, the camp relocated to present-day Fort Thomas, 5 miles upriver. Not until 1882 did Camp Thomas receive the designation of fort. A year later, Fort Thomas finally received funds to improve its buildings. The campaign against Geronimo ended in 1886, and the post was abandoned five years later.

GPS COORDINATES: N33°02.24' W109°57.84'
NEAREST TRAIL: South #25: Tripp Canyon Road

Fort Whipple

Fort Whipple is located 1 mile northeast of present-day Prescott. The site was known previously as Camp Clark and is also referred to as Prescott and Whipple Barracks. Troops occupied the new site on May 18, 1864, but it was eight years before the poor housing conditions were corrected. New log cabins were constructed; yet when the wood shrank, it left large gaps in the supposedly improved walls. The fort had a different name by 1902: Fort Whipple II. When the camp was abandoned in 1913, the Public Health

Arizona Territorial Infantry at Fort Whipple, circa 1898

Service took it over. Today, a veterans' administrative hospital occupies the land.
GPS COORDINATES: N34°33.25' W112°27.17'
NEAREST TRAIL: Central #24: Senator Highway

Fortuna

For a large number of people who ventured across the desert during the gold rush, life ended prematurely. Such was the fate of many migrating mine workers and their families who tried to reach Fortuna. The 150-mile stretch of desert trail they traversed was aptly named El Camino del Diablo, or the Devil's Highway.

The story of Fortuna begins when three men, Charles W. Thomas, William H. Holbert, and Laurent Albert, discovered gold in the Gila Mountains in 1894. They sold their claims about a year later to Charles D. Lane for $150,000. Lane, a financier from San Francisco, set up La Fortuna Gold Mining and Milling Company in 1896. La Fortuna housed anywhere from 80 to 100 mine laborers (primarily Mexicans and white Americans) and their families. There was a hotel, many saloons, and a freight line that linked Fortuna with Blaisdell on the Southern Pacific Railroad. The mining camp even had a hospital at one point. One problem for the camp was the lack of water in the dry Sonora Desert. However, a 12-mile pipeline and a 100-horsepower engine were put together to pump water in from the Gila River. Prostitutes and gamblers regularly made the trip down from Yuma (usually on or just after the day the miners were paid), and fights were common. The saloon did a roaring trade. The water in Fortuna supposedly tasted so wretched that the miners turned to stronger drinks.

In 1899, a cyanide treatment plant was constructed to treat the accumulated tailings, yielding another $5 per ton. One problem with the mine was that the vein was erratic and the ore was contained around an intersection of two short veins. In 1900, the productive vein was lost on a fault line and only a small segment was found after further exploration. But between 1896 and 1904, more than $2.5 million in bullion was sent from the Fortuna Mine to the Selby smelter in California's San Francisco Bay area. The gold was sent off from the mines in huge bars weighing as much as 400 pounds and worth about $115,000.

The Fortuna Mine had a few brief resurgences of activity since 1904, producing another $25,000 worth of gold. However most of this activity took place in the 20 years following the mine's initial closure in 1904. The Barry M. Goldwater Air Force Range incorporated the mine in 1954.
GPS COORDINATES: N32°33.18' W114°19.91'
TRAIL: South #2: Fortuna Mine Trail
MAP: Page 470

Galeyville

Galeyville is remembered more for its tough, lawless reputation than for its mining. Pennsylvania native John H. Galey founded the town in 1880 and opened the Texas Mining and Smelting Company with hopes of striking a rich silver vein. At its peak, Galeyville supported a population of 400 citizens and offered all the amenities of a budding Western town.

Cattle rustlers and outlaws also called Galeyville home. The most notable of these outlaws were Curly Bill Brocius and Johnny Ringo. Most people liked tall, handsome Curly Bill, even the sheriff. According to one story, Deputy Sheriff William Breckenridge requested Curly's presence while he was collecting taxes from the local thieves. The outlaw obliged and aided the officer in his debt-collecting duty. Accounts of Curly Bill's death remain a mystery but his legend in Galeyville lives on.

When his mines proved unproductive, the town's founder found himself in serious debt. With the mine closed and the smelter relocated to nearby Benson, John Galey eventually repaid his debt and moved on to better days.
GPS COORDINATES: N31°57.21' W109°13.05'
TRAIL: South #20: Pinery Canyon Trail
MAP: Pages 522–3

Globe

According to reports, the early Spanish conquistadors knew there were mineral deposits in and around the Pinal Mountains. In the 1820s, mountain men were also aware of the potential, but the strong Apache presence in the area prevented them from prospecting. A massacre of 19 Indians led by Colonel King Woolsey occurred at this site in 1864. There are several accounts of this event, one of which is that at the invitation of Woolsey, a group of Apaches joined the Americans for a supposed peace conference. According to one version, Woolsey and his men double-crossed the Indians and then gunned them down. In another version, Woolsey and his men poisoned the visiting Indians by lacing their food with strychnine. Having crawled to the edge of the creek for water, the natives stained the water red with their blood. This event has since been known as the Bloody Tanks Massacre.

The first mine of importance near Globe was established by prospectors in 1873. Two years later, Charles G. Mason located a vein of silver, staked his claim to the Globe Mine, and established the Globe Mining District. The camp soon formed around the district. One account of the origin of the town's name states that a lucky prospector found a large, round 9-inch ball of silver and the name Globe stuck. In another, a mine worker exclaimed that the discoveries were as "large as the whole globe." After that, silver was found in

Broad Street in Globe, circa 1890

many more places and prospectors poured into the area.

In 1876, the town of Globe was established, and by the following year it housed 1,000 residents. A reduction works was established at nearby Miami Wash, which made mining more mechanized and profitable. The town featured two newspapers, the *Arizona Silver Belt* and the *Globe Chronicle.* A stage line went into operation between Globe and Silver City, New Mexico. In the town's early days, miners extracted only silver from the mountains, discarding large amounts of copper. But as silver glutted the market—and with copper prices rising—the mining companies transferred much of their interest to copper ore.

One big problem was the lack of viable transportation to and from Globe. Miners transported the ore via ox trains, an expensive and slow process. The desperately needed railroad was delayed because the Indians did not want the line to run through their reservation. After many mines had closed, the Apaches agreed to let the railroad cross their land for $8,000 and 30 years of free rides. On December 1, 1898, the train made its first stop in Globe.

The town of Globe is still very vibrant, with busy streets and modern conveniences. There is no doubt that the railroad's presence had much to do with its success.

GPS COORDINATES: N33°23.81' W110°46.87'
NEAREST TRAIL: Central #39: Montana Mountain Trail

Goldfield

J. R. Morse, Orrin Merrill, and C. R. Hakes discovered gold east of Phoenix in 1892. A shanty-filled camp soon sprang up around the low-grade gold mines. However, as the gold boom continued, residents constructed more permanent structures, including a schoolhouse. The local minister even conducted well-attended services in the town's saloon. The body of gold that was discovered was in the shape of a funnel, and the deeper miners dug, the less gold there was to be found. As the promise of vast riches dwindled, the residents abandoned Goldfield in 1898. It was thought that around $3 million worth of gold was mined in Goldfield during its initial boom.

Former secretary of Arizona George Young redeveloped the mine around 1909 and renamed the town Youngsberg. He built a stamp mill and cyanide plant. But the town was once again deserted in 1926.

Today the town refuses to die. It survives as a tourist attraction along the road to Apache Lake. You can take a tour of the old mines, visit a museum dedicated to the history of the Superstition Mountains, and even witness a re-creation of a Wild West gunfight when you visit Goldfield.

GPS COORDINATES: N33°27.46' W111°29.23'
TRAIL: Central #38: Apache Trail
MAP: Pages 440–1

Goodwin

Only a few sparse remains left behind in the Bradshaw Mountains tell the tale of Goodwin. The Nonsuch Mining Company, based in Philadelphia, gave birth to the settlement in 1882 when it bought the Goodwin Mine. A mill, smelter, and stage stop were created to serve the miners. The town even grew large enough to support a hotel. The mining town, officially established in 1896, struggled for life. Eventually, the town gave in to the ghosts in the 1940s. Goodwin was named after John N. Goodwin, the first territorial governor of Arizona.

GPS COORDINATES: N34°21.31' W112°22.80'
TRAIL: Central #24: Senator Highway
MAP: Pages 402–3

Greenwood City

Jackson McCracken discovered silver and established the McCracken Silver Mine in 1874. Greenwood City was the town that grew around the mine, named for the lush cypress and magnolia trees along Big Sandy Creek. The mining company built a 10-stamp mill, which they acquired from the waning Moss Company in Hardyville to process the silver ore. Settlers arrived, and soon there was a great deal of activity in Greenwood City. At its peak the town boasted a population of 400, a clean, reasonably priced boardinghouse called the Davis House, and two outstanding saloons owned by Fatty Smith and John Cody. There was also a butcher, physician, barbershop, and various stores. Unfortunately, residents were forced to pay an exorbitant price for mail service; for some unknown reason, Greenwood City never had a post office. When a 20-stamp mill was built in Virginia City (adjacent to Signal), Greenwood City's population quickly declined, and the town was abandoned.

GPS COORDINATES: N34°30.43' W113°35.70'
TRAIL: Northwest #18: Seventeen Mile Road
MAP: Page 179

Gunsight

Named for a nearby mountain formation that closely resembles a gun sight, the Gunsight Mine was established in 1878. By 1892 the Silver Gert Mining Company owned much of the property, on which it constructed several buildings. It employed more than 40 men, and the mine produced $400,000 in silver ore. At its peak, the town of Gunsight was home to 1,500 people. A local rancher supplied residents with fresh vegetables and dairy products, and a stagecoach ran through the village three times a week. Today, only the ruins of old homes remain.

GPS COORDINATES: N32°12.27' W112°41.00'
TRAIL: South #3: El Camino del Diablo Trail
MAP: Pages 478–9

Hardyville

Few probably realize that the U.S. Postal Service improved greatly as a result of the genius of Hardyville's founder, William H. Hardy. When torn mailbags arrived in his town, Hardy sent them to be mended and had rivets added to the fabric carriers. After he consulted with the postmaster general in Washington, D.C., all postal bags were, and still are, constructed with these rivets.

Long before Hardy improved on the design of the modern-day postal bag, he had established a trading post and inn along the Colorado River. This port, also known as Hardy Landing, became an important supply route for Moss Gold Mine, Prescott, Camp Lincoln, and even Salt Lake City. A small settlement grew around the port, and it served as the county's first seat. Well liked and generous, "Captain" Hardy was known to give complimentary ferry rides to those who were down on their luck.

Although only about 20 full-time residents occupied Hardyville, many passersby kept the town bustling. Fires in 1872 and 1873 destroyed much of the town, but it managed to survive for a few more years. However, when the Atlantic & Pacific Railroad was built through Mohave County in 1883, Hardyville's port was deemed obsolete, and the town was deserted.

GPS COORDINATES: N35°02.33' W114°37.68' (approximately)
NEAREST TRAIL: Northwest #23: Moss Mine Trail

Harquahala

In the 1760s, Spanish explorers discovered gold in the Harquahala Mountains (the name means "running water high up" in the local Mojave tongue). Unsuccessful attempts were made to mine the gold both at that time and again in 1814. Hostile Pima Indians were successful in driving out most of the would-be prospectors. Inevitably, tales of gold in the Indians' territorty filtered through and caught the attention of passing military officers who managed to collect some surface gold before Apaches forced them out.

In 1863, Herman Ehrenberg mentioned to Henry Wickenburg that he had found a promising location in the Little Harquahala Mountains. Wickenburg explored the region and agreed that it was potentially rich. However on his return from the Little Harquahalas, he discovered an even richer vein, staked his claim as the Vulture Mine, and forgot all about the initial claim.

Historians credit Harry Walton, Mike Sullivan, and Robert Stein with staking the claims that became the Golden Eagle and Bonanza Mines. The three men owned two claims that were next to each other, with Walton and Stein owning one and Sullivan the other. As the story goes, Sullivan was out prospecting one day and ran across gold nuggets lying on the ground. He quickly filled his hat and pockets with the ore. Later, when he checked the claim stakes, Sullivan realized the claim was not his own but his neighbors'. Rather than relinquish the gold, he convinced Stein and Walton to combine the two claims in order to work them more efficiently. The two unsuspecting men knew nothing about the nuggets on their claim and agreed. Once the paperwork was done, Sullivan conveniently "found" the nuggets. Soon, the Bonanza and Golden Eagle Mines were luring prospectors from all over the Southwest to the settlement in the Little Harquahala Mountains.

Many mine owners during this time lost a portion of their profits when they shipped their gold to Phoenix. Bandits were common along these isolated trails, and many a robber made off with gold from the area's mines. When two men named Hubbard and Bowers owned the mine, Hubbard came up with the idea of casting 400-pound bars that would be too large to be easily carried by thieves. This scheme worked well until one day in 1890. Sheriffs Burke and Davis were transporting a load of gold to Sentinel when the bottom collapsed out of the flimsy wooden stage, and the 400-pound ingot fell out. The loss wasn't discovered until the stage had traveled for several miles; luckily the two men were able to recover the ingot from the bottom of a deep gully, though not without considerable difficulty.

The mines around Harquahala were very rich. The abundance of gold made many miners greedy. High grading—the practice of miners scraping off gold dregs from the arrastra beds—seemed an almost accepted activity in the eyes of those who administered the law in the Harquahala region. Children were known to sing loudly to stifle the noise as their fathers committed the crime. On several occasions the culprits were not charged even though they confessed to the crime.

The mines changed hands again and again and continued to produce ore in vast quantities. Eventually a group of Englishmen paid $1.25 million for the mines and recovered only a tenth of that sum in return. Ironically, the group sold out to the previous American owner for $7,000, who in turn sold the mines again for $40,000. Finally, the mines ran dry of worthwhile ore, and mining activities ceased in 1907.

GPS COORDINATES: N33°40.16' W113°35.33'
TRAIL: Central #11: Harquahala Mine Trail
MAP: Page 367

Harrisburg

In 1849, a group of pioneers traveled through the region in southwestern Arizona, later known as Harrisburg. At that time only a watering hole marked the site where they stopped to set up camp. Several months later, another train of settlers discovered their decomposed bodies and charred wagons and presumed they were the victims of an Indian attack. The group gathered the remains and buried them in a plot of land near the watering hole. (In 1936, the Arizona State Highway Department constructed a white quartz monument in honor of the victims.)

In 1886, Captain Charles Harris (also referred to as Horace E. Harris) and Arizona governor Frederick Tritle discovered gold ore at this site. Harris, a Canadian who served in the Civil War, named the booming town after himself. By 1888, prospectors located the vein that became the prosperous

Bonanza Mine, and one year later the peak of the gold rush hit this small town.

Between 1891 and 1893, mine owners George Bowers and A. G. Hubbard reaped $1.6 million from the extracted gold. Shortly after, the two sold the Bonanza and Harquahala Mines to a London company for $1.25 million, but because of a lack of water and spent mines, the town was virtually deserted by 1905.

GPS COORDINATES: N33°44.07' W113°32.47'
NEAREST TRAIL: Central #11: Harquahala Mine Trail

Harshaw

David Tecumseh Harshaw, a cattle rancher, was ordered in 1873 by Indian Agent Tom Jeffords to leave the area after Harshaw illegally grazed his herd on Indian land. Harshaw relocated to a region called Durasno and decided to become a prospector. Apparently prospecting was destined to be his calling. The one-time rancher prospered after he made a lucrative find. Locals renamed the town Harshaw after its wealthy citizen.

Around 1881, Harshaw sold the Hermosa Mine to a New York company that hired 150 men and constructed a 20-stamp mill. The town at one time had 30 buildings, ranging from hotels and saloons to stores and blacksmith shops. In 1881, several floods, a major fire, and the closing of the Hermosa Mine quieted Harshaw significantly. James Finley of Tucson purchased the mine in 1887, and Harshaw experienced a short rebirth until 1905.

GPS COORDINATES: N31°28.04' W110°42.42'
TRAIL: South #13: Harshaw Road
MAP: Page 507

Hilltop

The Hands family, originally from England, claimed partial responsibility for developing this region in the 1890s. These brothers, Frank, Alfred, and John, also initiated the early construction of trails that linked the mining settlements in this region. Hands Pass, named after them, is one such path. The Hands brothers acquired Hilltop Mine, formerly known as Ayers Camp, from its founder Jack Dunn who had established it in the early 1880s. The town of Hilltop developed around the mine after the brothers sold their interests to the Hilltop Metal Mining Company in 1913. Frank Hands and his wife, Grace, are buried very close to the southern end of South #21: Hands Pass Trail.

In 1917, developers constructed Kasper Tunnel through the mountain. The passage, approximately 1 mile long, allowed another side of Hilltop to emerge. The "new," developing east side of town grew even larger than the original west side because it was a more conducive place from which to ship the ore. In its prime, Hilltop hosted a dance hall, restaurant, pool hall, an impressive manager's house, and bunkhouses. In 1917, the town collectively purchased a motorized car and took great care of it, keeping it in its own garage. By the 1930s, the mining company greatly reduced activity, and the town began losing its residents. Various small groups attempted to continue mining through to the late 1940s, but the closure of the post office in 1945 marked the end of Hilltop. A few remnants of the town on the eastern side of the Kasper Tunnel survive on private land; permission is required to visit these. No buildings remain on the western slope—only several concrete footings and the outlet of the Kasper Tunnel.

GPS COORDINATES: N31°59.64' W109°16.73'
TRAIL: South #21: Hands Pass Trail
MAP: Page 526

Jerome

The Sinagua Indians roamed the hills around what is now known as Jerome, long before the United Verde Copper Company gained prominence in the area on and around Mingus Mountain. The natives collected and utilized blue azure residue for their body paints and pottery decorations. In the late 1500s and early 1600s, Spanish explorers took a minor interest in the area and collected some ore specimens to take back to Mexico. However, they were unimpressed and bypassed the ore because it was not gold.

In 1876 Al Sieber, General George Crook's scout, staked a claim on Mingus Mountain but did little to develop it. No one developed the mines until two ranchers, Morris Andrew Ruffner and Angus McKinnon, finally began production later in 1876. The cowboys soon decided to sell their claim to an interested party: the territorial governor of Arizona, Frederick Tritle, and his partner, Frederick F. Thomas. The governor gained much-needed financial backing from New Yorker Eugene Murray Jerome, who insisted the town be named after him. Under the direction of the United Verde Copper Company, the town of Jerome began to form. By 1883, Jerome bustled with 50 homes, 3 stores, several saloons, and about 400 residents, but that was only the beginning.

When Montana senator William A. Clark purchased the mine in 1884, Jerome experienced great changes. The multimillionaire spent more than $1 million over a 12-year period to renovate the mine and town. The entrepreneur constructed a standard-gauge railroad to ship the ore more efficiently, built a large hotel called Montana House, and erected a new smelter down valley in Clarkdale. By 1900, Jerome boasted the fourth largest population in Arizona. As often happens, competition soon appeared to Clark's dynasty. The United Verde Extension Mining Company (UVX) located a rich claim called Little Daisy in the mountains of Jerome. James Douglas, the mine's owner, opened a luxurious $200,000 hotel adjacent to the mine and constructed himself a sizable mansion. Of course,

Jerome, circa 1900

the simple, hardworking miners found the hotel too ritzy and refused to stay there.

A few problems arose within the town throughout the years. In 1917, 60 striking miners were forcibly carried out of town. Three ferocious fires at different times destroyed large parts of the town, which were then rebuilt bigger and better. An enormous dynamite blast in 1925 initiated a landslide that continues today, causing the town to shift downward one-half inch each month.

When the last of the Clark men died in 1935, the women of the family sold Jerome's mines to Phelps Dodge Corporation for $20.8 million. Those mines and the UVX Mine, which Phelps also purchased, continued to produce until 1953.

Thanks to the forethought of the Jerome Historical Society, the town did not meet the fate of so many and end up a ghost town. Museums, shops, and a state historical park remain to weave the tale of this once-booming mining town. As the community's chamber of commerce once stated, Jerome is a "town on the move."

GPS COORDINATES: N34°45.01' W112°06.87'

TRAILS: Northeast #15: Jerome-Perkinsville Road and Northeast #18: Mingus Mountain Loop Trail

MAP: Pages 260 & 267

Katherine

S. C. Bagg located a vein of gold in 1900 and the New Comstock Mining Company began working the Katherine Mine. However, it took the mine and town another 20 years to reach its boom. The Arizona-Pyramid Gold Mining Company purchased the Katherine Mine from New Comstock Mining Company in 1904. Due to inadequate transportation, the mine did not prove profitable for many years and temporarily closed in 1906.

The Katherine Gold Mining Company bought the mine in 1919 and built a new shaft as well as a 150-ton cyanide mill. With this resurgence of energy, the town of Katherine finally emerged. Miners and their families quickly relocated to the growing settlement. The company offered a free plot of land to the family with the first-born girl, under the stipulation that she be named Katherine.

In the 1930s, Katherine continued to have an active, busy community. But at the beginning of World War II, production halted and the town dwindled.

GPS COORDINATES: N35°13.40' W114°33.58'

NEAREST TRAILS: Northwest #26: Portland Mine Road and Northwest #27: Powerline Road

Kingman

The Atlantic & Pacific Railroad, laying tracks through northwestern Arizona, needed a railroad stop. The city of Kingman was created to fill the need. Previously in 1881, Henry P. Ewing and William Heimrod built a house on the site that would become Kingman, but the coming of the railroad in 1882 firmly established the town. Lewis Kingman, the locating engineer for the railroad, named the bustling new railroad stop in honor of himself. Before Lewis Kingman, though, there is evidence that the city was called either Shenfield Railroad Camp or Middleton. The name Kingman stuck, and the town steadily grew as an important shipping and shopping center. By 1887, the city's importance was clear and Kingman won the honor of Mohave County seat.

As time went on, Kingman also became an important hub for the airline industry. Early passenger and mail planes frequently stopped in Kingman. Charles Lindbergh, the famous pilot who was the first to solo the Atlantic, stopped in Kingman in 1928 to inaugurate a new airmail service. His arrival was a spectacular event and about 1,500 Arizonans welcomed him. An air base was later built during World War II at the site of present-day Mohave County Airport.

In addition to the railroad and the airlines, another important line of traffic blessed Kingman—Route 66. Kingman became a popular stop for travelers motoring between the gaming tables of Las Vegas, Nevada, and Phoenix, Arizona.

Charles Lindbergh wasn't the only star to touch Kingman. Clark Gable and Carole Lombard were married in the city. Andy Devine, one of Hollywood's greatest character actors, was born in Flagstaff but was raised in Kingman and called it his hometown. Kingman's main street is named after Devine, who starred in such memorable films as *Stagecoach* and *The Man Who Shot Liberty Valance.*

A parade along Kingman's main street in 1919

GPS COORDINATES: N35°11.42' W114°03.16'

NEAREST TRAIL: Northwest #19: Flag Mine Trail

Kofa

Before the founding of the King of Arizona Mine, the area around the S. H. Mountains saw little activity. The popular explanation for the name S. H. is that the rugged mountain silhouettes resembled a row of outhouses, and S. H. was the abbreviation for s***-house. A more genteel explanation was called for when the miners' wives began accompanying their men into the region. The story was revised: S. H. stood for Short Horn, possibly referring to the abundant sheep in the area. However, when the mine started producing great wealth, residents began calling the range the Kofa Mountains, making a name from an abbreviation of the King of Arizona Mine. The fabulously rich and profitable mine was responsible for attracting people into that desolate area of southwestern Arizona.

Charles E. Eichelberger established the King of Arizona Mine in 1896. He had been prospecting around Yuma in partnership with Epes Randolph, the superintendent of the Southern Pacific Railroad. Randolph grubstaked Eichelberger. However, Eichelberger found little early on and Randolph was slow to grubstake him again when the unlucky prospector returned empty-handed after a prolonged period of time. Eichelberger enlisted the help of H. B. Gleason and headed into an area of the S. H. Mountains he thought looked promising. After hunting for natural tanks of water in the mountains, Eichelberger was relaxing and noticed a soot-blackened Indian cave. He decided to investigate. He found a rich vein of gold, nearly 3 feet wide. The ore, assayed at $500 a ton, proved to be sitting on a very large vein. Randolph, Eichelberger's original partner, noticed the prosperous strike, and because the original contract was still valid, he was given a quarter share in the new mine.

Eichelberger, Randolph, and Gleason founded the King of Arizona Mining Company to raise much-needed funds. The company constructed a 5-stamp mill at Mohawk on the Gila River, 35 miles south of the mine. Access to water proved to be a problem, but underground water was found by drilling a 1,000-foot well and a new and larger mill was constructed 5 miles south of the mine. Before they drilled the well, the thirsty miners were forced to drink water that was carted in by mule team in old whiskey barrels.

Initially, the miners at Kofa slept in tents or caves. There was little protection from the elements, and men who worked nights faced the difficult task of sleeping in the hot Arizona sun during the day. But with the arrival of women, a small town sprang up. There was a boardinghouse, saloons, and even a school in town. A mix of Cornishmen, Mexicans, and Chinese moved in and populated the settlement.

Other claims in the region proved profitable, especially the nearby Polaris Mine, but no mine exceeded the profits of the King of Arizona. At the time, it was the richest single mine in the Southwest, producing $4.65 million throughout its duration. By 1910, the mine had closed and people had started to drift away. The post office, established in 1900, lasted until 1928. The area is still privately owned.

GPS COORDINATES: N33°16.13' W113°58.02'

TRAILS: Central #6: Engesser Pass Trail and Central #3: King Valley Road

MAP: Pages 346 & 355

Lochiel

Records are unclear, but Lochiel appears to be the same site as two other earlier settlements. In the early 1880s, post offices were established in southern Arizona less than 1 mile apart. One was named Luttrell after the owner of the Holland Company Smelting Works, Dr. J. M. Luttrell. The other was named La Noria (Spanish for "a well-water lifting device"). Both post offices closed in 1883. One year later, two of the region's early settlers, Colin and Brewster Cameron, named Lochiel for their hometown in Scotland. The two men secured the nearby San Rafael de la Zanja Land Grant in 1888 from its original owner, Manuel Bustello, who purchased it from the Mexican government in 1825. Around 1890, the U.S. government resurveyed the U.S.-Mexican border because the earlier survey was deemed inaccurate. The new border split the settlement down the middle, and neighbors suddenly found themselves living in different countries.

The green pastures of the San Rafael de la Zanja Land Grant, which refers to the ditch, or water basin of the Santa Cruz River, have been good grazing lands for centuries. The land was used mainly for cattle grazing. However, grazing cattle was not very easy around Lochiel because Apache Indians often came to kill them and Texan outlaws often came to rustle them. Settlers rounded up some of the offenders and publicly hung them in Tombstone. Other cattle rustlers came north from Mexico. Francisco Pancho Villa, a Mexican freedom fighter and rebel, was a notorious rustler who made a lot of money by "collecting" the community's cattle and selling them in the South. Supposedly, Lochiel was one of his favorite spots in which to "round up" cattle.

A century later, these same rolling pastures were featured in the making of the movies *Tom Horn, Monte Wash,* and *Oklahoma.* For the expensive *Oklahoma* set, 10 acres of corn were painstakingly grown and the film crew tied wax peaches on barren trees.

In the 1980s, Lochiel still had its one-room schoolhouse. The town also had a budget, a school board, and teachers intersted in working at the school. However the school lacked one crucial thing—students. Not a single child attended school in this fading desert community.

Lochiel finally did control its influx of illegal aliens with the construction of a U.S. customs house. But in time, officials saw the cost of maintaining it as unnecessary in a remote region. The guards at the border crossing stamped their last passport in 1986. The border fence has also disintegrated, as massive cottonwoods fell across it and sections of it were breached.

GPS COORDINATES: N31°20.06' W110°37.29'

TRAIL: South #12: Mexican Border Road

MAP: Pages 502–3

Mammoth

The town of Mammoth was named in the early 1870s for the Old Mammoth Mine above town. The gold ore deposits there were so rich they were said to be mammoth. In 1873, Charles Crimson and his company began working the mine. He soon traded it to Sam and William McIntyre for a herd of cattle. The McIntyres managed the mine for many years, creating a lucrative business for themselves.

The town housed a mill, through which tramway buckets shuttled ore from the mine above the town. Before the return journey, the ore buckets were then filled with drinking water for the thirsty miners. At its peak, Mammoth's population was an enormous 1,000, but the mine closed in the 1880s and the McIntyres relocated to Salt Lake City. Some mining occurs, but the residents of Mammoth number much fewer than they did a hundred years ago.

GPS COORDINATES: N32°43.26' W110°38.33'

TRAIL: South #29: Copper Creek Mining District Trail

MAP: Page 549

Mayer

In 1882, Joe Mayer established a store, saloon, and stage station in central Arizona at a site that bore his name. A busi-

Mayer, 1902

ness-minded man, he soon was earning thousands of dollars from traveling cattle drivers who stopped at his mercantile for supplies. Mayer chose his location well, and the small town was soon a hub for the surrounding agricultural community. Nearby mining, such as occurred at the Stoddard, Copper Mountain, and Poland Mines, increased the town's importance. In 1884, Joe Mayer added a two-story hotel, aptly named the Mayer Hotel. In 1902, a more elaborate hotel called the White House Hotel was constructed. It is not clear if Joe Mayer financed this enterprise. Mayer was always on the lookout for a new business venture, no matter how small. Around the same time as the White House Hotel was being built, Mayer developed the idea of selling cactus thorns as Indian souvenir toothpicks. The *Prescott-Journal Miner* seemed most impressed with the idea in an article they published about the novelty item.

Mayer gained even more importance when the Prescott & Eastern Railroad, the brainchild of Frank Murphy, reached the town in 1898. However, the railroad did not stop there. Frank Murphy had the wild idea of connecting Mayer to the rich mining district at Crown King. People laughed at the idea, calling the scheme Murphy's Impossible Railroad. Crown King was 2,000 feet higher than Mayer, and the proposed route through the mountains was steep and tortuous. But Murphy was undaunted; he had previous experience laying tracks across rugged terrain, and he thought this railroad would be difficult, but possible.

Murphy was not discouraged and advertised in newspapers in the East for workers to lay the grade. He offered double the going rate—a dollar a day. Construction started in 1901. First to be finished was a short spur from Poland Junction (to the north of Mayer) to the mines near Poland, although construction had to be delayed on this leg in 1902 when a dynamite blast revealed a significant gold deposit. Many of the construction workers, tempted by instant wealth, ceased their work and turned to prospecting, abandoning the railroad construction. It was some time before a new crew could be found. Yet with the amount of money Murphy was offering workers, he had little difficulty finding a new crew. Soon work was back on schedule and the line to Crown King completed. Along its route, there were switchbacks that were so tight, those in the caboose could look out and see the engine going in the opposite direction.

GPS COORDINATES: N34°23.94' W112°14.27'
TRAIL: Central #25: Mayer-Goodwin Road
MAP: Page 407

McCracken

In 1874, a party of prospectors led by "Hassayampa" Jackson McCracken and "Chloride Jack" Owens explored possible mining opportunities north of the Bill Williams River. Establishing the Owens District, the men staked several promising claims; one on top of McCracken Peak produced silver that assayed at $1,000 per ton. The discovery created a stir in Prescott and Mineral Park and initiated an influx of people eager to stake claims. McCracken (also recorded as McCrackin) boasted a tent city with very few permanent dwellings.

Nevada Senator John P. Jones, along with fellow senator William Stewart, financed the beginning of the town's mine. They had previously been involved with mining at the Comstock Lode. Many people knew the senators' names and saw their involvement at McCracken as a good omen. The senators bought the mill at Greenwood City (the site is found along Northwest #18: Seventeen Mile Road), which processed the silver. The nearby settlement of Signal provided most of the supplies for the camp.

The McCracken Mines closed in 1879 after producing a reported $1.5 million in silver. They have been worked sporadically since but with no where near the success of the initail boom.

GPS COORDINATES: N34°26.72' W113°46.47'
TRAIL: Northwest #16: McCracken Peak Trail
MAP: Page 174

Mineral Park

Resting amid the bustle of the Duval Mining Company's open pit mines is the town of Mineral Park. Well over 100 years ago, a parklike group of cedar trees in a field inspired

Mineral Park, 1884

Governor Hunt visiting Oatman, with the state car parked in the background, in 1912

the town's name. In 1870, prospectors established the Mayflower Mine, and many other claims soon followed. Two years later, 500 residents and an active town flourished at the foot of Ithaca Peak. Town dwellers proudly accepted the status of Mohave County seat in 1876 and welcomed the new Keystone Mill. The mill ran successfully for the next 10 years, but ironically, at that point Mineral Park lost its county seat ranking to Kingman.

Prior to this loss, the Atlantic & Pacific Railroad constructed a line that ran within 15 miles of the city. In 1884, Mineral Park's population jumped to 700 and seemed likely to continue to rise. However, mining activity was dramatically reduced in 1885 and so was the influx of people. Mining continued in the area but to a much lesser degree. Today, the activity of the Duval Mining Company continues to breathe life into Mineral Park but no one knows for how long.

GPS COORDINATES: N35°22.25' W114°9.16'
NEAREST TRAIL: Northwest #28: Packsaddle Mountain Loop Trail

Mohave City

In 1863, a group of California volunteers stationed at Fort Mohave on the Colorado River established Mohave City in order to service their needs. By 1864, the bustling town housed so many residents that it became the county's first seat. All of the conveniences of a city existed, including its share of prostitutes. Records indicate that more soldiers perished from sexually transmitted diseases than in the line of battle. In 1869, the U.S. government enlarged Fort Mohave to include the land where Mohave City was located. Officials commanded that residents evacuate within 30 days, and military troops moved into town, which from that point on was part of Fort Mohave.

GPS COORDINATES: N34°57.80' W114°37.90' (approximately)
NEAREST TRAIL: Northwest #24: Mossback Wash Trail

Mowry

Although claims in the area date back to early Spanish explorers, a Mexican cattle herder was the first to formally establish the Patagonia Mine in 1858. Two years later, a flamboyant army lieutenant, Sylvester Mowry, left the military, bought the claim for $20,000, and changed its name to Mowry Mine. Mowry sunk a great deal of money into the mines in the area building furnaces and smelting equipment. Under Mowry's leadership in the early 1860s, the mine became one of the richest in the nation. It produced $1.5 million worth of silver and lead and employed more than 100 workers.

General James H. Carleton arrested Lieutenant Mowry in 1862 for allegedly selling lead to the Southern army during the Civil War. Mowry was jailed in Fort Yuma. During the war, Apache Indians raided the mine, destroying the smelter and ruining most of the settlement. His mine was auctioned off for the meager price of $4,000. In Mowry's opinion, the mine's weekly profit was larger than the selling price.

When no solid evidence could be found against Mowry, the military released him in November 1862 and he moved to England. One possible reason why Mowry may have been wrongfully detained was his stance on the current status of Arizona. He saw the federal government as, by and large, ignoring the territory. He was outspoken about the need for Arizona to become a territory distinct from New Mexico and thereby controlling its own destiny. Most likely he offended some officials with his criticism. Mowry spent the rest of his life trying to raise capital in Europe to refurbish and reopen the looted mine. He died in 1871 at the age of 39.

New owners revamped the Mowry Mine and the town in 1891; a post office was established in 1905. Nothing remains except a few ruins and a small cemetery.

GPS COORDINATES: N31°25.71' W110°42.20'
TRAIL: South #13: Harshaw Road
MAP: Page 507

Oatman

In the 1850s, a family named Oatman camped at this site on the way to California. During the night, Apache Indians raided the camp, slaughtering six family members, beating the son, and kidnapping the two daughters. For several years the girls lived in captivity until one daughter, Olive, escaped (see page 97). The settlement earned its name from the brave young woman who endured great pains during her youth.

Originally named Vivian, the town originated in 1902 when Ben Taddock (also recorded as Paddock) established a gold mine. Five years later, the mine had produced ore worth $3 million, and people flocked to the once-desolate area. In 1908, prospectors made another find and named the claim Tom Reed Mine; that same year the town's post office opened. At this point the name Oatman became official. After United Eastern Mine opened in 1913, Oatman's population reached its peak at 10,000.

The extremely productive Tom Reed Mine closed in the 1930s, but the town has yet to fade away. Tourists continue to find their way into Oatman to admire its relics of the past, including the Oatman Hotel, which housed Clark Gable and Carole Lombard on their honeymoon. Wild burros roam the surrounding hills and the streets of Oatman—clues to this once-large town's mining past.

GPS COORDINATES: N35°01.53' W114°22.92'

NEAREST TRAILS: Northwest #24: Mossback Wash Trail and Northwest #25: Thumb Butte Trail

Octave

Although prospectors staked claims as early as 1864 at the central Arizona site of Octave, the town was not developed until the late 1890s when a group of eight men purchased it (hence the name Octave) and organized the Octave Gold Mining Company. The post office at Weaver—the remains are near the Weaver Cemetery—was transferred to Octave a year later. The town eventually developed a stage stop, a school, and general store. Although the mining company did not allow drinking, Octave's Jag-Town district had many saloons and prostitutes. The mine netted $50,000 a month for a while, and the town persisted until World War II began. Executive Order 208 closed all nonstrategic mines at that time. It is now privately owned and there is no access to the town site, though mining remains and buildings can be seen clearly from the public road.

Octave Mine, 1904

GPS COORDINATES: N34°08.32' W112°42.74'

TRAIL: Central #22: Stanton Ghost Town Trail

MAP: Page 397

Oracle

Albert Weldon, one of the early mining pioneers in this region of southern Arizona, had traveled west around Cape Horn in *The Oracle.* When he settled in the area, he gave the name Oracle to the region around the small adobe homestead where he prospected. He had arrived in the early 1880s when individual miners were operating on a small scale. Later, the Apache Mine began producing bigger returns.

Oracle continued to evolve slowly and by 1895, successful rancher Bill Neal and his wife built the comfortable Mountain View Hotel, which soon attracted many travelers en route to Tucson. Neal was the son of a black man and Cherokee woman. His Indian name was Bear Sitting Down. In his earlier years, he had spent time riding with Buffalo Bill Cody, who now was one of their regular guests. Buffalo Bill took an interest in the local mines until his death in 1917. Neal had previously worked in the freight business, and he provided his own stagecoaches to transport people to and from Tucson. Neal died in 1936 and his wife continued working at the hotel until she too passed away in 1950.

Freight teams in Oracle, circa 1895

GPS COORDINATES: N32°36.60' W110°46.52'

TRAIL: South #27: Oracle Control Road

MAP: Page 544

Oro Bella

George P. Harrington organized the Oro Belle Mining and Milling Company and established a mining camp in the valley of the Bradshaw Mountains in the 1890s. Originally called Harrington, the town supplied laborers for both the Oro Bella (sometimes called Oro Belle) and Gray Eagle Mines. The mines and the town were most active during the decade from 1900 to 1910. Both the town and the mine had problems. In 1905, the mining company felt that good-natured Harrington was too generous with its money so it hired another man, named Schlesinger, to run the mine. After Harrington's replacement severely cut back on the quality and quantity of food for the miners, an enraged mob confronted the new manager. The manager promptly quit, and the company quickly reinstated Harrington.

The town's post office closed its doors in 1918. There are still a few mining remains around the Oro Bella Mine. The town's saloon (with its bar still intact) was torn down and moved to nearby Crown King, where it can be visited today.

GPS COORDINATES: N34°10.30' W112°20.80' (approximately)

NEAREST TRAIL: Central #26: Crown King Backroad

MAP: Page 410

Palace Station

Originally from Missouri, Alfred B. Spence and his wife, Matilda, moved to the Bradshaw Mountains and built a cabin at this site in 1875. The two had previously lived in Groom Creek briefly, where they operated a sawmill. In 1877, the Spences' cabin became a stop along a new branch line of the Prescott and Phoenix Stage. The couple provided meals for travelers en route to the Peck Mine and feed for their horses. Elsie Spence, Alfred and Matilda's daughter, could remember some details of Palace Station's early years. She said that on the days the miners were paid, "fancy ladies" could often be seen at the station to relieve them of their hard-earned money. Palace Station's location was chosen because it was the halfway point between Prescott and the Peck Mine, which at the time was an important claim. The Spences' cabin originally had two rooms and a loft; it was extended a few years later. Alfred Spence died in 1908 and his wife sold the cabin two years later.

Palace Station became part of the Prescott National Forest in 1963, and the well-preserved cabin still stands. The forest service now uses the cabin for its personnel. Currently, Palace Station is home to one of Arizona's earliest pioneer cabins.

GPS COORDINATES: N34°22.59' W112°24.55'
TRAIL: Central #24: Senator Highway
MAP: Pages 402–3

Paradise

There are many stories about the origin of this town's romantic name. One tale states that a young couple named George and Reed Walker moved into the area and were so pleased that they named their new home site Paradise. However, the most widely recorded story states that men crossing the desert found their way to water at this site. Upon drinking the cool, refreshing water, they exclaimed that the spot must be paradise. Although prospecting began in the area in the 1880s, the town of Paradise was not established until 1901. The Chiricahua Developing Company was formed at this time, and a settlement began to grow. By 1904 the village boasted 13 saloons, several stores, a hotel, and a unique jail. The open-air facility consisted of a chain stretched between two trees; officials shackled prisoners to the chain. Later, a more permanent adobe building was constructed for a jail. The mines closed in 1907 but the town is still home to a few residents.

GPS COORDINATES: N31°56.09' W109°13.07'
TRAIL: South #20: Pinery Canyon Trail
MAP: Pages 522–3

Patagonia

In the mid-1800s, the area of southern Arizona around Patagonia was being used for cattle ranching. By the 1860s, rich ore found in the area drew a number of miners into the region. Mining soon became big business in southern Arizona. Founded in 1898 by Rollin Rice Richardson, the town originally known as Rollin was established next to the New Mexico & Arizona Railroad. It soon became a key shipping center for the region's cattle and mining industries. In 1899, a post office was established and the settlers voted to change the town's name to Patagonia (Spanish for "the place where the big-footed animals hold forth").

General merchandise store in Patagonia, circa 1900

The town continued to grow in the early 1900s, adding hotels, restaurants, and even an opera house. The train ran until 1962; the rails were taken up and the railroad's route through town was turned into a park. The depot (currently in use as the town hall), as well as the town's original schoolhouse and cemetery, may be viewed. Today, Patagonia is home to the Patagonia-Sonoita Creek Preserve, a cottonwood-willow riparian forest in which a wide variety of wildlife live. Bird-watching is especially popular in the area.

GPS COORDINATES: N31°32.89' W110°45.25'
TRAILS: South #13: Harshaw Road and South #16: Temporal Gulch Trail
MAP: Pages 507 & 514

Payson

Set beneath the shadows of the Mogollon Rim, Payson was first settled in 1876 when Bill Burch built a cabin in the area. In 1882 John and Frank Hise erected a home and opened the area's first general store. Illinois senator Louis Payson officially established a post office in 1884 at what was then called Union Park, Long Valley, or Green Valley. To show their gratitude, the settlers named the town Payson. In the late 1800s, Payson was by no means an easy place to get to or from. Roads from Payson leading to Globe and Flagstaff were very primitive and it took travelers five days to make the journey. The town began to grow and soon had two stores, two cafes, and two saloons, one of which was the popular Pioneer Saloon.

Payson schoolhouse, circa 1920

In its early years, Payson saw its share of rowdy frontier life. Although primarily set farther to the east, the Pleasant Valley War (see page 99) occasionally spilled over into the streets of Payson, causing the townspeople to either take sides or get out of the way. Another time, Texas cowboy Jack Lane rode through the streets, wildly firing his pistol and disturbing the town. However, he went too far by pointing his gun at a local cattleman named Tom Colcord. Colcord drew his pistol and shot Lane. The town was grateful to Colcord for quelling the disturbance and gave him a vote of confidence. Payson has been home to a number of cowboys throughout the years. Since 1884, the town has celebrated a festival called August Doin's, in which the town has a grand picnic and local cowboys compete in a number of events.

Payson changed forever in 1959 when Arizona 87 (also known as Beeline Highway) was paved. Phoenix was now only

two hours away and tourism took off as one of Payson's major industries. At the base of the Mogollon Rim, Payson has become a stopping point for recreationalists heading into Arizona's high country. Today, the town is home to a number of festivals including such annual events as the June Bug Blues Festival, the Fiddlers' Contest, and the Great Payson Jerky Jamboree.
GPS COORDINATES: N34°13.84' W111°19.47'
TRAIL: Central #34: Mazatzal Wilderness Trail
MAP: Page 432

Perkinsville
Along the banks of the Verde River sits the small ranching community of Perkinsville. The town was named after Marion Perkins, a rancher from Texas who purchased property owned by James Baker and John Campbell at the site. Perkins bought the ranch in 1899 and then returned to New Mexico to retrieve his cattle, which had been driven there from Texas. He finally settled at his new ranch in November 1900.

In 1912, the extension of a branch of the Santa Fe Railroad from Drake to Clarkdale crossed Perkins's ranch. Railroad officials built a station there and called it Perkinsville. The station still stands and may be seen from the road, but it is located on private property. Between 1925 and 1939, Perkinsville operated a post office.

Built in 1913, the single-lane steel bridge that now stands at Perkinsville once crossed the Gila River approximately 200 miles to the southwest. When a flood washed it out in 1915, a forest service work team brought the bridge to its current location and re-erected it across the Verde River. The Historic

The old Santa Fe Railroad depot in Perkinsville

American Buildings Survey classifies the overpass as technologically noteworthy—an early example of the most common truss-type bridge built in the United States.
GPS COORDINATES: N34°54.11' W112°11.48'
TRAIL: Northeast #13: Perkinsville Road
MAP: Pages 254–5

Phoenix
The first American to settle in the area where Phoenix is now located was John Y. T. Smith. In 1864, he planted hay in the Salt River Valley and sold it to troops at Camp McDowell. In 1867, Jack Swilling also recognized the valley's agricultural potential. He formed the Swilling Irrigating Canal Company and started irrigating the land. Within just a couple of years, ranches had been established, crops were

Phoenix, circa 1895

being harvested, and the population began to grow.

In 1870, residents formed a committee to decide what to call their new, prospering community. Swilling, who had previously served in the Confederate Army, suggested Stonewall, after General Stonewall Jackson. Salina was also suggested. Darrell Duppa looked over the valley and saw the crumbling remains of the Hohokam civilization. He noted that the community was rising from the ashes of a previous civilization and an idea struck him. He declared that the town should be named Phoenix after the mythological bird that consumed itself in a fiery mass, only to rise from its ashes more beautiful than before. The name stuck. The first lot, which was on the corner of Washington and Montezuma Streets, sold for $104 to Judge Berry of Prescott. The city was incorporated in 1881, and in 1889, Phoenix became the capital of Arizona.

After its incorporation, the settlement remained a relatively small farming community. By 1910 only 11,134 people lived in Phoenix. The population took off in 1926 when the Southern Pacific Railroad established a main line to the city. Phoenix flourished into a metropolis. Because of its warm climate, Phoenix became one of the fastest-growing cities in the United States in the years following World War II; today it is the seventh largest U.S. city, and manufacturing is its chief source of income.
GPS COORDINATES: N33°26.84' W112°04.55'

Planet/Eagle Landing
Many claim Planet was the first mine worked in Arizona by Americans and only the second copper mine in the state. Prospector Richard Ryland discovered the ore in 1863 during the copper boom of California. Eager investors hoped that Planet might reap them large rewards. Martin & Company quickly hired 200 Mexican mine workers, and a town grew around the mine. Small Eagle Landing on the Colorado River served as the shipping point for ore hauled from Planet en route to San Francisco.

At its peak in 1867, Planet bustled with 500 residents, and the *Arizona Miner* declared it the busiest camp in the territory after Wickenburg. Its unique status did not last long; in 1868, copper prices fell to 23¢ per pound, and mines everywhere closed. In 1883, the Matilda Mining Company deepened the mines, built roads, and constructed a new smelter in an attempt to revive the operation. However, the resurgence lasted only a year. From 1902 through World War II, several

companies reopened the Planet Mine but made no profit. The town's heyday passed long ago.
GPS COORDINATES: N34°14.85' W113°58.00' (approximately)
TRAIL: Northwest #7: Mineral Wash–Bill Williams River Trail
MAP: Page 155

Polhamus Landing

Much more is known about the man for whom this town was named than about the town itself. Although a native of New York City, Isaac Polhamus journeyed to California in 1846 at the age of 18. He began his long career as a river navigator with a steamboat company on the Sacramento River. After 10 years, the Colorado Steam Navigation Company recruited Polhamus. Captain Polhamus happily relocated to the small river landing of Yuma, where he resided for the next 66 years. In 1881, another tiny river landing was established on the Colorado, and officials named it after the well-respected captain. Polhamus, who never resided in the town that bears his name, died in Yuma at the age of 94.
GPS COORDINATES: N35°11.60' W114°34.10' (approximately)
NEAREST TRAILS: Northwest #25: Thumb Butte Trail and Northwest #27: Powerline Road

Portal

The settlement of Portal is descriptively named after the town's location at the mouth of Cave Creek Canyon and is thought to have been founded by the Duffener brothers around the turn of the twentieth century. The origin of the name is from the Spanish *el portal,* meaning "the entrance." Formerly of Paradise, the Duffeners were drawn to the area to pursue their mining interests. The tiny post office, opened in 1905, still operates today.
GPS COORDINATES: N31°54.78' W109°08.48'
NEAREST TRAIL: South #20: Pinery Canyon Trail

Prescott

The discovery of gold in 1838 brought national attention to Prescott. Further discoveries in 1861 attracted the notice of President Abraham Lincoln, who was looking for possible sources of funding for the North during the Civil War. He created the Arizona Territory in 1863. Secretary of the territory Richard McCormick proposed the name at a meeting on May 30, 1864. The first territorial governor, John Goodwin, established Prescott as the first territorial capital and began laying out the downtown streets.

Prescott after fire destroyed the town in 1900

By 1865, rapidly developing Prescott was described as being built exclusively of wood and inhabited almost entirely by Americans. Both of these facts made it unique among early communities in Arizona. Prescott lost its title as the capital of Arizona to Tucson in 1867 before it was permanently changed to Phoenix in 1889. In 1900, a devastating fire burned Prescott to the ground; but it was rebuilt, and many of the present buildings are reminders of its past. Today, the older residential streets are lined with tall trees and pitched-roof frame houses, including turreted Victorians. Prescott has many homes and businesses on the National Register of Historic Places, and its white granite courthouse, set on a green lawn with spreading trees, reflects the Midwestern and New England background of Prescott's pioneers.
GPS COORDINATES: N34°32.40' W112°28.08'
TRAIL: Central #24: Senator Highway

Quartzsite

The most interesting feature in Quartzsite may be in the cemetery, where a statue of a camel rests upon a stone pyramid. The monument honors Hi Jolly, the town's most famous resident.

In 1855, Lieutenant Edward Beale believed that camels would prove to be invaluable pack animals for the army. The military imported a herd of 75 dromedaries, along with several native herders, for the initial training. A Greek convert to Islam named Hadjii Ali worked as one of the camel herders. Soldiers on the mission Americanized the man's name, referring to him as Hi Jolly. As difficulties developed between the foreign beasts and U.S. soldiers, Beale's plan was abandoned. However, Hi Jolly, also known as Philip Tedro, remained in the Arizona desert and worked as a trail guide and prospector. The foreigner lived the rest of his days in Quartzsite and died in 1903 at the age of 75.

Quartzsite's old stage station, 1930

After miners discovered gold near the area, a small town, which was not more than a stage stop, arose. Originally called Tyson's Well for an early settler, the community was officially renamed Quartzsite after a post office was established in 1923.
GPS COORDINATES: N33°40.04' W114°12.97'
NEAREST TRAIL: Northwest #3: South Plomosa Range Trail

Redington

The Redfield brothers, Henry and Lem, lived in this area of southeast Arizona in 1875. In 1883, a stagecoach was robbed on the road from Florence to Globe. The bandits made off with $1,000 in gold and $2,000 in silver, killing a man during the holdup. People recalled seeing two men of the robbers' description on the road to the Redfield Ranch, some 75 miles away from the scene of the crime. Sheriff Doran and his posse decided to investigate the lead. When they arrived at the Redfield Ranch, the posse found the shotgun used in the robbery as well as a mail sack that was on the stage. As it turned out, Redfield was the mastermind behind the robbery. With further investigation, Doran found that the landowner had planned a number of other unsolved robberies in the area.

The people of Florence were outraged, but Sheriff Doran would not let them carry out there own retribution; rather he insisted that the case follow due process of law. However, the citizens of the town thought that Redfield, a rich man, would be able to buy his way out of conviction. So when Doran had briefly left the jailhouse, an angry mob lynched Lem Redfield.

When the post office was established in 1879, residents' first choice of the name of Redfield was denied; their second selection was Redington.

GPS COORDINATES: N32°25.67' W110°29.52'
TRAIL: South #31: Redington Road
MAP: Pages 554–5

Reef

The mining settlement of Reef became active in 1893 when prospectors discovered the first veins of gold and silver. The town continued to see activity until 1926. More than 100 people (some estimates go as far as 200 people) resided in Reef, which had a post office, a florist, a natural spring, and a phone line to Tombstone. Reef gained a mill for processing gold in 1899. When built, the mill was believed to be the most advanced of its kind, but workers utilized the factory for only six weeks before technical problems forced its closure. In 1903, workers dismantled the mill and moved down the mountain.

Reef opened its post office in 1900. In 1904, the name of the post office and town changed to Palmerlee after the new owner. By 1911, the town's name had changed again to Garces after the early explorer Fray Francisco Garcés.

During World War I, Reef turned to mining tungsten, and laborers constructed a tungsten-processing mill on the site of the original plant. Later, quartz was mined; light-colored piles of quartz may be seen along South #17: Carr Canyon Trail from the hiking trailhead opposite the Reef Town Site Campground.

GPS COORDINATES: N31°25.74' W110°17.39'
TRAIL: South #17: Carr Canyon Trail
MAP: Page 516

Reymert

On December 1, 1876, J. D. Reymert, a lawyer and the publisher of the *Pinal Drill* newspaper, discovered a rich silver vein about 12 miles southeast of Pinal. A new mining camp sprang to life. The camp eventually turned into a town and was named Reymert in honor of the man who found the silver vein. The Reymert Mining Company worked the vein on and off until the 1950s. During its years of operation, an estimated $700,000 worth of silver is said to have been extracted from the mine.

Anywhere from 100 to 5,000 people were said to have lived in the town. An 1890 census reported that 254 people lived in Reymert. The silver vanished in the 1950s, but a few residents lingered in the town until the 1960s.

Today, there is nothing left at the site of Reymert. Foundations onced showed the whereabouts of the assay house, blacksmith shop, boardinghouses, and the Wells, Fargo & Company station. However, the site was bulldozed in the 1970s, thus eradicating any indication of a town.

GPS COORDINATES: N33°13.80' W111°12.50'
TRAIL: Central #41: Box Canyon Trail
MAP: Page 452

Salome

At the age of 21, DeForest Hall, later known as Dick Wick Hall, traveled west from Iowa to the Arizona Territory. Settling in the Wickenburg area, Hall worked as a census bureau counter on the Hopi reservations, as a rancher, and as a construction worker. It wasn't until Hall became editor of the *Wickenburg News-Herald* that he earned the nickname Dick Wick.

When Dick and a friend struck gold a few miles west of town, a new settlement arose around the Glory Mine. Named for the wife of Dick's friend and business partner, Salome grew into a small but substantial town. Dick wanted his town to be well-known, so he opened a gas station in hopes of bringing in business. In order to advertise, the entrepreneur needed a theme—a mascot of some sort, which is how the Salome frog came into existence. With help from the *Saturday Evening Post,* Salome's cartoon mascot became famous.

Dick Wick Hall's gas station in Salome in 1927

Although the town dwindled years ago after Dick Wick's death in 1926, Salome "dances" one night out of the year. Commemorators gather annually to feast on barbecue, to square dance, and to celebrate Salome and its unforgotten heritage.

GPS COORDINATES: N33°46.87' W113°36.70'
TRAILS: Northwest #4: Desert Queen Mine Trail and Central #11: Harquahala Mine Trail
MAP: Pages 147 & 367

Sedona

Once inhabited only by fruit farmers, today Sedona boasts one of the top five arts communities in the country. Hundreds of years ago, Native American tribes—Hopi, Navajo, and Sinagua—lived in cliff dwellings at what is now Montezuma's Castle National Monument. In the 1870s, farmers settled in the region and planted apple and peach trees. By the turn of the century, about 15 families resided in the Oak Creek area year-round.

Two of the residents were T. Carl "T. C." and Sedona Schnebly, a couple from Missouri who moved to the area for a more peaceful way of life. In addition to running the town's first hotel, Carl also served as the town's first postmaster. When the burden of naming the town fell upon him, Carl initially came up with two names, Oak Creek Crossing and Schnebly Station, both of which were too long. Carl's brother

T. Carl "T. C." Schnebley's house and nearby tents used by campers, 1901

Ellsworth suggested that he call the town Sedona after his wife, and the name stuck.

Today, Sedona continues to grow, fueling the home construction industry. In addition, the town has become a hub for more than 150 resident artists, retirees, spiritual seekers, and those who wish to live a peaceful life. Since the 1920s, the area has welcomed Hollywood stars such as Jimmy Stewart, Henry Fonda, Rock Hudson, and Robert DeNiro, who have stayed there while filming feature movies. More than 40 art galleries call Sedona home, a testament to the inspirational beauty that prompts many people to relocate to the town. Some seeking a metaphysical experience claim that the red rocks encompassing the region contain "dynamic areas," or "vortices," that embody great amounts of spiritual energy.

Whatever the reason, more and more people are discovering this eclectic town, whose streets bear names like Doodlebug, Stutz Bearcat, Painted Cliffs, and Little Elf. It is easy to succumb to the beauty and wonder of Sedona.

GPS COORDINATES: N34°52.27' W111°45.62'

TRAILS: Northeast #23: Soldier Pass Road and Northeast #24: Schnebly Hill Road

MAP: Pages 276 & 277

Signal

Under the stern ruling hand of justice of the peace, Moses Levy, the citizens of Signal proved to be largely law-abiding. In 1874, prospectors discovered silver and established the McCracken Mine. Several small towns sprang up around it. Three years later, the Signal Silver Mining Company constructed a 10-stamp mill and Signal was born. Within just a few months the town had reached its peak with a population of 700 and more than 200 buildings. However, it dwindled significantly in 1879 when the mill and mine closed. Merchants in Signal often waited six months for their supplies to arrive because there was no convenient freighting route to the town. Despite these inconveniences, residents continued to inhabit the town for many years until the post office closed in 1932.

GPS COORDINATES: N34°28.26' W113°37.60'

TRAIL: Northwest #17: Signal Road

MAP: Pages 176–7

Stanton

The history of Stanton is inextricably linked with Charles P. Stanton, a conniving and ruthless man who single-handedly caused tremendous upset and violence in the settlement. The town of Stanton, originally called Antelope Station, boasted a general store and stage station. Most of the town's settlers were miners as well as a few merchants who moved in to provide services to the laborers. William Partridge, an Englishman, ran the stage station, and G. H. "Yaqui" Wilson owned the general store. Accounts vary, but the most prevalent one states that enmity arose between the two men when Wilson's pigs escaped into Partridge's garden. This trivial incident initiated a feud between the men that would eventually have tragic consequences.

Charles Stanton, originally from Ireland, relocated from Nevada to the gold camps in central Arizona. Previously the assayer at the Vulture Mine near Wickenburg, Stanton arrived in Antelope Station in the early 1870s. From the beginning, he was universally disliked; townspeople mockingly referred to him as the "Irish Lord." By unfair means Stanton had acquired a half-interest in the Leviathan Mine near Rich Hill. He used his earnings to build a cabin and open a small store. However, his aspirations went way beyond this simple contentment. Envious of Wilson's successful general store and the trade attached to Partridge's stage station, Stanton plotted to destroy the competition. The malicious man played upon the mutual dislike between the two men and eventually instigated a gunfight during which Partridge killed Wilson. The law found Partridge guilty of murder and sent him to Yuma Territorial Prison, where Wilson's ghost supposedly haunted him.

The old stage stop now used as a saloon in Stanton

However, Stanton could not immediately succeed in acquiring the two businesses. Unknown to the Irish Lord, Wilson had a silent partner named Timmerman, who claimed the store. Partridge's creditors claimed the stage station and sold it to Barney Martin. But Stanton was unfazed by this new turn of events. He hired a band of outlaws, led by Franciso Vega, who murdered Timmerman as he returned from Phoenix. Stanton then produced a will, allegedly written by Timmerman, that named him as the heir. Stanton, the town's postmaster, immediately changed the name from Antelope Station to Stanton.

Stanton could now run the town as he saw fit. The only person of importance left in the town apart from Stanton himself was Barney Martin. However, Martin supposedly received an intimidating threat, and he and his family soon departed for Phoenix. The unfortunate family never arrived and some weeks later their scorched bodies and burned wagon were found a few miles from Stanton. No one was ever charged with the murders, but the people around town had a pretty good idea who caused the family's death. There were many murders in the town at this time, and it seemed that each time only Stanton profited, though he did not live long enough to prosper from his deeds. In 1886, Cristo Lucero gunned down Stanton in his store because the man had insulted his sister. As Lucero was leaving town, he ran into Tom Pierson, a man not too fond of Stanton. Pierson told Lucero that he need not flee—in fact, he would probably receive a reward for his act of community service.

The town of Stanton closed down a few years later when the mines were exhausted. The post office closed first in 1890. Then a small resurgence of activity caused the post office to be reopened in 1894. The town had about 200 people for a few years before it dwindled again. The post office finally closed in 1905.

In 1950, the *Saturday Evening Post* bought the town site and awarded it to the winner of a jingle competition. Today the Lost Dutchman Mining Association, which has restored the remaining original buildings, owns Stanton. Partridge's stage station, now called the Hotel Stanton, still stands as does the store in which Charles Stanton was murdered.

GPS COORDINATES: N34°09.83' W112°43.83'
TRAIL: Central #22: Stanton Ghost Town Trail
MAP: Page 397

Stoddard

Located on the banks of the Agua Fria River, this copper mining town was named for the well-known mining developer Isaac Stoddard. When a new copper smelting mill was constructed at the site in 1880, a town grew around it. Its residents mainly worked for the nearby Stoddard and Binghampton Mines, and the town boasted all the necessary amenities. At the end of World War I, about 100 residents called Stoddard home, but when copper prices plummeted, so did the population. Only a few scattered remains are visible.

GPS COORDINATES: N34°25.46' W112°11.39'
NEAREST TRAIL: Central #25: Mayer-Goodwin Road

Sundad

Not much is known about the ghost town of Sundad. Originally a mining settlement, the site was once touted as being a suitable location for the state sanatorium. Another source indicates that the site was originally intended to be a desert health facility. However, these plans never got off the ground and Sundad faded into obscurity. Today the desolate town may be reached by traveling 1 mile down a spur off Central #15: Agua Caliente Road. Little is left—some small foundations, mine shafts, a tank, and the old bottle dump.

GPS COORDINATES: N33°10.85' W113°14.16'
TRAIL: Central #15: Agua Caliente Road
MAP: Page 377

Sunnyside

In sharp contrast to most mining towns of the time, Sunnyside boasted no saloons or gambling halls. The town did not even have a jail. Its founder, Samuel Donnelly, along with several of his followers, established the town in 1887 as a religious community. A former drinker, Donnelly had found sobriety at a Salvation Army meeting in San Francisco and followed his calling into the ministry. He did not advocate or adhere to any specific dogma or doctrine; rather he used the Bible solely as his and his followers' guide.

The community of 50 families formed a commune, with members working at various jobs and pooling their earnings. Residents spent their time singing hymns, reading the Bible, and working in the nearby Copper Glance Mine. Other income for the hardworking community was derived from cutting hay for Fort Huachuca, running a sawmill, and working on the railroad. Stores were not needed in Sunnyside —residents consolidated their goods, cooked, and ate in communal areas. The women prepared meals together and washed the laundry in large tubs. Idlers were not tolerated; anyone who would not contribute was asked to leave.

Sunnyside ghost town, 1969

Communal life seemed to work very well for the residents of this small town in southern Arizona. Visitors often remarked how happy everyone appeared. The violence, hard drinking, and prostitution often associated with mining camps of the era did not exist. Indeed, the residents practiced what they preached and often gave food, supplies, and money to people in need. Donnelly even contributed scholarship funds for students attending the University of Arizona. When visiting the universtiy, Donnelly met some struggling students who made $8.50 per month while being faced with bills and expenses of $13 per month. Donnelly was quick to donate $20 per month to each student.

Sunnyside ghost town today

Samuel Donnelly died in 1901, but the "Donnelites," as they were known, remained for several years. The little town received a post office on July 16, 1914, but it closed 20 years later when the mines were exhausted. The Donnelites dispersed, giving the mine to their creditors. John McIntyre came to Sunnyside as a three-year-old in 1893. He saw the town progress through many periods of history and took care of the site after the town folded. McIntyre died in the 1980s, and with him went the last link to the commune of Sunnyside.

GPS COORDINATES: N31°26.06' W110°24.23'
TRAIL: South #11: Sunnyside Trail
MAP: Page 498

Superior, circa 1920

Superior

Present-day Superior, named after Superior, Michigan, owes its more than 125 years of success to the Magma Copper Mine. Although the mine closed in 1996, its prosperity led to the continuation of the community. George Lobb, credited with developing the town in 1900, was often referred to as the Father of Superior. Today Superior is a modern industrial town. One of the town's main attractions is the Boyce Thompson Arboretum. Founded by mining tycoon Colonel William Boyce in the 1920s, it is the oldest arboretum in the American Southwest.

Hollywood has recently taken an interest in Superior. Both the horror film *The Prophecy* and Oliver Stone's *U-turn* have been set on Superior's old-fashioned streets.

GPS COORDINATES: N33°17.61' W111°05.85'

TRAILS: Central #39: Montana Mountain Trail and Central #40: Telegraph Canyon Trail

MAP: Pages 445 & 448–9

Swansea

The history of Swansea (originally known as Signal) began in 1886 when three prospectors searching for silver explored the region between the Buckskin and Rawhide Mountains. The men were not very happy with their find, which was some silver but mostly copper ore. Uninterested, the three moved on in hopes of better luck elsewhere.

Copper prices climbed in the early 1900s and one of the three prospectors, with a new partner, returned to the area to stake a claim. However, the cost of transporting ore remained high, making the prospect of mining in the area not very profitable. Luckily, in 1904, the Arizona & California Railroad decided to build a line west from Phoenix. The improved transportation was completed in 1907 and led to renewed interest in mining districts along the line.

In 1907, Newton Evans and Thomas Carrigan owned the mine at Swansea. Together they approached George Mitchell, a Welsh-born metallurgist and opportunist with a gift for promoting mines. Mitchell had arrived in the United States in the 1880s with his brother Robert and was involved in developing mines in Alaska and Mexico. The man's ethics were questionable, and he appeared to profit handsomely from his ventures while others lost considerably. His previous venture, the Mitchell Mining Company of Mexico, went bankrupt, but he personally gained more than $200,000.

Mitchell realized the site's potential and threw himself into developing Swansea with great enthusiasm. In 1908, he consolidated the claims as the Clara Consolidated Gold and Copper Mining Company and began selling shares. Mitchell's dreams were grandiose, and initially prospects seemed rosy. Using the money raised, Mitchell built an electricity plant, piped water from the Bill Williams River, and constructed grand houses for the mine managers and smaller cottages for the workers. The town of Swansea, with a population of 750, boasted a newspaper, restaurants, saloons, and a movie house. The town also featured an insurance salesman and a car dealership.

When the post office was registered, the name of the town was changed from Signal to Swansea, after Mitchell's hometown in Wales. Mitchell continued to attract outside investors; he took a profitable and much-publicized trip to France, during which he raised $2 million. He had a taste for the high life, and although he was able to bring in outside money, Mitchell proved to be just as good at spending it. His lavish 3,600-square-foot adobe home with its palm-lined entranceway and his luxury French car testified to that fact. One account of Mitchell's development of Swansea says the town was "an example of enthusiasm run wild, coupled with reckless stock selling and foolish construction of surface works before the development of enough ore to keep them busy."

With the completion of the railroad extension from Bouse to Swansea in 1910, Mitchell brought in machinery to construct a 700-ton smelter. Rather than cementing Swansea's status as a prosperous boomtown, the huge smelter hastened its demise. The smelter proved so inefficient that it cost 3¢ more to produce a pound of copper than the mineral's market value. Although the ore body was good, Mitchell had invested more funds in the amenities of Swansea than he did underground. The smelter was never run at full capacity, rendering it even less cost-effective.

In 1912, the mining company declared bankruptcy with debts of $712,000. Mitchell abandoned Swansea and became the manager of the Jerome Superior Copper Company. This enterprise went bankrupt after four years of his management. George Mitchell died in Los Angeles.

Rising copper prices revived interest briefly, and the mine at Swansea was worked under different owners until 1937 when the falling prices associated with the depression led to its closure. In its lifetime, the Clara Consolidated Gold and Copper Mining Company produced more than $5 million of copper.

GPS COORDINATES: N34°10.18' W113°50.73'

TRAILS: Northwest #6: Swansea Road and Northwest #11: Railroad Canyon Trail

MAP: Pages 152 & 164

Tip Top

In its current condition, this ghost town does not fit the grandeur that its name implies. Consisting only of skeletons of its former self, one would never guess it once boasted a population of 200.

In 1875, two men named Moore and Corning founded the Tip Top Silver Mine; nearly a year later, a camp began to grow around the claim. Most of the miners were former soldiers of the Civil War, but enmity did not prove to be a problem. Residents worried more about Indian attacks than past wartime grudges. But Tip Top was not immune to an occasional misfortune. One story reports that a centipede stung a slumbering man's toe. The distressed man ran to a local saloon, guzzled a liter of whiskey, and dropped dead. No one is certain whether it was the bite or the liquor that caused his death.

Although they had no church, Tip Top residents managed to participate in religious activities. When visiting preachers made their way into town, many of the men sat and listened attentively to the sermons. Inspired by the amount of beer consumed during the sermons, the residents were always generous when the collection plate was passed.

An old stone building in Tip Top in 1961

In 1895, silver prices dropped and so did the population of Tip Top.

GPS COORDINATES: N34°03.04' W112°14.78'

NEAREST TRAIL: Central #26: Crown King Backroad

Tombstone

On a hill overlooking the Tombstone town site lies Ed Schieffelin's grave. His epitaph simply reads: "This is my Tombstone." No one would dispute that fact. Schieffelin journeyed to the region in 1877 seeking silver. Soldiers from nearby Fort Huachuca labeled the prospector as a risk-taker, declaring that instead of silver, Schieffelin would certainly find his "tombstone."

But the headstrong man persevered and finally located his claim in August of that year, appropriately calling it the Tombstone Mine. Unsure of the ore's worth, Schieffelin carried the metal to an assayer, who valued it at $2,000 per ton. Enthusiastically, Ed, his brother, and Richard Gird founded four additional mines: Graveyard, Lucky Cuss, Tough Nut, and Contention.

Modoc stagecoach outside the Hotel Nobles in Tombstone, circa 1880

By 1879, the first home was built in Tombstone and within a short time a true mining town emerged. Arizona governor A. P. K. Stafford even invested in a reduction mill and two of the mines. Between 1880 and 1886, the mines produced more than $40 million in ore.

After mining, gambling was Tombstone's second-largest industry. By 1881, the town boasted 110 liquor licenses; saloons and gambling halls lined the main drag, Allen Street. With a population of around 15,000, crime became inevitable. On October 26, 1881, a legendary gunfight took place at the O.K. Corral (see page 82). Doc Holliday, Wyatt Earp, and his brothers Virgil and Morgan shot down three outlaws during the famous battle, which ironically lasted only a few seconds. Three years later, five men were hanged in Tombstone for the murder and robbery of a store clerk. After these incidents, the crime rate in the town diminished.

Tombstone's large population fluctuated greatly between 1880 and 1890 because of flooding in the mines. Many laborers were forced to relocate in order to find jobs. In 1901, Ed Schieffelin formed the Tombstone Consolidated Mining Company. It operated for 13 years until Phelps Dodge Corporation purchased it in 1914.

Today, the town has a new booming industry—tourism. More than 200,000 tourists visit Tombstone each year. Many original structures still stand to welcome onlookers; the red brick Cochise County Courthouse, City Hall, Bird Cage Theater, St. Paul's Episcopal Church, and Boot Hill Cemetery all bask in their original glory. Visitors may even pick up a copy of the *Tombstone Epitaph,* the town's newspaper. In addition to Ed Schieffelin's grave, visitors may also notice the grave of Dutch Annie, Tombstone's second most famous resident. Dutch Annie reigned as the town's prominent and well-loved queen of the red-light district. One thousand mourners, mainly businessmen and city officials, attended the woman's funeral. Although Tombstone has quieted since its heyday, the town's rich history stirs the imagination of all who wander its streets.

GPS COORDINATES: N31°42.80' W110°03.96'

NEAREST TRAIL: South #18: Mule Mountains Trail

Tortilla Flat

Tortilla Flat gets its name from the flat-top mountains in the area that looked like tortillas to early settlers. Major William Emory officially gave the area this name when he surveyed the region in 1853. Nearby Tortilla Butte was named 20 years later by a member of the Wheeler Survey named Arch Mavine.

When a new route was being built to Roosevelt Dam, Tortilla Flat became a freight station and camp along the way. The road reached Tortilla Flat in November 1904 and curiosity seekers traveled from Phoenix to view the construction of the new road. Mail service along the route began in 1904, although an 8-mile stretch in the middle continued to rely on horses and

mules for access. Officials promoted the road, now officially called the Apache Trail, as a tourist attraction in the 1920s.
GPS COORDINATES: N33°31.56' W111°23.37'
TRAIL: Central #38: Apache Trail
MAP: Pages 440–1

Tubac Presidio

In 1752, Spanish priests founded this mission and presidio, or garrison, whose name means "round house ruins." Tubac residents were plagued by the very same Indians from whom the mission's name was derived.

In the 1700s, Padre Eusebio Francisco Kino commissioned the construction of several missions. Three of these missions were built in the Tubac region: San Xavier del Bac, Tumacacori, and Guevavi. Although the last two exist only as ruins, San Xavier, or White Dove of the Desert, remains active today. Hostile Pima and Papago Indians terrorized the priests until they finally abandoned the missions.

In 1854, Charles D. Poston and Herman Ehrenberg established their mining headquarters at Tubac. Later known as the Father of Arizona, Poston became a leader of the town. With no priest nearby, he took on the role of baptizer and justice of the peace. By this time the town's population had grown to 1,000, four-fifths of whom were Mexican. The vast majority of Tubac's residents were illiterate and could not read the paper currency of the time. Therefore, a special form of "animal" money evolved, with pictures of pigs, roosters, and other animals that indicated the currency's value.

When soldiers abandoned Tubac Presidio during the Civil War, ranchers relocated to the garrison for protection against the Indians. Miners ceased operations when a string of attacks left many dead. However, after the military stationed a troop of California volunteers at this post in 1866, workers felt secure enough to return to the mines. Ten years later, Arizona's first Mormon settlers established camp in Tubac but did not stay long.

The stunning mission architecture, as well as ruins of the other two missions, can be viewed at Tubac.
GPS COORDINATES: N31°36.64' W111°02.70'
NEAREST TRAIL: South #12: Mexican Border Road

Tucson

A budding urban city, Tucson has a European history that dates back as far as the 1500s when Father Marcos de Niza visited the area. Originally called Presidio of San Jose de Tucson, the village served as a ranchiera and mission by 1763. Tucson is the second oldest European settlement in the United States, only younger than Santa Fe.

Tucson, a Piman word for "dark spring," became part of the Arizona Territory as a result of the Gadsden Purchase in 1853–54. Tucson won the Arizona capital from Prescott in 1867. It was lost to Phoenix in 1889. In 1912, the country embraced Arizona as its forty-eighth state.

Today, Tucson's population boasts around 1 million and continues to grow at a rapid rate. The city claims a large cultural and arts presence for its youthful population, which has a median age of 32. A growing high-tech manufacturing industry supports Tucson's strong economy while the University of Arizona at Tucson contributes a great number of students to the workforce. Resting upon its hearty foundation, Tucson continues to create history for itself.
GPS COORDINATES: N32°14.00' W110°57.09'
NEAREST TRAILS: South #27: Oracle Control Road and South #32: Buehman Canyon Trail

Streetcars and automobiles in Tucson, circa 1905

Venezia

Although a post office was not established in this mining camp until 1916, recorded activity dates back as early as the 1880s. An Italian settler named F. Scopel named the town after his hometown of Venice. By 1925 the small village supported only about 75 residents, a general store, and a stage line. However, mines in the area produced approximately $750,000 worth of gold.
GPS COORDINATES: N34°23.54' W112°24.90'
TRAIL: Central #24: Senator Highway
MAP: Pages 402–3

Vicksburg

Though many think that this town in southwestern Arizona was named after the town on the Mississippi River, its name actually has a much more local derivation. Located on present-day Arizona 72, Vicksburg was named after a storekeeper in the 1890s, Victor Satterdahl, who set up a post office in his store in 1906. Wells, Fargo & Company had a stage station in Vicksburg in 1907. Today, the town has a small, year-round population that swells every winter with visiting "snowbirds" from the north.
GPS COORDINATES: N33°44.62' W113°45.09'
TRAIL: Northwest #4: Desert Queen Mine Trail
MAP: Page 147

Virginia City

Area prospectors named Virginia City after the town in Nevada that bears the same name. Workers from Virginia City and its sister city, Signal, labored in the McCracken Mine and smelter. With a population of about 700 in 1877, the small camp had several buildings, including mill offices, a drugstore, a respectable hotel, and a restaurant. Today, nothing remains.
GPS COORDINATES: N34°27.10' W113°46.19' (approximately)
TRAIL: Northwest #16: McCracken Peak Trail
MAP: Page 174

Miners at Walker Mining District, 1898

Walker

In 1863, Captain Joseph R. Walker (see page 71), then age 65, led a party of prospectors from New Mexico through Arizona. The group set up camp in the area that would later be known as Prescott. During an exploration of the region, several men discovered gold and established a new camp. They named the settlement after their trusted guide, Walker. Located on Lynx Creek, the mining camp grew to a population of 2,700 and lasted for 80 years. A fire station is there today as well as the remains of a giant charcoal kiln nearby.

GPS COORDINATES: N34°27.40' W112°22.62'
TRAIL: Central #24: Senator Highway
MAP: Pages 402–3

Washington Camp

Prospectors staked claims in this region in the 1860s, but hostile Indians prevented development until the 1880s. At this time, Thomas Shane and his associate Mr. Capen brought life back to Washington Camp with the discovery of the Bonanza Mine. The claims changed hands often, until the Duquesne Mining and Reduction Company purchased many of the mines in the late 1880s. That is when the real boom began.

Duquesne and Washington Camp were less than 1 mile apart with more than 70 active mines and nearly 2,000 residents between the two. The two towns were extremely dependent on each other, as they were located in such a remote desert environment. The mining company constructed a smelter and reduction plant in Washington Camp along with its offices, a boardinghouse, and stores. A schoolhouse that served both towns was located at the midway point. The settlements flourished and survived into the early 1900s, but by 1920 the towns were deserted.

A brief mining resurgence in the early 1940s brought a momentary flicker back to the virtual ghost town of Washington Camp. A number of houses have remained occupied over the years while nature has slowly reclaimed the dozens of mine shafts.

GPS COORDINATES: N31°22.86' W110°41.44'
TRAIL: South #12: Mexican Border Road
MAP: Pages 502–3

Weaver

In 1863, a party guided by famous Southwest explorer Pauline Weaver (see page 71) camped for the night along Antelope Creek. The expedition was organized by Abraham Peeples to investigate rumors of gold in central Arizona. While at the camp, a Mexican named Alvaro climbed the rocky hill beside the creek and stumbled across a rich field of gold nuggets. This lucky find formed the basis of the Rich Hill Mining District.

Named for the explorer, Weaver was initially a tent city, as the initail rush of prospectors had little time to build anything but the makeshift dwellings. Gradually, the town acquired more permanent buildings and a reputation for thievery. Murders and shootings in Weaver were commonplace. Many of the thugs hired by Charles Stanton (see page 50) found refuge in the town. After the murder of storekeeper William Segna, a newspaper article called for Weaver to be closed. Many of the decent folk relocated to nearby Octave because the gold was beginning to run out and they were scared for their own well-being.

One of the more unusual incidents associated with Weaver concerned the local Indians. In December 1863, three Mexicans who made their living cutting grama grass had strayed farther than usual from the town. While working, they were surrounded by Indians who first demanded their firearms, then their guns, their burros, and finally their clothes. The Indians then took off, leaving the naked Mexicans to slink back home to Weaver.

Stanton's General Store in Weaver, circa 1880

The gold played out and by 1899 all the remaining people of Weaver had moved to Octave.

GPS COORDINATES: N34°09.22' W112°42.88'
TRAIL: Central #22: Stanton Ghost Town Trail
MAP: Page 397

White Hills

Local Hualapai Indians used the region's red iron oxide for face paint long before White Hills became a flourishing mining camp. In 1887, an Indian known as Hualapai Jeff located a sample of silver chloride. However, local white men told Jeff that the iron was worthless, so he paid no more attention to the ore.

In the winter of 1891, rancher Frank Robinson asked Hualapai Jeff to help him round up some cattle that had strayed over to White Hills. The men camped near Jeff's original silver claim, and the Indian once again picked up a good specimen. This time he kept it. Shortly after, Judge Henry Schaffer asked Hualapai Jeff if he knew of any good mineral deposits, and the man revealed his find. Recognizing the nearly pure silver, Schaffer offered Jeff $200 to show him the location of the deposits.

In 1892, Jeff led a party consisting of Schaffer, John Barnett, and John Sullivan back to the White Hills, or Secret Mining District, location. They staked the claims that would later become Horn Silver, Occident, Grand Army, Chief of the Hills, Treasurer, Norma, and Emma Mines. A separate party led by rancher John Robinson arrived 10 days later, and those men also staked claims.

News traveled rapidly and within two weeks of the find, a small town of 200 people, a store, four saloons, three restaurants, and a large number of tents grew around the mines. The demand for lots was so high that many would-be residents had to claim their land by sleeping on it. More than a few miners woke up in the company of the rattlesnakes that crawled under their bedding in the night. The town grew rapidly and soon supported a population of 1,500. In 1892, Postmaster Taggart gave the town the official name of White Hills, after the exposed rock of the region.

Many of the initial claims were not immediately worked, and in 1893 a Colorado consortium purchased all the claims except the Treasurer and Emma. The property was sold again in 1895, this time to an English company. Enthusiastically, the new owners constructed a 40-stamp mill and a power plant and laid water pipes to help solve the town's severe water shortage. However, even with spring water piped in daily, a lack of water continued to plague the town.

In addition to the water dilemma, White Hills experienced a rat infestation. To conquer the rodents, residents shipped in a large number of cats. When the felines reproduced, White Hills found itself overwhelmed with an enormous cat population. The solution: Use the felines as target practice. Unfortunately, the slain cats were left unburied, causing even more health problems for the mining town.

A surprise flash flood on the morning of August 5, 1899, swept the town away. Workers in the Grand Army Extension Mine narrowly escaped as the rising waters filled the mine. The schoolhouse and many homes floated away, and 2 feet of soil was deposited on the town's streets. The *Mohave County Miner* reported the flooding and stated, "We might call the affair too much of a good thing. For water sells at one dollar a barrel at White Hills. They just had a million dollar bath."

The town never really recovered and many residents relocated to nearby Chloride. A few miners remained and extracted a fair living from the mines. There have been various attempts to reopen the mines over the years, most of them short-lived.

GPS COORDINATES: N35°43.84' W114°23.15'
TRAIL: Northwest #29: White Hills Trail
MAP: Page 209

Wickenburg

Henry Heintzel fled from his homeland of Austria after government officials threatened to jail him for illegal mining. Upon arriving in the United States, Heintzel immediately changed his name to Wickenburg and struck out for the West. The new immigrant reached Yuma, Arizona, in 1862 but missed the party he was supposed to meet. Undaunted, Wickenburg traveled more than 200 miles alone and met the group in Peeples Valley.

After an unsuccessful prospecting trip, Wickenburg decided to search by himself for a while. According to the most recurrent story, the prospector noticed a group of vultures circling a tall peak. After he reached the base of the mountain, Wickenburg discovered a large gold strike. An honest man, Wickenburg included his partners' names in the claim and together they dug ore for the next 10 weeks.

Physically exhausted and unimpressed with the claim, Wickenburg's cohorts decided to leave the site. So the lone man persevered, digging the ore by hand and milling it in a crude arrastra. Finally, an assayer valued Wickenburg's claim at $100,000 per ton and investors began to take notice. Wickenburg hired workers for $15 per ton, but many of the unethical miners stole the highest-quality ore for themselves. Regardless, the Vulture Mine produced thousands of dollars worth of gold for its owner.

The Wickenburg stage office, circa 1890

In 1865, Wickenburg decided to change careers to ranching and sold his share of the mine to Benjamin Phelps for $85,000. Because of legal disputes concerning ownership, Wickenburg only received $20,000 for his mine, most of which he spent on litigation fees. Despondent but not broken, Wickenburg left the mining business for good and began life as a rancher.

Phelps owned the Vulture Mine for only a few years, but during this time the mine produced $2.5 million in gold. With so much valuable ore present, criminals were always close at hand. Officials kept the bullion in a "secure" location within town. However, one day three outlaws easily stole $75,000 in gold and escaped with the loot. A posse killed one of the outlaws, but the remaining two fled to Mexico. Luckily, the robbers did not prove to be too smart. After just a couple of months, one of the criminals returned to the area to retrieve his buried treasure, only to be shot and killed by officials. All of the gold was recovered.

Crime sprees were rampant in Wickenburg and in the Vulture Mine. If outlaws were not killing miners for gold, Indians were murdering their white enemies. Within 15 years, more than 400 whites died at the hands of hostile Indians.

The Vulture Mine changed ownership several times, and at one point no more ore could be located. McClyde, the mine's owner at the time, discovered a vein of high-quality ore within the rock pillars that supported the mine's roof. Desperate for new ore, McClyde began extracting the ore and it was not long before the mine's roof collapsed under the pressure. Today, passersby may easily view the result of this cave-in, or "glory hole."

Currently, Wickenburg is a popular resort area complete with guest ranches and hotels. The Vulture Mine closed operations as a result of a World War II ban on nonstrategic mining, but the ruins are quite visible. Also discernible are many of the old buildings, including the assay office, blacksmith shop, and two schoolhouses. A peek inside will even reveal many of the original antiques.

Unfortunately, Henry Wickenburg's demise was not as graceful as his town's. At the age of 85, the old man's savings had run dry and he sadly ended his life with a self-inflicted bullet wound to the head.

GPS COORDINATES: N33°58.13' W112°43.76'
TRAIL: Central #20: Buckhorn Creek Trail
MAP: Pages 390–1

Williams

Known as the Gateway to the Grand Canyon, the town of Williams was first settled in 1876, just about the same time that Flagstaff was founded. The name of the town came from the famous red-haired trapper "Old Bill" Williams (see page 69), who wandered and trapped the Arizona countryside. Williams remained a sleepy little settlement until the arrival of the railroad in 1882, which changed it forever.

The Southern Pacific and Santa Fe Railroads had been pushing their way into Grand Canyon country since the late 1870s. When the railroad reached Williams, the lumber and cattle industries moved in and began to become established. The railroad bolstered the town and the population rose to 500. By 1901, the railroad would introduce a new industry to Williams—tourism.

Williams became a popular tourist attraction after the Santa Fe Railroad linked the town to the awe-inspiring Grand Canyon. The opening of Route 66 (connecting Chicago and Los Angeles) during the 1920s further increased the number of visitors to Williams. Route 66 and the railroad became lifelines for the town.

But superhighways loomed in the future. Multilane highways bypassed Route 66 after 1956 when Congress approved the Federal Aid Highway Act, which required the federal government to substantially back the creation of a system of interstate and defense highways. Williams was the last town to be bypassed by the highways. The use of railroads had been steadily decreasing and the loss of Route 66 threatened the town's very existence. However, Williams surprised everyone by continuing to grow and, today, Williams is a high-class tourist area. The buildings in its historical downtown were built at the turn of the century and are among the best preserved in Arizona. The railroad to the Grand Canyon is still in use, firmly asserting that Williams is still the Gateway to the Grand Canyon.

GPS COORDINATES: N35°15.02' W112°11.25'
NEAREST TRAIL: Northeast #9: Bill Williams Mountain Loop Road

Winchester

The town of Winchester is possibly the most well-established, shortest-lived mining town in Arizona's history. Named for Josiah Winchester, the settlement grew rapidly after Dick Wick Hall found an enormous claim in the area. A major gold rush occurred in 1909 when Hall's ore assayed between $117,000 and $338,000 per ton.

Winchester boomed! Approaching a population of 2,000 in the first month, the town boasted two restaurants, a saloon, an accommodation house, and various stores, including a lumberyard. A telephone line linked the town to Vicksburg. Josiah Winchester, through zealous promotion, sold $2,500 worth of town lots on the first day alone, and the town was soon the largest on the Arizona & California Railroad. After only two months, the gold had run out and despondent Winchester residents departed.

GPS COORDINATES: N33°47.04' W113°43.86'
TRAIL: Northwest #4: Desert Queen Mine Trail
MAP: Page 147

Winslow

The first settler of Winslow is said to have been F. C. "Doc" Demerest. In 1880, Doc, who used to work in the hotel industry, set up his tent at the town's present site and began selling his wares. Winslow was not the earliest settlement in the area. Just 3 miles north of Winslow lay the small community of Sunset Crossing, established in 1876 by Mormon settlers.

The site of Sunset Crossing was critical because it was one of the few places that travelers could ford the hazardous Little Colorado River. A small fort was built to protect the early settlement and irrigation ditches were dug. But with the coming of the railroad, the sun set on that community and gave birth to Winslow as the important division point of the Atlantic & Pacific and the Santa Fe Railroads.

There are two theories on the source of Winslow's name. One suggests that the town was named after railroad executive

Santa Fe Pacific Depot in Winslow, circa 1890

General Edward Winslow. The other states that the town was named after local prospector Tom Winslow.

With the aid of the railroad and the stock-raising industry, Winslow became one of the largest towns in northern Arizona. Fred Harvey, the man who revolutionized dining on the railway (previously, dining on trains had been a very grim affair), built the Hotel La Posada within the city. La Posada, a reproduction of a Spanish hacienda, was a refreshing oasis for hungry travelers. More recently, this friendly community received another claim to fame. The Eagles spotlighted the town in the song "Take It Easy," with the lyric, "I was standin' on a corner in Winslow, Arizona / Such a fine sight to see."

GPS COORDINATES: N35°01.69' W110°41.82'

NEAREST TRAILS: Northeast #35: Chance Draw Trail and Northeast #38: Chevelon Crossing Road

Yuma

Although Spaniard Hernando de Alarcon was the first recorded explorer in the southwest corner of Arizona in 1540, various Indian tribes have inhabited this area for thousands of years. Fray Francisco Garcés built a mission there in 1775, but six years later, hostile Indians murdered all the male residents.

During the next 50 years, there were few incursions by whites. In 1829, famed trapper Kit Carson visited the region with his beaver pelts. By 1849, more than 60,000 settlers were moving through the district on their way to California. Hostile Indian attacks spurred the construction of Fort Yuma in 1850 to protect the emigrants. Three years later, Colorado City, named for the nearby river, was established adjacent to the garrison. When the town became the county seat in 1866, officials changed its name to Yuma.

Yuma, 1906

Despite the fact that mining did not support Yuma, the settlement grew steadily. Strategically located on the Colorado River, Yuma served as the main depot for many mining communities. In 1879, government officials opened the Yuma Territorial Prison, which operated until 1909. Now a popular tourist attraction, the penitentiary housed 3,000 inmates, including 29 women, during its existence. After the prison's closure, the local high school utilized the buildings and its nickname, "The Criminals," stuck.

Today, agriculture leads the town's economy, followed closely by manufacturing and tourism. A Canadian newspaper claims that nearly 80,000 "snowbirds" migrate to Yuma each year. St. Thomas Mission, Fort Yuma, and the famous prison, now the Arizona State Park, attract many tourists. Two wildlife refuges, Imperial and Kofa, can be found in the area surrounding Yuma. Visitors may also tour the Quartermaster Depot that served as the customs house until 1955.

Yuma's population of more than 65,000 continues to grow each year.

GPS COORDINATES: N32°43.07' W114°37.43'

NEAREST TRAILS: South #1: Tinajas Altas Pass Trail and South #2: Fortuna Mine Trail

Historic Trails

Apache Trail

The first people to travel along part of the route now known as the Apache Trail were early Native Americans. Most likely it was the Salado Indians who were traveling between the mountains and the Salt River Valley along what has become known as the Tonto, or Yavapai, Trail. In the 1600s and 1700s, Spanish explorers ventured into the Superstition Mountains, also called Sierra de la Espuma, or Mountains of Foam, in their quests for gold. Supposedly many Jesuit priests had acquired large caches of gold and were unwilling to pay the customary share to the king of Spain. According to some accounts, the priests hid the gold in several locations throughout the Southwest before they were recalled to Spain. The Superstition Mountains are reputed to be one of those hiding places.

Southern Pacific Railroad officials may have come up with the name of the trail during the completion of the Bowie to Globe branch of the railroad. The name Apache Trail was later extended to incorporate some 40 miles beyond Roosevelt Dam, on the road to Globe. The Apache Trail was designated Arizona's first historic and scenic highway in 1988.

Apparently, stagecoach drivers "invented" elaborate tales to entertain their passengers as they traveled along the Apache Trail. Landmarks along the trail, such as Mormon Flat, were said to be sites at which many Mormons were massacred by Native Americans. In another anecdote, Tortilla Flat was identified as the place where Mexican transients stopped to cook their dinner. Such events were only tall tales, but they made for interesting stories for many who traveled the Apache Trail.

Beale Wagon Road

> A year in the wilderness ended! During this time I have conducted my party from the Gulf of Mexico to the shores of the Pacific Ocean, and back again to the eastern terminus of the road through a country for a great part entirely unknown, and inhabited by hostile Indians, without the loss of a man.
>
> —*Journal of E. F. Beale, February 21, 1858*

Where the buffalo roam, where the *camels* and the antelope play? It might have happened, thanks to three men and a boat full of camels.

After the Mexican War ended in 1848, the United States possessed a new southwest territory that was ready to be surveyed and incorporated into the country. Congress also saw that the new land could provide better access to the burgeoning California. A federally funded supply route was soon commissioned.

A trek through Indian country was interesting enough, but the addition of camels made the event bizarre. Jefferson Davis, who was the secretary of war but would later become president of the Confederate States of America during the Civil War, proposed that camels be used for the expedition. Major Henry C. Wayne was ordered to investigate and import some camels from the Middle East in order to discern whether the animals could be used by the military. After some research, what first seemed like a ludicrous idea was deemed to be a pearl of wisdom. Dromedaries were docile, needed little water, and could carry excessive loads—these useful features were a perfect fit to the Southwest climate. Amiel Whipple (see page 72) had surveyed the Arizona area and excitedly told Congress that a road could be built. On May 1, 1856, Wayne and 33 camels landed in Powder Horn, Texas. Now all Davis needed was someone to handle the animals and to construct the highway.

Navy Lieutenant Edward Fitzgerald Beale (see page 73), the Western hero and companion of Kit Carson, was selected. On June 25, 1857, Beale and his party left San Antonio, Texas, and on October 18 arrived at the Colorado River. The expedition went without a hitch. No men were lost, and no one became ill along the way. Beale bragged that their medicine chest only encumbered their mission. The weather was even agreeable—Beale never once pitched his tent. He then commenced work on the wagon road, and for $210,000 he created a route to the Colorado River.

The importance of this route is disputed. Some historians argue that the road was more significant than the Oregon-California Trail, while others downplay the trail's importance, stating that it could never outdo the Oregon-California Trail because of the disruption of the Civil War and the trail's dangerous course through Indian country. In fact, the first immigrant party to try the trail had to turn back after Indians killed nine of its members. Nevertheless, the Beale Wagon Road was well traveled then and is well traveled today. Route 66, Interstate 40, and the Santa Fe Railroad all mirror Beale's trek. Later, from 1858 to 1859, Beale would create a wagon road that followed his camel expedition, but he extended it so that the road stretched from Los Angeles, California, to Fort Smith, Arkansas.

What became of the camels? The muleskinners hated the beasts. Beale fell in love with them. On September 21, 1857, he wrote in his diary: "I look forward to the day when every mail route across the continent will be conducted and worked altogether with this economical and noble brute." Even with such praise, camels would never come to be the pack animal of choice. The Civil War diverted attention from the Southwest's experiments with the animal. Troops were needed and no one gave the animals a second thought. They were released into the desert, where they were seen for many years. Eventually, some were rounded up, others were shot, and some just disappeared. However, there was one descendant of the original camel herd that lived until 1934 when she had to be put to sleep by the Los Angeles Zoo. Her name was Topsy. Fittingly, her ashes rest in the monument to Hadjii Ali (often called Hi Jolly) who cared for the camels during Beale's expedition. Like a distant mirage, camels faded from the Arizona deserts.

El Camino del Diablo

To many early travelers, El Camino del Diablo (the Devil's Highway) was hell on earth. This 250-mile trail meandered between Sonoita (near the present border between Arizona and Mexico) and Yuma, Arizona. Those who were prepared for the sweltering 120°F temperature had a good chance of survival. Those who were not prepared for the risky desert travel would forever remain as a part of that foreboding landscape. Approximately 50 marked graves dot the scorched countryside, while the graves of hundreds more remained unmarked. The great missionary and explorer Padre Eusebio Francisco Kino (see page 68) was the first to blaze this route. He used the trail to drive cattle and sheep and thereby introduced stock-raising to Arizona. Later, Sonorans braved this waterless stretch on their way to goldfields. The only hope travelers had of finding water was from moisture gathered in natural rock basins, such as Tule Tanks and Tinajas Altas. If both basins were empty and further water rations could not be found, death was inevitable. Today, parts of this old trail are used by the U.S. Border Patrol.

Crook's Wagon Trail

Unlike many other trails, the history of Crook's Wagon Trail does not involve the pursuit of Arizona gold but rather the end of war and the pursuit of peace. The story of the creation of the trail does not begin with General George Crook. It begins with the creation of the Military Department of Arizona in 1870 and General George Stoneman's neglect of the problems between settlers and Indians.

While plans for reservations were being drawn, Indians were constantly besieging the whites who had come to Arizona. Settlers, fearing for their lives and welfare, grumbled over the government's inability to solve the Indian problem. Soon the grumbling became a clamor for vigilante justice. General George Stoneman's idea that residents should handle their own problems seemed to encourage mob justice. A mob from Tucson massacred a group of Aravaipa Apaches who were living under army protection at Camp Grant. Those in charge in Washington were infuriated by what became known as the Camp Grant Massacre (see page 98), and General Stoneman was ousted.

General George Crook was sent to make peace with the Indians who refused to live on reservations. To aid his military actions, Crook constructed a road from Camp Verde to Camp Apache. Crook's Wagon Trail was born. The trail provided an essential communication link and supply route during General Crook's 1872–73 campaign in which he was able to attain peace treaties with the Apaches, Pimas, and Papagos. He was also able to make a peace treaty with Cochise's people and to establish a reservation for them on their own land—the Dragoon and Chiricahua Mountains.

The trail was used into the twentieth century, though much of the traffic was diverted when the railroad reached Holbrook in 1881. Today, Interstate 17 from Camp Verde to Strawberry roughly mirrors Crook's Wagon Trail. Milepost blazers, forgotten strands of telegraph wire, and sandstone grave markers can still be seen along the route and serve as ghostly reminders of Arizona's turbulent past.

Gila Trail

The Gila Trail bears the dusty footprints of some of the most colorful characters in U.S. and Mexican history. Francisco Vásquez de Coronado, Juan de Oñate, Fray Marcos de Niza, Alvar Nuñez Cabez de Vaca, Estavanico the Black (aka: Estabán, Esteván, or Little Steven), Olive Oatman, General Stephen Kearny, and Lieutenant Colonel Philip St. George Cooke all ventured on or crossed the Gila Trail. The story of this trail begins with the mysterious prehistoric Hohokam Indians who once lived in the area. They left behind pottery shards, signs of metallurgy, abandoned cliff dwellings, and numerous questions about the disappearance of this peaceful culture. The Gila Trail was originally worn by their footsteps along the Gila River.

After the Hohokam, the Pima Indians and then Spanish explorers and missionaries used the trail. It is interesting that the first European to set foot in Arizona wasn't Spanish, English, or French but a giant Negro slave named Estavanico the Black, who was scouting a path for Fray Marcos de Niza in his search for the Seven Cities of Cíbola (see page 67). After that expedition, Coronado and a band of about 225 conquistadors, 700 to 1,000 Indian servants, and a herd of livestock followed the trail in search of those same Seven Cities. Later, Padre Eusebio Francisco Kino (see page 68) used the trail to successfully establish missions and gain the friendship of the Pima Indians.

On May 11, 1846, Americans, burning with Manifest Destiny, would also use the trail in the Mexican War. During the war, General Stephen Kearny and guide Kit Carson were the first to lead an army regiment west along this route. But for a brief time the trail was named Cooke's Wagon Trail in honor of Lieutenant Colonel Philip Cooke. He marched his Mormon Battalion from New Mexico, blazed northwest on a trail known as Cooke's Cutoff, occupied Tucson, and then followed the Gila River to San Diego. Tucson was occupied without firing a shot because the troops at the Mexican garrison had fled after Cooke ordered them to surrender. Oddly enough, the only action the battalion saw was an attack by wild bulls (see page 77). They did, however, open a road of great value to the Southwest.

After the war, in 1848, President James K. Polk decided that California needed to be more closely linked to the Union. A new Gila Trail was born—one that differed from the route followed by the Spanish explorers along the Gila River. The new American Gila Trail followed Cooke's path, until a shortcut was found by the Butterfield Overland Mail, which used it to reach California. The shortcut ran through Apache Pass (just as Interstate 10 does today), and although miles were saved, lives were not. Apache Pass was a favorite ambush spot of the Apache Indians. A great number of wagon trains used this route as well as those bound for California gold.

Terror, violence, and reconciliation occurred along the trail. Olive and Mary Ann Oatman were kidnapped on the Gila Trail just after their brother was beaten and their parents and four siblings were slaughtered by Indians (see page 97). Another story tells of vigilante justice that ensued on the south side of the Gila River, 15 miles west of Gila Bend, at a place called Murderer's Camp. Details of the story have been clouded over time, but apparently a wealthy young man murdered his guardian. Witnesses to the crime executed the young man on the spot and buried him next to his victim. Explorer Amiel Whipple was also on this route when suddenly his surveying party was surrounded by hostile Yuma Indians. On the brink of what the explorers thought would be a massacre, one of the Indians recognized Whipple. Previously, while he was scouting the Colorado River, Whipple had rescued a lost, young Indian girl from certain death in the desert. Unknown to him at the time, the girl was the daughter of the Yuma chief. Instead of a massacre, the Yumas welcomed Whipple's party with open arms and gave the explorers much-needed food. The day on which they met as friends was Christmas Day.

On July 25, 1861, the ravages and upheaval of the Civil War touched the Gila Trail. Whoever controlled the trail controlled the flow of communications and wagons to California. Most important, whichever side could control and capture the California mines could keep its currency from deflating in the eyes of world powers. When Texas, in which the far eastern reaches of the trail lay, became the seventh state to secede, the battleground was set. Three hundred Union soldiers, under the command of Major Isaac Lynde, marched from their federal outpost to besiege Lieutenant Colonel John Robert Baylor's 258 Texans at Mesilla, New Mexico. The Texans prevailed. The territories of Arizona and New Mexico, already sympathetic to the Southern cause, joined the Confederacy. This did not bode well for the Gila Trail. Cochise and the Apaches had been fuming ever since the Bascom affair (see page 74), in which accusations of kidnapping and cattle rustling resulted in a number of deaths for both the Apaches and federal troops. With federal troops gone, the warring Apaches had free range over much of Arizona.

The Gila Trail suffocated beneath a blanket of fear—no one dared to challenge the Apache's reign. Baylor, now the confederate governor of Arizona, had his hands full and even with the creation of what later became the Arizona Rangers, he could not quell the Indians. Meanwhile, news of Arizona's rebellion from the Union had spread to nearby California. General James H. Carleton raised 2,000 Union soldiers and blazed his way through Arizona and into Tucson, thereby capturing the state for the Union. Unhappy that his troops had been assaulted by Indians along their march through Arizona, Carleton instructed Colonel J. R. West to free the eastern section of the Gila Trail from the grasp of the Mimbreños Apaches, who were led by Mangas Coloradas. The Gila Trail was eventually secured, but not until Mangas Coloradas was captured and murdered in prison.

With the trail open, and the Civil War simmering down in the East, travelers once again traversed the trail in 1869. The Butterfield Overland Mail Company's stages were brimming with passengers and mail. Eventually, the company would merge with William G. Fargo's firm—Wells, Fargo & Company. The completion of the Transcontinental Railroad and the line between San Diego and Tucson did not cripple the stagecoach industry. Coaches were needed to service small towns not linked to the railroad. Still, it was only a matter of time before this well-used trail was used as a railroad line. The respective owners of the Southern Pacific Railroad, the San Antonio Railroad, and the Texas & Pacific Railroad (owned by Jay Gould) decided to avoid a bitter railroad war and to cooperate in creating a line from Los Angeles to New Orleans, with spurs to Dallas and Marshal, Texas. In 1878, the Southern Pacific began laying tracks in Yuma that followed the Gila Trail. The railroad to Tucson was completed, and on March 20, 1880, the first train chugged into the city. A 38-gun salute and music from the cavalry band welcomed it. The driving of a silver spike signified the completion. The silver spike was molded from ore extracted from the Tough Nut Mine near Tombstone. Stagecoaches, freight wagons, and mule trains began to disappear from frontier Arizona. The trail was gradually paved to create US 80. The Federal Highway Act of 1956 incorporated the Gila Trail into the superhighway system that includes it as Interstate 8 from San Diego to Casa Grande, Arizona, and Interstate 10 to El Paso, Texas.

Leach's Wagon Road

Throughout the 1850s, the people of California were clamoring for a mail route in order to communicate with the East. Congress was busy surveying land routes for a transcontinental railroad, and to appease the Californians and buy a little more time, roads were constructed through Arizona. James B. Leach was the superintendent of a road that later became known as Leach's Wagon Road. This road started in El Paso and wound its way to Fort Yuma. The road basically followed Cooke's Wagon Road, except that Leach's Wagon Road started farther north in Arizona and missed Tucson entirely. The road reached the San Pedro River and then turned to follow the Gila River westward. Although the road saved about 30 miles from the trip to Fort Yuma, many citizens were upset that it bypassed Tucson. Leach's Wagon Road was completed in 1858 but saw little traffic because travelers preferred to stop in Tucson.

Mormon Wagon Road (Honeymoon Trail)

The Mormon Wagon Road was created in 1858 by Mormon missionary Jacob Hamblin who, as a result of his work with the Hopi Indians, frequently crossed from Utah into northern Arizona. Hamblin was instrumental in establishing several Mormon settlements along the Little Colorado River. He worked zealously and tirelessly with the Indians. For his service, Brigham Young dubbed him "Apostle to the Lamanites," referring to American Indians. He never killed an Indian during his years with the Hopi or when he was captured by the Navajos.

The Mormon Wagon Road ran south from Utah, crossed the Colorado at Lee's Ferry, followed the Little Colorado River, and then connected with the Beale Wagon Road (see page 58). The road was first traveled by wagons in 1873 and soon became known as the Honeymoon Trail when St. George Temple was opened and groups of Mormons traveled the path to get married. John D. Lee, whose name is often associated with the infamous Mountain Meadows Massacre, during which Mormons and Indians killed a group of emigrants en route to California, is also credited with helping to create the road. While hiding from the law, Lee explored the area of Lee's Ferry and worked as an Indian agent. Hamblin and Lee were once friends, but they had a tremendous falling out. Lee later referred to Hamblin as "the fiend of hell."

Southern Overland Trail

This almost forgotten road (sometimes called the Walker Trail) was built upon dreams of gold. In 1863, Joseph Reddeford Walker inspired the trail's creation when he found gold on the Hassayampa River, deep within an unmapped region of Arizona called the terra incognita. A direct route was proposed between Prescott and Flagstaff in order to improve travel and aid miners. However, the terrain proved to be fierce, and the native Apaches even fiercer. Captain Nathaniel J. Pishon decided to scout the proposed trail with 27 men and an experienced prospector named Robert Groom. Surprisingly, even after warnings from the Apaches, the journey went relatively smoothly and wagon trains started making the run. In fact, members of Arizona's first territorial government were brought to Prescott on this trail.

Nevertheless, the Southern Overland Trail proved to be dangerous and difficult. Shortly after completion of this route in 1864, alternative roads were being surveyed to avoid traveling the rough trail. Traffic began to dwindle, and by 1890, the road was just a memory. Then the memory faded—maps of the 1900s do not show it. But the road still exists and can be traveled. The Southern Overland Trail now serves as forest roads for the Kaibab National Forest.

The Steamboat Trade

For those lucky enough, wealth could be found in California during the gold rush of 1849. For those enterprising enough, wealth could be gleaned from those in search of the elusive California gold. When the massacre at John Glanton's ferry was vividly publicized, rumors began to spread of a possible gold mine in the ferry business. Lured by the prospect of wealth, George Alonzo Johnson sailed in from San Francisco and beat out his competition by re-establishing the ferry at the junction of the Gila and Colorado Rivers. The Yuma Indians, who were responsible for the massacre, still loomed in the area. Eventually, troops led by Major Samuel P. Heintzelman arrived to protect the ferry. Heintzelman, not one to pass up a good deal, soon realized the profitable prospect of ferrying and built Fort Yuma (in 1851) to completely encompass Johnson's ferry, thereby cutting Johnson out of the business. Disgruntled and understandably annoyed, Johnson and his partners sold their land to Heintzelman for $3,000 and a mule each. In the end, however, Johnson would have the last laugh.

As the years passed, Fort Yuma verged on disaster. Starvation constantly threatened those at the garrison because there was no substantial supply route. As he dropped off supplies for the fort near the mouth of the Colorado, the great Western humorist Lieutenant G. H. Derby wondered if steamships could steer up the river. The famous trapper Antoine Leroux, who had navigated the river by raft, said it could be done. There was a buzz of excitement about this opportunity; even Mormon leader Brigham Young wondered if steamships could make the journey. He saw the great possibilities that a sea route could have for new Mormon colonies. In November 1852, the first steamboat made its way up the Colorado River.

The *Uncle Sam,* powered by a 20-horsepower locomotive engine, sagged under 35 tons of freight. However, it carefully made its way to Fort Yuma, thanks to its captain, James Turnbell. Much to Heintzelman's chagrin, George Johnson financially backed Turnbell and the *Uncle Sam.* Running steamboats on the Colorado could be done—here was Johnson's gold mine. He launched the *General Jesup* to help the frumpish *Uncle Sam* service Fort Yuma.

In 1856, Johnson asked the California Legislature and the secretary of war (Jefferson Davis) for funding to see how far he could make it up the river in a steamboat. The funding was granted, but the honor went to Lieutenant Joseph Christmas Ives. Johnson was infuriated. Not to be denied, he secretly journeyed ahead of Ives in the *General Jesup.* Ives eventually caught wind of Johnson's lead and, seeing fame slipping from his fingertips, plowed on in his own steamship, the *Explorer.* The race was on. But the *Explorer* ran into difficulties, repeatedly striking the many sandbars along the river. Meanwhile, the *General Jesup* and Johnson had run into a submerged rock but still had a comfortable lead. They even had time to help Beale and his camels cross the Colorado River on the expedition's return journey back East. Johnson reached the head of Pyramid Canyon (north of present-day Bullhead City). He had traveled 300 miles and finally turned around triumphant: He proved that the Colorado was indeed navigable by steamboat. Ives reached the same conclusion after he ventured up to Black Canyon, but he was dismayed to discover that his own venture was overshadowed by Johnson and the *General Jesup.* With the Colorado deemed navigable, Fort Mohave was established farther up the river, which Johnson too would service.

In 1862, trappers Johnny Moss, Pauline Weaver, and Joseph Walker discovered silver in Eldorado Canyon, and Johnson's monopoly over the riverway paid off tenfold. Tons of equipment, ore, miners, and soldiers used Johnson's steamships, and the Colorado River became Arizona's lifeline. Johnson and his associates began to enjoy their new wealth and turned their attention away from their ships. As a result, business suffered. More steamships were needed, and there was a solid month's wait between trips up the river. Miners grumbled and protested about the monopoly. One of the most vocal was Samuel Adams, who then successfully created a rival company, the Union Line. Additional competition surfaced when Alphonzo Tilden put his own steamer in the river to better serve his Eldorado mines. Competition was fierce enough to pull Johnson away from his political endeavors and focus his attention on his steamships. In the end, Johnson proved to be the most ruthless. Firmly established as the freighter for both Fort Yuma and Fort Mohave, Johnson cut his shipping charges by half to root out his rivals. The only thing that could save them was to trade openly with Utah. But sandbars and low water prevented the opening of this route. Competition went belly-up; Johnson secured his monopoly and created more steamers to better serve the river. He was once again the king of the Colorado—until the arrival of the Southern Pacific Railroad.

The boom of the steamships was waning. In 1877, the Southern Pacific Railroad joined with Yuma, which cut deeply into Johnson's newly incorporated company, the Colorado Steam Navigation Company. Johnson's seafaring steamers, which carried freight from San Francisco to Yuma, were suddenly antiquated, slow, and expensive for travelers. Profits plummeted by 50 percent. In the wake of the great iron horse, Johnson and his partners knew they could not prevail. They sold their shares to the Western Development Company, which continued a light freight service up the Colorado River. But the increasing number of railroad tracks continued to cut away business. The river was now being dredged to remove silt and sandbars, but dredging and the use of ill-prepared canals doomed the waterways. In 1905, the Colorado flooded, broke loose from a canal, engulfed part of the Southern Pacific Railroad line, and turned the Salton Sink into the Salton Sea. It would take millions of dollars and three years of effort to return the river to its proper bed. The devastating erosion from this flood can be seen today. The construction of the Laguna Dam in 1909, just 13 miles above Yuma, signaled the end of steamships in Arizona.

Railroads

The Arizona Mineral Belt Rail Road Company

The Arizona Mineral Belt Rail Road Company was an ambitious project that sought to tap the successful mining camp of Globe. Construction began in 1883 and was led by Colonel J. W. Eddy, who would later be remembered for the famous Angel's Flight Road in Los Angeles. Backing the colonel was General A. A. McDonald, the manager of the Buffalo Mining Company in Globe, and the Atlantic & Pacific Railroad, which promised $5,000 per mile of track built. The Arizona Mineral Belt line was proposed to run south through the Mogollon Forest and Tonto Basin. One obstacle hampered the proposal—the descent of the 2,000-foot Mogollon Rim. A tunnel was dug near the rim, just east of Pine, and 35 miles of track were laid down before disaster struck. The Atlantic & Pacific Railroad failed to provide the funds needed, forcing the Arizona Mineral Belt to file for bankruptcy.

At the foreclosure sale on December 4, 1888, the Arizona Lumber and Timber Company bought the railroad for use in its logging operation and renamed it the Central Arizona Railway Company. Logs can still be hauled to the Flagstaff mills by way of this road.

The Atchison, Topeka & Santa Fe Railroad Company

Often called the Santa Fe Railway, this railroad was one of the largest in U.S. history and was influential in settling the Southwest. In 1859, the Atchison & Topeka Railroad Company was created in Kansas. Cyrus K. Holliday, the railroad's founder, had a vision. He sought to create a railroad that followed the famous trading route, the Santa Fe Trail, which started in Independence, Missouri, and ran to Santa Fe, New Mexico. Despite not having laid a single mile of track, the railway was renamed in 1863 as the Atchison, Topeka & Santa Fe (AT&SF) Rail Road Company. After further delays, the company finally began construction of the line in 1868, heading

An Atchison, Topeka & Santa Fe steam engine

west from Topeka. The railroad began operations in 1869 with 17 miles of track. In 1872 the railway reached Dodge City. Its arrival bolstered the town and established it as a railhead for shipping cattle east. After a battle with the Denver & Rio Grande Railway for control of Raton Pass, the gateway into the Territory of New Mexico, the AT&SF finally achieved its first major objective when it reached Santa Fe on February 9, 1880. However, the mountain ranges around Santa Fe meant that only a spur line was laid to the territorial capital. The main line continued southwest, reaching Albuquerque on April 10, 1880. In March 1881, the rails reached Deming, New Mexico, where they connected with the Southern Pacific to form a route through Arizona to California. However, the Atchison, Topeka & Santa Fe sought a more direct route from Albuquerque. The financial troubles of the Atlantic & Pacific Railroad provided such an opportunity (see below for the story of the Atlantic & Pacific Railroad).

Through a network of subsidiaries (amounting to 156 corporations in all), the scope of the Atchison, Topeka & Santa Fe continued to expand throughout the 1880s. By the early 1890s, the railroad operated a rail service that totaled 7,500 miles. But it could not escape the economic depression sweeping the country; after a financial crisis the railway was placed in receivership on Christmas Eve, 1893. It was sold at foreclosure and reorganized two years later as the Atchison, Topeka & Santa Fe Railway Company. The revitalized railroad expanded its operations for the next 40 years. In Arizona, it consolidated numerous small railroads into its system including the Western Arizona Railroad from Kingman to Chloride and the California, Arizona & Santa Fe Railway (which itself was a consolidation of 14 railroads spread throughout Arizona, California, and Nevada). By 1916, the railroad's operations extended from Chicago to San Francisco in the West and Galveston and New Orleans in the South. The railroad reached its zenith in 1937 when it operated 27,000 miles of track. Thereafter, more-efficient transportation (namely, the automobile) caused the Santa Fe to shrink.

In 1970, the railroad's passenger service was sold to Amtrack. In 1983, the Santa Fe tried to merge with the Southern Pacific Transportation Company to create the Santa Fe Southern Pacific Corporation, but the Interstate Commerce Commission rejected this proposal in 1987. Burlington Northern purchased the company in 1995; since then it has been known as the Burlington Northern Santa Fe Corporation.

The Atlantic & Pacific Railroad

Although it began slowly, the Atlantic & Pacific Railroad would eventually make significant contributions to trade and the settling of Arizona. The company was organized in 1866 to build a railroad from Springfield, Missouri, to Albuquerque, New Mexico, and then to the Pacific by way of the 35th parallel route first surveyed by Amiel W. Whipple in 1854. By 1873, after only 327 miles of track, in Missouri and eastern Oklahoma, financial difficulties forced the railroad into bankruptcy.

In early 1880, the Atchison, Topeka & Santa Fe Rail Road was laying tracks toward Albuquerque on its way to connecting with the Southern Pacific at Deming, New Mexico. However, it was keen to establish a more direct route to California. In January 1880, it joined with the St. Louis & San Francisco Railway Company to rescue the Atlantic & Pacific by financing the stalled expansion of its tracks westward from Albuquerque. The small town of Gallup, New Mexico (which was settled in 1880 as a Westward Overland Stagecoach stop), became the construction headquarters of the railway. In fact, the town was named after David L. Gallup, the railroad paymaster.

Laying tracks through Arizona was not an easy feat for the Atlantic & Pacific. Supplies had to be freighted by wagon from Maricopa, which was nearly 300 miles away. Water sources were needed, so storage reservoirs had to be constructed along the route. The line did have one thing going for it—an abundance of trees that could be used for railroad ties. Although construction was arduous, the surveys proved to be so good, that today the track continues along most of the original route's 575 miles. (Recently there was only a slight change in course to allow for double-tracking.)

While the Atlantic & Pacific was hard at work, the Southern Pacific Railroad beat it to the quick by completing its own line to Needles, California (named after a group of needlelike peaks in nearby Arizona). Although the Southern Pacific (see page 64) had built its line over the proposed route of the Atlantic & Pacific, begrudgingly, a compromise between the two was settled. The Atlantic & Pacific could lease that portion of the Southern Pacific line in order to enter California. Thus, the Thirty-Fifth Parallel Transcontinental Line was completed in August 1883, without the Southern Pacific losing its monopoly over railroad accesses to California.

In June 1897, after having been forced into bankruptcy for a second time, the Atlantic & Pacific was sold at foreclosure to the recently-reorganized Atchison, Topeka & Santa Fe Railway Company.

The Maricopa & Phoenix Railroad

The Maricopa & Phoenix Railroad almost vanished before tracks were even set. However, it was saved by the quick thinking of one man.

Interested in a railroad to bolster its community, Maricopa County gave the company a subsidy of $200,000. Time passed but work had not started on the line. H. R. Patrick, the surveyor for the project, knew that if work did not start by the end of October 1886, the subsidy would be dropped and the railroad would fail before it got started. No word about construction came from his supporters in San Francisco. So Patrick took a gamble and decided to do something about it. He set down a couple of stakes and built 300 feet of 6-inch grade. He saved the subsidy with only a day to spare. Construction commenced the following month, and on July 4, 1887, at a cost of $540,000, the line from Maricopa to Phoenix was completed.

In December 1895, a branch line was opened from Tempe to Mesa, bringing the railroad's total track to 42 miles. In April 1894, in anticipation of this expansion, the railway changed its name to The Phoenix, Tempe & Mesa Railway. Before the new line had carried its first passenger, the name was changed again. This time it was called The Maricopa & Phoenix & Salt River Valley Railway, perhaps in an effort to reflect further planned expansion. However, no further track was laid at this time.

Such a prosperous little railroad could not escape the eye of the mammoth Southern Pacific. The railroad's completion had piqued the interest of the Southern Pacific and it started buying up the company's stock. While the railroad continued to operate as a separate entity until 1910, it became a subsidiary of the Southern Pacific in 1901. In October 1908, the small railroad changed its title for the last time, reverting back to its original name, The Maricopa & Phoenix Railroad Company.

On February 1, 1910, The Maricopa & Phoenix became a part of the Arizona Eastern Railroad Company, which was an operating subsidiary of the Southern Pacific until September 1955. At that time, the railroad was merged into the Southern Pacific Railroad Company.

Southern Pacific Railroad and the Southern Transcontinental Railroad

The first transcontinental railroad changed the face of the West forever. The line opened travel, facilitated communication between East and West, and established a quicker route for trade.

As early as 1852, southern congressmen had proposed a southern railroad route to California. In 1853, Congress decided to sponsor the survey of four routes. Agreement could not be reached on the best route until the Civil War quashed any prospect of a southern route. In 1862, Congress passed the long-awaited Pacific Railroad Bill, which gave contracts for the line's construction to the Union Pacific and the Central Pacific, the latter of which was controlled by the Big Four merchants from California. The Big Four included Leland Stanford, a Sacramento wholesale grocer; Charles Crocker, a dry goods merchant; and Collis P. Huntington and Mark Hopkins, partners in a hardware store. These men all met by 1857, having already made fortunes from supplying the prospectors who flooded into California following the discovery of gold in 1848.

The Central Pacific's strategy for making a profit was not from running the line but, instead, selling it after completion. The trouble was that no one wanted to buy such an expensive project. In order to make a profit, the leaders of the Central Pacific decided they needed to maintain a monopoly on railroading to California. Even before the first transcontinental railway was completed in 1869, the Big Four acted to ensure that their monopoly was protected. In 1868, they acquired the Southern Pacific Railroad Company, quickly expanding its interests to control rail traffic from San Diego to Portland, Oregon.

A Southern Pacific locomotive

The Big Four then obtained the charter to build a southern transcontinental railroad. Thanks to the Gadsden Purchase of 1853–54 (which extended the U.S. border farther south), a Pacific railroad could be built. On May 23, 1877, the Southern Pacific reached the west bank of the Colorado River. To proceed east, however, the Big Four needed Congress to transfer the bankrupt Texas & Pacific Railroad, as well as any government subsidies, to their line. Jay Gould beat the Big Four to the punch when he acquired the Texas & Pacific. An understanding was reached between the two; together they would create the Southern Transcontinental Railroad.

Congress gave the Southern Pacific permission to build across the Fort Yuma Reservation, and steel track soon followed the old Gila Trail. The population of the area was sparse, and little shantytowns were built along the way to accommodate the workers. Immigrants, mostly Chinese and Irish, made up the workforce. Following in their wake were gamblers, saloon owners, and merchants. Towns were settled, but when the tracks out-distanced the town, the workers got up and left, leaving economic ruin behind them. Casa Grande began this way but managed to hang on and thrive when the trains began to roll through. Railroading history was made along the Southern Pacific. The steel track has the longest curve in history, 5 miles, and the longest portion of straight track, 47 miles.

On March 20, 1880, the first train chugged its way into Tucson. The train's welcome was a 38-gun salute and music from the cavalry band. The last spike, made of silver from the Tough Nut Mine near Tombstone, was driven into the rails in Tucson. Tracks had been laid at a rapid pace of 7 to 10 miles a day. Gould, on the other hand, was taking his time. After all, he and the Big Four had a deal; both railroads would meet in El Paso, Texas. So why rush? When there was no sign of Gould in El Paso, the Big Four steamed on. Controlling more track meant a bigger profit.

But they could not have done it without a little railroad company owned by Tom Peirce.

The Big Four's breach of agreement was not exactly a spur-of-the-moment decision. In 1880, they had bought a considerable share of Tom Peirce's railroad firm, the Galveston, Harrisburg and San Antonio. In order to cover more land, Peirce and the Big Four decided to meet at the western bank of the Pecos River. The Galveston, Harrisburg and San Antonio would build east while the Southern Pacific would build west. At 2:00 P.M. on January 12, 1883, the two railroads met. A year before, on January 1, 1882, Gould reached the town of Sierra Blanca but could not move westward because of the alliance between the Southern Pacific and the Galveston, Harrisburg, and San Antonio. The Big Four maintained its monopoly on railroading into California. Yuma, El Paso, Fort Worth, Casa Grande, and other cities along the railroad route exploded with people. (For more information on the historical route that the railroad roughly followed, see the Gila Trail on page 60.)

The United Verde & Pacific Railway Company

The United Verde & Pacific Railway Company was chartered in March 1894. Senator William Andrews Clark of Nevada spent $600,000 to lay the 26 miles of track that connected his copper mine in Jerome with the Santa Fe, Prescott & Phoenix Railway in the Chino Valley. The narrow-gauge railway began operating in January 1895 and was called the "crookedest railroad in the world" by the miners who rode along its 3-foot-wide tracks. With 126 curves along its route, the name described the railroad perfectly.

The hauling of coke for firing smelter furnaces was the primary function of the United Verde. Passengers (mainly miners) and other necessities were also carried to the booming town of Jerome. At the junction of the two railroads, the town of Jerome Junction shot up to service the freight and passengers transferring to the United Verde for the short journey east. Then in 1920, when the standard-gauge railroad was extended to Jerome from the east, the United Verde & Pacific Railway was abandoned and Jerome Junction was left for the ghosts.

United Verde & Pacific depot in Jerome, circa 1900

Stagecoach Lines

Butterfield Overland Mail

> Remember, boys, nothing on God's earth must stop the United States mail.
> —*John Butterfield*

When on March 3, 1857, John Butterfield and his business associates received a contract from the U.S. Congress to build a transcontinental stagecoach line, the Butterfield Overland Mail line began to take shape. One of Butterfield's associates was William G. Fargo, who would later play a key role in stagecoach history. However, the Butterfield Overland Mail was not the first transcontinental stagecoach line. That title belonged to the San Antonio and San Diego Mail line. Butterfield, instead, was taking the reins away from the ailing San Antonio and San Diego.

A stage standing in front of the Arizona Territorial Capitol in Prescott, 1877

Time was of the essence. Butterfield had only one year to get his stagecoaches rolling. A route was chosen that followed along the old Gila Trail (see page 60). However, Butterfield's route also crossed Texas and reached St. Louis and Memphis—a considerable extension from the previous San Antonio and San Diego route. From the Gila Trail, the Butterfield Overland Mail would stop in San Diego and then continue its way north to San Francisco. Butterfield hired Indian-friendly frontiersmen to work for the company. Trying to avoid using way stations, he paid farmers along the route to provide overnight room and board to passengers using his stagecoaches. In the sparsely populated Southwest, where hardly any farmers could be found, sod houses were used as way stations. Drivers were stationed along the route. All had to memorize their 60-mile routes because they would drive the stagecoach through day and night. An armed conductor, required to make a 120-mile run, would ride beside the driver to protect both passengers and mail with his life.

On September 15, 1858, the first Butterfield stage left San Francisco to make its way overland. Twenty-three days, 23 hours, and 30 minutes later, the stagecoach arrived in St. Louis. Regular mail had finally been provided across the continental United States. Two hundred dollars bought a ticket from St. Louis to San Francisco. Because hardly anyone was leaving California, a ticket from San Francisco to St. Louis cost only $100. Food was not provided, so it had to be either carried along or purchased at the way stations or farmhouses. Passengers also had to help the stagecoach if trouble arose;

A mail stage at Fort Apache in 1890

trouble could be anything from getting stuck in the mud to an Indian attack. The coach's speed depended on the smoothness of the road and ranged from three-and-a-half to nine miles an hour. For those who were hardy, the trip was exciting. For those of lesser stock, the trip was a grueling nightmare. One traveler remarked that he knew what hell was like because he had just spent 24 days there. Waterman L. Ormsby, a reporter for the *New York Herald,* made the rough journey and reported that during the ride he had subsisted on beans, salt pork, and black coffee. He slept very little, constantly breathed in trail dust, and lived in fear of an Indian attack.

Indian attacks rarely occurred, however. Apaches did attack a Butterfield Overland stagecoach when U.S. soldiers enraged Cochise in what is now known as the Bascom affair. Bascom falsely accused Cochise of cattle rustling and kidnapping. Soldiers arrested the warrior and six of his men. But Cochise escaped and sought revenge for his false arrest. Events got out of control quickly. Bascom hanged the six warriors that had been captured, one of whom was Cochise's brother. Cochise then ambushed a wagon train and burned its Mexican teamsters alive. A Butterfield stagecoach heard the news and, armed to the teeth, wound its way toward Apache Pass. Once there, it was promptly ambushed, but it evaded the Apache pursuers. Later, the station agent, C. W. Culver, the driver, J. F. Wallace, and a ranch hand named Welch went to propose a truce to the Indians. However, the warring Apaches would not hear of it. The Apaches attacked the three, killing Welch, capturing Wallace, and wounding Culver. Culver barely managed to escape with his life. Wallace wasn't so lucky. He was killed along with two other prisoners. Their bodies were mutilated beyond recognition.

In 1860, John Butterfield left the Butterfield Overland Mail after a successful career. William B. Dinsmore replaced him. In the 1860s, William G. Fargo's firm (Wells, Fargo & Company) took an interest in the mail route. Fargo's stagecoaches were running both mail and gold across the continent and gradually dominated the express business. By 1866, Butterfield Overland was absorbed into Wells, Fargo & Company.

San Antonio and San Diego Mail Line

In the 1800s, the vast Great Plains and daunting Rocky Mountains posed such obstacles to travel that they literally split the country in two. By the 1850s, California was clamoring for a decent line of communication with the eastern United States. So great were these land barriers that there was even talk of California splitting from the Union and becoming a separate country. Trade and communication between California and the eastern United States was a long and costly process; ships sailed down to Panama, paid a caravan to carry the freight and passengers to the other ocean, then another ship completed the journey to the destination port. In 1853, Congress decided to shorten and reduce the cost of the trip. Surveys were taken for a suitable land route for a transcontinental railroad. After careful consideration, four possible routes were chosen. But Congress could not decide which one to choose. The southern states wanted a route that started in Memphis or New Orleans; the northern states demanded that the route should go through St. Louis or Chicago; and Texas thought that a route running from Galveston would be very cost-effective. The U.S. Treasury certainly could not afford multiple routes. As the debate continued, California was becoming increasingly unhappy. Numerous petitions were signed, all revolving around the government's negligence. Finally, on March 3, 1857, Congress decided to subsidize a stagecoach route to facilitate communication between East and West and to give itself time to agree on the best railroad route. Bids were taken, and James Birch received the contract.

Birch quickly decided on a route that started in San Antonio, went through El Paso, and ended in San Diego. He chose this route because it was well traveled, well marked, and far enough to the south to avoid dealing with snow. In Arizona, the route followed the well-beaten Gila Trail (see page 60). (Today this route is essentially that of Interstate 10.) The only problem was the lack of way stations. Military forts could be used, but near El Paso the population was very sparse. Seven new sod house stations had to be built to accommodate the stagecoach line. Isaiah Woods, Birch's new employee in charge of purchasing, bought new stagecoaches. Instead of horses, he bought mules because he thought they would do better in the dryer climate. For this reason, the San Antonio and San Diego was soon nicknamed Jackass Mail. The line brought mail and

A Concord stagecoach advertised by Abbot Downing Company (its inventors) as having "pinstriping and retractable window covers," circa 1885

passengers overland in 38 days or less. For $200 a passenger could buy a one-way fare on the Jackass Mail. Conditions were rough; the new way stations that passengers had to sleep in were nothing more than hovels, and the food that Birch supplied was sometimes inedible. Although Birch succeeded in what he set out to do, he would not get to enjoy his success. On August 20, 1857, he concluded business in San Francisco and boarded the *Central America,* which was bound for New York. He would never arrive. The ship was lost at sea.

After his death, the San Antonio and San Diego had financial difficulties and eventually was acquired by the firm of Giddings & Doyle. In its hands the mail dwindled and the business was not as financially prosperous as it had hoped. Congress opened the bidding on another transcontinental stagecoach route. John Butterfield accepted the contract and started the famous Butterfield Overland Mail. Yet the honor of being the first to create a transcontinental stagecoach line will always belong to James Birch and his Jackass Mail.

People

Explorers, Mountain Men, and Surveyors

Coronado and the Seven Cities of Cíbola

A giant slave named Estavanico (also known as Estabán, Esteván, or Little Steven) was the first foreigner to set foot in Arizona. Estavanico's race is subject to debate; sources refer to him variously as a Negro, a Moor, and an Arab. Estavanico, Cabeza de Vaca, Castillo de Maldonado, and Dorantes de Carranza (the owner of Estavanico) were the only four men who survived a shipwreck off the coast of Florida. For eight years these four survivors traveled from the Florida Peninsula to Mexico City. Along the way they heard stories from the natives about the golden Seven Cities of Cíbola. They finally arrived in Mexico City and told the viceroy of their journey. Upon hearing these stories, the viceroy in Mexico City, Don Antonio de Mendoza, picked two people for a reconnaissance mission: Fray Marcos de Niza, a 38-year-old missionary who had previously served in Peru, and the former slave Estavanico. In March 1539, they set out. The plan was for Estavanico to scout ahead of Marcos de Niza and leave a trail of crosses behind him—the size of the cross would demonstrate the importance of Estavanico's findings.

Once out in the field, Estavanico donned a magnificent costume of colored feathers, bells and rattles, and brightly colored clothes. When he encountered Indians he proclaimed that he was a powerful medicine man, invincible to all attacks. When he approached a village, he had his arrival heralded by a magic gourd carried by one of his Indian followers. His strange behavior was never explained; perhaps it was a practice that he picked up during his sojourn from Florida or perhaps it was his newfound freedom that simply went to his head. Strangely enough, he was gathering followers, including a harem of Indian women. However, his days were numbered. Zuni Indians felled him outside of their city of Hawikuh (in present-day New Mexico). Whether the Indians were provoked is uncertain. The Zuni were peaceful, and scholars believe that they were curious as to how invincible Estavanico really was. His followers dashed back to Fray Marcos and told him the shocking news. But Marcos had found a giant cross set by the late Estavanico, proclaiming the Seven Cities of Gold. He rushed to Hawikuh, and when he saw how impressive the city was (he later explained that it was bigger than Mexico City), he believed it to be Cíbola. He scoured the city to no avail but, still convinced it was Cíbola, he raced back to the viceroy to report the good news.

Francisco Vásquez de Coronado then entered the scene. Seeking riches that would make even Cortés envious, Coronado and a band of about 225 conquistadors, 700 to 1,000 Indian servants, and a herd of livestock followed Estavanico's path in search of those same Seven Cities. The expedition set forth on February 23, 1540. They crossed the eastern Arizona mountains to the Little Colorado River from where they trekked to White River, near today's Fort Apache. However, as the men journeyed through what is now Arizona, their spirits sank. Only ruins and stories that refuted the mythical golden cities were found. After a brief skirmish with Cíbola Indians, and with starvation biting closely at their heels, the army found Marcos's Seven Cities on July 7, 1540. They were little more than crumbling pueblos about two stories high. Neither gold nor precious metals of any sort could be found. The army took the news hard, and Fray Marcos was devastated. He was sent back to Mendoza in August. The hardships of his journey had wracked his body and he slumped back to Mexico City a disheartened man.

To make matters worse, the Indians did not take kindly to the cavaliers. Upon seeing the soldiers, the warriors of Hawikuh prepared for war. Obviously, they were not happy to see an army of starving men outside their walls. The Zunis were, in fact, in the middle of a ritualistic celebration that could not be interrupted. A Zuni drew a line along the ground meaning that the Spanish were not welcome at this time. The Spanish saw the line—and the warriors going through their ritual on the other side—and took it as a challenge. Under the battle cry "Santiago y a ellos!" ("St. James and at them!"), the Spanish cavaliers took Hawikuh and the city's food.

Coronado had not given up on the golden cities. His journey had taken him out of Arizona and into the great plains of present-day Kansas. In April 1542, Coronado was finally forced to turn back because of dissension within his troops. The golden Seven Cities of Cíbola would forever remain an elusive legend.

Juan de Oñate y Salazar

In 1549, Juan de Oñate was born in Mexico into a prominent and very prosperous family. His father had fought in the conquest of New Galicia and had helped found the city of Zacatecas. Juan's wife was the granddaughter of Cortés, the celebrated explorer and conqueror of the Aztecs.

Juan decided to follow in the footsteps of his father, and in 1595 he was awarded the contract for the conquest and settlement of New Mexico. A year later his expedition, consisting of 400 men (130 of them with families), 83 wagons, and 7,000 head of cattle, set out from Mexico City, bound for New Mexico. In May 1598, after delays along the route, they settled along the Rio Grande below present-day El Paso. Oñate then set off with 60 men to "pacify the land" thereby founding the province of New Mexico.

Oñate struck out in search of riches. Indians had shown him a treasure in pearls, which immediately caught his attention. Following the trail of pearls and the lure of Indian tales, Oñate set out on an expedition to discover the South Sea in 1598 and made it as far as the Bill Williams Fork before he had to turn around.

During this expedition, he visited the pueblo people of Acoma and barely escaped with his life. He also saw the crosses erected during Estavanico's march through the Southwest. Later, Acoma was razed and most of its 800 inhabitants were killed in retribution for the killing of Oñate's nephew. Following a "trial," sentences were rendered on the survivors: Males over 25 years of age had one foot amputated and were ordered to serve 20 years of slavery; males 12 to 25 and all females older than 12 were also ordered into slavery for 20 years. Two Indian men from neighboring tribes each had one of their hands amputated and were told to return to their people and inform them of the danger of resisting the Spanish. This horrific punishment was intended to have a salutary effect on the inhabitants, ensuring that the authority of the Spanish conquistadors was unquestioned.

In June 1601, Oñate took 80 of his men and several friars and set out to the northeast from his New Mexican base. It is believed that this expedition reached what is now central Kansas where they fought a great battle with the Kaw (or Kansa) Indians. There they reported inflicting 1,000 casualties despite having to retreat.

Oñate arrived back at his New Mexican settlement to find that his colonists had retreated to Santa Barbara, Nueva Vizcaya. He ordered his nephew Vincente de Zaldivar, a soldier under his command and brother of the nephew killed at Acoma, to bring them back. The young man was successful in this task but inflicted great cruelty on the settlers.

Once again, in 1604, Oñate set out in search of the South Sea with dreams of pearls. In January 1605, having followed the Colorado River south, he reached the Gulf of California, becoming the first explorer to travel through Arizona from east to west. Despite having reached the South Sea and passing through many Indian settlements, he never found the pearls that he was after. He returned to New Mexico in April 1605, reduced to eating his horses for sustenance.

After his return, he moved the capital of the province to Santa Fe, where he ruled until 1608. Upon his return to Mexico, his failure to find treasure led to official charges of misconduct in office. He was convicted of the offense in 1614 but was granted a pardon shortly before his death in 1624.

Padre Eusebio Francisco Kino

Padre Eusebio Francisco Kino gained prominence in the Southwest because of his exploration, trail-blazing, devout religious genius, and missionary work.

Kino was born in the Austrian Alps near Trent on August 10, 1645. He was well educated and particularly excelled in mathematics. In 1663, he became very ill and doctors could only shrug their shoulders at Kino's malady. However, just when he reached death's door, Kino recovered. The recovery was so miraculous that Kino was imbued with faith and entered the Jesuit Order. He volunteered for missionary service in the Orient but instead was sent to the New World. On May 3, 1681, Kino landed on the shores of the Gulf of Mexico at Vera Cruz.

In 1683, Kino accompanied an exploration party and set out to create his first mission in lower California. Although the mission was a failure—the Indians became hostile to the encroaching Spaniards—Kino discovered that Baja California was not an island but a peninsula. He was reassigned to the Sonoran frontier in 1687 and continued there for the next 24 years. He often traveled 30 to 35 miles a day on horseback, usually with very little escort. He founded missions, including the precursor of San Xavier del Bac. He worked with the Pima Indians, and he introduced horses and cattle to the Indians at his missions. During this time the Pima were being ravaged by Apache raids, and Kino helped them defend their cattle and win a decided victory over the raiders.

Artist rendering of Padre Eusebio Francisco Kino

Kino converted a great number of Indians—about 30,000—and he baptized another 4,000. He later explained that he could have further spread the word of God but lacked priest co-workers and orders from the Church limited his progress.

Kino crossed into Arizona during 40 expeditions. Because of his efforts, the cultural influence of New Spain expanded up to the Gila River. He saw the Casa Grande Ruin, trailblazed the route of El Camino del Diablo (see page 59), and traveled as far as present-day Yuma. When he was 65, he rode out to Magdalena to dedicate a new chapel. During the Mass of Dedication, Padre Kino became ill. He died that night, on March 15, 1711.

Juan Bautista de Anza

Born in 1735, Juan Bautista de Anza became a third-generation Spanish frontier soldier when he joined the military at age 17. After only three years of service, he had risen to the rank of lieutenant. Military life suited young Anza and he was made captain of the Tubac Presidio by 1759.

As more and more world powers set their hooks into the New World, Spain began to grow worried about its claims. The Pacific coast needed to be controlled and protected from infringing English and Russian explorers. Anza heard his country's call. In 1774, he financed his own exploratory trip and proved that an overland route through Arizona to Alta California (right up to present-day San Francisco) was possible. On September 29, 1775, he left Sonora with 240 men and the blessing of Viceroy Bucareli to travel through Alta California. On March 27, 1776, the group founded San Francisco. Today, we can trace his steps using modern highways. The route north from Tubac along Interstate 19 mirrors his path through Arizona. From there, his route is followed by Interstate 10, joining Arizona 87 and 287, and then following the Gila River westward along Arizona 238. Anza then paralleled Old Highway 80 through to Yuma and the California border. He successfully opened up Alta California for settlement and missionaries. However, the Yuma revolt in 1781 (see page 95) closed the route and the Spanish never reopened it.

Officials were so impressed that Anza was made the governor of New Mexico in 1778. He strengthened Santa Fe in order to fight off the Apache and to consolidate the Spanish colonies. Leaving Santa Fe in 1787, Anza next became the commander and captain of the Tucson Presidio, a position he held until he died on December 19, 1788. Juan Bautista de Anza is buried in the floor of the church of Nuestra Senõra de la Asunción.

Fray Francisco Garcés

Francisco Garcés was born on April 12, 1748, in Aragon, Spain. He would eventually become one of the greatest missionaries in the Arizona area. As a young man, Garcés was very pious. He took holy orders when he was about sixteen, was ordained as a priest when he was twenty-five, and expressed a wish to work with the Indians of Sonora, Mexico. On June 30, 1768, the young priest arrived in Mexico, eager to spread the word of God.

He instantly took to his work. His friendly demeanor and unselfish attitude won him friendships with many Indians, and the priest was even welcomed by Indian chiefs. He set up missions, preached from the Bible, and cared for those suffering from a measles epidemic. Over the years, he visited the Pima, the Yuma, and the Papago. In 1774, he followed Captain Juan Bautista de Anza on his quest to open a route of communication between Sonora and the mission settlement at Monterey on the coast of California. Garcés had already made this harrowing trek once before in 1771. Garcés's adventures were extraordinary. He once traveled alone more than 2,100 miles visiting a number of Indian tribes.

His death came as a shock and a great tragedy. The missionary and the Yuma were on friendly terms. Yet after some miscommunications between the viceroy and the Yuma Indians—and some acts of cruelty inflicted by the Spanish soldiers on the Yuma—there was great distrust in the air. Garcés warned against setting up more missions in the area. But his warnings went unheeded, and missions were established. Garcés presided over a small band of troops and settlers. The Yuma attacked, descending on the mission and clubbing the settlers to death. Francisco Garcés died in July 1781. He was one of the few Spaniards to be buried by the Yuma, and piles of flowers were placed over his gravesite.

Bill Williams

Even though a town, a stream, and a mountain in Arizona are named after this bold explorer, there is little known about Bill Williams. William Shirley "Old Bill" Williams was born in 1787 and was brought up as a Methodist. So great was his faith that he became a missionary with the Osage Indians near St. Louis, where he translated part of the Bible into their language. He set up a trading post within the village and there he got this first taste of trapping and trading. Williams grew accustomed to and had great respect for the Indian culture. He also realized that his faith was increasingly dissolving into their paganism. When his Indian wife died, he gave up the Bible, grabbed a rifle, and disappeared into the Wild West.

Like a lone wolf, Bill Williams roamed the Rocky Mountains, making his living through trapping and trading. His unique signature was often displayed on his pelts: "Bill Williams, Master Trapper." Much of his solitary life is unrecorded and given to legend. After a very successful period of trapping, he would engage in wild stunts that were said to be astounding. At times he was known to drink and gamble all of his money away. He would wager $100 on his marksmanship, and there is a rumor that he once lost nearly $1,000 in just one game of seven-up. While in Taos, New Mexico, he tried setting up another trading post. But when he grew tired of the selling, he dumped his wares in the middle of town and took off for the wilderness. Before going, it is said that he stood by and merrily watched as the women of the town scrambled for the choicest pieces of calico cloth.

Williams traveled and trapped his way through Arizona, where he met up with another notable trapper, Antoine Leroux. Later, in 1851, in tribute to "Old Bill," Leroux and Richard H. Kern named both Bill Williams Mountain and Bill Williams Fork after him. Bill Williams's last expedition occurred in 1849. He led a party of 32 explorers into the Rockies and was besieged by terrible weather. Deep snow ended any possibility of travel, and the party was chilled by freezing temperatures. In the end, starvation claimed 11 members. Williams, John C. Frémont, and the remainder of the ill-fated party straggled into Taos. Ignoring rumors of cannibalism and murderous intentions, Williams struck back out in the spring to recover the party's lost scientific equipment. Somewhere between Pueblo, Colorado, and Taos, New Mexico, Bill Williams and Dr. Benjamin J. Kern were killed by Ute Indians.

Sylvester Pattie and James Ohio Pattie

Sylvester Pattie and James Pattie were a father-and-son team whose exciting and daring adventures are indicative of a period of time when the West was truly wild. On July 20, 1824, the 42-year-old Sylvester Pattie, along with his 20-year-old son James, left Council Bluffs with 114 men to hunt and trade in the area now called New Mexico. Their adventures were published in *Personal Narrative of James Ohio Pattie of Kentucky,* written by Timothy Flint as told to him by James Pattie. However, Flint embellished the story somewhat, clouding the truth about Pattie's endeavors. Whether true or false, the story makes for a good yarn.

While the Patties were waiting for the Mexican governor to give them a trapping license, a Mexican force galloped into town in pursuit of Apache raiders. The Patties joined the band when they learned that the Apache had kidnapped women and children. When the Apache were found, James Pattie rushed into the fray and rescued the beautiful maiden Jacova, who was the previous Mexican governor's daughter. James's bravery won him the trapping license as well as Jacova's heart; but James sought adventure, not romance. He set off into the wilderness, and for the next six years the Patties would trap, endure captivity, and suffer incredible hardships.

The Pattie party traveled along the Gila River and trapped

the tributaries just southwest of modern-day Phoenix. There they were ambushed, and Indians stampeded their horses, leaving the party stranded in the middle of an unforgiving terrain. On the verge of starvation, they stumbled up to the Santa Rita copper mining camp (near present-day Silver City), where they were fed, refreshed, and resupplied. Before the party had been ambushed, they had trapped a large number of beavers and hid their pelts so that they could return and reclaim them if they survived their journey to Santa Rita. James Pattie set off to reclaim their pelts, but Indians had found the largest cache and James returned with only a small number.

The Pattie party continued to trap along the Salt and Gila Rivers, and once again Indians attacked them. This time, though, the expedition suffered heavy losses. The three survivors, including James Pattie (his father had stayed in Santa Rita), joined up with another trapping group, which included such famous trappers as Ewing Young (see page 71), Tom "Peg-leg" Smith, George Yount, and Milton Sulette. In retribution for the slaughter, the group burned an Indian village and cut down many warriors in a swath of destruction. Scuffles between the trappers and Indians were becoming frequent; still, James Pattie was able to secure a fortune in pelts and return to his father. But the new Mexican governor in town accused Pattie of trapping without a license and stripped him of his pelts. Undaunted and aching for adventure, James Pattie and his father headed back into present-day Arizona.

In a grueling journey, the father-and-son team traveled through Arizona and eventually wound up in San Diego. The Mexican authorities were not happy to see them and immediately tossed them into prison. James Pattie was soon released because he knew how to treat small pox. He was entrusted to wander the vicinity to try to help those suffering from the rampant disease. His father, Sylvester Pattie, was not so lucky. He died within the confines of the Mexican prison. When given permission to leave, James Pattie sailed from Monterey to San Blass, making his way to Mexico City.

His final years are uncertain. After his stay in Mexico City, it is known that he reached New Orleans in 1830 and then returned to Augusta, Kentucky, where he had been born in 1804. In 1831, while Pattie was still in Kentucky, his adventures were published in Cincinnati. According to the county tax roles, he was still in Augusta in June 1833, but this is the last certain record of his location. It is thought probable that Pattie perished in a cholera epidemic that spread through Kentucky between 1832 and 1833, but his death was not officially recorded. There are unsubstantiated reports of him being in California as late as the 1850s.

Whatever his fate, two things are certain: He never garnered the fortune he sought, and his extraordinary adventures still live on.

Antoine Leroux

Antoine Leroux, born in 1801, was to become one of the best trappers, guides, and frontiersmen in the American West. He grew up in St. Louis, which was the eastern portal to the Wild West, with dreams of adventure. Leroux was educated and could fluently speak and write both French and English. This characteristic sets him apart from other mountain men who were often illiterate or could barely sign their names. Leroux was cool-tempered and composed, and he was a dead shot with a rifle. In 1822, the St. Louis newspaper advertised the Ashley-Henry Expedition, which was organized to find the source of the Missouri River. Leroux seized his chance to head out into the wilderness.

On the Missouri River expedition, Leroux learned the hardships mountain men faced. It was a dangerous profession with a great deal of adversity and very little gain. Financially, most mountain men barely got by, and many often wound up in the poorhouse during their later years. Leroux endured, though, as life on the frontier was to his liking. He crisscrossed the country, all the while heading south into the New Mexico Territory. He spoke of his journeys to the state senators who were considering a suitable route to the Pacific.

Leroux eventually settled in Taos, New Mexico, where he got married in 1833. His marriage entitled him to a Spanish land grant, whereby he received Los Lucero Ranch, which encompassed nearly half a million acres. From Taos he explored and trapped northward into the Rocky Mountains. But as time went on and rivers became trapped out, he set his eyes on Arizona country. Between 1825 and 1826, Leroux reached the Gila River and began trapping; there he continually ran into trouble with Indians and, often, barely escaped with his life.

In 1829, Leroux became a Mexican citizen so that he could easily obtain a trapping license. He became the president of the Santa Fe Town Council and, ironically, he verbally attacked foreigners who were trapping the Southwest. He also encountered and befriended notable figures such as Bill Williams (see page 69) and Kit Carson (see page 72). Carson was Leroux's assistant for a short period of time.

In 1846, when Colonel Stephen Kearny's party marched into Santa Fe with 2,000 troops, Leroux decided to aid their effort and joined Cooke's Mormon Battalion as their guide. Leroux, the Mexican citizen, successfully guided the American forces into Indian country, through hostile terrain, into Tucson, and finally into San Diego, California.

After the Mexican War, Leroux once again became an American citizen in 1848. He continued his work as a guide and was scouting for Major Benjamin Lloyd Beall when his dragoons fought the Apache in the Arkansas Valley between 1848 and 1849. Soon after, he scouted for another military expedition against the Ute. When he returned to New Mexico, he heard of John C. Frémont's and Bill Williams's ill-fated expedition into the Rocky Mountains in which 11 party members died. Frémont blamed the disaster on his guide, Bill Williams, a reclusive mountain man who had been killed by Indians and was unable to defend himself against the accusations. Antoine Leroux stepped forward to defend his departed friend.

Leroux continued his life as a guide. Edward F. Beale, of Beale Wagon Road fame (see page 58), used the intrepid scout when he traveled to California to assume his post as superintendent of Indian Affairs. When Leroux was 50, he guided the Sitgreaves Expedition as it explored the unknown region near Bill Williams Mountain and Flagstaff. On this trek, hostile Indians repeatedly attacked and Leroux was wounded. The expedition almost turned into a disaster as ambushes, starvation, and dying pack animals plagued the group. Leroux also accompanied Lieutenant A. W. Whipple when he was sent to explore the 35th parallel. Leroux was critical to the expedition's success, as he helped avoid conflicts with the Indians.

Later he settled down and returned to his home in New Mexico. Leroux was a prominent frontiersman, and in his old age, he lived quite comfortably thanks to the huge Spanish land grant that he had received. He died at the age of 60 of asthma complicated by wounds he had received during his adventures in Indian country.

Ewing Young

Ewing Young probably crisscrossed Arizona more than any other mountain man. He was born in Jonesboro, Tennessee, on the frontier in 1792 and as a young man trained as a carpenter. Ewing Young was persistent and single-minded in his quest to acquire wealth from trapping. By the time he was 30, he had traveled to Santa Fe and was trapping the Pecos River. Two years later, he was working on the San Juan River with his friend William Wolfskill.

In 1826, he made contact with the survivors of James Pattie's decimated trapping group. The two parties joined together and avenged themselves against the Indians who had attacked Pattie's party. The bolstered group traveled up the Colorado River, fought the Mojave Indians in a couple of skirmishes, and looped back to Santa Fe. There, Mexican authorities jailed him, confiscated his furs, and falsely accused him of trapping without a proper license. He was probably incarcerated because the authorities, who despised him and thought him a smuggling scoundrel, saw the opportunity to seize his furs. To avoid further confrontations, Young followed the lead of many trappers in the region and applied for Mexican citizenship. Wolfskill was still in the area and the two opened a store in Taos, New Mexico. However, the two eventually went their separate ways.

Young continued to cross Arizona on trapping expeditions, sometimes going into California to pursue furs, but each time returning to Taos. One expedition took him as far north as Oregon. On another, he joined up with Kit Carson (see page 72) to trap the Salt River. Along the way he and his men were accused by the California governor, José Figueroa, of stealing horses. The accusations were never followed up, but Young's expeditions were made more difficult because of the wild assertions.

In 1834, Young decided to settle in Oregon. He achieved great success at cattle ranching and in the wheat and lumber businesses. He is considered a major figure in early Oregon history. He died suddenly in 1841, apparently from a hemorhaging stomach ulcer.

Joseph Reddeford Walker

Destined for adventure as a trapper, explorer, and fortune seeker, Joseph Reddeford Walker was born on December 13, 1798, in eastern Tennessee's Roan County. Soft spoken, disciplined, and never a braggart, Walker stood at 6 feet tall. For four years he served as a sheriff in Jackson County, Missouri. He is best known, however, for his trailblazing skills and his exploring partnership with Captain Benjamin Bonneville.

Walker began as a surveyor on the Santa Fe Trail in 1826. For a while he trapped the surrounding lands but was never exceedingly successful. He, like many other mountain men, encountered his share of trouble with local Indians. Once, after being continually harassed, Walker and his party ambushed a group of Indians, surrounded them, and killed 39. The wounded were then put to the sword. Walker thought it was best to ensure the safety of the party. In 1833, he constructed a trading post on the Green River, possibly the first in Arizona. His travels also brought him through Utah and into California.

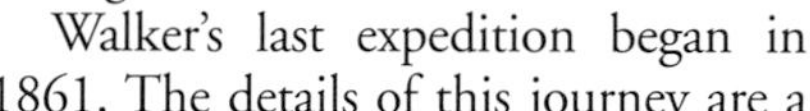

Joseph Reddeford Walker

Walker's last expedition began in 1861. The details of this journey are a bit obscure, but there are tales that say he was in the company of Kit Carson and Pauline Weaver as he was heading back to Arizona. What is true, though, is that Walker, though white-haired and in his 60s, led a party into the unexplored region of central Arizona, discovered a large vein of gold along the Hassayampa, and created the Southern Overland Trail (or the "Walker Trail").

The old pathfinder died in 1876 at the age of 78, widely respected for his intelligence and his command of western geography.

Pauline Weaver

In 1800, Pauline Weaver was born in Tennessee to a white father and Cherokee mother. He is known in Arizona history as a famous guide and mountain man. Although originally named Paulino, he soon became known as Pauline. For a brief time he worked for the Hudson's Bay Company as a trapper, but he left the company to venture west. In 1830, Pauline Weaver trekked into Arizona.

While in Arizona, he fell in love with the Arizona sun, which was much more to his liking than the snows of the North. Among other things, Weaver trapped to make a living. Lieutenant Colonel Cooke employed Weaver as a guide for his Mormon Battalion (see page 77). Weaver did a little prospecting as well. In 1861, he guided prospectors to Rich Hill and later to Weaver Diggings, where important gold strikes were made. In dealings with Indians, he was respectful and friendly; he often settled disputes between settlers and angry Indians. For negotiating a treaty to keep peace in the region of the gold diggings, he was awarded a grant of 2,800 acres around present-day Banning, California. Later, he gave most of the tract to the doctor who treated him when he fell ill.

Eventually, Weaver did run into some trouble with the Indians. While he was out trapping, some boys from the Apache-Mojave camp ravaged his planting fields. He complained to the Indians but was laughed out of their camp. Weaver wanted to

Pauline Weaver

show that he was not a man to be laughed at, so he complained to the commander at Fort Whipple. The incident exploded into a battle between Indians and soldiers, and the Apache-Mojave camp was wiped out.

Afterward, Weaver was eating his dinner when Aha-sa-ya-mo, an Indian girl, appeared in his camp and warned that the Tonto were planning his demise in retribution for the previous attack. Weaver escaped, but not before the Tonto severely wounded him. Troops from Fort Whipple later avenged the attack by assaulting the Tonto. Weaver was there during the battle and he saved Aha-sa-ya-mo from getting killed by a soldier. The Tonto survivors were rounded up and sent to the fort as prisoners. After four days, a guard sounded the alarm; the Tonto women and children were missing. Their escape is credited to Pauline Weaver.

Weaver never recovered from the wound he had received in the ambush, but he endured the pain silently. Around 1866, he was assigned as the scout and guide for Camp Lincoln. The old wound sapped his strength and the mountain man finally died in 1867. Signs of this famous trapper can still be seen: In 1832, he carved his name upon the Casa Grande Ruin. A monument in his honor was erected in Prescott.

Christopher "Kit" Carson

Kit Carson, born on December 24, 1809, would eventually become one of America's greatest folk heroes. Frontiersman, soldier, trapper, and Indian agent, Kit Carson was all of these. He was also an effective Indian fighter, although he had great respect for the Indian culture and way of life. The Comanche, Arapaho, and Kiowa all called Kit Carson their friend, often coming to him for advice. Once Carson was responsible for stopping a bloody battle between the Comanche and the Sioux. A deal was made with his help and the two bands halted their hostilities.

Christopher "Kit" Carson

His adventure-filled life began at the age of 15 when he ran away with a group of traders bound for Santa Fe. Along the way he learned to trap and trade, which he continued to do for 15 years. While trapping in 1842, he encountered John C. Frémont and agreed to serve as Frémont's guide in an exploration of the West. On his way back to Washington, D.C. to report on Frémont's exploration, Carson met another notable figure, General Stephen W. Kearny. Kearny pressed him into serving with the army, which was hoping to sweep away the Mexican influence from the Southwest during the Mexican War. From then on, Carson was the guide for Kearny's army. He also fought and carried dispatches back to Washington until the end of the war.

In the latest in a series of land grabs, Congress and the railroad companies were debating the acquisition of what is presently southern Arizona. Kit Carson had some words about the land in question. He described southern Arizona as being "so desolate, desert, and God-forsaken that a wolf could not make a living on it." The land was purchased anyway.

After the war, in 1854, he settled down briefly in Taos as an Indian agent. But the Civil War erupted and Kit Carson returned to the battlefield under the Union flag with the First New Mexico Volunteers. In 1863, Carson had to return to Indian affairs when he was commanded to send the Navajo to the Bosque Redondo Reservation in New Mexico. Carson's army of 700 soldiers and many Ute scouts arrived at Fort Defiance in Arizona as a show of force. The Navajo would not leave their native land, and tensions escalated. Hostilities soon turned into bloodshed. Strategically, Carson could not be beaten. He consistently outmaneuvered the Navajo. The Navajo stronghold in Canyon de Chelly was taken, and the Indians who survived the attack were forced to endure the grueling Long Walk to the reservation in New Mexico (see page 92).

In 1868, Carson was appointed superintendent of Indian affairs for the Colorado Territory, a post he held for only a short time. He died on May 23, 1868, and was buried in Taos, New Mexico.

Amiel W. Whipple

In 1816, A. W. Whipple was born in Greenwich, Massachusetts. His military career began in 1841 when he graduated from West Point. In 1851, he first traveled to Arizona as the assistant astronomer to the United States and Mexican Boundary Commission. On May 14, 1853, Jefferson Davis ordered Whipple to explore the 35th parallel route for a transcontinental railroad.

Whipple's party, guided by Antoine Leroux (see page 70), journeyed past the Little Colorado River to the site of Flagstaff and through the San Francisco Mountains. Along the way Whipple made notes, drew pictures, and surveyed the land for a promising railroad route. His notes, *Pacific Railroad Reports,* published in 1856, are a valuable document. He discovered various passes through which the railroad could be built, and more accessible land over which the railroad could travel. Yet his exploration was not without some problems. Whipple's surveying party was confronted and surrounded by very hostile Yuma Indians. On the brink of what the explorers thought to be a massacre, one of the Indians recognized Whipple. Previously, while he was scouting the Colorado River, Whipple had rescued a lost, young Indian girl from certain death in the desert. Unknown to him at the time, that girl happened to be the daughter of the Yuma chief. Soon the two parties were reconciled and the Yuma gave the explorers some much-needed food. The two groups met as friends on Christmas Day.

Major General Amiel W. Whipple

Despite Whipple proving the feasibility of a 35th parallel railroad, Congress was unable to agree on a route for the transcontinental railroad. At the time, tensions were building between the North and South and the antislave states were disinclined to support such a major improvement to the infrastructure of the southern states; soon after the start of the Civil War, a more northern route would be adopted for the first transcontinental railroad. However, the urgent need for an improved supply route through the Southwest was recognized, and as an interim measure, Congress funded a wagon road that would later be called "Beale Wagon Road" (see page 58).

After his Arizona adventure, Whipple served as the chief topographical engineer in General McDowell's Union Army during the Battle of Bull Run. For his bravery in the battle of Chancellorsville, he was promoted to the rank of major general. On May 4, 1863, he suffered a grievous wound while his forces lay in an exposed position. He died just three days later. In his honor, Fort Whipple and Whipple Valley are named after the great surveyor.

Lorenzo Sitgreaves

The first government exploration of northern Arizona was made by Captain Lorenzo Sitgreaves. Sitgreaves, born in 1810, was a West Point graduate. He served in the Black Hawk War in 1832, after which he joined the Corps of Topographical Engineers. There he successfully served, surveying the Florida reefs and constructing roads in Wisconsin. During the Mexican War, in the battle of Buena Vista, he was promoted to captain. Three years after the war ended, Sitgreaves arrived in Zuni, New Mexico, with orders to find a suitable railroad route to California. On September 24, 1851, Sitgreave's adventures in Arizona began.

The Sitgreaves Expedition set out along the Little Colorado River. The party was under the guidance of the famous trapper and scout Antoine Leroux (see page 70). Sheep were driven along with the group to provide sustenance. The sheep turned out to be a great boon because food was very scarce. By the seventeenth day of the expedition, the party was worse for wear. Many mules had died already, unable to endure the Arizona sun. The sheep and mules that survived were exhausted, their hooves cracked and worn from the journey.

As the party continued westward, their suffering grew worse. Water was increasingly scarce, and as they approached the Colorado River, the party made contact with Indians, probably Mojave, who tried to steal one of the explorers' horses. Later the party was ambushed; Antoine Leroux was wounded during the conflict, but the Indians were defeated.

When they reached the Colorado River, the party changed its bearing southward toward the Gulf of California. Starvation descended upon the expedition. Mules were dying. Only the essentials were kept—everything else was discarded. Just when things were looking as grim as possible, hostile Yuma Indians appeared. The situation looked even worse. The Yumas managed to pick off a straggling soldier. A firefight ensued, and only after several of the Indian warriors were killed were the Yuma routed. The party ultimately ended its journey at Fort Yuma, finally finding relief.

The expedition took about 10 weeks. Sitgreaves reported 700 miles of unknown territory. But the mission was not as successful as hoped. The report was sketchy at best and did little to assist in the selection of a railroad route. Still, his party had managed to survive a dangerous and grueling trek through Arizona in conditions that would have killed lesser men. After a series of promotions, Sitgreaves settled down and retired in Washington, D.C. He died May 14, 1888.

Edward F. Beale

Born in 1822, Edward Beale would go on to succeed in a number of professions ranging from naval officer and prominent explorer to bureaucrat and politician. Those who knew him described him as a thin, wiry man, who frankly voiced his thoughts. Status, wealth, and adventure drove Beale in his many exploits. Even though he is a prominent man in the history of the West, the strange episode involving camels in the Southwest desert overshadows his other accomplishments (see page 58). He played a heroic role in the Mexican War and carried the first sample of California gold to the East Coast, which helped inspire the gold rush.

Edward Beale

Beale's political life began in 1852 when he became California's first superintendent of Indian affairs; in that position he promoted a humanitarian approach toward relations with the Native Americans. Politics grew to be second nature for the war hero, and after leading the Law and Order Division in San Francisco, he became the superintendent for a transcontinental wagon road in 1857. This mission led to the creation of the Beale Wagon Road and the introduction of camels into the American Southwest. In about 1870, he purchased a home in Washington, D.C., spending half his time there and half in California. During the 1870s, he became involved in Republican politics, advocating the right to vote for African Americans. He also became one of President Ulysses S. Grant's friends. Beale died in Washington on April 21, 1893, at the age of 71.

King S. Woolsey and the Bloody Tanks Massacre

In the 1860s, the Tonto Apache were driving terror into the hearts of the ranchers who lived just south of Prescott. In January 1864, after Apache had stolen some cattle and horses from the ranchers, King S. Woolsey came by in a wagon with a full load of flour bound for Prescott. The settlers and ranchers pleaded their case to Woolsey and asked him to come back after his delivery and lead them against the rampaging Apache. Having no love for the Apache, Woolsey agreed. Together with 60 white men, 30 Pima, and 30 Maricopa Indians, Woolsey struck out for Tonto Basin. Along the way, the Pima sensed an ambush and melted into the hills. Woolsey and the rest continued. Soon the Tonto Apache surrounded them. Before the Apache could strike the first blow, Woolsey thought of a plan to double-cross them. He told the Apache, through Jack, his interpreter, that he

King Woolsey

wanted to make peace and had brought them gifts. Woolsey told his men that when he put his hand up to his hat, they should open fire. A group of Tonto Apache, reported as numbering between 20 and 30, came down to meet with Woolsey and two others from his group. As the meeting proceeded, a Maricopa Indian darted in and warned Woolsey that the Apache were planning a double-cross of their own. Woolsey placed his hand on his hat and his men killed the Tonto with just one white killed and several wounded. The conflict would go down in history as the Bloody Tanks Massacre. In the spring, Woolsey led another group on an Indian-hunting rampage to Squaw Canyon, where 14 Indians were killed with no white losses.

The notorious Bloody Tanks Massacre put Woolsey in the spotlight, though in his early years, he had lived the simple life of a mule driver. After moving to Arizona, he bought the Agua Caliente ranch near Yuma, where he started a flour mill. When the Civil War erupted, Woolsey's sympathies were with the Confederacy. He enlisted in their army, but came down with smallpox on the march eastward and saw no active service. In 1863, he joined the Walker party and prospected with Joseph Reddeford Walker (see page 71). He later established the Phoenix Flour Mills in 1878 and built the first road from Agua Caliente to Prescott. Woolsey also dipped into politics, getting elected five times to Arizona's Territorial Council and becoming the lieutenant colonel of volunteers. He ran for Congress in 1878 but was defeated.

Still, Woolsey was best known as an Indian fighter. His answer to the Apache problem was harsh and simple: extermination. A sudden heart attack claimed his life on June 29, 1879. He was 47 years old. At the time, Woolsey was the largest landowner in Maricopa County and considered one of the founders of Phoenix.

John Wesley Powell

John Wesley Powell was a Civil War veteran who lost his right arm at the Battle of Shiloh. However, this handicap did not prevent Powell from becoming one of the most influential explorers in the history of the West. After the war, Powell served as a professor of geology at Wesleyan University in Illinois as well as a museum curator. After spending time with a Ute Indian tribe in 1869, Powell conceived the idea of exploring the great rivers in the area by boat.

In May 1869, Powell led a group of 11 men down the Green River; they commenced in Green River, Wyoming, met the Colorado River, and traveled through the Grand Canyon. One man quit the expedition early, and three others refused to run the treacherous final rapids on the Colorado. Instead, the three men climbed out of the canyon only to be killed by Shivwitts Indians. On August 30, 1869, Powell and the remaining men arrived safely at the mouth of the Virgin River near the Mormon settlement of Callville.

Impressed by the expedition, Congress agreed to give Powell $10,000 for a second trip in 1871. Reportedly, Powell perched himself on a chair secured to the lead boat and recited poetry along the journey. The explorer also used this opportunity to conduct serious scientific research, mapping the Colorado Plateau region and creating a photographic catalog of the phenomenal scenery. He conducted further exploration of Arizona and Utah in 1874 and 1875.

Powell with Tau-Gu, great chief of the Paiute

Powell left his mark on Arizona by naming many landmarks in the state, including Marble Canyon, Vermillion Cliffs, Sunset Crater, and Glen Canyon. Later, Lake Powell, named after the intrepid explorer, filled in Glen Canyon.

In 1875, he became director of the federal Survey of the Rocky Mountain Region, which, with his support, was one of the agencies combined to form the U.S. Geological Survey in 1879. Powell was then appointed the first director of the Bureau of American Ethnology in 1879 in recognition of the ethnological studies he conducted during his western expeditions. President Garfield appointed him director of the U.S. Geological Survey in 1881; he held both positions for the remainder of his life. The explorer died on September 23, 1892, and is buried at Arlington National Cemetery.

American Indian Warriors

Cochise

Truthfulness, seriousness, and steadfast integrity—these were the traits of Cochise. Born in 1810, Cochise would go on to become a famous warrior and later chief of the Chiricahua Apache. He saw much war during his time, especially after a truce between the Mexicans and the Apache disintegrated. Casualities climbed on both sides of the conflict. Apache raided Mexican settlements and fought Mexican soldiers. Scalp hunters—mercenaries hired to eradicate the Indians—were close on Chiricahuan heels. Cochise's own father may have been killed by a scalp-hunting mercenary. Such bitter conflicts led to a continual and brutal grudge between the two factions. Later, Cochise married the daughter of Mangas Coloradas, which united the Chiricahuas with the Mimbreño Apache. Americans encountered Cochise and signed a peace agreement, while raids against the Mexicans continued relentlessly. However, American peace was a sham.

Lieutenant George Bascom, along with a small group of soldiers, appeared at Apache Pass in 1861 and asked to see Cochise. Cochise arrived, followed by his brother and five other warriors. They were initially welcomed into Bascom's tent. However, the lieutenant quickly accused Cochise of kidnapping a small boy and stealing cattle. In reality, it is likely that the boy had just run off, but Bascom never questioned the report. Cochise denied the accusations, suggested that the White Mountain Apache may have been responsible, and offered his assistance. Bascom had the group arrested. But Cochise escaped by cutting his way through the tent. Enraged at the arrest, Cochise besieged Apache Pass, killing several

Mexicans and capturing four Americans. Bascom hung his male Apache prisoners in retaliation and left their bodies until the elements stripped them to skeletons. The sight of his brother hanging from a tree enraged Cochise; he killed his prisoners and left their bodies mutilated beyond recognition.

From 1861 to 1872, the Chiricahua and the Mimbreño (the Mimbreño leader, Mangas Coloradas, was Cochise's father-in-law, who decided to join forces with the Chiricahua) inspired terror into the hearts of white men with a bloody cycle of vengeance and retaliation. Eventually, Cochise's rage abated but was soon rekindled after Mangas Coloradas was tricked and captured during a peace discussion.

All the while, Cochise's reputation as a deadly warrior grew. His horsemanship was said to be unparalleled and his skills with a lance were chilling. The war continued, and the embittered Cochise continued to distrust the Americans. He did accept one American, though, and called him "brother." Prospector and stagecoach driver Thomas Jeffords (see page 86) met with the legendary chief. When he entered the Apache camp he handed his weapons over to the warriors and asked to discuss matters with Cochise. Surprised by this courageous man, Cochise agreed. They talked for two days, and Cochise decided to let him continue delivering mail in Chiricahua territory. The mail personnel beneath Jeffords would also be spared the Apaches' wrath. After the meeting, Jeffords reported, "I found him to be a man of great natural ability, a splendid specimen of physical manhood, standing about six feet two, with an eye like an eagle. His religion was truth and loyalty."

However, the Apache continued their assaults on white men from an impregnable fortress in the Dragoon Mountains, which became known as Cochise's Stronghold. In 1872, General Oliver Howard sought peace with Cochise. He contacted Jeffords and asked to be guided to the Chiricahua chief. Jeffords agreed and Howard was able to parlay with Cochise for 11 days. He offered Cochise the reservation of his choosing. As a result of these discussions, an executive order in October 1872 granted the Chiricahua a large portion of southeastern Arizona as a reservation. Cochise promised to keep the peace on Apache Pass, and he did until his death, possibly from stomach cancer, on June 8, 1874. He was buried in secret in the Dragoon Mountains. Two years later, the 1872 executive order was revoked and the Chiricahua living on the reservation were relocated to San Carlos Reservation, otherwise known as Hell's Forty Acres.

Geronimo (Goyathlay)

Geronimo, born in 1829, was actually named Goyathlay. The origin of the name "Geronimo" is unknown, although some say that it comes from a mispronunciation of his name by Mexican soldiers. Others say that the name is a corruption of St. Jerome, the saint that soldiers called out for when Geronimo came barreling toward them. Geronimo first tasted war and revenge in 1858 when Mexican soldiers slaughtered women and children of the Bedonkohe Apaches. Geronimo's wife, Alope, and his three children died beneath the Mexican sword. Vengence for his people and his loved ones drove him to avenge these deaths. The Mexicans were not the only ones to witness Geronimo's fighting prowess. When Mangas Coloradas was captured through treachery, Geronimo joined Cochise to battle the Americans.

By the 1870s, most of the Apache bands had been settled in reservations. Geronimo joined his fellow Apache but soon found the conditions deplorable. He resisted with a group of followers, escaping from the San Carlos Reservation in 1878. They joined the Apache in Mexico but grew tired of fighting and returned to the reservation in 1880. When a religious gathering was suppressed, and the Indian shaman Nakaidoklini was killed, Geronimo escaped once again with his supporters. The following spring Geronimo came back, killed the chief of police, and led hundreds of Apache out of the San Carlos Reservation. The band raided American and Mexican settlements. In response, General Crook was called to apprehend the rampaging Apache. Using Apache scouts, he was able to do just that. The Apache were returned to San Carlos. Rumor circulated that the rebels were going to be executed, so they fled once again. Crook was right on their heels. Tirelessly, the army pursued the renegades, and Geronimo was forced to surrender. However, while being escorted back to the reservation, Geronimo and 30 followers escaped Crook's grasp, severely embarrassing the army. Even though Crook was not at fault, he was replaced by General Nelson Miles, who then sent 5,000 soldiers out after the Apache. On September 4, 1886, in Skeleton Canyon, Miles caught up with Geronimo and the great warrior surrendered for the last time.

Geronimo

Geronimo and his followers were sent to internment camps in Florida. Once there, they were forced to give up their way of life and made to don European dress and hairstyles. Life was difficult, and the men had to perform hard labor. Those who survived the camps were transferred to Fort Sill in present-day Oklahoma. Geronimo was reunited with one of his wives (he married two others after Alope's death) and he supported his family by farming, ranching, and selling pictures of himself. He became a celebrity and was at Teddy Roosevelt's inaugural parade and the St. Louis World's Fair. Yet he was still a prisoner of war. He longed to go back to his homeland, but never did. Pneumonia took him on February 17, 1909.

Mangas Coloradas (Red Sleeves)

Mangas Coloradas was a giant of a man, immense in stature and reputation alike. He stood more than 6 feet tall and possessed excellent skills as a leader and commander of his warriors. Born in 1795, he became known as a great chief of the Mimbreño Apache. He struck terror into the hearts of Mexicans, leading raids against them in retribution for wrongdoings against his people. In 1846, General Stephen Watts Kearny was heading toward California after taking Santa Fe, New Mexico. En route, he met Mangas Coloradas who wished peace between the Americans and the Apache and volunteered to do his part in the Mexican War. Although Kearny declined the offer, Mangas had made the first step toward peace. In 1852, Mangas continued to seek peace and agreed to a treaty proposed by Major John Greiner. However, Mexican settlements still suffered the unrelenting raids of the Mimbreño. Miners and prospectors who ventured near present-day Silver City, New Mexico, also felt Apache wrath. In 1861, when his son-in-law Cochise declared war against the United States, Mangas came to the aid of the Chiricahua Apache. Peace between the Mimbreño and the Americans was not to be.

The Civil War began in 1861 and American soldiers departed to fight in the East. A force from California under James H. Carleton marched into Arizona to wrestle the land away from the Confederacy. A contingent under Captain Thomas L. Roberts ventured into Apache Pass where the Mimbreño and the Chiricahua ambushed it. The battle went poorly for the combined Apache forces. They were shelled by howitzers, pelted by carbines, and charged by mounted cavalry. Mangas was shot in the chest during the conflict and was carried away by some of his warriors. Wounded, he was taken to Janos in Chihuahua, Mexico, where a Mexican doctor extracted the afflicting bullet under gunpoint. Mangas later recovered, but had grown tired of war, and once again sought peace with the Americans. Unfortunately, in January 1863, his pursuit of peace ended with bloody treachery.

Colonel J. R. West openly welcomed Mangas Coloradas to parlay at his camp. Upon his arrival, Mangas was immediately captured by American soldiers. Fort McLane became his prison, and he died there—although by what means is unclear. The official military version states that Mangas was shot when he attempted to escape. Another version is based on the statement of a soldier who said that he was under orders to murder the chief while he was in his cell. According to another, more brutal story, Mangas was tortured by hot bayonets, which were placed against his feet and legs, and then he was killed.

Victorio

Possibly the greatest Apache military strategist was most commonly known as Victorio. (He was also called Lucero, Biduya, and Beduiat.) Victorio, whose date of birth is most often stated to be 1825, but may have been as early as 1809, is perhaps the best-known chief of the Mimbreño Apache. Victorio was a burly man, not tall like Mangas Coloradas but "short and stout, with a heavy, firm-set lower jaw," as described by Indian Agent John Kimball. In the 1850s, Victorio joined up with Geronimo in raids against Mexico. He may have also fought beside Mangas Coloradas and Cochise at Apache Pass during their war against the United States.

After Mangas's capture and death in 1863, Victorio formed a band of Mimbreño Apache and Mescalero warriors and raided the Arizona countryside. In 1865, Victorio and his band agreed to settle down and move to a reservation if one could be provided. Waiting near Fort Craig they lived in peace, growing crops until 1877 when they were suddenly forced onto the infamous San Carlos Reservation.

San Carlos has often been described as 40 acres of hell. Summer heat frequently reached 110°F, and the unfortunate souls living there baked in the scorching sun. Victorio absconded from San Carlos twice; each time he returned. A chance visit to the reservation by officials was misinterpreted by Victorio as an indication that he was to be hung for crimes of murder and horse stealing. On August 21, 1879, Victorio and his followers bolted, this time never to return.

Victorio

The Black Range was their destination, and along the way they fought numerous skirmishes. The renegades moved south into Mexico but were pursued past the international border by Major Albert Payson Morrow. The two forces clashed and Morrow was repelled in a grim and bloody battle. Mexican militia were the next to feel Victorio's wrath; 30 militiamen fell beneath the Apaches. Victorio's band did not suffer a single loss. Raids continued through Mexico and Arizona as Victorio continued to outwit and elude his pursuers. However, he did have his close calls. Henry K. Parker, along with his Apache scouts, managed to trap Victorio in a canyon. Victorio's story may have ended there if Parker hadn't run out of ammunition. Like a shadow, the warrior slipped away. The chase continued. A war of attrition finally wore Victorio out. The army ransacked his supply camp and took hold of the region's water supply by securing the springs. Wearied and worn, Victorio tried to keep losses to a minimum. The tired band drifted into the Tres Castillos upthrust in Chihuahua and wandered into an ambush. Lieutenant Colonel Joaquin Terrazas and his Mexican militia annihilated the Apache, striking down 78 of them. Sixty-eight women and children were taken prisoner. When the smoke and dust cleared, only three militiamen had perished in the attack. Victorio was found dead. The circumstances of his death are unknown, but according to Apache legend, he killed himself at the final hour so that he would not fall into enemy hands.

Famous Soldiers and Battalions

Buffalo Soldiers

Buffalo Soldiers: the unsung heroes of the West. Often heralded as fierce warriors, these men were black soldiers segregated into four regiments, all commanded by white officers. The 9th, 10th, 24th, and 25th Regiments were authorized in 1866. For the next 25 years these regiments saw some of the bloodiest fighting in the West. They were nicknamed "Buffalo Soldiers" by the Indians against whom they fought. The nickname may have come about from the great amount of respect given to the soldiers and the buffalo alike or from the soldiers' thick, curly hair that reminded the Indians of a buffalo's coat.

The Buffalo Soldiers not only battled throughout the West, but also served in the Spanish-American War, following Teddy Roosevelt's famous charge up San Juan Hill. They fought in the Philippines and pursued the outlaw Pancho Villa into Mexico with General John Pershing. During their service, 23 Buffalo Soldiers received the Congressional Medal of Honor for bravery.

The Buffalo Soldiers also had a presence in Arizona. At Cedar Springs, the 24th and the 10th Regiments were escorting a pay wagon when outlaws ambushed them. The battle was fierce; the outlaws had set up a vicious ambush that subjected the soldiers to murderous crossfire. When most of the men were wounded, the company had to retreat. Although the bandits got the gold, Sergeant Brown and Corporal Mays were awarded the Medal of Honor. Nine soldiers were wounded, one of whom dragged himself 2 miles to a ranch house in search of help.

The Buffalo Soldiers also saw action during campaigns against notable Apache warriors Geronimo (see page 75) and Victorio (see page 76). They harried the Apache warriors by ambushing them and wearing them down. The campaigns were not easy; the Apache set ambushes, often with devastating results. In one ambush, five Buffalo Soldiers were killed, marking their highest loss until 1916.

The Buffalo Soldiers fought for honor and recognition at a time when America could not care less about the exploits of black soldiers, no matter how heroic. While they served, many Buffalo Soldiers received the recognition for which they yearned. But afterward, even those who were awarded Medals of Honor were denied work. Usually they ended up drifting into poverty or clustering into communities of other Buffalo Soldiers. The Buffalo Soldier units were finally integrated into the rest of the army during the Korean War.

Philip St. George Cooke and the Mormon Battalion

In 1846, thousands of Mormons were making their exodus from Illinois and Missouri and moving toward the promised land in Utah. At the same time, negotiations between the United States and Mexico had broken down and the Mexican War began. Mexican soldiers crossed the Rio Grande and President James K. Polk demanded that an army be raised to protect American soil and fully realize the country's westward expansion. Colonel Stephen Watts Kearny, later to become a general, was given the power to form an army to secure the Southwest. His army of 2,000 marched into Santa Fe, New Mexico, and took the area with little effort. In fact, not a single shot was fired when he took the town.

In a marvelous show of patriotism for a country that was persecuting them, 400 Mormons joined the cause. Unprepared, tired, and unruly, they were assigned to serve under Lieutenant Colonel Philip St. George Cooke and were charged with creating a supply road that would link New Mexico and California.

Lieutenant Cooke was born in Leesburg, Virginia, on June 13, 1809. His military career started when he was 18, right after he graduated from the U.S. Military Academy at West Point. He served in the Indian wars and had previously served with Kearny on a scouting mission into the Rocky Mountains. Cooke was one of Kearny's best officers as he was able-minded, stern, and experienced on the frontier. When Cooke saw the rabble he had to command, he knew he had his work cut out for him. Pauline Weaver (see page 71), the famous frontiersman, was to be his guide.

Spirits were low and distrust was in the air. Some sources say that even though they were marching through hostile Indian country, Cooke would not distribute ammunition for fear of a mutiny. Others say that a mutiny might have occurred if this troop had not fallen under the attentive eyes of the Mormon leader, Brigham Young, who charged the unruly bunch to be loyal. Water was scarce, and supplies were dwindling. After the troops changed their southerly march and began heading west toward Tucson, they came upon an abandoned ranch and a herd of wild cattle. What seemed as a boon to the hungry soldiers quickly changed to catastrophe—the cattle turned and attacked the battalion. No one was killed during the brief skirmish, but there were injuries. One private suffered a badly gashed leg after being gored and thrown; a sergeant also found himself in harm's way and suffered broken ribs. A burly bull charged Cooke, but a corporal saved his life by gunning down the beast. The bull, quite literally, died at Cooke's feet. Cooke, in his journal, recorded the skirmish as the battle of "Bull Run."

Word of the approaching battalion was traveling fast and Mexican forces in Tucson added 150 reinforcements to fight off any attack, thereby raising their forces to 200. To make matters worse for Cooke, the Mexicans were holed up in a defensible fort equipped with two brass cannons. Cooke's men knew little of tactics, and they had very little non-bovine combat experience. Still, the Mormons approached the fort ready for battle. The Mexican commander, Captain José Antonio Comaduran, tried to avoid a showdown. His messengers told Cooke that he could go around Tucson, but the city itself was off-limits. Cooke, however, needed to resupply his troops. In an act of gutsy bravado, Cooke demanded that the Mexicans surrender. The Mexicans refused. Two days later, the Mormon battalion descended on Tucson and were surprised to find that the Mexicans had pulled out the day before. Tuscon was occupied without firing a shot. Under Cooke's orders, there was no looting involved and the friendly townspeople welcomed the troops and even opened their food stores to them.

Cooke and his battalion endured great hardships as they trekked through Arizona and southern California. On January 29, 1847, they finally arrived in San Diego. For the troops that nearly mutinied, Cooke had only praise. They had survived the desert, had crossed streams that nearly swept some of them away, and had battled snowstorms as they pulled their wagons over the mountains of California. They helped create a major supply road to Arizona, the Gila Trail (see page 60), which would later be transformed into Interstate 10. Today, a statue in Salt Lake City stands in honor of Lieutenant Colonel Philip St. George Cooke and his hardy Mormon battalion.

General George Crook

George Crook, who became one of the most eminent Indian fighters of his time, was born on September 23, 1829. During early campaigns, he was repulsed by America's poor treatment of Indians and resolved to seek justice for those Indian tribes against whom he had fought. He also loved to hunt and fish and adored living in the wilderness. Proving himself to be an able soldier, he fought Indians in California, Oregon, and Washington. In the Civil War, Crook's next battlefield, he fought against the Cumberland guerrillas. He was captured and later released in a prisoner exchange. After the war he was once again sent to the Northwest to battle hostile Indians. Crook's success against the Snake, Paiute, and Pit Indians of Idaho won him the assignment of commanding the Department of Arizona, which he assumed on June 4, 1871. He replaced General George Stoneman who was partially to blame for the Camp Grant Massacre (see page 98).

The geographical obstacles combined with hostile Indians made military campaigns in Arizona difficult. But Crook was undaunted. His favorite method was to use Indians to catch Indians. Indian scouts, often drawn from rebellious bands, aided his pursuit of hostile Indians. The success of this upstart young officer irritated several senior officers. Still, he was promoted to brigadier general and left Arizona to command the Department of the Platte. On March 17, 1876, Crook ordered a strike against an Indian village beside the Powder River. Crook was there to supervise the battle, although his junior officer, Colonel Reynolds, was in command. Initially, the battle went very well for Reynolds. However, when the villagers launched a counterattack, the battle began to slip away from the Americans; the Indians even managed to retake the horses they had lost in the initial attack. Charges brought by Crook led to Reynolds being court-martialed and suspended, although the sentence was remitted subsequently by the secretery of war. Some felt that Crook's accusations were unjustified and simply an attempt at saving face. Others that Crook was doing his duty. Crook's next engagement was a hard-fought stalemate against the Sioux and the Cheyenne. In the face of a very large and fierce Sioux force, Crook decided to wait for reinforcements. His cautiousness was somewhat controversial and Crook's superiors wondered if the wait was strategically unsound. Reinforcements did arrive, and Crook pursued the Sioux toward the Black Hills in South Dakota. The march was long and full of hardships. The troops had to subsist on horse and mule meat. However, a minor victory was scored against the Sioux at Slim Buttes. Afterward, Crook was sent back into Arizona to quell the Apache rebellion.

General George Crook, circa 1890

In 1883, Crook and a company of cavalry, guided by about 200 Apache scouts, traveled through Mexico's Sierra Madres. He encountered the renegade Apache and requested that they return to the San Carlos Reservation. The gutsy move paid off and the Apache returned. On May 15, 1885, another rebellion took place on the San Carlos Reservation. Geronimo, the famous Indian leader, had fled with most of the Apache, particularly the Chiricahua. Crook eventually caught up with the Apache and began peace talks. However, Geronimo escaped, embarrassing the army. Crook requested that he be relieved of command and he was recalled to the Department of the Platte. There he worked until his death on March 21, 1890.

Ira Hayes

> Ira Hayes returned a hero—celebrated through the land,
> He was wined and speeched and honored—everybody shook his hand;
> But he was just a Pima Indian—no water, no home, no chance;
> At home nobody cared what Ira done—and when do the Indians dance?
> —*Peter LaFarge, "Ballad of Ira Hayes"*

Ira Hayes, one of America's many war heroes, was born on the Gila River Indian Reservation in Arizona on January 12, 1923. He was raised in the Pima tradition, but as a boy he relished listening to the stories recounted by World War I veteran Indians on the reservation. When America joined the Allies in World War II, Hayes enlisted in the Marine Corps Reserve in August 1944. There he was trained as a parachutist. His fellow soldiers dubbed him "the Chief."

Hayes's military tour of the Pacific began in March 1943 when the marines sailed to the Solomon Islands to join the U.S. Navy. General Douglas MacArthur's famous "island-hopping" tactic in the Pacific sector of World War II involved deploying troops from island to island, often suffering high casualties, to wrest each away from the Japanese. Hayes's unit saw combat in the assault on the tropical island Bougainville. Later, his company of parachutists was dissolved and Hayes was reassigned as a rifleman to Company E, Second Battalion, 28th Marine Division. On February 20, 1945, Company E was one of the first to land and begin the bloody assault on Iwo Jima. On February 23, the marines battled their way to the top of Mount Suribachi where, a day later, Hayes and five others raised a large American flag. Joe Rosenthal captured the moment in a photograph that later inspired the famous bronze statue in Arlington Cemetery.

> Well, they battled up Iwo Jima hill—two hundred and fifty men,
> But only twenty-seven lived—to walk back down again;
> When the fight was over—and Old Glory raised,
> Among the men who held it high was the Indian—Ira Hayes.
> —*Peter LaFarge, "Ballad of Ira Hayes"*

At the end of the campaign, Hayes returned a hero. He and the other two survivors (the other three marines had been killed in action) toured the United States. They gave speeches and re-enacted the famous flag-raising. Hayes did not enjoy the spotlight and quietly asked to return to duty; his request was denied. Guilt over his fallen comrades began to eat away at him. To dissolve these irrepressible feelings, he took to drinking excessively. Hayes's life began to take a tragic dive. He moved from the Gila River Reservation to Chicago where arrests and time in jail for drunkeness became an accustomed humiliation. Ira Hayes returned to the Gila River Reservation only to be found dead on January 23, 1955, just a mile from his parents' home. Ira Hayes died of exposure. He was given a hero's funeral in Arlington National Cemetery. The statue depicting the historic flag-raising had been dedicated the year before.

> Then Ira started drinkin' hard—jail was often his home;
> They let him raise the flag and lower it—as you would throw a dog a bone;
> He died drunk early one morning—alone in the land he'd fought to save;
> Two inches of water in a lonely ditch—was the grave for Ira Hayes.
>
> —*Peter LaFarge, "Ballad of Ira Hayes"*

William Price

William Redwood Price was born on May 20, 1838, in Cincinnati, Ohio. He was trained in civil engineering and successfully fought in the Civil War, during which he was promoted to major and breveted brigadier general. His military career continued in Arizona. He was primary field commander during the Hualapai War (or Walapai War) and succeeded in subduing the Hualapai (Walapai) Indians. The war lasted from 1867 to 1868 and Price was promoted to colonel for his success.

Price's next adventure lay in New Mexico. After being transferred to Fort Bayard, he led a patrol of scouts against cattle rustlers. The group roamed over the countryside, mapping the terrain and pursuing thieves. Price was once again transferred, and this time was assigned to fight with General Nelson Miles in his Red River campaign. Miles did not always agree with Price's command of his troops. In fact, Miles thought Price was incompetent and planned to bring him up on charges of dereliction, supposedly because Price led uneventful skirmishes and left wounded soldiers with rations and medical aid, but without any able-bodied soldiers to protect them. Charges were never brought, and Price was sent back to Arizona.

Price served for roughly three years in Arizona, almost until his death in 1881. Once again he policed the area, looking for renegades and hostile Indians. Accompanying him were notable scouts Dan O'Leary and Al Sieber. He retired two months before he died on December 30.

Arizona Rough Riders

On April 25, 1898, the United States declared war against Spain following the sinking of the U.S. battleship, *Maine.* In a show of patriotism, Arizona men signed up to fight in the conflict and two companies of cavalry troops were easily raised. The two companies, which were a part of the First U.S. Volunteer Cavalry, trained in San Antonio and became known as the Rough Riders. Captain William Owen "Buckey" O'Neill (see below), who was the mayor of Prescott, was put in charge of Company A. Captain James H. McClintock (see below), a newspaperman from Phoenix, led Company B. There were many other companies within the Rough Riders, but A and B were largely made up of Arizonans. Both O'Neill and McClintock served under Major Alexander O. Brodie. Theodore Roosevelt resigned as assistant secretary of the navy so he could become a lieutenant colonel and fight with the unit that he had helped create. Colonel Leonard Wood, who served in Arizona during the Apache Wars, was the overall commander of the force. The flag carried by the two units was created by women from Phoenix who pieced it together using ribbons and material. The bullet-riddled flag can be seen today in the Phoenix capitol building.

The Rough Riders were transferred to Tampa, Florida, and almost missed their transport to Cuba. They jumped aboard a troop transport, leaving their horses behind them. Because they had no horses they were called Wood's Weary Walkers. However, morale was high and the troops sang their war song, "There'll Be a Hot Time in the Old Town Tonight" as they sailed for Cuba. They participated in many major battles in the Cuba campaign, including the famous charge up San Juan Hill. Major Brodie was promoted during the conflict and served as Colonel Theodore Roosevelt's right-hand man. When Roosevelt was elected president in 1901, Brodie was made governor of the Arizona Territory. The Arizona Rough Riders helped win the war against the Spanish and launch the United States as a world power. A monument to O'Neill and the Arizona Rough Riders stands in Prescott.

James H. McClintock

James McClintock came to the Arizona Territory in 1879 when he was just 15. As he grew he was known to be a bit bluff, but an entertaining companion nonetheless. He learned the trade of a printer and became publisher of the *Phoenix Herald.* In 1887, he bought and began to publish the *Tempe News.* In addition to his publishing career, he taught school and was editorial correspondent of the *Los Angeles Times.* As relations between the United States and Spain crumbled, he demonstrated his patriotism by helping Buckey O'Neill and Alexander Brodie create the First U.S. Volunteer Cavalry, later known as the Rough Riders. James McClintock commanded Company B of this famous troop of soldiers. He was severely wounded in the battle at Las Guasimas, but he showed tremendous courage and was promoted to major. His military career continued, and in 1902 he became a colonel of the First Arizona Infantry.

James McClintock

McClintock literally made history when he set pen to paper and created *Arizona—The Youngest State,* the first complete history book of Arizona ever published. He also wrote *Mormon Settlement in Arizona.* He served as postmaster for Phoenix until his death on May 10, 1934.

William Owen "Buckey" O'Neill

Buckey O'Neill was born on February 2, 1860. It is not known where he came from, but he arrived in the Arizona Territory in 1879. He bounced from Tombstone to Phoenix, eventually winding up in Prescott in 1882. There he became the editor of the *Arizona Miner.* He also founded a paper

Buckey O'Neill

named *Hoof and Horn,* which was centered on the livestock industry.

Buckey O'Neill was a man of many accomplishments. He grew prosperous from onyx mines near Mayer and helped promote copper mining in the Grand Canyon. He served as the Yavapai County probate judge and school superintendent, tax collector, sheriff, and eventually the mayor of Prescott. When Buckey was sheriff, four cowboys robbed a train. Buckey and his posse tracked them into Utah and captured them after a gunfight. Writing fiction was one of Buckey's hobbies, and his stories were published both in the *Argonaut* and the *San Francisco Examiner.*

Relations between the United States and Spain faltered, leading to the Spanish-American War. Buckey, along with Alexander Brodie and James McClintock, founded the First U.S. Volunteer Cavalry. Buckey O'Neill, then the mayor of Prescott, was the first to enlist. He commanded Company A of the famous Rough Riders. On July 1, 1898, he was killed in action near San Juan Hill. It appears that O'Neill was a bit careless on the battlefield. When a compatriot pleaded with him to take cover, Buckey responded, "The Spanish bullet isn't molded that will kill me." Just then a Spanish bullet ended his life. Colonel Roosevelt (later to become president) mourned his loss, saying that Buckey O'Neill was an idol of the Arizona soldiers.

The Navajo Code Talkers

Navajo Code Talk is believed to be the only unbroken military code in the history of warfare. The idea of creating the code came from Philip Johnston, a veteran of World War I who learned the importance to the military of a code that was undecipherable. Johnston was the son of a missionary to the Navajo and was raised on the Navajo reservation where he became one of the few non-Navajo who spoke the language fluently.

The Navajo language is an extremely complex unwritten language. It has no alphabet or symbols, numerous dialects, complex syntax, subtle and unusual tonal variations, and is spoken only within the Navajo Nation. In 1942, the U.S. military believed that there were fewer than 30 non-Navajo who could speak it.

In February 1942, Johnston met with Major General Clayton B. Vogel, the commanding general of Amphibious Corps, Pacific Fleet, and his staff to demonstrate the value of the language as a military code. Johnston's presentation showed that under simulated combat conditions the Navajo could encode, transmit, and decode a three-line English message in 20 seconds. Conventional cryptographic facilities and techniques of the time required 30 minutes. General Vogel, although skeptical, gave the project the go-ahead, recommending the recruitment into the Marine Corps of at least 200 Navajo for the highly classified code-talker program.

Once the code talkers had completed training in the United States, they were sent to the Pacific for assignment to marine combat divisions. By August 1943, 191 Navajo had joined the marines under this program; it is estimated that the total number of Navajo who served as code talkers in World War II was between 375 and 420. The code talker's job was to transmit information on tactics and troop movements, orders, and other vital battlefield information over telephones and radios.

The Navajo Code Talk was transmitted as a meaningless string of Navajo words. When received, each word would be translated to its English equivalent. The first letter of each word would be used to form another word that was part of the message. Thus, the code for the word "bomb" would have been *shush* (bear), *ne-ahs-jah* (owl), *na-as-tso-si* (mouse), *shush* (bear). To avoid the need to spell out all words, about 450 frequently used military terms were assigned Navajo words.

The Navajo code talkers took part in every assault the U.S. Marines conducted in the Pacific from 1942 to 1945. They served in all six marine divisions, marine raider battalions, and marine parachute units, transmitting messages in their native language. The Japanese never broke the code. After the war, the Japanese chief of intelligence said that although they were able to decipher the codes used by the U.S. Army and Army Air Corps, they never cracked the code used by the marines.

In 1991, Senator Dennis DeConcini in his Senate resolution advocating a National Code Talkers Day, which is now celebrated every August 14, said, "Many Marines believe that Iwo Jima would never have been taken by American forces had it not been for the Navajo code talkers."

The Navajo Code Talk was so top secret that it was not declassified until 1968, 23 years after the end of the war.

Lawmen, Gunfighters, and Outlaws

Wyatt Earp

The controversial emblem of the West, Wyatt Berry Stapp Earp, was born on March 19, 1848, in Illinois. His father, Nicholas Porter Earp, had served in the Mexican War beneath Wyatt Berry Stapp, and young Wyatt was named in honor of his father's revered commander. Wyatt spent most of his early life in Illinois and Iowa. When the Civil War broke out in 1861, he dreamed of enlisting. Wyatt often ran off in hopes of joining, but his father would catch up to him and bring him back home. He was one of five rough-and-tumble brothers who were dubbed "the Fighting Earps." His siblings were James C. (1841–1926), Virgil W. (1843–1906), Morgan (1851–1882), and Warren B. (1855–1900). They had an older half-brother, Newton Jasper (1837–1928) and a younger sister, Adelia (b. 1861). Two other sisters, Virginia and Martha, died when very young. Both James and Virgil fought in the Civil War.

Wyatt worked on his father's farm but soon learned to hate the backbreaking labor. Upon Virgil's return from the Civil War, Wyatt left with him and took such jobs as loading freight wagons and working on the Union Pacific Railroad. The Earps, including Wyatt and Virgil, settled down on their father's farm in Lamar, Missouri. Wyatt married Urilla Sutherland there in 1870 and got his first taste of dispensing law and order when he was elected the local constable. Urilla died suddenly of typhoid just a year later. Grief-stricken and fleeing accusations of fraud, Wyatt left Lamar. In 1871, he wandered into controversy in present-day Oklahoma. Wyatt Earp's actions are unclear, but he was arrested for horse stealing. He jumped bail and fled into Kansas, where he may have worked briefly as a buffalo hunter.

Wyatt continued to drift from one frontier town to the next. In 1875, he became a policeman in Wichita where he gained a reputation as an excellent lawman. He rarely smiled, had nerves of steel, and never killed unless he had to. Once Wyatt imprisoned a drunken man, on whom he discovered a roll of bills adding up to $500. To the drunk's surprise, when he woke up Wyatt returned the money. The local newspaper, the *Beacon,* heralded Wyatt's honesty, noting that the drunk was lucky to be tossed into the Wichita prison because in any other jurisdiction the money would have disappeared. Yet Wyatt was by no means a saint and he often let his fists do the talking. In fact, Wyatt was eventually kicked off the force for assaulting the former marshal, Bill Smith.

Wyatt Earp

In 1876, Wyatt joined the police force in the wild and morally destitute Dodge City—the Babylon of the West. He frequently chased criminals and tracked them over the countryside. One such case involved robber Dave Rudabaugh, who escaped into Indian Territory (present-day Oklahoma) with Wyatt nipping at his heels. His trail led Wyatt to Fort Griffin, Texas. Once there, Wyatt met a slender, gambling dentist by the name of Doc Holliday, who had information that helped Wyatt find his man. The friendship between Doc and Wyatt would prove to be invaluable. In April 1877, Wyatt followed the gold rush to the Black Hills but was back in Dodge before the end of summer. In 1878, he spent a couple of months in Texas gambling, before returning to serve briefly as assistant city marshal to Charles Bassett.

Wyatt left Dodge City for good on September 9, 1879, to travel to Las Vegas, New Mexico, where he joined up with Doc Holliday and Morgan and Virgil Earp. The four, along with their families, soon moved to Tombstone, Arizona. Wyatt worked as a shotgun guard for Wells Fargo until July 1880, when he became the deputy sheriff of Tombstone. During this period, the Earps met the Clantons and the McLaury brothers, a miscreant bunch of cattle rustlers.

After their years of drifting, it soon became clear that the Earps had decided to put down roots in Tombstone. They invested in town property and acquired local mining claims. Wyatt also joined with his old friend Bat Masterson to acquire an interest in the gambling tables at the Oriental Saloon. After the town marshal was shot in October 1880, Virgil took over the job and expected to be confirmed to the post as soon as an election could be held but was disappointed when he lost. However, when the new marshal mysteriously disappeared, Virgil was appointed to take over the post.

From the first days when the Earps entered Tombstone, a feud began to develop between them and the Clantons and McLaurys. It exploded at the shoot-out at the O.K. Corral (see page 82) on October 26, 1881. The vendetta continued and on December 28, 1881, Virgil was ambushed by an unknown assassin. He was wounded and never regained full use of his left arm. In March of the following year, Morgan was fatally shot while playing pool at one of the saloons in town. In retribution, Wyatt, who had been deputized as a U.S. marshal after Virgil's shooting, tracked and gunned down two Clanton supporters. But Tombstone had finally had enough of the shooting and Wyatt was forced to leave.

He returned to drifting from town to town throughout the West. He roamed through Colorado, catching up with Holliday, and eventually following the gold rush to Idaho, where he bought a couple of saloons. By 1887, he was on the move again, this time to California, where he was elected marshal of Colton. From 1889 to 1890 Wyatt owned saloons in San Diego. Raising thoroughbreds in San Francisco was Earp's next venture. While there he refereed the Bob Fitzsimmons–Tom Sharkey prize fight, on the condition that he could wear his six-shooter. In a controversial decision, he awarded the win to Sharkey—a move that outraged Fitzsimmons's supporters. Perhaps it was the presence of his six-shooter, but he avoided anything more than being charbroiled in the newspaper and heralded as a cheat. His reputation sank and Wyatt became fed up.

After returning to Arizona briefly, he left with his third wife for the Alaska gold rush and opened a saloon in Nome in 1877. After returning from Alaska for the Nevada boom, he finally settled down in Los Angeles in 1906. He tried to attract the attention of the burgeoning Hollywood film industry but met with little success. During his time on the movie lots, he became friends with two cowboy stars of the era—Tom Mix and William S. Hart. He also endeavored to get his adventures published. In 1928, Stuart N. Larke took an interest in the project, but the fanciful acount of Wyatt's life did not appear until after his death at age 80, on January 18, 1929.

Doc Holliday

> Physically, Doc Holliday was a weakling who could not have whipped a healthy 15-year-old boy . . . this fact was perhaps why he was so ready to resort to a weapon of some kind whenever he got himself into difficulty. He was hot-headed and impetuous and very much given to both drinking and quarreling —absolutely unable to keep out of trouble for any great length of time. —*Bat Masterson*

John Henry "Doc" Holliday was born on August 14, 1851, the son of prosperous Southern parents. As such, it was only natural that he should take up a respected profession. During the 1870s, he studied dentistry, was quite good at the practice, and became a doctor of dental surgery. But shortly after he began his practice, he contracted tuberculosis. Like many sufferers of the disease, he moved out West to take advantage of the dry climate. Once there, he continued to practice dentistry, but his reputation as a dentist was overtaken by his notoriety as a hotheaded, calculating gunfighter. Eventually, Holliday quit dentistry altogether and survived solely on gambling.

He wandered and gambled throughout the West, stopping at Dallas and Fort Worth in Texas, Dodge City in Kansas, Denver, Leadville, and Pueblo in Colorado, and Tucson and Tombstone in Arizona. During his stay in Dallas, Doc had his first gunfight on January 2, 1875. Although no one was hurt in that episode, he was run out of a town two days later after he killed a man. He and partner John Joshua Webb then set up a saloon in Las Vegas, New Mexico, where his next gun battle would occur. Former army scout Mike Gordon was pleading with one of the saloon girls to give up her seamy way of life. She refused. Gordon threatened to tear the saloon down, went outside, and started firing at the building. After only two shots, Doc Holliday strolled out and shot him. One bullet from Doc's gun and Gordon was dead. However, fear of the law forced Doc to move once again.

Doc Holliday

Doc then met Kate "Big Nose" Elder, and his life would be changed forever. Elder was a dance hall girl and a prostitute; she was also the only woman to come into Doc Holliday's life. Together, they managed to get out of more than one scrape, as in the story of Ed Bailey. One day, Bailey challenged Holliday to a game of cards. To make victory certain, Ed continually cheated throughout the game. Doc warned him twice. The third time he put his cards down and swept the winnings into his hand. Bailey was enraged. He pulled his gun from underneath the table. Before a shot could be fired, Holliday pulled his knife and swiftly disemboweled the gambler. This time, Doc didn't run. After all, it was self-defense. Nevertheless, he was tossed into prison.

A mob outside was clamoring for his blood. Things looked grim, but Kate Elder was determined to save her lover's life. She set fire to a barn, creating a blaze that spread and threatened to consume the entire town. In the commotion she burst into the prison wielding a six-shooter. The guard was caught unaware and was quickly disarmed by the gun-toting Kate. Doc and Kate rode off into the night and disappeared from the scene. Though there is some possibility that the couple got married, we do know that they separated in 1881 after Kate Elder accused Holliday of participating in a brutal stage holdup.

Wyatt Earp also played an important role in Holliday's life. The two met when Doc gave Earp, who was a lawman in Dodge City at the time, information about a criminal named Dave Rudabaugh. Rudabaugh was a member of Billy the Kid's gang and was wanted for robbery. Later, Holliday saved Wyatt's life by ambushing a couple of gunmen who had the lawman pinned down. The two would later take part in the legendary shootout at the O.K. Corral (see below).

After the dust had settled in Arizona, Doc headed for Colorado. Perry Mallan immediately jailed him when he arrived in Denver and sought to return him to Arizona. According to rumor, Mallan was a Clanton-McLaury sympathizer and therefore unfriendly toward Holliday. Bat Masterson had recently been appointed city marshal of Trinidad, Colorado, and interceded on Holliday's behalf with the governor of Colorado, convincing him that Holliday would not receive a fair trial in Arizona. The governor denied his extradition. Holliday was released, left Denver, and wandered around Colorado, bouncing from saloon to saloon. Occasionally he got into some scuffles. However, his health was failing, as tuberculosis wracked his body. He retreated to Glenwood Springs, Colorado where he hoped that the natural springs and sulfur fumes could bolster his health. Tuberculosis eventually claimed the life of Doc Holliday on November 8, 1887.

The Clantons, the McLaurys and the Shoot-out at the O.K. Corral

The shoot-out at the O.K. Corral rattled the small town of Tombstone. In the center of the shoot-out was the bitter feud between two factions: the Earps versus the Clantons and McLaurys. At the end of the day, three men lay dead in the Arizona dust, and two more lives would be claimed in the aftermath.

The feud had its roots in the cattle-rustling activities of the Clantons and McLaurys. The Earps either infringed on their rustling or threatened to stop the crimes. Ike Clanton, in testimony about the shoot-out, accused the Earps of being involved in various shady dealings, including cattle rustling. The Earps were far from angelic, but they held positions of law enforcement, so it is more likely that they were going to put a stop to the cattle rustling. Ike Clanton was also a bit fidgety about some information that the Earps had on him. For a reward, Ike had tipped off Wyatt and his brother Virgil (the town marshal of Tombstone) about three very dangerous stagecoach robbers. If word got out, Ike would either be hanging from a tree or riddled with bullets. He was worried that Wyatt in particular would tell his friend Doc Holliday. Holliday was often seen gambling with notorious men—the underbelly of society. Tom and Frank McLaury then both testified that Doc had killed two people in an attempted stagecoach robbery. To Wyatt's relief, Doc was acquitted, but now the Earps had a score to settle with the McLaurys.

Hostilities continued to grow. Ike demanded to see Holliday. He figured that Doc knew of the bargain he had made with the law and feared that the dentist would expose him. On October 22, 1881, a hotheaded Holliday found Ike Clanton and verbally ripped him apart. The dispute would have escalated to gunplay if Virgil hadn't threatened to arrest the two. On October 26, Ike had a message that he wanted Virgil to give to Holliday: "The damned son of a bitch has got to fight." Virgil wanted nothing to do with it, wouldn't deliver the message, and told Ike that any disturbances would land him in jail. Fuming and very drunk, Ike Clanton wandered from saloon to saloon all night, wailing about the Earps and Holliday. Brandishing a shotgun, he went looking for them, but couldn't find anyone upon whom to vent his anger. The next morning Virgil Earp found the irate Ike, pistol-whipped him, and tossed him into prison for carrying a weapon within city limits. Wyatt found him in the recorder's court and told him, "You damn dirty cowthief. You have been threatening our lives, and I know it. I think I would be justified in shooting you down any place I would meet you." Tom McLaury showed up at the courthouse to check on his friend and found himself at the wrong place at the wrong time. Words about a showdown were exchanged between the two. Wyatt struck him, pistol-whipped him, and left him bloody and crumpled on the floor. Resentment grew to a fervent boil. John Behan, the sheriff of Cochise County, arrived on the scene and tried to settle things, but the Earps brushed him off.

At 2:00 P.M., October 26, 1881, Wyatt, Morgan, and Virgil Earp, along with the recently deputized Doc Holliday, approached the Clantons, McLaurys, and Billy Claiborne. The two factions were fuming and armed to the teeth. The Earps and the Clantons tell differing stories about the events that followed. Virgil proclaimed that he didn't want a firefight; he just wanted to have the Clanton faction disarmed and out of town. The Clantons say that the Earps fired first. Whatever happened, the outcome was the same—shooting began. Morgan Earp's shot clipped Billy Clanton in the wrist. Frank McLaury went down when Wyatt shot him in the stomach. Ike Clanton ran. Billy Claiborne ducked into a photography studio. Tom McLaury was shielded by his horse. Doc Holliday pulled a shotgun from beneath his long coat, darted around the animal, and blasted McLaury. Billy Clanton, wounded in the right wrist, drew with his left and shot Virgil in the leg. Frank McLaury, who was shot in the stomach, plugged Doc in the hip. But Frank went down for good when he was shot in the neck, either by Morgan or Holliday. Morgan was then shot in the shoulder by Billy Clanton. In a hail of gunfire from either Morgan or Wyatt, Billy Clanton went down. Tom McLaury, Frank McLaury, and Billy Clanton were dead. Before Billy died, he requested that his boots be taken off: "Get the doctor and put me to sleep . . . Pull off my boots. I always told my mother I'd never die with my boots on."

Billy Clanton and the McLaury Brothers lie dead after the shootout

The O.K. Corral after it burned to the ground in 1882

The battle wasn't over. Clanton supporters were vehement that the deaths of the McLaurys and Billy Clanton in the streets of Tombstone were acts of murder. They felt revenge had to be taken. On December 28, 1881, Virgil Earp was wounded by a shotgun blast as he exited a saloon. The gunman was never found. Virgil was lucky; he survived, though he never fully regained the use of his left arm. However, the Earp's luck was about to run out. On March 18, 1882, the Earps were playing pool. Just as Morgan Earp was reaching for the chalk, two shots rang out from the shadows of the saloon. Morgan went down with a fatal wound to his stomach; he died there surrounded by his family. The second bullet barely missed Wyatt. Virgil was still hurting from his previous wound, so the Earps decided he'd best get out of town. He was taken to the train depot. While waiting for the train, the Earps spotted Frank Stilwell—a known stagecoach robber and Clanton supporter. Wyatt also had a hunch that Stilwell was responsible for Morgan's murder. Stilwell spotted the Earps and ran. Wyatt and four others (including Doc Holliday) gave chase. Stilwell was cornered and riddled with bullets. His hands had powder burns, as if he'd recently fired a shotgun. With this last killing the dust finally settled in Tombstone.

Bat Masterson

Blue-eyed William Barclay "Bat" Masterson was known as a dapper lawman. Born November 1853 in Quebec, he was originally christened with the name Bartholomiew. He later changed it to William Barclay Masterson and used the nickname Bat.

When he was 18, Masterson and his brothers moved to Wichita, Kansas, and then to Dodge City the next year. He tried several professions, from railroad construction worker to buffalo hunter, from Indian fighter to civilian scout. In 1877, Masterson operated a saloon in Dodge City while also serving as an assistant sheriff to Charles Bassett. In September of that year, Masterson was appointed to the city police force. He later succeeded to the position of sheriff, which he held from January 1878 to January 1880. In 1879, while still sheriff of Dodge City, Masterson was recruited by the Atchison, Topeka & Santa Fe Railroad in its fight with the Denver & Rio Grande Railroad over the right of way through the Royal Gorge of the Arkansas River. He gathered 30 heavily armed men to assist him in this endeavor, but the dispute was settled without bloodshed and Masterson returned to Kansas. Shortly thereafter, he went back to Colorado to investigate mining

Bat Masterson (standing) with Wyatt Earp

opportunities that had come to his attention during his earlier visit, but returned disappointedly to Dodge City a few months later.

Masterson briefly stepped into Arizona history in 1881. He met up with his friends Wyatt Earp and Luke Short in Tombstone, Arizona. Short was a dapper fellow who enjoyed gambling, and the three became known as the "Dodge City Gang." Once, Masterson restrained Short from killing another gambler during a quarrel. Although Masterson held him back, Short returned later and shot the gambler to death.

Soon after, Masterson returned to Dodge to assist his brother in a dispute with Al Updegraff and A. J. Peacock. Within minutes of his arrival in town, Masterson became embroiled in one of Dodge City's most famous gunfights. Bullets flew wildly in all directions as the brothers confronted their rivals on an open street. By the time the sheriff arrived on the scene, Updegraff and a passerby lay injured. Updegraff later recovered and Masterson was fined $8 and told to leave town.

He was recruited from Dodge to become town marshal of Silverton, Colorado, in an effort to restore order to the town after two outlaws murdered the marshal on Blair Street. The town had become notoriously rowdy, and someone needed to take control. Under Masterson's rule, shoot-outs, drunken brawls, and the undesirable element disappeared from Silverton. However, Masterson did not close down the red-light district of Blair Street; he was known to enjoy the district's saloons, gambling, and girls.

In 1882, Masterson served as the marshal at Trinidad, Colorado. In 1884, he was appointed marshal of La Junta, Colorado, but served for only five weeks. He then returned to Dodge City, where he tried his hand as a sportswriter, briefly served as deputy sheriff, and refereed a prize fight. In 1886, when the saloons in Dodge were closed down, Masterson moved to Denver. He was married in 1891.

During the early days of Creede, Colorado, in 1892, Masterson arrived to manage the Denver Exchange, a high-class drinking and gambling establishment. Masterson was good at setting the rules and being in command. The ex-lawman tolerated no troublemakers and allowed no gunplay inside.

Masterson was always known for being well groomed and well dressed; he was considered a dandy, though no one is recorded to have told him so! When he was running the Denver Exchange, he usually wore an impeccable ensemble, such as a lavender corduroy suit, white shirt, and black string tie. A style of hat named after Masterson is still sold.

In 1902, Masterson moved to New York City, where Theodore Roosevelt appointed him deputy U.S. marshal. He became interested in writing and published a series of his articles, "Famous Gunfighters of the Western Frontier." He worked as a sportswriter for the *Morning Telegraph* and eventually served as the sports editor. For the next few years, he drank heavily and his fiery temper occasionally got him into trouble. Bat Masterson died at his desk of a heart attack in 1921.

Billy the Kid

Henry McCarty, also known as Billy the Kid, William Bonney, Henry Antrim, Kid Antrim, William Antrim, and simply the Kid, started his rise to infamy in Arizona. His early life is a mystery. He was born in 1859 in either New York or Indiana. The McCarty family then moved from place to place in Kansas before finally settling down in Silver City, New Mexico. McCarty got into trouble for petty theft, broke out of jail, and escaped to Arizona. While in eastern Arizona, he worked in Graham County, near Fort Grant, where he was picked on by Frank Cahill. However, Billy the Kid was not someone to be pushed around. Frank Cahill was shot in the stomach and became Billy's first murder victim, but not his last. Billy fled back to New Mexico where he got mixed up in the sordid Lincoln County War.

Tension in Lincoln County was steadily rising between two factions: the traders and the ranchers. Jimmy Dolan and John Riley represented the traders while the ranchers were led by John Tunstall and Alexander McSween. When Tunstall, who had hired Billy the Kid as a laborer and hired gun, was murdered, an explosion rocked Lincoln County. His death set off a bloody affair of bullets and vigilante justice. The Kid swore that Tunstall would be avenged. Dolan and Riley were powerful figures in the region; they controlled much of the government as well as the sheriff's office. The McSween faction knew that Sheriff Brady was not going to arrest those responsible for Tunstall's death; in fact, the sheriff started accosting the McSweens as well as the Kid. On their way to arrest McSween, Sheriff William Brady and Deputy George Hindman were ambushed and killed by Billy the Kid and a gang of followers.

Billy the Kid (aka William Bonny)

The vigilante force, known as the Regulators, declared open war on Dolan and Riley. The Dolan and Riley supporters were immediately hunted down and killed, with casualties escalating on both sides. The final showdown was on July 14, 1878. McSween and the Regulators were holed up in his house. Sheriff Peppin and his posse surrounded them. In the end, Alexander McSween was shot and killed, but Billy the Kid escaped.

Billy the Kid was not one of the deadliest gunfighters, nor was he one of the most successful. His life as a desperado was surprisingly short—only four years. But he had the devious flair of a showman. On January 10, 1880, he ran into Joe Grant while drinking at a saloon in Fort Sumner. As the story goes, Grant did not know the Kid but the Kid knew Grant. He also knew that Grant was out for him. Before a gunfight could occur, however, the Kid asked to see Grant's gun. Grant's revolver was very ornate with a pearl handle, and he agreed. The Kid opened the gun, saw there were only three bullets loaded, and spun the cylinder so that the next shot would land on an empty chamber. The Kid calmly gave back the gun and strolled out of the saloon. At that point, Grant found out that the man he was after was about to leave. He called the Kid out. The two drew their weapons. Grant's gun clicked harmlessly; the Kid's shot struck Grant in the head and killed him instantly.

Sheriff Pat Garrett eventually caught up with Billy the Kid. He tracked down the Kid and cornered him in a rock house that had only one exit, which was blocked by a dead horse. The Kid and his gang gave up and were arrested. On the day before he was to be hung, the Kid was led out, still chained, to the outhouse so that he could use the bathroom. The Kid produced a gun and shot the lawman escorting him. It is not known if he stole the gun from his victim or if it had been planted in the outhouse. Re-entering the jailhouse, he grabbed a shotgun and waited for Deputy Robert Olinger. The Kid yelled out, "Hello, Bob!" just before he killed him. He then leisurely rode out of town.

Sheriff Pat Garrett set out to capture Billy the Kid again. This time he resolved there would be no taking him to jail. On July 14, 1881, Garrett rode over to Pete Maxwell's house, near Fort Sumner, to ask if he'd seen the fugitive. By coincidence, the Kid was in the area and strolled into the same house to ask Maxwell if he could have a slab of meat. Garrett was in a darkened room when the Kid entered to ask who the stranger was. Garrett recognized the voice and fired twice. The Kid died without knowing who shot him, but from that day, the gunfighter has lived on in legend.

John Ringo

John Ringo (or Johnny Ringgold), who often had a six-shooter in his hand and a Shakespeare verse on his lips, is rumored to have been one of the deadliest gunfighters in his time. Yet, because much of his life remains a mystery, the wrath of Ringo's gun is only hearsay.

Gunman, gambler, cattle rustler, and lawman—the enigmatic Ringo was all of these. He was probably born in the early 1850s. He attended William Jewell College in Liberty, Missouri, which is probably where Ringo acquired his taste for Shakespeare. Then he ventured into Texas where it is likely that he fought in raging range wars. In 1877, he served some jail time in Austin but was freed and left for Shakespeare, New Mexico. From there he struck out into Arizona.

While in Safford, Arizona, Ringo was drinking heavily in a saloon, as he often did, and offered a drink to his companion Louis Hancock. Hancock refused, which enraged Ringo. He pistol-whipped Hancock and then shot him in the throat.

Ringo then lived in Tombstone for a while, just when the feud between the McLaurys and Clantons and the Earps was heating up. In fact, Ringo was an associate of the Clantons and the McLaurys and was involved with their cattle-rustling scheme. When Virgil Earp was wounded by a shotgun blast as he left the Oriental Saloon, just after the gunfight at the O.K. Corral, Ringo was believed to have been the culprit. It was also while in Tombstone that he managed to become a lawman; he was deputized by Sheriff John Behan for a short period of time.

John Ringo

On July 14, 1882, John Ringo's body was discovered in Turkey Creek Canyon. His death followed a two-week drinking spree with Frank Leslie, but the events that led to his death remain a mystery. A single bullet to the head killed him and suicide was proclaimed the cause of death. But Ringo's guns were holstered and fully loaded—and he had been scalped. Rumor named Frank Leslie as the killer, but Ringo's friend Pony Deal thought otherwise. He tracked down gambler Johnny O'Rourke and, in an act of vigilante justice, killed him. The real murderer was never determined.

Leaders, Ranchers, Settlers, and other Colorful Characters

Barry M. Goldwater

"Mr. Conservative" was born on January 1, 1909. At the time, Arizona was still a territory; it would become a state three years later. Goldwater graduated from Staunton Military Academy in 1928, honored as an outstanding cadet. He studied briefly at the University of Arizona and in 1929 entered the family business, Goldwater, Inc., after his father's death. He later regretted attending college for only a year, stating: "That was the biggest mistake of my life. . . . I've long had misgivings about my education being cut short." In 1931, he and Margaret Johnson entered a marriage that lasted for 51 years.

Barry M. Goldwater

Barry Goldwater was renowned for being earthy, freely speaking his mind, and contributing to the conservative cause. He was also famous for his skills inside the cockpit and was the first non-rated test pilot to fly such famous planes as the U-2, the SR-71, the B-1 Bomber, and the XV-15. During World War II, he was rejected for active duty because of age and sports-related knee injuries but persisted and was eventually assigned to develop gunnery techniques for the Air Training Command. From there he was launched into flying transport missions. When the war ended, Goldwater organized the Arizona Air National Guard. He served in the Air Force Reserve for 37 years until he retired in 1967. He loved to fly and continued to do so into his 80s.

Goldwater's esteemed political career started in 1949 when he was elected councilman for the City of Phoenix. In 1952, he entered in the U.S. Senate and continued there until 1964 when he ran for president against Lyndon Johnson. Things went poorly for Goldwater. Through the famous "Daisy" commercial, in which an image of a little girl counting petals is followed by a nuclear explosion, Johnson painted him as a right wing madman with his finger on the button. Goldwater lost in a landslide, but Arizona returned him to the Senate in 1968. Although Goldwater did not win the presidency, he set the stage for both Ronald Reagan and George Bush. Reagan, in fact, enacted many of Goldwater's ideas, including lower taxes, Pentagon reform, and deregulation of industry.

Goldwater championed Native American rights and was an honorary chief in many Arizona tribes. He came under fire when he broke from the traditional conservative line in his support for homosexual rights. He held fast to a simple political philosophy—respect individual freedom, and a smaller government is a better government. After the death of his first wife, he remarried in 1992. On May 29, 1998, he died at age 89. Following his death, Susan, his wife of eight years, and his family said, "He died as he lived: with dignity, courage and humility." An extensive, comprehensive library that belonged to Goldwater was given to the Arizona Historical Society.

Dick "Wick" Hall

Born in 1877, Dick "Wick" Hall went on to become one of Arizona's most notable humorists. He is famous for his writing, his pet frog, and as the co-founder of Salome, Arizona. He demonstrated his wit in *The Salome Sun,* which was distributed in the early 1920s. In the *Sun,* Hall sketched local figures, punned, exaggerated, satirized, and revealed his unique crackerbarrel philosophy. The paper received national attention, and his work was solicited by national magazines.

During his life, Hall worked as a rancher, postmaster, homesteader, and garage man. However, he is best known for his publications and his 7-year-old desert frog that regretted never learning how to swim. He also became famous for co-founding Salome and penning its motto: "Salome, Arizona—Where She Danced." He respectfully declined credit for the phrase, saying that it wasn't his fault that Mrs. Grace Salome Pratt (for whom the town was named) took her shoes off and tried to walk through the desert. He loved to make fun of the town that he helped found. He once wrote across the front of his gas station, "Smile, you don't have to stay here but we do." He was both honored and revered. After his death on April 28, 1926, friends, writers, miners, and cowboys created a monument to him made out of nuggets of the choicest ore.

Henry Clay Hooker

Colonel Henry Hooker had one of the most famous ranches in the West—the Sierra Bonita Ranch, just between Willcox and Fort Grant. The ranch was established in 1872 and its house stands today as one of Arizona's oldest ranch houses. His vast herd of 20,000 cattle roamed across his land—250,000 acres during its heyday. Hooker's brand, the Crooked H, is still in use. Under Hooker's care the ranch grew in fame and wealth. He employed a blacksmith, established a dairy herd, raised pigs and poultry, and grew vegetables to serve his guests. Among his guests were many celebrities including Wyatt Earp, George Crook, Nelson Miles, and Owen Wister. At this point in his life, Hooker was wealthy, but this hadn't always been the case.

Born in 1825, Hooker is rumored to have fought in the Civil War with the Union Army. He was called Colonel Hooker, although his role in the war is unconfirmed. After the Civil War, Hooker headed to California, where he just barely scraped by. On the verge of economic ruin he pulled his resources together and, as the story goes, came up with a crackpot scheme. He bought about 500 turkeys, several trained dogs, and hired a helper. He planned to drive the turkeys across the mountains into Carson City, Nevada, and sell them at a higher price than he paid for them. The turkey drive began with Hooker's remaining fortune riding on the birds' backs. Once, after the dogs pressed the turkeys down a very steep precipice, the birds took flight. All at once, Hooker saw his hopes scatter and descend into a valley. He ran after them, not about to give up without a fight. Luckily, the birds were rounded up. The rest of the trip went without a hitch. The money Hooker made in Carson City from selling the turkeys gave him enough funds to get a business rolling.

By 1869, Hooker secured a contract to supply Arizona's army posts and Indian agencies with beef. Just three years later he was able to buy the grand Sierra Bonita Ranch. From then on Hooker lived like a feudal baron of Arizona. Playwright Augustus Thomas, who was one of Hooker's many guests, used the ranch as the setting of his play *Arizona.* One of the characters is modeled after the resourceful cattleman. Hooker died and was buried in Los Angeles in 1907.

Thomas Jonathon Jeffords

Thomas Jeffords was a tall man, distinguished by long red hair that was accompanied by a sparse red beard. Indians often referred to him as "Red Whiskers" or "Sandy Whiskers." Jeffords was born in 1832. Early on, he made a life for himself as a boatman, captaining ships on the Great Lakes. In 1859, he gave up the waterways and headed for Taos, where he drove a Butterfield Overland Mail stagecoach. On the side, he prospected in the San Juan Mountains. The Butterfield route was dangerous, and Jeffords bore the arrow scars to prove it. During his service, 14 to 22 fellow stagecoach drivers were buried; all had been killed by Apache Indians. Mail was brought to a crippling halt as drivers feared for their lives. Something had to be done. Jeffords decided to take action and resolved to talk with the man who brought terror to the mailmen of Arizona, Apache chief Cochise (see page 74).

Relations between white settlers and Cochise's band of Apache had gone horribly wrong and the Chiricahua were on the warpath. Raids by the Indians had resulted in the capture, torture, and death of many whites. As was Cochise's intention, the methods used were instilling terror into the hearts of men throughout the local white communities. One common practice was to drag the helpless victim behind a running horse, dashing them against sharp, rocky terrain. Another was to strip a victim of his clothes, stake him down over an anthill, and leave him to die beneath the scalding sun. So when Jeffords sent smoke signals professing a desire to meet with the Chiricahua, Cochise was taken aback. A meeting was granted and Jeffords, alone, rode into camp, dismounted, and handed his weapons over to the Indians. He approached the wickiup in which Cochise was seated and took a place beside the war-

Thomas Jeffords photographed at his ranch shortly before his death

rior. The two sat in silence for a long time—Cochise quietly pondering and Jeffords wondering if he was going to live another day. The silence was finally broken and the two discussed matters for the next 24 hours. Jeffords's courage and frank honesty won over Cochise and the chief agreed to leave Jeffords and his mail carriers alone. The Chiricahua continued to terrorize Arizona, but Jeffords and his men were left in peace. Jeffords had many other visits with Cochise and he became known as "Chickasaw," or "Brother." Still, Jeffords later confessed that he was always wary of the Indian and never turned his back on him.

Jeffords's relationship with Cochise was often talked about, and Jeffords was repeatedly asked to set up meetings between the Apache chief and government officials. He tried once to get Cochise to visit New Mexico for peace talks, but the Apache wouldn't hear of it. In 1872, discussions culminated in Jeffords escorting General Oliver Otis Howard to the Chiricahua camp. Howard described his introduction to Cochise in his "Account of His Mission to the Apaches and Navajos" in the *Washington Daily Morning Chronicle,* November 10, 1872. "He gave me a grasp of the hand, and said very pleasantly: 'Buenas dias.'" For 11 days they talked of peace. As an incentive, Howard offered to let Cochise select the land for the Chiricahua reservation. Cochise settled for a reservation in the Dragoon Mountains. Cochise also demanded that Jeffords be the Indian agent.

Jeffords was a controversial Indian agent. He was accused of arming the Apaches and giving them more rations than the government allowed. There was not any sound evidence of either charge and Howard staunchly defended Jeffords's character. After Cochise's death, the Chiricahua were forced to relocate to the San Carlos Reservation. Jeffords, frustrated by his critics and government red tape, was relieved to no longer have to shoulder responsibility for the reservation.

After the Chiricahua relocation, Jeffords was a key player in parleying with the Apache leader Juh, who was leader of about 100 renegades in the Guadalupe Mountains. After that, and until his death, he tried a number of professions but avoided further involvement in Indian relations. He scouted for General Nelson Miles in his campaign against Geronimo, was a deputy sheriff at Tombstone, and made various unsuccessful attempts to strike it rich from mining. Jeffords retired to Owls Head, just 35 miles north of Tucson, where he died on February 19, 1914. In 1964, the Daughters of the American Colonists decorated his gravesite in Tucson.

Charles Debrille Poston

Charles Poston was an intelligent, highly literate man who wrote a great deal about Arizona, becoming known (partly through much self-promotion) as the "Father of Arizona." He was born in Kentucky on April 20, 1825, studied law, and was an apprentice newspaperman prior to moving west to take up a job in the customs house in San Francisco. In 1854, he was hired by a mining operation that wanted to establish a railway south of the border to Guaymas, Sonora. While investigating the plan, the British brig he was sailing aboard was wrecked in the Gulf of Mexico. Poston and his 25 companions struggled free of the wreckage, made their way ashore, and started overland. They made it to the lower reaches of the Colorado River, where Poston and another man in the group, Herman Ehrenberg, are credited with founding Colorado City, the predecessor of present-day Yuma.

While working for the mining syndicate, Poston was also charged with investigating mining prospects in the Santa Cruz Valley and at Ajo. Poston's report was enthusiastic about the area and led to the formation of the Sonora Exploring and Mining Company, which Poston supervised. He successfully raised the necessary finances in the East and set up headquarters at the abandoned presidio of Tubac, some 45 miles south of Tucson. He soon discovered ore in the area, and Tubac took off as silver filled the town's coffers. Poston, now in charge of an expanding community, assumed charge of all legal and civil affairs. He even produced a new currency. Poston was successful for several years, and Tubac flourished under his rule. Poston would later proclaim proudly, "We had no law but love and no occupation but labor; no government, no taxes, no public debt, no politics. It was a community in a perfect state of nature." However, the mine labored under the weight of faulty machinery, huge transportation costs, and capital shortages following the panic of 1857. The death knell sounded for the town in 1861. Civil War broke out in the East causing the recall of the soldiers from the area. At the same time Cochise and the Chiricahua went on the warpath terrorizing settlements throughout the district. Poston left hurriedly, but 40 settlers opted to stay. Tubac was encircled by 200 Apache on one side and a large band of Sonoran bandits on the other. A massacre was averted only when a rescue force arrived from Tuscon. Afterward, Tubac was abandoned.

Charles Poston

Poston moved to Washington, D.C., and entered political life, actively campaigning for the division of New Mexico and the establishment of the Territory of Arizona. By 1860, 10 bills to divide the Territory of New Mexico had been debated in Congress; all failed because of the growing sectional concerns that would soon culminate in the Civil War. Finally, a bill was passed and signed by President Lincoln on February 24, 1863 (see page 97). Poston had grandiose hopes of becoming the territory's first governor, but instead he was appointed superintendent of Indian affairs, a position he held from 1863 to 1864.

Poston settled down in Florence. He briefly tried to inspire sun worshiping and principles that followed the mysterious Persian prophet Zoroaster, but he could not gather enough funds. He moved to Phoenix where he died on June 25, 1902. In 1925 his remains were moved to the top of Poston Butte near Florence.

Roy Purcell

A tall, wiry, red-haired boy named Roy Purcell was born in 1936. He grew up in Utah and worked as a miner while studying for his master's degree in creative writing and fine arts at Utah State University. During that time, he was inspired to paint a giant mural upon the face of the Cerbat Mountains, near the small town of Chloride, Arizona. In 1966, while Purcell was working on this gigantic 2,000 square-foot exercise of abstract Modernism, he lived in a nearby cave. The mural, titled "The Journey," brought Purcell to national attention and now draws visitors from around the world to the remote location.

After the project was completed, Purcell became the director of the Mojave Museum of History and Arts where he started working with the medium for which he has become best known: etching. Next, he worked as director of the Southern Nevada Museum for four years before establishing himself as a freelance artist.

Purcell has maintained his passion for large-scale projects and his fascination with mankind's major historical and cultural journeys. Through his art he has portrayed the life of Christ, Moses and the Exodus, and the Mormon migration to Utah. His other subjects have included Western themes, desert images, world wildlife, and the legacy of the American Indian.

American Indian Tribes of Arizona

The presence of humans in the area we call Arizona can be traced as far back as 11,300 years. Ranchers in southern Arizona discovered the bones of a woolly mammoth containing the remnants of at least eight stone-tipped spears that had been thrust into its body by ice-age hunters.

During the period from approximately 1000 B.C. to A.D. 1500, four cultures flourished: the Hohokam in the south, the Patayan in the west, the Sinagua in the central and east, and the Anasazi in the north. The harsh terrain—mountains, deserts, canyons, and mesas—helped shape these cultures. With limited game for hunting and a small number of edible wild plants, the four tribes assimilated to an advanced agricultural way of life. Rooted villages took shape; tools, crafts, pottery, and art followed, with each society displaying distinct cultural characteristics.

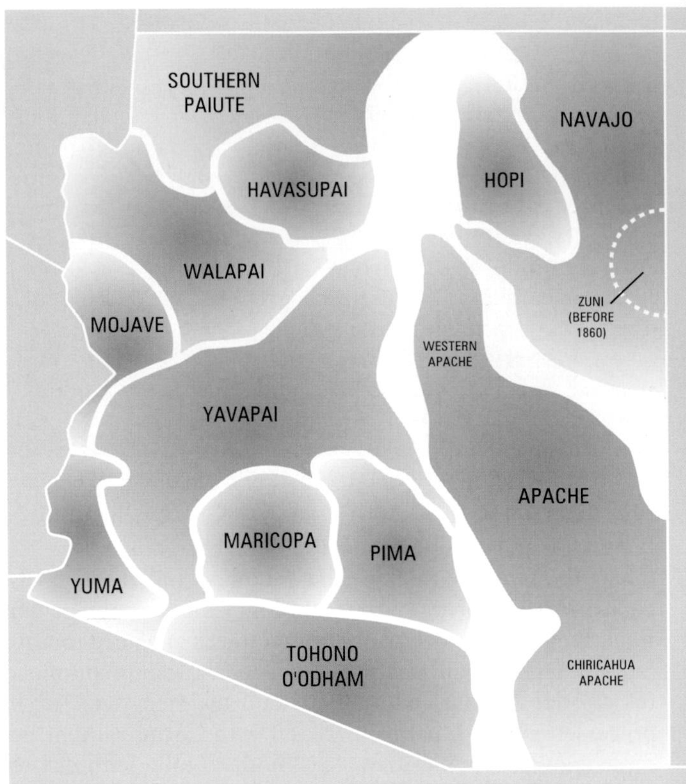

American Indian Lands, circa 1870

Details about the tribes of the Southwest between A.D. 1500 and 1600, are cloaked in mystery. There is evidence of a great drought, which could have caused the splintering of the major civilizations in the area. Important trade centers were no longer used, and settlements were abandoned. The history and the fate of these cultures remain the subject of speculation. Perhaps they were absorbed into the modern Indian tribes (1600 to present) entering the region, or perhaps the people of these cultures were forced to leave the area to survive the harsh droughts of the time. Marauding tribes from elsewhere in the Southwest could have also driven them out. Only as knowledge about these cultures increases will their fates be further understood.

There were a great number of migrations during the dissolution of the major Indian civilizations. The Pueblo, the Pima, and the Yuma settled in the region of present-day Arizona. The Navajo and Apache, migrating from the north, also moved into this region. When the early Spaniards arrived in the 1600s, many Indian tribes were spread across the land. Only the remains of ancient pueblos testified to the existence of previous civilizations, much to the disappointment of the conquistadors, who were looking for gold. Instead, they found a multitude of small tribes and heard a variety of languages.

Although the Apache thwarted attempts at extensive settlements, Spanish influence encroached into Indian land. The Spanish brought missionaries, silversmiths, horses, and other livestock; they left their Castilian dialect, a sense of empire, and Christianity. Spanish, and later Mexican, policy contrived to concentrate the small nomadic tribes. By the mid-1700s, several Indian groups were totally assimilated into the Spanish and Mexican cultures. Some tribes welcomed the change.

Others rose up in arms and revolted. The Pueblo drove the Spanish out of the Rio Grande area in the late 1600s. The land was later reclaimed, but the Apache, the Tarahumara, and the Upland Yuma (or the Yaquis) were unconquerable. Until the 1880s, when Americans moved onto their lands, these tribes continued their traditional ways of life and, to the settlers, were a fearful force with which to be reckoned.

The United States annexed the northern regions of New Spain in 1848, including much of present-day Arizona. The Americans brought with them forced assimilation and a reservation system that isolated the tribes. Suddenly, the groups were placed in a dependency role, and tribal law and government were secondary to state and federal law. Craft production steadily became economically important as tribes and families were integrated into the nation's economy. Tribal culture changed but was not eradicated. Not even epidemics could destroy the Indians. In 1883, the Hopi were devastated by smallpox and half of the population died. In the later 1900s, their population has regrown despite continued challenges to their culture from modern America.

Ancient Cultures

Anasazi

Current scholars have no idea what the Anasazi called themselves. The name Anasazi is actually derived from a Navajo word that can be translated as "ancient tribe," "ancient ones," or "enemy ancestors." It is not known why the Anasazi left their villages and sprawling pueblos, which were carved into the faces of cliffs. Scholars can only follow a trail of conjecture. Tree rings suggest that a great drought ravaged the area during the period of the Anasazi's disappearance (about A.D. 1300). There is also evidence that suggests the Anasazi began to concentrate in a smaller number of localities. Perhaps the land could not feed the rising population and the people were forced to leave.

Professor A. E. Douglass of the University of Arizona has dated the construction of the Anasazi ruins through tree trunks found in their structures. Tree ring width varies with rainfall, thereby creating a record of annual rainfall. This dating method has been very helpful in showing past droughts and suggesting reasons for the movement of people because of weather fluctuations. The Anasazi may, however, have been driven out or assimilated by the Ute or Navajo cultures, which were moving into the area. Or the disappearance of the Anasazi may have come about because of both scenarios. There is also evidence that some Anasazi settlements were burned shortly after the tribe's departure, although scholars are not certain who burned them.

Anasazi kiva

However, scholars do know that the Anasazi were an advanced culture. They were excellent craftsmen, especially when it came to baskets, pottery, and sandals. Moving away from a hunter-gatherer lifestyle, they developed an agricultural system that relied heavily on dry-farming techniques—a method that requires direct rainfall. The Anasazi employed stone masonry to create flat-roofed rooms, subterranean living quarters, and communal structures of ranging sizes. Subterranean ceremonial rooms called kivas appeared later in their culture as did middens—large trash areas that not only contained garbage, but the tribe's dead as well. Much evidence of this fascinating culture can still be seen.

Hohokam

The Hohokam culture can be traced back to 100 B.C. Hohokam is, in fact, the name given to this culture by the Pima Indians; it means "vanished ones" or "all used up." Scholars can only guess at what the Hohokam people called themselves.

The Hohokam dwelled mainly in the Gila and Salt River valleys, where they planted beans, corn, cotton, tobacco, and squash, lived in pithouses, and created quality pottery. To survive the desert climate, the Hohokam developed an irrigation system, a remarkable achievement considering that they had no beasts of burden. Large settlements, such as Snaketown, which was occupied for 1,500 years, arose in the Arizona desert. Snaketown consisted of at least 100 pithouses and covered 300 acres near Phoenix.

The tribe's culture flourished. Macaw parrots were kept as pets. A recreational game, similar to one created by the Toltecs and Mayans, was played. It involved a rubbery ball made from the desert bush guayule. The players aimed to knock the ball through rings using only their hips, elbows, and knees. The victors were rewarded with the losers' jewelry and clothing. After A.D. 1000, the Hohokam created a method of etching. Designs would be carved into shells over which acid from fermented saguaro cactus fruit would be poured. Because the shells were covered with an acid-resistant pitch, the acid would burn the designs into the shell. The Hohokam may have been the first in the world to use this process. Three hundred years later, Europeans were using a similar method to burn designs into chivalric armor.

Why, in the midst of such prosperity, did the Hohokam people disappear by A.D. 1450? Historians have concluded that the population of the area fell into decline by 1400, at a time when new customs were being adopted. Drought could have been the cause, or possibly raids from nomadic tribes. There is reason to believe that the Tohono O'odham (Papago) and Pima tribes are descendents of the Hohokam because of similarities in oral traditions and archaeological clues that have been found.

Patayan

The Patayan Indians, who dwelled in western Arizona beginning around A.D. 500, used hunting and gathering to supplement their farming. The Patayan are believed to be the ancestors of various Yuma-speaking tribes, including the Mojave, Havasupai, Cocopah, Maricopa, Hualapai, Yavapai, and today's Yuma. The Patayan created pottery, but little else is known about this culture because floods of the Colorado River have washed its ruins away. There are still a few sites in northwest Arizona that are accessible, and scholars are working now to uncover the mystery of the Patayan Indians.

Sinagua

Migrating from the north, the Sinagua settled in Arizona's Verde River valley in about A.D. 500. The Sinagua society was an agrarian society. Their farming techniques resembled those of the Hohokam, including the use of dams and irrigation systems. Their building design follows the Anasazi pueblo-type construction.

Sometime between 1064 and 1065, the eruption of a nearby volcano (today known as Sunset Crater) must have terrorized the populace. They fled the region but returned to discover that the volcano had left a newly enriched soil that could be easily farmed. Because of this, the Sinagua enjoyed a newfound prosperity, and their culture peaked around 1100. Masonry was used to create multiroom houses and Hohokam-style ball courts for a game that contained elements of both soccer and basketball. However, good fortune did not last.

A 23-year drought (between 1276 and 1299) ravaged the countryside. Settlements near Flagstaff were abandoned and the Sinagua centralized their dwellings. Excellently constructed and easily defensible cliff dwellings were built. However, by the 1400s, these too were vacated. Once again, scholars have only theories to explain this culture's disappearance. Overcrowding, water pollution, and disease have all been suggested as possible causes of the exodus. There is reason to believe that the Sinagua joined the Hopi. One Hopi legend detailing the arrival of a group of dark-skinned people from the south supports the theory. Sinagua cliff dwellings can still be seen, a silent testament to the culture.

Montezuma Castle, cliff dwellings built by the Sinagua

Modern American Indian Tribes

Apache

The term Apache refers to a large conglomerate of bands united by the Athapascan language. The groups moved into the Southwest later than other Indian cultures and instantly gained a fearful reputation as fierce warriors and raiders. The word itself is derived from the Zuni word *ápachu,* which means "enemy." The Apache call themselves N'dé, Indé, or Diné, all of which translate to "the people." However, for a brief stint in U.S. history, the label Apache was used to describe almost any Indian who rode a horse, wore a breechcloth, and was hostile toward Americans. Apache raids struck terror in Pueblo Indians, such as the Zuni, and Europeans too would come to dread these deadly fighters. For centuries their presence constrained Spanish and Mexican expansion northward. Settlements would often be targeted for raids, and any punitive action attempted by organized armed forces was repulsed using guerrilla tactics. When the Americans moved into present-day Arizona after winning the Mexican War, they too had to deal with these fearsome warriors.

Apache camp beside the San Carlos River

Yet there was more to Apache culture than raiding and warfare. The varied bands developed well-defined social structures, with lineage traced through the mother, complete with musical entertainment and a complex mythology. The society of the Apache was divided into several main tribes, including the Chiricahau and the Coyotero, or Western Apache. In the late 1800s, the Chiricahau resided throughout much of what is now New Mexico and eastern Arizona, while the Western Apache occupied the mountainous regions of central and eastern Arizona. Each of these tribes was further subdivided into bands of between 60 and 750, and local groups of about 35 to 200. The Chiricahau Apache consisted of three main bands, known as the Eastern, Southern, and Central Chiricahau. The Eastern group, the Mimbreño, counted among its leaders both Mangas Coloradas (see page 75) and Victorio (see page 76). The Central band produced the fiery warrior Cochise (see page 74), but it was from the Southern Chiricahau (also known as the Pinery Apache) that perhaps the best known Indian chief, Geronimo (see page 75), hailed. Leadership among the tribes was not hereditary, rather it was determined by force of personality and experience. Generally, the chiefs could only compel their followers to action in times of war.

The Apache were predominantly nonagricultural and relied on hunting (mainly deer and rabbits) and gathering for their subsistence, though some tribes did adopt seasonal farming practices. When food was scarce, as was often the case in the harsh climate of the American Southwest, bands resorted to raids on both European and neighboring Native American settlements.

Apache houses were usually domed huts known as wicki-ups. They consisted of pole frames covered with brush, grass, or reed mats, and often had a fire pit and smoke hole. The people generally dressed in deerskin, although they acquired cotton and wool clothes through trades and raids. Basket weaving among Apaches rose to quite an artful craft, producing varied coiled shapes of intricate design. Interestingly, they also invented a painted string instrument known as the Apache fiddle. Made from a yucca stalk, the sound box had a single string of sinew held onto a tuning fork that was played with a bow not unlike that of a violin.

The Apache were also a deeply religious people. They believed in an array of gods, the most powerful being Ussen, the Giver of Life. Mountain spirits, or *gaans,* were also important, especially in the elaborate ceremonies presided over by shamen. The major ceremony of this tribal culture is the Sunrise Dance *(Na'ii'es),* held for Apache females in the summer months of the year following a girl's first menstruation. Until recently, attempts by Westerners to convert the Apache to Christianity have been generally unsuccessful.

Early contact between white men and the Apache was peaceful. By 1600, however, Spanish settlements were beset by Apache raids. These continued unabated for several centuries, despite the efforts by Spanish and Mexican authorities to quell the belligerent Indians. The United States annexed Apache homelands in 1848 in accordance with the Treaty of Guadalupe Hidalgo and again through the Gadsden Purchase of 1853–54. Mistrust and betrayal between Indians and the hoards of white settlers following the allure of western mines soon sparked the Apache Wars, which would continue until Geronimo's final defeat in 1886. This conflict produced some of the most famous events in Native American history, including the Camp Grant Massacre (see page 98) and the Bloody Tanks Massacre (see page 73). Geronimo's uprising between 1881 and 1886 was the last sustained Indian resistance of its kind.

Today, the remaining Western Apache are congregated on the Fort Apache and San Carlos Reservations in Arizona. Most Chiricahau were moved to the Fort Sill Reservation in Oklahoma or to the Mescalero (another Apache tribe) Reservation in New Mexico. As of 1990, the Western Apache population numbered around 26,000 and the combined Chiricahu and Mescalero population was about 2,500. The people remain some of the poorest in the United States, eking out a living in the cattle and timber industries, and more recently through tourism and crafts.

Hopi

The Hopi Indians live in the plateau country of northern Arizona, surrounded completely by the Navajo Nation. They have resided in the same area for at least 500 years. The history of the Hopi is more peaceful than that of their neighbors, the Apache and Navajo. Indeed their very name derives from *hopituh,* meaning "the peaceful ones." Their cooperative nature and their relative isolation meant they avoided the bloody struggles that engulfed many nineteenth-century Native American tribes.

Hopi Indians, circa 1920

Many Hopi still live in the traditional multistoried stone homes of their ancestors, and farm the land with the same resourcefulness. Corn is the staple of the Hopi diet, but even this hardy crop must be grown near natural springs or with the aid of irrigation. The tribe also produced beans, squash, cotton, and tobacco—remarkable feats considering the hot and dry climate of the mesas.

Religion is very important to the Hopi. Spanish attempts to forcibly convert the Indians resulted in the only antiwhite revolt of their history, when they joined the Pueblo rebellion of 1680. Today, traditional ceremonies are an integral part of their social life, and many visitors flock to see their religious dance dramas or to buy their small kachina dolls. Unlike in most tribes, the spiritual shaman is also the political leader of Hopi clans. The "Hopi Way," a holistic philosophy which guides their relationship to nature and other people, has allowed this tribe to adapt to modern existence while maintaining much of their traditional culture.

Mojave (Mohave)

The Mojave Desert, named after this Southwestern tribe, is one of the harshest environments in the United States. Temperatures regularly exceed 100°F during the day, then drop sharply at night. The Mojave have adapted to the tough conditions by settling along the banks of the lower Colorado River, an area they occupy to this day. Mojave Indians call themselves the Aha Macave (meaning "people along the water"). Near the river they were able to farm corn, pumpkins, squash, melons, and (after Spanish influence permeated the area) wheat. The melting snows of the Rocky Mountains watered their lands annually, and they adjusted their crop cycles accordingly, producing double harvests of many crops. The Mojave supplemented their diet with local game, nuts, and protein-rich fish.

A Mojave woman on the Colorado River Indian Reservation

Traditionally, the Mojave lived in two types of dwellings constructed from brush and earth. For the winter months they built low rectangular houses; in the summer they made open flat-roofed structures. They dressed in sandals and rabbit skin robes. Both males and females took pride in body art, adorning their bodies in tattoos and body paint.

One of the Mojave's first

contacts with Europeans came when Spanish explorer Juan de Oñate met with them on January 25, 1605. The Mojave Indians regaled the conquistador with strange stories, which Oñate's companion Escobar jotted down in his journal. They told about a rich island on Lake Copalla where the natives wore gold bracelets, and another island whose fat, big-footed queen ruled over a tribe of bald-headed men. The stories kept getting more and more fantastic; the most bizarre was about a tribe that purposely slept underwater. By the time Oñate left, his head was full of outlandish visions of the New World and the Indians had eaten half of his party's horses.

However, much of the Mojave's contact with white men was less friendly. They became known as the "wild Indians" because of their frequent raids on Spanish settlers. With the Mexican cession of 1848 and the Californian gold rush of the following year, more Americans were traveling through Mojave territory. When Captain Lorenzo Sitgreaves (see page 73) surveyed the land in 1851, the Indians attacked, killing one member of the party and wounding another. Mojaves were also responsible for many ambushes and slaughters along the Beale Wagon Road (see page 58). In 1858, members of the tribe massacred a group of immigrants, killing nine and wounding sixteen. In response, Fort Mohave was created and the Indian raids were steadily reduced.

The Mojave never signed an official treaty with the government, but they continue to live on and have rights to their homeland on the Colorado River. A congressional act in 1934 created the Fort Mojave Indian Reservation and the Colorado River Indian Reservation. Today, most of the 2,900 Mojave live on these sites, along the Arizona-California border or on the Fort McDowell Reservation in Maricopa County, Arizona.

Navajo

The Navajo and their relatives the Apache are descendents of the Athapascan peoples who wandered from western Canada into the Southwest about a millennium ago. Like the Apache, the Navajo call themselves Diné, meaning "the people." They established their homeland between the Colorado, Rio Grande, and San Juan Rivers, in the Four Corners region of the modern United States. At first, the Navajo survived in the area by hunting and gathering, occasionally raiding Pueblo and Spanish settlements. However, the Navajo later adopted many Pueblo customs and crafts, such as farming and pottery making. Sheep and goats stolen from the Spanish were bred into large herds. These herds, combined with horses, gave the Navajo greater mobility.

Navajo weaver

Art and religion played key roles in tribal culture, and the two were often intertwined. Unique sand paintings were used to invoke spirits and relate to ancestors. In the absence of written records, oral chants related Navajo history and mythology from generation to generation. They brought to life fantastical images of the tribe's gods—creatures like the wily Coyote, the life-giving Earth Mother, and the far-seeing Spider Man. The Navajo also believed in malevolent ghosts, dead tribesmen who wander the land, bringing misfortune to the living.

Navajo rituals were lengthy and intricate. They varied from the Night Way Ceremony, used to cure illness, to the Enemy Way Ceremony, which freed a warrior from the ghosts of slain enemies. Most important was perhaps the *kinaaldá,* a significant event marking a girl's coming of age. This ceremony was essential before a female Navajo could be married.

The Navajo lived in conical or 8-sided structures known as hogans. The houses consisted of log frames covered in bark and earth with a single, east-facing doorway. The Navajo organized themselves into small outfits, usually made up of a large extended family. For most of their history, no nationwide leader existed. Only in its struggles with the U.S. Army did the Navajo Nation unite.

The Navajo had a long history of aggression, often retributive, against white settlers. Spaniards in the area often kidnapped Indian children for use as slaves. The Navajo would respond by stealing settlers' livestock. Attempts to restrail the raiding tribe usually proved futile, although in 1805 the Spanish killed 115 Navajo who were fortified in Canyon del Muerto. The site is now known as Massacre Cave.

The United States took control of Navajo land in 1848. By the 1860s, conflicts between the settlers and Indians had climaxed. The disputes arose around grazing rights in the area near Canyon de Chelly (see page 329), a sacred place to the Navajo. In 1860, the Indians, led by Manuelito, raided and almost conquered nearby Fort Defiance. Two years later, having driven Confederate troops from the area, the Union Army focused its efforts on the belligerent tribe. Using the harsh tactics of the Civil War, U.S. forces, led in the field by Colonel Christopher "Kit" Carson (see page 72) burned their way through Navajo farmlands and orchards, destroying livestock and homes. By 1866 at least 8,500 Indians had surrendered, the largest capitulation in Native American history.

The unfortunate captives were forced on a terrible 300-mile trek to Bosque Redondo in eastern New Mexico, a journey now known as the "Long Walk." More than 2,000 Navajo perished before they were allowed to return to their homeland two years later. The Navajo Nation now covers 16 million acres, mostly in northeastern Arizona. Almost 250,000 Indians call the reservation home. Navajo land is open to the public, and tourism and recreation help sustain the tribe's economy. Also important are the oil and mineral resources that are rich in this area. However, many Navajo make a living producing traditional crafts. Their jewelry and rug weaving are especially renowned.

The Navajo are a proud people but have also proved to be most patriotic. During World War II, 450 Navajo volunteered to serve in six marine battalions. Their language was an unbreakable code (see page 80), and the messages sent in that tongue were vital in the U.S. defeat of Japan.

Pai

The Pai Indians have a long history in Arizona. After excavating and studying pieces of pottery, scholars believe that they were living just east of the Colorado River as early as A.D. 700. They survived by hunting, gathering, and gardening along the banks of the Colorado River. During the 1300s, they spread eastward onto the Colorado Plateau. Around 1750, there was a great schism in the Pai civilization. Lore attributes the separation to a mudball fight between children. As parents ran to settle things between the children, hostilities arose among the adults as well. A group of Indians, the Yavapai, split off from the main Pai tribe and headed south. Settlers later dubbed the Pai Indians the Walapai (or Hualapai) to differentiate them from their southern enemies. In the years that followed, many heated and very bloody conflicts occurred between the two tribes.

For many decades, encounters between Pai Indians and white settlers were quite peaceful. Then a Prescott teamster murdered a Walapai Indian, Wauba Yuma, and the Walapai War (1868–69) exploded. Pitched battles and skirmishes between the Indians and Colonel William Price (see page 79) were common. Before long, the tribal chiefs were forced to surrender and the Walapais were relocated to the Colorado River Indian Reservation, where they stayed until 1875. Many of their leaders were imprisoned on Alcatraz and Angel Islands. However, throughout the conflict, a small band of Walapai along the Colorado River remained aloof. Americans referred to this group as the Havasupai to distinguish them from their warring brethren.

In the south, the Yavapai were finding trouble of their own. American gold miners began to enter their territory in search of wealth. The miners were promptly attacked, which caused retribution from the U.S. government. Beginning in 1872, the Yavapai fought a nine-year battle for their territory. The northern Walapai aided U.S. forces in destroying their mutual enemy. Eventually, the Yavapai were defeated and moved to the San Carlos Indian Reservation. In 1903, President Theodore Roosevelt created a large Yavapai reservation near the Verde and Salt Rivers. A reservation was formed for the Walapai on the Colorado Plateau, while the Havasupai were relocated to a small reservation at the bottom of Cataract Canyon. In 1975, their land was extended considerably in order to include traditional hunting grounds.

Culturally, the three Pai tribes are quite similar. Where possible, they survived in the dry climate by using irrigation or natural springs to provide water for their crops. They also prized the fruits of yucca plants and enjoyed the mescal hearts of the plentiful agave cacti. They wore and traded buckskin, and also hunted rabbits and wildcats. Generally their houses were pole-framed structures covered in brush, similar to Apache wickiups. Today they make a living in tourism, mining, and breeding livestock.

Pima

The Pima Indians, or Akimel O'odham ("the river people") as they call themselves, are perhaps the oldest continuous residents of present-day Arizona. They are likely descendents of the Hohokam (see page 89), which means "the vanished ones" in the Piman language. Aborigionally, the Pima culture was spread loosely over a wide range of land including the lower Colorado and the deserts south of the Gila River. Those who lived within the sparse deserts were commonly distinguished as the Papago (see page 94).

Pima Indians were peaceful villagers and successful farmers, diverting river water to irrigate their land. The men of the tribe did the farming and hunting. They grew corn, squash, kidney beans, tobacco, cotton, and later wheat and alfalfa, and killed rabbits and other small game. Men also built small houses that were essentially round structures with flat tops, framed by wooden poles and covered with grass and mud. Women gathered nuts, fruits, and seeds. They also weaved elaborate baskets, made polished red-and-black pottery, and outfitted their family with cotton and rabbit skin clothing.

A Pima woman, circa 1900

The Pima generally had peaceful relations with white men. Padre Eusebio Francisco Kino (see page 68) was the first European to encounter the tribe. He introduced cattle into the region and established a mission, Nuestra Señora de los Dolores, in order to spread Christianity. Soon the Pima were under the blanket of Spanish rule and were being exploited through agriculture and labor levies. Twice the Pima revolted, once in 1695 and again in 1751. The second rebellion, led by Luis Oacpicagigua, was the more organized of the two. Oacpicagigua had previously served with the Spanish in a campaign against other Indians of the Southwest. Seeing the Spanish spread further northward, he realized that they would soon be on the doorstep of the Pima and would subject them to forced labor. On November 20, 1751, Luis threw a party and afterward killed the 18 Spaniards who attended. The rebelling Indians then attacked Spanish settlements. The Pima hoped for an alliance with their longtime enemies, the Apache, but it never occurred. The Spanish army quelled the revolt, hanging the major players. Luis escaped by promising to rebuild the settlements.

The Pima Indians fell under U.S. jurisdiction with the Gadsden Purchase of 1853–54. They are one of the few tribes never to get into a conflict with American troops. Instead, they generally allied themselves with Americans fighting against the Apache. Indeed, the area of the Pima provided a welcome respite for the prospectors heading west to California. The Pima offered the weary travelers much-needed food and supplies. The first reservation in Arizona was set up for this tribe in 1859, when the Gila River Indian Reservation was created. Today they share this and the Salt River Reservation with the Maricopa. From these two sites, the tribe elects a council and a chief to oversee its affairs. The Pima Indians now number upward of 14,000 people. Now mostly Christian, they support themselves with craftwork and farming, despite continued disputes over their water supply.

Southern Paiute

The Paiute Indians, one of the Shoshonean tribes, included many bands scattered over the vast area from present-day Arizona to Oregon. They are generally studied as two separate groups, the Northern and Southern Paiute. The Southern Paiute lived along the Colorado River, in what is now southern Utah, Nevada, and northwestern Arizona. The bands moved often, following the availability of food. Male tribesmen chased small game, singing individual religious songs as they hunted. Women collected wild plant food. Baskets and pottery were essential as a means of storage.

Due to their nomadic nature, Paiute dwellings were temporary. Their architecture was similar to that of the Apache wickiup—huts of brush spread over pole frames. A village consisted of up to 10 of these houses. Each band elected its own leader; the tribe had no overall chief.

Religion and ceremonies were important to the Paiute. Funerals could last up to four days, with mourning rituals continuing for up to a year. Both sexes adorned themselves with tattoos and piercings. Indeed, the Southern Paiute believed that the dead could not pass into the next world without an ear piercing.

In the early 1800s, travelers on the Old Spanish Trail found their way into Southern Paiute territory. Priests arrived, seeking to convert the Indians. Neighboring Apache and Navajo tribes began to capture the unfortunate Paiute and sell them to white men. Disease and enslavement ravaged the tribe's population. By the time Brigham Young abolished Indian slavery in the 1850s, Mormons had seized most of their best land. The first Paiute reservation was established in 1872. Today, the Southern Paiute live on or near many reservations scattered around the Southwest.

One notable Paiute Indian, Wovoka (or Jack Wilson) from Nevada, is responsible for creating the Ghost Dance in 1888. This mystical religion uses chanting and dancing in a spiritual cleansing of self. It prophesies an end to the white man and his reign over the land, and an eventual return of the Indians and the buffalo. The religion caught on with many other tribes throughout the West and has even excited the curiosity of mystics outside of Indian cultures. Attempts to ban the Ghost Dance resulted in the last significant Indian violence of the century, culminating in the massacre of Wounded Knee (1890).

Paiute wickiups

Tohono O'odham (Papago)

The Tohono O'odham (meaning "desert people") are related to other O'odham, or Piman-speaking, tribes such as the Akimel O'odham (Pima Indians). Traditionally, they lived in what is now southern Arizona and northern Mexico. The name Papago, which means "bean people," was given to this tribe by neighboring Pima Indians, and it is by this name that they are often known.

Before they were placed on reservations, the Tohono O'odham migrated between two areas, depending on the season. In winter they lived in a mountain-spring village. During the summer they moved into a flood-farming village. These villages evolved over time into tightly knit communities, probably in response to hostilities from their longtime enemy, the Apache. When the Apache threat settled down in the late 1800s, the communities dispersed. However, the Tohono still held allegiance to one another and villages could be readily called upon in times of need. The Tohono were bolstered in the early 1800s when they absorbed the Subiapuris (another Piman-speaking tribe) after they had been ravaged by disease and Apache attacks.

Adobe dwelling built by the Tohono O'odham (Papago)

The first European to contact the Tohono O'odham was Padre Eusebio Francisco Kino. In the 1690s, Kino established missions with the Tohono O'odham, and heralded a new era of Spanish influence. The Tohono took to Kino's teaching and Christianity was absorbed into their traditional religion, thereby creating a Sonoran Catholicism, which is still widely practiced by the Tohono. Spaniards also introduced the tribe to a new way of life. The missionaries taught the Tohono how to herd cattle, farm wheat, and ride horses. Only once did the Indians resort to anti-European violence, when a small number joined the Akimel O'odham in the Pima revolt of 1751.

Tohono life changed with the Gadsden Purchase, when most of their territory fell under the domain of the United States. The Tohono allied themselves with the American newcomers to fight their mutual foe, the Apache. However, relations between the Tohono and the white settlers strained as American ranchers and prospectors continually moved into Tohono territory. In order to ease relations, reservations were set up for the tribe, starting with San Xavier in 1874.

The Gila Bend Reservation followed in 1884. These reservations were quite small—smaller than the land to which the Tohono were accustomed. In 1916, Woodrow Wilson solved the dilemma be creating the larger Papago Reservation, later renamed the Tohono O'odham Reservation. Currently, most of the 16,000 Tohono Indians live on this, the nation's second-largest reservation. Although many are forced to move in search of jobs, some economic opportunities exist in the form of the Desert Diamond Casino and extensive mineral mines.

Zuni Pueblo village, 1872

There are also Tohono living in northern Mexico, but they have fared worse than their brethren in Arizona. Mexican Tohono reservations remain very small and support only about 200 Indians.

Yuma (Quechan)

The Yuma, or Quechan, as they prefer to be called, trace their ancestral home to a sacred mountain near Needles, California, called Avikwamé. Sometime before Spanish explorers made contact with the tribe in 1540, they moved to the area around the confluence of the Colorado and Gila Rivers. Here they controlled the Yuma crossing, an important passage across the Colorado River.

Conditions in the region were harsh, with temperatures that often reached 120°F. The Yuma lived along the banks of the river, moving to higher lands to avoid the spring floods. Their dwellings varied from open, rectangular structures to Apache-like wickiups. They supplemented their diet of fish and wild plants by farming corn, beans, squash, and grasses in the silt left over from floods.

In the late 1700s, Spanish missionaries established two settlements near the Yuma crossing. Soldiers from the missions mistreated the Indians, stealing food supplies and Yuman land. On July 17, 1781, Chief Palma and his brother Ygnacio Palma led their people in a revolt. Local settlements were burned to the ground and about 95 priests, settlers, and soldiers were killed. The Yuma rebellion shut down the Spanish route into Alta California that had been created by Juan Bautista de Anza. Spanish soldiers tried to regain the lost land, but the Quechan fought them off and were never subdued.

A group of Yuma Indians, circa 1910

By the 1840s, Americans began to pass through Quechan territory. At first, the Yuma were able to exploit the situation, charging travelers for passage across the Colorado. However, non-Indian ferry companies soon challenged Quechan control of the crossing. When Yuma Indians attacked a rival ferryman, John C. Morehead, a California lawyer, raised a volunteer militia and destroyed Quechan crops and boats. Skirmishes between Indians and travelers became frequent. Those who traversed the Yuma crossing did so with trepidation. Fort Yuma was built in 1850 to quell the situation, but poor supplies and frequent attacks upon the fort caused its abandonment. Not until the following year did a stronger garrison return and secure the crossing.

In 1884, the Yuma Indians were provided a reservation along the Colorado River. Later, the Cocopah Reservation was established for them in 1917. Since then, the Quechan have had to continually battle for land. By the 1950s, the federal government had taken or sold 8,500 acres of Quechan territory. Twenty-five thousand acres of land were returned to the reservation in 1978, but the 1,000 remaining Indians still fight for water rights.

Zuni Pueblo

Ancestral Zunis first settled in the Zuni River Valley along the Zuni River, near St. Johns, Arizona. The Zuni Pueblo, also known as the A:shiwi, lived peacefully in the valley for many years, in six farming villages known as pueblos (the word refers to a group of Indians, their villages, and a style of house). Their homes were elaborate multistoried stone buildings interconnected by many ladders. When Spanish explorers made contact with the tribe in the 1500s, they found one settlement with 1,000 contiguous rooms. The rooms faced a large central plaza, where the Indians held ceremonial rituals.

The Zuni were successful farmers, a fact that enabled them to live such a complex village life. For spiritual guidance, they turned to *kachinas*, benevolent spirits whose presence permeated all aspects of tribal life. Masks worn in ceremonies and small idols were representative of these gods. The Indians summoned the spirits in rain dances, sometimes wrapping themselves in live snakes for the rituals.

Gradually, attacks by Apache and the Spanish forced Zuni villages to consolidate. Eventually, the whole tribe moved to the site of their sacred shrine, Halona. The present-day town of Zuni, New Mexico, still occupies this spot. Here the tribe managed a peaceful existence while the area changed hands from Spain to Mexico and, after 1848, to the United States. In 1877, an act of Congress created the Zuni Reservation. Traders and missionaries arrived in Zuni territory, and the tribe was encouraged to start raising livestock in order to exist in a new cash economy. Presently, the Zuni are the largest of the Pueblo Indian tribes, numbering at least 10,000.

Events

The Era of the Spanish and Mexican Missions and Presidios

The Spanish first crossed Arizona in pursuit of El Dorado, that distant glittering promise of gold and glory. Next came Christendom; fervent missionaries risked their lives to preach the Word. When hostile Indians were encountered, and missionaries were turning into martyrs, troop garrisons (presidios) were built to protect the missions and missionaries.

The era of missions and presidios started in 1629 when missions were established among the Hopi Indians. The Hopi did not take to Christianity, and several Franciscans were killed in their attempt to convert the Indians. The Pueblo Revolt in 1680 ended the Hopi missions. For seven years, all was quiet in Arizona. Then Padre Eusebio Francisco Kino arrived (see page 68).

Kino worked zealously in Arizona, coming in contact with tribes that lived near the Gila River. Along with the Gospel, he brought them cattle and sheep and taught them how to herd the animals. After Kino's death in 1711, mission work reached another lull. Missionaries continued to visit Arizona, and the height of the mission and presidio era was reached in 1767 when the Jesuits were expelled and the Franciscans took over.

Indian revolts, like the Pueblo revolt and the Pima revolt in 1751, were forcing the abandonment of settlements in northern New Spain. In 1766, the Marques de Rubi was given the assignment by the Spanish crown of investigating the problem. As a result of the Rubi recommendations, a new line of fortifications was established that consisted of 15 presidios situated at about 120-mile intervals from the Gulf of California on the west to the Gulf of Mexico on the east. They extended along what is now approximately the northern boundary of Mexico. Three of the presidios were located in present-day Arizona. Thanks to these presidios, missions were built with the idea of becoming permanent establishments. Resident priests could live at missions like Tumacácori and San Xavier and work with the local Indians.

Tubac was established as a presidio, named Presidio de San Ignacio de Tubac, with a garrison of 50 soldiers to protect the missions. After the Pima revolt, the garrison was moved north to Tucson in order to better protect the priests. Tubac was regarrisoned but was once again abandoned and the inhabitants moved to Tucson. The presidios proved to be critical to mission survival. The unprotected missions of La Purism Concepción and San Pedro y San Pablo de Bicuñer were both sacked by uprising Yuma Indians. Fray Francisco Garcés (see page 69), the Franciscan version of the great Padre Kino, was killed during the revolt.

While priests sought to Christianize, the presidios and missions helped New Spain get a foothold in the New World. Ranchers and farmers followed the presidios and tried to tame the land. The settlements also dissuaded Russian explorers who threatened New Spain in the West. Other world powers were also looking for a chunk of new territory. The Yuma revolt, however, closed off California to the Spanish, leaving it a veritable island. Missions within Arizona began to crumble as well. San Xavier was abandoned in 1828 and Tumacácori was deserted around 1848. The majority of the soldiers and missionaries were recalled to help fight the Mexican Revolution, leaving ranchers to fend for themselves. Many of them left the area.

San Xavier was kept well preserved by the local Indians and stands today. A Catholic mass is held there every Sunday. Presidio de San Ignacio de Tubac is now a state historical park where visitors can view Tubac's 1885 schoolhouse and a visitor center with exhibits.

The Mexican War—1846 to 1848

The annexation of Texas in 1845 set the stage for war between Mexico and the United States. Continued border disputes had fueled the animosity between the two nations. Mexico severed relations in March 1845. However, President James Polk would not be refused. He sent John Slidell on a secret mission to Mexico City, with orders to settle U.S. claims and purchase California and the New Mexico Territory (which included Arizona) for $30 million. Slidell's mission was not a complete secret. Mexican officials knew he was coming and he was rebuked at the door. The Mexicans would not even hear talk of their country's dismemberment. President Polk ordered Zachary Taylor to occupy the disputed territory between the Nueces and Rio Grande Rivers in Texas. Mexican troops crossed the Rio Grande and fired on American soldiers, killing 16. Polk proclaimed that Mexico had "invaded our territory and shed American blood on American soil." On May 11, Congress overwhelmingly supported a declaration of war.

Taylor began his march into the heart of Mexico. Colonel Stephen Kearny was to march through Mexican territory and take New Mexico (including Arizona) and California. Kearny's march went without a hitch. Mexican citizens welcomed the occupation and only a few resented it. (More information on Kearny's campaign can be found in the sections on Gila Trail [page 60] and on General George Cooke and the Mormon Battalion [page 77].) Taylor, however, fought several battles. He was victorious, but slowly trudged through Mexico. He was obviously in no rush to occupy the country. Polk then sent General Winfield Scott to take an army by sea and capture the seaport of Veracruz. After a siege of three weeks, the city fell. The door was open for Scott's occupation of Mexico City, which he took on September 14, 1847.

On February 2, 1848, Mexico signed the Treaty of Guadalupe Hidalgo, thereby signing over New Mexico, Utah, Nevada, California, western Colorado, Texas, and Arizona. For the territory the United States paid $15 million. The acquisition nearly vaulted the nation into civil war as discussions raged over which states should be slave states. Although the Compromise of 1850 settled the argument, the country slipped further into feelings of separation between North and South.

The Proposed Mormon State of Deseret—1849

The Mormons, after their exodus from Illinois and Missouri, settled down in the Salt Lake Valley and set their eyes on the horizon. They saw a boundless stretch of land that could be used and settled for the Mormon faith. Between 1849 and 1856, settlers were sent to establish communities in Wyoming, Idaho, Las Vegas (Nevada), and California. The

Brigham Young

proposed new Mormon state—the State of Deseret—encompassed a huge amount of land, roughly one-sixth the area of the United States. Everything north of the Gila River in today's Arizona was included within Deseret. Now all Deseret needed was a grant of statehood from Congress. But Congress refused. Instead, the Utah Territory, with its greatly reduced boundaries when compared to Deseret, was formed in the Compromise of 1850. Mormon political control was yanked from Arizona. However, Mormon settlements continued to be created during the 1870s and 1880s. Such towns as Fredonia, St. Johns, St. David, and Mesa were all created by Mormon settlers.

Oatman Massacre—1851

February 18, 1851, marks the day of the tragic Oatman Massacre and the beginning of one of Arizona's most famous captivity narratives. About 100 miles east of Yuma lies Oatman Flat, the site of the bloody affair. Royse Oatman and his family (his wife and seven children) were traveling across the Gila Trail (see page 60) when a small band of Yavapai Indians came out of the brush proclaiming friendship. To appease them, Royse handed out what food his family could spare. The Indians demanded more. They brandished their weapons and murdered six family members on the spot. They grabbed two daughters, Olive and Mary Ann, and carried them into the Arizona desert. Lorenzo, the oldest son, was knocked unconscious during the battle. He was later picked up by a wagon train and taken to Fort Yuma. He pleaded his case to General Heintzelman, but the general could not pursue the Indians because the incident had taken place beyond the U.S. border. Lorenzo never gave up hope of finding his sisters.

Olive Oatman with the mark tattooed by the Mojave medicine man visible on her chin

Olive and Mary Ann were enslaved and forced into hard labor. After enduring this suffering and the whip of their captors, they were sold to the Mojave Indians in northwest Arizona. The girls were inducted into the tribe, each one receiving a tattoo of five blue stripes between her chin and mouth. Life was better with the Mojave, but a drought ravaged the land. Olive was forced to watch her sister, Mary Ann, wither away from famine. When she died, Olive was left alone with her new tribe, although the chief and his wife accepted her as their own daughter. Unknown to Olive, she had not been forgotten by the settlers. Rumors of a white woman living with a tribe of Indians spread. Henry W. Grinnell decided to investigate. In 1856, he sent a Yuma messenger to find and ransom her. The messenger was successful and after a heartfelt good-bye, Olive Oatman left for Fort Yuma and returned to the welcome arms of her brother, Lorenzo. The two moved to Oregon where her fantastic story, *Captivity of the Oatman Girls* (published in 1857 by Reverend Royal Byron Stratton), paid for their education at the University of the Pacific. Lorenzo and his family settled in New York. In 1865, Olive married John Brant Fairchild, eventually settling in Sherman, Texas. Olive died in 1903, at age 66.

Gadsden Purchase—1853–54

To the west of the Union, California was burgeoning. California's success was the result of the 1849 gold rush and the sudden charge of immigrants looking to cash in. California was growing, creating the need for a line of communication between the East and the West. Citizens and railroad companies were pressuring Washington to create a link. Surveyors pointed out that the Gila Trail, which ran through Arizona, would be an excellent road on which to lay track. However, the land on which America wanted to build was in the hands of Mexico. President Franklin Pierce wanted to make a deal with Mexican president Antonio Lopez de Santa Anna. The good news for the United States was that Mexico was in a severe financial crunch. Pierce sent James Gadsden to Mexico City to work out a deal.

Gadsden had five different proposals for acquiring the needed land, each one with a different price. Santa Anna needed money to supply his army and was in no hurry to get into another war with the United States. He did not buckle under, however. Gadsden was made aware that he would only get enough land to make the railroad and that Mexico did not want to give up access to Baja California. A compromise was achieved and the purchase was signed on December 30, 1853. The treaty was not ratified until June 24, 1854, after the Mexican minister, Juan Nepomunceno Almonte, tinkered with the borders just a little bit more. Before the Gadsden Purchase, the border of the United States was along the Gila River. For $10 million the United States bought 9,000 square miles and the foundation for a railroad. The Gadsden Purchase set the present boundary between Arizona and Mexico.

Establishment of the Territory of Arizona—1863

After 1850, the area of present-day Arizona was included in the vast Territory of New Mexico, which covered New Mexico, southern Colorado, Arizona north of the Gila River, and a small fraction of southern Nevada. The territorial capital for such an enormous stretch of land was Santa Fe. As years passed, a desire for separation started to be expressed by Arizona citizens. Such sentiments can be found in the works of Arizona poet Sharlott Hall and statesman Charles Poston. Congress, however, was deeply involved in the Civil War and saw something else in Arizona—gold. The Union government badly needed gold to finance the war and to avoid currency depreciation. A southern stretch of Arizona and New Mexico had already supported the Confederacy, and the Union was not ready to allow the rest of the territory to fall into the hands of the enemy.

Congressman James H. Ashley of Ohio introduced the Arizona Organic Act on March 12, 1862; he called for a vertical division between Arizona and New Mexico. There was a lot of opposition to the bill; opponents said that there was hardly anyone within the territory loyal to the Union and that the new territory would divert money from the war effort. Still, the bill was passed with help from the lobbying efforts of Charles Poston, who consequently earned the name "Father of Arizona." In return for his efforts he hoped to be the territorial governor. Instead, the honor went to someone else and Poston was made an Indian agent. Sam Heintzelman was also a key player, who used his mining company and investors to pressure congressmen. Delegate John S. Watts of New Mexico was another influential proponent of the new territory. President Abraham Lincoln signed the bill on February 24, 1863, thus creating the Arizona Territory.

Camp Grant Massacre—1871

April 30, 1871, a day when Aravaipa Canyon was soaked in the blood of women and children, is one of the most tragic days in Arizona's history. A band of Aravaipa Apache had settled peacefully on a reservation near Camp Grant, at the point where Aravaipa Canyon intersects with the San Pedro River. Lieutenant R. E. Whitman was the officer in charge of the camp and it was his duty to protect and feed the Apache at Camp Grant. Although the Aravaipa desired peace, they were essentially prisoners of war.

Civilians in nearby Tucson claimed that the Aravaipa were escaping from the reservation to steal from and murder the townsfolk. Tension lay thick in the air. Apaches had held Arizona in the grip of terror and there were newly reported cases of people in Tucson being attacked by unknown Indians. Fingers were immediately pointed at the local reservation, Camp Grant. Lieutenant Whitman declared that the Aravaipa had never left the reservation. Whitman's superior, breveted Major General George Stoneman, was in charge of military policies in the Arizona Territory. He had previously moved the Third Cavalry away from Tucson, leaving the town without protection. This lack of protection along with continued Indian attacks left citizens scared and angry—a dangerous combination.

Farmers and ranchers were being massacred and their cattle plundered. During one raid, a mob of townsfolk pursued the raiders and killed a straggling Indian. Jesus M. Elias, an influential Mexican from Tucson, coldly regarded the body and identified the Indian as an Aravaipa Apache. The citizens decided to take action into their own hands.

A mob formed, consisting of Americans, Mexicans, and Papagos. In order to avoid suspicion, they departed Tucson one at a time and headed for Camp Grant. Someone saw the armed citizens approaching the camp and ran to tell Lieutenant Whitman. But he would arrive too late. Cloaked by the night, the mob stealthily approached the sleeping Aravaipa. In just 30 minutes the atrocity was over. Eight men and 110 women and children lay dead or dying at Camp Grant. Twenty-eight children were spared, only to be sold as slaves.

President Ulysses Grant was infuriated by the news. He notified Arizona authorities that those who took part in the bloody affair would be brought to justice; otherwise he'd place the territory under martial law. One hundred and four posse members were accused and brought to trial. The trial lasted five days and as the jury left the courtroom to deliberate a verdict, the judge instructed them to acquit the accused. After 19 minutes they returned. The jury foreman pronounced the verdict—not guilty.

Loring (Wickenburg) Massacre—1871

Writer Frederick Loring had just finished touring and surveying the lower Great Basin area, including Death Valley, Camp Mohave, and the Grand Canyon when, on November 5, 1871, he set out with five other men and a woman in a stage rolling out of Wickenburg. The stage also included Lieutenant George M. Wheeler, who was an important member of the surveying party. Just 8 miles from town, barely within sight of Wickenburg, the coach was ambushed. The attackers were brutally efficient. Six stagecoach riders died outright and another one died shortly after from wounds received in the attack. Only one person survived. Loring was cut down; the death of this up-and-coming author alerted Americans in the East of the harsh reality of the Arizona Territory. Just before he left on that fateful coach, Loring had his hair cut, joking that the Apaches would find it difficult to take his scalp.

The attackers were unknown, but scouts discovered signs of Yavapai Indians. After carefully figuring out who the perpetrators were, General Crook, along with a contingent of soldiers and scouts including the notable scout Al Sieber, discovered the whereabouts of the hostile Indians. They surprised the Apache and Crook's men killed 40 Apache warriors before defeating the rest of the group.

The Apache Insurrection—1877 to 1886

After General George Crook's Tonto Basin Campaign in 1872, the Apache bands were finally sent to reservations in Arizona and New Mexico. Reservation life was not a happy one. Rations dwindled and nostalgia for a previous way of life permeated the reservations. Rebellion and bloodshed loomed.

On September 2, 1877, Victorio rallied 300 Mimbreño from the San Carlos Reservation. They escaped and retreated into the nearby mountains and canyons. The number of his followers dwindled, and eventually he was left with only 80 warriors. After a failed negotiation, Victorio descended from the mountains and attacked. His band raided throughout Mexico, Texas, New Mexico, and Arizona. Both Mexican and American forces nipped at Victorio's heels. Yet he survived numerous skirmishes and evaded capture. Although he was gifted in the art of guerilla warfare, Victorio could not evade his pursuers forever. He was attacked by 350 Mexican troops in a two-day battle known as the Battle of Tres Castillos (Three Peaks). Legend has it that as his warriors died around him and the prospect of capture became a reality, Victorio took his own life.

On August 30, 1881, another rebellion was sparked on the San Carlos Reservation. A White Mountain Apache mystic, Nakaidoklini, was preaching that Indian warriors would return from their graves and annihilate the whites. At the time

Geronimo (front, third from right) and Natchez, son of Cochise (front, third from left), at a stop in Texas during their deportation to Florida

he was preaching, the number of soldiers stationed on the reservation grew. Violence broke out, and Nakaidoklini was killed. Fort Apache was briefly attacked by Indians, but they were quickly repulsed. A month later, Geronimo and fellow Apache Juh, Naiche, and Chato would lead another revolt. Seventy-four men followed them out of San Carlos, only to return in a raid designed to gather more followers and take the life of the chief of police. General Crook was once again called upon to deal with the runaway Apache. He used other Apache to track and relentlessly pursue Geronimo. Chato's camp was discovered and attacked. The battle's victor was uncertain, but it proved to Crook that he was closely behind the Apache. Talks began between the opposing sides, and the renegades agreed to return to the reservation.

In May 1885, Geronimo, Naiche, Nan, and 150 other Apache once again escaped the confines of the reservation after an alcoholic Apache drink *(tesquino)* was banned. Soldiers under General Crook tracked them down and finally on March 25, 1886, the renegades surrendered at Canyon de los Embudos. However, Geronimo escaped. Crook was relieved from duty, and General Nelson Miles took up the hunt for Geronimo. Five thousand soldiers relentlessly pursued the escaped Apache and his small band of followers. Geronimo surrendered for a final time on September 4, 1886, in Skeleton Canyon. He and his faithful followers were imprisoned. Geronimo never would return to his homeland; in 1909, he died a prisoner of war in Oklahoma.

The Pleasant Valley War—1883 to 1892

The Pleasant Valley War raged between the Tewksbury and Graham families. The Tewksburys lived on the Mogollon Rim in Pleasant Valley. For four years they lived a tranquil life raising horses, but things changed when the Grahams moved in nearby and started raising cattle. A strange thing about the Grahams' cattle was that the population grew incredibly fast. The Tewksburys soon learned that the Grahams were cattle rustlers. Pleasant Valley divided itself into two factions when the Tewksburys complained: those for the Grahams and those for the Tewksburys. The foundations for the feud were laid.

In 1883, John Gilliand and his nephew (both Graham supporters) were wounded by gunfire after a violent argument with Ed Tewksbury. After that incident, expectations of open war loomed. Instead, the situation cooled until 1887 when the Tewksburys started to raise sheep and let them graze over the valley. Feuds between cattle ranchers and sheepherders are infamous; the presence of the sheep riled up the Grahams. The boiling point had been reached. The Grahams and Blevins (who were solid Graham supporters) hired a gunman. The Tewksbury sheepherder was later drilled by gunfire. In August 1887, a Blevins brother lay dead and his companions were wounded after a meeting with Ed and Jim Tewksbury. William Graham was the next to fall when an avenging bullet fired by the brother-in-law of the murdered sheepherder struck him down. Two weeks later, the Tewksbury ranch house was attacked by a man identified as Andy Cooper, accompanied by John Blevins and a mob of Graham supporters. When the smoke cleared, John Tewksbury and William Jacobs were found dead. The war raged between the two factions and eventually the law noticed the blood and murder.

Sheriff Commodore Perry Owens rode up to the house of Eva Blevins on September 4, 1887. He was looking for the man called Andy Cooper, which it turned out was an alias used to throw lawmen off the trail of murders that followed the man from Texas through Pleasant Valley. Owens was a dead shot with the Winchester he had cradled in his arms. His sharp eyes spotted Andy by the front door. Andy drew his six-gun, Owens swung his rifle, and the two fired. Owens burst through the door and Andy fell bleeding into the arms of his mother. John Blevins appeared and fired at the sheriff but missed. Owens felled him with a shot to the shoulder. The steely eyed sheriff shot Mose Roberts and sent him crashing through the rear window. Sam Houston was the next to exit the house. The 16-year-old boy was armed with a six-gun, but before he could fire, the sheriff killed him with a clean shot to the head. John Blevins was the only one to survive Owens's wrath and precise shooting.

The feud simmered down in 1892 when Ed Tewksbury, the last of the Tewksburys, was found guilty of murdering Tom Graham. He was released from jail in 1896. Tuberculosis took him on April 4, 1904.

Establishment of the Civilian Conservation Corps

Designed to provide financial relief from the depression and to aid in a variety of conservation and public works projects, the Civilian Conservation Corps (CCC) arrived in Arizona during President Roosevelt's New Deal era. From the time of its formation in 1933 until 1939, the CCC established 28 camps in and made a major impact on Arizona. Various government agencies worked with the U.S. Army to coordinate and direct the work of those in the camps—mostly young men between the ages of 18 and 24 as well as local, experienced men who found themselves out of work. These skilled workers directed the young men, who were by and large without any particular skills. The 28 camps were spread across the state in order to adequately cover Arizona. They were located in national parks, national forests, federal grazing lands, and city parks.

Upon enlisting in the CCC, each man received a week's training in basic fire fighting. The years of the depression hap-

Civilian Conservation Corp camp near Sedona

pened to be extremely dry, and so the CCC was often called in to fight out-of-control forest fires. Additionally, they built nearly 400,000 erosion-control check dams, dug 3,000 reservoirs and wells, and helped fence off grazing lands. Archeologists were even helped by those in the CCC who aided with excavations. Within forests and parks, the CCC planted trees, stocked streams, constructed buildings, and ran telephone wires. Although the New Deal programs were designed to help all those suffering during the depression, programs often slighted Mexicans and African Americans. Few minorities were allowed to join the CCC until the early 1940s, when Anglo-America had started its return to a healthy economy.

With the onset of World War II, the United States found itself once more in a growing economy, and like many New Deal programs, the CCC had run its course. In July 1942, the CCC came to an end, but its impact on Arizona remains to this day. You can also still find the scattered remnants of CCC camps throughout the state.

Building the Hoover Dam

A testament to human ingenuity, engineering, and endurance stands on the Arizona-Nevada border in Black Canyon—the Hoover Dam. On September 30, 1930, while the depression devastated lives and sank the economy, the construction of Hoover Dam began. Work was hard to come by and many Americans were hungry and jobless. When word spread about the dam, workers came from all over the country to offer their services. Boulder City, Nevada, was created to house the employees and their families, and it is estimated that the city accommodated more than 4,000 workers during the construction. In order to build the dam, the mighty Colorado had to be diverted from the construction site. Four tunnels, 50 feet in diameter, were drilled through the canyon walls. For added support, the tunnels were then lined with concrete. In 1932, the Colorado changed its course as it spilled through these man-made openings. The holes were eventually closed when the dam was completed, but only after the Colorado River had flowed through the diversion tunnels for two years.

A boxcar of machinery on the cableway as the Hoover Dam nears completion

The construction of the dam was no easy task. In the summer, workers had to endure temperatures above 100°F; in the winter, frigid temperatures plagued the hardy workers. The job was dangerous. One particularly unnerving job was performed by the high-scalers. These men repelled down the canyon walls to chip away loose rock. They were agile and unafraid of being dangled by a slim rope over a deep crevice. Daredevils were drawn to this job, and soon contests arose about who could swing out the highest, the farthest, and who could perform the best stunts. The high-scalers were not the only ones at risk. Ninety-six people lost their lives during the dam's construction. Rocks or dropped tools falling from above would often end the life of a worker. In the face of this danger, the men began to improvise. They coated cloth hats with coal tar, creating crude but effective hard hats.

As time passed, the dam rose. The dam is, in fact, not a giant block of concrete. Individual columns, trapezoidal in shape, make up the dam. The shape allowed the heat to dissipate as the concrete cooled. Concrete was first poured on June 6, 1933. By the dam's completion there were 3.25 million cubic yards in place. This amount of concrete could pave a highway 16-feet wide from San Francisco to New York City. On May 29, 1935, the last concrete was poured. Turbines were then installed to turn the river's waters into electricity. Today, 17 turbines are housed in the Hoover power plant. They produce a maximum of 10,348,020,500 kilowatt-hours a year. Most of this power, about 56 percent, goes to southern California. Arizona receives 19 percent and Nevada gets 25 percent.

Lake Mead was formed by the Hoover Dam, which, when full, contains roughly 31,250,000 acre-feet of water (two year's worth of flow from the Colorado River), has a shoreline of over 550 miles, and covers an area of about 227 square miles. It is the largest man-made lake in the world, twice the size of Rhode Island. More than 6 million people visit the lake yearly. The waters are used for boating, skiing, swimming, and fishing.

The Development of a Reliable Communications Network

The Telegraph

In 1861, San Francisco was connected to the East by the first transcontinental telegraph line. The line was then extended throughout the West, linking major cities like Los Angeles and San Diego. Arizona, however, was not linked to the telegraph until 1873. There had been talk of doing so ever since 1866, and even General George Crook pleaded for its construction in 1871. Finally, a line from San Diego was extended to Yuma. From Yuma, the line snaked its way up to Prescott. As years passed, the telegraph continued eastward over the Gila River Valley and reached New Mexico in 1877. The telegraph

Western Union telegraph office, circa 1900

was mainly used by the military, but civilians could also receive messages. Once the telegraph was in place, businesses flourished. Goods could be ordered faster and the line increased the networking range of businesses. The telegraph became so popular that commercial telegraph companies were established to better serve the people. In 1877, for instance, there were about 1,000 miles of military telegraph lines. By 1882, there were only 532 miles operated by the military; the rest had been taken over by commercial enterprises. Eventually, all the military telegraph lines were bought up or replaced by commercial lines.

The Heliograph

Not as familiar as the telegraph, the heliograph proved to be an effective means of communication in the early days of the West. A heliograph works through reflection: the device uses mirrors to bounce sun rays in any direction. A shutter in the machine was used to block out the beam, allowing Morse Code messages to be sent. Of course, the heliograph could not be used at night or during storms; but the invention did prove useful. The heliograph was quick. It did not rely on messengers riding horses and there were no wires that Indians could cut, as they did to hamper military telegraphs. General Nelson A. Miles, the man who succeeded General George Crook, spearheaded the heliograph's use in Arizona. In August 1886, a network of 14 stations was created. Eventually that number would increase to 52 stations in the 1890s. The heliograph complemented the telegraph until forts were linked by the telephone.

Geography and Geology

The Geological Timeline

Lonely mountaintops that rise more than 10,000 feet above sea level, dry and searing deserts, howling and painted canyons—this is Arizona today. But it was not always so. Arizona is the product of 2 billion years of uplift, violent volcanic activity, a receding ocean, and the erosion of wind and water. Through deserts, mountaintops, and canyons, the forces of nature are slowly shaping the state's topography. The history of Arizona's landscape spans three eras: the Paleozoic, the Mesozoic, and the Cenozoic. These eras and their geological changes are responsible for the Arizona we see today.

The age of fishes, or the Paleozoic era, occurred between 550 and 240 million years ago. Arizona was, on the whole, featureless. A great western ocean advanced across the land, flooding nearly half of the area we now call Arizona. The ocean deposited sedimentary rock a few thousand feet deep in most places. The great, ancient sea deposited the dark, rich limestone that rims the Grand Canyon and makes up the southern mountain ranges. Within the waters lived corals, mollusks, and bony armored fish, all of which have been discovered through fossils in western Arizona.

From 240 to 63 million years ago was the Mesozoic era—the age of reptiles. Explosive volcanism erupted in the south, creating lava flows that traveled as far as southern Utah. These flows are also responsible for the ore deposits, particularly copper, found in the Bisbee area. Mountains in the central and eastern parts of the state began to rise, producing the Mogollon Highlands. The rising Sierra Nevadas cut the west and northwestern part of the state off from valuable moisture, and in response, desolate dunes rolled across the landscape. Briefly, seas once again trespassed across Arizona, this time coming from the northeast. Armored amphibians and crocodile-like creatures roamed the land. Their fossils can be found in the Chinle red beds of northern Arizona. Another formation, the Moenave Formation near Cameron, has also produced the skeletal remains of dinosaurs and ancient crocodiles. Near Black Mesa, in the Kayenta Formation, early mammals were discovered from this era of history.

The Cenozoic era, ranging from 63 million to about 10,000 years ago, brought the age of mammals. Mountain-building continued through continental uplift and faulting. Plateaus rose in the north while great basins sunk between mountain blocks in southern and western Arizona. Great, bubblelike swells of lava (known as batholithic lava formations) produced more mountains in the south. The San Francisco Volcano Field (see page 102) boiled to the surface and erupted. Erosion was all the while stripping away softer rock faces and leaving Kaibab limestone on the Coconino and Kaibab Plateaus. Navajo sandstone poked through on the Kaibito Plateau. The Grand Canyon was being continually cut away and volcanism poured basalt into the growing chasm. The Colorado River shifted its course and brought with it new erosion. Judging from the fossils left behind, mammals such as horses, rhinoceroses, antelopes, and a breed of extinct camels roamed the state. Early man arrived and hunted creatures like mammoths, ground sloths, camels, bison, horses, and horselike tapirs. From then on, the landscape has appeared much as it looks today.

The Regions

Arizona can be divided into three separate geological regions: the Colorado Plateau Province in the north, the Central Highlands (a transitional zone), and the Basin and Range Province in the south.

The Colorado Plateau

The spectacular Colorado Plateau spreads throughout northern Arizona. Volcanic mountains and cliff-rimmed buttes tower above canyons and valleys. The region, as a whole, is about 5,000 feet above sea level, although some areas spire past 9,000 feet. The plateau ends in the southwestern part of the state near cliffs that drop 1,500 feet. The illustrious Grand Canyon is a particular facet of the Colorado Plateau; it cuts a mile deep into the ground, revealing banks that vividly display their colorful geological history. The plateau exists as a great slab of sedimentary rock capped sporadically by new sedimentary and volcanic rock. In itself, the plateau can be subdivided into three regions: the Grand Canyon Region, the Mogollon Slope, and Navajo Country. The Grand Canyon Region is noted for plateaus, the highest one being the Kaibab Plateau. To the east of Flagstaff, the San Francisco Mountains cast their silent shadow. They include the highest point in the state (Humphreys Peak at 12,670 feet). Their peaks and crevices were carved by volcanic activity and glacial flows. The White Mountains and the Little Colorado River characterize the Mogollon Slope. A mile-wide crater known as Barringer Crater also lies within this region. The crater was once thought to have been produced by a vapor explosion, but scientists have discovered that the crater is the product of a meteor strike some 50,000 years ago. Similar to the Grand Canyon Region, Navajo Country dots the landscape with buttes and plateaus. The vivid red walls of Canyon de Chelly are one of the geological highlights seen in this area.

The Central Highlands

This rugged stretch of land separates the Colorado Plateau from the Basin and Range Province. Generally, a transitional zone is lower than the plateau, but there are some mountainous features that rise just as high as the cliffs of the Colorado Plateau. The majority of the landscape is made up of volcanic and sedimentary rocks. The region also displays three beautiful valleys that were wrought by faulting and erosion—the Chino, Tonto, and Verde.

The Basin and Range Province

Stunning mountains that shoot out of large, almost plainlike valleys characterize this area of Arizona. These mountains can reach as high as 10,000 feet. Mount Graham, the 10,713-foot giant, is the highest peak in this region. Some 9,000-footers also dot the Mountain Highlands in the southeast, but usually the craggy peaks of the southeast do not exceed 8,000 feet. Fissures and volcanic eruptions have laid a thick coating of volcanic rock across the Mountain Highlands. The streams in the basins and valleys that cover the region are most commonly tributaries of the Colorado River. Only a few basins are closed or have dry lakes. These extensive valleys slope and roll across the landscape, sometimes at elevations only 500 feet above sea level (near Yuma) and other times as high as 5,000 feet above sea level. Winds that howl over the land cause only a small portion of the erosion. Sheet flooding, where rain and streams sweep over the valley floor, is the major source of erosion. The Sonora region in the southwest does not quite reach the altitudes of the Mountain Highlands' peaks. Still, these craggy and rugged mountains, whose crests have been serrated by erosional forces, are impressive to behold.

Famous Geological Features of Arizona

The Grand Canyon

Of all Arizona's geological treasures, the most widely renowned is the Grand Canyon. Water, wind, and ice carved away the land to form the majestic canyon walls. About 60 to 70 million years ago, the area of the Grand Canyon was actually level and covered by an ancient sea. The sea deposited

The Grand Canyon

sand, which hardened into rock. As more and more sand was deposited, layering took place. As today's Grand Canyon gets deeper, older stone is revealed. As the ancient mountains rose and the ancient sea receded, rivers drained from mountain peaks and formed the ancestral Colorado River, which poured into Marble Canyon. As the Colorado Plateau began to lift, the river continued to cut its way through the landscape. About 5 million years ago, the river changed course to that of the present-day Colorado River. It is uncertain why this happened, but it is probable that the Colorado joined with another river. By that time, the canyon had already started to form and the erosive force of the Colorado hastened the canyon's creation. Today, Glen Canyon Dam has slowed the erosive force on the Grand Canyon. Also, the river now rolls over a solid rock bed, which will take more time to erode, but even now the awe-inspiring Grand Canyon continues to be shaped by forces of nature.

The San Francisco Volcano Field and Sunset Crater

On the southern margin of the Colorado Plateau lies the San Francisco Volcano Field. This 2,000-square-mile patch of Arizona is the result of several million years of volcanic activity. The most recent activity led to the formation of Sunset Crater in A.D. 1064–1065, when a massive eruption sprayed molten rock, which solidified in the air and rained down in small cylinders. A large lava flow, the Kana-A flow, spewed out from the fissure, killing all within its deadly path. As the years passed, debris from further eruptions accumulated around the volcanic vent and the crater was slowly born. In 1180, the Bonito lava flow spewed from the fissure. Around 1250, sulfur and iron were vented and collected on the sides of the crater. The sulfur, combined with the oxidized iron, created an eerie glow that inspired John Wesley Powell to name the fissure Sunset Crater in 1885. Spread sporadically across the region of the Sunset Crater are cinder cones of the San Francisco Volcano Field. These cinder cones are actually tiny volcanoes that formed around volcanic vents. Many of these cones contain crater lakes.

Looming above Sunset Crater and the volcanic field is San Francisco Mountain (or San Francisco Peaks). San Francisco Mountain is a very old volcano that takes after the notorious Mount St. Helens, Mount Hood, and Mount Fujiyama. The northeast face is said to have exploded, just as Mount St. Helens did, creating a roughly hewn valley. The valley was later smoothed by glacial activity. The explosion also caused the mountain to collapse in upon itself and fall into the emptied magma chamber. The highest point in the state can be found on one of this mountain's lonesome peaks; Humphreys Peak rises to 12,670 feet.

Mining

Early Mining

When Coronado struck out for the Seven Cities of Cíbola, he was seeking seven golden cities filled with enough riches to quench his avarice, propel him into fame, and make even Cortés jealous. When he marched through Arizona, however, he discovered only disappointment. The local Indians had not been mining precious metals or crafting gold into splendid artifacts. Yet early inhabitants did learn the importance of some resources that could be mined, such as coal and salt.

According to archeological evidence, there were crude mining enterprises by A.D. 1000. The Hopi Indians first discovered coal in Arizona within the Jeddito Valley, just south of Black Mesa. Early mining attempts were comparable to today's strip mining. There is also evidence of primitive underground mining. For 300 years the Hopi extracted around 100,000 tons of coal to use in heating and cooking, a remarkable achievement considering the primitive tools used.

Salt mining was another enterprise of early Indians. Veins of sodium chloride, the stuff of table salt, were sought out between A.D. 1200 and 1400, near present-day Camp Verde. Several mining levels were created, including a subsurface shaft.

Silver

Silver mining in Arizona goes as far back as early Spanish explorers. The first known prospector was Antonio de Espejo in 1582. He searched the Verde River for the lustrous ore. In 1604, Juan de Oñate also discovered a large amount of silver while he was searching the Santa Maria and Bill Williams Rivers. Padre Kino, the great missionary and explorer, also had his hand in helping the silver industry. Kino's silver discoveries led to further mining expeditions, especially in 1774 when the Spanish began mining gold and silver around the little settlement of Tucson. Mining waned, however, after the Mexican Revolution. Soldiers were recalled from the garrisons that protected miners and sent to wage war against Apache Indians and outlaws. Arizona mining trickled and almost disappeared until the arrival of the Americans.

The California gold rush of 1849 was coming to a halt during the mid-1850s, and in response, a great influx of miners surged into Arizona. The Mowry Mine, previously used by the Spanish, came into American hands in 1858. Silver and lead were extracted, and there is a claim that the lead used for a large portion of Confederate bullets came from this mine. The Cerro Colorado Mine, just southwest of Tucson, was another highly profitable silver mine. Silver was discovered and mined around Prescott, Wickenburg, Oatman (in the Cerbat Mountains), and Yuma. In 1876, silver discoveries resulted in the Silver King Mine just north of Superior and the McMillan Mine near Globe. Silver mining near Globe originated when a man by the name of Munson was traveling near the Apache Mountains and stumbled across a huge chunk of nearly pure silver. The giant piece of ore weighed over a ton. Since he was traveling alone, Munson left a note on the boulder saying simply, "This is Munson's Chunk." After securing the note to the boulder, he headed to Globe to purchase the supplies he needed to break up his lode. Munson returned, broke up the silver (a piece of which is pictured above), and hauled it to Florence where he sold it for $20,000. Understandably excited, Munson followed up the sale with a wild drinking spree. The party ended when he was thrown out of a saloon into the chilling temperatures of a cold winter's night. Although Munson died of exposure shortly thereafter, silver mining around Globe would thrive in the region for many years.

A 31-pound silver nugget found near Globe in 1895

The year 1878 marks Ed Schieffelin's discovery of silver at Tombstone. The Bonanza Silver Mine was created, and silver production bolstered the town until the mines flooded. Surprisingly, Tombstone did not fall by the wayside but still remains the "town too tough to die." Eventually, by the 1900s, silver mining would take a backseat to profitable copper mining, and silver would be just a welcome byproduct of the copper mining process.

Gold and Placer Mining

A "placer" is an easily obtainable deposit of ore that has been weathered out of its bedrock through forces of erosion. The ore can then be sifted out from the less valuable rock by a variety of methods, such as sluicing and panning. In dryer climates, such as Arizona, another method, called dry-washing, was used. Dry-washing was quite easy; a miner only had to lay the dust in a pan and then toss it up into the air. The wind would carry off the lighter ore. Granted, this is not a good way to sift through a large amount of ore, but it worked. Miners working in Gila City used this technique in 1858.

American mining, particularly placer mining, in Arizona was primarily a backwash from the California gold rush of 1849. Easily obtainable ore was mostly played out during the mid-1850s, and heavy equipment was needed to reach deeper ore deposits. Most miners did not have the finances for such an enterprise, so many went east across the Sierra Nevada. From there, tales of gold brought them to Arizona.

In 1857, the junction of the Sacramento Wash and the Colorado River was the point of Arizona's first placer deposit gold rush. The next hot spot was Gila City, just 20 miles east of Yuma, in 1858. A wildfire of discoveries shot up: Gold placers were discovered on Lynx Creek and at Weaver and Rich Hill in Yavapai County. The city of Wickenburg rose up in 1863 after the very profitable Vulture Mine was established. Gold was discovered and mined around Prescott, Oatman (in the Cerbat Mountains), and Yuma. As placer mines gave out, heavy equipment had to be moved in to reach underground ore. Prospectors either got up and moved on to the next boomtown or were hired as miners by those setting up the equipment. Gold, however, would not be as sought after once more-profitable copper deposits were discovered. In the end, gold would just be a favorable byproduct of copper mining.

Hydralic Mining in Yavapai County, circa 1900

Copper

The history of copper mining in Arizona is not as extensive as the history of mining gold and silver. However, copper eventually became Arizona's mining staple. The Arizona Mining and Trading Company's New Cornelia Mine in Ajo was the earliest major copper mine. American miners gained access to the Ajo district following the Gadsden Purchase in 1853–54, which included the area of Arizona south of the Gila River to the current Mexican border. The Arizona Mining and Trading Company became Arizona's first incorporated mining company when it was established in August 1854, only weeks after the Gadsden Purchase had been ratified. More and more copper mines were established in Arizona, including the Planet Copper Mine near the Bill Williams River. When silver deposits were finally exhausted or became uneconomic after the price of silver slumped, copper became a stronger resource. The creation of the second transcontinental railroad also encouraged the copper trade. In 1888, copper produced $5 million a year more than all other metals. By 1937, copper production was worth $37.8 million and Arizona became the U.S. leader in copper production, thereby dwarfing both gold and silver mining. Today there are hardly any gold or silver mines operating in the state.

United Verde Copper Company Mine in Jerome, circa 1900

Copper mine near Globe, circa 1920

Currently, the major copper producers in Arizona are in six counties: Pima, Pinal, Cochise, Greenlee, Gila, and Yavapai. The mining of copper is a very expensive process, and a few large companies rule the industry. Ore is moved out of open pit mines and then processed in large mills. Next, railroads transport the product. Even though there are hardly any silver and gold mines in Arizona, those metals are still being extracted because copper ore is made up of 17 percent copper, 0.5 percent gold, and 2 to 3 percent silver. Extensive copper production can lead to large amounts of these valuable byproducts.

Arizona's Lost Mine Legends

Lost Adams Diggings

Near Fort Defiance, by the Arizona–New Mexico state line, and just a bit north of Window Rock, the fabled Adams Mine is said to exist. The story begins with Henry Adams (sometimes called Jim Adams). He established a small trading post at Fort Defiance and was making a tidy profit by catering to Indians, particularly the Navajo. One day, three Navajo entered the general store and bought a large amount of goods. They paid for their purchases with a glittering mound of gold nuggets. Adams was astonished. Every time the three came into the store, they'd pay for their goods in gold dust or gold nuggets. Adams was determined to find out the source of their wealth.

Slowly, he gained the Indians' confidence and after many visits with the three Navajo, Adams was able to discuss the location of the gold. In fact, the Navajo trusted Adams so much that they agreed to show him where the gold was coming from. There was one catch—Adams had to be blindfolded during the trip. Adams agreed and the four rode off to the mouth of a canyon. When the blindfold came off he was in a cavernous room and the floor was glittering with gold. The sight was breathtaking, but it was also brief as the blindfold quickly came back on. A blast of cool air hit him in the face, which made him think that the cave had more than one entrance. He asked the Indians if he could take some gold with him. Politely, the Indians refused and led him out of the cave.

Curiosity, and probably greed, overtook Adams and he slid the blindfold away from his eyes. He saw three similar peaks in a triangular formation. The Indians realized he had peaked, and feeling betrayed, they re-covered his eyes and hustled him away. That was the last time they ever met. The sight of so much gold possessed Adams, and upon his return he immediately sold his shop and spent his days, and his money, looking for the Navajo gold. Each expedition proved futile. He arrived in Tucson brokenhearted, but his stories captured the attention of Judge Griscom. Griscom financed further searches but Adams continually came up empty-handed. The financing was cut and Adams was left bankrupt. The search for the fortune consumed Adams and left him broken and despondent. When no one else would finance his search, Adams shot himself in the head and died in Tucson.

Lost Dutchman Mine

The legend of the Lost Dutchman Mine is deeply rooted in the foreboding peaks of the Superstition Mountains. The mine exists in legend, deeply nestled in various stories with each one loosely clinging to the same set of characters. However, the tales force one to question whether it is merely a campfire legend. Legends are usually based on truth, and legendary treasures have been found. Some fiercely argue that the mine is not a legend. Every year or so somebody claims to have found the Lost Dutchman Mine and proves once and for all that the myth is a reality and that those who died in the Superstition Mountains in search of the Dutchman's legacy did not die in vain. Perhaps the mine has been discovered, perhaps not. Those discovering a probable Lost Dutchman Mine adamantly believe in their findings. Still, their findings do not dissuade other searchers. The mine enters the imagination and inspires people to continually wander the mountainsides in search of glory and the glittering El Dorado that is the Lost Dutchman Mine.

There are many stories of the Lost Dutchman Mine, but most start with the wealthy Don Miguel Peralta. A hired hand named Hector had fallen in love with Don Miguel's beautiful daughter, Maria. One night the two met in a fit of passion. But Maria had second thoughts and ended up fleeing from Hector's arms and running naked through the ranch. What happened next has been debated. Hector fled either to find his fortune on his own or to find enough gold to befriend Don Miguel and dismiss any harsh feelings between the two. Hector headed north and discovered riches in the Superstition Mountains—which would later become known as the Lost Dutchman Mine. He either returned to Don Miguel to show him the wealth, or he drowned in a river. An Indian scout (whom Don Miguel sent to track Hector) returned to report the mine's location. In either version, Don Miguel wound up with the mine and became wealthy. As the Mexican War was ending, the United States was set to take possession of the Superstition Mountains. Don Miguel planned to take a final shipment from the mine in one large swoop. A large expedition of around 400 people set out and packed away a huge quantity of gold. As the expedition wound around the rugged canyons on the return journey, it headed straight into an Apache ambush. The band was slaughtered, the gold was strewn on the ground, and the mules were butchered for meat. Only two Mexican boys survived. They had ducked behind some bushes as the slaughter came to a close.

The bodies of their comrades and glittering piles of gold surrounded the boys. According to alternate versions of the story, the boys either grew up and returned to the mine or they stumbled into a lone prospector—either way Jacob Waltz (sometimes called Walz or Walzer) entered into the story. He gained the trust of the two Mexicans and they showed him the mine. Then Waltz sent each of them to his grave with a bullet from his gun. With a bit of bloodshed and underhandedness, the Dutchman claimed the mine, and it remained his from the 1870s until his death in 1891.

Actually, Jacob Waltz was not Dutch, but German. He reportedly worked at Henry Wickenburg's sensational Vulture Mine briefly before he was fired for stealing. He met up with Jacob Wiser and the two became partners. Wiser disappears from the story as time goes on. There is a rumor that Waltz killed him. Waltz even supposedly bragged that he had his own graveyard set up within the mountains for those who were too curious. Instead of building mansions or flagrantly relishing in his wealth, Waltz only hauled out enough gold to fuel some drunken mischief. He did retire eventually and took to raising chickens along the Salt River. He befriended Julia Roberts, who owned an ice cream parlor, and helped her pay off some debts, totaling around $500. Gossip says that their meetings went beyond friendship. When Waltz became ill, he turned to Julia, but she was unable to nurse him back to health. Upon his deathbed, during his final moments, Waltz drew a map to his gold mine. Then he died. Waltz also told his secret to a German baker named Reinhart Petrash.

Julia and Reinhart set out for the Superstition Mountains. They searched for three months but came up empty-handed. Supposedly, Waltz told Reinhart that a fortune of gold nuggets lay laced along a vein of rose quartz. Perhaps the earthquake of 1877 buried the mine, or perhaps the map was a cruel hoax. When Waltz died, his death gave rise to one of the greatest lost mine legends in the West—the legend of the Lost Dutchman Mine.

Lost Frenchman's Gold

The arrival of three Frenchmen was enough to cause a bit of a stir in Yuma. But when they deposited $8,000 worth of gold at Hooper and Company, the town buzzed with gossip. Townsfolk wondered who these strangers were and, more important, where they found their gold. When the Frenchmen rode out of town, five Mexicans were bound and determined to find the source of their gold. They trailed the Frenchmen to Agua Caliente, south of the Eagle Tail Mountains. However, the Frenchmen were aware of their pursuers and repeatedly tried to lose the Mexicans. They would often double back, reverse their direction, or break camp and set out in the middle of the night. The Mexicans gave up eventually and returned to Yuma. But the Frenchmen never returned to reclaim their lofty deposit. Rumor spread that they had met a horrible fate within the Eagle Tail Mountains. The secret of their mine seemingly disappeared with them.

In 1868, four years after the Frenchmen first arrived in

Yuma, A. H. Peeples reported that he met three Frenchmen working a placer mine in the Harquahala Mountains, just north of the Eagle Tails. The next time he came through the area he found a skeleton and the remains of a burned camp. Perhaps the bones were the remains of a luckless Frenchman. Peeples was not certain what had happened.

The next mention of the Frenchmen comes from the reputed Indian fighter King S. Woolsey (see page 73). He was chasing a group of Apache through Tenhachape Pass in the Eagle Tail Mountains and his party stumbled upon a mound of rich ore. The odd thing was that the ore was in plain sight; no one had bothered to hide it. A possible explanation was that the three Frenchmen had dropped the ore in order to make a quick escape. From whom they were escaping is unknown—possibly from hostile Indians.

The legend resurfaced in 1889 when an aged Mexican hired Old Bill Bear to guide him around the Eagle Tail Mountains. The Mexican said that he had seen the Frenchmen when he was just a boy. He also had seen the location of the Frenchmen's profitable placer mine. But the Mexican was unable to find the mine. Time had erased the exact location from his memory.

Lost Jesuit Treasure

The expulsion of the Jesuits in 1767 created many tales of hidden Jesuit gold. The expulsion began with King Carlos III of Spain. He banished approximately 5,000 Jesuit priests in order to reform the Spanish Empire and to further create absolute power. Rumor has it that just before Spanish soldiers captured the Jesuits, they hid their gold in various caches around Arizona. Scholars have debunked this theory, stating that the Jesuit expulsion happened suddenly and secretly and that the Jesuits had no chance to hide anything. In addition, they say that Jesuit missions in Arizona were very poor. Still, the legend persists and modern fortune-seekers have destroyed many historical treasures in search of gold. Feuds flared up between prospectors; one notable feud sparked by the search of the Jesuit treasure was between Celeste Jones and Ed Piper during the late 1950s and early 1960s.

Celeste Jones was a black opera singer in pursuit of Jesuit gold rumored to be in the Superstition Mountains. Stories also say that she financed her expedition with money gleaned from a mystic sect originating in southern California. The target of her search was Weaver's Needle, and to better search its recesses a giant ladder was built alongside it. An employee of hers fell to his death in 1963 while building the monstrous ladder. (The forest service eventually removed the ladder.)

Ed Piper's camp was also near Weaver's Needle and he was in search of the famous Lost Dutchman Mine. Gunfire erupted in November 1959 between the two sides, and a mine worker named Robert Marie died after Piper felled him with a bullet. Piper said that Marie harassed him and that the shot was an act of self-defense; no charges were ever filed. Piper's men guarded their region bitterly, and shots between Piper and Celeste Jones were often exchanged, usually with very little damage done. A married couple hiking through the area found themselves in the wrong place when one of Piper's men, Vern Rowlee, attacked them. Rowlee was killed in the scuffle. The feud between Jones and Piper was finally extinguished only when Piper died from an illness. Neither ever found any Jesuit gold.

Lost Pick Mine

Somewhere north of Phoenix, within the deep recesses of the Black Canyon, lie the fabled riches of the Lost Pick Mine. A miner named Brown told the story as he lay on his deathbed. Brown and his friend Davies were loitering around the general store when a Yavapai Indian walked in and started buying equipment. He paid in gold nuggets, which immediately caught the attention of the two prospectors. When the Indian left, they questioned the manager. The manager told the two that the Indian would come into town once a year and every time would buy what he needed with an ample amount of gold nuggets. The prospectors decided to follow the Yavapai out of town in order to discover the source of his wealth.

Strangely, the Indian made no attempt to cover his tracks. They followed him across Skunk Creek, New River, and Agua Fria. Then the Indian turned into a side canyon and simply vanished. The prospectors, seeing their chances for wealth vanishing as well, desperately tried to find his trail. Instead, they found gold.

A rich vein of gold crisscrossed the hillside. The two prospectors went to work. Over the next several days they amassed a fortune, but in their greed they forgot about the Indian. A band of warriors descended upon them and Davies was killed in a volley of gunfire. Brown escaped by hiding in the brush. The warriors didn't search for Brown, but rather turned and left the scene. Brown left the site as well, but not before marking the claim by driving his pickax into the hillside.

Many years later he returned to reclaim the treasure. But he couldn't find it. The legend of the Lost Pick Mine began. Years after Brown's death, someone claimed to see a rusty pick sunk into an outcropping but did nothing about it. According to legend, great wealth is still waiting to be discovered.

Lost Six-shooter Mine

"Found gold ledge by rocks 15 feet high. Two rocks alike. Knocked off some pieces. Very rich. Dust in air too thick to tell exact location. Think it is above ravine I come up 7 miles." These are the last words of prospector named Perkins (sometimes called Jenkins, or P. J.). His body was found somewhere between Quartzsite and the Yuma County line, near the old Bouse-Parker wagon road. Searchers found him face down and partly covered with sand. His holster was filled with gold. What happened to Perkins and the location of his Six-shooter Mine have become a legend in Arizona.

In 1884, Perkins, who was the superintendent of the Planet Mines on the Bill Williams River, had led some prospective investors to their stagecoach stop at Tyson's Wells (today's Quartzsite). With his duty done, he left on his horse, but along the way was caught in a raging sandstorm. Perkins took shelter behind an outcropping of rocks. He peered through the sand and discovered a vein of gold. The gold was quite rich, and he shoveled some specimens into his holster. His six-shooter and overcoat were left as markers. Perkins struck out for home.

The next day, those waiting for him at the Planet Mines were worried. Perkins's horse arrived, but there was no sign of the superintendent. Searchers found his body and the legend of the Six-shooter Mine was born. Prospectors scoured the area but could not find anything resembling Perkins's discovery.

Lost Waterfall Gold

The legend of the Lost Waterfall Gold takes place in the Grand Canyon. As the story goes, a prospector named "Long Tom" Watson settled into a little shack in Flagstaff. The shack was cluttered with newspaper and other debris used for insulation. Watson also frequently used the paper as kindling. While poking around the cabin, he found an old letter, which he promptly opened. To his amazement the letter contained a treasure map and a description about what had happened to the previous owner.

The letter was the last testimony of a dying prospector to his brother. The prospector had found gold in the Grand Canyon. On his way out of the canyon he noticed that two gunmen were following him. Before the two thieves reached him, he hid the gold behind a small waterfall. A gunfight ensued and the prospector was wounded. Eventually the dying man was discovered and brought home, but the letter he dictated before he died was never sent to his brother. Watson decided to capitalize on his lucky find.

He set off for the canyon and spent months searching along river tributaries and in the Havasu Canyon. His search gradually led him to the Tanner Trail, where the disheartened Watson suddenly discovered a waterfall flowing into a spring. He eagerly reached into the waterfall and found an old sack that was full of gold. Quickly, he filled his pockets with the gold. But he slipped off a ledge, suffered a blow to the head, and broke his leg. Watson was able to drag himself onto his burro and hobble into Flagstaff. What happened to the gold is unknown. Watson did return to the spot but couldn't find the waterfall. Despondent, Watson committed suicide.

Animals

Mammals

Abert's Squirrel

Found in the mountains of Arizona, Abert's squirrels (also called tassel-eared squirrels) have grizzled gray, black, or reddish sides and backs, with white or black bellies. These tree squirrels live in ponderosa pine forests, feeding on the pine cones, bark, buds, and twigs of the trees. They build bulky nests of twigs high in the pines, where they sleep at night, court, mate, and raise their young. Abert's squirrels do not hibernate; they remain in their nests during cold weather and venture out to recover stored food below. Mating chases last all day in late winter, during which males frantically chase the females. A litter of about four young is usually born in April or May, after a gestation period of about 46 days.

Abert's squirrel

Antelope Squirrel

The two types of antelope squirrels found in Arizona are the white-tailed antelope squirrel, found in the northwestern part of the state, and Harris's antelope squirrel, found in the central, southern, and southwestern portions of the state. Both of these ground squirrels are pale buff in summer, but turn gray in winter, with a single white stripe along the sides of their body. Neither have stripes on their faces. These squirrels hold their tails vertically when running, as the American antelope or pronghorn does when it flees. Harris's antelope squirrels are slightly larger than white-tailed antelope squirrels. Both live in the burrows they dig. White-tailed antelope squirrels are most active in midmorning and late afternoon, becoming dormant during hot or dry periods. Harris's antelope squirrels remain active throughout the day, regardless of heat. Both of these omnivorous creatures eat seeds, nuts, and fruits, although they may also feed on insects. Water is generally metabolized from food. Their calls are easily recognized loud trills that sound like a mix between a bird and a katydid.

Antelope squirrel

Badger

Badgers measure about 2 feet long with short legs, clawed feet, and shaggy gray-brown coats. A white stripe reaches from midway on their pointy snouts back to their shoulders. They have bushy, short yellowish tails. Found in open grasslands, sagebrush, and brushy areas, badgers use their powerful legs and front claws to dig out ground squirrels and other rodents. They are most active at night and make burrowed homes in the ground.

Badger

Beaver

Beavers are very large rodents with thick brown fur, chunky bodies, short legs, rounded heads, small rounded ears, yellowish-orange front incisors, webbed hind feet, and flat, hairless, paddle-shaped tails. Their weight ranges from 30 to 60 pounds. Beavers, who live in lakes, streams, ponds, and rivers, eat bark and twigs. Because they do not hibernate, they collect large caches of twigs and branches to eat in their lodges during the winter. Beavers have thick layers of fat and waterproof fur, so icy waters do not bother them. Skin flaps close over their ears and nostrils when they are submerged. Their webbed feet aid in swimming. Their eyes have clear membrane covers that allow them to see in water and protect them from floating debris. A beaver can remain submerged for up to 15 minutes without needing to come up for air. Beavers build dams of

Beaver

sticks and mud across streams and slow rivers. They gnaw down trees, strip them, cut them into small sections, and weave them into dams, holding the logs in place with mud. They also build lodges with one or more entrances below water and the living chamber well above waterline. Beavers mate for life, which can be as long as 20 years. In the spring, furry beaver kits are born in the lodges with their eyes open.

The beaver population almost died out during the nineteenth century because of unregulated trapping for their fashionable fur (used primarily for hats), but the beaver population has been re-established and is thriving.

Bison

The bison has an imposing appearance, with its dark brown, shaggy hair, woolly mane, massive head, high shoulders, short legs, and long tufted tail. Bison are the largest terrestrial animals in North America. Cows range in weight from 800 to 1,000 pounds, and bulls can weigh well over 2,000 pounds. Both sexes have short, black, sharply curved horns with pointy tips. Bison are herd animals that graze in groups of at least a dozen but also in massive herds; they feed mainly on grasses and shrubs. In winter, they clear snow from vegetation with their hooves and heads. Most active in early morning and late afternoon, they rest in the midday heat, chewing cud or dust-bathing. Bison are good swimmers and so buoyant that their heads, humps, and tails remain above water. When frightened, bison will stampede, galloping at high speeds. Males may battle each other in an attempt to mate with a cow. Fights can involve butting, horn locking, shoving, and hooking. When butting, males walk to within 20 feet of each other, raise their tails, and charge. Their foreheads collide with the force of freight trains, and without apparent injury, they continue charging until one animal gives up.

Bison

Once the North American population of bison was estimated to be 70 million. However, around 1830, the federal government encouraged a mass extermination in an attempt to subdue the Indians, and nearly all the bison were killed. Today's bison population is estimated at 30,000. You are unlikely to encounter bison on the open range as you travel the routes in this book. They are primarily found in national parks, refuges, and game farms. Because they are unpredictable at all times, do not approach bison too closely for any reason.

Black Bear

Black bears can actually be black, brown, or cinnamon. Their bodies are powerful and densely furred, with slight shoulder humps, small rounded ears, small close-set eyes, and five dark, strongly curved front claws on each foot. Females range in weight from 120 to 200 pounds, and males range from 200 to 400 pounds. Nocturnal and solitary, black bears prefer forested habitats throughout the year, although they can sometimes be seen on open slopes searching for fresh greens. They usually make their dens in tree cavities, under logs, in brush piles, or under buildings; the dens are lined with leaves or grass. Black bears are omnivorous; they eat both plants and animals. They feast on grasses, sedges, berries, fruits, tree bark, insects, honey, eggs, fish, rodents, and even miscellaneous garbage. In the fall they go into a feeding frenzy to gain as much weight as possible to get them through their winter hibernation, often adding a 4-inch layer of fat to keep them warm and nourished. During hibernation, black bears crawl into their dens, and their bodies go dormant for the winter; they do not eat, drink, urinate, or defecate during their long sleep. Their kidneys continue to make urine, but it is reabsorbed into their bloodstream. They awaken by an internal clock in the spring and wander out in search of food. The black bear has a lumbering walk but can actually travel up to 30 miles per hour in a bounding trot. Black bears are powerful swimmers, able fishers, and agile tree climbers. They breed in the summer; the females undergo a phenomenon in which the fertilized egg passes into the uterus but changes very little until late fall, when it implants and then begins to grow quickly. Females commonly give birth to a litter of one to five young in January or February.

Black bear

Black-tailed Jackrabbit

Jackrabbits, also known as hares, are very similar in appearance to cottontails, but are larger and have longer ears, bigger feet, and longer hind legs. It is suggested that the name jackrabbit originated because their large ears resemble those of jackasses. Black-tailed jackrabbits have fur that is mottled gray and brown, grizzled with black. The tail has a black stripe above, which extends onto the rump, and a white border. Their very long ears are brown with black tips. Does (females) are larger than bucks, which is unusual in mammals. Their weight varies from four to eight pounds. In summer, jackrabbits eat mostly green plants, such as clover and flowers. In winter, they rely more on shrubs and dried vegetation. Their ears are so sensitive that they can detect the muted sound of a coyote as its fur brushes against the grass. When threatened, they first freeze, laying their ears back to be less conspicuous; their coats assist with camouflage. If this fails, they can move from a hiding place like lightning, running at speeds up to 35 miles per hour and changing direction instantly. If they are running at moderate speeds, every fourth or fifth leap is higher so they can get a broader view of their surroundings. Unlike cottontails, young hares are born fully furred, with their eyes open. The female puts each young hare into an individual

Black-tailed jackrabbit

form, or depression, in the ground, thus decreasing a predator's chance of taking her entire litter. She keeps her distance by day and comes several times to nurse at night so that she attracts less attention.

Bobcat

Bobcats are a reddish tawny color, grayer in winter, with dark spots on their bodies and legs. Their ears are slightly tufted; their bellies are usually buff and spotted. Bobcats get their name from their short, stubby, bobbed tails that have three horizontal, dark stripes. Females range in weight from 15 to 25 pounds, and males range from 20 to 35 pounds. The most common wildcat in North America, bobcats live in virtually every habitat below 10,000 feet—ranging from dry, rocky mountainsides to forests to brushy, arid lands. Bobcats have also been known to adapt to swamps and farmlands. Because of their secretive nature, bobcats are seldom seen or heard. When threatened, they make a cough-bark sound and during mating season they yowl. Bobcats are efficient predators with keen eyes and ears to help them locate prey in poor light. When hunting, they stalk and move at blinding speed for short distances, then pounce and make the kill. Their primary diet consists of rabbits and hares, ground squirrels, mice, birds, insects, lizards, and frogs. Generally solitary animals, bobcats come together mainly for mating. Litters of two or three kittens are born in April and May in maternity dens, which are usually in hollow logs or under rock ledges or fallen trees and lined with dry leaves. The bobcat population is currently stable, although trapping by humans once nearly eradicated the species.

Bobcat

Cottontail

One of the most abundant animals in nature, cottontails are very similar in appearance and behavior to jackrabbits, except that they tend to be smaller and have shorter ears, smaller feet, and shorter hind legs. They do not turn white in winter. Of the several types in Arizona, the buff-brown desert cottontail is found in grasslands as well as in creosote brush and desert areas. It will climb sloping trees and is known to use logs and stumps as lookout posts after dark. Nuttal's cottontail, also known as mountain cottontail, is grayish, with a white belly and black-tipped ears. It inhabits rocky wooded or brushy areas, often with sagebrush, throughout Arizona. It uses either dense vegetation for shelter or, when not available, it uses burrows and rocky crevices. Because of their vulnerability at birth, cottontails are born in maternal nests, which the pregnant female finds and prepares about a week before giving birth. She locates a suitable spot where brush or high grass provides protection, and makes a saucerlike depression in the ground, lining it with her own downy fur, soft grasses, and leaves. Adults may have three or four litters per year in a good habitat. Unlike hares, cottontails are born naked, with their eyes closed.

Cottontail

Coyote

The coyote is grayish brown with rusty or tan fur on its legs, feet, and ears. Canine in appearance, with pointed muzzles and bushy tails, coyotes range in weight from 30 to 50 pounds. Their tracks appear much like those of a domestic dog but in a nearly straight line; the hind feet usually come down in foreprints, with four toes per print. Coyotes rarely seek shelter and remain in dens only when they have pups. They are both carnivores and scavengers, and their opportunistic diet includes rabbits, mice, squirrels, birds, frogs, snakes, grasshoppers, fruits, berries, and sheep and other domestic livestock. In winter they often eat carrion from larger animals, especially deer, which is an important food source. They are vocal animals whose call is commonly heard at dusk or dawn, and consists of a series of barks and yelps, followed by a prolonged howl and short yaps. Coyotes howl as a means of communicating with one another; one call usually prompts other coyotes to join in, resulting in a chorus audible for significant distances. They are stealthy runners and can cruise at 25 to 35 miles per hour, making leaps as high as 14 feet. They hunt singly or in pairs, acting as a relay team to chase and tire their prey. Coyotes are monogamous and often mate for life. Their maternal dens are usually found or dug by the female under large boulders, in caves, on hillsides, or along river embankments. The openings, or mouths, of these dens usually measure several feet wide and are often marked by a mound of earth and tracks. A coyote might use the same den from year to year, unless it is disturbed. Coyotes breed in February, March, and April and give birth to a litter of four or more pups by May.

Coyote

The population of coyotes is flourishing, despite the popular demand for their fur in the 1970s and 1980s. Their main enemies are humans.

Elk

Elk are large, one-hoofed deer with brown bodies, tawny-colored rumps, thick necks, and sturdy legs. Cows range in weight from 500 to 600 pounds. Bulls range from 600 to 1,000 pounds and average about 6 feet in height. Only males have antlers, which they shed each year. Once widely ranged, elk are primarily mountain dwellers in the summer and valley dwellers in the winter. They remain in herds throughout the year and feed on grasses, shrubs, and trees. In the late summer and early fall, bulls display mating behavior caused by their high levels of testosterone: They begin thrashing bushes and "bugling"—making a sound that begins as a bellow, changes

Elk

to a shrill whistle or scream, and ends with a series of grunts. This vocalization broadcasts a bull's presence to other bulls and functions as a call of domination to the cows. Bulls become territorial and make great efforts to keep the cows together (a harem may consist of up to 60 cows), mating as they come into heat and keeping other bulls at a distance. Bulls often clash antlers in mating jousts but are seldom hurt. Calves are born in the late spring after a gestation period of about nine months. Elk calves are primarily brown with light spots until the early fall of their first year.

Gray Fox

Gray foxes are recognizable by their salt-and-pepper gray coats, rust-colored legs and feet, white throat and belly, black-tipped tail, and a dark streak down the spine. The gray fox weighs 7 to 13 pounds and is about 22 to 30 inches long with a 10- to 15-inch tail. This animal prefers heavier cover and is more nocturnal than the red fox, so it is rarely seen. It lives in wooded and brushy slopes in the valleys. It is the only fox that commonly climbs trees and has been known to rest, hide, or escape into them. Gray foxes sometimes raise their young in large, hollow trees, some of which have entrance holes as high as 20 feet. More often, dens are located among rocks, in cliffsides, or in hollow trees or logs. Because the gray fox's pelt is undesirably bristly, the animal has never been heavily hunted or trapped. Like other foxes, the gray fox's worst enemies are humans.

Gray fox

Javelina

The javelina, or collard peccary, is descended from large pigs that inhabited North America about 25 million years ago. At a height of about 2 feet, the javelina is smaller than domestic pigs and wild pigs, with straight tusks, an erectable mane, and a whitish collar. Average weight varies between 30 and 65 pounds. Javelinas have large heads and shoulders, relatively small legs and hindquarters, a piglike snout, and heavy, bristly, grizzled gray hair. Only the tips of their tusks protrude beyond their lips; in full, the tusks measure about 1 to 2 inches. Javelinas are becoming extremely common throughout the southern two-thirds of Arizona. They form herds, ranging from 6 to 30 animals, which may break up into temporary subherds for feeding purposes. These social animals will often stand side by side, head to tail, each grooming the other by rubbing its head along the rump, legs, and scent glands. Prickly pears are a favorite food, as they also provide a water source. Javelinas usually give birth to twins during the summer; they are born with yellowish or reddish hair. Humans should use caution, as families with young may charge when approached or disturbed.

Javelina

Kangaroo Rat

Kangaroo rats are so named for their upright hopping gait, their huge hind legs and feet, and a long furry tail on which they balance. The three types found in Arizona are Ord's kangaroo rat (most common), desert kangaroo rat (in the southeast), and banner-tailed kangaroo rat (in the southwest). Generally, they have buffy-reddish or blackish color above, with white underparts, and approximately 6- to 8-inch tails. Their large eyes enable them to see in minimal light. Kangaroo rats can survive in arid country without ever consuming water as a result of several amazing conservation features nature has given their bodies. Their nasal passages are elongated to cool the outgoing breath and recapture the moisture; their kidneys concentrate salts and urea between 10 and 20 times before eliminating them; and their feces are concentrated to contain 50 percent less water. These nocturnal creatures spend their days in their underground burrows with the opening plugged up, so as to maintain a stable temperature. Kangaroo rats eat seeds and when out foraging, can store up to a teaspoon in their cheeks for later caching. As a defense against predators (rattlesnakes, owls, badgers, skunks, foxes, coyotes), kangaroo rats kick sand into the face of their attacker. When pursued, the kangaroo rat speeds off in a zigzag pattern, changing course quickly, using its tail as a rudder—and sometimes leaping as far as 10 feet. Adults live a solitary existence except during mating, when males vie against each other for females. The reproductive season is concurrent with rainfall and new vegetative growth.

Kangaroo rat

Mule Deer

Gray in winter, the mule deer's coat changes to reddish-brown in summer. Some have a whitish throat and rump patch. Their tails are either black-tipped or black on top. Mule deer have large mulelike ears that move almost constantly. They are medium-sized deer with stocky bodies and long, slim, sturdy legs. Does range in weight from 100 to 180 pounds, and bucks range from 150 to 400 pounds. Only the buck has antlers; he sheds them in the winter and begins to grow another set in the spring. Summers are spent in mountain pastures, alpine meadows, and sometimes logged areas. The onset of winter drives them to lower slopes, where food supplies are more abundant. Summer forage includes grasses, sagebrush, serviceberry, and chokecherry. In winter they browse on twigs, shrubs, and acorns. Mule deer are mostly active in the mornings, evenings, and on moonlit nights. A social group general-

Mule deer

ly consists of the doe and her fawn or twins, while the bucks often remain solitary. During the November breeding season, bucks become increasingly active and intolerant of one another, sometimes engaging in conflict or vigorous fights, during which each tries, with antlers enmeshed, to force down the other's head. Injuries are rare, and usually the loser withdraws. Mule deer breed in mid-November; fawns usually arrive in June, July, and August, with spotted coats for camouflage. A doe giving birth for the first time normally produces a single fawn, whereas an older doe tends to have twins.

Porcupine

Porcupines have gray-brown, chunky bodies, high arching backs, and short legs. Yellowish hair covers long quills all over their backs, rumps, and tails. These rodents measure up to 2 feet in length, have an 8-inch tail, and range in weight from 10 to 28 pounds. Next to the beaver, they are the largest rodents in Arizona. Found throughout the state, even in very "scrubby" and desert areas, where they eat cactus and other available foods, porcupines are active year-round. They are slow-moving animals with poor eyesight, but are equipped with thousands of barbed quills for protection against predators. Contrary to popular belief, porcupines do not throw their quills; quills are released from the porcupine's body and penetrate the attacker's skin. Quills are hard to pull out, they readily work themselves in farther, which can produce painful and even fatal results. Porcupines are primarily nocturnal, but they can occasionally be seen resting in treetops during the day. They make their dens in logs or caves and use them for sleeping and birthing. Kits are born in May and June, after a gestation period of seven months. They are born headfirst, with quills aimed backward.

Porcupine

Prairie Dog

These heavily built ground squirrels have short legs and tails. Vocalized yaps earned it the name "dog". Prairie dogs are active during daylight hours only, and they are most energetic at dawn and dusk. They feed on grass, plants, and insects and have a particular fondness for grasshoppers. Black-tailed prairie dogs are found in the extreme southeast corner of Arizona. They are brownish-yellow on the back and sides, with whitish bellies, small ears, and black-tipped tails. Black-tailed prairie dogs are social animals that live in colonies, or "prairie dog towns," composed of several families. On purely a friendly level, they approach each other and touch noses and incisors to "kiss." They communicate by barking a variety of different sounds and groom each other socially—not as an act of courtship. Black-tailed prairie dogs retreat to their burrows for brief periods during warm summer days to escape the afternoon heat or for longer periods of time when the weather is severely cold. They do not hibernate but go dormant in bitter winter weather, arousing to feed during warm spells. They give birth in their burrows to one litter of deaf, blind, and hairless pups after a gestation period of about 30 days. Gunnison's prairie dogs are a yellowish color mixed with black, with slightly paler bellies and short white-tipped tails. The smallest of the prairie dog species in Arizona, they are found in the northern portion of the state. Gunnison's prairie dogs are less social than black-tailed prairie dogs; they form smaller communities that are considerably less developed. Their modes of communication include a distinctive danger call that is often repeated and gets louder as the urgency intensifies. Females typically give birth to one litter in May, after a gestation period of 27 to 33 days.

Black-tailed prairie dog

Pronghorn

Pronghorns are pale or reddish tan in color on the upper body and outer legs, with two white bands across the throat, a white rump patch, white chest, white lower sides, and white inner legs. The buck has vertical black markings from eyes to snout and on the cheek. Does range in weight from 75 to 110 pounds, and bulls range from 110 to 130 pounds. Both sexes have a set of horns; the doe's horns are seldom longer than 3 or 4 inches, but a buck's horns can grow as long as 20 inches, curving back and slightly inward. Horn sheaths are shed each year. Pronghorns are common and highly visible, preferring open rolling plains or grasslands. Active night and day, they alternate bits of sleep with watchful feeding. Pronghorns feed on grasses and forbs in summer and sagebrush and other shrubs in winter. They are the fastest animal in the Western Hemisphere and have been clocked at 80 miles per hour, although 45 miles per hour is more usual. Pronghorns run with their mouths open, not from exhaustion but to gasp extra oxygen. When it senses danger, a pronghorn snorts and erects the white hairs on its rump (twice as long as the body hairs), which creates a flash of white as it flees and warns other pronghorns of danger. If a surprise attack forces a pronghorn to fight rather than flee, it uses its sharp hooves, which can effectively drive off a coyote. Adult bucks establish territories in March and hold them through the September breeding season. Throughout the spring and summer, nonterritorial bucks gather into bachelor herds, while the does and fawns drift on and off the territories. By late September, terri-

Pronghorn

torial bucks attempt to hold groups of does and fawns on their territories for breeding and keep other bucks away. These territories are abandoned after the breeding season; horns are shed, and all ages and both sexes congregate on the winter range. The young are usually born in April, May, and June.

Pronghorn populations were reduced to fewer than 25,000 in the mid-1920s due to the fencing of range land, which hampered migration and foraging (pronghorns cannot leap fences like deer—they crawl under them instead). Most barbed-wire fences in pronghorn territory now have an unbarbed bottom wire to accommodate their movement. With management and transplantation of herds by game departments, the pronghorn population is steadily increasing; current estimates are over 500,000. There is, however, an endangered subspecies, the Sonoran pronghorn, in extreme southwestern Arizona.

Raccoon

Raccoons, who have salt-and-pepper coloring with black masks across their eyes and black-and-white ringed tails, appear slightly hunchbacked. They are about 2 feet long, with 10-inch tails. They range in weight from 10 to 25 pounds. Raccoons are found near water, living in dens in hollow trees, logs, rock crevices, or ground burrows. They feed mostly along streams, lakes, and ponds, and their favorite foods include fruits, nuts, grains, insects, eggs, and fish. While raccoons appear to wash their food before eating it, they are actually feeling for the edible parts. Raccoons do not hibernate in winter, although they may sleep for several days during cold weather. Raccoons give birth in April or May to litters of between two and seven young. Naturalists estimate that there are 15 to 20 times as many raccoons now as there were in the 1930s.

Raccoon

Ringtail

Also called ring-tailed cat, this nocturnal member of the raccoon family is Arizona's state mammal. The ringtail is appropriately named for the black and white rings encircling its bushy 15-inch tail. Their catlike bodies are yellowish brown or gray, with whitish buff below. Their heads resemble those of foxes, with big eyes and pointy ears. They inhabit rocky areas, canyons, and large trees with hollows, from deserts to lower mountain forests. Solitary and nocturnal, ringtails spend their days in a den—usually a crevice in rocks, padded with grass, moss, or leaves. They emerge at night to hunt insects, scorpions, lizards, snakes, birds and eggs, and small animals. Despite their short legs, ringtails are excellent climbers of trees and they have the traction to scale rock walls. They are particularly nimble on rock ledges and can turn around with a surefooted hop if the ledge runs out. When threatened, ringtails will scream at their predator and they might secrete a foul-smelling liquid. Females typically give birth to three or four young in May or June in their dens. They are born white, fuzzy, and stubby-tailed. Ringtails were once called miner's cats because of their propensity for catching and eating mice in and around mines.

Ringtail

River Otter

Dark brown in color, with silvery fur on their underparts, river otters have long, cylindrical bodies; small, rounded ears; large noses; small, beady eyes; long whiskers; and thick, furry tails. River otters are about 3 feet long, with 10- to 18-inch tails; they range in weight from 10 to 25 pounds. River otters live in large rivers, streams, and beaver ponds and feed primarily on fish, frogs, and aquatic invertebrates. River otters can stay under water for two to three minutes because their pulse slows and skin flaps close over their ears and nostrils. They have powerful feet and webbed toes to propel them through the water. Stiff whiskers help them hunt by feel under water. Cold waters do not bother them because their dense fur and oily underfur does not allow water to reach their skin. River otters tend to use beaver and muskrat burrows as their own. They are very playful animals that spend much time frolicking and chasing each other. Pups are born—furry, blind, and helpless—in litters of one to four in March, April, and May. The otters in Arizona are transplants from a Louisiana population brought through a re-establishment program.

River otter with trout

Rock Squirrel

Rock squirrels are the largest of the ground squirrels. They are 17 to 21 inches, with a 6- to 10-inch tail. Coloring is mottled gray-brown in front and darker behind, with buff bellies. Tails are long and bushy with sprinklings of brown and buff edges. True to its name, the rock squirrel dwells in rocky locales throughout Arizona—such as cliffs, canyon walls, talus slopes, and boulder piles—and digs its den in the ground below. Rock squirrels dine on berries, nuts, plants, and carrion and often collect food to transport and store in their dens. They are often seen sitting on or running among rocks, but they are also good tree climbers. Vocalizations include an alarm call, which is short and followed by a lower-pitched trill. They have a sharp, sometimes quavering, whistle. Females normally bear two litters during the year, one in late spring or early summer and the other in late summer or early fall.

Rock squirrel

Striped Skunk

A member of the weasel family, the striped skunk has a black coat, usually with two broad white stripes on the back, meet-

Striped skunk

ing at the head and tail. Striped skunks have a narrow vertical stripe on their foreheads, white caps, and bushy tails that can range from black to varying amounts of white. Striped skunks are typically 2 feet in length with 9-inch tails. The western spotted skunk has a smaller body, approximately 16 inches in length, with a 9-inch tail. Their bodies are black with small horizontal white stripes on the neck and shoulders and irregular stripes and spots on their sides. The contrast of a skunk's coloration and patterns with its environment demonstrates nature's protection; instead of blending, the boldness is a way of advertising to potential enemies that the skunk is not to be contended with. If appearance fails to be a deterrent, the skunk will face an intruder, arch and elevate its tail, chatter its teeth, and stomp the ground with its front feet in a show of aggression. Finally, the skunk will emit an oily, foul-smelling sulfurous spray from its anal glands, which is repulsive enough to drive predators away. When a direct hit is scored to the eyes, the irritating substance causes a temporary loss of vision. Their primary predator is the great horned owl. Both the striped skunk and the spotted skunk are omnivores with a widely varied diet, ranging from insects, small mammals, and eggs to seasonal fruits. They are primarily nocturnal and live in underground burrows that they have either dug themselves or taken over from other animals. Young are usually born in the spring to fiercely protective mothers. Skunks are currently the main carriers of rabies in the United States.

White-tailed Deer

White-tailed deer are grayish brown in winter and reddish brown in summer. Their tails are white below and brown above. They have small ears and a slim, graceful appearance. Does range in weight from 120 to 180 pounds, and bucks range from 150 to 400 pounds. Only the buck has antlers; he sheds them in the winter and begins to grow another set in the spring. White-tailed deer are occasionally found in farmlands, but they prefer a somewhat denser woodland habitat in riparian areas. These deer have adapted to live near human communities but are timid and elusive, primarily nocturnal. White-tailed deer forage on a variety of foods—including shrubs, trees, acorns, and grass—according to what is in season. They also enjoy garden vegetables (corn, peas, lettuce, apples, herbs) and other agricultural items. When nervous, the white-tailed deer snorts through its nose and stamps its hooves; when spooked, it raises its white tail, thus alerting other deer of danger. They are good swimmers, can run 30 to 40 miles per hour, and can jump 30 feet horizontally and more than 8 feet vertically. White-tailed deer breed in much the same manner as mule deer, except that buck fighting is less common.

White-tailed deer

Woodrat

Also known as the pack rat, woodrats are brownish gray above, with tawny-colored sides. Their feet, bellies, undersides of tail, and throats are white. They measure about 12 inches in length and have a 4- to 6-inch tail. The nickname "pack rat" was given because of the animal's tendency to accumulate all sorts of objects, such as cow pies, newspaper, aluminum cans, coins, and jewelry. Pack rats have a particular fondness for shiny objects. They line their "houses" with a collection of treasures, which serve as insulation to maintain consistent internal temperatures. Their houses are bulky, approximately 5 feet wide by 2 feet tall with a nest inside—constructed of various materials, mostly stacks of cacti, twigs, and cow droppings. Often the houses are built at the base of a cactus, the needles of which are used by the woodrat to cover its entrance. Only one adult inhabits each house. Badgers are the only animals that tear woodrat nests apart, but other predators include snakes, coyotes, owls, ringtails, and weasels. Woodrat diets consist of prickly pears, junipers, yuccas, chollas, and other leafy plants. They obtain water from the foods they consume. Woodrats are believed to communicate by drumming their hind feet. Females give birth to two to four litters per year, usually yielding two or three young per litter.

Desert woodrat

Desert woodrat nest

Reptiles

Arizona Coral Snake

Coral snakes are brightly colored small snakes with thin glossy bodies. They grow to about 24 inches in length and are distinctly marked with patterns of black and red rings, each separated by a yellow or white band. The head and tail are black. Generally, they are found in rocky, hilly areas in the desert and low mountains of Arizona. The venom of coral snakes is about twice as poisonous as that of the rattlesnake, yet they are of little threat to humans, partly because their small head and fangs prevent them from injecting much venom; also their nocturnal, burrowing lifestyle makes encounters with humans extremely rare. The venom is, however, effective at killing prey, which ranges from lizards to small snakes. When cornered, coral snakes coil and hide their heads while elevating and waving their tails, which are colored like

Arizona coral snake

their heads—as a decoy. Sometimes a snake might use its tail to "strike" and might emit a popping sound from its anal opening to frighten aggressors. To tell a coral snake from the similarly colored mountain king snakes, remember: "Red on black is a friend of Jack; red on yellow—fear this fellow," which means that if red bands touch black bands, the snake is OK; if red bands touch yellow bands, it's a coral snake.

Bullfrog

Bullfrogs grow to about 6 inches, which is large for a frog. They are yellowish green above, with dark mottling; their bellies are pale yellow. The bullfrog was introduced into Arizona from the eastern United States in order to supplement the diet of cowboys. Apparently, cowboys did not like the idea of eating frogs, so the appetizer never caught on. The frogs were let loose, and they eventually made their way into the waterways. Now bullfrogs are devouring practically everything in sight, including tarantulas, scorpions, and even birds. Bullfrogs have few predators and compete with native frogs and toads for food and space. There are some legislative proposals to exterminate bullfrogs.

Bullfrog

Chuckwalla

A harmless member of the iguana family, the stout-bodied chuckwalla is the second-largest lizard in the United States, second in size only to the Gila monster. Chuckwalla males grow to a length of 18 inches, while the females are slightly smaller. Adult males have reddish or gray backs and blackish heads, necks, and legs. Young chuckwallas have four or five broad bands across the body and three or four on the tail. Although these bands are usually lost in adulthood, females tend to retain them. Small scales cover the body, with larger scales protecting ear openings. Chuckwalla bodies have loose folds of sandpapery skin around the neck. Their tails are thick, long, and blunt. This lizard is able to change colors somewhat in response to changes in light, temperature, and other variables. This diurnal lizard emerges in the morning, and before seeking food, it basks in the sun until its optimum body temperature of 100°F is reached. On occasion, it is not unusual to see several chuckwallas sunning themselves at the same time. Strictly herbivorous, chuckwallas eat fruit, creosote bushes, leaves, buds, and flowers. When a chuckwalla senses danger, it scurries between rocks and lodges itself tightly in crevices by taking a breath and inflating itself—making forced extraction nearly impossible. If a predator in pursuit grabs a chuckwalla by its tail, the tail separates from the body and proceeds to wriggle, thus distracting the predator and giving the lizard a chance to escape. Another tail will grow back, smaller than the previous one. This phenomenon can occur several times. Females lay an average of eight eggs in rock crevices every year or perhaps every other year.

Chuckwalla

Collard Lizard

These robust lizards have bodies that measure 3 to 5 inches, with large heads, narrow necks, and long tails. Including tails, collard lizards reach lengths of about 12 inches. The males have blue-green bodies with yellow spots. The females are typically gray or brown with creamy spots. Found in rocky canyons, rocky ledges, and boulder-strewn areas, collard lizards seek out boulders to serve as areas for basking, warmth, and lookouts. They spring from boulders to seize lizards and insect prey with a rush. They are typically active from April through October. Collard lizards run from danger on their hind legs with tails in the air.

Collard lizard

Couch's Spadefoot Toad

Couch's spadefoot, also known as desert spadefoot, is a medium-small toad that grows to 3 inches. Its color is dull yellow to greenish yellow (male more yellow than female), with a network of brown to black spots or blotches (dark markings are more extensive in females). The eyes have vertical elliptical pupils. Spadefoot toads are named for their built-in digging tools—a black sickle-shaped spade on each hind leg, which they use to "swim" through mud. These peculiar little toads are almost entirely dependent on water; if exposed to the arid environment, unable to retreat to shelter, they dehydrate quickly and mummify. But, amazingly, these creatures are most abundant in the driest of areas. They spend dry parts of the year dormant in burrows (either self-dug or in those of other animals) near water ponds that are likely to form after a rainstorm. They may spend as much as two years underground, waiting for summer rains so they can emerge, if only for a few days, to feed and mate. When the rains begin, they tunnel upward at night, using their digging implements, and congregate by the thousands to rehydrate and absorb water directly through a porous skin patch on their bellies. During this time they participate in a feeding and breeding frenzy. Females produce hundreds of eggs at a time; which must metamorphose into air-breathing toads before their aquatic environment vanishes. The eggs of this species hatch at the fastest rate of any amphibian, becoming tadpoles within one day and maturing within about one week. The first tadpoles hatched produce a hormone that slows the growth of subsequent siblings, thus giving the eldest a greater chance of survival. The presence of dead tadpoles further stimulates the survivors to grow even quicker. Those that survive jump out of the drying ponds and begin digging their solitary burrows. Lifespan is 6 to 12 years.

Couch's spadefoot toad

Desert Tortoise

Desert tortoises have high-domed shells and stocky limbs that are covered with large conical scales. Adult males grow to about 15 inches and weigh 20 pounds; females are slightly smaller. These completely terrestrial creatures are masters at conserving water and energy in the harshest of conditions. They derive most of their water from food and then store up to a cup in their bladders for use during dry seasons. After heavy rains, tortoises will drink so much water that one tortoise was documented as having weighed 43 percent more after drinking! To minimize water loss they incur from breathing, desert tortoises hibernate in humid burrows, occupied by one to many individuals, as far as 30 feet underground—ideally beneath a wash. Their hard, domed shells serve as insulation against moisture loss and temperature fluctuation in addition to providing armorlike protection from predators. Tortoises breed after 15 years of age, at which time their eggs—which are the size and shape of Ping-Pong balls—hatch into fully formed self-sufficient young turtles. However, youngsters remain vulnerable to predators because their protective shells do not develop until after the first five years. It takes 15 to 20 years for one to reach maturity. Desert tortoises prefer rocky foothills; they live in burrows that they have dug in firm soil or between and under large rocks. They are a threatened species.

Desert tortoise

Garter Snake

There are several types of garter snakes found in Arizona. Among them are the wandering garter snake and the western terrestrial, both found in the northeastern portion of the state. The moderately slender bodies of adults range from 24 to 42 inches in length. They have light stripes down the sides of their bodies, with a distinctive light stripe down the back of some individuals. The color between the stripes is brownish, marked with dark spots. Underneath they are brownish, bluish, or gray, with reddish blotches. These snakes feed on fish, tadpoles, frogs, earthworms, snails, lizards, small mammals, and occasionally insects, birds, and carrion. When captured, they emit a foul-smelling fluid from vent glands.

Garter snake

Gila Monster

Gila monsters are large plump lizards, with short legs, massive heads, and thick tails. Adults can reach a length of 24 inches. They are brightly patterned in red, yellow, orange, and black, with shiny, beady, or wartlike scales. One type in Arizona has banded patterns with four broad double crossbands. Their tails are thick because that is where they store fat, and a thick tail indicates a well-fed Gila monster. Gila monsters possess potent venom, secreted by glands in the lower jaw. To inject the substance, they must bite their victim, using their strong jaws to break the skin so the venom is absorbed into the laceration. The venom and bite produce a painful wound, and if enough venom is absorbed into the nervous system, it can cause death. However, the venom is rarely fatal to humans although it causes swelling, followed by nausea and weakness. Gila monsters are found in shrubby deserts, canyons, and rocky foothills. They are nocturnal creatures that retreat to their burrows when it is very hot or cold. Generally they are slow-moving, but when threatened, Gila monsters will turn to face their attacker with their large mouths open, hissing loudly. They use taste and smell to track prey, frequently flicking their forked tongues to utilize their highly sensitive sense of smell. Their high-protein diet consists of reptile and bird eggs, nesting birds, and baby rodents. When drought limits the food supply, they can survive for several years on the fat stored in their tails. They typically give birth to three to eight offspring at a time, and their lifespan ranges from 20 to 30 years. Due to their unique nature and rapidly decreasing population, Gila monsters have been under governmental protection in Arizona since 1952. They are the only venomous animal protected by state law; they cannot be disturbed or killed.

Gila monster

Gopher Snake

This common snake, called a bullsnake in Arizona, is long, reaching 5 to 6 feet in length. The head is oval and slightly flattened, with a somewhat pointed snout and an enlarged scale on the front of the nose. Either yellow or cream colored, gopher snakes have smaller blotches on the sides, with a prominent dark stripe across the top of the head that reaches from eye to eye. Its habitats range from grassland, gravelly soil, coniferous forests, deciduous forests, riparian areas, and agricultural areas to sagebrush and rabbitbrush. Gopher snakes can appear threatening by mimicking the coiling and hissing of a rattlesnake; but the formidable-looking snake is harmless. These snakes are considered desirable to have around, because they consume large numbers of rodents. Diet includes assorted rodents, small rabbits, birds and their eggs, and occasionally lizards. Females lay from 5 to 20 eggs under rocks or in burrows.

Gopher snake

Horned Lizard

A member of the iguana family, the horned lizard is common throughout Arizona. It has sharp-pointed "horns" along the back of its head and is often referred to as a horned toad. About 3 or 4 inches in length, the horned lizard has a squat, somewhat flat body. Horned lizards can be brown or bluish

Short-horned lizard

gray, with the color matching the local soil. Their sides and quite short tail are edged with whitish spines. They inhabit rocky or sandy open areas, remaining active throughout the warm days but restricting activity to mornings when it is hot. Although most lizards rely on speed and break-away tails to avoid predators, the horned lizard is slow and sluggish. Instead, its defenses are camouflage and the ability to inflate itself like a blowfish. These lizards are far from sumptuous meals to predators—their spikelike scales make them difficult to swallow. Horned lizards feed on insects, primarily ants, but also are known to eat small snakes. Females give live birth to up to 30 offspring.

Regal horned lizard

King snake

The common king snake is a nonvenomous member of the Colubridae family, which includes gopher snakes, garter snakes, and whip snakes. Mature adults are 3 to 4 feet long and come in a variety of colors and patterns, usually chocolate brown to black. Common king snakes vary in pattern and color. Although most have a pattern of alternating black and white bands, these colors may vary to brown, white, cream, or pale yellow, depending on the region. Some individuals have black bellies, while others are nearly all black. The king snake was named because it eats other snakes—particularly rattlesnakes, copperheads, and coral snakes—and is immune to their toxic venom. They also eat lizards, birds and their eggs, small mammals, turtles, and frogs. They will even climb trees in pursuit of prey. King snakes use their keen sense of smell at night to locate food, then quickly bite and surround the victim with suffocating coils. They swallow their victims whole, while they are still alive. Generally regarded as a gentle snake, a king snake will hiss, strike, and vibrate its tail when threatened. If attacked, king snakes roll into a ball with their heads in the center and smear attackers with musk and feces. Females lay up to 20 eggs in the spring or summer; once the eggs are laid, she shows no further interest in her young.

King snake

Western Diamondback Rattlesnake

There are 11 species—all dangerous to man—of rattlesnakes found throughout Arizona, but the most common is the western diamondback. It is typically gray (although individual colors will vary, depending on how long it has been since the last molt), with darker diamond-shaped blotches along the back. The tail is ringed with black and white bands. It has a triangular head, narrow neck, and grows to an average length of about 6 feet, including the rattle on the end of its tail. The ridge-nosed rattlesnake, which is Arizona's state reptile, is smaller, growing to a length of only about 2 feet. The coloration of this woodland snake varies depending on the location of its residence, which is often near water. Western diamondback rattlesnakes inhabit prairie dog burrows or rocky crevices during winter and emerge for spring and summer activities. In hot summer weather they usually prowl at dusk and at night. Pores in their heads pick up scents and heat to help detect prey. The snake kills its prey by injecting it with venom through hollow fangs that snap downward and forward as the snake strikes. To human beings, a rattler's bite is painful and can cause infection and illness, although there have been few fatalities documented among bitten adults. They are relatively docile snakes; most frequently they lie still and allow danger to pass, only coiling and rattling if they know they've been seen and feel threatened. Often even then, they do not rattle. If left alone, they crawl away and seek a hiding place. Exercise caution in tall grass, rocky areas, and around prairie dog towns, especially in the mornings and evenings and after summer thunderstorms. Females give birth to as many as 15 live young in late summer.

Western diamondback rattlesnake

Sidewinder

Sidewinders are members of the rattlesnake family. They look much like other rattlesnakes but have a triangular horn over each eye. Their coloration gives a dusty appearance and blends with their environment; they range in color from sand to pale gray. They have rough scales with brown or gray blotches along their back and sides. Usually they reach a length ranging from 17 to 33 inches. The name sidewinder is derived from the unique way this snake moves: rippling sideways and keeping minimal contact between its body and the hot sand. Sidewinders leave parallel, J-shaped tracks in the sand. They are found in the deserts, sand dunes, and rocky hillsides of southern Arizona. Sidewinders are nocturnal, and adults feed primarily on kangaroo rats and pocket mice, while youngsters prefer lizards. Rodents are bitten, released, and tracked down, whereas lizards are held until the venom takes effect. Sidewinders mate April through May or sometimes in the fall. Females give birth to 5 to 18 young in late summer or fall.

Sidewinder

Sonoran Desert Toad

In Arizona, there are nine species of toads, including the Sonoran desert toad, which is also known as the Colorado River toad. It is olive green to dark brown, with white warts near the corners of its mouth. The largest of the species, it grows to about 6 inches. These amphibians are rather well protected against predators. The toads' skin produces toxins that react with mucous. If a dog mouths a toad, it will suffer severe discomfort with the possibility of paralysis and death. If a toad sits in a dog's water dish and the pet subsequently drinks the water, illness or death can result. Sonoran desert toads spend most of the year underground, having dug themselves in or usurped abandoned rodent burrows. Summer rains trigger emergence and signal the beginning of breeding season. After mating, toads feed on insects, spiders, smaller toads, and small vertebrates that are made abundant by the summer rains. After storing an adequate supply of fat, toads again burrow into the ground where they remain through winter.

Sonoran desert toad

Spiny Lizard

The Sonoran spiny lizard is the largest spiny lizard found in North American deserts—reaching up to 10 inches in length. The stocky lizard has sharp-tipped spiny scales, grayish to yellowish in color, with black triangular patches on the sides of the neck. Males have blue patches on the throat and on each side of the belly. Spiny lizards occur practically statewide, from low deserts to pinyon-juniper woodlands; they prefer a habitat with rocks, shrubs, and trees. Although good climbers, they are often found on the ground where they forage for insects, leaves, berries, and occasionally smaller lizards. They sometimes use the nests of woodrats, or pack rats, for shelter.

Spiny lizard

Whiptail Lizard

Western whiptails are slender lizards found throughout most of Arizona, except for the high mountain areas. They are yellow to grayish brown, sometimes with dark markings. Their underbellies are white or yellow. Adult males have a black throat and chest. Predators include birds, snakes, and small mammals. For protection, whiptails dig burrows that provide a safe retreat. Their agility and speed help them escape from danger; they travel up to 15 miles per hour. In addition, they have breakaway tails, which help them elude capture. Whiptails are constantly in motion—almost hyperactive. They are known to run upright on their hind legs, swiveling their head from side to side rapidly, sniffing the air with their forked tongue as they forage ceaselessly for termites, spiders, and insects. Some all-female species of whiptail lizards do not reproduce sexually but by parthenogenesis, which means that all of its offspring are female. Their eggs require no fertilization, and the offspring are exact and complete genetic duplicates of the mother.

Whiptail lizard

Woodhouse's Toad

A Woodhouse's toad can be 2 to 5 inches long, with a thick head, rounded snout, and wide waist (a hockey puck shape). The hind legs are short, and the body is grayish brown or yellowish brown with a prominent white stripe down the back. Woodhouse's toads have warty skins; the glands and warts produce the poison bufotalin (also bufonin or bufogin). Some people have been known to lick the toad because this toxin produces a temporary high. This practice is not advised! Predators include raccoons, skunks, snakes, and herons. Fish are also known to eat the tadpoles. Woodhouse's toads are active at night but can be seen in the daytime. The toads usually burrow into the soil beneath low mounds or hide in debris piles. Males have a vocal sac that they use during the springtime breeding season. They produce a sheeplike bleat, which is 4 to 10 seconds long and sounds like "waaaah." Males gather in small pools and attempt to attract females to mate in the water. Females lay strings of eggs as they walk or swim around.

Woodhouse's toad

Invertebrates

Ant lion

Ant lion larvae are sometimes referred to as doodlebugs because they have a clumsy, backward motion that leaves doodling tracks in the sand. When larvae hatch, they immediately begin digging individual ant traps with their sickle-shaped jaws. After they reach the bottom of their pitlike trap (approximately 2 by 2 inches), they open their jaws and wait for ants to slip on the edge of the pit and tumble inside—right into the ant lion larvae's mouth. Victims are then injected with venom and eaten by the ant lion larvae. Eventually, the larvae spin cocoons and metamorphose to emerge in late summer as winged dragonflylike creatures with one single mission: to mate. Adults die almost immediately after mating, but not before females lay their eggs directly onto the soil surface, where her larvae will hatch and repeat the life cycle.

Adult ant lion

Ant lion larva

Butterfly

There are many species of butterflies in Arizona. Dependent on plants for their survival, butterflies lay eggs on host

Acmon blue

American snout

Black swallowtail

Common buckeye

Monarch

Mourning cloak

plants, which then become food for the caterpillars after they hatch. The mature caterpillars spin cocoons on the host plants. After weeks or months a butterfly emerges to mate, sip flower nectar, lay eggs, and die. With wingspans of 4 to 6 inches, the giant swallowtail butterfly is the largest butterfly in the United States. The forewings have a diagonal band of yellow spots, and tails are edged with black and filled with yellow. The caterpillars, which are sometimes called orangedogs, feed mostly on citrus and prickly ash. Hairstreak butterflies are small, have cobalt blue wings with black margins dotted red and white. The hairstreaks fool predators into attacking a false head on the butterfly's hind wings, which it rubs up and down. Birds will bite the false head, allowing the butterfly to escape with minimal damage. Monarch butterflies have wings of a striking reddish brown with black veins and black borders with two rows of white dots. The wingspread may reach 4 inches. When monarch larvae feed on milkweed plants, they accumulate a poisonous substance in their bodies that makes them distasteful to birds and other predators. The birds learn to recognize the butterflies' bright pattern and avoid them. Tiger swallowtails are yellow with black stripes and have black wing margins. Some females are all black with a bluish iridescence. They are called swallowtails because they have long "tails" on their hind wings, which look a bit like the long, pointed tails of swallows (a type of bird). When it is very young, the caterpillar is camouflaged to look like bird droppings. Later, it develops distinctive eyespots that make it look like a snake, which scares off some predators.

Damselflies and Dragonflies

Damselflies and dragonflies belong to the Odonata order. These insects have biting mouthparts, short antennae, and very large eyes. Damselflies have broad heads with widely spaced eyes, while dragonflies have rounded heads with eyes that are closer together. Damselflies have two similar pairs of wings that they hold close to their bodies and fold together when at rest. Dragonflies' hind wings, which they hold outstretched when at rest, are broader than their forewings. Damselflies sit and wait for prey; dragonflies actively pursue their prey in the air. Both creatures lay their eggs on aquatic plants.

Damselfly

Dragonfly

Darkling Beetle

Also called stinkbugs, these desert beetles are blackish, about an inch long, and walk with their rear ends raised up in the air. This posture serves two purposes: (1) It gets the beetles up and away from the hot ground; and (2) it allows them to drink the drops of nighttime dew that collect on their backs by channeling the liquid into their mouths. Darkling beetles repel predators by spraying a foul-smelling liquid from their abdomens while standing on their heads and aiming directly at the target. The odor can remain in the air for 15 minutes. Not all enemies, however, are deterred by this kerosene-scented repellent. Black widow spiders tie the beetle down and stay out of range until the supply of spray has been depleted. Before consuming the insect, grasshopper mice press the beetle's abdomen into the soil to disarm the sprayer.

Darkling beetle

Giant Desert Centipede

Centipedes belong to an arthropod group called the Chilopods. Their name literally means "100 legs," although they do not actually have that many. At lengths of 6 to 9 inches, the giant desert centipede is North America's largest centipede. It is mostly brown with a bluish head and tail segments. It has a segmented body with a pair of legs attached to each segment. The first pair is slightly shorter than the body width, but the twentieth pair is twice as long as the body width. The last pair of legs faces backward, giving the impression that the centipede has a head on either end. Like many arthropods, centipedes can inflict a painful, but not fatal, venomous bite with the pincers at the end of their first pair of legs. They are not considered dangerous to humans although handling one is likely to be an unpleasant experience. Giant desert centipedes are most active at night, when they prey upon vertebrates such as small lizards and mice. During hot days they retreat to burrows in the arid desert.

Giant desert centipde

Harvester Ant

Ants are related to wasps and bees. They are social creatures, found in colonies with populations ranging from a few dozen to millions of members. All colonies have a queen—the large, fertile female—in addition to numerous, sterile, wingless females. The queen is the only one to reproduce. The cycle of a colony begins when the queen lays eggs that are both male and female; these hatch into winged ants, which leave the nest and mate; the males die and the females go on to become new

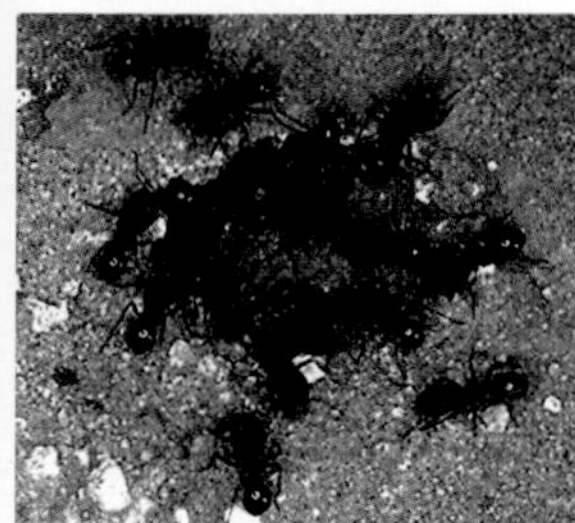
Harvester ants

queens, who build nests, lay eggs, and begin the cycle again. Individual ants can live as long as five years; queens live up to 15 years. Only old workers leave the nest, and when they are killed, a defensive scent is emitted that draws others from the colony to attack the killer of the worker. They will inject a venom that produces a painful sting. Most creatures will not eat harvester ants because of their venom, but an exception is the horned lizard, which has an antitoxin in its blood specific to harvester ants. Harvester ants get their name because a colony can collect as many as 7,000 seeds in one day. Some plants, such as datura, rely on harvester ants to gather and scatter their seeds before rodents eat them from the vine. Harvester ants do not eat datura seeds because of their thick seed coating.

Scorpion

Scorpions, venomous relatives of spiders, mites, and ticks, belong to the class Arachnida. They look a bit like miniature lobsters, with elongated bodies, four pairs of legs, pincers, and a segmented tail (actually the abdomen), which is tipped with a stinger. A scorpion stings by thrusting its "tail" forward over its head and impaling the prey held in its pincers. Scorpions are covered with several layers of wax in order to conserve body water. Of the 30 species of scorpions found in Arizona, the bark scorpion is considered the most venomous. Only 1 to 2 inches at maturity, it is a comparatively small scorpion. It may be distinguished from other less toxic species by its more slender tail segments and pincers. Bark scorpions are typically found under tree bark, leaves, and debris in mesquite, cottonwood, and sycamore groves in riparian areas. Devil scorpions, which have stockier bodies and shorter tails, are found under rocks, in washes, in open desert, in rocky terrain, and along riverbeds. The giant desert hairy scorpions, at lengths up to 6 inches, are the largest of the scorpion species. They are found in desert washes and open areas of desert floors throughout Arizona. Most scorpions are nocturnal predatory animals with diets that include crickets, spiders, centipedes, other scorpions, snakes, and mice. They locate prey by sensing vibrations. The primary purpose of a scorpion's venom is to capture prey—self-defense is secondary. A scorpion would much prefer to be left alone or to retreat than sting. Caution should be exercised when camping or participating in other outdoor activities; be sure that scorpions have not crawled into footwear, clothes, or sleeping bags. First aid for a scorpion bite should include cleaning the site with soap and water, applying a cool compress, elevating the affected limb to approximately heart level, and ingesting aspirin or Tylenol as needed for minor discomfort. Children or any patient experiencing severe symptoms from a bite should be taken to a health-care facility immediately.

Giant desert hairy scorpion

Sphinx Moth

Sphinx moths are also known as hummingbird moths for their ability to hover in front of flowers and sip the sweet nectar. The humming noise that is made by the rapid beating of wings, along with an extremely long proboscis (feeding tube) tongue, increases the similarity to hummingbirds. Sphinx moths are stout-bodied with long, narrow forewings and shorter hind wings; wingspans range from 2 to 8 inches. Many species pollinate flowers such as orchids, petunias, and evening primroses while sucking their nectar with a proboscis, which exceeds 10 inches in some species. Sphinx moths emerge at dusk from their hiding places and begin feeding on the nectar of flowers. Caterpillars of this group are known as hornworms because of sinister-looking barb on the rear; they are the culprits that eat all the leaves in tomato and petunia gardens. Sphinx moth larvae change into adult moths underground and then dig their way to the surface to mate. Females lay up to 1,000 eggs on the underside of food plants; the eggs will hatch within a few days. Sphinx moth males and females die after they have completed the reproductive process.

Sphinx moth

Tarantula

Desert tarantulas are large hairy spiders found throughout the Arizona deserts. Despite their multiple eyes, tarantulas are nearly blind, relying on smell and touch to help them "see." They have gray-brown bodies up to 3 inches long with 4-inch legs. Males have thinner, longer legs; the first pair has hooks that are used to hold the female's venomous fangs during mating. Males and females do not become sexually mature until about eight or nine years. Following copulation, the male scrambles away because females occasionally kill their suitors. Tarantulas are most active during their mating season, which lasts from June to October. The tarantula, which does not spin a web but catches its prey by pursuit, feeds on mice, lizards, and snakes. A bite from the quarter-inch fangs injects venom along with a digestive fluid to liquefy the victim's soft tissues. Then the tarantula sucks the body dry, leaving an empty shell. Tarantulas are timid creatures but will bite if provoked. To humans, their bites can be extremely painful but are not usually dangerous. Tarantulas live underground in burrows, where they are protected from extreme weather conditions. They can plug the entrance and go dormant, even going without food for up to two years and without water for seven months. Females may live to about 20 years but males live only half as long—they die after their one season of sexual activity.

Tarantula

Tarantula Hawk Wasp

These wasps are easily identified by their dark bodies, which have a black metallic appearance, and their bright orange wings. Females can be as long as 4 inches. Tarantula hawks are nectar feeders and can often be found in gatherings of a dozen or more feeding on plants. Their name is derived from their fascinating means of reproduction. After mating, a female is ready to lay her eggs. She seeks out a tarantula, immobilizes it with a paralyzing zap from her half-inch stinger, and then maneuvers the comatose victim to an underground chamber. Instead of killing the tarantula, the venom she injects causes only paralysis. Then she lays one large white egg on the spider, which hatches within five days. The larva then feeds on the spider, saving the vital organs for last so that the spider remains alive for about a month, or until the larva is ready to pupate. The larva then spins a cocoon, in which it spends the winter. When mature, it has transformed into an adult wasp to complete the cycle. The tarantula hawk wasp is the state insect of New Mexico.

Tarantula hawk wasp on top of a tarantula

Trap-door Spider

Trap-door spiders, relatives of tarantulas, are varied species of spiders that live in self-constructed underground lairs with carefully hidden entrances. These spiders have a special row of teeth adapted for digging. Their bodies are an inch or more in length and usually dull brown in color. The legs are relatively short. Trap-door spiders dig a tunnel in the ground and seal it with a hinged door. The burrow entrance usually has a door, the outer surface of which is camouflaged to blend in with the surrounding terrain. The spiders wait patiently behind the trap door until they sense prey passing nearby. Then they rush out to capture the prey and drag it down into the tunnel. They are timid and quickly retreat into the tube if frightened.

Male trap-door spider

Trap-door spider in its trap with the hinged door open

Velvet Ant

Velvet ants are actually hairy wasps, named for the wingless female's resemblance to an ant. Also known as cow killers and mule killers because of the female's long and painful sting, velvet ants are black with a dense velvety covering of white, yellow, golden, orange, or red hairs. Females measure to about an inch in length; males are smaller. As in all wasps, the males cannot sting. Females, however, can bite and sting. Some species of velvet ants are nocturnal, but many are active during the day. They are parasites, laying eggs in the nests of bees and other wasps. The female velvet ant enters the host's nest, punctures the host's cocoon, and lays an egg. The velvet ant larva feeds on the mature larvae, or pupae, of the host. After eating and growing, the larva metamorphoses, emerging as a woolly adult.

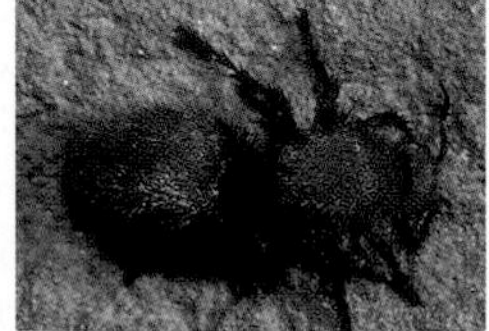
Velvet ant

Birds

American Kestrel

The American kestrel is a commonly seen bird of prey that was formerly known as the sparrow hawk. Kestrels can be spotted hovering in search of prey in the open country of the deserts, prairies, and farmland. The American kestrel is identified by two distinctive facial stripes. The male has a rusty back with blue-gray wings and crown. The female has a rusty back and rusty wings. The female's tail is rusty with black banding and the male's is solid rust with a black tip. At about 8 to 12 inches long, the American kestrel is the smallest falcon in North America. It is similar to a robin in size but fiercely preys on insects, small rodents, reptiles, and amphibians. It has a loud voice and, when excited, lets out a shrill "killy, killy, killy." Kestrels make their nests in the cavities of saguaros, trees, or in abandoned cavities of flickers.

American kestrel

Bald Eagle

The bald eagle is not really bald; it was named for its white head. The rest of its plumage is brown, except for its white tail. Bald eagles have large, heavy hooked bills and strong sharp claws called talons. They possess keen eyesight and can seek out prey while soaring high in the air or watching from a high perch; they swoop down to make the kill with their powerful talons. Eagles make their nests, or aeries, high in trees or on rocky ledges where other animals cannot reach, as young eagles remain helpless for a long period. Each year bald eagles add new material to their aerie. The largest known nest ever measured was 20 feet deep and nearly 10 feet wide.

Bald eagle

Common Raven

The common raven is entirely black and looks a bit like the American crow but is much larger. Common ravens are 20 to 27 inches long with thick black bills that are heavier than most birds of similar size. They have a wedge-shaped tail and shaggy throat feathers. When in flight, they often soar like hawks. Common ravens have an opportunistic diet, ranging from berries and other birds' eggs and nestlings to small vertebrates. In Arizona, they inhabit cliffs and canyons,

Common raven

where they build large nests of sticks or bones, lined with fur or plant materials on steep cliffs or in tall trees. Females usually lay four to seven eggs, which are green with brown spots. The Sonoran raven is a separate species that can be seen in southeastern Arizona.

Curve-billed Thrasher

Curve-billed thrashers are brownish gray with long down-curved bills and bright orange eyes. Their size ranges from 9 to 12 inches in length. Common year-round in Arizona deserts, these birds prefer extensive thickets of thorny shrubs and dense large cacti. Curve-billed thrashers are ground feeders and use their long curved bills to ferret out bugs. They vie with cactus wrens for food and nesting sites; thrashers have been known to tear up cactus wren nests. Curve-billed thrashers build cuplike nests in the protection of shiny chollas or in yuccas, where they lay two to four bluish green eggs.

Curve-bill thrasher

Gambel's Quail

The most common quail in Arizona is the desert-adapted Gambel's quail. These plump game birds are 10 to 12 inches and have a distinctive comma-shaped, forward-leaning black head plume, or "topknot." Their coloring is grayish-brownish gold. Males have a black face and throat with rusty sides, diagonal white stripes, and a buff-white belly. Females are somewhat drabber. Gambel's quail can withstand severe dehydration, losing up to half its body weight. When possible, they consume green, succulent plants that provide a water source, but when the plants they eat are dry—especially in winter—they will seek water, and large convoys of them can be found at waterholes. During the mating season, birds pair to mate and build nests on the ground beneath a cactus or low shrub. Females lay from 12 to 15 eggs. Due to their vulnerability in the ground nests, on average more than half the youngsters die within their first year.

Gambel's quail

Gila Woodpecker

Gila woodpeckers are medium-sized woodpeckers, about 8 to 10 inches in length. They have a tan head, throat, breast, and belly, a back strongly barred with black and white, and black wings barred and spotted with white; the white rump and upper tail has sparse dark barring, and the dark tail has barred central tail feathers. Very conspicuous, noisy birds, the Gila woodpeckers build nests in tree cavities. They may occupy the same nesting hole for more than one season until an owl, kestrel, snake, or large lizard appropriates it. Diet consists of insects and mistletoe berries in the winter. Females lay three to five eggs; the young can fly in about a month.

Gila woodpecker

Great Blue Heron

The great blue heron stands nearly 5 feet tall with blue-gray feathers, a long curving neck, and a straight yellow bill. Although its numbers are small in Arizona, this water bird is often seen. Great blue herons are occasionally mistaken for cranes because of their similarity in size and proportion. But in flight, cranes hold their necks outstretched while herons fold their necks back onto the shoulders. These birds are adept at catching aquatic fauna with a spearlike bill. Great blue herons nest in trees, in flimsy to elaborate stick-and-twig platforms, which are added to over years. These nests can be up to 4 feet in diameter to accommodate the heron pair as they incubate three to seven blue-green eggs.

Great blue heron

Greater Roadrunner

Perhaps Arizona's best-known bird, the greater roadrunner, about 20 to 24 inches in overall length, is a super-speedy, long-legged, crested bird with an oversized bill. These members of the cuckoo family are grayish brown, with streaks of black and white, tinged with shiny green. A blue and red patch is behind each eye. Roadrunners have long tails, which they sometimes flick vertically. They are shy and reclusive. Although they can fly, roadrunners prefer to run for cover instead of taking flight, sprinting up to 15 miles per hour when startled. They feed on a wide variety of desert life including insects, scorpions, lizards, snakes (including rattlesnakes), and rodents. Females lay three to five ivory-colored eggs in a flat stick nest lined with grass, usually in a thick shrub or cactus close to the ground. When food is scarce, older hatchlings selfishly devour it, leaving the younger hatchlings to starve. The siblings and parents then consume the dead hatchlings' bodies.

Greater roadrunner

Hummingbirds

The name hummingbird originated from the noise the birds' wings make in flight. Hummingbirds, only a few inches long, are the smallest of all birds. There are a number of types in Arizona, including black-chinned, Anna's, broad-tailed, and rufous. Hummingbirds feed on nectar, although they also regularly consume small insects. They obtain nectar by inserting their bills and tongues into a flower, thus accumulating pollen on their bills and heads; this pollen is then transferred from flower to flower. Hummingbirds are strong fliers and have exceptional flight characteristics for birds: They can hover and fly backward.

Hummingbird

The extremely rapid beating of their wings can reach 80 beats per second. Some hummingbirds save energy on cool nights by lowering their usually high body temperature until they become sluggish and unresponsive—a condition termed torpor. In contrast, during daylight hours, hummingbirds are often very active and can be highly aggressive, sometimes attacking much larger potential predators, such as hawks and owls.

Jays

The western scrub jay is commonly found in Arizona. This 11- to 12-inch crestless jay has sky blue upperparts, a long tail, and grayish buff underparts. It is found in the open country and dry habitat of Arizona. The western scrub jay is aggressively intolerant toward the Steller's jay and drives it away. The Steller's jay is the only western jay to have a crest. Because of its large size (10 to 12 inches), blue coloration, and crest, the Steller's jay is quite distinctive. Male and female Steller's jays look similar: The head and upper breast are brownish or grayish black to jet black. The underparts below the breast are greenish blue, turning brighter blue at the vent and under the tail. Wings are bright purplish blue to sky blue with narrow black barring; the rump and tail are bright blue with black barring that becomes more prominent toward the end. Under the wings and tail, the body is gray. Steller's jays prefer conifer forests in the mountains of Arizona. Like other jays, the Steller's jay consumes a wide variety of foods, including small vertebrates, seeds, berries, nuts, and especially acorns and pine seeds when available. They commonly take the eggs and nestlings of small birds, and they have even been observed attacking and eating adult birds. Normally a shy and wary bird, the Steller's jay can become accustomed to humans at campgrounds and picnic areas. They build bulky nests of sticks and twigs, which are lined with mud, grass, and conifer needles. The nests are found in conifer trees. Females typically lay four eggs.

Western scrub jay

Mourning Dove

Mourning doves are one of the most common wild doves native to North America. They are members of the same family as pigeons and bear a resemblance to them, except that mourning doves are grayish-brown, with thinner, pointed tails. Their outer tail feathers have white tips with a black marking midway so that the tail is edged with a black and white stripe. Both male and female mourning doves look alike, but females have more of an overall brown coloring. Mourning doves are named for their sad-sounding, long calls, most often heard in the mornings. This melancholy song has been compared to a person mourning the loss of a loved one. Mourning doves produce up to six broods per year—the most of any native bird. Typically, two eggs are laid in a nest made in an evergreen tree, although a wide variety of nest sites are used, including clumps of grass.

Mourning dove

Northern Cardinal

The northern cardinal, a member of the grosbeak family, grows to 9 inches. Males are bright red overall with a red crest and coral red bill surrounded by a mask of black that extends to a dark eye and includes the chin and throat. Legs and feet are dark red. The less showy females are buffy brown tinged with variable areas of red on the crest, head, and tail. In the 1800s, cardinals were much-sought-after cage birds, highly valued for their color and song. Thousands were trapped in the south in the winter and sent to northern markets, and thousands more were sent to Europe. This trade ceased with the passage of the Migratory Bird Treaty Act of 1918. Cardinals are noted for their loud, clear-whistled songs. Females will countersing, duetting with males, usually after the males have established territories and before nesting begins.

Northern cardinal

Northern Mockingbird

Northern mockingbirds are long streamlined gray birds reaching up to 9 inches in length, with white undersides and flashy white wing patches and outer tail feathers. The males and females look alike. Of all North American birds, the mockingbird is most famed for vocal imitations—its repertoire has been known to include more than 40 different sounds. These talented birds can also mimic sounds such as those of a barking dog, squeaky hinges, notes from a piano, and even a cackling hen. During the mating season the male will mark his territory with song. Mockingbirds sing incessantly, both night and day, hopping from one song post to another. They are known to be aggressive when defending their nests and territories. However, if you see them jumping up and down in the air, they may be catching a few insects.

Northern mockingbird

Orioles

Orioles are members of the blackbird family. The brightly colored hooded oriole is commonly found in Arizona. The male's head and underparts are bright yellowish orange; it has a black back, tail, and throat. Females are olive-gray with greenish yellow underparts. Two other orioles, Bullock's oriole and Scott's oriole, migrate to Arizona in the spring and summer for breeding. Bullock's oriole males are very brightly colored orange and black—distinguishable from other black and orange orioles by their black eye line. Scott's oriole males have solid black heads and

Hooded oriole

backs with lemon-yellow underparts. Females and their young are more subtly colored with an olive green to grayish back and yellowish breast. Orioles create beautifully woven hanging nests of plant fibers, suspended pouchlike from the very tips of tree branches. They eat insects, fleshy fruits, berries, nectar from hummingbird feeders, and nectar that they probe from flowers.

Owls

Great horned owls live throughout Arizona, especially in the desert on rocky cliffs or in saguaros in which they nest. They grow to 2 feet and have long ear tufts and yellow eyes. Coloring is brownish with a mottled appearance and a white strip along the throat. These birds have unique flight feathers that allow air to pass through quietly, resulting in near silent flight. At night you can sometimes hear their deep, resonating hoots. Great horned owls are skilled hunters, well equipped with sharp talons to grip rabbits, weasels, squirrels, skunks, and birds in a deadly lock. They have a wide range of vision: Their necks can swivel nearly 180 degrees, and they can practically see in the dark, although they locate their prey primarily with their extremely acute hearing. Also common in Arizona is the smaller barn owl, a lightly colored heart-shaped-faced owl, which is between 14 and 20 inches. Barn owls, also called monkey-faced owls, hiss when frightened.

Great horned owl

Phainopepla

The phainopepla is a slender elegant bird with lustrous feathers, a crest, and a long tail. Males are glossy black with two white wing patches that show in flight; females and juveniles are gray. Adults grow to about 8 inches. Male phainopeplas build a nest to attract females, who, if impressed, then lay and incubate the eggs. The pair disbands after their young are raised. In summer, phainopeplas seek relief from the hot Arizona deserts by migrating to southern Nevada and Utah and to the Pacific Coast. They usually breed in Arizona, often producing two broods. These birds eat mistletoe berries, which provide nutrition and water. When seasonal berries are not available, phainopeplas pluck insects from the air.

Phainopepla

Red-tailed Hawk

Arizona's most common hawk is the red-tailed hawk—a big, powerful bird that reaches lengths of about 24 inches. The red-tailed hawk goes through several color phases, which can make identification difficult. Generally, the bird has dark upperparts, light underparts, and a red tail. Females are larger than males. Red-tailed hawks like open country, fields, and mixed woodlands. These predatory birds perch in trees, overlooking open fields with a sit-and-wait hunting technique; then they swoop down on their prey, ripping it apart with their hooked beak and sharp talons. They are also known to dive after prey while soaring. Diet ranges from small rodents to medium-sized birds, amphibians, and reptiles. Red-tailed hawks normally make their nests in trees; bulkily constructed with sticks, the nests are usually added to each year. Both parents incubate the eggs, but only the female raises the young.

Red-tailed hawk

Red-winged Blackbird

Red-winged blackbirds are about 8 or 9 inches long. Males are black with crimson shoulder patches, bordered with yellow; females are mottled brown, with heavily streaked underparts and a faint red shoulder patch. The red coloration serves as a flag in courtship and also in aggression. In an experiment, males whose red shoulders were painted black soon lost their territories to rivals they had previously defeated. These birds inhabit marshes, wetlands, and open fields. Their nests—woven of dried grass and soft materials—are found among grasses or cattails.

Red-winged blackbird

Sparrows

The black-throated sparrow, previously called desert sparrow, thrives year-round in arid desert scrub conditions. These distinctive birds reach a length of about 5 inches, have a dark conical bill; black throat and mask; gray crown, back, and wings; white belly; and a long black tail with a small amount of white on outer tail feathers and outer corner. Both sexes are similar in appearance. The black-throated sparrows were named for their black throats, which resemble a V-shaped bib on their chest. They drink less water than any other seed-eating birds; they obtain most of their water from food supplies. After rains, they eat new vegetation and seeds. During dry seasons, they switch to juicy insects. To conserve water during very hot days, black-throated sparrows will retreat to cool underground rodent burrows. They can drink saltier water than other birds. Probably the most common sparrow found throughout Arizona during the winter months is the white-crowned sparrow—large flocks of them arrive during fall. White-crowned sparrows range from 6 to 7 inches in length. This bold, colorful, and vocal bird has a white crown ringed with black stripes, a white eyebrow, black eye line, gray face, gray back streaked with brown, and gray underparts. White-crowned sparrows scratch the ground to expose insects and seeds, although they also eat berries. Another very common and tame sparrow found in Arizona is the slightly smaller chipping sparrow, which is distinguished by its

White-crowned sparrow

rufous cap and black eye line. Chipping sparrows prefer woodland areas in the mountains.

Swifts

The white-throated swift is a 6- or 7-inch bird with a long forked tail and a black upperpart with white below that tapers down the belly. These remarkable little birds spend most of their lifetime in flight; they feed, drink, bathe, and even mate while flying! One of the fastest birds in the world—and certainly the one of the fastest in Arizona, white-throated swifts like open habitat, where they feed almost entirely on flying insects. They build nests within cracks or crevices of cliffs. The smallest swift in Arizona is Vaux's (rhymes with hawks) swift, about 4 inches in length and brown with light undersides. It builds its nest in hollow trees.

Tanagers

The colorful male western tanager is exotic and tropical looking with a red head, yellow body, black back, black wings, and black tail. The female is yellow-green above with yellow below. Her coloring is more subdued. Both males and females have horizontal bars on their wings; the top one is thin yellow and the bottom one is white. They eat insects and fruit and grow to about 7 inches in length. Found in coniferous mountain forests, the western tanager is a migratory bird that prefers conifer forests in the summer and southern warm spots in the winter. Western tanagers build frail cup nests made of twigs, grass, or other plant materials, on horizontal branches or in the fork of high trees. The summer tanager is another of the species found in Arizona. The male has a completely red body. The female has brownish to orange-yellow underparts, with an olive back and olive-gray wings and tail.

Western tanager

Summer tanager

Towhees

The spotted towhee, Abert's towhee, canyon towhee, and green-tailed towhee (though it is the least frequently seen) are all found in Arizona. These birds range from approximately 7 to 8 inches in length and are members of the sparrow family. The spotted towhee and Abert's towhee are found throughout Arizona, while the canyon towhee is found in central and southern Arizona. Towhees scratch the ground vigorously for insects and seeds. They nest low in a bush, on the ground under cover, or in a brushy pile in a cup nest made of leaves, grass, and bark shreds.

Spotted towhee

Turkey Vulture

This scavenger bird is predominantly black, with a featherless red head. Its legs and feet are orange and its hooked beak is yellow. Turkey vultures are large birds with bodies up to 32 inches and wingspans up to 6 feet. They soar over open areas, seldom flapping their wings, in search of carcasses they spot by utilizing their keen sight and smell. They gather for communal roosts on fence posts or in dead trees at night. Instead of building nests, turkey vultures lay their eggs in logs or under protective ledges.

Turkey vulture

Western Kingbird

Western kingbirds are 8 or 9 inches long, gray above, and white, gray, or yellow below, with whitish edges on the outermost tail feathers, and a blackish mask through the eye. They have a red spot (usually concealed) on the crown, which is flared in courtship displays or during confrontation with rivals. Cassin's kingbird, also found in Arizona at higher elevations, is similar in appearance but lacks the white outer tail feathers and has a darker breast and upperpart. Western kingbirds are somewhat social, as two or more pairs have been found nesting in the same tree, but they will attack hawks, crows, ravens, and other birds that fly near their nest; they will even ride on the larger bird's back and peck at its head. The western kingbird is mostly found in open country around ranches and towns. A large flycatcher, it perches upright on tall weeds, exposed branches, or wires before sweeping forward to catch insects in midair. Western kingbirds occasionally eat berries. An entertaining tumble display takes place during courtship when males fly to about 60 feet, then stall and tumble, free-falling toward the ground. Kingbirds build nests in cottonwood, oak, sycamore, and willow trees, on utility poles, water towers, and barns. Made of weed stems, twigs, and string, the nests are lined with sheep's wool, cotton, hair, and feathers. Four eggs are laid between April and July; incubation is usually 12 to 14 days. Fledglings can usually fly about two weeks after hatching.

Western kingbird

White-breasted Nuthatch

Arizona's white-breasted nuthatch is a small bird that is about 4 to 6 inches in length. It has bluish gray coloring on its back and a white breast; males have a black crown. This nuthatch, the only one with an entirely white face, lives in the mountains, in forests, and is a year-round resident of the Grand Canyon area. Nuthatches are the only tree-climbing birds that descend headfirst. While foraging on a tree trunk, it might pause in mid descent, arch its head, and call out noisily. Nuthatches clasp the trunk, gripping with their feet, which are equipped with a back claw to help them traverse the undersides of

White-breasted nuthatch

branches. They nest in natural cavities in trees or in abandoned woodpecker nests. They line the nests with bark, grass, fur, and feathers. Females lay five to eight eggs and incubate them for up to two weeks.

Wrens

The cactus wren, Arizona's state bird, is the largest wren in North America. At about 8 inches, this large speckled and striped wren has a brown head, white eye line, light colored underparts spotted with black, and a long white tail that is spotted with white. The cactus wren has a long beak, which it uses to search out termites and other insects from bark or cacti. Found mainly in the deserts of southern Arizona, the cactus ren builds domed ovular straw nests in a cholla or yucca. Females lay four to seven pinkish, speckled eggs from March to June. Bewick's wren grows to about 5 inches and is brown with white underparts. It has a long full tail with white corners. It usually holds its tail high up over the back. The bill is fairly long and pointed. It has a white eyebrow stripe. Bewick's wren is a very common bird and is seen throughout Arizona. The canyon wren, about 6 inches, is brown and buff, with a long, down-curved bill. It can be identified by its flight pattern, which consists of a quick raising and lowering of its hindquarters every few seconds. The agile canyon wren also has a slightly flattened body shape, which allows it to navigate through narrow crevices. Canyon wrens are usually found on open cliffs, in canyons, and on rocky slopes foraging for food—even throughout the hottest parts of the day—scanning ledges and crevices for insects and spiders. Canyon wrens nest on ledges, in crevices under rocks, or inside caves in cup-shaped nests of moss, twigs, and spider silk, lined with fur and feathers. Arizona's rock wren grows to about 6 inches and is grayish-brown, speckled with white above and has white undersides. This lightest colored of the Arizona wrens often bobs its head. Rock wrens build nests in cracks of rocks or under outcroppings and often lay a path of stones leading to their nests.

Cactus wren

Plants

Wildflowers

Broom Snakeweed

A member of the sunflower family, broom snakeweed is a low compact perennial half-shrub. The many stems are slender and multibranched, woody only at the base. The dark green leaves, about 3/4- to 1-inch long, grow at intervals along the stem, with smaller ones in clusters between the stem and main leaves. At the ends of its branches, broom snakeweed has small dense clusters of yellow flower heads that are covered by sticky resin at the tips of the many small branchlets. Broom snakeweed is an aggressive and obnoxious weed, covering millions of acres in northern Arizona. It is a poisonous plant, most toxic during leaf formation, that causes abortions in cattle and sheep. The plant is most common on overgrazed ranges. Height: to 2 feet.

Broom snakeweed

Buffalo Gourd

Also known as calabazilla, stinking gourd, or fetid gourd, buffalo gourd produces a 3- or 4-inch round gourd with yellow and green stripes. The gourd, which turns yellow when mature, is extremely bitter. The plant has foul-smelling, triangular, finely toothed leaves that are greenish gray above and whitish below. Flowers are funnel-shaped and yellow, up to 4 inches long. Gourds are edible before they dry; Native Americans used oil from the seeds for cooking. Buffalo gourd prefers dry, sandy, or gravelly soils of disturbed or waste areas. Height: The plant is a prostrate vine, usually growing flat on the ground but can attain lengths of up to 20 feet or more.

Buffalo gourd flowers

Buffalo gourd

Camphorweed

A member of the sunflower family, camphorweed is sometimes called telegraph plant because of its single-stemmed, erect appearance. Camphorweed is a tall, coarse, hairy, annual or sometimes biennial, with a strong odor. It is covered by long, spreading hairs filled with a sticky secretion. Flower heads grow to about 3/4 of an inch. In late summer you might spot the flowers of the camphorweed along roadsides throughout central and southern Arizona. Although it grows in dry soil, it attains its best growth in moist soil, as in and around the irrigated lands. Height: 2 to 6 feet.

Camphorweed

Common Mullein

Also known as flannel mullein, blanketweed, woolly mullein, and velvet plant, common mullein is a naturalized weed from Europe. It is an erect, stout, woolly biennial with matted layers of short, starlike hairs that cover the entire plant. Leaves form a woolly rosette on the ground in the first year, from which the stem arises in the second year. Its large woolly stem is very leafy. Greenish yellow flowers, which bloom from June to September, are crowded on a long, thick spike at the top of the plant, 1 to 3 feet long and 3/4 to 1 1/4 inches thick. Egg-shaped seed pods contain numerous tiny, dark brown seeds. Common mullein grows in dry

Common mullein

disturbed soil in waste places, along roadsides, railroad embankments, old dwellings, or fields. This widespread plant has no value as forage. Colonists and Native Americans lined their footwear with the leaves of this plant for warmth. Height: 2 to 6 feet.

Common Sunflower

Eight species of the common sunflower are found in Arizona, and it is the state flower of Kansas. Common sunflowers are tall, robust branched annuals, with coarse, rough stems. Hairy leaves are heart-shaped and pointed at the tip; the edges are usually toothed. Sunflowers have large 2- to 5-inch flower heads that bloom from March to October or November. The flower heads follow the sun as it moves across the sky during the day. The sunflower was introduced in Arizona and is native to the Great Plains area. This showy and somewhat ornamental plant is abundant in moist soils throughout most of the state along roadsides, waste places, abandoned fields, lowlands, and barren spots. It can be a pest near cultivated crops. Birds, rodents, and humans eat sunflower seeds. Native Americans have been known to make purple and black dye from the seeds, and yellow dye from the flowers. Height: 3 to 7 feet.

Common sunflower

Desert Globemallow

This year-round blooming plant is known by several other names, such as apricot mallow and desert mallow. Desert globemallows are bushy, somewhat woody perennials, covered by minute star-shaped hairs that may be very irritating to the eyes. Desert globemallows have bright orange or apricot flowers, with five petals each. These cup-shaped flowers grow along upper stems to 2 inches wide. Petals range in color from white, pink, peach, purple, or blue. The plant has erect branches and three-lobed, scalloped-edged leaves, which resemble the maple. Desert globemallow is the most drought-resistant member of the mallow family. It is found along roadsides, in sandy washes, and on rocky hillsides, sometimes among pinyons and junipers. Height: 1 to 4 feet.

Desert globemallow

Desert Lupine

Lupine in Latin means "wolfish," as members of this family were once believed to destroy the soil. The opposite is in fact true; many members of the pea family actually improve soil fertility through nitrogen fixation. Desert lupine, often called Coulter's lupine, is a favorite among bees. Like other peas, the plants have distinctive flowers with one petal on top and two on the bottom. They have 1/2-inch-long blue to lilac flowers that bloom on slender, erect stems January through May. The upper petal has a yellow spot, which changes to reddish after pollination. The two bottom petals are short and wide; they are hairy on the bottom edge and curve upward to a slender tip. When ripe, the seed pods explode, scattering their seed to the wind. This annual herb has dark green compound leaves with five to nine leaflets arranged like the spokes of a wheel. Lupines are toxic and should never be eaten. Height: to 16 inches.

Desert lupine

Desert Marigold

Also called wild marigold, paperdaisy, and desert baileya, desert marigolds are attractive spring annuals of the sunflower family. There are three species found in Arizona. Desert marigold grows in large clumps, with daisylike, brilliant yellow flowers—from five to many per head. The leaves and stems are a dull grayish green and are woolly and densely matted to protect the plant from ultraviolet rays and to help it retain water. Desert marigold is found on roadsides, slopes, sandy and gravely areas, and overgrazed land. Feeding on this plant has poisoned sheep and goats. Height: to 2 feet.

Desert marigold

Desert Trumpet

A perennial herb, desert trumpet is a member of the buckwheat family, of which there are 53 species in Arizona. Desert trumpet stems are inflated or flared just below the point of branching, vaguely reminiscent of several wind musical instruments. According to Dr. James L. Reveal of the University of Maryland, the swollen stem is due to high concentrations of carbon dioxide in the stem. If you look very carefully, you may see a small hole near the top of the inflated area, which is the entrance to a miniature food storage room and incubator for minute wasps. The female wasp packs the cavity with insect larvae and then lays her eggs upon them, thus ensuring a food supply for her young. Desert trumpets have tiny yellow flowers that bloom February to October. Height: to 3 feet.

Desert trumpet

Devil's Claw

Devil's claw, also called devil's horn, is a sticky, coarse, ground-hugging plant with purple, copper, and yellowish-rust-colored, snapdragonlike flowers. The flowers appear throughout the deserts and grasslands after seasonal rains. The fruit of the plant divides in half, revealing a black, woody shell with a horn-shaped "claw," which catches the passing wind (as well as passersby)

Devil's claw

and scatters the seeds. For more than 1,000 years, people have eaten devil's claw pods, and the Tohono O'odham, indigenous people of southern Arizona, used the dried claw for making baskets. Weavers strip the hooks and outer covering, weaving the tough fibers into distinctive designs onto lighter colored baskets. Devil's claw is found in sandy soil along roadsides, mesas, plains, and disturbed areas. Height: to 1 foot.

Fairy Duster

A member of the pea family, fairy duster is a low, thornless, densely branched shrub. It remains inconspicuous for much of the year, but when the spring bloom arrives, it sends out ball-shaped clusters of pink flowers, giving the plant its name. These light pink to orange puffs contain many flowers that are darker toward the center, from which long stamens radiate. It is a food source to a variety of desert animals, birds, and insects. Fairy dusters are a particular favorite of hummingbirds. Height: 8 inches to 4 feet.

Fairy duster

Filaree

Early Spanish settlers introduced filaree, a member of the geranium family, into the United States from Eurasia. Also called heron bill because of the way a ripening seed pod resembles a heron's beak, this plant is one of the earliest to bloom in the desert. Flowers are pinkish-violet, about 1/4- to 1/2-inch wide, with five petals that drop off the plant very quickly. The unusual needlelike fruits split into five one-seeded fruits at maturity. One seed is enclosed in each of these single, spindle-shaped, very hard fruits. The plant has red creeping stems that sprawl along the ground up to 20 inches, fernlike leaves, and small sword-shaped fruits. Mature seed pods turn into a spiral as they dry. But when moisture is available, the pod untwists, pushing the seed pod into the soil. Because of its abundance and high forage value, filaree is a very important plant on many Arizona ranges, particularly during the spring. Height: to 15 inches—it spreads horizontally.

Filaree

Filaree flower

Goldenrod

Also known as yellowweed, goldenrod is a genus in the sunflower family. It typically has a slender unbranched stem with short-stalked or stalkless leaves and small yellowish flower heads in complex clusters. It is one of the later-blooming plants, usually flowering around July to September. Medicinal applications of this plant include use as an astringent and diuretic for kidney stones. In powder form it has been used for cicatrization of ulcers. Height: 1 to 5 feet.

Goldenrod

Indian Paintbrush

Indian paintbrush flowers are small modified leaves called bracts, which have colorful tips of fiery orange, pink, maroon, red, or yellow, giving the appearance of a dipped paintbrush at the end of the stems. The roots of these plants are semiparasitic and steal food from other plants. Found most often in habitats with dry, open soil, sometimes with sagebrush, this plant blooms from May to September. Height: 1 to 3 feet.

Indian paintbrush

Jimson Weed

Also called sacred datura, all parts of this plant are poisonous and can prove fatal. Jimson weed has white, foul-smelling trumpet-shaped flowers that open after dusk and close the next morning. The fruit is round and thorny, with many small spines. Leaves are up to 6 inches long, greenish gray, and covered by tiny hairs. Jimson weed is often seen along roadsides and desert sandy flats. Height: to 24 inches.

Jimson weed

Mexican Poppy

Mexican poppy is also called desert poppy and Arizona poppy. The plant has brilliant yellow-orange flowers with pale green foliage that is prickly. The seeds have medicinal value and are used to mildly depress the central nervous system. Mexican poppy prefer a sunny location with a well-drained, sandy soil and it will adapt in very poor conditions. Cattle will graze on these plants. Height: to about 1 foot (spreads horizontally).

Mexican poppy

Milkvetch

There are hundreds of species of astragalus, or milkvetch, in Arizona. It is the largest genus of flowering plants in the state, and even experts disagree on which one is before them—the differences are slight and inconspicuous. Of the many types, Nuttall milkvetch is the most common. This member of the pea family is grayish green and thinly covered with straight gray hairs. Leaves are divided into pairs, the tips rounded, pointed, or with a slight notch—the largest of which are reddish. The plant has small drooping pealike flowers that are light purple, fading to nearly white, then drying blue. Two to six pealike

Milkvetch

Milkvetch seed pods

flowers, ranging from 1 to 3 inches long, cluster near the ends of stiff stalks. The warty seed pods grow to 2 inches and are somewhat square and flattened, with a notch in one edge. Nuttall milkvetch is found throughout the state on barren, dry, or disturbed soil along roadsides, waste places, river bottoms, mesas, slopes, and canyons, in southern and northern deserts, and in woodland ranges. Several species of this plant are toxic, especially to horses, which gives rise to its common name in the state, "loco weed." Height: less than 12 inches.

Pentstemon

Members of the snapdragon, or figwort, family, many species of pentstemon grow in Arizona. Pentstemon means "five stamens." Some of the plants are called beardtongue, which refers to the fact that one of the stamens is different from the rest. That one is covered with fine hairs and appears to have a beard. This stamen does not develop any pollen itself, but it probably helps to attract insects into the center of the flower where pollen from the other stamens can cover their bodies and be carried to the next flower. The flowers fall into two groups, each designed to accommodate their pollinators: One group produces brilliant red or scarlet narrowly tubular flowers to attract and feed hummingbirds; the other group has pale lilac flowers that are more designed for bees' bodies. Pentstemon's fruit is a dry, many-seeded capsule. Leaves are gray-green and oblong. It prefers moist grassland, roadsides, hillsides, and canyons. Height: to 4 feet.

Pentstemon

Prickly Poppy

This very branchy, pale green plant is covered with yellow prickles. Long, lobed, spiny leaves resembling thistles grow to 8 inches. Flowers are white and papery, with a single eye of yellow stamens and six broad, delicate, wrinkled petals. Seed pods are prickly and grow to 2 inches in length. All parts of this plant contain alkaloids that are poisonous. Prickly poppy grows wild throughout Arizona because no animals will eat it. Height: to 4 feet.

Prickly poppy

Purple Nightshade

One of 15 species of nightshade in Arizona, this woody member of the nightshade, or potato, family is a sticky, glandular perennial. Nightshade is a native subshrub with starlike deep purple flowers that have a crinkly appearance and a small cluster of yellow stamens in the center. Leaves are hairy and dark green. All parts of the plant are toxic. Purple nightshade occurs in several habitats, including chaparral and oak woodland. Height: 3 to 5 feet.

Purple nightshade

Salsify

Also called goat dandelion, this member of the sunflower family looks much like a tall, large dandelion after it goes to seed. Its yellow flowers bloom in the morning and close by noon. The plants are found in meadows and fields and along roadsides. Salsify was brought by European settlers to use as a garden vegetable; roots were soaked to remove the bitterness, then peeled and eaten raw or stewed. Their flavor is similar to that of oysters. Height: 1 to 3 feet.

Salsify

Thistle

There are 17 species of thistle in Arizona, all members of the sunflower family. Considered an obnoxious weed, Arizona thistle is characterized by a blaze of spiny-toothed red flowers, with grayish green, very hairy, spiny-toothed foliage. The slender flower heads measure about 2 inches long. The Latin name *Cirsium* means "a swollen vein," for which thistles were thought to be a remedy. Height: 2 to 4 feet.

Red thistle

Trees and Shrubs

Arizona Cypress

The Arizona cypress is a steeple-shaped evergreen with scaly, reddish brown bark and a pleasing aroma. Small yellow flowers become visible in the fall. The tiny and plentiful leaves are pale green to gray-green—giving an appearance that resembles a juniper, except the Arizona cypress has cones that are bigger than juniper fruits. These woody, spherical cones mature after two years and then split open, spilling tiny seeds. However, the cones remain on the tree for years. Arizona cypress is found in canyons, on slopes, in the high desert, and within hot interiors where it is valued as a windbreak tree. It is relatively drought resistant when established. The wood provided by the Arizona cypress is hard, heavy, and durable. Average height of an Arizona cypress is about 40 feet.

Arizona cypress

Arizona cypress fruit

Arizona Sycamore

Arizona sycamore are found along streams and in rocky canyons from 2,000 to 6,000 feet throughout central and southeast Arizona. The coloring and appearance of the bark changes as the tree ages. Its youthful, thin, brownish bark flakes off over time, exposing patches of whitish inner bark,

Arizona sycamore

which gives the tree a mottled appearance. Mature trees have white bark. The Arizona sycamore's leaves are large and maple-shaped; its swinging seed pods are sometimes called buttonballs. These dry, brownish pods, which hold innumerable seeds, remain on the trees until spring, when they separate and the downy seeds blow away in the breeze.

Arizona White Oak

The Arizona white oak, an evergreen that reaches heights of about 60 feet, has light gray fissured bark. The leaf undersides are densely matted with brownish fuzz. The leaf uppersides are smooth, dull, and bluish green. Arizona white oaks bloom in the spring with tiny flowers that are followed by light brown 1-inch acorns. Arizona white oaks are found in oak woodlands, foothills, mountains, and canyons throughout the state. Birds and animals rely on the fatty and nutritious acorns to sustain them through winter. Other oaks found throughout the state include emery oak (evergreen) and Gambel oak (deciduous).

Arizona white oak

Acorn

Blue Spruce

Blue spruce is primarily found in mixed conifer forests of Arizona at elevations between 6,000 and 11,000 feet. The pyramid-shaped tree ranges from 10 to 80 feet tall with branches that extend to the ground. The dark green or blue-green needles are square shaped (roll them between your fingers), with a pointed tip; they rise singly from the twig. Cones are 2 to 3 inches. Blue spruce bark is gray and is smooth in younger trees and lightly furrowed in older trees.

Blue spruce cones

Blue spruce

Brittlebush

Spanish missionaries in California's first churches called this common rounded leafy bush *incienso* for its former use as incense. Found on dry slopes and in desert washes, the deciduous shrub is a member of the sunflower family. These 2- to 5-foot plants have long, ovate silver-gray leaves and clusters of yellow flower heads that bloom in March to June. As its name suggests, brittlebush has breakable woody branches, and they contain a fragrant resin.

Brittlebush

Catclaw Acacia

Catclaw acacia is a low shrub that is a member of the pea family. It has curved thorns that lend this species its name. The stems are lined with sharp recurved "claws," which dig into whatever brushes against them. This shrub, or small tree, produces yellow blooms in spring that are densely formed on a cylindrical spike, about 2 1/2 inches long. The catclaw acacia also has twisted pods that grow to 6 inches. Catclaw patches are important to wildlife habitat. They are found on slopes, canyons, desert grasslands, and along washes and streams at elevations below 5,000 feet.

Catclaw acacia

Catclaw acacia pods

Creosote Bush

The yellow foliage of the creosote bush is followed by white fuzzy seed pods. The leaves are naturally varnished to slow evaporation and to conserve water. Stems are gray and ringed with black. This abundant evergreen shrub is covered with an aromatic resin (hence the name "creosote"). When older stems in the middle of the plant die off, new growth comes up around the edge. This process allows a plant, which is essentially a clone, to grow for a century or more. It is believed that the creosote produces a toxic substance that prevents other plants from growing too close, thereby in essence dictating local water rights. Only when the soil below a creosote bush has been cleansed by rain will other plants grow for a brief time beneath it. The sweet, refreshing smell of the desert after a rain results partly from wet creosote bush foliage. The plants are found primarily in the desert and on mesas below 4,500 feet.

Creosote bush

Desert Broom

This member of the sunflower family is found throughout Arizona. Early pioneers who used the branches as brooms named it. Desert broom is a deep green evergreen, about 9 to 10 feet tall, with needlelike leaves. The plant blooms from September through February with small white flowers in clusters.

Desert broom

The female shrub produces white silky seeds that are carried to new locations by the wind. Desert broom grows nearly everywhere throughout the state—along sandy washes, on hillsides, along streams, atop mesas, and alongside roads at elevations ranging from 1,000 to 5,500 feet. Some Native Americans have been known to chew the stems of this plant to ease toothaches.

Desert Willow

The desert willow is not a member of the willow family; it belongs to the bignonia family. Desert willow is an upright shrub or small tree that grows to a height of 25 feet. The trunk has a dark brown scaly bark; twigs are hairy and sticky. Narrow light green leaves with pointed ends grow from 3 to 6 inches. Desert willow flowers, which are pinkish purple, large, and fragrant, normally bloom from April to August. Long, brown, cigarlike pods, from 4 to 8 inches long, contain numerous flat, tan seeds. Desert willows grow along desert washes, creeks, stream banks, and drainages. This deciduous plant is tolerant to drought.

Desert willow

Douglas Fir

Douglas fir (which is actually a pine tree) is the largest of Arizona's trees. This conical evergreen has flattened needlelike leaves that are yellow-green or blue-green. When young, the trees are pyramid-shaped, but with age the crown becomes irregular. Bark is dark reddish brown and smooth on young trees; it becomes thick, furrowed, and corky on older trees. At the end of the twigs there is usually one, though sometimes more than one, cone-shaped, sharp-pointed, reddish brown oblong cone with three-pronged tongues sticking out between the cone scales. The cones are 3 to 4 inches long. Douglas firs are long-lived conifers that grow in vast forests in Arizona, often in pure stands, in well-drained soil at elevations from 6,000 to 9,000 feet. They are also found in canyons below 5,000 feet. Among the world's most important timber trees, Douglas firs are often used for reforestation. Height ranges from 100 to 130 feet in Arizona.

Douglas fir

Douglas fir cones

Four-wing Saltbush

Four-wing saltbush, also known as saltbrush, is a member of the goosefoot family. These shrubby bushes range from 2 to 5 feet with small, grayish green, densely branched stems. By the end of summer, its tiny yellow flowers produce conspicuous four-winged bracts, which are light green, papery, and distinctive. They become pale brown or nearly white when dry. The leaves are used as greens in salads or can be added to soup. The seeds can be ground and mixed with sugar and water to produce a drink called *pinhole*. Saltbush serves as an important food source for cattle, sheep, goats, deer, pronghorn, and rabbits, especially in the spring and winter when other forage is scarce. Some birds and animals also eat the seeds.

Four-wing saltbush

Fremont Cottonwood

Cottonwoods are deciduous members of the poplar family. The Fremont cottonwood is named for Major John Charles Frémont, an early explorer of the West. Frémont found these trees useful throughout his expeditions because their presence indicates nearby water and the trees provided shady resting spots. They are short-lived, fast-growing trees that produce an abundance of seeds. Male and female flowers bloom on separate trees in clusters of tiny petal-less flowers (catkins) in spring before leaves appear. The cotton-haired seeds, produced in small capsules, are carried to new locations by the wind. In suburban areas, this tree is sometimes prohibited because of the mess caused by the mass of "cotton" it yields. Fremont cottonwood foliage is dark, shiny green above and paler below, and turns dull yellow in the fall. Sometimes confused with aspens, the Fremont cottonwood is distinguished by larger, coarser, more deeply toothed triangular leaves; the trees are also larger than aspens and have coarser bark, except when young. The bark is whitish and smooth on young trees and thick, rough, splitting, and light gray or brownish on mature trees. Found along streams and in moist places below 6,000 feet, the Fremont cottonwood is important to riparian areas and coniferous forests. Mule deer and cattle often browse the twigs and foliage and Frémont referred to it as "sweet cottonwood" because its inner bark can be eaten by horses. This handsome hardwood usually reaches a height between 40 and 90 feet. Authentic Hopi kachinas are carved of cottonwood.

Freemont Cottonwood

Juniper

Members of the cypress family, both one-seed juniper and Utah juniper, are found throughout plateaus, plains, foothills, and the pinyon-juniper belt. Similar in appearance, they grow from 8 to 20 feet tall with rounded crowns. These trees often have several branches

Common juniper

as large as the main stem extending from ground level. The yellowish green foliage is pressed tightly to the twigs and is scale-shaped. Bark ranges from gray-brown to gray and grows whiter as the tree ages. It is fibrous and tends to shred in long strips. One-seed juniper has coppery cones, covered with a bluish waxy substance, about 1/4 inch in diameter, usually containing only one seed. The branches of one-seed juniper arise from the base of the trunk, giving the tree a globular appearance. The Utah juniper's branches arise all along the trunk. Its reddish brown cones are larger—up to 3/4 inch in diameter, usually with one or two seeds. Alligator juniper, another species, is the largest juniper in the state, reaching heights to 50 feet. It has bluish green foliage with four-seeded cones. Common juniper, also known as dwarf juniper, is a lower shrub that is an important erosion fighter. All juniper berries serve as an important food source to some birds and small wildlife.

Utah juniper

Alligator juniper

Mesquite

A member of the pea family, mesquite is a spiny deciduous shrub or small tree that grows up to 30 feet high. It is abundant throughout southern, central, and occasionally in northern Arizona, at elevations ranging from 1,000 to 5,000 feet. Three species of mesquite in Arizona are western honey mesquite, screwbean mesquite, and velvet mesquite. Of these, velvet mesquite is the most common. All three have bean pods, which are used by humans, wildlife, and livestock as a food source. Many birds, insects, and mammals eat the beans (some estimates are that 80 percent of a coyote's diet is mesquite beans in the late summer and fall). Native Americans relied on sweet mesquite pods as a dietary staple from which they dried, cooked, and ate the beans, made teas, syrup, and a ground meal called *pinole.* Mesquite produces small, fragrant, greenish yellow flowers that are crowded on stalked spikes. The bark separates into dark strips and the wood is hard, reddish brown, with thin yellow sapwood. Native Americans found a wide variety of applications for the bark, such as making baskets, fabrics, and medicine. Mesquite burns slowly and smokelessly, making it one of the best sources of firewood in the desert. It is a common tree along the watercourses, washes, and alluvial bottoms where groundwater is available. In some areas, the roots may penetrate to depths of 60 feet.

Velvet mesquite

Mormon Tea Bush

Also called Indian tea bush or desert jointfir, this erect shrub stands about 3 or 4 feet tall. The upright stems are parallel and smooth, with tiny scalelike leaves at the stem joints. They have an upside-down broomlike appearance. Both the male and female of this species develop cones up to 3/8 of an inch long. The tea bush grows at lower elevations in arid rocky areas, deserts, or grasslands. Cattle sometimes graze stems in the winter, and the branchlets can be steeped to make a noncaffeinated drink that is used to treat colds and congestion. The early pioneers brewed this tea, although Native Americans were first known to enjoy the beverage.

Mormon tea bush

Palo Verde

Palo verde is the state tree of Arizona. In Spanish, the name means "green pole" or "green stick." The palo verde is not a normal tree—it is actually a legume from the pea family. The two species native to Arizona are the blue palo verde, with blue-green branches and leaves, and the yellow, or foothill, palo verde, with yellow-green branches and leaves. They both have green bark and stems in which photosynthesis (the process plants use to make the "food" they need to grow) is carried out. The green bark enables the trees to continue photosynthesis even during its leafless stage. So that palo verdes can survive in their desert habitat, they have tiny leaves that help lower water loss through transpiration. The leaves drop off during dry periods, further reducing the need for water. After substantial rains, new leaves grow. Masses of yellow flowers bloom in spring. In midsummer, seed pods are full of hard, brown seeds. Most parts of the plants are browsed by wildlife; pocket mice and kangaroo rats bury the seeds to eat later. The wood is soft and makes poor firewood. These trees grow to 30 feet.

Palo verde

Pinyon (Piñon) Pine

The pinyon is a bushy evergreen with a short trunk and compact, rounded crown. The gray to red-brown bark is rough and scaly. Needles range from 3/4 to 3 inches long, usually two to a bundle, with blue-green foliage on the younger trees and dark yellow-green foliage on more mature ones. Singleleaf pinyon is very similar but its needles occur singly. Cones are 1 to 2 inches and have edible seeds, known as Indian nuts or pine nuts, that can be eaten raw or roasted. Pinyon pines rarely grow taller than 30 feet and they are the most drought resistant of all pines in Arizona. They are usually found in woodlands (often with junipers), mesas, and plateaus at elevations lower than 7,000 feet.

Pinyon pine

Pinyon pine cones

Ponderosa Pine

Also called western yellow pine, the ponderosa pine has long needles (5 to 11 inches), which grow in clusters of three from a single point. The bark of young trees is yellowish brown to cinnamon, whereas older trees develop orange flaky bark. The spiky red-brown cones are about 3 to 6 inches long. Seed cones provide an important food source for wildlife. Ponderosa pines can grow 60 to 125 feet tall and are usually found at altitudes of 6,000 to 8,500 feet. This is the most abundant large pine in Arizona.

Ponderosa pine

Ponderosa pine cones

Tamarisk

Often called salt cedar because the plant is fairly tolerant of saline soil and has foliage somewhat like that of junipers, tamarisk is found on riverbanks and moist sites throughout the state. Classified as a shrub or moderate-size tree, it has reddish bark, intricate feathery light green branches, and fragrant soft pink to nearly white blossoms in the spring. Tamarisk was introduced from Eurasia in the 1850s in an effort to control soil erosion, but the plant has since escaped and now dominates water supplies needed for the survival of native plants and animals. Dense thickets of tamarisk, a pioneer species, establish themselves on surfaces devoid of other plants. Mature specimens produce millions of seeds annually, which are widely distributed by the wind. Tamarisk produces most of its seeds at the same time river levels drop from spring highs. Consequently, as rivers dwindle, they expose large areas of wet sand and silt, which are ideal seedbeds. From a wildlife point of view, the tamarisk has little value and is usually considered detrimental to native plants and animals. The leaves, twigs, and seeds are extremely low in nutrients, and as a result, very few insects or wildlife will use them. Tamarisk is difficult to eradicate. It resprouts readily after cutting or burning. Research and many programs are now in place to reduce or eliminate tamarisk, and laws are being enacted to eliminate its sale and importation.

Tamarisk

Winter Fat

Winter fat is also called white sage, sweet sage, or winter sage, although it is not related to sage at all. The plant has many erect, woolly branches that arise from a woody base. It has flowering clusters that when gone to seed fluff out to look like cottonballs. The plant has a fuzzy, white, and hairy appearance due to the densely woolly leaves that cover the entire plant. Leaves are dry in the fall but remain on the plant throughout winter. Winter fat serves as an important winter food source for wildlife and livestock.

Winter fat

Cacti and Succulents

Banana Yucca

The most common yucca in Arizona, banana yucca is a medium-sized, usually stemless, plant. It has stiff broad blue-green leaves that stem from a basal rosette. Waxy reddish and white bell-shaped flowers grow on a short stem scarcely taller than the leaves. Flowers are followed by fat fleshy bananalike fruits, which grow to 5 inches. This species reproduces repeatedly in its lifetime. Dried roots can be soaked in water to produce a soapy lather. Native Americans ate the fruits, seeds, and flower buds raw, roasted, or dried. They wove the fibrous leaves to make mats, sandals, baskets, and cloth.

Banana yucca

Barrel Cactus

True to their name, barrel cacti are cylindrical or barrel-shaped and are among the largest cacti of the North American deserts. But they grow very slowly—a four-year old barrel cactus might only be 3 inches high. Once established, they can live to be 100 years old. Members of this genus have prominent ribs and are armed with heavy spines. Most have 1 1/2- to 2 1/2-inch yellow-green or red flowers growing in a crown near the top of the plant. They normally grow to heights of 2 to 3 feet but they have been known to reach heights up to 10 feet. Fruits become fleshy and often juicy when mature but are not usually considered edible. Barrel cacti usually grow along desert washes, on gravelly slopes, and beneath desert canyon walls. Most species bloom from April through June, depending on local conditions. Native Americans boiled young flowers in water to eat like cabbage and mashed the flowers for a drink. They also used the cactus as a cooking pot by cutting off the top, scooping out the pulp, and combining hot stones with food inside. The pulp has been used to make cactus candy, a popular treat.

Barrel cactus

Century Plant

Members of the agave family, century plants take many years to flower, although not a century. The plant actually lives about 25 years before it sends up a flowering stalk, which happens only once in its lifetime. The blossoming spike grows so large, so quickly that it entirely saps the plant's resources. New century plants are formed from the root system. Normally found on dry rocky desert slopes, this unique plant has a tall thin stalk from 10 to 14 feet high

Century plant

that grows from a thick basal rosette of gray-green leaves. The leaves are 10 to 18 inches long with sharp spines. The century plant provided Native Americans with a source of soap, food, fiber, medicine, and weapons.

Cholla

Pronounced "choy-ya," the cholla is a common cactus of the Arizona deserts. Both the prickly pear and cholla are shrubby cacti belonging to the genus *Opuntia,* which has the greatest number of species with more variation than any other cactus group. Of the more common Arizona chollas are the chainfruit cholla (the largest), teddybear cholla (also known as jumping cholla because the spiny joints detach easily, seeming to jump off and penetrate passersby), and staghorn cholla (forked branches resemble deer antlers). For the most part, cholla grows in well-drained sandy and gravelly soils in desert plant communities at lower elevations. Take care as you walk in the desert—the spikes can penetrate your shoe soles and are extremely painful to remove.

Staghorn cholla

Teddy bear cholla

Joshua Tree

The Joshua tree, the largest of the yuccas, is a member of the lily family. This picturesque spike-leafed evergreen grows in dry soils on plains, slopes, and mesas, often in groves. Joshua trees range from 15 to 40 feet in height with a diameter of 1 to 3 feet. Flowers are bell-shaped, 1 to 1 1/2 inches long, with six creamy yellow-green sepals. The flowers are crowded into 12- to 18-inch, many-branched clusters that have an unpleasant odor; they blossom mostly in the spring. Not all trees flower annually. Joshua tree fruit is elliptical, green-brown, 2 to 4 inches long, and somewhat fleshy. It dries and falls soon after maturity in late spring, revealing many flat seeds. Joshua trees (and most other yuccas) rely on the female pronuba moth (also called the yucca moth) for pollination. No other animal visiting the blooms transfers the pollen from one flower to another. In fact, the female yucca moth has evolved special organs to collect and distribute the pollen onto the surface of the flower. She then lays her eggs in the flower's ovaries, and when the larvae hatch, they feed on the yucca seeds. Without the moth's pollination, the Joshua tree could not reproduce, nor could the moth, whose larvae would have no seeds to eat. Although an old Joshua tree can sprout new plants from its roots, only the seeds produced in pollinated flowers can scatter far enough to establish a new stand. Joshua trees can live to between 100 and 300 years.

Joshua tree

Ocotillo

Not a cactus but a shrub, ocotillo is sometimes called coachwhip for its bare, 8- to 15-inch-long stems. Ocotillo are leafless most of the year, except immediately after rain, when the slender thorny branches sprout tiny green leaves. Ocotillo seize the opportunity to photosynthesize while the soil is moist, as the leaves quickly wither and drop as the ground dries out. This drought-responsive process may be repeated several times during warm months. Narrow oval leaves grow to 2 inches, appearing in bunches above the spines. Ocotillo blooms annually to produce dense spikes of bright red tubular blossoms in the late spring. Hummingbirds and other nectar feeders are attracted to the flowers. The Tohono O'odham ate the flowers like sweet candy and rubbed the flower stems on their cheeks for rouge. The ocotillo is one of the few flowering plants confined to the desert habitat.

Ocotillo

Organ Pipe Cactus

Organ Pipe National Monument in southwestern Arizona was established to preserve this species—the second-largest cactus in the United States (saguaro is largest), which grows as tall as 23 feet. It was named because the shape resembles the pipes of an organ. The plant has a cluster of slender branches that grow from a point at ground level, curving upward. In about July, these plants produce pale lavender, funnel-shaped blooms at night. The flowers are followed by round, edible, spiny red fruits. Fruits lose their spines at maturity, opening to display an edible red pulp. This fruit has provided a food source to Native Americans for centuries. The pulp can be eaten as is, made into jelly, or fermented into a beverage.

Organ pipe cactus

Prickly Pear Cactus

Prickly pear is the common name for plants of a genus of the cactus family. They typically have round pads with prickly spines. The pads, covered with a thick layer of wax to prevent water evaporation, are actually modified branches or stems that serve several functions including water

Desert prickly pear

Beavertail prickly pear

storage, photosynthesis, and flower production. Flowers may be red, purple, or yellow; the blooms appear from May to June and last only a few days. The flowers turn into a warty edible pear-shaped and spine-covered fruit with sweet flesh. The plants can be 5 feet tall.

Saguaro

The saguaro (pronounced "sahwaro") cactus is the state flower of Arizona. Some saguaros reach heights of 50 feet, making them the largest cacti in the United States. A saguaro has a tall, thick columnlike stem, 18 to 24 inches in diameter, with several large "arms" curving upward. Smooth waxy skin is covered with spines. Saguaros begin life nearby a "nurse" tree or shrub (perhaps a palo verde or mesquite), which provides a moist, shaded habitat. Ironically, the nurse plant will die when the growing saguaro outrivals and kills it off. Saguaros can increase their weight by up to a ton by absorbing water—and lots of it. But the cactus shrinks as it consumes the reservoir of water during drought. A combination of its slow growth and capacity to store large quantities of water enables the saguaro to flower every year, regardless of rainfall. The plant produces creamy white flowers during cool desert nights in May and June. The flowers close by noon the next day, never to reopen. Many petals form around a tube (about 4 inches long) lined with a mass of yellow stamens. In the bottom of this tube, sweet nectar accumulates. The somewhat skunky-smelling elixir, together with the colors of the flower, serves to attract birds, bats, and insects that pollinate the saguaro flower. After fertilization, green ovular fruits begin to form immediately. Just prior to the rainy season the ripened fruit will split apart to reveal a pulpy crimson flesh, which all desert creatures seem to relish. Several kinds of birds make their homes in the saguaro cactus by chiseling out holes in the trunk.

Saguaro cactus

Saguaro cactus flowers

Soaptree Yucca

An agave, the yucca has a tall, dense cluster of creamy whitish or greenish globe-shaped flowers atop stout, leafy stems. Numerous leaves grow from the base, up to 2 or 3 feet in length. Yuccas are members of the agave family and are pollinated by yucca moths. The moths, which cannot reproduce without yuccas, lay eggs during pollination and their larvae feed upon the seeds. Yuccas grow in sandy, rocky places, in dry mesas, and on slopes. The soaptree yucca derives its name from the material in its roots and trunk that people have used as soap. Native Americans ate the fruits, seeds, and flower buds raw, roasted, or dried. They wove the fibrous leaves to make mats, sandals, baskets, and cloth. Cattle enjoy the tender young stalks, and chopped trunks and leaves are still utilized as emergency cattle feed in times of drought.

Soaptree yucca

The Northwest Region

Trails in the Northwest Region

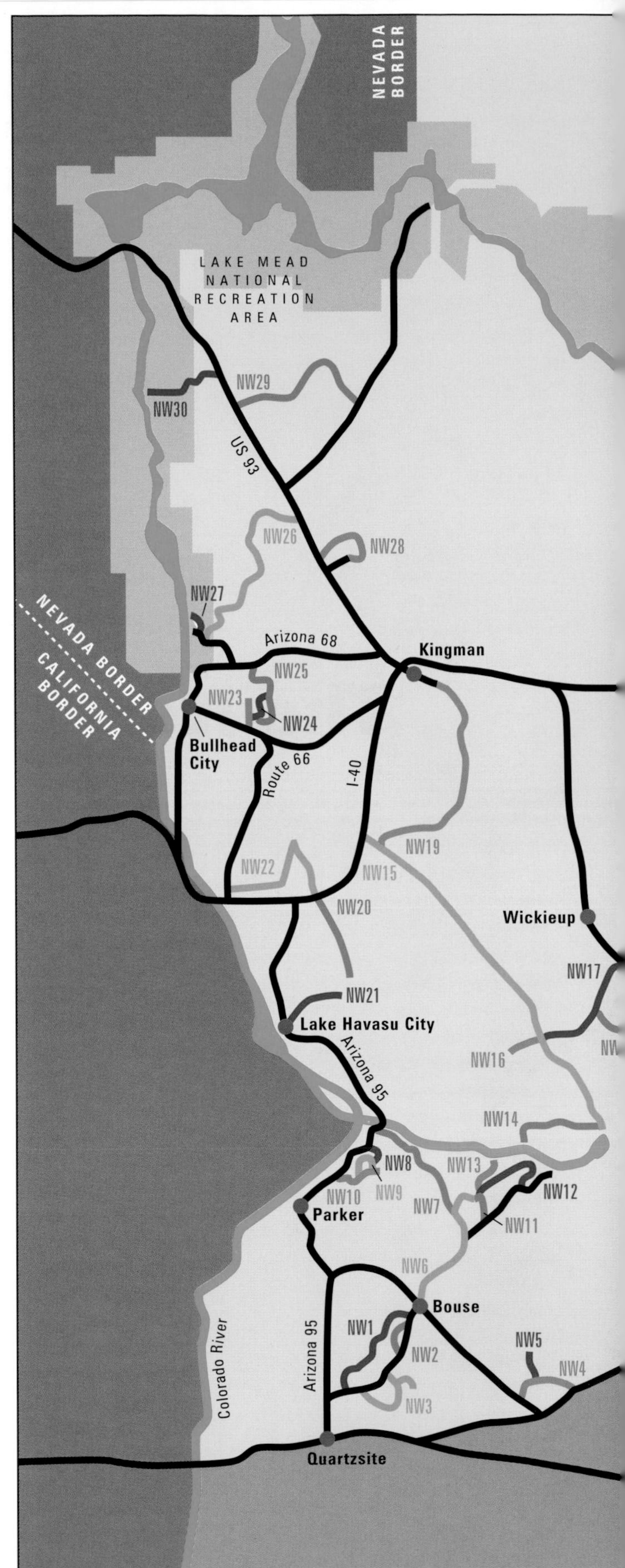

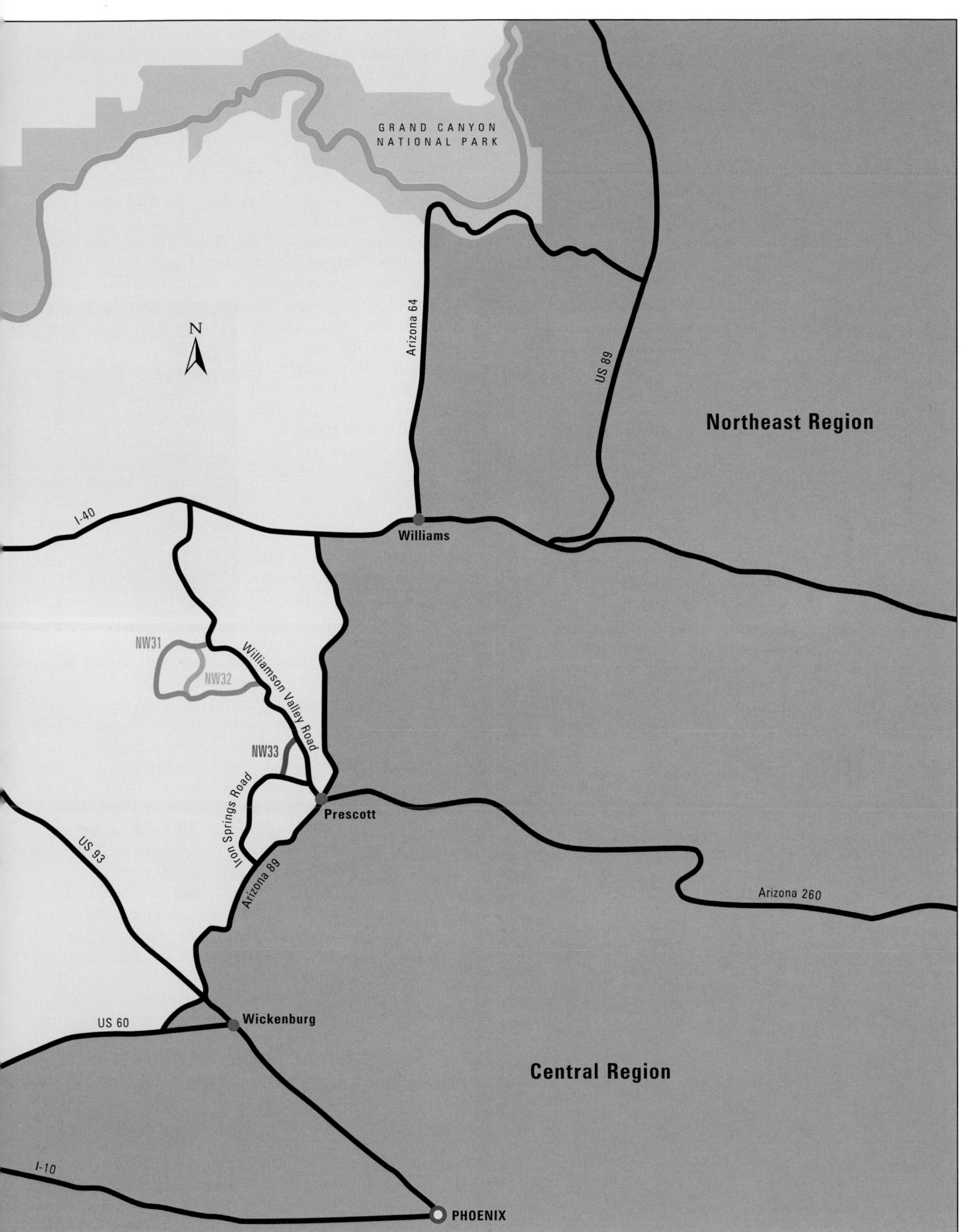
GRAND CANYON
NATIONAL PARK
N
Arizona 64
US 89
Northeast Region
I-40
Williams
NW31
NW32
Williamson Valley Road
NW33
Iron Springs Road
Prescott
US 93
Arizona 89
Arizona 260
US 60
Wickenburg
Central Region
I-10
PHOENIX

NORTHWEST REGION TRAIL #1

Four Peaks Mountain Trail

Starting Point:	Plomosa Road, 3.3 miles south of Bouse
Finishing Point:	Plomosa Road, 0.5 miles north of mile marker 7
Total Mileage:	14.8 miles
Unpaved Mileage:	14.8 miles
Driving Time:	2 hours
Elevation Range:	1,100–1,600 feet
Usually Open:	Year-round
Best Time to Travel:	Fall to spring
Difficulty Rating:	4
Scenic Rating:	8
Remoteness Rating:	+0

Special Attractions

- Rockhounding for jasper and hematite.
- Four Peaks Mountain and Plomosa Range scenery.
- Access to a network of 4WD trails.
- Many sand dunes to cross at the lower end of the trail.

History

Bouse, first settled in 1906, was originally named Brayton, after John Brayton, the owner of the nearby Harquahala Mine. It became Bouse when an official misread the application and accidentally registered the community as Bouse, which was the name of the person filing the form.

Thomas Bouse, after whom the town was accidentally named, arrived in the area in 1889. His wife, Katherine, and daughter joined him in 1892 after he had built the first two rooms of his home. More children were added to the family and more rooms to the house until the simple cabin he first built became a large, two-story home. Thomas Bouse died of a rattlesnake bite in 1929 and is buried in Bouse Cemetery. The homestead site, located a short distance out of Bouse on the Plomosa Road, is marked by a historical plaque.

Four Peaks Mountain

The Plomosa Range (Plomosa means "lead bearing") has had much mining activity over the years, mainly for gold. Early mines date back as far as the 1860s.

Description

To reach the start of the trail from the middle of Bouse, turn southwest on the paved Plomosa Road at the sign for the Bouse Community Park. This road is also known as the Quartzsite Scenic Route. Follow the paved road for 3.3 miles to the start of the trail.

The first part of the trail is well used because its smooth, gravelly surface attracts a lot of winter visitors in RVs. Consequently, there are many turnouts, small side trails, and areas used for RV parking in the first couple of miles. The route directions only list the major tracks to the left and right for the first few miles as new small tracks appear all the time. Remain on the main trail.

An easy sandy section of the trail

Two miles from the start, the trail passes through some low hills that are frequented by rock hounds. Chunks of hematite and rusty-colored jasper can be found around the slopes of the hills and the creek beds on either side of the trail.

From here the trail winds through the low hills of the Plomosa Range past many small mine workings. It passes along the eastern side of Four Peaks Mountain—the four distinct peaks are most visible from this side, the highest to the south end. After 3.8 miles a short track on the right climbs steeply to a mine shaft and tailings. The deep, perfectly square shaft is lined with timber as far as the eye can see.

From the junction with the Northwest #2: Plomosa Range Trail, the navigation becomes tricky. There are some well-used side trails along the south side of Four Peaks Mountain and it is easy to overshoot a turn. Keep a close eye on the directions and GPS coordinates to ensure you don't go wrong.

The scenery as the trail crosses through the Plomosa Range is very rugged and spectacular, with red soil, large saguaro cacti, and the southernmost peak of Four Peaks Mountain. The trail runs along a wash for a couple of miles and then leaves the wash to swing down through the sand dunes on the western side of the range. The right turn, 8.1 miles from the start of the trail, is easy to miss as there are no distinguishing features to mark it, and the trail straight ahead is well used. If you overshoot and continue past this point, it is possible to exit to Plomosa Road by keeping generally south, but it is an absolute maze of trails; many are used mainly by ATVs, and many are dead ends with brushy vegetation.

The final few miles of the trail cross through some sand dunes that have collected on the eastern side of the Plomosa Range. The sand is deep and loose, but the dunes are not high enough to cause many problems. In the warmer months you may need to deflate your tires. Watch for oncoming vehicles on the crests. The dunes are covered with saguaro and ocotillo and are exceptionally photogenic, especially in spring when the desert flowers are blooming. There are many small washes to cross and many faint tracks on the right and left on this final part of the trail. Only the major washes and tracks are noted in the route directions.

For the most part the trail is moderate. The surface is loose, especially in the washes and around the southern end of Four Peaks Mountain, but it lacks the fist-sized, rubbly boulders that make a lot of trails in the area more difficult.

The trail ends on Plomosa Road, 0.5 miles north of mile marker 7. Neither the topographic nor the BLM maps accurately show the trail on the east side of the Plomosa Range.

Current Road Information

Bureau of Land Management
Havasu Field Office
2610 Sweetwater Ave.
Lake Havasu City, AZ 86406
(520) 505-1200

Map References

BLM Blythe
USGS 1:24,000 Bouse, Ibex Peak, Bouse SW
1:100,000 Blythe
Maptech CD-ROM: Colorado River/Lake Havasu
Arizona Atlas & Gazetteer, p. 46

Route Directions

▼ 0.0			From Plomosa Road, 3.3 miles south of Bouse and the intersection with Arizona 72, turn west onto unmarked, single-lane dirt road. The turn is just south of a cattle guard. Zero trip meter.
	4.3 ▲		Trail ends back on Plomosa Road, 3.3 miles south of Bouse. Turn left for Bouse; turn right for Quartzsite.
			GPS: N33°53.67' W114°01.95'
▼ 0.3		SO	Track on left. The start of the trail is a popular RV winter parking area. Many small tracks and turnouts for the first 2.1 miles. Remain on the main trail.
	4.0 ▲	SO	Track on right.
▼ 0.4		SO	Track on left.
	3.9 ▲	SO	Track on right.
			GPS: N33°53.62' W114°02.38'
▼ 0.6		BL	Crossroads with well-used tracks coming in from the right; keep to the major left-hand track. Followed by track on left.
	3.7 ▲	BR	Track on right, then crossroads with well-used tracks coming in from left. Keep to the major right-hand track.
			GPS: N33°53.57' W114°02.65'
▼ 1.0		SO	Track on left.
	3.3 ▲	SO	Track on right.
▼ 2.1		SO	Trail passes through some low hills. Hematite and jasper can be found scattered in the hills on both sides of the trail.
	2.2 ▲	SO	Trail passes through some low hills. Hematite and jasper can be found scattered in the hills on both sides of the trail. Many small tracks and turnouts for the next 2.1 miles as the trail passes through a popular RV winter parking area. Remain on the main trail.
			GPS: N33°52.88' W114°03.95'
▼ 2.9		SO	Cross through wash.
	1.4 ▲	SO	Cross through wash.
			GPS: N33°52.51' W114°04.41'
▼ 3.0		SO	Cross through wash.
	1.3 ▲	SO	Cross through wash.
▼ 3.1		SO	Track on right. Four Peaks Mountain is ahead.
	1.2 ▲	SO	Track on left.
			GPS: N33°52.39' W114°04.51'
▼ 3.2		SO	Cross through wash.
	1.1 ▲	SO	Cross through wash.
▼ 3.5		SO	Faint tracks on left and right; then cross through wash.
	0.8 ▲	SO	Cross through wash; then faint tracks on left and right.
▼ 3.6		SO	Faint track on left; then cross through wash.
	0.7 ▲	SO	Cross through wash; then faint track on right.
▼ 3.7		SO	Faint track on left.
	0.6 ▲	SO	Faint track on right.
▼ 3.8		SO	Track on right goes to mine shaft and tailings. The four distinct peaks of Four Peaks Mountain are clearly visible to the right.
	0.5 ▲	BR	Track on left goes to mine shaft and tailings. The four distinct peaks of Four Peaks Mountain are clearly visible to the left.
			GPS: N33°51.80' W114°04.74'
▼ 4.1		SO	Track on right.
	0.2 ▲	SO	Track on left.
			GPS: N33°51.69' W114°04.45'
▼ 4.2		SO	Cross through wash; then faint track on left. Then cross through larger wash with tracks on left and right up and down wash.
	0.1 ▲	SO	Cross through large wash with tracks on left and right up and down the wash. Then faint track on right. Cross through second wash.
▼ 4.3		TR	Track on left and track straight ahead immediately lead to Northwest #2: Plomosa Range Trail. Zero trip meter.
	0.0 ▲		Continue to the northwest.
			GPS: N33°51.60' W114°04.27'
▼ 0.0			Continue to the southwest.
	4.1 ▲	TL	Two tracks on right immediately lead to Northwest #2: Plomosa Range Trail. Zero trip meter.
▼ 0.1		BR	Track on left; then cross through wash.
	4.0 ▲	SO	Cross through wash; then track on right.
▼ 0.3		SO	Track on right to old vehicle.
	3.8 ▲	SO	Track on left to old vehicle.
▼ 0.5		SO	Track on left.
	3.6 ▲	BL	Track on right.
			GPS: N33°51.29' W114°04.67'
▼ 0.8		BR	Cross through wash; then track on left.
	3.3 ▲	SO	Track on right; then cross through wash.
			GPS: N33°51.30' W114°04.93'
▼ 1.0		BR	Track on left.
	3.1 ▲	BL	Track on right. The largest peak of Four Peaks Mountain is ahead.
▼ 1.1		SO	Track on left; cross through small wash.
	3.0 ▲	SO	Cross through small wash; track on right.
▼ 1.2		TR	Cross through wash; then turn right; main track continues straight ahead. After the right turn, immediately bear left up red soil trail.
	2.9 ▲	TL	Track on left; continue straight ahead; then immediately turn left at T-intersection and cross through wash.

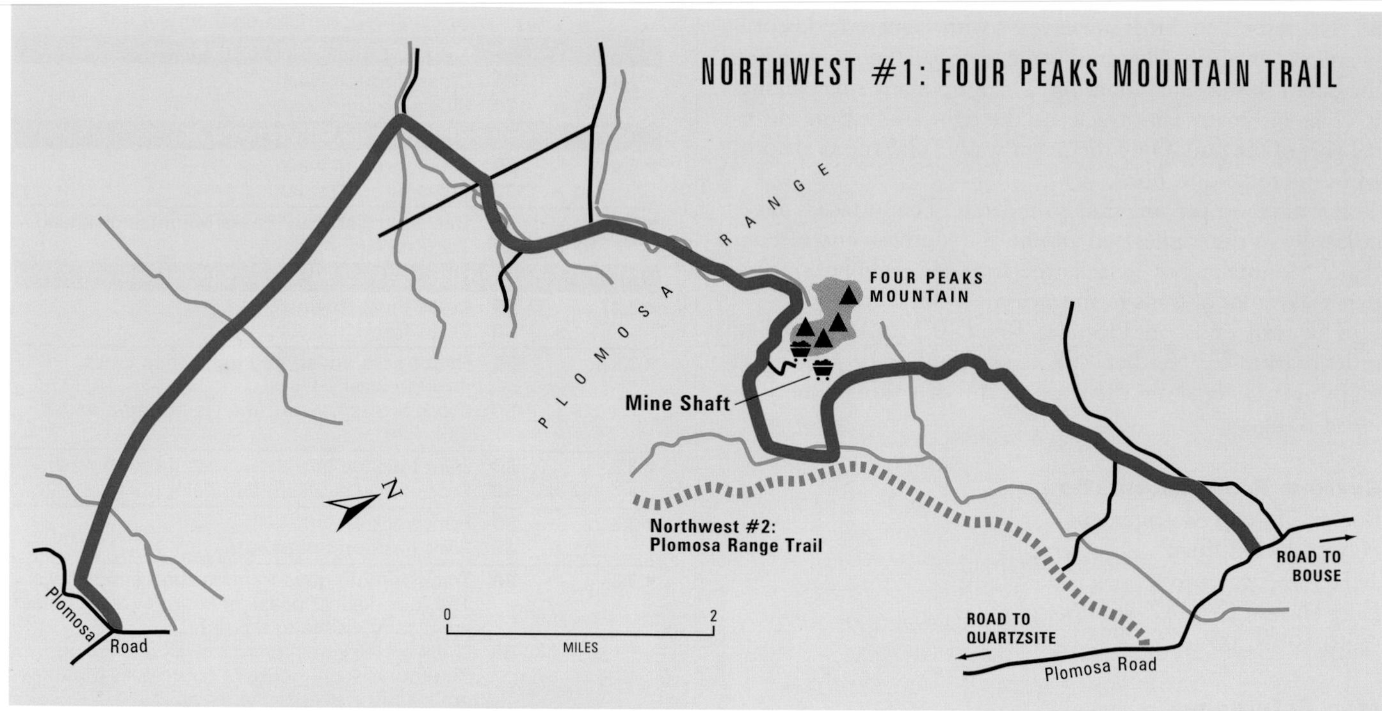

			GPS: N33°51.51′ W114°05.19′
▼ 1.3		TR	Mine with deep wooden shaft and concrete foundation on right at southern end of Four Peaks Mountain; then turn right again to rejoin main trail.
	2.8 ▲	TL	Turn left to pass by mine with deep wooden shaft and concrete foundation on left; then turn left again to rejoin main trail.
			GPS: N33°51.60′ W114°05.18′
▼ 1.6		SO	Cross through wash—there are many small washes to cross in this section.
	2.5 ▲	SO	Cross through wash.
▼ 1.8		SO	Track on right. Main trail follows alongside wash.
	2.3 ▲	BR	Track on left.
			GPS: N33°51.87′ W114°05.44′
▼ 2.3		SO	Enter wash.
	1.8 ▲	SO	Exit wash.
▼ 2.5		SO	Exit wash; then track on left. Many small wash crossings for the next 1.6 miles.
	1.6 ▲	SO	Track on right; then enter wash.
			GPS: N33°51.52′ W114°05.99′
▼ 3.5		BL	Cross through wash; then track on right; then cross through small wash.
	0.6 ▲	SO	Cross through small wash; then track on left; then cross through wash.
			GPS: N33°51.08′ W114°06.76′
▼ 3.6		SO	Track on right.
	0.5 ▲	SO	Track on left.
▼ 4.1		TR	Cross through wash; then turn right. Zero trip meter.
	0.0 ▲		Continue to the north. Many small wash crossings for the next 1.6 miles.
			GPS: N33°50.54′ W114°06.87′
▼ 0.0			Continue to the west.
	6.4 ▲	TL	T-intersection. Zero trip meter.
▼ 0.2		SO	Cross through wash.
	6.2 ▲	SO	Cross through wash.
▼ 0.4		SO	Cross through wash.
	6.0 ▲	SO	Cross through wash.
▼ 0.5		SO	Cross through wash.
	5.9 ▲	SO	Cross through wash.
▼ 0.6		TL	Crossroads.
	5.8 ▲	TR	Crossroads.
			GPS: N33°50.51′ W114°07.48′
▼ 0.7		BL	Small track on right goes to some diggings.
	5.7 ▲	SO	Small track on left is second entrance to diggings.
			GPS: N33°50.47′ W114°07.54′
▼ 0.8		SO	Track on right is second entrance to diggings. Survey marker on left.
	5.6 ▲	BR	Track on left goes to some diggings. Survey marker on right.
▼ 1.4		TL	Track swings sharp left; faint track straight on.
	5.0 ▲	TR	Track swings sharp right; faint track on left.
			GPS: N33°50.24′ W114°08.27′
▼ 1.5		SO	Cross through wash. Tracks on right down wash.
	4.9 ▲	SO	Cross through wash. Tracks on left down wash.
▼ 1.9		SO	Cross sand ridge.
	4.5 ▲	SO	Cross sand ridge.
▼ 2.7		SO	Cross double sand ridge.
	3.7 ▲	SO	Cross double sand ridge.
			GPS: N33°49.18′ W114°07.70′
▼ 3.1		SO	Cross sand ridge.
	3.3 ▲	SO	Cross sand ridge.
▼ 3.3		SO	Cross through wash.
	3.1 ▲	SO	Cross through wash.
▼ 3.6		SO	Cross through wash.
	2.8 ▲	SO	Cross through wash.
▼ 4.1		SO	Faint track on left; then cross through deep wash.
	2.3 ▲	SO	Cross through deep wash; then faint track on right.
			GPS: N33°48.01′ W114°07.40′

▼ 4.2	SO	Faint track on left.
2.2 ▲	SO	Faint track on right.
▼ 4.3	SO	Cross sand ridge.
2.1 ▲	SO	Cross sand ridge.
		GPS: N33°47.86' W114°07.23'
▼ 4.4	SO	Track on left.
2.0 ▲	SO	Track on right.
▼ 4.7	SO	Cross through wash.
1.7 ▲	SO	Cross through wash.
▼ 4.9	SO	Track on right.
1.5 ▲	SO	Track on left.
		GPS: N33°47.42' W114°06.92'
▼ 5.0	SO	Track on left.
1.4 ▲	SO	Track on right.
▼ 5.1	SO	Cross through wash.
1.3 ▲	SO	Cross through wash.
▼ 5.2	SO	Cross through wash; tracks on right and left up and down wash.
1.2 ▲	SO	Cross through wash; tracks on right and left up and down wash.
▼ 5.5	SO	Cross through wash.
0.9 ▲	SO	Cross through wash.
▼ 5.9	TL	T-intersection at graded dirt Old Plomosa Road.
0.5 ▲	TR	Turn onto unmarked, small, ungraded trail heading to the northwest. This turn is easy to miss.
		GPS: N33°46.79' W114°06.32'
▼ 6.0	SO	Small track on left; then cross through wash.
0.4 ▲	SO	Cross through wash; then small track on right.
▼ 6.4		Trail ends at the junction with the paved Plomosa Road, 0.5 miles north of mile marker 7. Turn is unmarked but numbered trail 822 is opposite the turn.
0.0 ▲		Trail commences on the paved Plomosa Road, 0.5 miles north of mile marker 7. The turn is unmarked, but numbered trail 822 is opposite the turn. Turn southwest on the graded Old Plomosa Road, which parallels the paved new road. Zero trip meter.
		GPS: N33°46.95' W114°05.87'

NORTHWEST REGION TRAIL #2

Plomosa Range Trail

Starting Point:	**Plomosa Road, 0.4 miles north of mile marker 15**
Finishing Point:	**Plomosa Road, 0.1 miles south of mile marker 12**
Total Mileage:	**6.4 miles**
Unpaved Mileage:	**6.4 miles**
Driving Time:	**1 hour**
Elevation Range:	**1,100–1,400 feet**
Usually Open:	**Year-round**
Best Time to Travel:	**Fall to spring**
Difficulty Rating:	**3**
Scenic Rating:	**8**
Remoteness Rating:	**+0**

Special Attractions

- Views of Four Peaks Mountain.
- Popular winter RV parking and camping area.

Description

This easy trail runs along the eastern edge of the Plomosa Range, giving views across the Plomosa Mountains.

To get to the start of the trail from the middle of Bouse, turn southwest on the paved Plomosa Road at the sign for the Bouse Community Park. The road is also known as the Quartzsite Scenic Route. Follow the paved road for 4.7 miles, then turn west on the narrow unmarked trail. The turn is 0.4 miles north of mile marker 15. The first couple of miles of the trail are smooth and wide enough that large RVs are able to traverse it. This aspect of the trail, and the many flat areas, make it a popular winter camping area for RVs, although there is a 14-day limit. There are many narrow trails and turnouts in the first few miles. Remain on the main trail.

The Plomosa Range

The trail intersects with the rougher Northwest #1: Four Peaks Mountain Trail, which crosses the range. The main trail then runs along a ridge top, which is easy and smooth. One nice thing about this trail is the absence of the fist-sized, rubbly boulders that make many of Arizona's trails difficult. The surface is loose in places, and has some minor ruts, but is well within the capabilities of a stock SUV. A couple of the descents through the dry washes are slightly rougher.

The trail, which then rejoins the paved Plomosa Road, is a pleasant alternative route for exploring the area around the range.

Current Road Information

Bureau of Land Management
Havasu Field Office
2610 Sweetwater Ave.
Lake Havasu City, AZ 86406
(520) 505-1200

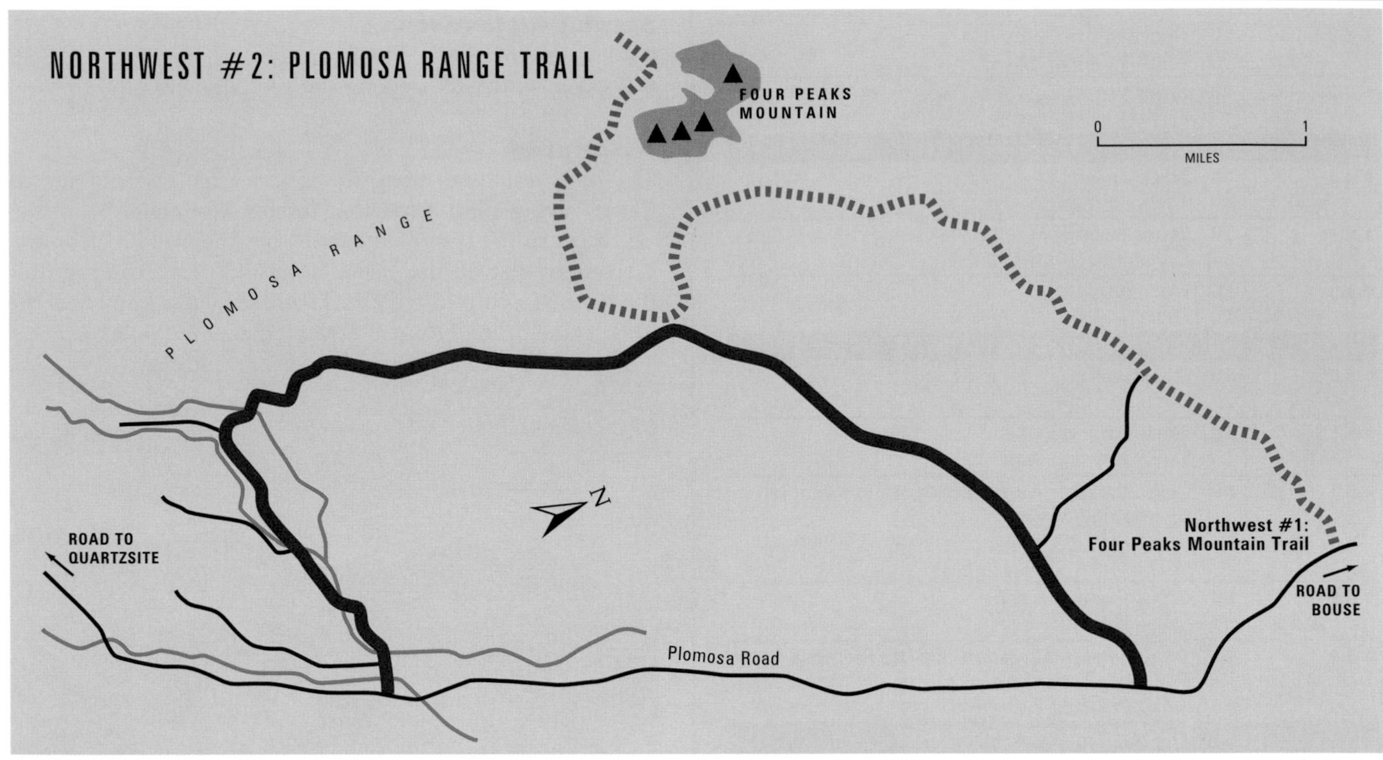

Map References

BLM Blythe
USGS 1:24,000 Bouse, Ibex Peak
1:100,000 Blythe
Maptech CD-ROM: Colorado River/Lake Havasu
Arizona Atlas & Gazetteer, p. 46

Route Directions

Mileage		Direction	Description
▼ 0.0			On Plomosa Road, 0.4 miles north of mile marker 15, 4.7 miles south of Bouse, turn west on small, ungraded, unmarked dirt road and zero trip meter. There is a small track opposite. Many small trails on the right and left; remain on main trail for the first 2.5 miles.
	2.5 ▲		Trail finishes back on Plomosa Road. Turn left for Bouse; turn right for Quartzsite.
			GPS: N33°52.76′ W114°01.70′
▼ 2.5		BL	Track on right leads to Northwest #1: Four Peaks Mountain Trail. Zero trip meter.
	0.0 ▲		Continue to the northeast. Many small trails on the right and left; remain on the main trail for the final 2.5 miles.
			GPS: N33°51.66′ W114°04.19′
▼ 0.0			Continue to the southeast.
	2.4 ▲	BR	Track on left leads to Northwest #1: Four Peaks Mountain Trail. Zero trip meter.
▼ 0.1		SO	Faint track on left.
	2.3 ▲	BL	Faint track on right.
			GPS: N33°51.48′ W114°04.23′
▼ 0.4		SO	Track on left.
	2.0 ▲	SO	Track on right.
			GPS: N33°51.27′ W114°04.29′
▼ 0.6		SO	Track on left.
	1.8 ▲	BR	Track on right.
▼ 1.4		SO	Track on right.
	1.0 ▲	BR	Track on left.
			GPS: N33°50.37′ W114°04.64′
▼ 2.2		SO	Cross through wash.
	0.2 ▲	SO	Cross through wash.
			GPS: N33°49.84′ W114°04.73′
▼ 2.3		SO	Track on right.
	0.1 ▲	BR	Track on left.
			GPS: N33°49.74′ W114°04.73′
▼ 2.4		SO	Track on right. Zero trip meter.
	0.0 ▲		Continue to the northwest.
			GPS: N33°49.67′ W114°04.68′
▼ 0.0			Continue to the east.
	1.5 ▲	BR	Track on left. Zero trip meter.
▼ 0.3		SO	Track on right.
	1.2 ▲	SO	Track on left.
▼ 0.4		SO	Faint track on left and right.
	1.1 ▲	SO	Faint track on left and right.
▼ 0.6		BL	Cross through wash; then track on right.
	0.9 ▲	BR	Track on left; then cross through wash.
			GPS: N33°49.76′ W114°04.04′
▼ 0.9		SO	Track on left; then cross through wash.
	0.6 ▲	BL	Cross through wash; then track on right.
▼ 1.2		SO	Cross through wide wash.
	0.3 ▲	SO	Cross through wide wash.
▼ 1.3		SO	Two tracks on right.
	0.2 ▲	BR	Two tracks on left.
▼ 1.4		SO	Cross through wash.
	0.1 ▲	SO	Cross through wash.
▼ 1.5			Trail ends at the junction with the paved Plomosa Road. Turn right for Quartzsite; turn left for Bouse.
	0.0 ▲		Trail commences on the paved Plomosa Road, 0.1 miles south of mile marker 12. Turn west on unmarked, ungraded dirt road and zero trip meter. There is a turnout opposite.
			GPS: N33°49.89′ W114°03.19′

NORTHWEST REGION TRAIL #3

South Plomosa Range Trail

Starting Point:	Plomosa Road, mile marker 8
Finishing Point:	Plomosa Road, 0.3 miles northeast of mile marker 3
Total Mileage:	16.2 miles
Unpaved Mileage:	16.2 miles
Driving Time:	2.5 hours
Elevation Range:	1,000–2,000 feet
Usually Open:	Year-round
Best Time to Travel:	October to May
Difficulty Rating:	4
Scenic Rating:	9
Remoteness Rating:	+0

Special Attractions

- Remains of the Southern Cross Mine.
- Views of Haystack Peak and Ibex Peak.
- Winding, remote desert trail through the Plomosa Range.
- Bouse Fisherman intaglio.

History

Quinn Pass, located approximately 1.5 miles north of the northern end of this trail, was for many years the home of Thomas Quinn. Originally from New Jersey, Quinn prospected in the Plomosa Range and lived north of the pass in a cabin that bears his name.

The Bouse Fisherman is an intaglio, or geoglyph, an etching inscribed in the desert floor by Native Americans many years ago. It is one of a series of geoglyphs that can be found along the Colorado River. The most well known is at Blythe; there are others south of Quartzsite and near Yuma. The Bouse Fisherman is thought to represent Kumastamho, the creator, as he plunges his spear into the desert to create the Colorado River. The ancient story tells of Kumastamho as he made his way north through the desert, searching for water. His first attempts were unsuccessful; the water drained away to the more fertile, well-watered lands to the north. On his third attempt he struck water that drained to the south and the desert areas. With his spear tip, he made a path for the water, creating the path of the Colorado River.

A stone ruin at Southern Cross Mine with Ibex Peak (on right) and Haystack Peak in the background

Climax Mine shaft with the trail behind

The intaglio is large and has been fenced off by the BLM to protect it. At first, it can be difficult to see the lighter-colored edges against the desert pavement, but it is still possible to make out most of the figure, the spear raised above his head, and two fish in the water below.

The Bouse Fisherman is 0.2 miles southwest of the northern end of the trail and is marked by a small sign. There is a large parking area. To reach the intaglio, hike 0.2 miles along the old vehicle trail. Coordinates for the intaglio are GPS: N33°47.45' W114°05.57'.

Description

This highly scenic trail winds through the southern end of the Plomosa Range, south of the paved Plomosa Road. The well-formed, ungraded trail is well used and easy to follow. A fairly deep wash at the start of the trail forms a natural barrier to RVs, so this trail does not have the large network of faint trails and campsites that make navigation tricky on many of the other trails in the Plomosa Range.

The trail winds through a pathway in the range, passing close to dramatic, steep red walls as it climbs into the hills. Close to the northern end, a spur trail leads 2.8 miles to the remains of the Southern Cross Mine. There are a few small stone ruins, extensive diggings, adits, shafts, and a large wooden ore hopper—all located near the foot of Ibex Peak.

The main trail climbs through a tight, scenic canyon past the many diggings of the Climax Mine before exiting the south side of the range onto the wide, gently sloping bajada. The trail finishes back on the paved Plomosa Road. If you drive the route in the reverse direction, take care not to miss the start of the formed trail where it turns southeast off the old graded, gravel Plomosa Road.

Current Road Information

Bureau of Land Management
Havasu Field Office
2610 Sweetwater Ave.
Lake Havasu City, AZ 86406
(520) 505-1200

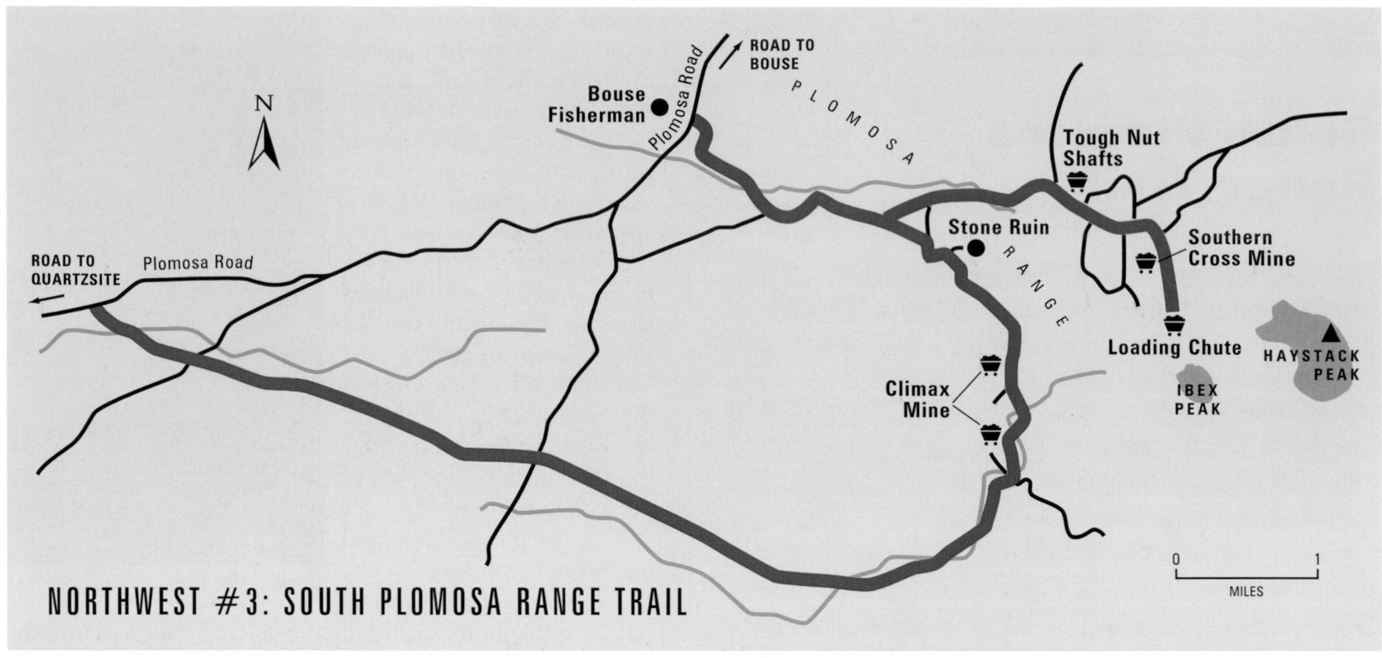

Map References

BLM Blythe
USGS 1:24,000 Ibex Peak, Plomosa Pass, Bouse SW
1:100,000 Blythe
Maptech CD-ROM: Colorado River/Lake Havasu
Arizona Atlas & Gazetteer, p. 46
Arizona Road & Recreation Atlas, p. 38 & p. 72

Route Directions

▼ 0.0		From the center of Bouse, proceed south on Plomosa Road for 11 miles to mile marker 8. The start of trail is immediately north of mile marker 8. Zero trip meter and turn northeast on unmarked, formed, well-used trail. Cross through wash.
1.7 ▲		Trail finishes at the intersection with the paved Plomosa Road. Turn right for Bouse; turn left for Quartzsite.
		GPS: N33°47.45′ W114°05.40′
▼ 0.3	SO	Cross through wash.
1.4 ▲	SO	Cross through wash.
▼ 0.5	SO	Track on left.
1.2 ▲	SO	Track on right.
▼ 0.6	SO	Cross through wash.
1.1 ▲	SO	Cross through wash.
▼ 0.8	BL	Track on right.
0.9 ▲	BR	Track on left.
▼ 1.1	SO	Cross through wash.
0.6 ▲	SO	Cross through wash.
▼ 1.2	SO	Cross through wash.
0.5 ▲	SO	Cross through wash.
▼ 1.7	BR	Track straight on is the spur trail to the Southern Cross Mine. Zero trip meter.
0.0 ▲		Continue to the northwest.
		GPS: N33°46.95′ W114°04.08′

Spur to Southern Cross Mine

▼ 0.0		1.7 miles from the north end of the trail, zero trip meter and proceed to the east on the formed trail.
▼ 0.2	SO	Cross through wash.
▼ 0.3	SO	Track on right returns to main trail.
		GPS: N33°47.04′ W114°03.80′
▼ 0.5	SO	Cross through wash.
▼ 0.7	SO	Faint track on right.
▼ 0.9	SO	Cross through wash.
▼ 1.0	SO	Faint track on left.
▼ 1.2	SO	Two tracks on left. Tough Nut Shafts are on the left. Ibex Peak is ahead on the right. Haystack Peak is ahead on the left.
		GPS: N33°47.17′ W114°02.99′
▼ 1.3	SO	Cross through wash; tracks on left and right in wash.
▼ 1.4	SO	Two tracks on left.
▼ 1.5	SO	Track on right.
▼ 1.6	SO	Track on left on ridge.
▼ 1.7	SO	Cross through wash; then track on right; then bear right at track on left.
		GPS: N33°46.98′ W114°02.48′
▼ 1.8	BL	Cross through wash; then track on right; then stone ruin straight ahead. Bear left at stone ruin. This is the Southern Cross Mine. Concrete foundations on left; diggings and tailings on right.
		GPS: N33°46.93′ W114°02.41′
▼ 1.9	BR	Concrete foundations on left; then bear right. Track on left.
▼ 2.0	TR	T-intersection. Turn right and cross through wash.
▼ 2.2	SO	Track on left and track on right to concrete foundations and mine diggings.
		GPS: N33°46.90′ W114°02.26′
▼ 2.3	SO	Two tracks on left to tailings.
▼ 2.4	SO	Deep shaft on left immediately beside trail.
		GPS: N33°46.75′ W114°02.23′
▼ 2.5	TL	Track on right to adits and diggings.
		GPS: N33°46.64′ W114°02.20′
▼ 2.6	SO	Cross through wash.
▼ 2.8		Spur ends at the wooden loading chute and shaft near the base of Ibex Peak.
		GPS: N33°46.46′ W114°02.17′

Continuation of Main Trail

Mileage		Directions
▼ 0.0		Continue around the loop.
5.5 ▲	BL	Track on right is the spur trail to the Southern Cross Mine. Zero trip meter.
		GPS: N33°46.95' W114°04.08'
▼ 0.3	BR	Second entrance to spur trail on left.
5.2 ▲	BL	First entrance to spur trail on right.
		GPS: N33°46.80' W114°03.78'
▼ 0.4	SO	Cross through wash.
5.1 ▲	SO	Cross through wash.
▼ 0.5	BR	Track on left goes to stone ruin and wooden memorial marker on hillside above.
5.0 ▲	BL	Track on right goes to stone ruin and memorial marker on hillside above.
		GPS: N33°46.76' W114°03.68'
▼ 0.7	SO	Cross through wash.
4.8 ▲	SO	Cross through wash.
▼ 0.9	SO	Cross through wash.
4.6 ▲	SO	Cross through wash.
▼ 1.0	SO	Cross through wash.
4.5 ▲	SO	Cross through wash.
▼ 1.1	SO	Cross through wash.
4.4 ▲	SO	Cross through wash.
▼ 1.4	SO	Timber-braced adit of the Climax Mine on right of trail; then saddle.
4.1 ▲	SO	Saddle; then timber-braced adit of the Climax Mine on left of trail. Ibex Peak is ahead.
		GPS: N33°46.15' W114°03.21'
▼ 1.5	BL	Faint track on right.
4.0 ▲	SO	Faint track on left.
▼ 1.6	SO	Cross through wash.
3.9 ▲	SO	Cross through wash.
▼ 1.7	SO	Cross through wash.
3.8 ▲	SO	Cross through wash.
▼ 1.8	SO	Cross through two washes.
3.7 ▲	SO	Cross through two washes.
▼ 1.9	SO	Track on right goes into Climax Mine.
3.6 ▲	SO	Track on left goes into Climax Mine.
		GPS: N33°45.75' W114°03.19'
▼ 2.0	SO	Cross through wash; then track on right to Climax Mine.
3.5 ▲	SO	Track on left to Climax Mine; then cross through wash.
▼ 2.1	SO	Track on right goes to mine workings. There is a deep shaft on right at intersection.
3.4 ▲	SO	Track on left goes to mine workings. There is a deep shaft on left at intersection.
▼ 2.2	TR	Intersection. Well-used track on left crosses through wash, faint track straight on. Turn right and cross through wash.
3.3 ▲	TL	Cross through wash; then intersection. Well-used track ahead crosses through wash, faint track on right.
▼ 2.5	SO	Cross through wash.
3.0 ▲	SO	Cross through wash.
		GPS: N33°45.26' W114°03.32'
▼ 2.8	SO	Faint track on right.
2.7 ▲	SO	Faint track on left.
▼ 2.9	SO	Faint track on right; then cross through wash.
2.6 ▲	SO	Cross through wash; then faint track on left.
▼ 3.0	SO	Track on left.
2.5 ▲	SO	Track on right.
▼ 3.4	SO	Cross through wash.
2.1 ▲	SO	Cross through wash.
▼ 3.5	SO	Track on left.
2.0 ▲	SO	Track on right.
▼ 3.6	SO	Cross through wash; then track on left.
1.9 ▲	SO	Track on right; then cross through wash.
▼ 5.5	SO	Intersection. Equally used tracks on left, right, and straight on over open area of desert pavement. Zero trip meter.
0.0 ▲		Continue to the east.
		GPS: N33°45.48' W114°06.27'
▼ 0.0		Continue to the west.
3.4 ▲	SO	Intersection. Equally used tracks on left, right, and straight on over open area of desert pavement. Zero trip meter.
▼ 2.1	SO	Cross wide, graded dirt road.
1.3 ▲	SO	Cross wide, graded dirt road.
		GPS: N33°45.91' W114°08.56'
▼ 2.6	SO	Cross through wide wash.
0.8 ▲	SO	Cross through wide wash.
▼ 2.8	TL	Turn left onto graded dirt road running parallel to paved Plomosa Road, which is just beyond.
0.6 ▲	TR	Turn right onto small, unmarked, well-used, formed trail to the northeast. There is a No Camping marker at the turn.
		GPS: N33°46.18' W114°09.22'
▼ 3.4		Trail ends at intersection with the paved Plomosa Road. Turn left for Quartzsite; turn right for Bouse.
0.0 ▲		Trail starts on the paved Plomosa Road, 3.2 miles northeast of Arizona 95, 0.3 miles northeast of mile marker 3. Turn east on wide, graded gravel Old Plomosa Road, which runs parallel to the paved road and zero trip meter.
		GPS: N33°46.07' W114°09.78'

NORTHWEST REGION TRAIL #4

Desert Queen Mine Trail

Starting Point:	**Arizona 72 in Vicksburg**
Finishing Point:	**US 60 in Salome**
Total Mileage:	**9.9 miles**
Unpaved Mileage:	**7.5 miles**
Driving Time:	**1.5 hours**
Elevation Range:	**1,400–2,200 feet**
Usually Open:	**Year-round**
Best Time to Travel:	**September to May**
Difficulty Rating:	**3**
Scenic Rating:	**8**
Remoteness Rating:	**+0**

Special Attractions

- Remains of the historic Desert Queen Mine.

History

This trail passes through, or close to, the site of three interesting settlements of the past and present. The first is Vicksburg. Situated on Arizona 72, the town was named after Victor Satterdahl, a storekeeper in the 1890s who set up a post office in his store in 1906. Wells Fargo had a stage station in Vicksburg in 1907. Today Vicksburg has a small, year-round population that swells every winter with visiting "snowbirds" from the north.

Winchester Peak, situated to the southeast of the trail, is named after Josiah Winchester, who owned the Desert Mine just southeast of the Desert Queen Mine around 1910. He was also the founder of the nearby, short-lived town of Winchester. Dick Wick Hall can also lay claim to the founding of Winchester, having set off the major rush for the region by announcing his assay returns of between $117 and $338 per ton on the streets of Phoenix in 1909.

Winchester boomed! Approaching a population of 2,000 in just the first month, the town boasted two restaurants, a saloon, an accommodation house, various stores (including a lumberyard), and a telephone line to Vicksburg. Through zealous promotion, Josiah Winchester sold $2,500 worth of town lots on the first day of sales, and the town was soon the largest settlement on the Arizona & California Railroad. However, after only two months the gold ran out and the town was abandoned.

Salome, at the east end of the trail, was established in 1904 by Dick Wick Hall, his brother Ernest, and Charles W. Pratt as a speculative venture; they were counting on the probable route of the new railroad going through the town. Salome is also the home of an interesting motto. The slogan seen around town and on the city limit signs reads, "Salome, where she danced." This slogan supposedly arose because Charles's wife, Grace Salome Pratt, "danced" across the hot sand, burning her feet.

Dick Wick Hall opened a gas station in the desert close to Salome on the route from Phoenix to Los Angeles. Promoting his station with billboards that made fun of the rotten condition of the road with its holes and humps, he soon had a following among regular travelers of the route. Later he spread his quick wit through his own newspaper, *The Salome Sun.* His most famous character was the Salome frog who couldn't swim... after all, because he was a desert frog he didn't need to! But the poor frog lamented not being able to swim. Through his paper, Hall also boasted about the town's lengthy golf course. It was so lengthy that it rented camping gear and maps for its endless desert fairways. Salome still retains many images of Dick Wick Hall and his most famous creation, the frog. Visitors will enjoy checking out the Salome Restaurant and viewing their collection of newspaper clippings and memorabilia.

An old cabin at the Desert Queen Mine

The loading hopper at the Desert Queen Mine

In an effort to improve the rutted roads for the new automobiles of the early 1900s, organizers held road races (one of which was called the Cactus Derby) from Los Angeles to Phoenix as early as 1905. Salome was on the route. Drivers averaged an amazing 15 to 17 miles an hour and carried extra gas and spare parts strapped to every conceivable part of their vehicles. Promoters predicted that one day there would be an all-weather surfaced road through the desert.

Description

This moderate, narrow trail runs north from Vicksburg, close to the town site of Winchester, and past the Desert Queen Mine—one of the major gold-producing mines of the area. Initially, the trail is a graded road, but after it passes the county materials site it drops to a small, formed trail. It follows along Calcite Wash, passing close to the Desert Queen Mine after 2.3 miles. The mine is listed as being privately owned, but there appears to be no restrictions on access. Like all mining claims, its status may change.

A small track on the right leads 0.4 miles into the site of the mine, past an old cabin, and along a narrow section of shelf road to the mine hole and wooden loading hopper. Be careful as you approach the hopper: There is a big shaft on the left just as the trail opens out at the mine. Some workings of the mine are also visible to the right.

Past the Desert Queen Mine, the trail winds through the Granite Wash Mountains. There are a few ditchy gullies and washes to cross, and the trail is rough in spots, but it is mainly easy. Close to the Calcite Mine, navigation can be difficult as there are so many side tracks, but generally speaking the main trail is the correct one. The trail follows Calcite Wash, running along the small ridge above the wash but dropping down to cross through it often. Past the mine the trail crosses the open plain of McMullen Valley to reach Salome. A memorial to Dick Wick Hall is passed just before the end of the trail.

Current Road Information

Bureau of Land Management
Havasu Field Office
2610 Sweetwater Ave.
Lake Havasu City, AZ 86406
(520) 505-1200

Map References

BLM Salome

USGS 1:24,000 Vicksburg, Hope, Harcuvar, Salome
1:100,000 Salome

Maptech CD-ROM: Colorado River/Lake Havasu

Arizona Atlas & Gazetteer, p. 47

Arizona Road & Recreation Atlas, p. 39 & p. 73

Route Directions

Mileage		Description
▼ 0.0		From Arizona 72 in Vicksburg, zero trip meter and turn north on unmarked gravel road that immediately crosses the railroad. The turn is opposite the paved road that cuts across back to US 60.
1.2 ▲		Trail ends on Arizona 72 in Vicksburg. Turn right for Bouse; turn left for Wickenburg.
		GPS: N33°44.66' W113°45.12'
▼ 0.2	BL	Graded gravel road on right.
1.0 ▲	SO	Graded gravel road on left.
▼ 1.1	SO	Cross through Calcite Wash.
0.1 ▲	SO	Cross through Calcite Wash.
▼ 1.2	BR	Bear right on smaller graded road immediately before La Paz County Materials Site. Zero trip meter.
0.0 ▲		Continue to the southwest.
		GPS: N33°45.68' W113°44.51'
▼ 0.0		Continue to the northeast.
1.2 ▲	SO	Continue past La Paz County Materials Site onto wider graded road. Zero trip meter.
▼ 0.3	SO	Enter Calcite Wash.
0.9 ▲	SO	Exit Calcite Wash.
▼ 0.4	BR	Fork in wash; keep to the right.
0.8 ▲	SO	Track on right in wash.
▼ 0.8	SO	Track on right and track on left.
0.4 ▲	SO	Track on right and track on left.
		GPS: N33°46.34' W113°44.10'
▼ 0.9	SO	Track on right.
0.3 ▲	SO	Track on left.
▼ 1.0	SO	Two tracks on right.
0.2 ▲	SO	Two tracks on left.
▼ 1.1	SO	Track on right goes into the remains of the Desert Queen Mine.
0.1 ▲	SO	Track on left goes into the remains of the Desert Queen Mine.
		GPS: N33°46.61' W113°43.96'
▼ 1.2	BR	Well-used track on left. Zero trip meter.
0.0 ▲		Continue to the south.
		GPS: N33°46.71' W113°43.93'
▼ 0.0		Continue to the north.
1.3 ▲	SO	Well-used track on right. Zero trip meter.
▼ 0.4	BL	Bear left and dip down to cross through wash.
0.9 ▲	SO	Dip down to cross through wash.
		GPS: N33°47.04' W113°43.75'
▼ 0.7	BR	Bear right up Calcite Wash.
0.6 ▲	BL	Bear left out of Calcite Wash.
		GPS: N33°47.30' W113°43.80'
▼ 0.8	BR	Fork in wash; track on left; keep to the right.
0.5 ▲	SO	Track on right.
▼ 0.9	BR	Rise up out of wash.
0.4 ▲	BL	Drop down to travel along wash.
		GPS: N33°47.38' W113°43.64'
▼ 1.0	SO	Cross through wash.
0.3 ▲	SO	Cross through wash.
▼ 1.3	SO	Track on left is Northwest #5: Glory Hole Mine Trail, which turns sharply back. Turn is unmarked. Zero trip meter.
0.0 ▲		Continue to the west.
		GPS: N33°47.41' W113°43.23'
▼ 0.0		Continue to the southeast. Small diggings on hill to the left and right on saddle at intersection.
2.2 ▲	BL	Track on right is Northwest #5: Glory Hole Mine Trail. Turn is unmarked. Small diggings on hill to the left and right on saddle at intersection. Zero trip meter.
▼ 0.1	SO	Cross through wash.
2.1 ▲	SO	Cross through wash.
▼ 0.2	SO	Track on left.
2.0 ▲	SO	Track on right.
▼ 0.5	SO	Track on right enters wash.
1.7 ▲	SO	Track on left enters wash.
		GPS: N33°47.24' W113°42.72'
▼ 0.6	SO	Cross diagonally through wash.
1.6 ▲	SO	Cross diagonally through wash.

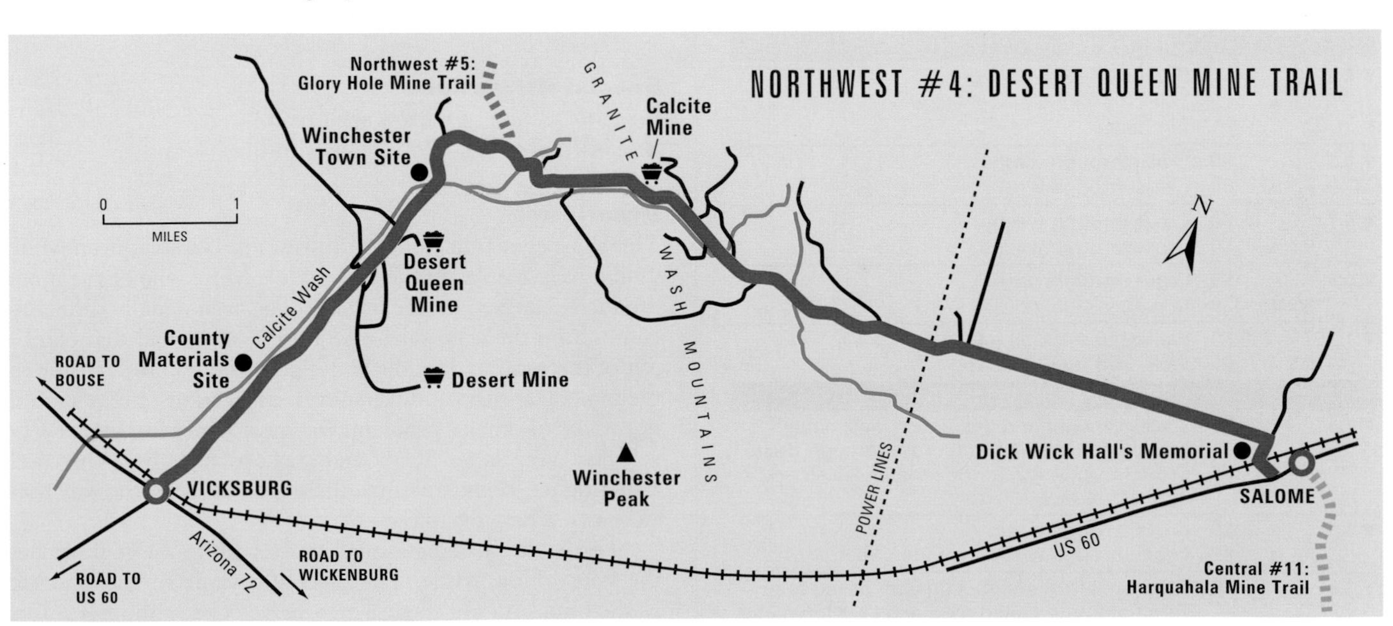

			GPS: N33°47.29' W113°42.66'
▼ 0.7		SO	Track on left.
	1.5 ▲	SO	Track on right.
▼ 0.8		SO	Cross through Calcite Wash.
	1.4 ▲	SO	Cross through Calcite Wash.
▼ 0.9		SO	Cross through Calcite Wash.
	1.3 ▲	SO	Cross through Calcite Wash.
▼ 1.0		SO	Cross through Calcite Wash.
	1.2 ▲	SO	Cross through Calcite Wash.
▼ 1.3		SO	Cross through Calcite Wash.
	0.9 ▲	SO	Cross through Calcite Wash.
			GPS: N33°47.38' W113°42.03'
▼ 1.5		SO	Enter wash. Calcite Mine is on the left. Some workings on the left; then track on left climbs the hill to mine shafts.
	0.7 ▲	BL	Calcite Mine is on the right. Track on right climbs hill to mine shafts; then workings on the right. Exit wash.
			GPS: N33°47.31' W113°41.86'
▼ 1.55		TR	Exit wash; track on left and track straight on. Turn right, staying close to the wash and then cross through wash.
	0.65 ▲	TL	Cross through wash; then turn left and enter wash. Tracks on right and straight on.
			GPS: N33°47.26' W113°41.81'
▼ 1.6		BR	Bear right and enter wash; track on left out of wash.
	0.6 ▲	BL	Bear left out of wash. Track on right out of wash.
			GPS: N33°47.25' W113°41.71'
▼ 1.7		SO	Cross through wash.
	0.5 ▲	SO	Cross through wash.
▼ 1.8		SO	Cross through wash. More diggings of the Calcite Mine on the left, and track on right; then cross through wash.
	0.4 ▲	SO	Cross through wash; then track on left. Diggings of the Calcite Mine on right; then cross through wash a second time.
			GPS: N33°47.19' W113°41.53'
▼ 1.9		SO	Cross through wash; then track on left.
	0.3 ▲	SO	Track on right; then cross through wash.
			GPS: N33°47.12' W113°41.39'
▼ 2.2		SO	Track on left and well-used track on right. Zero trip meter.
	0.0 ▲		Continue to the west.
			GPS: N33°47.09' W113°41.16'
▼ 0.0			Continue toward Salome.
	1.6 ▲	SO	Track on right and well-used track on left. Zero trip meter.
▼ 0.3		SO	Cross through wash.
	1.3 ▲	SO	Cross through wash.
▼ 0.7		SO	Cross through wash.
	0.9 ▲	SO	Cross through wash.
▼ 0.8		SO	Cross through wash.
	0.8 ▲	SO	Cross through wash.
▼ 1.1		SO	Well-used track on left.
	0.5 ▲	BL	Well-used track on right.
			GPS: N33°46.98' W113°40.05'
▼ 1.3		SO	Tracks on right and left along power lines; continue straight on and cross through wash.
	0.3 ▲	SO	Cross through wash; then tracks on left and right along power lines.
▼ 1.5		SO	Cross through wash.
	0.1 ▲	SO	Cross through wash.
▼ 1.6		TR	Track on left; then junction with paved road. Turn right onto paved road and zero trip meter.
	0.0 ▲		Continue west on dirt road.
			GPS: N33°46.99' W113°39.45'
▼ 0.0			Continue on paved road, ignoring turns on right and left.
	2.4 ▲	TL	Turn left off paved road at right-hand bend and head west on unmarked, single-track trail; then track on right.
▼ 2.2		TR	Turn onto paved Center Street in Salome. Dick Wick Hall's memorial is immediately on the right.
	0.2 ▲	TL	Dick Wick Hall's memorial is on the left; then turn left at T-intersection onto Hall Avenue. Continue due west, ignoring turns on right and left.
			GPS: N33°47.00' W113°37.03'
▼ 2.4			Cross over railroad. Trail ends at the junction with US 60 in Salome.
	0.0 ▲		From the western edge of Salome, turn north on paved Center Street at the sign for the historical marker on US 60 and zero trip meter. Immediately cross over railroad.
			GPS: N33°46.76' W113°37.00'

NORTHWEST REGION TRAIL #5

Glory Hole Mine Trail

Starting Point:	**Northwest #4: Desert Queen Mine Trail, 3.6 miles north of Vicksburg**
Finishing Point:	**Glory Hole Mine**
Total Mileage:	**2.1 miles**
Unpaved Mileage:	**2.1 miles**
Driving Time:	**45 minutes (one-way)**
Elevation Range:	**2,000–2,400 feet**
Usually Open:	**Year-round**
Best Time to Travel:	**September to May**
Difficulty Rating:	**5**
Scenic Rating:	**8**
Remoteness Rating:	**+0**

Special Attractions

- Scenic section of narrow shelf road.
- Short trail to the Glory Hole Mine.

Description

This short spur trail from Northwest #4: Desert Queen Mine Trail travels 2 miles to the Glory Hole Mine, one of the more productive mines of the region. The trail's main difficulty comes from the very narrow section of shelf road that climbs out of the wash to a saddle and descends down the far side to the mine. It is steep and has some loose sections, but it should not cause too many problems for most high-clearance 4WD vehicles. Very large SUVs and pickups may find this trail rather tight—there are some ditchy gullies along the way that can catch a long overhang.

Shortly after passing a small timber cabin, the trail reaches the Glory Hole Mine. The final 200 yards of the trail are washed out and are too narrow for vehicles, although ATVs are able to continue to the mine. There is a small turning point at the 2-mile mark—be prepared to do a many point turn, especially if you are in a long vehicle.

There are tailings piles, shafts, adits, and concrete foundations to the left at the Glory Hole Mine, which is set in a very pretty, small, tight valley.

Current Road Information

Bureau of Land Management
Havasu Field Office
2610 Sweetwater Ave.
Lake Havasu City, AZ 86406
(520) 505-1200

Map References

BLM Salome
USGS 1:24,000 Harcuvar
1:100,000 Salome
Maptech CD-ROM: Colorado River/Lake Havasu
Arizona Atlas & Gazetteer, p. 47

Route Directions

▼ 0.0		From Northwest #4: Desert Queen Mine Trail, 3.6 miles north of Vicksburg, zero trip meter and turn northwest on unmarked, rough, single-track trail. There is no sign or marking at the intersection, but it is on a small saddle.
		GPS: N33°47.41' W113°43.23'
▼ 0.2	SO	Cross through wash with pour off to the left.
▼ 0.5	BR	Enter wash. Tracks on left down wash.
		GPS: N33°47.74' W113°43.58'
▼ 1.0	BL	Bear left out of wash (turn can be hard to spot, but track is visible further up rise to the left).
		GPS: N33°48.16' W113°43.56'
▼ 1.2	SO	Trail climbs up narrow, rough shelf road. Mine shaft on left of trail.
		GPS: N33°48.30' W113°43.64'
▼ 1.3	SO	Saddle, with views to the north.
		GPS: N33°48.38' W113°43.65'
▼ 1.6	SO	Bottom of descent. Stone marker on left, recording a mining claim filed in 1968. Small timber hut on left and concrete foundations.
		GPS: N33°48.44' W113°43.87'
▼ 1.8	SO	Track on left.
		GPS: N33°48.58' W113°43.87'
▼ 2.0	SO	Final turning point.
		GPS: N33°48.63' W113°43.76'
▼ 2.1		Trail ends approximately 200 yards before the Glory Hole Mine.
		GPS: N33°48.69' W113°43.68'

A view of the saguaros along the spur trail to Glory Hole Mine

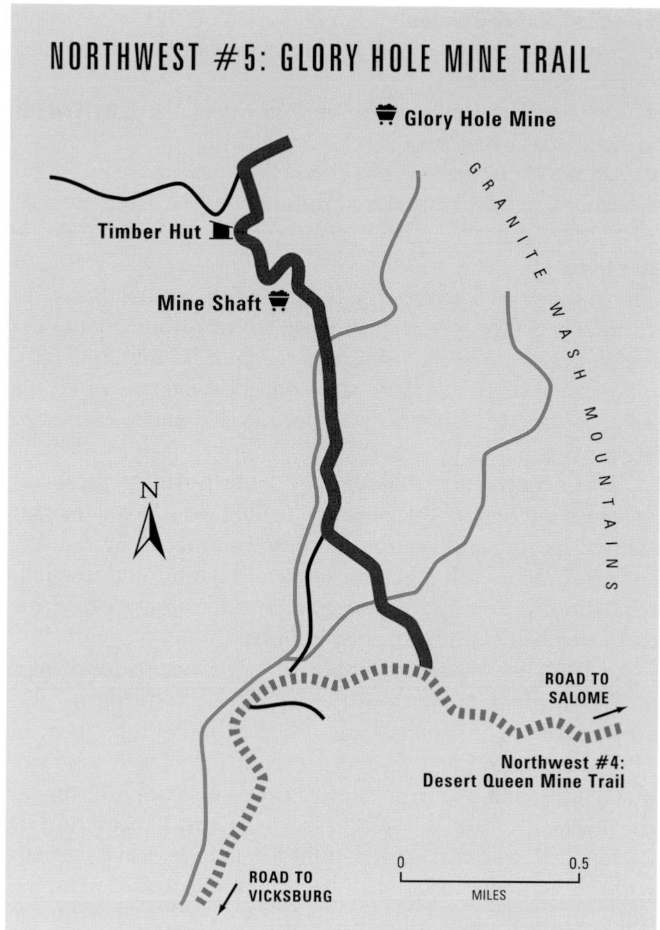

NORTHWEST REGION TRAIL #6

Swansea Road

Starting Point:	**Arizona 72 in Bouse**
Finishing Point:	**Swansea ghost town**
Total Mileage:	**24.6 miles**
Unpaved Mileage:	**23.8 miles**
Driving Time:	**1.5 hours**
Elevation Range:	**900–1,900 feet**
Usually Open:	**Year-round**
Best Time to Travel:	**November to April**
Difficulty Rating:	**1**
Scenic Rating:	**9**
Remoteness Rating:	**+1**

Special Attractions

- Extensive remains of the buildings and mines of Swansea town site.
- Access to and views of the sand dunes of the East Cactus Plain Wilderness Area.
- Access to a network of 4WD and ATV trails.
- Remote, lightly traveled trail through rugged desert scenery.

History

The history of Swansea (originally called Signal) began in 1886, when three prospectors in search of silver explored the region between the Buckskin and Rawhide Mountains. They found some silver, but most of the ore body was copper. At the time, copper was not worth mining, so they moved on, hoping for better luck elsewhere.

When copper prices climbed in the early 1900s, there was renewed interest in the Swansea region, which was further spurred by the construction of a line being built by the Arizona & California Railroad west from Phoenix. With the railroad running through Bouse, Swansea's location enabled the town to profit from the nearby railroad.

In 1907, Swansea was a company town, with three owners in the company: Newton Evans, Thomas Carrigan, and George Mitchell. Mitchell was added to the group when, in 1907, Evans and Carrigan approached Mitchell, a Welsh-born metallurgist and opportunist, with the prospect of investing in the mines.

Mitchell, who had arrived in the United States in the 1880s with his brother Robert, had been involved with developing mines in Alaska and Mexico. His ethics were questionable; he appeared to profit handsomely from his dealings but others were not so lucky. His previous venture, the Mitchell Mining Company of Mexico, went bankrupt, but he personally gained more than $200,000.

Tailings and workers' cottages at Swansea ghost town

Seeing the potential of the site, Mitchell threw himself into the development of Swansea with great enthusiasm. In 1908 he consolidated claims as the Clara Consolidated Gold and Copper Mining Company and started selling shares. His dreams were grandiose, and initially prospects seemed rosy. Using the money raised, Mitchell built an electricity plant, grand houses for the mine managers, and small cottages for the workers. He also piped in water pumped from the Bill Williams River. Swansea, with a population of 500, boasted a newspaper, restaurants, saloons, and a movie house. It also had insurance salesmen and a car dealership. What the hardworking, poorly paid miners thought of these businesses is not recorded.

The old dust chamber at Swansea ghost town

When the post office was registered, the name of the town was changed from Signal to Swansea, after Mitchell's hometown in Wales. Mitchell continued attracting outside investors. He took a profitable and much-publicized trip to France on which he raised $2 million. He had a taste for the high life, and although he was able to bring in outside money, he was also pretty good at spending it. His lavish 3,600-square-foot adobe home with its palm-lined entranceway and luxury French car testified to his ability to spend money.

With the completion of the railroad extension from Bouse to Swansea in 1910, Mitchell was able to start the next phase of his plans. Machinery was brought in to construct a 700-ton smelter. Ironically, rather than cementing Swansea's status as a prosperous boomtown, the huge smelter hastened its demise. The smelter was so inefficient that it cost three cents more to produce a pound of copper than it could be sold for. Although the ore body was good, Mitchell had invested more money in the surface and amenities of Swansea than he did underground and the smelter was never run at full capacity, rendering it even less cost-effective.

In 1911 the company was declared bankrupt with debts of $71,200. Mitchell left Swansea and went on to become the manager of the Jerome Superior Copper Company, which also went bankrupt after four years of his management.

Rising copper prices caused a brief revival of interest in the region, and Swansea was worked under different owners until 1937 when the falling prices associated with the depression led to its closure. It had produced more than $5 million in copper.

Description

This road offers easy access into a remote and highly scenic area of southwestern Arizona. Swansea town site at the end of the trail should be on every ghost town aficionado's list of places to visit. The town site is extensive and well preserved, with many buildings and mine remains.

The wide road is graded gravel all the way and suitable for passenger vehicles in dry weather. The major hazards are patches of soft road and a couple of loose, deep sand traps that are impassable in wet weather. The road can also be washboardy. It leaves Bouse and follows close to the line of the old Bouse to Swansea railroad. The railroad property is closed to vehicles, but a keen eye will be able to see the old grade where it crosses the road on a couple of occasions.

The trail initially crosses Cactus Plain, with panoramic

views north to the Buckskin Mountains. There are many wash crossings along the road; only the major ones are mentioned in the route directions. There are also many small 4WD trails that lead off in both directions. Again, only the major ones are mentioned; many of the others go just a short distance to a campsite. The BLM Arizona Access Guide–Cactus Plain shows all of these small trails in detail.

The trail runs alongside the East Cactus Plain Wilderness Area. There is a parking area and hiking access immediately after the aqueduct. The wilderness area encompasses more than 14,000 acres of sand dunes characterized by dense desert vegetation.

Swansea is one of the best-preserved and most extensive ghost towns in Arizona. The BLM has marked designated trails through the town site to avoid multiple trails that would scar the landscape. The setting is perfect for photographers and ghost town aficionados to explore. The town is located in a very scenic spot, with the low hills set against the backdrop of the larger Buckskin and Rawhide Mountains. You can drive or hike around many of the remains on the marked trails. Many frequent it on weekends and weekdays during the winter, but in summer it is deserted. Extreme summer temperatures keep most people away.

The BLM publishes a free brochure on Swansea, which includes a detailed map of the town site. It is available at BLM offices or at the information boards at Swansea. It is also included on the Arizona Access Guide–Cactus Plain. Facilities are limited in Swansea. There are a couple of campsites that have picnic tables under shade ramadas 0.3 miles past the end of the trail, but there is no water.

Passenger vehicles can make the trip with care; the final section of the road, as it climbs over the ridge and then drops down to Swansea, is slightly rough, but still reasonable. Watch your vehicle's temperature over this section. Trails past the town site are for high-clearance or 4WD vehicles only.

If you are planning to do much exploration around Swansea and the surrounding trails, you may need to carry extra fuel. Note that fuel is not available in Bouse; the nearest gas station is approximately 27 miles away at either Quartzsite or Hope.

Current Road Information

Bureau of Land Management
Havasu Field Office
2610 Sweetwater Ave.
Lake Havasu City, AZ 86406
(520) 505-1200

Map References

BLM Blythe, Salome, Alamo Lake
USGS 1:24,000 Bouse, Bouse Hills West, Powerline Well, Planet, Swansea
1:100,000 Blythe, Salome, Alamo Lake
Maptech CD-ROM: Colorado River/Lake Havasu
Arizona Atlas & Gazetteer, pp. 46, 47
Arizona Road & Recreation Atlas, p. 38 & p. 72
Recreational Map of Arizona
Other: Arizona Access Guide–Cactus Plain

Route Directions

Mileage		Direction
▼ 0.0		From the center of Bouse, at mile marker 27 on Arizona 72, turn northeast on paved Main Street opposite Plomosa Road and immediately cross over railroad. Turn is sign-posted to the Museum Assay Office. Continue straight on and pass the museum on the right. Zero trip meter.
2.4 ▲		Cross over railroad; trail ends on Arizona 72 in Bouse. Turn right for Parker; turn left for Wickenburg; continue straight on for Quartzsite.
		GPS: N 33°55.93' W 114°00.29'
▼ 0.2	TL	Turn onto the paved Rayder Drive, remain on Rayder Drive, ignoring turns to the right and left.
2.2 ▲	TR	Turn onto Main Street and continue south to Arizona 72, passing the Museum Assay Office on the left.
		GPS: N33°55.93' W114°00.29'
▼ 0.8	SO	Paved road on left is Saguaro Drive at the edge of Bouse. Continue straight ahead on graded dirt road.
1.6 ▲	SO	Edge of Bouse; pavement begins. Paved road on right is Saguaro Drive. Continue straight ahead on Rayder Drive, ignoring turns to the right and left.
		GPS: N33°56.56' W114°00.37'
▼ 2.0	SO	Faint track on right goes to Barber Gene Mine.
0.4 ▲	SO	Faint track on left goes to Barber Gene Mine.
		GPS: N33°57.48' W113°59.91'
▼ 2.4	BL	Graded road on right is Butler Valley Road. Information board at junction. This is Bouse Y Limited Use Area. Zero trip meter.
0.0 ▲		Continue to the southwest. Road is now Rayder Drive.
		GPS: N33°57.80' W113°59.85'
▼ 0.0		Continue to the northwest. Road is now Swansea Road.
5.2 ▲	BR	Graded road on left is Butler Valley Road. Information board at junction. This is Bouse Y Limited Use Area. Zero trip meter.
▼ 0.3	SO	Private drive on left. Old railroad grade crosses road, driveway follows it on left.
4.9 ▲	SO	Private drive on right. Old railroad grade crosses road, driveway follows it on right.
		GPS: N33°58.07' W113°59.86'
▼ 0.5	SO	Cross through wash; then track on left.
4.7 ▲	SO	Track on right; then cross through wash.
▼ 1.0	SO	Track on left and small track on right to Thompson Well.
4.2 ▲	SO	Track on right and small track on left to Thompson Well.
		GPS: N33°58.65' W113°59.70'
▼ 3.1	SO	Track on right.
2.1 ▲	SO	Track on left.
▼ 3.9	SO	Old railroad grade crosses road.
1.3 ▲	SO	Old railroad grade crosses road.
		GPS: N34°00.30' W113°57.56'
▼ 5.0	SO	Old railroad grade crosses road. Track on right.
0.2 ▲	SO	Old railroad grade crosses road. Track on left.
▼ 5.2	SO	Cross over large Central Arizona Canal Project Aqueduct on concrete bridge. Zero trip meter.
0.0 ▲		Continue to the southwest.
		GPS: N34°01.04' W113°56.52'
▼ 0.0		Continue to the northeast on Swansea Road.
4.8 ▲	SO	Cross over large Central Arizona Canal Project Aqueduct on concrete bridge. Zero trip meter.

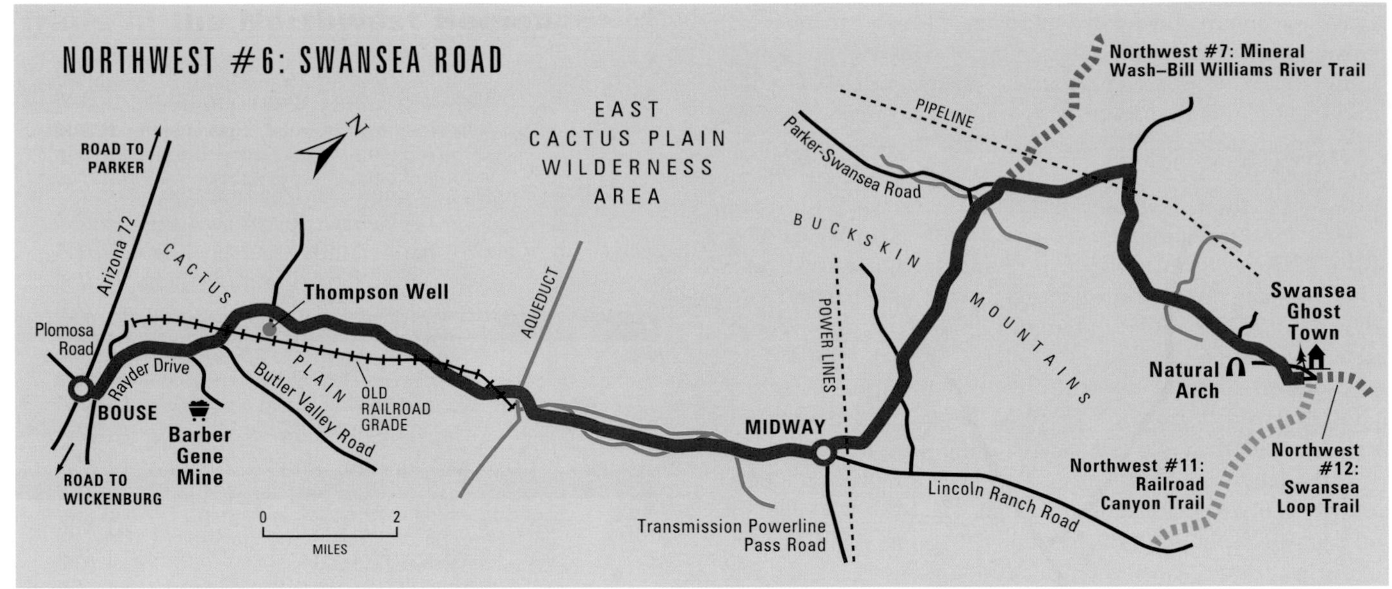

▼ 0.2		SO	Information board on left for East Cactus Plain Wilderness Area.
	4.6 ▲	SO	Information board on right for East Cactus Plain Wilderness Area.
▼ 0.4		SO	Track on right is government property.
	4.4 ▲	SO	Track on left is government property.
▼ 0.8		SO	Cross through wash.
	4.0 ▲	SO	Cross through wash.
▼ 3.4		SO	Cross through wash.
	1.4 ▲	SO	Cross through wash.
▼ 4.3		SO	Cross through wash.
	0.5 ▲	SO	Cross through wash.
▼ 4.8		BL	Midway. BLM information board at intersection. Graded road on right is Transmission Powerline Pass Road over Butler Pass. Immediately left off this road is Lincoln Ranch Road. Zero trip meter.
	0.0 ▲		Continue to the southwest.
			GPS: N34°04.21' W113°53.19'
▼ 0.0			Continue to the north and immediately cross through wide wash.
	5.3 ▲	BR	Cross through wide wash; then arrive at Midway. BLM information board at intersection. Graded road on left is Transmission Powerline Pass Road over Butler Pass. Also, immediately left off this road is Lincoln Ranch Road. Zero trip meter.
▼ 0.3		SO	Pass underneath power lines; tracks on right and left underneath power lines.
	5.0 ▲	SO	Pass underneath power lines; tracks on left and right underneath power lines.
▼ 1.5		SO	Faint track on left.
	3.8 ▲	SO	Faint track on right.
▼ 1.6		SO	Track on right.
	3.7 ▲	SO	Track on left.
			GPS: N34°05.58' W113°53.48'
▼ 2.1		SO	Track on left.
	3.2 ▲	SO	Track on right.
▼ 4.6		SO	Track on left.
	0.7 ▲	SO	Track on right.
▼ 4.8		SO	Cross through wash.
	0.5 ▲	SO	Cross through wash.
▼ 5.3		TR	Intersection of graded gravel road. Turn right, remaining on Swansea Road. Graded gravel road ahead and on left. Northwest #7: Mineral Wash–Bill Williams River Trail is straight ahead; Parker-Swansea Road is on left. Zero trip meter.
	0.0 ▲		Continue to the south, passing a sign—Bouse 20 miles.
			GPS: N34°08.25' W113°55.59'
▼ 0.0			Continue to the northeast.
	6.6 ▲	TL	Intersection of graded gravel road. Turn left, remaining on Swansea Road. Graded gravel road ahead and on right. Northwest #7: Mineral Wash–Bill Williams River Trail is on the right; Parker-Swansea Road is straight on. Zero trip meter.
▼ 1.3		SO	Aboveground gas pipeline crosses road; tracks on right and left along pipeline.
	5.3 ▲	SO	Aboveground gas pipeline crosses road; tracks on right and left along pipeline.
▼ 2.0		SO	Track on left.
	4.6 ▲	SO	Track on right.
			GPS: N34°09.85' W113°54.72'
▼ 2.2		SO	Faint track on left.
	4.4 ▲	SO	Faint track on right.
▼ 2.4		SO	Aboveground gas pipeline crosses road; tracks on right and left along pipeline.
	4.2 ▲	SO	Aboveground gas pipeline crosses road; tracks on right and left along pipeline.
▼ 2.7		SO	Track on left.
	3.9 ▲	SO	Track on right.
			GPS: N34°09.53' W113°54.13'
▼ 4.5		SO	Cross over wash on bridge.
	2.1 ▲	SO	Cross over wash on bridge.
			GPS: N34°09.44' W113°52.48'
▼ 5.1		SO	Views ahead to the tailings piles at Swansea.
	1.5 ▲	SO	Final views back to Swansea.
▼ 5.9		SO	Track on left; then cross over wash.
	0.7 ▲	SO	Cross over wash; then track on right.
▼ 6.0		SO	Natural arch on right of trail.
	0.6 ▲	SO	Natural arch on left of trail.
			GPS: N34°09.89' W113°51.30'
▼ 6.4		SO	Cross through wash.
	0.2 ▲	SO	Cross through wash.

▼ 6.5		SO	Track on right.
	0.1 ▲	SO	Track on left.
▼ 6.6		SO	Swansea town site information board. Track on left. Zero trip meter.
	0.0 ▲		Continue to the southwest.
			GPS: N34°10.23' W113°50.73'
▼ 0.0			Continue on into Swansea town site.
	0.3 ▲	SO	Swansea town site information board. Track on right. Zero trip meter.
▼ 0.1		SO	Remains of adobe and concrete Company Store on left with the workers' cottages behind. The General Office is at the left-hand bend.
	0.2 ▲	SO	The General Office is at the right-hand bend; remains of adobe and concrete Company Store on right with the workers' cottages behind.
			GPS: N34°10.14' W113°50.61'
▼ 0.2		SO	Workers' cottages on left.
	0.1 ▲	SO	Workers' cottages on right.
▼ 0.3		SO	Trail finishes at the information board on left. Continuing straight ahead at this point leads 0.1 miles to the start of Northwest #11: Railroad Canyon Trail and Northwest #12: Swansea Loop Trail.
	0.0 ▲		Trail commences at the information board on right, 0.1 miles south of the end of Northwest #11: Railroad Canyon Trail and Northwest #12: Swansea Loop Trail.
			GPS: N34°10.24' W113°50.50'

NORTHWEST REGION TRAIL #7

Mineral Wash–Bill Williams River Trail

Starting Point:	**4-way intersection with Northwest #6: Swansea Road, Parker-Swansea Road, and Mineral Wash Road**
Finishing Point:	**Arizona 95, 2.8 miles north of Parker Dam Road**
Total Mileage:	**16.2 miles**
Unpaved Mileage:	**16.2 miles**
Driving Time:	**2 hours**
Elevation Range:	**500–1,800 feet**
Usually Open:	**Year-round**
Best Time to Travel:	**October to May**
Difficulty Rating:	**5**
Scenic Rating:	**9**
Remoteness Rating:	**+0**

Special Attractions

- Fording the Bill Williams River many times.
- Bird-watching in the Bill Williams River National Wildlife Refuge.
- Varied, remote desert scenery from arid mountains to riparian valleys.

History

The Bill Williams River National Wildlife Refuge, dedicated in January 1941, protects a part of the dwindling native riparian habitat in Arizona. It follows a 9-mile stretch of the Bill Williams River down to the confluence with the Colorado River. Today the Bill Williams River is not free flowing. The Alamo Dam, constructed in 1968, regulates the flow.

The refuge is named after William Shirley Williams, known as Bill Williams, a reclusive mountain man who wandered extensively in the Southwest. Born in 1871 in North Carolina, Williams spent his early years in St. Louis. As a young man, he was a Methodist preacher. When he proposed to a young lady in his congregation, not only was he summarily turned down, but he was humiliated when the woman laughed in his face. Williams left St. Louis and headed west, aiming to bring Christianity to the Osage Indians. In an interesting turnabout of affairs, he failed to convert the Indians to Christianity; rather, the Indians converted him to their lifestyle and he lived among them for many years. He married an Osage woman who bore him two daughters.

Looking into Mineral Wash with its striking red rock formations

His wife died at a young age, and Williams became even more reclusive. He turned to the mountains for solace, working as a trapper. He moved further and further west, traveling through the northern Arizona mountains as he did so. He worked for a while as a guide on the Santa Fe Trail and accompanied Colonel John Frémont on one of his expeditions. Wild Bill's nickname was well earned. He is most often described as a tall, gangly redheaded man, eccentric to the point of insanity, with wild woolly hair, a luxuriant beard, and questionable hygiene.

His death and final resting place remain a mystery. Some accounts tell of his being killed by Indians, others of his freezing to death on a lonely mountain pass. A popular tale has him lying in an unmarked grave in the mountains that bear his name, the Bill Williams Mountains, in northwest Arizona.

Description

Most people who visit the Swansea region will travel via the well-used Northwest #6: Swansea Road or the Parker-Swansea Road. However, for those with high-clearance 4WDs who want a little more driving excitement, there are two alternative routes into and out of the region. One is from the north, via Northwest #14: Rawhide Mountains Trail; the other is through the Bill Williams River National Wildlife Refuge and along Mineral Wash.

The Mineral Wash–Bill Williams River Trail leaves from the intersection of the graded Parker-Swansea Road and Northwest #6: Swansea Road. Initially, it is a well-graded road as it travels to join Planet Ranch Road. It runs along a wide, gravelly wash in a canyon (a branch of Mineral Wash), passing alongside Planet Peak and the smaller Squaw Peak. This first part of the trail is also known as the Swansea Cutoff Road. After 6.8 miles, the trail enters the main Mineral Wash and travels down an extremely pretty canyon with high, red walls that contrast with the green palo verde growing along the sides.

The trail then enters into the Bill Williams River National Wildlife Refuge. No camping or campfires are permitted within the reserve, so if you plan on camping along the trail you will need to take this into account. There are some suitable sites near the south end of the trail outside of the refuge; once you start to enter the wash, sites are very limited.

The difficulty rating for this trail comes from the many deep crossings of the Bill Williams River. The trail runs alongside the river, passing through dense vegetation, so that, at first, the river channel is not seen at all. The initial water crossings are offshoots of the river that have flowed into depressions in the riverbed. Under normal conditions they can be up to 24 inches deep, but local conditions can alter the depths. The crossings are wide, in some cases extending out of sight around a bend, and the muddy water obscures the bottom. The bottom is generally firm, so if you are satisfied that the depth of the water is within safe limits for your vehicle, you can proceed. If in doubt, consider walking through first, although this idea is not particularly appealing given the muddy water! At the very least, use a long stick to determine the depth in a few places before proceeding. There are normally six distinct crossings within 0.6 miles. In between the water crossing, the trail is sandy and continues through the tamarisk, cottonwood, and willow. Tamarisk, the curse of Arizona waterways, started to take hold in the region with the damming of the Colorado River. Also known as salt cedar, tamarisk was used as a quick fix to stabilize riverbanks. However, it has gotten out of control and has spread rapidly within the region. Active management within the refuge has kept the spread of tamarisk to a minimum and it is less prevalent there than in other riparian areas.

After the first stretch of river crossings, the trail opens out and runs along a sandy trail past some red rock formations—the most attractive stretch of scenery along this part of the trail. There are two more crossings of the main channel of the Bill Williams River before you leave the refuge, but these are

Crossing through a pool of water along the trail

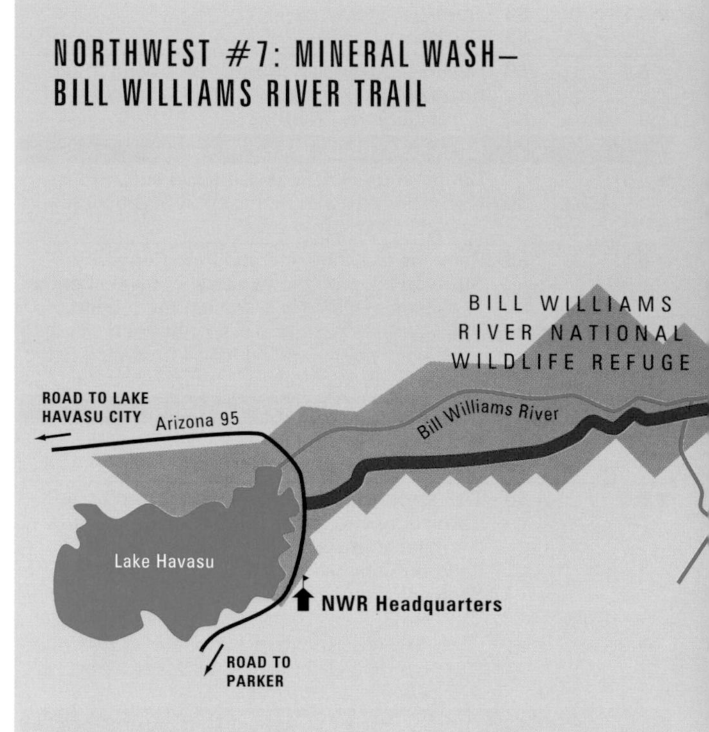

generally shallow. They are also out in open areas and the water is clear so it is easy to assess the depth.

The trail finishes on Arizona 95, 0.8 miles north of the NWR headquarters. The headquarters has information on the refuge; for bird-watchers, there are detailed lists of the 288 species of birds that you can expect to see in the refuge. The refuge is one of the premier bird-watching locations in Arizona. In addition to birds, you may be lucky enough to spot beaver, raccoon, bobcat, gray fox, mountain lion, coyote, desert bighorn sheep, javelina, and mule deer. Hunting in season is permitted south of the trail for dove, quail, cottontail, and desert bighorn sheep.

The Bill Williams River is dammed upstream at Alamo Lake, but the river flows year-round. In summer it may go underground for a while, but the constant flow is responsible for the luxuriant vegetation. The regulated flow is also partly responsible for the decline in the native fish, which do not thrive in these conditions. Summer travelers will need to take extra care—Mineral Wash often washes out following summer storms and may be impassable. In spring and summer, be very careful before proceeding across the river; the depth may be deceptive.

Current Road Information

Bureau of Land Management
Havasu Field Office
2610 Sweetwater Ave.
Lake Havasu City, AZ 86406
(520) 505-1200

Bill Williams NWR
60911 Hwy 95
Parker, AZ 85344
(520) 667-4144

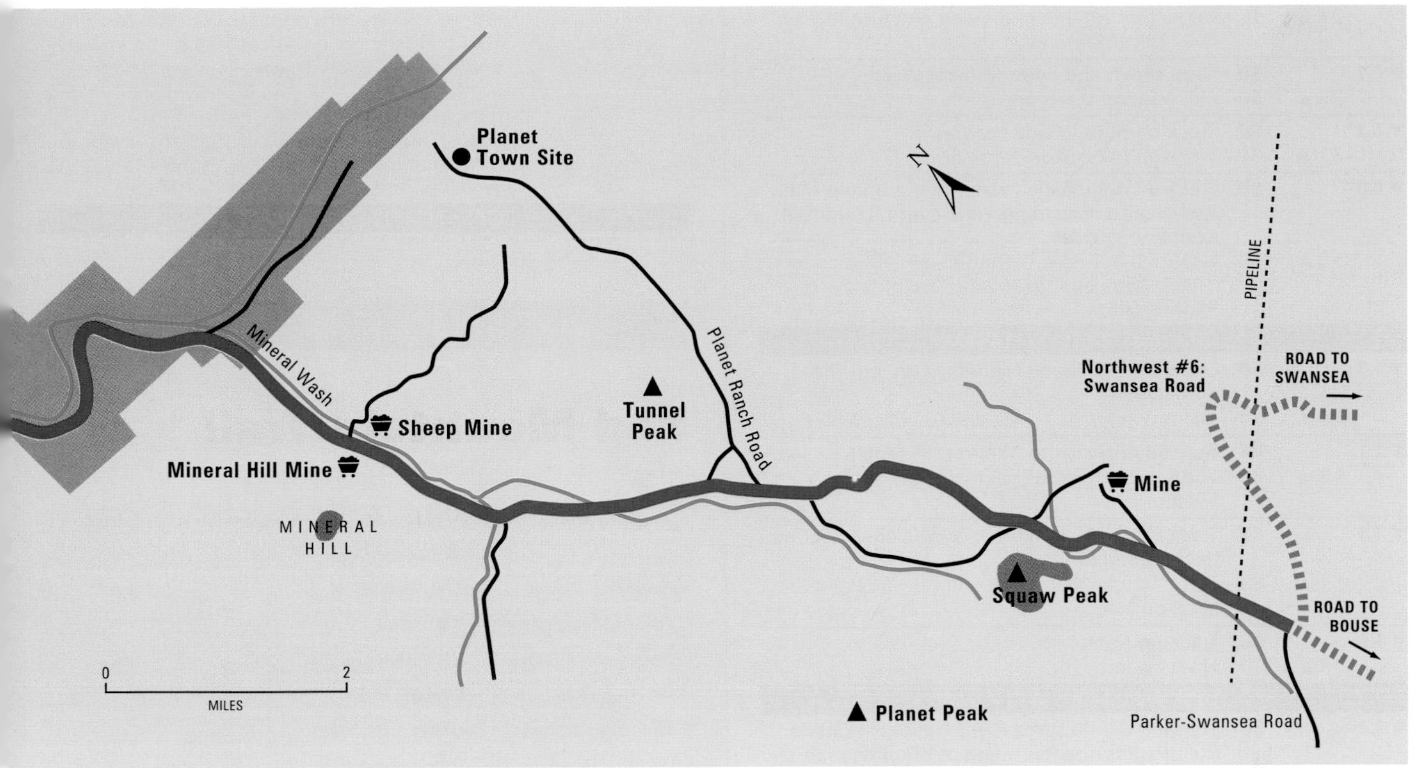

Map References

BLM Alamo Lake, Parker
USGS 1:24,000 Planet, Osborne Well, Monkeys Head
1:100,000 Alamo Lake, Parker
Maptech CD-ROM: Colorado River/Lake Havasu
Arizona Atlas & Gazetteer, p. 46
Arizona Road & Recreation Atlas, p. 38 & p. 72
Recreational Map of Arizona
Other: Arizona Access Guide–Cactus Plain

Route Directions

▼ 0.0			From Northwest #6: Swansea Road, 17.7 miles from Bouse, 6.9 miles from Swansea, zero trip meter and turn northwest on graded gravel road signed to Mineral Wash 8 miles.
	1.2 ▲		Trail ends at the intersection with Northwest #6: Swansea Road and the Parker-Swansea Road. Continue straight ahead for Bouse; turn left to continue to Swansea; turn right to exit to Parker.
			GPS: N34°08.26′ W113°55.58′
▼ 0.4		SO	Cross over gas pipeline. Track on right and track on left along pipeline.
	0.8 ▲	SO	Cross over gas pipeline. Track on right and track on left along pipeline.
▼ 1.0		SO	Enter wash.
	0.2 ▲	SO	Exit wash.
▼ 1.2		SO	Exit wash; track on right up wash goes 0.4 miles to a mine. Zero trip meter.
	0.0 ▲		Continue to the southeast.
			GPS: N34°09.40′ W113°55.99′
▼ 0.0			Continue to the northwest.
	3.5 ▲	SO	Enter wash; track on sharp left goes up wash for 0.4 miles to mine. Zero trip meter.
▼ 0.3		SO	Track on right is the second entrance to mine.
	3.2 ▲	SO	Track on left is the first entrance to mine.
▼ 0.8		SO	Enter wash.
	2.7 ▲	SO	Exit wash.
▼ 1.0		SO	Exit wash.
	2.5 ▲	SO	Enter wash.
▼ 1.1		SO	Two tracks on right.
	2.4 ▲	SO	Two tracks on left.
			GPS: N34°10.20′ W113°56.60′
▼ 1.2		SO	Track on left.
	2.3 ▲	SO	Track on right.
▼ 1.4		SO	Enter wash.
	2.1 ▲	SO	Exit wash.
▼ 3.2		SO	Track on left.
	0.3 ▲	SO	Track on right.
			GPS: N34°11.47′ W113°57.84′
▼ 3.4		SO	Small track on left; then small track on right.
	0.1 ▲	SO	Small track on left; then small track on right.
▼ 3.5		BL	Graded road on right is Planet Ranch Road. Zero trip meter.
	0.0 ▲		Continue up wash to the southeast.
			GPS: N34°11.66′ W113°58.09′
▼ 0.0			Continue down wash to the northwest.
	2.1 ▲	BR	Graded road on left is Planet Ranch Road. Zero trip meter.
▼ 0.5		BL	Track on right down side wash. Remain in main wash.
	1.6 ▲	SO	Track on left down side wash. Remain in main wash.
			GPS: N34°12.03′ W113°58.48′
▼ 1.5		SO	Exit wash. Track on right continues in wash.
	0.6 ▲	SO	Enter wash. Track on left in wash.
▼ 2.1		TR	Turn right and immediately cross through Mineral Wash. Zero trip meter.
	0.0 ▲		Continue on Mineral Wash Road to the south.
			GPS: N34°12.87′ W113°59.85′
▼ 0.0			Continue on Mineral Wash Road to the north.

2.4 ▲ TL Cross through Mineral Wash and turn left on rise. Zero trip meter.

▼ 0.2 SO Drop down and enter Mineral Wash.
2.2 ▲ SO Exit Mineral Wash up rise.

▼ 0.3 SO Track on right in side canyon.
2.1 ▲ SO Track on left in side canyon.

▼ 0.9 SO Track on right leaves wash to the Sheep Mine and gives a rewarding view over Mineral Hill. Continue in wash.
1.5 ▲ SO Continue in wash; then track on left goes to Sheep Mine and gives a rewarding view over Mineral Hill.

GPS: N34°13.59′ W114°00.08′

▼ 1.0 SO Entrance to Mineral Hill Mines on left—no admittance.
1.4 ▲ SO Second entrance to Mineral Hill Mines on right.

▼ 1.1 BR Second entrance to Mineral Hill Mines on left.
1.3 ▲ BL Entrance to Mineral Hill Mines on right—no admittance.

▼ 1.3 SO Track on right; then track on left; then second track on right.
1.1 ▲ SO Track on left; then track on right; then second track on left.

▼ 1.6 SO Track on right.
0.8 ▲ SO Track on left.

GPS: N34°14.21′ W114°00.36′

▼ 2.4 SO Entering Bill Williams River National Wildlife Refuge. Information board at boundary. Zero trip meter.
0.0 ▲ Continue up Mineral Wash into BLM land.

GPS: N34°14.95′ W114°00.44′

▼ 0.0 Continue into Bill Williams River National Wildlife Refuge. Small arch on right at top of cliff.
3.8 ▲ SO Exiting Bill Williams River National Wildlife Refuge into BLM land. Information board at boundary. Small arch on left at top of cliff. Zero trip meter.

▼ 0.2 SO Track on right to power lines (opposite old pipeline remains) and track on left.
3.6 ▲ SO Track on left to power lines (opposite old pipeline remains) and track on right.

▼ 0.3 BL Track on left is dead end.
3.5 ▲ SO Track on right is dead end.

▼ 0.5 BL Bear left and run alongside river.
3.3 ▲ BR Bear right and leave river.

▼ 0.8 SO Start of river crossings.
3.0 ▲ SO End of river crossings.

GPS: N34°15.53′ W114°00.96′

▼ 1.4 SO End of first stretch of crossings.
2.4 ▲ SO Start of multiple river crossings.

GPS: N34°15.90′ W114°01.29′

▼ 2.5 SO Ford through Bill Williams River.
1.3 ▲ SO Ford through Bill Williams River.

▼ 2.6 SO Ford through Bill Williams River.
1.2 ▲ SO Ford through Bill Williams River.

▼ 3.2 SO Cross through wash.
0.6 ▲ SO Cross through wash.

▼ 3.8 SO Gate. Zero trip meter.
0.0 ▲ Continue to the south.

GPS: N34°16.40′ W114°03.16′

▼ 0.0 Continue to the north.
3.2 ▲ SO Gate. Zero trip meter.

▼ 3.1 SO Information board on left.
0.1 ▲ SO Information board on right.

▼ 3.2 Trail ends at intersection with Arizona 95. Turn left for Parker; turn right for Lake Havasu City.
0.0 ▲ Trail commences on Arizona 95 at the intersection with the Bill Williams Highway, 0.8 miles north of the Bill Williams River National Wildlife Refuge HQ and 2.8 miles north of the intersection with Parker Dam Road. Zero trip meter and turn southeast on graded dirt road into the Bill Williams River National Wildlife Refuge.

GPS: N34°17.68′ W114°05.78′

NORTHWEST REGION TRAIL #8

Red Mountain Trail

Starting Point:	**Arizona 95, 2.9 miles south of the turn to Parker Dam**
Finishing Point:	**Gray Eagle Mine**
Total Mileage:	**3.8 miles**
Unpaved Mileage:	**3.8 miles**
Driving Time:	**1 hour**
Elevation Range:	**400–1,200 feet**
Usually Open:	**Year-round**
Best Time to Travel:	**Fall to spring**
Difficulty Rating:	**6**
Scenic Rating:	**8**
Remoteness Rating:	**+1**

Special Attractions

- Challenging trail through a rugged mountain range.
- Rockhounding around mine tailings dumps.
- Gray Eagle Mine.

Description

This short trail starts on Arizona 95, 2.9 miles south of the turn to Parker Dam. The turn is unsigned and easy to miss. It is opposite the Castle Rock Shores RV Park, immediately south of the Gas Market. Turning south, the trail runs alongside the RV storage fence line. There are many turns off the trail but generally the most used trail is the correct one; however, it pays to follow the directions closely. The trail initially passes through Buckskin Mountain State Park, but neither the trail nor the park are marked or signed in any way. Also, the trail is not shown in its entirety on the topographic maps of the region.

The trail twists and turns around Giers Mountain

The trail winds along a well-used road, running along the western boundary of the Gibraltar Mountain Wilderness Area through the Buckskin Moun-

An open mine adit beside the trail

tains. It then swings sharp right and climbs up the side of the hill. At this point, a disused jeep trail goes a short distance to an old mine. There are tailings and shafts nearby on the hillside, and rock hounds will enjoy picking up small, colorful specimens of copper rock. The scenery is rugged, and the area is sparsely vegetated with palo verde, creosote bush, and the occasional saguaro.

The climbs present the greatest challenge of the trail. Although the trail is not long or particularly steep, the surface is very loose and rubbly, and it is hard to get adequate traction in places. This is not the place for road tires! Some of the wash crossings can be gully-like, and some sections of the trail, which are normally narrow, are made narrower by washouts; even so, this trail should be suitable for all but the very longest or very widest vehicles. The newer, lower-to-the ground, super-sized SUVs may struggle a bit. Experienced drivers, well versed in picking a line for their vehicles will enjoy the trail, but there are tight spots and often the best line takes you close to the edge of the drop.

The hardest section comes after the mine, as the trail climbs up the edge of the hill to a saddle before dropping to the Gray Eagle Mine. Run in reverse, the climb from the Gray Eagle Mine may halt some vehicles as it has some difficult ledges. The ledge surfaces are extremely loose and gravelly, challenging the driver with the worst traction of the trail.

The trail finishes at the junction of Northwest #9: Gray Eagle Mine Trail. The mine is at the junction—a small stone cabin remains, and many tailings and workings are scattered around the nearby desert.

Current Road Information

Bureau of Land Management
Havasu Field Office
2610 Sweetwater Ave.
Lake Havasu City, AZ 86406
(520) 505-1200

Map References

BLM Parker
USGS 1:24,000 Gene Wash, Cross Roads
1:100,000 Parker
Maptech CD-ROM: Colorado River/Lake Havasu
Arizona Atlas & Gazetteer, p. 46
Other: Arizona Access Guide–Cactus Plain

Route Directions

▼ 0.0		From Arizona 95, 2.9 miles south of the turn to Parker Dam, turn south immediately south of the Gas Market on the well-used, narrow trail alongside the RV storage fence line. Zero trip meter.
3.8 ▲		Trail finishes on Arizona 95 at the Gas Market. Turn right for the Parker Dam; turn left for Parker.
		GPS: N34°15.41' W114°08.82'
▼ 0.1	BL	Track on right; then trail heads up wash.
3.7 ▲	BR	Trail leaves wash; then track on left.
▼ 0.2	TL	Track on right; climb out of wash.
3.6 ▲	TR	Track on left; enter wash.
▼ 0.6	BR	Two faint tracks on left.
3.2 ▲	BL	Two faint tracks on right.
▼ 0.8	BL	Track on right.
3.0 ▲	BR	Track on left.
		GPS: N34°14.80' W114°09.06'
▼ 0.9	SO	Track on left.
2.9 ▲	SO	Track on right.
▼ 1.1	BR	Faint track on left goes toward arch.
2.7 ▲	SO	Faint track on right goes toward arch.
		GPS: N34°14.58' W114°09.04'
▼ 1.2	SO	Cross through wash. Loose, rutted terrain; difficult climb out of wash.
2.6 ▲	SO	Loose, rutted terrain for the descent; then cross through wash.
▼ 1.6	SO	Cross through wash. Giers Mountain is on the left.
2.2 ▲	SO	Cross through wash. Giers Mountain is on the right.
▼ 1.7	BR	Trail enters wash.
2.1 ▲	BL	Exit wash.
▼ 1.8	SO	Exit wash. Loose, scrabbly descent into wash.
2.0 ▲	SO	Enter wash. Loose, scrabbly climb out of wash.
▼ 1.9	SO	Crest of rise.
1.9 ▲	SO	Crest of rise.
▼ 2.3	SO	Start to cross through wide wash.

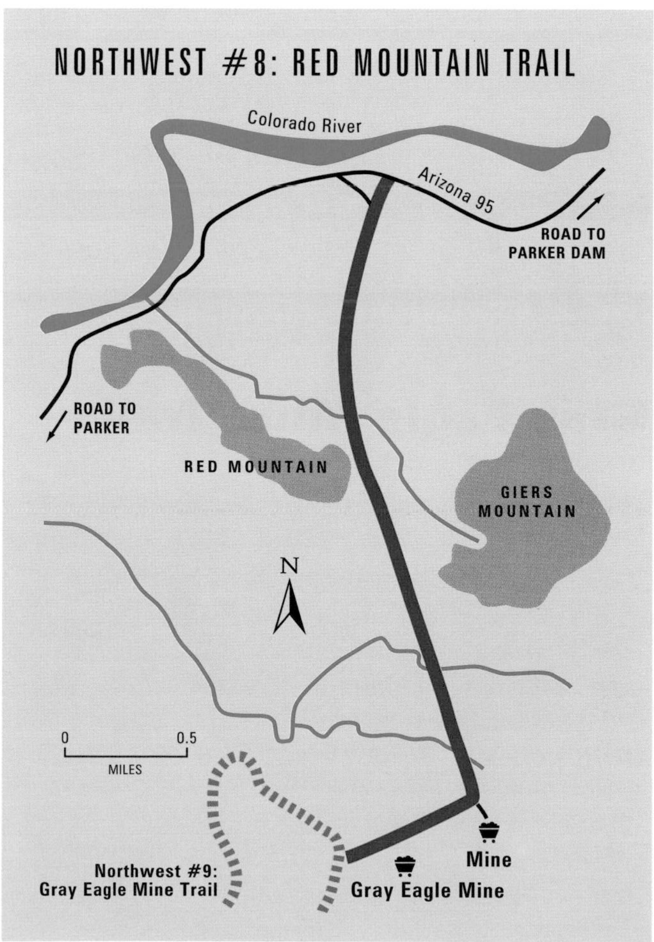

		Vehicles travel to the right down wash.
1.5 ▲	SO	Exit wash crossing.
		GPS: N34°13.71' W114°08.75'
▼ 2.5	SO	Exit wash crossing.
1.3 ▲	SO	Start to cross through wide wash. Vehicles travel to the left down wash.
▼ 2.8	SO	Cross through wash.
1.0 ▲	SO	Cross through wash.
▼ 2.9	SO	Cross through wash.
0.9 ▲	SO	Cross through wash.
▼ 3.0	SO	Cross through wash.
0.8 ▲	SO	Cross through wash.
▼ 3.1	TR	Turn sharp right and start to climb up ridge. Disused track straight ahead goes short distance to mine.
0.7 ▲	TL	End of descent from ridge; turn sharp left on main trail. Disused track on right goes short distance to mine.
		GPS: N34°13.08' W114°08.48'
▼ 3.3	SO	Crest of ridge; turnout on right and views in both directions. Mine shafts at crest. Difficult descent ahead from crest with large boulders and a tight line.
0.5 ▲	SO	Crest of ridge; turnout on left and views in both directions. Mine shafts at crest. Descend from ridge.
		GPS: N34°13.04' W114°08.65'
▼ 3.8		Trail ends at the junction with Northwest #9: Gray Eagle Mine Trail at the Gray Eagle Mine. Remains of a small stone cabin, shafts, and tailings on the left. Turn left for the quickest exit to the county road (Northwest #10: Nellie Mine Road); turn right to continue around the Gray Eagle Mine Trail.
0.0 ▲		Trail commences along Northwest #9: Gray Eagle Mine Trail, 1.2 miles from the western end of the trail at the Gray Eagle Mine. Zero trip meter and turn northeast on the rough trail. Trail immediately climbs a ridge with large boulders and a tight line.
		GPS: N34°12.84' W114°09.10'

NORTHWEST REGION TRAIL #9

Gray Eagle Mine Trail

Starting Point:	**Northwest #10: Nellie Mine Road, 3 miles from Arizona 95**
Finishing Point:	**Northwest #10: Nellie Mine Road, 4.1 miles from Arizona 95**
Total Mileage:	**3.6 miles**
Unpaved Mileage:	**3.6 miles**
Driving Time:	**45 minutes**
Elevation Range:	**800–900 feet**
Usually Open:	**Year-round**
Best Time to Travel:	**Fall to spring**
Difficulty Rating:	**4**
Scenic Rating:	**8**
Remoteness Rating:	**+1**

The loading chute at Gray Eagle Mine

Special Attractions

- Gray Eagle Mine.
- Rugged, remote trail through the spectacular Buckskin Mountains.
- Rockhounding in old mine sites.

Description

This is a short, winding trail that travels through the very rugged terrain of Billy Mack Mountain. It offers good views of the area and is an easy, undulating trail suitable for all stock vehicles. The trail starts and finishes from the graded Northwest #10: Nellie Mine Road. The eastern entrance to the trail is easier to find as it has a small marker post at the junction. The western entrance is unmarked.

Much of the trail travels in a narrow, gravelly, smooth wash. Part of the time it runs in a narrow canyon with palo verde trees growing up the sides. There are a few rocky sections, but the formed trail is generally easygoing, if a bit rough in places. This is an easier trail than Northwest #8: Red Mountain Trail but runs through similar scenery.

The Gray Eagle Mine is located 2.4 miles along the trail. The remains of an old stone cabin can be seen at the junction with Northwest #8: Red Mountain Trail; a short distance further along, a short spur leads to more mining remains.

From the mine, the trail climbs up a narrow shelf road out of the wash and then wraps back and rejoins Northwest #10: Nellie Mine Road.

Current Road Information

Bureau of Land Management
Havasu Field Office
2610 Sweetwater Ave.
Lake Havasu City, AZ 86406
(520) 505-1200

Map References

BLM Parker
USGS 1:24,000 Cross Roads
1:100,000 Parker
Arizona Atlas & Gazetteer, p. 46
Other: Arizona Access Guide–Cactus Flat

Route Directions

Mileage		Directions
▼ 0.0		Trail commences on Northwest #10: Nellie Mine Road, 3 miles east of Arizona 95. Zero trip meter and turn north on unmarked trail.
2.4 ▲		Trail finishes on Northwest #10: Nellie Mine Road. Turn right to return to Arizona 95.
		GPS: N34°11.98' W114°10.27'
▼ 0.1	SO	Two tracks on left; track on right; then cross through wash. Vehicles travel up and down wash.
2.3 ▲	SO	Cross through wash; track on left; then two tracks on right. Vehicles travel up and down wash.
▼ 0.2	SO	Faint track on left.
2.2 ▲	SO	Faint track on right.
▼ 0.3	SO	Cross through wash; then track on left.
2.1 ▲	SO	Track on right; then cross through wash.
		GPS: N34°12.24' W114°10.25'
▼ 0.6	SO	Cross through wash.
1.8 ▲	SO	Cross through wash.
▼ 0.9	SO	Cross through wash; track on left down wash.
1.5 ▲	SO	Cross through wash; track on right down wash.
		GPS: N34°12.56' W114°09.76'
▼ 1.1	BL	Enter wash canyon; track on right in wash.
1.3 ▲	BR	Track on left; bear right and exit wash.
▼ 1.6	BR	Second wash joins; bear right up wash.
0.8 ▲	BL	Bear left following vehicle tracks down wash.
▼ 1.8	BR	Exit wash.
0.6 ▲	SO	Re-enter wash.
		GPS: N34°13.22' W114°09.57'
▼ 1.9	SO	Re-enter wash.
0.5 ▲	BL	Bear left on formed trail and exit wash.
▼ 2.3	SO	Exit wash.
0.1 ▲	SO	Enter wash.
▼ 2.4	BR	Track on left is Northwest #8: Red Mountain Trail. The Gray Eagle Mine is directly ahead; remains of old stone cabin and tailings on the left. Zero trip meter.
0.0 ▲		Continue toward Northwest #10: Nellie Mine Road.
		GPS: N34°12.84' W114°09.11'
▼ 0.0		Continue past the Gray Eagle Mine. Immediately, small track on left to mine; followed by large adit on left.
1.2 ▲	BL	Large adit on right; followed by small track on right to mine. Track on right is Northwest #8: Red Mountain Trail. The Gray Eagle Mine is on the right; remains of an old stone cabin and tailings. Zero trip meter.
▼ 0.1	BR	Track on left goes to mining remains. Bear right and descend to wash.
1.1 ▲	SO	Exit from wash; then track on right goes to mining remains.
▼ 0.2	SO	Cross through wash.
1.0 ▲	SO	Cross through wash.
▼ 0.6	SO	Track on right.
0.6 ▲	SO	Track on left.
▼ 0.7	SO	Track on left; then faint track on right.
0.5 ▲	SO	Faint track on left; then track on right.
		GPS: N34°12.36' W114°09.22'
▼ 0.9	BR	Track on left; bear right and cross through wash.
0.3 ▲	BL	Cross through wash; then track on right.
		GPS: N34°12.19' W114°09.21'
▼ 1.0	SO	Enter wash.
0.2 ▲	SO	Exit wash.
▼ 1.1	TR	Wash forks. Track on left goes to Eagle Nest Mine.
0.1 ▲	TL	Wash forks. Track on right goes to Eagle Nest Mine.
		GPS: N34°12.13' W114°09.15'
▼ 1.2		Trail ends on Northwest #10: Nellie Mine Road, near the end of the trail. Turn right for Arizona 95.
0.0 ▲		Trail commences at the junction with Northwest #10: Nellie Mine Road, 4.1 miles from the junction with Arizona 95. Turn northwest on roughly graded dirt road at the BLM sign for Gray Eagle Mine Trail. Zero trip meter.
		GPS: N34°12.06' W114°09.15'

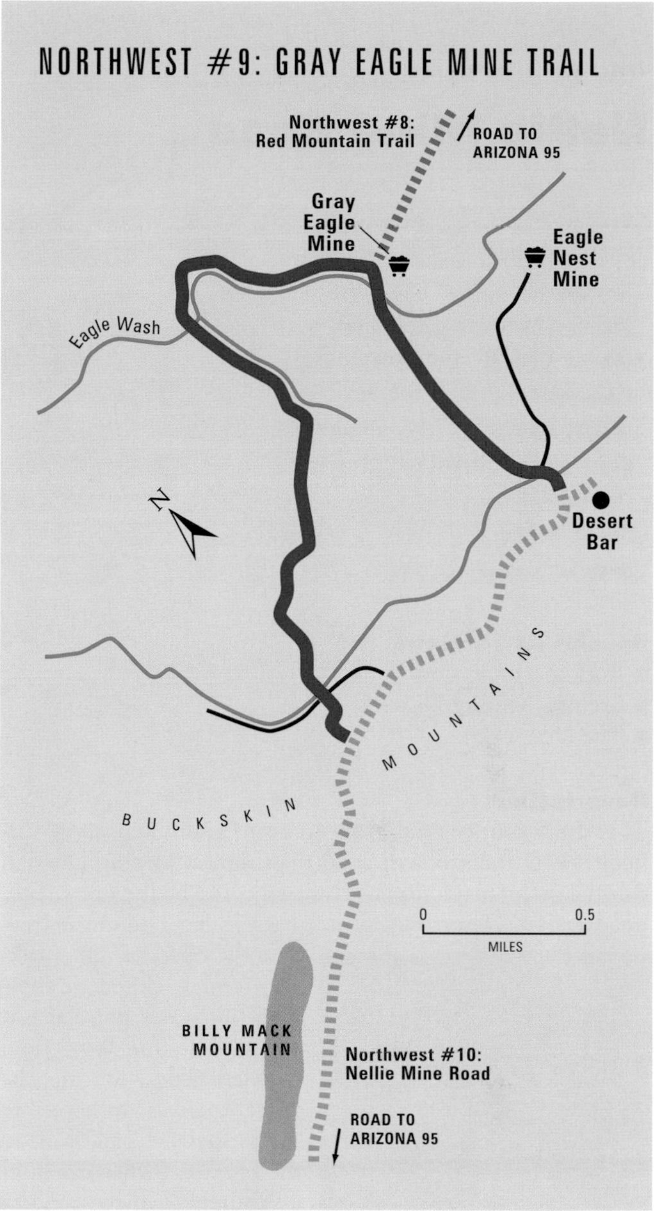

NORTHWEST REGION TRAIL #10

Nellie Mine Road

Starting Point:	**Arizona 95**
Finishing Point:	**Desert Bar**
Total Mileage:	**4.2 miles**
Unpaved Mileage:	**4.2 miles**
Driving Time:	**30 minutes**
Elevation Range:	**400–900 feet**
Usually Open:	**Year-round**
Best Time to Travel:	**Fall to spring**
Difficulty Rating:	**1**
Scenic Rating:	**7**
Remoteness Rating:	**+0**

Special Attractions

- Rockhounding sites.
- Cienega Mining District.
- The Desert Bar.

Description

This short county road gives access to additional, more difficult 4WD trails as well as to the Cienega Mining District. But the major attraction of this trail could be the unmarked, unadvertised Desert Bar, situated at the very end of the trail. It only operates on weekends and is closed in summer, but it is a popular watering hole for locals and travelers alike. During the week, there is no access to the property. In addition to the bar, the owner has built a "church" (which is nothing more than a board front) on his property. It is hard to miss as you come down the wash.

An old abandoned truck along the trail

The Nellie Mine Road goes past an area popular with RV travelers in the winter and past the active Billy Mack Mine. There are numerous old mining claims in these hills, and many are popular fossicking areas for rock hounds. Northwest #9: Gray Eagle Mine Trail leads off from this route and loops around and rejoins the Nellie Mine Road.

Current Road Information

Bureau of Land Management
Havasu Field Office
2610 Sweetwater Ave.
Lake Havasu City, AZ 86406
(520) 505-1200

A church front at the desert bar at the end of the trail

Map References

BLM Parker
USGS 1:24,000 Cross Roads
1:100,000 Parker
Maptech CD-ROM: Colorado River/Lake Havasu
Arizona Atlas & Gazetteer, p. 46
Arizona Road & Recreation Atlas, p. 38 & p. 72
Other: Arizona Access Guide–Cactus Flat

Route Directions

▼ 0.0		Trail commences on Arizona 95, 1 mile north of the Riverside Drive stoplight on the northern edge of Parker. The turn is unmarked; turn southeast on the graded road and zero trip meter.
3.0 ▲		Trail ends at junction with Arizona 95; turn left for Parker; turn right for Parker Dam.
		GPS: N34°11.43' W114°12.55'
▼ 0.6	BR	Graded dirt road on left is Cienega Springs Road, which goes to Billy Mack Mine. Bear right, following the sign pole for Nellie Mine Road. Many small tracks on right and left; remain on main graded road.
2.4 ▲	BL	Graded dirt road on right is Cienega Springs Road, which goes to Billy Mack Mine.
▼ 0.9	SO	Two tracks on left and two tracks on right at information board. Mining adits on the right are the start of the Cienega Mining District.
2.1 ▲	SO	Two tracks to left and two tracks on right at information board. Mining adits on left. Many small tracks on right and left; remain on main road.
		GPS: N34°11.04' W114°11.98'
▼ 1.1	SO	Cross through wash; then track on right.
1.9 ▲	SO	Track on left; then cross through wash.
▼ 1.4	BL	Track on right.
1.6 ▲	SO	Track on left.
		GPS: N34°10.99' W114°11.53'
▼ 1.6	SO	Track on right goes to diggings on Lion Hill.
1.4 ▲	SO	Track on left goes to diggings on Lion Hill.
▼ 1.8	SO	Track on left.
1.2 ▲	SO	Track on right.
▼ 1.9	SO	Memorial cross on the flank of Billy Mack Mountain on left.
1.1 ▲	SO	Memorial cross on the flank of Billy Mack Mountain on right.

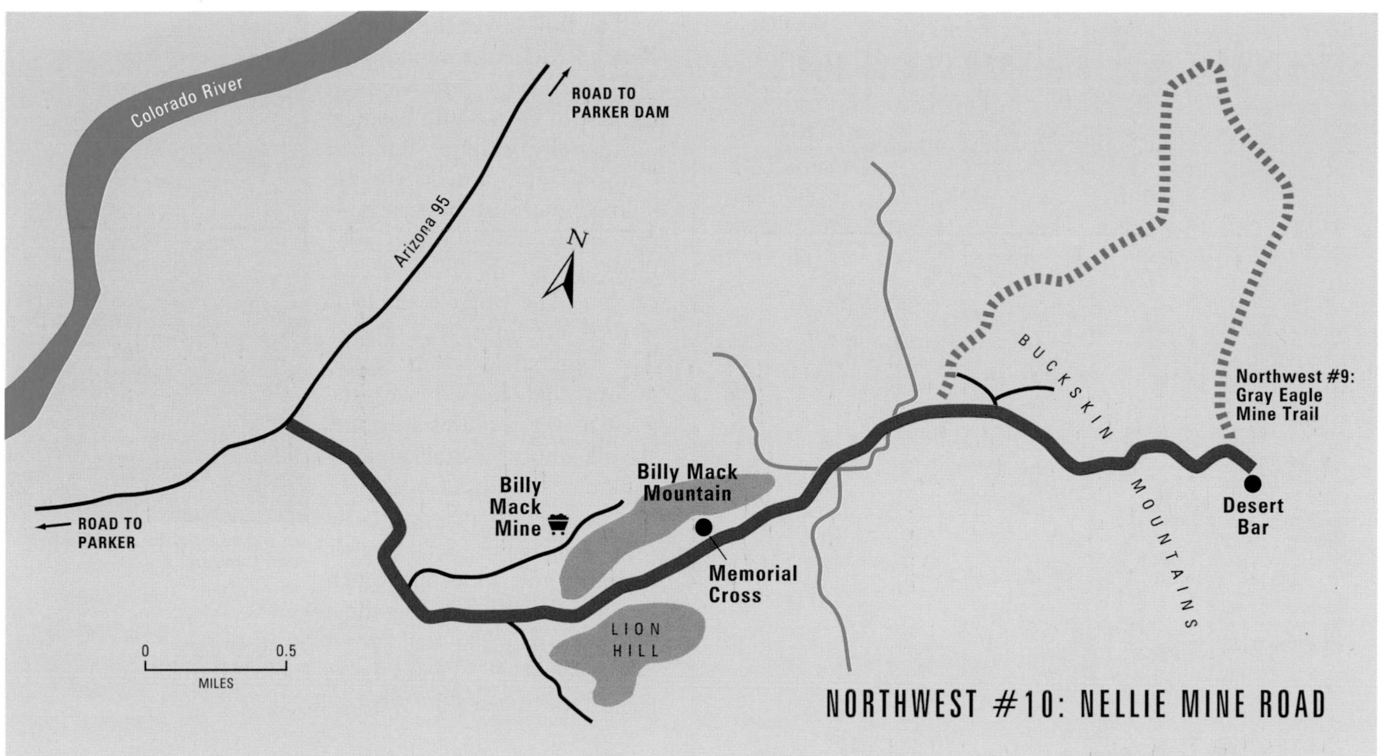

▼ 2.3		BR	Track on left.
	0.7 ▲	SO	Track on right.
			GPS: N34°11.57′ W114°10.72′
▼ 2.6		SO	Track on left; then cross through wash.
	0.4 ▲	SO	Cross through wash; then track on right.
▼ 2.7		SO	Two tracks to left.
	0.3 ▲	SO	Two tracks to right.
▼ 2.8		SO	Cross through wash; then track on left.
	0.2 ▲	SO	Track on right; then cross through wash.
▼ 3.0		SO	Track on left is Northwest #9: Gray Eagle Mine Trail. Zero trip meter.
	0.0 ▲		Continue to the west.
			GPS: N34°11.99′ W114°10.27′
▼ 0.0			Continue to the east and cross through wash.
	1.2 ▲	SO	Cross through wash; then track on right is the other end of Northwest #9: Gray Eagle Mine Trail. Zero trip meter.
▼ 0.2		SO	Three tracks on left. One goes to a cross on top of a hillock.
	1.0 ▲	SO	Three tracks on right. One goes to a cross on top of a hillock.
▼ 0.7		SO	Track on left.
	0.5 ▲	SO	Track on right.
▼ 1.1		SO	Track on left is the other end of Northwest #9: Gray Eagle Mine Trail; there is a post marking the route.
	0.1 ▲	SO	Track on right is Northwest #9: Gray Eagle Mine Trail; there is a post marking the route.
			GPS: N34°12.06′ W114°09.15′
▼ 1.2			Track on right; then trail ends in wash at the Desert Bar.
	0.0 ▲		Trail commences at the end of the public access road to the Desert Bar. This property is only open on weekends; please do not trespass at other times. Zero trip meter and proceed west along the graded road.
			GPS: N34°12.06′ W114°08.99′

NORTHWEST REGION TRAIL #11

Railroad Canyon Trail

Starting Point:	**Lincoln Ranch Road, 5.4 miles from Midway and 4.7 miles southwest of junction with Johnson Ranch Road**
Finishing Point:	**Northwest #12: Swansea Loop Trail in Swansea**
Total Mileage:	**4.1 miles**
Unpaved Mileage:	**4.1 miles**
Driving Time:	**30 minutes**
Elevation Range:	**1,400–1,600 feet**
Usually Open:	**Year-round**
Best Time to Travel:	**November to April**
Difficulty Rating:	**3**
Scenic Rating:	**7**
Remoteness Rating:	**+1**

Special Attractions

- Final section of historic railroad grade from Bouse to Swansea.
- Can be driven as part of a loop drive from Swansea.

Description

This short trail follows part of the railroad grade from Bouse to Swansea. The train operated from 1910 to 1937, transporting workers, copper ore, and supplies to and from Swansea.

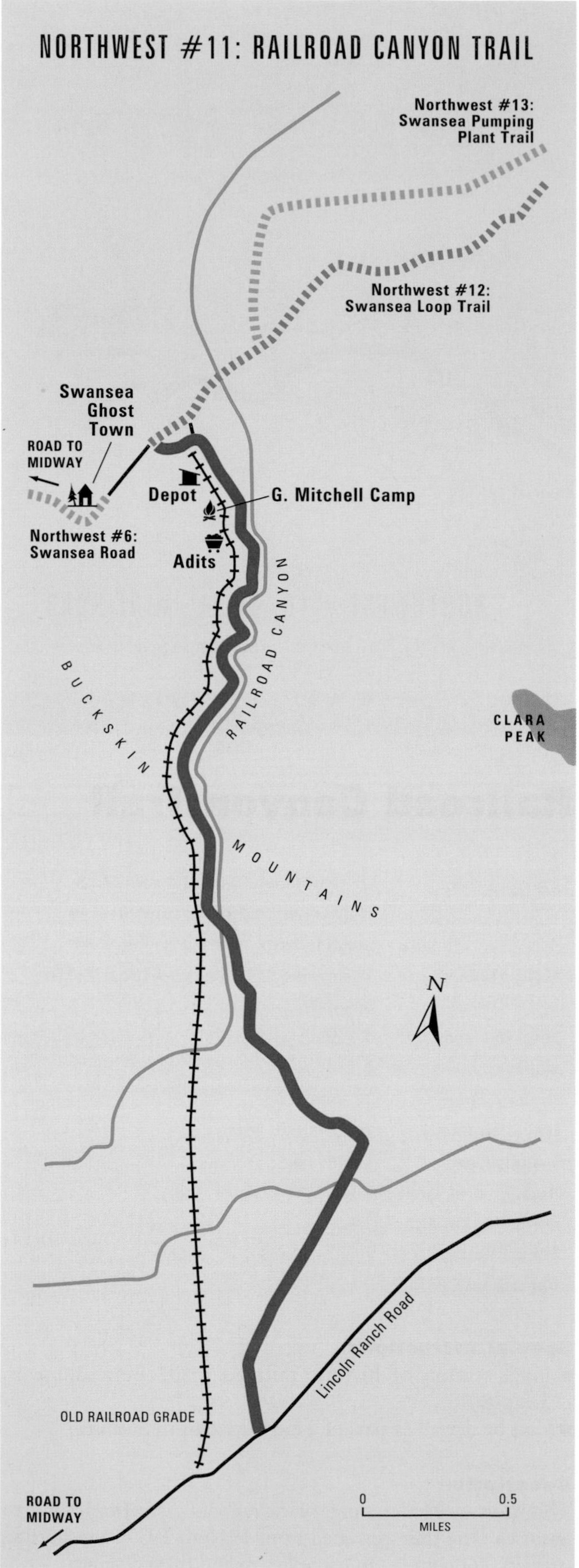

NORTHWEST #11: RAILROAD CANYON TRAIL

Northwest #13: Swansea Pumping Plant Trail
Northwest #12: Swansea Loop Trail
Swansea Ghost Town
ROAD TO MIDWAY
Depot
G. Mitchell Camp
Northwest #6: Swansea Road
Adits
RAILROAD CANYON
BUCKSKIN MOUNTAINS
CLARA PEAK
N
Lincoln Ranch Road
OLD RAILROAD GRADE
ROAD TO MIDWAY
0 0.5 MILES

The trail leaves the Lincoln Ranch Road and runs along an undulating ridge, with views to the east of Clara Peak. It enters the gravelly wash of Railroad Canyon and immediately the railroad grade can be seen built up on an embankment, running around the edge of the canyon. The original grade is washed out in several places. The original wooden trestle bridges that crossed over the wash at several points are gone, leaving only the built-up embankments on either side.

An old railway foundation in Railroad Canyon

The trail is an easy, fairly smooth drive. The section after it leaves the Johnson Ranch Road has some interesting moguls and can become very greasy in wet weather. The trail ends in Swansea at the junction with Northwest #12: Swansea Loop Trail, 0.1 miles north of the end of Northwest #6: Swansea Road.

Current Road Information

Bureau of Land Management
Havasu Field Office
2610 Sweetwater Ave.
Lake Havasu City, AZ 86406
(520) 505-1200

Map References

BLM Alamo Lake
USGS 1:24,000 Swansea
1:100,000 Alamo Lake
Maptech CD-ROM: Colorado River/Lake Havasu
Arizona Atlas & Gazetteer, p. 47
Arizona Road & Recreation Atlas, p. 39 & p. 73
Other: Arizona Access Guide–Cactus Plain

Route Directions

Mileage		Direction	
▼ 0.0			From Lincoln Ranch Road, 4.7 miles southwest of the junction with Johnson Ranch Road and 5.4 miles northeast of Midway, turn northeast on the small, well-used, formed trail. Trail is marked with a wooden marker post for Railroad Canyon; zero trip meter. Cross through wash.
	4.1 ▲		Cross through wash; trail ends at the junction with Lincoln Ranch Road. Turn right for Midway; turn left to return to Swansea via Northwest #12: Swansea Loop Trail.
			GPS: N34°07.56′ W113°49.28′
▼ 0.7		SO	Cross through wash.
	3.4 ▲	SO	Cross through wash.
▼ 0.9		SO	Cross through wash.
	3.2 ▲	SO	Cross through wash.
▼ 1.6		SO	Views ahead into Railroad Canyon. Clara Peak is on the right.
	2.5 ▲	SO	Clara Peak is on the left.
▼ 1.8		BR	Enter Railroad Canyon wash and bear right

			down wash. Lesser-used track on left in wash.
	2.3 ▲	BL	Lesser-used track on right in wash; keep to the left in wash; then exit wash and bear left up to ridge. Marker post at junction.
			GPS: N34°08.89' W113°49.70'
▼ 2.2		SO	Railroad grade enters on left.
	1.9 ▲	SO	Railroad grade leaves on right.
			GPS: N34°09.04' W113°49.82'
▼ 3.5		SO	Two small adits on left.
	0.6 ▲	SO	Two small adits on right.
▼ 3.6		BL	Bear left out of wash; trail ahead in wash joins Northwest #12: Swansea Loop Trail; G. Mitchell Camp on left with picnic table and shade ramada.
	0.5 ▲	BR	G. Mitchell Camp on right with picnic table and shade ramada; then drop down into wash and bear right up wash. Track on left in wash joins Northwest #12: Swansea Loop Trail.
			GPS: N34°10.28' W113°50.00'
▼ 3.7		BL	Adobe railroad depot on left. Bear left past the depot, track on right.
	0.4 ▲	BR	Adobe railroad depot on right. Bear right past the depot, track on left.
			GPS: N34°10.34' W113°50.13'
▼ 3.9		BL	Bear left at fork; then small track on left down wash.
	0.2 ▲	BR	Small track on right down wash; then bear right at fork.
			GPS: N34°10.43' W113°50.26'
▼ 4.0		SO	Cross through wash.
	0.1 ▲	SO	Cross through wash.
▼ 4.1			Trail ends at the junction with Northwest #12: Swansea Loop Trail, 0.1 miles south of the information board in Swansea. Turn left for Midway; turn right to continue around the Swansea Loop Trail.
	0.0 ▲		Trail commences 0.1 miles south of the information board in Swansea. Zero trip meter and turn northeast on well-used, formed trail. There is a marker post for Railroad Canyon at the junction. The left fork at this intersection is Northwest #12: Swansea Loop Trail signed for Swansea Pumping Plant.
			GPS: N34°10.38' W113°50.40'

NORTHWEST REGION TRAIL #12

Swansea Loop Trail

Starting Point:	**Swansea Ghost Town**
Finishing Point:	**Lincoln Ranch Road**
Total Mileage:	**12 miles**
Unpaved Mileage:	**12 miles**
Driving Time:	**1.5 hours**
Elevation Range:	**800–1,400 feet**
Usually Open:	**Year-round**
Best Time to Travel:	**November to April**
Difficulty Rating:	**3**
Scenic Rating:	**9**
Remoteness Rating:	**+1**

Red rock formations contrast with the white wash trail as it approaches Bill Williams River

Special Attractions

- The Bill Williams River.
- Spectacular views to the Rawhide Mountains.
- Access to a network of 4WD trails.

Description

When combined with part of the graded gravel Lincoln Ranch Road and Northwest #11: Railroad Canyon Trail, this trail makes a complete loop. The trail runs through some wild and rugged country south of the Bill Williams River, coming within 0.1 miles of the river at the apex of the trail.

The trail is marked from Swansea as going to the Swansea Pumping Plant, a spur trail (Northwest #13: Swansea Pumping Plant Trail), which leads off the main loop trail. The trail is well formed and easy to follow. It has some scrabbly sections and some moderately steep grades as it descends to cross through a large wash; but it is well within the capabilities of most high-clearance 4WDs.

A view of the dry landscape as the trail descends to cross a wash

For the first few miles the trail runs along a ridge top, offering great views to the north over the Rawhide Mountains and the Bill Williams River Valley. It descends toward the river, traveling in a gravelly wash between high red canyon walls. Closer to the Bill Williams River, the vegetation gets denser, and the short sandy section running parallel to the river can be quite brushy because of the close-growing tamarisk.

The trail loops back to join Lincoln Ranch Road by following the El Paso Gas Pipeline Road. This part of the trail is wider and more frequently used, and for a couple of miles it follows a roller-coaster ride over the ridge tops and down to cross through the washes.

The trail joins the graded Johnson Ranch Road, called Rankin Ranch Road on some maps, 3.1 miles after leaving the river. The left turn at this point goes a couple of miles back to the river and the Johnson Ranch. Some maps show a small

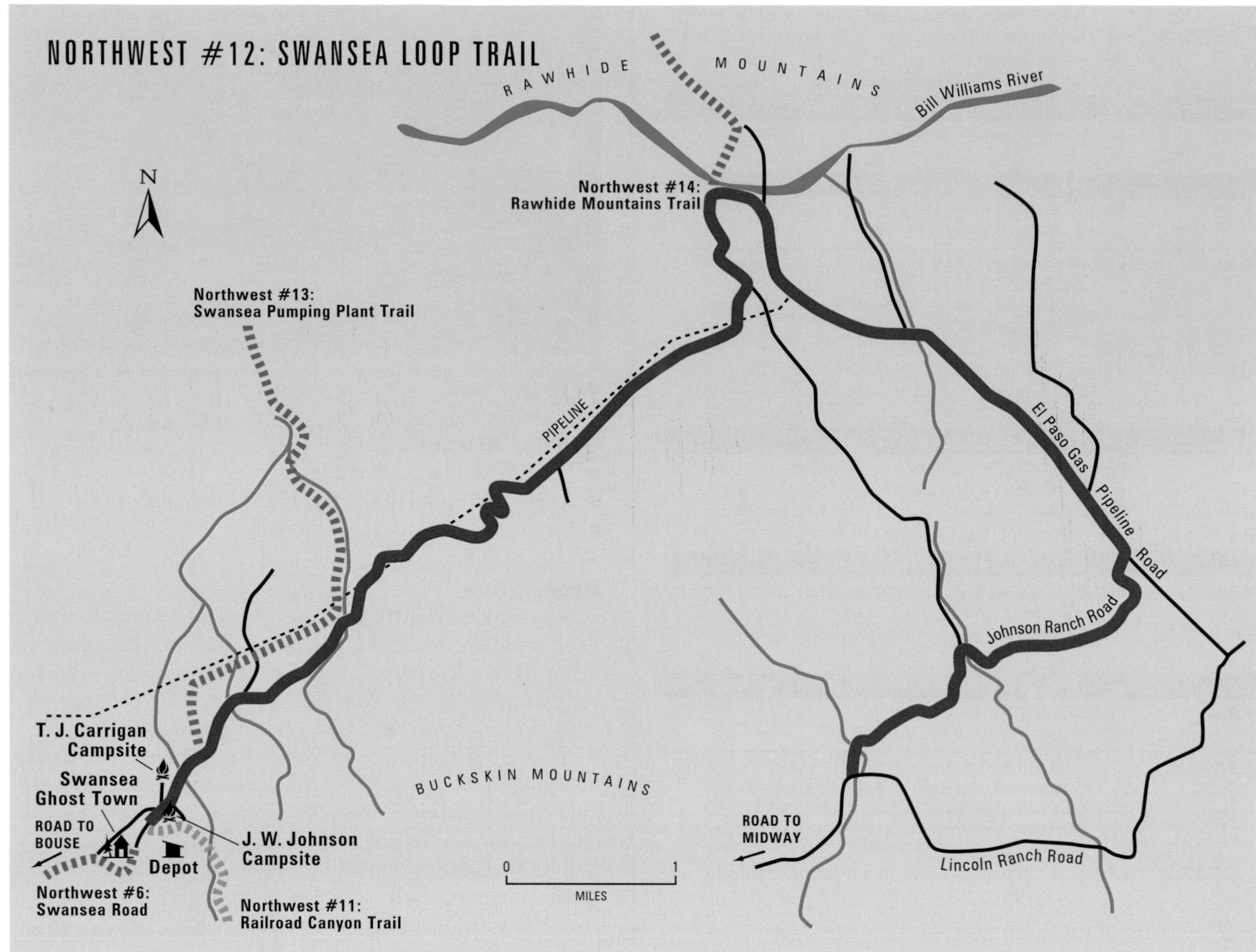

trail that goes past this point and then doubles back to run close to the river, eventually joining Northwest #14: Rawhide Mountains Trail. This trail is becoming very overgrown and is seldom used. Camping opportunities close to the river are extremely limited and not particularly appealing.

The trail follows the graded Johnson Ranch Road out to join Lincoln Ranch Road. From here it is 4.7 miles to the south end of Northwest #11: Railroad Canyon Trail. This trail takes you back to Swansea or to Midway (10.1 miles) to join the graded Northwest #6: Swansea Road to exit the region to Bouse or Parker.

Current Road Information

Bureau of Land Management
Havasu Field Office
2610 Sweetwater Ave.
Lake Havasu City, AZ 86406
(520) 505-1200

Map References

BLM Alamo Lake
USGS 1:24,000 Swansea, Reid Valley
1:100,000 Alamo Lake
Maptech CD-ROM: Colorado River/Lake Havasu
Arizona Atlas & Gazetteer, p. 47
Arizona Road & Recreation Atlas, p. 39 & p. 73
Other: Arizona Access Guide–Cactus Plain

Route Directions

▼ 0.0 From the northern end of Northwest #6: Swansea Road, at the information board, zero trip meter and continue along the road for another 0.1 miles. At the fork in the trail, zero trip meter and bear left onto the Swansea Loop Trail, signed to the Swansea Pumping Plant. To the right is Northwest #11: Railroad Canyon Trail. Continue to the northeast. Table and shade ramada immediately on right is J. W. Johnson Campsite. Swansea company houses are on the left.

0.5 ▲ Trail ends in Swansea, 0.1 miles north of the information board at the end of Northwest #6: Swansea Road. The track on left is Northwest #11: Railroad Canyon Trail. Continue south to exit to Bouse or Parker via graded dirt road.

GPS: N34°10.39′ W113°50.41′

▼ 0.1 TR Intersection. Track on left; track ahead goes to T. J. Carrigan Campsite and picnic table with shade ramada. Turn right following marker for

		Swansea Pumping Plant and cross through wash.
0.4 ▲	TL	Cross through wash; then intersection. Track on right goes to T. J. Carrigan Campsite and picnic table with shade ramada. Track ahead.
▼ 0.2	TL	Track on right goes to railroad depot.
0.3 ▲	TR	Track on left goes to railroad depot.
		GPS: N34°10.48' W113°50.28'
▼ 0.4	SO	Cross through wash.
0.1 ▲	SO	Cross through wash.
▼ 0.5	SO	Track on left is Northwest #13: Swansea Pumping Plant Trail. Zero trip meter and continue following marker for Bill Williams River.
0.0 ▲		Continue toward Swansea.
		GPS: N34°10.75' W113°50.09'
▼ 0.0		Continue to the northeast.
5.5 ▲		Track on right is Northwest #13: Swansea Pumping Plant Trail. Zero trip meter.
▼ 0.3	SO	Cross through wash.
5.2 ▲	SO	Cross through wash.
▼ 0.4	SO	Track on right; then faint track on left.
5.1 ▲	SO	Faint track on right; then track on left.
▼ 0.6	SO	Enter wash.
4.9 ▲	SO	Exit wash.
▼ 1.1	SO	Exit wash.
4.4 ▲	SO	Enter wash.
▼ 1.4	SO	Gas pipeline crosses trail; track on right and track on left along pipeline.
4.1 ▲	SO	Gas pipeline crosses trail; track on right and track on left along pipeline.
		GPS: N34°11.57' W113°49.10'
▼ 1.5	SO	Cross through wash; track on right in wash follows pipeline.
4.0 ▲	SO	Cross through wash; track on left in wash follows pipeline.
▼ 1.7	SO	Cross through wash.
3.8 ▲	SO	Cross through wash.
▼ 2.1	SO	Cross through wash; gas pipeline crosses trail; tracks on left and right along pipeline.
3.4 ▲	SO	Cross through wash; gas pipeline crosses trail; tracks on left and right along pipeline.
▼ 2.5	SO	Trail starts to descend to cross wide wash. Views to the right over the wash canyon.
3.0 ▲	SO	End of climb out of wash; views to the left over the wash canyon.
		GPS: N34°11.99' W113°48.28'
▼ 2.6	TR	Two tracks on left along pipeline.
2.9 ▲	BL	Two tracks on right along pipeline.
▼ 2.7	BL	Enter wash and bear left down wash; track on right in wash; track on left along pipeline.
2.8 ▲	BR	Exit wash; track straight on continues in wash; second track on right follows pipeline.
		GPS: N34°12.09' W113°48.26'
▼ 2.8	TR	Turn right and exit wash up ridge.
2.7 ▲	TL	Enter wash and turn left up wash.
▼ 3.0	SO	Top of climb out of wash; continue alongside pipeline.
2.5 ▲	SO	Descend into wash; views ahead and to the right down wash.
▼ 3.2	SO	Cross through wash; then faint track on left. Trail crosses through many washes for the next 1.7 miles.
2.3 ▲	SO	Faint track on right; then cross through wash.
		GPS: N34°12.31' W113°47.87'
▼ 4.6	BL	Bear left on crest; track continues straight ahead. Views down to wash and then over toward Bill Williams River and Rawhide Mountains.
0.9 ▲	BR	At top of crest bear right; track on left along pipeline.
▼ 4.9	TL	Enter wash and turn left down wash. Track on right up wash.
0.6 ▲	TR	Exit wash to the right; track continues in wash straight ahead. Trail crosses through many washes for the next 1.7 miles.
		GPS: N34°13.25' W113°46.71'
▼ 5.5	TR	Track on right in wash is private property; then second track on right is El Paso Gas Pipeline Road. Turn sharp right onto this road and zero trip meter. Track straight on is the start of Northwest #14: Rawhide Mountains Trail; the Bill Williams River is 0.1 miles along the start of it.
0.0 ▲		Proceed to the south.
		GPS: N34°13.72' W113°46.94'
▼ 0.0		Proceed to the southeast through dense vegetation.
2.9 ▲	TL	Track ahead is the start of Northwest #14: Rawhide Mountains Trail; the Bill Williams River is 0.1 miles along the start of it. Zero trip meter and turn sharp left. The track on left in wash is private property.
▼ 0.2	BR	Two tracks on left.
2.7 ▲	SO	Two tracks on right.
▼ 0.3	TR	Track on left goes to pipeline bridge.
2.6 ▲	TL	Track straight on goes to pipeline bridge.
▼ 0.9	SO	Track on right beside gas pressure valves.
2.0 ▲	SO	Track on left beside gas pressure valves.
▼ 1.3	SO	Cross through wash.
1.6 ▲	SO	Cross through wash.
▼ 1.6	BR	Cross over wash on causeway; then track on left. Tracks rejoin almost immediately; left-hand fork has track on left leading off from it.
1.3 ▲	SO	Tracks rejoin; cross over wash on causeway.
▼ 1.7	SO	Tracks rejoin.
1.2 ▲	BL	Track on right; tracks rejoin almost immediately; right-hand fork has track on right leading off from it.
		GPS: N34°12.99' W113°45.58'
▼ 2.2	SO	Cross through wash.
0.7 ▲	SO	Cross through wash.
▼ 2.5	SO	Cross over wash.
0.4 ▲	SO	Cross over wash.
▼ 2.6	SO	Cross over wash.
0.3 ▲	SO	Cross over wash.
▼ 2.9	SO	Graded road on left. Trail now joins the wider Johnson Ranch Road. Zero trip meter.
0.0 ▲		Continue northwest, following the pipeline.
		GPS: N34°12.19' W113°44.58'
▼ 0.0		Continue to the southeast.
3.1 ▲	SO	Graded road on right. Trail leaves the wider Johnson Ranch Road. Zero trip meter.
▼ 0.4	BR	Track on left is El Paso Gas Pipeline Road; bear right away from pipeline.
2.7 ▲	SO	Track on right is El Paso Gas Pipeline Road. Trail now follows close to the pipeline.
		GPS: N34°11.88' W113°44.32'
▼ 0.6	SO	Cross through wash.
2.5 ▲	SO	Cross through wash.
▼ 0.8	SO	Cross through wash.
2.3 ▲	SO	Cross through wash.
▼ 1.0	SO	Cross through wash.
2.1 ▲	SO	Cross through wash.

▼ 1.9		BL	Enter wash. Track on right down wash.
	1.2 ▲	BR	Track on left down wash. Exit wash.
			GPS: N34°11.32' W113°45.34'
▼ 2.1		SO	Exit wash.
	1.0 ▲	SO	Enter wash.
▼ 2.3		SO	Cross through wash.
	0.8 ▲	SO	Cross through wash.
▼ 2.4		SO	Enter wash.
	0.7 ▲	SO	Exit wash.
▼ 2.6		SO	Exit wash.
	0.5 ▲	SO	Enter wash.
▼ 2.9		SO	Cross through wash.
	0.2 ▲	SO	Cross through wash.
▼ 3.1			Trail ends at the junction with the graded gravel Lincoln Ranch Road. Track on left is marked with a wooden marker post—Lincoln Ranch Road. Turn right for Midway.
	0.0 ▲		From Lincoln Ranch Road, 4.7 miles past the south end of Northwest #11: Railroad Canyon Trail and 10.1 miles northwest of Midway, zero trip meter and turn northwest onto graded gravel road. Lincoln Ranch Road continues east at this point and is marked with a marker post. The road you take is unmarked except for a primitive road sign.
			GPS: N34°10.70' W113°46.03'

NORTHWEST REGION TRAIL #13

Swansea Pumping Plant Trail

Starting Point:	**Northwest #12: Swansea Loop Trail, 0.5 miles northeast of Swansea**
Finishing Point:	**Swansea Pumping Plant**
Total Mileage:	**3.8 miles**
Unpaved Mileage:	**3.8 miles**
Driving Time:	**45 minutes (one-way)**
Elevation Range:	**900–1,300 feet**
Usually Open:	**Year-round**
Best Time to Travel:	**November to April**
Difficulty Rating:	**4**
Scenic Rating:	**9**
Remoteness Rating:	**+1**

Special Attractions

- Historic Swansea Pumping Plant.
- Scenic trail in deep red-walled canyon.
- Access to the Bill Williams River.

Description

This short trail runs down an extremely pretty canyon to the Bill Williams River and the site of the Swansea Pumping Plant. The pump supplied Swansea with water from the Bill Williams River.

A view of the climb back out of the wash

The trail's main difficulty comes from a loose, moderately steep descent down to the wash and then the very deep gravel in the wash that runs down to the river. In hotter weather especially, watch engine temperatures on the return trip when you are climbing up the wash.

The wide wash has no close vegetation but is lined with palo verde trees. In April, the mass of yellow blossoms against the red walls of the canyon makes for a very colorful scene. Small barrel cacti grow precariously on the sheer rock walls.

The trail ends at a turnaround, 0.1 miles before the Bill Williams River. You can hike the short distance down the wash to the river. The river normally flows year-round but can disappear into the sand in the hotter months. The wash is lined with dense vegetation.

To reach the pumping plant, walk through the fence and after about 20 yards, bear right out of the wash. You will need to scramble up the bank on a small foot track. The pump is on the rise on the north side of the wash. A concrete tank and some footings remain.

Current Road Information

Bureau of Land Management
Havasu Field Office
2610 Sweetwater Ave.
Lake Havasu City, AZ 86406
(520) 505-1200

Map References

BLM Alamo Lake
USGS 1:24,000 Swansea
1:100,000 Alamo Lake
Maptech CD-ROM: Colorado River/Lake Havasu
Arizona Atlas & Gazetteer, p. 47
Other: Arizona Access Guide–Cactus Plain

Route Directions

▼ 0.0			From Northwest #12: Swansea Loop Trail, 0.5 miles northeast of Swansea, turn north on the Swansea Pumping Plant Trail at the marker and zero trip meter. Trail is well used and formed.
			GPS: N34°10.75' W113°50.07'
▼ 0.4		SO	Cross through wash.

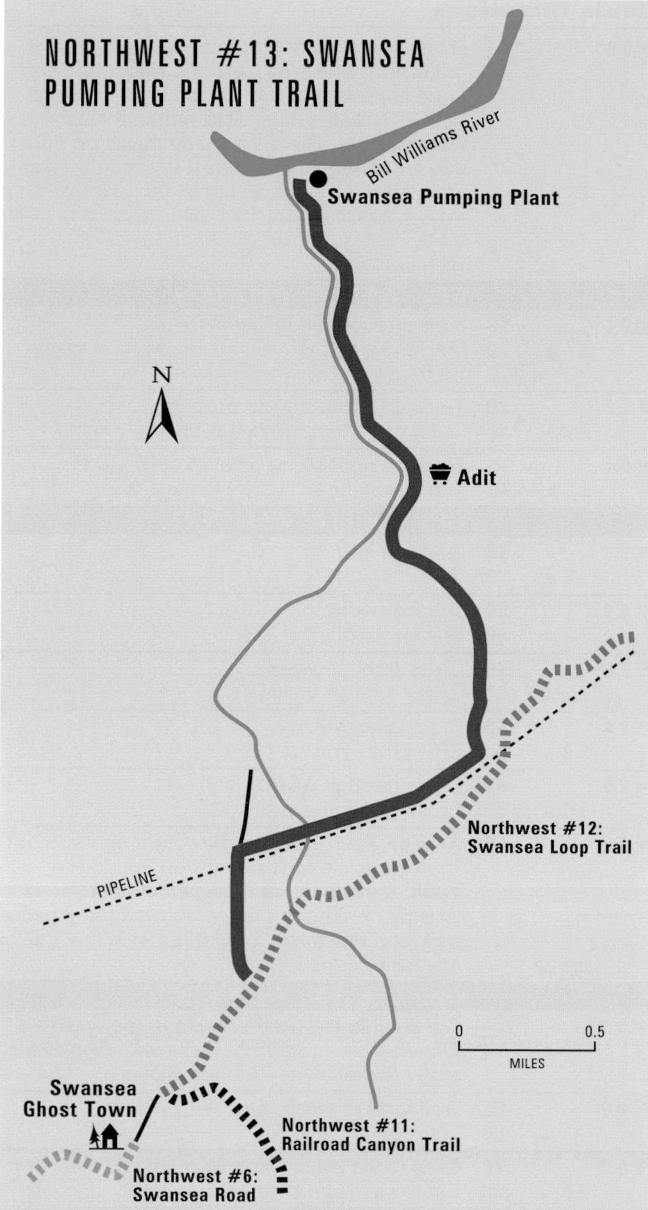

▼ 0.5	TR	Track on left follows along pipeline. Turn right and follow alongside pipeline.
		GPS: N34°11.16' W113°50.13'
▼ 0.6	SO	Cross through wash.
▼ 0.7	SO	Cross through wash.
▼ 1.4	TL	Enter wash and turn left down wash at the marker for Swansea Pumping Plant. Trail continues ahead along pipeline. Zero trip meter.
		GPS: N34°11.49' W113°49.18'
▼ 0.0		Continue down wash to the northwest.
▼ 0.9	SO	Exit wash up rise.
▼ 1.1	BR	Enter wash and bear right down wash. Mine adit on right.
		GPS: N34°12.37' W113°49.46'
▼ 2.4		Trail ends at a turning circle in the wash. From here, hike down the wash to the Bill Williams River and from there to Swansea Pumping Plant.
		GPS: N34°13.30' W113°49.95'

NORTHWEST REGION TRAIL #14

Rawhide Mountains Trail

Starting Point:	Northwest #12: Swansea Loop Trail, 6 miles from Swansea, 2.9 miles from junction with JW Ranch Road
Finishing Point:	Northwest #15: Alamo Lake Road
Total Mileage:	16.3 miles
Unpaved Mileage:	16.3 miles
Driving Time:	1.5 hours
Elevation Range:	800–2,400 feet
Usually Open:	Year-round
Best Time to Travel:	November to April
Difficulty Rating:	3 (5 at river crossing)
Scenic Rating:	9
Remoteness Rating:	+1

Special Attractions

- Fording the Bill Williams River.
- Trail connecting two major travel areas—Cactus Plain and the Rawhide Mountains.
- Varied scenery through the Rawhide Mountains.

Description

The trail commences along Northwest #12: Swansea Loop Trail, 6 miles from Swansea. It immediately crosses the wide, sandy wash of the Bill Williams River and fords the river. The crossing in normal conditions is about 100 yards wide and it can be up to 24 inches deep. The bottom is firm. The river depth can vary, and it has the potential to be much higher in winter and after summer flooding. If in doubt, walk the crossing first.

Once over the crossing, the trail takes a roller-coaster ride alongside the pipeline for a few miles before turning off to proceed up a wide, sandy wash. Although unmarked, the turn is relatively easy to spot as it will be the only very wide wash encountered since you crossed the river. Once you are in the wash, the navigation becomes tricky for the next few miles.

The trail climbs through the Rawhide Mountains as seen from Northwest #12: Swansea Loop Trail

Checking the depth and soundness of the riverbed of the Bill Williams River before driving across is always a good idea

There are many branching tracks in the wash, and the most-used trail is not necessarily the correct one. Keep to the left in the wash so that you don't miss the exit: up the bank to the left, 1.2 miles from the entry point. The trail remains faint as it winds through creosote bushes, but there are a few side trails to confuse the navigator.

After the next major intersection (where the trail turns east), it is well defined and easy to follow as it runs along a ridge with a deep wash on each side. From there it remains well defined to the end of the trail; however, if you take one of the unmarked turns you will be convinced to follow the directions closely. A GPS unit is extremely handy on this trail.

The trail offers attractive views along its length: over Fools Peak and the Rawhide Mountains, and from the top of the saddle further afield to the Arrastra Mountains to the east and the Bill Williams Mountains to the west. For those with more time to explore, there are a number of side trails that lead to some of the old mines in the region. The trail surface and difficulty rates a 3. It is rated a 5 at the initial crossing of the Bill Williams River, which must be negotiated to complete the trail.

The eastern end of trail is called McGuffie Mine Road on some maps.

Current Road Information

Bureau of Land Management
Havasu Field Office
2610 Sweetwater Ave.
Lake Havasu City, AZ 86406
(520) 505-1200

Map References

BLM Alamo Lake
USGS 1:24,000 Swansea, Centennial Wash, Rawhide Wash, Artillery Peak
1:100,000 Alamo Lake
Maptech CD-ROM: Colorado River/Lake Havasu
Arizona Atlas & Gazetteer, p. 47
Arizona Road & Recreation Atlas, p. 39 & p. 73
Other: Arizona Access Guide–Cactus Plain

Route Directions

Mileage		Directions
▼ 0.0		From Northwest #12: Swansea Loop Trail, 6 miles from Swansea, zero trip meter and continue northwest along the sandy trail toward the Bill Williams River. Trail enters the sandy river channel. There are many tracks on right and left. Continue northwest toward the river.
3.8 ▲		Trail ends at the intersection with Northwest #12: Swansea Loop Trail. Bear right to continue to Swansea; bear left to exit via Lincoln Ranch Road.
		GPS: N34°13.72' W113°46.94'
▼ 0.1	SO	Ford through Bill Williams River.
3.7 ▲	SO	Ford through Bill Williams River; then many tracks up and down wide wash.
▼ 0.2	SO	Track on left to private property.
3.6 ▲	SO	Track on right to private property.
▼ 0.4	TL	Track on right along pipeline.
3.4 ▲	TR	Track straight on along pipeline.
		GPS: N34°14.07' W113°46.72'
▼ 0.8	SO	Track on left.
3.0 ▲	SO	Track on right.
▼ 0.9	SO	Track on right.
2.9 ▲	SO	Track on left.
▼ 1.6	SO	Cross through wash.
2.2 ▲	SO	Cross through wash.
▼ 2.4	SO	Cross over wash.
1.4 ▲	SO	Cross over wash.
▼ 2.9	SO	Cross through wash.
0.9 ▲	SO	Cross through wash.
▼ 3.8	TR	At wide wash crossing, turn right up wash, following vehicle tracks. Track on left down wash; trail along the pipeline continues straight on. This is the first turn off the pipeline trail for a few miles. Zero trip meter.
0.0 ▲		Continue to the southeast.
		GPS: N34°16.88' W113°48.00'
▼ 0.0		Continue to the northeast along the wash.
4.7 ▲	TL	Exit wash and turn onto well-used formed trail along the pipeline. Zero trip meter.
▼ 0.2	BL	Trail forks in wash; bear left.
4.5 ▲	SO	Track on left in wash.
▼ 1.2	BL	Keep to the left in wash. Bear left and exit wash.
3.5 ▲	BR	Enter wash and bear right.
		GPS: N34°17.66' W113°47.22'
▼ 1.4	SO	Cross through wash.
3.3 ▲	SO	Cross through wash.
▼ 1.6	SO	Faint track on right.
3.1 ▲	SO	Faint track on left.
▼ 1.7	TR	Crossroads. Turn right onto equally used, small, formed trail. Immediately track on right.
3.0 ▲	TL	Track on left; then crossroads. Turn left at the crossroads onto equally used, small, formed trail.
		GPS: N34°18.08' W113°47.05'
▼ 1.9	SO	Cross through wash.
2.8 ▲	SO	Cross through wash.
▼ 2.1	SO	Cross through wash and enter a gap in the hills.
2.6 ▲	SO	Leaving the hills; cross through wash.
▼ 2.4	SO	Cross through wash.
2.3 ▲	SO	Cross through wash.
▼ 3.6	BR	Enter wash and bear right, crossing wash.
1.1 ▲	BL	Bear left and exit wash; tracks continue down wash.

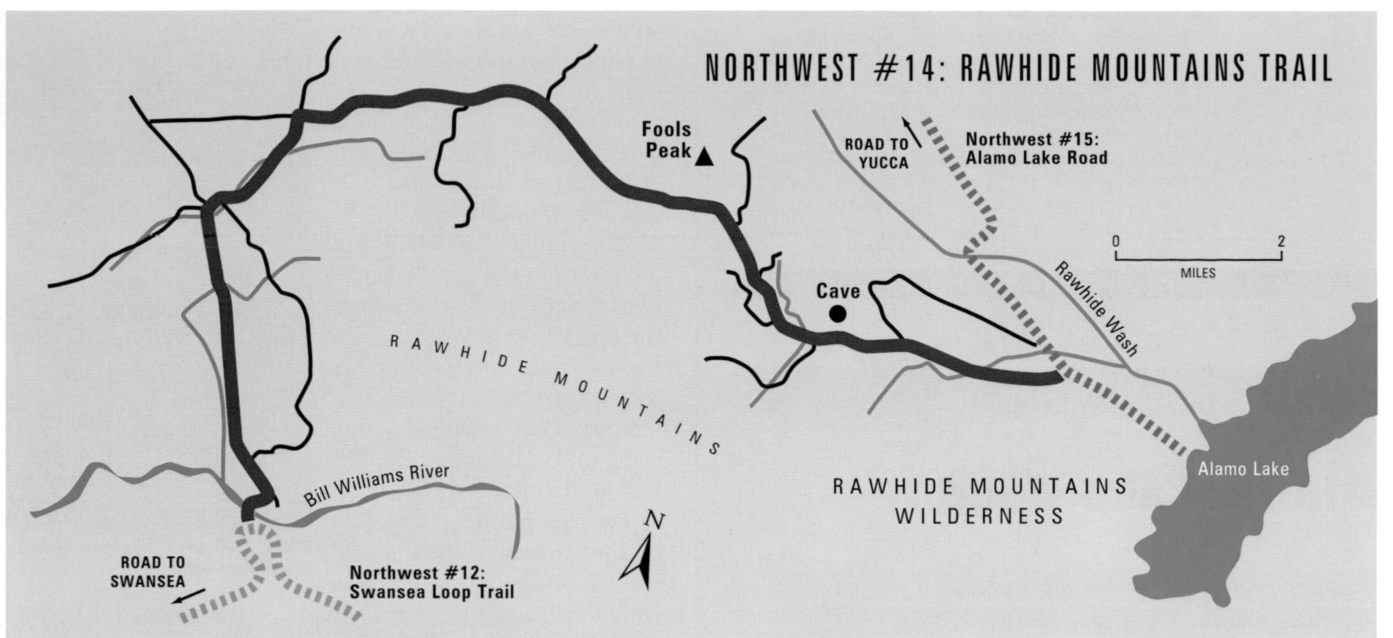

			GPS: N34°18.49′ W113°45.15′
▼ 3.8		SO	Exit wash; then well-used track on right.
	0.9 ▲	BR	Well-used track on left; bear right and enter wash.
			GPS: N34°18.48′ W113°44.91′
▼ 3.9		SO	Faint track on right; cross through wash.
	0.8 ▲	SO	Cross through wash; faint track on left.
▼ 4.2		SO	Cross through wash.
	0.5 ▲	SO	Cross through wash.
▼ 4.3		SO	Cross through wash.
	0.4 ▲	SO	Cross through wash.
▼ 4.7		SO	Well-used track on left opposite abandoned caravan. Zero trip meter.
	0.0 ▲		Continue to the west.
			GPS: N34°18.55′ W113°43.99′
▼ 0.0			Continue to the east.
	2.9 ▲	SO	Well-used track on right opposite abandoned caravan. Zero trip meter.
▼ 0.3		SO	Cross through wash.
	2.6 ▲	SO	Cross through wash.
▼ 0.8		SO	Cross through wash.
	2.1 ▲	SO	Cross through wash.
▼ 1.2		SO	Cross through wash.
	1.7 ▲	SO	Cross through wash.
▼ 1.4		SO	Saddle. The dark-colored cone of Fools Peak is on the left. Views ahead to the Arrastra Mountain Wilderness on the far side of the Alamo Lake Valley.
	1.5 ▲	SO	Saddle. The dark-colored cone of Fools Peak is on the right. Views ahead to the Aubrey Peak Wilderness, with the Bill Williams Mountains in distance and the closer Rawhide Mountains.
			GPS: N34°17.73′ W113°42.84′
▼ 1.7		SO	Cross through wash.
	1.2 ▲	SO	Cross through wash.
▼ 2.1		SO	Cross through wash.
	0.8 ▲	SO	Cross through wash.
▼ 2.5		SO	Cross through wash.
	0.4 ▲	SO	Cross through wash.
▼ 2.7		SO	Cross through wash.
	0.2 ▲	SO	Cross through wash.

▼ 2.9		SO	Well-used trail on left. Zero trip meter.
	0.0 ▲		Continue to the northwest.
			GPS: N34°17.56′ W113°41.43′
▼ 0.0			Continue to the south.
	4.9 ▲	BL	Well-used trail on right. Zero trip meter.
▼ 0.3		SO	Cross through wash.
	4.6 ▲	SO	Cross through wash.
▼ 0.4		SO	Cross through wash.
	4.5 ▲	SO	Cross through wash.
▼ 0.6		SO	Track on right and track on left.
	4.3 ▲	SO	Track on right and track on left.
▼ 0.7		SO	Cross through wash.
	4.2 ▲	SO	Cross through wash.
▼ 1.3		BL	Track on right.
	3.6 ▲	BR	Track on left.
			GPS: N34°16.60′ W113°40.72′
▼ 1.6		SO	Cross through wash.
	3.3 ▲	SO	Cross through wash.
▼ 1.7		SO	Cross through wash; then track on right. Rawhide Mountains Wilderness is now on the right of the trail.
	3.2 ▲	SO	Track on left; then cross through wash; end of Rawhide Mountains Wilderness.
			GPS: N34°16.46′ W113°40.22′
▼ 1.9		SO	Cross through wash.
	3.0 ▲	SO	Cross through wash.
▼ 2.2		SO	Large cave on left set back from trail.
	2.7 ▲	SO	Large cave on right set back from trail.
			GPS: N34°16.47′ W113°39.76′
▼ 2.4		SO	Cross through wash.
	2.5 ▲	SO	Cross through wash.
▼ 2.8		SO	Track on left
	2.1 ▲	BL	Track on right.
			GPS: N34°16.52′ W113°39.09′
▼ 3.7		BL	Enter wash and bear left down main wash channel.
	1.2 ▲	BR	Bear right out of wash.
			GPS: N34°16.27′ W113°38.21′
▼ 4.2		SO	Exit wash.
	0.7 ▲	SO	Enter wash.

▼ 4.9		Trail ends on Northwest #15: Alamo Lake Road, 1.5 miles west of Alamo Lake. Continue east to Alamo Lake; turn left to exit to Yucca or Wickenburg via Northwest #17: Signal Road.
0.0 ▲		Trail commences on Northwest #15: Alamo Lake Road, 1.5 miles west of the end of the trail at Alamo Lake. The road is unmarked, but there is a Rawhide Mountains Wilderness Area sign at the junction. Zero trip meter and turn west on well-used, formed dirt trail.
		GPS: N34°16.44' W113°36.92'

NORTHWEST REGION TRAIL #15

Alamo Lake Road

Starting Point:	**I-40 at exit 25 (Yucca)**
Finishing Point:	**Alamo Lake**
Total Mileage:	**53.9 miles**
Unpaved Mileage:	**50.9 miles**
Driving Time:	**1.25 hours**
Elevation Range:	**1,200–3,200 feet**
Usually Open:	**Year-round**
Best Time to Travel:	**October to May**
Difficulty Rating:	**1**
Scenic Rating:	**8**
Remoteness Rating:	**+0**

Special Attractions

- Access to Alamo Lake and Alamo Lake National Wildlife Refuge.
- Joshua tree forest.
- Rockhounding for onyx and rhyolite.

Description

This well-used, graded dirt road is the primary access road to the west side of Alamo Lake. Alamo Lake State Park, a popular spot, is on the east side of the lake; however a national wildlife area on the west is just as popular with fishermen. It is primarily included as an easy, scenic trail to a seldom-used part of Alamo Lake. Many other 4WD trails in the area start or finish from this road.

Alamo Lake with the Rawhide Mountains in the background

Baker Well with a Joshua tree in the foreground

The trail leaves Yucca and for several miles travels across Dutch Flat. The first section of the trail passes through a thick Joshua tree forest. Further down, there are views of McCracken Peak before the trail starts to wind through the low hills around Rawhide Wash.

For rock hounds, the gullies on the east side of the trail immediately south of the junction with Northwest #17: Signal Road can yield some interesting specimens of onyx and rhyolite. The site has been picked over through the years, but there are still rocks to be found.

The trail is graded dirt all the way and suitable for passenger vehicles in dry weather. As it is heavily used, it can be very washboardy, although it is regularly graded. Campers can find some pleasant spots near the McCracken Hills. There are some other popular sites near the lake.

Current Road Information

Bureau of Land Management
Kingman Field Office
2475 Beverly Ave.
Kingman, AZ 86401
(520) 692-4400

Map References

BLM Needles, Bagdad, Alamo Lake
USGS 1:24,000 Yucca, Yucca SE, Creamery Canyon, Dutch Flat NW, Beecher Canyon, Dutch Flat SE, Groom Spring, Signal, Rawhide Wash, Artillery Peak
1:100,000 Needles, Bagdad, Alamo Lake
Maptech CD-ROM: Colorado River/Lake Havasu
Arizona Atlas & Gazetteer, pp. 36, 37, 47
Arizona Road & Recreation Atlas, p. 39 & p. 73
Recreational Map of Arizona

Route Directions

▼ 0.0		From I-40 at exit 25 (Yucca), proceed to east side of freeway and zero trip meter. Follow sign for Alamo Road and immediately turn right on paved road.
2.6 ▲		Trail ends at exit 25 (Yucca) on I-40.
		GPS: N34°51.87' W114°08.67'
▼ 1.1	SO	Cattle guard.
1.5 ▲	SO	Cattle guard.
▼ 1.2	SO	Track on right.
1.4 ▲	SO	Track on left.
▼ 1.4	SO	Graded road on right is Apache Road.
1.2 ▲	SO	Graded road on left is Apache Road.

▼ 2.0		SO	Graded road on right.
	0.6 ▲	SO	Graded road on left.
▼ 2.1		SO	Graded road on right.
	0.5 ▲	SO	Graded road on left.
▼ 2.6		SO	Graded road on left is Northwest #19: Flag Mine Trail. Zero trip meter.
	0.0 ▲		Continue to the west.
			GPS: N34°50.99' W114°06.60'
▼ 0.0			Continue to the east and cross over Mackenzie Wash.
	8.7 ▲	SO	Cross over Mackenzie Wash; then graded road on right is Northwest #19: Flag Mine Trail. Zero trip meter.
▼ 0.4		SO	Road turns to graded dirt.
	8.3 ▲	SO	Road is now paved.
▼ 0.7		SO	Graded road on right.
	8.0 ▲	SO	Graded road on left.
▼ 1.3		SO	Track on left; then track on right.
	7.4 ▲	SO	Track on left; then track on right.
▼ 1.6		SO	Track on left.
	7.1 ▲	SO	Track on right.
▼ 2.5		SO	Track on left; then track on right.
	6.2 ▲	SO	Track on left; then track on right.
▼ 3.1		SO	Major graded road on left and right is Knox Drive.
	5.6 ▲	SO	Major graded road on left and right is Knox Drive.
			GPS: N34°49.13' W114°03.81'
▼ 4.7		SO	Two tracks on left and track on right; then cattle guard.
	4.0 ▲	SO	Cattle guard; then two tracks on right and track on left.
▼ 5.8		SO	Track on right.
	2.9 ▲	SO	Track on left.
▼ 6.9		SO	Track on left and track on right. There are many signed subdivision roads on the left and right for the next 11.3 miles.
	1.8 ▲	SO	Track on left and track on right.
▼ 8.7		SO	Graded road on left is La Cienega Ranch Road. Zero trip meter.
	0.0 ▲		Continue to the northwest.
			GPS: N34°45.99' W113°58.94'
▼ 0.0			Continue to the southeast.
	8.1 ▲	SO	Graded road on right is La Cienega Ranch Road. Zero trip meter.
▼ 1.1		SO	Cross through Cow Creek.
	7.0 ▲	SO	Cross through Cow Creek.
▼ 3.6		SO	Track on right.
	4.5 ▲	SO	Track on left.
▼ 4.0		SO	Track on right.
	4.1 ▲	SO	Track on left.
▼ 4.5		SO	Track on left.
	3.6 ▲	SO	Track on right.
▼ 8.1		SO	Well on left; then graded road on right is Cattle Crossing Road. Zero trip meter.
	0.0 ▲		Continue to the northwest.
			GPS: N34°40.00' W113°53.47'
▼ 0.0			Continue to the southeast.
	7.3 ▲	SO	Graded road on left is Cattle Crossing Road; then well on right. Zero trip meter.
▼ 5.9		SO	Planet Ranch Road on right.
	1.4 ▲	SO	Planet Ranch Road on left. There are now many signed subdivision roads on the left and right for the next 11.3 miles.
			GPS: N34°36.36' W113°48.86'
▼ 7.0		SO	Track on right.
	0.3 ▲	SO	Track on left.
▼ 7.1		SO	Cross through wash; then track on right to corral.
	0.2 ▲	SO	Track on left to corral; then cross through wash.
▼ 7.2		SO	Track on right to Stouts Well.
	0.1 ▲	SO	Track on left to Stouts Well.
▼ 7.3		SO	Major graded road on left is Chicken Springs Road to Wickieup. Zero trip meter.
	0.0 ▲		Continue to the west.
			GPS: N34°35.46' W113°47.62'
▼ 0.0			Continue to the east toward Alamo Lake.
	4.4 ▲		Major graded road on right is Chicken Springs Road to Wickieup. Zero trip meter.
▼ 0.3		SO	Track on left.
	4.1 ▲	SO	Track on right.
▼ 2.1		SO	Cross through wash.
	2.3 ▲	SO	Cross through wash.
▼ 3.3		SO	Corral on left and track on right to tank.
	1.1 ▲	SO	Corral on right and track on left to tank.
			GPS: N34°33.10' W113°45.34'
▼ 4.4		SO	Graded road on left is Coyote Wells Road. Zero trip meter.
	0.0 ▲		Continue to the northwest.
			GPS: N34°32.25' W113°44.72'
▼ 0.0			Continue to the southeast.
	4.9 ▲	SO	Graded road on right is Coyote Wells Road. Zero trip meter.
▼ 1.4		SO	Cross through wash.
	3.5 ▲	SO	Cross through wash.
▼ 2.2		SO	Cross through wash.
	2.7 ▲	SO	Cross through wash.
▼ 3.4		SO	Cattle guard; then track on right.
	1.5 ▲	SO	Track on left; then cattle guard.
			GPS: N34°29.30' W113°43.83'
▼ 4.7		SO	Cross through wash.
	0.2 ▲	SO	Cross through wash.
▼ 4.9		SO	Graded road on left is Northwest #17: Signal Road; track on right is Northwest #16: McCracken Peak Trail. Zero trip meter and continue along Alamo Lake Road.
	0.0 ▲		Continue to the northwest.
			GPS: N34°28.20' W113°42.93'
▼ 0.0			Continue to the southeast.
	4.0 ▲		Graded road on right is Northwest #17: Signal Road; track on left is Northwest #16: McCracken Peak Trail. Zero trip meter and continue along Alamo Lake Road.
▼ 0.1		SO	Track on left.
	3.9 ▲	SO	Track on right.
			GPS: N34°28.14' W113°42.94'
▼ 0.2		SO	Cross through wash.
	3.8 ▲	SO	Cross through wash.
▼ 1.0		SO	Cross through wash.
	3.0 ▲	SO	Cross through wash.
▼ 1.2		SO	Track on left.
	2.8 ▲	SO	Track on right.
			GPS: N34°27.22' W113°43.15'
▼ 1.7		SO	Track on left and track on right.
	2.3 ▲	SO	Track on left and track on right.
			GPS: N34°26.78' W113°43.36'
▼ 3.8		SO	Cross through wash.
	0.2 ▲	SO	Cross through wash.
▼ 4.0		SO	Track on right at Baker Well. Well and corrals

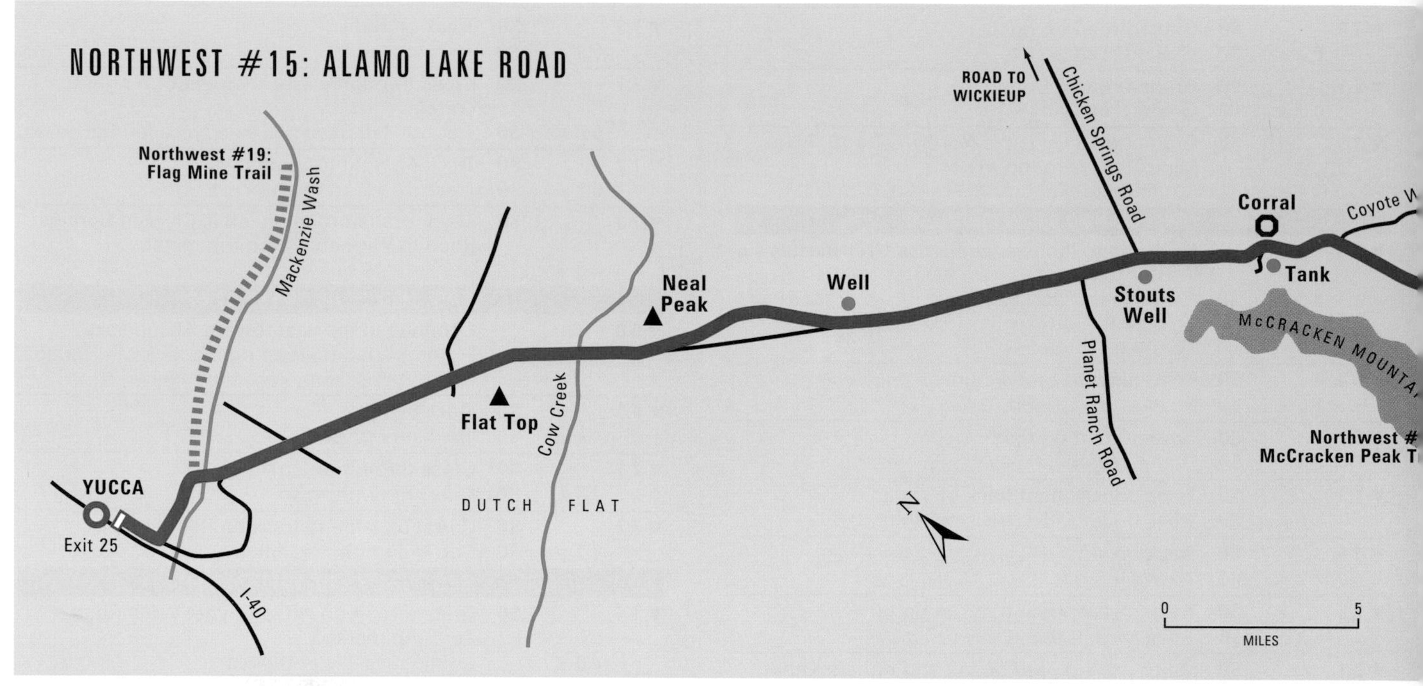

			are visible on the right of the trail; then track on left. Zero trip meter.
	0.0 ▲		Continue toward Yucca.
			GPS: N34°24.92′ W113°44.37′
▼ 0.0			Continue toward Alamo Lake.
	3.5 ▲	SO	Track on right; then track on left at Baker Well. Well and corrals are visible on the left of the trail.
▼ 0.1		SO	Track on right under power lines. Pass under power lines. Aubrey Peak Wilderness Area on right.
	3.4 ▲	SO	Track on left under power lines. Pass under power lines. Aubrey Peak Wilderness Area on left.
			GPS: N34°24.78′ W113°44.43′
▼ 2.4		SO	Cross through wash.
	1.1 ▲	SO	Cross through wash.
▼ 2.8		SO	Cross through wash; then track on right.
	0.7 ▲	SO	Track on left; then cross through wash.
▼ 2.9		SO	Cross through wash.
	0.6 ▲	SO	Cross through wash.
▼ 3.5		SO	Cattle guard. Zero trip meter.

Rawhide Wash crossing typifies the landscape near Alamo Lake

	0.0 ▲		Continue to the northwest.
			GPS: N34°22.24′ W113°42.60′
▼ 0.0			Continue to the southeast.
	8.9 ▲	SO	Cattle guard. Zero trip meter.
▼ 0.3		SO	Cross through wash.
	8.6 ▲	SO	Cross through wash.
▼ 0.9		SO	Cross through Maggie Wash.
	8.0 ▲	SO	Cross through Maggie Wash.
▼ 2.0		SO	Cross through Maggie Wash.
	6.9 ▲	SO	Cross through Maggie Wash.
▼ 2.5		SO	Cross through wash; track on left down wash. Trail is following alongside Maggie Wash.
	6.4 ▲	SO	Cross through wash; track on right down wash. Trail is following alongside Maggie Wash.
			GPS: N34°20.57′ W113°40.89′
▼ 3.3		SO	Cross through wash.
	5.6 ▲	SO	Cross through wash.
▼ 3.5		SO	Track on left.
	5.4 ▲	SO	Track on right.
▼ 3.6		SO	Track on right.
	5.3 ▲	SO	Track on left.
			GPS: N34°19.77′ W113°40.43′
▼ 4.0		SO	Cross through wash.
	4.9 ▲	SO	Cross through wash.
▼ 4.2		SO	Tracks on right and left on crest.
	4.7 ▲	SO	Tracks on right and left on crest.
			GPS: N34°19.45′ W113°39.84′
▼ 5.6		SO	Cross through wash.
	3.3 ▲	SO	Cross through wash.
▼ 6.2		SO	Cross through wash.
	2.7 ▲	SO	Cross through wash.
▼ 6.6		SO	Cross through wash.
	2.3 ▲	SO	Cross through wash.
▼ 6.9		SO	Cross through Rawhide Wash.
	2.0 ▲	SO	Cross through Rawhide Wash.
			GPS: N34°17.74′ W113°38.36′
▼ 7.1		SO	Cross through wash; then two roads on right and one on left.

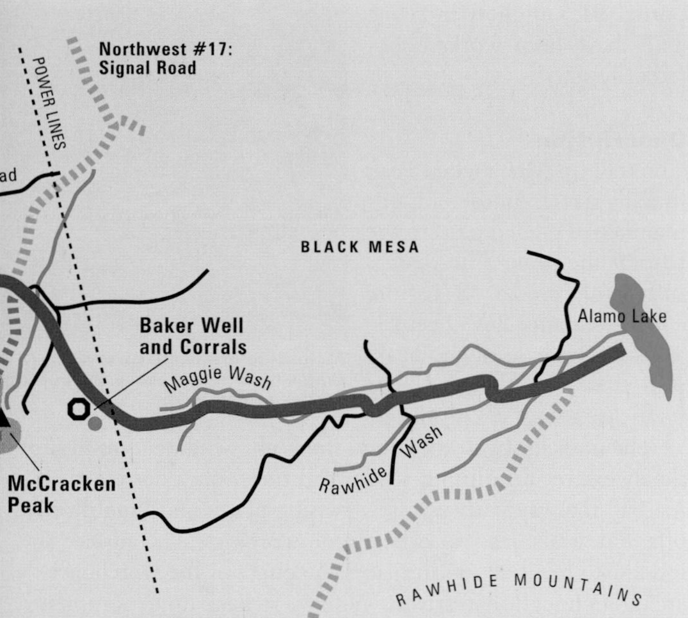

	1.8 ▲	SO	Two roads on left and one on right; then cross through wash.
▼ 7.3		SO	Cross through wash.
	1.6 ▲	SO	Cross through wash.
▼ 7.6		SO	Old road on left.
	1.3 ▲	SO	Old road on right.
▼ 8.1		SO	Graded dirt road on left.
	0.8 ▲	SO	Graded dirt road on right.
			GPS: N34°17.01′ W113°37.58′
▼ 8.2		SO	Cross through wash.
	0.7 ▲	SO	Cross through wash.
▼ 8.3		SO	Cross through wash.
	0.6 ▲	SO	Cross through wash.
▼ 8.6		SO	Cross through wide wash.
	0.3 ▲	SO	Cross through wide wash.
▼ 8.9		SO	Track on right is Northwest #14: Rawhide Mountains Trail. Zero trip meter. Rawhide Mountains Wilderness Area begins on right.
	0.0 ▲		Continue to northwest.
			GPS: N34°16.46′ W113°36.94′
▼ 0.0			Continue to the east.
	1.5 ▲	BR	Track on left is Northwest #14: Rawhide Mountains Trail. Zero trip meter. Rawhide Mountains Wilderness Area ends on left.
▼ 0.1		SO	Track on left.
	1.4 ▲	SO	Track on right.
▼ 0.7		SO	Entering Alamo Lake National Wildlife Refuge.
	0.8 ▲	SO	Exiting Alamo Lake National Wildlife Refuge.
			GPS: N34°16.23′ W113°36.18′
▼ 1.3		SO	Track on left is dead end.
	0.2 ▲	SO	Track on right is dead end.
▼ 1.5			Trail ends at the edge of Alamo Lake. There are a couple of trails that lead to the lake's edge through the tamarisk. Some cleared areas are suitable for camping. The exact ending of the trail varies with the water level.
	0.0 ▲		From Alamo Lake, zero trip meter and proceed north along the graded dirt road.
			GPS: N34°15.85′ W113°35.40′

NORTHWEST REGION TRAIL #16

McCracken Peak Trail

Starting Point:	**Intersection of Northwest #15: Alamo Lake Road and Northwest #17: Signal Road**
Finishing Point:	**McCracken Peak**
Total Mileage:	**4.7 miles**
Unpaved Mileage:	**4.7 miles**
Driving Time:	**1 hour (one-way)**
Elevation Range:	**2,200–3,400 feet**
Usually Open:	**Year-round**
Best Time to Travel:	**November to May**
Difficulty Rating:	**5**
Scenic Rating:	**8**
Remoteness Rating:	**+0**

Special Attractions

- Historic McCracken Silver Mine.
- Panoramic views from McCracken Peak.
- Rockhounding for quartz crystals.

History

In 1874 a party of prospectors led by "Hassayampa" Jackson McCracken and "Choride Jack" Owens explored the arid and remote hills north of the Bill Williams River. They staked several promising claims, but the richest one was near the top of McCracken Peak; it rewarded them with silver that assayed at $1,000 per ton. As usual, the discovery brought in a rush of people all eager to stake their own claims. The camp of McCracken was a tent city with very few permanent dwellings. The mill at Greenwood City (the site is found along Northwest #18: Seventeen Mile Road) processed the silver, and the nearby settlement of Signal provided most of the supplies for the camp.

The McCracken mines closed in 1879 after producing a re-

Mine shaft at the top of McCracken Peak with the narrow twisting trail leading back down

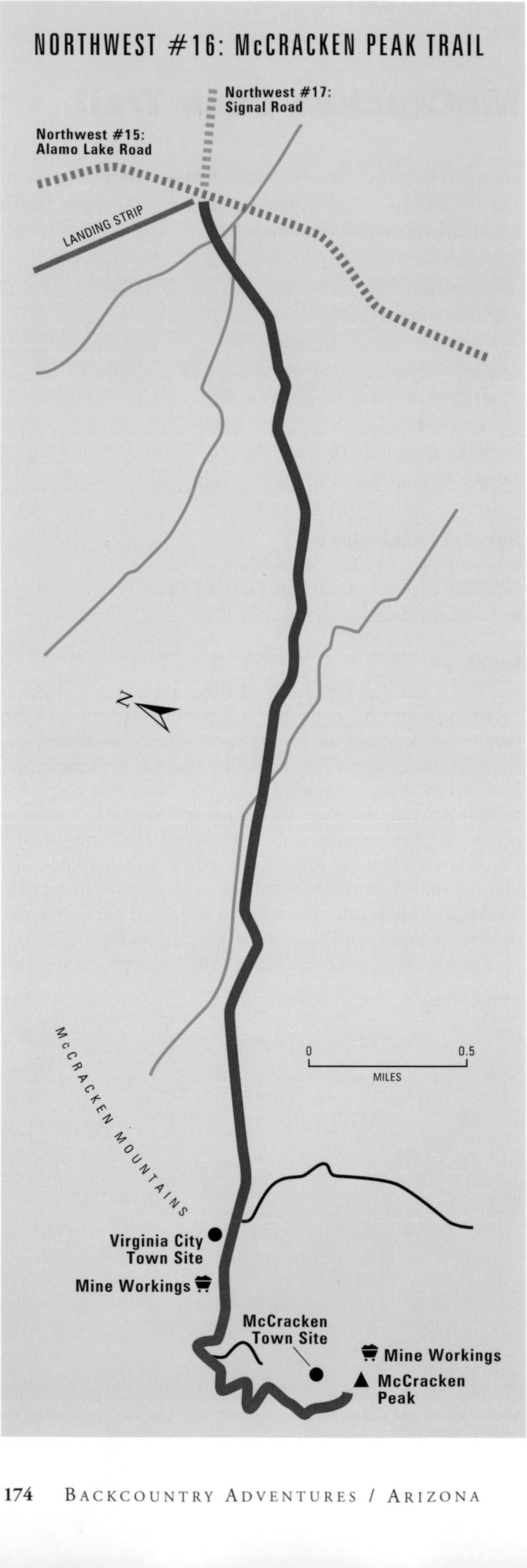

NORTHWEST #16: McCRACKEN PEAK TRAIL

Northwest #17: Signal Road
Northwest #15: Alamo Lake Road
LANDING STRIP
N
McCRACKEN MOUNTAINS
0 0.5 MILES
Virginia City Town Site
Mine Workings
McCracken Town Site
Mine Workings
McCracken Peak

ported $1.5 million in silver. They have been worked sporadically since.

A close-up of the quartz crystal seams to be found above the cutting on McCracken Peak

Description

The trail up McCracken Peak initially travels on the old, unmaintained graded road to the base of the peak. The road is sufficiently eroded to require a high-clearance 2WD vehicle as far as the base of the peak; past that it is definitely for high-clearance 4WDs only.

The trail climbs steeply up to the peak, winding around on a network of old mining roads. You travel on a narrow shelf road all the way with very few passing places and long drop-offs. Side trails lead to other mine workings. The surface is loose with low traction in places. A couple of the switchbacks are tight enough that drivers will have to back up to complete the turn.

Near the top, the trail passes through a cutting with an adit and large shaft on the right. Those who scramble up to the top of the ridge on the right of the cutting are often rewarded by finding some pretty quartz crystals. A seam of the crystals comes to the surface at this point.

Immediately past the ridge, there is a short section of trail that is extremely narrow and unstable. At the time of writing it was safe to pass, but it may not be in the future. A large boulder on the cliff side forces vehicles close to the edge, and a loose surface, off-camber tilt to the trail increases the difficulty. There is an extremely long drop down from the shelf road at this point, so if you are in any doubt about the safety of passing by the boulder, park your vehicle at the cutting and walk the remaining 0.1 miles to the peak.

There is a small concrete block hut at the top of the peak and panoramic views west to the Arrastra Mountain Wilderness and east over the Casteneda Hills to the Bill Williams Mountains.

Current Road Information

Bureau of Land Management
Kingman Field Office
2475 Beverly Ave.
Kingman, AZ 86401
(520) 692-4400

Map References

BLM Alamo Lake
USGS 1:24,000 Signal, McCracken Peak
1:100,000 Alamo Lake
Maptech CD-ROM: Colorado River/Lake Havasu
Arizona Atlas & Gazetteer, p. 47
Arizona Road & Recreation Atlas, p. 39 & p. 73 (incomplete)

Route Directions

▼ 0.0 SO At the intersection of Northwest #15: Alamo Lake Road, which is graded dirt, and

Northwest #17: Signal Road, zero trip meter and turn southwest on roughly graded dirt road. A landing strip also joins the intersection (at first glance, it resembles a road). The junction is marked with road signs for Signal Road and Alamo Road.

		GPS: N34°28.17' W113°42.96'
▼ 0.1	SO	Cross through wash.
▼ 0.2	SO	Cross through wash.
▼ 0.3	SO	Cross through wash.
▼ 0.4	SO	Cross through wash.
▼ 1.9	SO	Cross through wash.
		GPS: N34°27.44' W113°44.82'
▼ 2.3	SO	Gate.
▼ 3.2	SO	Track on left.
		GPS: N34°27.14' W113°46.12'
▼ 3.5	SO	Flat area surrounded by mine workings at base of hill. Zero trip meter.
		GPS: N34°27.10' W113°46.34'
▼ 0.0		Continue to the southwest.
▼ 0.2	SO	Track on right.
▼ 0.3	BR	Trail forks; track on left.
		GPS: N34°27.04' W113°46.58'
▼ 0.6	BR	Trail forks; track on left goes 0.3 miles to mine adit and continues past it. Bear right and keep climbing.
		GPS: N34°26.95' W113°46.59'
▼ 0.8	SO	Timber-supported adit visible down to the left.
▼ 1.0	BR	Track on left runs around hill and goes 0.3 miles to more diggings, a stone wall, and a wooden loading hopper and continues past them.
		GPS: N34°26.71' W113°46.58'
▼ 1.1	BL	Pass through a cutting with adit and large shaft on the right; then washed-out section on shelf road. This is currently passable, but check before proceeding.
		GPS: N34°26.64' W113°46.56'
▼ 1.2		Top of McCracken Peak. Small concrete block hut on top.
		GPS: N34°26.66' W113°46.51'

NORTHWEST REGION TRAIL #17

Signal Road

Starting Point:	**Northwest #15: Alamo Lake Road, 36 miles southeast of Yucca**
Finishing Point:	**US 93, 7 miles south of Wickieup**
Total Mileage:	**17.9 miles (including spur to town site)**
Unpaved Mileage:	**17.9 miles**
Driving Time:	**1 hour**
Elevation Range:	**1,600-2,200 feet**
Usually Open:	**Year-round**
Best Time to Travel:	**October to May**
Difficulty Rating:	**1**
Scenic Rating:	**7**
Remoteness Rating:	**+0**

Special Attractions

- Ghost town of Signal.
- The Big Sandy River.
- Scenic trail through the Poachie Range.

History

The story of Signal is intertwined with that of the McCracken mines, located a few miles away. Signal sprang into existence in 1877 and was quickly established as the milling town for the silver extracted from the mines. The isolated settlement boasted 800 people and 200 buildings, and in its heyday it was a thriving, yet orderly, settlement. The stores supplied not only the people of Signal but the many prospectors and miners working the neighboring McCracken mines, as well as others prospecting in nearby hills. Five stores were needed to supply the population, three restaurants, and thirteen saloons. Signal even had its own brewery. Goods came via rail from San Francisco to Yuma, where they were then brought up the Colorado River by barge as far as Aubrey Landing. They were then loaded on to mule teams for the final 35 miles of desert travel to Signal. Storekeepers had to order goods six months in advance; inevitably, fresh goods were scarce.

Big Sandy River crossing

The town's respectability was mainly attributed to the strictness of the local justice of the peace, Moses Levy, whose legendary sentences had the effect of quelling even the most rambunctious miners.

The mill at Signal operated around the clock while the boom lasted. However, like most mining booms, this one subsided quickly. The ore played out at the McCracken mines and by the mid-1880s, Signal's population had dwindled. About 300 people stayed on, but the number gradually declined over the years.

Today the traveler can see some remains of the mill site as well as a small wooden building. The graveyard, the most noteworthy feature at Signal, can be found a short distance away. There are stories of a second graveyard at Signal. The Chinese cemetery has been said to have existed further down the wash of the Big Sandy River, but no trace remains of the unmarked site, so these stories cannot be verified.

Description

This graded dirt road connects US 93 with Northwest #15: Alamo Lake Road. After it passes the town site of Signal, the trail follows the course of the Big Sandy River and crosses through the northern end of the Poachie Range.

The site of Signal is just off the main trail, 5.1 miles from the western end. The turn is poorly marked by a hand-painted sign that directs travelers down a side trail. A couple of timber buildings and mining remains clearly visible. However, a little more exploration and a short hike are required to find the

An old stone ruin at Signal overlook on the Big Sandy River

stone ruins and graveyard. It helps to have a handheld GPS unit with the coordinates entered. The fenced graveyard contains several unidentified graves that are marked with piles of rock. There are also some more recent graves in the cemetery.

The entire trail is a reasonable graded road. The crossings of the Big Sandy River usually present no problem to a passenger vehicle. The typical depth of the river is fairly shallow, only a couple of inches. However, conditions can change quickly—do not attempt to cross the wash when it is flooded. The water normally runs in a small channel in the wide, sandy wash.

The final part of the trail rises up to cross the Poachie Range before finishing at US 93.

Current Road Information

Bureau of Land Management
Kingman Field Office
2475 Beverly Ave.
Kingman, AZ 86401
(520) 692-4400

Map References

BLM Bagdad, Alamo Lake
USGS 1:24,000 Signal, Signal Mountain, Greenwood Peak
1:100,000 Bagdad, Alamo Lake
Maptech CD-ROM: Colorado River/Lake Havasu
Arizona Atlas & Gazetteer, pp. 47, 37
Arizona Road & Recreation Atlas, p. 39 & p. 73
Recreational Map of Arizona

Route Directions

▼ 0.0			From Northwest #15: Alamo Lake Road, at the 4-way intersection with Signal Road, and Northwest #16: McCracken Peak Trail, 36 miles southeast of Yucca, zero trip meter and turn northeast on the graded dirt Signal Road at the sign.
	5.1 ▲		Trail ends at the 4-way intersection with Northwest #15: Alamo Lake Road, and Northwest #16: McCracken Peak Trail. Turn right for Yucca; turn left for Alamo Lake; and continue straight ahead to visit McCracken Peak.
			GPS: N34°28.20' W113°42.96'
▼ 0.9		SO	Track on right.
	4.2 ▲	SO	Track on left.
▼ 1.1		SO	Cross through wash.
	4.0 ▲	SO	Cross through wash.
▼ 2.6		SO	Pass under power lines; track on right and track on left under power lines.
	2.5 ▲	SO	Pass under power lines; track on right and track on left under power lines.
			GPS: N34°28.72' W113°40.09'
▼ 3.4		SO	Graded road on left is Coyote Wells Road; then cattle guard.
	1.7 ▲	SO	Cattle guard; then graded road on right is Coyote Wells Road.
			GPS: N34°28.49' W113°39.32'
▼ 3.7		SO	Track on left; then cattle guard.
	1.4 ▲	SO	Cattle guard; then track on right.
▼ 4.3		SO	Track on right.
	0.8 ▲	SO	Track on left.
▼ 4.6		SO	Cattle guard; then track on left.
	0.5 ▲	SO	Track on right; then cattle guard.
▼ 5.0		SO	Track on right.
	0.1 ▲	SO	Track on left.
▼ 5.1		SO	Track on right goes to Signal town site, marked with old sign board and daubed fence post. Turn is opposite a corral on the left and entrance to ranch. Zero trip meter. Also two tracks on left.
	0.0 ▲		Continue along graded road to the southwest.
			GPS: N34°28.39' W113°37.81'

Spur to Signal Town Site

▼ 0.0		From Signal Road, at the hand-painted sign to Signal, zero trip meter and turn southeast on small dirt road.
		GPS: N34°28.39' W113°37.81'
▼ 0.1	SO	Two tracks on right.

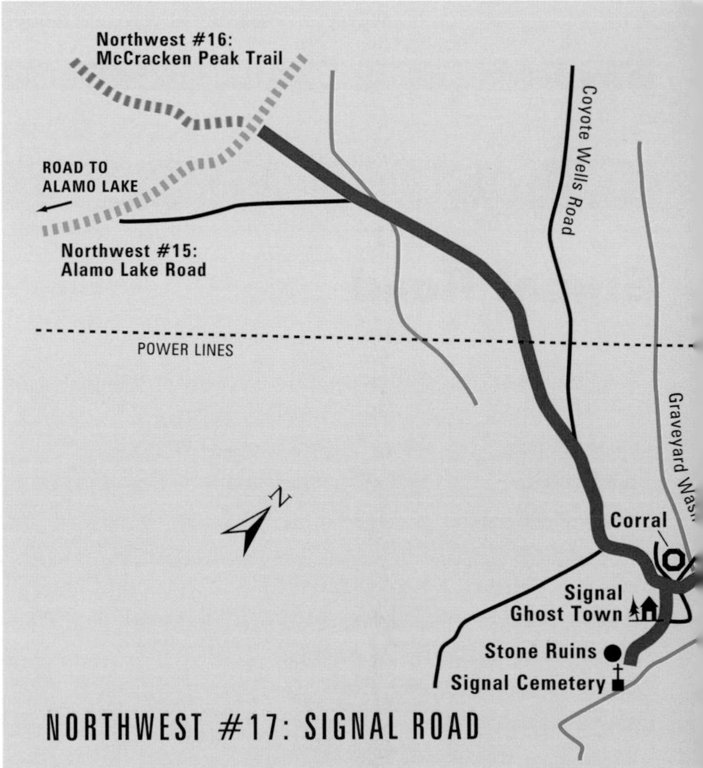

▼ 0.2		BR	Signal town site. Old corrugated iron cabin and mine workings on hill to the left over wash.
			GPS: N34°28.27′ W113°37.58′
▼ 0.3		BL	Two tracks on right and one on left; take major track heading southeast and enter wash at a junction in the wash. Take the right-hand wash.
			GPS: N34°28.19′ W113°37.56′
▼ 0.5			Keep right in the wash and the vehicle trail ends where it is washed out and impassable.
			GPS: N34°28.04′ W113°37.48′
			From here, hike west along the old vehicle trail that leaves the wash. After 0.1 miles you will come to some stone ruins at GPS: N34°28.00′ W113°37.58′. From the ruins, the trail is less clear but stay to the left, close to the wash, and you will reach the cemetery after another 0.2 miles. The cemetery is at GPS: N34°27.83′ W113°37.48′.

Continuation of Main Trail

▼ 0.0			Continue along graded road to the northeast.
	3.7 ▲	SO	Track on left goes to Signal town site, marked with old sign board and daubed fence post. Turn is opposite a corral on the right and entrance to ranch. Zero trip meter. Also two tracks on right.
▼ 0.1		SO	Track on right.
	3.6 ▲	SO	Track on left.
▼ 0.2		SO	Cross through Graveyard Wash.
	3.5 ▲	SO	Cross through Graveyard Wash.
▼ 0.6		SO	Track on left.
	3.1 ▲	SO	Track on right.
▼ 2.3		SO	Graded dirt road, the High Road, on left.
	1.4 ▲	SO	Graded dirt road, the High Road, on right.
			GPS: N34°30.06′ W113°36.53′
▼ 3.1		SO	Cattle guard.
	0.6 ▲	SO	Cattle guard.
▼ 3.2		SO	Start to cross Big Sandy River wash and river channel.
	0.5 ▲	SO	Exit Big Sandy River wash.
▼ 3.5		SO	Exit Big Sandy River wash; then small track on right.
	0.2 ▲	SO	Small track on left; then start to cross Big Sandy River wash and river channel.
			GPS: N34°30.75′ W113°35.70′
▼ 3.6		SO	Track on right.
	0.1 ▲	SO	Track on left.
▼ 3.7		SO	Graded road on right is Northwest #18: Seventeen Mile Road. Zero trip meter.
	0.0 ▲		Continue to the southwest.
			GPS: N34°30.92′ W113°35.57′
▼ 0.0			Continue to the north.
	8.1 ▲	SO	Graded road on left is Northwest #18: Seventeen Mile Road. Zero trip meter.
▼ 1.1		SO	Track on right.
	7.0 ▲	SO	Track on left.
▼ 1.2		SO	Cross through Big Sandy River wash and river channel.
	6.9 ▲	SO	Cross through Big Sandy River wash and river channel.
▼ 1.8		SO	Graded road on left; then track on right.
	6.3 ▲	SO	Track on left; then graded road on right.
			GPS: N34°32.35′ W113°34.74′
▼ 2.1		SO	Cattle guard.
	6.0 ▲	SO	Cattle guard.
▼ 3.1		SO	Track on right is driveway.
	5.0 ▲	SO	Track on left is driveway.
▼ 3.4		SO	Cross over pipeline.
	4.7 ▲	SO	Cross over pipeline.
▼ 3.6		SO	Track on left; then ford through Big Sandy River.
	4.5 ▲	SO	Ford through Big Sandy River; then track on right.

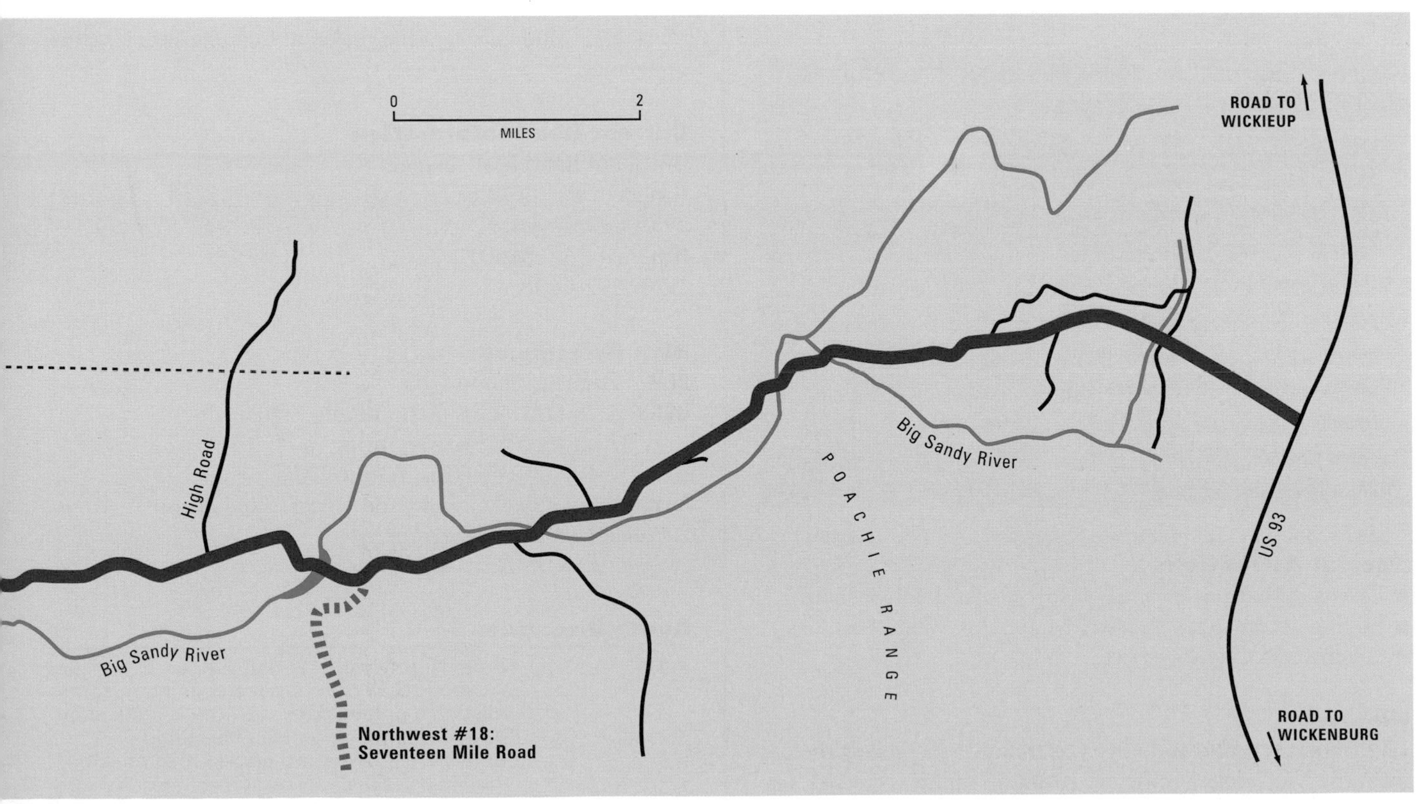

		GPS: N34°33.93' W113°34.53'
▼ 3.8	SO	Track on left; then cattle guard.
4.3 ▲	SO	Cattle guard; then track on right.
▼ 3.9	SO	Track on right.
4.2 ▲	SO	Track on left.
▼ 4.1	SO	Cross through wash.
4.0 ▲	SO	Cross through wash.
▼ 4.6	SO	Two tracks on right.
3.5 ▲	SO	Two tracks on left.
▼ 4.9	SO	Track on right.
3.2 ▲	SO	Track on left.
▼ 5.5	SO	Track on left.
2.6 ▲	SO	Track on right.
▼ 5.9	SO	Track on right.
2.2 ▲	SO	Track on left.
		GPS: N34°35.61' W113°33.34'
▼ 6.9	SO	Cross through wash; track on right and track on left down wash.
1.2 ▲	SO	Cross through wash; track on right and track on left down wash.
▼ 8.1		Trail ends at junction of US 93. Turn left for Wickieup; turn right for Wickenburg.
0.0 ▲		Trail commences on US 93, 7 miles south of Wickieup, 0.1 miles south of mile marker 132. Zero trip meter and turn southwest on graded dirt road at the sign for Signal Road.
		GPS: N34°36.57' W113°31.41'

NORTHWEST REGION TRAIL #18

Seventeen Mile Road

Starting Point:	**Northwest #17: Signal Road, 8.1 miles west of US 93**
Finishing Point:	**US 93, 0.8 miles northwest of mile marker 144**
Total Mileage:	**13.1 miles**
Unpaved Mileage:	**13.1 miles**
Driving Time:	**1 hour**
Elevation Range:	**1,600–3,300 feet**
Usually Open:	**Year-round**
Best Time to Travel:	**October to May**
Difficulty Rating:	**2**
Scenic Rating:	**8**
Remoteness Rating:	**+0**

Special Attractions

- Easy trail that passes through spectacular desert scenery.
- Hiking access to the Arrastra Mountains Wilderness.
- Greenwood City town site.

History

Like Signal, Greenwood City was founded to process the ore from the McCracken mines. A 10-stamp mill was erected, settlers arrived, and there was soon an active town. At its peak, there were 400 inhabitants, a clean and reasonably priced boardinghouse called Davis House, two saloons, a butcher, a physician, a barbershop, and various other stores. For some unknown reason, Greenwood City never had a post office. After a mill was built in Virginia City (adjacent to Signal), Greenwood City declined and was quickly abandoned.

Description

This scenic graded road crosses through the Poachie Range between Northwest #17: Signal Road and US 93. The trail passes very close to the site of Greenwood City. There are some stone foundations, but little is left of this once-thriving town. Much of the trail runs along the ridge tops, giving excellent views over the Arrastra Mountains Wilderness and the Big Sandy River Valley. The vegetation is a diverse combination of ocotillo, yucca, and cholla mixed with small juniper trees.

Yuccas and granite outcrops combine to form a striking landscape

As the trail enters the Poachie Range, large granite boulders and outcrops dot the landscape. As it descends down the range to join US 93, there are views of the Burro Creek Bridge, north toward Wickieup, and east toward the mining town of Bagdad and the Aquarius Mountains.

The road is graded its entire length, but a few rough sections and moderate grades make a high-clearance vehicle preferable.

Current Road Information

Bureau of Land Management
Kingman Field Office
2475 Beverly Ave.
Kingman, AZ 86401
(520) 692-4400

Map References

BLM Bagdad, Alamo Lake
USGS 1:24,000 Greenwood Peak, Signal Mt., Arrastra Mt., Kaiser Spring
1:100,000 Bagdad, Alamo Lake
Maptech CD-ROM: Colorado River/Lake Havasu
Arizona Atlas & Gazetteer, p. 47
Arizona Road & Recreation Atlas, p. 39 & p. 73

Route Directions

▼ 0.0		From Northwest #17: Signal Road, 8.1 miles west of US 93, zero trip meter and turn southeast on a graded dirt road. Turn is marked by a road sign for Seventeen Mile Road. Immediately, there is a graded road on left.
7.7 ▲		Trail ends at the intersection with Northwest

#17: Signal Road. Turn left to continue to Signal; turn right to exit to US 93.

GPS: N34°30.89' W113°35.57'

▼ 0.2 SO Two tracks on left.
7.5 ▲ SO Two tracks on right.

▼ 0.5 SO Small track on right goes to the site of Greenwood City. The unmarked turn is at the base of the hill. Also track on left.
7.2 ▲ SO Small track on left goes to the site of Greenwood City. The unmarked turn is at the base of the hill. Also track on right.

Intersection is at:

GPS: N34°30.49' W113°35.57'

Greenwood City is at:

GPS: N34°30.45' W113°35.71'

▼ 0.7 BR Two tracks on left.
7.0 ▲ BL Two tracks on right.

GPS: N34°30.32' W113°35.47'

▼ 1.8 SO Track on left.
5.9 ▲ SO Track on right.

▼ 2.1 SO Cross through wash.
5.6 ▲ SO Cross through wash.

▼ 3.0 SO Cross through wash.
4.7 ▲ SO Cross through wash.

▼ 4.2 SO Cross through wash. Arrastra Mountains Wilderness on right.
3.5 ▲ SO Cross through wash. Arrastra Mountains Wilderness on left.

▼ 4.6 SO Cross through wash.
3.1 ▲ SO Cross through wash.

▼ 5.6 SO Cattle guard.
2.1 ▲ SO Cattle guard.

▼ 7.7 SO Track on left and right down and up wash. Each has a sign for the end of Mohave County Road Maintenance. Zero trip meter.
0.0 ▲ Continue to the southwest.

GPS: N34°28.59' W113°29.18'

▼ 0.0 Continue to the northeast.
1.5 ▲ SO Track on left and right up and down wash. Each has a sign for the end of Mohave County Road Maintenance. Zero trip meter.

▼ 0.4 SO Track on right on left-hand bend.
1.1 ▲ SO Track on left on right-hand bend.

GPS: N34°28.45' W113°28.80'

▼ 1.1 SO Cross through wash.
0.4 ▲ SO Cross through wash.

▼ 1.3 SO Cross through wash.
0.2 ▲ SO Cross through wash.

▼ 1.5 SO Corral on right and well on right. Zero trip meter.
0.0 ▲ Continue to the west.

GPS: N34°28.43' W113°27.62'

▼ 0.0 Continue to the east.
3.9 ▲ SO Corral on left and well on left. Zero trip meter.

▼ 0.1 SO Track on right.
3.8 ▲ SO Track on left.

▼ 2.6 SO Cross through wash.
1.3 ▲ SO Cross through wash.

GPS: N34°29.76' W113°25.53'

▼ 2.7 SO Track on left.
1.2 ▲ SO Track on right.

▼ 3.2 SO Cross through wash.
0.7 ▲ SO Cross through wash.

▼ 3.4 SO Cross through wide Black Canyon Wash.
0.5 ▲ SO Exit wash crossing.

▼ 3.5 SO Exit wash crossing.
0.4 ▲ SO Cross through wide Black Canyon Wash.

▼ 3.6 BL Track on right.
0.3 ▲ BR Track on left.

▼ 3.9 Cattle guard; then trail ends at intersection with US 93. Turn right for Wickenburg; turn left for Wickieup.
0.0 ▲ Trail commences on US 93, 0.8 miles northwest of mile marker 144. Zero trip meter and turn west onto the graded dirt road at the sign for Seventeen Mile Road.

GPS: N34°30.71' W113°24.97'

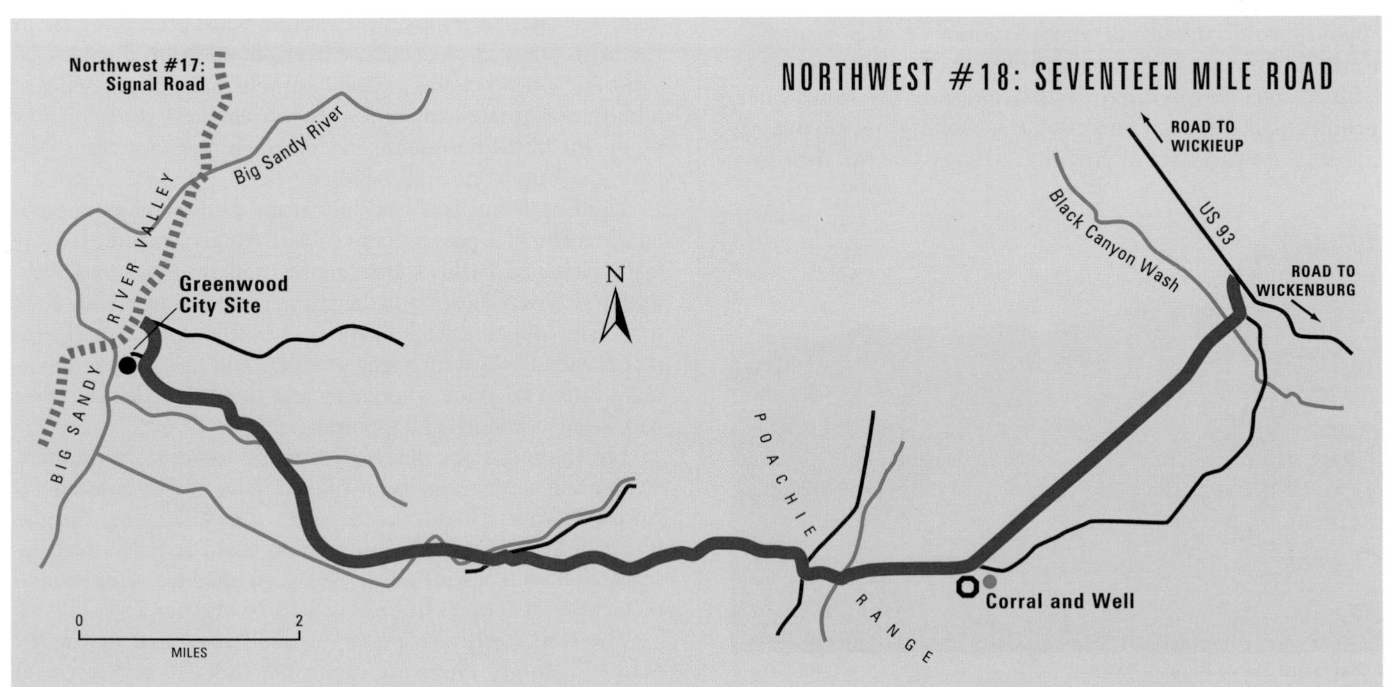

Flag Mine Trail

Starting Point:	**Hualapai Mountain Road at Hualapai Mountain Park**
Finishing Point:	**Northwest #15: Alamo Lake Road**
Total Mileage:	**34 miles**
Unpaved Mileage:	**32.1 miles**
Driving Time:	**5 hours**
Elevation Range:	**2,000–7,000 feet**
Usually Open:	**April to November**
Best Time to Travel:	**April to November**
Difficulty Rating:	**5**
Scenic Rating:	**9**
Remoteness Rating:	**+0**

Special Attractions

- Extensive section of shelf road.
- Picnicking, hiking, and camping at Hualapai Mountain Park.
- Old mining buildings of the Boriana Mine.
- Long, moderately challenging trail.

History

Hualapai Mountain Park, the pretty and popular refuge at the start of this trail, was developed during the 1930s by the Civilian Conservation Corps, which constructed the small stone cabins, picnic areas, and hiking trails. The word *hualapai* (pronounced wal-a-pie) means "pine tree folk" and comes from the name of the Indian tribe that once inhabited this area.

The Hualapai Indians, along with the Yavapai and Havasupai, have occupied northern Arizona for more than 800 years. They were primarily hunters and gatherers and had little contact with Western civilization until the 1840s when prospectors, trappers, and pioneers looking for ranchlands moved into this part of Arizona. Miners saw the tribe as a labor source, and many Hualapai worked in the mines of the region. Still, many other Hualapai despised the encroachment on their land and war broke out. Lt. Colonel William Price secured a surrender from the Hualapai people in 1867. Many of their leaders were sent to San Francisco where they were imprisoned on Alcatraz and Angel Islands. The majority of the tribe was forcibly relocated to the Colorado River bottom. Because they were mountain people, many of them sickened and died. They sent word to General George Crook that they would rather die fighting in their mountain territory then die slowly along the river bottom. Today the Hualapai people occupy a reservation on the south rim of the Grand Canyon.

The shelf road above Boriana Mine

The closed portal of the American Flag Mine

The Flag Mine, or American Flag Mine, as it is sometimes called, was discovered in 1871 by a group of Cornishmen, who established a small settlement with a post office. Although the mines in the area were small, they were worked steadily until the late 1880s. (There is another settlement in Arizona called American Flag; that one is located along South #27: Oracle Control Road on the north side of the Santa Catalina Mountains.)

The Boriana Mine was a hard-rock mine that was operational for some time during the early 1900s.

Description

This trail commences at the Hualapai Mountain Park, a peaceful sky island far above the arid plains surrounding Kingman. The park offers excellent camping and picnicking facilities, with many areas to choose from. In addition there are 16 stone and timber cabins available for rent year-round. Miles of hiking trails invite exploration. In winter there is often snow on the top of the mountain, and although there is access to the park, the Flag Mine Trail is closed.

The Flag Mine Trail leads out from the park along a graded dirt road that passes many private cabins as it heads away from Hualapai Peak. The standard quickly drops to a well-used trail that almost immediately starts to follow a wide shelf road. The longest stretch of the trail travels along a shelf road that is wide enough for a single vehicle and has adequate passing places. The grade is very easy and the surface for the most part is fairly smooth and granitic.

The trail passes by the Flag Mine, 3.5 miles from the start. A large adit can be seen in the hillside. The trail then intersects Antelope Wash Road, which passes the Wild Cow Springs Recreation Site. This pleasant campground at 6,200 feet has shady sites set in a wide gully. A fee is charged for camping and picnicking. It is open from May 1 to November 1.

The trail continues along the shelf road just below the crest of a ridge. There are expansive views to the east over

Big Sandy River Valley to Aquarius Mountains, and further along over the pretty Moss Basin. To the west there are views over Wabayuma Peak and the wilderness area and surrounding canyons.

As the trail leaves Moss Basin, there are some rough spots; the roughest occurs where the trail starts to switchback down the south side of Moss Basin and farther south where there are some steep, loose-surfaced sections.

As the trail starts to descend the southern side of the range, the extensive remains of the Boriana Mine can be seen in Boriana Canyon. You can gaze down into the canyon and see the single-width shelf road descending to the mine far below.

The trail follows Mackenzie Creek through the jumbled rocks and prolific vegetation of Boriana Canyon before becoming a graded dirt road at private property. It is an easy run to join Northwest #15: Alamo Lake Road, a few miles east of Yucca and I-40.

Camping along the trail is limited because of the shelf road, but there are a few small, pleasant sites tucked into the vegetation close to the trail. The best camping can be found in the developed campgrounds at Wild Cow Springs and Hualapai Peak.

This trail is marked as road #2123 on the BLM map of the region.

Current Road Information

Bureau of Land Management
Kingman Field Office
2475 Beverly Ave.
Kingman, AZ 86401
(520) 692-4400

Map References

BLM Valentine, Bagdad, Needles
USGS 1:24,000 Hualapai Peak, Dean Peak, Wabayuma Peak, Creamery Canyon, Yucca SE
1:100,000 Valentine, Bagdad, Needles
Maptech CD-ROM: Colorado River/Lake Havasu
Arizona Atlas & Gazetteer, pp. 36, 37
Arizona Road & Recreation Atlas, pp. 32, 33 & pp. 66, 67
Recreational Map of Arizona (incomplete)

Route Directions

▼ 0.0		From Kingman, take Hualapai Mountain Road 9.7 miles to the boundary of the Mohave County Hualapai Mountain Park. Zero trip meter and continue on the paved road into the park.
1.9 ▲		Trail ends at the boundary of the Mohave County Hualapai Mountain Park. Continue along the paved road to Kingman.
		GPS: N35°06.54' W113°53.97'
▼ 0.1	SO	Road on right to Camp Stephens.
1.8 ▲	SO	Road on left to Camp Stephens.
▼ 0.7	SO	Road on right to Deer Canyon Picnic Area.
1.2 ▲	SO	Road on left to Deer Canyon Picnic Area.
▼ 0.9	SO	Ranger station and camper registration on right—fee charged for camping.
1.0 ▲	SO	Ranger station and camper registration on left—fee charged for camping.
		GPS: N35°06.08' W113°53.09'
▼ 1.1	BL	Road on right is park entrance to picnicking and camping areas.
0.8 ▲	BR	Road on left is park entrance to picnicking and camping areas.
		GPS: N35°05.97' W113°53.02'
▼ 1.2	SO	Track on right goes to recreation area.
0.7 ▲	SO	Track on left goes to recreation area.
▼ 1.3	SO	Track on right goes to recreation area.
0.6 ▲	SO	Track on left goes to recreation area.
▼ 1.5	SO	Track on left.
0.4 ▲	SO	Track on right.
▼ 1.6	SO	Leaving county park into private property.
0.3 ▲	SO	Entering Mohave County Hualapai Mountain Park.
▼ 1.7	SO	Crumb Road on right; then Ponderosa Drive on left.
0.2 ▲	SO	Ponderosa Drive on right; then Crumb Road on left.
▼ 1.8	SO	Road on right.
0.1 ▲	SO	Road on left.
▼ 1.9	TR	Turn right onto Flag Mine Road at BLM sign for Wild Cow Springs Recreation Site. Zero trip meter.
0.0 ▲		Continue to the northwest.
		GPS: N35°05.56' W113°52.46'
▼ 0.0		Continue to the south. Road is now graded gravel.
3.1 ▲	TL	Turn left onto paved Hualapai Mountain Road opposite the Pine Lake Fire Department. Zero trip meter.
▼ 0.2	SO	Road is now graded dirt. Remain on Flag Mine Road; there are many driveways on the right and left for next 0.5 miles.
2.9 ▲	SO	Road is now paved.
▼ 0.3	SO	Track on right is Ridge Road (dead end).
2.8 ▲	SO	Track on left is Ridge Road (dead end).
		GPS: N35°05.44' W113°52.57'
▼ 0.4	SO	Track on left is Halmar Road.
2.7 ▲	SO	Track on right is Halmar Road.
▼ 0.7	BR	Two tracks on left to viewpoint, bear right on wide shelf road.
2.4 ▲	BL	Two tracks on right to viewpoint; bear left, remaining on Flag Mine Road. There are many driveways on the right and left for next 0.5 miles.
		GPS: N35°05.19' W113°52.35'

Boriana Mine, near the southern end of the trail

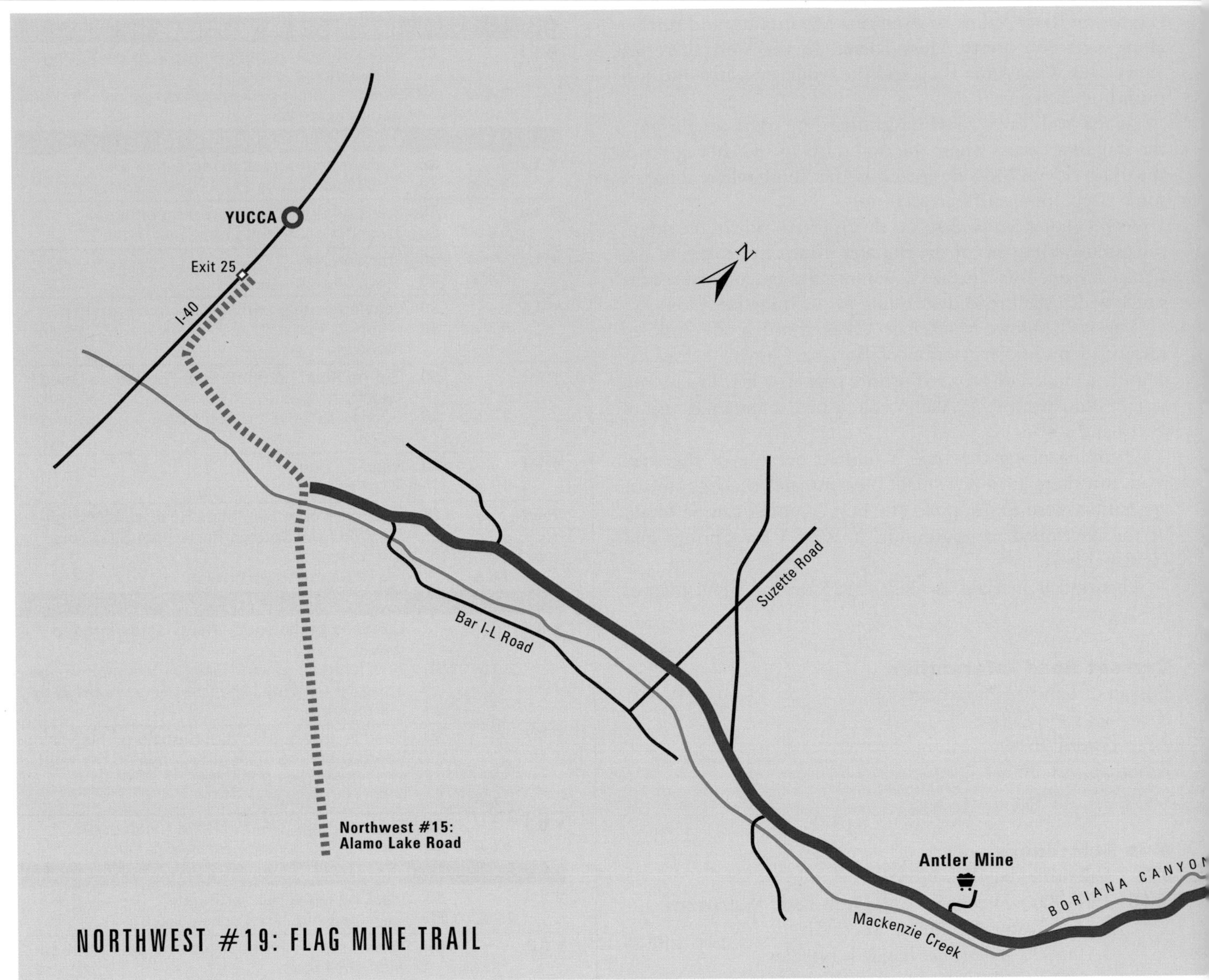

▼ 1.6	BL	Track on right is short, steep dead end. Adit of the Flag Mine on right.
1.5 ▲	BR	Track on left is short, steep dead end. Adit of the Flag Mine on left.
		GPS: N35°04.62' W113°52.88'
▼ 1.8	SO	Track on left.
1.3 ▲	SO	Track on right.
▼ 2.0	SO	Turnouts on right and left.
1.1 ▲	SO	Turnouts on right and left.
▼ 2.8	SO	Track on left.
0.3 ▲	SO	Track on right.
▼ 3.1	BR	Track on left is Antelope Wash Road to Wild Cow Springs Recreation Site. BLM sign at intersection. Zero trip meter.
0.0 ▲		Continue west toward Kingman.
		GPS: N35°04.14' W113°52.13'
▼ 0.0		Continue southeast toward Yucca.
5.3 ▲	SO	Track on right is Antelope Wash Road to Wild Cow Springs Recreation Site. BLM sign at intersection. Zero trip meter.
▼ 0.7	SO	Cross through wash.
4.6 ▲	SO	Cross through wash.

▼ 0.8	SO	Faint track on left; then cross over wash.
4.5 ▲	SO	Cross over wash; then faint track on right.
▼ 2.0	SO	Track on left to camping area.
3.3 ▲	SO	Track on right to camping area.
		GPS: N35°03.57' W113°53.37'
▼ 2.3	SO	Faint track on left; then corral on left.
3.0 ▲	SO	Corral on right; then faint track on right.
		GPS: N35°03.31' W113°53.40'
▼ 2.4	SO	Faint track on right.
2.9 ▲	SO	Faint track on left.
▼ 2.5	BR	Track on left. Shelf road starts.
2.8 ▲	BL	Track on right. End of shelf road.
		GPS: N35°03.17' W113°53.52'
▼ 2.7	SO	Track on right.
2.6 ▲	SO	Track on left.
▼ 3.3	SO	Track on right; then cattle guard.
2.0 ▲	SO	Cattle guard; then track on left.
		GPS: N35°03.12' W113°54.13'
▼ 4.6	SO	Small track on right.
0.7 ▲	SO	Small track on left.
		GPS: N35°02.27' W113°54.49'

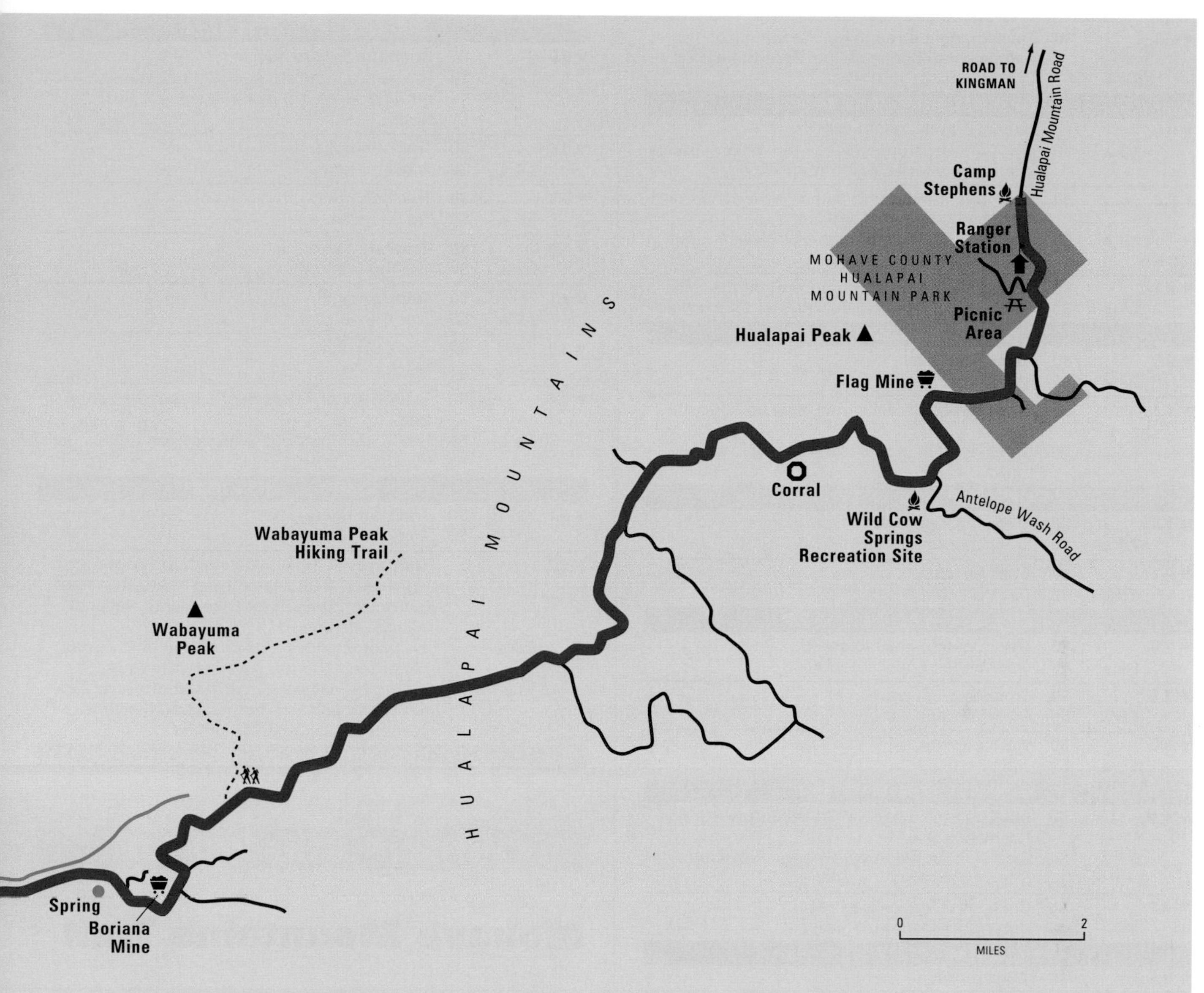

▼ 5.3	SO	Well-used track on left. Zero trip meter.
0.0 ▲		Continue to the north.
		GPS: N35°01.74′ W113°54.23′
▼ 0.0		Continue to the south.
7.5 ▲	SO	Well-used track on right. Zero trip meter.
▼ 2.4	SO	Track on left.
5.1 ▲	SO	Track on right.
		GPS: N35°00.43′ W113°53.62′
▼ 2.9	SO	Start of switchbacks.
4.6 ▲	SO	End of switchbacks.
▼ 3.2	BL	Track on right.
4.3 ▲	BR	Track on left.
▼ 3.5	SO	End of switchbacks.
4.0 ▲	SO	Start of switchbacks.
		GPS: N34°59.94′ W113°53.98′
▼ 5.1	SO	Cattle guard.
2.4 ▲	SO	Cattle guard.
▼ 7.0	SO	Track on left.
0.5 ▲	SO	Track on right.
		GPS: N34°57.61′ W113°54.81′
▼ 7.1	SO	Cattle guard.
0.4 ▲	SO	Cattle guard.
▼ 7.5	SO	Wabayuma Peak hiking trailhead on right at information board. Small parking area on left. Hiking trail enters wilderness area. Zero trip meter.
0.0 ▲		Continue to the north.
		GPS: N34°57.20′ W113°54.90′
▼ 0.0		Continue to the south.
2.8 ▲	SO	Wabayuma Peak hiking trailhead on left at information board. Small parking area on right. Zero trip meter.
▼ 1.4	BR	Track on left through fence line.
1.4 ▲	BL	Track on right through fence line.
		GPS: N34°56.64′ W113°54.78′
▼ 1.7	BR	Two tracks on left through fence line. Trail starts to descend to Boriana Canyon.
1.1 ▲	BL	Two tracks on right through fence line.
		GPS: N34°56.42′ W113°54.62′
▼ 2.7	SO	Track on right goes to Boriana Mine. End of shelf road.
0.1 ▲	SO	Track on left goes to Boriana Mine. Shelf road begins and climbs out of Boriana Canyon.

▼	▲		
▼ 2.8		SO	Track on right through gate is the main entrance into Boriana Mine. Zero trip meter.
	0.0 ▲		Continue to the northeast.
			GPS: N34°56.09′ W113°54.99′
▼ 0.0			Continue to the southwest.
	9.2 ▲	SO	Track on left through gate is the main entrance into Boriana Mine. Zero trip meter.
▼ 0.2		SO	Track on right through gate is old washed-out entrance to Boriana Mine.
	9.0 ▲	SO	Track on left through gate is old washed-out entrance to Boriana Mine.
▼ 0.3		SO	Track on left goes to spring, just off the trail.
	8.9 ▲	SO	Track on right goes to spring, just off the trail.
			GPS: N34°55.98′ W113°55.29′
▼ 0.5		SO	Cross over wash.
	8.7 ▲	SO	Cross over wash.
▼ 1.5		SO	Cross through Mackenzie Creek on concrete ford.
	7.7 ▲	SO	Cross through Mackenzie Creek on concrete ford.
			GPS: N34°55.30′ W113°55.96′
▼ 1.8		SO	Cross through wash.
	7.4 ▲	SO	Cross through wash.
▼ 2.3		SO	Track on left.
	6.9 ▲	SO	Track on right.
			GPS: N34°54.62′ W113°56.28′
▼ 2.4		SO	Track on right goes to corral.
	6.8 ▲	SO	Track on left goes to corral.
▼ 2.6		SO	Cross through wash.
	6.6 ▲	SO	Cross through wash.
▼ 3.3		SO	Track on right.
	5.9 ▲	SO	Track on left.
			GPS: N34°53.89′ W113°56.76′
▼ 4.1		SO	BLM sign the other way to Wild Cow Springs Recreation Site.
	5.1 ▲	SO	BLM sign for Wild Cow Springs Recreation Site straight on.
▼ 4.2		SO	Cross over Mackenzie Creek.
	5.0 ▲	SO	Cross over Mackenzie Creek.
			GPS: N34°53.22′ W113°57.19′
▼ 4.8		SO	Track on left.
	4.4 ▲	BL	Track on right.
▼ 5.2		SO	Cross through wash. Antler Mine on right.
	4.0 ▲	SO	Cross through wash. Antler Mine on left.
▼ 5.3		SO	Two tracks on right to the Antler Mine.
	3.9 ▲	SO	Two tracks on left to the Antler Mine.
			GPS: N34°52.68′ W113°58.17′
▼ 5.9		SO	Track on left opposite house. Trail is now graded dirt road.
	3.3 ▲	SO	Track on right opposite house. Trail is now a formed trail.
▼ 6.2		SO	Cattle guard.
	3.0 ▲	SO	Cattle guard.
▼ 6.6		SO	Graded road on left.
	2.6 ▲	SO	Graded road on right.
▼ 7.2		SO	Cattle guard.
	2.0 ▲	SO	Cattle guard.
▼ 7.4		SO	Track on left.
	1.8 ▲	SO	Track on right.
▼ 8.2		SO	Track on right.
	1.0 ▲	SO	Track on left.
▼ 9.2		SO	Graded road on right is Suzette Road; also track on left. Zero trip meter at sign for Suzette Road.
	0.0 ▲		Continue to the northeast.
			GPS: N34°52.31′ W114°02.24′
▼ 0.0			Continue toward Yucca.
	4.2 ▲	SO	Graded road on left is Suzette Road; also track on right. Zero trip meter at sign for Suzette Road.
▼ 0.6		SO	Track on right.
	3.6 ▲	SO	Track on left.
▼ 0.9		SO	Track on right.
	3.3 ▲	SO	Track on left.
▼ 1.9		SO	Graded road on right.
	2.3 ▲	SO	Graded road on left.
▼ 2.1		SO	Track on right.
	2.1 ▲	SO	Track on left.
▼ 3.0		SO	Track on right.
	1.2 ▲	SO	Track on left.
▼ 3.4		SO	Track back on left is Bar I-L Road. Also small track on left.
	0.8 ▲	BL	Small track on right. Also track on right is Bar I-L Road.
			GPS: N34°51.27′ W114°05.89′
▼ 4.1		SO	Track on right.
	0.1 ▲	SO	Track on left.
▼ 4.2			Trail ends at the junction with the paved Northwest #15: Alamo Lake Road. Turn right for Yucca; turn left for Lake Alamo National Wildlife Refuge.
	0.0 ▲		Trail commences at the junction of Boriana Mine Road and the paved Northwest #15: Alamo Lake Road, 3 miles east of Yucca. Zero trip meter and turn northeast on the wide, graded dirt Boriana Mine Road.
			GPS: N34°50.99′ W114°06.60′

NORTHWEST REGION TRAIL #20

Mohave Mountains Trail

Starting Point:	I-40 at exit 13
Finishing Point:	Mohave Mountains
Total Mileage:	12.6 miles
Unpaved Mileage:	12.6 miles
Driving Time:	2 hours (one-way)
Elevation Range:	1,200–3,400 feet
Usually Open:	Year-round
Best Time to Travel:	Fall to spring
Difficulty Rating:	3
Scenic Rating:	7
Remoteness Rating:	+1

Special Attractions

- Stone ruin at Scotts Well.
- Wide variety of Mohave Desert scenery.

Description

The large, blocky Mohave Mountains are intersected by narrow washes that cut into them. This trail travels up one main

Stone ruins at Scotts Well

wash and two smaller spurs to the slopes of the mountain. There are no trails that climb over the mountains because of the steep face on the northern side.

Mohave Mountains Trail leaves from I-40 at exit 13 and proceeds south, initially along a roughly graded, dirt road. After 4.6 miles the trail passes an active mining property. After this the trail drops in standard to a lumpy, ungraded trail that runs along a slight ridge, affording views ahead of the Mohave Mountains. On the return trip, the gently sloping ridge gives views back to the Black Mountains.

The trail then enters a gravelly wash with many side trails that lead right and left. Remain in the main wash until 10.9 miles from the start of the trail. Here the wash forks; the left-hand, smaller canyon leads along a twisty trail that runs partly in the wash and partly along a formed trail to finish at private property where there is a small stone cabin ruin and a tank at Scotts Well. This pretty, narrow canyon has some scattered Joshua trees. Some sections in the wash can be a bit brushy with some close-growing tamarisk, but a small fire has reduced the worst of it. The second spur continues up the main canyon for another 1.8 miles. It is possible to continue a short distance past that point, but the trail is used mainly by ATVs and is very narrow and scratchy for a vehicle.

The Mohave Mountains represent somewhat of a crossover between the Mohave and Sonoran desert vegetation. The canyons on the south side have a population of Joshua trees (the representative plant of the Mohave Desert communities), while the northern slope has vegetation characteristic of the Sonoran Desert, including saguaro cacti. A keen eye will spot a couple of saguaros growing on the northern side of the mountain up the slopes of the main wash. Wildlife includes Gambel's quail, coyote, and bighorn sheep.

Current Road Information

Bureau of Land Management
Havasu Field Office
2610 Sweetwater Ave.
Lake Havasu City, AZ 86406
(520) 505-1200

Map References

BLM Needles
USGS 1:24,000 Franconia, Buck Mts., Crossman Peak
1:100,000 Needles
Maptech CD-ROM: Colorado River/Lake Havasu
Arizona Atlas & Gazetteer, p. 36
Arizona Road & Recreation Atlas, p. 38 & p. 72

Route Directions

▼ 0.0 From I-40 at exit 13, zero trip meter at the top of the exit ramp and turn south on the

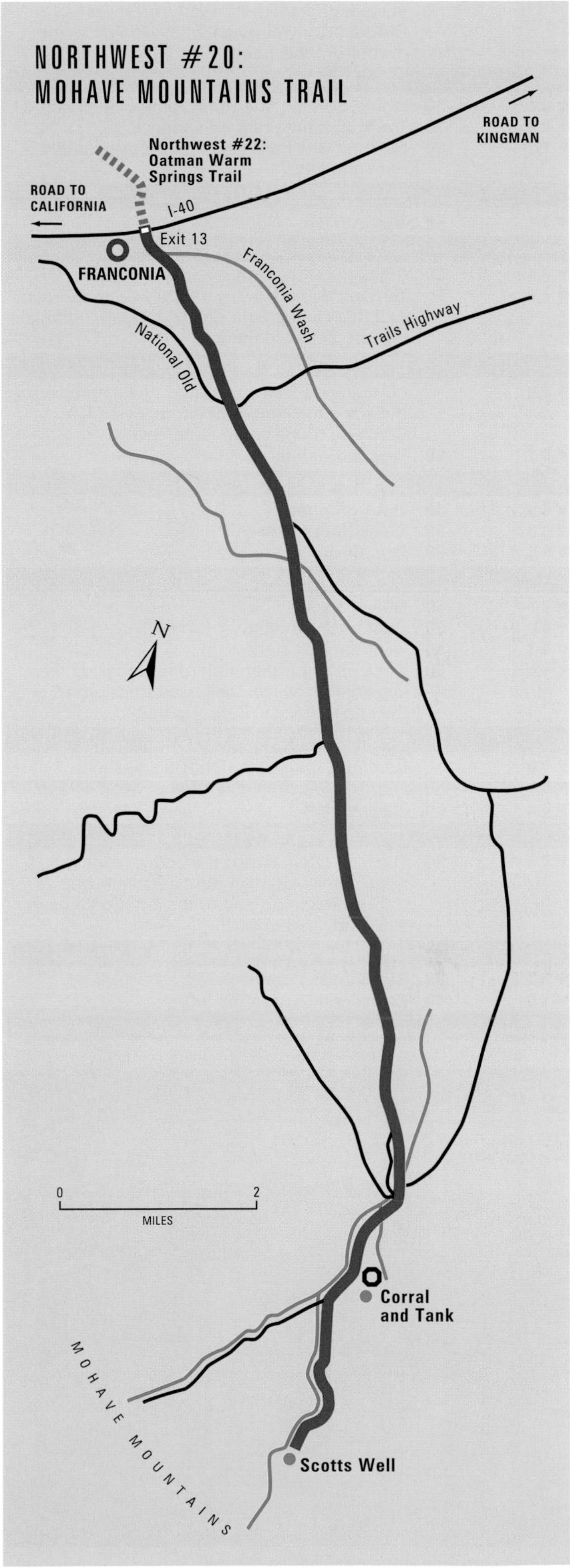

NORTHWEST #20:
MOHAVE MOUNTAINS TRAIL

ROAD TO KINGMAN
Northwest #22: Oatman Warm Springs Trail
ROAD TO CALIFORNIA
I-40
Exit 13
FRANCONIA
Franconia Wash
National Old
Trails Highway
N
0 2 MILES
Corral and Tank
MOHAVE MOUNTAINS
Scotts Well

		unsigned, graded dirt road. Northwest #22: Oatman Warm Springs Trail leads off to the north from this point.
		GPS: N34°44.02' W114°15.42'
▼ 0.1	SO	Pipeline on left and right; remain on main trail.
▼ 0.6	SO	Track on right along power lines.
▼ 1.9	SO	National Old Trails Highway crosses on the right and left.
		GPS: N34°42.73' W114°14.19'
▼ 3.1	BR	Track on left.
		GPS: N34°41.85' W114°13.33'
▼ 3.4	SO	Cross through wash.
▼ 4.6	TL	Turn left directly in front of fenced property of AL\FAR Mining. Sign directs through traffic to the left. Zero trip meter.
		GPS: N34°40.62' W114°12.60'
▼ 0.0		Continue on lesser standard trail. Immediately, there is a track on right and track on left. Continue to the south-southeast.
▼ 0.1	SO	Pass through fence line.
		GPS: N34°40.51' W114°12.58'
▼ 0.5	SO	Track on right.
▼ 0.9	SO	Cross through wash.
▼ 2.6	SO	Pass through wire gate.
		GPS: N34°38.53' W114°11.56'
▼ 2.7	SO	Quarry on left.
▼ 4.0	SO	Faint track on right.
▼ 4.3	SO	Faint track on right.
▼ 4.4	SO	Track on right; then trail runs alongside the large, sandy wash. Well-used track on left at the edge of wash. Zero trip meter.
		GPS: N34°37.01' W114°10.96'
▼ 0.0		Continue southeast alongside wash.
▼ 0.1	SO	Track on left. Trail now runs in wash course.
▼ 0.4	SO	Track on left.
		GPS: N34°36.68' W114°10.84'
▼ 0.5	SO	Track on left in wash; then crossroads in wash. Small track on right and well-used tracks straight on and to the left. Continue straight ahead in wash.
		GPS: N34°36.58' W114°10.80'
▼ 0.7	BR	Fork in wash; track on left.
▼ 1.6	SO	Corral and tank on the left.
		GPS: N34°35.68' W114°11.20'
▼ 1.9	BL	Fork in wash; track on right is spur trail that goes 1.8 miles up the wash.
		GPS: N34°35.52' W114°11.36'
▼ 2.4	SO	Exit wash through small stone walling.
▼ 2.5	SO	Re-enter wash.
		GPS: N34°34.95' W114°11.21'
▼ 2.8	SO	Exit wash.
		GPS: N34°34.75' W114°11.15'
▼ 3.0	SO	Re-enter wash.
▼ 3.4	SO	Exit wash.
		GPS: N34°34.27' W114°11.29'
▼ 3.6		Trail ends at a gate and stone ruin on private property. Old mine ruin and tank.
		GPS: N34°34.15' W114°11.34'

Joshua trees growing in the wash beside the trail

NORTHWEST REGION TRAIL #21

Falls Springs Wash Trail

Starting Point:	**Arizona 95, north of Lake Havasu City**
Finishing Point:	**Falls Springs Wash**
Total Mileage:	**10.1 miles**
Unpaved Mileage:	**5 miles**
Driving Time:	**45 minutes (one-way)**
Elevation Range:	**300–3,100 feet**
Usually Open:	**Year-round**
Best Time to Travel:	**Fall to spring**
Difficulty Rating:	**4**
Scenic Rating:	**6**
Remoteness Rating:	**+0**

Special Attractions

- Northernmost point of the saguaro cactus distribution.
- Well-used trail traveling up a wash.
- Bison Falls.

Description

This trail leaves from the eastern side of Lake Havasu City's limits along a well-used, dirt trail marked by an information board. It is an easy ride as it travels along the ridge before dropping to enter Falls Springs Wash. The wash is smooth as it climbs steadily up to the south side of the Mohave Mountains. The vegetation is the ubiquitous creosote bush, ocotillo, and some fairly large, scattered saguaro—this is the northernmost point of their distribution.

The trail then turns right into a narrow and twisty side canyon. The left turn at this point dead-ends 2 miles further at a locked gate marking the start of the trail up to the radio towers.

Continue along the main trail for 0.9 miles; it arrives at the bottom of the small, rocky Bison Falls. A constructed stone dam halfway up the falls testifies to the efforts of early miners to secure a water supply in this harsh landscape.

Two trails climb around the falls, one on either side. They

Falls Springs Wash approaching the Mohave Mountains

rejoin almost immediately. Both are very rocky and narrow. Neither one is much harder than the other; the left-hand one is steeper and looser, but the right-hand one is extremely narrow just before it rejoins the other and has a rocky section at the bottom.

At the top of Bison Falls there is a short, narrow, brushy section. However, it soon opens out again and the trail continues in the wash. A well-used track to the left goes 0.6 miles along a narrow ridge top and a shelf road to some old diggings. Nothing remains except the shaft and tailings. The main trail continues in the wash until it forks at the very end of the trail. The left-hand fork goes a short distance to the few remains of an old mining camp; all that is left are the tumbled stone walls of a cabin at the top of the small pour-off and some tin can dumps. The right-hand fork at the end of the trail soon turns into a loose, rubbly 4WD trail that climbs steeply and may result in vehicle damage.

Current Road Information

Bureau of Land Management
Havasu Field Office
2610 Sweetwater Ave.
Lake Havasu City, AZ 86406
(520) 505-1200

Map References

BLM Needles
USGS 1:24,000 Lake Havasu City South, Lake Havasu City North, Crossman Peak
1:100,000 Needles
Maptech CD-ROM: Colorado River/Lake Havasu
Arizona Atlas & Gazetteer, pp. 36, 46
Arizona Road & Recreation Atlas, p. 38 & p. 72
Other: Lake Havasu City Sheriff's Office Off-road Map, Arizona Access Guide–Lake Havasu

Route Directions

Mileage	Action	Directions
▼ 0.0		From Arizona 95, north of Lake Havasu City, turn east on Industrial Boulevard at the stoplight and zero trip meter. Industrial Boulevard is 1 mile south of Wal-Mart on Arizona 95. Continue east—Industrial Boulevard turns into Havasupai Boulevard.
		GPS: N34°29.61 W114°21.50'
▼ 3.1	TR	Continue along Kiowa Boulevard.
▼ 5.1	TL	Turn onto Bison Boulevard. Follow paved road to the end where it turns into a dirt single-lane trail. Zero trip meter at the information board.
▼ 0.0		Trail heads out from the information board at the end of Bison Boulevard.
		GPS: N34°31.27' W114°16.32'
▼ 0.4	SO	Track on left.
▼ 1.0	SO	Track on left.
		GPS: N34°31.78' W114°15.40'
▼ 1.2	BL	Bear left at concrete foundation in large open area, heading down toward wash.
▼ 1.4	BR	Ignore small tracks on left and right; remain on main trail. Bear right up wash under power lines.
		GPS: N34°31.95' W114°15.24'
▼ 2.1	SO	Track on right and small track on left.
		GPS: N34°32.27' W114°14.53'
▼ 2.2	SO	Small track on right.
▼ 2.6	BR	Wash forks; well-used track on left goes 2 miles to a locked gate. Zero trip meter.
		GPS: N34°32.57' W114°14.13'
▼ 0.0		Continue to the northeast.
▼ 0.9	TR	Trail forks in front of Bison Falls with old concrete dam in the wash. Both ways join up fairly quickly. Both are narrow and rocky—the right fork is slightly easier, but it is narrower.
		GPS: N34°32.66' W114°13.32'

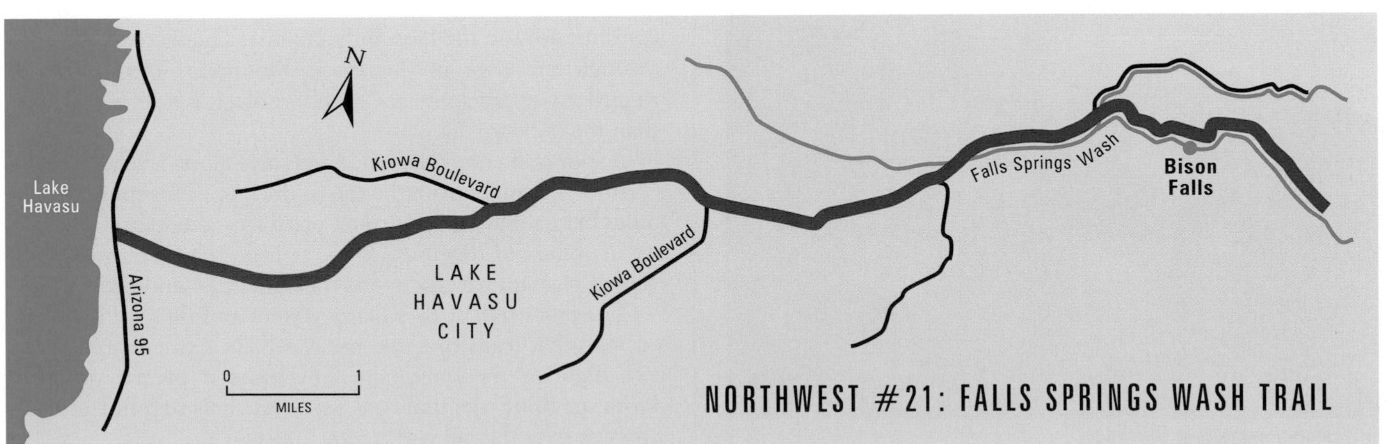

▼ 1.0	SO	Tracks rejoin at top of pour-off.
▼ 1.7	SO	Track on left climbs 0.6 miles along the ridge, then along a narrow shelf road to some diggings. There is a view back to Lake Havasu.
		GPS: N34°32.63' W114°12.67'
▼ 2.3	TL	Fork in wash.
		GPS: N34°32.32' W114°12.15'
▼ 2.4		Trail ends at small pour-off in the wash. Immediately above the pour-off on the left, there is a small stone ruin—part of an old mining camp. No diggings, just the ruin and tin can dumps. Hiking trail continues to the mine, visible above the head of the valley.
		GPS: N34°32.34' W114°12.49'

NORTHWEST REGION TRAIL #22

Oatman Warm Springs Trail

Starting Point:	**Route 66, 0.7 miles south of Golden Shores**
Finishing Point:	**I-40 at exit 13**
Total Mileage:	**29.9 miles**
Unpaved Mileage:	**29.9 miles**
Driving Time:	**2.5 hours**
Elevation Range:	**600–2,000 feet**
Usually Open:	**Year-round**
Best Time to Travel:	**Fall to spring**
Difficulty Rating:	**3 (spur could be classed as a 4)**
Scenic Rating:	**8**
Remoteness Rating:	**+1**

Special Attractions

- Oatman Warm Springs.
- Trail running along the edge of the Warm Springs Wilderness.
- Far-reaching views of the Black and Mohave Mountains.
- Wildflower-viewing in spring.

An off-camber section of the trail

Description

This trail combines a long, interesting drive, a short walk, and wide-ranging views. It leaves from the community of Golden Shores along a wide, graded (though often washboardy) road. The turnoff for the trail proper is 6.4 miles along this road. The turn is well used but very narrow, and with no marker it is easy to miss. If you come to a windmill, a stone tower, and a dwelling on the graded road, you have gone 1 mile too far.

The trail runs along a ridge for much of the first leg, giving 360° views ahead over the Black Mountains and back over the Mohave Mountains. Although the trail is easy for a 4WD vehicle, it is very lumpy and you will be forced to go slowly. Take your time. Fast speeds risk tire damage and make for a very uncomfortable ride for the vehicle's occupants. Vegetation is sparse along the rocky ridge top—a mix of creosote bush, large ocotillo, palo verde, and barrel cactus. The trail is at its best in spring when the ocotillo are waving their red flaglike blooms and the yellow flowers of the palo verde are out. You are likely to see wildlife along this trail, Gambel's quail are prolific, coyotes roam the slopes, and there are wild burros that have strayed down the mountains from the mines around Oatman.

Viewpoint at the Talc Mine looking back down on the distant trail

The section of trail that leads off as a spur to Oatman Warm Springs is slightly tougher than the rest of the trail because it has a couple of loose, steep hills; but anyone who has come this far is unlikely to have trouble. This short spur ends at a small turnaround on the boundary of Warm Springs Wilderness. From here, hike past the gate along the old trail for approximately 1 mile to Oatman Warm Springs. A cold spring is reached first at approximately 0.3 miles. Coordinates for the warm springs are GPS: N34°53.80' W114°18.48'. The springs are small and not suitable for bathing because no pool has been built, but the hike is pleasant and goes through some wonderful wilderness scenery.

From the springs, retrace your steps to the main trail and continue around the loop to Franconia. The second leg winds through the edge of the Black Mountains through some rugged mountain scenery. On the whole, it is a smoother road than the outward leg.

A spur trail enters the wilderness area along a vehicle access corridor, 2.5 miles from the top of the loop. This spur goes 1.3 miles before ending on a small platform raised above the valley at some old diggings. There is little to see, although the view is pleasant. Access to the trail is narrow and brushy.

The main trail crosses many washes and then joins a graded road that leads to a talc mine, which is just visible to the left, high on the mountain. The mine is private property. From the mine, the trail runs across the flats to join I-40 after crossing over the railroad tracks.

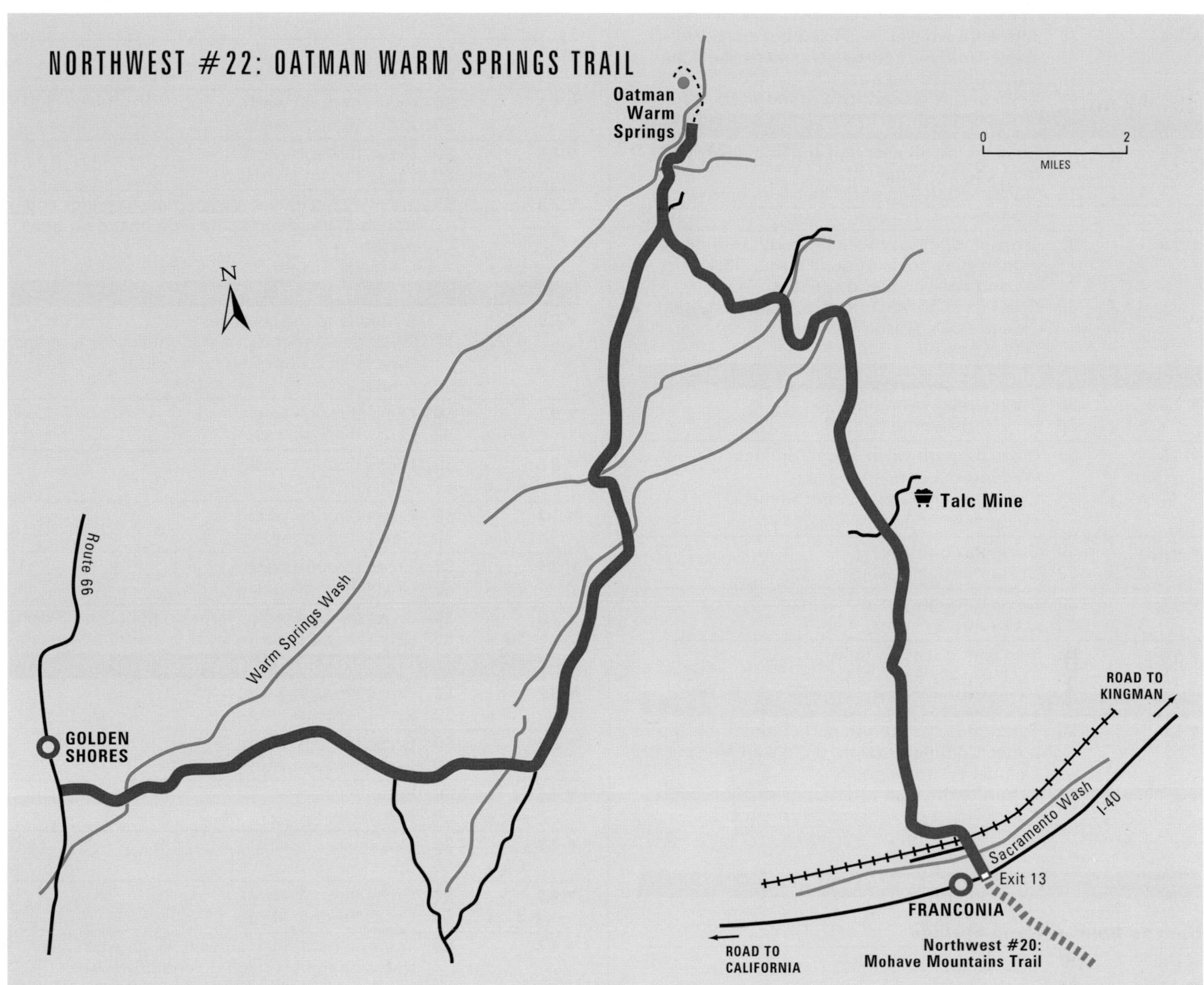

Current Road Information
Bureau of Land Management
Kingman Field Office
2475 Beverly Ave.
Kingman, AZ 86401
(520) 692-4400

Map References
BLM Needles
USGS 1:24,000 Warm Springs SW, Warm Springs, Warm Springs SE, Franconia
1:100,000 Needles
Maptech CD-ROM: Colorado River/Lake Havasu
Arizona Atlas & Gazetteer, p. 36
Arizona Road & Recreation Atlas, pp. 32, 38 & pp. 66, 72

Route Directions

▼ 0.0		From Route 66, 0.7 miles south of the community of Golden Shores, turn east on wide, graded dirt road and zero trip meter. Turn is unmarked, but the road runs just north of the radio tower, which is a short, white square building.
6.4 ▲		Trail finishes on Route 66, 0.7 miles south of the community of Golden Shores. Turn left for Topock and I-40; turn right for Oatman.
		GPS: N34°46.12' W114°28.61'
▼ 0.9	TL	Turn left in front of fenced enclosure. Track on right; then cross through Warm Springs Wash.
5.5 ▲	TR	Cross through Warm Springs Wash; then turn right in front of fenced enclosure. Track straight on.
▼ 2.2	SO	Track on left.
4.2 ▲	SO	Track on right.
▼ 4.9	SO	Cross through wash.
1.5 ▲	SO	Cross through wash.
▼ 5.1	SO	Track on right.
1.3 ▲	SO	Track on left.
▼ 5.5	SO	Track on right.
0.9 ▲	SO	Track on left.
▼ 6.2	SO	Cross through wash; then private entrance on right.
0.2 ▲	SO	Private entrance on left; then cross through wash.

▼ 6.4 TL Turn onto smaller, well-used but unmarked single-lane trail and zero trip meter. Track on right opposite the turn.

0.0 ▲ Continue on graded road to the west.

GPS: N34°45.81′ W114°21.71′

▼ 0.0 Continue on smaller trail and immediately tracks on right and left.

8.0 ▲ TR Tracks on left and right; then turn onto larger graded road.

▼ 0.9 BL Track on right is private property; bear left and immediately cross through wash. Tracks on left and right up and down wash.

7.1 ▲ SO Cross through wash; tracks on left and right up and down wash. Then track on left is private property.

GPS: N34°46.63′ W114°21.26′

▼ 1.6 SO Survey marker on right.

6.4 ▲ SO Survey marker on left.

▼ 3.5 SO Cross through wash. Warm Springs Wilderness boundary on left.

4.5 ▲ SO Cross through wash. Warm Springs Wilderness boundary finishes on right.

▼ 4.3 SO Cross through wash.

3.7 ▲ SO Cross through wash.

▼ 4.4 SO Cross through wash.

3.6 ▲ SO Cross through wash.

▼ 5.4 BL Two faint tracks on right.

2.6 ▲ BR Two faint tracks on left.

GPS: N34°49.90′ W114°20.05′

▼ 8.0 SO Track on right is return part of loop. Zero trip meter. Continue straight on to start the spur to Oatman Warm Springs.

0.0 ▲ TR Return to the start of the spur and turn right (as you are now looking) to continue on around the loop on well-used, single-track dirt road. Zero trip meter.

GPS: N34°52.09′ W114°19.12′

Spur to Oatman Warm Springs

▼ 0.0 Start of spur to Oatman Warm Springs.

▼ 0.1 SO Track on right.

▼ 0.3 SO Trail descends to join the large Warm Springs Wash.

▼ 0.5 SO End of descent. Enter large wash channel.

▼ 0.8 SO Cross through wash.

▼ 1.1 SO Cross through wash.

▼ 1.5 UT Spur ends at turnaround and gate blocking vehicle travel into the wilderness area. From here, hike the short distance to the springs.

GPS: N34°53.10′ W114°18.59′

Continuation of Main Trail

▼ 0.0 TL Return to the start of the spur and turn left (as you are now looking) to continue on around the loop on well-used, single-track dirt road. Zero trip meter.

2.5 ▲ TR Track on left is return part of loop; turn right and start the spur to Oatman Warm Springs. Zero trip meter.

GPS: N34°52.09′ W114°19.12′

▼ 0.1 SO Cross through wash.

2.4 ▲ SO Cross through wash.

▼ 0.4 SO Track on right on saddle.

2.1 ▲ SO Track on left on saddle.

GPS: N34°51.78′ W114°19.03′

▼ 0.5 SO Cross through wash.

2.0 ▲ SO Cross through wash.

▼ 1.1 SO Cross through wash.

1.4 ▲ SO Cross through wash.

▼ 1.3 SO Cross through wash.

1.2 ▲ SO Cross through wash.

▼ 1.5 SO Cross through wash.

1.0 ▲ SO Cross through wash.

▼ 2.5 BR Track on left enters a wilderness corridor and travels 1.3 miles to some diggings. Zero trip meter.

0.0 ▲ Continue toward Oatman Warm Springs.

GPS: N34°51.04′ W114°17.46′

▼ 0.0 Continue to the southeast.

4.7 ▲ BL Track on right enters a wilderness corridor and travels 1.3 miles to some diggings. Zero trip meter.

▼ 0.1 SO Cross through wash.

4.6 ▲ SO Cross through wash.

▼ 0.6 SO Cross through wash.

4.1 ▲ SO Cross through wash.

▼ 1.3 SO Cross through wash.

3.4 ▲ SO Cross through wash.

▼ 2.4 SO Cross through wash.

2.3 ▲ SO Cross through wash.

▼ 2.8 SO Cross through wash. Track on right down wash.

1.9 ▲ SO Cross through wash. Track on left down wash.

GPS: N34°49.63′ W114°16.60′

▼ 3.2 SO Cross through wash.

1.5 ▲ SO Cross through wash.

▼ 3.4 SO Cross through wash.

1.3 ▲ SO Cross through wash.

▼ 4.1 SO Enter wash.

0.6 ▲ SO Exit wash.

▼ 4.3 SO Exit wash.

0.4 ▲ SO Enter wash.

▼ 4.5 SO Cross through wash.

0.2 ▲ SO Cross through wash.

▼ 4.7 SO Track on right; then cross through wash with tracks on right and left up and down wash; immediately followed by major track on left that goes to private property. A talc mine is visible up the mountain to the left. Zero trip meter.

0.0 ▲ Continue toward wash, bearing right at narrow track on left in the wash.

GPS: N34°48.17′ W114°16.25′

▼ 0.0 Continue to the southeast. Trail standard improves slightly.

2.1 ▲ BL Wider track on right goes to private property. Bear left on narrower track toward wash and zero trip meter.

▼ 0.4 SO Cross through wash. Trail now follows along the wide sandy wash, crossing it often in the next 1.4 miles.

1.7 ▲ SO Cross through wash.

▼ 1.8 SO Cross through wash. Trail swings away from wash.

0.3 ▲ SO Cross through wash. Trail now follows along the wide sandy wash, crossing it often in the next 1.4 miles.

GPS: N34°46.63′ W114°16.39′

▼ 2.1 TR T-intersection with well-used graded trail. Turn right and zero trip meter.

0.0 ▲ Continue toward Oatman Warm Springs.

GPS: N34°46.49′ W114°16.26′

▼ 0.0 Continue toward Franconia.

	3.2 ▲	TL	Turn left on roughly graded trail and zero trip meter.
▼ 0.7		SO	End of Warm Springs Wilderness on left.
	2.5 ▲	SO	Warm Springs Wilderness starts on right.
▼ 1.1		SO	Faint track on right after small hillock. Views of Mohave Mountains ahead.
	2.1 ▲	SO	Faint track on left. Keep right of the hill on main trail.
▼ 1.7		SO	Tracks on left and right along transmission line.
	1.5 ▲	SO	Tracks on left and right along transmission line.
▼ 2.0		SO	Start to cross wide wash. Many tracks on right and left for the next 0.6 miles; remain on main trail.
	1.2 ▲	SO	Exit wash.
▼ 2.6		SO	Track on right; exiting wash channel.
	0.6 ▲	SO	Trail enters wash channel. Many tracks on right and left for the next 0.6 miles; remain on main trail.
▼ 2.7		BR	Track on right; then track to left.
	0.5 ▲	BL	Bear left after the railroad crossing. Remain on main trail; many tracks on right and left.
▼ 2.8		TR	Stop sign at railroad crossing; turn right after crossing. Track on left.
	0.4 ▲	TL	Turn left and cross over railroad crossing. Stop sign at crossing. Track straight ahead.
			GPS: N34°44.48' W114°15.51'
▼ 2.9		TL	Turn left, heading toward freeway; cross wide, sandy Sacramento Wash.
	0.3 ▲	TR	Turn right away from freeway; cross wide, sandy Sacramento Wash.
▼ 3.2			Track on right; then trail ends at the junction with I-40, just east of Franconia.
	0.0 ▲		Trail starts at exit 13 on I-40, just east of Franconia. Exit freeway, zero trip meter, and proceed north on wide, graded dirt road toward the railroad crossing. Northwest #20: Mohave Mountains Trail leads off to the south at this point. Immediately there is a turn to the left. Exit is signed—Franconia Road.
			GPS: N34°44.14' W114°15.49'

NORTHWEST REGION TRAIL #23

Moss Mine Trail

Starting Point:	**Silver Creek Road, 4.5 miles from Route 66 and Oatman**
Finishing Point:	**Moss Mine**
Total Mileage:	**2 miles**
Unpaved Mileage:	**2 miles**
Driving Time:	**20 minutes (one-way)**
Elevation Range:	**2,000–2,200 feet**
Usually Open:	**Year-round**
Best Time to Travel:	**Fall to spring**
Difficulty Rating:	**3**
Scenic Rating:	**8**
Remoteness Rating:	**+0**

Stone ruin near Moss Mine with a mine gantry visible further up the wash

Special Attractions

- Extensive remains of Moss Mine.
- Access to a network of other 4WD trails.
- Can be combined with Northwest #24: Mossback Wash Trail and Northwest #25: Thumb Butte Trail to make a full-day tour.

History

John Moss, who was responsible for opening up the Moss Mine and hence this area of Arizona for mining, was a colorful character. He was born in 1823 in Utica, Iowa. By the time he was in his early twenties he was already prospecting for gold in Eldorado Canyon, Nevada. When Eldorado Canyon became too crowded for him, he crossed the river and began prospecting in Mohave County.

Most mentions of John Moss refer to him as Captain Moss. The title seems to have been honorary, as there is no record of military service in his career. He was always friendly to the local Indians, learning to speak their language and winning their trust and friendship in return. This friendship with the Mojave Indians accounts for the version of his discovery of Moss Mine that paints him in the most favorable light. Supposedly, in 1863 the Mojave leader, Chief Iretaba, grateful to Moss for his friendship, showed him some outcroppings of rock likely to be productive. Moss noticed the glint of gold and was quick to establish his claim.

The alternative version of the discovery of the mine tells of a prospector who came to Moss to ask his opinion of some ore he had found. Moss proclaimed it valueless, but wheedled the location of the ore out of the man. He then quickly staked the claim, driving off the original discoverer when he returned.

The Moss Mine was truly amazing. John Moss extracted more than $200,000 worth of gold from a hole 10-feet square by 10-feet deep. He then sold the claim to Dahren Black, who was backed by a consortium from the East. Later, the Gold Giant Mining and Milling Company from Los Angeles became the operator but soon discovered that the only gold was in the original small hole. When that played out, the company sunk many holes trying to locate the lode, but they never found it for the simple reason that there wasn't one! John Moss's original hole is to the right of the headframe. The surrounding holes were the attempts to find more riches.

Another of John Moss's discoveries was the Mossback Mine, just over the hill from the Moss Mine. Moss also tried to establish the first town site in Mohave County. As a result of his find other mines sprang up along Silver Creek. The settlement became known as Fort Silver, although it had nothing to do with the military directly. It may have been known as "Fort" because the soldiers from Fort Mohave prospected here while on furlough. They constructed a rock cabin, which they used as a base while they explored the hills.

John Moss is perhaps best remembered for something other than mining. He was well respected among the Mojave and was concerned about the bloodshed between Indians and the white settlers. He thought that if the Indians realized the sheer number of white people, they would see the futility of their attacks and would stop.

His friendship with Chief Iretaba enabled him to persuade the chief to accompany him to Washington to meet President Abraham Lincoln. The chief was gone far longer than the planned three months, and he did indeed meet the president. As part of Moss's campaign to convince Iretaba that the white population was more numerous than he ever imagined, every time their train passed through a town at night, Moss would wake his friend to show him the lights and would try to convince him that they were traveling through one large city rather than isolated settlements.

After leaving Mohave County, Moss moved to Colorado, where he had a checkered career involving a diamond-mining scam. In spite of all the wealth he had accumulated over the years, he ultimately died in poverty.

Description

This short spur trail leads along a rutty trail to the remains of the Moss Mine. The major attraction is the mine, which has some interesting ruins of stone buildings, many adits and shafts, and a steel headframe. The ruins make an excellent subject for photographers.

There are many side trails leading from Moss Mine and along some of the washes, and a keen explorer will be able to find one of several different routes through to Northwest #24: Mossback Wash Trail. However, these unmapped trails can be confusing to follow and it is easy to get bushed. Make sure you are carrying at least a topographic map and compass if you are planning to attempt any of these routes.

Moss Mine gantry

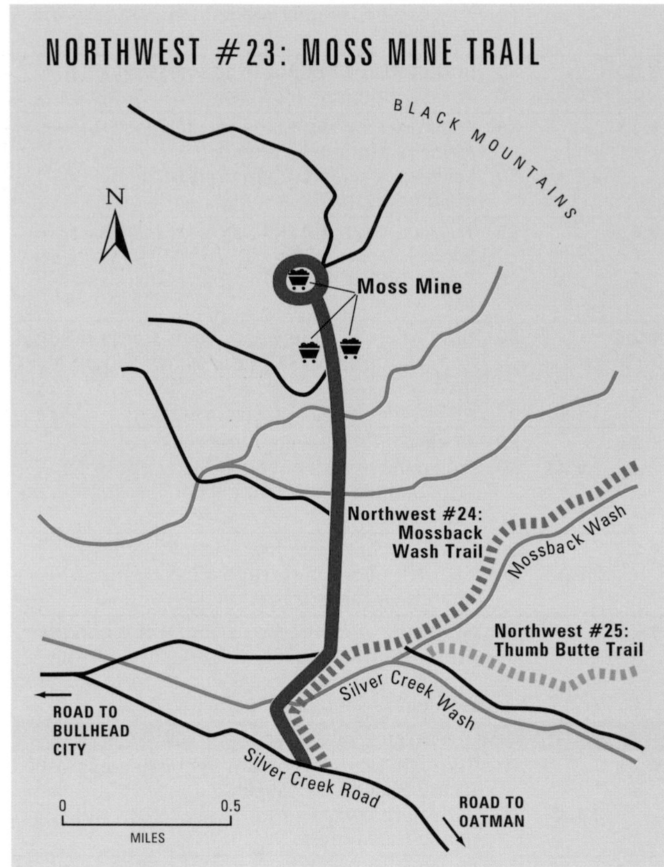

Current Road Information

Bureau of Land Management
Kingman Field Office
2475 Beverly Ave.
Kingman, AZ 86401
(520) 692-4400

Map References

BLM Davis Dam
USGS 1:24,000 Oatman
1:100,000 Davis Dam
Maptech CD-ROM: Colorado River/Lake Havasu
Arizona Atlas & Gazetteer, p. 36

Route Directions

▼ 0.0		Proceed along Silver Creek Road for 4.5 miles from Route 66 and Oatman. Then turn north onto an unmarked trail that leaves along a wash. Zero trip meter. Immediately bear right, staying on the better-used major track. Lesser-used track on left.
		GPS: N35°04.70' W114°26.94'
▼ 0.1	BR	Enter main Silver Creek Wash. Vehicles travel left down wash as well. Trail immediately forks; bear right following main use of trail.
		GPS: N35°04.79' W114°26.93'
▼ 0.2	SO	Two tracks on left and two tracks on right down and up wash. Remain on main trail toward the far side of the wash.
▼ 0.3	BL	Track on right up wash is Northwest #24: Mossback Wash Trail. Also track on left out of

wash. Continue straight on up small side wash to the north.

GPS: N35°04.92' W114°26.72'

▼ 0.5	SO	Crest ridge at head of wash.
▼ 0.8	SO	Two tracks on left.
▼ 0.9	SO	Cross through wash.
▼ 1.1	SO	Track on left.
▼ 1.2	SO	Cross through wash; tracks on right and left up wash.
		GPS: N35°05.63' W114°26.62'
▼ 1.3	SO	Track on left up wash. Stone remains of the Moss Mine on both sides of the trail. Adit down in wash on left. Many small tracks on right and left around mine. Remain on main trail.
		GPS: N35°05.81' W114°26.67'
▼ 1.5	BL	Track on right is end of small loop at the end of the trail. Zero trip meter.
		GPS: N35°05.94' W114°26.71'
▼ 0.0		Start of loop at end of trail.
▼ 0.2	BR	Steel headframe on right and many adits in the hillside. Bear right before the headframe and swing up ridge. Climb up ridge for view back over Moss Mine.
		GPS: N35°05.97' W114°26.82'
▼ 0.4	TR	T-intersection. Track on left and faint track straight on.
		GPS: N35°06.02' W114°26.65'
▼ 0.5		End of trail at the end of the small loop.
		GPS: N35°05.94' W114°26.71'

NORTHWEST REGION TRAIL #24

Mossback Wash Trail

Starting Point:	**Northwest #25: Thumb Butte Trail, 8.5 miles from the northern end**
Finishing Point:	**Silver Creek Road, 4.5 miles from Oatman and Route 66**
Total Mileage:	**5.6 miles**
Unpaved Mileage:	**5.6 miles**
Driving Time:	**1 hour**
Elevation Range:	**2,000–2,500 feet**
Usually Open:	**Year-round**
Best Time to Travel:	**Fall to spring**
Difficulty Rating:	**4**
Scenic Rating:	**8**
Remoteness Rating:	**+1**

Special Attractions

- Viewing wild burros and bighorn sheep.
- Spectacular scenery in the Black Mountains.
- Mossback Mine and German Soldiers Caves.

Description

This narrow, winding single track meanders through some spectacular Black Mountains scenery before dropping into Mossback Wash. It leaves from Northwest #25: Thumb Butte Trail along a wash, before climbing out and winding its way over ridges, dropping often to cross through narrow gully washes.

The caves at Mossback Mine where German soldiers hid

After 2.6 miles, the trail passes Mossback Mine, another of John Moss's claims. The mine has large tailings heaps and adits. Nearby are caves reputed to be the hideout of some German prisoners of war from World War II who escaped from the camp in Kingman.

The trail comes very close to meeting Northwest #25: Thumb Butte Trail at the mine, just as the main trail drops into Mossback Wash. From here to the end, the trail, which runs along Mossback Wash, is easy, gravelly, and smooth. Sections are fairly narrow, but even the widest vehicle will have no trouble fitting through.

The trail ends at the junction with Silver Creek Wash and shares the exit to the main dirt Silver Creek Road with Northwest #23: Moss Mine Trail. From the Silver Creek Road, it is 4.5 miles to Route 66 and Oatman.

Current Road Information

Bureau of Land Management
Kingman Field Office
2475 Beverly Ave.
Kingman, AZ 86401
(520) 692-4400

Map References

BLM Davis Dam
USGS 1:24,000 Oatman
1:100,000 Davis Dam
Maptech CD-ROM: Colorado River/Lake Havasu
Arizona Atlas & Gazetteer, p. 36

Route Directions

▼ 0.0		Trail starts on Northwest #25: Thumb Butte Trail, 8.5 miles from the northern junction with Arizona 68; at an unmarked junction in the wash. Turn west in the wash and zero trip meter.
4.0 ▲		Trail ends at the junction with Northwest #25: Thumb Butte Trail. Turn left in the wash to exit to Arizona 68; turn right to return to Silver Creek Road via the Thumb Butte Trail.
		GPS: N35°07.33' W114°25.13'
▼ 0.5	BL	Bear left out of wash and swing up hill. Track continues in wash and is a difficult route out via Pass Canyon.
3.5 ▲	BR	Descend hill and bear right up wash. Track on left down wash is a difficult route out via Pass Canyon.
		GPS: N35°07.14' W114°25.63'
▼ 0.7	TR	Cross through wash; then track on left.

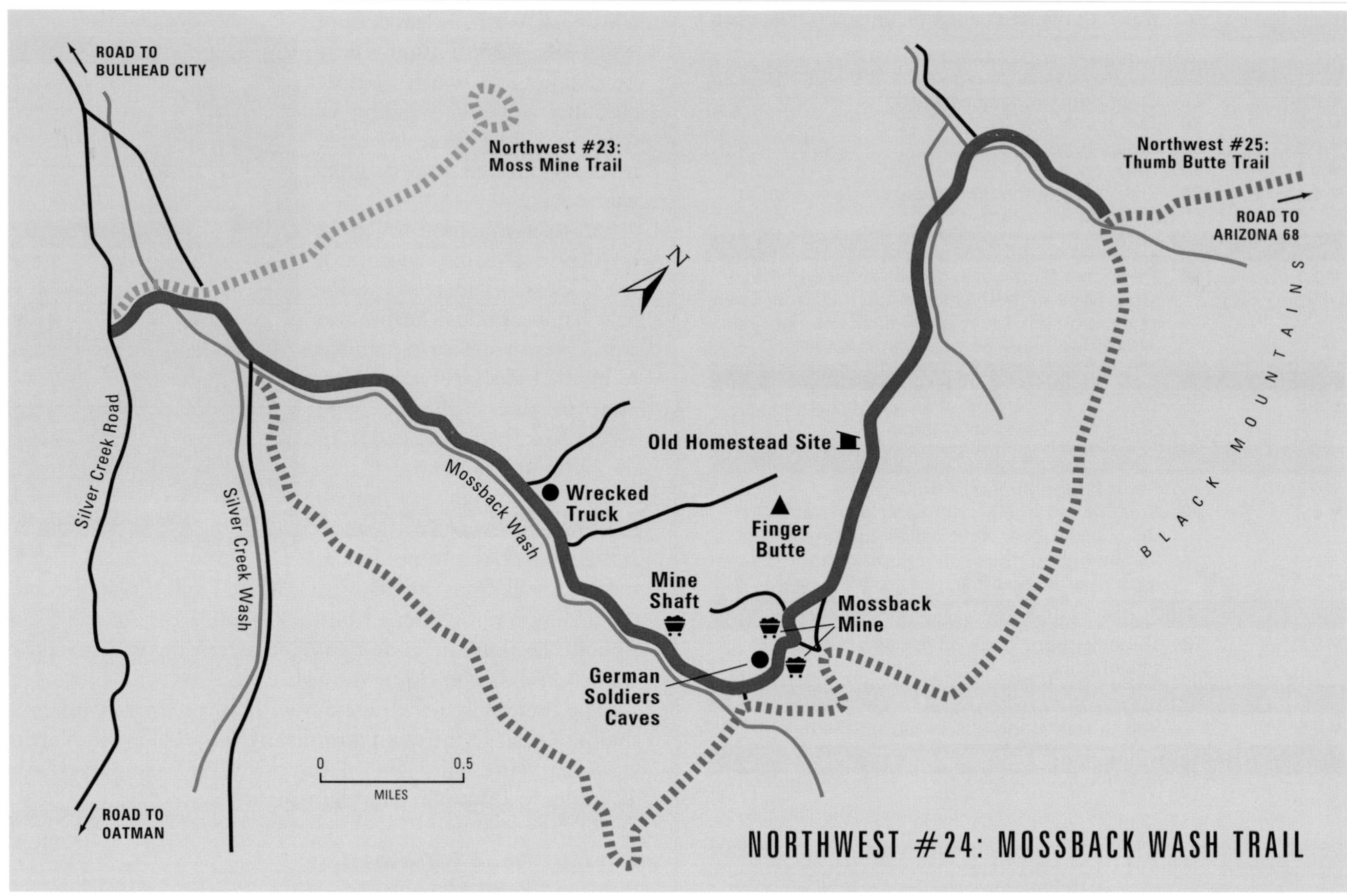

	3.3 ▲	TL	Turn sharp left; track continues straight on; then cross through wash.
			GPS: N35°07.05′ W114°25.54′
▼ 0.9		SO	Descend ridge and head up the wash.
	3.1 ▲	SO	Exit wash and climb up ridge to the right.
▼ 1.3		BR	Exit wash to the right and climb ridge.
	2.7 ▲	BL	Descend small ridge and bear left, entering wash.
			GPS: N35°06.73′ W114°25.15′
▼ 1.6		SO	Cross through wash. Tracks up and down wash.
	2.4 ▲	SO	Cross through wash. Tracks up and down wash.
▼ 1.7		SO	Pass through forest thicket, by the site of old homestead and past a spring.
	2.3 ▲	SO	Pass through forest thicket, by the site of old homestead and past a spring.
			GPS: N35°06.40′ W114°25.03′
▼ 1.9		SO	Cross through wash.
	2.1 ▲	SO	Cross through wash.
▼ 2.3		SO	Track on right.
	1.7 ▲	BR	Track on left.
			GPS: N35°06.06′ W114°24.60′
▼ 2.4		SO	Track on left.
	1.6 ▲	SO	Track on right.
▼ 2.5		BL	Two tracks on right.
	1.5 ▲	BR	Two tracks on left.
▼ 2.6		TR	Track on left; then turn right at T-intersection and enter wash. Track on left leads a short distance to join Northwest #25: Thumb Butte Trail. Second track on left up wash. Mossback Mine is on the right.
	1.4 ▲	TL	Track on right; then second track on right, which joins Northwest #25: Thumb Butte Trail. Turn left and exit wash; then track on right.
			GPS: N35°05.82′ W114°24.50′
▼ 2.7		SO	Track on left and the German Soldiers Caves on right; then track on left.
	1.3 ▲	SO	Track on right; then another track on right and the German Soldiers Caves on left. The Mossback Mine is on the left.
▼ 2.8		BL	Track on right; then track on left.
	1.2 ▲	BR	Track on right; then track on left. Bear right up wash.
▼ 2.9		SO	Track on left up wash.
	1.1 ▲	BL	Track on right up wash.
			GPS: N35°05.59′ W114°24.47′
▼ 3.2		SO	Mine shaft on right up bank.
	0.8 ▲	SO	Mine shaft on left up bank.
▼ 3.8		SO	Track on right.
	0.2 ▲	SO	Track on left.
▼ 4.0		SO	Two tracks on right marked by an old orange wrecked truck on right of wash. Zero trip meter.
	0.0 ▲		Continue toward Mossback Mine.
			GPS: N35°05.40′ W114°25.51′
▼ 0.0			Continue along in the wash.
	1.6 ▲	SO	Two tracks on left marked by an old orange wrecked truck on left of wash. Zero trip meter.
▼ 0.3		BL	Track on right at fork in wash.
	1.3 ▲	SO	Track on left is previous track rejoining.
▼ 0.5		SO	Track on right is previous track rejoining.

1.1 ▲	BR	Track on left at fork in wash.
▼ 1.1	TR	T-junction with the larger Silver Creek Wash. Track on left goes 0.1 miles to the start of Northwest #25: Thumb Butte Trail. Turn right and join Silver Creek Wash.
0.5 ▲	BL	Track on right runs up Silver Creek Wash and goes 0.1 miles to the start of Northwest #25: Thumb Butte Trail. Bear left into the smaller Mossback Wash.
		GPS: N35°04.95' W114°26.49'
▼ 1.3	TL	Track on right is Northwest #23: Moss Mine Trail. Also track straight on, leading out of wash. Remain in Silver Creek Wash and turn left.
0.3 ▲	TR	Remain in Silver Creek Wash and turn right. Track straight ahead is Northwest #23: Moss Mine Trail; also track on left out of wash.
		GPS: N35°04.92' W114°26.72'
▼ 1.4	SO	Two tracks on left and two tracks on right up and down main wash. Continue straight ahead to north side of wash.
0.2 ▲	SO	Two tracks on left and two tracks on right down and up wash. Remain on main trail toward far side of wash.
▼ 1.5	BL	Bear left up smaller side wash. Bear extreme right into main Silver Creek Wash, up the south side.
0.1 ▲	BR	Enter main Silver Creek Wash. Vehicles travel left down wash as well. Trail immediately forks; bear right following main trail.
		GPS: N35°04.79' W114°26.94'
▼ 1.6		Track on right; then trail ends at the junction with major graded dirt Silver Creek Road. Turn left for Route 66 and Oatman; turn right for Bullhead City.
0.0 ▲		Trail starts on Silver Creek Road, 4.5 miles northwest of Route 66 and Oatman. Turn north onto an unmarked trail that leaves along a wash. Zero trip meter. Immediately bear right, staying on the better-used major track. Lesser-used track on left.
		GPS: N35°04.70' W114°26.94'

NORTHWEST REGION TRAIL #25

Thumb Butte Trail

Starting Point:	Arizona 68, 19.5 miles west of junction with US 93
Finishing Point:	Silver Creek Wash, 0.1 miles east of Northwest #24: Mossback Wash Trail
Total Mileage:	14.5 miles
Unpaved Mileage:	14.5 miles
Driving Time:	3 hours
Elevation Range:	2,000–2,700 feet
Usually Open:	Year-round
Best Time to Travel:	Fall to spring
Difficulty Rating:	5
Scenic Rating:	8
Remoteness Rating:	+1

Special Attractions

- Spectacular scenery in the Black Mountains.
- Old mine remains.
- Thumb Butte.
- Wild burros.

Description

This extremely pretty route takes the backcountry traveler along the western side of the Black Mountains, through rugged terrain, gravelly washes, and remnants of the mining era. The trail leaves Arizona 68 to the west of Union Pass on an unmarked but well-used gravel road, 19.5 miles west of Kingman. A series of turns leads to increasingly smaller and less traveled roads, passing around the distinctive rock spire of Thumb Butte.

The road shown on most maps of the region as leading south from Arizona 68 is closed to public access by a mining claim; but an alternate route around exists: Follow the coal slurry pipeline as it travels up a loose desert wash to the junction with the original road. Take care you don't miss the turn—a sharp right out of the wash just past the wash wall. Vehicle tracks that continue in the wash are traveling east to rejoin Arizona 68.

Bullhead Jeep Club exploring the trail

Once on the formed vehicle trail, you will find the road rough and rocky. The trail crosses many washes as it winds its way south, often traveling in a wash bed that can be narrow in places. Vegetation seen along the trail includes creosote bush, Mohave yucca, cholla, and a few barrel cacti. The rugged Black Mountains make a spectacular backdrop to the stony trail. This is the Mohave Desert at its best.

The junction with Northwest #24: Mossback Wash Trail is reached 8.5 miles from the start. This shorter trail loops around and comes close to rejoining the Thumb Butte Trail. The main trail continues to the south, skirting the boundary of the Finger Butte Mount Nut Wilderness Area. Camping is limited because of the rugged terrain and rocky soils, but it is possible to find a few isolated spots.

The trail comes close to joining Northwest #24: Mossback Wash Trail a second time at the Mossback Mine. The final part of the trail is slightly more difficult and travel is very slow, so anyone not wanting to tackle this harder section down

The rockiest and most difficult section of the trail

Grapevine Wash could go out on the Mossback Wash Trail for a slightly faster, easier exit. From this second convergence with the Mossback Wash Trail, the Thumb Butte Trail is lesser used and a bit rougher. There are a couple of loose, rubbly descents, in particular the one to Grapevine Wash. The exit leading from the junction of Grapevine Canyon travels in the wash. The formed trail at this point leads to some interesting scenery and a short vehicle access corridor into the wilderness area; however, it is not the through route as it appears on the maps because of gated private property. Instead, the trail travels west down Grapevine Wash. Some drivers may not like this section—it can be quite brushy in places, and squeezing through a couple of tight spots in the wash will require some careful wheel placement over large boulders. The trail widens out as it goes downstream, and the end is wide and gravelly.

The trail ends where Grapevine Wash joins Silver Creek Wash, which in turn is 0.1 miles from the junction with Northwest #24: Mossback Wash Trail. From here, it is another 0.4 miles along the wash to the graded dirt Silver Creek Road that leads to Oatman. If you travel the trail in reverse, it can be tricky finding the right entrance to Grapevine Canyon. Follow the reverse directions at the start of the Mossback Wash Trail and instead of turning up Mossback Canyon, continue for 0.1 miles in the main Silver Creek Wash. Grapevine Canyon is the next side canyon leading to the east. It is smaller than the start of Mossback Wash, but usually there are vehicle tracks leading up the wash. A GPS is extremely useful for finding the route along this trail.

The trail follows down the west side of the Black Mountains

Current Road Information

Bureau of Land Management
Kingman Field Office
2475 Beverly Ave.
Kingman, AZ 86401
(520) 692-4400

Map References

BLM Davis Dam
USGS 1:24,000 Union Pass, Oatman
1:100,000 Davis Dam
Maptech CD-ROM: Colorado River/Lake Havasu
Arizona Atlas & Gazetteer, p. 36

Route Directions

▼ 0.0		From Arizona 68, 19.5 miles west of the junction with US 93, turn south onto gravel road at the unmarked junction and zero trip meter. The trail swings away from the highway up a rise.
0.9 ▲		Trail ends at the junction with Arizona 68. Turn left for Bullhead City; turn right for Kingman.
		GPS: N35°11.13' W114°27.26'
▼ 0.1	TL	Smaller track on right at the top of a rise.
0.8 ▲	TR	Smaller track on left. Turn right and descend rise to the highway.
▼ 0.2	SO	Track on left; then track on right. Thumb Butte is directly ahead.
0.7 ▲	SO	Track on left; then track on right.
▼ 0.4	SO	Cross through wash.
0.5 ▲	SO	Cross through wash.
▼ 0.6	SO	Track on left.
0.3 ▲	SO	Track on right.
▼ 0.7	SO	Track on left.
0.2 ▲	SO	Track on right.
▼ 0.8	SO	Track on left at small mine hole; then track on right. Cross through wash.
0.1 ▲	SO	Cross through wash. Track on left; then track on right at small mine hole.
▼ 0.9	TR	Turn onto unmarked, graded road. Zero trip meter. Views to the right to Bullhead City.
0.0 ▲		Continue toward Arizona 68. Thumb Butte is to the right.
		GPS: N35°10.76' W114°26.71'
▼ 0.0	SO	Continue on slightly smaller graded road.
7.6 ▲	TL	Turn onto unmarked graded road. Zero trip meter. Views to the left to Bullhead City.
▼ 0.1	BR	Track on left.
7.5 ▲	BL	Track on right.
▼ 0.2	SO	Track on right.
7.4 ▲	SO	Track on left.
▼ 0.4	SO	Enter wash; then track on left.
7.2 ▲	SO	Track on right; then exit wash.
▼ 0.8	SO	Track on left; then exit wash.
6.8 ▲	SO	Enter wash; then track on right.
▼ 0.9	SO	Track on right; then cross through wide wash. Track on left up wash.
6.7 ▲	SO	Track on right up wash; then track on left.
▼ 1.0	SO	Exit wash crossing.
6.6 ▲	SO	Cross through wide wash.
▼ 1.2	BL	Track on right. Bear left down wash.
6.4 ▲	BR	Track on left.
		GPS: N35°09.89' W114°27.45'

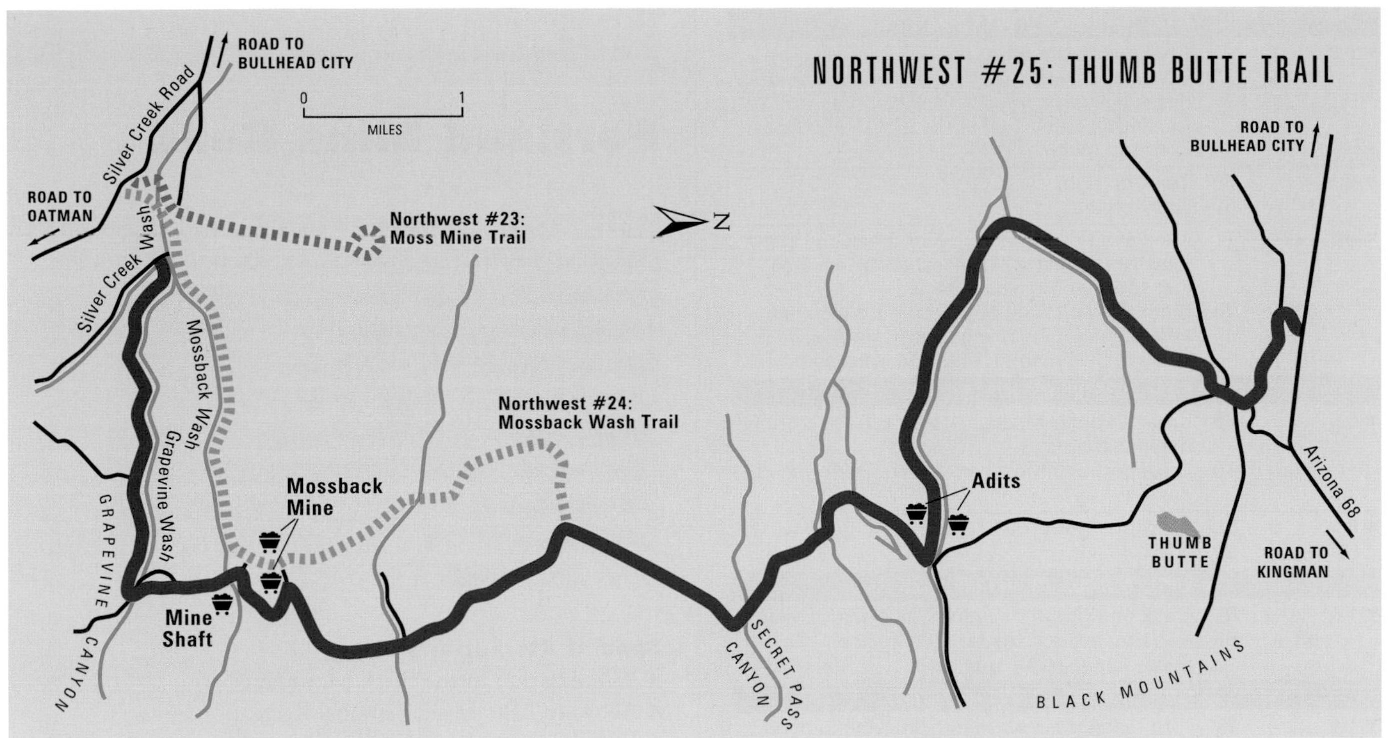

▼ 1.8		TL	Turn out of wash.
	5.8 ▲	TR	Turn right and enter wash.
			GPS: N35°09.43' W114°27.61'
▼ 2.2		TL	T-intersection. Track on right. Turn left up the wash. Trail is following along a poorly marked pipeline (high-pressure coal slurry pipeline).
	5.4 ▲	BR	Track on left. Bear right and leave the wash and pipeline.
▼ 3.2		BL	Faint track on right. Wrap around the wash diversion around pipeline.
	4.4 ▲	BR	Swing right around the wash diversion around pipeline. Faint track on left.
			GPS: N35°09.09' W114°26.19'
▼ 4.0		SO	Small mine adits on right and left.
	3.6 ▲	SO	Small mine adits on right and left.
			GPS: N35°09.37' W114°25.52'
▼ 4.2		SO	Track on left.
	3.4 ▲	BL	Track on right.
			GPS: N35°09.37' W114°25.33'
▼ 4.3		TR	Exit wash. Track straight on continues up wash.
	3.3 ▲	TL	Enter wash. Track on right continues up wash.
			GPS: N35°09.37' W114°25.29'
▼ 4.5		SO	Cattle guard.
	3.1 ▲	SO	Cattle guard.
▼ 4.9		SO	Cross through wash.
	2.7 ▲	SO	Cross through wash.
▼ 5.0		SO	Cross through wash.
	2.6 ▲	SO	Cross through wash.
▼ 5.1		SO	Cross through wash.
	2.5 ▲	SO	Cross through wash.
▼ 5.4		SO	Cross through wash; then proceed up small wash.
	2.2 ▲	SO	Exit small wash; then cross through wash.
▼ 5.6		SO	Exit wash.
	2.0 ▲	SO	Enter wash.
▼ 5.9		SO	Cross through wash.
	1.7 ▲	SO	Cross through wash.
▼ 6.1		SO	Enter wide wash crossing.
	1.5 ▲	SO	Exit wash crossing.
▼ 6.2		SO	Exit wash crossing.
	1.4 ▲	SO	Enter wide wash crossing.
▼ 7.1		SO	Enter wash.
	0.5 ▲	SO	Exit wash.
▼ 7.4		SO	Tailings on right.
	0.2 ▲	SO	Tailings on left.
▼ 7.6		TL	Join second wash and turn left. Zero trip meter. Track on right is Northwest #24: Mossback Wash Trail.
	0.0 ▲		Continue to the north in wash.
			GPS: N35°07.33' W114°25.13'
▼ 0.0			Continue to the east in wash.
	2.3 ▲	TR	Turn into well-used wash and zero trip meter. Track continuing straight on in the wash is Northwest #24: Mossback Wash Trail.
▼ 0.5		SO	Exit wash.
	1.8 ▲	SO	Enter wash.
			GPS: N35°07.12' W114°24.69'
▼ 1.3		SO	Cross through wash. Track on right down wash.
	1.0 ▲	SO	Cross through wash. Track on left down wash.
			GPS: N35°06.58' W114°24.15'
▼ 1.4		SO	Enter wash.
	0.9 ▲	SO	Exit wash.
▼ 1.5		BR	Exit wash; old trail into wilderness area on the left is now closed to vehicles.
	0.8 ▲	BL	Enter wash and bear left. Old trail into wilderness area on the right is now closed to vehicles.
			GPS: N35°06.40' W114°24.02'
▼ 2.3		TL	Turn sharp left up ridge. Mossback Mine is ahead. Continuing on at this point joins Northwest #24: Mossback Wash Trail at Mossback Mine. Zero trip meter.
	0.0 ▲		Continue to the northeast.

▼	▲		
			GPS: N35°05.91′ W114°24.40′
▼ 0.0			Continue to the east.
	1.4 ▲	TR	Descend ridge and turn sharp right. Turning left at this point joins Northwest #24: Mossback Wash Trail at the Mossback Mine. Zero trip meter.
▼ 0.1		SO	Track on right.
	1.3 ▲	SO	Track on left.
▼ 0.5		TL	Mine shaft on left at junction. Track on right joins Northwest #24: Mossback Wash Trail just south of Mossback Mine.
	0.9 ▲	TR	Mine shaft on right at junction. Continuing on at this point joins Northwest #24: Mossback Wash Trail just south of the Mossback Mine.
			GPS: N35°05.63′ W114°24.38′
▼ 0.6		SO	Cross through Mossback Wash. Track on right down wash.
	0.8 ▲	SO	Cross through Mossback Wash. Track on left down wash.
▼ 0.9		BL	Track on right.
	0.5 ▲	SO	Track on left.
			GPS: N35°05.33′ W114°24.25′
▼ 1.3		BL	Track on right; then enter Grapevine Canyon.
	0.1 ▲	BR	Exit Grapevine Canyon; then track on left. Climb loose, rocky section.
			GPS: N35°05.09′ W114°24.17′
▼ 1.4		TR	Turn down main wash in Grapevine Canyon. Do not exit main wash up well-used trail on the far side (dead-ends 0.6 miles further in wilderness corridor). Zero trip meter.
	0.0 ▲		Continue away from Grapevine Canyon.
			GPS: N35°05.07′ W114°24.13′
▼ 0.0			Continue down wash.
	2.3 ▲	TL	Turn left out of wash. Track continues up wash; also track on right (dead-ends 0.6 miles further in wilderness corridor). Zero trip meter.
▼ 0.8		SO	Faint track on left up wash. Remain on best-used trail and pick the best line through for your vehicle.
	1.5 ▲	BL	Faint track on right up wash. Remain on best-used trail and pick the best line through for your vehicle.
			GPS: N35°05.01′ W114°24.93′
▼ 1.3		SO	Faint track on right up wash. Remain on best-used trail.
	1.0 ▲	BR	Faint track on left up wash. Remain on best-used trail.
			GPS: N35°04.96′ W114°25.44′
▼ 1.6		TR	Tailings piles of mine on left; then T-intersection. Track on right continues down wash; track on left.
	0.7 ▲	TL	Track on right exits wash to mine. Remain in wash; then pass tailings piles of mine on right.
			GPS: N35°04.84′ W114°25.72′
▼ 2.3			Trail ends at the junction with the major Silver Creek Wash. Turn right for Northwest #24: Mossback Wash Trail, Moss Mine, and the graded dirt road to Oatman.
	0.0 ▲		Trail starts at the junction of the major Silver Creek Wash and Grapevine Canyon Wash. There are no signs. To get to the start, follow the reverse directions from the start of Northwest #24: Mossback Wash Trail. Thumb Butte Trail starts a further 0.1 miles to the east down the main Silver Creek Wash. Zero trip meter and proceed east up Grapevine Canyon in the wash, following the vehicle tracks.
			GPS: N35°04.91′ W114°26.39′

NORTHWEST REGION TRAIL #26

Portland Mine Road

Starting Point:	**US 93, 0.3 miles south of mile marker 45**
Finishing Point:	**Princess Cove Road**
Total Mileage:	**31.8 miles**
Unpaved Mileage:	**31.8 miles**
Elevation Range:	**800–3,800 feet**
Driving Time:	**5 hours**
Usually Open:	**Year-round**
Best Time to Travel:	**Fall to spring**
Difficulty Rating:	**4**
Scenic Rating:	**9**
Remoteness Rating:	**+1**

Special Attractions

- Winding trail in the Black Mountains.
- Access to Lake Mead National Recreation Area.
- Wild burros and bighorn sheep.
- Views of Lake Mohave and the Newberry Mountains.

History

The Portland Mine Road, as it is known, was put in by the miners working the Portland Mine. This gold mine is still sporadically worked by investors.

The wild burros that abound in the region are descended from the burros the miners used as pack animals and for transport. When the miners left the region in the 1860s, they turned their burros loose. The animals are descended from African burros, and many show the characteristic cross-shaped dark stripe across the shoulders and down their back; others have dark stripes on their legs. The burros are rounded up yearly, and many are taken to Kingman for adoption. It is necessary to keep their numbers in check as they compete with the native bighorn sheep for food.

At the lower end of the trail, the settlement of Katherine

Lost Cabin Well

Landing and the Katherine Mine both took their name from the sister of Kingman's Stanley C. Bagg. Bagg was the man who discovered the mine in 1920. The mine was active until 1942, although after 1929 it had very limited production.

Description

The Portland Mine Road is one of a number of designated vehicle access trails within the Lake Mead Recreation Area. The long trail leaves from US 93, 3 miles south of the Pierce Ferry Road. Initially, it follows the wide, graded dirt Cottonwood Road that leads to several subdivisions. The turn is well marked from US 93.

After 8.1 miles, the trail turns off onto an ungraded, smaller trail. The trail leads down to Lost Cabin Wash; there is a well at the head of the wash. You will have the best chance of finding a shady campsite along this section of the trail as it passes through stands of juniper trees, Mohave yucca, and creosote bush.

The first part of the trail runs down the shallow canyon of Lost Cabin Wash, within the Black Mountains. The wash is loose and gravelly, and the soil acts like sand, with the ability to bog down a vehicle. Your engine will work hard—in hot weather watch out for overheating. The trail continues in the wash, passing the currently unmarked turn for Jeep Cove (currently open to vehicles although this status may change), and then swings up the ridge to the Portland Mine. The road runs around the fenced perimeter of the mine before dropping to run along the equally gravelly Portland Wash.

A rutted section of the trail

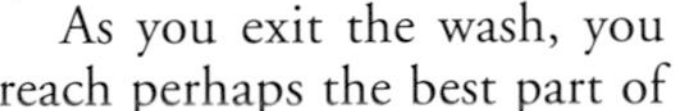

As you exit the wash, you reach perhaps the best part of the trail as it runs along a ridge with views of Lake Mohave, the Eldorado and Newberry Mountains, and the Black Mountains. This is also the roughest part of the trail; it is loose, rutty, and washed out in places, especially on the many steep descents that cross through dry washes. In places these descents can be narrow, but currently, with a careful driver, even the widest vehicles can travel the road. However, conditions can change after every rainstorm. The road is not actively maintained; most of the maintenance comes from trail users. If in doubt, walk the trail first. Many times, some minor work on the road will make it passable again and keep the trail open for other users in time to come.

There is very little shade along this trail, especially along the ridge tops in the recreation area. It can be uncomfortably hot in summer months. Winter is an excellent time to visit; temperatures are mild, it is easier to see wildlife, and there are very few visitors.

Vehicle-based camping within the Lake Mead National Recreation Area is allowed in designated primitive spots only.

Deep loose sand where the trail follows along in Lost Cabin Wash

Current Road Information

Bureau of Land Management
Kingman Field Office
2475 Beverly Ave.
Kingman, AZ 86401
(520) 692-4400

Lake Mead National Recreation Area
601 Nevada Hwy.
Boulder City, NV 89005
(702) 293-8907

Map References

BLM Davis Dam
USGS 1:24,000 Grasshopper Junction NW, Spirit Mt. NE, Spirit Mt. SE, Grasshopper Junction
1:100,000 Davis Dam
Maptech CD-ROM: Colorado River/Lake Havasu
Trails Illustrated, Lake Mead National Recreation Area
Arizona Atlas & Gazetteer, p. 28
Arizona Road & Recreation Atlas, p. 32 & p. 66
Other: Lake Mead National Recreation Area Map

Route Directions

Mileage		Direction
▼ 0.0		On US 93, 0.3 miles south of mile marker 45, zero trip meter and turn west across cattle guard onto graded dirt road at the sign for Cottonwood Road. Immediately track on left. Remain on the major graded dirt road, ignoring tracks on left and right, which lead mainly into subdivided lots.
8.1 ▲		Trail ends on US 93, 3 miles south of Pierce Ferry Road. Turn right for Kingman; turn left for Hoover Dam.
		GPS: N35°29.40' W114°19.48'
▼ 2.9	BR	Track on left is Cheryl Avenue; remain on the main Cottonwood Road.
5.2 ▲	SO	Track on right is Cheryl Avenue; remain on the main Cottonwood Road.
▼ 8.1	BL	Turn onto unmarked, graded dirt road, which heads southwest, initially staying close to Cottonwood Road. Zero trip meter.
0.0 ▲		Continue on Cottonwood Road toward US 93.
		GPS: N35°29.45' W114°28.39'
▼ 0.0		Continue on smaller trail. There are many small, shallow wash crossings for the next 3.2 miles.

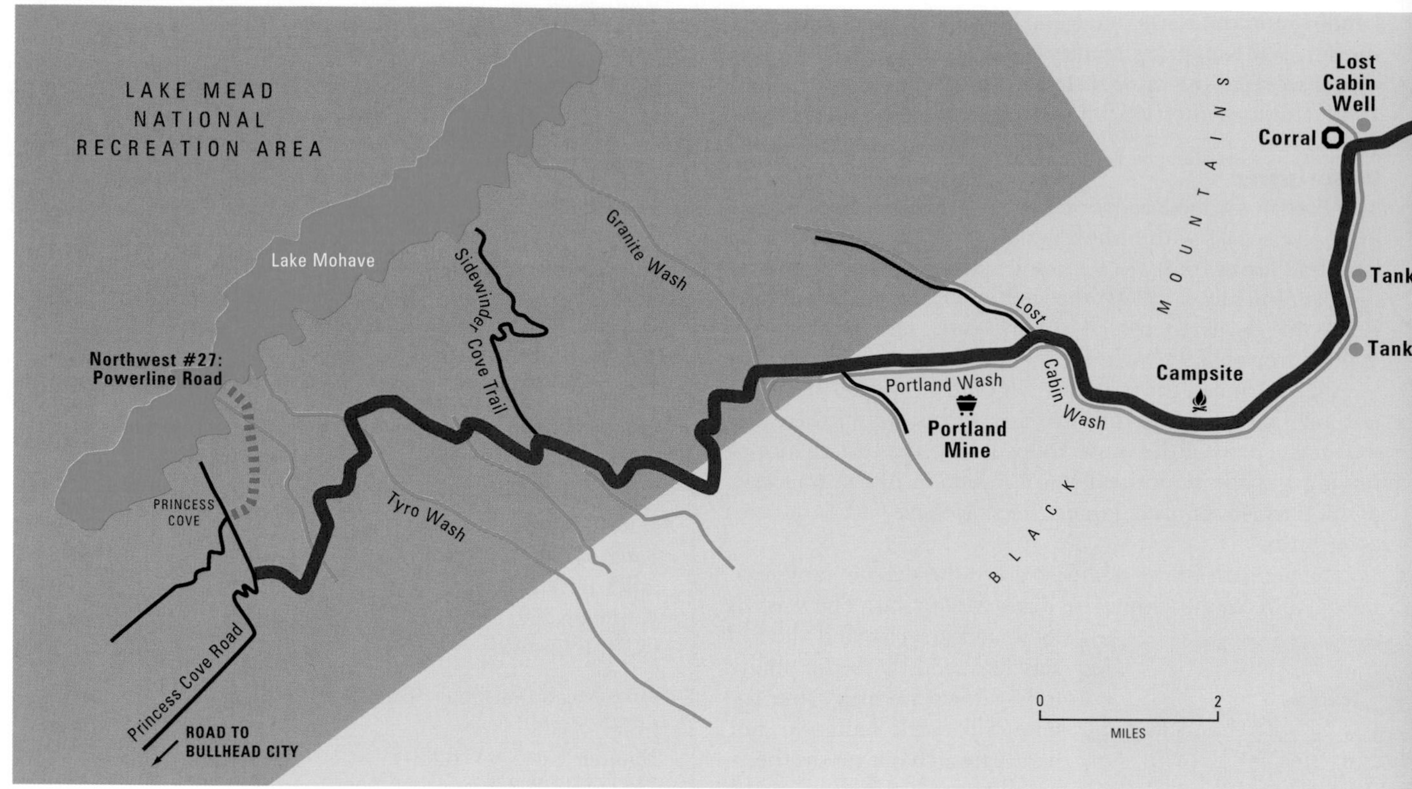

	3.2 ▲	SO	Turn onto wide graded road and zero trip meter.
▼ 1.4		SO	Track on right and track on left.
	1.8 ▲	SO	Track on left and track on right.
			GPS: N35°28.29′ W114°28.64′
▼ 3.1		SO	Track on right goes short distance to Lost Cabin Well; track on left.
	0.1 ▲	SO	Track on right; track on left goes short distance to Lost Cabin Well.
			GPS: N35°27.06′ W114°29.48′
▼ 3.2		TL	T-intersection. Track on right goes short distance to Lost Cabin Well. Zero trip meter.
	0.0 ▲		Continue to the northeast away from the wash. There are many small, shallow wash crossings for the next 3.2 miles.
			GPS: N35°26.94′ W114°29.51′
▼ 0.0			Continue on to the southeast, traveling in Lost Cabin Wash. Corral on right.
	6.5 ▲	TR	Corral on left; then track ahead goes short distance to Lost Cabin Well. Swing right, out of Lost Cabin Wash.
▼ 0.1		SO	Pass through fence line.
	6.4 ▲	SO	Pass through fence line.
▼ 1.5		SO	Tank on left.
	5.0 ▲	SO	Tank on right.
▼ 2.1		SO	Tank on left.
	4.4 ▲	SO	Tank on right.
▼ 4.0		SO	Campsite on right out of wash.
	2.5 ▲	SO	Campsite on left out of wash.
			GPS: N35°24.19′ W114°27.94′
▼ 4.5		SO	Small track on left.
	2.0 ▲	SO	Small track on right.
▼ 6.0		SO	Trail enters narrow gap.
	0.5 ▲	SO	Trail leaves narrow gap.
			GPS: N35°23.59′ W114°29.76′
▼ 6.4		SO	Track on right continues down Lost Cabin Wash to Jeep Cove. Trail leaves Lost Cabin Wash and climbs up ridge.
	0.1 ▲	SO	Track on left follows Lost Cabin Wash to Jeep Cove.
▼ 6.5		TR	Track straight on goes into Portland Mine. Zero trip meter.
	0.0 ▲		Continue away from the mine and descend down the ridge to join Lost Cabin Wash.
			GPS: N35°23.25′ W114°29.96′
▼ 0.0			Trail follows along the fence line marking the boundary of the Portland Mine on the left.
	2.2 ▲	TL	T-intersection. Track on right goes into Portland Mine. Zero trip meter.
▼ 0.8		SO	Trail leaves fence line and enters Portland Wash.
	1.4 ▲	SO	Exit Portland Wash and follow along the fence line marking the boundary of the Portland Mine on the left.
▼ 1.2		SO	Drill hole on left.
	1.0 ▲	SO	Drill hole on right.
▼ 2.1		SO	Track on left up wash.
	0.1 ▲	SO	Track on right up wash.
			GPS: N35°21.62′ W114°30.93′
▼ 2.2		SO	Entering Lake Mead National Recreation Area on unimproved road. Zero trip meter.
	0.0 ▲		Continue out of the Lake Mead National Recreation Area.
			GPS: N35°21.56′ W114°31.06′
▼ 0.0			Continue into Lake Mead National Recreation Area.
	5.6 ▲	SO	Leaving Lake Mead National Recreation Area. Zero trip meter.
▼ 0.7		BL	Swing left out of wash and climb up ridge.
	4.9 ▲	BR	Descend down ridge and enter Portland Wash.
			GPS: N35°21.07′ W114°31.56′
▼ 0.8		SO	Cross through Granite Wash.
	4.8 ▲	SO	Cross through Granite Wash.

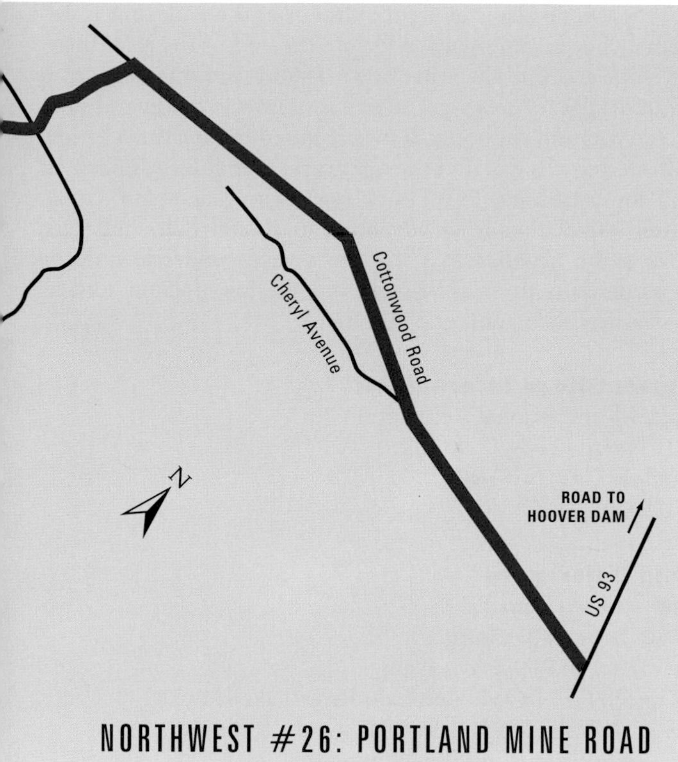

▼ 1.4		SO	Descend down from ridge-rutted, washed-out descent.
	4.2 ▲	SO	Ascend ridge-rutted, washed-out climb.
▼ 1.6		SO	Cross through wash.
	4.0 ▲	SO	Cross through wash.
▼ 2.0		SO	Cross through wash.
	3.6 ▲	SO	Cross through wash.
▼ 4.2		SO	Cross through wash.
	1.4 ▲	SO	Cross through wash.
▼ 4.5		SO	Enter wash.
	1.1 ▲	SO	Exit wash.
▼ 5.1		SO	Exit wash; then washed-out climb from wash.
	0.5 ▲	SO	Washed-out descent; then enter wash.
▼ 5.6		SO	Sidewinder Cove Trail on right descends to the lake. Zero trip meter.
	0.0 ▲		Continue along ridge.
			GPS: N35°18.74′ W114°32.47′
▼ 0.0			Continue along ridge.
	6.2 ▲	SO	Sidewinder Cove Trail on left descends to the lake. Zero trip meter.
▼ 0.1		SO	Small track on left.
	6.1 ▲	SO	Small track on right.
▼ 0.4		SO	Old bulldozer line on right.
	5.8 ▲	SO	Old bulldozer line on left.
			GPS: N35°18.52′ W114°32.74′
▼ 0.7		SO	Rutted descent around head of wash.
	5.5 ▲	SO	Rutted ascent around head of wash.
▼ 1.2		SO	Cross through wash.
	5.0 ▲	SO	Cross through wash.
▼ 2.4		SO	Cross through wash.
	3.8 ▲	SO	Cross through wash.
▼ 2.8		SO	Start to cross wide Tyro Wash.
	3.4 ▲	SO	Exit Tyro Wash.
			GPS: N35°17.50′ W114°33.99′
▼ 3.0		SO	Exit Tyro Wash.
	3.2 ▲	SO	Start to cross wide Tyro Wash.
▼ 3.8		SO	Enter wash.
	2.4 ▲	SO	Exit wash.
▼ 4.0		SO	Exit wash.
	2.2 ▲	SO	Enter wash.
▼ 4.5		SO	Cross through wash.
	1.7 ▲	SO	Cross through wash.
▼ 4.7		SO	Cross over wash.
	1.5 ▲	SO	Cross over wash.
▼ 4.8		SO	Cross over wash.
	1.4 ▲	SO	Cross over wash.
▼ 5.2		SO	Cross over wash.
	1.0 ▲	SO	Cross over wash.
▼ 5.5		SO	Cross over wash.
	0.7 ▲	SO	Cross over wash.
▼ 5.6		SO	Cross through wash.
	0.6 ▲	SO	Cross through wash.
▼ 6.1		SO	Cross through wash.
	0.1 ▲	SO	Cross through wash.
▼ 6.2			Trail ends at the junction with the major gravel road to Princess Cove. Turn left for Bullhead City; turn right for Princess Cove.
	0.0 ▲		Trail starts at the junction with the major gravel road to Princess Cove, opposite mile marker 3. Road is signed to the Portland Mine Road, Recreation Road #5.
			GPS: N35°15.79′ W114°33.18′

NORTHWEST REGION TRAIL #27

Powerline Road

Starting Point:	**Princess Cove Road, 0.7 miles past mile marker 3**
Finishing Point:	**Lake Mohave**
Total Mileage:	**2.2 miles**
Unpaved Mileage:	**2.2 miles**
Driving Time:	**45 minutes (one-way)**
Elevation Range:	**650–900 feet**
Usually Open:	**Year-round**
Best Time to Travel:	**Fall to spring**
Difficulty Rating:	**6**
Scenic Rating:	**8**
Remoteness Rating:	**+0**

Special Attractions

- Challenging trail for smaller stock vehicles.
- Access to Lake Mohave.
- Views of the Newberry Mountains.

Description

This road is not the complete track designated as Recreation Road #2. Although it is only the spur that gives access to the lake, it is the most interesting part of the trail. The trail com-

Trail ends on a narrow peninsula jutting into Lake Mohave

mences on Princess Cove Road, 3.7 miles from the junction with the paved Katherine Landing–Cabinsite Point Road. It is one of a series of designated vehicle trails within the Lake Mead Recreation Area; all are marked by yellow arrows and route numbers. The short, challenging trail winds down to a narrow point jutting out into Lake Mohave. You will have to share the view with a pylon, but it is still a magnificent point.

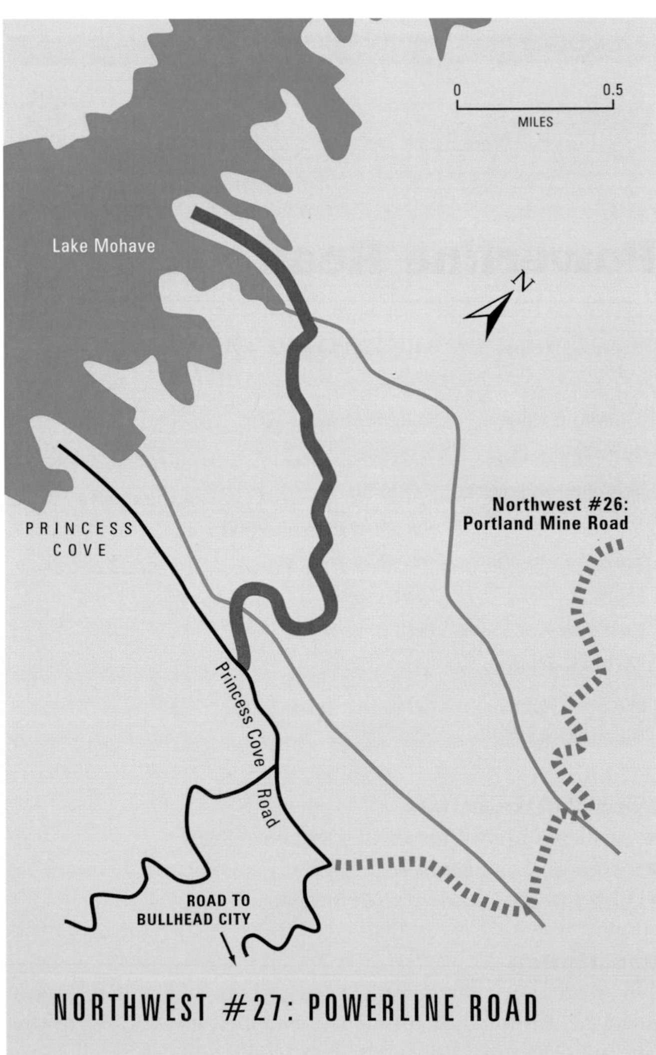

There is no shade along the trail or at the end, so it is extremely hot in summer. Just before the end of the trail, there is vehicle access to the water down a short wash that leads to a pleasant spot for a swim. The trail is narrow in places and subject to ruts and washouts. It is best suited for smaller vehicles; full-sized trucks will find the tight turns and gullies difficult as will lower-clearance 4WDs or ones with side steps. Good wheel articulation is an advantage as several holes and ruts have to be negotiated. There are several moderately steep, loose descents to cross washes, and the low-traction surface makes tires with good grip essential.

Current Road Information

Lake Mead National Recreation Area
601 Nevada Hwy.
Boulder City, NV 89005
(702) 293-8907

Map References

BLM Davis Dam
USGS 1:24,000 Spirit Mt. SE
1:100,000 Davis Dam
Maptech CD-ROM: Colorado River/Lake Havasu
Trails Illustrated, Lake Mead National Recreation Area
Arizona Atlas & Gazetteer, p. 36
Arizona Road & Recreation Atlas, p. 32 & p. 66
Other: Lake Mead National Recreation Area Map

Route Directions

▼ 0.0		Trail begins on Princess Cove Road, 3.7 miles from the junction with the paved Katherine Landing–Cabinsite Point Road, 0.7 miles past mile marker 3. Zero trip meter and turn west at the sign for Powerline Road, Lake Mead Recreation Road #2.
		GPS: N35°15.95' W114°33.88'
▼ 0.1	BR	Cross through wash. Track on left follows wash to lake.
▼ 0.2	BL	Trail forks; track on right.
▼ 0.4	SO	Tracks rejoin.
▼ 0.5	SO	Cross over wash; the crossing is narrow and washing out.
▼ 0.7	SO	Cross through wash.
▼ 0.9	TR	Track continues ahead and goes 0.8 miles to a promontory over Lake Mohave. This route avoids the more difficult sections of the main trail.
		GPS: N35°16.35' W114°34.13'
▼ 1.0	SO	Track on left goes to pylon. Main trail has tricky off-camber descent with holes and a loose surface.
▼ 1.1	SO	Cross through wash.
▼ 1.4	SO	Track on left to pylon.
▼ 1.5	SO	Track on left is easier route down to the wash. Main trail descends difficult section with large ruts. If the easier route is taken, swing right in the wash to rejoin the main trail.
		GPS: N35°16.61' W114°34.63'
▼ 1.7	SO	Cross through wash. Vehicles can travel a short distance to the left down the wash to the lake.
		GPS: N35°16.66' W114°34.70'
▼ 2.2		Trail ends on the promontory over Lake Mohave.
		GPS: N35°16.62' W114°35.22'

NORTHWEST REGION TRAIL #28

Packsaddle Mountain Loop Trail

Starting Point:	**US 93, 0.9 miles north mile marker 52**
Finishing Point:	**Chloride, 4.4 miles from US 93**
Total Mileage:	**16.5 miles**
Unpaved Mileage:	**16.5 miles**
Driving Time:	**2.5 hours**
Elevation Range:	**3,600–6,300 feet**
Usually Open:	**Year-round**
Best Time to Travel:	**Fall to spring**
Difficulty Rating:	**2 to the Cherum Peak trailhead, 4 from there to Chloride**
Scenic Rating:	**9**
Remoteness Rating:	**+0**

Special Attractions

- Chloride town site and many historic mining remains.
- Network of 4WD trails around Chloride, leading to other mining remains.
- Hiking trail to Cherum Peak.
- Long, winding shelf road with panoramic views.

History

From as early as the 1840s, men searched for minerals in the mountains around Chloride. However, the first real mention on paper comes with the formation of the Chloride Mining District in 1863. Miners traveled from afar to these remote and uninhabited regions to seek their fortunes. Even the last stage of the trip—from Yuma, up the Colorado River to the site of Hardyville, now submerged under water near Laughlin, and the long desert trek through Hualapai country—was a feat in its own right.

Gaining its name from the silver chloride that most were seeking, the town had its own post office by 1870; but the re-

Big Wash lies below the shelf road on Packsaddle Mountain

The remains of an old mine tramway along the trail

al rush came at the turn of the twentieth century. This rush, which raised Chloride's population from 700 to 2,000, was the biggest Arizona had seen since Tombstone in 1879–1880. The Butterfield Stagecoach operated out of Chloride from 1868 to 1919. Near the turn of the century, the Atchison, Topeka & Santa Fe Railroad Company raced day and night to build the connecting railroad from nearby Kingman to Chloride. The railroad was in service until 1935. The Tennessee, Diana, Mollie Gibson, Merrimac, and Elkhart Mines were shipping not only silver but also gold, lead, copper, turquoise, barium, and zinc to the processing plant. As many as 75 mines were active between 1900 and 1920.

As in many mining communities across the country, tales of fortunes gained and lost were common in Chloride. One of interest concerned Andy Flynn, a railroad brakeman, cowboy, and prospector for 11 years. The story was recounted by the *San Francisco Chronicle.* Having worked the nearby White Hills silver mines and witnessed the ore removed there, he staked his own claim, the Mollie Gibson. With a borrowed $50 he worked to find out what exactly he had claimed. After six weeks he was out of money and had insufficient food to continue his efforts. Desperate, Flynn walked to Kingman after attempts to get further cash in Chloride failed. With no other options Andy went to work for the railroad and was financially able to return to his diggings one month later. This time, after some blasting, he was surprised to find a promising-looking ore body. Much to his disbelief the ore was assayed at $600 a ton. Within days he was offered $20,000 for his claim. He scoffed at the offer, realizing he had struck it rich. One month later he sold just half his claim for $75,000 and continued to extract ore at the rate of nearly $3,000 a month.

Chloride was a distribution point for surrounding mines and ranches as far away as Eldorado Canyon. Various stores, the weekly *Arizona Arrow*, and more than a dozen saloons were all testimony to the town's success. The Tennessee Mine went through stages of success; a company invested in a flotation plant (set just below the mine) that was better than the previous one. By 1948 the Tennessee Mine had produced more than $7 million and was the deepest mine in Mohave County. When the mines finally ceased to produce in the late 1940s, Chloride was winding down as a town.

Never reaching the status of ghost town, Chloride has managed to attract enough residents who enjoy a relaxed approach to life and businesses that promote the colorful past in the few remaining buildings.

In 1966 Roy Purcell, a student from the University of Utah, decided to drop out of college and take a job with the Duval Mine in Mineral Park. In the way of the hippie culture of the time, Roy was looking for inner answers, and his answers were expressed in the creation of murals. An old miner supplied the automotive paint, and Roy spent most of the summer of 1966 living in a cave, painting his now-famous murals. The murals led to a commission from the Kingman Museum, and Purcell became a full-time artist. Purcell returned to Chloride in 1976 to touch up the murals, which today are one of the town's biggest attractions.

Description

The trail leaves US 93, 15.5 miles north of the junction with Arizona 68. The well-used dirt road initially follows alongside Big Wash, gradually climbing as it makes its way to the Cerbat Mountains. There are a few primitive campsites along this stretch, set within the juniper, Mohave yucca, and cactus. Six miles from the start, the trail starts to climb in earnest, switchbacking its way up the side of the range. This long section of shelf road is usually wide enough for two vehicles to pass easily. The trail is graded, but it can be rough in spots. All along the fairly steep climb, there are views back along Big Wash and then higher up over Detrital Valley to the Black Mountains. Near the Packsaddle Recreation Area, there is a distant view across the Hualapai Valley to the Music Mountains.

The small Packsaddle Recreation Area is reached in 8 miles. It has three small sites—each equipped with a picnic table and fire ring. There is a pit toilet but no water. The walk-in sites can accommodate only small tents, but they are more sheltered than those at Windy Point Recreation Area, 1.3 miles farther along.

From Packsaddle the trail runs along the ridge top, through jumbled boulders and windswept vegetation. There are views to Chloride, 2,000 feet below. The Windy Point Recreation Area has some lovely campsites with great views west over Detrital Valley. These seven sites are more exposed than the ones at Packsaddle. Most of them are only large enough for small tents, although there are a couple of larger ones. A fee is charged for camping. The sites have picnic tables and fire rings but no water.

Roy Purcell's murals from the 1960s

Two miles further, the hiking trailhead to Cherum Peak is reached, and the BLM's trail maintenance ends. At this point 2WD vehicles should turn around and return to US 93. High-clearance 4WDs can continue to Chloride. The trail descends a series of switchbacks, which run along a single-lane shelf road; the road has a rougher, looser surface and steeper grade than the ascent from Big Wash. There are limited passing places.

The trail passes the turnoffs first to the Samoa Mine and then to the Rainbow Mine, with its wooden chute. It then passes directly by the tailings, adits, tramway, and loading hopper of another unnamed mine.

The road passes other turns to mining remains before passing by the distinctive rock paintings done by Roy Purcell. Directly beside the trail, these distinctive murals are impossible to miss. A sign on the rocks says, "The Journey, Images from an inner search for self." The trail standard improves from this point to allow passenger vehicle access to the murals. Tracks on the right and left lead to some of Chloride's famous mines.

The trail ends on the eastern edge of Chloride, at the start of the paved road. Continue into town to explore some of the shops that sell antiques, memorabilia, and rocks and to visit the saloon or cafe. There are many interesting old buildings to photograph.

The end of the trail is marked CR 125 to Chloride, which is 13.5 miles from the junction with Arizona 68.

Current Road Information

Bureau of Land Management
Kingman Field Office
2475 Beverly Ave.
Kingman, AZ 86401
(520) 692-4400

Map References

BLM Davis Dam
USGS 1:24,000 Grasshopper Junction, Chloride
1:100,000 Davis Dam
Maptech CD-ROM: Colorado River/Lake Havasu
Arizona Atlas & Gazetteer, p. 28
Arizona Road & Recreation Atlas, p. 32 & p. 66
Recreational Map of Arizona

Route Directions

▼ 0.0		Trail commences on US 93, 15.5 miles north of the junction with Arizona 68, 0.9 miles north of mile marker 52. Zero trip meter and turn northeast on graded dirt road at the sign for Big Wash Road. Immediately cross cattle guard.
8.4 ▲		Trail ends on US 93. Turn right for Hoover Dam; turn left for Kingman.
		GPS: N35°25.06' W114°16.38'
▼ 0.2	SO	Track on left.
8.2 ▲	SO	Track on right.
▼ 0.4	SO	Track on left.
8.0 ▲	SO	Track on right.

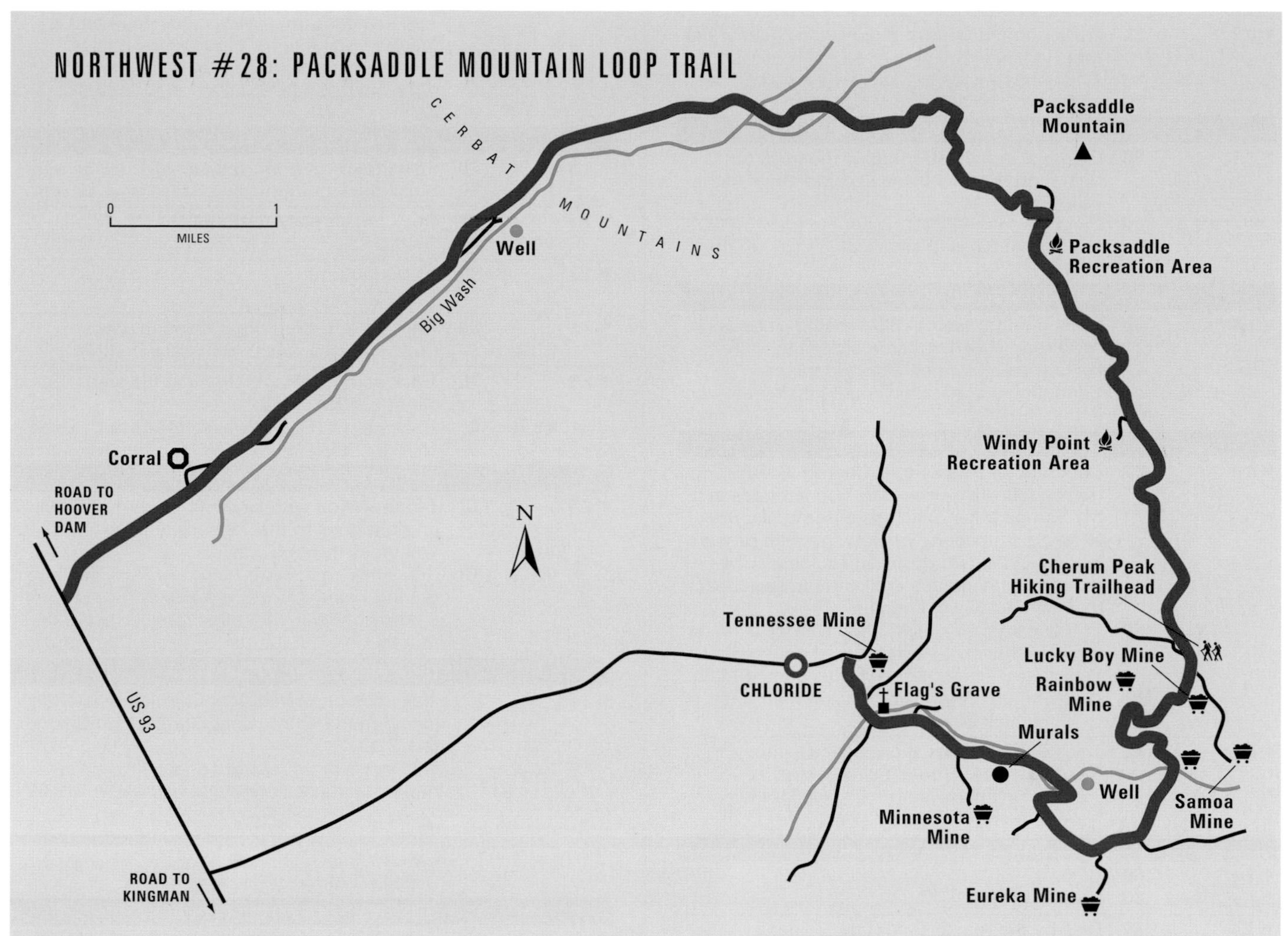

Mileage		Description
▼ 0.9	SO	Track on left goes to corral and tank.
7.5 ▲	SO	Track on right goes to corral and tank.
▼ 1.4	SO	Track on right.
7.0 ▲	SO	Track on left.
▼ 2.3	SO	Track on right.
6.1 ▲	SO	Track on left.
▼ 3.0	SO	Track on right.
5.4 ▲	SO	Track on left.
▼ 3.2	SO	Cattle guard.
5.2 ▲	SO	Cattle guard.
		GPS: N35°27.08' W114°13.84'
▼ 3.4	SO	Track on right goes to well.
5.0 ▲	SO	Track on left goes to well.
▼ 3.5	SO	Track on right.
4.9 ▲	SO	Track on left.
▼ 4.0	SO	Track on right.
4.4 ▲	SO	Track on left.
▼ 4.2	SO	Track on right.
4.2 ▲	SO	Track on left.
▼ 4.9	SO	Campsite on right.
3.5 ▲	SO	Campsite on left.
▼ 5.0	SO	Track on right.
3.4 ▲	SO	Track on left.
▼ 5.2	SO	Cross over wash; trail starts to climb.
3.2 ▲	SO	Cross over wash.
▼ 5.6	SO	Cross over wash; then campsite on right.
2.8 ▲	SO	Campsite on left; then cross over wash.
▼ 6.2	SO	Start of switchbacks and wide shelf road.
2.2 ▲	SO	End of switchbacks and shelf road.
▼ 7.3	SO	Cattle guard. Views over Detrital Wash to the Black Mountains.
1.1 ▲	SO	Cattle guard. Views over Detrital Wash to the Black Mountains.
▼ 8.0	SO	Track on left. Views to the left over the Hualapai Valley to the Music Mountains.
0.4 ▲	SO	Track on right. Views to left over the Hualapai Valley to the Music Mountains and views ahead down Big Wash.
▼ 8.4	SO	Packsaddle Recreation Site on right and left. Zero trip meter at sign.
0.0 ▲		Continue toward Big Wash. Start of switchbacks and shelf road.
		GPS: N35°27.13' W114°10.15'
▼ 0.0		Trail starts to descend. Views on right to Chloride.
1.3 ▲	SO	Packsaddle Recreation Site on left and right. Zero trip meter at sign.
▼ 1.3	SO	Track on right goes to Windy Point Recreation Site. Zero trip meter.
0.0 ▲		Continue toward Packsaddle Recreation Site.
		GPS: N35°26.23' W114°09.46'
▼ 0.0		Continue to the southeast along the top of the ridge.
1.8 ▲	SO	Track on left goes to Windy Point Recreation Site. Zero trip meter.

▼ 0.9		BL	Track on right goes to radio tower; gate at bottom.
	0.9 ▲	SO	Track on left goes to radio tower; gate at bottom.
			GPS: N35°25.62' W114°09.24'
▼ 1.5		SO	Diggings immediately below the track on right, and remains of small cabin down in the valley.
	0.3 ▲	SO	Diggings immediately below the track on the left, and remains of small cabin down in the valley.
			GPS: N35°25.13' W114°09.13'
▼ 1.8		SO	Track on right; end of BLM road maintenance. 4WD road ahead; other vehicles turn here. Parking area on right. Zero trip meter.
	0.0 ▲		Continue on graded dirt road; parking area on left.
			GPS: N35°24.99' W114°08.99'
▼ 0.0		BR	Continue on smaller trail. Cherum Peak hiking trail on left. Also vehicle trail on left goes to the Samoa Mine. Diggings of the Lucky Boy Mine are immediately below the road on the left. Trail standard drops and is looser and more roughly graded and starts to switchback down a narrow shelf road.
	2.4 ▲	SO	End of climb. Diggings of the Lucky Boy Mine are immediately below the road on the right. Vehicle trail on right goes to the Samoa Mine; then Cherum Peak hiking trail on right. Start of BLM maintained road.
▼ 0.8		BL	Track on right goes short distance into Rainbow Mine. Wooden chute remains.
	1.6 ▲	BR	Track on left goes short distance into Rainbow Mine. Wooden chute remains.
			GPS: N35°24.71' W114°09.40'
▼ 1.2		SO	Gate.
	1.2 ▲	SO	Gate.
▼ 1.4		SO	Pass by the remains of mine. Tailings, tramway, and loading chute on left.
	1.0 ▲	SO	Pass by the remains of mine. Tailings, tramway, and loading chute on right.
			GPS: N35°24.46' W114°09.07'
▼ 1.5		SO	Track on left goes into mine. Concrete foundations on right.
	0.9 ▲	SO	Track on right goes into mine. Concrete foundations on left.
▼ 2.1		SO	Faint track on left.
	0.3 ▲	BL	Faint track on right.
▼ 2.2		SO	Faint track on right.
	0.2 ▲	SO	Faint track on left.
▼ 2.4		BR	Track on left goes to Eureka Mine. Zero trip meter.
	0.0 ▲		Continue toward the top of the ridge.
			GPS: N35°23.96' W114°09.60'
▼ 0.0			Continue toward Chloride.
	2.6 ▲	BL	Track on right goes to Eureka Mine. Zero trip meter.
▼ 0.4		SO	Track on left.
	2.2 ▲	BL	Track on right.
▼ 0.7		SO	Cross through wash. Falls on right.
	1.9 ▲	SO	Cross through wash. Falls on left.
			GPS: N35°24.28' W114°09.78'
▼ 1.0		SO	Faint track on right alongside of tailings; then cross through wash.
	1.6 ▲	SO	Cross through wash; then faint track on left alongside of tailings.
▼ 1.4		SO	Roy Purcell's murals on the rocks on the left. Trail standard improves at this point and is graded—suitable for passenger vehicles.
	1.2 ▲	SO	Roy Purcell's murals on the rocks on the right. Trail standard is 4WD only from this point.
			GPS: N35°24.48' W114°10.25'
▼ 1.5		SO	Small track on right; then small track on left.
	1.1 ▲	SO	Small track on right; then small track on left.
▼ 1.6		BR	Track on left goes to the Minnesota Mine.
	1.0 ▲	BL	Track on right goes to the Minnesota Mine.
▼ 1.9		SO	Track on right.
	0.7 ▲	SO	Track on left.
▼ 2.1		SO	Track on left; then cross through wash.
	0.5 ▲	SO	Cross through wash; then track on right.
▼ 2.3		SO	Track on right. Flag's Grave at the start: "Good ole dog, 1991–1998."
	0.3 ▲	SO	Track on left. Flag's Grave at the start: "Good ole dog, 1991–1998."
			GPS: N35°24.72' W114°11.15'
▼ 2.5		TL	T-intersection with larger graded road. Track on right goes to the Tennessee Mine. Turn left and cross through wash.
	0.1 ▲	TR	Cross through wash; then turn from the larger graded road onto a smaller one. Turn is at the painted boulder with directional arrow to the murals.
			GPS: N35°24.88' W114°11.23'
▼ 2.6			Trail ends on the edge of Chloride where the paved road begins. Continue through Chloride to US 93.
	0.0 ▲		Trail starts at the eastern end of the paved main street in Chloride, 4.4 miles from US 93. Cross cattle guard and zero trip meter and continue on the graded dirt road to the east past the information sign for the Tennessee Schuylkill Mine.
			GPS: N35°24.92' W114°11.35'

NORTHWEST REGION TRAIL #29

White Hills Trail

Starting Point:	**US 93, 0.4 miles north of mile marker 29**
Finishing Point:	**Pierce Ferry Road (Mohave CR 25)**
Total Mileage:	**22.2 miles**
Unpaved Mileage:	**16.9 miles**
Driving Time:	**1.75 hours**
Elevation Range:	**2,400–4,900 feet**
Usually Open:	**Year-round**
Best Time to Travel:	**Fall to spring**
Difficulty Rating:	**3**
Scenic Rating:	**7**
Remoteness Rating:	**+1**

Special Attractions

- Historic sites of White Hills and Cyclopic.
- Joshua tree forest.
- Views of Hualapai Valley and the White Hills.

History

Long before White Hills was a flourishing mining camp, local Hualapai Indians would scour the region for the iron oxide, which they used to make paint. In 1887, an Indian known as Hualapai Jeff was searching the White Hills area when he came across a sample of silver chloride. He kept the ore, and when he was next in town, he asked about the value of his find. He was told it was worthless iron, so he discarded it.

In the winter of 1891, a rancher named Frank Robinson asked Hualapai Jeff to help him round up some cattle that had strayed over to White Hills in a snowstorm. The men camped near the spot where Jeff had found the silver. Once again Jeff picked up a good specimen. This time he kept it. Shortly after, Judge Henry Schaffer asked him if he knew of any good mineral deposits and Jeff showed him his find. Recognizing nearly pure silver, the judge offered Jeff $200 (a large sum of money at the time) if he would show him the location of the deposits.

In 1892, Jeff led the judge's party of John Barnett and John Sullivan to the White Hills location, where they staked the claims that would become a number of mines: the Horn Silver, the Occident, the Grand Army, the Chief of the Hills, the Treasurer, the Norma, and the Emma. A separate party led by rancher John Robinson arrived 10 days later and also staked claims.

The news had traveled rapidly and within two weeks of the find there was a small town of 200 people, with a store, four saloons, three restaurants, and a large number of tents. The demand for lots was so great that would-be residents had to claim their land by sleeping on it. With no permanent housing, many a miner woke up in the company of rattlesnakes that had crawled under the bedding in the night.

A washed out section of the trail as it climbs the ridge

The town, set on the edge of the Detrital Valley, grew rapidly and soon had a population of 1,500. The first post office was opened in 1892 by a man named Taggart, who gave the town its official name of White Hills, after the exposed rock of the region.

Many of the initial claims of the judge's party were not immediately worked, and in 1893, all the claims except the Treasurer and the Emma were sold to a consortium from Colorado. This proved a good move for the town, and by 1895, it boasted running water, electricity, and flush toilets. The town was a law abiding one, with a wide main street lined on both sides with businesses. The biggest problem for the population was the scarcity of water, which sold for a dollar a barrel.

White Hills had a very concentrated number of profitable mines in its relatively small area. The ore quality varied, but the consortium's Grand Army Mine produced ore that assayed at 3,000 ounces of silver and 10 ounces of gold per ton. Other profitable mines were the Horn Silver and the Occident.

Joshua trees beside the trail basking in the late afternoon sun

On the morning of August 5, 1889, the town was swept away in a surprise flash flood caused by heavy rain. Men working in the Grand Army Extension Mine escaped just in time, as the rising waters filled the mine. The schoolhouse and many houses were swept away, and two feet of soil was deposited on the streets of the town. The local paper, *The Mohave County Miner*, reported the flood. One sentence of its story said, "We might call their affair too much of a good thing. For water sells at one dollar a barrel at White Hills. They just had a million dollar bath."

The town never really recovered; many residents moved themselves and their houses to nearby Chloride. A few miners remained and extracted a fair living from the mines. There have been various attempts to reopen the mines over the years, although most of them were short-lived.

The small settlement of Cyclopic, located at the far end of the trail, was never as large as White Hills. It was established in the early 1890s by three prospectors, Robert Patterson, Sol Rowe, and a man named Glenn. In 1896 they leased the site to a company from Seattle that continued to work it profitably for many years. Unlike White Hills, where silver was the predominate ore, Cyclopic was known for gold. One of the early miners, Stanley Bagg, named the town after the Cyclops, a mythological one-eyed giant. A post office was established in 1905, and the town and mine continued until 1917.

Description

The White Hills Road is sign-posted from US 93 at the small settlement of Boulder Inn. There is a crossover on the divided highway at this point. The initially paved road runs in a plumb line across the Detrital Valley toward the White Hills. The settlement of White Hills was located on the western edge of the White Hills. Today it can be found on either side of the road that runs through the subdivision. Most of the site is privately owned. Please respect the landowners' wishes and stay on the road. There is little left to see in any case—mine diggings, tailings piles, adits, and a few pieces of rusted mine equipment.

The trail runs through the subdivision on a wide gravel road. There are many turns to the right and left on this first part of the route; most of them lead to private property. Remain on the major graded road until it finishes at a T-intersection marked Cyclopic Boulevard. Turn left and travel through the subdivision to the end, at which point the trail starts in earnest, climbing up a rise on a rough, single-track trail.

Immediately, you will see Joshua trees and be treated to wide-ranging Mohave Desert views as the rough track undulates across the western slope of the White Hills. The trail joins a wash and enters the White Hills before leaving the wash at a corral and starting to climb up the ridge.

There are many trails leading off the main trail; most are small but others can look like the main trail, which can make finding the route somewhat confusing. A GPS unit is an asset in picking the correct route. The road surface deteriorates as the trail climbs up on the ridge heading toward the mining settlement of Cyclopic. It can be severely washed out, which can make travel harder for wide vehicles; but it should be passable. The trail descends to Cyclopic, where an old water tank marks the northernmost boundary of the settlement. Little is left in Cyclopic—extensive diggings, tailings heaps, water tanks, and some concrete foundations.

Once past Cyclopic, the trail gradually improves in standard as it passes alongside Table Mountain Plateau and Archibald Corral. The trail ends at the paved Pierce Ferry Road. From here it is 16.2 miles to US 93.

The trail offers some excellent views across the Hualapai Valley to Garnet Mountain. The Mohave Desert vegetation, dense Joshua tree forest, and historic mining sites add interest to a trip in this seldom-traveled region. The naturally gravelly, loose trail is easily traveled by stock vehicles, although future washouts may render the trail more difficult.

Current Road Information

Bureau of Land Management
Kingman Field Office
2475 Beverly Ave.
Kingman, AZ 86401
(520) 692-4400

Map References

BLM Boulder City
USGS 1:24,000 White Hills West, White Hills East, Senator Mt., Gold Basin, Mt. Tipton NW
1:100,000 Boulder City
Maptech CD-ROM: Colorado River/Lake Havasu
Arizona Atlas & Gazetteer, p. 28
Arizona Road & Recreation Atlas, p. 32 & p. 66
Recreational Map of Arizona (incomplete)

Route Directions

Mileage			Directions
▼ 0.0			From US 93, 0.4 miles north of mile marker 29, just south of Boulder Inn, turn east on White Hills Road at the sign. Information board and historical marker at the turn. Zero trip meter. Remain on the paved road, ignoring small tracks on left and right.
	8.8 ▲		Trail ends at US 93 immediately south of Boulder Inn. Turn right for Hoover Dam; turn left for Kingman.
			GPS: N35°41.99' W114°28.43'
▼ 5.3		SO	Road turns to wide, graded dirt road. The site of White Hills is to the north of the road, with some mines on the south side of the road. Continue straight on the major dirt road, ignoring the tracks on left and right, which lead to houses. Continue straight on until the trail reaches a T-intersection.
	3.5 ▲	SO	The site of White Hills is to the north of the road, immediately before the point where the road becomes paved. Mining sites are on either side of the road.
▼ 8.8		TL	T-intersection of White Hills Road and Cyclopic Blvd. (signs for both roads). Turn left onto Cyclopic Blvd. Small track continues ahead. Zero trip meter.
	0.0 ▲		Continue through the subdivision; remain on main trail, ignoring tracks on right and left that lead to houses.
			GPS: N35°44.01' W114°19.10'
▼ 0.0			Continue north on Cyclopic Blvd.
	0.8 ▲	TR	Turn onto the major dirt White Hills Road, marked with a street sign. Zero trip meter.
▼ 0.1		SO	Rolling Ridge Drive on right.
	0.7 ▲	SO	Rolling Ridge Drive on left.
▼ 0.3		SO	Santa Cruz Drive on left and right.
	0.5 ▲	SO	Santa Cruz Drive on left and right.
▼ 0.4		SO	Cross through wash; followed by Escondido Drive on right and left.
	0.4 ▲	SO	Escondido Drive on right and left; then cross through wash.
			GPS: N35°44.36' W114°19.07'
▼ 0.8		SO	Crossroads. Zero trip meter.
	0.0 ▲		Continue on wider graded road through housing subdivision.
			GPS: N35°44.70' W114°18.87'
▼ 0.0			Continue on narrower trail and climb up hill.
	1.3 ▲	SO	Crossroads. Zero trip meter.
▼ 0.1		SO	Cross through wash.
	1.2 ▲	SO	Cross through wash.
▼ 0.2		SO	Cross through wash.
	1.1 ▲	SO	Cross through wash.
▼ 0.3		SO	Faint track on right.
	1.0 ▲	SO	Faint track on left.
▼ 0.6		SO	Cross through wash.
	0.7 ▲	SO	Cross through wash.
▼ 0.8		SO	Cross through wash.
	0.5 ▲	SO	Cross through wash.
▼ 1.0		SO	Enter wash channel.
	0.3 ▲	SO	Exit wash channel.
			GPS: N35°45.62' W114°18.64'
▼ 1.3		TR	Crossroads with slightly wider trail. Take the first right. Zero trip meter.
	0.0 ▲		Continue on narrower trail.
			GPS: N35°45.75' W114°18.50'
▼ 0.0			Continue to the northeast.
	2.4 ▲	TL	Crossroads with narrower trail. Take the first left and zero trip meter.
▼ 0.5		SO	Track along wash rejoins. Continue in wash.
	1.9 ▲	BL	Track forks; right-hand track travels in the wash.
▼ 0.8		BL	Swing left out of wash; corral on right.
	1.6 ▲	BR	Join the wash; corral on left.
▼ 1.0		SO	Cross through wash; then track on right.
	1.4 ▲	SO	Track on left; then cross through wash.
			GPS: N35°45.93' W114°17.59'
▼ 1.2		SO	Cross through wash.
	1.2 ▲	SO	Cross through wash.
▼ 1.4		SO	Pass through fence line.
	1.0 ▲	SO	Pass through fence line.

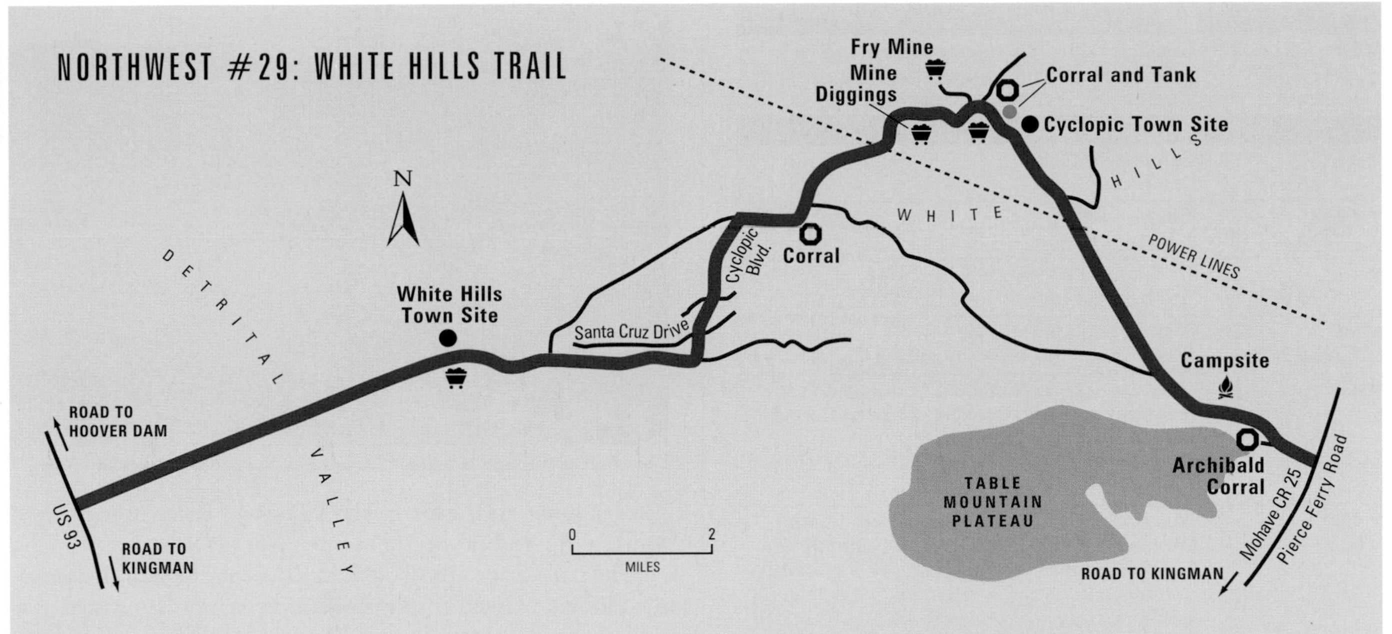

▼ 1.8	SO	Cross through wash.
0.6 ▲	SO	Cross through wash.
▼ 2.0	SO	Track on left.
0.4 ▲	SO	Track on right.
		GPS: N35°46.55′ W114°17.00′
▼ 2.4	BR	Large track on left along power lines. Bear right and follow power lines. Zero trip meter.
0.0 ▲		Continue away from the power lines.
		GPS: N35°46.66′ W114°16.55′
▼ 0.0		Continue along power lines.
2.0 ▲	BL	Wide track continues on right along power lines. Bear left away from power lines. Zero trip meter.
▼ 0.1	BL	Track on right at pylon.
1.9 ▲	BR	Track on left at pylon.
▼ 0.2	BL	Track on right up wash; bear left and start to climb up ridge.
1.8 ▲	SO	Bottom of ridge; track on left up wash.
▼ 0.7	SO	Crossroads on saddle. Track on right leads toward old mine diggings.
1.3 ▲	SO	Crossroads on saddle. Track on left leads to old mine diggings. Trail now descends from ridge.
		GPS: N35°47.02′ W114°16.10′
▼ 1.0	SO	Mine diggings on right.
1.0 ▲	SO	Mine diggings on left.
		GPS: N35°47.03′ W114°15.93′
▼ 1.1	SO	Track on right goes to a viewpoint over diggings and a network of small trails around them.
0.9 ▲	SO	Track on left goes to a viewpoint over diggings and a network of small trails around them.
		GPS: N35°47.05′ W114°15.84′
▼ 1.6	BL	Swing away from wash. Track on right goes to more diggings.
0.4 ▲	BR	Track on left goes to more diggings. Follow line of wash.
		GPS: N35°47.02′ W114°15.24′
▼ 1.7	SO	Track on right.
0.3 ▲	SO	Track on left.
▼ 1.9	TR	T-intersection. Track on left goes to Fry Mine.
0.1 ▲	TL	Track straight on goes to Fry Mine.
		GPS: N35°47.21′ W114°15.05′
▼ 2.0	TR	Track on left. Old water tank and corral at T-intersection. Zero trip meter.
0.0 ▲		Continue away from Cyclopic.
		GPS: N35°47.21′ W114°14.99′
▼ 0.0		Continue toward Cyclopic.
2.1 ▲	TL	Old water tank and corral at junction. Zero trip meter.
▼ 0.1	SO	Track on right into diggings. Trail is now traveling through the old diggings of Cyclopic. Numerous tracks on right and left into the various diggings.
2.0 ▲	SO	Track on left into diggings.
▼ 0.4	SO	Concrete foundations on right.
1.7 ▲	SO	Concrete foundations on left. Trail is now traveling through the old diggings of Cyclopic. Numerous tracks on right and left into various diggings.
▼ 0.6	SO	Cross through wash.
1.5 ▲	SO	Cross through wash.
▼ 0.7	SO	Cross through wash. Track on right up wash.
1.4 ▲	SO	Cross through wash. Track on left up wash.
		GPS: N35°46.74′ W114°14.43′
▼ 1.5	SO	Track on right.
0.6 ▲	SO	Track on left.
▼ 1.7	SO	Cross through wash; then track on left.
0.4 ▲	SO	Track on right; then cross through wash.
		GPS: N35°46.12′ W114°13.65′
▼ 2.1	SO	Crossroads under power lines. Zero trip meter.
0.0 ▲		Continue toward Cyclopic.
		GPS: N35°45.78′ W114°13.48′
▼ 0.0		Continue toward Pierce Ferry Road. Numerous small wash crossings for next 4.8 miles.
4.8 ▲	SO	Crossroads under power lines. Zero trip meter.
▼ 2.2	SO	Pass through fence line.
2.6 ▲	SO	Pass through fence line.
▼ 2.3	SO	Track on right goes to Butcher Camp. Main trail is now roughly graded.
2.5 ▲	SO	Track on left goes to Butcher Camp. Main trail is now a lesser standard.

			GPS: N35°44.04' W114°12.06'
▼ 2.8		SO	Track on right. Trail now follows along with Table Mountain Plateau on the right.
	2.0 ▲	BR	Track on left. Trail leaves Table Mountain Plateau.
			GPS: N35°43.64' W114°11.70'
▼ 3.4		SO	Campsite on left.
	1.4 ▲	SO	Campsite on right.
▼ 4.0		SO	Track on left.
	0.8 ▲	SO	Track on right.
▼ 4.1		SO	Track on right to Archibald Corral.
	0.7 ▲	SO	Track on left to Archibald Corral.
▼ 4.2		SO	Pass through fence line.
	0.6 ▲	SO	Pass through fence line. Archibald Corral on left.
▼ 4.3		BL	Track on right to Archibald Corral; then second track on right. Looking ahead at Cerbat Mountains to the south.
	0.5 ▲	BR	Track on left; then second track on left to Archibald Corral.
▼ 4.8			Trail ends at the paved Pierce Ferry Road (Mohave CR 25). Turn right for Kingman.
	0.0 ▲		Trail starts on the paved Pierce Ferry Road, immediately north of mile marker 17, 16.2 miles from the junction with US 93. Turn northwest on narrow, roughly graded dirt road and zero trip meter. Numerous wash crossings for next 4.8 miles. Table Mountain Plateau is on the left.
			GPS: N35°42.99' W114°09.73'

NORTHWEST REGION TRAIL #30

Eldorado Jeep Trail

Starting Point:	**US 93, 0.1 miles south of mile marker 20**
Finishing Point:	**Colorado River**
Total Mileage:	**13 miles**
Unpaved Mileage:	**13 miles**
Driving Time:	**1 hour (one-way)**
Elevation Range:	**700–3,100 feet**
Usually Open:	**Year-round**
Best Time to Travel:	**Fall to spring**
Difficulty Rating:	**3**
Scenic Rating:	**7**
Remoteness Rating:	**+1**

Special Attractions

- Old gold, silver, and copper mining remains.
- Colorado River access and camping in the Lake Mead National Recreation Area.
- Chance to see bighorn sheep and wild burros.

History

The Eldorado Jeep Trail runs down a canyon that is unnamed on the topographic maps of the region. It likely takes its name from the Eldorado Mountains on the far side of the Colorado River in Nevada. Eldorado Canyon, a well-known gold and

Descending through the Black Mountains toward the Colorado River

silver mining area, exits to the Colorado River immediately south of the end of this trail on the Nevada side.

The trail's exit to the Colorado River may be near the site of the Eldorado Camp, a short-lived army camp that existed as a military outpost for a few months in 1867. The camp, which was located on the west side of the Colorado River, just north of Eldorado Canyon, was founded to protect the miners in Eldorado Canyon from Indian attacks and to assist in the safe passage of steamboats upstream to Utah. However, when the first soldiers arrived to establish the camp on January 1, 1867, they found no steamboats, only three miners and a few scattered peaceful Paiute. But orders were orders, so the troops constructed the outpost and sat back waiting for further instructions. They were eventually recalled seven months later.

Description

This trail leads off from the southbound lane of the main divided US 93, 0.9 miles south of the signed Temple Bar Road. The junction is unmarked, but it is 0.1 miles south of mile marker 20. There is an informal crossing of the divided highway for vehicles traveling north. The trail immediately leads away from the highway. It travels through BLM land for the first stretch as it follows along the wash line, sometimes traveling in the wash. The vegetation is sparse—mainly creosote bush and tall Mohave yuccas.

The trail following the wash through a narrow gap in the Black Mountains

The trail leads toward the Black Mountains and for the first 3.2 miles is fairly wide and easy. It then turns off onto a smaller, single-lane trail, marked as the Eldorado Jeep Trail. Trails open for vehicle travel within the national recreation area are marked with a route number and yellow arrow. Travel on unmarked trails is not permitted. The trail now gradually descends toward Lake Mohave, twisting through the Black Mountains.

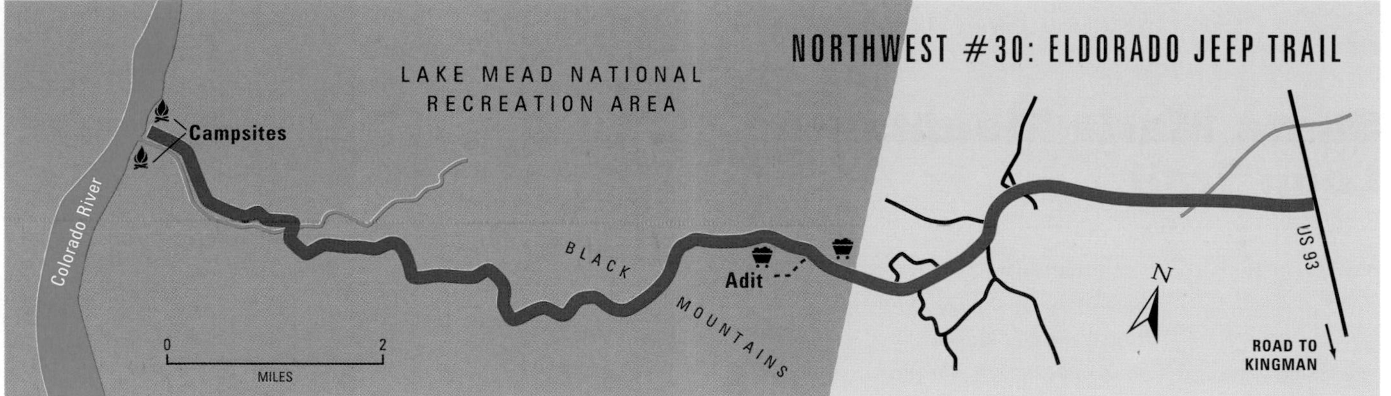

The remains of some old mines can be seen. They have been unused for a long time. Sharp-eyed travelers should watch for bighorn sheep on the cliffs, especially in the early mornings and evenings. Somewhat easier to spot are the small herds of wild burros that roam the area around Lake Mohave.

Vehicle-based camping is restricted to designated primitive sites in the Lake Mead National Recreation Area. The only camping area along this trail is at the very end. As the trail continues to descend through the recreation area, there are views over Lake Mohave to the Eldorado Mountains on the far side. The trail ends at a designated primitive camping area (currently no fee) on the Colorado River. There are no facilities—only two or three small sites set within the tamarisks in the wash. Do not camp here if there is any danger of flash flooding. There are many fish to be caught in Lake Mohave, including large-mouth bass, rainbow trout, bullhead catfish, crappie, and bluegill.

The trail surface is gravelly, loose, and similar to sand in how it affects vehicles, which will tend to bog down in the deep, loose areas of the washes. In the hot summer air, watch engine temperatures when you climb back up the trail. On the return trip, 4WD will be necessary for traction.

Current Road Information

Bureau of Land Management
Kingman Field Office
2475 Beverly Ave.
Kingman, AZ 86401
(520) 692-4400

Lake Mead National Recreation Area
601 Nevada Hwy.
Boulder City, NV 89005
(702) 293-8907

Map References

BLM Boulder City
USGS 1:24,000 Householder Pass, Mojave Mine, Fire Mt.
1:100,000 Boulder City
Maptech CD-ROM: Colorado River/Lake Havasu
Arizona Atlas & Gazetteer, p. 28
Trails Illustrated, Lake Mead National Recreation Area
Other: Lake Mead National Recreation Area Map

Route Directions

▼ 0.0		From the junction of US 93, 0.1 miles south of mile marker 20, turn southwest on unmarked trail. Zero trip meter. Immediately cross cattle guard and pass under power lines.
		GPS: N35°45.143' W114°30.145'
▼ 0.9	SO	Cross through wash.
▼ 1.2	SO	Cross through wash.
▼ 1.6	SO	Cross through wash.
▼ 2.0	SO	Enter wash.
▼ 2.6	SO	Track on left.
		GPS: N35°44.82' W114°32.97'
▼ 2.7	BR/SO	Trail forks; track on left, immediately followed by track on right.
▼ 2.8	SO	Cross through wash.
▼ 2.9	SO	Track on right.
▼ 3.0	SO	Cross through wash. Vehicles travel left and right down the wash.
▼ 3.2	BR	Track on left goes to diggings, immediately followed by fork. Track on left goes toward TV towers. Bear right at fork at sign "Eldorado Jeep Trail." Zero trip meter.
		GPS: N35°44.34' W114°33.26'
▼ 0.0		Continue along the small trail. Road is now marked as Lake Mead Recreation Area #54.
▼ 0.1	SO	Second entrance to track on left.
▼ 0.5	SO	Small track on right.
▼ 0.7	SO	Small track on left.
		GPS: N35°43.89' W114°33.82'
▼ 0.9	SO	Track on right on small saddle. Track starts to descend down wash, which quickly becomes narrower and starts to twist.
▼ 1.3	SO	Entering Lake Mead National Recreation Area. Zero trip meter.
		GPS: N35°43.80' W114°34.59'
▼ 0.0		Continue into recreation area.
▼ 0.2	SO	Old mining remains on right.
		GPS: N35°43.85' W114°34.65'
▼ 0.3	SO	Old mine shaft on right.
▼ 0.4	SO	Foot trail on left to old diggings; then old diggings on right of track.
▼ 0.9	TL	Track on right; turn in front of large mine adit, following the wash downstream. Track on right is dead end.
▼ 6.3	SO	Narrow section of trail in canyon.
▼ 6.6	BL	Trail joins another wash; bear left down wash, heading downhill.
		GPS: N35°43.34' W114°39.99'
▼ 8.0	SO	Colorado River comes into view.
▼ 8.5		Trail ends at designated primitive campsites on the Colorado River.
		GPS: N35°43.83' W114°41.62'

NORTHWEST REGION TRAIL #31

Santa Maria Mountains Loop Trail

Starting Point:	**Williamson Valley Road (CR 5), 22 miles north of the intersection with Iron Springs Road in Prescott**
Finishing Point:	**Williamson Valley Road (CR 5), 14 miles north of the starting point**
Total Mileage:	**35.3 miles**
Unpaved Mileage:	**35.3 miles**
Driving Time:	**2.5 hours**
Elevation Range:	**4,600–6,500 feet**
Usually Open:	**Year-round**
Best Time to Travel:	**Dry weather**
Difficulty Rating:	**2**
Scenic Rating:	**8**
Remoteness Rating:	**+1**

Special Attractions

- Long trail passing through a variety of forest vegetation.
- Excellent backcountry camping.
- Old Walnut Creek Cemetery and Walnut Creek Station.

Description

This long trail follows a wide loop through the Santa Maria Mountains in the Prescott National Forest. The main attraction of this lightly traveled trail is the range of forest scenery through which it passes. Initially, it travels through open ranchland as it heads toward the forest boundary. As the trail starts to climb into the forest, the landscape changes to low hills vegetated with pinyon, juniper, and a variety of low shrubs. As the elevation increases, tall ponderosa pines and oaks dominate. Most of the loop is lightly traveled and you may spend a couple of days, especially around the apex of the loop, without seeing another vehicle.

Walnut trees surround the old Walnut Creek Guard Station

Small stone building that covers a flowing spring near Merritt Spring

The trail starts off as a graded road and can be driven in a passenger vehicle as far as Camp Wood and the south end of Northwest #32: Walnut Creek Road. There is excellent camping around this intersection in the large, shady areas underneath the pines. Also at this intersection is Merritt Spring, set back in a clearing. At the back of the clearing is an old fruit orchard, indicating that somebody must have made a home here. There is no camping in the immediate area around the spring.

Once past Camp Wood, the trail drops in standard to become a single-lane trail, rough enough to need high clearance, although 4WD is not necessary under normal conditions. It is rutted and less used after it passes the entrance to the 7 Up Ranch. The trail continues to wind through the forest for a few miles before descending from a saddle to follow alongside the south fork of Walnut Creek. This section of the trail has good views to the north over Juniper Mesa.

The trail joins the larger graded road that runs beneath Juniper Mesa alongside Walnut Creek. The old Walnut Creek Guard Station is passed immediately after the north end of Northwest #32: Walnut Creek Road. The site is now jointly managed by the National Forest Service and an educational institution. It is not open to the public. The station and creek take their names from the native Arizona walnut trees in the area.

Shortly after Walnut Creek Guard Station, there is a narrow, faint trail to the north that leads 0.3 miles to the old Walnut Creek Cemetery. This trail can be a little tricky to find. Keep bearing left at the many forks in the trail and you will find the cemetery, surrounded by a fence. The coordinates of the site are given in the route directions, which will make it easier to locate.

Like other trails in this region, the Santa Maria Mountains Loop Trail should be driven in dry weather only. Light snow is possible during winter months.

Current Road Information

Prescott National Forest
Chino Valley Ranger District
735 North Hwy 89
PO Box 485
Chino Valley, AZ 86323
(520) 636-2302

Map References

BLM Prescott
USFS Prescott National Forest: Chino Valley Ranger District
USGS 1:24,000 Simmons, Seepage Mt., Camp Wood, Juniper Mts., Indian Peak
1:100,000 Prescott
Maptech CD-ROM: Flagstaff/Sedona/Prescott
Arizona Atlas & Gazetteer, p. 40
Arizona Road & Recreation Atlas, pp. 33, 34 & pp. 67, 68
Recreational Map of Arizona (incomplete)

Route Directions

▼ 0.0 From Prescott, take Iron Springs Road out of town; then turn north on Williamson Valley Road. Follow the paved road for 22 miles and turn west on unmarked road, which turns to graded dirt after the cattle guard. Zero trip meter at the intersection. There is a sign after the cattle guard, marking the road as FR 21 to Camp Wood.
4.8 ▲ Trail ends at the intersection with the paved Williamson Valley Road. Turn right for Prescott.

GPS: N34°49.94' W112°38.81'

▼ 0.5 SO Track on left.
4.3 ▲ SO Track on right.

▼ 1.8 SO Cross through Hitt Wash on concrete ford.
3.0 ▲ SO Cross through Hitt Wash on concrete ford.

▼ 2.5 SO Cattle guard.
2.3 ▲ SO Cattle guard.

▼ 3.5 SO Cattle guard.
1.3 ▲ SO Cattle guard.

GPS: N34°49.21' W112°41.97'

▼ 4.8 SO Entering Prescott National Forest at sign. Then track on right is FR 9805B. Zero trip meter.
0.0 ▲ Continue to the northeast.

GPS: N34°48.78' W112°43.32'

▼ 0.0 Continue to the southwest.
3.4 ▲ SO Track on left is FR 9805B. Leaving Prescott National Forest at sign. Zero trip meter.

▼ 0.8 SO Cattle guard.
2.6 ▲ SO Cattle guard.

▼ 1.1 SO Cross over creek on bridge.
2.3 ▲ SO Cross over creek on bridge.

GPS: N34°48.43' W112°44.39'

▼ 1.6 SO Track on right.
1.8 ▲ SO Track on left.

▼ 2.2 SO Track on right is FR 9807B; then cattle guard.
1.2 ▲ SO Cattle guard; then track on left is FR 9807B.

GPS: N34°48.86' W112°45.45'

▼ 2.3 SO Cross over Pine Creek on bridge.
1.1 ▲ SO Cross over Pine Creek on bridge.

▼ 2.4 SO Ranch road on left.
1.0 ▲ SO Ranch road on right.

▼ 3.4 SO Track on left is FR 666 through gate; then well. Zero trip meter.
0.0 ▲ Continue to the east.

GPS: N34°48.72' W112°46.59'

▼ 0.0 Continue to the west.
6.6 ▲ SO Well; then track on right is FR 666 through gate. Zero trip meter.

▼ 0.6 SO Cattle guard; then track on right is FR 9821B.
6.0 ▲ SO Track on left is FR 9821B; then cattle guard.

GPS: N34°48.75' W112°47.26'

▼ 0.7 SO Cross over creek on bridge.
5.9 ▲ SO Cross over creek on bridge.

▼ 1.0 SO Cross through creek; then track on right is FR 9871B.
5.6 ▲ SO Track on left is FR 9871B; then cross through creek.

GPS: N34°48.53' W112°47.60'

▼ 1.1 SO Cross over creek on bridge.
5.5 ▲ SO Cross over creek on bridge.

▼ 1.5 SO Cattle guard.
5.1 ▲ SO Cattle guard.

▼ 1.9 SO Trail #21 on left for hikers, horses, mountain bikes, dirt bikes, and ATVs—no vehicles. Johnson Mountain is on the right.
4.7 ▲ SO Trail #21 on right for hikers, horses, mountain bikes, dirt bikes, and ATVs—no vehicles. Johnson Mountain is on the left.

GPS: N34°48.06' W112°48.13'

▼ 3.0 SO Cross through wash; camping area on left.
3.6 ▲ SO Cross through wash; camping area on right.

▼ 3.1 SO Track on left is FR 9874B.
3.5 ▲ SO Track on right is FR 9874B.

GPS: N34°47.75' W112°49.36'

▼ 3.6 SO Track on right is FR 9872B.
3.0 ▲ SO Track on left is FR 9872B.

GPS: N34°47.69' W112°49.89'

▼ 3.9 SO Track on right is FR 6869B.
2.7 ▲ SO Track on left is FR 6869B.

▼ 5.9 SO Graded road on left is FR 705 to Cottonwood Canyon. Continue on, following the sign for Camp Wood.
0.7 ▲ SO Graded road on right is FR 705 to Cottonwood Canyon. Continue on, following the sign to Prescott.

GPS: N34°48.01' W112°51.91'

▼ 6.3 SO Track on right is FR 9877B.
0.3 ▲ SO Track on left is FR 9877B.

GPS: N34°48.05' W112°52.45'

▼ 6.4 SO Trail #5 on left for hikers, horses, mountain bikes, dirt bikes, and ATVs—no vehicles. Then cattle guard.
0.2 ▲ SO Cattle guard. Then Trail #5 on right for hikers, horses, mountain bikes, dirt bikes, and ATVs—no vehicles.

▼ 6.6 SO Graded road on right is Northwest #32: Walnut Creek Road, FR 95, to Camp Wood Station. Zero trip meter.
0.0 ▲ Continue to the northeast.

GPS: N34°48.05' W112°52.72'

▼ 0.0 Continue to the southwest, following the sign to the 7 Up Ranch. Merritt Spring is immediately after the intersection on left. Also on left is Trail #9 for hikers, horses, mountain bikes, dirt bikes, and ATVs—no vehicles.
2.5 ▲ SO Merritt Spring on right. Also on right is Trail #9 for hikers, horses, mountain bikes, dirt bikes, and ATVs—no vehicles. Then graded road on left is Northwest #32: Walnut Creek Road, FR 95, to Camp Wood Station. Zero trip meter.

▼ 0.4 SO Track on right to a stone building covering a flowing spring.
2.1 ▲ SO Track on left to a stone building covering a flowing spring.

GPS: N34°48.01' W112°53.16'

▼ 1.7 SO Track on right.
0.8 ▲ SO Track on left.

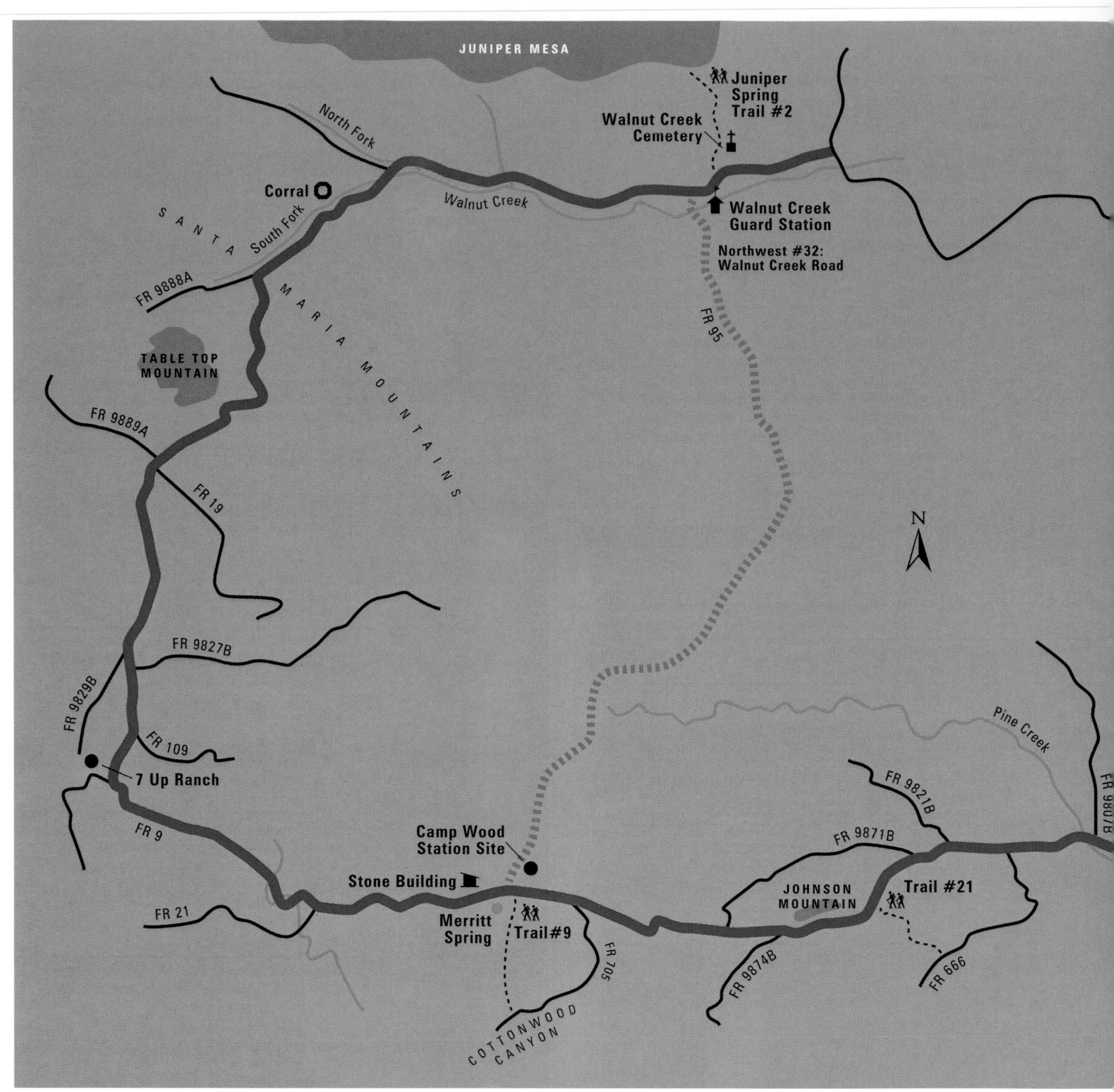

▼ 2.1	SO	Trail #9836 on left for hikers, horses, mountain bikes, dirt bikes, and ATVs—no vehicles.
0.4 ▲	SO	Trail #9836 on right for hikers, horses, mountain bikes, dirt bikes, and ATVs—no vehicles.
		GPS: N34°47.83' W112°54.77'
▼ 2.5	TR	Turn right onto graded dirt road, FR 9, to 7 Up Ranch. FR 21 continues ahead. Zero trip meter.
0.0 ▲		Continue to the northeast on FR 21.
		GPS: N34°47.80' W112°55.12'
▼ 0.0		Continue to the west on FR 9.
3.1 ▲	TL	T-intersection with FR 21. Turn left onto graded dirt road following the sign for Prescott. Road is now FR 21. Zero trip meter.
▼ 0.2	SO	Cross through wash.
2.9 ▲	SO	Cross through wash.
▼ 0.4	SO	Cross through wash.
2.6 ▲	SO	Cross through wash.
▼ 0.5	SO	Cross through wash.
2.5 ▲	SO	Cross through wash.
▼ 0.8	SO	Cross through wash.
2.3 ▲	SO	Cross through wash.
▼ 1.0	SO	Cross through wash.
2.1 ▲	SO	Cross through wash.
▼ 1.6	SO	Track on left.
1.5 ▲	SO	Track on right.
▼ 1.7	SO	Cross through wash.
1.4 ▲	SO	Cross through wash.

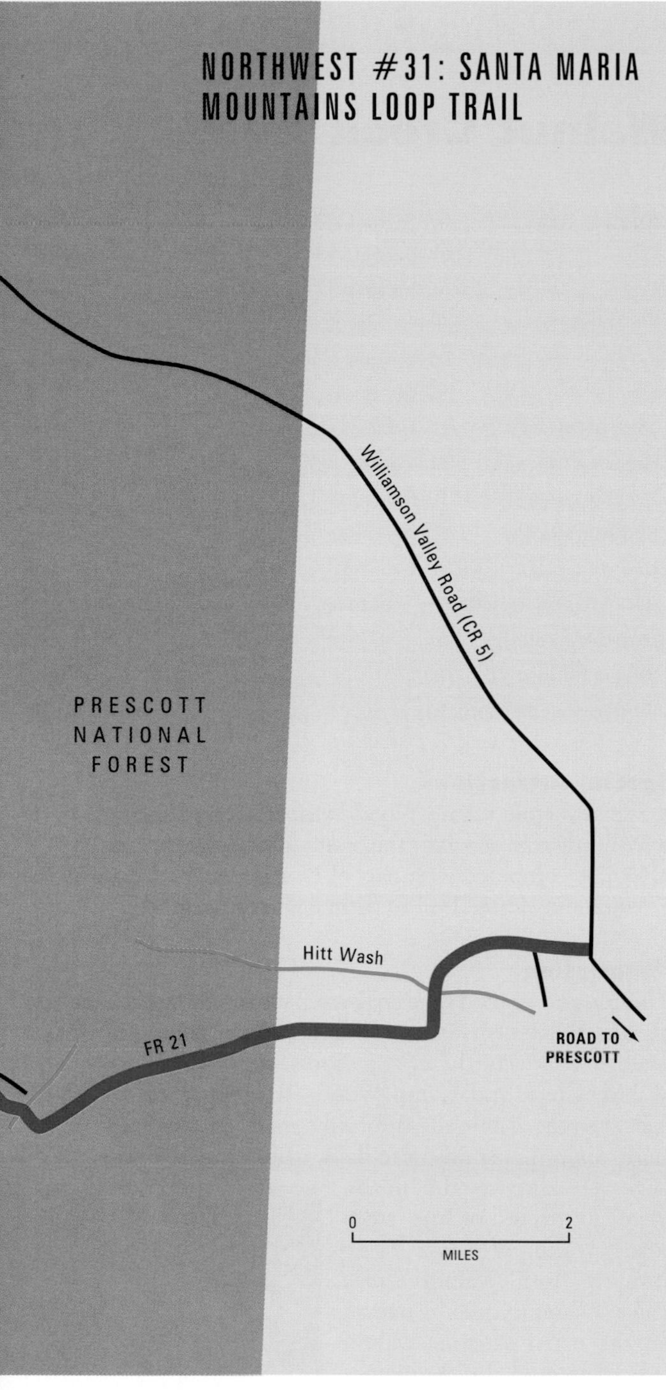

Mileage		Direction
▼ 1.9	SO	Cattle guard.
1.2 ▲	SO	Cattle guard.
▼ 2.0	SO	Track on left.
1.1 ▲	SO	Track on right.
▼ 2.4	SO	Cross through wash; then track on left.
0.7 ▲	SO	Track on right; then cross through wash.
▼ 3.1	TR	Turn right in front of 7 Up Ranch gates and zero trip meter.
0.0 ▲		Continue to the east on FR 9.
		GPS: N34°48.98′ W112°57.75′
▼ 0.0		Continue to the north on FR 9.
4.1 ▲	TL	Turn left, remaining on FR 9. The 7 Up Ranch gates are on the right. Zero trip meter.
▼ 0.3	SO	Track on left is FR 9828B.
3.8 ▲	SO	Track on right is FR 9828B.
		GPS: N34°49.24′ W112°57.73′
▼ 0.5	SO	Track on right is FR 109.
3.6 ▲	SO	Track on left is FR 109.
		GPS: N34°49.35′ W112°57.68′
▼ 1.3	SO	Track on right.
2.8 ▲	SO	Track on left.
▼ 1.5	SO	Track on right is FR 9827B.
2.6 ▲	SO	Track on left is FR 9827B.
		GPS: N34°50.20′ W112°57.57′
▼ 1.8	SO	Track on left is FR 9829B.
2.3 ▲	SO	Track on right is FR 9829B.
		GPS: N34°50.43′ W112°57.60′
▼ 2.1	SO	Cross through wash.
2.0 ▲	SO	Cross through wash.
▼ 2.5	SO	Cattle guard.
1.6 ▲	SO	Cattle guard.
▼ 2.8	SO	Cross through wash.
1.3 ▲	SO	Cross through wash.
▼ 3.5	SO	Cross through wash.
0.6 ▲	SO	Cross through wash.
▼ 3.7	SO	Track on left; then cross through wash.
0.4 ▲	SO	Cross through wash; then track on right.
▼ 4.0	SO	Track on right is FR 19.
0.1 ▲	SO	Track on left is FR 19.
▼ 4.1	SO	Track on left is FR 9889A. There is a vehicle travel information sign at the intersection. Zero trip meter.
0.0 ▲		Continue to the southwest.
		GPS: N34°52.37′ W112°57.40′
▼ 0.0		Continue to the northeast.
5.4 ▲	SO	Track on right is FR 9889A. There is a vehicle travel information sign at the intersection. Zero trip meter.
▼ 0.8	SO	Cattle guard.
4.6 ▲	SO	Cattle guard.
▼ 1.2	SO	Saddle. Table Top Mountain on left.
4.2 ▲	SO	Saddle. Table Top Mountain on right.
▼ 1.7	SO	Track on right.
3.7 ▲	SO	Track on left.
▼ 2.4	SO	Cross through wash.
3.0 ▲	SO	Cross through wash.
		GPS: N34°53.67′ W112°56.18′
▼ 2.6	SO	Cross through wash.
2.8 ▲	SO	Cross through wash.
▼ 3.2	BR	Track on left is FR 9888A.
2.2 ▲	BL	Track on right is FR 9888A.
		GPS: N34°54.36′ W112°56.28′
▼ 3.5	SO	Track on left through gate.
1.9 ▲	SO	Track on right through gate.
▼ 3.6	SO	Track on right.
1.8 ▲	SO	Track on left.
▼ 3.7	SO	Cross through wash.
1.7 ▲	SO	Cross through wash.
▼ 4.8	SO	Corral on left.
0.6 ▲	SO	Corral on right.
▼ 5.0	SO	Cross through South Fork Walnut Creek.
0.4 ▲	SO	Cross through South Fork Walnut Creek.
▼ 5.1	SO	Cattle guard.
0.3 ▲	SO	Cattle guard.
▼ 5.4	TR	T-intersection; turn right onto wider graded dirt road following the sign to Walnut Creek Station. Zero trip meter. Juniper Mesa is directly ahead.

▼	▲		
	0.0 ▲		Continue to the southwest.
			GPS: N34°55.55' W112°54.51'
▼ 0.0			Continue to the east.
	3.6 ▲	TL	Turn left onto narrower, roughly graded road, FR 9, following the sign to 7 Up Ranch. Track ahead goes to a locked gate in 3 miles.
▼ 0.2		SO	Cross through wash; then cattle guard.
	3.4 ▲	SO	Cattle guard; then cross through wash.
▼ 0.3		SO	Track on left.
	3.3 ▲	SO	Track on right.
▼ 0.4		SO	Cross through wash.
	3.2 ▲	SO	Cross through wash.
▼ 1.3		SO	Cross over creek on bridge.
	2.3 ▲	SO	Cross over creek on bridge.
▼ 1.6		SO	Cross through wash.
	2.0 ▲	SO	Cross through wash.
▼ 1.8		SO	Ranch entrance on right.
	1.8 ▲	SO	Ranch entrance on left.
▼ 2.2		SO	Track on right.
	1.4 ▲	SO	Track on left.
▼ 2.5		SO	Ranch entrance on right.
	1.1 ▲	SO	Ranch entrance on left.
▼ 2.8		SO	Ranch entrance on right.
	0.8 ▲	SO	Ranch entrance on left.
▼ 3.3		SO	Exiting the Box L Ranch; then track on left.
	0.3 ▲	SO	Track on right; then entering the Box L Ranch; remain on county road.
			GPS: N34°55.40' W112°51.02'
▼ 3.6		BL	Track on right is Northwest #32: Walnut Creek Road, FR 95. Zero trip meter.
	0.0 ▲		Continue to the west, following the sign toward Oro Ranch.
			GPS: N34°55.36' W112°50.68'
▼ 0.0			Continue to the northeast, road is now marked Yavapai CR 125 following the sign to Prescott.
	1.8 ▲	BR	Track on left is Northwest #32: Walnut Creek Road, FR 95. Zero trip meter.
▼ 0.1		SO	Walnut Creek Guard Station on right.
	1.7 ▲	SO	Walnut Creek Guard Station on left.
			GPS: N34°55.41' W112°50.61'
▼ 0.3		SO	Juniper Spring Trail #2 for hikers and horses on left; then cattle guard.
	1.5 ▲	SO	Cattle guard; then Juniper Spring Trail #2 for hikers and horses on right.
			GPS: N34°55.58' W112°50.47'
▼ 0.6		SO	Cross through wash; then small, faint track on left goes 0.5 miles to the old Walnut Creek Cemetery—coordinates for cemetery are GPS: N34°55.79' W112°50.43'. The spur is 3-rated; keep left at the intersections.
	1.2 ▲	SO	Small, faint track on right goes 0.5 miles to the old Walnut Creek Cemetery—coordinates for cemetery are GPS: N34°55.79' W112°50.43'. The spur is 3-rated; keep left at the intersections. Cross through wash.
▼ 1.8			Trail ends at the intersection with the graded dirt road, CR 5. Turn right for Prescott.
	0.0 ▲		Trail commences on CR 5, 36 miles north of Prescott and 14 miles north of the south end of the trail. Zero trip meter and turn southwest on graded dirt road marked Yavapai CR 125. Junction is 0.2 miles north of the single-lane steel bridge over Walnut Creek. Immediately after the turn, the road is sign-posted to Walnut Creek Station.
			GPS: N34°55.91' W112°48.98'

NORTHWEST REGION TRAIL #32

Walnut Creek Road

Starting Point:	**Northwest #31: Santa Maria Mountains Loop Trail, 1.8 miles from the north end of the loop**
Finishing Point:	**Northwest #31: Santa Maria Mountains Loop Trail, 14.8 miles from the south end of the loop**
Total Mileage:	**10.4 miles**
Unpaved Mileage:	**10.4 miles**
Driving Time:	**1 hour**
Elevation Range:	**5,200–5,800 feet**
Usually Open:	**Year-round**
Best Time to Travel:	**Dry weather**
Difficulty Rating:	**2**
Scenic Rating:	**8**
Remoteness Rating:	**+1**

Special Attractions

- Site of the old Camp Wood National Forest Station.
- Winding trail through the Santa Maria Mountains.
- Can be combined with part of Northwest #31: Santa Maria Mountains Loop Trail to form a shorter loop trail.

Description

This roughly graded road makes a pleasant alternative to driving the full Northwest #31: Santa Maria Mountains Loop Trail. It connects the two national forest guard stations of Walnut Creek and Camp Wood. Traveling from the north end, the road is initially smoothly graded as it crosses private land, climbing up onto the flank of the Santa Maria Mountains. Looking to the north, there are views of the steep edge of Juniper Mesa rising abruptly from Walnut Creek Valley. Walnut Creek is named for the native Arizona walnut trees that grow in abundance along its course.

As it enters the forest, the trail becomes a single-track road and is not as smooth; a high-clearance vehicle is needed for some of the wash crossings and a few rocky sections, mainly toward the south end. The trail climbs steadily upward, leaving the pinyon and juniper vegetation to enter an area of ponderosa pines. There are many pleasant campsites among the

One of the many creek crossings along this trail

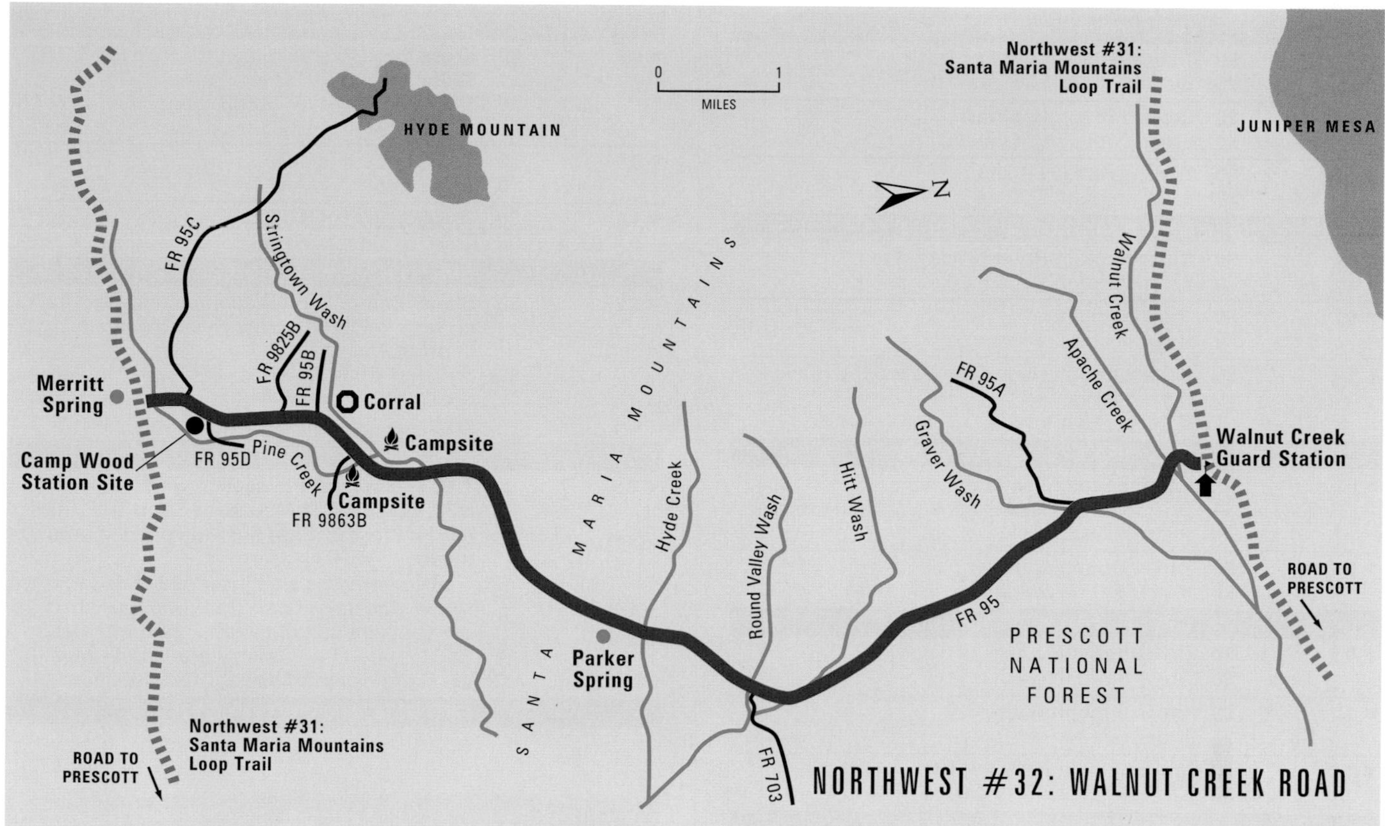

pines, mainly toward the south end of the trail.

The trail passes by the site of Camp Wood National Forest Station, which was actively used by rangers into the 1990s. Only the foundations of the building remain in the clearing because the station was dismantled by the forest service. Opposite the Camp Wood site, a road leads up toward the Hyde Fire Lookout.

The trail ends where it rejoins Northwest #31: Santa Maria Mountains Loop Trail at Merritt Spring, 14.8 miles from the south end. Like other trails in this region, Walnut Creek Road should be driven in dry weather only. Light snow is possible during winter months.

Current Road Information

Prescott National Forest
Chino Valley Ranger District
735 North Hwy. 89
PO Box 485
Chino Valley, AZ 86323
(520) 636-2302

Map References

BLM Prescott
USFS Prescott National Forest: Chino Valley Ranger District
USGS 1:24,000 Indian Peak, Seepage Mt., Camp Wood
1:100,000 Prescott
Maptech CD-ROM: Flagstaff/Sedona/Prescott
Arizona Atlas & Gazetteer, p. 40
Arizona Road & Recreation Atlas, p. 34 & p. 68
Recreational Map of Arizona

Route Directions

▼ 0.0		From Northwest #31: Santa Maria Mountains Loop Trail (CR 125), 1.8 miles from the north end, zero trip meter and turn southwest on the narrow, roughly graded dirt road, FR 95. Road is signed to Camp Wood; then cross through wash.
5.4 ▲		Cross through wash; then trail ends at the intersection with Northwest #31: Santa Maria Mountains Loop Trail (CR 125). Turn right to exit to Prescott; turn left to continue around the loop.
		GPS: N34°55.36' W112°50.68'
▼ 0.2	SO	Cross through Walnut Creek.
5.2 ▲	SO	Cross through Walnut Creek.
▼ 0.3	SO	Cross through Apache Creek.
5.1 ▲	SO	Cross through Apache Creek.
▼ 0.6	SO	Cattle guard.
4.8 ▲	SO	Cattle guard.
▼ 0.9	SO	Track on right.
4.5 ▲	SO	Track on left.
▼ 1.2	SO	Track on right is FR 95A; then cross through Graver Wash.
4.2 ▲	SO	Cross through Graver Wash; then track on left is FR 95A.
		GPS: N34°54.48' W112°50.55'
▼ 1.3	SO	Track on right; then cattle guard; then track on left.
4.1 ▲	SO	Track on right; then cattle guard; then track on left.
▼ 2.3	SO	Cattle guard.
3.1 ▲	SO	Cattle guard.
▼ 3.7	SO	Cross through creek.
1.7 ▲	SO	Cross through creek.

Mileage		Directions
		GPS: N34°52.55′ W112°49.43′
▼ 3.9	SO	Track on left.
1.5 ▲	SO	Track on right.
▼ 4.0	SO	Cross through Hitt Wash.
1.4 ▲	SO	Cross through Hitt Wash.
▼ 4.3	SO	Track on left is FR 703.
1.1 ▲	SO	Track on right is FR 703.
		GPS: N34°52.01′ W112°49.42′
▼ 4.4	SO	Cross through Round Valley Wash.
1.0 ▲	SO	Cross through Round Valley Wash.
▼ 5.2	SO	Track on right.
0.2 ▲	SO	Track on left.
▼ 5.4	SO	Cross through Hyde Creek. Zero trip meter at the crossing.
0.0 ▲		Continue to the north.
		GPS: N34°51.25′ W112°50.05′
▼ 0.0		Continue to the south.
3.5 ▲	SO	Cross through Hyde Creek. Zero trip meter at the crossing.
▼ 0.4	SO	Parker Spring on left.
3.1 ▲	SO	Parker Spring on right.
		GPS: N34°50.98′ W112°50.25′
▼ 0.5	SO	Cross through wash.
3.0 ▲	SO	Cross through wash.
▼ 1.2	SO	Cross through wash.
2.3 ▲	SO	Cross through wash.
▼ 1.3	SO	Track on right is FR 9821B to mine tailings.
2.2 ▲	SO	Track on left is FR 9821B to mine tailings.
		GPS: N34°50.43′ W112°50.98′
▼ 1.6	SO	Track on right.
1.9 ▲	SO	Track on left.
▼ 1.9	SO	Cross through wash.
1.6 ▲	SO	Cross through wash.
▼ 2.0	SO	Cattle guard.
1.5 ▲	SO	Cattle guard.
▼ 2.3	SO	Cattle guard.
1.2 ▲	SO	Cattle guard.
▼ 2.5	SO	Cross through Pine Creek; then track on left.
1.0 ▲	SO	Track on right; then cross through Pine Creek.
		GPS: N34°49.93′ W112°51.81′
▼ 2.6	SO	Track on left.
0.9 ▲	SO	Track on right.
▼ 2.7	SO	Cross through wash.
0.8 ▲	SO	Cross through wash.
▼ 3.0	SO	Cross through Pine Creek; campsites on either side of the trail.
0.5 ▲	SO	Cross through Pine Creek; campsites on either side of the trail.
		GPS: N34°49.54′ W112°51.97′
▼ 3.1	SO	Track on left is FR 9863B.
0.4 ▲	SO	Track on right is FR 9863B.
▼ 3.5	SO	Stringtown Wash on right; corral on right; then track on right is FR 95B. Zero trip meter.
0.0 ▲		Continue to the northeast.
		GPS: N34°49.29′ W112°52.35′
▼ 0.0	SO	Continue to the southwest.
1.5 ▲	SO	Track on left is FR 95B; then corral on left; Stringtown Wash on left. Zero trip meter.
▼ 0.3	SO	Track on left.
1.2 ▲	SO	Track on right.
▼ 0.4	SO	Track on right is FR 9825B; then cattle guard.
1.1 ▲	SO	Cattle guard; then track on left is FR 9825B.
		GPS: N34°48.96′ W112°52.45′
▼ 0.5	SO	Cross through creek; then track on left is FR 9865B.
1.0 ▲	SO	Track on right is FR 9865B; then cross through creek.
▼ 0.9	SO	Cross through creek.
0.6 ▲	SO	Cross through creek.
▼ 1.0	SO	Track on left is FR 95D.
0.5 ▲	SO	Track on right is FR 95D.
		GPS: N34°48.40′ W112°52.57′
▼ 1.2	SO	Site of Camp Wood Station on left; then track on right is FR 95C to the Hyde Mountain Lookout Trail.
0.3 ▲	SO	Track on left is FR 95C to the Hyde Mountain Lookout Trail; then site of Camp Wood Station on right.
		GPS: N34°48.30′ W112°52.69′
▼ 1.5		Trail ends at the intersection with Northwest #31: Santa Maria Mountains Loop Trail. Turn left for Prescott; turn right to continue around the loop.
0.0 ▲		Trail commences along Northwest #31: Santa Maria Mountains Loop Trail, 14.8 miles from the southern end of the trail. Zero trip meter and turn north on roughly graded dirt road, FR 95, sign-posted to Walnut Creek Station.
		GPS: N34°48.05′ W112°52.72′

NORTHWEST REGION TRAIL #33

Tonto Wash Trail

Starting Point:	**Iron Springs Road, 10 miles north of Prescott**
Finishing Point:	**Williamson Valley Road, 15.2 miles north of Prescott**
Total Mileage:	**16.2 miles**
Unpaved Mileage:	**15.5 miles**
Driving Time:	**1.5 hours**
Elevation Range:	**4,600–5,000 feet**
Usually Open:	**Year-round**
Best Time to Travel:	**Dry weather only**
Difficulty Rating:	**2**
Scenic Rating:	**7**
Remoteness Rating:	**+0**

Special Attractions

- Pleasant, easy trail that crosses through ranchland and Prescott National Forest.
- Views of Granite Mountain.

Description

This easy trail follows the broad valleys of Tonto Wash and Long Canyon, passing close to Tonto Mountain. The majority of the trail lies within Prescott National Forest; the rest passes through the open ranchland of Arizona's cattle country.

Most of Tonto Wash Trail is an easy graded road. Only a couple of rough rutted sections make high-clearance preferable. There are excellent views of the gray peak of Granite Mountain to the northeast and the Santa Maria Mountains to the north. Camping is a bit restricted because of private property, but there are many side forest roads leading off from the main trail where it is possible to find a secluded site.

Current Road Information

Prescott National Forest
Bradshaw Ranger District
344 South Cortes St.
Prescott, AZ 86303
(520) 771-4700

Maps References

BLM Prescott
USFS Prescott National Forest: Bradshaw Ranger District
USGS 1:24,000 Skull Valley, Mt. Josh, Simmons, Sullivan Buttes
1:100,000 Prescott
Maptech CD-ROM: Flagstaff/Sedona/Prescott
Arizona Atlas & Gazetteer, p. 40
Arizona Road & Recreation Atlas, p. 40 & p. 74

Route Directions

▼ 0.0		Leave Prescott to the northwest along Iron Springs Road. Enter the Prescott National Forest and proceed for 10 miles to Tonto Road. Turn northwest down the graded dirt Tonto Road and zero trip meter.
2.7 ▲		Trail ends at the intersection with Iron Springs Road. Turn left for Prescott; turn right for Skull Valley.
		GPS: N34°33.87' W112°39.95'
▼ 0.1	SO	Cattle guard.
2.6 ▲	SO	Cattle guard.
▼ 0.2	SO	Track on left.
2.5 ▲	SO	Track on right.
▼ 0.5	SO	Cross through wash.
2.2 ▲	SO	Cross through wash.
▼ 0.6	SO	Cattle guard; then pass under railroad track; then track on left and track on right.
2.1 ▲	SO	Track on left and track on right; then pass under railroad track; then cattle guard.
		GPS: N34°34.22' W112°40.49'
▼ 1.4	SO	Cross through wash.
1.3 ▲	SO	Cross through wash.
▼ 2.2	SO	Entering Prescott National Forest over cattle guard.
0.5 ▲	SO	Leaving Prescott National Forest over cattle guard.
		GPS: N34°35.56' W112°40.16'
▼ 2.7	SO	Graded road on left is FR 65, sign-posted for Tonto Spring and Tank Creek Mesa. Zero trip meter.
0.0 ▲		Continue to the south.
		GPS: N34°36.06' W112°40.17'
▼ 0.0		Continue to the north.
4.4 ▲	SO	Graded road on right is FR 65, sign-posted for Tonto Spring and Tank Creek Mesa. Zero trip meter.

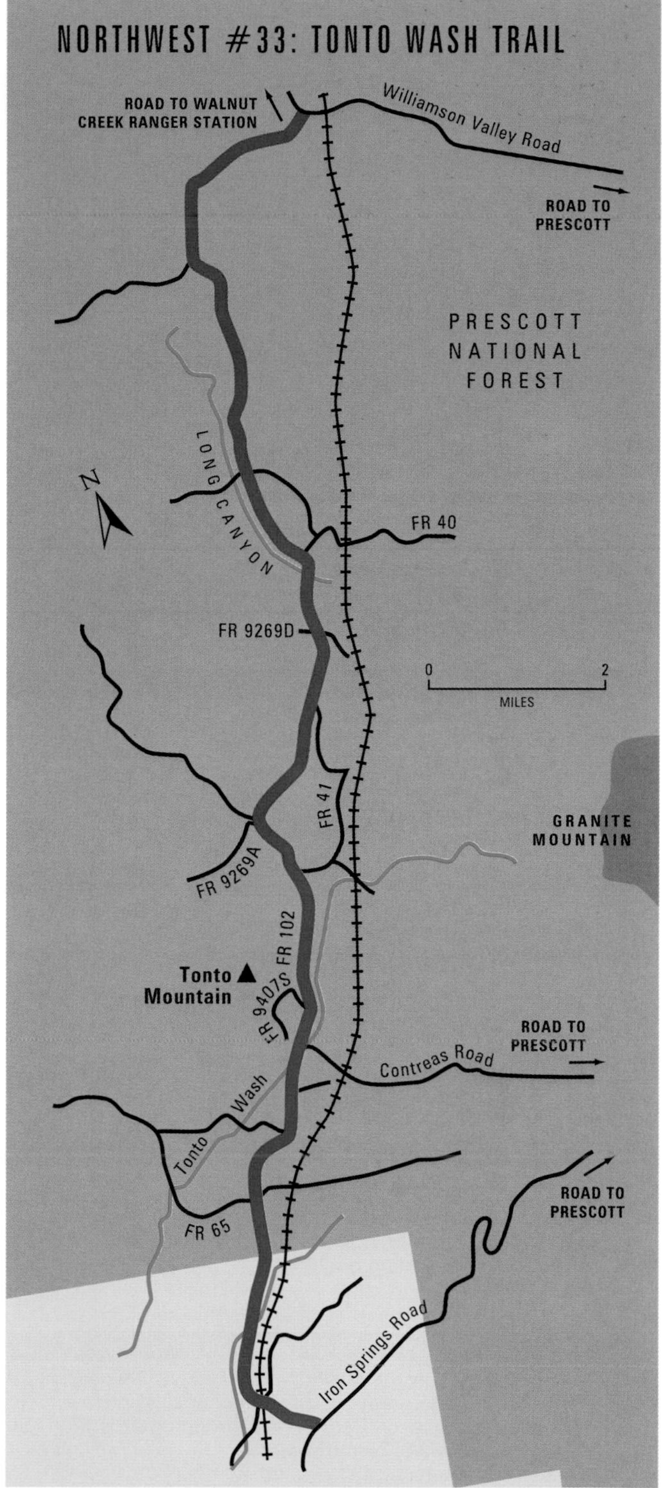

▼ 0.1	SO	Track on right.
4.3 ▲	SO	Track on left.
▼ 0.4	SO	Cattle guard.
4.0 ▲	SO	Cattle guard.
▼ 0.5	BR	Tonto Ranch Road on left.
3.9 ▲	BL	Tonto Ranch Road on right.
		GPS: N34°36.48' W112°39.97'
▼ 0.9	SO	Graded road on left.
3.5 ▲	SO	Graded road on right.

A monsoonal storm gathers over Granite Mountain

▼ 1.3 SO Track on right.
3.1 ▲ SO Track on left.

▼ 1.4 SO Cattle guard.
3.0 ▲ SO Cattle guard.

GPS: N34°37.14' W112°39.47'

▼ 1.6 SO Track on left.
2.8 ▲ SO Track on right.

▼ 1.8 SO Graded road on right is Contreas Road to Prescott. Continue toward Fair Oaks Road.
2.6 ▲ SO Graded road on left is Contreas Road to Prescott. Continue following sign to Skull Valley.

GPS: N34°37.45' W112°39.25'

▼ 1.9 BL Track on right to ranch; then cross through Tonto Wash.
2.5 ▲ BR Cross through Tonto Wash; then track on left to ranch.

▼ 2.3 SO Track on left is FR 9407S.
2.1 ▲ SO Track on right is FR 9407S.

GPS: N34°37.88' W112°39.05'

▼ 2.7 SO Ranch entrance on right.
1.7 ▲ SO Ranch entrance on left.

▼ 3.5 SO Track on left.
0.9 ▲ SO Track on right.

▼ 3.7 SO Entering ranch property; remain on road. Track on right is FR 41. Continue straight on, remaining on FR 102.
0.7 ▲ SO Leaving ranch property. Track on left is FR 41. Continue straight on, remaining on FR 102.

GPS: N34°39.13' W112°38.99'

▼ 4.4 TR 4-way intersection. Turn right, remaining on main graded road. Ahead goes to private property. Track on left through gate is FR 9269A. Zero trip meter.
0.0 ▲ Continue to the southeast.

GPS: N34°39.66' W112°39.31'

▼ 0.0 Continue to the northeast.
4.3 ▲ TL 4-way intersection. Turn left, remaining on main graded road. Graded road on right goes to private property. Track ahead through gate is FR 9269A. Zero trip meter.

▼ 1.4 SO Cross through wash; then track on right is FR 41.
2.9 ▲ SO Track on left is FR 41; then cross through wash.

GPS: N34°40.69' W112°38.38'

▼ 2.1 SO Cross through wash; then track on right. Track on left is FR 9269D.
2.2 ▲ SO Track on right is FR 9269D. Track on left; then cross through wash.

GPS: N34°41.26' W112°38.19'

▼ 2.2 SO Cattle guard; then track on right.
2.1 ▲ SO Track on left; then cattle guard.

▼ 2.8 SO Cross through wash.
1.5 ▲ SO Cross through wash.

▼ 2.9 SO Track on right is FR 40.
1.4 ▲ SO Track on left is FR 40.

GPS: N34°41.96' W112°38.17'

▼ 3.3 SO Track on left.
1.0 ▲ SO Track on right.

▼ 3.5 SO Track on left.
0.8 ▲ SO Track on right.

▼ 4.0 SO Track on left.
0.3 ▲ SO Track on right.

▼ 4.3 SO Track on left; then cattle guard, entering ranch property. Second track on left after cattle guard into ranch. Leaving Prescott National Forest. Zero trip meter.
0.0 ▲ Continue to the south.

GPS: N34°43.11' W112°38.74'

▼ 0.0 Continue to the north.
2.4 ▲ SO Entering Prescott National Forest. Track on right into ranch. Then cattle guard and second track on right. Zero trip meter.

▼ 0.9 SO Gravel road on right.
1.5 ▲ SO Gravel road on left.

▼ 1.1 SO Ranch road on right and left.
1.3 ▲ SO Ranch road on right and left.

▼ 2.0 SO Graded dirt road on right.
0.4 ▲ SO Graded dirt road on left.

▼ 2.4 TR T-intersection. Turn right onto graded dirt road, following the sign toward Camp Wood and Walnut Creek. Zero trip meter.
0.0 ▲ Continue to the southeast.

GPS: N34°45.04' W112°38.81'

▼ 0.0 Continue to the north.
2.4 ▲ TL Turn left onto graded dirt road, following the sign to Skull Valley. Zero trip meter.

▼ 0.7 SO Road turns to paved.
1.7 ▲ SO Road turns to graded dirt.

▼ 2.4 Trail ends at the intersection with Williamson Valley Road, FR 5. Turn right for Prescott; turn left for Walnut Creek Ranger Station.
0.0 ▲ Trail commences on Williamson Valley Road, FR 5, 15.2 miles from Prescott. Zero trip meter and turn southwest on paved road. The intersection is marked for Fair Oaks Road and is north of the railroad, immediately north of a cattle guard.

GPS: N34°46.40' W112°37.11'

The Northeast Region

Trails in the Northeast Region

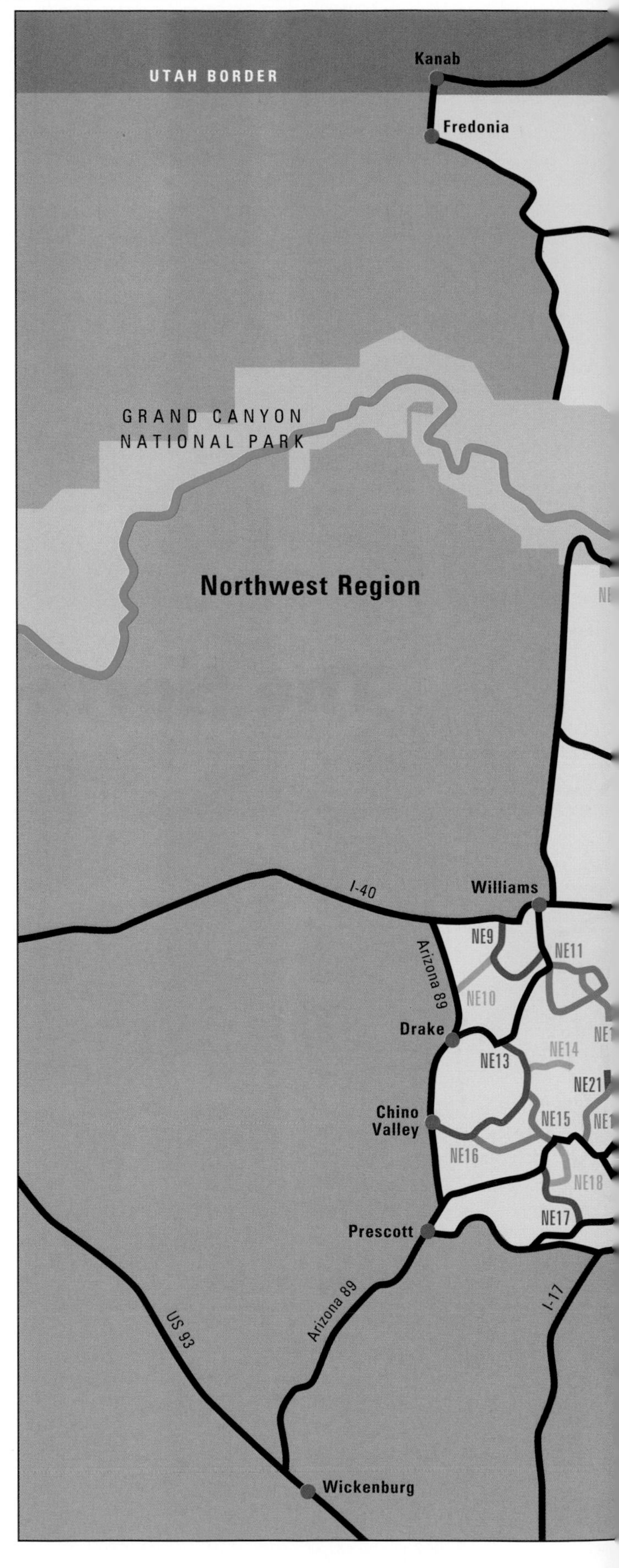

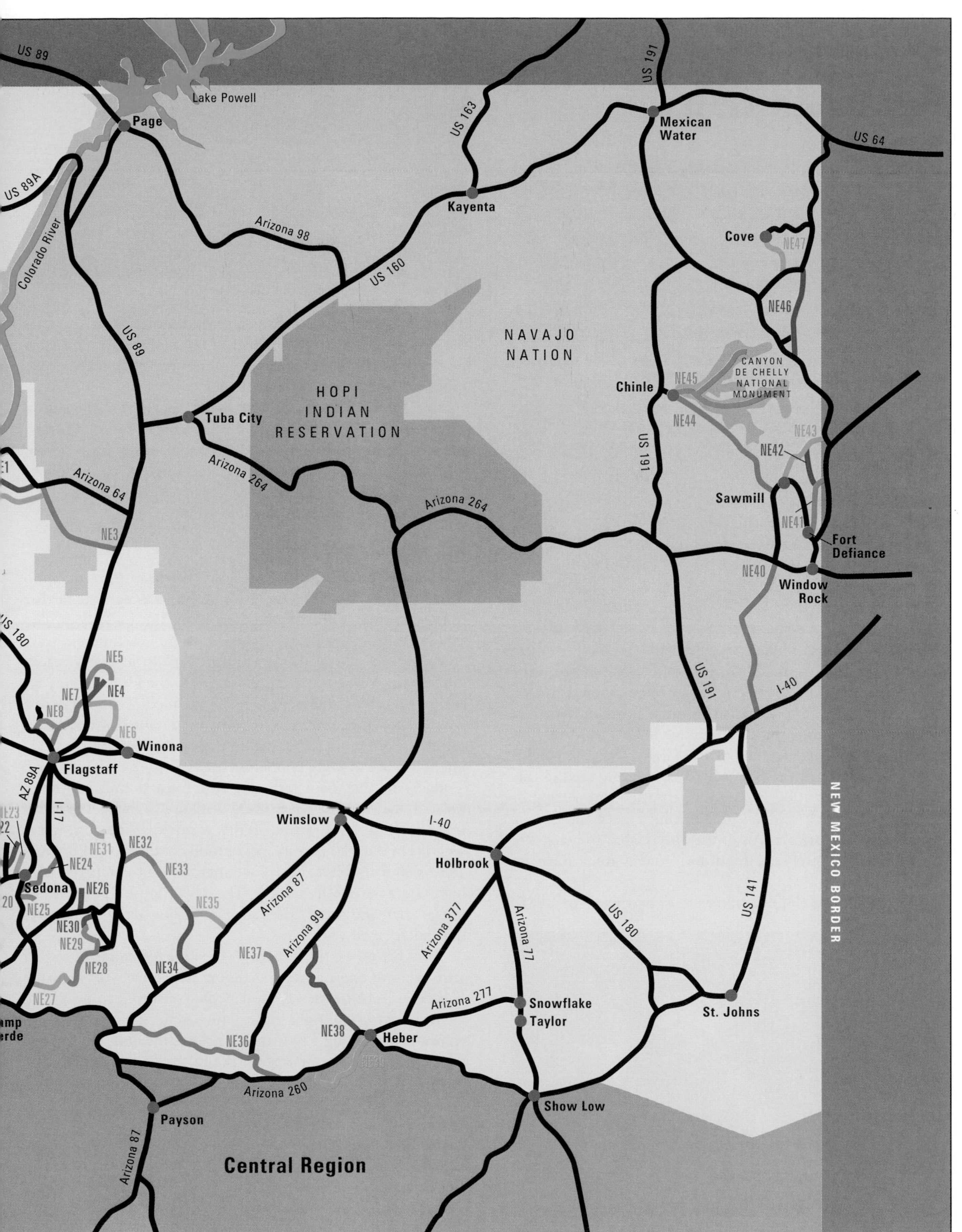
US 89
Lake Powell
Page
US 89A
Colorado River
Arizona 98
US 163
Kayenta
US 191
Mexican Water
US 64
Cove
NE47
NE46
US 160
US 89
NAVAJO NATION
HOPI INDIAN RESERVATION
CANYON DE CHELLY NATIONAL MONUMENT
Chinle
NE45
NE44
US 191
NE43
NE42
Sawmill
NE41
Fort Defiance
NE40
Window Rock
Tuba City
Arizona 264
Arizona 64
NE3
Arizona 264
US 180
NE5
NE4
NE7
NE8
NE6
Winona
Flagstaff
AZ 89A
I-17
US 191
I-40
Winslow
I-40
NE32
NE31
NE33
NE24
Sedona
NE26
NE25
NE30
NE29
NE28
NE35
Arizona 87
Arizona 99
Holbrook
Arizona 377
Arizona 77
US 180
US 141
NE37
NE34
NE27
Arizona 277
Snowflake
Taylor
St. Johns
NE38
Heber
NE36
Arizona 260
Show Low
Payson
Arizona 87
Central Region
NEW MEXICO BORDER

NORTHEAST REGION TRAIL #1

Hull Cabin Trail

Starting Point:	**Northeast #2: Coconino Rim Trail, 1.3 miles south of Arizona 64**
Finishing Point:	**Arizona 64, 0.6 miles west of mile marker 276**
Total Mileage:	**13.7 miles**
Unpaved Mileage:	**13.7 miles**
Driving Time:	**1 hour**
Elevation Range:	**6,300–7,500 feet**
Usually Open:	**April to December**
Best Time to Travel:	**Dry weather**
Difficulty Rating:	**2**
Scenic Rating:	**8**
Remoteness Rating:	**+0**

Special Attractions

- Hull Cabin Historic District.
- Trail travels beneath curving Coconino Rim.
- Can be combined with Northeast #2: Coconino Rim Trail to create a loop.

History

The Hull brothers, Phillip and William, established their ranch south of the Grand Canyon in 1884. Initially, they raised cattle but later switched to sheep. When the Atlantic & Pacific Railroad was constructed through northern Arizona, the enterprising brothers started a stage line to carry tourists from the railroad in Flagstaff to the Grand Canyon. Phillip died of a heart attack in 1888, but William continued to run the ranch and tourist business until he started prospecting in the canyon. Another settler, Captain John Hance, set up tent cabins a short distance north of the Hull Cabin to house the tourists. He also provided food and guided tours into the Grand Canyon.

The cabins and Hull Tank were constructed in 1888.

Hull Cabin is set in a clearing among the ponderosa pines

The trail runs parallel with the Coconino Rim

The cabins are built of round logs, V-notched at the corners—a time-consuming construction technique. The barn is constructed of hand-hewn ponderosa pine logs, dovetailed at the corners.

The National Forest Service, which purchased the site in 1907, used it until 1940 as a summer ranger station. The forest service has recently restored the cabin, using logs, siding, and shingles of the same type as the original construction. Hull Cabin Historic District was listed on the National Register of Historic Places in October 1984.

Description

Northeast #1: Hull Cabin Trail joins Northeast #2: Coconino Rim Road with Arizona 64, exiting onto the highway farther to the east than Northeast #2: Coconino Rim Road does. The trail leaves from beside the Grandview Fire Lookout and travels down the side of the Coconino Rim through ponderosa pine forest. A side trail leads 0.4 miles to the Hull Cabins, actually two cabins and a barn, which are used occasionally as a work center in the summer months by the forest service. The cabins are often photographed in their pretty setting—a clearing in a grove of large ponderosa pines.

Back on the main trail, the soft formed trail continues through the trees. Deep ruts bear evidence to the fact that this trail should only be driven in dry weather. With rain, many sections of the trail become very muddy and are often impassable, even for 4WDs. In dry weather the trail is suitable for a high-clearance 2WD vehicle. The trail may be passable for longer than the travel dates suggest. In low snowfall years it may be open all year.

After 6.1 miles, the trail leaves the pine forest and enters an area of more open lower vegetation as it travels through the Upper Basin below the swooping curve of the Coconino Rim. Many tracks to the right lead to the base of the rim. The trail travels briefly along Lee Canyon before finishing on Arizona 64, 1 mile west of the eastern boundary of the Kaibab National Forest.

Current Road Information

Kaibab National Forest
Tusayan Ranger District
PO Box 3088
Tusayan, AZ 86023
(520) 638-2443

Map References

BLM Cameron
USFS Kaibab National Forest: Tusayan Ranger District
USGS 1:24,000 Grandview Point, Grandview Point NE, Hellhole Bend
1:100,000 Cameron
Maptech CD-ROM: Flagstaff/Sedona/Prescott
Arizona Atlas & Gazetteer, p. 32
Arizona Road & Recreation Atlas, pp. 28, 29 & pp. 62, 63
Recreational Map of Arizona

Route Directions

Mileage		Directions
▼ 0.0		From Northeast #2: Coconino Rim Trail, immediately east of Grandview Fire Lookout, zero trip meter and turn northeast on graded dirt road, FR 307, at the sign for Hull Cabin.
1.4 ▲		Trail ends on Northeast #2: Coconino Rim Trail, immediately east of Grandview Fire Lookout. Turn right to exit to Arizona 64 and Grand Canyon National Park; turn left to travel along Northeast #2: Coconino Rim Trail.
		GPS: N35°57.37' W111°57.23'
▼ 0.2	SO	Arizona Trail on left; then cattle guard; then Arizona Trail on right.
1.2 ▲	SO	Arizona Trail on left; then cattle guard; then Arizona Trail on right.
▼ 0.7	SO	Trail starts to descend Coconino Rim.
0.7 ▲	SO	Top of the Coconino Rim.
▼ 1.2	SO	Hull Tank on left.
0.2 ▲	SO	Hull Tank on right.
▼ 1.4	SO	Track on left is FR 851, which goes through gate, 0.4 miles to Hull Cabin. Zero trip meter.
0.0 ▲		Continue to the southwest.
		GPS: N35°58.05' W111°56.37'
▼ 0.0		Continue to the east.
2.3 ▲	SO	Track on right is FR 851, which goes through gate, 0.4 miles to Hull Cabin. Zero trip meter.
▼ 0.2	BR	Track on left is FR 2805; bear right, remaining on FR 307.
2.1 ▲	BL	Track on right is FR 2805; bear left, remaining on FR 307.
		GPS: N35°58.10' W111°56.19'
▼ 0.8	SO	Track on left; then track on right; then cross over wash.
1.5 ▲	SO	Cross over wash; then track on left; then track on right.
▼ 1.3	SO	Small track on left.
1.0 ▲	SO	Small track on right.
▼ 1.8	SO	Cross over wash.
0.5 ▲	SO	Cross over wash.
▼ 1.9	SO	Track on right.
0.4 ▲	SO	Track on left.
▼ 2.3	SO	Track on left is FR 2805. Zero trip meter.
0.0 ▲		Continue to the northwest on FR 307.
		GPS: N35°57.58' W111°54.12'
▼ 0.0		Continue to the southeast on FR 307.
3.4 ▲	BL	Track on right is FR 2805. Zero trip meter.
▼ 0.3	SO	Track on left is FR 854; then cross through wash.
3.1 ▲	SO	Cross through wash; then track on right is FR 854.
▼ 0.6	SO	Cross through wash.
2.8 ▲	SO	Cross through wash.
▼ 0.9	SO	Closure gate.
2.5 ▲	SO	Closure gate.
		GPS: N35°57.30' W111°53.41'
▼ 1.0	BR	Track on left is FR 683; bear right, remaining on FR 307.
2.4 ▲	BL	Track on right is FR 683; bear left, remaining on FR 307.
		GPS: N35°57.33' W111°53.32'
▼ 1.2	SO	Track on left to Trash Dam.
2.2 ▲	SO	Track on right to Trash Dam.
▼ 1.3	SO	Track on right.
2.1 ▲	SO	Track on left.
▼ 1.4	SO	Track on right and track on left.
2.0 ▲	SO	Track on left and track on right.
▼ 1.8	SO	Track on right.
1.6 ▲	SO	Track on left.
▼ 2.1	SO	Track on right.
1.3 ▲	SO	Track on left.

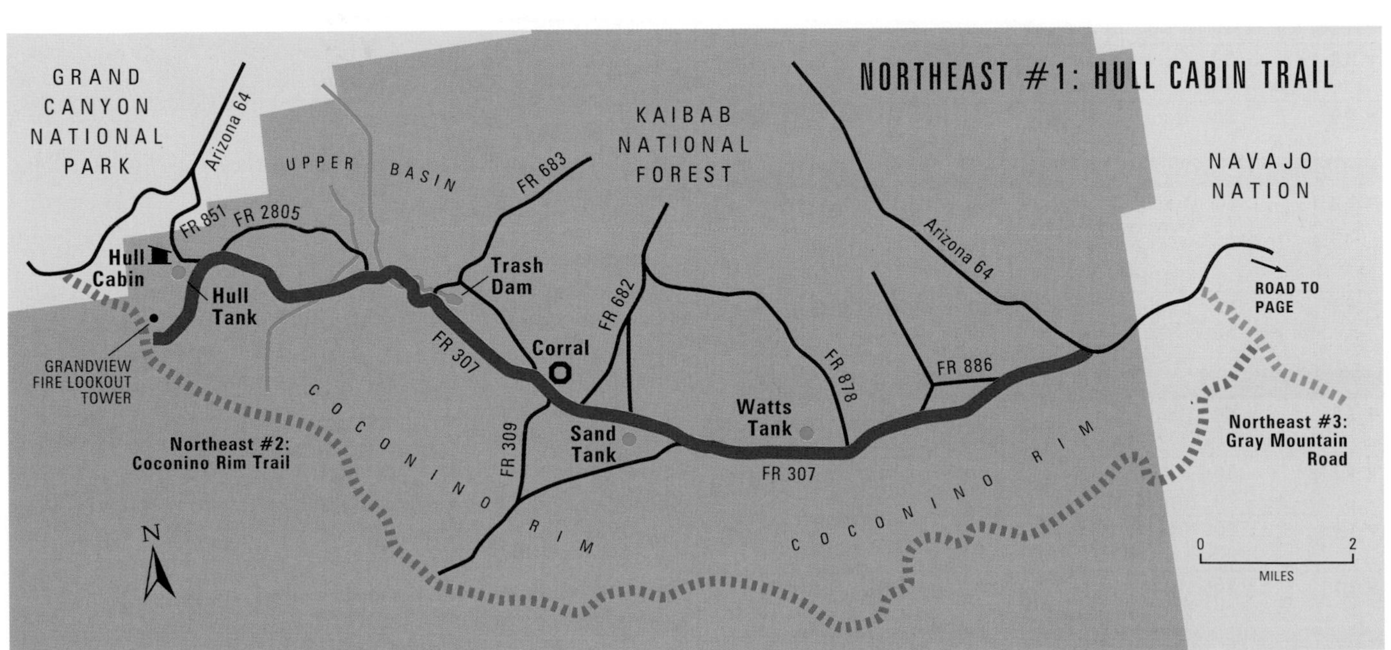

▼ 2.2 SO Track on right.
1.2 ▲ SO Track on left.

▼ 2.4 SO Cattle guard; then track on left and track on right is FR 784.
1.0 ▲ SO Track on left is FR 784 and track on right; then cattle guard.

GPS: N35°56.34' W111°52.43'

▼ 3.0 SO Track on left.
0.4 ▲ SO Track on right.

▼ 3.1 SO Corral on left; track on right is FR 309.
0.3 ▲ SO Corral on right; track on left is FR 309.

GPS: N35°56.01' W111°51.85'

▼ 3.4 SO Track on left is FR 682. Zero trip meter.
0.0 ▲ Continue to the west.

GPS: N35°55.81' W111°51.53'

▼ 0.0 Continue to the east.
3.6 ▲ SO Track on right is FR 682. Zero trip meter.

▼ 0.7 SO Sand Tank on right and track on left; then cattle guard.
2.9 ▲ SO Cattle guard; then Sand Tank on left and track on right.

▼ 1.5 SO Track on left is FR 877.
2.1 ▲ SO Track on right is FR 877.

GPS: N35°55.25' W111°50.04'

▼ 1.6 SO Track on right.
2.0 ▲ SO Track on left.

▼ 2.1 SO Two tracks on right.
1.5 ▲ SO Two tracks on left.

▼ 2.6 SO Track on right.
1.0 ▲ SO Track on left.

▼ 3.0 SO Watts Tank on left.
0.6 ▲ SO Watts Tank on right.

GPS: N35°54.92' W111°48.43'

▼ 3.6 SO Track on left is FR 878; also track on right. Zero trip meter.
0.0 ▲ Continue to the southwest.

GPS: N35°54.82' W111°47.83'

▼ 0.0 Continue to the northeast.
3.0 ▲ SO Track on right is FR 878; also track on left. Zero trip meter.

▼ 0.5 SO Small track on left.
2.5 ▲ SO Small track on right.

▼ 0.8 SO Track on left.
2.2 ▲ SO Track on right.

▼ 0.9 SO Track on left is FR 791.
2.1 ▲ SO Track on right is FR 791.

GPS: N35°55.01' W111°46.90'

▼ 1.0 SO Track on left; then track on right; then cross over wash.
2.0 ▲ SO Cross over wash; then track on left; then track on right.

▼ 1.4 SO Cattle guard; then track on left is FR 2815.
1.6 ▲ SO Track on right is FR 2815; then cattle guard.

GPS: N35°55.05' W111°46.35'

▼ 1.6 SO Cattle guard; then track on right.
1.4 ▲ SO Track on left; then cattle guard.

▼ 1.7 SO Track on right.
1.3 ▲ SO Track on left.

▼ 1.9 SO Track on right.
1.1 ▲ SO Track on left.

▼ 2.1 SO Well-used track on left is FR 886.
0.9 ▲ BL Well-used track on right is FR 886.

GPS: N35°55.28' W111°45.63'

▼ 2.6 SO Track on right.
0.4 ▲ SO Track on left.

▼ 2.9 SO Track on right.
0.1 ▲ SO Track on left.

▼ 3.0 Track on right; then cattle guard and closure gate. Trail ends at the T-intersection with Arizona 64. Turn right for Page and Flagstaff; turn left for the Grand Canyon National Park.
0.0 ▲ Trail commences on Arizona 64, 0.6 miles west of mile marker 276, 1 mile from the eastern boundary of the Kaibab National Forest. Zero trip meter and turn east on graded dirt road marked FR 307. Cattle guard and closure gate; then immediately track on left.

GPS: N35°55.37' W111°44.64'

NORTHEAST REGION TRAIL #2

Coconino Rim Trail

Starting Point:	**Northeast #3: Gray Mountain Road, 1.7 miles from Arizona 64**
Finishing Point:	**Arizona 64 (East Rim Drive, Grand Canyon National Park), 0.4 miles east of mile marker 252**
Total Mileage:	**21 miles**
Unpaved Mileage:	**21 miles**
Driving Time:	**2.5 hours**
Elevation Range:	**7,000–7,500 feet**
Usually Open:	**April to December**
Best Time to Travel:	**Dry weather**
Difficulty Rating:	**3**
Scenic Rating:	**7**
Remoteness Rating:	**+0**

Special Attractions

- Grandview Fire Lookout and views into Grand Canyon National Park.
- Wildlife viewing—deer, elk, bush turkeys, javelina, antelope.
- Cross-country ski area in winter.

Description

This trail explores the Kaibab National Forest along the edge of the Coconino Rim. In this region, the rim is lightly vegetated with pinyons and junipers, and is very different from the more open section that Northeast #3: Gray Mountain Road passes through. Initially, the trail leaves Northeast #3: Gray Mountain Road, and for the first 2 miles it follows small tracks within the Navajo Nation. Navigation can be tricky; there are many small trails very close together. Some of them rejoin the main trail after a short distance, but most go to dwellings. Should you find yourself on one of these, turn around and retrace your steps. The trail does not directly pass by any dwellings.

The national forest boundary is marked by a sign and a cat-

The rim of the Grand Canyon from the Grandview Fire Lookout

tle guard; past this point, the trail is slightly wider and smoother. The trail is very rutted in places and in wet weather can be impassable. It is often open longer than the dates given and is closed naturally as a result of snowfall.

Near the western end of the trail is the intersection with Northeast #1: Hull Cabin Trail, which can be driven in conjunction with this one to create a loop. The Grandview Fire Lookout Tower is rarely manned. The number of joy flights over the Grand Canyon and surrounding area has made it redundant—the pilots normally report the fires. You are welcome to climb the tower to see the view, but the cabin at the top is usually locked. The climb up the tower is worthwhile. There are views over the tree tops to the rim of the Grand Canyon and the Coconino Rim. To the south are the San Francisco Peaks. The 80-foot-tall steel tower was erected in 1936 to replace an older, wooden tower. At its base is a two-room bungalow, which was the living quarters for the lookouts. Both the Vishnu Hiking Trail and the Tusayan Mountain Bike Trail commence from the tower.

Arizona Trail access and Grandview Fire Lookout

The final section of the trail enters Grand Canyon National Park before finishing on the East Rim.

Current Road Information

Kaibab National Forest
Tusayan Ranger District
PO Box 3088
Tusayan, AZ 86023
(520) 638-2443

Map References

BLM Cameron
USFS Kaibab National Forest: Tusayan Ranger District
USGS 1:24,000 Hellhole Bend, Grandview Point NE, Grandview Point
1:100,000 Cameron

Maptech CD-ROM: Flagstaff/Sedona/Prescott
Arizona Atlas & Gazetteer, pp. 32, 31
Arizona Road & Recreation Atlas, pp. 28, 34, 35 & pp. 62, 68, 69
Recreational Map of Arizona

Route Directions

Mileage		Direction	
▼ 0.0			From Northeast #3: Gray Mountain Road, 1.7 miles south of Arizona 64, zero trip meter and turn southwest on well-used, unmarked trail.
	2.5 ▲		Trail ends at the intersection with Northeast #3: Gray Mountain Road, 1.7 miles south of Arizona 64. Turn left to exit to Arizona 64; turn right to continue along Northeast #3: Gray Mountain Road to Arizona 89.
			GPS: N35°55.31' W111°41.86'
▼ 0.1		BR	Two tracks on left; then track on right.
	2.4 ▲	BL	Track on left; then two tracks on right.
▼ 0.3		BL	Trail forks; keep left.
	2.2 ▲	SO	Track on left.
			GPS: N35°55.13' W111°42.07'
▼ 0.5		BL/BR	Track on right into private property; then immediately bear right, leaving the second track on your left.
	2.0 ▲	SO/BR	Track on right; then immediately bear right; track on left into private property.
▼ 0.6		SO	Track on right and track on left.
	1.9 ▲	SO	Track on right and track on left.
▼ 0.7		TR	Track on left and track straight on; then track on right.
	1.8 ▲	TL	Track on left; then crossroads; track on right and track straight on.
			GPS: N35°54.85' W111°42.32'
▼ 0.9		BR	Track on right; then trail forks; bear right at fork.
	1.6 ▲	SO	Track on right; then track on left.
			GPS: N35°54.86' W111°42.57'
▼ 1.0		BR	Track on left.
	1.5 ▲	BR	Track on right.
▼ 1.1		SO	Track on right; then track on left.
	1.4 ▲	SO	Track on right; then track on left.
			GPS: N35°54.74' W111°42.71'
▼ 1.3		SO	Track on left.
	1.2 ▲	BL	Track on right.
			GPS: N35°54.58' W111°42.77'
▼ 1.6		SO	Trail forks.
	0.9 ▲	SO	Trail rejoins.
▼ 1.7		SO	Trail rejoins.
	0.8 ▲	SO	Trail forks.
▼ 1.8		SO	Track on left.
	0.7 ▲	SO	Track on right.
▼ 1.9		SO	Well-used track on left.
	0.6 ▲	BL	Well-used track on right.
			GPS: N35°54.14' W111°43.02'
▼ 2.0		SO	Track on left.
	0.5 ▲	SO	Track on right.
▼ 2.4		BR	Track on left.
	0.1 ▲	BL	Track on right.
			GPS: N35°53.83' W111°43.44'
▼ 2.5		SO	Cattle guard; entering Kaibab National Forest. Zero trip meter.
	0.0 ▲		Continue to the southeast into the Navajo Nation.
			GPS: N35°53.85' W111°43.52'
▼ 0.0			Continue to the northwest; trail is now marked FR 310.

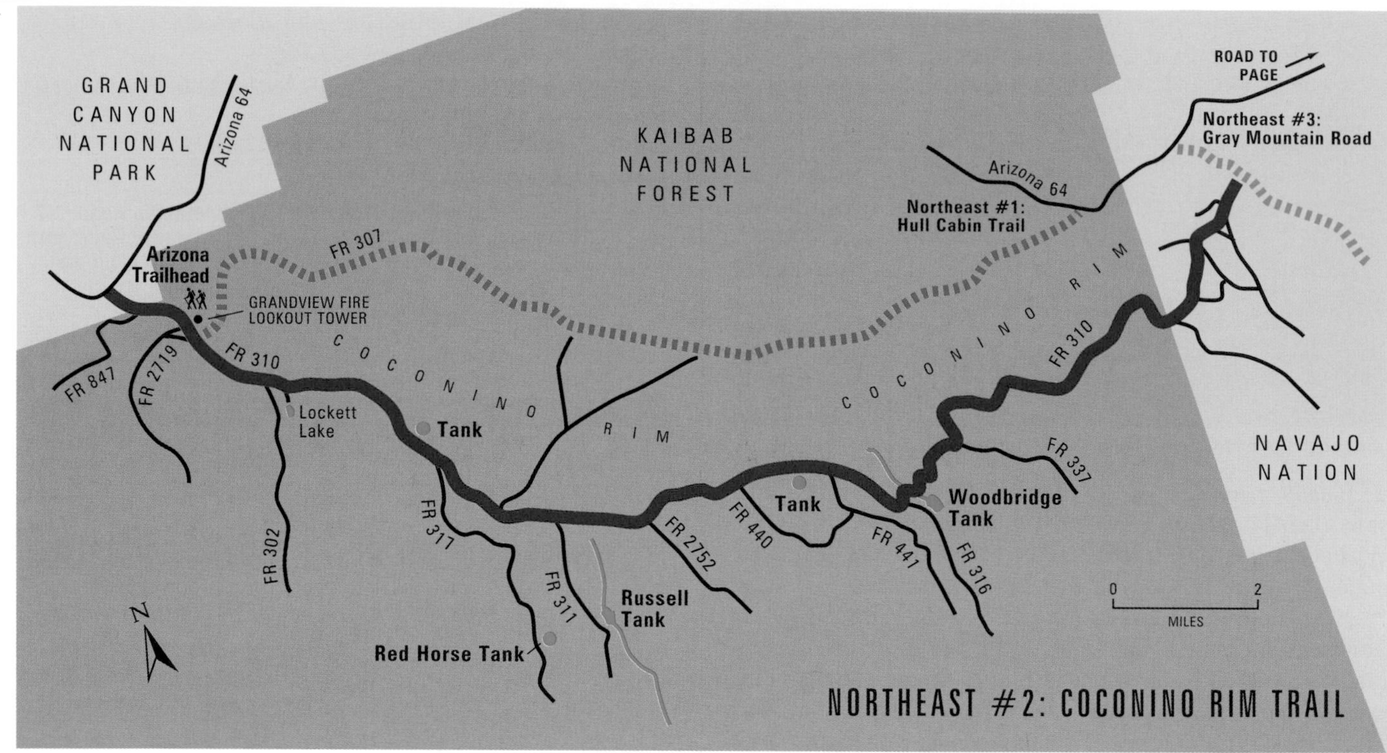

Mileage		Description
4.7 ▲	SO	Cattle guard; leaving Kaibab National Forest. Zero trip meter.
▼ 0.5	SO	Track on left.
4.2 ▲	SO	Track on right.
▼ 1.1	SO	Track on left.
3.6 ▲	SO	Track on right.
▼ 1.3	SO	Track on left.
3.4 ▲	SO	Track on right.
▼ 1.5	SO	Faint track on right.
3.2 ▲	SO	Faint track on left.
▼ 1.7	SO	Track on left.
3.0 ▲	SO	Track on right.
▼ 1.9	SO	Faint track on left.
2.8 ▲	SO	Faint track on right.
▼ 3.1	SO	Track on right.
1.6 ▲	SO	Track on left.
		GPS: N35°53.77' W111°46.06'
▼ 3.4	SO	Track on left.
1.3 ▲	SO	Track on right.
▼ 4.1	BL	Track straight on.
0.6 ▲	BR	Track on left.
		GPS: N35°53.74' W111°47.02'
▼ 4.7	TR	T-intersection. Turn right, remaining on FR 310. Track on left is FR 337. Zero trip meter.
0.0 ▲		Continue to the northeast.
		GPS: N35°53.22' W111°47.06'
▼ 0.0		Continue to the west.
1.3 ▲	TL	Turn left, remaining on FR 310. Track straight ahead is FR 337. Zero trip meter.
▼ 0.2	SO	Wire gate; then track on left.
1.1 ▲	SO	Track on right; then wire gate.
▼ 0.3	SO	Track on left.
1.0 ▲	SO	Track on right.
▼ 0.5	SO	Track on right.
0.8 ▲	SO	Track on left.
▼ 0.8	SO	Track on right.
0.5 ▲	SO	Track on left.
▼ 1.1	SO	Cross through wash; then Woodbridge Tank on left.
0.2 ▲	SO	Woodbridge Tank on right; then cross through wash.
		GPS: N35°52.82' W111°48.00'
▼ 1.3	TR	T-intersection. Turn right, remaining on FR 310. Road on left is FR 316. Zero trip meter.
0.0 ▲		Continue to the northeast.
		GPS: N35°52.71' W111°48.04'
▼ 0.0		Continue to the west; trail is now smoother and roughly graded.
5.1 ▲	TL	Turn left, remaining on FR 310. Track ahead is FR 316. Zero trip meter.
▼ 1.1	SO	Track on left is FR 441; also track on right.
4.0 ▲	SO	Track on right is FR 441; also track on left.
		GPS: N35°53.32' W111°48.89'
▼ 1.6	SO	Game tank on left.
3.5 ▲	SO	Game tank on right.
▼ 2.4	SO	Track on left is FR 440.
2.7 ▲	SO	Track on right is FR 440.
		GPS: N35°53.55' W111°50.27'
▼ 3.7	SO	Track on left.
1.4 ▲	SO	Track on right.
▼ 3.9	SO	Track on left is FR 2752.
1.2 ▲	BL	Track on right is FR 2752.
		GPS: N35°53.46' W111°51.78'
▼ 4.5	SO	Track on left.
0.6 ▲	SO	Track on right.
▼ 4.7	SO	Russell Wash section of the Arizona Trail crosses the main trail.
0.4 ▲	SO	Russell Wash section of the Arizona Trail crosses the main trail.
		GPS: N35°53.67' W111°52.58'
▼ 5.0	SO	Cattle guard.
0.1 ▲	SO	Cattle guard.

▼ 5.1		SO	Graded road on left is FR 311 to Russell Tank. Zero trip meter. There is no sign in this direction.
	0.0 ▲		Continue to the east, following the sign to Woodbridge.
			GPS: N35°53.79' W111°52.97'
▼ 0.0			Continue to the west.
	4.8 ▲	SO	Graded road on right is FR 311 to Russell Tank. Zero trip meter.
▼ 0.8		SO	Track on right.
	4.0 ▲	SO	Track on left.
▼ 1.3		SO	Track on right.
	3.5 ▲	SO	Track on left.
▼ 2.0		SO	Track on left is FR 317 to Red Horse Tank. Continue straight on, following the sign to Grandview and cross cattle guard; closure gate at cattle guard.
	2.8 ▲	SO	Closure gate and cattle guard; then track on right is FR 317 to Red Horse Tank. Continue straight on, following the sign to Russell Tank.
			GPS: N35°54.90' W111°54.37'
▼ 2.4		SO	Game tank on right.
	2.4 ▲	SO	Game tank on left.
			GPS: N35°55.25' W111°54.66'
▼ 2.6		SO	Track on left is FR 729.
	2.2 ▲	SO	Track on right is FR 729.
▼ 3.2		SO	Track on left is FR 735.
	1.6 ▲	SO	Track on right is FR 735.
			GPS: N35°55.86' W111°54.92'
▼ 3.5		SO	Cattle guard.
	1.3 ▲	SO	Cattle guard.
▼ 3.6		SO	Track on left is FR 728.
	1.2 ▲	SO	Track on right is FR 728.
▼ 4.1		SO	Track on left is FR 712.
	0.7 ▲	SO	Track on right is FR 712.
			GPS: N35°56.24' W111°55.71'
▼ 4.6		SO	Track on left is FR 301 to Lockett Lake. No sign in this direction.
	0.2 ▲	SO	Track on right is FR 301 to Lockett Lake.
			GPS: N35°56.43' W111°56.25'
▼ 4.8		SO	Track on left is FR 302 to Bucklar and Camp 36 Tank. Zero trip meter.
	0.0 ▲		Continue to the east, following the sign to Russell Tank.
			GPS: N35°56.50' W111°56.46'
▼ 0.0			Continue to the west, following sign to Grandview Fire Lookout.
	1.3 ▲	SO	Track on right is FR 302 to Bucklar and Camp 36 Tank. Zero trip meter.
▼ 0.6		SO	Track on right.
	0.7 ▲	SO	Track on left.
▼ 0.8		SO	Track on left.
	0.5 ▲	SO	Track on right.
▼ 1.0		SO	Track on left; then cattle guard.
	0.3 ▲	SO	Cattle guard; then track on right.
▼ 1.3		SO	Graded road on right is FR 307, Northeast #1: Hull Cabin Trail. Graded dirt road on left is FR 2719. Zero trip meter.
	0.0 ▲		Continue to the southeast on FR 310, following the sign to Russell Tank.
			GPS: N35°57.37' W111°57.23'
▼ 0.0			Continue to the northwest on FR 310, following the sign to Grand Canyon National Park.
	1.3 ▲	SO	Graded dirt road on left is FR 307, Northeast #1: Hull Cabin Trail. Graded dirt road on right is FR 2719. Zero trip meter.
▼ 0.1		SO	Grandview Fire Lookout on right and Arizona Trail on right.
	1.2 ▲	SO	Grandview Fire Lookout on left and Arizona Trail on left.
			GPS: N35°57.44' W111°57.28'
▼ 0.6		SO	Track on left.
	0.7 ▲	SO	Track on right.
▼ 0.7		SO	Track on left is FR 847. Leaving Kaibab National Forest.
	0.6 ▲	SO	Entering Kaibab National Forest. Track on right is FR 847.
			GPS: N35°57.75' W111°57.83'
▼ 0.8		SO	Cattle guard; entering Grand Canyon National Park.
	0.5 ▲	SO	Cattle guard; leaving Grand Canyon National Park.
▼ 1.3			Trail ends on Arizona 64, East Rim Drive in Grand Canyon National Park. Turn right for Page; turn left for Grand Canyon south rim.
	0.0 ▲		Trail commences on Arizona 64, East Rim Drive in Grand Canyon National Park, 2.1 miles southeast of the turn to Grandview Point. Zero trip meter and turn south on graded dirt road. The turn is signed for the Arizona Trail. Turn is 0.4 miles east of mile marker 252.
			GPS: N35°58.09' W111°58.29'

NORTHEAST REGION TRAIL #3

Gray Mountain Road

Starting Point:	**US 89 at Gray Mountain**
Finishing Point:	**Arizona 64 (Navahopi Road), 1.8 miles east of the Kaibab National Forest boundary**
Total Mileage:	**22.2 miles**
Unpaved Mileage:	**20.3 miles**
Driving Time:	**2.25 hours**
Elevation Range:	**4,900–7,100 feet**
Usually Open:	**Year-round**
Best Time to Travel:	**Dry weather**
Difficulty Rating:	**2**
Scenic Rating:	**9**
Remoteness Rating:	**+1**

Special Attractions

- Remote, lightly traveled trail through the Navajo Nation.
- Spectacular deep Burro Canyon.
- Views of the San Francisco Volcanic Field.

Description

This lightly traveled trail follows Indian Road 6150 as it travels up onto the plateau of Gray Mountain. The road is also marked on some maps as the Gray Mountain Truck Trail. It leaves US 89 at the settlement of Gray Mountain and follows a paved road to the west. This is the only road leaving to the west, so although it is not marked, it is easy to find. After a couple of miles, the route turns onto a graded

Navajo hogan (private property—please view only from the trail)

dirt road, suitable for high-clearance vehicles. It travels across an open plain covered with sagebrush toward the rise of the Coconino Rim. One pretty point along the trail is the crossing of Tappan Wash, which is a moderately deep, rocky canyon at this point.

The road climbs onto the Coconino Rim, crossing a narrow saddle with deep drops into Burro Canyon to the north and Tappan Wash to the south. This is the best view along the trail. Once up on the rim the road runs across the plateau of Gray Mountain, a sparsely vegetated, wind-blown plateau, dissected with deep canyons and light-colored gullies.

The road is graded all the way but is subject to ruts and bulldust. It is impassable after rain. The road is mostly unmarked, but it follows the main graded road for most of the way, so it is easy to navigate. The final section of the trail descends the Coconino Rim to Arizona 64. As it descends, the Little Colorado River Gorge can be seen to the north.

Remember that all land within the Navajo Nation is privately owned. Remain on the main route as you pass through. The side trails noted in the route directions are included for navigational purposes and are not necessarily open for travel; most of them lead to dwellings. Hiking and camping require specific permits. Please check requirements and restrictions before traveling. Refer to the section on travel etiquette in the Navajo Nation for more details. The area is used by the Navajo people for grazing and you are likely to encounter flocks of sheep and goats. Be sure you drive slowly to avoid startling them.

Current Road Information

Navajo Nation Parks and Recreation
PO Box 9000
Window Rock AZ, 86515
(520) 871-6647

Map References

BLM Cameron
USGS 1:24,000 Gray Mt., Cameron South, Coconino Point SE, Willows Camp, Hellhole Bend
1:100,000 Cameron
Maptech CD-ROM: Flagstaff/Sedona/Prescott
Arizona Atlas & Gazetteer, p. 32
Arizona Road & Recreation Atlas, p. 35 & p. 69

Route Directions

▼ 0.0			From US 89 at the settlement of Gray Mountain, zero trip meter and turn west on the paved road in the middle of Gray Mountain. The road is unmarked, but it is the only road leading out to the west. Immediately cross cattle guard. Remain on the paved road, ignoring tracks on right and left.
	1.9 ▲		Trail ends at the T-intersection with US 89 in Gray Mountain. Turn left for Page; turn right for Flagstaff.
			GPS: N35°44.72' W111°28.40'
▼ 1.9		TL	On a right-hand bend, turn left opposite mile marker 2 onto graded dirt road marked Navajo Highway 6150. Zero trip meter.
	0.0 ▲		Continue to the east.
			GPS: N35°46.00' W111°29.90'
▼ 0.0			Continue to the west.
	6.0 ▲	TR	T-intersection with paved road; zero trip meter and turn right. Remain on the paved road into Gray Mountain, ignoring tracks on left and right.
▼ 0.3		SO	Track on left and track on right.
	5.7 ▲	SO	Track on left and track on right.
▼ 0.5		SO	Track on left; then track on right.
	5.5 ▲	SO	Track on left; then track on right.
▼ 0.6		SO	Track on right.
	5.4 ▲	SO	Track on left.
▼ 1.0		SO	Pass under power lines.
	5.0 ▲	SO	Pass under power lines.
▼ 1.2		BL	Cross over Cedar Wash; then track on right.
	4.8 ▲	BR	Track on left; then cross over Cedar Wash.

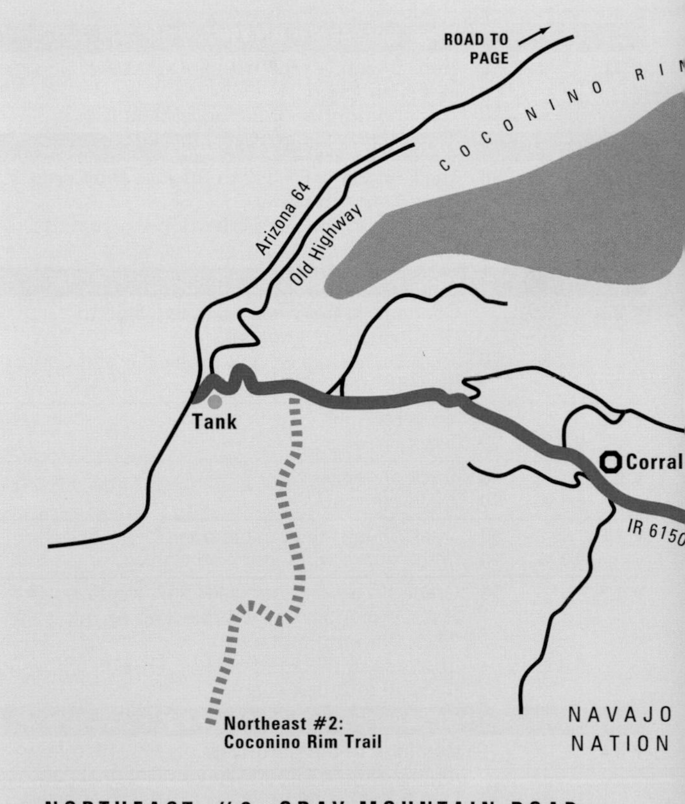

		GPS: N35°46.52′ W111°31.15′
▼ 1.4	SO	Track on left under power lines.
4.6 ▲	SO	Track on right under power lines.
▼ 1.8	SO	Track on right.
4.2 ▲	SO	Track on left.
▼ 2.0	SO	Track on left.
4.0 ▲	SO	Track on right.
▼ 2.1	SO	Cross through Needmore Wash.
3.9 ▲	SO	Cross through Needmore Wash.
▼ 2.4	SO	Track on left.
3.6 ▲	SO	Track on right.
▼ 2.5	SO	Track on left.
3.5 ▲	SO	Track on right.
▼ 2.6	SO	Track on right.
3.4 ▲	SO	Track on left.
▼ 2.8	SO	Graded road on left and track on right.
3.2 ▲	SO	Graded road on right and track on left.
		GPS: N35°46.90′ W111°32.51′
▼ 3.3	SO	Track on left; then road descends to cross through Tappan Wash.
2.7 ▲	SO	Track on right as road climbs away from wash.
▼ 3.5	SO	Cross through Tappan Wash.
2.5 ▲	SO	Cross through Tappan Wash.
		GPS: N35°46.97′ W111°33.15′
▼ 3.8	SO	Track on left.
2.2 ▲	SO	Track on right.
▼ 4.1	SO	Track on right.
1.9 ▲	SO	Track on left.
▼ 5.1	SO	Track on left and track on right.
0.9 ▲	BR	Track on left; bear right, remaining on main dirt road; then track on right.
		GPS: N35°47.55′ W111°34.46′
▼ 5.2	SO	Track on left.
0.8 ▲	SO	Track on right.
▼ 5.3	SO	Cross through wash.
0.7 ▲	SO	Cross through wash.
▼ 5.8	SO	Small track on right.
0.2 ▲	SO	Small track on left.
▼ 6.0	BL	Graded road on right. There is a stone corral on the left. Zero trip meter.
0.0 ▲		Continue to the east.
		GPS: N35°47.78′ W111°35.39′
▼ 0.0		Continue to the west.
9.2 ▲	SO	Graded road on left. There is a stone corral on the right. Zero trip meter.
▼ 0.3	SO	Track on right; then cross through wash.
8.9 ▲	BR	Cross through wash; then track on left.
▼ 0.4	SO	Track on left.
8.8 ▲	SO	Track on right.
▼ 1.9	SO	Saddle between two canyons. Burro Canyon on the right and Tappan Wash on the left.
7.3 ▲	SO	Saddle between two canyons. Burro Canyon on the left and Tappan Wash on the right.
		GPS: N35°47.48′ W111°36.99′
▼ 2.4	SO	Top of Gray Mountain.
6.8 ▲	SO	Top of Gray Mountain.
▼ 3.1	SO	Track on right.
6.1 ▲	SO	Track on left.
▼ 3.5	SO	Track on right.
5.7 ▲	SO	Track on left.

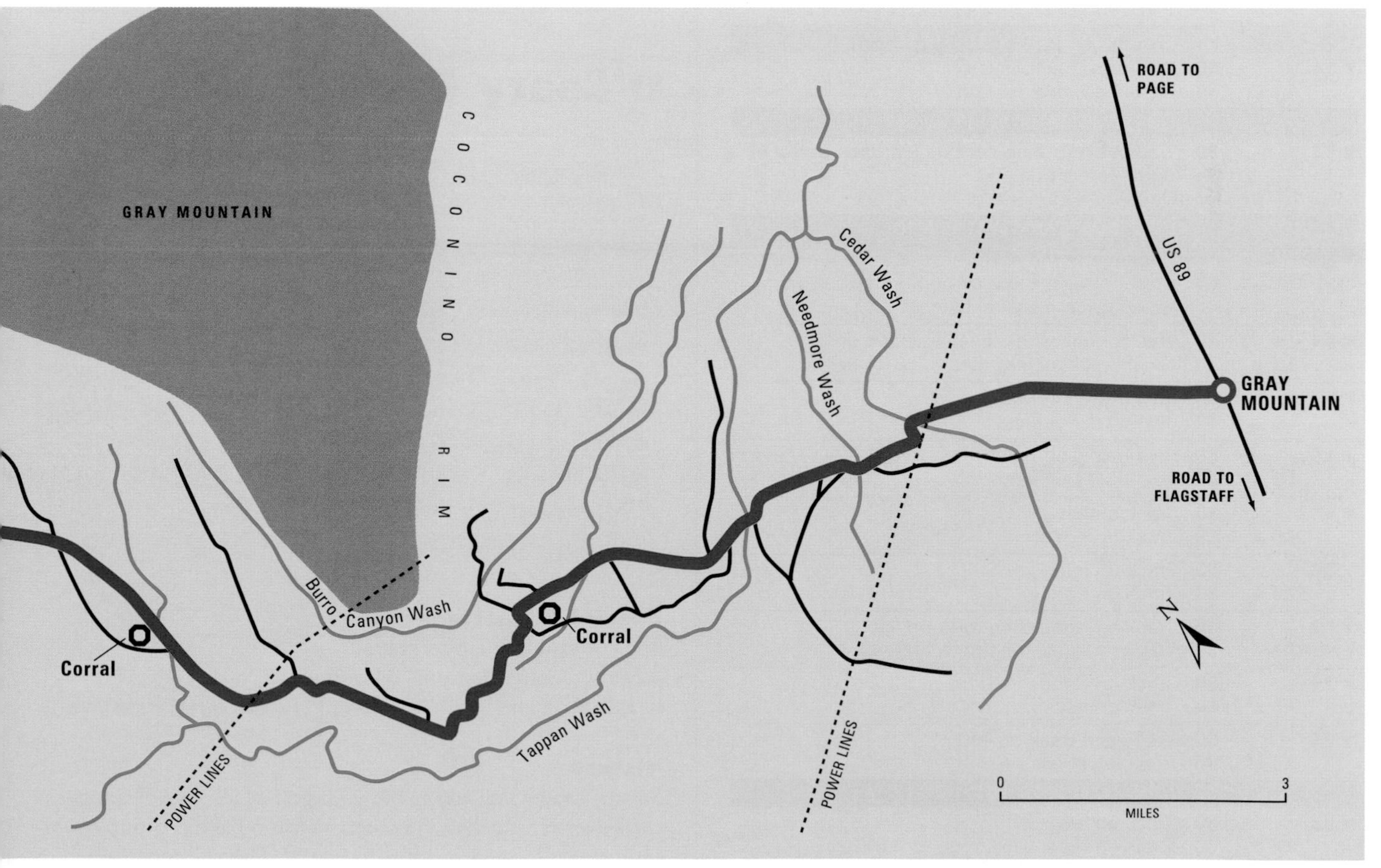

▼ 3.7	SO	Track on right.
5.5 ▲	SO	Track on left.
▼ 4.0	SO	Track on right.
5.2 ▲	SO	Track on left.
▼ 4.2	SO	Small track on left.
5.0 ▲	SO	Small track on right.
▼ 4.6	SO	Pass under power lines; small track on right.
4.6 ▲	SO	Pass under power lines; small track on left.
		GPS: N35°48.92' W111°38.60'
▼ 5.5	SO	Cross through wash; track on left.
3.7 ▲	SO	Track on right; cross through wash.
▼ 5.7	SO	Track on left to corral; then cross through wash.
3.5 ▲	SO	Cross through wash; then track on right to corral.
▼ 5.9	SO	Track on left.
3.3 ▲	SO	Track on right.
▼ 6.3	SO	Track on left.
2.9 ▲	SO	Track on right.
▼ 6.7	SO	Two tracks on right; track on left.
2.5 ▲	SO	Track on right; two tracks on left.
▼ 6.9	SO	Track on right.
2.3 ▲	SO	Track on left.
▼ 7.0	SO	Small track on left.
2.2 ▲	SO	Small track on right.
▼ 7.2	SO	Track on right and track on left.
2.0 ▲	SO	Track on left and track on right.
▼ 8.1	SO	Track on right.
1.1 ▲	SO	Track on left.
▼ 8.3	SO	Track on right.
0.9 ▲	SO	Track on left.
		GPS: N35°52.04' W111°39.66'
▼ 8.6	SO	Track on left.
0.6 ▲	SO	Track on right.
		GPS: N35°52.30' W111°39.86'
▼ 9.1	SO	Well-used track on left.
0.1 ▲	SO	Well-used track on right.
		GPS: N35°52.69' W111°40.06'
▼ 9.2	SO	Track on left; then dam on left; then corral on right. Zero trip meter.
0.0 ▲		Continue to the south.
		GPS: N35°52.83' W111°40.10'
▼ 0.0		Continue to the north.
3.4 ▲	SO	Corral on left; then dam on right; then track on right. Zero trip meter.
▼ 0.1	SO	Track on left; then small track on right.
3.3 ▲	SO	Small track on left; then track on right.
▼ 0.4	SO	Two tracks on right.
3.0 ▲	SO	Two tracks on left.
▼ 1.5	SO	Two tracks on right.
1.9 ▲	SO	Two tracks on left.
▼ 1.9	SO	Track on left.
1.5 ▲	SO	Track on right.
▼ 2.0	SO	Track on left.
1.4 ▲	SO	Track on right.
▼ 2.2	SO	Track on right; then track on left.
1.2 ▲	SO	Track on right; then track on left.
▼ 2.4	SO	Track on right.
1.0 ▲	SO	Track on left.
▼ 2.6	SO	Well-used track on left.
0.8 ▲	SO	Well-used track on right.
		GPS: N35°54.76' W111°41.32'
▼ 2.9	SO	Track on left.
0.5 ▲	SO	Track on right.
▼ 3.0	SO	Track on right; then track on left.
0.4 ▲	SO	Track on right; then track on left.
		GPS: N35°54.99' W111°41.63'
▼ 3.1	SO	Track on right.
0.3 ▲	SO	Track on left.
▼ 3.4	SO	Track on left is Northeast #2: Coconino Rim Road; track on right. Zero trip meter.
0.0 ▲		Continue to the northwest.
		GPS: N35°55.31' W111°41.85'
▼ 0.0		Continue toward Arizona 64.
1.7 ▲	SO	Track on left; track on right is Northeast #2: Coconino Rim Trail. Zero trip meter.
▼ 0.3	SO	Track on right; then track on left.
1.4 ▲	SO	Track on right; then track on left.
▼ 1.3	SO	Tank on left.
0.4 ▲	SO	Tank on right.
▼ 1.4	TL	T-intersection with paved Old Highway.
0.3 ▲	TR	Turn right onto graded dirt road.
		GPS: N35°55.90' W111°42.41'
▼ 1.7	TR	Turn right and cross cattle guard; then trail ends at the T-intersection with Arizona 64.
0.0 ▲	TL	From Arizona 64, 18 miles west of the intersection with US 89, zero trip meter and turn southeast on small road across a cattle guard and then immediately turn left at the T-intersection onto the paved Old Highway. Turn is immediately west of roadside trading stands, but intersection is unmarked.
		GPS: N35°55.86' W111°42.76'

NORTHEAST REGION TRAIL #4

O'Leary Peak Trail

Starting Point:	**US 89, 6 miles north of Flagstaff, 0.1 miles south of mile marker 427**
Finishing Point:	**Gate of O'Leary Peak Fire Lookout**
Total Mileage:	**8.7 miles**
Unpaved Mileage:	**8.1 miles**
Driving Time:	**1 hour (one-way)**
Elevation Range:	**6,900–8,200 feet**
Usually Open:	**Year-round**
Best Time to Travel:	**Year-round**
Difficulty Rating:	**2**
Scenic Rating:	**10**
Remoteness Rating:	**+0**

Special Attractions

- Twisting black cinder trail.
- Sunset Crater National Monument.
- Trail passes beside Bonito Lava Flow and offers views over it.

History

Sunset Crater Volcano is the youngest of all the volcanoes included within the San Francisco Volcano Field, a group of volcanic peaks located north of Flagstaff. The volcano erupted in

A.D. 1064. The Indian tribes who inhabited the area at the time would have seen the eruption, the results of which lie around the surrounding area today as a carpet of black cinders. Molten rock spewed from a weakness in the earth's crust with such force that it created a thousand-foot-high cone of cinders and debris. The finale to the eruptions at Sunset Crater occurred in 1250 when iron- and sulphur-rich cinders fell around the summit of the cone. The iron cinders around the cone are oxidized red, which inspired John Wesley Powell to give the crater its name in 1892.

This trail passes alongside the Bonito Lava Flow, a jagged black stream of cooled lava that flowed out of the base of Sunset Crater more than a hundred years after its initial eruption. The flow hardened and covered nearly 2 square miles of the landscape. The flow of black basalt, the most common volcanic rock to be found on the earth's surface, is composed mainly of silica but also contains many tiny mineral grains, mainly iron- and magnesium-rich minerals that give it its dark color. The quick cooling of the flow prevented the minerals from forming larger structures. The texture of the flow, with its uneven surface, comes from the bubbles of gas trapped within the cooling lava. The geological term for these bubbles is *vesicles.*

Sunset Crater was nearly obliterated in 1928. A movie company had plans to dynamite the slopes of the cone to create a landslide effect for a film. Local citizens stepped in to halt the move, and as a result, President Herbert Hoover created the national monument in 1930.

O'Leary Peak and O'Leary Basin are named after Dan O'Leary, a guide and interpreter for General George Crook.

Description

This trail travels through the edge of the Cinder Hills OHV Area and Sunset Crater National Monument to climb O'Leary Peak, one of the volcanic peaks contained within the San Francisco Volcano Field.

The trail leaves US 89 north of Flagstaff at the same point as Northeast #6: Cinder Hills Loop Trail but diverges from this trail after 0.5 miles. Initially, the trail follows a well-graded road through ponderosa pines that cover the black cinder hills. It crosses the paved road to Sunset Crater National Monument just inside the western edge of the monument boundary. You will have to pass through the entrance booth to

One of the contorted mounds created by the Bonito Lava Flow

Sunset Crater viewed from the spur trail

continue along the trail, but normally there is no fee required if you just wish to pass through.

The route turns away from the paved road almost immediately, following the rougher trail to O'Leary Peak. It passes directly alongside the Bonito Lava Flow, characterized by hardened waves of black basalt. The flow is clearly defined as it rises above the trail.

Once away from the lava flow, the trail ascends O'Leary Peak. It is not possible to drive all the way to the fire lookout because there is a locked gate 1.3 miles from the top. You can park and hike the final section to the tower. The shelf road to the gate is wide and gives a spectacular view over the lava flow to pink-tipped Sunset Crater.

A second short spur, a much smaller, 3-rated trail, travels over the ridge top of Robinson Mountain to end at a viewpoint over Bonito Park and the San Francisco Peaks.

Current Road Information

Coconino National Forest
Peaks Ranger District
5075 North Hwy 89
Flagstaff, AZ 86004
(520) 526-0866

Sunset Crater National Monument
Route 3 Box 149
Flagstaff, AZ 86004
(520) 526-0502

Map References

BLM Flagstaff
USFS Coconino National Forest: Peaks Ranger District
USGS 1:24,000 Sunset Crater West, O'Leary Peak
1:100,000 Flagstaff
Maptech CD-ROM: Flagstaff/Sedona/Prescott
Arizona Atlas & Gazetteer, pp. 42, 32

Route Directions

▼ 0.0		From US 89, 6 miles north of Flagstaff, zero trip meter and turn northeast on FR 776 signposted to the Cinder Hills OHV Area. Road is graded dirt. Turn is 0.1 miles south of mile marker 427.
0.5 ▲		Trail ends on US 89 north of Flagstaff. Turn left for Flagstaff.
		GPS: N35°19.70' W111°32.68'
▼ 0.5	TL	Turn left onto the graded road, FR 414.

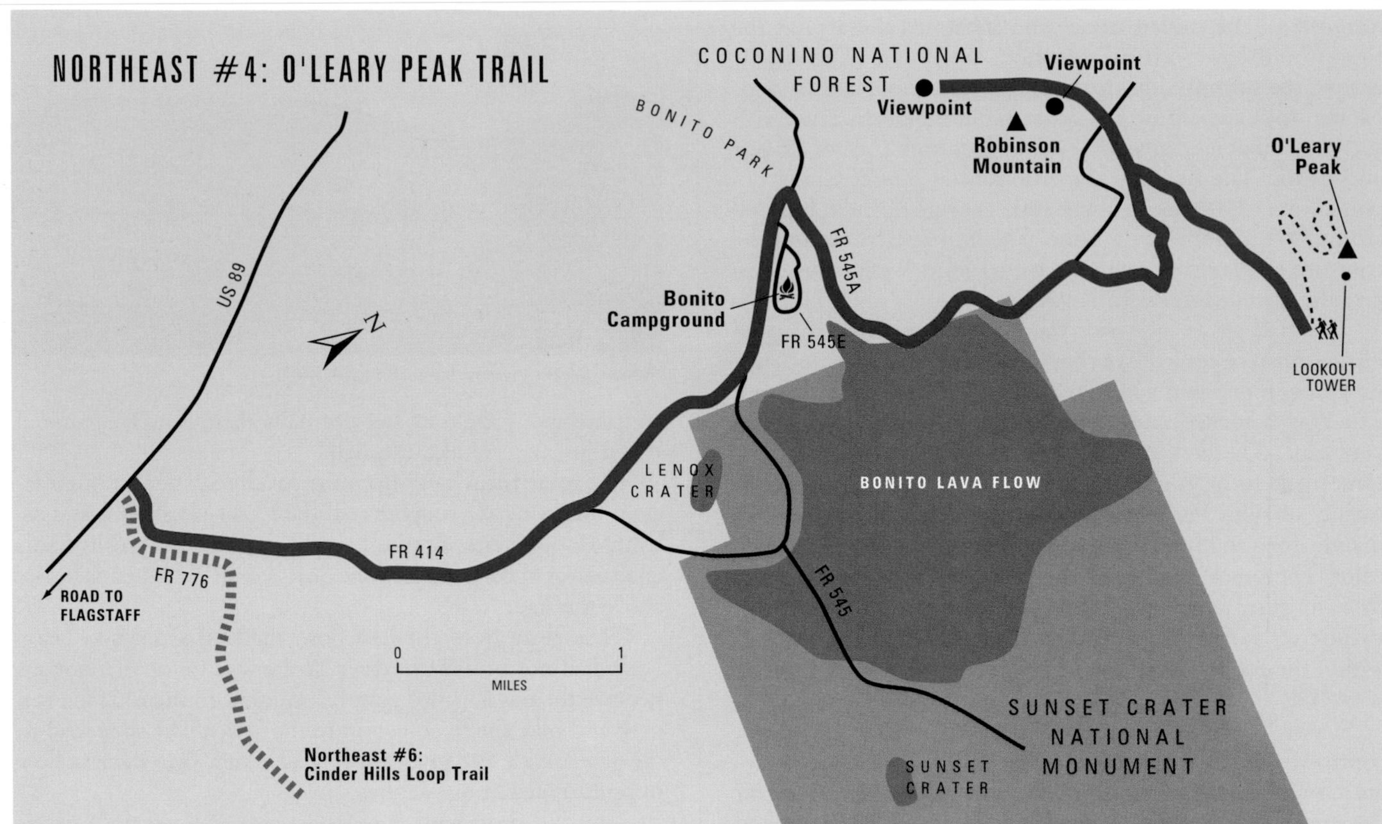

			Northeast #6: Cinder Hills Loop Trail continues ahead. Zero trip meter.
	0.0 ▲		Continue to the west.
			GPS: N35°19.93′ W111°32.22′
▼ 0.0			Continue to the northwest.
	2.5 ▲	TR	Turn right onto graded road, FR 776. Track on left is Northeast #6: Cinder Hills Loop Trail. Zero trip meter.
▼ 0.1		SO	Track on right.
	2.4 ▲	SO	Track on left.
▼ 0.2		SO	Graded road on right is FR 9143C.
	2.3 ▲	SO	Graded road on left is FR 9143C.
			GPS: N35°20.14′ W111°32.11′
▼ 0.4		SO	Track on left.
	2.1 ▲	SO	Track on right.
▼ 0.5		SO	Track on left.
	2.0 ▲	SO	Track on right.
▼ 0.6		SO	Track on right.
	1.9 ▲	BR	Track on left.
▼ 0.7		SO	Track on right.
	1.8 ▲	SO	Track on left.
▼ 0.8		SO	Track on left is FR 9141U (no vehicles), and track on right goes into OHV area (ATVs only).
	1.7 ▲	SO	Track on right is FR 9141U (no vehicles), and track on left goes into OHV area (ATVs only).
			GPS: N35°20.54′ W111°31.84′
▼ 1.5		BL	Well-used track on right. Bear left, remaining on FR 414.
	1.0 ▲	SO	Well-used track on left. Continue straight on, remaining on FR 414.
			GPS: N35°21.18′ W111°31.80′
▼ 2.5		TL	Join paved road to Sunset Crater and turn left. Zero trip meter.
	0.0 ▲		Continue to the southeast.
			GPS: N35°21.96′ W111°32.14′
▼ 0.0			Continue to the northwest.
	0.6 ▲	TR	Leave paved road turning right onto small, formed unmarked trail, which is 0.1 miles beyond the trail marked FR 414. Zero trip meter.
▼ 0.5		SO	Exit Sunset Crater National Monument; then track on right is FR 545E into Bonito NFS Campground.
	0.1 ▲	SO	Track on left is FR 545E into Bonito NFS Campground. Enter Sunset Crater National Monument.
			GPS: N35°22.22′ W111°32.66′
▼ 0.6		TR	Turn right at Bonito Park onto graded dirt road, FR 545A.
	0.0 ▲		Continue to the southeast along paved road toward the entrance to Sunset Crater National Monument.
			GPS: N35°22.29′ W111°32.75′
▼ 0.0			Continue to the east. Camping and campfires are prohibited from this point.
▼ 0.6		SO	Edge of the Bonito Lava Flow on the right.
▼ 1.2		SO	Track on left.
▼ 2.3		SO	Start of wide shelf road up O'Leary Peak.
▼ 2.6		BR	Track on left is spur to viewpoint on right-hand switchback. Remain on main trail.
			GPS: N35°23.47′ W111°32.30′
▼ 3.7		UT	Trail ends at the locked gate to the lookout tower. Turn around at the gate. From here it is a 1.3-mile hike to the fire lookout.
			GPS: N35°23.84′ W111°31.28′

Spur to Viewpoint

▼ 0.0			Turn west on small unmarked trail on the right-hand switchback.

		GPS: N35°23.47′ W111°32.30′
▼ 0.3	BL	Track on right on left-hand bend.
		GPS: N35°23.45′ W111°32.53′
▼ 0.5	SO	Viewpoint at top of steep hill; track on right.
		GPS: N35°23.34′ W111°32.71′
▼ 0.8	SO	Track on right.
		GPS: N35°23.14′ W111°32.83′
▼ 1.4		Trail ends at second viewpoint.
		GPS: N35°22.90′ W111°32.91′

NORTHEAST REGION TRAIL #5

O'Leary Basin Trail

Starting Point:	**FR 545 on the eastern edge of Sunset Crater National Monument**
Finishing Point:	**Sunset Crater Road, FR 545, 0.1 miles east of US 89, 15 miles north of Flagstaff**
Total Mileage:	**13.6 miles**
Unpaved Mileage:	**13.6 miles**
Driving Time:	**1.5 hours**
Elevation Range:	**6,300–7,500**
Usually Open:	**Year-round**
Best Time to Travel:	**Year-round**
Difficulty Rating:	**3**
Scenic Rating:	**10**
Remoteness Rating:	**+0**

Special Attractions

- Views of Sunset Crater.
- Trail travels on the black lava dunes of the San Francisco Volcano Field.
- One of the less traveled trails within this region.

Description

This trail travels through the black lava dunes that surround Sunset Crater National Monument but outside of the popular OHV area. If anything, this trail has the most impressive scenery of all those that pass through this unique region, and the trail is infinitely quieter than the busy trails within the OHV area.

The trail winds along the side of the black volcanic O'Leary Peak

The trail leaves paved FR 545 at the eastern edge of Sunset Crater National Monument and travels as a formed single-track trail across the black cinder "dunes" on the edge of the monument. The surface, similar to loose sand, is very smooth and soft in places.

Sunset Crater up ahead

This undulating trail winds in a large loop around the north face of the jutting volcanic cones of O'Leary Peak, passing along the edge of O'Leary Basin through ponderosa pines that grow out of the black cinders.

Around the west side of O'Leary Peak the trail becomes rougher and more eroded. It follows a smaller track, FR 9124C, descending to rejoin FR 545 near the intersection with US 89.

There are exceptional views all along the trail of the San Francisco Peaks, Sunset Crater, O'Leary Peak, and over O'Leary Basin. There are some good campsites as well, especially those on beds of black cinders. Light snow, which can make the trail temporarily impassable, is possible during the winter months.

Current Road Information

Coconino National Forest
Peaks Ranger District
5075 North Hwy 89
Flagstaff, AZ 86004
(520) 526-0866

Sunset Crater National Monument
Route 3 Box 149
Flagstaff, AZ 86004
(520) 526-0502

Map References

BLM Flagstaff
USFS Coconino National Forest: Peaks Ranger District
USGS 1:24,000 Sunset Crater East, Strawberry Crater, O'Leary Peak
1:100,000 Flagstaff
Maptech CD-ROM: Flagstaff/Sedona/Prescott
Arizona Atlas & Gazetteer, p. 32
Arizona Road & Recreation Atlas, p. 35 & p. 69

Route Directions

▼ 0.0	From FR 545 at the eastern edge of Sunset Crater National Monument, zero trip meter and turn northeast on small dirt road marked FR 546.
4.6 ▲	Trail ends at the intersection with paved FR 545 at the eastern edge of Sunset Crater National Monument. Turn left for Wupatki National Monument; turn right for Flagstaff.

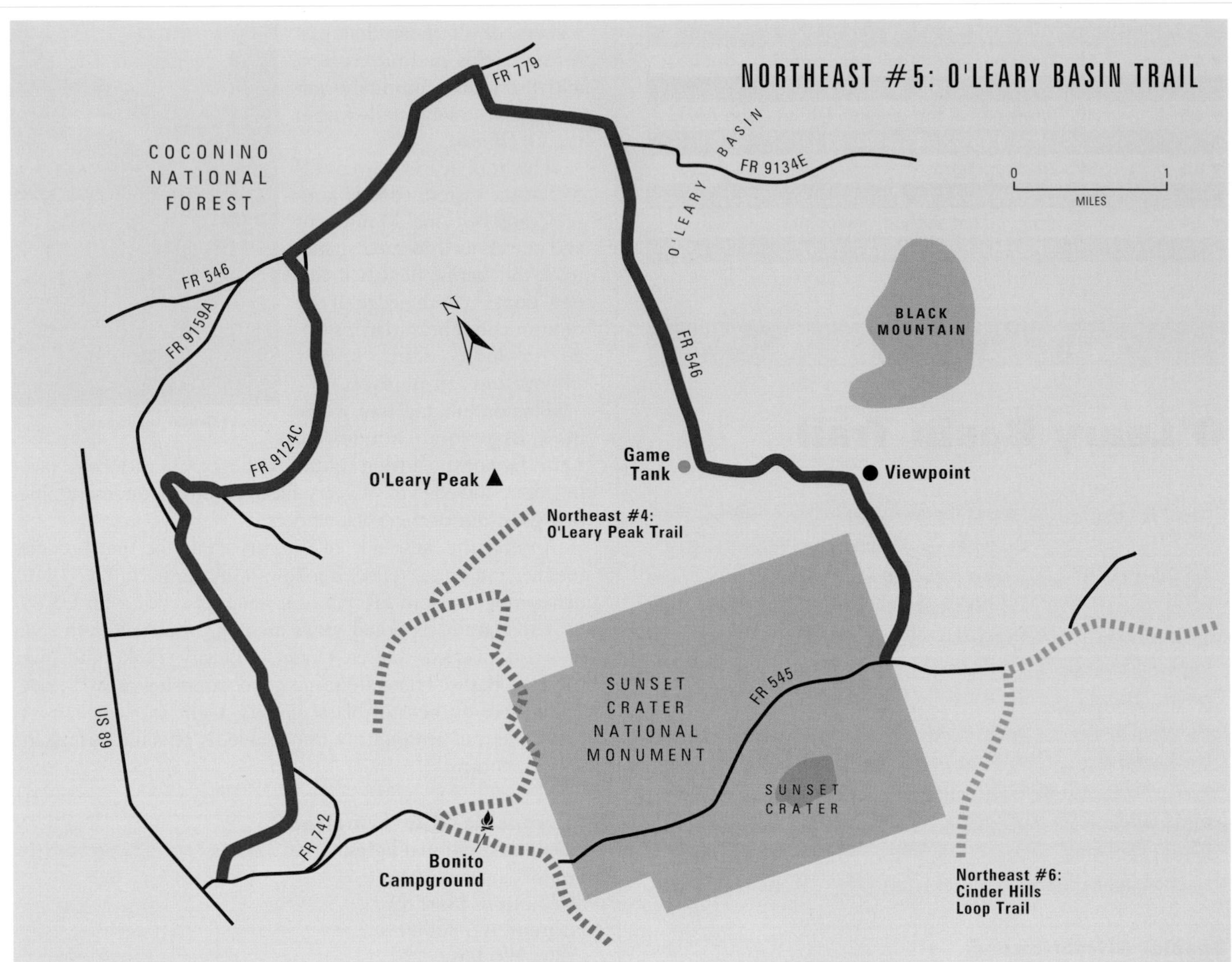

Mileage		Directions
		GPS: N35°22.36' W111°29.33'
▼ 0.6	SO	Trail crosses open black lava dune.
4.0 ▲	SO	Trail crosses open black lava dune.
▼ 1.3	BL	Track on right is viewpoint over Black Mountain.
3.3 ▲	BR	Track on left is viewpoint over Black Mountain.
		GPS: N35°23.40' W111°29.10'
▼ 2.5	SO	Game tank on left.
2.1 ▲	SO	Game tank on right.
		GPS: N35°23.81' W111°30.11'
▼ 3.0	SO	Track on left.
1.6 ▲	SO	Track on right.
▼ 4.6	SO	Track on right is FR 9134E. Zero trip meter.
0.0 ▲		Continue to the south.
		GPS: N35°25.71' W111°29.92'
▼ 0.0		Continue to the north.
2.9 ▲	SO	Track on left is FR 9134E. Zero trip meter.
▼ 1.1	TL	T-intersection; FR 546 continues to the left; track on right is FR 779.
1.8 ▲	TR	Turn right, remaining on FR 546. Track ahead is FR 779.
		GPS: N35°26.37' W111°30.71'
▼ 1.4	SO	Track on left.
1.5 ▲	SO	Track on right.
▼ 2.0	SO	Cattle guard.
0.9 ▲	SO	Cattle guard.
▼ 2.2	SO	Track on left.
0.7 ▲	SO	Track on right.
▼ 2.8	SO	Track on left.
0.1 ▲	SO	Track on right.
		GPS: N35°25.69' W111°32.31'
▼ 2.9	TL	Turn left onto smaller trail, FR 9124C. FR 546 continues ahead. Zero trip meter.
0.0 ▲		Continue to the east.
		GPS: N35°25.68' W111°32.38'
▼ 0.0		Continue to the south.
4.4 ▲	TR	T-intersection with FR 546. Turn right onto the slightly larger trail. Zero trip meter.
▼ 0.1	SO	Small track on right.
4.3 ▲	SO	Small track on left.
▼ 0.5	SO	Track on left.
3.9 ▲	SO	Track on right.
▼ 1.2	SO	Track on left.
3.2 ▲	SO	Track on right.
▼ 2.0	SO	Track on right; then track on left.
2.4 ▲	SO	Track on right; then track on left.
		GPS: N35°24.51' W111°33.47'
▼ 2.1	SO	Start to descend shelf road.
2.3 ▲	SO	End of climb.

▼ 2.6		SO	End of descent.
	1.8 ▲	SO	Start to climb shelf road.
▼ 2.8		BL	Trail forks; bear left on unmarked trail. Track on right is FR 9159A. Both tracks are equally used.
	1.6 ▲	SO	Track on left is FR 9159A; continue straight on FR 9124C.
			GPS: N35°24.29' W111°33.81'
▼ 3.7		SO	Track on right.
	0.7 ▲	SO	Track on left.
▼ 4.4		TR	T-intersection with graded dirt road, FR 742. Turn right and zero trip meter.
	0.0 ▲		Continue to the west.
			GPS: N35°22.92' W111°33.58'
▼ 0.0			Continue to the south toward US 89.
	1.7 ▲	TL	Turn left at the marker for FR 545B onto smaller formed trail. Zero trip meter.
▼ 0.4		SO	Track on left.
	1.3 ▲	SO	Track on right.
▼ 1.7			Trail ends at the T-intersection with the paved road to Sunset Crater, FR 545, immediately east of US 89.
	0.0 ▲		Trail commences on the Sunset Crater Road, FR 545, immediately east of US 89, 15 miles north of Flagstaff. Turn north on wide graded dirt road. Turn is opposite an information board.
			GPS: N35°22.36' W111°34.42'

NORTHEAST REGION TRAIL #6

Cinder Hills Loop Trail

Starting Point:	**US 89, 6 miles north of Flagstaff, 0.1 miles south of mile marker 427**
Finishing Point:	**Townsend-Winona Road, 5.5 miles east of US 89**
Total Mileage:	**18.9 miles**
Unpaved Mileage:	**18.5 miles**
Driving Time:	**2 hours**
Elevation Range:	**6,500–7,300 feet**
Usually Open:	**Year-round**
Best Time to Travel:	**Year-round**
Difficulty Rating:	**3**
Scenic Rating:	**9**
Remoteness Rating:	**+0**

Special Attractions

- Very unusual and spectacular black cinder hills.
- Popular ATV and dirt bike area.
- Excellent backcountry camping.

Description

Cinder Hills OHV Area lies within the Coconino National Forest and is specifically managed for vehicle recreation. Thirteen thousand five hundred acres have been designated for use by dirt bikes, ATVs, and 4WD vehicles. The area has a dense network of designated routes as well as open areas of unrestricted use where there is little vegetation. Surrounding the main vehicle-use area is a larger resource area of 53,000 acres in which vehicle use is limited to a lesser number of designated routes.

A black cinder trail traveling through the ponderosa pine trees

This trail passes through both regions and gives an excellent introduction to the scenically unique area of the Cinder Hills, part of the San Francisco Volcano Field. The region is a study in contrasts; the black volcanic cinders provide a driving surface that is similar to sand. The green of the vegetation contrasts with the black ground to give an almost surreal effect. Photographers will appreciate the opportunity to obtain some unusual photos of a unique landscape.

Initially, the trail follows the main graded route through the OHV area. There are many side trails on the right and left, particularly past the first main staging and camping area on the edge of Cinder Lake. The dry, black volcanic expanse of Cinder Lake is a major play area for those with dirt bikes, ATVs, and sand rails. The graded road follows the edge and has a firm surface suitable for passenger vehicles when it is dry. The area is extremely popular at all times of the year and especially on weekends, so be on the lookout for fast-moving vehicles. Only the major trails suitable for vehicles have been mentioned in the route directions; it is not possible to list the many trails made by ATVs and dirt bikes.

The route briefly joins the paved road through Sunset Crater National Monument before turning off onto a designated forest route outside the main OHV area. Here the trail is narrower, less frequently used, and has a softer surface. There are fewer, more secluded campsites along this section of the trail. The trail continues to meander along the edge of the OHV area before dropping south to finish on the Townsend-Winona Road.

Note that no glass containers are allowed in the OHV area.

The black cinder surface of Cinder Lake provides a favorite location for off-road vehicles

Current Road Information

Coconino National Forest
Peaks Ranger District
5075 North Hwy 89
Flagstaff, AZ 86004
(520) 526-0866

Sunset Crater National Monument
Route 3 Box 149
Flagstaff, AZ 86004
(520) 526-0502

Map References

BLM Flagstaff
USFS Coconino National Forest: Peaks Ranger District
USGS 1:24,000 Sunset Crater West, Sunset Crater East, Winona
1:100,000 Flagstaff
Maptech CD-ROM: Flagstaff/Sedona/Prescott
Arizona Atlas & Gazetteer, p. 42
Arizona Road & Recreation Atlas, p. 35 & p. 69
Other: Cinder Hills OHV Area—free map put out by Coconino National Forest

Route Directions

Mileage		Direction
▼ 0.0		From US 89, 6 miles north of Flagstaff, zero trip meter and turn northeast on FR 776 signposted to the Cinder Hills OHV Area. Road is graded dirt. Turn is 0.1 miles south of mile marker 427.
4.9 ▲		Trail ends on US 89 north of Flagstaff. Turn left for Flagstaff.
		GPS: N35°19.70′ W111°32.68′
▼ 0.5	BR	Track on left is Northeast #4: O'Leary Peak Trail, FR 414. Many small tracks for ATV and dirt bike use on left and right for next 4.9 miles.
4.4 ▲	SO	Track on right is Northeast #4: O'Leary Peak Trail, FR 414.
		GPS: N35°19.93′ W111°32.22′
▼ 1.3	SO	Cinders Hill OHV Area. Major staging and camping area on right and left.
3.6 ▲	SO	Cinders Hill OHV Area. Major staging and camping area on right and left.
		GPS: N35°19.71′ W111°31.45′
▼ 1.4	SO	Cinder Lake on right.
3.5 ▲	SO	Cinder Lake on left.
▼ 1.9	SO	Graded road on right is FR 777 to Little Cinder Basin.
3.0 ▲	SO	Graded road on left is FR 777 to Little Cinder Basin.

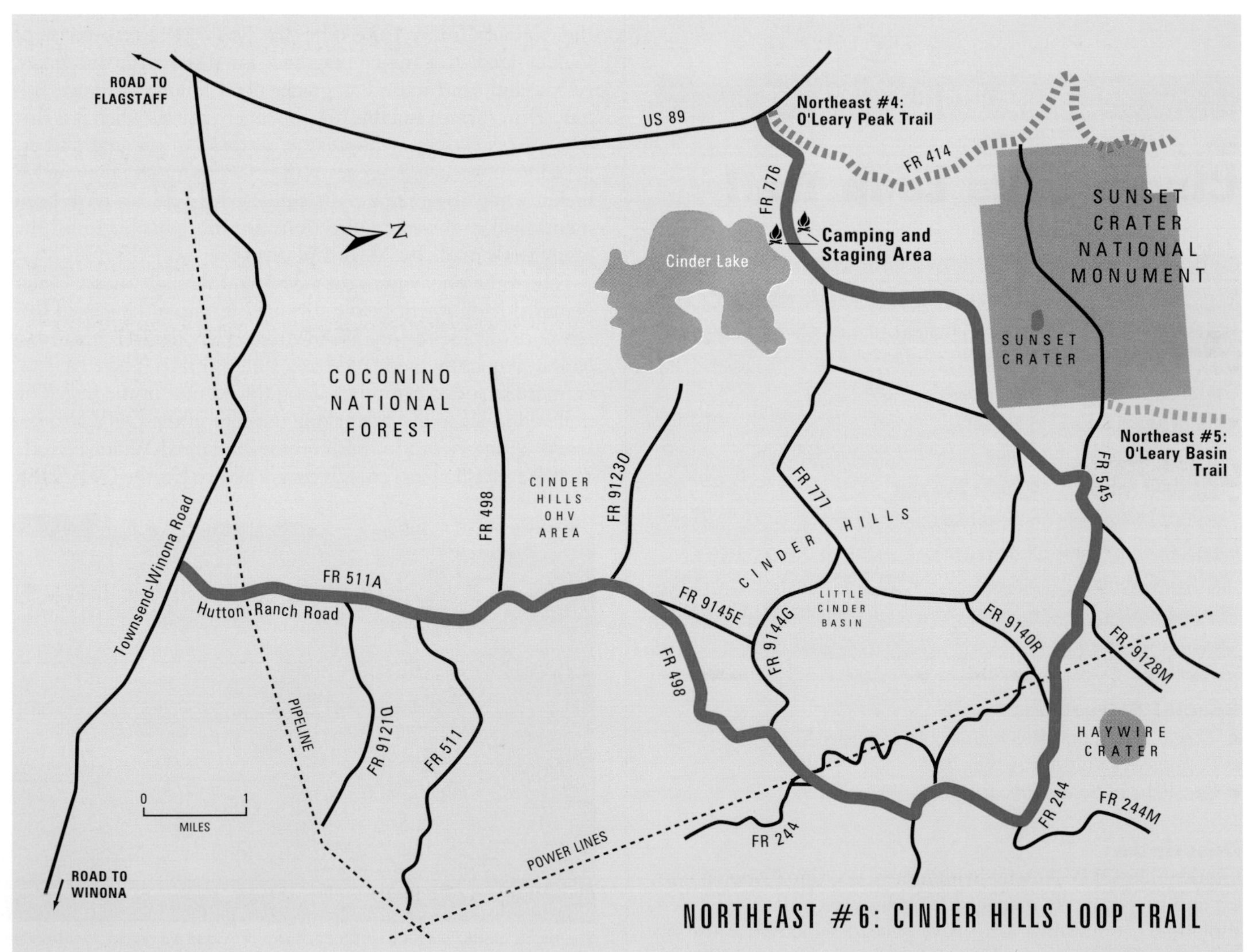

Mileage		Direction	Description
			GPS: N35°20.03' W111°30.85'
▼ 3.0		SO	Information sign on left.
	1.9 ▲	SO	Information sign on right.
▼ 4.7		SO	Track on right is FR 9140X.
	0.2 ▲	SO	Track on left is FR 9140X.
			GPS: N35°21.49' W111°29.14'
▼ 4.9		SO	Track on right is FR 777 to Little Cinder Basin. Sign on left of trail for FR 545 ahead and US 89 back. Zero trip meter.
	0.0 ▲		Continue to the south.
			GPS: N35°21.60' W111°28.93'
▼ 0.0			Continue to the north.
	0.7 ▲	SO	Track on left is FR 777 to Little Cinder Basin. Sign on right of trail for US 89 ahead. Zero trip meter.
▼ 0.3		SO	Unloading area on right.
	0.4 ▲	SO	Unloading area on left.
▼ 0.5		SO	Enter no-camping area.
	0.2 ▲	SO	Camping permitted past this point.
▼ 0.7		TR	T-intersection with paved FR 545. Turn right and zero trip meter.
	0.0 ▲		Continue to the south. Many small tracks on right and left for next 4.9 miles.
			GPS: N35°22.12' W111°28.51'
▼ 0.0			Continue to the east.
	0.4 ▲	TL	Turn left onto graded dirt road FR 776, entering the Cinder Hills OHV Area. Turn is immediately before a national parks entrance fee sign for Sunset Crater. Zero trip meter.
▼ 0.4		TR	Turn right onto small trail marked FR 244. Zero trip meter.
	0.0 ▲		Continue to the southwest.
			GPS: N35°22.20' W111°28.07'
▼ 0.0			Continue to the east.
	2.0 ▲	TL	T-intersection with paved FR 545. Turn left onto paved road. Zero trip meter.
▼ 0.2		SO	Track on left.
	1.8 ▲	SO	Track on right.
▼ 0.7		SO	Track on left is FR 9128M.
	1.3 ▲	SO	Track on right is FR 9128M.
			GPS: N35°21.97' W111°27.30'
▼ 1.5		SO	Track on left under power lines.
	0.5 ▲	SO	Track on right under power lines.
▼ 1.6		SO	Track on right.
	0.4 ▲	BR	Track on left.
			GPS: N35°21.71' W111°26.43'
▼ 1.9		SO	Track on right.
	0.1 ▲	SO	Track on left.
▼ 2.0		SO	Track on right is FR 9140R to Little Cinder Basin and FR 777. The blue arrows mark this trail. Zero trip meter. Haywire Crater is on the left.
	0.0 ▲		Continue to the northwest.
			GPS: N35°21.68' W111°25.98'
▼ 0.0			Continue to the southeast.
	3.2 ▲	SO	Track on left is FR 9140R to Little Cinder Basin and FR 777. Zero trip meter. Haywire Crater is on the right.
▼ 1.0		BR	Track on left is FR 244M. Bear right, remaining on FR 244.
	2.2 ▲	BL	Track on right is FR 244M. Bear left, remaining on FR 244.
			GPS: N35°21.33' W111°25.02'
▼ 1.9		SO	Track on right.
	1.3 ▲	SO	Track on left.
			GPS: N35°20.59' W111°25.44'
▼ 2.3		BR	Track on left.
	0.9 ▲	BL	Track on right.
▼ 3.2		BR	FR 244 continues to the left. Bear right onto well-used unmarked trail and zero trip meter.
	0.0 ▲		Continue to the north.
			GPS: N35°19.61' W111°25.63'
▼ 0.0			Continue to the southwest; trail is marked with white arrows on blue posts.
	4.4 ▲	SO	FR 244 on right; continue straight on and join FR 244. Zero trip meter.
▼ 0.1		SO	Pass under power lines; then track on left and track on right. Road is now marked FR 498.
	4.3 ▲	SO	Track on left and track on right; then pass under power lines.
▼ 0.7		SO	Track on left through gate and track on right is FR 9144G. Continue straight on, remaining on FR 498.
	3.7 ▲	SO	Track on right through gate and track on left is FR 9144G. Continue straight on, remaining on FR 498.
			GPS: N35°19.22' W111°26.23'
▼ 1.1		SO	Track on left.
	3.3 ▲	SO	Track on right.
▼ 1.8		SO	Track on left is FR 9144X.
	2.6 ▲	BL	Track on right is FR 9144X. Remain on FR 498.
			GPS: N35°18.61' W111°28.83'
▼ 2.7		SO	Track on left is FR 9145E; then almost immediately track on right is FR 9145E.
	1.7 ▲	BL	Track on left is FR 9145E; then almost immediately track on right is FR 9145E.
			GPS: N35°18.27' W111°27.71'
▼ 2.8		SO	Track on right is marked with blue arrow.
	1.6 ▲	BR	Bear right, remaining on FR 498; track on left is marked with blue arrow.
			GPS: N35°18.26' W111°27.73'
▼ 2.9		BL	Track on right is FR 9143T.
	1.5 ▲	SO	Track on left is FR 9143T.
			GPS: N35°18.20' W111°27.84'
▼ 3.1		BL	Fork; both unmarked. Track on right is FR 9123O. Bear left across open cinder area; there is a blue arrow after the junction.
	1.3 ▲	BR	Fork; both unmarked. Track on left is FR 9123O. Bear right into the trees.
			GPS: N35°17.97' W111°27.96'
▼ 3.4		SO	Track on right and track on left along gas pipeline.
	1.0 ▲	SO	Track on right and track on left along gas pipeline.
			GPS: N35°17.81' W111°27.93'
▼ 3.6		SO	Track on left.
	0.8 ▲	BL	Track on right.
▼ 4.0		SO	Track on left.
	0.4 ▲	SO	Track on right.
▼ 4.1		BL	Trail forks.
	0.3 ▲	SO	Track on left rejoins.
			GPS: N35°17.15' W111°27.87'
▼ 4.3		TL	Trail rejoins; then turn left onto well-used unmarked track. Ahead is FR 498.
	0.1 ▲	TR	Turn right; then trail forks; bear right (tracks rejoin shortly).
			GPS: N35°17.03' W111°27.95'
▼ 4.4		TL	Track on right is FR 498. Turn left onto unmarked trail, which is FR 511A, and zero trip meter.

0.0 ▲		Continue to the northwest.
		GPS: N35°16.97′ W111°27.89′
▼ 0.0		Continue to the southeast. Many tracks and campsites on right and left; remain on main trail for next 0.8 miles.
3.3 ▲	BR	Bear right onto FR 498 at well-used, unmarked intersection and zero trip meter.
▼ 0.5	SO	Enclosure contains aspens damaged by fire and being encouraged to regrow.
2.8 ▲	SO	Enclosure contains aspens damaged by fire and being encouraged to regrow.
▼ 0.8	SO	Track on left is FR 511 at edge of private property. Continue straight on, joining FR 511. Road is now graded.
2.5 ▲	BL	At edge of private property bear left, leaving FR 511 and joining the well-used FR 511A. Road is now formed trail. Many tracks and campsites on right and left; remain on main trail for next 0.8 miles.
		GPS: N35°16.24′ W111°27.82′
▼ 1.6	SO	Cattle guard; then track on left is FR 9121Q; track on right.
1.7 ▲	SO	Track on right is FR 9121Q; track on left; then cattle guard.
		GPS: N35°15.62′ W111°28.08′
▼ 1.8	SO	Track on right.
1.5 ▲	SO	Track on left.
▼ 2.1	SO	Track on left.
1.2 ▲	SO	Track on right.
▼ 2.3	SO	Graded road on right and left.
1.0 ▲	SO	Graded road on left and right.
▼ 3.3		Cattle guard; then trail ends at the T-intersection with the Townsend-Winona Road. Turn right for Flagstaff; turn left for Winona.
0.0 ▲		Trail commences on the Townsend-Winona Road, 5.5 miles east of the intersection with US 89 (north of Flagstaff), 0.2 miles east of mile marker 426. Zero trip meter and turn northeast onto the graded dirt Hutton Ranch Road across a cattle guard.
		GPS: N35°14.21′ W111°28.56′

NORTHEAST REGION TRAIL #7

Schultz Pass Trail

Starting Point:	**US 89, 1.3 miles south of the Sunset Crater National Monument turn-off**
Finishing Point:	**US 180, 3 miles north of Flagstaff**
Total Mileage:	**11.4 miles**
Unpaved Mileage:	**10.7 miles**
Driving Time:	**45 minutes**
Elevation Range:	**7,200–8,200 feet**
Usually Open:	**March to November**
Best Time to Travel:	**March to November**
Difficulty Rating:	**2**
Scenic Rating:	**8**
Remoteness Rating:	**+0**

Special Attractions

- Pleasant backcountry trail over the south side of the San Francisco Peaks.
- Views of the cinder hills that form part of the San Francisco Volcanic Field.
- Many backcountry campsites and access to hiking trails.

Description

Schultz Pass is a well-known backcountry drive, which is often combined with a visit to Sunset Crater and can be combined with one or two of the trails within the Cinder Hills OHV Area to make a full-day's tour. The graded road winds over the southern flanks of the San Francisco Peaks through some pretty alpine scenery along the south side of the Kachina Peaks Wilderness. In spring and early summer, there are fields of colorful wildflowers, and in the fall, scattered aspens contrast with pines. The northern end of the road has views over the Cinder Hills area to the east where the undulating black hills can be seen. This area is also part of the San Francisco Volcanic Field.

Bike trail that follows alongside Schultz Creek

The road climbs steadily to the top of Schultz Pass (named for Charley H. Schultz, a sheepherder) before descending alongside Schultz Creek toward Flagstaff. Originally, the route served as a shortcut from the outlying settlements to Flagstaff. Northeast #8: Freidlein Prairie Trail leads from the top of the pass and offers a smaller, rougher alternate route down the south side of the mountain. The Schultz Creek Trail, a single-track trail for hikers, horses, and mountain bikes, parallels the road for much of the way, running closer to the creek below the road. Because the final few miles of the trail run through watershed, no camping is allowed. There are a couple of places to pitch a tent near the north end of the trail, but better camping can be found in the Cinder Hills OHV Area on the east side of US 89.

Current Road Information

Coconino National Forest
Peaks Ranger District
5075 North Hwy 89
Flagstaff, AZ 86004
(520) 526-0866

Map References

BLM Flagstaff
USFS Coconino National Forest: Peaks Ranger District
USGS 1:24,000 Sunset Crater West, Humphreys Peak, Flagstaff West
1:100,000 Flagstaff

Maptech CD-ROM: Flagstaff/Sedona/Prescott
Arizona Atlas & Gazetteer, p. 42
Arizona Road & Recreation Atlas, p. 35 & p. 69
Recreational Map of Arizona

Route Directions

▼ 0.0		From US 89, 1.3 miles south of the turn to Sunset Crater National Monument and 14 miles north of Flagstaff, zero trip meter and turn west on the graded dirt road at the sign for Schultz Pass (FR 420). Immediately, there is a track on right, FR 553. Continue straight on, following the sign for Schultz Pass. Seasonal closure gate.
6.6 ▲		Track on left is FR 553; then trail ends at the T-intersection with US 89. Turn right for Flagstaff; turn left for the Grand Canyon.
		GPS: N35°21.22′ W111°34.13′
▼ 0.1	SO	Track on right; then track on left and second track on right.
6.5 ▲	SO	Track on left; then track on right and second track on left.
▼ 0.3	SO	Track on left.
6.3 ▲	SO	Track on right.
▼ 0.7	SO	Track on left; then trailhead for Deer Hill Trail for pack animals, hikers, and mountain bikes.
5.9 ▲	SO	Trailhead for Deer Hill Trail for pack animals, hikers, and mountain bikes; then track on right.
		GPS: N35°20.72′ W111°34.46′
▼ 1.2	SO	Track on left and track on right.
5.4 ▲	SO	Track on right and track on left.
▼ 1.7	SO	Track on right.
4.9 ▲	SO	Track on left.
▼ 1.9	SO	Track on left.
4.7 ▲	SO	Track on right.
▼ 2.3	SO	Track on right.
4.3 ▲	SO	Track on left.
▼ 2.4	SO	Track on right.
4.2 ▲	SO	Track on left.
▼ 2.5	SO	Cross over creek.
4.1 ▲	SO	Cross over creek.
		GPS: N35°19.32′ W111°35.29′
▼ 2.6	SO	Track on right.
4.0 ▲	SO	Track on left.
▼ 3.0	SO	Track on left is FR 420D.
3.6 ▲	SO	Track on right is FR 420D.
		GPS: N35°18.88′ W111°35.35′
▼ 3.1	SO	Two tracks on right; then track on left.
3.5 ▲	SO	Track on right; then two tracks on left.
▼ 3.5	SO	Track on right.
3.1 ▲	SO	Track on left.
▼ 3.7	SO	Track on left.
2.9 ▲	SO	Track on right.
▼ 3.8	SO	Track on right; then track on left.
2.8 ▲	SO	Track on right; then track on left.
▼ 4.2	SO	Well-used track on right.
2.4 ▲	SO	Well-used track on left.
		GPS: N35°17.87′ W111°35.71′
▼ 4.4	SO	Track on right.
2.2 ▲	SO	Track on left.
▼ 5.2	SO	Cross over gas pipeline; tracks on right and left along pipeline.
1.4 ▲	SO	Cross over gas pipeline; tracks on left and right along pipeline.

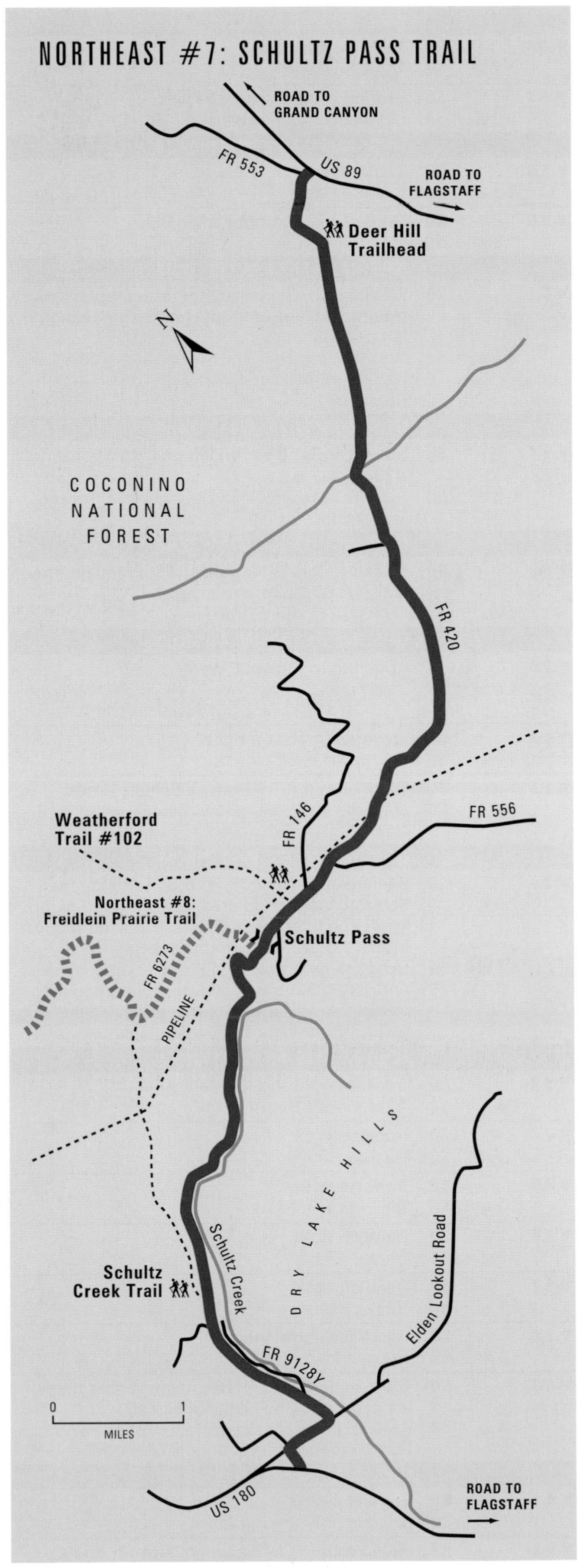

		GPS: N35°17.46' W111°36.61'
▼ 5.5	SO	Track on left.
1.1 ▲	SO	Track on right.
▼ 5.8	SO	Graded road on left is FR 556.
0.8 ▲	SO	Graded road on right is FR 556.
		GPS: N35°17.31' W111°37.16'
▼ 5.9	SO	Cattle guard.
0.7 ▲	SO	Cattle guard.
▼ 6.0	SO	Graded road on right is FR 146.
0.6 ▲	SO	Graded road on left is FR 146.
		GPS: N35°17.24' W111°37.42'
▼ 6.1	SO	Weatherford Trail #102 for hikers, horses, and mountain bikes on right. Trailhead parking on left.
0.5 ▲	SO	Weatherford Trail #102 for hikers, horses, and mountain bikes on left. Trailhead parking on right.
		GPS: N35°17.21' W111°37.54'
▼ 6.4	SO	Schultz Pass. Track on left goes to Sunset Trail #23.
0.2 ▲	SO	Schultz Pass. Track on right goes to Sunset Trail #23.
		GPS: N35°17.15' W111°37.86'
▼ 6.6	SO	Track on right is Northeast #8: Freidlein Prairie Trail, FR 6273. Zero trip meter.
0.0 ▲		Continue to the northeast.
		GPS: N35°17.12' W111°38.00'
▼ 0.0		Continue to the southwest.
4.8 ▲	SO	Track on left is Northeast #8: Freidlein Prairie Trail, FR 6273. Zero trip meter.
▼ 0.2	BL	Well-used track on right.
4.6 ▲	BR	Well-used track on left.
▼ 2.8	SO	Track on right. Trail leaves Schultz Creek.
2.0 ▲	SO	Track on left. Trail follows alongside Schultz Creek.
		GPS: N35°15.57' W111°39.75'
▼ 3.0	SO	Well-used track on right; then cattle guard. Entering watershed area, camping and campfires prohibited. Schultz Creek Trail on left for hikers, horses, and mountain bikes.
1.8 ▲	SO	Schultz Creek trail on right for hikers, horses, and mountain bikes. Leaving watershed area, camping and campfires permitted. Cattle guard; then well-used track on left.
		GPS: N35°15.44' W111°39.84'
▼ 3.2	SO	Track on right through fence line.
1.6 ▲	SO	Track on left through fence line.
▼ 3.4	SO	Track on right.
1.4 ▲	SO	Track on left.
▼ 3.5	SO	Track on right.
1.3 ▲	SO	Track on left.
▼ 3.6	SO	Track on right.
1.2 ▲	SO	Track on left.
▼ 3.7	SO	Track on right.
1.1 ▲	SO	Track on left.
▼ 3.8	SO	Two tracks on right.
1.0 ▲	SO	Two tracks on left.
▼ 4.0	SO	Track on left is FR 9128Y; then closure gates, leaving Coconino National Forest.
0.8 ▲	SO	Closure gates, entering Coconino National Forest; then track on right is FR 9128Y.
		GPS: N35°14.62' W111°39.66'
▼ 4.1	SO	Road is paved.
0.7 ▲	SO	Road is now graded dirt.
▼ 4.3	BR	Paved road on left is Elden Lookout Road.
0.5 ▲	BL	Paved road on right is Elden Lookout Road.
▼ 4.6	BL	Weatherford Road on right.
0.2 ▲	BR	Weatherford Road on left. Remain on main paved road.
▼ 4.8		Trail ends at the intersection with US 180. Turn left for Flagstaff.
0.0 ▲		Trail starts at the intersection of US 180, 0.6 miles north of mile marker 218, 3 miles north of Flagstaff. Zero trip meter and turn north on the paved Schultz Pass Road.
		GPS: N35°14.22' W111°39.98'

NORTHEAST REGION TRAIL #8

Freidlein Prairie Trail

Starting Point:	**Snowbowl Road, 2.3 miles north of the intersection with US 180**
Finishing Point:	**Northeast #7: Schultz Pass Trail**
Total Mileage:	**6.4 miles**
Unpaved Mileage:	**6.4 miles**
Driving Time:	**45 minutes**
Elevation Range:	**8,000–8,700 feet**
Usually Open:	**March to late November**
Best Time to Travel:	**March to late November**
Difficulty Rating:	**3**
Scenic Rating:	**8**
Remoteness Rating:	**+0**

Special Attractions

- Small trail that winds around the flank of the San Francisco Peaks.
- Spring wildflowers and splashes of golden aspens in the fall.

Description

This short trail is one of only a few smaller trails that travel the southern side of the San Francisco Peaks, which at 12,643 feet are the highest mountains in Arizona and part of the San Francisco Volcanic Field. The towering San Francisco Mountains

Passing through the pines below Schultz Peak (at over 8,000 feet)

The San Francisco Peaks rise above the aspen

are sacred to many Indian tribes and are known by several names. To the Navajo, they are Dok'o'sliid, "the sacred mountain of the west." The Hopi name is Nuvateekia-ovi, "the place of snow on the very top." The Hopi believe that their gods (kachinas) live on the peaks for part of each year and that they bring rain to the mesa area where the Hopi live.

This trail runs around the southern end of the Kachina Peaks Wilderness, which encompasses the peaks area, and through pine forests interspersed with stands of aspens, which typically change color around late November and early December. In spring, the area has patches of wildflowers, mainly irises.

The route chosen does not show up on all maps; it diverts to exit onto Northeast #7: Schultz Pass Trail on top of the pass. It is rough and rutted enough to make 4WD preferable, but it should not cause any problems in dry weather.

Current Road Information

Coconino National Forest
Peaks Ranger District
5075 North Hwy 89
Flagstaff, AZ 86004
(520) 526-0866

Map References

BLM Flagstaff
USFS Coconino National Forest: Peaks Ranger District
USGS 1:24,000 Humphreys Peak
1:100,000 Flagstaff
Maptech CD-ROM: Flagstaff/Sedona/Prescott
Arizona Atlas & Gazetteer, p. 42

Route Directions

▼ 0.0			From the Arizona Snowbowl Road, 2.3 miles north of the intersection with US 180, zero trip meter and turn east on FR 522 onto the well-used formed dirt trail. Seasonal closure gate at intersection.
	3.7 ▲		Trail ends on the Arizona Snowbowl Road, 2.3 miles north of US 180. Turn left to exit to the highway and Flagstaff; turn right to continue to the Arizona Snowbowl.
			GPS: N35°17.48' W111°42.35'
▼ 0.1		BL	Track on right.
	3.6 ▲	SO	Track on left.
▼ 0.8		SO	Track on left to corral.
	2.9 ▲	SO	Track on right to corral.
▼ 0.9		SO	Track on right.
	2.8 ▲	SO	Track on left.
▼ 1.4		SO	Track on right.
	2.3 ▲	SO	Track on left.
▼ 1.7		SO	Track on right.
	2.0 ▲	SO	Track on left.
▼ 2.5		SO	Track on right to campsite.
	1.2 ▲	SO	Track on left to campsite.
▼ 3.6		SO	Pass through fence line.
	0.1 ▲	SO	Pass through fence line.
			GPS: N35°17.77' W111°39.07'
▼ 3.7		TR	Well-used track ahead is closed to vehicles 0.1 miles farther on. Turn sharp right onto FR 6273 (unmarked). Zero trip meter.
	0.0 ▲		Continue to the southwest.
			GPS: N35°17.80' W111°39.04'
▼ 0.0			Continue to the south.
	2.7 ▲	TL	Well-used track ahead is closed to vehicles 0.1 miles farther on; turn sharp left and continue on FR 522. Zero trip meter.
▼ 0.8		BL	Hiking trail on right.
	1.9 ▲	BR	Hiking trail on left.
			GPS: N35°17.15' W111°39.11'
▼ 2.0		BR	Track on left.
	0.7 ▲	BL	Track on right.
			GPS: N35°17.43' W111°38.22'
▼ 2.6		SO	Cross over gas pipeline. Tracks on left and

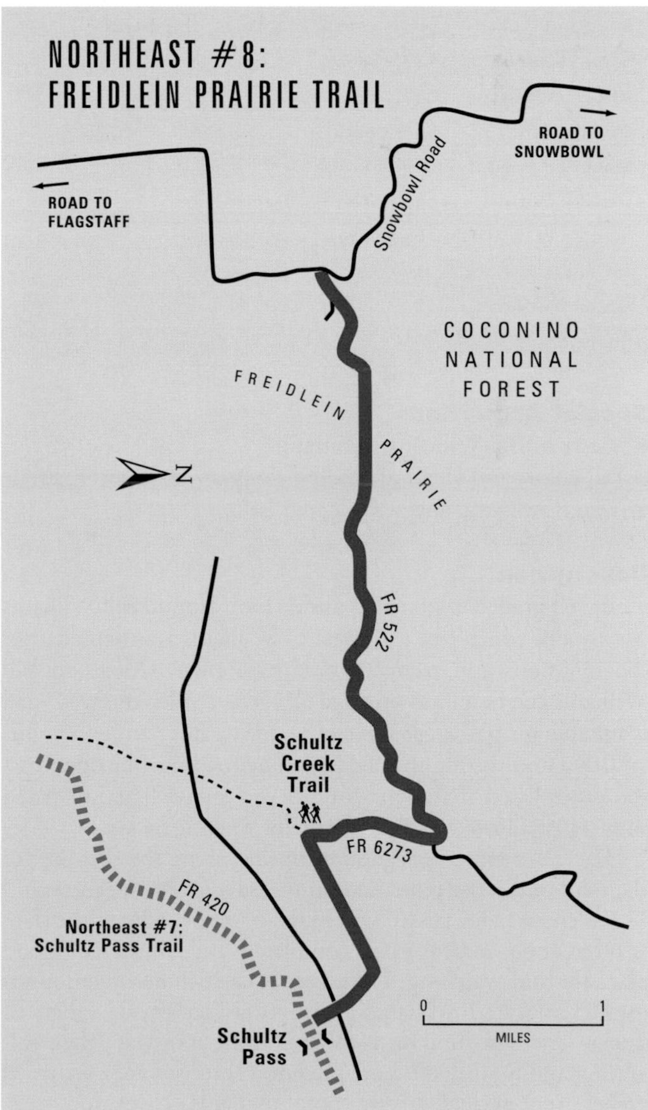

right along pipeline.

0.1 ▲ SO Cross over gas pipeline. Tracks on left and right along pipeline.

GPS: N35°17.25' W111°38.04'

▼ 2.7 Trail ends at the T-intersection with Northeast #7: Schultz Pass Trail. Turn right to return to Flagstaff; turn left to exit to US 89.

0.0 ▲ Trail commences on Northeast #7: Schultz Pass Trail, 6.6 miles southwest of US 89, 0.1 miles north of the entrance to the Museum of Northern Arizona. Zero trip meter and turn northwest on formed dirt trail, FR 6273.

GPS: N35°17.12' W111°38.00'

NORTHEAST REGION TRAIL #9

Bill Williams Mountain Loop Road

Starting Point:	**CR 73, 0.2 miles south of mile marker 179**
Finishing Point:	**I-40 at exit 157, Devil Dog Road**
Total Mileage:	**17.4 miles**
Unpaved Mileage:	**17.4 miles**
Driving Time:	**1.5 hours**
Elevation Range:	**6,400–7,200 feet**
Usually Open:	**Early April to December**
Best Time to Travel:	**Early April to December**
Difficulty Rating:	**1**
Scenic Rating:	**8**
Remoteness Rating:	**+0**

Special Attractions

- Views of Bill Williams Mountain.
- Fall colors and views of wildlife along an easy loop road.
- Waterfowl watching at Coleman Lake.

Description

This well-graded road makes a wide loop around Bill Williams Mountain, which like the town of Williams was named after the infamous and reclusive mountain man. (More on Bill Williams can be found on page 69.) The cinder-surfaced road is suitable for passenger vehicles in dry weather and is a popular drive from spring through fall. The road may be open past the dates listed if there is little or no snow. It is not gated shut—just allowed to close naturally when it snows.

There are some very good campsites along the first part of the road under the pine trees on the edge of the meadows.

Coleman Lake, passed within the first few miles of the trail, is often more marshy than completely full, but it is a good place for bird-watching. The presence of duck nesting mounds created by waterfowl habitat projects attract a wide variety of ducks. The best time for birding is April and May when migrating and nesting birds are present. Observers may see eared grebes, ring-necked ducks, coots, mallards, cinnamon teals,

Bill Williams Mountain viewed from the meadows along the trail

ruddy ducks, buffleheads, pintails, and others.

The road travels through a mix of forest and open prairie and crosses through some private property as it nears I-40. Please respect the landowners' property and remain on the road. There are good views of Bill Williams Mountain all along the trail.

The Stage Station Mountain Bike Loop, an 8-mile loop through rolling terrain, starts and finishes from this road. An old cabin, a stage stop on the route between Williams and Prescott, gives the loop its name.

Current Road Information

Kaibab National Forest
Williams Ranger District
742 South Clover Rd.
Williams, AZ 86046
(520) 635-4707

Map References

BLM Williams
USFS Kaibab National Forest: Williams Ranger District
USGS 1:24,000 Williams South, May Tank Pocket, Matterhorn, McLellan Reservoir
1:100,000 Williams
Maptech CD-ROM: Flagstaff/Sedona/Prescott
Arizona Atlas & Gazetteer, p. 41
Arizona Road & Recreation Atlas, p. 34 & p. 68
Recreational Map of Arizona

Route Directions

▼ 0.0 From CR 73 (Perkinsville Road), 0.2 miles south of mile marker 179, 6.3 miles south of Williams, zero trip meter and turn southwest onto graded dirt road, FR 108, signed to Coleman Lake and I-40.

5.9 ▲ Trail ends on CR 73. Turn left for Williams.

GPS: N35°09.85' W112°09.39'

▼ 0.1 SO Cattle guard and closure gate; then track on left.

5.8 ▲ SO Track on right; then cattle guard and closure gate.

▼ 0.6	SO	Track on right is FR 401.
5.3 ▲	SO	Track on left is FR 401.
		GPS: N35°09.67' W112°09.97'
▼ 1.2	SO	Track on left is FR 593.
4.7 ▲	SO	Track on right is FR 593.
		GPS: N35°09.18' W112°10.16'
▼ 1.5	SO	Cattle guard; then track on left is FR 590; then Coleman Lake on right.
4.4 ▲	SO	Track on right is FR 590; then cattle guard.
		GPS: N35°08.94' W112°10.24'
▼ 2.1	SO	Track on right through gate. Road leaves Coleman Lake.
3.8 ▲	SO	Coleman Lake on left; then track on left through gate.
▼ 2.8	SO	Small track on right.
3.1 ▲	SO	Small track on left.
▼ 3.1	SO	Track on right.
2.8 ▲	SO	Track on left.
▼ 3.8	SO	Track on right.
2.1 ▲	SO	Track on left.
▼ 4.4	SO	Track on left.
1.5 ▲	SO	Track on right.
▼ 4.5	SO	Cross over wash.
1.4 ▲	SO	Cross over wash.
▼ 4.9	SO	Track on left.
1.0 ▲	SO	Track on right.
▼ 5.5	SO	M.C. Tank on left.
0.4 ▲	SO	M.C. Tank on right.
		GPS: N35°06.94' W112°12.99'
▼ 5.9	SO	Track on left is FR 186 to D.T. Tank. Zero trip meter.
0.0 ▲		Continue to the northeast on FR 108, following the sign to Perkinsville Road.
		GPS: N35°06.71' W112°13.28'
▼ 0.0		Continue to the southwest, following the sign to Dutch Kid Tank and I-40.
6.9 ▲	SO	Track on right is FR 186 to D.T. Tank. Zero trip meter.
▼ 0.6	SO	Track on right; then cross over creek.
6.3 ▲	SO	Cross over creek; then track on left.
▼ 0.9	SO	Track on right is FR 42.
6.0 ▲	SO	Track on left is FR 42.
		GPS: N35°06.83' W112°14.11'
▼ 1.9	SO	Track on left is FR 41.

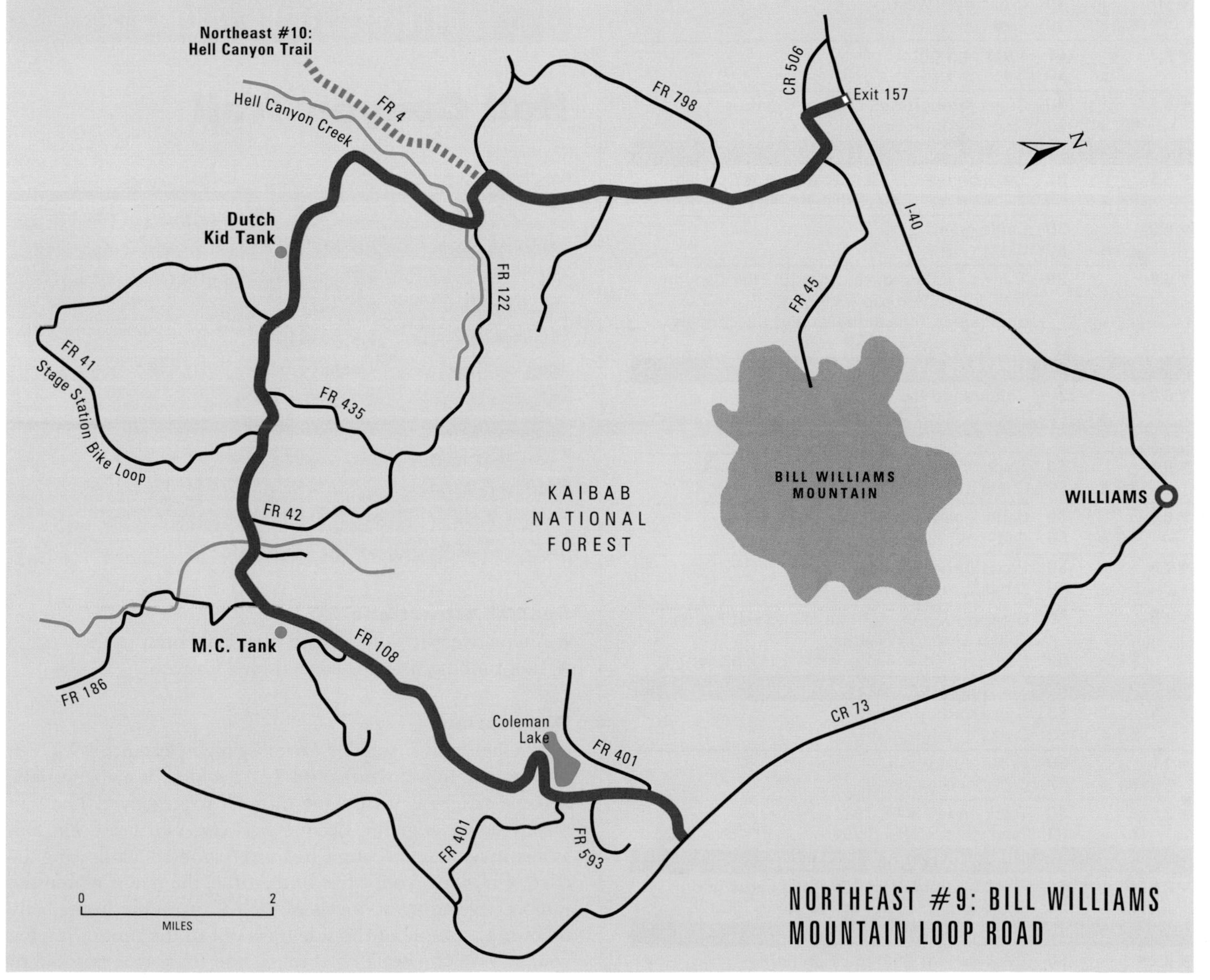

	5.0 ▲	SO	Track on right is FR 41.
			GPS: N35°07.20' W112°15.04'
▼ 2.3		SO	Cattle guard; then track on right is FR 435.
	4.6 ▲	SO	Track on left is FR 435; then cattle guard.
			GPS: N35°07.27' W112°15.44'
▼ 3.1		SO	Cross over creek; then track on left is FR 41, also marked as the Stage Station Bike Loop.
	3.8 ▲	SO	Track on right is FR 41, also marked as the Stage Station Bike Loop; then cross over creek.
			GPS: N35°07.57' W112°16.13'
▼ 3.8		SO	Track on right and track on left; then Dutch Kid Tank on left.
	3.1 ▲	SO	Dutch Kid Tank on right; then track on right and track on left.
			GPS: N35°07.86' W112°16.77'
▼ 4.0		SO	Cross through creek; then track on right is FR 532; then track on left.
	2.9 ▲	SO	Track on right; then track on left is FR 532; then cross through creek.
▼ 4.5		SO	Track on left.
	2.4 ▲	SO	Track on right.
▼ 5.2		SO	Track on right is FR 446.
	1.7 ▲	SO	Track on left is FR 446.
			GPS: N35°08.80' W112°17.42'
▼ 5.7		SO	Cross over wash.
	1.2 ▲	SO	Cross over wash.
▼ 6.3		SO	Track on right.
	0.6 ▲	SO	Track on left.
▼ 6.4		SO	Cross through Hell Canyon Creek.
	0.5 ▲	SO	Cross through Hell Canyon Creek.
			GPS: N35°09.52' W112°16.53'
▼ 6.5		BL	Track on right is FR 122; then track on left.
	0.4 ▲	BR	Track on right; then track on left is FR 122.
▼ 6.6		SO	Cattle guard.
	0.3 ▲	SO	Cattle guard.
▼ 6.9		SO	Track on left is Northeast #10: Hell Canyon Trail, FR 4. Zero trip meter.
	0.0 ▲		Continue to the southeast and descend to cross through Hell Canyon.
			GPS: N35°09.68' W112°16.89'
▼ 0.0			Continue to the northwest.
	4.6 ▲	SO	Track on right is Northeast #10: Hell Canyon Trail, FR 4. Zero trip meter.
▼ 0.1		SO	Track on left; then cross through creek.
	4.5 ▲	SO	Cross through creek; then track on right.
▼ 0.6		SO	Cattle guard.
	4.0 ▲	SO	Cattle guard.
▼ 1.0		SO	Cross through wash.
	3.6 ▲	SO	Cross through wash.
▼ 1.5		SO	Graded road on right goes into Hat Ranch. Follow sign to Williams.
	3.1 ▲	BR	Graded road on left goes into Hat Ranch.
			GPS: N35°10.89' W112°16.38'
▼ 1.6		SO	Cross through wash.
	3.0 ▲	SO	Cross through wash.
▼ 2.1		SO	Cross over wash.
	2.5 ▲	SO	Cross over wash.
▼ 2.5		SO	Track on left is FR 798.
	2.1 ▲	SO	Track on right is FR 798.
			GPS: N35°11.75' W112°16.05'
▼ 2.8		SO	Track on right is FR 455; then cattle guard.
	1.8 ▲	SO	Cattle guard; then track on left is FR 455.
			GPS: N35°11.94' W112°15.92'
▼ 3.2		SO	Track on left; then track on right.
	1.4 ▲	SO	Track on left; then track on right.
▼ 3.5		SO	Track on right.
	1.1 ▲	SO	Track on left.
▼ 3.7		SO	Cross over creek on bridge; then track on right is FR 45. No camping past this point.
	0.9 ▲	SO	Track on left is FR 45; then cross over creek on bridge. Camping permitted past this point.
			GPS: N35°12.82' W112°16.08'
▼ 3.9		BL	Track on right; remain on main graded road.
	0.7 ▲	BR	Track on left; remain on main graded road.
▼ 4.2		TR	Turn right, remaining on FR 108; follow sign to I-40. Paved road ahead is CR 506.
	0.4 ▲	TL	T-intersection; paved road on right is CR 506. Turn left, remaining on graded dirt road FR 108.
			GPS: N35°12.78' W112°16.56'
▼ 4.6			Trail ends at the intersection with I-40, exit 157.
	0.0 ▲		Trail commences on I-40, exit 157, Devil Dog Road. Proceed to the south side of the freeway and zero trip meter at cattle guard, and proceed south on graded dirt road. No camping for the first mile.
			GPS: N35°13.12' W112°16.57'

NORTHEAST REGION TRAIL #10

Hell Canyon Trail

Starting Point:	**Northeast #9: Bill Williams Mountain Loop Road, 4.6 miles south of I-40**
Finishing Point:	**Arizona 89, 8.9 miles south of Ash Fork, 0.2 miles south of mile marker 355**
Total Mileage:	**9.9 miles**
Unpaved Mileage:	**9.9 miles**
Driving Time:	**1 hour**
Elevation Range:	**5,100–6,500 feet**
Usually Open:	**Year-round**
Best Time to Travel:	**Dry weather**
Difficulty Rating:	**3**
Scenic Rating:	**7**
Remoteness Rating:	**+0**

Special Attractions

- Alternative exit from Kaibab National Forest to the west.
- Trail running near the edge of Hell Canyon.

Description

This rough trail is suitable for most high-clearance 4WDs in dry weather. In wet weather it is best avoided, as many sections become extremely greasy and difficult to negotiate. The trail travels down a gentle decline between Northeast #9: Bill Williams Mountain Loop Road and Arizona 89, following the edge of Hell Canyon. Most of the time, the trail is within the juniper vegetation, so views of Hell Canyon are limited. By following a couple of the side trails out to the rim, or leaving your vehicle and walking through the trees, it is possible to

Views of Bill Williams Mountain as you crest the last rise before intersecting with Northeast #9: Bill Williams Mountain Loop Road

view the rugged, dark gray-black depths of Hell Canyon. The canyon is composed of the dark lava predominant in this region, which is probably how it got its name.

Navigation is very easy, although the trail is narrow at times and lightly used. There are few side trails to confuse the navigator. For the most part the trail heads straight in a southwesterly direction. As it descends, there are views ahead to Big Black Mesa and Prescott National Forest.

There are a few suitable campsites, mainly at the top and bottom of the trail, and at the edge of Hell Canyon.

Current Road Information

Kaibab National Forest
Williams Ranger District
742 South Clover Rd.
Williams, AZ 86046
(520) 635-4707

Map References

BLM Williams
USFS Kaibab National Forest: Williams Ranger District
USGS 1:24,000 McLellan Reservoir, Matterhorn, Meath Spring
1:100,000 Williams
Maptech CD-ROM: Flagstaff/Sedona/Prescott
Arizona Atlas & Gazetteer, p. 41
Arizona Road & Recreation Atlas, p. 34 & p. 68

Route Directions

Mileage		Direction
▼ 0.0		From Northeast #9: Bill Williams Mountain Loop Road, 4.6 miles south of I-40, zero trip meter and turn southwest on small formed trail, FR 4.
2.7 ▲		Trail ends at the intersection with Northeast #9: Bill Williams Mountain Loop Road. Turn left for I-40; turn right to continue around the loop to CR 73.
		GPS: N35°09.68' W112°16.89'
▼ 0.8	SO	Cattle guard and closure gate.
1.9 ▲	SO	Cattle guard and closure gate.
▼ 1.1	SO	Track on right.
1.6 ▲	SO	Track on left.
▼ 1.6	SO	Track on left. Trail drops toward Hell Canyon.
1.1 ▲	SO	Track on right.
		GPS: N35°08.82' W112°18.18'
▼ 2.4	SO	Track on left.
0.3 ▲	SO	Track on right.
▼ 2.7	SO	Cattle guard. Zero trip meter.
0.0 ▲		Continue to the northeast.
		GPS: N35°08.12' W112°18.92'
▼ 0.0		Continue to the southwest.
4.3 ▲	SO	Cattle guard. Zero trip meter.
▼ 0.3	SO	Track on left.
4.0 ▲	SO	Track on right.
▼ 2.7	SO	Track on left.
1.6 ▲	SO	Track on right.
		GPS: N35°06.74' W112°21.15'
▼ 3.0	SO	Pass under power lines; track on left and track

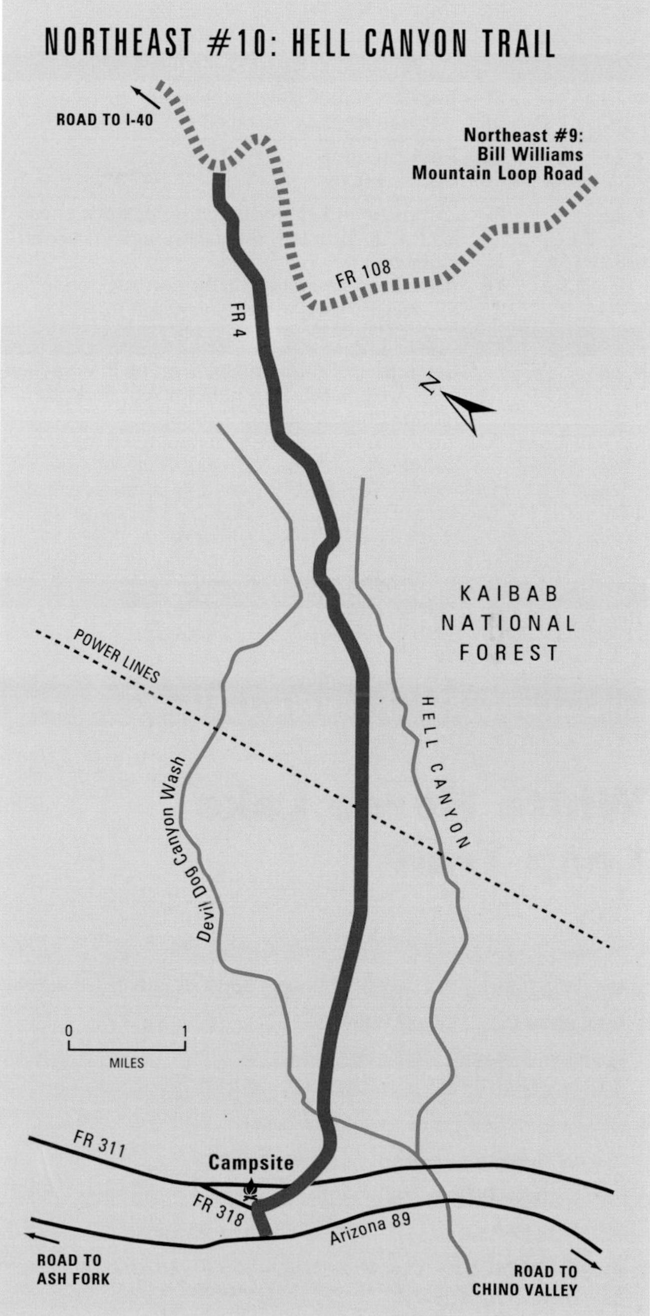

▼	▲		
			on right under power lines.
	1.3 ▲	SO	Pass under power lines; track on left and track on right under power lines.
▼ 4.3		SO	Track on left is FR 322. Zero trip meter.
	0.0 ▲		Continue to the northeast.
			GPS: N35°06.40' W112°22.62'
▼ 0.0			Continue to the southwest; track on right.
	2.9 ▲	SO	Track on left; then track on right is FR 322. Zero trip meter.
▼ 1.0		SO	Track on left.
	1.9 ▲	SO	Track on right.
			GPS: N35°06.12' W112°23.54'
▼ 1.5		SO	Cross through Devil Dog Canyon Wash.
	1.4 ▲	SO	Cross through Devil Dog Canyon Wash.
			GPS: N35°05.92' W112°24.06'
▼ 1.8		SO	Cross through wash.
	1.1 ▲	SO	Cross through wash.
▼ 2.1		BR	Track on left, FR 311, follows pipeline.
	0.8 ▲	BL	Track on right, FR 311, follows pipeline.
			GPS: N35°05.80' W112°24.70'
▼ 2.2		BL	Track on right follows pipeline.
	0.7 ▲	BR	Track on left follows pipeline.
▼ 2.4		SO	Track on right.
	0.5 ▲	SO	Track on left.
▼ 2.6		TL	Campsite and cinder pit on right; track ahead is FR 318. Turn left, remaining on FR 4 toward highway.
	0.3 ▲	TR	Campsite ahead and cinder pit. Track on left is FR 318. Turn right, remaining on FR 4.
			GPS: N35°06.09' W112°25.07'
▼ 2.9			Cattle guard; then trail ends at the intersection with Arizona 89. Turn right for Ash Fork; turn left for Chino Valley.
	0.0 ▲		Trail commences on Arizona 89, 8.9 miles south of Ash Fork, 0.2 miles south of mile marker 355. Zero trip meter and turn east across cattle guard onto small formed trail marked FR 4. There is no sign on the highway.
			GPS: N35°05.87' W112°25.28'

NORTHEAST REGION TRAIL #11

White Horse Lake Loop Trail

Starting Point:	**CR 73 at mile marker 178**
Finishing Point:	**CR 73, 0.1 miles north of mile marker 176**
Total Mileage:	**28 miles**
Unpaved Mileage:	**28 miles**
Driving Time:	**2.75 hours**
Elevation Range:	**6,300–7,300 feet**
Usually Open:	**April to December**
Best Time to Travel:	**Dry weather**
Difficulty Rating:	**2**
Scenic Rating:	**8**
Remoteness Rating:	**+0**

Special Attractions

- Fishing and camping at White Horse Lake and fishing at J. D. Dam Lake.
- J. D. cabins and grave.
- Long trail traveling through the Kaibab National Forest.

History

White Horse Lake was constructed in 1934–1935 as a community lake for the people of Williams. Runoff from snowmelt nearly breached the dam, but it was saved by a quick and concerted effort by the people of Williams. In 1951 the dam was enlarged to double its original size.

J. D. Dam Lake is the older of the two along this trail. It was constructed by local rancher J. D. Douglas, who is buried a short distance from the trail near the remains of three log cabins that he built. He died in 1884 at the age of 64. The site also has a later cabin constructed of railroad sleepers, which is still used by the forest service. Visitors are welcome but are asked to respect the privacy of the occupants.

Description

This trail passes by two popular fishing spots within the Kaibab National Forest. From the start of the trail on CR 73 to White Horse Lake, the trail is an easy 1-rated gravel road. There are many side trails leading off from this road, including the start of Northeast #12: Sycamore Point Trail.

White Horse Lake is set in a shallow dish among ponderosa pines. Along the lake shore, there is a developed campground operated by the forest service. Near the lake, camping is restricted to these developed sites, but there are many options for backcountry camping nearby. There is a boat launch and the lake is stocked with trout, bluegill, and catfish.

Tule Tank Wash crossing

From CR 73 to White Horse Lake the road can be busy. Once past the lake the road becomes more suitable for high-clearance vehicles and sees a lot less traffic as it travels through pine forest as a narrower, single-track road. The road bisects Northeast #12: Sycamore Point Trail again at J. D. Dam Lake, a slightly smaller but very pretty lake that offers excellent blue-ribbon trout fishing. Reeds and water lilies in the water and the surrounding pine forest make an attractive scene. There is abundant bird life and the area is noisy with bird calls. The land immediately surrounding the lake is for day use only, but camping is permitted outside of a fence line a short distance from the lakeshore. There is a boat-launching point, which was renovated in 1989.

Past J. D. Dam, the trail drops in standard again to become a formed single-track trail. The next couple of miles are recommended for dry weather travel only; they become extremely muddy when wet.

Once you are past Tule Tank, the worst of the mud is over

Bird life abounds at the picturesque J. D. Dam Lake

and the trail continues to gently climb its way back to CR 73. It crosses open Pine Flat and the start of several hiking trails before finishing back on CR 73, less than 2 miles south of its starting point. There is excellent camping to be found along the southern section of the trail.

Current Road Information

Kaibab National Forest
Williams Ranger District
742 South Clover Rd.
Williams, AZ 86046
(520) 635-4707

Kaibab National Forest
Chalender Ranger District
742 South Clover Rd.
Williams, AZ 86046
(520) 635-2676

Map References

BLM Williams, Flagstaff
USFS Kaibab National Forest: Williams and Chalender Ranger Districts
USGS 1:24,000 Williams South, Davenport Hill, White Horse Lake, Sycamore Point, May Tank Pocket
1:100,000 Williams, Flagstaff
Maptech CD-ROM: Flagstaff/Sedona/Prescott
Arizona Atlas & Gazetteer, p. 41
Arizona Road & Recreation Atlas, p. 34 & p. 68
Recreational Map of Arizona

Route Directions

Mileage	Reverse	Action	Directions
▼ 0.0			From CR 73, 8 miles south of Williams at mile marker 178, zero trip meter and turn east on graded dirt road, FR 110, at the sign for White Horse Lake.
	7.0 ▲		Trail ends back on CR 73, 8 miles south of Williams. Turn right for Williams.
			GPS: N35°08.53' W112°08.86'
▼ 0.4		SO	Cattle guard.
	6.6 ▲	SO	Cattle guard.
▼ 1.0		SO	Track on right is FR 165.
	6.0 ▲	SO	Track on left is FR 165.
			GPS: N35°08.46' W112°07.90'
▼ 1.9		SO	Track on right is FR 706 to Summit Mountain Trailhead.
	5.1 ▲	SO	Track on left is FR 706 to Summit Mountain Trailhead.
			GPS: N35°08.12' W112°07.11'
▼ 2.2		SO	Track on right is FR 147.
	4.8 ▲	SO	Track on left is FR 147.
			GPS: N35°07.88' W112°06.87'
▼ 2.3		SO	Track on left is FR 747.
	4.7 ▲	SO	Track on right is FR 747.
▼ 3.7		SO	Cattle guard.
	3.3 ▲	SO	Cattle guard.
▼ 4.0		SO	Track on right is FR 730.
	3.0 ▲	SO	Track on left is FR 730.
▼ 4.3		SO	Track on right is FR 736.
	2.7 ▲	SO	Track on left is FR 736.
			GPS: N35°07.55' W112°04.95'
▼ 4.5		SO	Graded road on right is FR 740.
	2.5 ▲	SO	Graded road on left is FR 740.
			GPS: N35°07.57' W112°04.69'
▼ 4.7		SO	Track on left is FR 747. Take this trail and then turn right onto FR 14 to reach J. D. cabins and grave.
	2.3 ▲	SO	Track on right is FR 747. Take this trail and then turn right onto FR 14 to reach J. D. cabins and grave.
▼ 4.8		SO	Small track on right.
	2.2 ▲	SO	Small track on left.
▼ 5.1		SO	Track on left is FR 422.
	1.9 ▲	SO	Track on right is FR 422.
			GPS: N35°07.60' W112°04.06'
▼ 5.2		SO	Corral on left.
	1.8 ▲	SO	Corral on right.
▼ 5.5		SO	Track on right is FR 742.
	1.5 ▲	SO	Track on left is FR 742.
			GPS: N35°07.35' W112°03.78'
▼ 5.6		SO	Track on left.
	1.4 ▲	SO	Track on right.
▼ 6.4		SO	Track on right is FR 11.
	0.6 ▲	SO	Track on left is FR 11.
▼ 7.0		TL	Turn left onto FR 109, following the sign for White Horse Lake and J. D. Dam. Ahead is Northeast #12: Sycamore Point Trail, FR 110. Zero trip meter.
	0.0 ▲		Continue to the northwest.
			GPS: N35°06.29' W112°02.89'
▼ 0.0			Continue to the northeast and cross cattle guard.
	1.6 ▲	TR	Cattle guard; then T-intersection; turn right onto FR 110, following the sign to Williams. Zero trip meter. Track on left is Northeast #12: Sycamore Point Trail, FR 110.
▼ 1.0		SO	Small track on right.
	0.6 ▲	SO	Small track on left.
▼ 1.6		TR	Turn right onto graded road FR 12, following the sign to J. D. Dam and Sycamore Point. Zero trip meter. White Horse Lake Campground is straight ahead, 0.6 miles.
	0.0 ▲		Continue to the southeast.
			GPS: N35°06.67' W112°01.51'
▼ 0.0			Continue to the east.
	4.7 ▲	TL	T-intersection; turn left onto graded road FR 109, following the sign to Williams. Graded road on right goes 0.6 miles to White Horse Lake Campground.
▼ 0.4		SO	Track on right is FR 765.

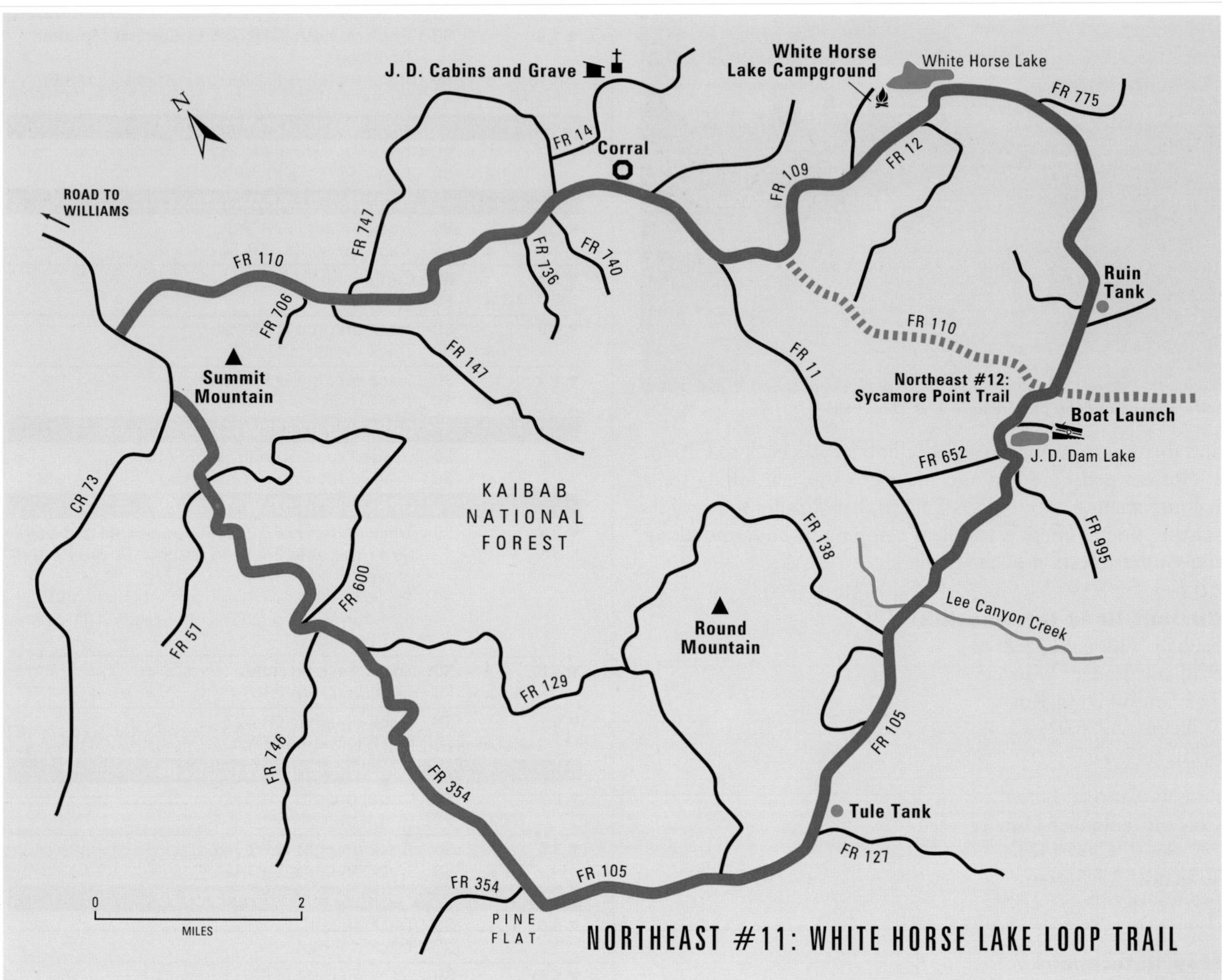

NORTHEAST #11: WHITE HORSE LAKE LOOP TRAIL

	4.3 ▲	SO	Track on left is FR 765.
			GPS: N35°06.68′ W112°01.09′
▼ 1.0		SO	Track on left.
	3.7 ▲	SO	Track on right.
▼ 1.4		SO	Track on left is FR 771.
	3.3 ▲	SO	Track on right is FR 771.
			GPS: N35°06.49′ W112°00.16′
▼ 1.5		SO	Track on left is FR 775.
	3.2 ▲	SO	Track on right is FR 775.
▼ 1.6		SO	Track on right.
	3.1 ▲	SO	Track on left.
▼ 2.2		SO	Track on right is FR 786.
	2.5 ▲	SO	Track on left is FR 786.
			GPS: N35°05.80′ W111°59.78′
▼ 2.5		SO	Cattle guard; then track on left.
	2.2 ▲	SO	Track on right; then cattle guard.
▼ 3.0		SO	Track on left.
	1.7 ▲	SO	Track on right.
▼ 3.8		SO	Track on right.
	0.9 ▲	SO	Track on left.
▼ 3.9		SO	Ruin Tank on left.
	0.8 ▲	SO	Ruin Tank on right.
			GPS: N35°04.61′ W112°00.58′

▼ 4.0		SO	Track on left.
	0.7 ▲	SO	Track on right.
▼ 4.7		TR	T-intersection. Turn right onto FR 105, following the sign to J. D. Dam. Track on left is Northeast #12: Sycamore Point Trail, FR 110. Zero trip meter.
	0.0 ▲		Continue to the southeast.
			GPS: N35°04.21′ W112°01.27′
▼ 0.0			Continue to the west.
	0.5 ▲	TL	Turn left on FR 12, following the sign to White Horse Lake. Ahead is Northeast #12: Sycamore Point Trail, FR 110. Zero trip meter.
▼ 0.1		SO	Track on right is FR 110 and the continuation of Northeast #12: Sycamore Point Trail.
	0.4 ▲	SO	Track on left is FR 110 and the continuation of Northeast #12: Sycamore Point Trail.
▼ 0.3		SO	Cattle guard.
	0.2 ▲	SO	Cattle guard.
▼ 0.5		SO	Graded road on left over cattle guard to J. D. Dam boat launch. Zero trip meter.
	0.0 ▲		Continue to the northeast.
			GPS: N35°04.17′ W112°01.75′
▼ 0.0			Continue to the west. Track on right is FR 720.
	7.4 ▲	SO	Track on left is FR 720; then graded road on

right over cattle guard to J. D. Dam boat launch. Zero trip meter.

▼ 0.2		SO	Cross through wash.
	7.2 ▲	SO	Cross through wash.
▼ 0.3		BL	Track on right is FR 652.
	7.1 ▲	BR	Track on left is FR 652.
			GPS: N35°04.02' W112°01.96'
▼ 0.4		SO	Parking area on left; trail is now small formed trail.
	7.0 ▲	SO	Parking area on right; trail is now roughly graded.
▼ 0.5		SO	Track on left is FR 995.
	6.9 ▲	SO	Track on right is FR 995.
▼ 1.6		SO	Track on left is FR 990.
	5.8 ▲	SO	Track on right is FR 990.
			GPS: N35°03.46' W112°02.95'
▼ 1.8		SO	Track on right is FR 11. Continue on FR 105 and cross through wash.
	5.6 ▲	BR	Cross through wash; then track on left is FR 11. Continue on FR 105.
			GPS: N35°03.42' W112°03.14'
▼ 2.1		SO	Cross through Lee Canyon creek.
	5.3 ▲	SO	Cross through Lee Canyon creek.
			GPS: N35°03.33' W112°03.41'
▼ 2.4		SO	Track on left is FR 986; then track on right is FR 646.
	5.0 ▲	SO	Track on left is FR 646; then track on right is FR 986.
▼ 2.5		SO	Cattle guard; then track on right is FR 138. Round Mountain Bike Loop starts from the intersection. Continue on FR 105 and cross through creek.
	4.9 ▲	SO	Cross through creek; then track on left is FR 138. Round Mountain Bike Loop starts from the intersection. Continue on FR 105 and cross cattle guard.
			GPS: N35°03.24' W112°03.80'
▼ 2.7		SO	Track on right is FR 642.
	4.7 ▲	SO	Track on left is FR 642.
▼ 3.2		SO	Cross through creek.
	4.2 ▲	SO	Cross through creek.
▼ 3.4		SO	Track on right is FR 640; then cross through creek.
	4.0 ▲	SO	Cross through creek; then track on left is FR 640.
			GPS: N35°02.69' W112°04.39'
▼ 4.3		SO	Tule Tank on left.
	3.1 ▲	SO	Tule Tank on right.
			GPS: N35°02.27' W112°05.27'
▼ 4.5		SO	Track on left is FR 127.
	2.9 ▲	BL	Track on right is FR 127. Bear left, remaining on FR 105.
			GPS: N35°02.14' W112°05.45'
▼ 5.5		SO	Track on right is FR 138.
	1.9 ▲	SO	Track on left is FR 138.
			GPS: N35°02.23' W112°06.46'
▼ 5.9		SO	Track on left is FR 125. Continue on FR 105.
	1.5 ▲	SO	Track on right is FR 125. Continue on FR 105.
			GPS: N35°02.37' W112°06.94'
▼ 6.6		SO	Track on left through fence line; then cross through creek.
	0.8 ▲	SO	Cross through creek; then track on right through fence line.
▼ 7.1		BR	Cattle guard; then bear right. Track on left is FR 936.
	0.3 ▲	BL	Track on right is FR 936; bear left over cattle guard.
▼ 7.4		SO	Track on left is FR 354. Zero trip meter.
	0.0 ▲		Continue to the southeast. Road is now FR 105.
			GPS: N35°03.03' W112°08.12'
▼ 0.0			Continue to the northwest. Road is now FR 354.
	3.5 ▲	BL	Track on right is FR 354. Zero trip meter.
▼ 0.4		SO	Two tracks on right.
	3.1 ▲	SO	Two tracks on left.
▼ 0.7		SO	Track on right is FR 620.
	2.8 ▲	SO	Track on left is FR 620.
			GPS: N35°03.66' W112°08.25'
▼ 0.8		SO	Cross through creek.
	2.7 ▲	SO	Cross through creek.
▼ 1.1		SO	Track on left.
	2.4 ▲	SO	Track on right.
▼ 1.2		SO	Cross through creek.
	2.3 ▲	SO	Cross through creek.
▼ 1.3		SO	Cross through creek.
	2.2 ▲	SO	Cross through creek.
▼ 1.7		SO	Cross over creek on bridge.
	1.8 ▲	SO	Cross over creek on bridge.
			GPS: N35°04.43' W112°08.45'
▼ 3.1		SO	Graded road on right is FR 129 to Round Mountain.
	0.4 ▲	BR	Graded road on left is FR 129 to Round Mountain.
			GPS: N35°05.30' W112°08.35'
▼ 3.5		SO	Graded road on left is FR 746. Zero trip meter.
	0.0 ▲		Continue to the southeast.
			GPS: N35°05.66' W112°08.60'
▼ 0.0			Continue to the northwest.
	3.3 ▲	SO	Graded road on right is FR 746. Zero trip meter.
▼ 0.2		SO	Track on right is FR 600.
	3.1 ▲	SO	Track on left is FR 600.
			GPS: N35°05.72' W112°08.72'
▼ 0.7		SO	Cross through wash.
	2.6 ▲	SO	Cross through wash.
▼ 0.9		SO	Track on left is FR 904.
	2.4 ▲	SO	Track on right is FR 904.
			GPS: N35°06.17' W112°08.61'
▼ 1.3		BR	Track on left is FR 902.
	2.0 ▲	BL	Track on right is FR 902.
			GPS: N35°06.28' W112°08.95'
▼ 1.9		SO	Track on left.
	1.4 ▲	SO	Track on right.
▼ 2.1		SO	Cattle guard.
	1.2 ▲	SO	Cattle guard.
▼ 2.2		SO	Cattle guard.
	1.1 ▲	SO	Cattle guard.
▼ 2.4		SO	Track on right is FR 600. Track on left is FR 57, the Overland Trail to Davenport.
	0.9 ▲	SO	Track on right is FR 57, the Overland Trail to Davenport. Track on left is FR 600.
			GPS: N35°07.19' W112°08.91'
▼ 2.8		SO	Closure gate.
	0.5 ▲	SO	Closure gate.
▼ 3.1		SO	Track on right is FR 195.
	0.2 ▲	SO	Track on left is FR 195.
			GPS: N35°07.67' W112°08.69'
▼ 3.3			Trail ends back on CR 73. Turn right for Williams.
	0.0 ▲		From CR 73, 0.1 miles north of mile marker 176, zero trip meter and turn north on graded dirt road, FR 354, sign-posted to Pine Flat.
			GPS: N35°07.83' W112°08.72'

NORTHEAST REGION TRAIL #12

Sycamore Point Trail

Starting Point:	**Northeast #11: White Horse Lake Loop Trail, 7 miles from CR 73 along the north end**
Finishing Point:	**Sycamore Point**
Total Mileage:	**7.5 miles**
Unpaved Mileage:	**7.5 miles**
Driving Time:	**1 hour**
Elevation Range:	**6,000–7,000 feet**
Usually Open:	**April to December**
Best Time to Travel:	**Dry weather**
Difficulty Rating:	**2**
Scenic Rating:	**10**
Remoteness Rating:	**+0**

Special Attractions

- Exceptional views of Sycamore Canyon from Sycamore Point.
- Can be used to shorten Northeast #11: White Horse Lake Loop Trail.
- Shady campsites under ponderosa pines.

Description

Sycamore Point is an easily accessible, not-to-be-missed viewpoint with stunning vistas more than 1,000 feet down a sheer drop into beautiful Sycamore Canyon, part of the wilderness area. The view of the folded red Coconino Sandstone cliffs that form Sycamore Canyon is one that will never be forgotten.

The view from Sycamore Point into Sycamore Canyon

The access trail to the point leaves Northeast #11: White Horse Lake Loop Trail 7 miles from the northern exit onto CR 73 and cuts across the loop, bypassing White Horse Lake to intersect with it again at J. D. Dam Lake. This first part of the trail travels in the cool shade of a ponderosa pine forest. There is an excellent chance of seeing elk as well as mule deer and many smaller forest creatures.

Past the second intersection with Northeast #11: White Horse Lake Loop Trail, the road is one-way only as it travels through open forest out to the point. The trail ends in a small loop on Sycamore Point.

Sycamore Point has some shade at the turnaround point, and there is room to camp and picnic near the edge of the canyon.

Current Road Information

Kaibab National Forest
Williams Ranger District
742 South Clover Rd.
Williams, AZ 86046
(520) 635-4707

Map References

BLM Williams
USFS Kaibab National Forest: Williams Ranger District
USGS 1:24,000 White Horse Lake, Sycamore Point
1:100,000 Williams
Maptech CD-ROM: Flagstaff/Sedona/Prescott
Arizona Atlas & Gazetteer, p. 41
Arizona Road & Recreation Atlas, p. 34 & p. 68
Recreational Map of Arizona

Route Directions

▼ 0.0		Trail commences on Northeast #11: White Horse Lake Loop Trail, 7 miles from the northern end of the trail. Zero trip meter and turn southeast on small roughly graded trail marked FR 110. There is a sign at the intersection for White Horse Lake Campground 3 miles to the north.
2.9 ▲		Trail ends at the intersection with Northeast #11: White Horse Lake Loop Trail. Turn right for White Horse Lake; turn left to exit to Williams.
		GPS: N35°06.29' W112°02.89'
▼ 0.1	SO	Closure gate.
2.8 ▲	SO	Closure gate.
▼ 1.1	SO	Track on right is FR 660.
1.8 ▲	SO	Track on left is FR 660.
		GPS: N35°05.42' W112°02.52'
▼ 1.5	SO	Cattle guard.
1.4 ▲	SO	Cattle guard.
▼ 2.1	SO	Track on right is FR 653.
0.8 ▲	SO	Track on left is FR 653.
		GPS: N35°04.74' W112°01.72'
▼ 2.2	SO	Track on left.
0.7 ▲	SO	Track on right.
▼ 2.5	SO	Track on left.
0.4 ▲	SO	Track on right.
▼ 2.8	TL	Turn left at T-intersection onto graded road FR 105, which is part of Northeast #11: White Horse Lake Loop Trail.
0.1 ▲	TR	Turn right onto small roughly graded road FR 110, leaving Northeast #11: White Horse Lake Loop Trail.
		GPS: N35°04.25' W112°01.37'
▼ 2.9	SO	Track on left is FR 12, continuation of Northeast #11: White Horse Lake Loop Trail. Zero trip meter and continue on FR 110, following the sign to Sycamore Point.
0.0 ▲		Track on right is FR 12, continuation of Northeast #11: White Horse Lake Loop Trail. Continue to the west on FR 110.
		GPS: N35°04.21' W112°01.27'

NORTHEAST #12: SYCAMORE POINT TRAIL

Northeast #11: White Horse Lake Loop Trail
FR 109
White Horse Lake Campground
White Horse Lake
FR 110
FR 660
KAIBAB NATIONAL FOREST
FR 105
FR 12
J. D. Dam Lake
FR 721
FR 795
FR 729
N
FR 110
FR 760
SYCAMORE CANYON
Sycamore Point
0 1
MILES

▼ 0.0		Continue to the southeast on FR 110.
▼ 0.2	SO	Track on right is FR 721.
		GPS: N35°04.06' W112°01.08'
▼ 0.4	SO	Track on left is FR 795.
▼ 0.8	SO	Track on left is FR 795; then second track on left is FR 729 and track on right.
		GPS: N35°03.83' W112°00.55'
▼ 1.8	SO	Track on left is FR 760; then cross through wash.
		GPS: N35°03.24' W111°59.65'
▼ 2.6	SO	Track on right.
▼ 2.9	SO	Small track on right.
▼ 4.5	BR	Start of final loop.
		GPS: N35°01.50' W111°58.69'
▼ 4.6		Trail ends at Sycamore Point.
		GPS: N35°01.43' W111°58.65'

NORTHEAST REGION TRAIL #13

Perkinsville Road

Starting Point:	**Arizona 89 in Chino Valley**
Finishing Point:	**Intersection of CR 71 with FR 173, 25 miles south of Williams**
Total Mileage:	**29.8 miles**
Unpaved Mileage:	**28.2 miles**
Driving Time:	**1.5 hours**
Elevation Range:	**4,000–5,400 feet**
Usually Open:	**Year-round**
Best Time to Travel:	**Year-round**
Difficulty Rating:	**1**
Scenic Rating:	**8**
Remoteness Rating:	**+0**

Special Attractions

- Historic town of Perkinsville and the United Verde & Pacific Railroad.
- Views of the Sycamore Canyon Wilderness.
- Campsites along the Verde River.

History

Perkinsville is a small ranching community along the Verde River. It is named after Marion Perkins, a rancher from Texas, who purchased the existing property at the site owned by James Baker and John Campbell. Perkins purchased the ranch in 1899 and then returned to New Mexico for his cattle, which had been driven from Texas. He finally settled at his new ranch in November 1900.

Government Wash

In 1912, the Santa Fe Railroad extended a branch from Drake to Clarkdale, which crossed Perkins's ranch. A station was built and named Perkinsville. It is still standing and can be glimpsed from the road, but it is located on private property. Perkinsville had a post office between 1925 and 1939.

The single-lane steel bridge at Perkinsville was originally constructed in another location. Built in 1913, it crossed the Gila River some 200 miles to the southwest, but the bridge was washed out in a flood in 1915. It was brought to its current location and erected across the Verde River by a forest service work team. The bridge is classified by the Historic American

Buildings Survey as "technologically noteworthy," being an early example of the most common truss-type bridges built in America.

Description

The long Perkinsville Road is a highly scenic route that offers some impressive panoramas as it travels through the Prescott National Forest in mainly open country. The trail leaves Chino Valley north of Prescott and initially follows a paved road as it runs east across open ranchland to the forest boundary. To the south is Woodchute Mountain. The trail enters Prescott National Forest and runs along a ridge top, which drops off to expose the red rocks of the Sycamore Canyon Wilderness to the northeast. Bill Williams Mountain is to the west, and the San Francisco Peaks can be seen on the horizon to the north.

A short series of switchbacks drops the trail swiftly down to join the Jerome-Perkinsville Road a short distance south of the old settlement of Perkinsville.

At Perkinsville—situated on the Verde River—the railroad, river, and road come together. The Verde Canyon Railroad, which takes tourists on a scenic trip from Clarkdale through Verde Canyon, winds along the river at this point to finish its outbound trip at Perkinsville; it then retraces its route to Clarkdale. There is a single-lane steel bridge over the river, and tracks on the right and the left lead to a small number of campsites set in the riparian area.

From Perkinsville, the trail climbs gradually again, passing the start of Northeast #14: Henderson Flat Trail to finish at the intersection of CR 71 and FR 173, 25 miles south of Williams, at the start of the paved road.

Current Road Information

Prescott National Forest
Chino Valley Ranger District
735 North Hwy 89
PO Box 485
Chino Valley, AZ 86323
(520) 636-2302

Map References

BLM Prescott
USFS Prescott National Forest: Chino Valley Ranger District
USGS 1:24,000 Chino Valley North, King Canyon, Munds Draw, Perkinsville, Hell Point
1:100,000 Prescott
Maptech CD-ROM: Flagstaff/Sedona/Prescott
Arizona Atlas & Gazetteer, p. 41
Arizona Road & Recreation Atlas, p. 34 & p. 68
Recreational Map of Arizona

Route Directions

▼ 0.0			From Arizona 89 in Chino Valley, zero trip meter and turn east on the paved road signed Perkinsville Road, CR 70. The turn is immediately south of mile marker 329. Remain on main paved road.
	6.2 ▲		Trail ends at the T-intersection with Arizona 89 in Chino Valley. Turn left for Prescott; turn right for Ash Fork.
			GPS: N34°46.26' W112°27.13'
▼ 1.4		SO	Road on left and right; then cattle guard. Road turns to graded dirt and initially crosses private property; remain on county road.
	4.8 ▲	SO	Cattle guard; then road is paved. Road on right and left after cattle guard; remain on main paved road into Chino Valley.
			GPS: N34°46.34' W112°25.61'
▼ 2.3		SO	Graded road on right is M. A. Perkins Trailway; road on left to ranch.
	3.9 ▲	SO	Graded road on left is M. A. Perkins Trailway; road on right to ranch.
▼ 3.2		SO	Graded road on right.
	3.0 ▲	SO	Graded road on left.

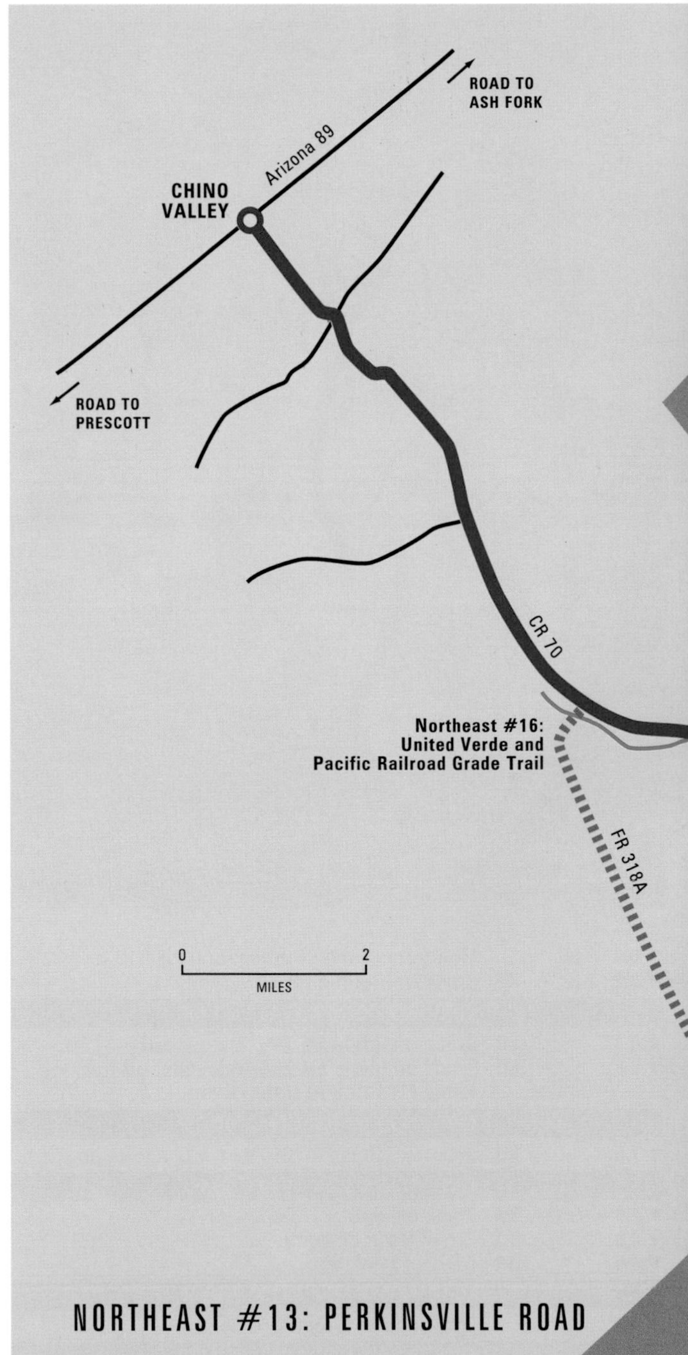

▼ 5.2 SO Cattle guard.

1.0 ▲ SO Cattle guard.

▼ 6.2 SO Graded road right is Northeast #16: United Verde and Pacific Railroad Grade Trail, FR 318A. Zero trip meter.

0.0 ▲ Continue to the west.

GPS: N34°45.83′ W112°20.45′

▼ 0.0 Continue to the northeast.

4.0 ▲ SO Graded road on left is Northeast #16: United Verde and Pacific Railroad Grade Trail, FR 318A. Zero trip meter.

▼ 1.1 SO Cattle guard. Entering state land.

2.9 ▲ SO Cattle guard. Leaving state land.

▼ 1.3 BR Graded road on left. Bear right and cross over creek on bridge.

2.7 ▲ BL Cross over creek on bridge; then bear left; graded road on right.

GPS: N34°46.56′ W112°19.36′

▼ 1.8 BL Graded road on right.

2.2 ▲ BR Graded road on left.

▼ 2.5 SO Track on left; then cattle guard; then ranch road on right.

1.5 ▲ SO Ranch road on left; then cattle guard; then track on right.

GPS: N34°46.97′ W112°18.36′

▼ 2.6 SO Track on right to ranch.

1.4 ▲ SO Track on left to ranch.

▼ 3.8 SO Track on left is FR 163.

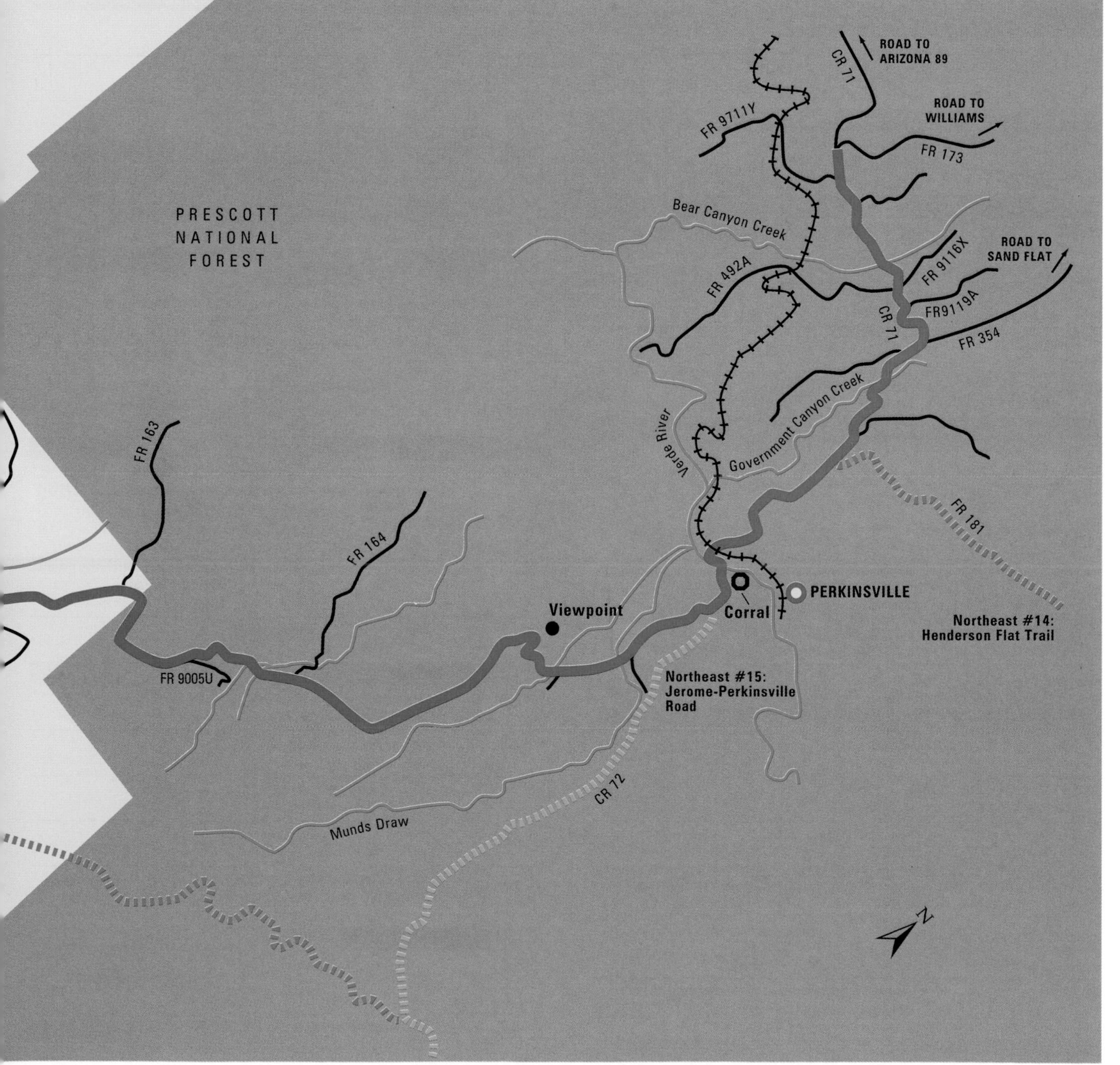

A view of the trail with the Sycamore Canyon Wilderness in the background

0.2 ▲ SO Track on right is FR 163.

GPS: N34°47.93′ W112°17.59′

▼ 4.0 SO Entering Prescott National Forest over cattle guard. Zero trip meter.
0.0 ▲ Continue to the southwest.

GPS: N34°48.04′ W112°17.33′

▼ 0.0 Continue to the northeast; track on left.
7.3 ▲ SO Track on right; then leaving Prescott National Forest over cattle guard. Zero trip meter.

▼ 0.7 SO Track on right.
6.6 ▲ SO Track on left.

▼ 1.0 SO Track on left.
6.3 ▲ SO Track on right.

▼ 1.6 SO Track on right is FR 9005U.
5.7 ▲ SO Track on left is FR 9005U.

GPS: N34°47.91′ W112°16.28′

▼ 1.8 SO Track on left.
5.5 ▲ SO Track on right.

▼ 2.2 SO Track on left.
5.1 ▲ SO Track on right.

▼ 2.6 SO Cattle guard.
4.7 ▲ SO Cattle guard.

▼ 2.9 SO Cross through two washes.
4.4 ▲ SO Cross through two washes.

▼ 3.0 SO Cross through wash.
4.3 ▲ SO Cross through wash.

▼ 3.3 SO Track on left is FR 164.
4.0 ▲ SO Track on right is FR 164.

GPS: N34°48.83′ W112°15.03′

▼ 3.4 SO Pass under power lines.
3.9 ▲ SO Pass under power lines.

▼ 4.1 SO Cattle guard.
3.2 ▲ SO Cattle guard.

▼ 4.3 SO Track on left is FR 9001J.
3.0 ▲ SO Track on right is FR 9001J.

GPS: N34°49.09′ W112°14.01′

▼ 4.5 SO Cattle guard.
2.8 ▲ SO Cattle guard.

▼ 4.8 SO Two tracks on left to corral.
2.5 ▲ SO Two tracks on right to corral.

▼ 7.3 SO Viewpoint on left toward Sycamore Canyon Wilderness. Zero trip meter.
0.0 ▲ Continue to the south.

GPS: N34°51.45′ W112°13.29′

▼ 0.0 Continue to the north and descend switchback.
3.5 ▲ SO Top of switchback; then viewpoint on right toward Sycamore Canyon Wilderness. Zero trip meter at viewpoint.

▼ 0.3 SO Cross through wash.
3.2 ▲ SO Cross through wash.

▼ 1.1 SO Cross through wash; then track on right. Cattle guard; then track on left.
2.4 ▲ SO Track on right; then cattle guard. Track on left; then cross through wash.

▼ 2.0 SO Cross through Munds Draw.
1.5 ▲ SO Cross through Munds Draw.

GPS: N34°52.06′ W112°12.26′

▼ 2.2 SO Track on right is FR 9899D.
1.3 ▲ SO Track on left is FR 9899D.

GPS: N34°52.20′ W112°12.28′

▼ 2.5 SO Track on left.
1.0 ▲ SO Track on right.

▼ 3.0 SO Cross through wash.
0.5 ▲ SO Cross through wash.

▼ 3.4 SO Cross over wash.
0.1 ▲ SO Cross over wash.

▼ 3.5 TL T-intersection. Northeast #15: Jerome-Perkinsville Road, CR 72, to Jerome on right. Turn left, remaining on CR 70. Zero trip meter. There is no signpost in this direction.
0.0 ▲ Continue to the southwest.

GPS: N34°53.30′ W112°11.87′

▼ 0.0 Continue to the northwest.
3.6 ▲ TR Turn right onto graded road, sign-posted to Chino Valley. Ahead is Northeast #15: Jerome-Perkinsville Road, CR 72, to Jerome. Zero trip meter.

▼ 0.6 SO Corral on right; then cross over Verde River on steel bridge.
3.0 ▲ SO Cross over Verde River on steel bridge; then corral on left.

GPS: N34°53.70′ W112°12.27′

▼ 0.7 TL Track on left is FR 9004M; cross over aqueduct; then turn left over cattle guard. Track on right goes to Perkinsville Railroad Station (located on private property).
2.9 ▲ TR Cattle guard; then turn right and cross over aqueduct. Track straight on goes to Perkinsville Railroad Station (located on private property);then track on right is FR 9004M.

▼ 1.0 SO Cross over railroad; then track on left.
2.6 ▲ SO Track on right; then cross over railroad.

GPS: N34°53.70′ W112°12.57′

▼ 1.3 SO Cross through wash.
2.3 ▲ SO Cross through wash.

▼ 2.5 SO Track on left.
1.1 ▲ SO Track on right.

▼ 2.7 SO Track on left.
0.9 ▲ SO Track on right.

▼ 3.0 SO Cattle guard.
0.6 ▲ SO Cattle guard.

▼ 3.6 SO Track on right is Northeast #14: Henderson Flat Trail, FR 181. Zero trip meter.
0.0 ▲ Continue to the south.

GPS: N34°55.59′ W112°12.33′

▼ 0.0 Continue to the north.
2.2 ▲ SO Track on left is Northeast #14: Henderson Flat Trail, FR 181. Zero trip meter.

▼ 0.7 SO Track on right is FR 9004T.
1.5 ▲ SO Track on left is FR 9004T.

Mileage		Direction
		GPS: N34°56.16′ W112°12.60′
▼ 1.4	SO	Cross over Government Canyon Creek on bridge.
0.8 ▲	SO	Cross over Government Canyon Creek on bridge.
		GPS: N34°56.63′ W112°12.75′
▼ 2.1	SO	Track on left; then cattle guard.
0.1 ▲	SO	Cattle guard; then track on right.
▼ 2.2	BL	Graded road on right is FR 354 to Sand Flat. This road is also part of the Great Western Trail. Zero trip meter.
0.0 ▲		Continue to the south on CR 70.
		GPS: N34°57.31′ W112°12.75′
▼ 0.0		Continue to the west on CR 71.
3.0 ▲	BR	Graded road on left is FR 354 to Sand Flat. This road is also part of the Great Western Trail. Zero trip meter.
▼ 0.2	SO	Cross through wash.
2.8 ▲	SO	Cross through wash.
▼ 0.5	SO	Two tracks on left.
2.5 ▲	SO	Two tracks on right.
▼ 0.6	SO	Cross through wash.
2.4 ▲	SO	Cross through wash.
▼ 0.7	SO	Track on right is FR 9119A; then cross through wash.
2.3 ▲	SO	Cross through wash; then track on left is FR 9119A.
		GPS: N34°57.35′ W112°13.37′
▼ 1.0	SO	Track on left is FR 492A to Bear Siding and Verde River. Track on right is FR 9116X.
2.0 ▲	SO	Track on right is FR 492A to Bear Siding and Verde River. Track on left is FR 9116X.
		GPS: N34°57.50′ W112°13.64′
▼ 1.3	SO	Track on right; then cross over Bear Canyon Creek on bridge.
1.7 ▲	SO	Cross over Bear Canyon Creek on bridge; then track on left.
▼ 1.7	SO	Cross over creek on bridge; then track on left.
1.3 ▲	SO	Track on right; then cross over creek on bridge.
▼ 1.5	SO	Track on right; then cattle guard.
1.5 ▲	SO	Cattle guard; then track on left.
▼ 2.3	SO	Track on right.
0.7 ▲	SO	Track on left.
▼ 2.6	SO	Cross over wash; then track on left is FR 9711Y.
0.4 ▲	SO	Track on right is FR 9711Y; then cross over wash.
		GPS: N34°57.74′ W112°15.39′
▼ 2.8	SO	Road turns to paved.
0.2 ▲	SO	Road turns to graded dirt.
▼ 3.0	SO	Trail ends immediately after the paved road where the graded road on the left from Drake and Arizona 89 enters. This intersection is signed to Drake. Turn left for Arizona 89; continue straight ahead on the paved road to Williams.
0.0 ▲		Trail commences on FR 173 (Perkinsville Road), 25 miles south of Williams at the intersection of CR 71 and Perkinsville Road. Zero trip meter at the intersection and continue southeast on paved Perkinsville Road, following the sign to Perkinsville and Jerome. Graded road on the right is the road to Drake and is sign-posted.
		GPS: N34°57.96′ W112°15.76′

NORTHEAST REGION TRAIL #14

Henderson Flat Trail

Starting Point:	**Northeast #13: Perkinsville Road, 3 miles north of the Verde River crossing at Perkinsville**
Finishing Point:	**Sycamore Basin Hiking Trailhead #63**
Total Mileage:	**12.5 miles**
Unpaved Mileage:	**12.5 miles**
Driving Time:	**1.25 hours (one-way)**
Elevation Range:	**4,200–5,000 feet**
Usually Open:	**Year-round**
Best Time to Travel:	**Dry weather**
Difficulty Rating:	**3**
Scenic Rating:	**9**
Remoteness Rating:	**+1**

Special Attractions

- Access to Sycamore Canyon hiking trails.
- Spectacular red rock scenery.

Description

One of the most scenic and popular wilderness areas within Arizona is the Sycamore Canyon Wilderness, with its striking red rock canyons and mountains. Although there are more than 70 places with the name Sycamore in Arizona alone, Sycamore Canyon near Sedona is probably the best known. The canyon is 25 miles long and up to 7 miles across at its widest point. Scattered throughout are many cliff dwellings left behind by early Indians. Many people travel to Sedona to view the area, but a quieter yet equally pretty access comes in from the west side, through Prescott National Forest.

This trail leaves Northeast #13: Perkinsville Road to travel a roughly graded, single-track trail toward the wilderness boundary. The trail winds through the predominant pinyon and juniper vegetation, crossing through a number of small canyons as it travels toward Henderson Flat. The red bluffs of Sycamore Canyon come into view. The trail continues past the cabin at Henderson Flat to finish at the trailhead for the Sycamore Basin Hiking Trail #63, which is the main trail leading into the Sycamore Canyon Wilderness.

Rock formations reach skyward as the trail nears Sycamore Canyon

The road surface, especially at the far end, gradually turns into red clay. The addition of water turns the clay into a thick, greasy mess that quickly fills tire treads and

A summer thunderstorm darkens the sky above Sycamore Canyon

makes traction impossible. Traveling along this trail in wet weather is not recommended. There are a couple of nice camping spots, particularly near the trailhead at the end.

Current Road Information

Prescott National Forest
Chino Valley Ranger District
735 North Hwy 89
PO Box 485
Chino Valley, AZ 86323
(520) 636-2302

Map References

BLM Prescott
USFS Prescott National Forest: Chino Valley Ranger District
USGS 1:24,000 Perkinsville, Sycamore Basin
1:100,000 Prescott
Maptech CD-ROM: Flagstaff/Sedona/Prescott
Arizona Atlas & Gazetteer, p. 41
Arizona Road & Recreation Atlas, p. 34 & p. 68

Route Directions

Mileage		Directions
▼ 0.0		From Northeast #13: Perkinsville Road, 3 miles north of the Verde River crossing at Perkinsville, zero trip meter and turn northeast on FR 181 signed to Henderson Flat. Trail is roughly graded dirt road.
		GPS: N34°55.59' W112°12.33'
▼ 0.6	SO	Cattle guard; entering canyon.
▼ 0.7	SO	Cross through wash.
▼ 0.9	SO	Track on left.
▼ 1.2	BL	Track on right is FR 9000P.
		GPS: N34°56.01' W112°11.53'
▼ 2.6	SO	Track on right.
▼ 2.8	SO	Track on right; then cross through wash.
▼ 3.1	SO	Track on left through fence.
		GPS: N34°56.48' W112°09.92'
▼ 3.6	SO	Cattle guard.
▼ 3.8	SO	Track on right is FR 639. Zero trip meter.
		GPS: N34°56.39' W112°09.57'
▼ 0.0		Continue to the east.
▼ 0.7	SO	Track on right is FR 9710R.
		GPS: N34°56.71' W112°09.01'
▼ 0.8	SO	Track on right.
▼ 0.9	SO	Track on right.
▼ 1.6	SO	Cattle guard.
▼ 2.3	BL	Small track on right and viewpoint over the Sycamore Canyon Wilderness.
		GPS: N34°57.75' W112°07.94'
▼ 2.6	SO	Track on left; entering the line of Railroad Draw.
▼ 2.8	SO	Cross through Railroad Draw.
		GPS: N34°57.78' W112°07.87'
▼ 3.3	SO	Track on right is FR 639. Zero trip meter.
		GPS: N34°57.81' W112°07.51'
▼ 0.0		Continue to the east.
▼ 0.2	SO	Lonesome Pocket Hiking Trail #61 on left to Sand Flat; then entrance to old cabin on left and track on right; water catchment on left. This is Henderson Flat.

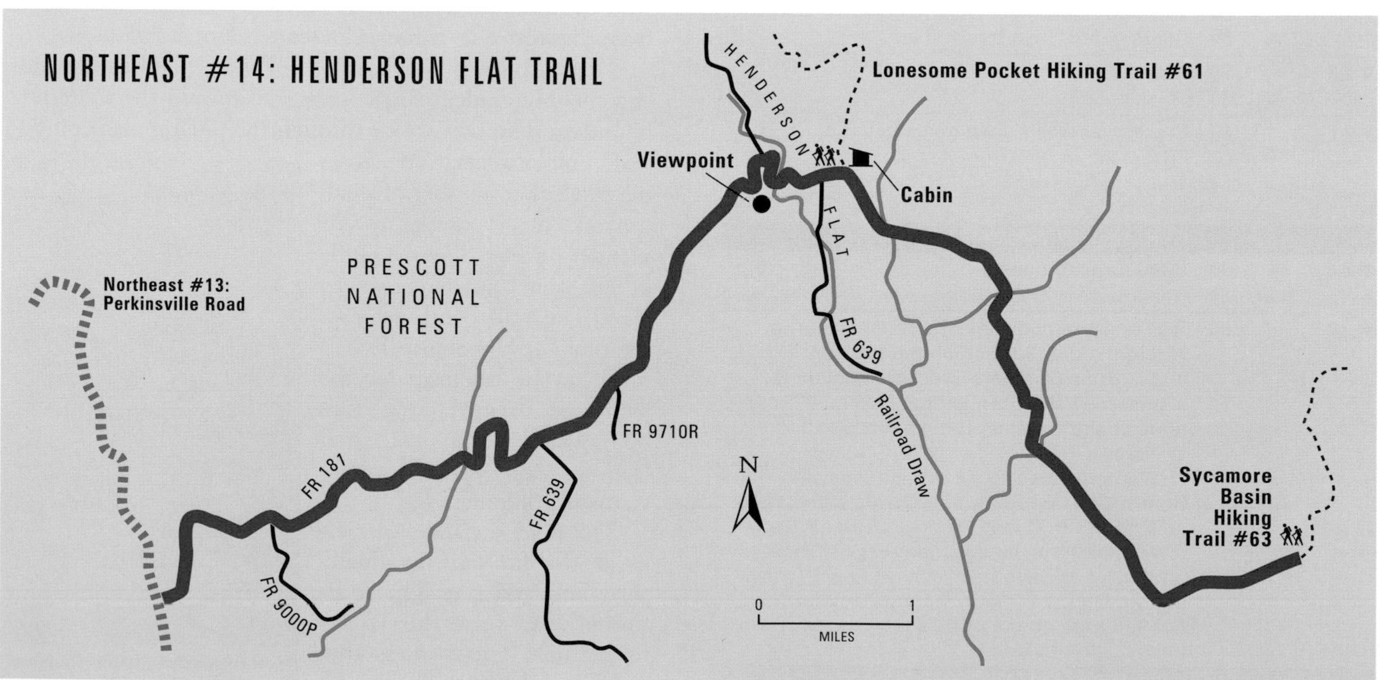

		GPS: N34°57.78' W112°07.34'
▼ 0.3	SO	Cattle guard.
▼ 0.6	SO	Cross through wash.
▼ 0.9	SO	Track on left.
▼ 1.0	SO	Cross through wash.
▼ 1.3	SO	Cross through wash.
▼ 1.6	SO	Cross through wash.
▼ 2.9	SO	Cross through wash.
		GPS: N34°56.19' W112°06.11'
▼ 3.0	SO	Cross through wash.
▼ 3.8	SO	Cross through wash; then track on right; then track on left.
▼ 4.4	SO	Track on right; then cattle guard; then cross through wash.
		GPS: N34°55.24' W112°05.25'
▼ 4.7	SO	Track on right.
▼ 5.4	BR	The trail finishes at Sycamore Basin Hiking Trailhead #63 into Sycamore Canyon Wilderness. The main trail continues as a smaller formed trail for a short distance before finishing at the wilderness boundary.
		GPS: N34°55.51' W112°04.27'

NORTHEAST REGION TRAIL #15

Jerome-Perkinsville Road

Starting Point:	Northeast #13: Perkinsville Road, immediately south of Perkinsville
Finishing Point:	Jerome
Total Mileage:	14.8 miles
Unpaved Mileage:	14.8 miles
Driving Time:	1.25 hours
Elevation Range:	4,000–6,000 feet
Usually Open:	Year-round
Best Time to Travel:	Dry weather
Difficulty Rating:	2
Scenic Rating:	8
Remoteness Rating:	+0

Special Attractions

- Many varied views, including the Woodchute Wilderness, Jerome, and the Verde Valley.
- Route follows a section of the historic United Verde & Pacific Railroad.
- Rockhounding for Perkinsville agate.

Description

This graded dirt road travels through fascinating scenery between Perkinsville and the former ghost town of Jerome. The trail travels on ridge tops and on a section of the old United Verde & Pacific Railroad grade as it makes its final descent into Jerome.

The trail, which also forms part of the Great Western Trail, is roughly graded along its length, although a few rough spots make it more suitable for high-clearance vehicles.

Six miles south of Perkinsville, rock hounds may be able to find some samples of agate by scouring in the washes and areas surrounding them.

Negotiating an old railroad cutting

From the intersection with Northeast #16: United Verde and Pacific Railroad Grade Trail, the route follows along the old railroad bed into Jerome. The shelf road is wide enough for two vehicles to pass with care and the gentle grade winds around Woodchute Mountain before passing through a cutting and the highest point of the railroad (5,935 feet). On the south side of the cutting is First View. Travelers in this direction get their first view of Jerome and the Verde Valley. From here, the trail winds its way down to Jerome, passing through property still owned by Phelps Dodge. It passes by the entrance of the Gold King Mine, Museum, and Ghost Town before finishing in the center of Jerome.

The road can be negotiated by any high-clearance vehicle in dry weather, but 4WD or chains are recommended for winter travel when there might be a sprinkling of snow on the higher elevations.

Current Road Information

Prescott National Forest
Chino Valley Ranger District
735 North Hwy 89
PO Box 485
Chino Valley, AZ 86323
(520) 636-2302

Prescott National Forest
Verde Ranger District
300 East Hwy 260
PO Box 670
Campe Verde, AZ 86322
(520) 567-4121

Map References

BLM Prescott
USFS Prescott National Forest: Chino Valley and Verde Ranger Districts
USGS 1:24,000 Perkinsville, Munds Draw, Clarkdale
1:100,000 Prescott
Maptech CD-ROM: Flagstaff/Sedona/Prescott
Arizona Atlas & Gazetteer, p. 41
Arizona Road & Recreation Atlas, p. 34 & p. 68
Recreational Map of Arizona

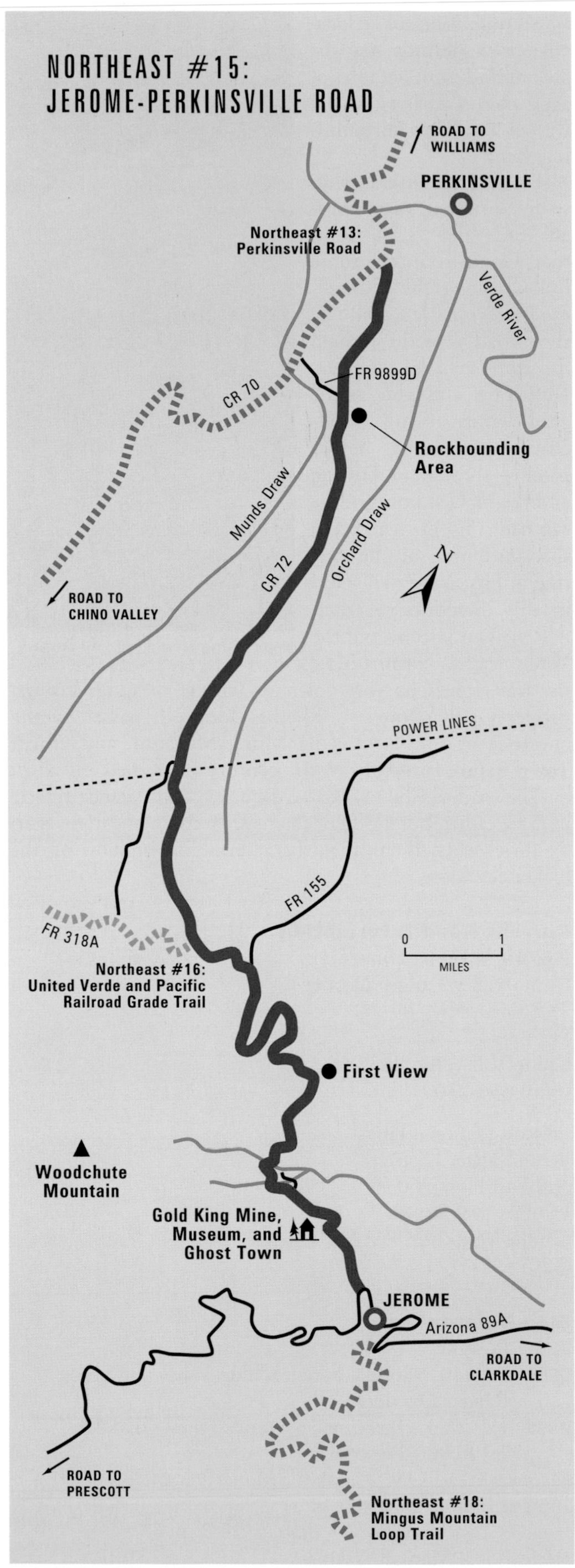

Route Directions

▼ 0.0			From the intersection of Northeast #13: Perkinsville Road, CR 70, and CR 72 immediately south of Perkinsville, zero trip meter and turn southeast on graded dirt road CR 72, following the sign to Jerome. The route is designated as part of the Great Western Trail.
	1.5 ▲		Trail ends at the intersection of CR 70 and CR 72, Northeast #13: Perkinsville Road, immediately south of Perkinsville. Continue north to exit to Williams or Drake; turn left to exit to Chino Valley.
			GPS: N34°53.30′ W112°11.87′
▼ 1.5		SO	Track on right is FR 9899D to Chino Valley. Zero trip meter.
	0.0 ▲		Continue to the northwest, following the sign to Drake and Williams.
			GPS: N34°52.02′ W112°11.53′
▼ 0.0			Continue to the southeast and cross cattle guard. Around this cattle guard is the agate rockhounding area.
	6.0 ▲	BR	Cattle guard; then track on left is FR 9899D to Chino Valley. Zero trip meter at intersection. Around this cattle guard is an agate rockhounding area.
▼ 0.7		SO	Cattle guard; then track on right.
	5.3 ▲	SO	Track on left; then cattle guard.
▼ 2.7		SO	Track on right.
	3.3 ▲	SO	Track on left.
▼ 4.1		SO	Cattle guard; then track on right. Pass under power lines; then track on left under power lines.
	1.9 ▲	SO	Track on right under power lines; then pass under power lines. Track on left; then cattle guard.
			GPS: N34°48.44′ W112°11.40′
▼ 4.4		SO	Track on right.
	1.6 ▲	SO	Track on left.
▼ 4.7		SO	Track on left.
	1.3 ▲	SO	Track on right.
▼ 5.4		SO	Track on left.
	0.6 ▲	SO	Track on right.
▼ 6.0		BL	Track on right is Northeast #16: United Verde and Pacific Railroad Grade Trail, FR 318A. Zero trip meter.
	0.0 ▲		Continue to the northwest, following sign to Williams and Chino Valley.
			GPS: N34°47.11′ W112°10.34′
▼ 0.0			Continue to the east.
	3.8 ▲	BR	Track on left is Northeast #16: United Verde and Pacific Railroad Grade Trail, FR 318A. Zero trip meter.
▼ 0.8		BR	Track on left is FR 155.
	3.0 ▲	SO	Track on right is FR 155.
			GPS: N34°47.14′ W112°09.69′
▼ 2.5		SO	Pass through cutting.
	1.3 ▲	SO	Pass through cutting.
			GPS: N34°47.03′ W112°09.11′
▼ 3.8		SO	Cattle guard; then track on left. First View of the Verde Valley, Cottonwood and Clarkdale, and then Jerome. Zero trip meter at sign.
	0.0 ▲		Continue to the west on FR 318.
			GPS: N34°46.59′ W112°08.50′
▼ 0.0			Continue to the south.
	3.5 ▲	SO	First View of Jerome and the Verde Valley; then track on right; then cattle guard. Signpost in other direction for First View. Zero trip meter.
▼ 0.2		SO	Cutting; then view of Jerome.
	3.3 ▲	SO	Cutting.

▼ 1.2	SO	Track on right; then cutting.
2.3 ▲	SO	Cutting; then track on left.
▼ 1.3	SO	Cross over creek.
2.2 ▲	SO	Cross over creek.
		GPS: N34°45.69' W112°08.59'
▼ 1.6	SO	Cross over creek on bridge.
1.9 ▲	SO	Cross over creek on bridge.
▼ 1.9	SO	Track on left.
1.6 ▲	BL	Track on right.
▼ 2.0	SO	Track on left.
1.5 ▲	SO	Track on right.
▼ 2.7	TL	Entrance to the Gold King Mine, Museum, and Ghost Town on right.
0.8 ▲	TR	Entrance to the Gold King Mine, Museum, and Ghost Town ahead. Turn right in front of the entrance.
		GPS: N34°45.45' W112°07.74'
▼ 3.3	SO	Cross old railroad; mine entrance on right and road on left.
0.2 ▲	SO	Mine entrance on left and road on right; cross old railroad.
▼ 3.5		Trail ends in Jerome on Arizona 89A at the fire station. Continue ahead for Clarkdale; turn right for Prescott.
0.0 ▲		In Jerome on Arizona 89A, at the fire station, on a sharp switchback in the main street, zero trip meter and turn west on Perkinsville Road. The road goes to the Gold King Mine, Museum, and Ghost Town.
		GPS: N34°45.11' W112°07.01'

NORTHEAST REGION TRAIL #16

United Verde and Pacific Railroad Grade Trail

Starting Point:	**Northeast #13: Perkinsville Road, 6.2 miles east of Chino Valley**
Finishing Point:	**Northeast #15: Jerome-Perkinsville Road, 7.3 miles north of Jerome**
Total Mileage:	**13.1 miles**
Unpaved Mileage:	**13.1 miles**
Driving Time:	**1 hour**
Elevation Range:	**5,000–5,600 feet**
Usually Open:	**Year-round**
Best Time to Travel:	**Dry weather**
Difficulty Rating:	**2**
Scenic Rating:	**8**
Remoteness Rating:	**+0**

Special Attractions

- Trail that follows the route of the United Verde & Pacific Railroad.
- Views of Jerome and the Verde Valley.
- Long, extremely scenic shelf road.

The trail commences along the dead straight course of the old railroad grade

History

The United Verde & Pacific Railroad was once described as the "crookedest line in the world" because it had 126 curves along its 26.3-mile length. The 3-foot-wide railroad was constructed in 1894 by Senator William Andrews Clark, the owner of the United Verde Copper Company, a rich mine in Jerome. The railroad connected Jerome to Chino Valley (then called Jerome Junction) and the Santa Fe, Prescott & Phoenix Railway. Jerome Junction was originally called simply Junction when it was established in 1895, but the name was changed to the less confusing Jerome Junction in 1914. The station was used by both railroads.

The line was not without its problems. Heavy rain often caused washouts, which in 1905 and 1906 were severe enough to stop the trains. No trains into Jerome meant no coke for the smelters, and production was curtailed on several occasions. Rockfalls along the line often had to be cleared as well.

Wooden trestles were built to cross the gullies and to create an acceptable grade, but frequent fires started by engine sparks often delayed the train. Twenty-three trestles were replaced between 1898 and 1901 by the built-up grade that you see today. The project cost a quarter of a million dollars.

The trail bears evidence of the sidings and turnaround points for the railroad. Near the eastern end of the trail, an open area beside the road is Horseshoe Siding, which is believed to be the site of a sawmill that milled timber from Woodchute Mountain. Timber was used to fire the smelters before coke was brought in.

The United Verde & Pacific Railroad closed in 1920, and Jerome Junction was renamed Chino Valley in 1923.

Description

For the most part, this trail follows along the path of the United Verde & Pacific Railroad as it travels between Chino Valley and Jerome. The trail leaves from Northeast #13: Perkinsville Road, turning south on the small graded dirt road, FR 318A. There is a forest road number post at the

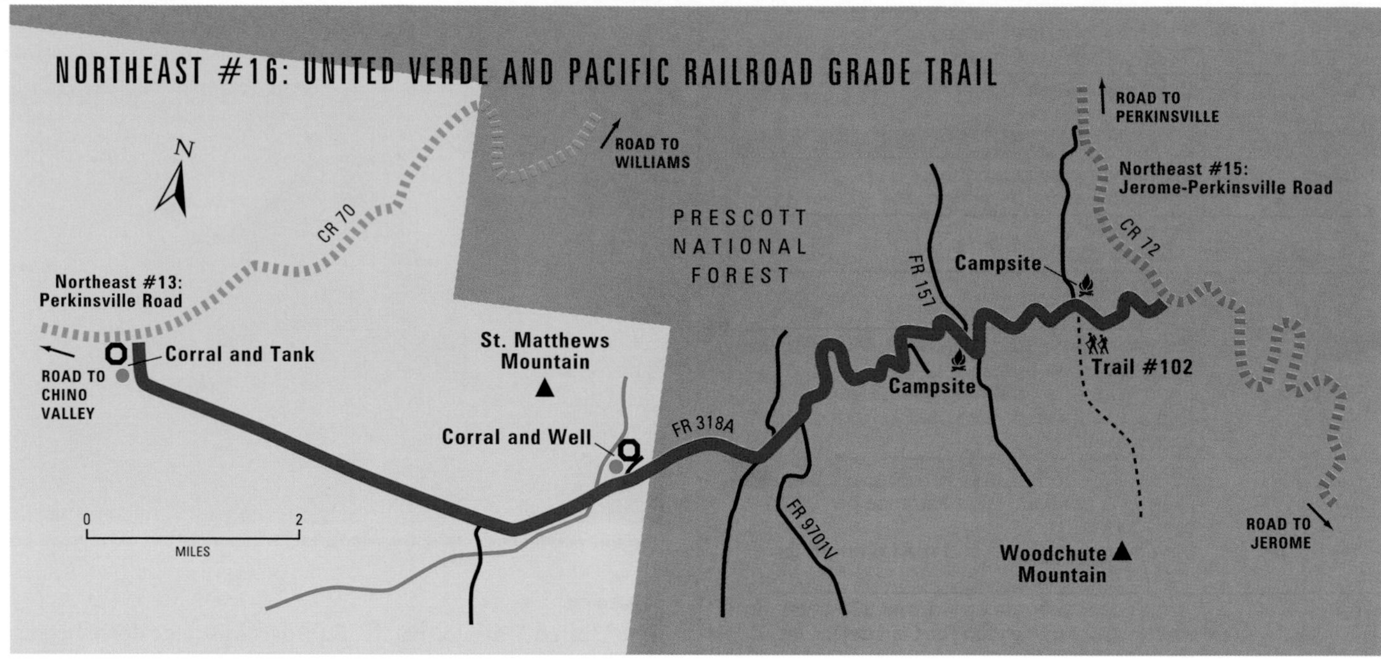

intersection, and a large corral can be seen a short distance down the road. Initially, the trail crosses the broad flat plain, joining the railroad grade to head in a straight line toward Woodchute Mountain.

Past the intersection of FR 9701V (which appears on the Prescott National Forest Map as FR 642), the trail becomes narrower and starts to wind along a shelf road around the north face of Woodchute Mountain. It closely follows the original railroad grade, and you will pass through many of the cuttings made for the train. The grade is easy and the shelf road is wide enough for a single vehicle; there are good passing places.

Surprisingly, given that the trail is mainly a shelf road, there are a couple of good campsites where you can pull off the trail and enjoy the panoramic view north toward the Sycamore Canyon Wilderness and the San Francisco Peaks north of Williams.

The trail ends at the intersection with Northeast #15: Jerome-Perkinsville Road, which then continues to follow the path of the railroad grade into Jerome.

Current Road Information

Prescott National Forest
Chino Valley Ranger District
735 North Hwy 89
PO Box 485
Chino Valley, AZ 86323
(520) 636-2302

Map References

BLM Prescott
USFS Prescott National Forest: Chino Valley Ranger District
USGS 1:24,000 King Canyon, Prescott Valley North, Munds Draw
1:100,000 Prescott
Maptech CD-ROM: Flagstaff/Sedona/Prescott
Arizona Atlas & Gazetteer, p. 41
Arizona Road & Recreation Atlas, p. 34 & p. 68

Route Directions

▼ 0.0		From Northeast #13: Perkinsville Road, 6.2 miles east of Chino Valley, zero trip meter and turn south on graded dirt road marked FR 318A.
5.3 ▲		Trail ends at the intersection with Northeast #13: Perkinsville Road. Turn right for Williams; turn left for Chino Valley and Prescott.
		GPS: N34°45.83' W112°20.45'
▼ 0.1	SO	Corral and tank on right.
5.2 ▲	SO	Corral and tank on left.
▼ 0.4	SO	Join railroad grade.
4.9 ▲	SO	Leave railroad grade.
▼ 1.7	SO	Cattle guard.
3.6 ▲	SO	Cattle guard.
▼ 2.2	SO	Cattle guard.
3.1 ▲	SO	Cattle guard.
▼ 2.4	SO	Track on right to dam.
2.9 ▲	SO	Track on left to dam.
▼ 2.8	SO	Cattle guard.
2.5 ▲	SO	Cattle guard.
▼ 3.7	SO	Track on right.
1.6 ▲	SO	Track on left.
		GPS: N34°44.70' W112°16.81'
▼ 4.9	SO	Cross over wash; corral and well on left.
0.4 ▲	SO	Cross over wash; corral and well on right.
▼ 5.1	SO	Cattle guard; then track on left.
0.2 ▲	SO	Track on right; then cattle guard.
▼ 5.3	SO	Entering Prescott National Forest at sign. Zero trip meter.
0.0 ▲		Continue to the west.
		GPS: N34°45.28' W112°15.24'
▼ 0.0		Continue to the east on FR 318A.

1.5 ▲	SO	Leaving Prescott National Forest. Zero trip meter.
▼ 0.4	SO	Track on left under power lines.
1.1 ▲	SO	Track on right under power lines.
▼ 0.6	SO	Track on left.
0.9 ▲	SO	Track on right.
▼ 1.1	SO	Track on right through wire gate.
0.4 ▲	SO	Track on left through wire gate.
▼ 1.2	SO	Track on left.
0.3 ▲	SO	Track on right.
▼ 1.5	SO	Track on right is FR 9701V, part of the Great Western Trail. Zero trip meter.
0.0 ▲		Continue to the southwest, remaining on FR 318A. End of shelf road.
		GPS: N34°45.80' W112°13.84'
▼ 0.0		Continue to the northeast, remaining on FR 318A. Start of shelf road.
3.2 ▲	SO	Track on left is FR 9701V, part of the Great Western Trail. Zero trip meter.
▼ 0.9	SO	Cattle guard.
2.3 ▲	SO	Cattle guard.
▼ 1.2	SO	Cross over creek.
2.0 ▲	SO	Cross over creek.
▼ 1.4	SO	Track on left.
1.8 ▲	SO	Track on right.
▼ 1.8	SO	Cross over wash; then track on right.
1.4 ▲	SO	Track on left; then cross over wash.
▼ 2.1	SO	Track on right.
1.1 ▲	SO	Track on left.
▼ 2.7	SO	Cross over creek; dam on right.
0.5 ▲	SO	Cross over creek; dam on left.
		GPS: N34°46.59' W112°12.50'
▼ 3.2	SO	Track on left is FR 157. Zero trip meter. Campsite at intersection.
0.0 ▲		Continue to the northwest.
		GPS: N34°46.56' W112°12.29'
▼ 0.0		Continue to the southeast.
3.1 ▲	SO	Track on right is FR 157. Zero trip meter. Campsite at intersection.
▼ 0.1	SO	Track on right; then cross over creek.
3.0 ▲	SO	Cross over creek; then track on left.
▼ 0.4	SO	Cattle guard.
2.7 ▲	SO	Cattle guard.
▼ 1.4	SO	Cross over creek.
1.7 ▲	SO	Cross over creek.
▼ 1.7	SO	Track on left; campsite at intersection.
1.4 ▲	SO	Track on right; campsite at intersection.
		GPS: N34°46.97' W112°11.22'
▼ 1.8	SO	Trail on right (#102) for hiking and horses only. The open area on the left is Horseshoe Siding.
1.3 ▲	SO	Trail on left (#102) for hiking and horses only. The open area on the right is Horseshoe Siding.
		GPS: N34°46.97' W112°11.18'
▼ 3.1		Trail ends at the intersection with Northeast #15: Jerome-Perkinsville Road. Turn left to continue to Perkinsville; turn right to continue to Jerome.
0.0 ▲		Trail commences at the intersection with Northeast #15: Jerome-Perkinsville Road, 7.3 miles from Jerome. Zero trip meter and proceed southwest on FR 318A. Trail is a shelf road.
		GPS: N34°47.11' W112°10.34'

NORTHEAST REGION TRAIL #17

Goat Peak Trail

Starting Point:	**Arizona 89A, west of Jerome, opposite Potato Patch Campground**
Finishing Point:	**FR 372, 1 mile west of Cherry**
Total Mileage:	**14.6 miles**
Unpaved Mileage:	**14.5 miles**
Driving Time:	**1.5 hours**
Elevation Range:	**5,200–7,500 feet**
Usually Open:	**March to November**
Best Time to Travel:	**Dry weather**
Difficulty Rating:	**2**
Scenic Rating:	**8**
Remoteness Rating:	**+0**

Special Attractions

- Mingus Lake.
- Long, scenic ridge top trail.
- Backcountry campsites and developed camping on Mingus Mountain.

Description

This trail connects the small settlement of Cherry with Mingus Mountain to the north. It leaves from Arizona 89A west of Jerome and travels up Mingus Mountain to within a mile of Mingus Lake, which is a small but pretty lake that is a popular spot for fishing or relaxing on a hot summer day. Initially, the trail travels on a wide, graded dirt road past many well-used backcountry campsites. In addition, there is a campground on Mingus Mountain. The trail then travels along FR 132, which is definitely for dry weather travel only. The road becomes totally impassable in wet weather, and a sign at the start warns that wet weather travel is prohibited and violators are subject to prosecution.

The northern end of the trail passes through cool ponderosa pine country on Mingus Mountain, but as it descends it enters the lower vegetation zone—manzanita and small oak trees predominate. Much of the trail travels along a ridge top, and there are great views to the west over the Prescott National Forest as well as Goat Peak. After passing below the summit of Goat Peak, the trail drops down farther to follow along a creek before joining FR 372 near Cherry.

Mingus Lake, a popular spot for fishing or just relaxing

Current Road Information
Prescott National Forest
Verde Ranger District
300 East Hwy 260
PO Box 670
Campe Verde, AZ 86322
(520) 567-4121

Map References
BLM Prescott
USFS Prescott National Forest: Verde Ranger District
USGS 1:24,000 Hickey Mt., Cottonwood, Cherry
1:100,000 Prescott
Maptech CD-ROM: Flagstaff/Sedona/Prescott
Arizona Atlas & Gazetteer, p. 41
Arizona Road & Recreation Atlas, p. 40 & p. 74

Route Directions

Mileage		Direction	
▼ 0.0			From Arizona 89A west of Jerome, zero trip meter on the saddle at the entrance to Summit Picnic Area and Potato Patch Campground and turn east on paved FR 104 sign-posted to Mingus Springs Camp. Summit Picnic Area is immediately on the left. The road is also marked for the Great Western Trail.
	1.4 ▲		Trail finishes at the intersection with Arizona 89A. Turn right for Jerome; turn left for Prescott.
			GPS: N34°42.44′ W112°08.94′
▼ 0.1		SO	Road turns to graded gravel.
	1.3 ▲	SO	Road is now paved.
▼ 1.4		TR	Turn right onto FR 413, following the sign for Cherry. Road straight on goes 0.6 miles to Mingus Lake. Zero trip meter.
	0.0 ▲		Continue to the west.
			GPS: N34°41.88′ W112°08.29′
▼ 0.0			Continue to the south.
	2.1 ▲	TL	T-intersection; turn left onto FR 104, following the sign to Arizona 89A. Road on right goes 0.6 miles to Mingus Lake. Zero trip meter.
▼ 1.9		SO	Track on left.
	0.2 ▲	SO	Track on right.
▼ 2.1		TR	Cattle guard; then turn right onto FR 105/FR 132, following the sign to Cherry. Northeast #18: Mingus Mountain Loop Trail is straight ahead. Zero trip meter.
	0.0 ▲		Continue to the northwest.
			GPS: N34°40.39′ W112°09.02′
▼ 0.0			Continue to the south.
	9.0 ▲	TL	Turn left onto FR 413. Track on right is FR 413, Northeast #18: Mingus Mountain Loop Trail. Zero trip meter.
▼ 0.4		SO	Track on right is FR 105 to Mingus Springs Camp. Tank on left. Continue on FR 132.
	8.6 ▲	SO	Track on left is FR 105 to Mingus Springs Camp. Tank on right. Continue on FR 132.
			GPS: N34°40.08′ W112°09.18′
▼ 0.7		SO	Cross through wash.
	8.3 ▲	SO	Cross through wash.
			GPS: N34°39.86′ W112°08.92′
▼ 1.0		SO	Track on left.
	8.0 ▲	SO	Track on right.
▼ 1.1		SO	Track on right.
	7.9 ▲	SO	Track on left.
▼ 1.6		SO	Trail #9029 on right for hikers, horses, and mountain bikes.
	7.4 ▲	SO	Trail #9029 on left for hikers, horses, and mountain bikes.
			GPS: N34°39.52′ W112°08.35′
▼ 1.7		SO	Track on left.
	7.3 ▲	SO	Track on right.
▼ 3.4		SO	Entering private land. Track on left; then Brindle Pup Mine on left.
	5.6 ▲	SO	Brindle Pup Mine on right; then track on right. Leaving private land.
			GPS: N34°38.74′ W112°07.01′
▼ 3.8		SO	Leaving private land; then track on left.
	5.2 ▲	SO	Track on right; then entering private land.
▼ 4.2		SO	Cross through wash.
	4.8 ▲	SO	Cross through wash.
▼ 5.9		SO	Cattle guard; then track on left through fence line.
	3.1 ▲	SO	Track on right through fence line; then cattle guard.
			GPS: N34°38.16′ W112°05.26′
▼ 6.6		SO	Track on right.
	2.4 ▲	BR	Track on left.

▼ 6.7	SO	Turnout on left under Goat Peak.
2.3 ▲	SO	Turnout on right under Goat Peak.
		GPS: N34°37.80′ W112°04.78′
▼ 6.9	SO	Track on left.
2.1 ▲	SO	Track on right.
▼ 7.7	SO	Closure gate; then cattle guard.
1.3 ▲	SO	Cattle guard; then closure gate.
		GPS: N34°37.01′ W112°04.77′
▼ 8.0	BR	Track on left at wash.
1.0 ▲	BL	Track on right at wash.
▼ 8.1	SO	Cross through wash.
0.9 ▲	SO	Cross through wash.
▼ 8.6	SO	Track on left.
0.4 ▲	SO	Track on right.
▼ 8.8	SO	Track on right.
0.2 ▲	SO	Track on left.
▼ 9.0	SO	Cross through Cherry Creek; then track on right is FR 9004A. Zero trip meter.
0.0 ▲		Continue to the north and cross through Cherry Creek.
		GPS: N34°36.09′ W112°04.36′
▼ 0.0		Continue to the south; then track on left.
2.1 ▲	SO	Track on right; then track on left is FR 9004A. Zero trip meter.
▼ 0.2	SO	Track on left.
1.9 ▲	SO	Track on right.
▼ 1.1	SO	Graded road on left.
1.0 ▲	BL	Graded road on right.
		GPS: N34°36.02′ W112°03.51′
▼ 1.3	SO	Track on left.
0.8 ▲	SO	Track on right.
▼ 2.1		Trail ends at the intersection with FR 372. Turn left for Cherry; turn right for Dewey.
0.0 ▲		Trail starts on FR 372, 1 mile west of Cherry. Zero trip meter and turn north on FR 132 at the sign for the Great Western Trail, following the sign for Mingus Mountain.
		GPS: N34°35.14′ W112°03.43′

NORTHEAST REGION TRAIL #18

Mingus Mountain Loop Trail

Starting Point:	**Arizona 89A, on the east side of Jerome**
Finishing Point:	**Northeast #17: Goat Peak Trail, 2.1 miles south of intersection with FR 104**
Total Mileage:	**16.6 miles**
Unpaved Mileage:	**16.6 miles**
Driving Time:	**2.5 hours**
Elevation Range:	**4,800–6,900 feet**
Usually Open:	**April to November**
Best Time to Travel:	**Dry weather**
Difficulty Rating:	**5**
Scenic Rating:	**9**
Remoteness Rating:	**+0**

A narrow section of shelf road, 2,000 feet above the Verde Valley

Special Attractions

- Historic mining town of Jerome.
- Very long section of narrow shelf road.
- Panoramic views over Verde Valley and the Red Rock Secret Mountain Wilderness.
- Old mining adits and tailings.

History

Mingus Mountain and the Jerome region have been visited by humans looking for minerals in the ground for more than a thousand years. The Sinagua Indians sought copper ore, argillite, azurite, and malachite for ornaments, tools, and as trading items.

The Spanish explorers who passed through the region in the 1500s were looking for gold, so they ignored the rich copper deposits there. These deposits first attracted interest in 1876, but it was a few more years before investors could be persuaded to commit funds to the remote, inaccessible location. In 1882, the Atlantic & Pacific Railroad came within 60 miles of the region, making the deposits a more attractive proposition and a group of investors formed the United Verde Copper Company. The town of Jerome, named after Eugene Murray Jerome, one of the investors, was formed and continued to expand, despite its precarious location on the steep slopes of Mingus Mountain. The site of the town caused many problems. For a start, it had been built on the flattest section of ground on Cleopatra Hill, which happened to be near the smelter. Thus, the town was covered with smoke and the immediate area denuded of vegetation. Because of the steep slopes, landslip was, and still is, a continual problem. The original underground mine was unable to be worked after a fire in 1894, which burned for an incredible 33 years. To reach the rich ore body, ways were found around these problems. The smelter was relocated and the mine converted to an open-pit operation, which necessitated rerouting the twisting United Verde & Pacific Railroad, which connected the town to Jerome Junction (now Chino Valley) near Prescott.

Jerome continued to thrive, and in 1900 it was the fourth largest town in Arizona. In 1917, it was affected by labor disputes. The Industrial Workers of the World (known as the Wobblies) were in dispute with another union and a strike resulted. The Wobblies were unpopular in much of Jerome, and some of the townspeople took action, rounding up the Wobblies and deporting them out of town.

In 1935, mining giant Phelps Dodge purchased the United Verde Copper Company and continued churning out copper, recouping the initial investment in only five years. The mines finally closed in 1953.

For a time Jerome was quiet enough to be described as a ghost town, but over the years it has been redefining itself as a center for the arts, a tourist town, and a historical center. It is now a thriving little place, packed on weekends with sightseers eager to explore the history and attractions of Jerome.

Description

This trail is not for the faint-hearted, as for most of its length it runs along an extremely narrow shelf road with precipitous drops. It leaves the former ghost town of Jerome on narrow unpaved streets along the mountainside. There is no sign on the highway, and it is easy to miss the turn as well as the subsequent ones to the start of the shelf road; at first glance they look like private driveways. Once you reach the cattle guard with the yellow national forest marker, it is obvious that you are on the correct trail.

The trail leaves the outskirts of Jerome and immediately starts climbing along a narrow, rough shelf road. At the first saddle, you get a good view of the trail ahead and the last easy turning point for many miles. The shelf road is narrow, and passing places are extremely limited. If you see an oncoming vehicle and you are close to a passing point, pull in and wait. Uphill vehicles have the right of way, but common sense should always prevail. The trail continues as a shelf road for the next 13 miles as it winds around the steep eastern slope of Mingus Mountain. The first section of the shelf road is by far the narrowest and roughest; after the intersection with FR 493 the trail gradually widens until two vehicles can pass with care. Don't be surprised if you see hang gliders soaring above you on the east side of Mingus Mountain. A launch pad is located on the top of the mountain.

Jerome Town Hall

Originally, the trail was cut by miners, the evidence of which can be seen in the tailings heaps and adits along the way. The trail surface is rough in places, but not exceptionally so, and there are several miles of smooth travel along red clay soils that become very greasy in wet weather.

The views are stunning all along this trail; initially, they look back to the houses straggling down the mountainside in Jerome and then later over the Verde Valley with the communities of Cottonwood and Clarkdale more than 2,000 feet below. Higher up still, you can see over the path of Northeast #19: Bill Gray–Buckboard Road to the red rock country near Sedona.

Initially, the shelf road is open and has low vegetation, but farther up the trail passes through patches of pine forest. Several hiking trails intersect the vehicle route, most of which climb up Mingus Mountain. Campers should note that there are no campsites near Jerome along this trail, but that there are many excellent ones in the ponderosa pines near the intersection with Northeast #17: Goat Peak Trail. This trail should not be attempted when it is wet or if there is snow or ice on the trail. Muddy sections, or lack of traction caused by snow or ice, make this trail extremely dangerous because of the low margin for error. Even in dry weather, care needs to be taken and the sightseeing should be left to the passengers.

Current Road Information

Prescott National Forest
Verde Ranger District
300 East Hwy 260
PO Box 670
Campe Verde, AZ 86322
(520) 567-4121

Map References

BLM Prescott
USFS Prescott National Forest: Verde Ranger District
USGS 1:24,000 Cottonwood, Hickey Mt.
1:100,000 Prescott
Maptech CD-ROM: Flagstaff/Sedona/Prescott
Arizona Atlas & Gazetteer, p. 41
Arizona Road & Recreation Atlas, p. 40 & p. 74

Route Directions

▼ 0.0			From Arizona 89A on the east side of Jerome, turn east onto small Gulch Road; this turn is hard to spot—it is on a switchback on the east side of town and initially passes houses. The turn is opposite East Avenue and is immediately a graded narrow dirt road as it descends down into the gulch.
	0.5 ▲		The trail ends on Arizona 89A on the east side of Jerome. Turn left to visit Jerome; turn right for Clarkdale.
			GPS: N34°44.83' W112°06.64'
▼ 0.3		TR	Turn onto unmarked dirt street that looks like a private drive and bear left.
	0.2 ▲	TL	Turn onto larger street.
▼ 0.5		SO	Cattle guard; leaving Jerome. Zero trip meter.
	0.0 ▲		End of shelf road; continue into the edge of Jerome.
			GPS: N34°44.53' W112°06.60'
▼ 0.0			Continue south up rough shelf road.
	7.7 ▲	SO	Cattle guard; entering Jerome. Zero trip meter.
▼ 0.3		BR	Track on left at saddle. Continue on FR 413 past primitive road sign.
	7.4 ▲	BL	Track on right at saddle. Trail is descending toward Jerome.
			GPS: N34°44.59' W112°06.24'
▼ 0.6		SO	Track on right and mine tailings on right up the hill.
	7.1 ▲	SO	Track on left and mine tailings on left up the hill.
			GPS: N34°44.46' W112°06.47'
▼ 1.8		SO	Track on right.
	5.9 ▲	BR	Track on left.
			GPS: N34°43.80' W112°06.99'

▼ 2.1 SO Cross over Mescal Gulch on bridge.
5.6 ▲ SO Cross over Mescal Gulch on bridge.

GPS: N34°43.63' W112°07.16'

▼ 2.3 SO Adit on right.
5.4 ▲ SO Adit on left.

GPS: N34°43.52' W112°06.98'

▼ 2.4 SO Cross through creek fed by spring. Mine tailings on left.
5.3 ▲ SO Mine tailings on right. Cross through creek fed by spring.

▼ 3.1 SO Cross over wash.
4.6 ▲ SO Cross over wash.

▼ 3.6 SO Trail levels off and runs around Mingus Mountain. Cottonwood and Clarkdale are visible far below.
4.1 ▲ SO Trail starts to descend toward Jerome.

▼ 4.1 SO Mine on left below trail.
3.6 ▲ SO Mine on right below trail.

GPS: N34°43.42' W112°06.15'

▼ 4.8 SO Cross over wash; small tailings pile on the right.
2.9 ▲ SO Cross over wash; small tailings pile on the left.

GPS: N34°43.11' W112°06.10'

▼ 5.5 SO Adit on left and mine below the trail.
2.2 ▲ SO Adit on right and mine below the trail.

GPS: N34°42.88' W112°05.67'

▼ 5.7 SO Adit on right.
2.0 ▲ SO Adit on left.

▼ 5.9 SO Cross over creek.
1.8 ▲ SO Cross over creek.

▼ 6.3 SO Cross over creek on bridge.
1.4 ▲ SO Cross over creek on bridge.

GPS: N34°42.57' W112°05.93'

▼ 7.0 SO Track on left; first track on right is Trail #106 to viewpoint. Also second small track on right. Trail #106 is hiking only and is blocked to vehicles after a short distance.
0.7 ▲ SO Track on left; then second track on left is Trail #106 to viewpoint. Trail #106 is hiking only and is blocked to vehicles after a short distance. Track on right.

GPS: N34°42.34' W112°05.61'

▼ 7.3 SO Cross over creek.
0.4 ▲ SO Cross over creek.

▼ 7.7 SO Track on left is FR 493. Zero trip meter.
0.0 ▲ Continue to the northwest on FR 413.

GPS: N34°42.02' W112°05.77'

▼ 0.0 Continue to the southeast on FR 413.
5.0 ▲ BL Bear left, remaining on upper trail. Track on right is FR 493. Zero trip meter.

▼ 0.3 SO Cross over creek.
4.7 ▲ SO Cross over creek.

▼ 0.6 SO Cross over creek.
4.4 ▲ SO Cross over creek.

▼ 1.4 SO Copper Chief Spring on right.
3.6 ▲ SO Copper Chief Spring on left.

GPS: N34°41.48' W112°06.17'

▼ 2.5 BR Track on left.
2.5 ▲ SO Track on right.

GPS: N34°40.95' W112°05.89'

▼ 2.6 SO Track on right.
2.4 ▲ SO Track on left.

▼ 3.0 SO Seasonal closure gate.
2.0 ▲ SO Seasonal closure gate.

▼ 3.7 SO Track on left through gate.
1.3 ▲ SO Track on right through gate.

GPS: N34°40.50' W112°05.69'

▼ 4.4 SO Cattle guard; then Coleman Trail #108 on right

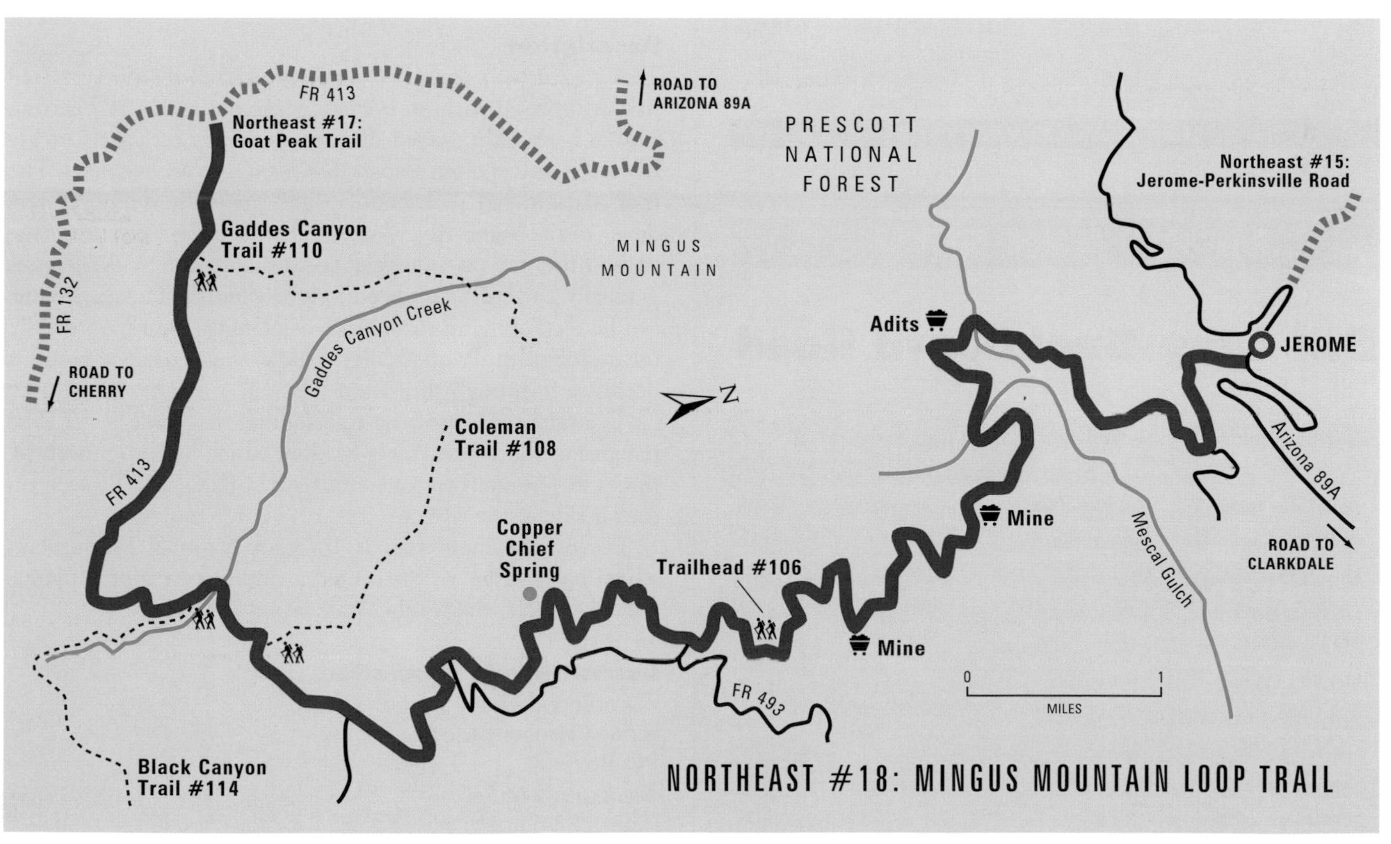

NORTHEAST #18: MINGUS MOUNTAIN LOOP TRAIL

to Mingus Mountain Lookout for hikers, horses, and mountain bikes only.

	0.6 ▲	SO	Coleman Trail #108 on left to Mingus Mountain Lookout for hikers, horses, and mountain bikes only; then cattle guard.
			GPS: N34°40.12' W112°06.14'
▼ 4.9		SO	Cross over Gaddes Canyon creek.
	0.1 ▲	SO	Cross over Gaddes Canyon creek.
▼ 5.0		SO	Track on right is Trail #110; then Black Canyon Trail #114 on left. Zero trip meter.
	0.0 ▲		Continue to the north.
			GPS: N34°39.98' W112°06.55'
▼ 0.0			Continue to the south.
	3.4 ▲	SO	Black Canyon Trail #114 on right; then track on left is Trail #110. Zero trip meter.
▼ 1.0		SO	Shelf road ends.
	2.4 ▲	SO	Start of shelf road.
▼ 2.2		SO	Track on left.
	1.2 ▲	SO	Track on right.
▼ 2.7		SO	Track on left is FR 9003V, Gaddes Canyon Trail #110 on right for hikers and horses.
	0.7 ▲	SO	Track on right is FR 9003V, Gaddes Canyon Trail #110 on left for hikers and horses.
			GPS: N34°40.15' W112°08.35'
▼ 2.8		SO	Cross through creek.
	0.6 ▲	SO	Cross through creek.
▼ 3.1		SO	Track on right; then second track on right is FR 9003T.
	0.3 ▲	SO	Track on left is FR 9003T; then second track on left.
			GPS: N34°40.31' W112°08.71'
▼ 3.4		SO	Track on left; then trail ends at the intersection with Northeast #17: Goat Peak Trail, FR 413. Also track on right. Turn left to continue along Goat Peak Trail to Cherry; turn right to exit to Arizona 89A.
	0.0 ▲		Trail commences on Northeast #17: Goat Peak Trail, FR 413, 2.1 miles south of the intersection with FR 104. Zero trip meter and turn southeast on FR 413. The trail is a smooth graded road at this point. Track on right and track on left.
			GPS: N34°40.39' W112°09.02'

NORTHEAST REGION TRAIL #19

Bill Gray–Buckboard Road

Starting Point:	**Northeast #20: Boynton Pass Trail, 2.5 miles north of Arizona 89A**
Finishing Point:	**Arizona 89A, south of Clarkdale**
Total Mileage:	**18.5 miles**
Unpaved Mileage:	**16.7 miles**
Driving Time:	**1.25 hours**
Elevation Range:	**3,400–4,400 feet**
Usually Open:	**Year-round**
Best Time to Travel:	**Dry weather**
Difficulty Rating:	**2**
Scenic Rating:	**8**
Remoteness Rating:	**+0**

Special Attractions

- Views of Verde Valley and Mingus Mountain.
- Tuzigoot National Monument.

History

Tuzigoot, a small national monument set slightly above the Verde River, contains the stone remains of twelfth-century Sinagua Indian dwellings. Tuzigoot, which is an Apache word for "crooked water," was home to approximately 200 people and originally had 110 rooms in several 3-story complexes.

The Sinagua (Spanish for "without water") lived in the Verde Valley and nearby plateau. Originally pithouse dwellers and farmers dependent on rain to grow their crops, they integrated with the Hohokam Indians; the blending of cultures changed their farming techniques and their dwellings. The Sinagua adopted the Hohokam irrigation system and began to build aboveground stone houses.

The Verde River flows near Tuzigoot National Monument

The building of the hilltop houses began around 1150, and Tuzigoot probably reached its present size in the 1300s. The Sinagua were not as skillful at building as the Anasazi—the walls at Tuzigoot are large but often poorly constructed. However, the structures have stood for more than 600 years. The Sinagua abandoned the valley around 1400.

Description

This graded road connects Northeast #20: Boynton Pass Trail to Cottonwood without ever touching the highway. The trail surface is roughly graded dirt that becomes extremely greasy when wet and is often impassable, even to 4WD vehicles. The trail starts in red rock country and gradually wraps its way down to the Verde River Valley. The differing views from the ends of the trail provide great contrasts. As the road descends gradually toward Clarkdale along a wide shelf road, Jerome can be seen clinging to the side of Mingus Mountain on the other side of the Verde Valley. Below, the Verde River cuts a deep swath through the valley.

The final section of the trail follows the Verde River. The remains of the Tapco Power Station, which used to power the mines in Jerome, Prescott, and Crown King, can be seen on the far side of the river.

Just off the main trail is Tuzigoot National Monument, which has a small visitor center, a display of regional plants, and a wheelchair-accessible walk around the ruins.

Current Road Information

Coconino National Forest
Sedona Ranger District
PO Box 300
Sedona, AZ 86336
(520) 282-4119

Map References

BLM Sedona
USFS Coconino National Forest: Sedona Ranger District
USGS 1:24,000 Page Springs, Loy Butte, Clarkdale
1:100,000 Sedona
Maptech CD-ROM: Flagstaff/Sedona/Prescott
Arizona Atlas & Gazetteer, p. 41
Arizona Road & Recreation Atlas, p. 34 & p. 68
Recreational Map of Arizona
Other: Beartooth Maps—Sedona

Route Directions

▼ 0.0		From Northeast #20: Boynton Pass Trail, 2.5 miles north of Arizona 89A, zero trip meter and turn northwest on the graded dirt road, sign-posted to Bill Gray Road and Sycamore Pass, FR 525C.
3.0 ▲		Trail ends on Northeast #20: Boynton Pass Trail. Turn right to exit to Arizona 89A; turn left to continue along the Boynton Pass Trail to Sedona.
		GPS: N34°51.02' W111°54.94'
▼ 0.5	BR	Track on left is FR 525A; then cross through wash and immediately bear right. Unmarked graded road on left.
2.5 ▲	SO	Unmarked graded road on right. Cross through wash; then track on right is FR 525A.
		GPS: N34°50.92' W111°55.54'
▼ 0.8	SO	Track on left to private property.
2.2 ▲	SO	Track on right to private property.
▼ 1.1	SO	Track on right; then cross through Spring Creek.
1.9 ▲	SO	Cross through Spring Creek; then track on left.
		GPS: N34°51.19' W111°56.01'
▼ 1.4	SO	Track on right.
1.6 ▲	SO	Track on left.
▼ 2.0	SO	Track on left is FR 9554.
1.0 ▲	SO	Track on right is FR 9554.
		GPS: N34°51.69' W111°56.62'
▼ 2.2	SO	Track on right.
0.8 ▲	SO	Track on left.
▼ 3.0	BL	Bear left onto Bill Gray Road at the sign.

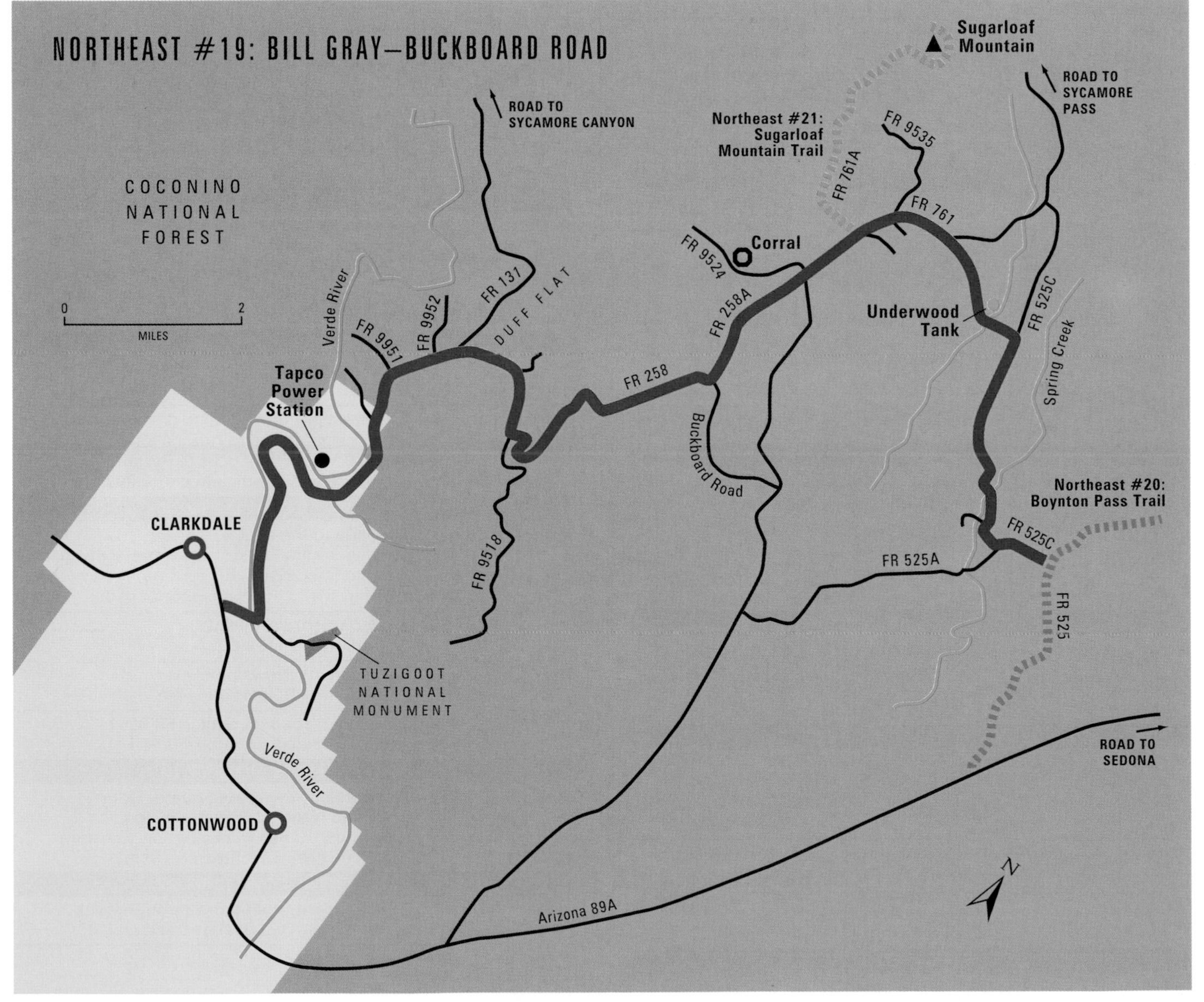

Tuzigoot National Monument

			Graded road on right goes to Sycamore Pass. Zero trip meter.
	0.0 ▲		Continue to the south on FR 525C.
			GPS: N34°52.62′ W111°56.86′
▼ 0.0			Continue to the west on FR 761 and cross cattle guard.
	2.5 ▲	BR	Cattle guard; then graded road on left goes to Sycamore Pass. Zero trip meter.
▼ 0.4		SO	Cross through wash.
	2.1 ▲	SO	Cross through wash.
▼ 0.5		SO	Track on right to Underwood Tank and track on left.
	2.0 ▲	SO	Track on left to Underwood Tank and track on right.
▼ 0.6		SO	Track on right is FR 9553.
	1.9 ▲	SO	Track on left is FR 9553.
▼ 0.9		SO	Track on right; then cattle guard; then private road on left.
	1.6 ▲	SO	Private road on right; then cattle guard; then track on left.
▼ 1.2		SO	Graded road on left.
	1.3 ▲	SO	Graded road on right.
			GPS: N34°53.01′ W111°57.99′
▼ 1.4		SO	Cattle guard; then track on right.
	1.1 ▲	SO	Track on left; then cattle guard.
▼ 2.1		SO	Track on right over cattle guard is FR 9535 and track on left is FR 9534.
	0.4 ▲	SO	Track on left over cattle guard is FR 9535 and track on right is FR 9534.
			GPS: N34°52.85′ W111°58.93′
▼ 2.5		SO	Track on left; track on right is Northeast #21: Sugarloaf Mountain Trail, FR 761A. Zero trip meter.
	0.0 ▲		Continue to the north.
			GPS: N34°52.50′ W111°59.11′
▼ 0.0			Continue to the south.
	0.6 ▲	SO	Track on right; track on left is Northeast #21: Sugarloaf Mountain Trail, FR 761A. Zero trip meter.
▼ 0.6		BR	Small track on right to corral is FR 9524; then bear right on FR 258A sign-posted to Buckboard Road. Zero trip meter. Graded road on left goes to Arizona 89A.
	0.0 ▲		Continue to the north.
			GPS: N34°51.96′ W111°59.36′
▼ 0.0			Continue to the south.
	1.7 ▲	SO	Graded road on right goes to Arizona 89A; then track on left is FR 9524 to corral. Zero trip meter and continue straight on.
▼ 1.0		SO	Two tracks on right; then cattle guard.
	0.7 ▲	SO	Cattle guard; then two tracks on left.
▼ 1.1		SO	Track on right.
	0.6 ▲	SO	Track on left.
▼ 1.5		SO	Track on right; then track on left.
	0.2 ▲	SO	Track on right; then track on left.
▼ 1.7		TR	T-intersection with Buckboard Road. Turn right, following the sign to Duff Flat Road. Zero trip meter.
	0.0 ▲		Continue to the north on FR 258A.
			GPS: N34°50.53′ W111°59.52′
▼ 0.0			Continue to the southwest on FR 258.
	4.7 ▲	BL	Bear left, leaving Buckboard Road for FR 258A, following the sign to Bill Gray Road. Zero trip meter.
▼ 0.1		SO	Track on right.
	4.6 ▲	SO	Track on left.
▼ 0.8		SO	Gas pipeline crosses.
	3.9 ▲	SO	Gas pipeline crosses.
▼ 1.2		SO	Track on left; trail starts to descend toward Clarkdale.
	3.5 ▲	SO	Track on right; end of climb.
▼ 2.3		SO	Track on left to tank.
	2.4 ▲	SO	Track on right to tank.
▼ 3.3		SO	Track on left is FR 9518; then second track on left.
	1.4 ▲	SO	Track on right; then second track on right is FR 9518.
			GPS: N34°48.96′ W112°01.09′
▼ 3.6		SO	Pipeline and power line cross.
	1.1 ▲	SO	Pipeline and power line cross.
▼ 4.0		SO	Well-used track on right. End of descent; now crossing Duff Flat.
	0.7 ▲	SO	Well-used track on left. Trail starts to climb.
			GPS: N34°49.50′ W112°01.50′
▼ 4.2		SO	Track on left.
	0.5 ▲	SO	Track on right.
▼ 4.7		TL	T-intersection. Turn left onto graded dirt road, FR 131, sign-posted to Arizona 89A. Zero trip meter. Road on right goes to Sycamore Canyon.
	0.0 ▲		Continue to the northeast on FR 258.
			GPS: N34°49.31′ W112°02.24′
▼ 0.0			Continue to the south.
	5.6 ▲	TR	Turn right onto FR 258, sign-posted Buckboard Road to Bill Gray Road. Zero trip meter. Road ahead is FR 131 to Sycamore Canyon.
▼ 0.3		SO	Track on right is FR 9952.
	5.3 ▲	SO	Track on left is FR 9952.
▼ 0.4		SO	Track on left follows pipeline.
	5.2 ▲	SO	Track on right follows pipeline.
▼ 0.8		SO	Graded dirt road on right is FR 9951.
	4.8 ▲	SO	Graded dirt road on left is FR 9951.
			GPS: N34°48.78′ W112°02.73′
▼ 1.2		SO	Track on left; then cattle guard. Exiting Coconino National Forest; no sign.
	4.4 ▲	SO	Cattle guard; then track on right. Entering Coconino National Forest; no sign.
			GPS: N34°48.43′ W112°02.58′
▼ 1.3		BL	Track on right; then cross through wash.
	4.3 ▲	BR	Cross through wash; then track on left.
▼ 1.4		SO	Track on right.
	4.2 ▲	BR	Track on left.

▼ 1.7		SO	Cross through wash.
	3.9 ▲	SO	Cross through wash.
▼ 2.4		SO	Cross through wash.
	3.2 ▲	SO	Cross through wash.
▼ 3.4		BL	Two tracks on right.
	2.2 ▲	BR	Two tracks on left.
▼ 3.5		SO	Track on right.
	2.1 ▲	SO	Track on left.
▼ 3.6		SO	Track on right and track on left.
	2.0 ▲	SO	Track on right and track on left.
▼ 3.7		SO	Track on right.
	1.9 ▲	SO	Track on left.
▼ 4.0		SO	Track on left.
	1.6 ▲	SO	Track on right.
▼ 4.2		SO	Road becomes paved. Remain on paved road.
	1.4 ▲	SO	Road turns to graded dirt.
▼ 5.6		TR	T-intersection. Turn right onto paved road. Zero trip meter. Road on the left goes 0.7 miles to Tuzigoot NM.
	0.0 ▲		Continue to the north.
			GPS: N34°46.10' W112°02.29'
▼ 0.0			Continue to the west and cross over the Verde River on bridge.
	0.4 ▲	TL	Bridge over Verde River; then turn left on paved Sycamore Canyon Road. Road ahead goes 0.7 miles to Tuzigoot NM. Zero trip meter.
▼ 0.4			Trail ends at the T-intersection with Arizona 89A immediately south of Clarkdale. Turn left for Sedona; turn right for Jerome and Clarkdale.
	0.0 ▲		Trail starts on Arizona 89A immediately to the south of Clarkdale. Zero trip meter and turn northeast on paved road sign-posted to Tuzigoot National Monument.
			GPS: N34°45.99' W112°02.71'

NORTHEAST REGION TRAIL #20

Boynton Pass Trail

Starting Point:	**Long Canyon Road, FR 152D**
Finishing Point:	**Arizona 89A, 0.5 miles southwest of mile marker 365**
Total Mileage:	**10.5 miles**
Unpaved Mileage:	**9 miles**
Driving Time:	**45 minutes**
Elevation Range:	**4,000–4,800 feet**
Usually Open:	**Year-round**
Best Time to Travel:	**Dry weather**
Difficulty Rating:	**2**
Scenic Rating:	**9**
Remoteness Rating:	**+0**

Special Attractions

- Palatki and Honanki Ruins and rock art.
- Very scenic road over Boynton Pass through red rock country.
- Boynton Canyon Vortex and Blue Door Vortex.

The Palatki cliff dwellings

History

Palatki Ruins are a southern Sinagua cliff dwelling that was occupied from A.D. 1100 to 1300. Along with the Honanki Ruins, Palatki Ruins were first reported by Dr. Jesse Walter Fewkes of the Smithsonian Institution. He named the sites in the Hopi language: Palatki means "red house" and Honanki means "bear house." The sites are the two largest cliff dwellings in the Sedona area.

Palatki consists of two separate dwellings with many pictographs. The structures are pressed against natural alcoves in the cliff face, which acts as one wall for the buildings and provides a degree of protection from the elements. The walls are made from stones, held together by a mortar and clay plaster. The site, which has been stabilized by the forest service, also contains an agave roasting pit and many pictographs, including clan symbols and Barrier Canyon figures.

In addition to the remains of Indian occupation, the Palatki site also houses the remains of a later settler of the site, Charles Willard, who became the founder of Clarkdale. The remains of his stone dwelling and a number of catchments can be seen.

Description

This road leaves Sedona and travels through red rock country over Boynton Pass. Initially, the road is paved as it passes close to a resort and residential areas. It passes several hiking trailheads that lead into the wilderness areas to the north. The Boynton Canyon Trailhead also gives access to one of Sedona's more famous vortices—the Boynton Canyon Vortex. Some believe that a vortex is an outflowing of the earth's energy at a specific point and that each vortex has a unique energy. Vortices are often used as meditation sites and are thought to have spiritual qualities. The Boynton Canyon Vortex, a masculine-feminine vortex, is reputed to enhance the senses—in particular, psychic senses and past life memories. To reach the vortex from the parking area at the trailhead, take Boynton Canyon Trail #47 and then fork right onto Vista Trail, which goes to a 30-foot-high knoll. The energy is believed to be strongest around the knoll.

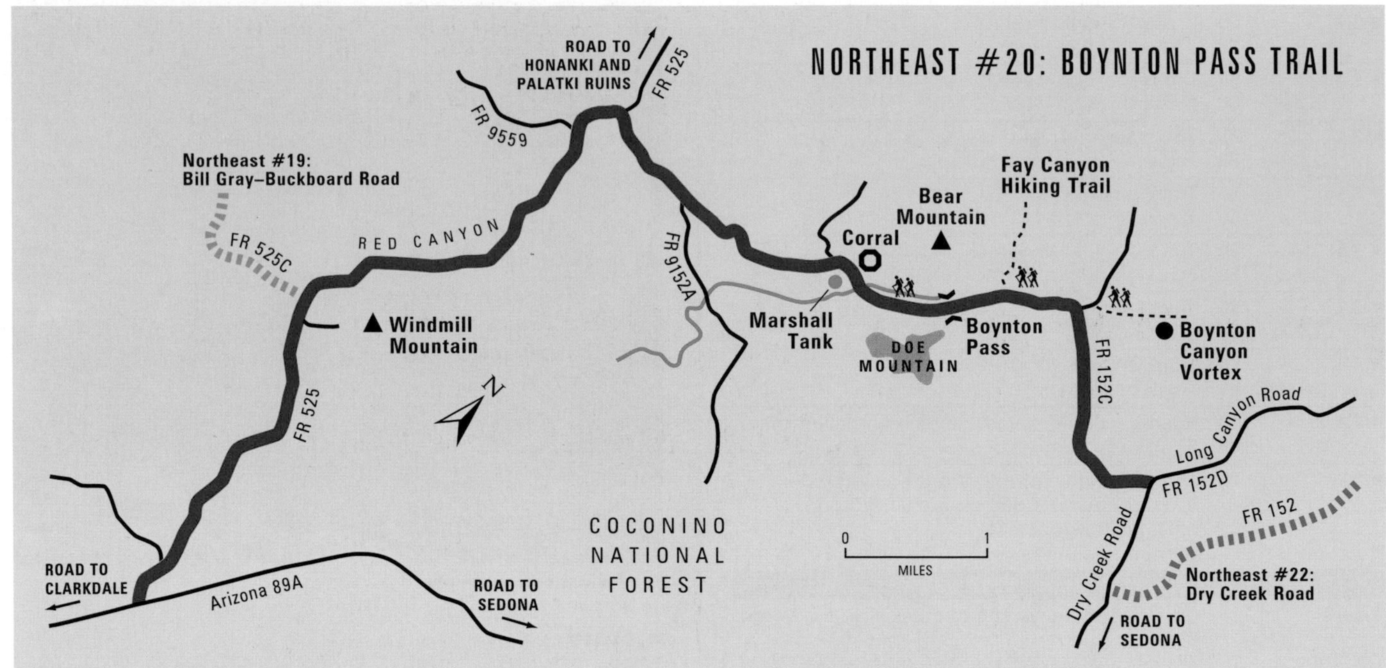

The road turns to rough graded dirt as it travels over Boynton Pass. A high-clearance vehicle is preferred, and like all roads in this region it is not suitable for wet weather travel. As the road crests the gentle pass, there are views back toward Sedona.

There are two Sinagua Indian ruins located just off the main trail. They are well sign-posted up FR 525. A small fee is charged to visit the closer Palatki Ruins, which are run by the forest service. The hiking trail to the pictographs and an intact agave roasting pit is approximately 0.2 miles long. Immediately past the pit, at the end of the trail, there is a tall vertical crack in the rock, which some people believe to be the Blue Door Vortex. People come from all over the world to visit the vortex.

A second hiking trail leads to the ruins of a five-room cliff dwelling. Honanki Ruins are larger and more spread out than the Palatki Ruins but they are not as well preserved. There is no fee at this site, but as at the Palatki Ruins, visitors are restricted to opening hours. Call ahead for days and hours, which are subject to change; at the time of writing the ruins were only open from Friday to Sunday. The main trail continues down Red Canyon to finish on Arizona 89A.

Current Road Information

Coconino National Forest
Sedona Ranger District
PO Box 300
Sedona, AZ 86336
(520) 282-4119

Map References

BLM Sedona
USFS Coconino National Forest: Sedona Ranger District
USGS 1:24,000 Wilson Mt., Loy Butte, Page Springs
1:100,000 Sedona
Maptech CD-ROM: Flagstaff/Sedona/Prescott
Arizona Atlas & Gazetteer, p. 42
Arizona Road & Recreation Atlas, pp. 34, 35 & pp. 68, 69
Recreational Map of Arizona
Other: Beartooth Maps—Sedona

Route Directions

▼ 0.0		From Arizona 89A in Sedona, turn north up Dry Creek Road through West Sedona. Remain on paved Dry Creek Road for 2.7 miles, passing the start of Northeast #22: Dry Creek Road after 1.9 miles. At the T-intersection of Boynton Pass Road (FR 152C) and Long Canyon Road (FR 152D), zero trip meter and turn southwest on paved Boynton Pass Road, following the sign to Palatki and Honanki Ruins.
1.5 ▲		Trail ends at the intersection of Boynton Pass Road and Long Canyon Road (FR 152D). Turn south on Long Canyon Road, which leads to Dry Creek Road and West Sedona.
		GPS: N34°53.92′ W111°49.69′
▼ 1.5	TL	At T-intersection, turn left. Zero trip meter. Paved road on right goes 0.3 miles to the trailhead of Boynton Canyon Trail #47. This area is the site of the Boynton Canyon Vortex.
0.0 ▲		Continue to the southeast on paved road.
		GPS: N34°54.38′ W111°50.98′
▼ 0.0		Continue to the southwest on graded dirt road.
3.7 ▲	TR	Turn right onto paved Boynton Pass Road. Zero trip meter. Paved road ahead goes 0.3 miles to the trailhead of Boynton Canyon Trail #47. This area is the site of the Boynton Canyon Vortex.
▼ 0.3	SO	Track on left is FR 9587.
3.4 ▲	SO	Track on right is FR 9587.
		GPS: N34°54.19′ W111°51.29′
▼ 0.5	SO	Fay Canyon Hiking Trailhead parking on right; then track on left is FR 9586.
3.2 ▲	SO	Track on right is FR 9586; then Fay Canyon Hiking Trailhead parking on left.
		GPS: N34°54.10′ W111°51.43′

▼ 0.7	SO	Track on left.
3.0 ▲	SO	Track on right.
▼ 0.8	SO	Boynton Pass is at the saddle.
2.9 ▲	SO	Boynton Pass is at the saddle.
		GPS: N34°53.85′ W111°51.64′
▼ 1.2	SO	Doe Mountain Hiking Trail #60 on left and Bear Mountain Trail #54 on right. Trailhead parking on right; then cross cattle guard.
2.5 ▲	SO	Cross cattle guard; then Doe Mountain Hiking Trail #60 on right and Bear Mountain Trail #54 on left. Trailhead parking on left.
		GPS: N34°53.61′ W111°51.88′
▼ 1.4	SO	Track on left is FR 9584 and track on right.
2.3 ▲	SO	Track on right is FR 9584 and track on left.
		GPS: N34°53.52′ W111°52.08′
▼ 1.5	SO	Cross through wash.
2.2 ▲	SO	Cross through wash.
▼ 1.6	SO	Track on right past corral on right.
2.1 ▲	SO	Track on left past corral on left.
▼ 1.7	SO	Track on left past Marshall Tank; then cattle guard; then track on right.
2.0 ▲	SO	Track on left; then cattle guard; then track on right past Marshall Tank.
▼ 1.9	SO	Well-used graded road on left is FR 9583, which goes 0.2 miles to a viewpoint overlooking Boynton Pass. The road continues a short distance to private property.
1.8 ▲	SO	Well-used graded road on right is FR 9583, which goes 0.2 miles to a viewpoint overlooking Boynton Pass. The road continues a short distance to private property.
		GPS: N34°53.41′ W111°52.53′
▼ 2.1	SO	Track on left.
1.6 ▲	SO	Track on right.
▼ 2.3	SO	Track on right.
1.4 ▲	SO	Track on left.
▼ 2.7	SO	Private road on right; then cross through wash.
1.0 ▲	SO	Cross through wash; then private road on left.
▼ 2.9	SO	Well-used track on left is FR 9152A (shown on forest map as 152A).
0.8 ▲	SO	Well-used track on right is FR 9152A (shown on forest map as 152A).
		GPS: N34°53.16′ W111°53.55′
▼ 3.2	SO	Track on right.
0.5 ▲	SO	Track on left.
▼ 3.3	SO	Private paved road on right.
0.4 ▲	SO	Private paved road on left.
▼ 3.7	TL	T-intersection. Turn left onto graded road FR 525. Zero trip meter. Turn right here to go to Palatki Ruins (1.8 miles) and to Honanki Ruins (4 miles).
0.0 ▲		Continue to the east on FR 152C.
		GPS: N34°53.29′ W111°54.33′
▼ 0.0		Continue to the south on FR 525.
2.8 ▲	TR	Turn right onto FR 152C, Boynton Pass Road. Zero trip meter. Continue straight to go to Palatki Ruins (1.8 miles) and to Honanki Ruins (4 miles).
▼ 0.2	SO	Track on right.
2.6 ▲	SO	Track on left.
▼ 0.3	SO	Track on right is FR 9559.
2.5 ▲	SO	Track on left is FR 9559.
		GPS: N34°52.98′ W111°54.49′
▼ 0.9	SO	Track on right.
1.9 ▲	SO	Track on left.
▼ 1.1	SO	Track on right is FR 9558.
1.7 ▲	SO	Track on left is FR 9558.
		GPS: N34°52.33′ W111°54.29′
▼ 1.4	SO	Track on left is FR 9576.
1.4 ▲	SO	Track on right is FR 9576.
		GPS: N34°52.08′ W111°54.21′
▼ 1.6	SO	Track on right.
1.2 ▲	SO	Track on left.
▼ 1.9	SO	Track on left is FR 9575.
0.9 ▲	SO	Track on right is FR 9575.
▼ 2.4	SO	Track on left follows pipeline.
0.4 ▲	SO	Track on right follows pipeline.
▼ 2.6	SO	Pipeline trail on right.
0.2 ▲	SO	Pipeline trail on left.
▼ 2.8	SO	Graded road on right is Northeast #19: Bill Gray–Buckboard Road. Zero trip meter.
0.0 ▲		Continue to the northwest.
		GPS: N34°51.02′ W111°54.94′
▼ 0.0		Continue to the southeast and cross cattle guard.
2.5 ▲	BR	Cattle guard; then graded road on left is Northeast #19: Bill Gray–Buckboard Road. Zero trip meter.
▼ 0.1	SO	Track on left is FR 9574.
2.4 ▲	SO	Track on right is FR 9574.
▼ 1.5	SO	Track on left is FR 9573.
1.0 ▲	SO	Track on right is FR 9573.
		GPS: N34°49.85′ W111°54.41′
▼ 2.2	SO	Graded road on right is FR 761B.
0.3 ▲	BR	Graded road on left is FR 761B.
		GPS: N34°49.25′ W111°54.23′
▼ 2.3	SO	Track on right.
0.2 ▲	SO	Track on left.
▼ 2.5		Cattle guard; then trail ends on Arizona 89A. Turn right for Clarkdale; turn left for Sedona.
0.0 ▲		Trail commences on Arizona 89A, 0.5 miles southwest of mile marker 365 between Sedona and Clarkdale. Zero trip meter and turn west on graded dirt road sign-posted FR 525. After the turn, there is a sign for Boynton Pass and other directional signs.
		GPS: N34°48.97′ W111°54.18′

NORTHEAST REGION TRAIL #21

Sugarloaf Mountain Trail

Starting Point:	**Northeast #19: Bill Gray–Buckboard Road, 5.5 miles from the eastern end**
Finishing Point:	**Sugarloaf Mountain**
Total Mileage:	**3.7 miles**
Unpaved Mileage:	**3.7 miles**
Driving Time:	**45 minutes (one-way)**
Elevation Range:	**4,400–5,200 feet**
Usually Open:	**Year-round**
Best Time to Travel:	**Year-round**
Difficulty Rating:	**3**
Scenic Rating:	**8**
Remoteness Rating:	**+0**

Special Attractions

- Rarely used trail offering excellent views over the red rocks west of Sedona.

Description

This short, rough-surfaced trail provides a distant view of the red rock country west of Sedona. The trail, which leaves Northeast #19: Bill Gray–Buckboard Road, is initially narrow but quite eroded. As it gradually climbs around the side of Black Mountain, it becomes a shelf road that is wide enough for a single vehicle and has adequate places to pass other vehicles.

The panoramic views are excellent: back to the east over the Boynton Pass area and north toward Sycamore Pass and the Red Rock Secret Mountain Wilderness. Although this trail is shown as a loop on many maps, private property has blocked it at the point indicated. There are a couple of good camping spots a short distance from the trail on some of the side trails. Like most of the trails in the area, this one should not be attempted in wet weather. The red soil becomes extremely greasy and the road is likely to be impassable.

A view toward Sugarloaf Mountain, typical of the expansive scenic views along this trail

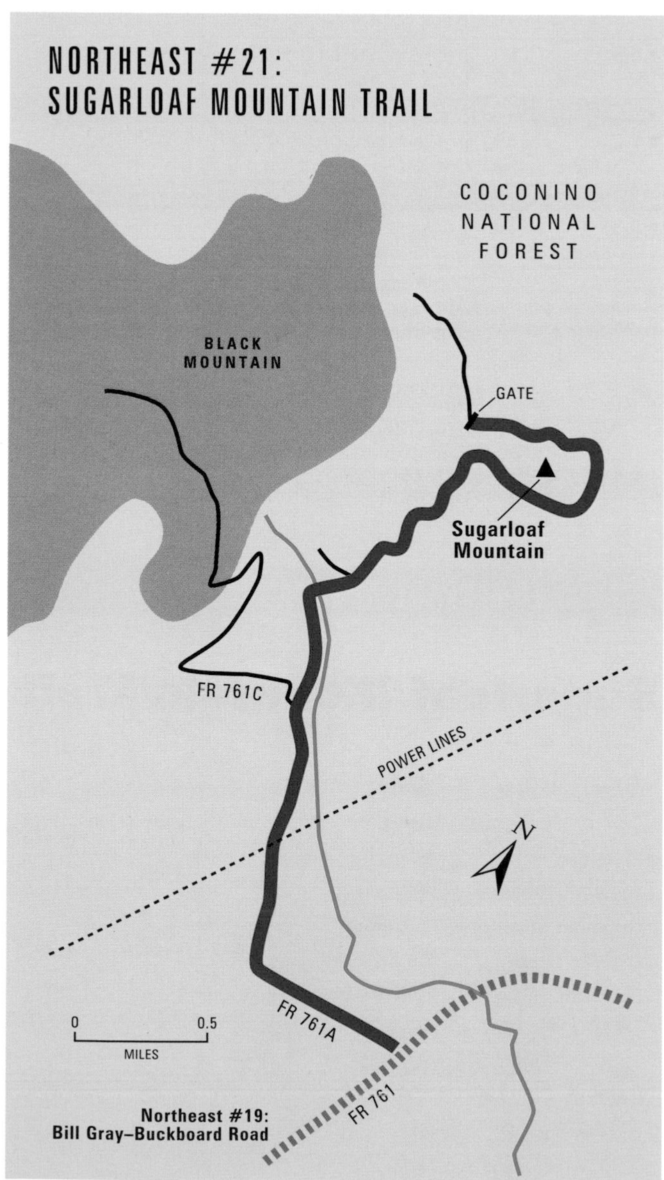

Current Road Information

Coconino National Forest
Sedona Ranger District
PO Box 300
Sedona, AZ 86336
(520) 282-4119

Map References

BLM Prescott, Sedona
USFS Coconino National Forest: Sedona Ranger District
USGS 1:24,000 Loy Butte, Sycamore Basin
1:100,000 Prescott, Sedona
Maptech CD-ROM: Flagstaff/Sedona/Prescott
Arizona Atlas & Gazetteer, p. 41
Arizona Road & Recreation Atlas, p. 34 & p. 68
Other: Beartooth Maps—Sedona

Route Directions

▼ 0.0		From Northeast #19: Bill Gray–Buckboard Road, 2.5 miles northwest of the intersection of FR 525C and FR 761, zero trip meter and turn west on small formed trail marked FR 761A.
		GPS: N34°52.50' W111°59.11'
▼ 0.9	BR	Track on right; then two tracks on left, one of which is FR 95241. Bear right. Do not follow track on right along power lines.
		GPS: N34°52.94' W111°59.89'
▼ 1.3	SO	Track on left is FR 761C, which climbs up Black Mountain. Zero trip meter.
		GPS: N34°53.32' W112°00.08'
▼ 0.0		Continue to the north.
▼ 0.4	SO	Cross through wash.
▼ 0.6	SO	Track on left.
		GPS: N34°53.79' W112°00.15'
▼ 1.7	SO	Track on right.
		GPS: N34°54.30' W111°59.50'
▼ 1.8	SO	Track on right.
▼ 2.4		Road is closed at this point. There is a turning point immediately before the gate.
		GPS: N34°54.39' W112°00.04'

NORTHEAST REGION TRAIL #22

Dry Creek Road

Starting Point:	**Dry Creek Road**
Finishing Point:	**Vultee Arch and Dry Creek Hiking Trailheads**
Total Mileage:	**4.2 miles**
Unpaved Mileage:	**4.2 miles**
Driving Time:	**45 minutes**
Elevation Range:	**4,600–4,800 feet**
Usually Open:	**Year-round**
Best Time to Travel:	**Dry weather**
Difficulty Rating:	**2**
Scenic Rating:	**9**
Remoteness Rating:	**+0**

Special Attractions

- Stunning views of red rock country.
- Access to a number of popular hiking trails.
- Historic cowboy cabin located a short distance from the main trail.

Description

This high-clearance road is immensely popular with photographers who like the diversity of the red rock scenery along its length. At sunset especially, the rocks take on a luminescent quality as the red color deepens. The scene often produces some wonderful atmospheric photographs.

The trail is roughly graded dirt along its entire length. There are many pull-ins at viewpoints along the trail, but because of the popularity of the area, camping is not allowed. The trail meanders alongside Dry Creek for much of the way, and the pull-ins can be used for picnicking or just relaxing amid some of the most beautiful scenery in Arizona.

Red sandstone granules from Brins Mesa settle on the road below

A short 4-rated spur trail leads to an old cabin perched above Dry Creek. Only the final section of this spur is 4-rated; those who do not wish to tackle the rougher section can park before the crossing of Dry Creek and walk the final short distance. The old timber cabin consists of two connected rooms. Behind the cabin there is an underground dugout visible to the southwest. There is private property nearby. Please respect the signs. The coordinates of the cabin are: N34°54.99' W111°48.74'.

The bed of Dry Creek runs parallel to the road—beware of flash floods

The trail passes the start of many hiking trails that lead into the Red Rock Secret Mountain Wilderness before finishing at the trailhead to Vultee Arch. This popular easy hike (1.7 miles) with a gentle gradient climbs to the natural arch, which is named after Gerard and Sylvia Vultee, pioneer aviators who died in a plane crash in 1938. The crash site is farther north on East Picket Mesa.

Current Road Information

Coconino National Forest
Sedona Ranger District
PO Box 300
Sedona, AZ 86336
(520) 282-4119

Map References

BLM Sedona
USFS Coconino National Forest: Sedona Ranger District
USGS 1:24,000 Wilson Mt.
1:100,000 Sedona
Maptech CD-ROM: Flagstaff/Sedona/Prescott
Arizona Atlas & Gazetteer, p. 42
Arizona Road & Recreation Atlas, p. 35 & p. 69
Other: Beartooth Maps—Sedona

Route Directions

▼ 0.0		From the intersection of Arizona 89A in West Sedona, turn north on the paved Dry Creek Road and zero trip meter. Proceed for 1.9 miles; then turn northeast on FR 152 signposted Dry Creek Road to Vultee Arch Trail. Road is graded dirt road. Zero trip meter.
		GPS: N34°53.26' W111°49.31'
▼ 0.2	SO	Track on left goes 0.1 miles to excellent viewpoint.
▼ 0.5	SO	Track on left to excellent viewpoint.
		GPS: N34°53.64' W111°49.11'
▼ 1.3	SO	Devils Bridge Trailhead #120 and parking on right; then cross through wash.
		GPS: N34°54.18' W111°48.80'
▼ 1.9	SO	Track on left.
		GPS: N34°54.68' W111°48.59'
▼ 2.2	SO	Cross through wash.
		GPS: N34°54.88' W111°48.50'
▼ 2.2	SO	Track on left goes 0.3 miles to old timber

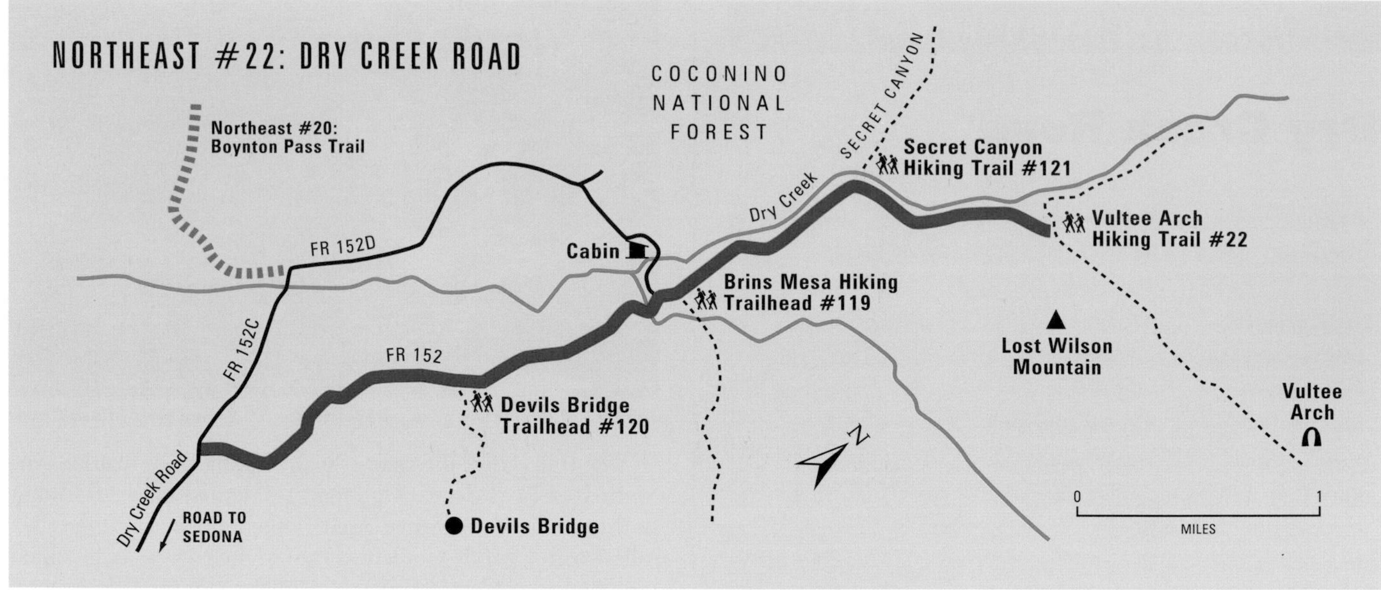

		cabin. To reach it, take this side trail; at 0.2 miles there is a rough rocky crossing of Dry Creek; then bear left up onto slickrock platform above Dry Creek.
		GPS: N34°54.92' W111°48.53'
▼ 2.4	SO	Brins Mesa Hiking Trailhead #119 and parking on right. Zero trip meter.
		GPS: N34°55.01' W111°48.49'
▼ 0.0		Continue to the north.
▼ 0.1	SO	Track on left to viewpoint.
		GPS: N34°55.10' W111°48.49'
▼ 0.9	SO	Secret Canyon Hiking Trailhead #121 on left; then track on left to Dry Creek.
		GPS: N34°55.78' W111°48.34'
▼ 1.8		Trail ends at the hiking trailheads for Dry Creek Trail and Vultee Arch Trail #22.
		GPS: N34°56.24' W111°47.62'

NORTHEAST REGION TRAIL #23

Soldier Pass Road

Starting Point:	**Arizona 89A, 1.2 miles west of the intersection with Arizona 179**
Finishing Point:	**Hiking trail to Soldier Pass**
Total Mileage:	**2.5 miles**
Unpaved Mileage:	**1 mile**
Driving Time:	**45 minutes (one-way)**
Elevation Range:	**4,400–4,600 feet**
Usually Open:	**Year-round**
Best Time to Travel:	**Year-round**
Difficulty Rating:	**4 (main trail); 5 (Devils Kitchen)**
Scenic Rating:	**8**
Remoteness Rating:	**+0**

Special Attractions

- Devils Kitchen—a natural sinkhole.
- Popular, short rugged trail used by 4WD tour companies.
- Natural rock tanks of Seven Sacred Ponds.

Description

This very short trail is maintained by Red Rock Jeep Tours in conjunction with the Coconino National Forest, and you can expect to meet some of the tour jeeps along the trail as well as private vehicles. The trail does not go all the way to Soldier Pass but stops a short distance before it. It is suitable for high-clearance 4WD vehicles, because it is rough and sandy for most of the way. The main trail is rated a 4 for difficulty, but the short spur to the Devils Kitchen sinkhole rates a 5 because of the rough slickrock and short, steep sections.

The trail passes the side trail to Devils Kitchen, a very large and spectacular natural sinkhole, which is so regular it looks manmade. Farther along are the Seven Sacred Ponds—small natural rock holes that contain water year-round. These pools were important to local Indian tribes in the past and to local wildlife today.

The trail ends at a turnaround and the start of the hiking trail to Soldier Pass,

At the Seven Sacred Ponds

which was used by General George Crook during the Apache Campaign in 1871–72. There is limited parking at the end of the trail. If you plan on hiking to the pass, you would be better off parking at the trailhead rather than obstructing the turnaround point.

Current Road Information

Coconino National Forest
Sedona Ranger District
PO Box 300
Sedona, AZ 86336
(520) 282-4119

Map References

BLM Sedona
USFS Coconino National Forest: Sedona Ranger District
USGS 1:24,000 Sedona, Wilson Mt.
1:100,000 Sedona
Maptech CD-ROM: Flagstaff/Sedona/Prescott
Arizona Atlas & Gazetteer, p. 42
Other: Beartooth Maps—Sedona

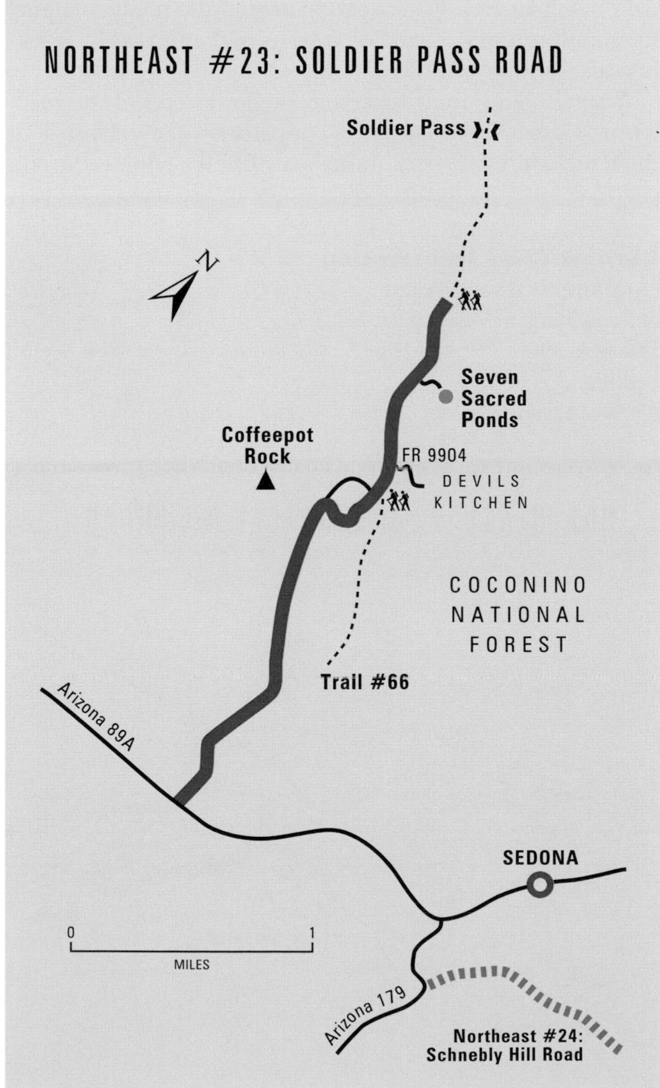

Route Directions

▼ 0.0		From Arizona 89A, 1.2 miles west of the intersection with Arizona 179, zero trip meter and turn north on Soldier Pass Road, which is a paved street. Remain on Soldier Pass Road, ignoring turns to the right and left.
		GPS: N34°51.77′ W111°46.95′
▼ 1.3	TR	Turn right onto Rim Shadows Drive, following the sign for Soldier Pass Trail.
		GPS: N34°52.93′ W111°47.15′
▼ 1.5	BR	Bear right, following the sign for Soldier Pass Trail. Canyon Shadows Drive is the first right; take the second right; then immediately turn left through gateway for Soldier Pass Trailhead. Parking area is closed 6 P.M. to 8 A.M.
		GPS: N34°52.99′ W111°47.02′
▼ 1.6	SO	Parking area for Soldier Pass Road. Hiking Trail #66 on right. Soldier Pass Road, FR 9904, continues ahead out the back of the parking area. Zero trip meter.
		GPS: N34°53.06′ W111°46.99′
▼ 0.0		Continue to the north.
▼ 0.2	SO	Track on right is FR 9904, which goes 0.3 miles to Devils Kitchen, a natural sinkhole. This spur is rated 5. Zero trip meter.
		GPS: N34°53.19′ W111°47.02′
▼ 0.0		Continue to the north and pass the Teacup Hiking Trail on the left.
▼ 0.2	BR	Trail forks and rejoins almost immediately.
		GPS: N34°53.32′ W111°47.13′
▼ 0.3	SO	Track on right goes 0.1 miles to the Seven Sacred Ponds. The pools are immediately below the slickrock platform. Zero trip meter.
		GPS: N34°53.45′ W111°47.14′
▼ 0.0		Continue to the northwest.
▼ 0.3	SO	Cross through wash.
		GPS: N34°53.69′ W111°47.22′
▼ 0.4		Vehicle trail ends at turnaround.
		GPS: N34°53.77′ W111°47.21′

NORTHEAST REGION TRAIL #24

Schnebly Hill Road

Starting Point:	I-17 at exit 320
Finishing Point:	Arizona 179, south of Sedona
Total Mileage:	11.4 miles
Unpaved Mileage:	10.5 miles
Driving Time:	1 hour
Elevation Range:	4,300–6,600 feet
Usually Open:	Year-round
Best Time to Travel:	Year-round
Difficulty Rating:	2
Scenic Rating:	9
Remoteness Rating:	+0

Special Attractions

- Unequaled view of red rock country above Sedona.
- Deep Bear Wallow Canyon.

History

The red rock country around Sedona has seen a long history of human settlement, stretching back thousands of years. The earliest inhabitants appear to date back to 8000 B.C. when humans hunted in the valley. Indians used the hot springs in Oak Creek Canyon and the Sedona area as a trading place for goods from the south. In the 1500s, the Spanish explorers passed through the valley.

The earliest permanent settlement in the area was in Oak Creek Canyon. In 1876 John James Thompson took up squatters' rights in an area known as Indian Gardens. The Indians, who had planted the thriving gardens of corn and vegetables that Thompson found there, had been relocated to the San Carlos Reservation. Thompson's small farming settlement soon attracted other families.

A view of the trail down in Bear Wallow Canyon

The Schnebly family name is inextricably linked with Sedona. The town was named in 1902 after Sedona Schnebly, the wife of the first postmaster, Carl Schnebly, who had come from Missouri. The original name suggested for the town was Schnebly Station, but the post office would not accept the name because it was too long. When Carl's brother, Ellsworth, suggested the name Sedona after his sister-in-law, the post office accepted it.

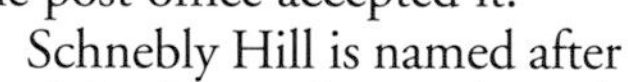

Schnebly Hill is named after Theodore Carlton Schnebly, one of the first settlers in the Oak Creek Canyon area. In 1902 Schnebly constructed a rough road up Bear Wallow Canyon over the Mogollon Rim.

Description

This popular route linking I-17 and Sedona is best suited for a high-clearance vehicle because of the rockiness of the road around Bear Wallow Canyon. The best direction for travel is east to west because the descent into Bear Wallow Canyon gives the better views.

Initially, the trail passes through the ponderosa pine forest of Coconino National Forest on Schnebly Hill. There are many tracks off to the right and left on this section, most of which enter the Woods Wildlife Area. Motorized vehicles are not allowed within the wildlife area between December 15 and April 1 to protect the winter habitat for elk and other animals. Travel on Schnebly Hill Road is permitted year-round.

The Schnebly Hill Vista is reached at 5.4 miles, where there is a large pull-in. It is a good place to stop and appreciate the view. From the viewpoint, you can look down Casner Canyon to the highway far below. Wilson Mountain is ahead. Sedona can be glimpsed in the valley, 1,800 feet below.

Foxboro Lake, high above Sedona in the Coconino National Forest

Past the vista point, the trail is not recommended for passenger vehicles as it is rough and rocky, but a high-clearance vehicle will have no problems. The trail winds down a wide shelf road, providing unparalleled views of the red rock country that has made Sedona world famous. This road is extremely popular with jeep tours that operate out of Sedona as well as with individuals, and it can be busy. It descends gradually along an even grade, leaving behind the ponderosa pine forest and entering a band of vegetation dominated by prickly pears, century plants, and junipers.

Several hiking trails lead from the lower end of the road. There is also a viewpoint for Snoopy Rock—the small rock to the southeast that looks unmistakably like the famous cartoon character lying on his back on the roof of his kennel.

Current Road Information

Coconino National Forest
Sedona Ranger District
PO Box 300
Sedona, AZ 86336
(520) 282-4119

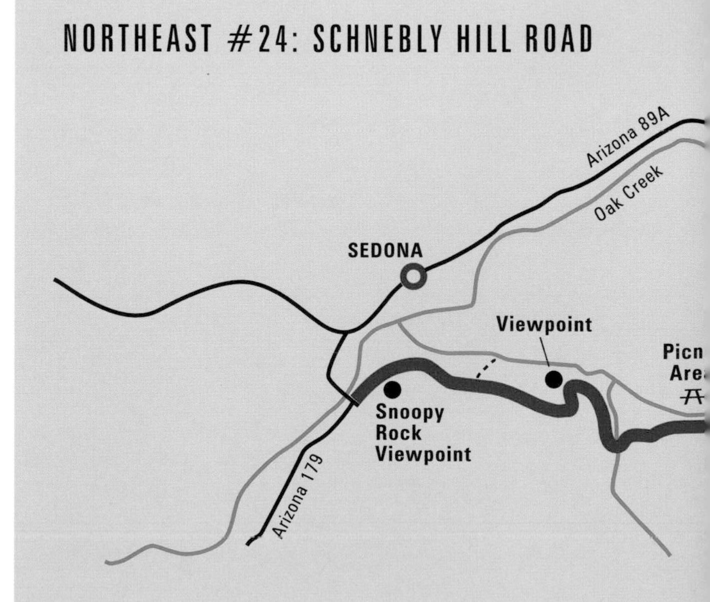

Coconino National Forest
Mormon Lake Ranger District
4373 South Lake Mary Rd.
Flagstaff, AZ 86001
(520) 774-1182

Map References

BLM Sedona
USFS Coconino National Forest: Sedona and Mormon Lake Ranger Districts
USGS 1:24,000 Munds Park, Munds Mt., Sedona
1:100,000 Sedona
Maptech CD-ROM: Flagstaff/Sedona/Prescott
Arizona Atlas & Gazetteer, p. 42
Arizona Road & Recreation Atlas, p. 35 & p. 69
Recreational Map of Arizona
Other: Beartooth Maps—Sedona

Route Directions

▼ 0.0		From I-17 at exit 320, proceed to the west side of the freeway; zero trip meter and proceed west on Schnebly Hill Road, FR 153. The road turns to dirt immediately after a cattle guard. Bear immediately left after the cattle guard, following the sign for Sedona.
5.4 ▲		Bear right over the cattle guard to finish at exit 320 on I-17.
		GPS: N34°54.73′ W111°38.48′
▼ 0.2	SO	Track on right.
5.2 ▲	SO	Track on left.
▼ 0.5	SO	Track on left into Woods Wildlife Area.
4.9 ▲	SO	Track on right into Woods Wildlife Area.
▼ 0.7	SO	Graded road on right.
4.7 ▲	SO	Graded road on left.
▼ 0.8	SO	Track on right.
4.6 ▲	SO	Track on left.
▼ 1.1	SO	Track on left.
4.3 ▲	SO	Track on right.
▼ 1.5	SO	Graded road on left.
3.9 ▲	SO	Graded road on right.
		GPS: N34°53.84′ W111°39.45′
▼ 2.2	SO	Graded road on left; then Foxboro Lake on left; then track on right and track on left into Woods Wildlife Area.
3.2 ▲	BL	Track on right into Woods Wildlife Area and track on left; then Foxboro Lake on right; then graded road on right.
		GPS: N34°53.88′ W111°40.06′
▼ 2.6	SO	Two tracks on left.
2.8 ▲	SO	Two tracks on right.
▼ 2.8	SO	Track on left into Woods Wildlife Area.
2.6 ▲	SO	Track on right into Woods Wildlife Area.
		GPS: N34°53.69′ W111°40.36′
▼ 3.1	SO	Track on left; no motorized access.
2.3 ▲	SO	Track on right; no motorized access.
		GPS: N34°53.48′ W111°40.58′
▼ 3.2	SO	Track on right is FR 153E. Closed to vehicles from December 15 to April 1 to minimize disturbance to big-game winter habitat.
2.2 ▲	SO	Track on left is FR 153E. Closed to vehicles from December 15 to April 1 to minimize disturbance to big-game winter habitat.
		GPS: N34°53.44′ W111°40.62′
▼ 3.4	SO	Track on left is FR 801 into Woods Wildlife Area; then track on right.
2.0 ▲	SO	Track on left; then track on right is FR 801 into Woods Wildlife Area.
		GPS: N34°53.30′ W111°40.76′
▼ 3.5	SO	Track on left is closed to vehicles from December 15 to April 1.
1.9 ▲	SO	Track on right is closed to vehicles from December 15 to April 1.
▼ 3.9	SO	Track on left is FR 153A into Woods Wildlife Area; closed to vehicles from December 15 to April 1.
1.5 ▲	SO	Track on right is FR 153A into Woods Wildlife Area; closed to vehicles from December 15 to April 1.
▼ 5.0	SO	Cattle guard.
0.4 ▲	SO	Cattle guard.

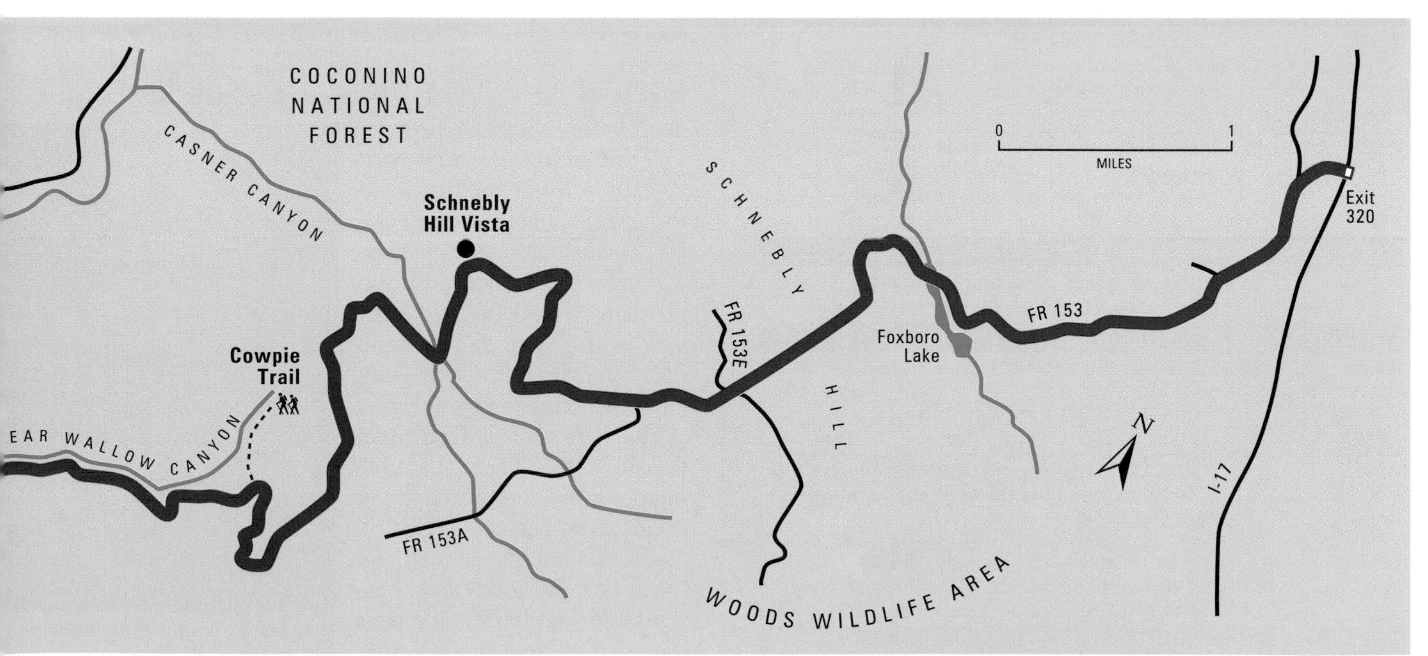

▼ 5.4		SO	Schnebly Hill Vista on the right. Camping and fires prohibited past this point. Zero trip meter.
	0.0 ▲		Continue to the east.
			GPS: N34°53.39' W111°42.15'
▼ 0.0			Continue to the west. Not recommended for passenger vehicles past this point.
	5.1 ▲	SO	Schnebly Hill Vista on the left. Zero trip meter.
▼ 0.4		SO	Cross through wash.
	4.7 ▲	SO	Cross through wash.
			GPS: N34°53.05' W111°42.13'
▼ 0.7		SO	Turnout on right.
	4.4 ▲	SO	Turnout on left.
▼ 1.1		SO	Saddle between Casner Canyon and Bear Wallow Canyon.
	4.0 ▲	SO	Saddle between Casner Canyon and Bear Wallow Canyon.
▼ 1.6		SO	Closure gate.
	3.5 ▲	SO	Closure gate.
			GPS: N34°52.52' W111°42.41'
▼ 2.6		SO	Pull-in on left is parking for Cowpie Trail on the right.
	2.5 ▲	SO	Pull-in on right is parking for Cowpie Trail on the left.
			GPS: N34°52.32' W111°42.74'
▼ 3.4		SO	Cross over wash.
	1.7 ▲	SO	Cross over wash.
▼ 4.1		SO	Picnic tables on right below road alongside creek. Hiking trail on far side.
	1.0 ▲	SO	Picnic tables on left below road alongside creek. Hiking trail on far side.
			GPS: N34°52.08' W111°44.05'
▼ 4.5		SO	Cross through wash.
	0.6 ▲	SO	Cross through wash.
			GPS: N34°51.90' W111°44.44'
▼ 4.8		SO	Viewpoint on right over Sedona.
	0.3 ▲	SO	Viewpoint on left over Sedona.
			GPS: N34°52.05' W111°44.73'
▼ 5.1		SO	Road becomes paved. Trailhead parking for Huckaby and Margs Draw Trails on right (hiking, horses, mountain bikes). Zero trip meter.
	0.0 ▲		Continue to the east.
			GPS: N34°51.96' W111°44.87'
▼ 0.0			Continue to the west.
	0.9 ▲	SO	Road turns to graded dirt. Trailhead parking for Huckaby and Margs Draw Trails on left (hiking, horses, mountain bikes). Zero trip meter.
▼ 0.2		SO	Munds Mountain Wilderness on left and hiking trail on right.
	0.7 ▲	SO	Munds Mountain Wilderness on right and hiking trail on left.
			GPS: N34°51.97' W111°45.03'
▼ 0.3		SO	Pull-in on left is viewpoint for Snoopy Rock.
	0.6 ▲	SO	Pull-in on right is viewpoint for Snoopy Rock.
			GPS: N34°51.92' W111°45.18'
▼ 0.4		SO	Track on right and track on left; then cattle guard.
	0.5 ▲	SO	Cattle guard; then track on left and track on right.
▼ 0.9			Trail ends at the intersection with Arizona 179 in Sedona, immediately south of the bridge over Oak Creek.
	0.0 ▲		From Arizona 179, zero trip meter and turn northeast on the paved Schnebly Hill Road at the well-marked intersection, immediately south of the bridge over Oak Creek in Sedona.
			GPS: N34°51.74' W111°45.64'

NORTHEAST REGION TRAIL #25

Broken Arrow Trail

Starting Point:	**Arizona 179, south of Sedona, 1.3 miles from intersection with Arizona 89A**
Finishing Point:	**Chicken Point**
Total Mileage:	**3.1 miles (round-trip)**
Unpaved Mileage:	**2.6 miles**
Driving Time:	**2 hours**
Elevation Range:	**4,200–4,600 feet**
Usually Open:	**Year-round**
Best Time to Travel:	**Year-round**
Difficulty Rating:	**7**
Scenic Rating:	**9**
Remoteness Rating:	**+0**

Special Attractions

- Challenging and scenic sand and slickrock trail.
- Submarine Rock and other prominent rock formations.
- Exceptional views from Chicken Point and all along the trail.
- Devils Dining Room—a natural sinkhole.

Description

This extremely popular short trail encompasses the best of Sedona—panoramic views, red rock formations, and a challenging 4WD trail. You won't find solitude along this trail. It is heavily used by individuals and by Pink Jeep Tours, one of Sedona's popular Jeep tour companies. Pink Jeep Tours helps to maintain the trail in conjunction with the Coconino National Forest.

Although this trail is very short, it is extremely rugged; the main challenge comes from the extensive slickrock. The trail is best suited to small or mid-sized SUVs with high clearance. Vehicles with long overhangs will probably connect with the slickrock ledges—and vehicle underbodies bend before slickrock does.

The trail lets you know what you are in for at the first slickrock step, which is actually easier than it looks; most vehicles will slowly advance with no problem. If you don't like the look of this step, or you think that your front or rear overhangs will catch, go no farther as there are more difficult sections to come. There is a turning point before the step if you decide to go back.

The trail, a mix of sand and slickrock steps, winds its way toward Chicken Point. Side trails lead to the large natural sink-

These steps are the most difficult part of the trail

Chicken Point at the southern end of the trail

hole of Devils Dining Room and the aptly named Submarine Rock. The viewpoint at Chicken Point is a large slickrock platform that looks out to the southwest over the red rock cliffs.

A portion of the return trip takes a detour to allow one-way travel on this part of the ascent. A highlight of the return trip, a slickrock knob that makes a tight natural "roundabout," is a great place from which to photograph Submarine Rock.

The most challenging part of the trail is the end of the one-way section, which descends a very steep, ledgy slickrock hill. This section is not easy in wet weather, when slickrock lives up to its name. This hill is rated a 7 for difficulty; the rest of the trail is rated a 6. You can view this hill from the bottom at the start of the one-way section by walking the hundred yards to the base of the hill. If you don't feel comfortable piloting your vehicle down the hill, turn back at this point. Please respect the one-way system, which is designed to reduce congestion on the trail. Do not continue to Chicken Point if you do not wish to tackle the steep downhill.

Once down the hill, the trail retraces its path back to Arizona 179.

Current Road Information

Coconino National Forest
Sedona Ranger District
PO Box 300
Sedona, AZ 86336
(520) 282-4119

Map References

BLM Sedona
USFS Coconino National Forest: Sedona Ranger District
USGS 1:24,000 Sedona, Munds Mt.
1:100,000 Sedona
Maptech CD-ROM: Flagstaff/Sedona/Prescott
Arizona Atlas & Gazetteer, p. 42
Other: Beartooth Maps—Sedona

Route Directions

▼ 0.0 From the intersection of Arizona 179 and Arizona 89A, proceed south on Arizona 179 for 1.3 miles; then turn southeast on Morgan Road at the sign for Broken Arrow Estates.

Zero trip meter. Remain on paved Morgan Road, ignoring roads on right and left.

GPS: N34°50.92' W111°45.90'

▼ 0.5 SO Road turns to graded dirt; then cattle guard.

▼ 0.6 SO Parking area on left for Margs Draw Trailhead. Hiking trail on the right. Road is now designated FR 179F and is a 4WD road.

GPS: N34°50.73' W111°45.40'

▼ 0.8 SO Climb up large rock step; then cross through wash. This is the start of the 4WD section.

GPS: N34°50.56' W111°45.28'

▼ 0.9 SO Track on right goes 0.1 miles to the large natural sinkhole of Devils Dining Room. Zero trip meter.

GPS: N34°50.50' W111°45.26'

▼ 0.0 Continue to the southeast on the main trail.

▼ 0.1 BR Start of one-way section.

GPS: N34°50.45' W111°45.15'

▼ 0.2 SO End of one-way section.

▼ 0.4 SO Hiking trail crosses vehicle trail. Submarine Rock is on the left, among the junipers.

GPS: N34°50.29' W111°44.96'

▼ 0.5 BL Start of one-way section. Track on right is end of loop. Walk a short distance to the right to

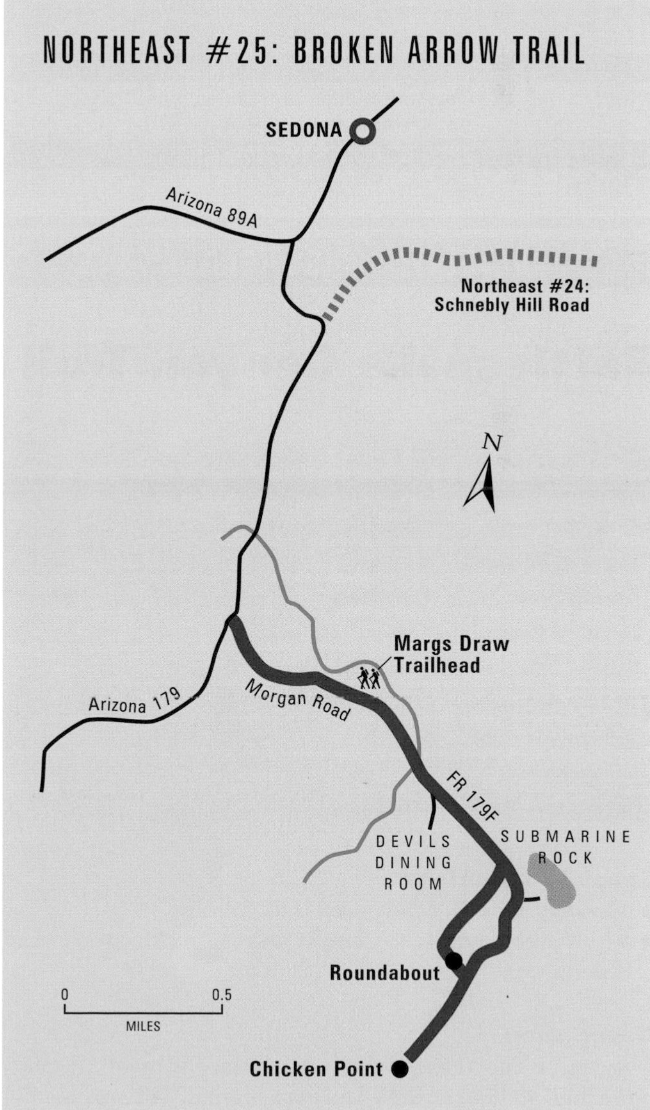

		view the final steep descent, which is the most difficult section of the trail. You can turn around here if you do not want to descend the rock steps. Past this point, the trail is one-way.
▼ 0.6	BR	Track on left goes 0.2 miles to a viewpoint on the top of Submarine Rock. Zero trip meter.
		GPS: N34°50.21' W111°44.89'
▼ 0.0		Continue to the southeast.
▼ 0.4	BL	Track on right is start of return loop. Zero trip meter.
		GPS: N34°49.97' W111°45.05'
▼ 0.0		Continue to the south.
▼ 0.3	UT	Chicken Point. Make a U-turn and return along the trail the way you came.
		GPS: N34°49.76' W111°45.23'
▼ 0.6	BL	Track on right. Zero trip meter.
		GPS: N34°49.97' W111°45.05'
▼ 0.0		Continue to the north.
▼ 0.1	SO	Steep climb up slickrock to a "roundabout" around a large rock.
		GPS: N34°50.03' W111°45.09'
▼ 0.2	TR	Trail does a sharp right turn at a high point, then twists on slickrock with some tight turns.
		GPS: N34°50.05' W111°45.14'
▼ 0.3	SO	Hiking trail on left.
▼ 0.5	SO	Very steep, short downhill section. Most difficult section of trail.
		GPS: N34°50.23' W111°44.99'
▼ 0.6	TL	Two-way section of trail resumes. Turn left and retrace your steps to Arizona 179.
		GPS: N34°50.24' W111°44.94'

NORTHEAST REGION TRAIL #26

Rattlesnake Canyon Trail

Starting Point:	**FR 239, 2.1 miles south of junction with I-17**
Finishing Point:	**Stoneman Lake Road, FR 213**
Total Mileage:	**4.4 miles**
Unpaved Mileage:	**4.4 miles**
Driving Time:	**1.25 hours**
Elevation Range:	**6,200–6,700 feet**
Usually Open:	**January 1–August 15**
Best Time to Travel:	**January 1–August 15**
Difficulty Rating:	**5**
Scenic Rating:	**8**
Remoteness Rating:	**+0**

Special Attractions

- Moderately rated, lightly used trail.
- Views over Rattlesnake Canyon and red rock country near Sedona.

Description

This trail is short, but because the surface is rough, it takes more than an hour to drive less than 5 miles. The trail is contained within the Rattlesnake Quiet Area, which is closed to vehicles between August 15 and December 31 to allow for non-motorized hunting, hiking, and horseback riding.

The descent into Rattlesnake Canyon is rough and rocky

The main difficulty of the trail comes from the large rocks embedded in the surface. At some sections, particularly as the trail descends to cross through Rattlesnake Canyon, you will need to place your wheels carefully. If you have low-hanging brush bars or side steps, you should be particularly careful.

South of the Rattlesnake Canyon crossing, there is an excellent viewpoint to the southwest down the canyon. Other great views are to be found earlier on the trail as it crosses through an open area where you can look west toward the red rock country around Sedona, and across Horse Mesa to Lee Mountain.

This trail sees little use, and in places it can be faint and hard to follow, particularly around an open area 1.1 miles from the start of the trail.

Current Road Information

Coconino National Forest
Beaver Creek Ranger District
PO Box 300
Sedona, AZ 86336
(520) 567-4121

Map References

BLM Sedona
USFS Coconino National Forest: Beaver Creek Ranger District
USGS 1:24,000 Stoneman Lake
1:100,000 Sedona
Maptech CD-ROM: Flagstaff/Sedona/Prescott
Arizona Atlas & Gazetteer, p. 42
Arizona Road & Recreation Atlas, p. 35 & p. 69

The trail is indistinct because of its light use

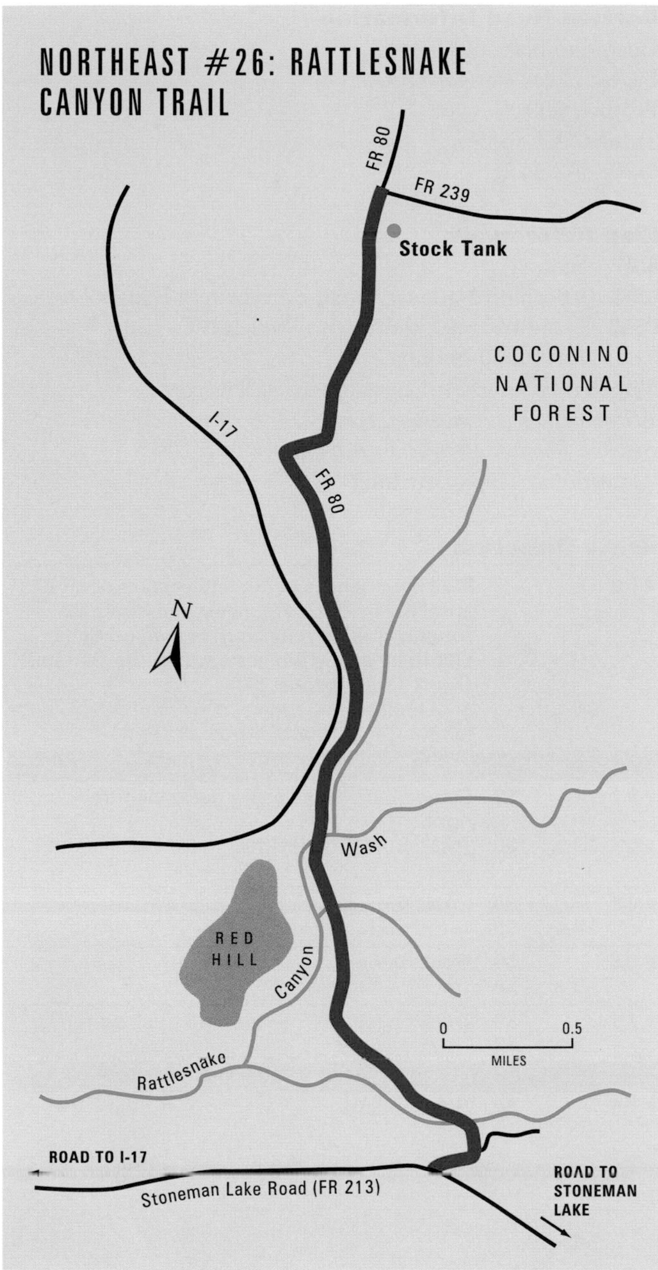

Route Directions

▼ 0.0 From I-17, exit 315, proceed to the east side of the interstate and head south along FR 80 for 2.1 miles. Zero trip meter at the intersection of FR 80 and FR 239 and proceed to the south. Enter Rattlesnake Quiet Area through gate.
4.4 ▲ Trail finishes at the intersection of FR 239 and FR 80. Bear left to exit to I-17.

GPS: N34°49.47′ W111°35.65′

▼ 0.1 SO Stock tank on left.
4.3 ▲ SO Stock tank on right.

▼ 1.1 BL Faint track on right; continue on small faint trail.
3.3 ▲ BR Faint track on left; continue on main trail, which is faint at this point.

GPS: N34°48.53′ W111°35.78′

▼ 1.8 SO Gate on right; trail is beside the freeway.
2.6 ▲ SO Gate on left; trail is beside the freeway.

▼ 1.9 SO Gate.
2.5 ▲ SO Gate.

GPS: N34°47.93′ W111°35.37′

▼ 2.3 SO Trail follows alongside the edge of a tributary of Rattlesnake Canyon.
2.1 ▲ SO Trail follows alongside the edge of a tributary of Rattlesnake Canyon.

GPS: N34°47.56′ W111°35.34′

▼ 2.7 SO Cross through Rattlesnake Canyon wash.
1.7 ▲ SO Cross through Rattlesnake Canyon wash.

GPS: N34°47.29′ W111°35.33′

▼ 2.9 SO Wire gate. Red Hill is on the right.
1.5 ▲ SO Wire gate. Red Hill is on the left.

GPS: N34°47.19′ W111°35.32′

▼ 3.0 SO Cross through wash.
1.4 ▲ SO Cross through wash.

▼ 3.4 SO Faint track on left.
1.0 ▲ SO Faint track on right.

▼ 4.0 SO Cross through wash.
0.4 ▲ SO Cross through wash.

GPS: N34°46.45′ W111°34.50′

▼ 4.1 SO Track on left goes sharply back to the left.
0.3 ▲ BL Trail forks; take left-hand fork down to cross wash.

GPS: N34°46.41′ W111°34.42′

▼ 4.3 SO Faint track on left.
0.1 ▲ SO Faint track on right.

▼ 4.4 Cross cattle guard; information board for the Palatkwapi Indian Trail immediately on right and seasonal closure gate. Trail ends at the intersection with paved Stoneman Lake Road. Turn left for Stoneman Lake; turn right for I-17.
0.0 ▲ Trail commences on paved Stoneman Lake Road, FR 213, 5.1 miles east of I-17, exit 306. Zero trip meter and turn northwest through seasonal closure gate and across a cattle guard. There is an information board for the old Palatkwapi Indian Trail immediately after the gate. Proceed northeast on formed lumpy trail, FR 80. The route marker is a few hundred yards along the trail.

GPS: N34°46.27′ W111°34.56′

NORTHEAST REGION TRAIL #27

Cedar Flat Road

Starting Point:	**Intersection of FR 618 and FR 214, 4 miles north of the General Crook Trail (Arizona 260)**
Finishing Point:	**Intersection with Northeast #28: Home Tank Draw Trail (FR 214)**
Total Mileage:	**10.8 miles**
Unpaved Mileage:	**10.8 miles**
Driving Time:	**1 hour**
Elevation Range:	**3,900–6,000 feet**
Usually Open:	**May to October**
Best Time to Travel:	**Dry weather**
Difficulty Rating:	**1**
Scenic Rating:	**9**
Remoteness Rating:	**+0**

The easy trail runs high above West Clear Creek Canyon

Special Attractions

- Views into West Clear Creek Canyon and south to the Verde Valley.
- Connects to Northeast #28: Home Tank Draw Trail.

Description

This trail, basically a continuation of Northeast #28: Home Tank Draw Trail, connects with it to form a loop that returns to more-used roads. However, this portion of the loop is a highly scenic trail in its own right for those without the high-clearance 4WD necessary to tackle the rocky Home Tank Draw Trail. Cedar Flat Road, a wide, graded dirt road, can be driven by passenger vehicles in dry weather.

The highlight of the trail is the section of wide shelf road near the western end, which has panoramic views into West Clear Creek Canyon and south to the Verde Valley. These views are best appreciated when driving the trail in the reverse direction.

The remainder of the trail crosses the wide plateau of Cedar Ridge to connect with the start of Northeast #28: Home Tank Draw Trail.

Current Road Information

Coconino National Forest
Beaver Creek Ranger District
PO Box 300
Sedona, AZ 86336
(520) 567-4121

Map References

BLM Sedona
USFS Coconino National Forest: Beaver Creek Ranger District
USGS 1:24,000 Buckhorn Mt., Walker Mt.
1:100,000 Sedona
Maptech CD-ROM: Flagstaff/Sedona/Prescott
Arizona Atlas & Gazetteer, p. 42
Arizona Road & Recreation Atlas, p. 41 & p. 75
Recreational Map of Arizona

Route Directions

Mileage		Directions
▼ 0.0		Trail commences at the intersection of FR 618 and FR 214. Zero trip meter and turn east on roughly graded road. Turn is marked Cedar Flat Road and is 4 miles north of the General Crook Trail (Arizona 260).
5.0 ▲		Trail ends at the intersection with FR 618. Turn left for Camp Verde; turn right for I-17.
		GPS: N34°34.28' W111°44.10'
▼ 0.1	SO	Cattle guard and closure gate; then track on right.
4.9 ▲	SO	Track on left; then cattle guard and closure gate.
▼ 0.2	SO	Cross through wash.
4.8 ▲	SO	Cross through wash.
▼ 0.8	SO	Track on right.
4.2 ▲	SO	Track on left.
▼ 1.5	SO	Track on left is FR 9201S and track on right.
3.5 ▲	SO	Track on right is FR 9201S and track on left.
		GPS: N34°34.33' W111°42.66'
▼ 2.6	SO	Track on left.

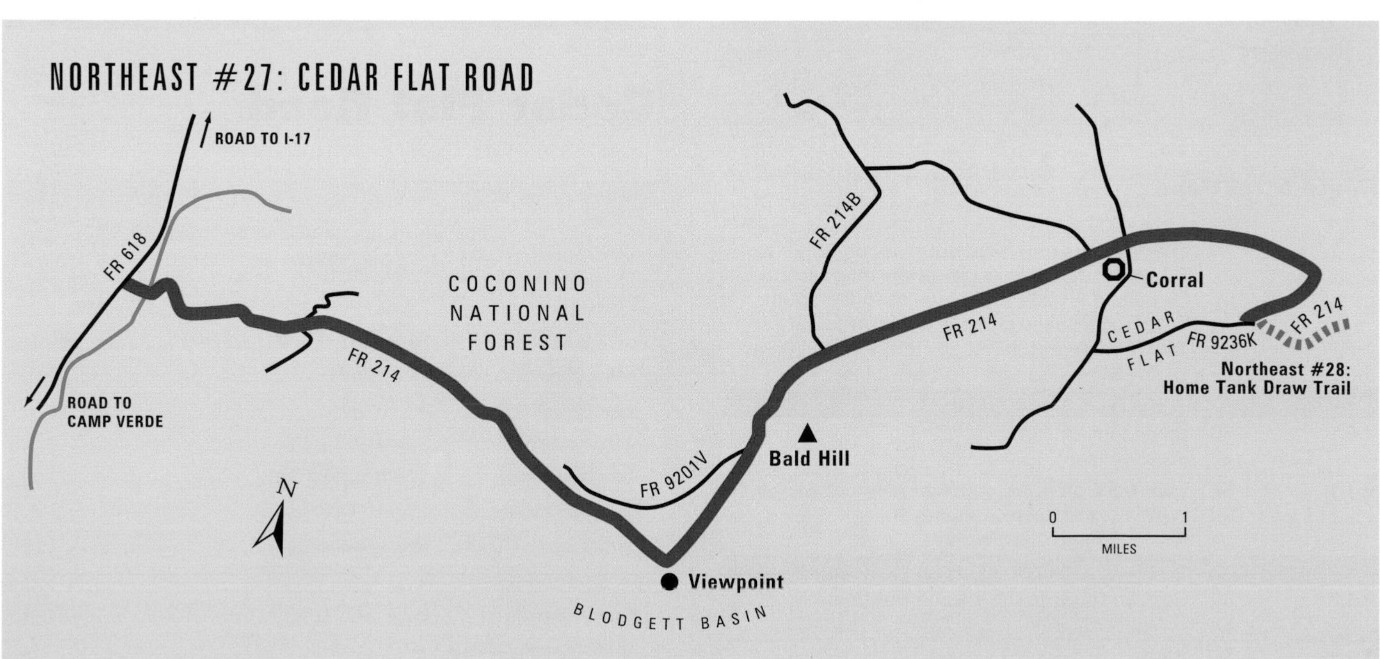

Mileage			Directions
	2.4 ▲	SO	Track on right.
▼ 2.7		SO	Track on left.
	2.3 ▲	SO	Track on right.
▼ 3.2		SO	Track on right.
	1.8 ▲	SO	Track on left.
▼ 3.9		SO	Track on right goes to Blodgett Basin Trail #31 (initially suitable for vehicles); then cattle guard.
	1.1 ▲	SO	Cattle guard; then track on left goes to Blodgett Basin Trail #31 (initially suitable for vehicles).
			GPS: N34°33.78' W111°40.33'
▼ 4.9		SO	Viewpoint on right on left-hand bend into West Clear Creek Canyon.
	0.1 ▲	SO	Viewpoint on left on right-hand bend into West Clear Creek Canyon.
▼ 5.0		SO	Track on right is FR 214A; then track on left through gate. Zero trip meter.
	0.0 ▲		Continue to the northwest.
			GPS: N34°33.58' W111°39.25'
▼ 0.0			Continue to the northeast.
	5.8 ▲	SO	Track on left is FR 214A; then track on right through gate. Zero trip meter.
▼ 0.9		SO	Track on left is FR 9201V; then track on right.
	4.9 ▲	SO	Track on left; then track on right is FR 9201V.
			GPS: N34°34.35' W111°38.88'
▼ 1.1		SO	Track on left is FR 9201W.
	4.7 ▲	SO	Track on right is FR 9201W.
			GPS: N34°34.53' W111°38.89'
▼ 1.8		SO	Cattle guard; then track on left is FR 214B, also marked Walker Basin Trail #81 (hiking); then track on right is FR 9263N; then cattle guard.
	4.0 ▲	SO	Cattle guard; then track on left is FR 9263N; then track on right is FR 214B, also marked Walker Basin Trail #81 (hiking); then cattle guard.
			GPS: N34°35.10' W111°38.51'
▼ 3.9		SO	Track on left through wire gate.
	1.9 ▲	SO	Track on right through wire gate.
▼ 4.0		SO	Cattle guard.
	1.8 ▲	SO	Cattle guard.
▼ 4.1		SO	Corral on right at Cedar Flat; then cattle guard; then track on right and track on left.
	1.7 ▲	SO	Track on right and track on left; then cattle guard; then corral on left at Cedar Flat.
			GPS: N34°36.30' W111°36.51'
▼ 5.0		SO	Track on right.
	0.8 ▲	SO	Track on left.
▼ 5.2		SO	Track on left.
	0.6 ▲	SO	Track on right.
▼ 5.3		TR	Two tracks on left; remain on main trail. Trail is now a roughly graded road.
	0.5 ▲	TL	Two tracks on right. Remain on main trail.
			GPS: N34°36.46' W111°35.18'
▼ 5.8			Trail finishes at the intersection with Northeast #28: Home Tank Draw Trail, FR 214. Turn left over the cattle guard and continue northeast to continue along the Home Tank Draw Trail.
	0.0 ▲		Trail commences at the western end of Northeast #28: Home Tank Draw Trail, FR 214. Zero trip meter and turn north on unmarked trail. To the south is FR 9236K.
			GPS: N34°36.02' W111°35.39'

NORTHEAST REGION TRAIL #28

Home Tank Draw Trail

Starting Point:	**Intersection of FR 229 and Northeast #29: Apache Maid Fire Lookout Trail (FR 620)**
Finishing Point:	**Eastern end of Northeast #27: Cedar Flat Road**
Total Mileage:	**14.1 miles**
Unpaved Mileage:	**14.1 miles**
Driving Time:	**2 hours**
Elevation Range:	**5,900–6,600 feet**
Usually Open:	**May to October**
Best Time to Travel:	**Dry weather**
Difficulty Rating:	**4**
Scenic Rating:	**8**
Remoteness Rating:	**+1**

Special Attractions

- Little-used trail that passes through interesting scenery in the Coconino National Forest.
- Alternative entry and exit to the Apache Maid Fire Lookout.

Description

This trail sees surprisingly little traffic considering that it is a very scenic (although fairly slow) alternative route into the Coconino National Forest. For the most part, the lumpy, rock-embedded surface ensures a slow pace. The rocks are not difficult to negotiate; a little care with wheel placement is all that is needed. Between the rocky sections, the trail is smooth although there are deep ruts caused by wet weather travel. This is not a good place to be in wet weather.

A typical view of the meadows dotted with pines

The single-track trail runs alongside Jacks Canyon for a short way and crosses through the very pretty Brady Canyon before running through open countryside, which is dotted with alligator junipers and oaks. Elk can often be seen in the area. There are many small trails leading off from the main trail, but it is fairly easy to remain on track, despite the limited route markers.

The trail finishes at the eastern end of Northeast #27: Cedar Flat Road, which is the way to Camp Verde. This trail is 1-rated so it is dealt with separately, but the two trails combine to form a complete route.

Current Road Information
Coconino National Forest
Beaver Creek Ranger District
PO Box 300
Sedona, AZ 86336
(520) 567-4121

Coconino National Forest
Long Valley Ranger District
HC 31 Box 68
Happy Jack, AZ 86024
(520) 527-3640

Map References
BLM Sedona
USFS Coconino National Forest: Beaver Creek Ranger District
USGS 1:24,000 Apache Maid Mt., Happy Jack, Buckhorn Mt.
1:100,000 Sedona
Maptech CD-ROM: Flagstaff/Sedona/Prescott
Arizona Atlas & Gazetteer, p. 42
Arizona Road & Recreation Atlas, p. 41 & p. 75

Route Directions

▼	▲		
▼ 0.0			From the intersection of FR 229 and FR 620, Northeast #29: Apache Maid Fire Lookout Trail, zero trip meter and turn southeast on formed trail marked FR 229.
	3.3 ▲		Trail ends at the intersection of FR 229 and FR 620, Northeast #29: Apache Maid Fire Lookout Trail. Turn left to exit via Mullican Canyon; turn right to exit via the graded road.
			GPS: N34°42.76' W111°31.22'
▼ 0.1		SO	Cattle guard.
	3.2 ▲	SO	Cattle guard.
▼ 0.5		SO	Cross through Jacks Canyon wash.
	2.8 ▲	SO	Cross through Jacks Canyon wash.
			GPS: N34°42.58' W111°30.83'
▼ 1.1		BR	Track on left and faint track on right.
	2.2 ▲	SO	Track on right and faint track on left.
			GPS: N34°42.29' W111°30.48'
▼ 1.6		SO	Track on left is second entrance to FR 229. Continue ahead on FR 214.
	1.7 ▲	SO	Track on right is FR 229. Continue straight on to join FR 229.
			GPS: N34°41.98' W111°30.06'
▼ 2.0		BL	Cattle guard; then faint track on right.
	1.3 ▲	BR	Faint track on left; then cattle guard.
			GPS: N34°41.78' W111°29.68'
▼ 2.1		SO	Track on right to stock tank.
	1.2 ▲	SO	Track on left to stock tank.
▼ 2.2		SO	Cross through wash.
	1.1 ▲	SO	Cross through wash.
			GPS: N34°41.68' W111°29.48'
▼ 3.2		SO	Cross through wash.
	0.1 ▲	SO	Cross through wash.
▼ 3.3		TR	Track ahead is FR 83. Turn right, remaining on FR 214, and zero trip meter. Route markers at intersection.
	0.0 ▲		Continue to the northeast.
			GPS: N34°40.84' W111°29.02'
▼ 0.0			Continue to the west.
	4.4 ▲	TL	Track on right is FR 83. Turn left, remaining on FR 214, and zero trip meter. Route markers at intersection.

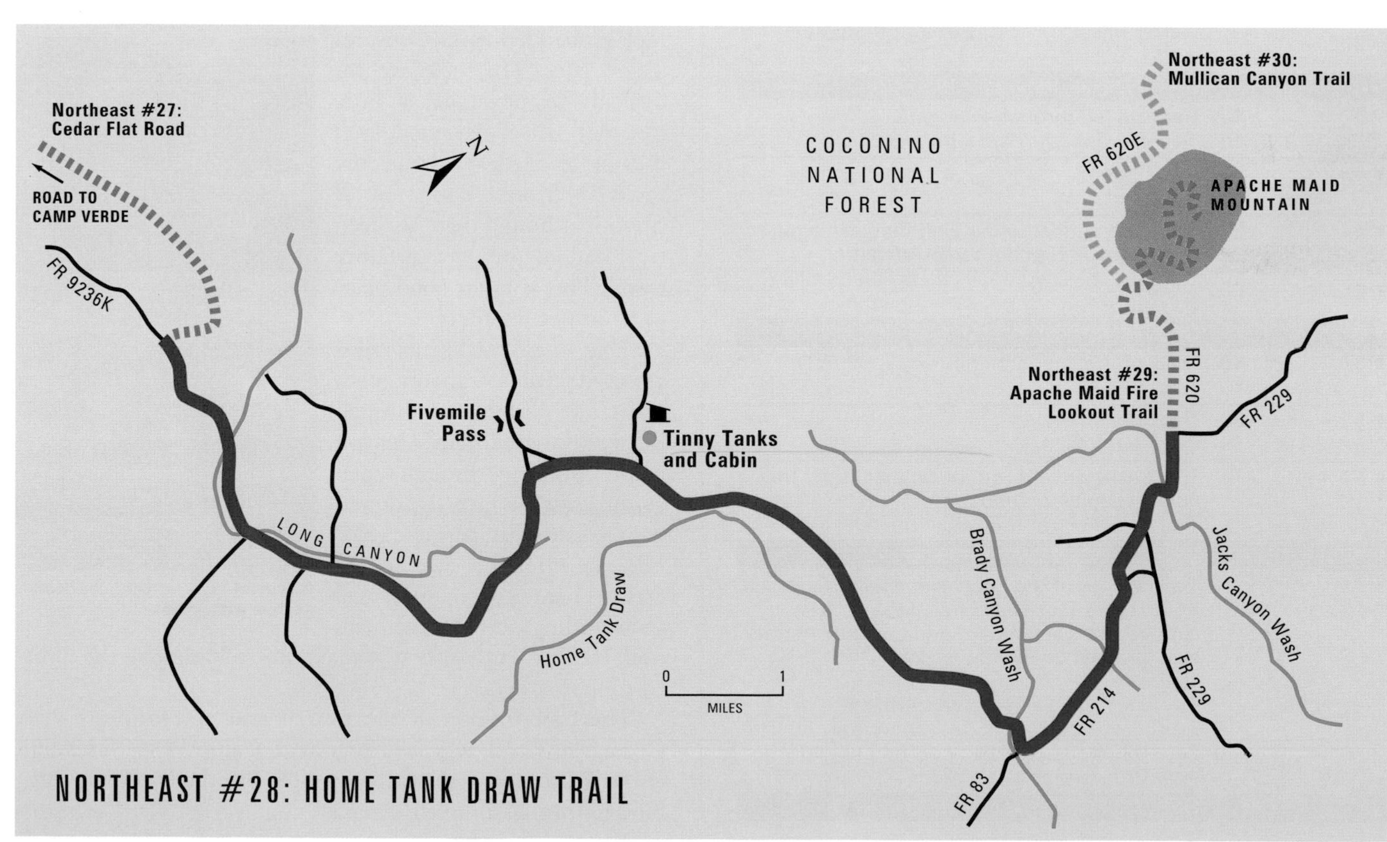

▼ 0.2 SO Cross through Brady Canyon.
4.2 ▲ SO Cross through Brady Canyon.

GPS: N34°40.85' W111°29.24'

▼ 1.6 SO Cattle guard; then track on right.
2.8 ▲ SO Track on left; then cattle guard.

GPS: N34°40.17' W111°30.32'

▼ 2.5 SO Pass through wire gate.
1.9 ▲ SO Pass through wire gate.

GPS: N34°40.07' W111°31.26'

▼ 3.7 SO Cross over creek.
0.7 ▲ SO Cross over creek.

▼ 3.9 SO Faint track on right.
0.5 ▲ BR Faint track on left.

GPS: N34°39.20' W111°32.25'

▼ 4.4 BL Track on right to Tinny stock tanks and cabin; bear left and cross cattle guard. Zero trip meter. The intersection is unmarked.
0.0 ▲ Continue to the northeast.

GPS: N34°39.04' W111°32.69'

▼ 0.0 Continue to the south; track on left.
6.4 ▲ BR Track on right; then cross cattle guard; then track on left to Tinny stock tanks and cabin. Bear right, remaining on main trail. Zero trip meter. The intersection is unmarked.

▼ 0.1 SO Cross through wash; then track on right. This section can be muddy.
6.3 ▲ SO Track on left; then cross through wash. This section can be muddy.

▼ 0.2 SO Track on right.
6.2 ▲ SO Track on left.

▼ 0.6 SO Track on right through gate.
5.8 ▲ SO Track on left through gate.

GPS: N34°38.51' W111°33.01'

▼ 1.0 BL Two tracks on right; road through gates goes to Fivemile Pass and stock tanks. Bear left, remaining on main trail.
5.4 ▲ BR Two tracks on left; road through gates goes to Fivemile Pass and stock tanks. Bear right, remaining on main trail.

GPS: N34°38.22' W111°33.07'

▼ 1.6 TR Track on left; turn right after cattle guard.
4.8 ▲ TL Cattle guard; then turn left. Track continues ahead after cattle guard.

GPS: N34°37.95' W111°32.44'

▼ 2.0 BR Track on left.
4.4 ▲ SO Track on right.

GPS: N34°37.61' W111°32.27'

▼ 2.1 SO Track on right.
4.3 ▲ SO Track on left.

▼ 2.3 SO Stock tank on left.
4.1 ▲ SO Stock tank on right.

▼ 2.6 BR Well-used track on left; bear right and cross cattle guard.
3.8 ▲ BL Cattle guard; then well-used track on right.

GPS: N34°37.09' W111°32.16'

▼ 3.3 SO Pass through fence line.
3.1 ▲ SO Pass through fence line.

▼ 3.6 SO Track on right to stock tank.
2.8 ▲ SO Track on left to stock tank.

▼ 3.8 SO Track on left.
2.6 ▲ SO Track on right.

GPS: N34°36.43' W111°33.12'

▼ 3.9 SO Pass through wire gate.
2.5 ▲ SO Pass through wire gate.

▼ 4.0 SO Cross through wash.
2.4 ▲ SO Cross through wash.

▼ 4.1 SO Cross through wash.
2.3 ▲ SO Cross through wash.

GPS: N34°36.25' W111°33.41'

▼ 4.4 SO Track on left.
2.0 ▲ BL Track on right.

GPS: N34°36.04' W111°33.52'

▼ 4.5 SO Track on left; then cross through wash.
1.9 ▲ SO Cross through wash; then track on right.

GPS: N34°36.02' W111°33.55'

▼ 5.2 SO Cross through wash.
1.2 ▲ SO Cross through wash.

▼ 5.8 SO Well-used track on left.
0.6 ▲ BL Well-used track on right.

GPS: N34°36.02' W111°34.84'

▼ 5.9 SO Track on left.
0.5 ▲ SO Track on right.

▼ 6.4 Trail ends at the T-intersection at the eastern end of the Northeast #27: Cedar Flat Road. Turn right to continue down Cedar Flat Road to Camp Verde. Track on left is FR 9236K. Stock tank at the intersection.
0.0 ▲ Trail commences at the eastern end of the easier Northeast #27: Cedar Flat Road. Zero trip meter and turn east over the cattle guard onto FR 214, which is unmarked but has a yellow road sign: "Not maintained for low clearance vehicles." The trail that continues to the west at that point is FR 9236K. There is a stock tank at the intersection.

GPS: N34°36.02' W111°35.39'

NORTHEAST REGION TRAIL #29

Apache Maid Fire Lookout Trail

Starting Point:	**Intersection of Northeast #28: Home Tank Draw Trail (FR 229) and FR 620**
Finishing Point:	**Apache Maid Fire Lookout**
Total Mileage:	**4 miles**
Unpaved Mileage:	**4 miles**
Driving Time:	**30 minutes**
Elevation Range:	**6,500–7,200 feet**
Usually Open:	**May to October**
Best Time to Travel:	**May to October**
Difficulty Rating:	**2**
Scenic Rating:	**9**
Remoteness Rating:	**+0**

Special Attractions

- Panoramic 360-degree views from the Apache Maid Fire Lookout.
- Connects with other 4WD trails within the Coconino National Forest.

The view from the Apache Maid Fire Lookout

Description

This short trail climbs up the twisting road to the Apache Maid Fire Lookout in the Coconino National Forest. The trail, maintained by the forest service as access for the tower, is normally slightly rutted but is generally suitable for high-clearance vehicles.

The lookout tower, which was built in 1961 to protect the Beaver Creek Watershed, is manned during the fire season. Usually, you are welcome to climb the tower with the lookout's permission. The gate to the tower is closed when the tower is not manned and at night. There are No Camping signs on the far side of the gate, but there are some good campsites scattered among the oaks and pines along this trail.

Current Road Information

Coconino National Forest
Beaver Creek Ranger District
PO Box 300
Sedona, AZ 86336
(520) 567-4121

Map References

BLM Sedona
USFS Coconino National Forest: Beaver Creek Ranger District
USGS 1:24,000 Apache Maid Mt.
1:100,000 Sedona
Maptech CD-ROM: Flagstaff/Sedona/Prescott
Arizona Atlas & Gazetteer, p. 42
Arizona Road & Recreation Atlas, p. 41 & p. 75

Route Directions

▼ 0.0			From the intersection of FR 229 and FR 620, zero trip meter and turn west on formed trail marked FR 620. Northeast #28: Home Tank Draw Trail leads off to the east.
	1.5 ▲		Trail ends at the intersection of Northeast #28: Home Tank Draw Trail (FR 229) and FR 620.
			GPS: N34°42.76' W111°31.22'
▼ 0.3		SO	Track on right.
	1.2 ▲	SO	Track on left.
▼ 0.4		SO	Track on left opposite dam; then track on right to dam.
	1.1 ▲	SO	Track on left to dam; then track on right opposite dam.
▼ 0.8		SO	Track on right.
	0.7 ▲	SO	Track on left.
▼ 1.0		SO	Track on right is FR 620D.
	0.5 ▲	SO	Track on left is FR 620D.
			GPS: N34°42.94' W111°32.19'
▼ 1.3		BR	Track on left; then cross over creek.
	0.2 ▲	BL	Cross over creek; then track on right.
▼ 1.5		SO	Track on left is Northeast #30: Mullican Canyon Trail, FR 620E; track on right to camping area. Zero trip meter.
	0.0 ▲		Proceed southeast on FR 620.
			GPS: N34°42.85' W111°32.55'
▼ 0.0			Continue to the northwest on FR 620.
▼ 0.6		SO	Closure gate; no camping beyond closure gate.
▼ 2.5			Trail ends at Apache Maid Fire Lookout. There is a picnic table at the top.
			GPS: N34°43.53' W111°32.99'

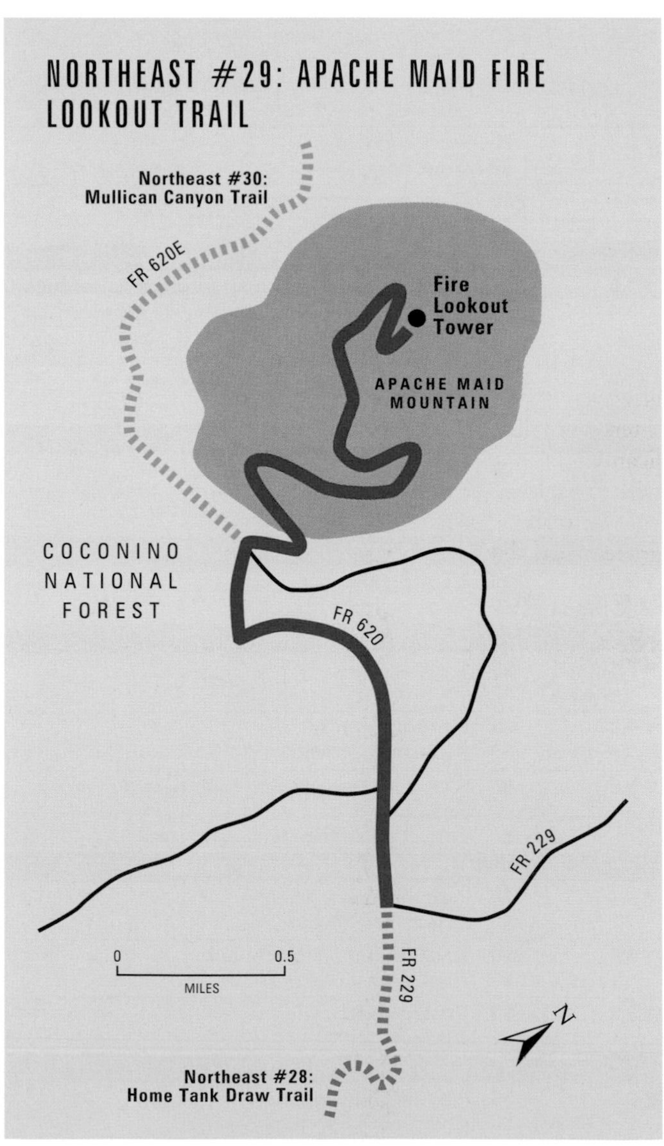

NORTHEAST REGION TRAIL #30

Mullican Canyon Trail

Starting Point:	**Northeast #29: Apache Maid Fire Lookout Trail, 1.5 miles from the intersection with FR 229**
Finishing Point:	**Intersection of FR 229 and FR 644, immediately north of the Watershed Camp Station**
Total Mileage:	**6.5 miles**
Unpaved Mileage:	**6.5 miles**
Driving Time:	**1 hour**
Elevation Range:	**6,000–6,600 feet**
Usually Open:	**May to October**
Best Time to Travel:	**Dry weather**
Difficulty Rating:	**3**
Scenic Rating:	**8**
Remoteness Rating:	**+0**

Special Attractions

- Rugged and scenic Mullican Canyon.
- Views of Apache Maid Mountain.

Description

This short trail runs between Northeast #29: Apache Maid Fire Lookout Trail and FR 229. The trail, which is rough and rutted in places, describes a wide loop around Apache Maid Mountain. Initially, it runs over the open plateau, falling off gradually toward Wet Beaver Creek and Hog Hill. After the intersection with FR 9243H, the trail dips gradually into Mullican Canyon, a narrow, fairly shallow canyon that is rimmed with the black lava rocks that abound in this region.

The trail standard gradually improves until it joins the graded road that completes the loop to FR 229.

A small stock tank at the head of Mullican Canyon

Current Road Information

Coconino National Forest
Beaver Creek Ranger District
PO Box 300
Sedona, AZ 86336
(520) 567-4121

Map References

BLM Sedona
USFS Coconino National Forest: Beaver Creek Ranger District
USGS 1:24,000 Apache Maid Mt., Stoneman Lake
1:100,000 Sedona
Maptech CD-ROM: Flagstaff/Sedona/Prescott
Arizona Atlas & Gazetteer, p. 42
Arizona Road & Recreation Atlas, p. 41 & p. 75

Route Directions

▼ 0.0		From Northeast #29: Apache Maid Fire Lookout Trail, (FR 620), zero trip meter and turn west on the small formed trail marked FR 620E.
0.8 ▲		Trail ends at Northeast #29: Apache Maid Fire Lookout Trail, 1.5 miles from the start. Turn left to visit the lookout; turn right to exit the forest.
		GPS: N34°42.85' W111°32.55'
▼ 0.4	BR	Track on left is FR 9238M.
0.4 ▲	SO	Track on right is FR 9238M.
		GPS: N34°42.71' W111°33.03'
▼ 0.5	SO	Cross through wash.
0.3 ▲	SO	Cross through wash.
▼ 0.8	TR	Turn right onto FR 9243H. FR 620E continues ahead. Zero trip meter.
0.0 ▲		Continue to the east.
		GPS: N34°42.75' W111°33.37'
▼ 0.0		Continue to the north.
2.0 ▲	TL	Turn left onto FR 620E. Zero trip meter. Track on right is also 620E.
▼ 0.7	SO	Trail is following alongside Mullican Canyon Creek.
1.3 ▲	SO	Trail is following alongside Mullican Canyon Creek.
▼ 0.8	SO	Stock tank on left.
1.2 ▲	SO	Stock tank on right.
		GPS: N34°43.47' W111°33.60'
▼ 1.0	SO	Cross through Mullican Canyon wash.
1.0 ▲	SO	Cross through Mullican Canyon wash.
		GPS: N34°43.54' W111°33.83'
▼ 2.0	SO	Pass through gate; private property on left. Zero trip meter. Trail is now marked as FR 242H.
0.0 ▲		Continue to the south. Standard improves at this point—still a formed trail but a lot smoother.
		GPS: N34°43.98' W111°34.53'
▼ 0.0		Continue to the north and cross through small wash.
1.5 ▲	BL	Cross through small wash; then private property on right; pass through gate. Trail is now marked FR 9243H. Zero trip meter.
▼ 0.8	SO	Stock tank on right.
0.7 ▲	SO	Stock tank on left.
▼ 1.1	SO	Track on right is FR 644A; then cross through wash.

The trail heading toward Hog Hill

▼	▲		
	0.4 ▲	SO	Cross through wash; then track on left is FR 644A.
▼ 1.2		SO	Track on right is FR 644B; bear left, remaining on FR 242H.
	0.3 ▲	BR	Track on left is FR 644B; bear right, remaining on FR 242H.
			GPS: N34°44.69′ W111°33.98′
▼ 1.5		TR	T-intersection with FR 644. Turn right onto FR 644 and zero trip meter. Faint track ahead.
	0.0 ▲		Continue to the south.
			GPS: N34°44.96′ W111°33.93′
▼ 0.0			Continue to the northeast.
	2.2 ▲	TL	Turn left from FR 644 onto FR 644A and zero trip meter. Faint track on right.
▼ 0.5		SO	Track on right to campsite.
	1.7 ▲	SO	Track on left to campsite.
▼ 0.6		SO	Track on right.
	1.6 ▲	SO	Track on left.
▼ 0.7		SO	Track on left.
	1.5 ▲	SO	Track on right.
▼ 1.1		SO	Track on right is FR 644E and track on left.
	1.1 ▲	SO	Track on left is FR 644E and track on right.
			GPS: N34°44.82′ W111°32.89′
▼ 1.2		SO	Track on right.
	1.0 ▲	SO	Track on left.
▼ 1.4		SO	Track on right; then cross over creek on bridge.
	0.8 ▲	SO	Cross over creek on bridge; then track on left.
			GPS: N34°44.73′ W111°32.58′
▼ 1.5		SO	Cross over creek.
	0.7 ▲	SO	Cross over creek.
▼ 2.2			Trail ends at the T-intersection with FR 229, immediately north of the Watershed Camp Station. Turn left for I-17.
	0.0 ▲		Trail commences on FR 229, immediately north of Watershed Camp Station, 9 miles east of I-17, exit 306. Zero trip meter and turn southwest on graded FR 644.
			GPS: N34°45.19′ W111°31.87′

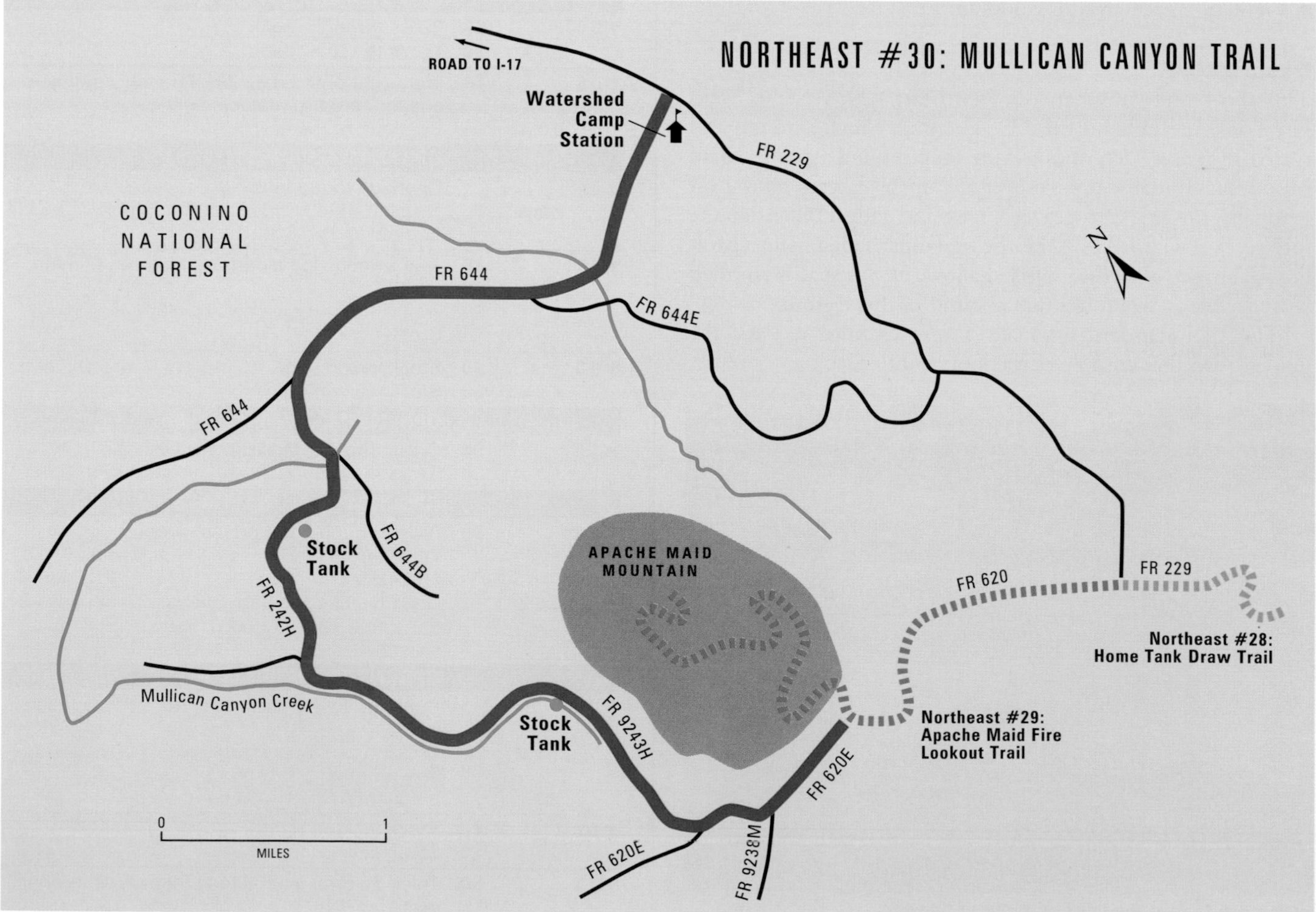

NORTHEAST #30: MULLICAN CANYON TRAIL

ROAD TO I-17
Watershed Camp Station
FR 229
COCONINO NATIONAL FOREST
FR 644
FR 644E
FR 644
Stock Tank
FR 644B
FR 242H
APACHE MAID MOUNTAIN
FR 620
FR 229
Northeast #28: Home Tank Draw Trail
Mullican Canyon Creek
Stock Tank
FR 9243H
Northeast #29: Apache Maid Fire Lookout Trail
FR 620E
0 1 MILES
FR 620E
FR 9238M
N

NORTHEAST REGION TRAIL #31

Coulter Hill Trail

Starting Point:	**Mormon Lake Road, immediately south of mile marker 8**
Finishing Point:	**Lake Mary Road, near Lower Lake Mary**
Total Mileage:	**18.1 miles**
Unpaved Mileage:	**17.6 miles**
Driving Time:	**1.25 hours**
Elevation Range:	**6,800–7,500 feet**
Usually Open:	**April to October**
Best Time to Travel:	**April to October**
Difficulty Rating:	**2**
Scenic Rating:	**7**
Remoteness Rating:	**+0**

Special Attractions

- Elk can often be seen in the area.
- Open area of Antelope Park.
- The mainly dry area of Mormon Lake.

History

A lake in this region was first noted in 1864 when one called Carleton Lake appeared on a map made by General James Henry Carleton. Oral histories contradict the presence of a lake and say that Mormon Lake was not formed until Mormons came to the area and clogged the natural drainage channels to the basin with their farming and grazing activities. However it formed, Mormon Lake is recognized as the largest natural lake in Arizona. The lake is shallow and for much of the time, especially in recent years, it has been marshland or dry. However, at one time it was deep enough for a boat tour company to operate.

In the late 1870s, Brigham Young was encouraging Mormons to settle in Arizona, partly for colonization and expansion and partly to provide a refuge for polygamous families that were being hounded in Utah. There was an active Mormon settlement in the area, then known as Pleasant Valley, including a dairy built by Hyrum Judd at Dairy Springs, near the present-day campground. The cows grazed near Mormon Lake, and butter and cheese were produced to supply the towns of Brigham City, Sunset, and Joseph. The dairy closed in 1886 and Judd and his family moved to Mexico to avoid prosecution for polygamy.

Old Coulter Cabin

Description

This roughly graded, narrow dirt road travels between Mormon Lake and Lower Lake Mary. Much of the route passes through the Pinegrove Quiet Area, which is closed to vehicles from August to January to protect elk habitat and allow for non-motorized quiet recreation. The trails that lead into the quiet area are clearly marked.

A stand of aspens makes Weimer Springs a particularly scenic spot

The main Coulter Hill Trail is a roughly graded dirt road with patches of gravel. It travels through the pine forest, which is dotted with small stands of aspens. In early spring, wild irises carpet many of the open meadows along the way and in November and December the brilliant fall colors of aspens and oaks contrast with the dark green of the ponderosa pines.

FR 236 goes past Coulter Cabin, a forest service guard station, at 10.3 miles from the start of the trail. To reach the cabin, turn down FR 236 and proceed for 0.3 miles before turning right down an unmarked small track that goes to the cabin. You can walk past the gate on the trail to see the old cabin plus the new guard station, which is often occupied in summer months.

The trail finishes on Lake Mary Road, just to the northwest of Lower Lake Mary.

Current Road Information

Coconino National Forest
Mormon Lake Ranger District
4373 South Lake Mary Rd.
Flagstaff, AZ 86001
(520) 774-1182

Map References

BLM Sedona, Flagstaff
USFS Coconino National Forest: Mormon Lake Ranger District
USGS 1:24,000 Mormon Lake, Mormon Mt., Lower Lake Mary
1:100,000 Sedona, Flagstaff
Maptech CD-ROM: Flagstaff/Sedona/Prescott
Arizona Atlas & Gazetteer, p. 42
Arizona Road & Recreation Atlas, p. 35 & p. 69

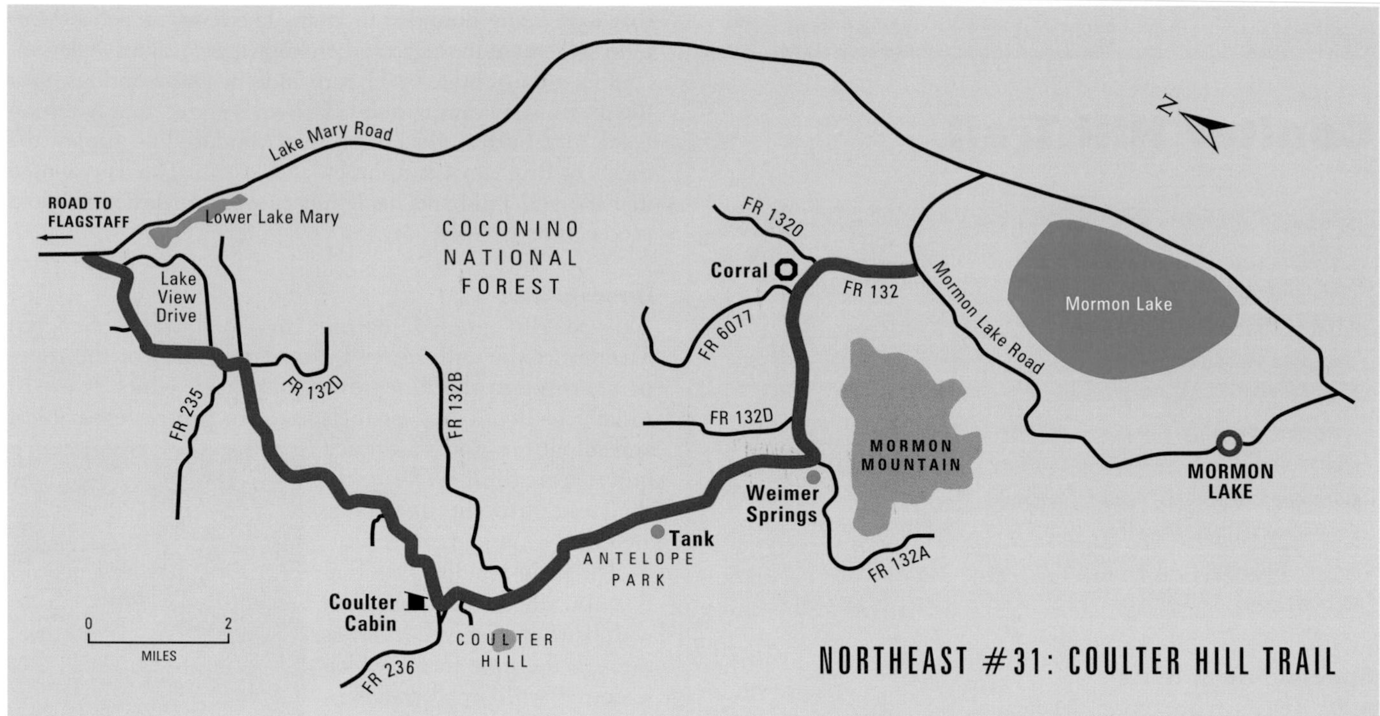

Route Directions

Mileage		Directions
▼ 0.0		From Mormon Lake Road, north of the settlement of Mormon Lake, and immediately south of mile marker 8, zero trip meter and turn west on graded dirt road, FR 132, following the sign to Weimer Springs and Antelope Park.
4.2 ▲		Trail ends on Mormon Lake Road, north of the settlement of Mormon Lake. Turn right for Mormon Lake; turn left for Flagstaff.
		GPS: N34°58.88' W111°28.56'
▼ 0.1	SO	Track on right is FR 9466Y into Pinegrove Quiet Area, which extends on the right side of the trail.
4.1 ▲	SO	Track on left is FR 9466Y into Pinegrove Quiet Area.
▼ 0.2	SO	Track on left is FR 9459C.
4.0 ▲	SO	Track on right is FR 9459C.
▼ 0.4	SO	Track on right is FR 9459 and track on left.
3.8 ▲	SO	Track on left is FR 9459 and track on right.
▼ 0.6	SO	Track on left.
3.6 ▲	SO	Track on right.
▼ 0.7	SO	Track on right.
3.5 ▲	SO	Track on left.
▼ 0.9	SO	Track on left is FR 9466X.
3.3 ▲	SO	Track on right is FR 9466X.
		GPS: N34°59.63' W111°29.10'
▼ 1.1	SO	Track on left; then track on right is FR 9459A.
3.1 ▲	SO	Track on left is FR 9459A; then track on right.
▼ 1.3	SO	Track on right is FR 1320.
2.9 ▲	SO	Track on left is FR 1320.
▼ 1.4	SO	Cattle guard.
2.8 ▲	SO	Cattle guard.
▼ 1.7	SO	Corral on right; then track on right is FR 6077.
2.5 ▲	SO	Track on left is FR 6077; then corral on left.
		GPS: N34°59.87' W111°29.79'
▼ 2.4	SO	Track on right.
1.8 ▲	SO	Track on left.
▼ 2.6	SO	Track on left.
1.6 ▲	SO	Track on right.
▼ 3.4	SO	Track on right is FR 132D.
0.8 ▲	SO	Track on left is FR 132D.
		GPS: N34°58.99' W111°31.32'
▼ 3.9	SO	Track on left is FR 9466X.
0.3 ▲	SO	Track on right is FR 9466X.
▼ 4.2	BR	Graded road on left is FR 132A to Munds Park and Mormon Mountain. Bear right, remaining on FR 132, and zero trip meter.
0.0 ▲		Continue to the east.
		GPS: N34°58.48' W111°31.65'
▼ 0.0		Continue to the north, following the sign to Antelope Park and Lake Mary. Weimer Springs on left.
3.3 ▲	BL	Weimer Springs on right; then graded road on right is FR 132A to Munds Park and Mormon Mountain. Bear left, remaining on FR 132, and zero trip meter.
▼ 0.2	SO	Track on right.
3.1 ▲	SO	Track on left.
▼ 0.3	SO	Track on right.
3.0 ▲	SO	Track on left.
▼ 1.0	SO	Track on right.
2.3 ▲	SO	Track on left.
▼ 1.3	SO	Track on right.
2.0 ▲	SO	Track on left.
▼ 2.0	SO	Entering Antelope Park.
1.3 ▲	SO	Leaving Antelope Park.
▼ 2.3	SO	Track on left is FR 9410X.
1.0 ▲	SO	Track on right is FR 9410X.
		GPS: N34°59.55' W111°33.54'
▼ 2.4	SO	Cattle guard; then tank on left.
0.9 ▲	SO	Tank on right; then cattle guard.
▼ 2.5	SO	Track on right.
0.8 ▲	SO	Track on left.
▼ 2.6	SO	Track on right; then cross over creek.
0.7 ▲	SO	Cross over creek; then track on left.

▼ 2.7 SO Leaving Antelope Park.
0.6 ▲ SO Entering Antelope Park.

▼ 3.3 SO Small graded road on left is FR 133. Zero trip meter.
0.0 ▲ Continue to the east.

GPS: N35°00.07' W111°34.46'

▼ 0.0 Continue to the west.
2.4 ▲ SO Small graded road on right is FR 133. Zero trip meter.

▼ 0.1 SO Track on right.
2.3 ▲ SO Track on left.

▼ 0.3 SO Track on right.
2.1 ▲ SO Track on left.

▼ 0.4 SO Track on right.
2.0 ▲ SO Track on left.

▼ 0.9 SO Track on right.
1.5 ▲ SO Track on left.

▼ 1.1 SO Track on left is FR 9412G.
1.3 ▲ SO Track on right is FR 9412G.

GPS: N35°00.29' W111°35.47'

▼ 1.3 SO Track on right is FR 132B.
1.1 ▲ SO Track on left is FR 132B.

GPS: N35°00.36' W111°35.63'

▼ 2.2 SO Track on left to Lockett Ranch. Hard-to-spot, old metal sign at intersection.
0.2 ▲ SO Track on right to Lockett Ranch. Hard-to-spot, old metal sign at intersection.

GPS: N35°00.92' W111°36.27'

▼ 2.3 BL Track on right; then cattle guard.
0.1 BR Cattle guard; then track on left.

▼ 2.4 BR Graded dirt road on left is FR 236. Bear right, remaining on FR 132. Zero trip meter.
0.0 ▲ Continue to the southeast.

GPS: N35°01.08' W111°36.38'

▼ 0.0 Continue to the northwest.
4.9 ▲ BL Graded dirt road on right is FR 236. Bear left, remaining on FR 132. Zero trip meter.

▼ 0.1 SO Second entrance to FR 236 on left.
4.8 ▲ SO Road on right is FR 236.

▼ 0.9 SO Track on right is FR 132K.
4.0 ▲ SO Track on left is FR 132K.

GPS: N35°01.76' W111°36.08'

▼ 1.2 SO Track on left is FR 9487X.
3.7 ▲ SO Track on right is FR 9487X.

▼ 1.8 SO Track on left.
3.1 ▲ SO Track on right.

▼ 2.3 SO Track on right.
2.6 ▲ SO Track on left.

▼ 2.7 BL Well-used track on right.
2.2 ▲ BR Well-used track on left.

GPS: N35°03.11' W111°36.00'

▼ 3.1 SO Cattle guard.
1.8 ▲ SO Cattle guard.

▼ 3.2 SO Track on left is FR 9483W.
1.7 ▲ SO Track on right is FR 9483W.

GPS: N35°03.50' W111°36.44'

▼ 3.8 SO Track on left; then track on right.
1.1 ▲ SO Track on left; then track on right.

▼ 4.1 SO Track on left; then track on right.
0.8 ▲ SO Track on left; then track on right.

▼ 4.9 TL Graded road on right is FR 132D; also small track straight on. Zero trip meter.
0.0 ▲ Continue to the south, following the sign for Weimer Springs and Mormon Mountain.

GPS: N35°04.79' W111°35.54'

▼ 0.0 Continue to the west, following the sign for Lake Mary Road and Flagstaff; graded road on right is FR 296A.
3.3 ▲ TR Graded road on left is FR 296A; then 4-way intersection. Graded road ahead is FR 132D. Small track on left. Turn right, remaining on FR 132. Zero trip meter.

▼ 0.3 BR Track on left is FR 235.
3.0 ▲ BL Track on right is FR 235.

GPS: N35°05.01' W111°35.71'

▼ 0.5 SO Lake View Drive on right.
2.8 ▲ SO Lake View Drive on left.

▼ 1.0 SO Track on left.
2.3 ▲ SO Track on right.

▼ 1.9 SO Track on right.
1.4 ▲ SO Track on left.

▼ 2.0 SO Track on left.
1.3 ▲ SO Track on right.

▼ 2.2 SO Cattle guard.
1.1 ▲ SO Cattle guard.

▼ 2.3 SO Track on left.
1.0 ▲ SO Track on right.

▼ 2.8 SO Track on right; then road becomes paved.
0.5 ▲ SO Road turns to graded dirt; then track on left.

GPS: N35°06.74' W111°35.53'

▼ 3.2 SO Graded road on right.
0.1 ▲ SO Graded road on left.

▼ 3.3 Trail finishes at the intersection with Lake Mary Road. Turn left for Flagstaff; turn right for Mormon Lake.
0.0 ▲ Trail starts on the Lake Mary Road immediately north of mile marker 338. Zero trip meter and turn southwest on the graded primitive road, FR 132. Turn is not marked apart from a primitive road sign. There are mailboxes at the intersection.

GPS: N35°07.10' W111°35.69'

NORTHEAST REGION TRAIL #32

Mormon to Kinnikinick Lakes Trail

Starting Point:	**Lake Mary Road at Mormon Lake**
Finishing Point:	**Kinnikinick Lake**
Total Mileage:	**8.7 miles**
Unpaved Mileage:	**8.5 miles**
Driving Time:	**45 minutes**
Elevation Range:	**7,100–7,300 feet**
Usually Open:	**March to November**
Best Time to Travel:	**March to November**
Difficulty Rating:	**2**
Scenic Rating:	**8**
Remoteness Rating:	**+0**

Mud Lake

Special Attractions

- Kinnikinick Lake—trout fishing and camping.
- Mormon Lake—duck hunting in season.
- Mud Lake.
- Can be driven as a loop with Northeast #34: Long Lake Road and Northeast #33: Soldier and Kinnikinick Lakes Trail.

Description

This 2-rated trail is rough enough that a high-clearance vehicle is recommended to negotiate a few embedded rocks and vehicle ruts caused by wet-weather travel. It goes from the paved Lake Mary Road at Mormon Lake to Kinnikinick Lake.

Mormon Lake, the largest natural lake in Arizona, encompasses more than 5,000 acres. Early in the 1900s, the lake was consistently deep enough for sailing, which became a popular activity. There was even a boat tour company. In 1924 the lake started to dry up, and now it is mostly dry. Some years it remains marshy enough to attract wildfowl, and it is a popular area for duck hunting. The small community of Mormon Lake sells gas and has a post office, country store, lodge, and restaurant.

At the end of the trail Kinnikinick Lake, which is stocked annually, is a popular spot for trout fishing. There is also a small national forest campground along the lake shore (fee area), which is open from May to October. From the lake, the trail winds through open forest, passing shallow Mud Lake, which is set just below the densely wooded and aptly named Pine Hill. Along the east side of Pine Hill, there are many shady campsites to be found.

Current Road Information

Coconino National Forest
Mormon Lake Ranger District
4373 South Lake Mary Rd.
Flagstaff, AZ 86001
(520) 774-1182

Map References

BLM Sedona
USFS Coconino National Forest: Mormon Lake Ranger District
USGS 1:24,000 Mormon Lake, Kinnikinick Lake
1:100,000 Sedona
Maptech CD-ROM: Flagstaff/Sedona/Prescott
Arizona Atlas & Gazetteer, p. 42
Arizona Road & Recreation Atlas, p. 35 & p. 69
Recreational Map of Arizona

Route Directions

Mileage			Directions
▼ 0.0			Trail commences at the intersection of FH 3 (Lake Mary Road) and FR 125 on the east side of Mormon Lake, 0.4 miles north of mile marker 316. Zero trip meter and turn southeast on paved FR 125, following the sign for Kinnikinick Lake.
	4.5 ▲		Trail ends at the T-intersection with FH 3 (Lake Mary Road) on the east side of Mormon Lake. Turn left for Mormon Lake; turn right for Flagstaff.
			GPS: N34°55.50′ W111°25.82′
▼ 0.2		SO	Cattle guard and seasonal closure gate. Road turns to graded dirt.
	4.3 ▲	SO	Cattle guard and seasonal closure gate. Road is now paved.
			GPS: N34°55.39′ W111°25.77′
▼ 0.4		SO	Track on left.
	4.1 ▲	SO	Track on right.
▼ 0.6		BL	Small track on right goes to Wallace Lake; then second track on right, FR 9483, over cattle guard.
	3.9 ▲	BR	Track on left over cattle guard is FR 9483; then second small track on left goes to Wallace Lake.
			GPS: N34°55.06′ W111°25.50′
▼ 0.8		SO	Track on left.
	3.7 ▲	SO	Track on right.
▼ 1.4		SO	Track on right is FR 104 and track on left.
	3.1 ▲	SO	Track on left is FR 104 and track on right.
			GPS: N34°55.29′ W111°24.82′
▼ 1.5		SO	Cross over Ashurst Run.
	3.0 ▲	SO	Cross over Ashurst Run.
			GPS: N34°55.36′ W111°24.72′
▼ 1.7		SO	Cattle guard.
	2.8 ▲	SO	Cattle guard.
▼ 2.0		SO	Track on left is FR 9117V.
	2.5 ▲	SO	Track on right is FR 9117V.
			GPS: N34°55.61′ W111°24.19′
▼ 2.8		SO	Track on right and track on left.
	1.7 ▲	SO	Track on right and track on left.
▼ 3.1		SO	Track on left; then track on right.
	1.4 ▲	SO	Track on left; then track on right.
▼ 3.4		SO	Track on right and left under power lines. Track on left is closed to motorized vehicles from April 20 to June 15 to protect wildlife.
	1.1 ▲	SO	Track on right and left under power lines. Track on right is closed to motorized vehicles from April 20 to June 15 to protect wildlife.
			GPS: N34°56.10′ W111°22.75′
▼ 3.5		SO	Cattle guard.
	1.0 ▲	SO	Cattle guard.
▼ 4.0		SO	Track on right is FR 9468H.
	0.5 ▲	SO	Track on left is FR 9468H.
			GPS: N34°56.33′ W111°22.32′
▼ 4.5		TR	Turn right onto FR 82, following the sign to Kinnikinick Lake. FR 125 continues ahead to

		Twin Arrows. Small track on left is closed to motorized vehicles from April 20 to June 15 to protect wildlife. Zero trip meter.
0.0 ▲		Continue to the southwest.
		GPS: N34°56.46′ W111°21.72′
▼ 0.0		Continue to the southeast. Many small tracks on right and left for next 0.5 miles, mainly to campsites.
3.7 ▲	TL	Turn left onto FR 125, following the sign to Mormon Lake. FR 125 to the right goes to Twin Arrows. Small track ahead, which is closed to motorized vehicles from April 20 to June 15 to protect wildlife. Zero trip meter.
▼ 0.5	SO	Track on left.
3.2 ▲	SO	Track on right. Many small tracks on right and left for next 0.5 miles, mainly to campsites.
▼ 0.8	SO	Track on right. Pine Hill on the right.
2.9 ▲	SO	Track on left. Pine Hill on the left
		GPS: N34°55.95′ W111°21.21′
▼ 1.0	SO	Cattle guard.
2.7 ▲	SO	Cattle guard.
▼ 1.2	SO	Track on right.
2.5 ▲	SO	Track on left.
▼ 1.3	SO	Cross over creek; then track on right. Pine Hill is the small tree-covered hill to the northwest. Mud Lake on the right.
2.4 ▲	SO	Track on left; then cross over creek. Mud Lake on the left. Pine Hill is the small tree-covered hill to the northwest.
		GPS: N34°55.51′ W111°20.84′
▼ 2.1	SO	Track on left; then cattle guard.
1.6 ▲	SO	Cattle guard; then track on right.
▼ 2.9	SO	Track on left; then cross over creek.
0.8 ▲	SO	Cross over creek; then track on right.
▼ 3.3	SO	Track on left.
0.4 ▲	SO	Track on right.
▼ 3.7	SO	Cattle guard; then track on right is Northeast #33: Soldier and Kinnikinick Lakes Trail, FR 82. Zero trip meter.
0.0 ▲		Continue to the northwest and cross cattle guard.

Mormon Lake, now rarely more than marshland

		GPS: N34°53.84′ W111°19.08′
▼ 0.0		Continue to the southeast toward Kinnikinick Lake; small track on left.
0.5 ▲	SO	Small track on right; then track on left is Northeast #33: Soldier and Kinnikinick Lakes Trail, FR 82. Zero trip meter.
▼ 0.3	BL	Small track on right; then second track on right.
0.2 ▲	BR	Track on left; then second smaller track on left.
▼ 0.4	SO	Track on right and Kinnikinick NFS Campground on the left.
0.1 ▲	SO	Kinnikinick NFS Campground on the right and track on left.
▼ 0.5		Trail ends at Kinnikinick Lake boat ramp. Return the way you came, or take Northeast #33: Soldier and Kinnikinick Lakes Trail to the south.
0.0 ▲		At Kinnikinick Lake boat ramp, zero trip meter and proceed south on the roughly graded road away from the lake. There is a picnic site at the end.
		GPS: N34°53.82′ W111°18.66′

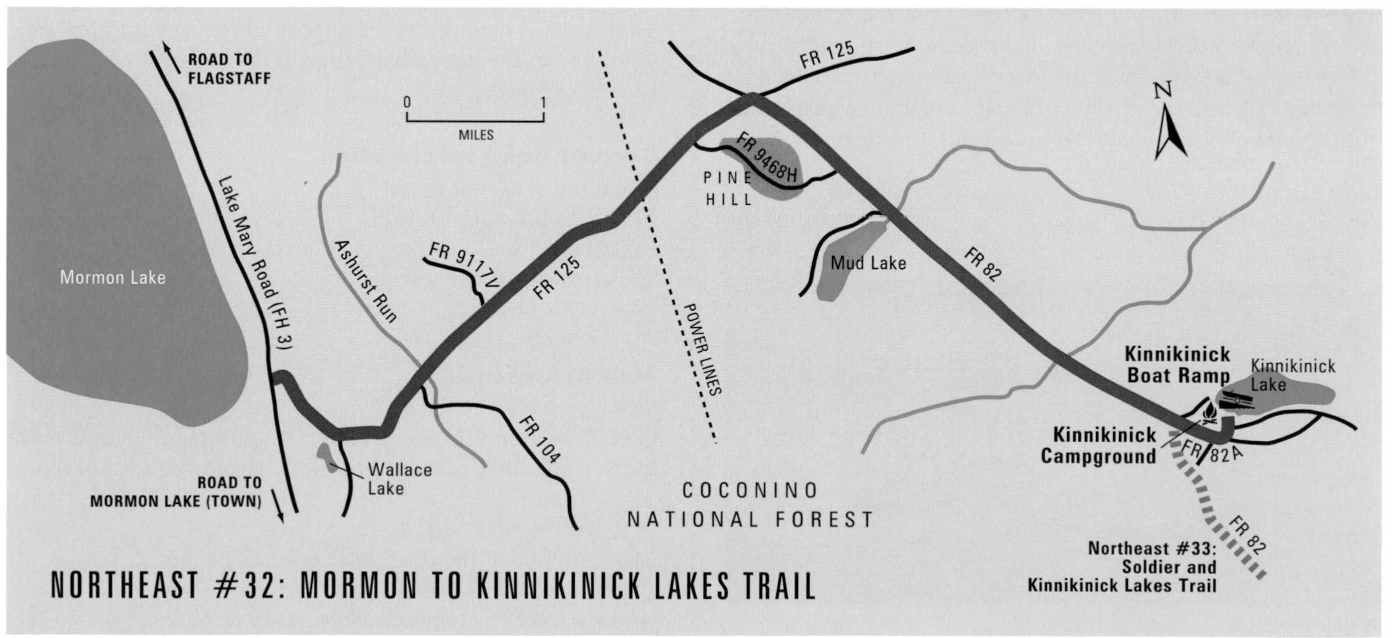

NORTHEAST REGION TRAIL #33

Soldier and Kinnikinick Lakes Trail

Starting Point:	**Long Lake, at the intersection with Northeast #34: Long Lake Road**
Finishing Point:	**Kinnikinick Lake, at the intersection with Northeast #32: Mormon to Kinnikinick Lakes Trail**
Total Mileage:	**9.4 miles**
Unpaved Mileage:	**9.4 miles**
Driving Time:	**1.5 hours**
Elevation Range:	**6,700–7,200 feet**
Usually Open:	**March to December**
Best Time to Travel:	**Dry weather**
Difficulty Rating:	**3**
Scenic Rating:	**7**
Remoteness Rating:	**+0**

Special Attractions

- Elk can often be seen grazing in the open meadows.
- Trout fishing in the stocked waters of Kinnikinick and Soldier Lakes.
- Rough but scenic trail that crosses open meadows.

Description

A rough but scenic trail that links two lakes best describes this route, which follows part of FR 82. It commences at the north end of Northeast #34: Long Lake Road, at Long Lake, and is a continuation of the graded, 1-rated road from Arizona 87. Although this trail shares the same forest route number as Long Lake Road, the similarity ends there. This trail crosses the rough plateau strewn with lava rocks to the north and is definitely not suitable for low-clearance or passenger vehicles. The trail leaves behind the expanse of Long Lake and passes around the top end of Soldier Lake. Although not directly visible from the main trail, Soldier Lake can be reached by driving 0.1 miles along a side trail. Fishermen can angle for bass and catfish there. Only boats powered by single electric motors are permitted on Soldier Lake.

Kinnikinick Lake

The volcanic rock along the trail often provides a rough road

Immediately past Soldier Lake, the route is extremely rocky and rough. Lava boulders and rocks make for a rough, slow ride as the trail winds its way along the side of Jaycox Mountain, which is more of a small rise than a mountain. However, it provides enough elevation for good views west over the Coconino National Forest to the Hutch Mountain area. This section of the trail is also the most vegetated as it meanders through junipers and pinyon pines. Jaycox Mountain is named after Henry H. Jaycox, a scout on two of King S. Woolsey's expeditions in 1864. He camped in a spot known as Jaycox Tank.

Once past Jaycox Mountain, the trail passes through more open country. Large grassy meadows, lightly scattered with pinyons and junipers, provide a very good chance of seeing elk herds that often come to the meadows to graze. The area north of Cow Lake is often fruitful. Elk also often come to drink at Kinnikinick Lake. This section of the trail, as it crosses the open meadows, can be impassable and is best avoided in wet weather.

The trail finishes at Northeast #32: Mormon to Kinnikinick Lakes Trail, FR 82. Turn right onto the graded dirt road to go to Kinnikinick Lake (only 0.5 miles away), another good spot for catfish and trout fishing. There is a national forest campground at Kinnikinick Lake, which is open from May to October (fee required), and undeveloped campsites at Long Lake. These places are suggested for tent campers who might otherwise have a hard time finding a flat spot along the lava rock–studded trail.

Current Road Information

Coconino National Forest
Blue Ridge Ranger District
HC 31 Box 300
Happy Jack, AZ 86024
(520) 477-2255

Map References

BLM Sedona
USFS Coconino National Forest: Blue Ridge Ranger District
USGS 1:24,000 Chavez Mt. West, Jaycox Mt., Kinnikinick Lake
1:100,000 Sedona
Maptech CD-ROM: Flagstaff/Sedona/Prescott
Arizona Atlas & Gazetteer, p. 42
Arizona Road & Recreation Atlas, p. 35 & p. 69

Route Directions

Mileage	Action	Directions
▼ 0.0		From the northern end of Northeast #34: Long Lake Road (at the northern end of Long Lake), at the intersection of FR 82 and the small FR 9719P, zero trip meter and turn west on the more frequently used FR 82. FR 82 is unmarked at this point.
5.6 ▲		Trail ends at the north end of Long Lake at the northern end of Northeast #34: Long Lake Road. Continue on along FR 82 to connect with Arizona 87.
		GPS: N34°48.04' W111°13.24'
▼ 0.1	SO	Cattle guard.
5.5 ▲	SO	Cattle guard.
▼ 0.9	SO	Track on left is FR 653, which goes 0.1 miles to Soldier Lake and on to Soldier Annex Lake.
4.7 ▲	SO	Track on right is FR 653, which goes 0.1 miles to Soldier Lake and on to Soldier Annex Lake.
		GPS: N34°48.07' W111°14.17'
▼ 1.0	SO	Track on right is FR 126A to Crater Lake. Continue on FR 82.
4.6 ▲	SO	Track on left is FR 126A to Crater Lake. Continue on FR 82.
		GPS: N34°48.08' W111°14.29'
▼ 1.2	SO	Stock tank on right.
4.4 ▲	SO	Stock tank on left.
▼ 1.4	SO	Well-used track on left.
4.2 ▲	SO	Well-used track on right.
▼ 1.8	SO	Cross through Sawmill Wash.
3.8 ▲	SO	Cross through Sawmill Wash.
		GPS: N34°48.42' W111°15.05'
▼ 2.0	SO	Track on right.
3.6 ▲	SO	Track on left.
		GPS: N34°48.55' W111°15.19'
▼ 2.3	SO	Stock tank on right.
3.3 ▲	SO	Stock tank on left.
▼ 3.3	SO	Well-used track on left.
2.3 ▲	SO	Well-used track on right.
		GPS: N34°49.31' W111°16.24'
▼ 4.4	SO	Cattle guard. Views ahead to the San Francisco Peaks.
1.2 ▲	SO	Cattle guard.
		GPS: N34°50.01' W111°16.92'
▼ 5.2	SO	Small track on right; then track on left.
0.4 ▲	SO	Track on right; then small track on left.
		GPS: N34°50.67' W111°17.23'
▼ 5.6	BR	Bear right, remaining on FR 82. Track on left is FR 82B. Zero trip meter. There is a seep at the intersection, which can be muddy.
0.0 ▲		Continue to the southeast.
		GPS: N34°50.88' W111°17.45'
▼ 0.0		Continue to the north.
3.8 ▲	BL	Bear left, remaining on FR 82. Track on right is FR 82B. Zero trip meter. There is a seep at the intersection, which can be muddy.
▼ 0.3	SO	Track on right; then pass through wire gate.
3.5 ▲	SO	Pass through wire gate; then track on left.
		GPS: N34°51.15' W111°17.48'
▼ 1.4	SO	Track on right.
2.4 ▲	SO	Track on left.
▼ 3.0	SO	The seasonal Cow Lake is on the right.
0.8 ▲	SO	The seasonal Cow Lake is on the left.
▼ 3.3	SO	Well-used track on left is FR 124.
0.5 ▲	SO	Well-used track on right is FR 124.
		GPS: N34°53.38' W111°18.98'

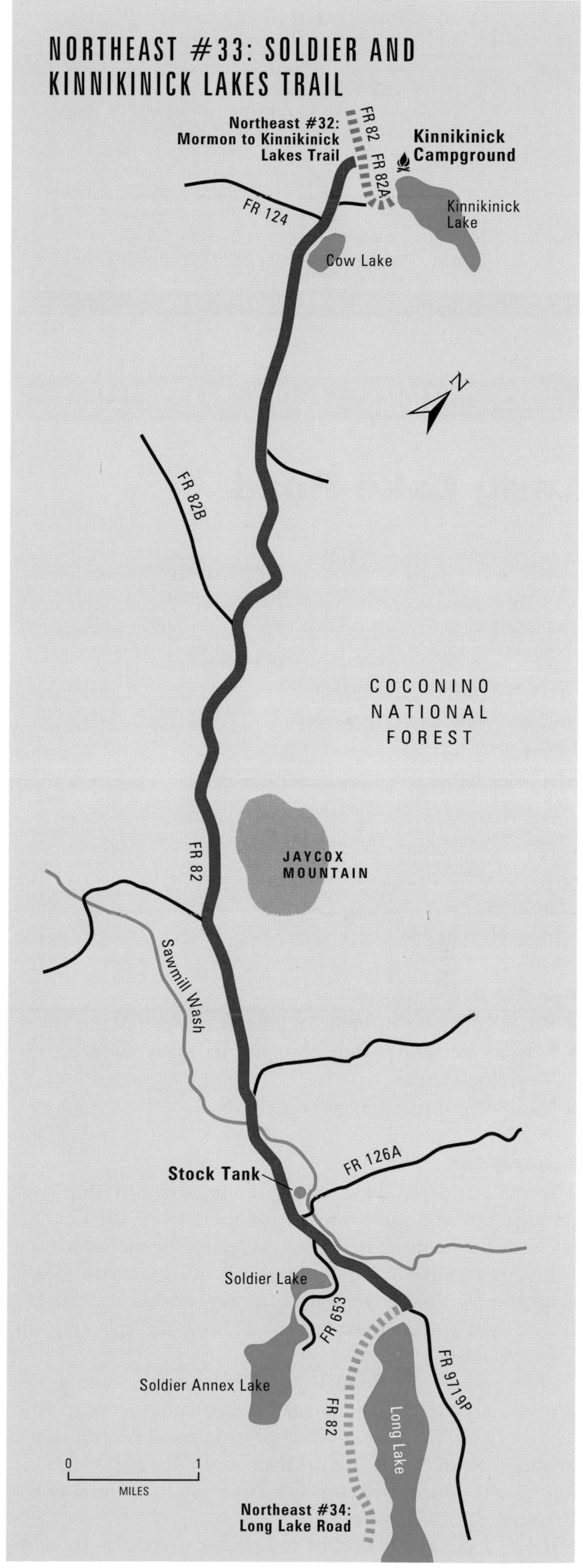

▼ 3.4		SO	Cattle guard; then track on right.
	0.4 ▲	SO	Track on left; then cattle guard.
▼ 3.8			Trail ends at the T-intersection of FR 82 and FR 82A, Northeast #32: Mormon to Kinnikinick Lakes Trail. Kinnikinick Lake is visible to the right, 0.5 miles down FR 82A.
	0.0 ▲		Trail commences along Northeast #32: Mormon to Kinnikinick Lakes Trail at the intersection of FR 82 and FR 82A, 0.5 miles west of Kinnikinick NFS Campground. Immediately west of a cattle guard, zero trip meter and turn southeast on the formed trail, marked FR 82.
			GPS: N34°53.84' W111°19.08'

NORTHEAST REGION TRAIL #34

Long Lake Road

Starting Point:	**Arizona 87, 0.2 miles northeast of the Blue Ridge Ranger Station**
Finishing Point:	**Northeast #33: Soldier and Kinnikinick Lakes Trail, at Long Lake**
Total Mileage:	**16.2 miles**
Unpaved Mileage:	**16.2 miles**
Driving Time:	**1 hour**
Elevation Range:	**6,700–6,900 feet**
Usually Open:	**April to October**
Best Time to Travel:	**Dry weather**
Difficulty Rating:	**1**
Scenic Rating:	**7**
Remoteness Rating:	**+0**

Special Attractions

- Varied fishing opportunities at Long and Soldier Annex Lakes.
- Easy scenic trail passing through the open forest on the Mogollon Plateau.
- Undeveloped camping at Long Lake.

Description

The trail to Long Lake travels along a graded dirt road through a pinyon-juniper forest and meadows in the Coconino National Forest. The trail is easygoing for the most part, with only a couple of slightly rough patches. In dry weather, it is suitable for a passenger vehicle. In wet weather, the dirt sections crossing open meadows can become difficult even for 4WD vehicles.

The trail crosses through Jacks Canyon at a more gentle gradient and at a less dramatic place than Northeast #35: Chavez Draw Trail, but is pretty nevertheless. There are many smaller trails to explore off the main trail. One of the nicest is the Chavez Draw Trail which follows a formed road down Chavez Draw to Arizona 87.

Long Lake at the end of the trail is a popular spot for

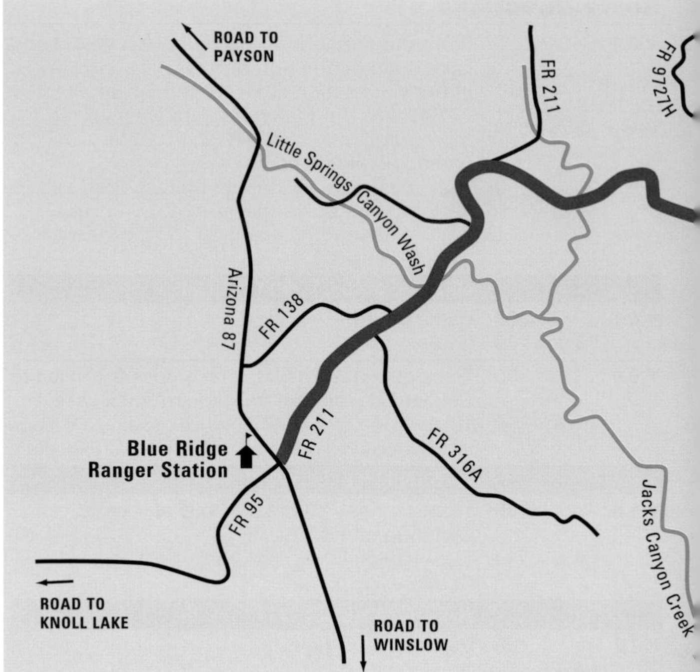

trout fishing. Periodically, the lake is stocked with trout, but fishermen can also catch bass and catfish. There are some primitive campsites spread along the lakeshore as well as a boat ramp. The smaller Soldier Annex Lake on the west side of the trail is reached by a rocky high-clearance road. This lake is not stocked with trout, but there is fishing for catfish and bluegill. The third lake of the group is the smallest—Soldier Lake, which is a short distance farther on, just off Northeast #33: Soldier and Kinnikinick Lakes Trail. Only boats powered by single electric motors are allowed on Soldier and Soldier Annex Lakes.

Most years this area of the Coconino National Forest can receive up to 100 inches of snow, causing the closure of forest roads and trails. Exact closure dates depend on snowfall, and the trails can be open past the dates given above.

Long Lake, popular with fishermen

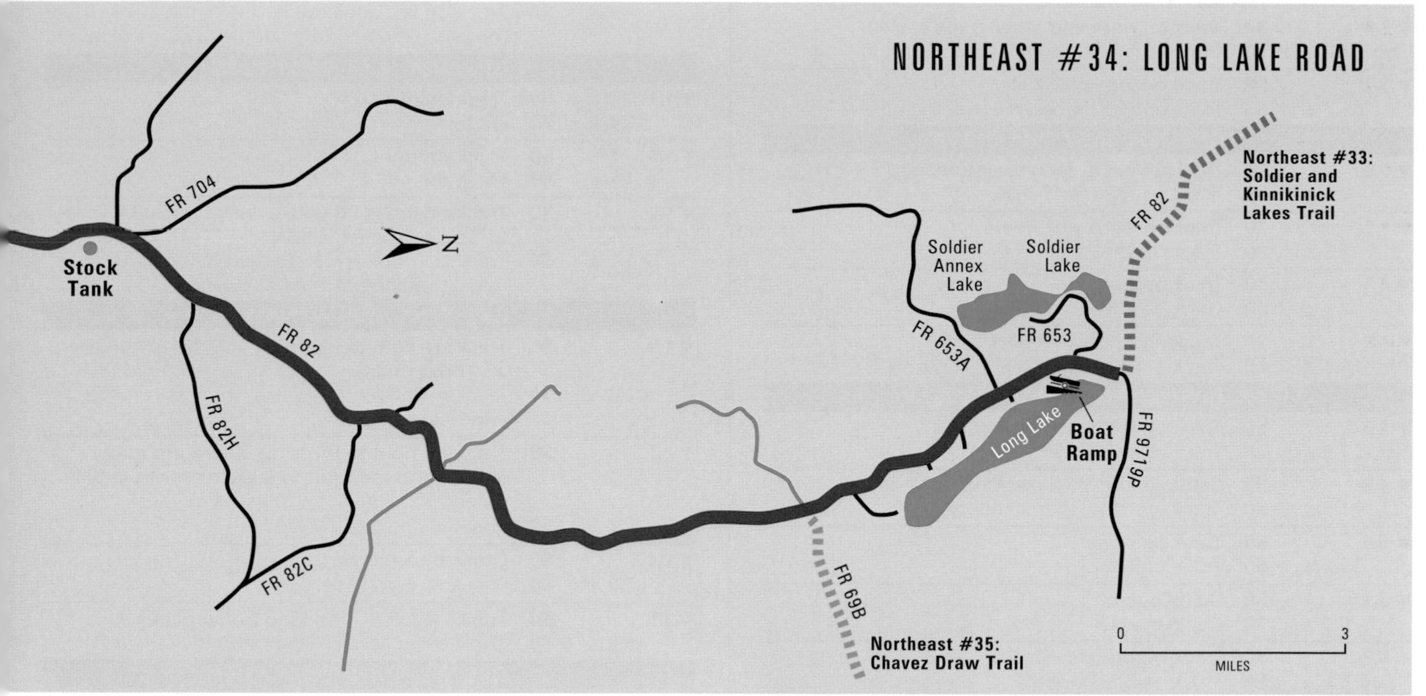

Current Road Information
Coconino National Forest
Blue Ridge Ranger District
HC 31 Box 300
Happy Jack, AZ 86024
(520) 477-2255

Map References
BLM Sedona
USFS Coconino National Forest: Blue Ridge Ranger District
USGS 1:24,000 Blue Ridge Reservoir, Hay Lake, Chavcz Mt. West
1:100,000 Sedona
Maptech CD-ROM: Flagstaff/Sedona/Prescott
Arizona Atlas & Gazetteer, p. 42
Arizona Road & Recreation Atlas, p. 41 & p. 75
Recreational Map of Arizona

Route Directions

▼ 0.0			From Arizona 87, 0.2 miles northeast of the Blue Ridge Ranger Station, zero trip meter and turn west on the graded gravel road, FR 211, marked to Long Lake. The turn is opposite FR 95 to Knoll Lake.
	3.0 ▲		Trail ends at the intersection with Arizona 87. Turn right for Payson; turn left for Winslow. The Blue Ridge Ranger Station is 0.2 miles to the right.
			GPS: N34°36.80′ W111°11.18′
▼ 0.1		SO	Track on right to county work station.
	2.9 ▲	SO	Track on left to county work station.
▼ 0.2		SO	Cattle guard and work station on right.
	2.8 ▲	SO	Cattle guard and work station on left.
▼ 1.3		SO	Track on right is FR 316A.
	1.7 ▲	SO	Track on left is FR 316A.
▼ 1.4		SO	Arizona Hiking Trail crosses the road.
	1.6 ▲	SO	Arizona Hiking Trail crosses the road.
			GPS: N34°37.43′ W111°12.45′
▼ 1.5		SO	Track on left is FR 138.
	1.5 ▲	SO	Track on right is FR 138.
			GPS: N34°37.49′ W111°12.52′
▼ 1.7		SO	Cross through Little Springs Canyon wash.
	1.3 ▲	SO	Cross through Little Springs Canyon wash.
▼ 2.4		SO	Track on right is FR 9726J; then track on left.
	0.6 ▲	SO	Track on right; then track on left is FR 9726J.
			GPS: N34°38.02′ W111°13.27′
▼ 2.6		SO	Track on right.
	0.4 ▲	SO	Track on left.
▼ 2.9		SO	Track on left.
	0.1 ▲	SO	Track on right.
▼ 3.0		BR	Graded road ahead is FR 211 to FH 3. Bear right onto FR 82, following the sign for Long Lake. Zero trip meter.
	0.0 ▲		Continue to the southeast.
			GPS: N34°37.94′ W111°13.84′
▼ 0.0			Continue to the north.
	6.4 ▲	TL	Graded road on right is FR 211 to FH 3. Turn left onto FR 211. Zero trip meter.
▼ 0.8		SO	Track on left; then cross through Jacks Canyon Creek.
	5.6 ▲	SO	Cross through Jacks Canyon Creek; then track on right.
			GPS: N34°38.66′ W111°13.59′
▼ 1.2		SO	Track on right to campsite.
	5.2 ▲	SO	Track on left to campsite.
▼ 1.5		SO	Arizona Hiking Trail crosses road.
	4.9 ▲	SO	Arizona Hiking Trail crosses road.
			GPS: N34°39.18′ W111°13.98′
▼ 1.7		SO	Cattle guard.
	4.7 ▲	SO	Cattle guard.
▼ 2.3		SO	Track on left is FR 9727H.
	4.1 ▲	SO	Track on right is FR 9727H.
			GPS: N34°39.63′ W111°13.58′
▼ 3.4		SO	Stock tank on right.
	3.0 ▲	SO	Stock tank on left.

▼ 3.6 SO Track on right and small track on left.
2.8 ▲ SO Track on left and small track on right.

▼ 3.7 SO Track on left is FR 704.
2.7 ▲ SO Track on right is second entrance to FR 704.

GPS: N34°40.82' W111°13.70'

▼ 3.8 SO Track on left is second entrance to FR 704.
2.6 ▲ SO Track on right is FR 704.

▼ 4.1 SO Track on right.
2.3 ▲ SO Track on left.

▼ 4.3 SO Track on right.
2.1 ▲ SO Track on left.

▼ 4.5 SO Track on right is FR 82H.
1.9 ▲ SO Track on left is FR 82H.

GPS: N34°41.37' W111°13.25'

▼ 4.8 SO Track on left.
1.6 ▲ SO Track on right.

▼ 4.9 SO Cattle guard; then track on left.
1.5 ▲ SO Track on right; then cattle guard.

▼ 5.0 SO Track on right.
1.4 ▲ SO Track on left.

▼ 5.7 SO Cattle guard.
0.7 ▲ SO Cattle guard.

▼ 6.2 SO Track on right is FR 82C.
0.2 ▲ SO Track on left is FR 82C.

GPS: N34°42.66' W111°12.26'

▼ 6.4 TR Road ahead goes to Hay Lake Ranch. Zero trip meter.
0.0 ▲ Continue to the southeast on FR 82.

GPS: N34°42.88' W111°12.37'

▼ 0.0 Continue to the northeast on FR 82.
3.9 ▲ TL Road on right goes to Hay Lake Ranch. Zero trip meter.

▼ 0.3 SO Cattle guard.
3.6 ▲ SO Cattle guard.

▼ 0.6 SO Track on right is FR 9718G; then cross over creek. Route number is hard to read and may be incorrect.
3.3 ▲ SO Cross over creek; then track on left is FR 9718G. Route number is hard to read and may be incorrect.

GPS: N34°43.25' W111°11.93'

▼ 0.7 SO Cattle guard; then track on right.
3.2 ▲ SO Track on left; then cattle guard.

▼ 1.6 SO Track on right is FR 9718N.
2.3 ▲ SO Track on left is FR 9718N.

▼ 2.4 SO Track on right.
1.5 ▲ SO Track on left.

▼ 2.8 SO Track on left; then cattle guard.
1.1 ▲ SO Cattle guard; then track on right.

▼ 3.9 SO Track on right is Northeast #35: Chavez Draw Trail, FR 69B. Small track on left. Zero trip meter.
0.0 ▲ Continue to the southeast toward Arizona 87.

GPS: N34°45.93' W111°11.90'

▼ 0.0 Continue to the northwest toward Long Lake.
2.9 ▲ SO Track on left is Northeast #35: Chavez Draw Trail, FR 69B. Small track on right. Zero trip meter.

▼ 0.4 SO Track on right is marked by a faded forest route marker.
2.5 ▲ SO Track on left is marked by a faded forest route marker.

▼ 0.7 SO Track on left.
2.2 ▲ SO Track on right.

▼ 1.0 SO Track on right goes to shore of Long Lake where there is parking and a couple of campsites.
1.9 ▲ SO Track on left goes to shore of Long Lake where there is parking and a couple of campsites.

GPS: N34°46.68' W111°12.38'

▼ 1.1 SO Track on right.
1.8 ▲ SO Track on left.

▼ 1.4 SO Track on right.
1.5 ▲ SO Track on left.

▼ 1.8 SO Track on left is FR 653A, which goes 0.5 miles to Soldier Annex Lake.
1.1 ▲ SO Track on right is FR 653A, which goes 0.5 miles to Soldier Annex Lake.

GPS: N34°47.19' W111°13.01'

▼ 1.9 SO Track on right to camping area by Long Lake and boat ramp.
1.0 ▲ SO Track on left to camping area by Long Lake and boat ramp.

▼ 2.1 SO Track on right to lakeside. There are many small tracks on right to lakeside for next 0.8 miles.
0.8 ▲ SO Track on left to lakeside.

▼ 2.4 SO Cross through wash.
0.5 ▲ SO Cross through wash.

▼ 2.6 SO Track on left is FR 653 to Soldier Lake.
0.3 ▲ SO Track on right is FR 653 to Soldier Lake.

GPS: N34°47.78' W111°13.37'

▼ 2.9 Trail ends at the intersection of FR 9719P and FR 82, Northeast #33: Soldier and Kinnikinick Lakes Trail, at the north end of Long Lake. Turn left to follow the 3-rated Soldier and Kinnikinick Lakes Trail.
0.0 ▲ Trail commences on FR 82 at the north end of Long Lake, at the intersection of Northeast #33: Soldier and Kinnikinick Lakes Trail, FR 82, and the smaller FR 9719P. Zero trip meter and proceed south down the roughly graded dirt road that runs along the west side of Long Lake. For the next 0.8 miles there are many small tracks on the left that lead to the lakeshore.

GPS: N34°48.04' W111°13.24'

NORTHEAST REGION TRAIL #35

Chavez Draw Trail

Starting Point:	**Arizona 87, 4.7 miles south of the northern Coconino National Forest boundary, 0.2 miles south of mile marker 311**
Finishing Point:	**Northeast #34: Long Lake Road, 2 miles south of Long Lake**
Total Mileage:	**9 miles**
Unpaved Mileage:	**9 miles**
Driving Time:	**1 hour**
Elevation Range:	**6,200–6,700 feet**
Usually Open:	**Year-round**
Best Time to Travel:	**Dry weather in spring and fall**
Difficulty Rating:	**3**
Scenic Rating:	**8**
Remoteness Rating:	**+0**

Special Attractions

- Scenic Jacks Canyon.
- Moderate trail providing access to Long, Soldier, and Soldier Annex Lakes.

History

This trail follows a short section of what is known as the Palatkwapi Trail. The name is derived from a Hopi word meaning "red land to the south," a description of the area from which a number of their people came before they settled on the Hopi Mesas. The trail, which runs from Montezuma Castle and the Verde Valley to the Hopi Mesas, was used primarily as a trading route. Pottery, cotton, and parrots from the south were common trade items. Later, the trail was used by Antonio de Espejo, a Spanish explorer who was searching for gold. In 1863, Lt. Col. J. Francisco Chavez, who guided the Arizona territorial governors party to Prescott, traveled along part of the Palatkwapi Trail on his return trip. Chavez Draw and Chavez Pass are named after him. In 1950, highway construction engineers searching for the best route for the new freeway, I-17, picked a similar route down the Mogollon Rim.

A bumpy descent into Jacks Canyon caused by the large imbedded rocks

Description

Jacks Canyon is one of a number of canyons that cuts deep paths across the Mogollon Plateau. Chavez Draw drains into Jacks Canyon, and this trail follows the path of much of Chavez Draw. The trail leaves Arizona 87 a few miles south of the north boundary of the Coconino National Forest and travels as a rough formed trail that quickly descends into the scenic and rugged Jacks Canyon. It leaves the canyon, traveling alongside Chavez Draw and crossing it often in the next few miles.

The trail is impassable following heavy rain because of the long sections of deep, red mud at the higher end of Chavez Draw. It is best to avoid the trail when wet. Not only are you very likely to get stuck but you are also likely to damage the track and surrounding meadows and vegetation.

Once past the intersection with the Chavez Pass Road, the trail standard gradually improves until it is a roughly graded dirt road. It finishes at Northeast #34: Long Lake Road, immediately south of Long Lake.

Current Road Information

Coconino National Forest
Blue Ridge Ranger District
HC 31 Box 300
Happy Jack, AZ 86024
(520) 477-2255

Map References

BLM Sedona
USFS Coconino National Forest: Blue Ridge Ranger District
USGS 1:24,000 Quayle Hill, Chavez Mt. East, Chavez Mt. West
1:100,000 Sedona
Maptech CD-ROM: Flagstaff/Sedona/Prescott
Arizona Atlas & Gazetteer, pp. 43, 42
Arizona Road & Recreation Atlas, p. 41 & p. 75
Recreational Map of Arizona

Route Directions

Mileage		Direction
▼ 0.0		From Arizona 87, 32 miles south of Winslow, 4.7 miles south of the national forest boundary, 0.2 miles south of mile marker 311, zero trip meter and turn west on roughly formed dirt road marked FR 69 to Chavez Pass and Long Lake.
5.4 ▲		Trail ends on Arizona 87, 32 miles south of Winslow.
		GPS: N34°43.08′ W111°05.36′
▼ 0.1	BR	Track on right; then immediately bear right, remaining on the main rocky trail.
5.3 ▲	BL	Bear left, remaining on the main rocky trail; then track on left.
▼ 0.2	SO	Track on left.
5.2 ▲	SO	Track on right.
		GPS: N34°43.28′ W111°05.46′
▼ 1.0	SO	Track on left.
4.4 ▲	SO	Track on right.
▼ 1.2	SO	Trail forks; take either one.
4.2 ▲	SO	Trails rejoin.
▼ 1.4	SO	Trails rejoin.
4.0 ▲	SO	Trail forks; take either one.
▼ 1.5	SO	Lumpy descent into Jacks Canyon.
3.9 ▲	SO	Trail exits Jacks Canyon.
▼ 1.6	SO	Track on left.
3.8 ▲	SO	Track on right.
▼ 1.7	SO	Cross through Jacks Canyon Wash.
3.7 ▲	SO	Cross through Jacks Canyon Wash.
		GPS: N34°44.46′ W111°05.41′
▼ 1.8	SO	Cattle guard; then cross through Chavez Draw; then track on right. Jacks Canyon leaves on right. Trail now follows Chavez Draw.
3.6 ▲	SO	Track on left; then cross through Chavez Draw. Jacks Canyon leaves on left; then cattle guard.
▼ 2.2	SO	Cross through Chavez Draw.
3.2 ▲	SO	Cross through Chavez Draw.
▼ 2.3	SO	Cross through wash.
3.1 ▲	SO	Cross through wash.
▼ 2.4	SO	Cross through wash.
3.0 ▲	SO	Cross through wash.
▼ 2.5	SO	Faint track on left.
2.9 ▲	SO	Faint track on right.
▼ 2.6	SO	Cross through wash.

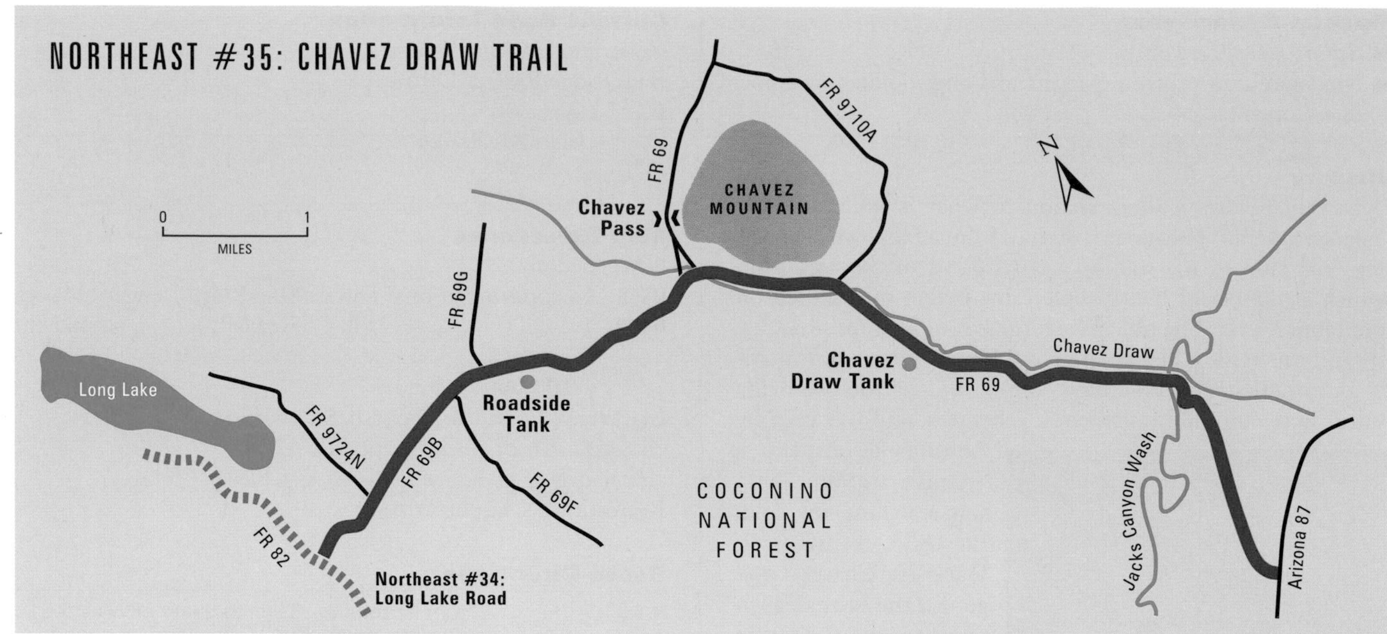

2.8 ▲	SO	Cross through wash.
▼ 2.8	SO	Cross through wash.
2.6 ▲	SO	Cross through wash.
▼ 3.4	SO	Cross through wash.
2.0 ▲	SO	Cross through wash.
▼ 3.5	SO	Track on right is FR 9729.
1.9 ▲	SO	Track on left is FR 9729.
		GPS: N34°45.28′ W111°07.00′
▼ 3.7	SO	Chavez Draw Tank on left; then track on left is FR 9722M (sign is obliterated and hard to read).
1.7 ▲	SO	Track on right is FR 9722M (sign is obliterated and hard to read). Chavez Draw Tank on right.
		GPS: N34°45.42′ W111°07.12′
▼ 4.1	SO	Cross through Chavez Draw.
1.3 ▲	SO	Cross through Chavez Draw.
▼ 4.3	BR	Track on left is FR 9721H.
1.1 ▲	SO	Track on right is FR 9721H.
		GPS: N34°45.92′ W111°07.38′
▼ 4.5	SO	Track on right is FR 9710A.
0.9 ▲	SO	Track on left is FR 9710A.
		GPS: N34°46.01′ W111°07.48′
▼ 4.7	SO	Track on left.
0.7 ▲	BL	Track on right.
▼ 5.3	SO	Entering motor travel restricted area at sign—travel only on designated roads.
0.1 ▲	SO	Leaving motor travel restricted area at sign.
		GPS: N34°46.39′ W111°08.26′
▼ 5.4	BL	Equally used track on right is FR 69. Bear left on FR 69B and zero trip meter.
0.0 ▲		Continue to the southeast.
		GPS: N34°46.44′ W111°08.34′
▼ 0.0		Continue to the northwest.
3.6 ▲	SO	Equally used track on left is second entrance to FR 69. Keep straight on and zero trip meter.
▼ 0.1	SO	Cross through Chavez Draw.
3.5 ▲	SO	Cross through Chavez Draw.
▼ 0.2	TL	T-intersection. Turn left and cross cattle guard, remaining on FR 69B. Track on right joins FR 69.
3.4 ▲	TR	Cattle guard; then turn right, remaining on FR 69B. Track ahead is first entrance to FR 69.
		GPS: N34°46.46′ W111°08.51′
▼ 0.3	SO	Cattle guard.
3.3 ▲	SO	Cattle guard.
▼ 0.4	SO	Leaving motor travel restricted area.
3.2 ▲	SO	Entering motor travel restricted area at sign—travel only on designated roads.
▼ 1.5	SO	Roadside Tank on left.
2.1 ▲	SO	Roadside Tank on right.
		GPS: N34°46.42′ W111°09.89′
▼ 1.8	SO	Track on right is FR 69G.
1.8 ▲	SO	Track on left is FR 69G.
▼ 2.1	SO	Track on left is FR 69F.
1.5 ▲	SO	Track on right is FR 69F.
		GPS: N34°46.46′ W111°10.48′
▼ 2.5	SO	Track on left.
1.1 ▲	SO	Track on right.
▼ 2.7	SO	Track on right; then cross over Chavez Pass Ditch.
0.9 ▲	SO	Cross over Chavez Pass Ditch; then track on left.
		GPS: N34°46.24′ W111°11.11′
▼ 2.9	SO	Small track on right.
0.7 ▲	SO	Small track on left.
▼ 3.0	SO	Track on right is FR 9724N and small track on left.
0.6 ▲	SO	Track on left is FR 9724N and small track on right.
		GPS: N34°46.10′ W111°11.38′
▼ 3.6		Trail ends at the intersection with Northeast #34: Long Lake Road, FR 82. Turn left to exit to Arizona 87 along graded gravel road; turn right to continue to Long Lake. Small track continues straight on.
0.0 ▲		Trail commences at the intersection of Northeast #34: Long Lake Road, FR 82, and FR 69B, 2 miles south of Long Lake and 15 miles north of Arizona 87. Zero trip meter and turn northeast on graded dirt road, following the sign to Chavez Pass.
		GPS: N34°45.93′ W111°11.90′

NORTHEAST REGION TRAIL #36

The Mogollon Rim Road

Starting Point:	**Arizona 87, 0.1 miles east of mile marker 281**
Finishing Point:	**Arizona 260, opposite the Mogollon Rim Visitor Center**
Total Mileage:	**41.3 miles**
Unpaved Mileage:	**38.1 miles**
Driving Time:	**3 hours**
Elevation Range:	**7,200–7,900 feet**
Usually Open:	**April to October**
Best Time to Travel:	**April to October**
Difficulty Rating:	**1**
Scenic Rating:	**9**
Remoteness Rating:	**+0**

Special Attractions

- Trail follows part of the historic route of the General George Crook Trail.
- Spectacular views of the rocky Mogollon Rim and the panoramic views to the south.
- Excellent, cool country camping opportunities.
- Access to many backcountry vehicle and hiking trails.

History

The present-day Mogollon Rim Road follows much of the original route put through by General George Crook as a military supply route to connect Fort Whipple at Prescott to Fort Apache and Camp Verde. The trail was constructed in 1872 as a wagon road and has been upgraded several times since. The military camps of Fort Whipple and Fort Apache were established to protect early settlers in the region against the frequent attacks from Apache Indians. The Apache were hunters and gatherers who resisted the takeover of their lands and efforts to confine them to the reservations. Far more skilled than the settlers at living in the trackless wilderness, they launched many successful surprise attacks.

General Springs Cabin

General George Crook arrived in the Arizona Territory in 1871 as commander of the area's military. His original journey from Fort Apache to Fort Whipple formed the basis of the trail that was constructed in 1872. When completed, the trail was only the third major route constructed in northern Arizona. Today, a few old trees and rocks still bear the marks of the original blazes, which indicated the mileage along the trail. Many landmarks are named according to the mileage, such as Thirteen Mile Rock and Twentynine Mile Lake. Today the trail is popular for hiking and is well marked with cream and orange chevrons.

Approximately 15 miles from the western end and a short distance to the north of the main trail is the site of General Springs Cabin. The small wooden cabin, built between 1914 and 1915 by Louis Fisher, was used for many years as a guard station. It sits beside springs used by General Crook as a source of water along the trail and reputedly was the spot at which he had a very narrow escape from the Apaches. The cabin, which was restored in 1989, is now listed as a historic site. Camping is prohibited in the immediate area around the cabin, but it makes for an exceedingly pretty picnic spot.

A rock precipice along the Mogollon Rim

Opposite the turn to the cabin is the start of the Tunnel Hiking Trail. This trail leads down to the top of an ambitious project—a tunnel intended to burrow through the rock of the Mogollon Rim to connect the large town of Flagstaff to the rich mines of Globe. The Atlantic & Pacific Railroad already ran through Flagstaff in 1886 en route to the Pacific coast from Albuquerque. A proposal for the 160-mile Mineral Belt Railroad to Globe was floated, and construction started through some incredibly rough terrain. The tunnel, which is situated at the mouth of General Springs Canyon, a low point in the rim, was to have been bored 3,100 feet through the rim. However, the promoters ran out of money after laying 40 miles of track and after tunneling only 70 feet into the rim.

Description

The Mogollon (pronounced "muggy-own") Rim is a 200-mile-long escarpment that cuts across the middle of Arizona, separating the lower desert country from the ponderosa pine and cedar forests of the upper elevations, and the scorching desert climate from the cooler, temperate zones. This "backbone of Arizona" forms the southern edge of the Colorado Plateau that extends to the north and east into Utah and New Mexico and is the result of a fault line that uplifted approximately 15 to 20 million years ago. It is named after Juan Ignacio Flores Mogollon, who was the governor of New Mexico from 1712 to 1715. Subsequent volcanic activity has deposited lava over the plateau and parts of the rim. Every summer, thousands of people from Phoenix and the valley escape to the cooler climes above the rim.

The first part of the Rim Road—a national recreation route—follows a section of the General Crook Trail, which

Overlooking Dude Creek, the site of Arizona's worst wildfire

was blazed by Crook in the 1870s. The trail is a narrow graded gravel and dirt road for its entire length and although uneven in places, when it is dry it is suitable for a carefully driven passenger vehicle. Most of the trail runs through a cool ponderosa pine forest. There are many places along its length when it runs right at the edge of the rim, giving excellent views not only of the rugged rim itself but down to the lower elevations. Take care if you walk out on the edge of the rim, especially in wet conditions. Some of the trees at the edge carry memorial plaques to those who accidentally fell.

Backcountry campsites abound; some of the best are set under large pine trees right on the edge of the rim. One of the best is at Hi-View Point, an exceptionally beautiful scenic overlook set right on the rim. There are also developed national forest campgrounds at Kehl Spring, just off the trail at Knoll Lake, Bear Canyon Lake, several sites at Woods Canyon Lake, and along the final couple of miles of the trail.

Many smaller vehicle trails lead from the main rim road. Many to the south lead to additional, more secluded viewpoints and campsites on the rim. To the north, there are graded roads that will take a passenger vehicle back to Arizona 87 and smaller 4WD trails that lead to equally spectacular scenery.

Other sites worth seeing just off the main trail include the General Springs Cabin, a restored forest cabin set on the edge of a flat grassy area next to General Springs. This area makes an excellent picnic spot. A passenger vehicle can negotiate the 0.4-mile spur to the cabin with care. Knoll Lake, Bear Canyon Lake, and Woods Canyon Lake are all just a few miles from the trail.

The eastern end of the trail within the Apache-Sitgreaves National Forest runs within the popular Rim Lakes Recreation Area. Inside this area, motorized travel is permitted on numbered roads only, ATVs are not permitted, and camping restrictions apply. In much of the area, camping is only permitted at designated backcountry campsites or developed campgrounds. The trail finishes on Arizona 260, opposite the Mogollon Rim Visitor Center.

The trail is closed each winter because of snow, but the dates are dependent on snowfall. Most years it is closed for a shorter period of time than the approximate dates given above.

Current Road Information

Coconino National Forest
Blue Ridge Ranger District
HC 31 Box 300
Happy Jack, AZ 86024
(520) 477-2255

Coconino National Forest
Long Valley Ranger District
HC 31 Box 68
Happy Jack, AZ 86024
(520) 527-3640

Apache-Sitgreaves National Forest
Chevelon Ranger District
PO Box 968
Overgaard, AZ 85933
(520) 535-4481

Map References

BLM Payson, Show Low
USFS Coconino National Forest: Long Valley and Blue Ridge Ranger Districts; Apache-Sitgreaves National Forest: Chevelon Ranger District (also shown on Tonto National Forest)
USGS 1:24,000 Pine, Kehl Ridge, Dane Canyon, Knoll Lake, Promontory Butte, Woods Canyon
1:100,000 Payson, Show Low
Maptech CD-ROM: Flagstaff/Sedona/Prescott; East Central Arizona/White Mountains
Arizona Atlas & Gazetteer, pp. 50, 51
Arizona Road & Recreation Atlas, p. 41 & p. 75
Recreational Map of Arizona

Route Directions

▼ 0.0		From Arizona 87, 0.1 miles east of mile marker 281, 2.5 miles east of the intersection with Arizona 260, zero trip meter and turn southeast on FR 300 at the sign for Rim Road and Knoll Lake. Immediately cross cattle guard and continue on graded gravel road and pass Baker Lake on right.
3.4 ▲		Pass Baker Lake on left; then cattle guard; then trail finishes at the intersection with Arizona 87. Turn right for Winslow; turn left for Pine.
		GPS: N34°27.31' W111°23.75'
▼ 0.1	TL	Track ahead is FR 218A to Milk Ranch Point; small track on right. Turn left onto FR 300, following the sign for the Rim Road and Knoll Lake.
3.3 ▲	TR	Track on left is FR 218A to Milk Ranch Point; small track ahead. Turn right toward Arizona 87.
▼ 1.3	SO	Track on right to lookout tower; then track on left.
2.1 ▲	SO	Track on right; then track on left to lookout tower.
		GPS: N34°27.22' W111°22.80'
▼ 1.7	SO	Track on left.
1.7 ▲	SO	Track on right.
▼ 1.8	SO	Track on right.
1.6 ▲	SO	Track on left.

▼ 2.1		SO	Cattle guard.
	1.3 ▲	SO	Cattle guard.
▼ 2.2		SO	Track on right.
	1.2 ▲	SO	Track on left.
▼ 2.3		SO	Track on left.
	1.1 ▲	SO	Track on right.
▼ 2.4		SO	Track on left.
	1.0 ▲	SO	Track on right.
▼ 2.6		SO	Track on left and track on right.
	0.8 ▲	SO	Track on left and track on right.
▼ 2.9		SO	Track on left and track on right.
	0.5 ▲	SO	Track on left and track on right.
▼ 3.2		SO	Track on right; then track on left.
	0.2 ▲	SO	Track on right; then track on left.
▼ 3.4		SO	Cross roads. Graded road on right is FR 218; graded road on left is FR 147 to Potato Lake. Zero trip meter.
	0.0 ▲		Continue to the west on FR 300, following the sign for Arizona 87.
			GPS: N34°26.75' W111°21.04'
▼ 0.0			Continue to the east on FR 300, following the sign to Knoll Lake and Kehl Spring.
	3.6 ▲	SO	Cross roads. Graded road on left is FR 218; graded road on right is FR 147 to Potato Lake. Zero trip meter.
▼ 0.3		SO	Cattle guard; then Lee Johnson Spring on right; track on right into spring.
	3.3 ▲	SO	Lee Johnson Spring on left; track on left into spring; then cattle guard.
			GPS: N34°26.50' W111°20.87'
▼ 0.9		SO	Track on left and track on right.
	2.7 ▲	SO	Track on left and track on right.
▼ 1.7		SO	Track on right. Trail enters previously logged area.
	1.9 ▲	SO	Track on left.
▼ 1.8		SO	Track on right.
	1.8 ▲	SO	Track on left.
▼ 1.9		SO	Track on left is FR 308 to Potato Lake. Track on right goes out to a viewpoint along the rim. Continue on, following the sign to Kehl Spring.
	1.7 ▲	SO	Track on right is FR 308 to Potato Lake. Track on left goes out to a viewpoint along the rim. Continue on, following the sign to Arizona 87. This viewpoint gives an excellent unobscured view of the rocky rim.
			GPS: N34°25.56' W111°19.81'
▼ 2.0		SO	View on right over rim.
	1.6 ▲	SO	View on left over rim.
▼ 2.1		SO	Track on right.
	1.5 ▲	SO	Track on left.
▼ 2.3		SO	Track on right.
	1.3 ▲	SO	Track on left.
▼ 2.7		SO	Track on right.
	0.9 ▲	SO	Track on left.
▼ 3.1		SO	Kehl Spring on left; then Kehl Spring Campground on left.
	0.5 ▲	SO	Kehl Spring Campground on right; then Kehl Spring on right.
			GPS: N34°26.09' W111°18.97'
▼ 3.3		SO	Track on left.
	0.3 ▲	SO	Track on right.
▼ 3.6		SO	Graded road on left is FR 141; small track on right. Zero trip meter.
	0.0 ▲		Continue to the northwest on FR 300, following sign to Baker Butte Lookout.
			GPS: N34°26.22' W111°18.51'
▼ 0.0			Continue to the southeast on FR 300, following sign to Knoll Lake.
	4.4 ▲	SO	Graded road on right is FR 141; small track on left. Zero trip meter.
▼ 0.1		SO	Track on left.
	4.3 ▲	SO	Track on right.
▼ 0.2		SO	Track on right.
	4.2 ▲	SO	Track on left.
▼ 0.4		SO	Track on left and track on right.
	4.0 ▲	SO	Track on left and track on right.
▼ 1.2		SO	Excellent large campsite on right on edge of rim. This is Hi-View Point.
	3.2 ▲	SO	Excellent large campsite on left on edge of rim. This is Hi-View Point.
			GPS: N34°26.23' W111°17.59'
▼ 1.7		SO	Track on left is FR 320.
	2.7 ▲	SO	Track on right is FR 320.
			GPS: N34°26.40' W111°17.20'
▼ 2.6		SO	Track on right.
	1.8 ▲	SO	Track on left.
▼ 2.8		SO	Cattle guard; then track on left is FR 501.
	1.6 ▲	SO	Track on right is FR 501; then cattle guard.
			GPS: N34°26.73' W111°16.20'
▼ 2.9		SO	Track on right.
	1.5 ▲	SO	Track on left.
▼ 3.0		SO	Track on right.
	1.4 ▲	SO	Track on left.
▼ 3.1		SO	Track on left.
	1.3 ▲	SO	Track on right.
▼ 3.6		SO	Graded road on left is FR 123 to Battleground Ridge and Battleground Monument.
	0.8 ▲	SO	Graded road on right is FR 123 to Battleground Ridge and Battleground Monument.
			GPS: N34°27.10' W111°15.53'
▼ 3.8		SO	Track on right.
	0.6 ▲	SO	Track on left.
▼ 4.1		SO	Track on right.
	0.3 ▲	SO	Track on left.
▼ 4.4		SO	Track on left goes 0.4 miles to General Springs Cabin and is also the Arizona Trail and Fred Haught Hiking Trail #22. Small track on right is start of Tunnel Hiking Trail and Colonel Devin Trail #290 also on right. Historical marker at the intersection for Battle of Big Dry Wash. Zero trip meter.
	0.0 ▲		Continue to the south.
			GPS: N34°27.23' W111°14.99'
▼ 0.0			Continue to the north.
	4.1 ▲	SO	Track on right goes 0.4 miles to General Springs Cabin and is also the Arizona Trail and Fred Haught Hiking Trail #22. Track on left rejoins and is start of Tunnel Hiking Trail and Colonel Devin Trail #290 also on left. Historical marker at the intersection for Battle of Big Dry Wash. Zero trip meter.
▼ 0.2		SO	Track on right rejoins.
	3.9 ▲	SO	Small track on left.
▼ 0.7		SO	Track on left is FR 393; then track on right.
	3.4 ▲	SO	Track on left; then track on right is FR 393.
			GPS: N34°26.85' W111°14.51'
▼ 1.0		SO	Graded road on left is FR 95 to Fred Haught Ridge and Arizona 87.
	3.1 ▲	SO	Graded road on right is FR 95 to Fred Haught Ridge and Arizona 87.
			GPS: N34°26.67' W111°14.30'

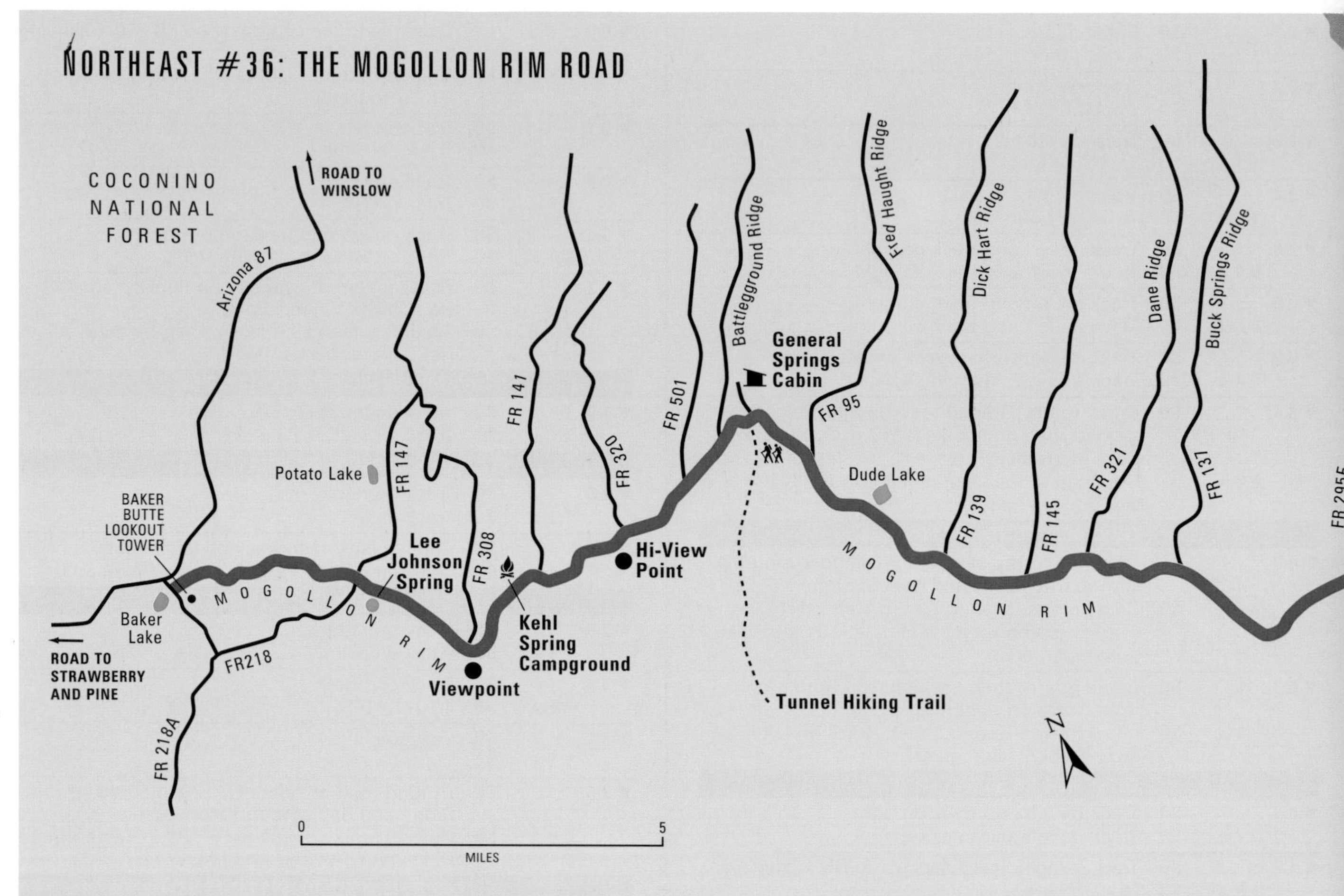

▼ 1.1 SO Track on left is FR 398 and track on right.
3.0 ▲ SO Track on right is FR 398 and track on left.

▼ 2.0 SO Cattle guard.
2.1 ▲ SO Cattle guard.

▼ 2.3 SO Track on left.
1.8 ▲ SO Track on right.

▼ 2.5 SO Track on left to Dude Lake, just off the main trail.
1.6 ▲ SO Track on right to Dude Lake, just off the main trail.

GPS: N34°25.80' W111°13.60'

▼ 3.9 SO Houston Brothers Hiking Trail #171 on left.
0.2 ▲ SO Houston Brothers Hiking Trail #171 on right.

GPS: N34°25.15' W111°12.92'

▼ 4.1 SO Graded road on left is FR 139 to Dick Hart Ridge and Arizona 87. Zero trip meter.
0.0 ▲ Continue to the west following the sign to Arizona 87.

GPS: N34°25.05' W111°12.81'

▼ 0.0 Continue to the east on FR 300, following the sign for Knoll Lake.
6.4 ▲ SO Graded road on right is FR 139 to Dick Hart Ridge and Arizona 87. Zero trip meter.

▼ 0.3 SO Cattle guard.
6.1 ▲ SO Cattle guard.

▼ 0.7 SO Track on left.
5.7 ▲ SO Track on right.

▼ 1.1 SO Track on left.
5.3 ▲ SO Track on right.

▼ 1.4 SO Graded gravel road on left is FR 145, but there is no trail number.
5.0 ▲ SO Graded gravel road on right is FR 145, but there is no trail number.

GPS: N34°24.49' W111°11.74'

▼ 2.2 SO Graded road on left is FR 321 to Dane Ridge and Arizona 87.
4.2 ▲ SO Graded road on right is FR 321 to Dane Ridge and Arizona 87.

GPS: N34°24.61' W111°10.89'

▼ 2.3 SO Short section of rough ground; passenger vehicles will need to take it very carefully.
4.1 ▲ SO Short section of rough ground; passenger vehicles will need to take it very carefully.

▼ 3.7 SO Graded road on left is FR 137 to Buck Springs Ridge and Arizona 87.
2.7 ▲ SO Graded road on right is FR 137 to Buck Springs Ridge and Arizona 87.

GPS: N34°24.23' W111°09.61'

▼ 3.8 SO Cattle guard.
2.6 ▲ SO Cattle guard.

▼ 5.2 SO Two tracks on right.
1.2 ▲ SO Two tracks on left.

▼ 5.3 SO Track on left.
1.1 ▲ SO Track on right.

▼ 5.7 SO Track on left.
0.7 ▲ SO Track on right.

▼ 6.4 SO Graded road on left is FR 295E, which goes to Knoll Lake. Zero trip meter.
0.0 ▲ Continue to the west on FR 300, following sign to Arizona 87.

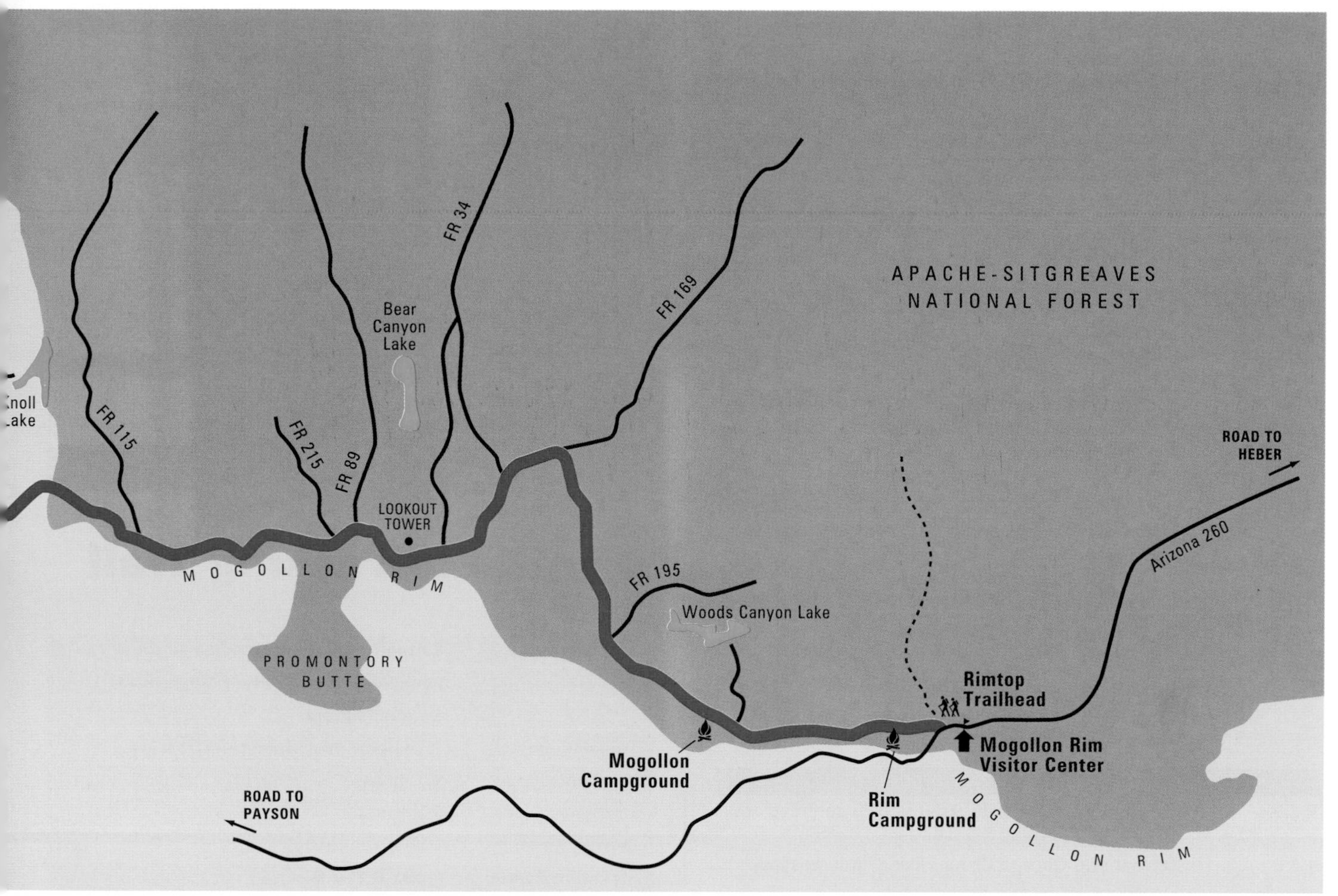

			GPS: N34°23.50′ W111°07.55′
▼ 0.0			Continue to the east on FR 300, following sign to Arizona 260.
	7.4 ▲	SO	Graded road on right is FR 295E, which goes to Knoll Lake. Zero trip meter.
▼ 0.9		SO	Track on left.
	6.5 ▲	SO	Track on right.
▼ 1.2		SO	Track on left.
	6.2 ▲	SO	Track on right.
▼ 2.0		SO	Babe Haught Hiking Trail #143 on right; then track on left.
	5.4 ▲	SO	Track on right; then Babe Haught Hiking Trail #143 on left.
			GPS: N34°24.15′ W111°05.76′
▼ 2.4		SO	Entering Apache-Sitgreaves National Forest; then closure gates. Entering motor-travel restricted area.
	5.0 ▲	SO	Closure gates; then entering Coconino National Forest. Leaving motor-travel restricted area.
			GPS: N34°24.07′ W111°05.40′
▼ 3.8		SO	Graded road on left is FR 115, Chaco Loop (12 miles). Route is also a snowmobile route in winter.
	3.6 ▲	BL	Graded road on right is FR 115, Chaco Loop (12 miles). Route is also a snowmobile route in winter.
			GPS: N34°23.23′ W111°04.51′
▼ 4.3		SO	Pass under power lines.
	3.1 ▲	SO	Pass under power lines.
▼ 4.7		SO	Horton Spring Hiking Trail #292 on right.
	2.7 ▲	SO	Horton Spring Hiking Trail #292 on left.
			GPS: N34°22.88′ W111°03.62′
▼ 4.9		SO	Cattle guard.
	2.5 ▲	SO	Cattle guard.
▼ 7.1		SO	Track on left is FR 215.
	0.3 ▲	SO	Track on right is FR 215.
			GPS: N34°22.47′ W111°01.62′
▼ 7.4		SO	Graded road on left is FR 89 to Bear Canyon Lake. Zero trip meter.
	0.0 ▲		Continue to the northwest on FR 300, following sign to Knolls Lake.
			GPS: N34°22.60′ W111°01.37′
▼ 0.0			Continue to the southeast on FR 300, following sign to Woods Canyon Lake.
	3.9 ▲	SO	Graded road on right is FR 89 to Bear Canyon Lake. Zero trip meter.
▼ 0.1		SO	Track on right is FR 76 to Promontory Butte.
	3.8 ▲	SO	Track on left is FR 76 to Promontory Butte.
			GPS: N34°22.53′ W111°01.25′
▼ 0.5		SO	See Canyon Hiking Trail #184 on right.
	3.4 ▲	SO	See Canyon Hiking Trail #184 on left.
			GPS: N34°22.33′ W111°01.00′
▼ 0.9		SO	Track on left is FR 208 and track on right.
	3.0 ▲	SO	Track on right is FR 208 and track on left.
			GPS: N34°22.02′ W111°00.85′
▼ 1.0		SO	Promontory Lookout Tower on left.
	2.9 ▲	SO	Promontory Lookout Tower on right.
▼ 1.6		SO	Graded road on left is FR 84, Bear Loop.

▼	▲		
	2.3 ▲	SO	Graded road on right is FR 84, Bear Loop.
			GPS: N34°21.94' W111°00.15'
▼ 2.2		SO	Track on right is FR 9354 into NFS camping area.
	1.7 ▲	SO	Track on left is FR 9354 into NFS camping area.
▼ 3.0		TR	Graded road ahead is FR 34.
	0.9 ▲	TL	Graded road on right is FR 34.
			GPS: N34°22.74' W110°59.07'
▼ 3.1		SO	Track on left.
	0.8 ▲	SO	Track on right.
▼ 3.6		SO	Track on right is FR 9354 into NFS camping area.
	0.3 ▲	SO	Track on left is FR 9354 into NFS camping area.
▼ 3.9		SO	Graded road on left is FR 169 to Chevelon Canyon Lake. Zero trip meter.
	0.0 ▲		Continue to the northwest on FR 300, following the sign to Bear Canyon Lake.
			GPS: N34°22.77' W110°58.15'
▼ 0.0			Continue to the southeast on FR 300, following the sign to Woods Canyon Lake.
	4.9 ▲	SO	Graded road on right is FR 169 to Chevelon Canyon Lake. Zero trip meter.
▼ 0.1		SO	Closure gates.
	4.8 ▲	SO	Closure gates.
▼ 2.7		SO	Graded road on left is FR 195 to NFS camping area; then tank on right.
	2.2 ▲	SO	Tank on left; then graded road on right is FR 195 to NFS camping area.
			GPS: N34°20.48' W110°58.30'
▼ 2.9		SO	Track on right is FR 9350 to NFS camping area.
	2.0 ▲	SO	Track on left is FR 9350 to NFS camping area.
▼ 3.0		SO	General George Crook Hiking Trail crosses road.
	1.9 ▲	SO	General George Crook Hiking Trail crosses road.
			GPS: N34°20.18' W110°58.16'
▼ 4.3		SO	Mogollon Campground on right (fee area).
	0.6 ▲	SO	Mogollon Campground on left (fee area).
			GPS: N34°19.33' W110°57.27'
▼ 4.9		SO	Closure gates; then join paved road. Paved road on left goes to Woods Canyon Lake. Zero trip meter.
	0.0 ▲		Continue to the northwest, following sign for Knolls Lake.
			GPS: N34°19.01' W110°56.69'
▼ 0.0			Continue to the southeast toward Arizona 260.
	3.2 ▲	BL	Bear left onto graded dirt road, FR 300. Paved road continues to Woods Canyon Lake. Zero trip meter.
▼ 0.1		SO	Parking area on right for Rim Lakes Vista Trail. Paved hiking trail, #622, suitable for wheelchairs next to the parking area.
	3.1 ▲	SO	Parking area on left for Rim Lakes Vista Trail. Paved hiking trail, #622, suitable for wheelchairs next to the parking area.
▼ 0.5		SO	Parking area on right for Rim Lakes Vista Trail.
	2.7 ▲	SO	Parking area on left for Rim Lakes Vista Trail.
▼ 1.3		SO	Parking area for Military Sinkhole Trail and Vista on right.
	1.9 ▲	SO	Parking area for Military Sinkhole Trail and Vista on left.
			GPS: N34°18.56' W110°55.52'
▼ 2.5		SO	Rim NFS Campground on right (fee area).
	0.7 ▲	SO	Rim NFS Campground on left (fee area).
			GPS: N34°18.39' W110°54.37'
▼ 2.9		SO	Hiking trail crosses left and right.
	0.3 ▲	SO	Hiking trail crosses left and right.
▼ 3.1		SO	Closure gate; then Rimtop Trailhead on left.
	0.1 ▲	SO	Rimtop Trailhead on right; then closure gate.
▼ 3.2			Trail ends at the intersection with Arizona 260, opposite the Mogollon Rim Visitor Center. Turn left for Heber; turn right for Payson.
	0.0 ▲		Trail commences on Arizona 260, 0.6 miles west of mile marker 283, opposite the Mogollon Rim Visitor Center. Zero trip meter and turn north on paved road, following the sign for Woods Canyon Lake. There is a sign at the turn for the Rim Lakes Recreation Area.
			GPS: N34°18.17' W110°53.73'

NORTHEAST REGION TRAIL #37

Hamilton Crossing Trail

Starting Point:	**Arizona 99 (FR 34), 6 miles south of the boundary of the Apache-Sitgreaves National Forest**
Finishing Point:	**Viewpoint near Hamilton Crossing**
Total Mileage:	**9.7 miles**
Unpaved Mileage:	**9.7 miles**
Driving Time:	**1 hour (one-way)**
Elevation Range:	**6,500–6,800 feet**
Usually Open:	**March to November**
Best Time to Travel:	**March to November**
Difficulty Rating:	**4**
Scenic Rating:	**8**
Remoteness Rating:	**+0**

Special Attractions

- Panoramic views over Clear Creek.
- Rough, moderately challenging trail.

Description

This trail within the Apache-Sitgreaves National Forest travels to the edge of steep Clear Creek Canyon and overlooks the site of historic Hamilton Crossing, which was originally a stock crossing of Clear Creek Canyon. The trail initially follows well-graded FR 63 before turning off onto FR 63B, a lumpy formed trail. This extremely twisty trail winds through oaks, cypress, pines, and junipers as it travels along the plateau. The embedded rocks make for a rough, slow ride for the first couple of miles. After that, there are some smoother sections, but these have deep wheel ruts. The trail can be impassable when wet; the red soil becomes very greasy. A couple of short, loose sections and rock ledges may cause some vehicles to lose traction, but this trail is moderately rated and suitable for any high-clearance 4WD.

The trail ends on the rim of Clear Creek Canyon. A trail to the left goes approximately 100 yards to a campsite on

The view into Clear Creek Canyon from the trail's end

the rim. A short hiking trail goes 50 yards farther out to the very edge to give an unobstructed view into the canyon, 400 feet below. Take care on the edge when on foot—the surface is very loose and there is little margin for error. Most people stop at this campsite, but vehicles can proceed for 0.2 miles to other viewpoints and to a second, much rockier, campsite. Past this, the trail deteriorates into a serious hiking trail. It quickly descends the side of the cliff to Hamilton Crossing. The trail is very steep, loose, and washed out in places. A view of Hamilton Crossing can be obtained from the first switchback.

Current Road Information

Apache-Sitgreaves National Forest
Chevelon Ranger District
PO Box 968
Overgaard, AZ 85933
(520) 535-4481

Map References

BLM Holbrook
USFS Apache-Sitgreaves National Forest: Chevelon Ranger District
USGS 1:24,000 Grama Draw, Hamilton Crossing
1:100,000 Holbrook
Maptech CD-ROM: East Central Arizona/White Mountains
Arizona Atlas & Gazetteer, p. 43
Arizona Road & Recreation Atlas, p. 42 & p. 76

Route Directions

▼ 0.0		From FR 34, 6 miles south of the boundary of the Apache-Sitgreaves National Forest, zero trip meter and turn northwest on FR 63. There is a camping area at the intersection.
		GPS: N34°34.51' W110°53.93'
▼ 0.1	SO	Track on left to campsite.
▼ 0.2	SO	Cattle guard.
▼ 0.3	BL	Track on right.
▼ 0.6	SO	Track on right.
▼ 0.9	SO	Track on right.
▼ 1.0	BR	Track on left over cattle guard is FR 70. Bear right, remaining on FR 63.
		GPS: N34°34.97' W110°54.74'
▼ 1.3	SO	Track on right.
▼ 1.7	SO	Track on right.
▼ 1.8	SO	Track on left.
▼ 2.4	SO	Track on right.
▼ 2.6	SO	Track on left.
▼ 3.3	SO	Track on right.
▼ 3.5	BL	Track on right is FR 63; bear left onto smaller formed trail marked FR 63B and zero trip meter.
		GPS: N34°37.00' W110°55.85'
▼ 0.0		Continue to the northwest on FR 63B. Trail immediately splits into three, but they all rejoin almost immediately.
▼ 0.2	SO	Game water tank on right.
		GPS: N34°37.14' W110°56.01'
▼ 0.6	SO	Track on left.
▼ 3.1	SO	Fence line on right; then track on right through wire gate. Continue on and swing away from the fence. Zero trip meter.
		GPS: N34°38.48' W110°57.43'
▼ 0.0		Continue to the north.
▼ 0.1	SO	Pass through wire gate; then track on left.
▼ 0.4	BL	Equally used track on right. Keep heading west.
		GPS: N34°38.73' W110°57.67'
▼ 2.9	BR	Small track on left goes 50 yards to a campsite on the edge of Clear Creek Canyon. Park and hike for 100 yards along the faint hiking trail along the edge for the best, unobstructed view into Clear Creek Canyon. The Coconino National Forest is on the far side, and the San Francisco Peaks can be seen in the distance.
		GPS: N34°38.93' W110°59.58'
▼ 3.1		Trail ends at second camp spot and another viewpoint into Clear Creek Canyon. Steep, unstable foot trail leaves from this point. Hamilton Crossing can be seen down in the canyon to the northwest.
		GPS: N34°39.02' W110°59.68'

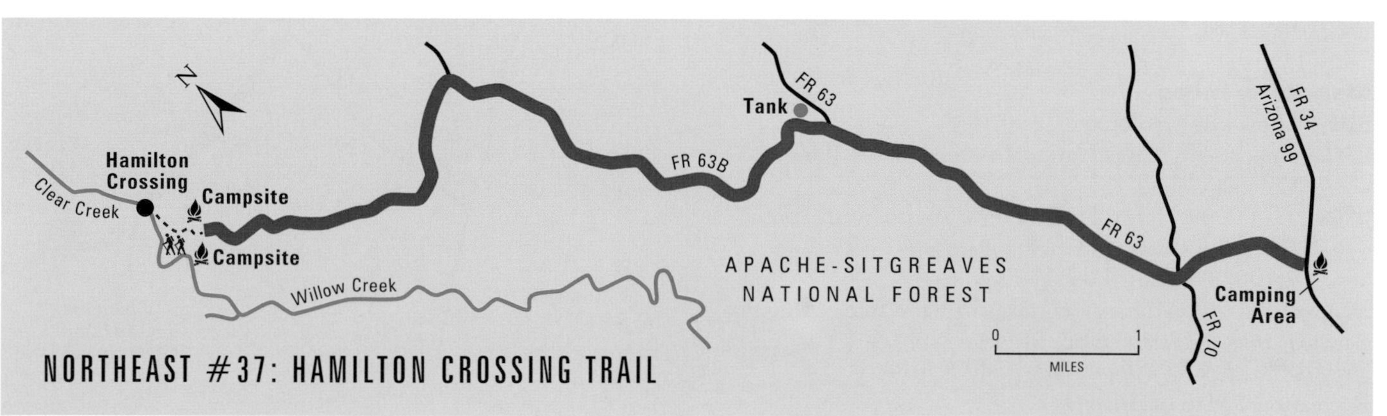

NORTHEAST REGION TRAIL #38

Chevelon Crossing Road

Starting Point:	**Arizona 260, 1 mile northwest of Heber**
Finishing Point:	**Arizona 99 (FR 34), 28 miles south of Winslow**
Total Mileage:	**24 miles**
Unpaved Mileage:	**24 miles**
Driving Time:	**1.25 hours**
Elevation Range:	**4,600–6,700 feet**
Usually Open:	**April to October**
Best Time to Travel:	**April to October**
Difficulty Rating:	**1**
Scenic Rating:	**8**
Remoteness Rating:	**+0**

Special Attractions

- The deep gorge of Chevelon Canyon.
- Access to many backcountry campsites and roads within the Apache-Sitgreaves National Forest.
- Elk may be seen in the area.

Description

This smooth backcountry road winds through pine forests on the Mogollon Plateau in the Apache-Sitgreaves National Forest. The trail is not suitable for vehicles more than 35 feet long because of the winding road and tight curves at Chevelon Crossing. The trail is a well-used, graded gravel road, which can become very washboardy.

Chevelon Crossing is a scenic and historic canyon area. Next to the crossing is a U.S. Forest Service campground that was built originally by the Civilian Conservation Corps in the 1930s. There is water in the canyon year-round.

Current Road Information

Apache-Sitgreaves National Forest
Heber Ranger District
PO Box 968
Overgaard, AZ 85933
(520) 535-4481

Map References

BLM Show Low, Holbrook
USFS Apache-Sitgreaves National Forest: Heber Ranger District
USGS 1:24,000 Heber, Hanks Draw, Potato Wash South, Chevelon Crossing, Chevelon Butte
1:100,000 Show Low, Holbrook
Maptech CD-ROM: East Central Arizona/White Mountains
Arizona Atlas & Gazetteer, pp. 51, 43
Arizona Road & Recreation Atlas, p. 42 & p. 76
Recreational Map of Arizona

Route Directions

▼ 0.0		From Arizona 260, 1 mile northwest of Heber and 0.4 miles northwest of mile marker 303, zero trip meter and turn northwest on graded gravel road, FR 504.
5.0 ▲		Trail ends on Arizona 260. Turn left for Heber; turn right for Payson and Winslow.
		GPS: N34°26.35' W110°37.09'
▼ 0.1	SO	Tracks on left and right along power lines.
4.9 ▲	SO	Tracks on left and right along power lines.
▼ 0.2	SO	Track on right.
4.8 ▲	SO	Track on left.
▼ 0.3	SO	Track on left.
4.7 ▲	SO	Track on right.
▼ 0.4	SO	Cattle guard; then track on right.
4.6 ▲	SO	Track on left; then cattle guard.
▼ 0.5	SO	Track on left.
4.5 ▲	SO	Track on right.
▼ 0.7	SO	Track on right.
4.3 ▲	SO	Track on left.
▼ 1.2	SO	Graded road on right to private property and track on left.
3.8 ▲	SO	Graded road on left to private property and track on right.
▼ 1.7	SO	Track on left is FR 93.
3.3 ▲	SO	Track on right is FR 93.
▼ 1.8	SO	Road on right is FR 95.
3.2 ▲	SO	Road on left is FR 95.
		GPS: N34°27.73' W110°38.04'
▼ 1.9	SO	Track on right.
3.1 ▲	SO	Track on left.
▼ 2.3	SO	Cattle guard; then track on right to corral.

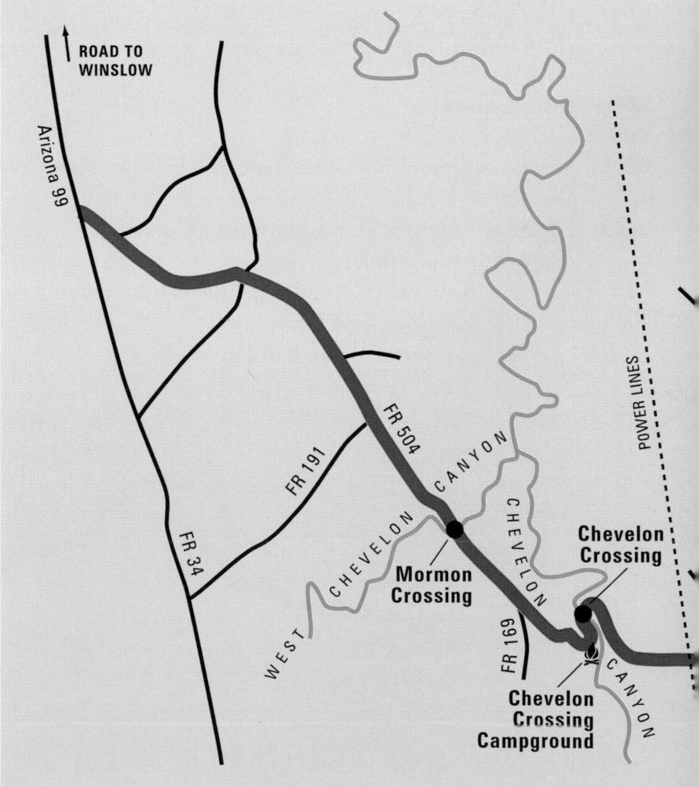

Mileage		Directions
2.7 ▲	SO	Track on left to corral; then cattle guard.
		GPS: N34°27.99′ W110°38.52′
▼ 2.9	SO	Crossing through Brookbank Canyon; cross over wash. Track on right down canyon.
2.1 ▲	SO	Crossing through Brookbank Canyon; cross over wash. Track on left down canyon.
▼ 3.1	SO	Track on right.
1.9 ▲	SO	Track on left.
▼ 3.2	SO	Track on right; then track on left.
1.8 ▲	SO	Track on right; then track on left.
▼ 3.3	SO	Track on right.
1.7 ▲	SO	Track on left.
▼ 3.6	SO	Track on right.
1.4 ▲	SO	Track on left.
▼ 4.2	SO	Track on right; then track on left.
0.8 ▲	SO	Track on right; then track on left.
▼ 4.5	SO	Track on left is FR 9554B.
0.5 ▲	SO	Track on right is FR 9554B.
▼ 4.6	SO	Track on right is FR 228.
0.4 ▲	SO	Track on left is FR 228.
		GPS: N34°29.26′ W110°40.43′
▼ 5.0	SO	Graded road on left is FR 99, Wildcat Road. Zero trip meter.
0.0 ▲		Continue to the southeast on FR 504 toward Heber.
		GPS: N34°29.51′ W110°40.73′
▼ 0.0		Continue to the northwest on FR 504 toward Chevelon Canyon.
5.5 ▲	SO	Graded road on right is FR 99, Wildcat Road. Zero trip meter.
▼ 1.0	SO	Track on right.
4.5 ▲	SO	Track on left.

A view of Chevelon Canyon Creek

Mileage		Directions
▼ 1.3	SO	Track on left.
4.2 ▲	SO	Track on right.
▼ 1.6	SO	Track on right; then cattle guard.
3.9 ▲	SO	Cattle guard; then track on left.
▼ 1.9	SO	Track on left.
3.6 ▲	SO	Track on right.
▼ 2.1	SO	Track on right.
3.4 ▲	SO	Track on left.
▼ 2.4	SO	Track on left.
3.1 ▲	SO	Track on right.

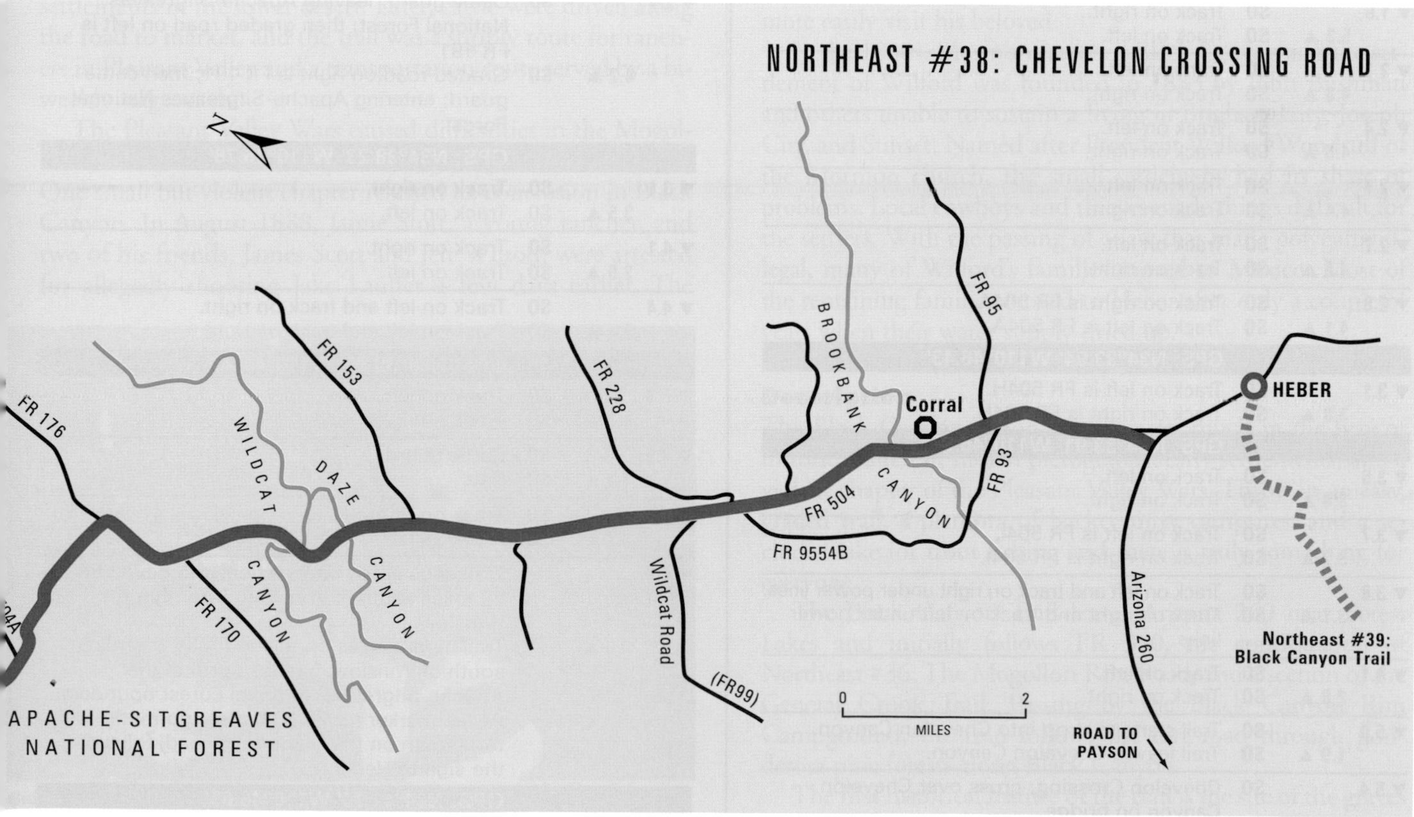

NORTHEAST #38: CHEVELON CROSSING ROAD

N
FR 176
FR 153
FR 228
FR 95
BROOKBANK
Corral
HEBER
FR 93
CANYON
FR 504
FR 9554B
WILDCAT
DAZE
CANYON
CANYON
FR 170
Wildcat Road
(FR99)
Arizona 260
Northeast #39: Black Canyon Trail
0 2
MILES
ROAD TO PAYSON
APACHE-SITGREAVES NATIONAL FOREST

The Polimana Pictographs near the east end of the trail

of Jamie Stott, James Scott, and Jeff Wilson. To reach the site, turn down a small formed trail marked with auto tour number 7. Take the side trail, which immediately forks; follow the right-hand fork for 1 mile. When you reach two Closed Road signs at the end of the vehicle trail, you are there. The graves are just past the second sign on the right, hidden in the trees and surrounded by a wooden fence. The coordinates of the graves are—GPS: N34°18.34' W110°44.00'.

Black Canyon Lake, a long narrow lake ringed by tall pine trees, is located just off the main trail. The Three Oak Hiking Trail leaves from the parking area. The lake is stocked with trout and is a popular fishing spot. No camping is allowed at the lake, but there are two large informal camping areas nearby: the West Camping Area and the South Camping Area. There are no facilities, but there are plenty of large sites set among the trees on the edge of a large, open area.

The next stop along the trail is the Baca Ranch and graves. Nothing remains of the ranch, but the graves—in a small stand of aspens—can easily be seen. The historic Black Canyon Ranch and the site of the township of Wilford are passed before the short hiking trail to the Black Canyon Rock Shelter is reached. The shelter is on the far side of the canyon and can be seen without hiking up to it. There are a few pictographs at the shelter.

The final stop on the trail is the Polimana Pictographs. They are located right beside the main trail, but you will need to hike up a short, steep climb to view them closely. The pictographs were painted by the Mogollon Indians.

The Chevelon-Heber Ranger Districts publish a free auto tour guide for this trail; in the guide, the auto tour marker posts refer to points of interest discussed.

Current Road Information

Apache-Sitgreaves National Forest
Heber Ranger District
PO Box 968
Overgaard, AZ 85933
(520) 535-4481

Map References

BLM Show Low
USFS Apache-Sitgreaves National Forest: Heber Ranger District
USGS 1:24,000 O W Point, Brookbank Point, Hanks Draw, Heber
1:100,000 Show Low
Maptech CD-ROM: East Central Arizona/White Mountains
Arizona Atlas & Gazetteer, p. 51
Arizona Road & Recreation Atlas, p. 42 & p. 76
Recreational Map of Arizona

Route Directions

Mileage		Directions
▼ 0.0		From Arizona 260, 7 miles east of the intersection with Arizona 288, 0.1 miles east of mile marker 291, zero trip meter and turn south over cattle guard on graded dirt road marked FR 300. Immediately past the turn, the road is marked to Rim Road and Black Canyon Lake. There is a message board on the right.
2.3 ▲		Trail ends at the T-intersection with Arizona 260. Turn right for Heber; turn left for Payson.
		GPS: N34°20.02' W110°45.13'
▼ 0.1	SO	Track on left.
2.2 ▲	SO	Track on right.
▼ 0.3	SO	Track on left.
2.0 ▲	SO	Track on right.
▼ 0.6	SO	Track on left through camp area; then two tracks on right; then track on left.
1.7 ▲	SO	Track on right; then two tracks on left; then track on right through camp area.
▼ 0.7	SO	Graded road on left is FR 9555Y; track on right.
1.6 ▲	SO	Track on left; graded road on right is FR 9555Y.
		GPS: N34°19.35' W110°45.00'
▼ 0.9	SO	Track on left.
1.4 ▲	SO	Track on right.
▼ 1.0	SO	Track on right.
1.3 ▲	SO	Track on left.
▼ 1.4	SO	Track on right.
0.9 ▲	SO	Track on left.
▼ 1.8	BL	Track on right is FR 196.
0.5 ▲	BR	Track on left is FR 196.
		GPS: N34°18.45' W110°45.27'
▼ 1.9	SO	Track on left.
0.4 ▲	SO	Track on right.
▼ 2.2	SO	Track on right is FR 168.
0.1 ▲	SO	Track on left is FR 168.
		GPS: N34°18.24' W110°44.88'
▼ 2.3	TL	Turn onto graded road FR 86, following the sign to Black Canyon Lake. FR 300 continues ahead. Black Canyon Rim NFS Campground at intersection. Zero trip meter.
0.0 ▲		Continue to the west.
		GPS: N34°18.23' W110°44.74'
▼ 0.0		Continue to the north.
1.7 ▲	TR	T-intersection; turn right onto FR 300 following the sign to Arizona 260. Black Canyon Rim NFS Campground at intersection. Zero trip meter.
▼ 0.1	SO	Campground entrance on right. Closure gate.
1.6 ▲	SO	Closure gate. Campground entrance on left.
▼ 0.8	SO	Track on left.
0.9 ▲	SO	Track on right.
▼ 0.9	SO	Track on left.
0.8 ▲	SO	Track on right.
▼ 1.5	SO	Track on left.
0.2 ▲	SO	Track on right.

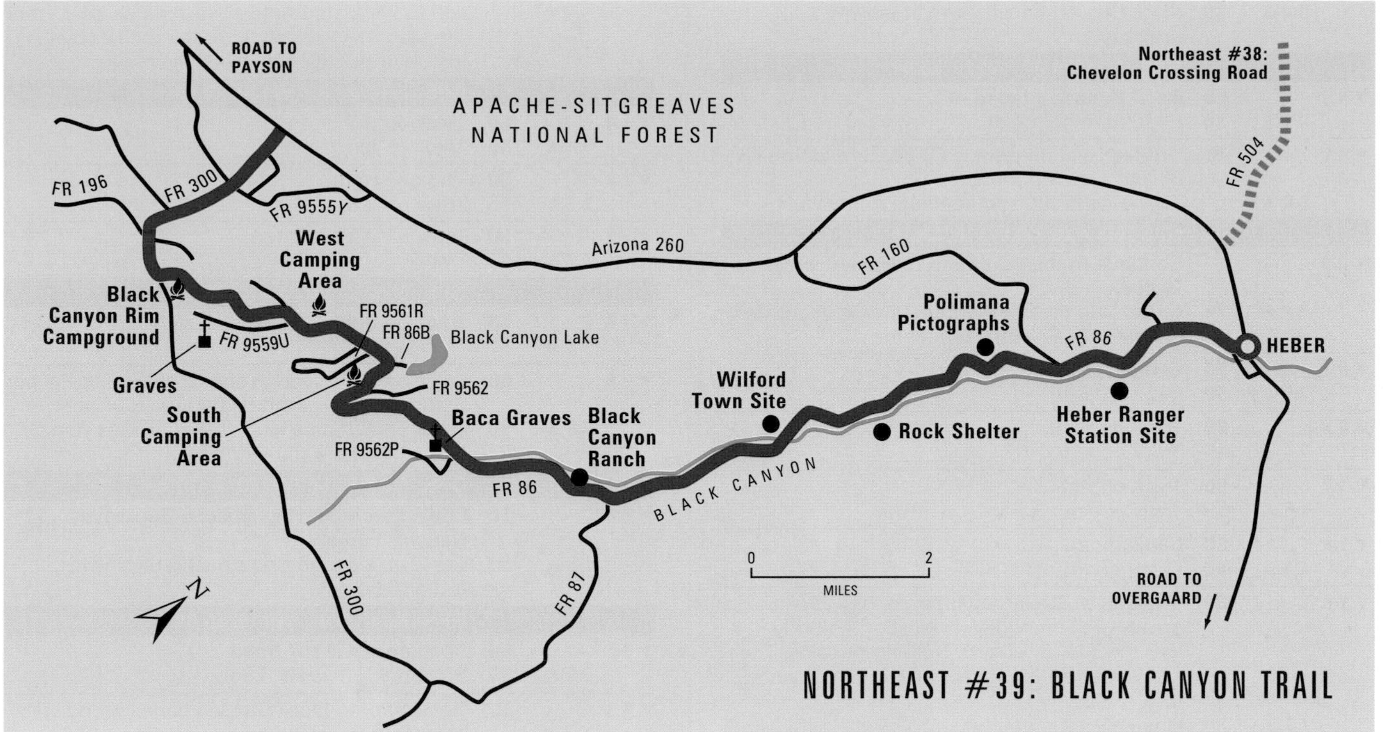

▼ 1.7 **SO** Track on right is FR 9559U, which goes to the graves of Stott, Scott, and Wilson. Track is marked by auto tour stop 7 sign. Zero trip meter.
0.0 ▲ Continue to the west.

GPS: N34°18.98′ W110°43.26′

▼ 0.0 Continue to the east.
1.1 ▲ **SO** Track on left is FR 9559U, which goes to the graves of Stott, Scott, and Wilson. Track is marked by auto tour stop 7 sign. Zero trip meter.

▼ 0.1 **SO** Track on right; then track on left. Area is marked as West Camping Area. Many tracks right and left for next 0.3 miles, mainly to campsites.
1.0 ▲ **SO** Track on right; then track on left.

▼ 0.4 **SO** End of main camping area.
0.7 ▲ **SO** Many tracks on right and left for next 0.3 miles, mainly to campsites. Area is marked as West Camping Area.

▼ 0.6 **SO** Track on right.
0.5 ▲ **SO** Track on left.

GPS: N34°19.30′ W110°42.75′

▼ 0.8 **SO** Track on right.
0.3 ▲ **SO** Track on left.

▼ 0.9 **SO** Track on right is FR 9561R.
0.2 ▲ **SO** Track on left is FR 9561R.

GPS: N34°19.37′ W110°42.42′

▼ 1.1 **BR** Track on left is FR 86B, which goes to Black Canyon Lake (0.25 miles). Zero trip meter.
0.0 ▲ Continue to the west on FR 86.

GPS: N34°19.38′ W110°42.23′

▼ 0.0 Continue to the east toward Heber.
4.1 ▲ **BL** Track on right is FR 86B, which goes to Black Canyon Lake (0.25 miles). Zero trip meter.

▼ 0.2 **SO** South Camping Area on right; FR 9561S.
3.9 ▲ **SO** South Camping Area on left; FR 9561S.

▼ 0.3 **SO** Track on right to camping area.
3.8 ▲ **SO** Track on left to camping area.

▼ 0.4 **SO** Track on right to camping area.
3.7 ▲ **SO** Track on left to camping area.

▼ 0.7 **SO** Closure gate; then track on left is FR 9562.
3.4 ▲ **SO** Track on right is FR 9562; then closure gate.

GPS: N34°18.77′ W110°42.28′

▼ 0.8 **SO** Track on right.
3.3 ▲ **SO** Track on left.

▼ 1.6 **SO** Track on left.
2.5 ▲ **SO** Track on right.

▼ 1.7 **SO** Track on right is FR 9562F.
2.4 ▲ **SO** Track on left is FR 9562F.

GPS: N34°19.28′ W110°41.62′

▼ 1.9 **SO** Track on left.
2.2 ▲ **SO** Track on right.

▼ 2.0 **SO** Two tracks on left.
2.1 ▲ **SO** Two tracks on right.

▼ 2.2 **SO** The Baca graves are on the right surrounded by a fence; also track on right.
1.9 ▲ **SO** The Baca graves are on the left surrounded by a fence; also track on left.

GPS: N34°19.35′ W110°41.13′

▼ 2.3 **SO** Cross through wash; then Baca Meadow on right. Track on right is FR 9562P.
1.8 ▲ **SO** Track on left is FR 9526P. Baca Meadow on left; cross through wash.

GPS: N34°19.38′ W110°40.98′

▼ 2.7 **SO** Track on right.
1.4 ▲ **SO** Track on left.

▼ 3.2 **SO** Cattle guard; then track on right.
0.9 ▲ **SO** Track on left; then cattle guard.

▼ 3.5 **SO** Track on left. Road becomes paved.
0.6 ▲ **SO** Track on right. Road turns to graded dirt.

GPS: N34°20.04′ W110°40.04′

▼ 3.7 **SO** Black Canyon Ranch on left (private property).

▼	▲		
	0.4 ▲	SO	Black Canyon Ranch on right (private property).
			GPS: N34°20.07′ W110°39.88′
▼ 4.0		SO	Road turns to graded dirt.
	0.1 ▲	SO	Road turns to paved.
▼ 4.1		TL	Graded road on right is FR 87. Turn left on FR 86 and zero trip meter.
	0.0 ▲		Turn onto FR 86 and continue to the west.
			GPS: N34°20.23′ W110°39.46′
▼ 0.0			Continue to the north and cross over creek on bridge.
	3.2 ▲	TR	Cross over creek on bridge; then graded road on left is FR 87. Zero trip meter.
▼ 0.2		SO	Cattle guard.
	3.0 ▲	SO	Cattle guard.
▼ 0.8		SO	Track on right.
	2.4 ▲	SO	Track on left.
▼ 1.7		SO	Track on right.
	1.5 ▲	SO	Track on left.
▼ 1.8		SO	Cattle guard.
	1.4 ▲	SO	Cattle guard.
▼ 1.9		SO	Cross over Black Canyon on bridge. Open grassy area immediately west of the bridge was the site of Wilford. Nothing remains. The site is marked by marker post 6 on the auto tour.
	1.3 ▲	SO	Open grassy area immediately west of the bridge was the site of Wilford. Nothing remains. The site is marked by marker post 6 on the auto tour. Cross over Black Canyon on bridge.
			GPS: N34°21.87′ W110°38.68′
▼ 2.0		SO	Track on right.
	1.2 ▲	SO	Track on left.
▼ 2.4		SO	Track on left is FR 9596F.
	0.8 ▲	SO	Track on right is FR 9596F.
			GPS: N34°22.25′ W110°38.65′
▼ 2.6		SO	Track on right.
	0.6 ▲	SO	Track on left.
▼ 3.2		SO	Track on right at auto tour marker 3 goes a short distance to a parking area. Follow the blue diamond markers a short distance on foot to Black Canyon Creek and the rock shelter. Zero trip meter.
	0.0 ▲		Continue to the west.
			GPS: N34°22.83′ W110°38.18′
▼ 0.0			Continue to the east.
	4.4 ▲	SO	Track on left at auto tour marker 3 goes a short distance to a parking area. Follow the blue diamond markers on foot a short distance to Black Canyon Creek and the rock shelter. Zero trip meter.
▼ 0.5		SO	Track on left to corral.
	3.9 ▲	SO	Track on right to corral.
▼ 0.6		SO	Cattle guard.
	3.8 ▲	SO	Cattle guard.
▼ 0.9		SO	Track on left.
	3.5 ▲	SO	Track on right.
▼ 1.2		SO	Polimana Pictographs on the left. Park close to auto tour marker 2 and take the short, steep hiking trail for approximately 100 yards up the cliff to the pictographs. They can be seen from the road immediately after the marker by looking up underneath the rock overhang.
	3.2 ▲	SO	Polimana Pictographs on the right. Park close to auto tour marker 2 and take the short, steep hiking trail for approximately 100 yards up the cliff to the pictographs. They can be seen from the road immediately after the marker by looking up underneath the rock overhang.
			GPS: N34°23.82′ W110°37.81′
▼ 1.4		SO	Track on right.
	3.0 ▲	SO	Track on left.
▼ 1.7		SO	Track on right.
	2.7 ▲	SO	Track on left.
▼ 2.2		SO	Track on left is FR 160.
	2.2 ▲	SO	Track on right is FR 160.
			GPS: N34°24.46′ W110°37.14′
▼ 2.6		SO	Track on right.
	1.8 ▲	SO	Track on left.
▼ 2.8		SO	Track on right goes to site of old Heber Ranger Station. Road is marked by auto tour post 1.
	1.6 ▲	SO	Track on left goes to site of old Heber Ranger Station. Road is marked by auto tour post 1.
			GPS: N34°24.88′ W110°36.71′
▼ 2.9		SO	Cattle guard; leaving Apache-Sitgreaves National Forest.
	1.5 ▲	SO	Cattle guard; entering Apache-Sitgreaves National Forest.
			GPS: N34°24.93′ W110°36.69′
▼ 3.5		SO	Road on left is Hill Road.
	0.9 ▲	SO	Road on right is Hill Road.
▼ 4.3		TL	Turn left onto Black Canyon Lane immediately before wash crossing.
	0.1 ▲	TR	Turn right onto Black Canyon Road and proceed west.
▼ 4.4			Trail ends at the intersection with Arizona 260 in Heber. Turn left for Payson; turn right for Overgaard.
	0.0 ▲		Trail commences from Arizona 260 in Heber. Zero trip meter and turn south on graded dirt road at the sign for FR 86, Black Canyon Lane.
			GPS: N34°25.90′ W110°36.02′

NORTHEAST REGION TRAIL #40

Defiance Plateau Trail

Starting Point:	**I-40, exit 343 (Querino Road)**
Finishing Point:	**Arizona 264, 5.1 miles west of St. Michaels**
Total Mileage:	**32.3 miles**
Unpaved Mileage:	**32.2 miles**
Driving Time:	**1.5 hours**
Elevation Range:	**6,100–7,800 feet**
Usually Open:	**Year-round**
Best Time to Travel:	**Dry weather**
Difficulty Rating:	**2**
Scenic Rating:	**7**
Remoteness Rating:	**+0**

Special Attractions

- Oak Ridge Fire Lookout Tower.
- Long trail through open forest along Defiance Plateau.
- Alternative route to Window Rock from the south.

Description

Most people who enter the Navajo Nation from the south travel via Indian Road 12, from I-40 to Window Rock. However, a little-known dirt road parallels this paved route to the west, traveling through open forest on Defiance Plateau.

The trail is used as a main access to the settlement of Pine Springs and by many Navajo who live on the plateau. Consequently, the route stays open year-round but may be snow-covered in winter and impassable after summer monsoons. In dry weather, it is suitable for high-clearance 2WDs.

From I-40 to Pine Springs the road is wide and well graded, although there are a few sand traps and rutted sections that might be uncomfortable for those traveling in a passenger vehicle. The remains of the old Pine Springs Trading Post are on the west side of the road; only the walls still stand.

St. Michaels Mission

Past Pine Springs, the trail continues to be wide but is only roughly graded with a loose surface and deep, powder-fine sand traps. Take care: The edges of the road are very soft and sandy and it would be easy to get bogged down. The vegetation on Defiance Plateau is mainly pinyon-juniper at the lower elevations; as the trail gradually climbs, there are dense stands of ponderosa pines. There are many side tracks leading from the main one, most of which lead to dwellings. Only the major ones and ones that do not immediately lead to houses are mentioned in the route directions. The side trails are mentioned for navigation purposes only; most are not open to public travel.

The fire lookout tower on Oak Ridge is manned during daylight hours in the fire season. Visitors are usually welcome to climb the tower when it is manned but must ask permission from the lookout first. From the top, there is a good view of Defiance Plateau, an unbroken flat expanse of vegetation. Other fire lookout towers can be seen to the north.

The trail ends at Arizona 264, a paved road a short distance to the west of St. Michaels and Window Rock. St. Michaels Mission and Museum warrant a visit.

Current Road Information

Navajo Nation Parks and Recreation
PO Box 9000
Window Rock, AZ 86515
(520) 871-6647

Map References

BLM Sanders, Ganado
USGS 1:24,000 Burntwater Wash, Pine Springs, Antelope Lake, Joe Woody Well, West of Window Rock
1:100,000 Sanders, Ganado

Maptech CD-ROM: Northeast Arizona/Navajo County
Arizona Atlas & Gazetteer, pp. 45, 35
Arizona Road & Recreation Atlas, p. 37 & p. 71
Recreational Map of Arizona

Route Directions

▼ 0.0			From exit 343 on I-40, Querino Road, proceed to the north side of the freeway exit. Zero trip meter at cattle guard and continue northwest on paved road.
	1.7 ▲		Trail ends at exit 343 on I-40.
			GPS: N35°15.58' W109°16.72'
▼ 0.1		SO	Road is now graded dirt. Track on left and right.
	1.6 ▲	SO	Track on left and right. Road is now paved.
▼ 0.6		TR	Turn right at T-intersection onto Big Arrow Road (unmarked); track ahead into private property.
	1.1 ▲	TL	Turn left on unmarked graded road; track on right into private property.
			GPS: N35°15.83' W109°17.24'
▼ 0.7		SO	Two graded roads on left.
	1.0 ▲	SO	Two graded roads on right.
▼ 0.8		SO	Graded road on right and many tracks on right and left into private property.
	0.9 ▲	SO	Graded road on left and many tracks on right and left into private property.
▼ 1.3		SO	Track on right; then cross over Querino Wash on bridge.
	0.4 ▲	SO	Cross over Querino Wash on bridge; then track on left.
			GPS: N35°16.30' W109°16.54'
▼ 1.7		TL	Turn left onto graded dirt road. The Querino Trading Post is at the intersection and there is a wooden sign for Pine Lake and Burnt Water. Zero trip meter.
	0.0 ▲		Continue to the southwest.
			GPS: N35°16.43' W109°16.24'
▼ 0.0			Continue to the northwest.
	2.9 ▲	TR	T-intersection at the Querino Trading Post; turn right onto graded dirt road and zero trip meter.
▼ 0.1		SO	Track on right.
	2.8 ▲	SO	Track on left.
▼ 0.6		SO	Two tracks on right.
	2.3 ▲	SO	Two tracks on left.
▼ 0.7		SO	Track on right.
	2.2 ▲	SO	Track on left.
▼ 1.3		SO	Two tracks on right.
	1.6 ▲	SO	Two tracks on left.
▼ 1.8		SO	Track on right.
	1.1 ▲	SO	Track on left.
▼ 2.0		SO	Track on right.
	0.9 ▲	SO	Track on left.
▼ 2.9		SO	Graded road on right; graded road on left and track on left. Continue straight on, following the sign for Pine Springs. Zero trip meter.
	0.0 ▲		Continue to the southeast.
			GPS: N35°18.72' W109°17.66'
▼ 0.0			Continue to the north.
	6.4 ▲	SO	Graded road on left; graded road on right and track on right. Zero trip meter.
▼ 0.1		SO	Track on left.
	6.3 ▲	SO	Track on right.
▼ 0.2		SO	Track on left.
	6.2 ▲	SO	Track on right.

▼ 0.9 SO Track on left and track on right.
5.5 ▲ SO Track on left and track on right.

▼ 1.2 SO Graded road on right and track on left.
5.2 ▲ SO Graded road on left and track on right.

▼ 1.5 SO Track on left.
4.9 ▲ SO Track on right.

▼ 2.7 BL Graded road on right.
3.7 ▲ SO Graded road on left.

GPS: N35°21.15′ W109°17.52′

▼ 3.1 SO Track on right.
3.3 ▲ SO Track on left.

▼ 4.0 SO Major graded road on left.
2.4 ▲ BL Major graded road on right.

GPS: N35°22.31′ W109°17.79′

▼ 4.3 SO Track on left.
2.1 ▲ SO Track on right.

▼ 4.6 SO Track on right.
1.8 ▲ SO Track on left.

▼ 4.8 SO Track on right and track on left.
1.6 ▲ SO Track on left and track on right.

▼ 5.2 SO Track on left.
1.2 ▲ SO Track on right.

▼ 5.8 SO Track on right.
0.6 ▲ SO Track on left.

▼ 6.3 SO Pine Springs. Water tower on left; track on left and track on right.
0.1 ▲ SO Water tower on right; track on left and track on right. Leaving Pine Springs.

GPS: N35°24.24′ W109°16.80′

▼ 6.4 BL Bear left at fork onto Oak Ridge Road. Pine Springs Road continues ahead. Zero trip meter.
0.0 ▲ Continue to the south.

GPS: N35°24.37′ W109°16.73′

▼ 0.0 Continue to the north.
9.3 ▲ Bear right onto Pine Springs Road and enter Pine Springs. Zero trip meter.

▼ 0.2 SO Track on right.
9.1 ▲ SO Track on left.

▼ 0.6 SO Track on right.
8.7 ▲ SO Track on left.

▼ 0.9 SO Track on left.
8.4 ▲ SO Track on right.

▼ 1.0 SO Track on left and track on right.
8.3 ▲ SO Track on right and track on left.

▼ 1.6 SO Track on right.

Crossing through mature pines on the quiet Defiance Plateau

7.7 ▲ SO Track on left.

▼ 1.7 SO Graded road on right.
7.6 ▲ SO Graded road on left.

▼ 3.6 SO Two tracks on right; then track on left.
5.7 ▲ SO Track on right; then two tracks on left.

▼ 4.1 SO Track on right.
5.2 ▲ SO Track on left.

▼ 5.2 SO Track on right.
4.1 ▲ SO Track on left.

▼ 5.9 SO Track on right.
3.4 ▲ SO Track on left.

▼ 6.4 SO Two tracks on right and track on left; then cross through wash.
2.9 ▲ SO Cross through wash; then track on right and two tracks on left.

GPS: N35°30.02′ W109°18.06′

▼ 6.5 SO Track on left to Antelope Well.
2.8 ▲ SO Track on right to Antelope Well.

▼ 6.6 SO Track on left.
2.7 ▲ SO Track on right.

▼ 7.1 SO Track on left.
2.2 ▲ SO Track on right.

▼ 7.6 SO Track on left to well and tank.
1.7 ▲ SO Track on right to well and tank.

GPS: N35°31.18′ W109°18.66′

▼ 7.8 SO Track on right.
1.5 ▲ SO Track on left.

▼ 7.9 SO Track on left and track on right.
1.4 ▲ SO Track on right and track on left.

▼ 8.0 SO Two tracks on left.
1.3 ▲ SO Two tracks on right.

▼ 8.2 SO Two tracks on right.
1.1 ▲ SO Two tracks on left.

▼ 8.7 SO Track on left.
0.6 ▲ SO Track on right.

▼ 9.2 SO Track on right.
0.1 ▲ SO Track on left.

▼ 9.3 TR Major staggered intersection. Turn right at the sign for Banana Wash Road at major graded road intersection. Graded road straight on is South Summit Road; bear right, remaining on the major graded road. Zero trip meter.
0.0 ▲ Continue to the southeast.

GPS: N35°32.48′ W109°19.34′

▼ 0.0 Continue to the northeast; second track on left.
6.0 ▲ TL Track on right; then South Summit Road goes to the right. Bear left; then turn left on Oak Ridge Road. Banana Wash Road signed to Antelope is straight on at this point. Zero trip meter.

▼ 0.1 SO Track on right.
5.9 ▲ SO Track on left.

▼ 0.2 SO Track on right.
5.8 ▲ SO Track on left.

▼ 0.5 SO Track on right and track on left.
5.5 ▲ SO Track on left and track on right.

▼ 1.0 SO Track on right.
5.0 ▲ SO Track on left.

▼ 1.6 SO Track on left.
4.4 ▲ SO Track on right.

▼ 1.9 SO Track on left.
4.1 ▲ SO Track on right.

▼ 2.0 SO Track on right.
4.0 ▲ SO Track on left.

▼ 2.2 SO Track on left.

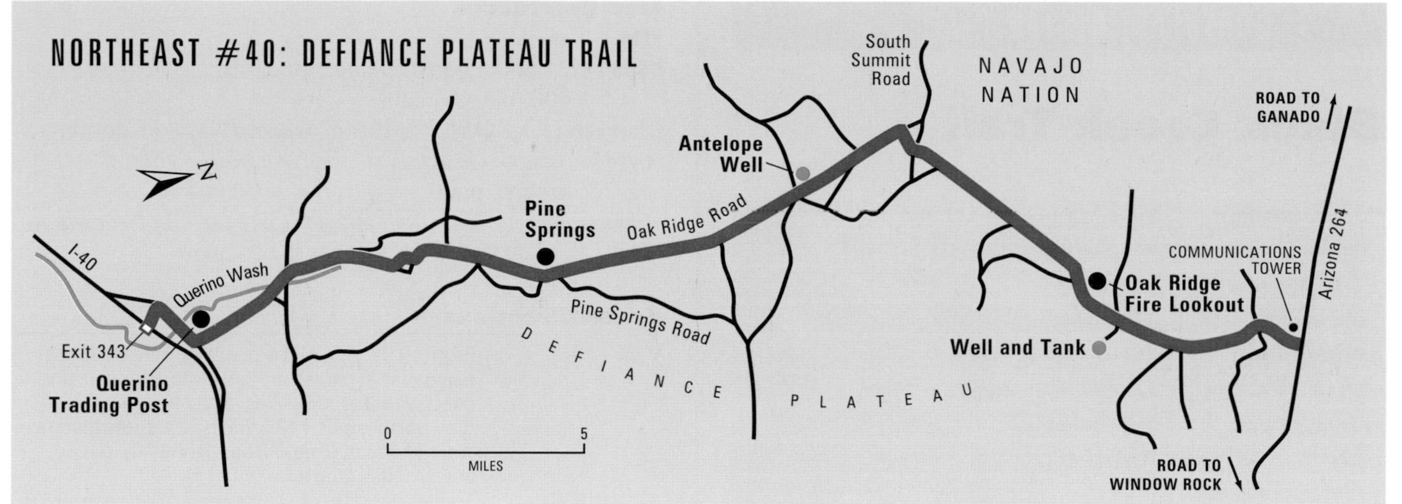

3.8 ▲ SO Track on right.

▼ 2.4 SO Track on right.
3.6 ▲ SO Track on left.

▼ 2.7 SO Track on left.
3.3 ▲ SO Track on right.

▼ 2.8 SO Track on left.
3.2 ▲ SO Track on right.

▼ 2.9 SO Two tracks on right and track on left.
3.1 ▲ SO Track on right and two tracks on left.

▼ 3.5 SO Track on right.
2.5 ▲ SO Track on left.

▼ 3.6 SO Two tracks on right and track on left.
2.4 ▲ SO Two tracks on left and track on right.

▼ 3.8 SO Track on right; then cross over gas pipeline.
2.2 ▲ SO Cross over gas pipeline; then track on left.

GPS: N35°34.89′ W109°16.36′

▼ 4.3 SO Track on left.
1.7 ▲ SO Track on right.

▼ 5.3 SO Track on left.
0.7 ▲ SO Track on right.

▼ 5.7 SO Track on left.
0.3 ▲ SO Track on right.

▼ 6.0 SO Track on right; then track on left signed to Oak Ridge Lookout. Zero trip meter.
0.0 ▲ Continue to the southwest.

GPS: N35°36.07′ W109°14.48′

▼ 0.0 Continue to the northeast.
6.0 ▲ SO Track on right signed to Oak Ridge Lookout; then track on left. Zero trip meter.

▼ 0.1 SO Track on right.
5.9 ▲ SO Track on left.

▼ 0.3 SO Track on right.
5.7 ▲ SO Track on left.

▼ 0.5 SO Pass under power lines; then track on right and track on left alongside gas pipeline.
5.5 ▲ SO Track on right and track on left alongside gas pipeline; then pass under power lines.

GPS: N35°36.27′ W109°13.97′

▼ 1.3 SO Track on right to well and tank and track on left.
4.7 ▲ SO Track on left to well and tank and track on right.

GPS: N35°36.79′ W109°13.41′

▼ 1.8 SO Track on left.
4.2 ▲ SO Track on right.

▼ 1.9 SO Track on right.
4.1 ▲ SO Track on left.

▼ 2.2 SO Track on right.
3.8 ▲ SO Track on left.

▼ 2.6 SO Two tracks on right.
3.4 ▲ SO Two tracks on left.

▼ 2.9 SO Two tracks on right.
3.1 ▲ SO Two tracks on left.

▼ 3.1 SO Track on right.
2.9 ▲ SO Track on left.

▼ 3.2 SO Track on right and track on left.
2.8 ▲ SO Track on right and track on left.

▼ 3.4 SO Track on left.
2.6 ▲ SO Track on right.

▼ 3.8 SO Track on left.
2.2 ▲ SO Track on right.

▼ 4.1 SO Track on right.
1.9 ▲ SO Track on left.

▼ 4.3 SO Track on right and track on left.
1.7 ▲ SO Track on right and track on left.

▼ 4.7 SO Track on left and track on right.
1.3 ▲ SO Track on left and track on right.

▼ 4.8 SO Track on left.
1.2 ▲ SO Track on right.

▼ 5.0 SO Track on left.
1.0 ▲ SO Track on right.

▼ 5.3 SO Track on left and track on right.
0.7 ▲ SO Track on left and track on right.

▼ 5.4 SO Track on right to communications tower.
0.6 ▲ SO Track on left to communications tower.

GPS: N35°40.33′ W109°12.48′

▼ 5.5 SO Track on right and track on left to communications tower.
0.5 ▲ SO Track on left and track on right to communications tower.

▼ 5.6 SO Track on right and track on left.
0.4 ▲ SO Track on left and track on right.

▼ 6.0 Trail ends at the T-intersection with paved Arizona 264. Turn right for St. Michaels and Window Rock; turn left for Ganado.
0.0 ▲ From Arizona 264, 5.1 miles west of St. Michaels and 1.5 miles west of mile marker 468, zero trip meter and turn south over cattle guard on graded dirt road toward communications towers.

GPS: N35°40.72′ W109°12.25′

NORTHEAST REGION TRAIL #41

Black Creek Trail

Starting Point:	**Intersection of IR 112 and IR 7**
Finishing Point:	**IR 12 near Red Lake**
Total Mileage:	**11.6 miles**
Unpaved Mileage:	**11.2 miles**
Driving Time:	**45 minutes**
Elevation Range:	**7,000–7,200 feet**
Usually Open:	**Year-round**
Best Time to Travel:	**Dry weather**
Difficulty Rating:	**1**
Scenic Rating:	**8**
Remoteness Rating:	**+0**

Special Attractions

- Easy trail running along a wide, scenic valley.
- Camping and fishing at Red Lake.

Description

This graded road runs along Black Creek Valley, parallel to paved Indian Road 12. It is a well-used road because it accesses several houses. The valley is wide and shallow, and the meandering, often dry Black Creek is to the east. The Chuska Mountains are to the east of the valley, just across the state line in New Mexico.

The trail ends on Indian Road 12 a short distance into New Mexico, at the entrance to Red Lake, a popular fishing and camping place. For more information on Red Lake, refer to Northeast #42: Red Valley Trail.

Current Road Information

Navajo Nation Parks and Recreation
PO Box 9000
Window Rock, AZ 86515
(520) 871-6647

Black Creek Valley with the Chuska Mountains in the distance

Map References

BLM Ganado
USGS 1:24,000 Fort Defiance, Buell Park
1:100,000 Ganado
Maptech CD-ROM: Northeast Arizona/Navajo County
Arizona Atlas & Gazetteer, p. 35; *New Mexico Atlas & Gazetteer,* p. 20
Arizona Road & Recreation Atlas, p. 37 & p. 71; *New Mexico Road & Recreation Atlas,* p. 10 & p. 34

Route Directions

▼ 0.0		From IR 12, 1.7 miles north of Fort Defiance, turn west at the stop light onto IR 7 and proceed west for 1.5 miles. Zero trip meter and turn north on IR 112, which is a short distance west of Black Creek. Road is initially paved; cross cattle guard.
10.6 ▲		Trail ends at the 4-way intersection with IR 7. Cross cattle guard and then turn left onto IR 7; proceed for 1.5 miles to stoplight. Turn right at stoplight for Fort Defiance.
		GPS: N35°45.62' W109°04.30'
▼ 0.3	SO	Road is now graded dirt. Many tracks on right and left to houses. Remain on main road.
10.3 ▲		Road is now paved.
▼ 1.7	SO	Track on right to well and tank.
8.9 ▲	SO	Track on left to well and tank.
		GPS: N35°46.98' W109°03.35'
▼ 2.4	SO	Well-used track on left and small track on right.
8.2 ▲	SO	Well-used track on right and small track on left.
▼ 2.9	SO	Track on left.
7.7 ▲	SO	Track on right.
▼ 4.6	SO	Track on right.
6.0 ▲	SO	Track on left.
▼ 4.9	SO	Two tracks on right and track on left.
5.7 ▲	SO	Two tracks on left and track on right.
▼ 5.5	SO	Track on right.
5.1 ▲	SO	Track on left.
▼ 5.7	SO	Track on right.
4.9 ▲	SO	Track on left.
▼ 6.9	SO	Track on right.
3.7 ▲	SO	Track on left.
		GPS: N35°51.40' W109°02.97'
▼ 7.0	SO	Graded road on right.
3.6 ▲	SO	Graded road on left.
		GPS: N35°51.50' W109°03.05'
▼ 7.8	SO	Track on right.
2.8 ▲	SO	Track on left.
▼ 8.1	SO	Cross over irrigation ditch; tracks on left and right along ditch.
2.5 ▲	SO	Cross over irrigation ditch; tracks on left and right along ditch.
▼ 9.1	SO	Track on left.
1.5 ▲	SO	Track on right.
▼ 9.6	SO	Cross over irrigation ditch.
1.0 ▲	SO	Cross over irrigation ditch.
▼ 10.6	TR	Trail intersection with large graded dirt road. Also road ahead. Zero trip meter and turn right toward the town of Navajo.
0.0 ▲		Continue to the south.
		GPS: N35°54.51' W109°02.79'
▼ 0.0		Continue to the northeast.

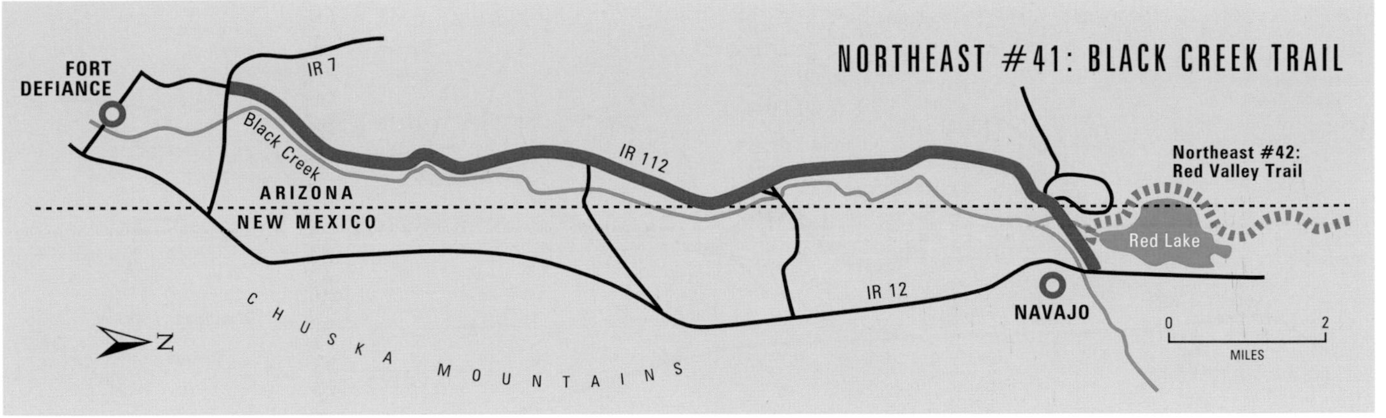

Mileage		Action	Directions
	1.0 ▲	TL	Turn left onto graded dirt road at unmarked intersection. Also track on right over cattle guard. Zero trip meter.
▼ 0.1		SO	Track on right; then cross over Black Creek.
	0.9 ▲	SO	Cross over Black Creek; then track on left.
▼ 0.4		SO	Track on right.
	0.6 ▲	SO	Track on left.
▼ 0.5		SO	Cross over drainage ditch.
	0.5 ▲	SO	Cross over drainage ditch.
▼ 0.9		SO	Track on left goes across the dam wall of Red Lake and is the start of Northeast #42: Red Valley Trail.
	0.1 ▲	SO	Track on right goes across the dam wall of Red Lake and is the start of Northeast #42: Red Valley Trail.
			GPS: N35°54.99' W109°01.95'
▼ 1.0			Trail ends at the intersection with IR 12. Turn right for Fort Defiance.
	0.0 ▲		The trail starts on IR 12, 13.3 miles north of Fort Defiance. The trail begins in New Mexico but crosses into Arizona almost immediately. The state line is unmarked. Zero trip meter.
			GPS: N35°55.05' W109°01.90'

NORTHEAST REGION TRAIL #42

Red Valley Trail

Starting Point:	**Northeast #41: Black Creek Trail, IR 112, near Red Lake**
Finishing Point:	**Intersection with Northeast #43: Sawmill Navajo Trail, IR 72**
Total Mileage:	**7.5 miles**
Unpaved Mileage:	**7.5 miles**
Driving Time:	**1 hour**
Elevation Range:	**7,100–7,300 feet**
Usually Open:	**Year-round**
Best Time to Travel:	**Dry weather**
Difficulty Rating:	**3**
Scenic Rating:	**8**
Remoteness Rating:	**+0**

Special Attractions

Fishing for catfish at Red Lake.
Camping opportunities near Red Lake.

Description

Red Lake is very popular with fishermen. It is one of the best places to catch catfish in the Navajo Nation. The lake, set in a wide valley under the shadow of the Chuska Mountains to the east in New Mexico, has several miles of grassy shoreline interspersed with marshy banks and some rocky outcrops. This trail commences by crossing the rutted track that leads across

Red Lake, noted for its catfish

the top of the dam at the south end of the lake. The deep ruts show that this area is extremely muddy and best avoided in wet weather—a good policy for the entire trail.

Once on the west side of the dam wall, the trail runs northward around the lakeshore. There are numerous pull-ins for fishermen and campers. A tribal fishing permit is essential if you are planning to fish; for night fishing, a camping permit is required as well.

The north end of the lake is quieter than the south. The trail, which gradually travels along Red Valley, is unmarked once it leaves the lake; a plethora of small trails crisscross the main trail. For the most part, the best-used trail is the correct one, but there are a couple of turns that will keep navigators on their toes. In particular the 4-way intersection at the zero trip meter point approximately halfway along the trail is easily missed, especially in the reverse direction.

The trail continues up Red Valley, giving views over the

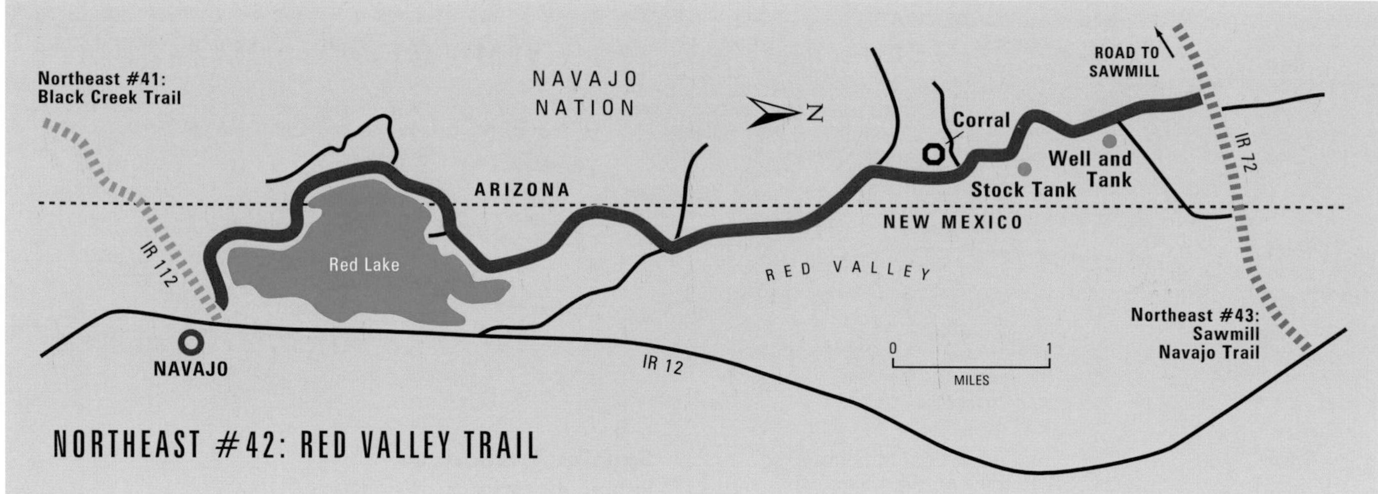

Chuska Mountains to the east and Sonsela Buttes to the north. It finishes at the intersection with Northeast #43: Sawmill Navajo Trail, Indian Road 72. From here, Indian Road 12, a paved road, is 1.8 miles to the east.

Current Road Information

Navajo Nation Parks and Recreation
PO Box 9000
Window Rock, AZ 86515
(520) 871-6647

Map References

BLM Ganado,
USGS 1:24,000 Buell Park, Sonsela Buttes
1:100,000 Ganado
Maptech CD-ROM: Northeast Arizona/Navajo County
Arizona Atlas & Gazetteer, p. 35; *New Mexico Altas & Gazetteer,* p. 20

Route Directions

▼ 0.0		0.1 miles from the western end of Northeast #41: Black Creek Trail at Red Lake, zero trip meter and turn west across the cattle guard and start to cross the dam wall at the south end of Red Lake.
4.0 ▲		Cattle guard; then trail ends at the intersection with Northeast #41: Black Creek Trail. Turn right to follow Black Creek Trail to Fort Defiance. Turn left and travel 0.1 miles to join IR 12, the paved road to Fort Defiance.
		GPS: N35°54.99' W109°01.95'
▼ 0.5	BR	Bear right off dam wall and wrap north along the lakeshore.
3.5 ▲	BL	Bear left and start to cross the dam wall.
▼ 1.0	BL	Track on right stays close to lakeshore and goes to pull-ins and fishing spots. Bear left up hill.
3.0 ▲	BR	Track on left stays close to lakeshore and goes to pull-ins and fishing spots. Bear right and continue along the lakeshore.
		GPS: N35°55.46' W109°02.60'
▼ 1.1	SO	Track on left and track on right on crest of hill.
2.9 ▲	SO	Track on left and track on right on crest of hill.
▼ 1.2	SO	Track on right.
2.8 ▲	SO	Track on left.
▼ 1.7	BR	Track on left through gate; bear right, remaining along lakeshore.
2.3 ▲	SO	Track on right through gate; continue on around the lakeshore.
		GPS: N35°55.88' W109°02.96'
▼ 1.8	BR	Track on left.
2.2 ▲	BL	Track on right.
▼ 2.1	SO	Track on right.
1.9 ▲	SO	Track on left.
		GPS: N35°56.20' W109°02.76'
▼ 2.3	SO	Track on right on slight rise.
1.7 ▲	SO	Track on left on slight rise.
▼ 2.4	SO	Track on right.
1.6 ▲	SO	Track on left.
		GPS: N35°56.33' W109°02.51'
▼ 2.7	BL	Two tracks on right; bear left across cattle guard; then track on right.
1.3 ▲	BR	Track on left; then cattle guard; then bear right past two tracks on left.
		GPS: N35°56.47' W109°02.31'
▼ 2.9	SO	Track on right.
1.1 ▲	SO	Track on left.
▼ 3.3	SO	Track on right.

The trail heading toward the Chuska Mountains

▼	▲		
	0.7 ▲	BR	Track on left.
▼ 3.4		SO	Cattle guard.
	0.6 ▲	SO	Cattle guard.
▼ 3.9		BL	Track on right.
	0.1 ▲	SO	Track on left.
▼ 4.0		TL	4-way intersection. Turn left onto slightly larger trail. Zero trip meter. Intersection is unmarked.
	0.0 ▲		Continue to the southwest.
			GPS: N35°57.49′ W109°02.42′
▼ 0.0			Continue to the north; track on right.
	2.9 ▲	BR	Bear right onto well-used trail; track on left; then turn immediately right onto well-used, smaller trail heading southwest. Zero trip meter.
▼ 0.1		BR	Track on left.
	2.8 ▲	SO	Track on right.
▼ 0.4		SO	Track on right and track on left.
	2.5 ▲	SO	Track on left and track on right.
▼ 0.7		SO	Faint track on right.
	2.2 ▲	SO	Faint track on left.
▼ 0.9		SO	Faint track on right.
	2.0 ▲	SO	Faint track on left.
▼ 1.3		BR	Track on left; bear right and cross cattle guard.
	1.6 ▲	BL	Cross cattle guard; then bear left past track on right.
			GPS: N35°58.62′ W109°02.94′
▼ 1.7		BR	Track on left to corral and sheds.
	1.2 ▲	SO	Track on right to corral and sheds.
▼ 1.9		SO	Track on left and track on right.
	1.0 ▲	SO	Track on right and track on left.
			GPS: N35°59.09′ W109°02.74′
▼ 2.2		SO	Track on right; then cattle guard.
	0.7 ▲	SO	Cattle guard; then track on left.
▼ 2.3		SO	Stock tank on right.
	0.6 ▲	SO	Stock tank on left.
▼ 2.4		SO	Track on right and track on left.
	0.5 ▲	SO	Track on left and track on right.
▼ 2.7		SO	Track on left.
	0.2 ▲	BL	Track on right.
▼ 2.9		SO	Well and tank on right; track on right and track on left. Zero trip meter.
	0.0 ▲		Continue to the south.
			GPS: N35°59.93′ W109°03.31′
▼ 0.0			Continue to the north.
	0.6 ▲	SO	Well and tank on left; track on right and track on left. Zero trip meter.
▼ 0.2		SO	Track on right.
	0.4 ▲	SO	Track on left.
▼ 0.4		SO	Track on left.
	0.2 ▲	SO	Track on right.
▼ 0.6		SO	Trail ends at the intersection with Northeast #43: Sawmill Navajo Trail (IR 72). Turn right to exit to IR 12; turn left to continue along the trail to Sawmill. There is also a track straight ahead.
	0.0 ▲		Trail starts on Northeast #43: Sawmill Navajo Trail (IR 72), 1.8 miles from the intersection with IR 12 (the eastern end of the trail). Zero trip meter and turn south on the unmarked, formed trail. A well and tank can be seen a short distance down the trail. There is also a track to the north.
			GPS: N36°00.40′ W109°03.58′

NORTHEAST REGION TRAIL #43

Sawmill Navajo Trail

Starting Point:	**IR 12, 0.2 miles north of mile marker 49**
Finishing Point:	**IR 7 at Sawmill**
Total Mileage:	**12.3 miles**
Unpaved Mileage:	**12.3 miles**
Driving Time:	**1 hour**
Elevation Range:	**7,200–8,000 feet**
Usually Open:	**Year-round**
Best Time to Travel:	**Dry weather**
Difficulty Rating:	**2**
Scenic Rating:	**8**
Remoteness Rating:	**+1**

Special Attractions

■ Great views traveling along a ridge top in the Navajo Nation.

Description

This trail travels through some of the forest areas of the Navajo Nation. The trail leaves Indian Road 12, 7 miles north of the small settlement of Navajo, which is just to the south of Red Lake. The well-used, single-track trail crests a rise and then runs across open Red Valley before entering the forest. Much of the trail travels along a ridge top, giving views east over red rock buttes and the Chuska Mountains. The surface is very rutted and eroded and only suitable for travel in dry weather. The final section of the trail follows a graded dirt road as it emerges from the forest at the settlement of Sawmill.

Crossing Defiance Plateau

Current Road Information

Navajo Nation Parks and Recreation
PO Box 9000
Window Rock, AZ 86515
(520) 871-6647

Map References

BLM Canyon de Chelly, Ganado
USGS 1:24,000 Sonsela Buttes, Buell Park, Sawmill
1:100,000 Canyon de Chelly, Ganado
Maptech CD-ROM: Northeast Arizona/Navajo County
Arizona Atlas & Gazetteer, p. 35; *New Mexico Atlas & Gazetteer,* p. 20
Recreational Map of Arizona

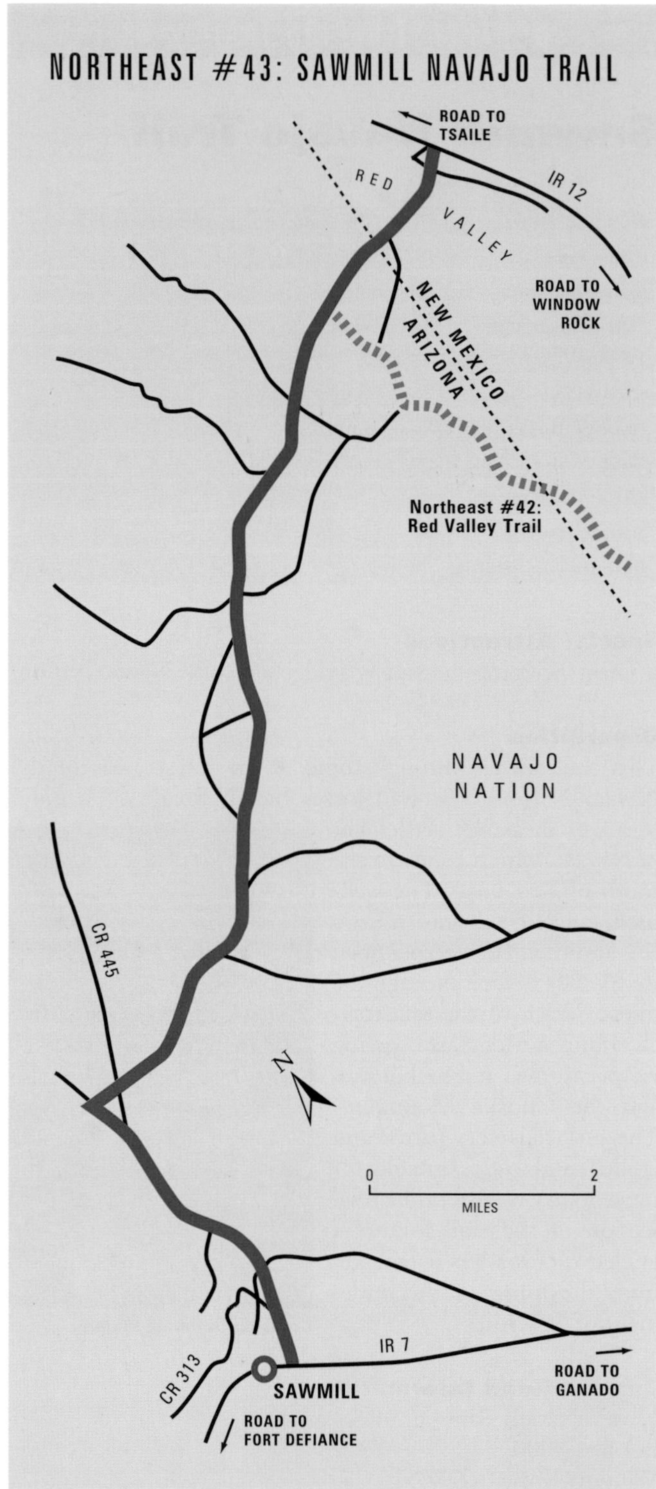

Route Directions

▼ 0.0		Trail commences on IR 12, 7.3 miles north of Navajo. Zero trip meter and turn southwest across cattle guard. Intersection is unmarked but is 0.2 miles north of mile marker 49. Small track opposite.
1.8 ▲		Cattle guard; then trail ends at T-intersection with IR 12. Turn right for Window Rock; turn left for Tsaile.
		GPS: N36°01.02′ W109°01.71′
▼ 0.1	SO	Track on right to house.
1.7 ▲	SO	Track on left to house.
▼ 0.2	SO	Track on right and track on left on top of rise.
1.6 ▲	SO	Track on right and track on left on top of rise.
		GPS: N36°00.88′ W109°01.88′
▼ 0.3	SO	Track on left.
1.5 ▲	SO	Track on right.
▼ 0.5	SO	Track on left.
1.3 ▲	SO	Track on right.
▼ 0.7	SO	Track on left.
1.1 ▲	SO	Track on right.
▼ 0.9	SO	Track on right.
0.9 ▲	SO	Track on left.
▼ 1.0	SO	Faint track on left; then track on right.
0.8 ▲	SO	Track on left; then faint track on right.
▼ 1.3	SO	Track on left.
0.5 ▲	SO	Track on right.
▼ 1.4	SO	Track on right.
0.4 ▲	SO	Track on left.
▼ 1.6	SO	Track on right; then cross through wash.
0.2 ▲	SO	Cross through wash; then track on left.
▼ 1.7	SO	Track on left.
0.1 ▲	SO	Track on right.
▼ 1.8		Track on left is Northeast #42: Red Valley Trail. Zero trip meter.
0.0 ▲		Continue to the northeast.
		GPS: N36°00.40′ W109°03.58′
▼ 0.0		Continue to the southwest.
2.7 ▲		Track on right is Northeast #42: Red Valley Trail. Zero trip meter.
▼ 0.7	BL	4-way intersection. Bear left, leaving two tracks on the right.
2.0 ▲	BR	4-way intersection. Bear right, leaving two tracks on the left.
		GPS: N36°00.03′ W109°04.16′
▼ 0.8	SO	Track on left and track on right.
1.9 ▲	SO	Track on left and track on right.
		GPS: N35°59.95′ W109°04.19′
▼ 1.5	SO	Track on right.
1.2 ▲	SO	Track on left.
▼ 2.1	BL	Track on right.
0.6 ▲	SO	Track on left.
		GPS: N35°59.37′ W109°05.42′
▼ 2.6	SO	Track on right.
0.1 ▲	SO	Track on left.
▼ 2.7	SO	Well-used track on left and track on right in small clearing. Zero trip meter.
0.0 ▲		Continue to the north.
		GPS: N35°58.97′ W109°05.77′
▼ 0.0		Continue to the south.
4.7 ▲	SO	Well-used track on right and track on left in small clearing. Zero trip meter.
▼ 0.3	SO	Track on right.
4.4 ▲	SO	Track on left.
▼ 1.0	SO	Track on right.
3.7 ▲	SO	Track on left.
▼ 1.2	SO	Track on left.
3.5 ▲	SO	Track on right.
▼ 1.9	SO	Track on left; then well-used track on right.
2.8 ▲	SO	Well-used track on left; then track on right.
		GPS: N35°57.52′ W109°06.88′
▼ 2.1	SO	Track on right.

	2.6 ▲	SO	Track on left.
▼ 2.2		SO	Track on right.
	2.5 ▲	BR	Track on left.
▼ 2.3		SO	Track on left.
	2.4 ▲	SO	Track on right.
▼ 2.6		SO	Track on left.
	2.1 ▲	BL	Track on right.
			GPS: N35°57.04' W109°07.26'
▼ 3.0		SO	Track on left.
	1.7 ▲	SO	Track on right.
▼ 3.2		SO	Well-used track on left and small track on right.
	1.5 ▲	SO	Small track on left and well-used track on right.
			GPS: N35°56.77' W109°07.81'
▼ 3.8		SO	Track on left.
	0.9 ▲	BL	Track on right.
▼ 4.5		SO	Two tracks on left.
	0.2 ▲	SO	Two tracks on right.
▼ 4.7		BL	Join larger graded dirt road. Graded dirt road on right is marked CR 445. Zero trip meter.
	0.0 ▲		Continue to the east.
			GPS: N35°56.31' W109°09.35'
▼ 0.0			Continue to the west.
	0.2 ▲	BR	Bear right onto smaller graded dirt road. Larger graded dirt road, CR 445, continues around to the left. Zero trip meter.
▼ 0.2		TL	T-intersection with large, graded gravel road. Zero trip meter.
	0.0 ▲		Continue to the east.
			GPS: N35°56.31' W109°09.61'
▼ 0.0			Continue to the south toward Sawmill.
	2.9 ▲	TR	Turn right onto graded gravel road and zero trip meter. Intersection is unmarked.
▼ 0.1		SO	Track on right.
	2.8 ▲	SO	Track on left.
▼ 0.3		SO	Track on left.
	2.6 ▲	SO	Track on right.
▼ 0.4		SO	Track on left.
	2.5 ▲	SO	Track on right.
▼ 0.8		SO	Track on right.
	2.1 ▲	SO	Track on left.
▼ 1.2		SO	Track on right and track on left.
	1.7 ▲	SO	Track on right and track on left.
▼ 1.5		SO	Graded road on right.
	1.4 ▲	SO	Graded road on left.
▼ 2.0		SO	Well-used track on left and graded road on right.
	0.9 ▲	SO	Graded road on left and well-used track on right.
			GPS: N35°54.59' W109°09.11'
▼ 2.4		SO	Graded road on right is CR 313.
	0.5 ▲	SO	Graded road on left is CR 313.
			GPS: N35°54.26' W109°09.21'
▼ 2.9			Cattle guard; then trail finishes on IR 7 at Sawmill. Turn left for Fort Defiance; turn right for Ganado.
	0.0 ▲		Trail commences on IR 7 at Sawmill. Zero trip meter and turn north on wide graded dirt White Clay Road marked with a road sign. Also sign to White Clay. Immediately cross cattle guard. Turn is 0.2 miles east of mile marker 14.
			GPS: N35°53.81' W109°09.35'

NORTHEAST REGION TRAIL #44

Fluted Rock Road

Starting Point:	**IR 7, 2.5 miles southwest of Sawmill**
Finishing Point:	**Canyon de Chelly Visitor Center**
Total Mileage:	**31.1 miles**
Unpaved Mileage:	**20.6 miles**
Driving Time:	**3 hours**
Elevation Range:	**5,500–8,100 feet**
Usually Open:	**Year-round**
Best Time to Travel:	**Dry weather**
Difficulty Rating:	**2**
Scenic Rating:	**9**
Remoteness Rating:	**+0**

Special Attractions

- South Rim Drive of Canyon de Chelly National Monument.
- Shady forest drive.
- Excellent photo opportunities from many overlooks into Canyon de Chelly.
- Optional 4-rated climb up to Fluted Rock Fire Lookout.

Description

Canyon de Chelly National Monument is one of the biggest attractions within the Navajo Nation and deservedly so. The paved South Rim Drive takes visitors past many overlooks into the canyon, where they can peer down into the red-walled chasm and see farmland and the vehicle trail far below. It also offers glimpses of some of the famous rock formations and ruins, such as Spider Woman Rock and White House Ruin. The rim drive does not equal the trail along the floor of the canyon for a real feel of the nature and life in the canyon, but it complements it well. For those with limited time, it makes a stunning introduction to Canyon de Chelly.

A view into Canyon de Chelly where it joins Canyon del Muerto, with Dog Rock in the foreground

Fluted Rock

The trail starts on Arizona 7, a short distance west of the settlement of Sawmill. Most of the road early on is wide graded dirt. It is very rutted, and in wet weather the clay quickly becomes impassable, even to 4WD vehicles. The section from Sawmill to the South Rim Drive runs mainly through a shady pine forest.

One highlight along this section is the accurately named Fluted Rock. The folds of the rock resemble organ pipes or the fluted edge of a piecrust; hence the name. A short side trail rewards drivers of high-clearance 4WDs with a spectacular view from the top of the rock. The 4-rated trail climbs the north face of Fluted Rock, crossing a loose rocky surface and expanses of the rock itself to the fire lookout perched on the top. When the lookout is manned in fire season, you are usually welcome to climb into the tower. Do be sure that you have the lookout's permission first. As the tower is small, only two visitors at any one time can climb up. The view from the tower is one of the best in the region. The red rock face of the Chuska Mountains can be seen stretching from north to south. Fluted Rock Lake, a small body of water, can be seen to the north in a clearing in the trees, and there are expansive views over the forest toward Canyon de Chelly, although the canyon itself is not distinguishable.

The trail joins the paved South Rim Drive of Canyon de Chelly close to its final point—the overlook of Spider Woman Rock. There are many turns along the trail to overlooks into the canyon. The overlook of White House Ruin is also the trailhead for White House Ruin Trail (1.5 miles each way) and a strenuous hike that descends to the floor of the canyon to the ruin. This is the only trail into the canyon that visitors may take unaccompanied by a Navajo guide.

The trail finishes at Canyon de Chelly National Monument Visitor Center, where you can arrange guide services for journeys into the canyon. There are also interpretive displays. The rangers are active in organizing walks and excellent interpretive talks, many of which are by local Navajo.

Current Road Information

Navajo Nation Parks and Recreation
PO Box 9000
Window Rock, AZ 86515
(520) 871-6647

Map References

BLM Ganado, Canyon de Chelly
USGS 1:24,000 Sawmill, White Rock Wash, Spider Rock, Three Turkey Canyon, Del Muerto, Chinle
1:100,000 Ganado, Canyon de Chelly
Maptech CD-ROM: Northeast Arizona/Navajo County
Arizona Atlas & Gazetteer, p. 35
Arizona Road & Recreation Atlas, pp. 37, 31 & pp. 71, 65
Recreational Map of Arizona

Route Directions

▼ 0.0		From IR 7, 2.5 miles southwest of Sawmill, at a major fork in the road, zero trip meter and turn west on wide graded dirt road. The wide graded road to the south goes to Ganado. The intersection is unmarked. There are some picnic tables under the trees on the right at the intersection.
3.3 ▲		Trail ends at major intersection with graded dirt road on the right that goes to Ganado. Turn right for Ganado; bear left to continue to Sawmill.
		GPS: N35°52.52′ W109°12.14′
▼ 0.6	SO	Track on right.
2.7 ▲	SO	Track on left.
▼ 1.0	SO	Track on right.
2.3 ▲	SO	Track on left.
▼ 1.2	SO	Track on right.
2.1 ▲	SO	Track on left.
▼ 1.6	SO	Track on left.
1.7 ▲	SO	Track on right.
		GPS: N35°52.73′ W109°13.79′
▼ 2.1	SO	Track on right; then track on left.
1.2 ▲	SO	Track on right; then track on left.
		GPS: N35°53.00′ W109°14.25′
▼ 2.3	SO	Track on left and track on right.
1.0 ▲	SO	Track on left and track on right.
▼ 2.8	SO	Track on right; then track on left. Fluted Rock on right.
0.5 ▲	SO	Track on right; then track on left. Fluted Rock on left.

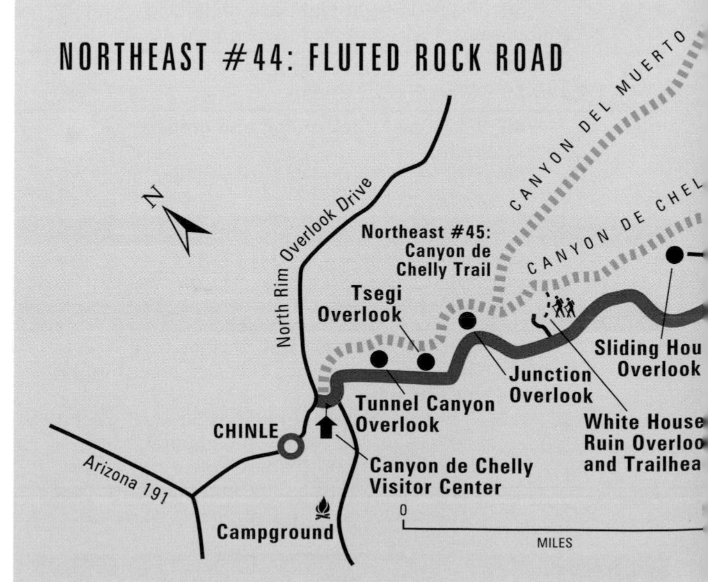

Mileage		Directions
▼ 3.1	SO	Track on left.
0.2 ▲	SO	Track on right.
▼ 3.3	SO	Track on left and graded road on right goes to Fluted Rock Fire Lookout. An old sign marks the turn. Small track on left. Zero trip meter.
0.0 ▲		Continue to the east.
		GPS: N35°52.92′ W109°15.49′
▼ 0.0		Continue to the west.
0.7 ▲	SO	Graded road on left goes to Fluted Rock Fire Lookout. An old sign marks the turn. Track on right; small track on right. Zero trip meter.
▼ 0.2	SO	Track on left.
0.5 ▲	SO	Track on right.
▼ 0.6	SO	Track on right and track on left under power lines.
0.1 ▲	SO	Track on left and track on right under power lines.
▼ 0.7	SO	Graded dirt road on left is IR 9450. Smaller track on right. Zero trip meter.
0.0 ▲		Continue to the south.
		GPS: N35°53.51′ W109°15.82′
▼ 0.0		Continue to the north.
12.1 ▲	SO	Graded road on right is IR 9450. Smaller track on left; continue straight on. Zero trip meter.
▼ 0.2	SO	Track on left.
11.9 ▲	SO	Track on right.
▼ 0.7	SO	Track on left.
11.4 ▲	SO	Track on right.
▼ 1.3	SO	Small track on right.
10.8 ▲	SO	Small track on left.
▼ 1.6	SO	Track on left.
10.5 ▲	SO	Track on right.
▼ 2.4	SO	Track on left.
9.7 ▲	SO	Track on right.
▼ 2.6	SO	Track on right.
9.5 ▲	SO	Track on left.
▼ 2.7	SO	Track on right.
9.4 ▲	SO	Track on left.
▼ 3.3	SO	Track on left.
8.8 ▲	SO	Track on right.
▼ 4.0	SO	Track on left and track on right.
8.1 ▲	SO	Track on left and track on right.
		GPS: N35°57.08′ W109°15.41′
▼ 4.1	SO	Track on right.
8.0 ▲	SO	Track on left.
▼ 4.2	SO	Track on right.
7.9 ▲	SO	Track on left.
▼ 4.3	SO	Track on right.
7.8 ▲	SO	Track on left.
▼ 4.6	SO	Track on left.
7.5 ▲	SO	Track on right.
▼ 4.8	SO	Track on right.
7.3 ▲	SO	Track on left.
▼ 5.1	SO	Track on right.
7.0 ▲	SO	Track on left.
▼ 5.4	SO	Track on left; then track on right.
6.7 ▲	SO	Track on left; then track on right.
▼ 5.5	SO	Track on right and track on left.
6.6 ▲	SO	Track on right and track on left.
		GPS: N35°57.66′ W109°16.84′
▼ 6.0	SO	Track on left.
6.1 ▲	SO	Track on right.
▼ 6.2	SO	Track on right.
5.9 ▲	SO	Track on left.
▼ 6.3	SO	Track on left.
5.8 ▲	SO	Track on right.
▼ 6.4	SO	Track on right.
5.7 ▲	SO	Track on left.
▼ 6.7	SO	Track on left and track on right.
5.4 ▲	SO	Track on left and track on right.
▼ 6.9	SO	Track on right; then track on left.
5.2 ▲	SO	Track on right; then track on left.
▼ 7.1	SO	Track on right.
5.0 ▲	SO	Track on left.
▼ 7.2	SO	Track on right.
4.9 ▲	SO	Track on left.
▼ 7.4	SO	Track on left.
4.7 ▲	SO	Track on right.
▼ 7.6	SO	Track on right.
4.5 ▲	SO	Track on left.
▼ 7.7	SO	Track on right and track on left.

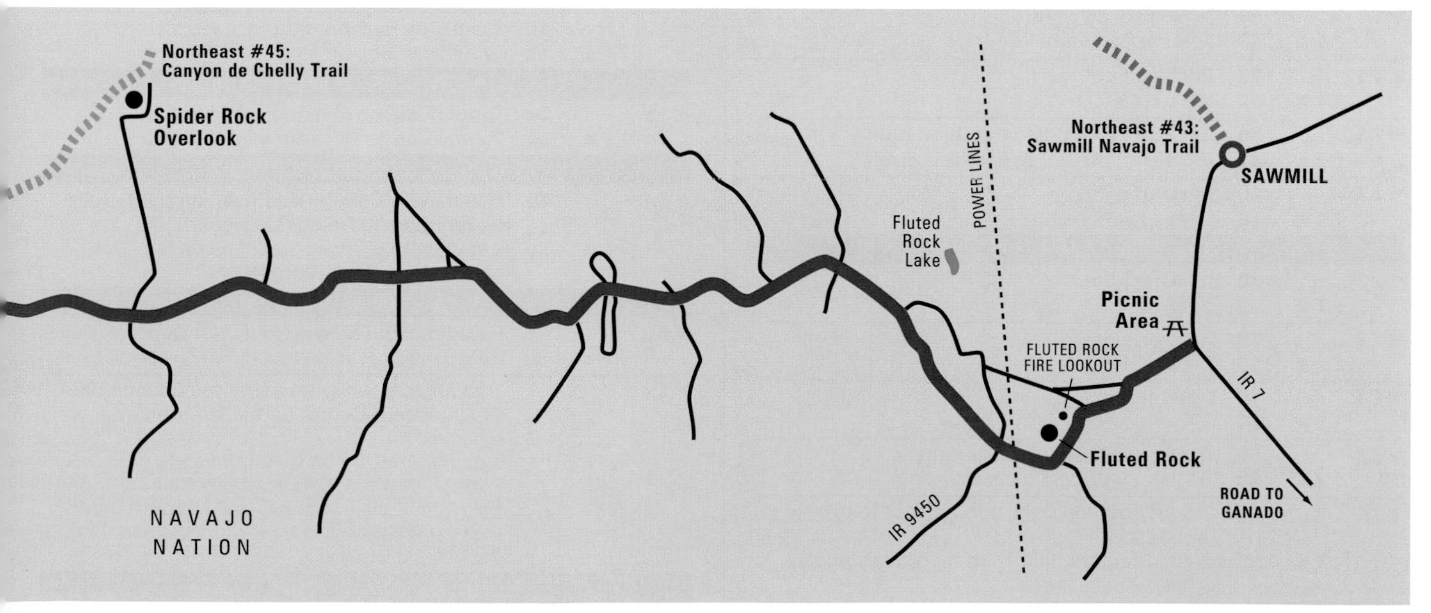

▼	▲		
	4.4 ▲	SO	Track on right and track on left.
▼ 7.9		SO	Track on right and track on left.
	4.2 ▲	SO	Track on right and track on left.
▼ 8.0		SO	Track on left and track on right.
	4.1 ▲	SO	Track on left and track on right.
▼ 8.2		SO	Track on right.
	3.9 ▲	SO	Track on left.
▼ 8.5		SO	Three tracks on right.
	3.6 ▲	SO	Three tracks on left.
▼ 8.7		SO	Track on left.
	3.4 ▲	SO	Track on right.
▼ 8.9		SO	Two tracks on right and two tracks on left; road starts to descend.
	3.2 ▲	SO	Two tracks on right and two tracks on left.
			GPS: N35°59.49' W109°19.30'
▼ 9.5		SO	Track on right.
	2.6 ▲	SO	Track on left.
▼ 10.6		SO	Track on left; then track on right.
	2.5 ▲	SO	Track on left; then track on right.
▼ 11.0		SO	Track on right.
	1.1 ▲	SO	Track on left.
▼ 11.2		SO	Track on left.
	0.9 ▲	SO	Track on right.
▼ 11.3		SO	Track on right.
	0.8 ▲	SO	Track on left.
▼ 11.9		SO	Track on left.
	0.2 ▲	SO	Track on right.
▼ 12.1		SO	Major graded road on right and major graded road on left. The intersection is unmarked. Zero trip meter.
	0.0 ▲		Continue to the southeast.
			GPS: N36°01.70' W109°20.77'
▼ 0.0			Continue to the northwest.
	4.5 ▲	SO	Major graded road on right and major graded road on left. The intersection is unmarked. Zero trip meter.
▼ 0.4		SO	Track on right and track on left.
	4.1 ▲	SO	Track on right and track on left.
▼ 0.7		SO	Track on right.
	3.8 ▲	SO	Track on left.
▼ 0.9		SO	Track on left and track on right.
	3.6 ▲	SO	Track on left and track on right.
▼ 1.0		SO	Two tracks on right.
	3.5 ▲	SO	Two tracks on left.
▼ 1.1		SO	Track on right.
	3.4 ▲	SO	Track on left.
▼ 1.8		SO	Track on left and two tracks on right.
	2.7 ▲	SO	Track on right and two tracks on left.
▼ 2.2		SO	Track on right.
	2.3 ▲	SO	Track on left.
			GPS: N36°02.94' W109°22.48'
▼ 2.3		SO	Track on right.
	2.2 ▲	SO	Track on left.
▼ 2.5		SO	Track on right.
	2.0 ▲	SO	Track on left.
▼ 2.7		SO	Track on right.
	1.8 ▲	SO	Track on left.
▼ 2.8		SO	Track on left and track on right.
	1.7 ▲	SO	Track on right and track on left.
▼ 3.1		SO	Graded road on right; road on left to private property.
	1.4 ▲	SO	Graded road on left; road on right to private property.
			GPS: N36°03.59' W109°22.98'
▼ 3.3		SO	Track on left.
	1.2 ▲	SO	Track on right.
▼ 3.6		SO	Track on left.
	0.9 ▲	SO	Track on right.
▼ 4.5		SO	Paved road on right goes to Spider Rock Overlook (4.3 miles). Join paved road and continue straight on. Zero trip meter.
	0.0 ▲		Continue to the southeast, following the sign to Fort Defiance.
			GPS: N36°04.22' W109°24.41'
▼ 0.0			Continue to the northwest; graded road on left. Remain on paved road, ignoring turns to right and left, most of which go to private property.
	2.3 ▲	SO	Graded road on right; then paved road on left goes to Spider Rock Overlook (4.3 miles). Continue straight on graded dirt road. Zero trip meter.
▼ 2.3		SO	Paved road on right goes to Sliding House Overlook (1.6 miles). Zero trip meter.
	0.0 ▲		Continue to the southeast.
			GPS: N36°05.78' W109°25.93'
▼ 0.0			Continue to the northwest.
	3.4 ▲	SO	Paved road on left goes to Sliding House Overlook (1.6 miles). Zero trip meter.
▼ 3.4		SO	Paved road on right goes to White House Ruin Overlook and to hiking trailhead (0.7 miles). Zero trip meter.
	0.0 ▲		Continue to the east.
			GPS: N36°07.31' W109°28.73'
▼ 0.0			Continue to the west.
	1.4 ▲	SO	Paved road on left goes to White House Ruin Overlook and to hiking trailhead (0.7 miles). Zero trip meter.
▼ 1.4		SO	Paved road on right goes to Junction Overlook (0.1 miles), which overlooks the junction of Canyon de Chelly and Canyon del Muerto. Zero trip meter.
	0.0 ▲		Continue to the east.
			GPS: N36°08.22' W109°29.60'
▼ 0.0			Continue to the west.
	3.4 ▲	SO	Paved road on left goes to Junction Overlook (0.1 miles), which overlooks the junction of Canyon de Chelly and Canyon del Muerto. Zero trip meter.
▼ 1.2		SO	Tsegi Overlook on right.
	2.2 ▲	SO	Tsegi Overlook on left.
			GPS: N36°08.32' W109°30.68'
▼ 1.6		SO	Tunnel Canyon Overlook on right.
	1.8 ▲	SO	Tunnel Canyon Overlook on left.
			GPS: N36°08.57' W109°30.97'
▼ 3.1		SO	Entrance to Canyon de Chelly on right. Road on left goes to free campground.
	0.3 ▲	SO	Entrance to Canyon de Chelly on left. Road on right goes to free campground.
			GPS: N36°08.57' W109°30.97'
▼ 3.3		SO	Paved road on right is North Rim Overlook Drive.
	0.1 ▲	SO	Paved road on left is North Rim Overlook Drive.
▼ 3.4			Trail ends at the entrance to the Canyon de Chelly Visitor Center on the left. Continue on to Chinle.
	0.0 ▲		Trail commences at the entrance to the Canyon de Chelly Visitor Center, which is on the right. Zero trip meter and proceed northeast on the paved road toward the entrance to Canyon de Chelly.
			GPS: N36°09.20' W109°32.35'

NORTHEAST REGION TRAIL #45

Canyon de Chelly Trail

Starting Point:	**Canyon de Chelly Visitor Center**
Finishing Point:	**Canyon de Chelly/Canyon del Muerto**
Total Mileage:	**Approximately 18 miles (one-way) for Canyon de Chelly, add approximately 12 miles (one-way) for Canyon del Muerto**
Unpaved Mileage:	**All unpaved**
Driving Time:	**3 hours minimum for both canyons**
Elevation Range:	**5,500–6,200 feet**
Usually Open:	**May to October**
Best Time to Travel:	**May to October**
Difficulty Rating:	**5**
Scenic Rating:	**10**
Remoteness Rating:	**+0**

Special Attractions

- A rare chance to explore a beautiful canyon in the company of a Navajo guide.
- Many cliff dwellings, pictographs, and petroglyphs.
- Personal guided tour of the canyon in your own vehicle.

History

Canyon de Chelly is best known for its strikingly red, sheer cliffs streaked by desert varnish. Two forces—stream cutting and land uplifting—created the cliff walls of this marvelous canyon. The canyon walls are made of sandstone from the de Chelly Formation, which is more than 200 million years old. The canyon depth ranges from 30 feet to 1,000 feet. Canyon del Muerto, the principal tributary of Canyon de Chelly, received its name when James Stevenson, with a Smithsonian Institution expedition, found the remains of prehistoric Indian burials. The name means "canyon of the dead."

Canyon de Chelly is actually a Spanish corruption of the Navajo word *tsegi* (or *tseyi*), which means "rock canyon" or "in the rock." Over time the pronunciation of the word "de Chelly" has changed from "day shay-yee" to "d'SHAY." Chinle, the name of the town just west of the canyon, comes from another Navajo word, *ch'inli'*, which simply refers to the mouth of the canyon. In 1882, this town began as a trading post but over the years has grown into a larger town, currently serving as the gateway to Canyon de Chelly.

Mummy Cave Ruin in Canyon del Muerto

Canyon de Chelly is as rich in history as it is in beauty. The ruins and rock art of a people referred to as Basketmakers can be found there. These people lived from about 200 B.C. to about A.D. 750. The Basketmaker people made way for the cliff-dwelling Pueblo people, who lived between A.D. 750 and 1300. Drought then ravaged the land, and it is possible that this drought drove the Pueblo people to abandon their cliff dwellings. A myriad of other conjectures have been offered to explain their disappearance, including overcrowding, disease, and war. They scattered across the Southwest, becoming the ancestors for some of Arizona's and New Mexico's Pueblo Indians. The Navajo (see page 92), the next people to inhabit this colorful canyon, arrived around A.D. 1700. Their tranquility was destroyed first by other Indians, then by encroaching Spanish settlers, and finally by the U.S. Army. A year after their defeat in 1863, the Navajo were forced out of their homeland in a bitter march known as "The Long Walk." On June 1, 1868, a peace treaty signed between the Navajo and the United States permitted them to return to their homeland, beautiful Canyon de Chelly.

White House Ruin in Canyon de Chelly

Description

Canyon de Chelly is one of the most spectacular and awe-inspiring settings in Arizona. Part of its magic arises from the towering red sandstone walls and spires, the ancient ruins, and a sandy, winding trail; but Canyon de Chelly is more than just scenery. The Diné, as the Navajo people call themselves, continue to live in the canyon and the surrounding area, and the glimpse that we are allowed into their lives enhances an already special experience.

This trail is different from all the others in this book in that you are not permitted to enter the canyon unless a Navajo guide accompanies you. This requirement includes vehicle touring, hiking, and horseback riding. The only exception to this rule is the White House Ruin Trail, accessed from the South Rim Drive.

There are a variety of tours available. It is possible to sign up for a vehicle tour run by one of the hotels or to hire horses or hike for an hour or several days. For people wishing to enter the canyon via vehicle, the best way is undoubtedly to hire a guide to accompany you in your own 4WD vehicle. The advantages of this arrangement over the hotel-run tours are obvious: flexibility, a more personalized experience, and the fun of driving your own vehicle. The cost is reasonable, and for a family it is

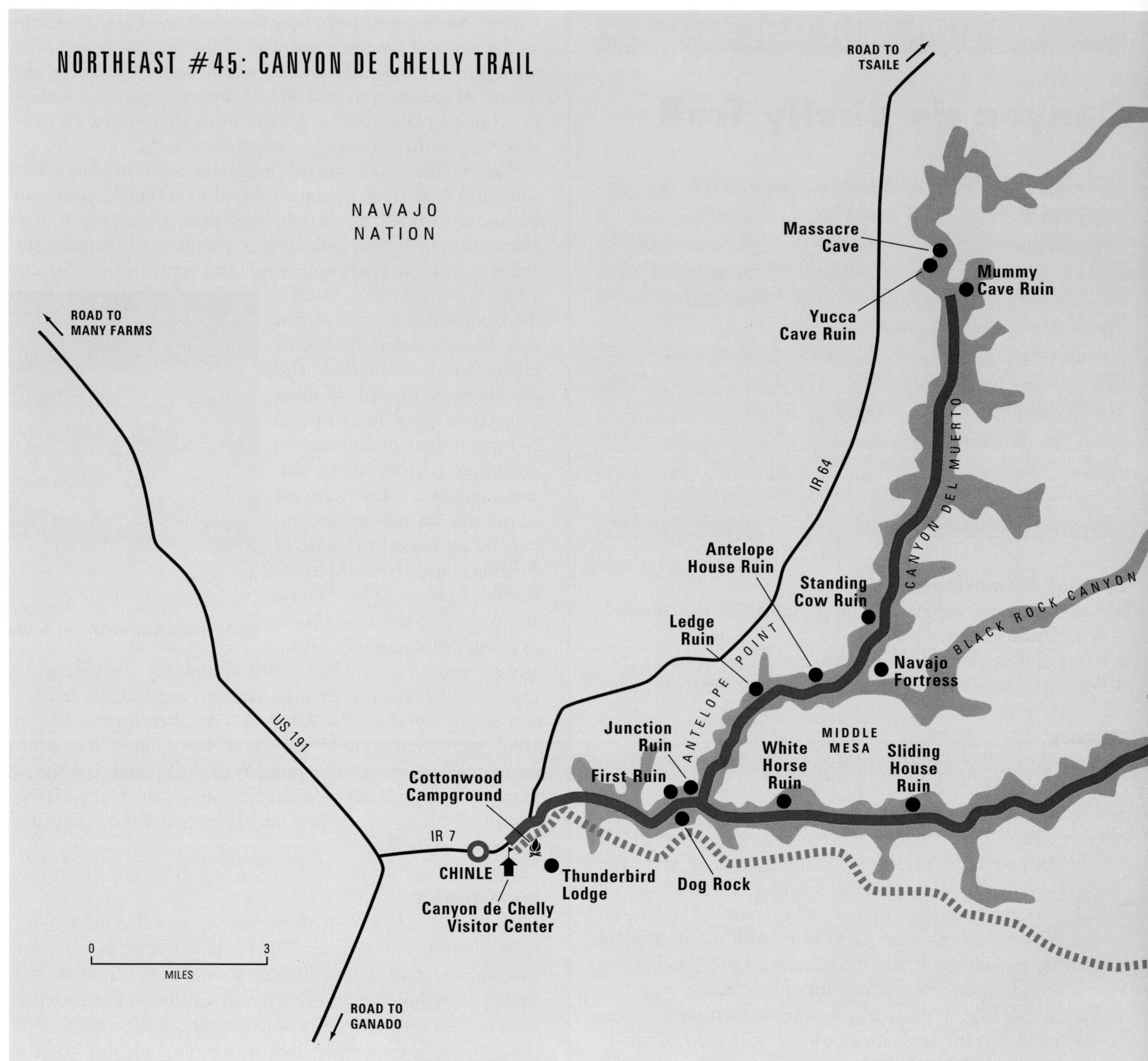

generally less than the hotel tours. Note that pets are not allowed within the canyon, even if confined to a vehicle.

You can arrange for a Navajo guide at the Canyon de Chelly Visitor Center, where you can also see displays on life within the canyon and its history. Usually you do not need to book ahead. The guides are waiting at the center; but if you are visiting on a long weekend or have limited time, it is possible to call ahead. Visitors wanting to take multiday hiking trips must call ahead.

The minimum amount of time required is three hours, which is barely enough to scratch the surface of what the canyon offers. Six hours allows for a leisurely tour to the end of Canyon del Muerto and back and partway up Canyon de Chelly. Both canyons have a lot to offer.

Mile-by-mile details of the trails within both canyons are not given here; they would be redundant because the Navajo guide directs you along the route and explains the features that you will see. Only an overview is given here.

The trail commences a short distance past the visitor center, turning off the paved road into the sandy mouth of the canyon. This first section is what gives the trail its difficulty rating of 5. The sand is very loose and extremely deep and limits this trail to high-clearance 4WD vehicles only. Lower tire pressures are recommended. At this stage the canyon is shallow, but it quickly deepens as you progress.

The intersection of Canyon de Chelly and Canyon del Muerto is reached after 4 miles and you have the choice of continuing in Canyon de Chelly or taking the Canyon del Muerto trail.

In Canyon del Muerto the track becomes easier and the sand

less deep. The trail turns to a formed dirt trail that winds through the deepening canyon, past many cliff dwellings, rock formations, petroglyphs, and pictographs. Your guide will direct you to the best ones. At many of the larger ruins, such as Antelope House Ruin, people (often children) sell jewelry and souvenirs. If you buy from the people in the canyon, all the profits go directly to the Navajo themselves. However, quality can vary widely. The vehicle trail in Canyon del Muerto ends at Mummy Cave, one of the largest ancient Pueblo ruins in the canyon.

Canyon de Chelly is still used by the Navajo for farming, and the trail passes alongside many of the small traditional fields, most planted with corn. Many plots have either a traditional hogan or a smaller, summer shade shelter. The farms in the canyon, which are often only occupied during the summer months, are passed down through the daughters of the family. Farms have to be actively worked if the owner is to retain the holding; another person who has a traditional claim to the area can take possession of any unworked plot. Flocks of sheep and goats and other livestock roam the canyons.

The spur that travels up Canyon de Chelly passes the famous White House Ruin as well as the base of Spider Woman Rock. In either case, you return the way you came in.

Guides charge $15 per hour, with a minimum of three hours. A gratuity is appropriate. One guide can escort multiple vehicles, although for maximum benefit it helps if they are equipped with CB radios to share the commentary.

Current Road Information

Canyon de Chelley National Monument
PO Box 588
Chinle, AZ 86503-0588
(520) 674-5500

Maps References

BLM Canyon de Chelly
USGS 1:24,000 Chinle, Del Muerto, Three Turkey Canyon, Mummy Cave Ruins, Spider Rock
1:100,000 Canyon de Chelly
Maptech CD-ROM: Northeast Arizona/Navajo County
Arizona Atlas & Gazetteer, p. 35
Arizona Road & Recreation Atlas, p. 31 & p. 65
Recreational Map of Arizona
Other: Canyon de Chelly National Monument Park Map

NORTHEAST REGION TRAIL #46

Tunitcha Mountains Trail

Starting Point:	**IR 13, 12.1 miles northeast of the intersection with IR 12**
Finishing Point:	**IR 12, 8 miles south of intersection of IR 12 and IR 64**
Total Mileage:	**18 miles**
Unpaved Mileage:	**18 miles**
Driving Time:	**2 hours**
Elevation Range:	**7,400–9,000 feet**
Usually Open:	**Year-round**
Best Time to Travel:	**Dry weather**
Difficulty Rating:	**2**
Scenic Rating:	**9**
Remoteness Rating:	**+0**

Special Attractions

- Optional 3-rated spur to Roof Butte Fire Lookout.
- Easy trail that travels along the picturesque Tsaile Creek.
- Tsaile Butte and the Tunitcha Mountains.
- Views of Shiprock from the north end of the trail.
- View golden aspen on the north end of the trail in early fall.

Description

This roughly graded road takes you through the green Tunitcha Mountains, part of the larger north-south Chuska Mountains. Along the way, the trail passes through the peaceful rural landscape of the Navajo Nation, offers views of Shiprock and Tsaile Butte, and has an optional 3-rated climb to the fire lookout at Roof Butte.

The trail commences by leaving Indian Road 13 and climbing around the north face of Roof Butte, easily picked out by the communications masts on its summit. As it climbs, the distinctive shape of isolated Shiprock, with its resemblance to a sailing ship in full sail, can be seen just over the border in New Mexico. This section also passes through many stands of aspen; in fall their golden leaves contrast with the green pines to form a tapestry of color.

A lush meadow fed by Tsaile Creek

After 2 miles, a well-used unmarked trail leads north and swiftly climbs to the top of Roof Butte and the communications masts and fire lookout there. This rocky 3-rated spur trail stops at the end of a ridge (1.6 miles); but on the way you will have a clear view of the main trail ahead, winding its way along the valley close to Tsaile Creek. There is a fire lookout on Roof Butte, and when it is manned you are usually welcome to climb the tower with the lookout's permission. This tower is only a few feet above the ground; the height and aspect of Roof Butte obviate the need for a tall tower.

Back on the main trail, the track follows the Tsaile Creek valley, crossing the creek on occasion. Along the way you are likely to see flocks of grazing sheep and goats, either accompanied by mounted shepherds or, more likely, guarded only by shaggy sheepdogs. Small side trails that lead to private property are noted in the route directions only for navigational purposes. Those that lead only to private property have been omitted. Many Navajo live in the peaceful areas off this trail, and you can see their traditional hogans, corrals, and other buildings along the way. Don't be surprised if people stop to see if you are all right or if you need directions along the way. This lightly traveled road sees few visitors.

The end of the spur trail on Roof Butte overlooking Tsaile Creek

NORTHEAST #46: TUNITCHA MOUNTAINS TRAIL

TSAILE
CR 443
IR 12
TSAILE BUTTE
0 2 MILES
Wheatfields Lake

The trail turns toward prominent Tsaile Butte and travels on a smooth gravel road for the last few miles before rejoining Indian Road 12 a few miles south of Tsaile Lake. Campers may take advantage of the campground at Tsaile Lake, and fishermen may fish for trout. Tsaile means "water entering the rock." The town of Tsaile is close to the head of the canyon.

One advantage of this trail is the section of paved road that approaches the north end. If you approach from Chinle, the 12 miles of road that run from Indian Road 12 at Lukachukai (which means "field of reeds") to the start of the trail is one of the most dramatic and picturesque stretches in Arizona. This road climbs through a gap in the red rock face of the Chuska Mountains, passing pillars and cliffs of red sandstone—a landscape more commonly associated with the Sedona region. This stretch used to be a rough, narrow dirt road, but when the trail was surveyed, it was in the middle of extensive works to widen and pave the road. Some of the quiet, intimate character will be lost, but this stretch of road will still rate highly for scenic value in anyone's eyes.

Current Road Information

Navajo Nation Parks and Recreation
PO Box 9000
Window Rock, AZ 86515
(520) 871-6647

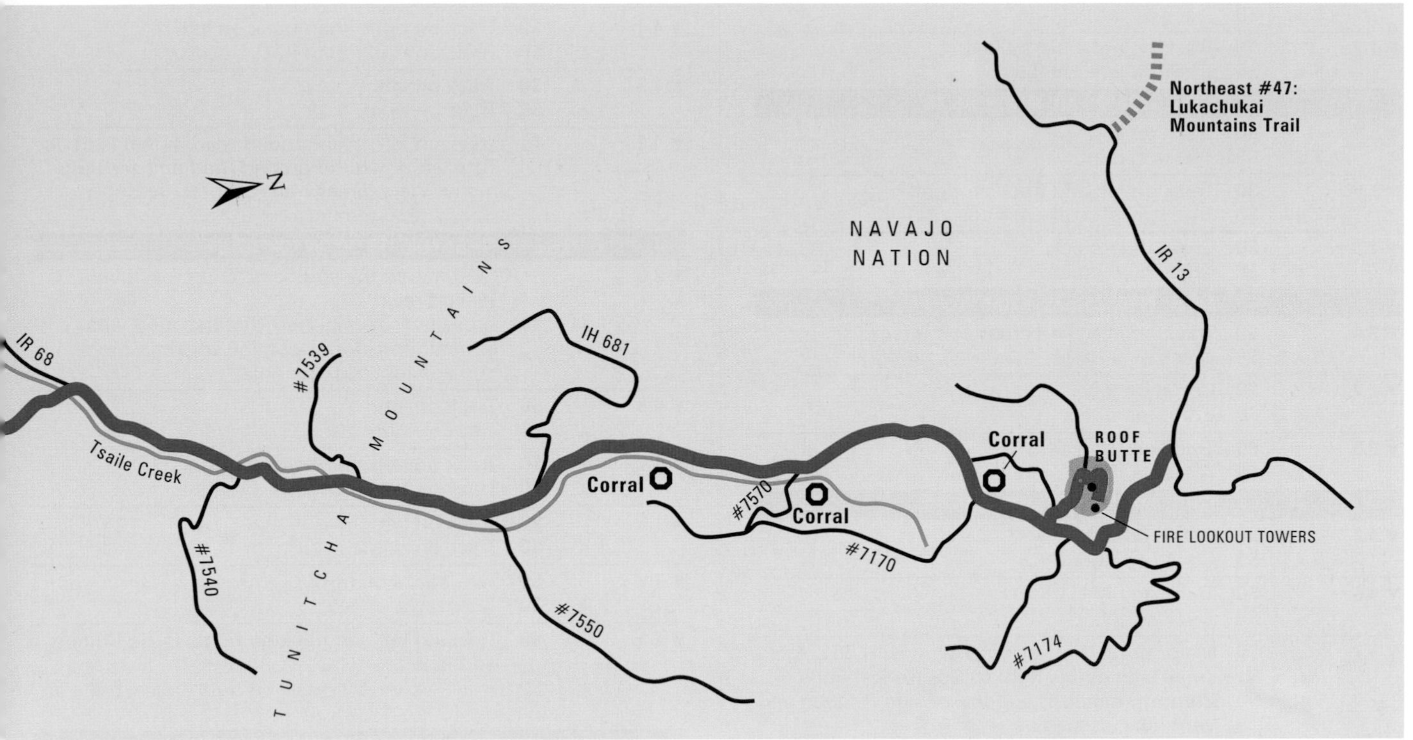

Map References

BLM Canyon de Chelly
USGS 1:24,000 Roof Butte, Tsaile Butte, Tsaile, Lower Wheatfields
1:100,000 Canyon de Chelly
Maptech CD-ROM: Northeast Arizona/Navajo County
Arizona Atlas & Gazetteer, p. 27
Arizona Road & Recreation Atlas, p. 31 & p. 65
Recreational Map of Arizona

Route Directions

▼ 0.0		From IR 13, 12.1 miles northeast of the intersection with IR 12, zero trip meter and turn north across cattle guard on graded dirt road. IR 7500 is painted on a tree at the intersection.
2.0 ▲		Trail ends at the T-intersection with paved IR 13. Turn left for Lukachukai and Tsaile; turn right for Red Rocks.
		GPS: N36°28.40′ W109°05.92′
▼ 1.1	SO	Spring on left; then track on right.
0.9 ▲	SO	Track on left; then spring on right.
▼ 1.2	SO	Track on left.
0.8 ▲	SO	Track on right.
▼ 1.3	SO	Track on left is #7174.
0.7 ▲	SO	Track on right is #7174.
		GPS: N36°27.65′ W109°04.98′
▼ 1.4	SO	Track on left.
0.6 ▲	SO	Track on right.
▼ 1.6	SO	Track on right; then track on left.
0.4 ▲	SO	Track on right; then track on left.
▼ 1.7	SO	Track on left.
0.3 ▲	SO	Track on right.
▼ 2.0	BL	Track on right goes to Roof Butte Fire Lookout (1.6 miles). Zero trip meter. There is no sign, but the turn is well used and in a small clearing. There is a wooden post at the intersection.
0.0 ▲		Continue to the northeast.
		GPS: N36°27.19′ W109°05.29′

Spur to Roof Butte Fire Lookout

▼ 0.0		Turn north on the unmarked well-used trail and zero trip meter. Immediately small track on left.
		GPS: N36°27.19′ W109°05.29′
▼ 0.1	BR	Track on left.
▼ 0.8	SO	Track on left.
		GPS: N36°27.56′ W109°05.85′
▼ 1.2	SO	Closure gate; open when the tower is manned.
		GPS: N36°27.59′ W109°05.63′
▼ 1.4	SO	Communications towers on right. The fire lookout is on the right.
▼ 1.6	UT	Spur ends at farther towers. Retrace your steps back to the main trail.
		GPS: N36°27.61′ W109°05.55′

Continuation of Main Trail

▼ 0.0		Continue to the southwest.
5.7 ▲	BR	Track on left goes to Roof Butte Fire Lookout (1.6 miles). Zero trip meter. There is no sign but the turn is well used and in a small clearing. There is a wooden post at the intersection.
▼ 0.6	SO	Graded dirt road on left is #7170; corral on right.
5.1 ▲	SO	Graded dirt road on right is #7170; corral on left.
		GPS: N36°26.66′ W109°05.63′
▼ 0.8	SO	Track on right and track on left.
4.9 ▲	SO	Track on right and track on left.
▼ 1.0	SO	Track on right.
4.7 ▲	SO	Track on left.
▼ 1.1	SO	Track on right.

4.6 ▲ SO Track on left.

▼ 1.2 SO Track on right is #7500-N.
4.5 ▲ SO Track on left is #7500-N.

GPS: N36°26.48' W109°06.18'

▼ 1.4 SO Track on left.
4.3 ▲ SO Track on right.

▼ 1.5 SO Track on left and track on right.
4.2 ▲ SO Track on left and track on right.

▼ 2.3 SO Cross over creek.
3.4 ▲ SO Cross over creek.

GPS: N36°25.57' W109°06.33'

▼ 2.4 SO Track on left; then cross over creek.
3.3 ▲ SO Cross over creek; then track on right.

▼ 2.7 SO Corral on left.
3.0 ▲ SO Corral on right.

▼ 2.9 SO Track on left is #7570.
2.8 ▲ SO Track on right is #7570.

GPS: N36°25.09' W109°06.15'

▼ 4.2 SO Corral on left.
1.5 ▲ SO Corral on right.

▼ 4.6 SO Track on right.
1.1 ▲ SO Track on left.

▼ 5.7 SO Major graded road on the right is IH 681. A small sign points right to Geese Nest Pond. Zero trip meter. The highway sign is faded and very difficult to read.
0.0 ▲ Continue to the northwest.

GPS: N36°22.76' W109°06.12'

▼ 0.0 Continue to the southeast; track on left.
4.8 ▲ BR Track on right and major graded road on the left is IH 681. A small sign points right to Roof Butte. Zero trip meter.

▼ 0.4 SO Track on left.
4.4 ▲ SO Track on right.

▼ 0.5 SO Well-used track on left is #7550.
4.3 ▲ BL Well-used track on right is #7550.

GPS: N36°22.30' W109°05.99'

▼ 0.8 SO Track on right.
4.0 ▲ SO Track on left.

▼ 1.3 SO Track on right.
3.5 ▲ SO Track on left.

▼ 1.6 SO Track on left; then track on right is #7539.
3.2 ▲ SO Track on left is #7539; then track on right.

GPS: N36°21.35' W109°06.48'

▼ 1.9 SO Cross over Tsaile Creek.
2.9 ▲ SO Cross over Tsaile Creek.

GPS: N36°21.12' W109°06.55'

▼ 2.1 SO Track on left.
2.7 ▲ SO Track on right.

▼ 2.2 SO Track on right.
2.6 ▲ SO Track on left.

▼ 3.0 SO Track on left is #7540.
1.8 ▲ SO Track on right is #7540.

GPS: N36°20.34' W109°06.77'

▼ 3.1 SO Cross over Tsaile Creek.
1.7 ▲ SO Cross over Tsaile Creek.

▼ 3.2 SO Track on left.
1.6 ▲ SO Track on right.

▼ 3.9 SO Track on right.
0.9 ▲ SO Track on left.

▼ 4.2 SO Track on left.
0.6 ▲ SO Track on right.

▼ 4.4 SO Track on right; then track on left.
0.4 ▲ SO Track on right; then track on left.

▼ 4.5 SO Track on left.
0.3 ▲ SO Track on right.

▼ 4.8 TL Track on left; then graded road on left is IR 68. Turn left down the graded road and zero trip meter. View directly ahead to Tsaile Butte.
0.0 ▲ Continue to the northeast.

GPS: N36°18.90' W109°07.81'

▼ 0.0 Continue to the southeast and cross over Tsaile Creek.
3.1 ▲ TR Cross over creek; then T-intersection with graded road. Turn right and zero trip meter. Immediately track on right.

▼ 0.8 SO Track on left.
2.3 ▲ SO Track on right.

▼ 1.1 SO Track on left; then track on right.
2.0 ▲ SO Track on left; then track on right.

▼ 1.8 SO Track on left.
1.3 ▲ SO Track on right.

▼ 1.9 SO Two tracks on right.
1.2 ▲ SO Two tracks on left.

▼ 2.1 SO Track on left and track on right. Tsaile Butte is on the left.
1.0 ▲ SO Track on left and track on right. Tsaile Butte is on the right.

GPS: N36°17.14' W109°07.64'

▼ 2.8 SO Track on left; then track on right.
0.3 ▲ SO Track on left; then track on right.

▼ 3.0 SO Track on right.
0.1 ▲ SO Track on left.

▼ 3.1 BL Graded road on right is CR 443. Zero trip meter.
0.0 ▲ Continue to the northwest.

GPS: N36°16.34' W109°08.05'

▼ 0.0 Continue to the southeast.
2.4 ▲ BR Graded road on left is CR 443. Zero trip meter.

▼ 0.3 SO Track on left.
2.1 ▲ SO Track on right.

▼ 0.5 SO Track on left.
1.9 ▲ SO Track on right.

▼ 1.0 SO Track on left.
1.4 ▲ SO Track on right.

▼ 1.6 SO Pinnache Lake on right (dry).
0.8 ▲ SO Pinnache Lake on left (dry).

GPS: N36°15.09' W109°07.80'

▼ 2.2 SO Graded road on left.
0.2 ▲ BL Graded road on right; bear left, remaining on IR 19. There is a faded route marker past the junction.

▼ 2.3 SO Cross over wash; then track on left.
0.1 ▲ SO Track on right; then cross over wash.

▼ 2.4 Trail ends at the intersection with paved IR 12. Turn right for Tsaile; turn left for Wheatfields Lake.
0.0 ▲ Trail starts on IR 12. Zero trip meter and turn north on graded dirt road marked #7500. The dirt road has been realigned and the turn is now 0.2 miles north of the original marker to Roof Butte, 0.2 miles north of Wheatfields Chapter house and approximately 3 miles north of Wheatfields Lake.

GPS: N36°14.43' W109°07.72'

NORTHEAST REGION TRAIL #47

Lukachukai Mountains Trail

Starting Point:	**IR 13, 8.5 miles northeast of the intersection with IR 12**
Finishing Point:	**IR 33, in Cove**
Total Mileage:	**11.2 miles**
Unpaved Mileage:	**11.2 miles**
Driving Time:	**1.5 hours**
Elevation Range:	**6,400–9,000 feet**
Usually Open:	**Year-round**
Best Time to Travel:	**Dry weather**
Difficulty Rating:	**3**
Scenic Rating:	**10**
Remoteness Rating:	**+1**

Special Attractions

- The red rock of the Lukachukai Mountains.
- Aspen viewing in the fall.
- Extremely scenic smaller trail.

Description

This lightly traveled trail is smaller and rougher than many in the Navajo Nation. It also travels through some of the most breathtaking scenery in the Navajo Nation—the red sandstone cliffs and buttes of the Lukachukai Mountains.

The trail leaves Indian Road 13 just south of Buffalo Pass and for the first 1.6 miles travels through the pine and aspen forest. The shallow pan of Big Lake is passed, and briefly the trail passes through an open area in the forest that has many small natural ponds, some of which are carpeted with water lilies.

The trail drops in standard from a roughly graded road to a smaller, formed, singletrack. It starts to descend through more aspens and pines, twisting its way through the red rock canyons on the north side of the Lukachukai Mountains along a shelf road that is only wide enough for one vehicle. The trail surface is definitely suitable for dry weather only, and the route should not be attempted in wet weather. Navigation can be a little tricky as the trail descends; none of the tracks are marked and there are many side trails. Pay close attention to the route description to avoid going the wrong way.

The shelf road provides some fabulous views of the Carrizo Mountains

As the road descends, the view to the northwest opens up to reveal a glorious panorama of contrasting colors: the red sandstone of the mountains, the dark green of the oaks and junipers, and the muted yellow of the plain below. Far below, the settlement of Cove sits cradled in the natural bowl formed by the mountains. To reach it, the trail descends steeply along a series of switchbacks and through a gap in the bowl, the roughest and most uneven part of the trail. Black Rock, to the north, is easily recognizable by its dark color among all the red pinnacles that surround it. Shiprock, visible to the east, stands alone on the plains in New Mexico.

The trail ends at paved Indian Road 33 in Cove. From this point, the road is paved all the way back to the main highway to Shiprock.

Current Road Information

Navajo Nation Parks and Recreation
PO Box 9000
Window Rock, AZ 86515
(520) 871-6647

Map References

BLM Canyon de Chelly, Rock Point
USGS 1:24,000 Lukachukai, Cove
1:100,000 Canyon de Chelly, Rock Point
Maptech CD-ROM: Northeast Arizona/Navajo County
Arizona Atlas & Gazetteer, p. 27
Arizona Road & Recreation Atlas, p. 31 & p. 65

Route Directions:

▼ 0.0		From IR 13, 8.5 miles from the intersection with IR 12, zero trip meter and turn northwest on graded dirt road, just south of Buffalo Pass Picnic Ground. Road is unmarked.
3.3 ▲		Trail ends on IR 13. Turn left for Red Rocks; turn right for Lukachukai and Tsaile.
		GPS: N36°28.06′ W109°09.27′
▼ 0.1	SO	Track on right along power lines.
3.2 ▲	SO	Track on left along power lines.
▼ 0.2	SO	Track on right; then track on left.
3.1 ▲	SO	Track on left; then track on right.
▼ 0.5	SO	Well-used track on right and small track on left.
2.8 ▲	SO	Small track on right and well-used track on left. Continue straight on, following the homemade sign on the tree to Lukachukai.
		GPS: N36°28.42′ W109°09.64′
▼ 0.8	SO	Track on left.
2.5 ▲	SO	Track on right.
▼ 0.9	SO	Track on right; then track on left is #7565.
2.4 ▲	SO	Track on right is #7565; then track on left.
		GPS: N36°28.43′ W109°10.06′
▼ 1.1	SO	Track on left.
2.2 ▲	SO	Track on right.
▼ 1.6	SO	Track on left.
1.7 ▲	SO	Track on right.
▼ 1.7	SO	Track on right.
1.6 ▲	SO	Track on left.
▼ 1.8	SO	Track on left.
1.5 ▲	SO	Track on right.
▼ 1.9	SO	The depression on the left is Big Lake (often dry).
1.4 ▲	SO	The depression on the right is Big Lake (often dry).
		GPS: N36°28.68′ W109°10.73′
▼ 2.1	SO	Cross over creek.

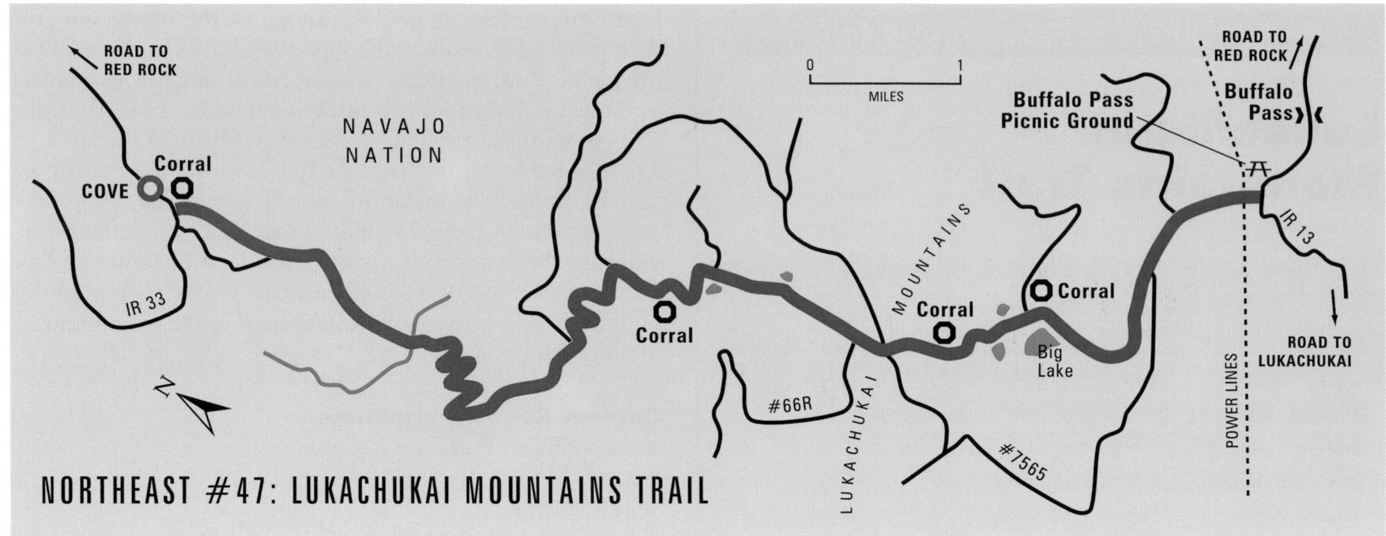

	1.2 ▲	SO	Cross over creek.
▼ 2.2		SO	Track on right past corral.
	1.1 ▲	SO	Track on left past corral.
▼ 2.3		SO	Track on right and track on left.
	1.0 ▲	SO	Track on left and track on right.
▼ 2.4		SO	Pond on right.
	0.9 ▲	SO	Pond on left.
▼ 2.5		SO	Pond on left.
	0.8 ▲	SO	Pond on right.
▼ 2.7		SO	Track on right is #N4.
	0.6 ▲	SO	Track on left is #N4.
▼ 2.8		SO	Corral on right.
	0.5 ▲	SO	Corral on left.
▼ 3.3		SO	4-way intersection. Small track on left; well-used tracks straight on and to the right. A homemade sign is affixed to an aspen at the intersection. Zero trip meter and continue straight up the hill, following the sign to Cove and Boundary Butte.
	0.0 ▲		Continue to the east.
			GPS: N36°29.51' W109°11.47'
▼ 0.0			Continue to the west.
	3.4 ▲	SO	4-way intersection. Small track on right; well-used tracks straight on and to the left. Continue straight uphill and zero trip meter.
▼ 0.1		SO	Track on left.
	3.3 ▲	SO	Track on right.
▼ 0.2		SO	Track on left is #66-R.
	3.2 ▲	SO	Track on right is #66-R.
▼ 0.3		SO	Track on right.
	3.1 ▲	SO	Track on left.
▼ 0.7		SO	Track on right.
	2.7 ▲	SO	Track on left.
▼ 0.8		SO	Pond on right.
	2.6 ▲	SO	Pond on left.
▼ 0.9		SO	Track on right.
	2.5 ▲	SO	Track on left.
▼ 1.2		SO	Pond on left; then track on right.
	2.2 ▲	SO	Track on left; then pond on right.
▼ 1.4		SO	Two tracks on right; trail starts to head downhill.
	2.0 ▲	SO	Two tracks on left; top of hill.
▼ 1.8		SO	Track on right and corral on left.
	1.6 ▲	SO	Track on left and corral on right.
			GPS: N36°30.77' W109°11.85'
▼ 2.3		SO	Track on right.
	1.1 ▲	SO	Track on left.
▼ 3.4		SO	Well-used roughly graded narrow trail to the right. Intersection is unmarked. Zero trip meter and continue straight on.
	0.0 ▲		Continue to the east.
			GPS: N36°31.09' W109°12.48'
▼ 0.0			Continue to the west.
	4.5 ▲	SO	Well-used roughly graded narrow trail to the left. Intersection is unmarked. Zero trip meter and continue straight on.
▼ 0.3		SO	Track on left.
	4.2 ▲	SO	Track on right.
▼ 0.5		SO	Track on right.
	4.0 ▲	SO	Track on left.
▼ 1.1		SO	Track on left.
	3.4 ▲	SO	Track on right.
			GPS: N36°31.53' W109°13.31'
▼ 2.5		SO	Cross through wash.
	2.0 ▲	SO	Cross through wash.
			GPS: N36°31.89' W109°13.05'
▼ 2.8		SO	Track on left and track on right.
	1.7 ▲	SO	Track on left and track on right.
▼ 3.1		SO	Track on right.
	1.4 ▲	SO	Track on left.
▼ 3.3		SO	Track on right.
	1.2 ▲	SO	Track on left.
▼ 3.4		SO	Track on right.
	1.1 ▲	SO	Track on left.
▼ 3.7		SO	Track on right; then track on left.
	0.8 ▲	SO	Track on left; then track on right.
▼ 3.9		SO	Track on right.
	0.6 ▲	SO	Track on left.
▼ 4.4		SO	Corral and track on right.
	0.1 ▲	SO	Corral and track on left.
▼ 4.5		TR	Trail ends at the T-intersection with the paved road in Cove. A very large arch is ahead and slightly to the south. Turn right to exit to Red Rock and IR 63.
	0.0 ▲		From IR 33 in Cove, zero trip meter and turn southeast over cattle guard onto graded dirt road, marked IH N336. The sign is clear and easy to read.
			GPS: N36°33.48' W109°13.04'

The Central Region

Trails in the Central Region

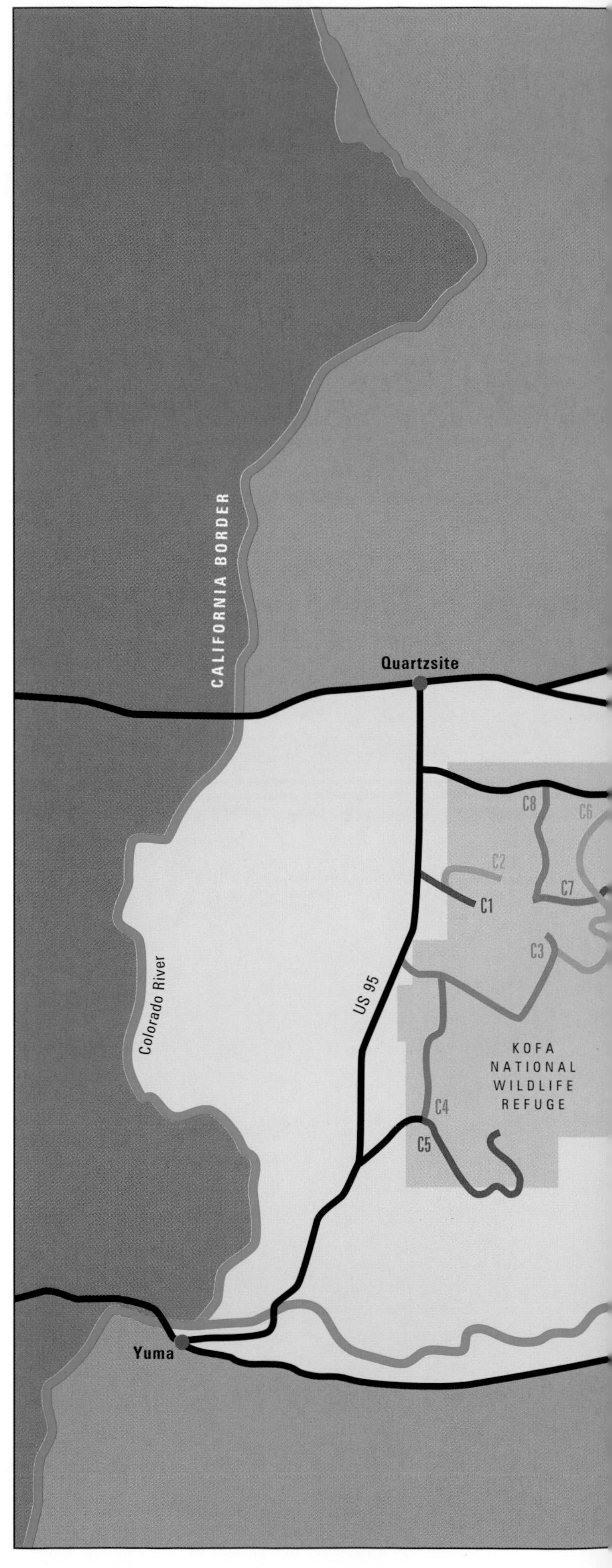

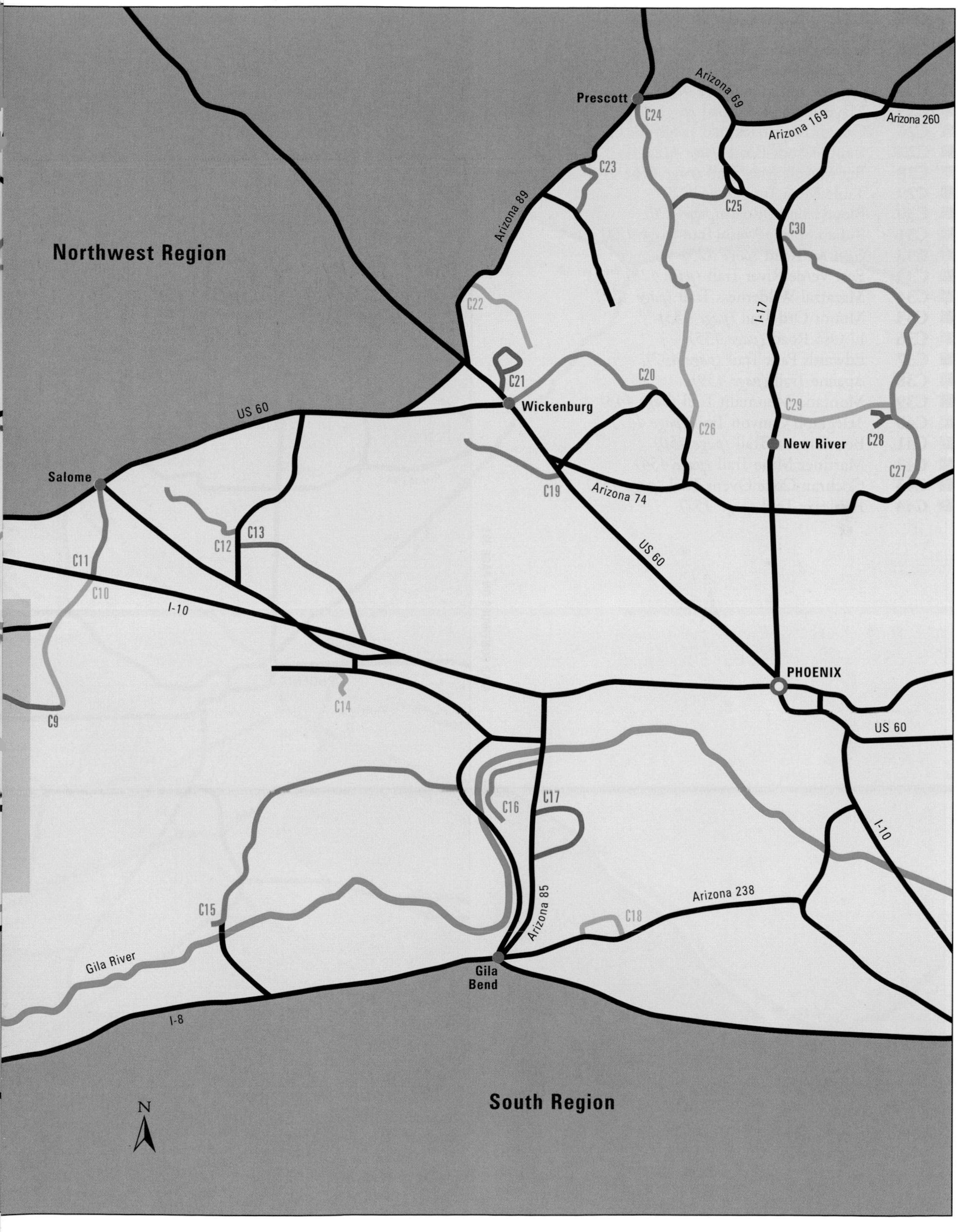

Northwest Region

Prescott

Arizona 69

Arizona 169

Arizona 260

Arizona 89

C24

C23

C25

C30

C22

I-17

C21

C20

Wickenburg

US 60

C29

C28

C26

New River

Salome

C27

C19

Arizona 74

C13

C12

US 60

C11

C10

I-10

PHOENIX

C14

C9

US 60

C16

C17

I-10

Arizona 238

Arizona 85

C15

C18

Gila River

Gila Bend

I-8

South Region

N

MAP CONTINUES ON PAGE 340

Palm Canyon Road

Starting Point:	**US 95, 17.9 miles south of Quartzsite, between mile markers 85 and 86**
Finishing Point:	**Palm Canyon**
Total Mileage:	**6.7 miles**
Unpaved Mileage:	**6.7 miles**
Driving Time:	**30 minutes (one-way)**
Elevation Range:	**1,400–2,300 feet**
Usually Open:	**Year-round**
Best Time to Travel:	**November to April**
Difficulty Rating:	**1**
Scenic Rating:	**7**
Remoteness Rating:	**+0**

Special Attractions

- Native Arizona palms in a natural setting.
- Rugged canyon in the Kofa Mountains.

Description

This graded gravel road provides access to Palm Canyon, from where a short hike leads to views over what is possibly the only community of native palms in Arizona. The trail itself is suitable for passenger vehicles, and it is possible to park overnight at the hiking trailhead at the end of the road. This area has sweeping views west over the La Posa Plain to the Trigo Mountains and Chocolate Mountains and is especially lovely at sunset. There are no facilities or picnic tables at the trailhead.

The California fan palms, from which the canyon derives its name, are thought to be remnants from an era when Arizona was a lot cooler and wetter than it currently is. The cooler air within the canyon, lack of direct sunlight, and slightly moister conditions have allowed the trees to survive.

The rhyolite cliffs at Palm Canyon

The hiking trail to view the palms is a rough but well-defined path that climbs up into the canyon for approximately 0.5 miles to a viewing point. From here, the palms can be seen high in a narrow side canyon on the north side of the main Palm Canyon. There are approximately 40 trees in the main grove, and although some were damaged by fire in 1954, most are surviving well and younger trees are starting to shoot up. If you wish to climb to the trees, expect an arduous scramble over very large boulders. Be alert for rattlesnakes and watch where you place hands and feet. The trees are not visible until you are directly below them.

The grove of palm trees growing deep in Palm Canyon

Photographers should be aware that the trees are only in sunlight for a short period around the middle of the day; the rest of the time they are in shade. A telephoto lens is necessary if you want a good photo from the viewpoint.

Current Road Information

Kofa National Wildlife Refuge
356 West 1st St.
Yuma, AZ 85364
(520) 783-7861

Map References

BLM Trigo Mts.
USGS 1:24,000 Livingston Hills NW, Stone Cabin, Palm Canyon
1:100,000 Trigo Mts.
Maptech CD-ROM: Southwest Arizona/Yuma
Arizona Atlas & Gazetteer, p. 54
Arizona Road & Recreation Atlas, p. 44 & p. 78
Recreational Map of Arizona
Other: Kofa NWR Map (free leaflet put out by the NWR showing designated travel routes)

Route Directions

▼ 0.0		From US 95, 17.9 miles south of Quartzsite, 0.7 miles south of mile marker 84, zero trip meter and turn east onto the graded gravel road at the sign for Kofa National Wildlife Refuge, Palm Canyon.
		GPS: N33°23.33' W114°12.95'
▼ 0.7	SO	Cross over the pipeline; tracks on right and left at pipeline.
▼ 3.1	SO	Entering Kofa NWR. Information board and maps available at entrance. Track on right at marker post 19 is Central #2: Kofa Queen Canyon Trail. Zero trip meter.
		GPS: N33°22.28' W114°09.79'

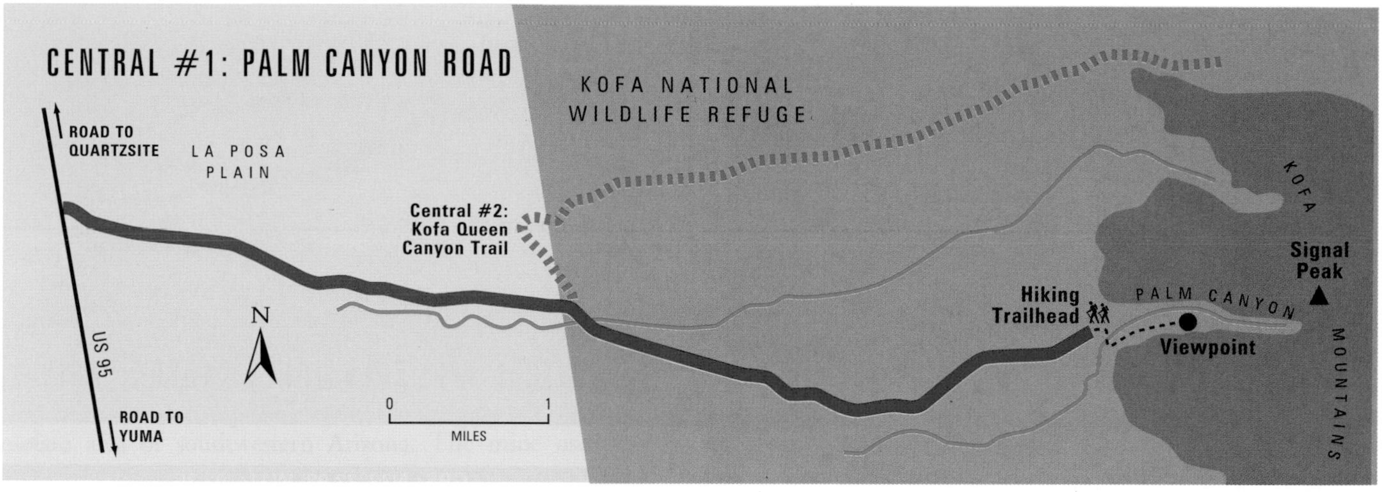

▼ 0.0		Continue toward Palm Canyon.
▼ 0.1	SO	Cross through wash.
▼ 2.1	SO	Cross through wash.
▼ 3.0	SO	Cross through wash.
▼ 3.6		Trail ends at the turning area and the start of the hiking trail into the canyon.
		GPS: N33°21.61' W114°06.31'

CENTRAL REGION TRAIL #2

Kofa Queen Canyon Trail

Starting Point:	**Central #1: Palm Canyon Road**
Finishing Point:	**Closure sign in Kofa Queen Canyon**
Total Mileage:	**8.7 miles**
Unpaved Mileage:	**8.7 miles**
Driving Time:	**1.25 hours (one-way)**
Elevation Range:	**1,500–3,200 feet**
Usually Open:	**Year-round**
Best Time to Travel:	**November to April**
Difficulty Rating:	**3**
Scenic Rating:	**8**
Remoteness Rating:	**+0**

Special Attractions

- Scenic Kofa Queen Canyon and the remains of the Kofa Queen Mine.
- Views of La Posa Plain.
- Easy winding trail that travels up a wash.

Description

This spur trail is one of the few within the Kofa National Wildlife Refuge that travels up one of the high-walled red canyons that penetrate into the rugged Kofa Range. The trail leads off from Central #1: Palm Canyon Road, where it enters the Kofa National Wildlife Refuge. For the first 4 miles, the trail is smooth and easygoing as it ascends the bajada, the gently sloping fan on the west side of the range. For campers, the large campsite over the rise to the right at the 4.3-mile mark is easily the best—large, flat, and gravelly, with a measure of privacy from the main trail and great sunset views to the west.

At the mouth of Kofa Queen Canyon, the trail drops into the gravelly wash and remains in it to the end of the trail. Like all the designated roads within the national wildlife refuge, most of the old side trails are closed to vehicle use. This trail runs up a vehicle access corridor into the wilderness area. A couple of potentially confusing forks in the wash either rejoin the main trail immediately or are closed to vehicles a few yards farther on, so navigation is easy.

The trail passes a prominent rock pillar in the wash; the column is being undercut by erosion and eventually it will be a true balanced rock. Bighorn sheep like the habitat within the canyon and can often be seen in the early morning and evening high up on the canyon walls.

The wash is generally loose and gravelly, with only a few sections of rough boulders to contend with. The last mile, however, is quite brushy, and most vehicles will collect a few light scratches.

A large rock formation in Kofa Queen Wash

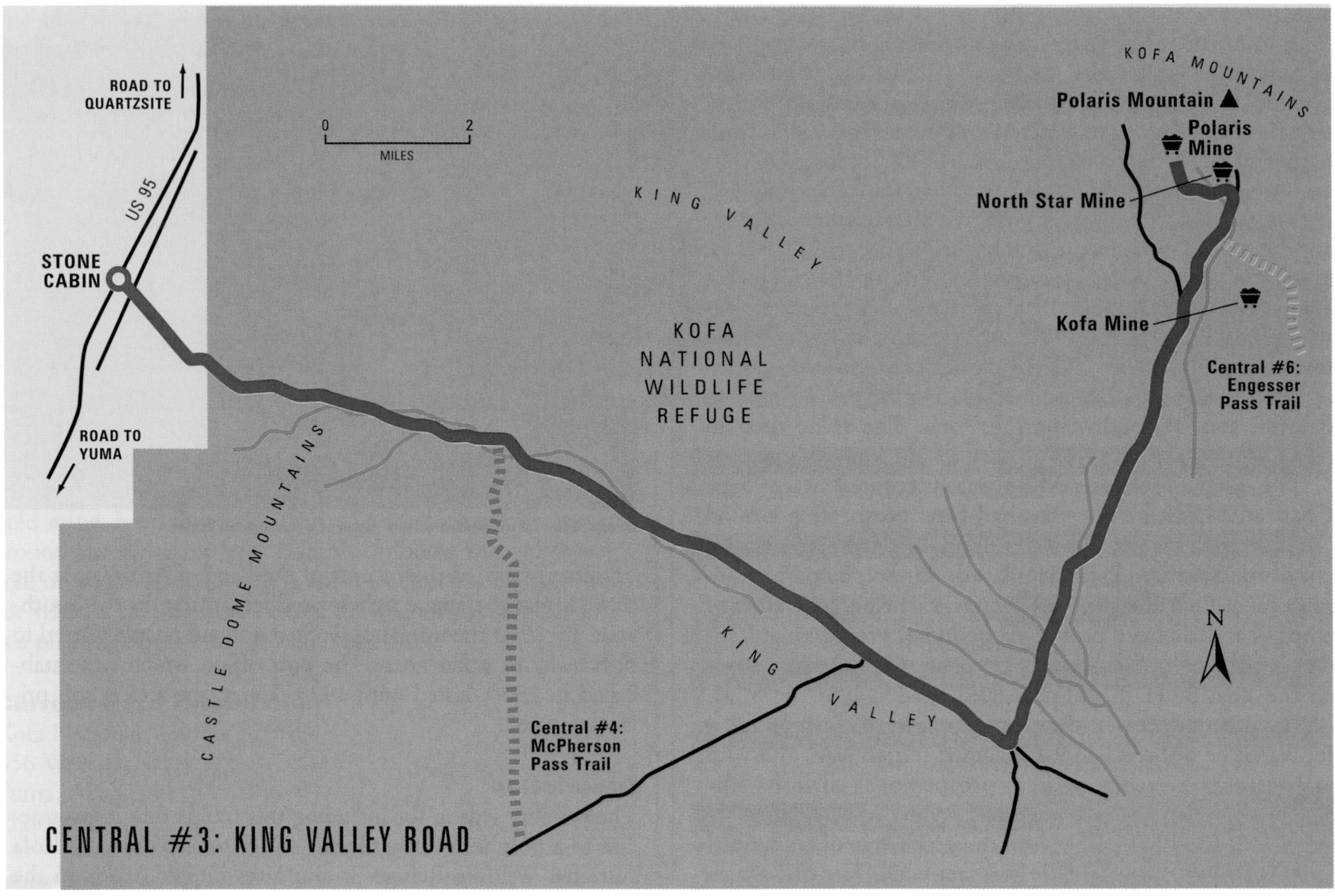

Map References

BLM Trigo Mts., Little Horn Mts.

USGS 1:24,000 Stone Cabin, Arch Tank, Kofa Deep Well, Charlie Died Tank, Kofa Butte
1:100,000 Trigo Mts., Little Horn Mts.

Maptech CD-ROM: Southwest Arizona/Yuma

Arizona Atlas & Gazetteer, p. 54

Arizona Road & Recreation Atlas, p. 44 & p. 78

Recreational Map of Arizona

Other: Kofa NWR Map (free leaflet put out by the NWR showing designated travel routes)

Route Directions

▼ 0.0		From US 95, 26.1 miles south of Quartzsite at Stone Cabin, 0.3 miles south of mile marker 77, zero trip meter and turn east on the graded dirt road at the sign for Kofa National Wildlife Refuge, King Valley.
2.1 ▲		Trail ends on US 95. Turn right for Quartzsite; turn left for Yuma.
		GPS: N33°16.03' W114°14.33'
▼ 0.3	SO	Cross pipeline; tracks on right and left along pipeline.
1.8 ▲	SO	Cross pipeline; tracks on right and left along pipeline.
▼ 1.4	SO	Cross through wash.
0.7 ▲	SO	Cross through wash.
▼ 1.7	SO	Entering the Kofa NWR at sign. Information boards and maps on right.
0.4 ▲	SO	Leaving the Kofa NWR. Information boards and maps on left.
		GPS: N33°14.99' W114°12.96'
▼ 2.1	SO	Track on left at marker post 42. Zero trip meter.
0.0 ▲		Continue to the west.
		GPS: N33°14.78' W114°12.58'
▼ 0.0		Continue to the east.
3.8 ▲	SO	Track on right at marker post 42. Zero trip meter.
▼ 2.0	SO	Cross through wash.
1.8 ▲	SO	Cross through wash.
▼ 2.3	SO	Cross through wash.
1.5 ▲	SO	Cross through wash.
▼ 2.7	SO	Cross through wash.
1.1 ▲	SO	Cross through wash.
▼ 3.4	SO	Cross through wash.
0.4 ▲	SO	Cross through wash.
▼ 3.6	SO	Cross through wash.
0.2 ▲	SO	Cross through wash.
▼ 3.8	SO	Track on right at marker post 60 is Central #4: McPherson Pass Trail. Zero trip meter.
0.0 ▲		Continue to the northwest.
		GPS: N33°14.06' W114°08.80'
▼ 0.0		Continue to the southeast.
5.7 ▲	SO	Track on left at marker post 60 is Central #4: McPherson Pass Trail. Zero trip meter.
▼ 2.2	SO	Cross through wash.
3.5 ▲	SO	Cross through wash.
▼ 3.1	SO	Cross through wash.
2.6 ▲	SO	Cross through wash.

▼	▲		
▼ 5.7		SO	Track on right at marker post 76 joins Central #4: McPherson Pass Trail. Zero trip meter.
	0.0 ▲		Continue to the northwest.
			GPS: N33°11.71' W114°03.35'
▼ 0.0			Continue to the southeast.
	2.2 ▲	SO	Track on left at marker post 76 joins Central #4: McPherson Pass Trail. Zero trip meter.
▼ 1.6		SO	Cross through wash. Castle Dome is visible on the right.
	0.6 ▲	SO	Cross through wash.
			GPS: N33°11.04' W114°01.84'
▼ 2.2		BL	Track ahead and on right at marker post 79. Zero trip meter.
	0.0 ▲		Continue to the northwest. Castle Dome is visible to the south.
			GPS: N33°10.74' W114°01.26'
▼ 0.0			Continue on graded road to the northeast.
	6.4 ▲	BR	Track on left and ahead at marker post 79. Zero trip meter.
▼ 0.2		SO	Cross through wash.
	6.2 ▲	SO	Cross through wash.
▼ 0.7		SO	Cross through wash.
	5.7 ▲	SO	Cross through wash.
▼ 1.0		SO	Cross through wash.
	5.4 ▲	SO	Cross through wash.
▼ 1.2		SO	Cross through wash.
	5.2 ▲	SO	Cross through wash.
▼ 1.4		SO	Cross through wide wash.
	5.0 ▲	SO	Cross through wide wash.
▼ 2.6		SO	Cross through wash.
	3.8 ▲	SO	Cross through wash.
▼ 5.5		SO	Concrete footings on right.
	0.9 ▲	SO	Concrete footings on left.
			GPS: N33°15.34' W113°59.31'
▼ 6.4		SO	Track on left at marker post 64. Zero trip meter.
	0.0 ▲		Continue to the south.
			GPS: N33°16.10' W113°58.92'
▼ 0.0			Continue to the north.
	1.1 ▲	SO	Track on right at marker post 64. Zero trip meter.
▼ 0.7		SO	Cross through wash.
	0.4 ▲	SO	Cross through wash.
▼ 1.0		SO	Entering private property; remain on designated roads.
	0.1 ▲	SO	Leaving private property.
▼ 1.1		BL	Track on right at marker post 65 is Central #6: Engesser Pass Trail. The King of Arizona (Kofa) Mine is a short distance down this trail, which is accessible to passenger vehicles as far as the mine. Zero trip meter.
	0.0 ▲		Continue to the south.
			GPS: N33°16.96' W113°58.45'
▼ 0.0			Continue to the north.
▼ 0.1		SO	Re-entering the Kofa NWR.
▼ 0.3		SO	Cross through wash.
▼ 0.6		TL	Turn in front of the entrance to the North Star Mine, which is private property, no access. You can get a good view of the workings from the gate.
			GPS: N33°17.48' W113°58.31'
▼ 0.7		SO	Cross through wash.
▼ 0.9		SO	Cross through wash.
▼ 1.2		SO	Cross through wash.
▼ 1.4			Trail ends at a small turning area overlooking a mine on the slope.
			GPS: N33°17.68' W113°59.16'

CENTRAL REGION TRAIL #4

McPherson Pass Trail

Starting Point:	**Castle Dome Road, marker post 75, at the start of Central #5: Big Eye Wash Trail**
Finishing Point:	**Central #3: King Valley Road, marker post 60**
Total Mileage:	**15.4 miles**
Unpaved Mileage:	**15.4 miles**
Driving Time:	**2.5 hours**
Elevation Range:	**1,300–2,000 feet**
Usually Open:	**Year-round**
Best Time to Travel:	**October to April**
Difficulty Rating:	**3**
Scenic Rating:	**9**
Remoteness Rating:	**+1**

Special Attractions

- Castle Dome Mines Museum.
- Wildlife viewing within Kofa National Wildlife Refuge.
- Interesting trail through rugged Sonoran desert scenery.
- Hull Mine.
- McPherson Pass.

History

The Castle Dome Mines date back to Indian and Spanish times. Ancient trails, worn in the desert pavement, record the pathways used by these early miners. They carried the ore south to an old adobe furnace on the Gila River. However, the major activity in the Castle Dome region took place after 1863, when Conner and Jacob Snively formed the Castle Dome Mining District. After discarding the high-quality galena, which contained as much as 70 percent lead, the men extracted silver.

A supply and shipping point for the ore was set on the Colorado River, due west from the mining district. Initially,

Teddy bear chollas dot the landscape with Castle Dome in the background

there were plans to build a 17-mile railroad from the mines to the river. The route was surveyed but was never constructed. The town, known as Castle Dome Landing and later as Castle Dome City, was the first stop upriver from Yuma. It had a store, post office, saloon, and hotel. Later a small smelter was built. Many people traveled north upriver from Yuma to attend celebrations and sports days. Mexican Independence Day in September was a particularly big occasion. In the 1880s, the county that now bears the name Yuma was nearly named Castle Dome, as Castle Dome had a larger population than Yuma. Today the waters of Martinez Lake cover the site of Castle Dome City.

In 1865, Castle Dome was quiet. Although there was plenty of lead left in the hills, no one seemed interested in mining it. A gold strike in central Arizona drew miners away to seek richer pickings in the mines around Wickenburg and Prescott. However, in the early 1870s William B. Hooper and James M. Barney, both from Yuma, began shipping ore to San Francisco smelters to process the lead. Although transportation was difficult and expensive, it was possible to realize a fair profit from the rich ore. In 1877, a group from San Francisco invested in the mines and began buying up nearby claims. Some old prospectors saw the buyout as a perfect opportunity to get rid of claims that they knew were nearly exhausted.

Castle Dome, like most mining towns, was rowdy. Although there were a number of fights and shootings, it did not experience as much violence as the Fortuna Mine, southeast of Yuma. But it did have its share of trouble. One incident started in May 1881 when Rafael Gutierrez was killed by an outlaw calling himself Blanco Flores. Officers investigating the incident quickly determined that Blanco Flores was a fugitive, using an alias for his real name, Florencia Sanchez. A reward of $50 was offered for his capture. Sanchez evaded the law for a while by working on a ferry on the Colorado River. However, he was eventually recognized and shot to death while attempting to avoid capture.

The Castle Dome Mining District continued to produce but at a lesser rate than it had in its early years. In 1943, the Arizona Lead Company reactivated the Castle Dome Mine, and between 1943 and 1946 the company produced 60,000 tons of lead, most of which was used for bullets in World War II. In 1948, the mine changed hands again, and the new owner, the Joplin Lead Company, produced another 30,000 tons of lead by 1953. Today the Castle Dome Mine is privately owned and is the site of the Castle Dome Mines Museum.

Hull Mine portal

The Hull Mine, a short distance north of the Castle Dome Mines Museum, produced mostly silver but was never profitable. Investors poured $18 million into the mine, but it only returned a couple of million. The mine is privately owned with liens still current on the property.

The Kofa National Wildlife Refuge, established in 1939 primarily to protect the desert bighorn sheep, encompasses 660,000 acres of the Sonoran Desert. The sheep are thriving, and some are regularly relocated to other areas in the Southwest to replenish populations that have died out.

Description

McPherson Pass Trail commences 8 miles from US 95 along the graded dirt Castle Dome Road. The road to the start of the trail is well used, as many people take it to visit the Castle Dome Mines Museum, which is located on the site of the historic Castle Dome Mine, now on private property. The museum is well worth a visit. You can view the interesting and historic mining relics that the owners have collected, primarily from the Castle Dome Mines but also from other mines in the Kofa National Wildlife Refuge. The refuge management has been removing mining equipment from some of the mines in order to retain the wilderness feel of the landscape. Much of the equipment has been relocated to the museum. There is a small entrance fee to the museum, which is housed in the old mining company headquarters building.

Crossing a wide stony wash

Less than a mile north of the museum, the trail passes close to the Hull Mine. The mine is on private property, but currently it seems possible to visit it and view the enormous adit descending into the hillside. North of the Hull Mine, the trail becomes narrower and more rough as it crosses the bajada on the west side of the Castle Dome Mountains. The rounded peak of Castle Dome is clearly visible to the east as the trail starts to wind into the range toward the gap of McPherson Pass. This is the roughest part of the trail, but it is still easily negotiated by high-clearance 4WDs.

The trail descends from the pass and then leaves the range to swing across the bajada on the eastern side of the Castle Dome Mountains, crossing many washes before it joins Central #3: King Valley Road, 5.9 miles east of US 95.

Current Road Information

Kofa National Wildlife Refuge
356 West 1st St.
Yuma, AZ 85364
(520) 783-7861

Map References

BLM Trigo Mts.
USGS 1:24,000 Castle Dome Peak, Arch Tank
1:100,000 Trigo Mts.

Maptech CD-ROM: Southwest Arizona/Yuma
Arizona Atlas & Gazetteer, p. 54
Arizona Road & Recreation Atlas, p. 44 & p. 78
Other: Kofa NWR Map (free leaflet put out by the NWR showing designated travel routes)

Route Directions

▼ 0.0		From US 95 at mile marker 55, turn northeast on Castle Dome Road at the sign for Kofa National Wildlife Refuge, Castle Dome. Proceed for 8 miles to the junction of McPherson Pass Trail and Central #5: Big Eye Wash Trail at marker post 75. Zero trip meter and continue northeast on the wide, graded dirt road, following the sign for McPherson Pass. Central #5: Big Eye Wash Trail is to the right at marker post 75.
0.6 ▲		Trail finishes at marker post 75, at the junction with Central #5: Big Eye Wash Trail. Turn left to travel the Big Eye Wash Trail; continue straight ahead on the wide graded road for 8 miles to US 95.
		GPS: N33°02.13' W114°10.92'
▼ 0.1	SO	Smaller track on right cuts across to Central #5: Big Eye Wash Trail.
0.5 ▲	BR	Smaller track on left cuts across to Central #5: Big Eye Wash Trail.
▼ 0.6	SO	Entrance to Castle Dome Mines Museum on left. Zero trip meter.
0.0 ▲		Continue toward US 95.
		GPS: N33°02.63' W114°10.54'
▼ 0.0		Continue toward McPherson Pass.
0.8 ▲	SO	Entrance to Castle Dome Mines Museum on right. Zero trip meter.
▼ 0.2	SO	Cross through wash.
0.6 ▲	SO	Cross through wash.
▼ 0.8	BR	Cross through wash; then track on left goes through gate into the Hull Mine. Zero trip meter.
0.0 ▲		Continue toward the Castle Dome Mines Museum and cross through wash.
		GPS: N33°03.32' W114°10.37'
▼ 0.0		Continue on the designated road toward McPherson Pass.
8.3 ▲	BL	Track on right goes through gate into the Hull Mine. Zero trip meter.
▼ 0.2	SO	Tailings from the Hull Mine on the left.
8.1 ▲	SO	Tailings from the Hull Mine on the right.
▼ 0.5	SO	Cross through wash.
7.8 ▲	SO	Cross through wash.
▼ 0.8	SO	Cross through wash.
7.5 ▲	SO	Cross through wash.
▼ 1.3	SO	Cross through wash.
7.0 ▲	SO	Cross through wash.
▼ 1.6	SO	Cross through wash.
6.7 ▲	SO	Cross through wash.
		GPS: N33°04.74' W114°10.38'
▼ 1.9	SO	Grave on right, "Little Frank," 9/14/1996.
6.4 ▲	SO	Grave on left, "Little Frank," 9/14/1996.
		GPS: N33°04.93' W114°10.50'
▼ 2.3	SO	Start to cross wide wash path with many channels. Trail remains in the general line of the wash until McPherson Pass, crossing and entering it many times.
6.0 ▲	SO	Exit wide wash channel.
▼ 2.6	SO	Exit wide wash channel.

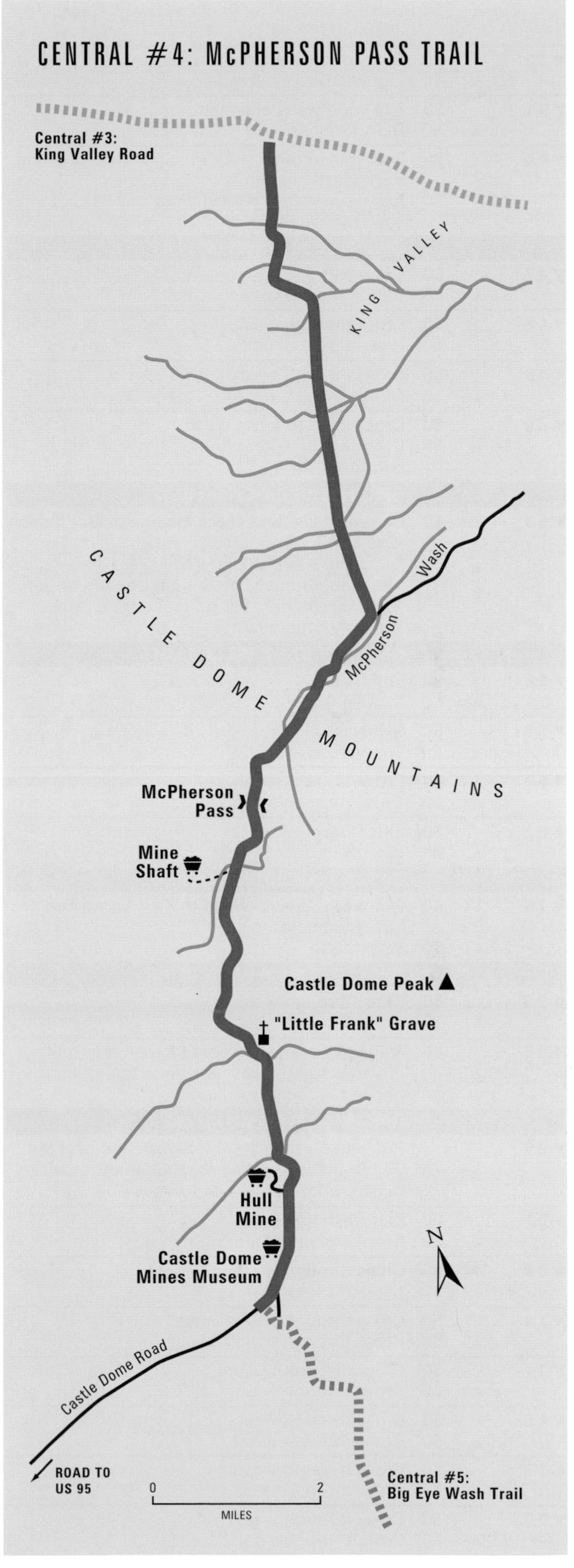

5.7 ▲ SO Start to cross wide wash path with many channels.

▼ 3.2 SO Start to cross wide wash path.
5.1 ▲ SO Exit wide wash channel.

▼ 4.1 SO Exit wide wash channel.
4.2 ▲ SO Start to cross wide wash channel.

▼ 4.5 SO Foot trail to mine shaft up hill on left. Entering main wash channel.
3.8 ▲ SO Exit main wash channel. Foot trail to mine shaft up hill on right.

GPS: N33°06.77' W114°10.41'

▼ 4.7 SO Exit wash.
3.6 ▲ SO Entering main wash channel.

▼ 4.8 SO Cross through wash.
3.5 ▲ SO Cross through wash.

▼ 4.9 SO Cross through wash.
3.4 ▲ SO Cross through wash.

▼ 5.0 SO Drop down to cross wash.
3.3 ▲ BR Cross wash, exiting to the right, and climb over rise.

GPS: N33°07.06' W114°10.12'

▼ 5.5 SO Exit wash line and cross the rise of McPherson Pass.
2.8 ▲ SO Cross the rise of McPherson Pass; then enter wash. Trail remains in the general line of the wash for the next 3.2 miles, crossing and entering it many times.

GPS: N33°07.50' W114°10.04'

▼ 5.6 SO Enter wash.
2.7 ▲ SO Exit wash.

▼ 5.8 SO Exit wash.
2.5 ▲ SO Enter wash.

▼ 6.0 SO Cross through wash.
2.3 ▲ SO Cross through wash.

▼ 6.2 SO Enter wash.
2.1 ▲ BR Bear right out of wash.

GPS: N33°07.92' W114°09.90'

▼ 7.6 SO Exit wash. Views ahead to King Valley and the Kofa Mountains.
0.7 ▲ SO Enter wash.

GPS: N33°08.88' W114°08.72'

▼ 7.9 SO Cross through wash.
0.4 ▲ SO Cross through wash.

▼ 8.3 BL Trail forks at marker post 53. Zero trip meter.
0.0 ▲ Proceed southwest. Trail starts to enter the gap in the range.

GPS: N33°09.23' W114°08.21'

▼ 0.0 Proceed northwest; enter wash and bear left.
5.7 ▲ BR Bear right and exit wash; then track on left at marker post 53. Zero trip meter.

▼ 0.1 BL Exit wash to left.
5.6 ▲ BR Enter wash and bear right in wash.

▼ 0.6 SO Cross through wash.
5.1 ▲ SO Cross through wash.

▼ 1.0 SO Cross through two washes.
4.7 ▲ SO Cross through two washes.

▼ 1.1 SO Cross through wash.
4.6 ▲ SO Cross through wash.

▼ 1.6 SO Cross through wash.
4.1 ▲ SO Cross through wash.

▼ 1.7 SO Cross through wash.
4.0 ▲ SO Cross through wash.

▼ 2.2 SO Cross through wash.
3.5 ▲ SO Cross through wash.

GPS: N33°11.22' W114°08.47'

▼ 2.5 SO Cross through wash.
3.2 ▲ SO Cross through wash.

▼ 2.8 SO Cross through wash.
2.9 ▲ SO Cross through wash.

▼ 3.8 SO Cross through wash.
1.9 ▲ SO Cross through wash.

▼ 4.5 SO Cross through wash.
1.2 ▲ SO Cross through wash.

▼ 5.1 SO Cross through wash.
0.6 ▲ SO Cross through wash.

▼ 5.7 Trail ends on Central #3: King Valley Road at marker post 60. Turn right for the King of Arizona (Kofa) Mine and Central #6: Engesser Pass Trail; turn left for US 95.
0.0 ▲ Trail commences on Central #3: King Valley Road, 5.9 miles east of US 95. Turn southeast on formed dirt trail at marker post 60 and zero trip meter.

GPS: N33°14.06' W114°08.80'

CENTRAL REGION TRAIL #5

Big Eye Wash Trail

Starting Point:	**Castle Dome Road, marker post 75, at the start of Central #4: McPherson Pass Trail**
Finishing Point:	**Gate before trail to Big Eye Mine**
Total Mileage:	**14.5 miles**
Unpaved Mileage:	**14.5 miles**
Driving Time:	**2 hours (one-way)**
Elevation Range:	**1,200–2,400 feet**
Usually Open:	**Year-round**
Best Time to Travel:	**November to April**
Difficulty Rating:	**3**
Scenic Rating:	**9**
Remoteness Rating:	**+1**

Special Attractions

- Cabins and remains of Big Eye Mine.
- Colorado Mine and graves.
- Scenic desert trail within the remote Castle Dome Mountains.
- Wildlife-viewing opportunities.

History

Not too much is known about the Big Eye and Colorado Mines. Like most of the mines at the southern end of the Castle Dome Mountains, they contained both silver and gold. The Castle Dome Mining District was very productive; between 1863 and 1959 the area yielded a total of 9,500 to 10,000 ounces of placer and lode gold. The Big Eye Mine, worked until the 1950s, was a major producer of lode gold. Although it is not apparent from the surface, there are several miles of underground workings. The last owner, Pauline

Taylor, a sister of the Yuma County sheriff, died in 1982, and her ashes were scattered in the area.

Adams Well, situated a couple of miles northeast of the trail, was excavated by Samuel Adams in the 1860s. Supposedly, it was the only water supply in the Castle Dome Mountains at the time. Adams, originally from Pennsylvania, was renowned for his efforts to promote the Colorado River as a suitable waterway for ocean-going vessels. A few miles west of Adams Well is a natural water tank called Chain Tank, so named because a prospector installed a chain to aid people in climbing up to the tank. When animals, however, tried to reach the water, many fell into the tank and contaminated the water supply. In 1955, a tunnel was dug near the water level to allow the animals that had fallen in to escape.

Description

This trail is a spur within the Kofa National Wildlife Refuge. All the trails within the refuge are incredibly scenic and remote. This one is no exception. It travels through classic Sonoran desert scenery and vegetation; in spring the wildflowers and cacti bring splashes of color to the region.

The trail leaves from a point southwest of the Castle Dome Mines Museum and turns off the graded Castle Dome Road to become a formed, single-track trail. It runs southeast along the western face of the Castle Dome Mountains, passing the wooden-lined shafts and adits of the Colorado Mine. Across from the mine remains, on the right-hand side of the trail, there is a short row of graves marked with simple wooden crosses.

Offering many panoramic views to the south and west over Castle Dome Plain before it tucks into the Castle Dome Mountains, the trail winds across the cactus-strewn bajadas within the red-colored range. The remains of the Copper Cup Mine are passed on the left as the trail passes to the right of Thumb Butte, a distinctively shaped peak. The trail then drops down into the wide, gravelly Big Eye Wash. The vehicle trail ends at a locked gate. From here it is a short hike up the old vehicle trail to the Big Eye Mine, which is just over the saddle out of sight from the end of the existing vehicle trail. The hike is well worth the effort. There is an old timber cabin in good condition with many interesting tools and furnishings. The NWR has placed a visitors book in the cabin. To reach the mine itself, climb up on the slope behind the cabin to the west of the old water tank; then hike north along the foot trail to the ridge. From here you can look down to see the mine workings. Alternatively, continue past the cabin on the old vehicle trail to reach the bottom of the workings.

The main cabin at Big Eye Mine

Colorado Mine shaft

There is a good chance you will see some wildlife along this trail, especially at dawn and dusk. Bighorn sheep, desert mule deer, desert kit fox, coyote, badger, and many reptiles and desert tortoises make their homes in the refuge.

The trail is smooth for most of the way, although sections in the wash can be gravelly and there are a few lumpy and rough spots on the latter stages of the trail. Camping is permitted anywhere in the refuge within 100 feet of the designated roads, and there are many pleasant spots to choose from. They are all fairly exposed, but the great views make up for the lack of shade.

Current Road Information

Kofa National Wildlife Refuge
356 West 1st St.
Yuma, AZ 85364
(520) 783-7861

Map References

BLM Yuma, Trigo Mts.
USGS 1:24,000 Castle Dome Peak, Red Bluff Mt. NW, Salton Tanks, Slumgullion Pass
1:100,000 Yuma, Trigo Mts.
Maptech CD-ROM: Southwest Arizona/Yuma
Arizona Atlas & Gazetteer, p. 54
Arizona Road & Recreation Atlas, p. 44 & p. 78
Other: Kofa NWR Map (free leaflet put out by the NWR showing designated travel routes)

Route Directions

▼ 0.0		From US 95 at mile marker 55, turn northeast on the paved Castle Dome Road at the sign for Kofa National Wildlife Refuge, Castle Dome. Proceed for 8 miles to the junction of Central #4: McPherson Pass Trail and Big Eye Wash Trail at marker post 75. Zero trip meter and turn southeast on formed trail. Ahead is the start of Central #4: McPherson Pass Trail.
		GPS: N33°02.13' W114°10.91'
▼ 0.1	SO	Track on left rejoins Central #4: McPherson Pass Trail; then cross through wide wash.
▼ 0.3	SO	Cross through wash.
▼ 0.6	SO	Closed vehicle trail on left—hiking access to old mine remains.
		GPS: N33°01.83' W114°10.52'
▼ 0.7	SO	Cross through wash.
▼ 1.2	SO	Cross through wash.
▼ 2.0	SO	Cross through two washes.
▼ 2.2	SO	Cross through wash.

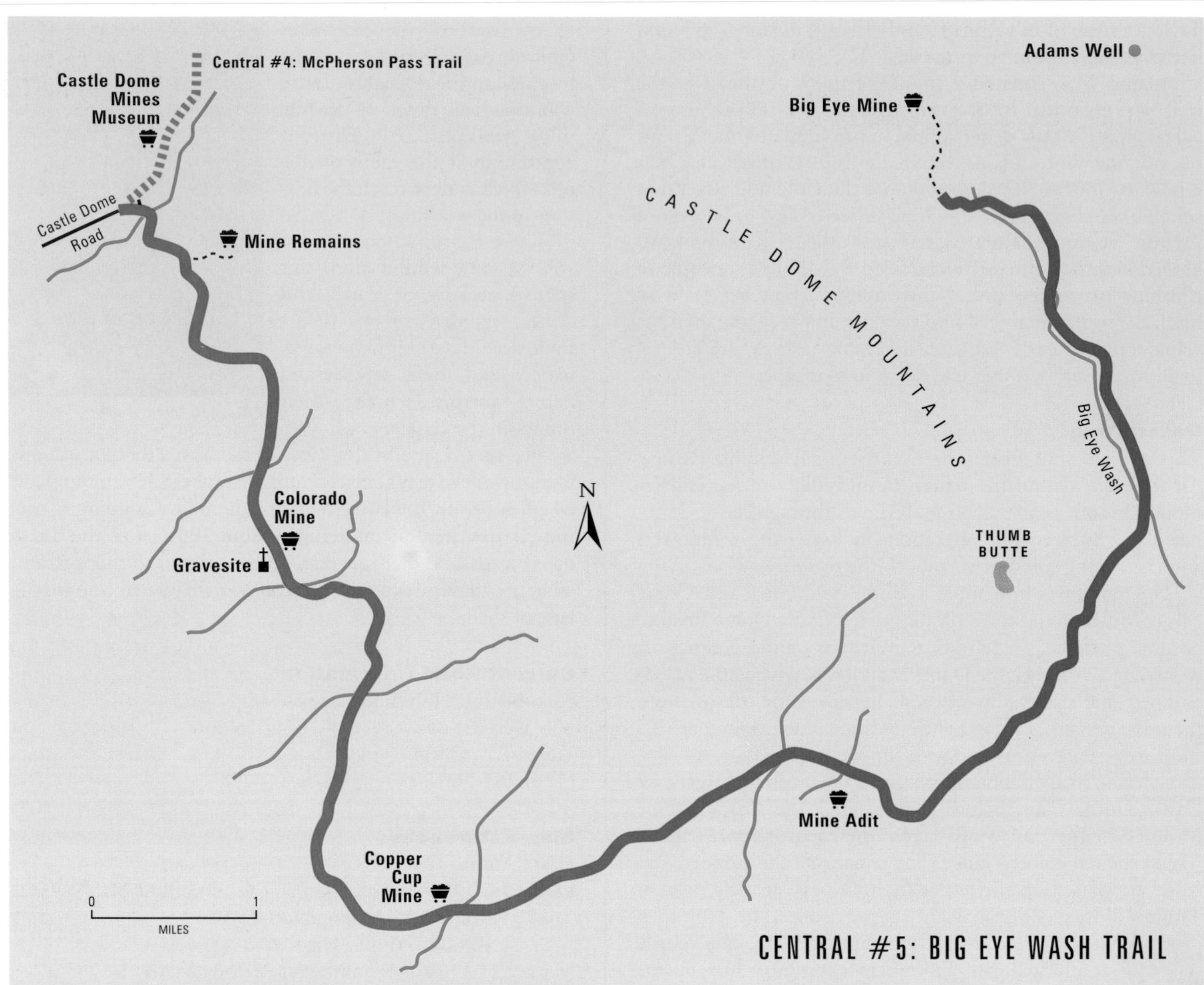

		GPS: N33°00.68′ W114°10.11′
▼ 2.7	SO	Colorado Mine on left. Shafts, tailings, and adits on both sides of the trail. Four graves to the right of the trail. Zero trip meter at the wooden-lined, large shaft on the left.
		GPS: N33°00.32′ W114°10.08′
▼ 0.0		Continue to the southeast
▼ 0.3	SO	Cross through wash.
▼ 0.9	SO	Cross through wash.
▼ 1.0	SO	Cross through wash.
▼ 1.1	SO	Cross through wash.
▼ 1.4	SO	Cross through wide wash.
		GPS: N32°59.49′ W114°09.50′
▼ 2.6	SO	Cross through two washes.
▼ 2.9	SO	Cross through wash.
▼ 3.0	SO	Cross through two washes.
▼ 3.3	SO	Cross through wash.
		GPS: N32°58.29′ W114°09.25′
▼ 3.5	SO	Copper Cup Mine on left of trail. Many tailings heaps remain. The distinctively shaped Thumb Butte is directly ahead.
		GPS: N32°58.36′ W114°09.01′
▼ 3.6	SO	Cross through wide wash.
▼ 4.2	SO	Cross through wash.
▼ 5.6	SO	Cross through wash.
▼ 5.7	SO	Cross through wide wash.
▼ 6.1	SO	Cross through wash.
▼ 6.2	SO	Cross through wash; then adit in hillside on right.
		GPS: N32°59.01′ W114°06.44′
▼ 6.5	SO	Enter wash.
▼ 6.6	SO	Exit wash.
▼ 6.8	SO	Enter wash.
		GPS: N32°58.78′ W114°05.96′
▼ 7.1	SO	Exit wash.
▼ 9.1	SO	Enter Big Eye Wash. Trail follows the line of the wash.
		GPS: N33°00.39′ W114°04.58′
▼ 9.7	BL	Exit main wash channel.
		GPS: N33°00.81′ W114°04.72′
▼ 10.6	SO	Track on left; remain in wash channel.
▼ 11.2	SO	Exit wash.
▼ 11.3	BL	Closed track on right.
▼ 11.4	SO	Enter wash, traveling through a gap in the range.
▼ 11.8		Trail ends at a gate to the old vehicle trail to the Big Eye Mine. Mine is just over the saddle a short way along the trail.
		GPS: N33°02.05′ W114°05.81′

CENTRAL REGION TRAIL #6

Engesser Pass Trail

Starting Point:	**Central #3: King Valley Road, marker post 65**
Finishing Point:	**Pipeline Road, marker post 14**
Total Mileage:	**42.4 miles**
Unpaved Mileage:	**42.4 miles**
Driving Time:	**2.5 hours**
Elevation Range:	**1,300–2,600 feet**
Usually Open:	**Year-round**
Best Time to Travel:	**November to April**
Difficulty Rating:	**4**
Scenic Rating:	**8**
Remoteness Rating:	**+1**

Special Attractions

- Historic King of Arizona (Kofa) Mining District.
- Panoramic views over King Valley, the Tank Mountains, and the Kofa Mountains.
- Rugged Engesser Pass.
- Wildlife-viewing and remote desert experience.

History

In 1939 a Civilian Conservation Corps (CCC) camp was established at New Water Well under the leadership of Ray Tanner. The corps consisted primarily of young Native American men. Its mission in the area was to protect and conserve the surface water that flows from the Kofa Mountains into the Colorado River drainage. The CCC constructed Kofa Cabin along with several earthen and rock reservoirs in the area, including Four Peaks Dam.

Description

This long trail makes a wide loop through the Kofa National Wildlife Refuge and encompasses a wide variety of scenery. It commences at the east end of Central #3: King Valley Road in the historic Kofa Mining District. The remains of the Kofa Mine can be seen from the start of the trail; however, the area is privately owned and there is no admittance to the mines.

Kofa Butte in the distance

Initially, the trail is wide and smooth as it climbs around the edge of the Kofa Mountains. It crosses the gently sloping bajadas, giving panoramic views over King Valley. Farther along, the trail gets rougher; the section around Engesser Pass has an uneven surface, and there are a few loose, low-traction climbs. The trail is well used, but some sections in the wash are tight and slightly brushy for wider vehicles. Some drivers may spin their tires on the short, steep climb out of a wash crossing to Engesser Pass.

If the U.S. Air Force is looking for part of one of its planes...

Past Engesser Pass (named after a miner who prospected in the region), the trail is easy again and runs along a long ridge with spectacular views into the wash below. There are a couple of campsites along this section with no shade but spectacular views.

At a T-intersection, a track to the left goes 5.7 miles along a wash and on an increasingly rough trail to Yaqui Tanks. Yaqui Tanks are named after an Indian who discovered that the tanks were a reliable place to catch bighorn sheep. He had quite a profitable business selling the meat to the miners at the Kofa Mine. The track out to the tanks is narrow and very brushy in places. It ends at a good viewpoint of Kofa Butte.

Continuing on the Engesser Pass Trail, the road takes a roller-coaster ride over the ridges and down into the washes, culminating in the spectacular view from Red Rock Pass. The pass is not particularly high or steep, but the view down the narrow shelf road, north over the Little Horn Mountains, is one of the best on the trail.

Rock hounds can find some nice specimens of chalcedony and rhyolite on the desert pavement and in the washes, but these are strictly for admiring only—no collecting of any sort is allowed in the refuge.

Shortly after Red Rock Pass the standard improves as the trail passes by Craven Well to finish on Pipeline Road. If you are driving the trail in the reverse direction, Pipeline Road leaves US 95 seven miles south of Quartzsite and is signed to the Kofa National Wildlife Refuge, Crystal Hill. The section of trail from marker post 34 to marker post 14 is also known as Red Rock Pass Road.

Current Road Information

Kofa National Wildlife Refuge
356 West 1st Street
Yuma, AZ 85364
(520) 783-7861

Map References

BLM Little Horn Mts.

USGS 1:24,000 Kofa Butte, Charlie Died Tank, Engesser Pass, Hoodoo Well, Cholla Tank, Owl Head
1:100,000 Little Horn Mts.

Maptech CD-ROM: Southwest Arizona/Yuma; Colorado River/Lake Havasu

Arizona Atlas & Gazetteer, pp. 54, 55

Arizona Road & Recreation Atlas, pp. 44, 45 & pp. 78, 79

Other: Kofa NWR Map (free leaflet put out by the NWR showing designated travel routes)

Route Directions

▼ 0.0		From the east end of Central #3: King Valley Road, at marker post 65, turn east on roughly graded dirt road and cross through wash. Zero trip meter.
1.4 ▲		Trail ends at the intersection with Central #3: King Valley Road, at marker post 65. Turn left to exit to US 95.
		GPS: N33°16.95' W113°58.46'
▼ 0.2	BL	Track on right leads into the Baker Mine (on right) and on to the Kofa Mine. Both mines are private and there is no admittance. Bear left, remaining on the designated road. Initially, the trail is crossing private property.
1.2 ▲	BR	Track on left leads into the Baker Mine (on right) and on to the Kofa Mine. Both mines are private and there is no admittance. Bear right, remaining on the designated road.
		GPS: N33°16.80' W113°58.31'
▼ 0.3	SO	Tracks on right into private property; mine diggings on both sides of the road.
1.1 ▲	SO	Tracks on left into private property; mine diggings on both sides of the road.
▼ 0.5	SO	Track on right is private. Trail enters the Kofa NWR.
0.9 ▲	SO	Trail leaves the Kofa NWR into private property. Track on left is private.
▼ 0.7	SO	Track on right goes into private property.
0.7 ▲	BR	Track on left goes into private property.
▼ 1.1	SO	Cross through wash. Kofa Butte is the large, red-colored butte on the left.
0.3 ▲	SO	Kofa Butte is the large, red-colored butte on the right. Cross through wash.
▼ 1.4	SO	Track on left at marker post 21. Zero trip meter.
0.0 ▲		Continue to the northwest.
		GPS: N33°16.25' W113°57.28'
▼ 0.0		Continue to the southeast and cross through wash.
9.7 ▲	SO	Cross through wash; then track on right at marker post 21. Zero trip meter.
▼ 0.3	SO	Cross through wash.
9.4 ▲	SO	Cross through wash.
▼ 0.4	BL	Track on right is not a designated road. Bear left, remaining on the designated road.
9.3 ▲	BR	Track on left is not a designated road. Bear right, remaining on designated road.
		GPS: N33°15.92' W113°57.38'
▼ 0.6	SO	Cross through wide wash.
9.1 ▲	SO	Cross through wide wash.
▼ 0.8	SO	Cross through wide Yaqui Wash.
8.9 ▲	SO	Cross through wide Yaqui Wash.
▼ 1.2	SO	Cross through wash.
8.5 ▲	SO	Cross through wash.
▼ 1.3	SO	Cross through wide wash.
8.4 ▲	SO	Cross through wide wash.
▼ 1.9	SO	Cross through wash.
7.8 ▲	SO	Cross through wash.
▼ 2.0	SO	Cross through wide wash.
7.7 ▲	SO	Cross through wide wash.
		GPS: N33°14.61' W113°56.69'
▼ 2.1	BL	Bear right up wash.
7.6 ▲	BR	Bear left and exit wash.
▼ 3.5	SO	Exit up out of wash.
6.2 ▲	SO	Drop down to enter wash.
		GPS: N33°14.20' W113°55.40'
▼ 3.6	SO	Start to cross wide wash.
6.1 ▲	SO	Exit wide wash.
▼ 3.7	SO	Exit wide wash; then cross second wash.
6.0 ▲	SO	Cross through wash; then start to cross second wide wash.
▼ 4.1	SO	Cross through wide wash.
5.6 ▲	SO	Cross through wide wash.
▼ 4.9	SO	Cross through wash.
4.8 ▲	SO	Cross through wash.
▼ 5.3	SO	Enter wash.
4.4 ▲	SO	Exit wash.
▼ 5.5	SO	Exit wash.
4.2 ▲	SO	Enter wash.
		GPS: N33°13.03' W113°54.31'
▼ 6.6	SO	Cross through wash.
3.1 ▲	SO	Cross through wash.
▼ 6.7	SO	Cross through wash.
3.0 ▲	SO	Cross through wash.
▼ 7.0	SO	Cross through wide wash.
2.7 ▲	SO	Cross through wide wash.
▼ 7.9	SO	Cross through wash.
1.8 ▲	SO	Cross through wash.
▼ 8.2	SO	Cross through wash; then enter wash.
1.5 ▲	SO	Exit wash; then cross through wash.
		GPS: N33°11.88' W113°52.50'
▼ 8.3	SO	Exit wash.
1.4 ▲	SO	Enter wash.
▼ 9.3	SO	Cross through wash.
0.4 ▲	SO	Cross through wash.
▼ 9.6	SO	Enter wide wash.
0.1 ▲	SO	Exit wide wash.
▼ 9.7	SO	Track on right at marker post 62. Courthouse Mountain is on the right. Zero trip meter.
0.0 ▲		Continue on toward the Kofa Mining District.
		GPS: N33°12.81' W113°51.45'
▼ 0.0		Continue on toward Engesser Pass.
4.8 ▲	SO	Track on left at marker post 62. Courthouse Mountain is on the left. Zero trip meter.
▼ 0.1	SO	Exit wash.
4.7 ▲	SO	Enter wash.
▼ 0.3	BL	Enter wash.
4.5 ▲	BR	Bear right out of wash.
		GPS: N33°13.04' W113°51.36'
▼ 2.5	SO	Exit wash.
2.3 ▲	SO	Enter wash.
		GPS: N33°13.65' W113°49.78'
▼ 2.6	SO	Cross through wash; then short, steep climb up to Engesser Pass.
2.2 ▲	SO	Engesser Pass; then short, steep descent to cross through wash.
		GPS: N33°13.74' W113°49.73'

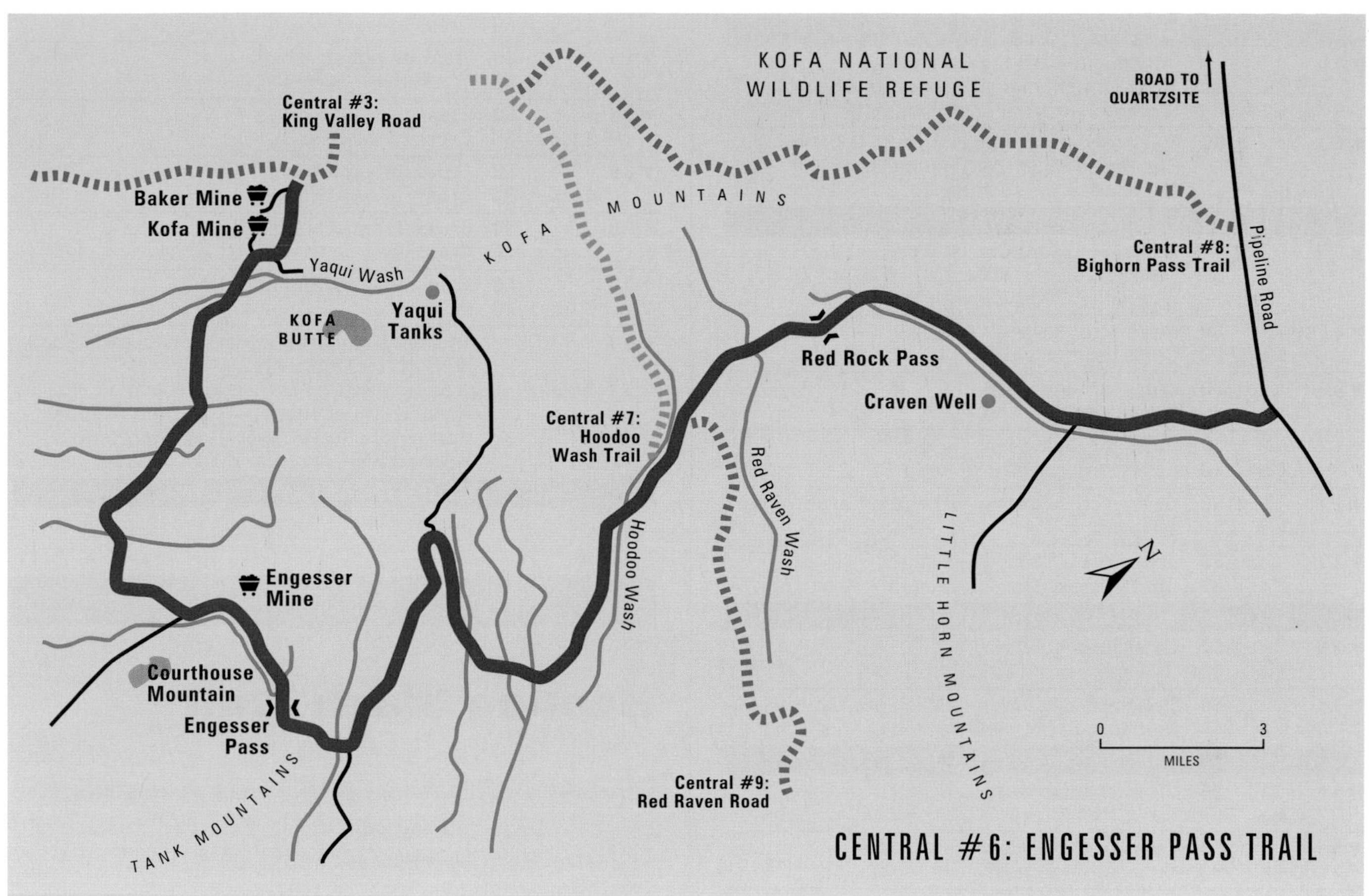

▼ 3.0		SO	Cross through wash.
	1.8 ▲	SO	Cross through wash.
▼ 3.5		SO	Cross through wash.
	1.3 ▲	SO	Cross through wash.
▼ 3.8		SO	Cross through wash.
	1.0 ▲	SO	Cross through wash.
▼ 4.1		SO	Cross through wash.
	0.7 ▲	SO	Cross through wash.
▼ 4.7		SO	Cross through wash.
	0.1 ▲	SO	Cross through wash.
			GPS: N33°14.33′ W113°48.14′
▼ 4.8		SO	Track on right at marker post 48. Zero trip meter.
	0.0 ▲		Continue to the southeast.
			GPS: N33°14.42′ W113°48.12′
▼ 0.0			Continue to the northeast.
	4.6 ▲	SO	Track on left at marker post 48. Zero trip meter.
▼ 0.1		SO	Cross through wash.
	4.5 ▲	SO	Cross through wash.
▼ 4.6		TR	T-intersection at marker post 47. Track on left goes 5.7 miles to Yaqui Tanks. Zero trip meter.
	0.0 ▲		Continue to the southeast.
			GPS: N33°16.96′ W113°51.18′
▼ 0.0			Continue to the east.
	8.8 ▲	TL	Turn left at marker post 47. Track continues straight ahead for 5.7 miles to Yaqui Tanks. Zero trip meter.
▼ 2.0		SO	Cross through wash.
	6.8 ▲	SO	Cross through wash.
			GPS: N33°16.80′ W113°49.15′
▼ 2.4		SO	Cross through wash.
	6.4 ▲	SO	Cross through wash.
▼ 3.0		SO	Cross through wash.
	5.8 ▲	SO	Cross through wash.
▼ 3.5		SO	Cross through wash.
	5.3 ▲	SO	Cross through wash.
			GPS: N33°17.66′ W113°47.93′
▼ 5.8		SO	Cross through wash.
	3.0 ▲	SO	Cross through wash.
▼ 6.0		SO	Enter Hoodoo Wash.
	2.8 ▲	SO	Exit Hoodoo Wash.
			GPS: N33°19.25′ W113°49.21′
▼ 6.6		BL	Bear left out of main wash channel.
	2.2 ▲	BR	Bear right and enter main wash channel.
▼ 6.7		SO	Exit wash path.
	2.1 ▲	SO	Enter wash path.
▼ 7.3		SO	Start to cross wide, multichanneled Hoodoo Wash.
	1.5 ▲	SO	Exit Hoodoo Wash.
▼ 7.5		SO	Exit wash crossing.
	1.3 ▲	SO	Start to cross wide, multichanneled Hoodoo Wash.
▼ 7.6		SO	Cross through wash.
	1.2 ▲	SO	Cross through wash.
▼ 8.4		SO	Start to cross wide wash.
	0.4 ▲	SO	Exit wash.
			GPS: N33°20.67′ W113°50.84′
▼ 8.5		SO	Exit wash.
	0.3 ▲	SO	Start to cross wide wash.
▼ 8.8		SO	Track on left at marker post 36 is Central #7: Hoodoo Wash Trail. Zero trip meter.
	0.0 ▲		Continue to the southeast.

			GPS: N33°20.96′ W113°51.07′
▼ 0.0			Continue toward Craven Well.
	0.3 ▲	SO	Track on right at marker post 36 is Central #7: Hoodoo Wash Trail. Zero trip meter.
▼ 0.3		SO	Track on right at marker post 34 is Central #9: Red Raven Road. Zero trip meter.
	0.0 ▲		Continue to the southeast.
			GPS: N33°21.09′ W113°51.35′
▼ 0.0			Continue toward Craven Well.
	7.4 ▲	SO	Track on left at marker post 34 is Central #9: Red Raven Road. Zero trip meter.
▼ 0.6		SO	Cross through wash.
	6.8 ▲	SO	Cross through wash.
▼ 0.9		SO	Cross through wash.
	6.5 ▲	SO	Cross through wash.
▼ 1.2		SO	Cross through wash.
	6.2 ▲	SO	Cross through wash.
▼ 2.1		SO	Start to cross through wide Red Raven Wash.
	5.3 ▲	SO	Exit wash.
▼ 2.2		SO	Exit wash.
	5.2 ▲	SO	Start to cross through wide Red Raven Wash.
			GPS: N33°22.84′ W113°52.37′
▼ 2.6		SO	Cross through wash.
	4.8 ▲	SO	Cross through wash.
▼ 3.4		SO	Red Rock Pass—short section of shelf road.
	4.0 ▲	SO	Red Rock Pass—short section of shelf road.
			GPS: N33°23.92′ W113°52.32′
▼ 4.8		SO	Cross through wash.
	2.6 ▲	SO	Cross through wash.
▼ 5.0		SO	Cross through wash.
	2.4 ▲	SO	Cross through wash.
▼ 5.4		SO	Cross through wash.
	2.0 ▲	SO	Cross through wash.
			GPS: N33°25.53′ W113°51.99′
▼ 5.7		SO	Cross through wash.
	1.7 ▲	SO	Cross through wash.
▼ 6.2		SO	Cross through wash.
	1.2 ▲	SO	Cross through wash.
▼ 6.5		SO	Cross through wide wash.
	0.9 ▲	SO	Cross through wide wash.
▼ 7.2		SO	Cross through wash.
	0.2 ▲	SO	Cross through wash.
▼ 7.4		SO	Two tracks on right to Craven Well. Zero trip meter at the second entrance (which is the main one). Well and tanks are visible immediately on right of the trail.
	0.0 ▲		Continue to the southwest.
			GPS: N33°26.38′ W113°50.28′
▼ 0.0			Continue toward Pipeline Road.
	5.4 ▲	SO	Two tracks on left to Craven Well. Zero trip meter at the first entrance (which is the main one). Well and tanks are visible immediately on left of the trail.
▼ 0.1		SO	Cross through wash; then enter wash.
	5.3 ▲	SO	Exit wash; then cross through wash.
▼ 0.4		SO	Exit wash.
	5.0 ▲	SO	Enter wash.
▼ 0.6		SO	Cross through wide wash.
	4.8 ▲	SO	Cross through wide wash.
▼ 0.8		SO	Cross through wash.
	4.6 ▲	SO	Cross through wash.
▼ 1.1		SO	Cross through wash.
	4.3 ▲	SO	Cross through wash.
▼ 1.2		SO	Cross through wash.
	4.2 ▲	SO	Cross through wash.
▼ 1.6		SO	Track on right is closed.
	3.8 ▲	BR	Track on left is closed.
▼ 3.3		SO	Cross through wash.
	2.1 ▲	SO	Cross through wash.
▼ 3.6		SO	Cross through wash.
	1.8 ▲	SO	Cross through wash.
▼ 5.0		SO	Cross through wash.
	0.4 ▲	SO	Cross through wash.
▼ 5.3		SO	Pass under power lines.
	0.1 ▲	SO	Pass under power lines.
▼ 5.4			Trail ends at marker post 14 on Pipeline Road. Turn left for Quartzsite.
	0.0 ▲		Trail commences at marker post 14 on Pipeline Road, 25 miles east of US 95. Turn south at the sign for Craven Well, Red Rock Dam, and Hoodoo Well. Zero trip meter.
			GPS: N33°30.41′ W113°47.76′

CENTRAL REGION TRAIL #7

Hoodoo Wash Trail

Starting Point:	**Central #6: Engesser Pass Trail, marker post 36**
Finishing Point:	**Wilbanks Cabin**
Total Mileage:	**9 miles**
Unpaved Mileage:	**9 miles**
Driving Time:	**1 hour**
Elevation Range:	**2,300–3,300 feet**
Usually Open:	**Year-round**
Best Time to Travel:	**November to April**
Difficulty Rating:	**3**
Scenic Rating:	**7**
Remoteness Rating:	**+1**

Special Attractions

- Easy trail that runs along wide Hoodoo Wash.
- Historic Wilbanks Cabin.
- Can be combined with Bighorn Pass for a loop trail.

History

The two-room Wilbanks Cabin was constructed by Jack Wilbanks in 1934 after their original cabin, built on the opposite side of Hoodoo Wash, burned down. It was home to Jack, his wife, Martha Lewis Wilbanks, and their three daughters. The Wilbanks family raised cattle in the area beginning in 1931. The family relocated to Vicksburg in 1939 and used the cabin as a weekend retreat. The Wilbanks family continued to raise cattle in the area until 1945 when they sold their interest in the ranch to the Crowder Cattle Company and moved to Parker. Livestock grazing on the Kofa refuge ceased in 1976 when the Kofa Game Range became the Kofa National Wildlife Refuge.

Wilbanks Cabin with its ocotillo roof

Description

The Hoodoo Wash Trail runs down the wide, gravelly wash to finish at Wilbanks Well and Cabin. The trail is easier and smoother than many of the trails in the region. The main factor to contend with is the loose, gravelly surface. The wash runs in a fairly shallow canyon, which allows for better views than in narrower washes. Vehicles are also less likely to be scratched.

The Wilbanks Cabin is a well-preserved wooden structure located next to a well that also bears the family name. Look at the underside of the verandah roof to see the ocotillo sticks that form the roof lining. This typical roofing and shade material was commonly used in southwestern deserts. The visitors book in the cabin reflects the relatively few travelers the cabin attracts.

The wells found along the trail are primarily for animals, and each has an attached game tank. Some have water tanks with faucets, but the water is not potable and should not be relied upon. The faucets may be removed when supplies are low. Note that you are not permitted to camp within 0.25 miles of any water source in Arizona.

Current Road Information

Kofa National Wildlife Refuge
356 West 1st St.
Yuma, AZ 85364
(520) 783-7861

Map References

BLM Little Horn Mts.
USGS 1:24,000 Hoodoo Well, Kofa Butte
1:100,000 Little Horn Mts.
Maptech CD-ROM: Southwest Arizona/Yuma
Arizona Atlas & Gazetteer, p. 54
Arizona Road & Recreation Atlas, p. 44 & p. 78
Other: Kofa NWR Map (free leaflet put out by the NWR showing designated travel routes)

Route Directions

Mileage	Reverse	Direction	Description
▼ 0.0			The trail commences on Central #6: Engesser Pass Trail, 12.8 miles south of Pipeline Road. Zero trip meter and turn south at marker post 36.
	0.4 ▲		Trail ends at the junction with Central #6: Engesser Pass Trail at marker post 36. Turn right to continue along the Engesser Pass Trail; turn left to exit to Pipeline Road.
			GPS: N33°20.96′ W113°51.07′
▼ 0.2		BL	Cross through wide Hoodoo Wash; then track on right.
	0.2 ▲	SO	Track on left; then cross through wide Hoodoo Wash.
▼ 0.4		TR	Turn on rise. Track straight ahead goes 0.1 miles to Hoodoo Cabin and Well. Zero trip meter.
	0.0 ▲		Continue toward Central #6: Engesser Pass Trail.
			GPS: N33°20.64′ W113°51.27′
▼ 0.0			Continue toward Wilbanks Cabin.
	8.2 ▲	TL	Turn on rise. Track on right goes 0.1 miles to Hoodoo Cabin and Well. Zero trip meter.
▼ 0.1		BL	Smaller track on right.
	8.1 ▲	SO	Smaller track on left.
▼ 0.7		SO	Cross through two washes.
	7.5 ▲	SO	Cross through two washes.
▼ 1.0		SO	Cross through wash.
	7.2 ▲	SO	Cross through wash.
▼ 1.9		SO	Enter Hoodoo Wash.
	6.3 ▲	SO	Exit wash.
			GPS: N33°21.25′ W113°52.81′
▼ 7.3		BR	Bear right out of wash.
	0.9 ▲	BL	Enter Hoodoo Wash and bear left down wash.
			GPS: N33°20.75′ W113°58.15′
▼ 7.5		SO	Trail re-enters Hoodoo Wash.

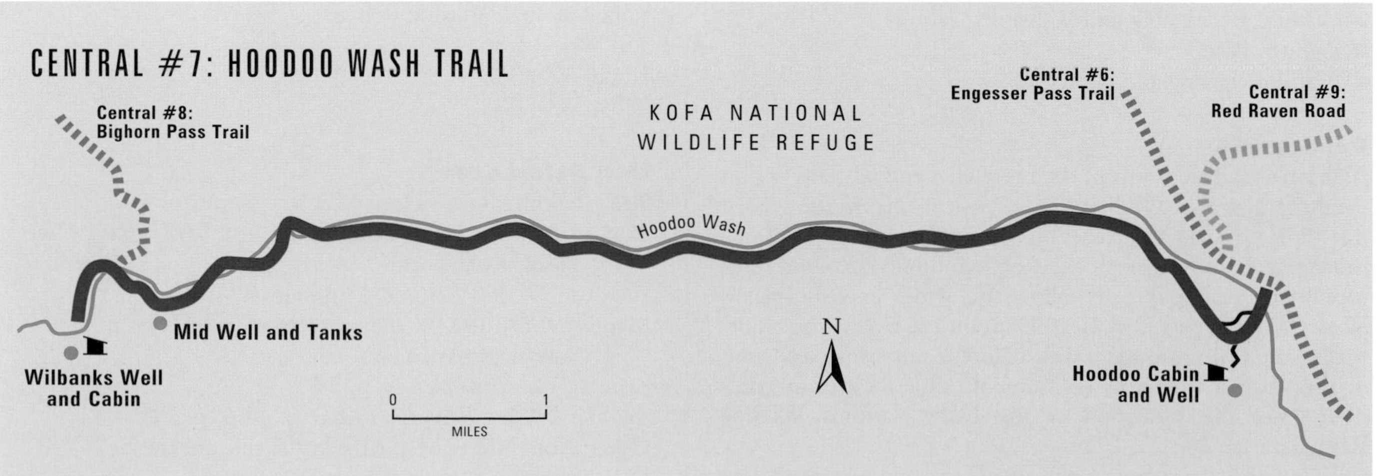

	0.7 ▲	SO	Trail exits Hoodoo Wash.
▼ 7.8		SO	Mid Well and Tanks on the left.
	0.4 ▲	SO	Mid Well and Tanks on the right.
			GPS: N33°20.54' W113°58.70'
▼ 8.1		BR	Fork in wash; left goes to Wilbanks Well, bypassing marker post 31 and the turn to Central #8: Bighorn Pass Trail.
	0.1 ▲	SO	Track in wash on right bypasses marker post 31.
			GPS: N33°20.64' W113°58.99'
▼ 8.2		SO	Track on right in Hoodoo Wash at marker post 31 is Central #8: Bighorn Pass Trail. Zero trip meter.
	0.0 ▲		Continue toward Hoodoo Well.
			GPS: N33°20.68' W113°59.02'
▼ 0.0			Continue to Wilbanks Cabin.
▼ 0.4			Trail ends at Wilbanks Well and Cabin.
			GPS: N33°20.36' W113°59.23'

CENTRAL REGION TRAIL #8

Bighorn Pass Trail

Starting Point:	**Pipeline Road, marker post 16**
Finishing Point:	**Central #7: Hoodoo Wash Trail, marker post 31**
Total Mileage:	**17.6 miles**
Unpaved Mileage:	**17.6 miles**
Driving Time:	**3.5 hours**
Elevation Range:	**700–3,300 feet**
Usually Open:	**Year-round**
Best Time to Travel:	**November to April**
Difficulty Rating:	**5**
Scenic Rating:	**8**
Remoteness Rating:	**+1**

Special Attractions

- Moderately challenging rocky trail through spectacular Kofa Range.
- Historic Kofa Cabin and Wilbanks Cabin.
- Bighorn Pass.
- Wildlife-viewing and photography.

Description

Bighorn Pass Trail is one of the more challenging trails within the Kofa National Wildlife Refuge. It leaves from the graded dirt Pipeline Road and passes by the small stone Kofa Cabin a mile later. It runs through the Kofa Mountains along a ridge top before descending to follow the wide, gravelly Alamo Wash. You will pass Owl Head Dam on the right, which normally contains some water, just before a short spur leads out of the wash to the Kofa Monument. This rock cairn commemorates the formation of the Kofa National Wildlife Refuge on January 25, 1939.

The trail continues in Alamo Wash for another mile before swinging out of the wash and onto the ridge again. The turn is easy to miss as the intersection is somewhat obscured by a tree, and misleading tire tracks continue in the wash because people have missed the turn. The trail is rocky as it climbs over the ridge tops; there are several low-traction sections with moderately steep climbs. Sections of the trail in the wash can be lumpy, while other sections have loose, deep gravel. Traversing some of these loose sections can be very similar to driving in deep sand. The upper sections of the wash, as you near Bighorn Pass, are narrow and can be a little brushy. The scenery around Bighorn Pass, with views over the Kofa Mountains, is the most spectacular of the trail. The roller-coaster aspect of the trail at this point adds to the fun. Bighorn Pass itself is easily missed, as it is one of the many saddles along this stretch of trail. The area around Bighorn Pass is a good spot to look for the bighorn sheep that are native to the refuge. Dawn and dusk are prime times for viewing.

Kofa Cabin

Most of the wells in the refuge are active, and they supply game tanks. Some of the tanks have faucets, but the water is not potable. Remember that you are not permitted to camp within 0.25 miles of a water source anywhere in Arizona. This restriction ensures that animals have access to the water points. However, there are many pleasant campsites to be found within the permitted area—100 feet of the designated trail. On topographic maps, this trail is named Wilbanks Road.

Current Road Information

Kofa National Wildlife Refuge
356 West 1st St.
Yuma, AZ 85364
(520) 783-7861

Map References

BLM Salome, Little Horn Mts.
USGS 1:24,000 New Water Well, New Water Mts., Owl Head, Kofa Butte
1:100,000 Salome, Little Horn Mts.
Maptech CD-ROM: Colorado River/Lake Havasu; Southwest Arizona/Yuma
Arizona Atlas & Gazetteer, p. 54
Arizona Road & Recreation Atlas, p. 44 & p. 78
Other: Kofa NWR Map (free leaflet put out by the NWR showing designated travel routes)

Route Directions

▼ 0.0		From Pipeline Road at marker post 16, turn southwest at the sign for Kofa Cabin and New Water Well. Zero trip meter.
1.1 ▲		Trail ends on Pipeline Road at marker post 16. Turn left to exit to US 95.
		GPS: N33°30.76′ W113°51.08′
▼ 0.9	SO	Cross through wash.
0.2 ▲	SO	Cross through wash.
▼ 1.0	SO	Cross through wash.
0.1 ▲	SO	Cross through wash.
▼ 1.1	BL	Track on right goes 0.4 miles to New Water Well. Zero trip meter and bear left. Kofa Cabin is on the left.
0.0 ▲		Continue toward Pipeline Road.
		GPS: N33°30.28′ W113°52.09′
▼ 0.0		Continue to the southwest past the cabin.
0.4 ▲	BR	Kofa Cabin is on the right; then track on left goes 0.4 miles to New Water Well. Zero trip meter.
▼ 0.3	SO	Cross through Alamo Wash.
0.1 ▲	SO	Cross through Alamo Wash.
▼ 0.4	BL	Track on right at marker post 12. Zero trip meter.
0.0 ▲		Continue to the northeast.
		GPS: N33°30.10′ W113°52.48′
▼ 0.0		Continue to the south.
6.3 ▲	BR	Track on left at marker post 12. Zero trip meter.
▼ 0.4	SO	Cross through wash.
5.9 ▲	SO	Cross through wash.
▼ 0.5	SO	Cross through wash.
5.8 ▲	SO	Cross through wash.
▼ 1.7	SO	Cross through wash.
4.6 ▲	SO	Cross through wash.
		GPS: N33°28.90′ W113°53.50′
▼ 3.4	SO	Cross through wash.
2.9 ▲	SO	Cross through wash.
		GPS: N33°27.68′ W113°54.50′
▼ 3.8	SO	Cross through wash.
2.5 ▲	SO	Cross through wash.
▼ 4.1	BR	Enter Alamo Wash and swing right up the wide, gravelly wash.
2.2 ▲	BL	Bear left and exit wash.
		GPS: N33°27.35′ W113°55.08′
▼ 4.8	SO	Two small arches high on the rock to the left.
1.5 ▲	SO	Look back to the right to see two small arches high on the rock.
▼ 6.2	SO	Owl Head Dam on right, located behind the remains of a metal fence.
0.1 ▲	SO	Owl Head Dam on left, located behind the remains of a metal fence.
		GPS: N33°25.78′ W113°55.07′
▼ 6.3	SO	Unmarked track on right goes 0.1 miles to Kofa Monument. Zero trip meter.
0.0 ▲		Continue along Alamo Wash.
		GPS: N33°25.73′ W113°55.07′
▼ 0.0		Continue along Alamo Wash.
7.8 ▲	SO	Unmarked track on left goes 0.1 miles to Kofa Monument. Zero trip meter.
▼ 1.0	BL	Bear left out of wash and climb up ridge. Tire marks continue in the wash. This turn is easy to miss.
6.8 ▲	BR	Drop down off the ridge and bear right into Alamo Wash.
		GPS: N33°24.97′ W113°55.15′
▼ 1.3	SO	Cross through wash.
6.5 ▲	SO	Cross through wash.
▼ 1.6	SO	Re-enter Alamo Wash.
6.2 ▲	SO	Exit wash.

A view of the trail traveling along the Alamo Wash

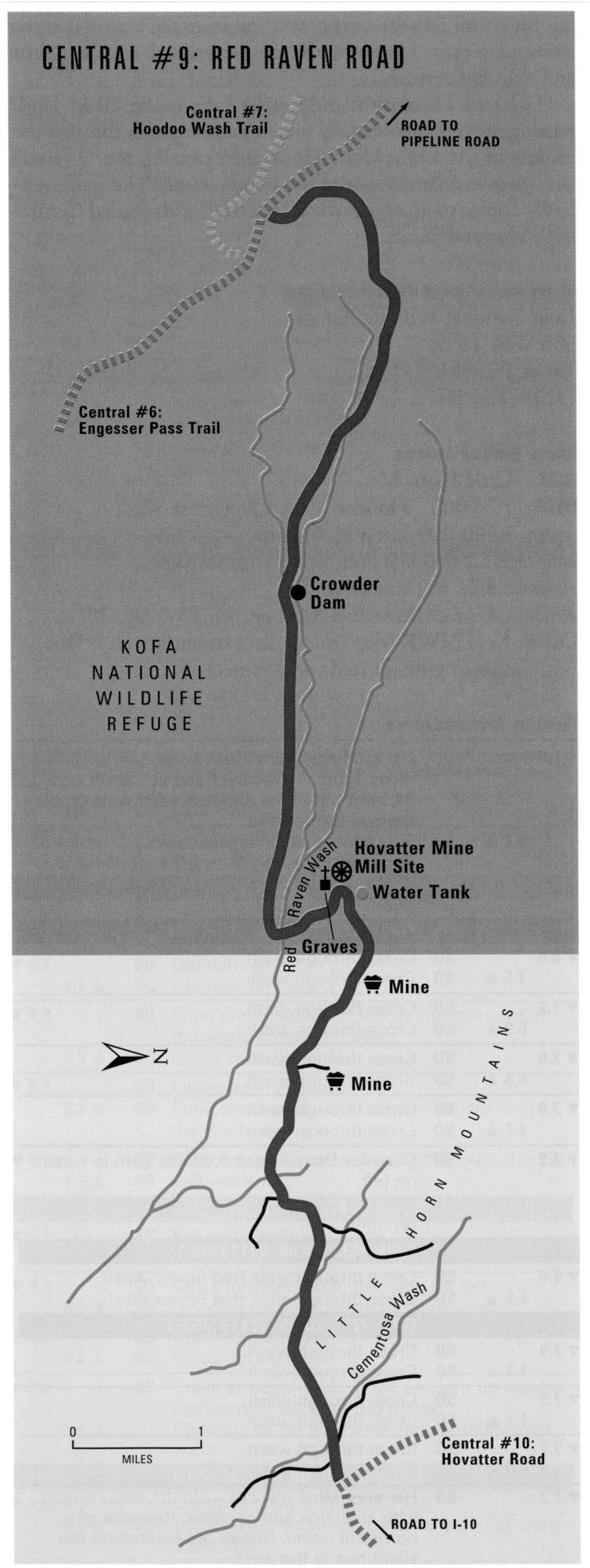

	0.9 ▲	SO	Hovatter Mine mill site—old driveway edged with saguaros and ocotillos. Remains of a burnt-out trailer. Graves are located on the slight rise to the west.
			GPS: N33°21.24′ W113°45.96′
▼ 7.3		SO	Hovatter Mine mill site water tank; then cross through wash.
	0.8 ▲	SO	Cross through wash; then Hovatter Mine mill site water tank.
			GPS: N33°21.30′ W113°45.91′
▼ 7.4		SO	Cross through wash.
	0.7 ▲	SO	Cross through wash.
▼ 7.5		SO	Cross through wash.
	0.6 ▲	SO	Cross through wash.
▼ 8.1		SO	Exiting Kofa NWR into BLM land. Small mine on left. Zero trip meter.
	0.0 ▲		Continue northwest into the Kofa NWR. Trail becomes narrower and rougher.
			GPS: N33°21.28′ W113°45.14′
▼ 0.0			Continue southeast into BLM lands. Trail is wider at this point and has been roughly graded in the past.
	4.1 ▲	SO	Entering Kofa NWR at sign; maps available at entrance point. Small mine on right. Zero trip meter.
▼ 0.1		SO	Small track on left goes to mine; then cross through wash.
	4.0 ▲	SO	Cross through wash; then small track on right goes to mine.
▼ 0.7		SO	Small track on left goes to mine. Numerous stone walls remain.
	3.4 ▲	SO	Small track on right goes to mine. Numerous stone walls remain.
			GPS: N33°20.84′ W113°44.55′
▼ 0.8		SO	Cross through wash.
	3.3 ▲	SO	Cross through wash.
▼ 1.5		SO	Cross through wash.
	2.6 ▲	SO	Cross through wash.
▼ 1.6		SO	Cross through wash.
	2.5 ▲	SO	Cross through wash.
▼ 1.7		SO	Small track on right.
	2.4 ▲	SO	Small track on left.
▼ 2.1		SO	Two small tracks on left.
	2.0 ▲	SO	Two small tracks on right.
			GPS: N33°20.97′ W113°43.31′
▼ 2.5		SO	Cross through wash.
	1.6 ▲	SO	Cross through wash.
▼ 3.9		SO	Cross through Cementosa Wash; then track on left. The track you are on is marked in the other direction as 001.
	0.2 ▲	SO	Track on right; continue straight on at trail marker 001 and cross through Cementosa Wash.
			GPS: N33°21.02′ W113°41.48′
▼ 4.0		SO	Track on right.
	0.1 ▲	SO	Track on left.
▼ 4.1			Trail ends at the intersection with the wider, graded dirt Central #10: Hovatter Road. Turn right to exit to I-10.
	0.0 ▲		Trail starts 20.4 miles south from I-10 along Central #10: Hovatter Road. Bear left onto smaller trail at white painted cairn with marker post. Zero trip meter and continue to the southwest.
			GPS: N33°21.04′ W113°41.23′

CENTRAL REGION TRAIL #10

Hovatter Road

Starting Point:	**I-10 at exit 53**
Finishing Point:	**Oakland Mine**
Total Mileage:	**21.4 miles**
Unpaved Mileage:	**21.1 miles**
Driving Time:	**1.5 hours**
Elevation Range:	**1,300–2,400 feet**
Usually Open:	**Year-round**
Best Time to Travel:	**November to April**
Difficulty Rating:	**1**
Scenic Rating:	**7**
Remoteness Rating:	**+0**

Special Attractions

- Prominent Coyote Peak.
- Panoramic views across the Ranegras Plain to four mountain ranges.

Description

This easy trail, suitable for most passenger vehicles in dry weather, leaves from I-10 at exit 53 (Hovatter Road) and travels across the flat Ranegras Plain. There are panoramic views along this section—north to the Little Harquahala Mountains, west to the New Water Mountains, south to the Little Horn Mountains, and east to the Eagletail Mountains. The road is named after the Hovatters, a family that lived at the homestead site now contained within the Kofa National Wildlife Refuge along Central #9: Red Raven Road.

There is a section of deep powder sand (3.9 miles from the north end of the trail) that becomes totally impassable when wet. This stretch is 0.5 miles long and is situated where the road crosses the otherwise unnoticeable Upper Bouse Wash.

Coyote Peak is a prominent feature along the trail. The conical hill rises abruptly from the flat Ranegras Plain. At the southern end of the trail is the Bob Crowder Dam, dedicated to a pioneer Arizona cattleman who hailed from Texas.

The open-cut Oakland Mine with its heap of red tailings

Once the trail crosses from La Paz to Yuma County, the smoothly graded road becomes rough and is less maintained. Passenger vehicles will have a harder time than 4WDs, but they can still travel the trail with a little care and common sense.

The trail ends at a large, open-pit Oakland Mine that is undergoing revegetation. You can either exit the way you came in or continue west along Central #9: Red Raven Road into the Kofa National Wildlife Refuge.

Current Road Information

Bureau of Land Management
Phoenix Field Office
2015 West Deer Valley Rd.
Phoenix, AZ 85027
(623) 580-5500

Map References

BLM Little Horn Mts., Salome
USGS 1:24,000 Hope SE, Hope SW, Coyote Peak, Cementosa Wash
1:100,000 Little Horn Mts., Salome
Maptech CD-ROM: Southwest Arizona/Yuma; Colorado River/Lake Havasu
Arizona Atlas & Gazetteer, p. 55
Arizona Road & Recreation Atlas, p. 45 & p. 79
Recreational Map of Arizona

Route Directions

▼ 0.0			From I-10, exit 53, proceed south and zero trip meter at the cattle guard immediately after the freeway bridge.
0.3 ▲			Trail ends at the south side of I-10 at exit 53. Take the freeway east for Phoenix, west for Quartzsite.
			GPS: N33°36.40' W113°37.20'
▼ 0.3		TL	Cross over aqueduct; immediately swing right, remaining on paved road. Turn left onto graded dirt road toward communications towers. Turn is unmarked but is opposite a dead-end road sign. Zero trip meter.
0.0 ▲			Continue on paved road.
			GPS: N33°36.18' W113°37.33'
▼ 0.0			Continue on graded dirt road.
9.4 ▲		TR	Turn onto paved road and immediately swing left over aqueduct, remaining on paved road. Zero trip meter.
▼ 0.7		SO	Communications towers on right.
8.7 ▲		SO	Communications towers on left.
▼ 0.8		SO	Faint track on left at right-hand bend.
8.6 ▲		SO	Faint track on right at left-hand bend.
▼ 0.9		SO	Cross through wash.
8.5 ▲		SO	Cross through wash.
▼ 1.0		SO	Enter wash.
8.4 ▲		SO	Exit wash.
▼ 1.1		SO	Exit wash.
8.3 ▲		SO	Enter wash.
▼ 1.6		SO	Cross through wash. Black Rock Hill on right.
7.8 ▲		SO	Cross through wash. Black Rock Hill on left.

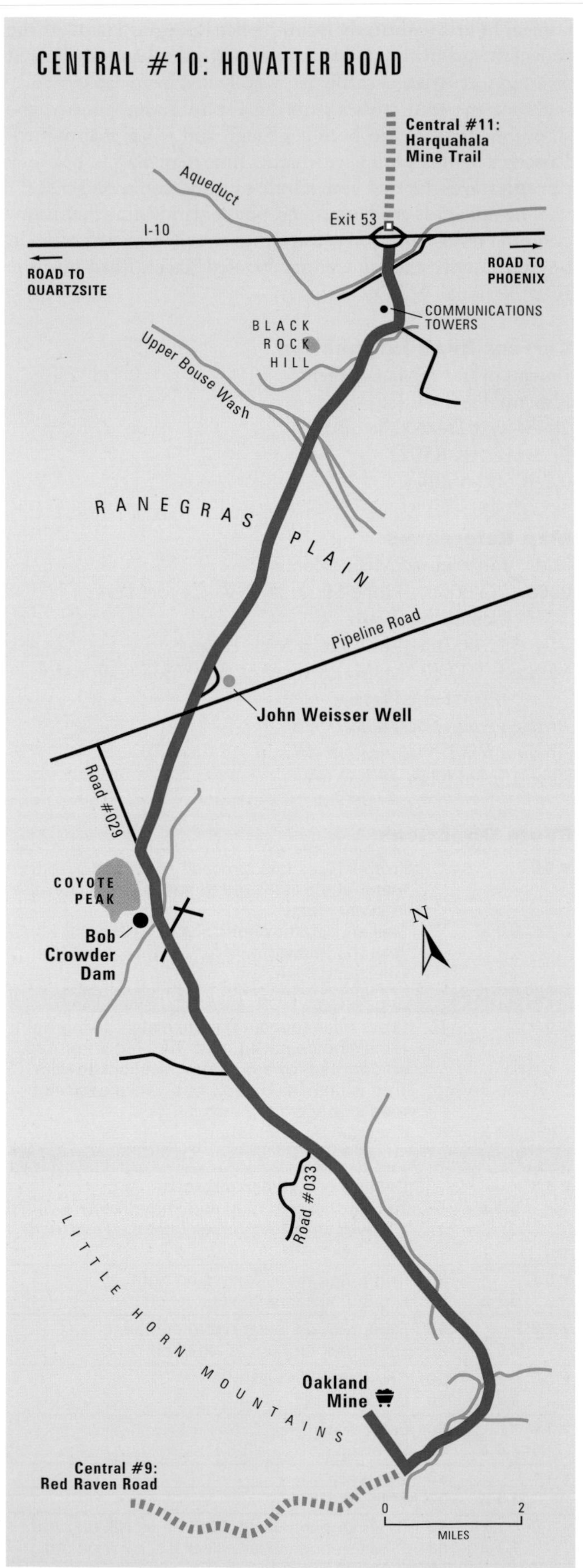

▼ 2.6		SO	Cattle guard.
	6.8 ▲	SO	Cattle guard.
▼ 3.6		SO	Long section of deep sand traps crossing Upper Bouse Wash.
	5.8 ▲	SO	Long section of deep sand traps crossing Upper Bouse Wash.
▼ 6.7		BR	Track on left goes to corral and John Weisser Well.
	2.7 ▲	SO	Track on right goes to corral and John Weisser Well.
▼ 6.9		SO	Track on left goes to corral and John Weisser Well.
	2.5 ▲	BL	Track on right goes to corral and John Weisser Well.
▼ 7.0		SO	Pass under power lines.
	2.4 ▲	SO	Pass under power lines.
▼ 7.2		SO	Track on left and track on right along pipeline. This is the continuation of Pipeline Road to US 95.
	2.2 ▲	SO	Track on left and track on right along pipeline. This is the continuation of Pipeline Road to US 95.
			GPS: N33°31.22′ W113°41.79′
▼ 9.4		SO	Wide graded road to the right is #029. Zero trip meter at junction.
	0.0 ▲		Continue toward freeway.
			GPS: N33°29.44′ W113°43.06′
▼ 0.0			Continue toward Coyote Peak.
	8.6 ▲	BR	Road forks, with wide graded road leading off to the left. Road on left is #029. Bear right, remaining on Road #001. Zero trip meter.
			GPS: N33°28.72′ W113°43.06′
▼ 0.8		SO	Track on right onto dam wall. Bob Crowder Dam on right at the southern end of Coyote Peak.
	7.8 ▲	SO	Track on left onto dam wall.
▼ 0.9		SO	Track on left goes to corral.
	7.7 ▲	SO	Track on right goes to corral.
▼ 1.1		SO	Narrow track on right at start of dam wall.
	7.5 ▲	SO	Narrow track on left at start of dam wall. Bob Crowder Dam at the southern end of Coyote Peak.
			GPS: N33°28.41′ W113°42.99′
▼ 3.4		SO	Narrow track on right.
	5.2 ▲	SO	Narrow track on left. Coyote Peak is the cone-shaped hill directly in front.
▼ 4.5		SO	Cattle guard.
	4.1 ▲	SO	Cattle guard.
▼ 4.8		SO	Track on right is #033.
	3.8 ▲	SO	Track on left is #033.
			GPS: N33°25.40′ W113°41.63′
▼ 7.8		SO	Cross through wash.
	0.8 ▲	SO	Cross through wash.
▼ 8.2		SO	Track on right.
	0.4 ▲	SO	Track on left.
▼ 8.3		SO	Track on right.
	0.3 ▲	SO	Track on left.
▼ 8.6		SO	Entering Yuma County; sign pointing the other way for La Paz County. Zero trip meter.
	0.0 ▲		Continue into La Paz County.
			GPS: N33°22.30′ W113°39.81′
▼ 0.0			Continue into Yuma County.
	2.1 ▲	SO	Entering La Paz County at sign. Zero trip meter.
▼ 0.4		SO	Cross through wash.
	1.7 ▲	SO	Cross through wash.

Mileage	Reverse	Dir.	Description
▼ 1.0		SO	Cross through wash.
	1.1 ▲	SO	Cross through wash.
▼ 1.1		SO	Cross through wash.
	1.0 ▲	SO	Cross through wash.
▼ 1.2		BR	Smaller track on left.
	0.9 ▲	SO	Smaller track on right.
▼ 1.5		SO	Cross through wash.
	0.6 ▲	SO	Cross through wash.
▼ 2.0		SO	Small track on right.
	0.1 ▲	SO	Small track on left.
▼ 2.1		BR	Smaller track on left is Central #9: Red Raven Road. Trail has a white painted cairn at the intersection but is otherwise unmarked. Zero trip meter.
	0.0 ▲		Continue to the east.
			GPS: N33°21.04′ W113°41.23′
▼ 0.0			Continue toward Oakland Mine.
▼ 0.3		SO	Small track on right; then small track on left.
▼ 0.9		SO	Main entrance to old open-pit Oakland Mine on right. Area is now closed for revegetation.
▼ 1.0			Trail ends at turnaround. Small trail continues but is closed where it enters the Kofa National Wildlife Refuge.
			GPS: N33°21.85′ W113°41.67′

CENTRAL REGION TRAIL #11

Harquahala Mine Trail

Starting Point:	**I-10 at exit 53**
Finishing Point:	**US 60 in Salome**
Total Mileage:	**12.1 miles**
Unpaved Mileage:	**9.8 miles**
Driving Time:	**1 hour**
Elevation Range:	**1,600–2,200 feet**
Usually Open:	**Year-round**
Best Time to Travel:	**September to June**
Difficulty Rating:	**1**
Scenic Rating:	**7**
Remoteness Rating:	**+0**

Special Attractions

- Historic Harquahala Mining District.
- Harquahala Cemetery.
- Easy desert drive suitable for passenger vehicles.
- Salome—made famous by Dick Wick Hall.

History

Reports as early as the 1760s state that Spanish prospectors knew of gold in the Harqua Halas, as it was often spelled in earlier days. The Indian name translates as "running water high up." Attempts were made to mine the gold, but the local Pima Indians were very successful in driving out most of the would-be prospectors. Tales of the gold filtered through and finally caught the attention of passing military officers. They managed to collect some surface gold before being forced out by the Apache.

Harquahala Cemetery

In 1863, Herman Ehrenberg mentioned to Henry Wickenburg that he had found a promising location in the Little Harquahala Mountains. Wickenburg explored the region and also found it to be potentially rich. However, on his way back, he discovered the Vulture Mine, which made him forget all about the Little Harquahala Mountains.

Harry Walton, Mike Sullivan, and Robert Stein are credited with discovering what became the Harquahala Mine. The three men owned two adjacent claims, with Walton and Stein owning one, and Sullivan the other. According to the story, Mike Sullivan, out prospecting one day, was overjoyed to find a number of gold nuggets on the ground. He filled his hat and his pockets with the find, but when he checked the claim stakes he discovered he had inadvertently strayed onto his neighbors' claim. Rather than relinquish the gold, he convinced Stein and Walton that they should combine their claims to work them more efficiently. Knowing nothing about the nuggets on their claim, the two men agreed to the merger. Once the paperwork was complete, Sullivan "found" the nuggets and the three men established the Harquahala Mine.

Two other rich areas in the region, the Bonanza and Golden Eagle veins, drew in prospectors from far and wide. Harrisburg developed in the 1880s with the construction of a mill to process ore from the mines, and the inevitable rush began. The Bonanza and Golden Eagle Mines gained notoriety and changed hands several times with ever-growing returns.

Many mines suffered losses when shipping gold to Phoenix. Outlaws regularly held up stagecoaches known to be carrying gold, and they made off with the bars. One later owner of the Harquahala Mine came up with the idea of casting bars too large to be easily carried. This idea worked well until one day in 1890. As Sheriffs Burke and Davis were transporting a load to Sentinel, the bottom fell out of the flimsy wooden stage and the 400-pound ingot followed. The loss wasn't

Remains of an old adobe building at the original Harquahala settlement

Looking south across Ranegras Plain to the Eagletail Mountains

discovered for a few miles, but luckily the gold was recovered (not without considerable difficulty, however, as it had to be retrieved from the bottom of a deep gully).

High grading—the practice of employed miners making off with choice pieces of ore—seemed an almost accepted activity in the eyes of the law in the Harquahala region. On several occasions culprits were not charged, even though they confessed their crimes.

The mines continued to produce ore in enormous quantities and changed hands again and again until a group of Englishmen paid $1.25 million for the mine although they recovered only $125,000 in return. Ironically, the group sold out to the previous American owner for $7,000; he, in turn, sold the mines again for $40,000. Finally, the mines ran dry and the main activities ceased by 1907.

Description

This graded gravel road passes the historic Harquahala Mining District. The road is well maintained and suitable for passenger vehicles. It leaves I-10 and heads north, traveling through the rugged and scenic Little Harquahala Mountains. After 4 miles the trail passes close to the old Harquahala Mine. Many of the workings can be seen from the road; the old adobe building that is part of the original settlement is just over a rise out of sight from the road. Much of the area is on private property or under mining claim. Please respect posted restrictions. Many of the remains at the Harquahala Mine date from activity after 1907. There are many old steps, retaining walls, and a fireplace.

One interesting feature along the trail is the old cemetery, which is found alongside the graded road. There are approximately 30 graves, marked by piles of stones. There are no headstones or names.

A short distance farther along, a side trail (0.5 miles) goes to the remains of the Golden Eagle Mine. Tailings, shafts, and a wooden hopper can be seen. A high-clearance 2WD vehicle is required for this side trail.

The trail ends in the town of Salome on US 60. This town was made famous by comedian Dick Wick Hall, who was also active in promoting the mines around Winchester. A memorial to Dick Wick Hall can be found in town. Refer to Northwest #4: Desert Queen Mine Trail for the exact location.

Current Road Information

Bureau of Land Management
Phoenix Field Office
2015 West Deer Valley Rd.
Phoenix, AZ 85027
(623) 580-5500

Map References

BLM Salome
USGS 1:24,000 Hope SE, Harrisburg Valley, Salome
1:100,000 Salome
Maptech CD-ROM: Colorado River/Lake Havasu
Arizona Atlas & Gazetteer, pp. 47, 54
Arizona Road & Recreation Atlas, p. 39 & p. 73
Recreational Map of Arizona

Route Directions

Mileage			Directions
▼ 0.0			From I-10 at exit 53 (Hovatter Road), proceed to the north side of the freeway and zero trip meter at cattle guard. Continue to the north.
	3.2 ▲		Trail ends at I-10, exit 53. Westbound goes to Quartzsite, eastbound to Phoenix.
			GPS: N33°36.69' W113°37.13'
▼ 0.6		SO	Track on left.
	2.6 ▲	SO	Track on right.
▼ 1.8		SO	Major graded road on left; small track on right. Continue to north.
	1.4 ▲	SO	Major graded road on right; small track on left.
			GPS: N33°38.31' W113°36.69'
▼ 2.6		SO	Track on left.
	0.6 ▲	SO	Track on right.
▼ 3.0		SO	Cross through wash.
	0.2 ▲	SO	Cross through wash.
▼ 3.2		BL	Graded road on right goes into quarry; also small track on right. Zero trip meter.
	0.0 ▲		Continue to the south.
			GPS: N33°39.51' W113°36.13'
▼ 0.0			Continue to the north.
	1.7 ▲	BR	Graded road on left goes into quarry; also small track straight ahead. Bear right, remaining on graded road. Zero trip meter.
▼ 0.4		SO	Track on left.
	1.3 ▲	BL	Track on right.
▼ 0.8		SO	Cross through wash; then track on left. Cross through second wash. Old buildings of Harquahala Mine are visible ahead and to the right.
	0.9 ▲	SO	Cross through wash; then track on right. Cross through second wash. Old buildings of Harquahala Mine are visible to the left.
▼ 1.0		SO	Mine building on rise to the right. Old adobe building is behind the rise, not visible from the road.
	0.7 ▲	SO	Mine building on rise to the left. Old adobe building is behind the rise, not visible from the road.
			GPS: N33°40.23' W113°35.60'
▼ 1.2		SO	Track on right.
	0.5 ▲	SO	Track on left.
▼ 1.3		SO	Cemetery on left at left-hand bend.
	0.4 ▲	SO	Cemetery on right at right-hand bend.
			GPS: N33°40.49' W113°35.45'
▼ 1.5		BL	Two tracks on right. Northernmost track on right goes toward the Golden Eagle Mine. Bear left, remaining on graded gravel road.

Junctions are unmarked.

	0.2 ▲	BR	Two tracks on left. Northernmost track goes toward the Golden Eagle Mine. Bear right, remaining on graded gravel road. Junctions are unmarked.
			GPS: N33°40.66' W113°35.35'
▼ 1.7		SO	Graded track on right goes to Golden Eagle Mine. Small track on left. Zero trip meter.
	0.0 ▲		Continue to the southeast.
			GPS: N33°40.93' W113°35.46'
▼ 0.0			Continue to the northwest.
	4.9 ▲	BR	Small track on right; then graded track on left goes to Golden Eagle Mine. Zero trip meter.
▼ 0.1		SO	Faint track on left.
	4.8 ▲	SO	Faint track on right.
▼ 0.2		SO	Faint track on left and faint track on right.
	4.7 ▲	SO	Faint track on left and faint track on right.
▼ 0.6		SO	Small track on right.
	4.3 ▲	SO	Small track on left.
▼ 0.8		SO	Track on right and track on left; then cross through wash.
	4.1 ▲	BR	Cross through wash; then track on right and track on left.
			GPS: N33°41.60' W113°35.47'
▼ 1.0		SO	Cross through wash.
	3.9 ▲	SO	Cross through wash.
▼ 1.3		SO	Track on left.
	3.6 ▲	SO	Track on right.
▼ 1.7		SO	Track on right is private.
	3.2 ▲	SO	Track on left is private.
▼ 1.9		SO	Track on right; then second track on right.
	3.0 ▲	SO	Track on left; then second track on left.
			GPS: N33°42.48' W113°35.84'
▼ 2.1		SO	Track on left.
	2.8 ▲	SO	Track on right.
▼ 2.2		SO	Track on right goes to diggings.
	2.7 ▲	SO	Track on left goes to diggings.
			GPS: N33°42.74' W113°36.04'
▼ 2.5		SO	Track on right goes to diggings.
	2.4 ▲	SO	Track on left goes to diggings.
▼ 2.8		SO	Cross through wash.
	2.1 ▲	SO	Cross through wash.
▼ 2.9		SO	Track on right.
	2.0 ▲	SO	Track on left.
▼ 3.4		SO	Faint track on left; then cross through wash.
	1.5 ▲	SO	Cross through wash; then faint track on right.
▼ 3.5		SO	Cross through wash.
	1.4 ▲	SO	Cross through wash.
▼ 3.6		SO	Track on left.
	1.3 ▲	SO	Track on right.
▼ 3.7		SO	Track on right and track on left.
	1.2 ▲	SO	Track on right and track on left.
			GPS: N33°43.91' W113°36.02'
▼ 4.0		SO	Cross through wash.
	0.9 ▲	SO	Cross through wash.
▼ 4.4		SO	Track on left.
	0.5 ▲	SO	Track on right.
▼ 4.5		SO	Track on left.
	0.4 ▲	SO	Track on right.
▼ 4.6		SO	Cross through wash.
	0.3 ▲	SO	Cross through wash.
▼ 4.9		SO	Road is paved. Track on left and paved Monroe Street on right. Entering outskirts of Salome. Zero trip meter.

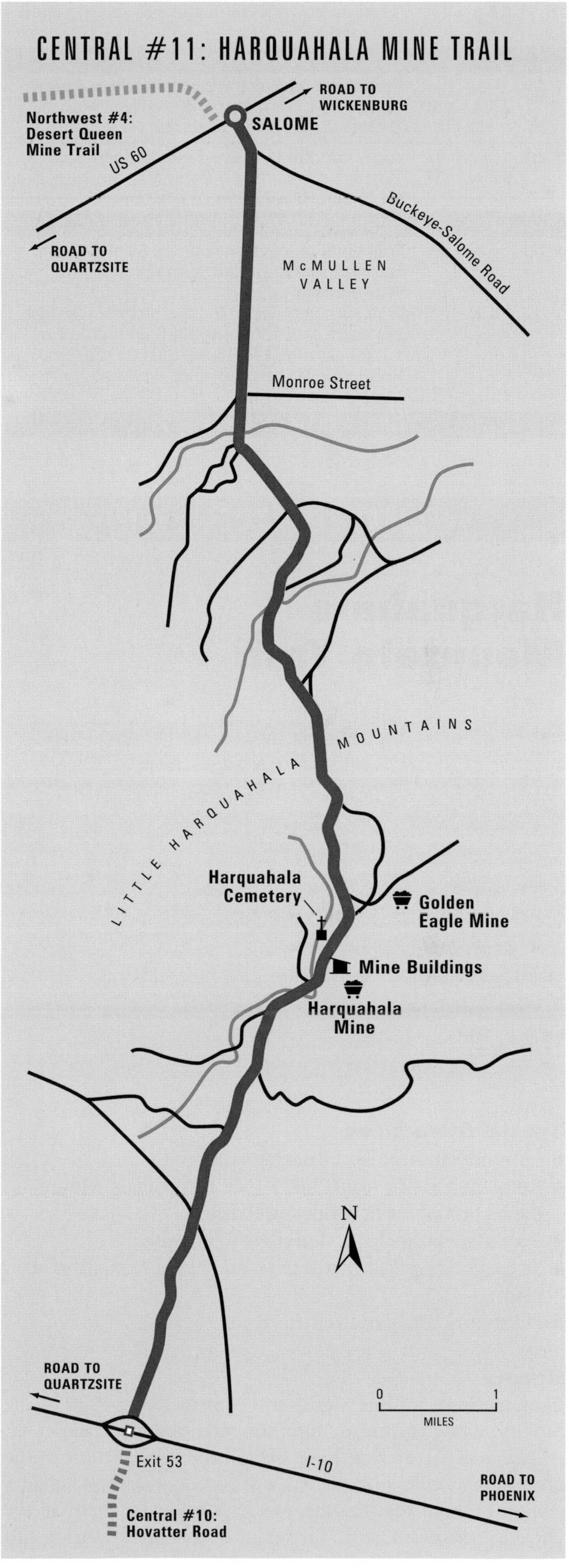

	0.0 ▲		Continue toward Harquahala Mine on graded dirt road.
			GPS: N33°44.80′ W113°36.57′
▼ 0.0			Continue into Salome on Harquahala Road.
	2.3 ▲	SO	Road turns to graded gravel. Paved Monroe Street on left; track on right.
▼ 2.1		TL	Turn onto the Buckeye-Salome Road.
	0.2 ▲	TR	Turn onto Harquahala Road at street sign. Sign for Indian Hills Airpark at junction.
			GPS: N33°46.76′ W113°36.57′
▼ 2.3			Trail ends at junction with US 60 in Salome. Turn left for Quartzsite; turn right for Wickenburg.
	0.0 ▲		Trail starts on US 60 in Salome near the eastern edge of town. Zero trip meter and turn southeast onto the paved Buckeye-Salome Road beside the post office and zero trip meter.
			GPS: N33°46.91′ W113°36.73′

CENTRAL REGION TRAIL #12

Harquahala Mountain Trail

Starting Point:	**Eagle Eye Road, 8 miles from junction with Buckeye-Salome Road**
Finishing Point:	**Harquahala Mountain**
Total Mileage:	**10.3 miles**
Unpaved Mileage:	**10.3 miles**
Driving Time:	**1.5 hours (one-way)**
Elevation Range:	**1,900–5,600 feet**
Usually Open:	**Year-round**
Best Time to Travel:	**Year-round**
Difficulty Rating:	**5**
Scenic Rating:	**9**
Remoteness Rating:	**+0**

Special Attractions

- Historic Smithsonian Observatory.
- Panoramic views from 5,691-foot Harquahala Mountain, the highest point in southwest Arizona.
- Access to Harquahala Mountain Wilderness.
- Steep, exciting trail that travels along long sections of shelf road.
- Harrisburg town and cemetery.

History

Harquahala Peak Observatory was constructed in 1920 by the Smithsonian Institute to monitor solar activity. Charles G. Abbott was the driving force behind the construction of the observatory. Following the work of Samuel Pierpont Langley, Abbott believed that the sun was responsible for many of the climate changes on earth. He reasoned that by measuring and observing the amount of energy from the sun that reached the earth (known as the solar constant), it would be possible to more accurately predict the weather. To record the observations, clear skies and low humidity were needed—conditions that made Arizona an obvious potential location. Abbott was impressed with the Harquahala Mountain site, citing the good pack trail to the summit and the clear skies in the region.

Smithsonian Observatory behind a well

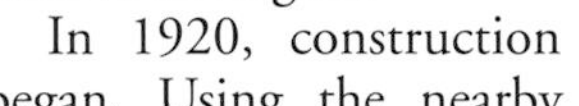

In 1920, construction began. Using the nearby settlement of Wenden as a base, the construction team used burros to pack building materials up the 5-mile trail to the summit. Progress was fairly slow, as it was an hour's drive from Wenden and then a grueling 3-hour hike to the observatory site up grades that climbed as much as 1,000 feet per mile. Abbott oversaw the construction and remained to run the small observatory. His cousin, Frederick Greeley, joined him as his assistant.

The daily life of the two men must have been hard and monotonous. The hot desert sun scorched the mountain peak, and their daily recordings and subsequent mathematical calculations were slow and tedious. Sensitive mercury thermometers and other instruments measured the energy from both the sun's direct and indirect rays as well as the heat from the atmosphere around the sun. Once the daily readings were collected, they were formulated by hand and reports were sent to Washington to be compared with reports from an observatory in Chile. The information was first used for weather forecasting in 1923.

Early life at the observatory was plagued by mishaps; the water tank leaked, freak winds smashed precious instruments, and the building was found to be unstable. Water had to be packed in by burros. However, all these obstacles were overcome, the building was shored up, and water tanks were rebuilt. A reclusive miner named Ellison, who was prospecting nearby, was the only regular outside companion. In addition, he and his mule provided a grocery and water service as needed.

Dr. Abbott left the observatory in 1921 to return to Washington. His place was taken by Dr. Alfred Moore who brought his wife, Chella, with him. The standard of living for the researchers improved gradually; a refrigerator was added and in 1922 a telephone line down the valley to Mr. Ellison gave Moore and his wife more reliable communication than the earlier methods, which included Morse code.

In 1925 the observatory was abandoned in favor of a new location on Table Mountain in California. The old observatory is listed on the National Register of Historic Places.

If you approach the Harquahala Mountain Trail from Salome, the paved Buckeye-Salome Road takes you through the small settlement of Harrisburg. Founded in 1886 around the mines in the nearby hills, Harrisburg is currently home to a few residents. A short distance out of town is the cemetery, where there is a monument to pioneers slain by Indians. During the California gold rush in 1849, a wagon party stopped for the night at a waterhole near the site of present-day Harrisburg. The group was attacked by Indians, who left no survivors. The sun-bleached skeletons were not discovered for many months until another group of emigrants chanced upon them. They buried the bones on a small knoll—the site of the present cemetery. When Harrisburg sprang into life, this knoll became the official burial place for the community. The memorial you see today was placed by the Arizona State Highway Department.

From the top of Harquahala Mountain, you can look west to Socorro Peak, which houses the Socorro Mine (thought to be the earliest of the mines in the Harquahalas, dating back to 1882). A family from Socorro, New Mexico, discovered the mine.

The Alaska Mine, located just off the main Harquahala Mountain Trail, was a gold mine discovered in 1920 and worked for a brief time.

Description

This trail has been upgraded by the BLM in recent times, but it is still a steep, rough, exciting drive leading to the reward of the highest summit in southwest Arizona. The start of the trail is well marked from the paved Eagle Eye Road. The first few miles are easygoing as the trail travels along a graded dirt road snaking toward Blue Tank Canyon. A track on the left goes to the scattered remains of the Alaska Mine, 1.2 miles from the start of the trail. A few miles into the canyon, the trail starts to climb and it doesn't stop climbing until it reaches the summit of Harquahala Mountain, 6.8 miles later. The shelf road continues all the way to the top.

The early switchbacks, along a smooth surface, are easy as the trail climbs up to run along a ridge top. There are views back over Blue Tank Canyon and west over the Harrisburg Valley. After 8 miles the grade becomes a lot steeper and the trail rougher. To climb up the grades a 4WD is necessary. Vehicles with less aggressive tires may spin. The shelf road is wide enough for one vehicle, although at times, passing places are limited because of rubble on the sides of the trail. Remember that uphill vehicles have the right of way; however as always, courtesy and common sense should prevail. In hotter months, keep an eye on your engine temperature. The constant steep grade can warm up a vehicle very quickly.

Trail climbing the southern ridge of Harquahala Mountain

At the top there are parking areas, a couple of picnic tables (although no shade), and the corrugated iron shed that housed the old Smithsonian Observatory. The trail continues for another 0.3 miles to the hiking trailhead into the Harquahala Mountain Wilderness Area.

The Harquahala Mountain Wilderness Area, designated in 1990, consists of 22,880 acres and contains part of one of western Arizona's largest mountain ranges. Harquahala Peak, on which the observatory stands, is 5,691 feet high. A popular trail for foot and pack use only travels down into Browns Canyon, a remote community of desert grassland, chaparral, and rare cacti.

In winter there can be snow at the top of the mountain. Do not attempt this trail if there is snow or ice on the ground! On the return trip, use the lowest available gear for the steepest parts. Watch for overheating brakes.

To reach the start of the trail from Salome, take the Buckeye-Salome Road southeast for 26 miles. The site of Harrisburg ghost town is located 5 miles from the start of the road and is marked by a sign. Another 0.2 miles along the paved road, an unmarked primitive dirt road on the right goes 0.6 miles to the Harrisburg Cemetery. The coordinates for the cemetery are GPS: N33°44.10' W113°32.45'. Continue on the paved road for another 20.6 miles, then turn east on the paved Eagle Eye Road, which is sign-posted to Aguila. Proceed along Eagle Eye Road for 8 miles before turning northwest on a graded dirt road at the BLM sign for Harquahala Mountain Road.

Current Road Information

Bureau of Land Management
Phoenix Field Office
2015 West Deer Valley Rd.
Phoenix, AZ 85027
(623) 580-5500

Map References

BLM Salome
USGS 1:24,000 Weldon Hill, Harquahala Mt.
1:100,000 Salome
Maptech CD-ROM: Colorado River/Lake Havasu
Arizona Atlas & Gazetteer, p. 47
Arizona Road & Recreation Atlas, p. 39 & p. 73

Route Directions

▼ 0.0	From Eagle Eye Road, turn northwest up the small graded Harquahala Mountain Road and zero trip meter.
	GPS: N33°43.66' W113°17.59'

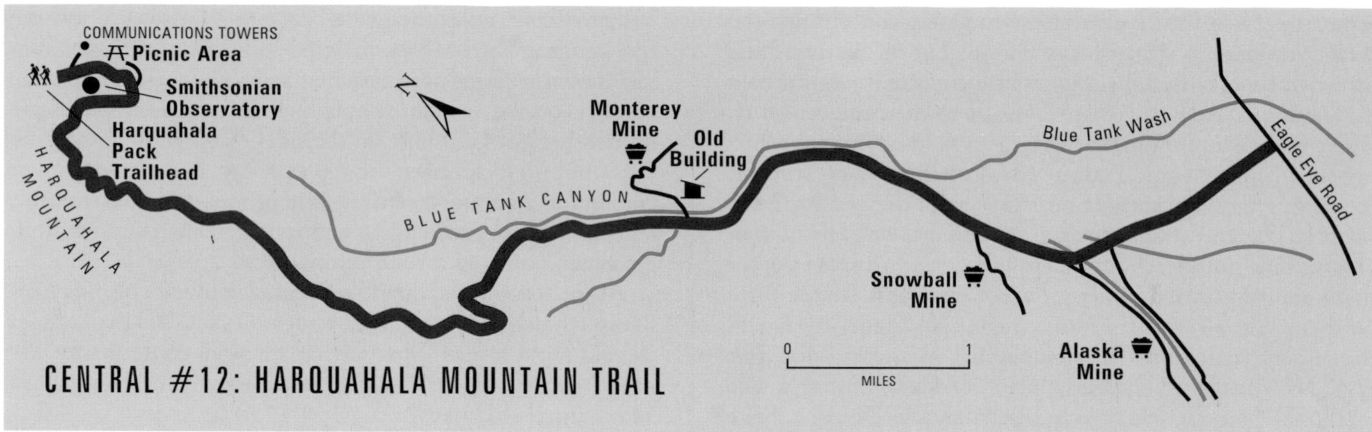

▼ 0.1	SO	Track on right (looks like new parking area and toilets are going in).
▼ 0.2	SO	Second entrance to track on right; then cross through wash.
▼ 0.5	SO	Cross through wash.
▼ 1.0	SO	Cross through wash.
▼ 1.1	SO	Track on left; then cross through wash. Second track on left goes to the Alaska Mine.
		GPS: N33°44.15' W113°18.68'
▼ 1.2	SO	Track on left goes to the Alaska Mine (0.6 miles).
		GPS: N33°44.22' W113°18.76'
▼ 1.5	SO	Track on right.
▼ 1.7	SO	Track on left goes to the Snowball Mine (0.2 miles); only a few diggings remain.
		GPS: N33°44.65' W113°18.86'
▼ 2.2	SO	Trail starts to enter Blue Tank Canyon. Blue Tank Wash is on the right.
▼ 2.4	SO	Cross through wash.
		GPS: N33°45.33' W113°18.88'
▼ 3.5	BL	Trail forks; bear left, remaining on better-used trail. Track on right dips down to cross through the wash. Zero trip meter. Track on right has old building 0.1 miles ahead and continues up the hill to the Monterey Mine.
		GPS: N33°45.83' W113°19.64'
▼ 0.0		Continue to the northwest. Trail starts to climb.
▼ 0.1	SO	Cross through wash.
▼ 0.8	SO	Small stone walls on right.
		GPS: N33°46.16' W113°19.94'
▼ 1.3	SO	Cross through wash.
▼ 1.7	SO	Start of switchbacks and shelf road.
▼ 4.5	SO	Steepest section of switchbacks. Watch for overheating in hot weather.
▼ 6.1	SO	Track on right.
		GPS: N33°48.44' W113°20.71'
▼ 6.4	SO	Picnic tables and parking area on right.
		GPS: N33°48.61' W113°20.66'
▼ 6.5	SO	Old Smithsonian Observatory on left of trail; two parking areas on right.
		GPS: N33°48.69' W113°20.74'
▼ 6.6	BL	Top of the peak at communications towers. Bear left past the towers.
		GPS: N33°48.73' W113°20.78'
▼ 6.7	BL	Track on right.
		GPS: N33°48.76' W113°20.87'
▼ 6.8		Trail ends at a turnaround on the edge of the Harquahala Mountain Wilderness Area, at the start of the Harquahala Pack Trail.
		GPS: N33°48.78' W113°20.96'

CENTRAL REGION TRAIL #13

Big Horn Mountains Trail

Starting Point:	**Eagle Eye Road, 0.8 north of mile marker 3**
Finishing Point:	**Indian School Road, 4.8 miles from Tonopah**
Total Mileage:	**24.1 miles**
Unpaved Mileage:	**24.1 miles**
Driving Time:	**3 hours**
Elevation Range:	**1,300–2,100 feet**
Usually Open:	**Year-round**
Best Time to Travel:	**September to June**
Difficulty Rating:	**3**
Scenic Rating:	**8**
Remoteness Rating:	**+0**

Special Attractions

- Vehicle corridor passing between two wilderness areas.
- Hiking access to Hummingbird Springs Wilderness and Big Horn Mountains Wilderness.
- Very scenic trail passing through remote desert area.

Description

This moderate trail passes between two wilderness areas: Big Horn Mountains Wilderness to the south and Hummingbird Springs Wilderness to the north. The trail leaves from paved Eagle Eye Road. Initially, it is small and hard to follow in places, but as other trails gradually join the main trail, it becomes well defined and easy to follow. The portion of the trail that travels the vehicle corridor through the wilderness areas is the only trail that does so. Inevitably, it sees more vehicle traffic.

Along the length of the trail there are wide-ranging views into the wilderness, especially to the south. Big Horn Peak is visible. The name Big Horn Mountains, after the abundant mountain sheep, was first used in the 1850s.

The trail is well used and is not brushy. There are a couple of eroded gullies, but nothing that should cause problems for most high-clearance SUVs. One gully may be tight for longer

A well and stock tank along the trail

vehicles or those with long or low overhangs.

One popular hiking trail leads from the trail to Hummingbird Spring. In addition to this one, there are many other opportunities for hiking as well. The spring was named after the nearby Hummingbird Mine that was owned by E. Cartwright. Past this trailhead, the vehicle trail is smoother and sees slightly more use. The final section of the trail runs across the flat Tonopah Desert, passing by Burnt Mountain. It crosses the aqueduct before passing under I-10 to finish on Indian School Road near Tonopah. People wishing to explore further in this region should be aware that in many places access across the aqueduct is restricted, and thus, some of the trails that show up on topographic maps are not accessible.

Current Road Information

Bureau of Land Management
Phoenix Field Office
2015 West Deer Valley Rd.
Phoenix, AZ 85027
(623) 580-5500

Map References

BLM Salome, Little Horn Mts.
USGS 1:24,000 Weldon Hill, Little Horn Peak, Hummingbird Spring, Burnt Mt., Saddle Mt.
1:100,000 Salome, Little Horn Mts.
Maptech CD-ROM: Colorado River/Lake Havasu; Southwest Arizona/Yuma
Arizona Atlas & Gazetteer, pp. 56, 55
Arizona Road & Recreation Atlas, pp. 39, 45 & pp. 73, 79

Route Directions

▼	▲		
▼ 0.0			From Eagle Eye Road, 0.8 miles north of mile marker 3, turn east on unmarked, formed, single-track road and zero trip meter.
	5.1 ▲		Trail ends on paved Eagle Eye Road. Turn left for I-10; turn right for Aguila.
			GPS: N33°39.69' W113°18.00'
▼ 0.2		BR	Fence line on left; stay on the south side.
	4.9 ▲	BL	Fence line on right.
▼ 0.4		BL	Bear left, following corral's fence line and proceed northeast.
	4.7 ▲	BR	Swing right, following corral's fence line on right and proceed west.
			GPS: N33°39.63' W113°17.60'
▼ 0.6		BR	Track on left enters corral.
	4.5 ▲	BL	Track straight on enters corral.
▼ 1.3		SO	Cross through wash.
	3.8 ▲	SO	Cross through wash.
▼ 1.7		SO	Cross through wash.
	3.4 ▲	SO	Cross through wash.
▼ 2.0		BR	Track on left; remain on main trail.
	3.1 ▲	BL	Track on right; remain on main trail.
			GPS: N33°40.70' W113°16.40'
▼ 2.2		SO	Cross through wash.
	2.9 ▲	SO	Cross through wash.
▼ 2.3		SO	Cross through wash.
	2.8 ▲	SO	Cross through wash.
▼ 2.4		BL	Faint track on right; remain on better trail.
	2.7 ▲	BR	Faint track on left; remain on better trail.
			GPS: N33°40.63' W113°16.00'
▼ 2.5		BR	Faint track on left.
	2.6 ▲	BL	Faint track on right.
			GPS: N33°40.66' W113°15.84'
▼ 2.7		SO	Faint track on left.
	2.4 ▲	SO	Faint track on right.
▼ 2.9		SO	Faint track on left; then cross through wash.
	2.2 ▲	SO	Cross through wash; then faint track on right.
			GPS: N33°40.61' W113°15.52'
▼ 3.4		SO	Cross through wash.
	1.7 ▲	SO	Cross through wash.
▼ 4.1		SO	Cross through wide wash.
	1.0 ▲	SO	Cross through wide wash.
			GPS: N33°40.14' W113°14.39'
▼ 4.2		SO	Cross through wash.
	0.9 ▲	SO	Cross through wash.
▼ 4.7		SO	Cross through two washes.
	0.4 ▲	SO	Cross through two washes.
▼ 4.9		SO	Cross through wash.
	0.2 ▲	SO	Cross through wash.
▼ 5.0		SO	Cross through wash.
	0.1 ▲	SO	Cross through wash.
▼ 5.1		SO	Well-used track on right. Continue straight on and zero trip meter. The junction is unmarked, but a well is visible straight ahead.
	0.0 ▲		Continue to the west.
			GPS: N33°39.95' W113°13.28'
▼ 0.0			Continue toward well.
	3.8 ▲	SO	Well-used track on left. Continue straight on and zero trip meter.

The trail following the wash at its head toward Sugarloaf Mountain

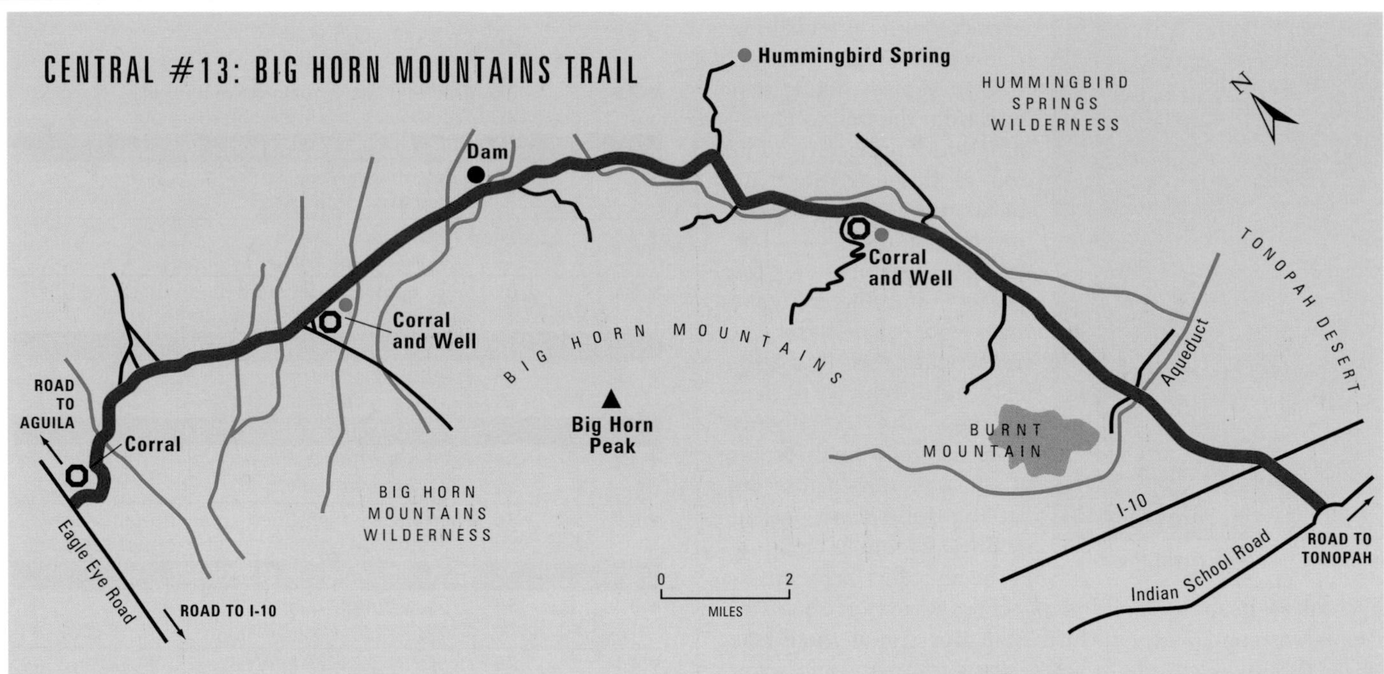

▼ 0.1		SO	Cross through wash; then track on right.
	3.7 ▲	BR	Track on left; then cross through wash.
▼ 0.3		SO	Well, concrete tank, and corrals on right.
	3.5 ▲	SO	Well, concrete tank, and corrals on left.
			GPS: N33°39.97' W113°13.00'
▼ 0.9		SO	Cross through wash.
	2.9 ▲	SO	Cross through wash.
▼ 1.3		SO	Cross through wash.
	2.5 ▲	SO	Cross through wash.
▼ 1.4		SO	Cross through wash; then Big Horn Mountains Wilderness begins on the right.
	2.4 ▲	SO	Big Horn Mountains Wilderness ends; then cross through wash.
			GPS: N33°40.06' W113°11.73'
▼ 1.6		SO	Cross through wash.
	2.2 ▲	SO	Cross through wash.
▼ 1.8		SO	Small track on right.
	2.0 ▲	SO	Small track on left.
▼ 2.3		SO	Cross through wash.
	1.5 ▲	SO	Cross through wash.
▼ 2.4		SO	Cross through wash.
	1.4 ▲	SO	Cross through wash.
▼ 2.8		SO	Cross through wash.
	1.0 ▲	SO	Cross through wash.
			GPS: N33°40.03' W113°10.27'
▼ 3.0		SO	Cross through wash.
	0.8 ▲	SO	Cross through wash.
▼ 3.2		SO	Cross over old dam wall; dam on left.
	0.6 ▲	SO	Cross over old dam wall; dam on right.
			GPS: N33°40.01' W113°09.85'
▼ 3.5		SO	Hummingbird Springs Wilderness starts on the left. Then cross through wide wash.
	0.3 ▲	SO	Cross through wide wash. Hummingbird Springs Wilderness ends on right.
			GPS: N33°40.06' W113°09.55'
▼ 3.8		SO	Entering wilderness corridor; Hummingbird Springs Wilderness on north of road for next 4.8 miles. Zero trip meter at sign.
	0.0 ▲		Continue away from the wilderness corridor.
			GPS: N33°39.93' W113°09.25'
▼ 0.0			Continue into wilderness corridor. Trail immediately forks; bear left past track on right.
	3.8 ▲	SO	Track on left; then Big Horn Mountains Wilderness on south of trail for next 2.4 miles. Zero trip meter at sign.
▼ 0.9		SO	Cross through wash.
	2.9 ▲	SO	Cross through wash.
▼ 1.2		SO	Narrow section of trail where it is washing out. You will need to pass very close to the palo verde on the left to squeeze past.
	2.6 ▲	SO	Narrow section of trail where it is washing out. You will need to pass very close to the palo verde on the right to squeeze past.
▼ 1.4		SO	Cross through wash.
	2.4 ▲	SO	Cross through wash.
▼ 1.6		SO	V-shaped, washed-out gully with tight, steep entrance and exit. If you are in a longer vehicle, be careful not to get caught in the middle.
	2.2 ▲	SO	V-shaped, washed-out gully with tight, steep entrance and exit. If you are in a longer vehicle, be careful not to get caught in the middle.
			GPS: N33°39.41' W113°07.65'
▼ 1.9		SO	Cross through wash.
	1.9 ▲	SO	Cross through wash.
▼ 2.1		SO	Track on left.
	1.7 ▲	BR	Track on right.
			GPS: N33°39.13' W113°07.22'
▼ 2.2		SO	Faint track on right to old dam.
	1.6 ▲	SO	Faint track on left to old dam.
▼ 2.4		SO	Track on right to old dam; then second track on right up rise.
	1.4 ▲	BR	Track on left up rise; then second track on left to old dam.
▼ 2.9		SO	Cross through wide wash.
	0.9 ▲	SO	Cross through wide wash.
▼ 3.3		SO	Cross through wide wash. Old dam and corrals on right.

0.5 ▲	SO	Cross through wide wash. Old dam and corrals on left.
		GPS: N33°38.55' W113°06.59'
▼ 3.5	BL	Track on right.
0.3 ▲	SO	Track on left.
		GPS: N33°38.64' W113°06.34'
▼ 3.7	SO	Cross through wash.
0.1 ▲	SO	Cross through wash.
▼ 3.8	TR	Turn right before sign for Hummingbird Springs Wilderness. Turn is in the wash. Track on left goes 1.3 miles to the start of the hiking trail to Hummingbird Spring. Zero trip meter.
0.0 ▲		Continue to the west.
		GPS: N33°38.63' W113°06.06'
▼ 0.0		Continue to the south and cross through wash.
1.0 ▲	TL	Turn left before sign for Hummingbird Springs Wilderness. Turn is in the wash. Track on right goes 1.3 miles to the start of the hiking trail to Hummingbird Spring. Zero trip meter.
▼ 0.2	SO	Track on right.
0.8 ▲	SO	Track on left.
		GPS: N33°38.41' W113°06.12'
▼ 1.0	SO	Track on right. Sign for Hummingbird Springs Wilderness and Big Horn Mountains Wilderness. Road passes through a wilderness corridor for the next 4.4 miles. Zero trip meter.
0.0 ▲		Continue to the north.
		GPS: N33°37.78' W113°06.21'
▼ 0.0		Continue into wilderness corridor.
1.5 ▲	BR	Track on left; bear right and pass sign for Hummingbird Springs Wilderness; wilderness is to the north of the road for the next 4.8 miles. Zero trip meter.
▼ 0.1	SO	Cross through wash.
1.4 ▲	SO	Cross through wash.
▼ 0.4	SO	Cross through wash.
1.1 ▲	SO	Cross through wash.
▼ 0.7	SO	Cross through wash.
0.8 ▲	SO	Cross through wash.
▼ 0.8	SO	Cross through wide wash.
0.7 ▲	SO	Cross through wide wash.
▼ 1.4	BR	Track on right goes past well.
0.1 ▲	SO	Track on left goes past well.
▼ 1.5	SO	Corral and well on right. Zero trip meter.
0.0 ▲		Continue to the west.
		GPS: N33°37.01' W113°04.90'
▼ 0.0		Continue to the east.
1.3 ▲	SO	Corral and well on left. Zero trip meter.
▼ 1.3	SO	Track on left goes 2.1 miles along a wilderness corridor to game and wildlife area. Zero trip meter.
0.0 ▲		Continue to the northwest.
		GPS: N33°36.16' W113°04.07'
▼ 0.0		Continue to southeast.
1.6 ▲	SO	Track on right goes 2.1 miles along a wilderness corridor to game and wildlife area. Zero trip meter.
▼ 1.6	SO	Track on right; then pass through wire gate. Leaving wilderness corridor.
0.0 ▲		Continue to the northwest. Burnt Mountain is on the left.
		GPS: N33°34.83' W113°03.40'
▼ 0.0		Continue to the southeast. Burnt Mountain is on the right.
4.7 ▲	SO	Pass through wire gate; then track on left. Trail is now passing through a wilderness corridor, with the Big Horn Mountains Wilderness to the left and the Hummingbird Springs Wilderness to the right. Zero trip meter.
▼ 0.1	SO	Cross through wash.
4.6 ▲	SO	Cross through wash.
▼ 1.3	SO	Track on right. Trail is following along power lines.
3.4 ▲	BR	Track on left.
		GPS: N33°33.66' W113°03.17'
▼ 1.8	SO	Cross through wash.
2.9 ▲	SO	Cross through wash.
▼ 2.4	SO	Small track on right; then pass through wire gate.
2.3 ▲	SO	Pass through wire gate; then small track on left.
		GPS: N33°32.63' W113°02.79'
▼ 2.5	SO	Tracks on left and right are for authorized vehicles along the top of the aqueduct.
2.2 ▲	SO	Tracks on left and right are for authorized vehicles along the top of the aqueduct.
▼ 2.6	SO	Cross over aqueduct.
2.1 ▲	SO	Cross over aqueduct.
▼ 3.2	SO	Track on left.
1.5 ▲	SO	Track on right.
		GPS: N33°32.00' W113°02.56'
▼ 4.3	SO	Track on left.
0.4 ▲	SO	Track on right.
▼ 4.7	TL	Turn left onto graded dirt road that parallels I-10. Zero trip meter.
0.0 ▲		Continue to the northwest.
		GPS: N33°30.87' W113°01.81'
▼ 0.0		Continue to the east.
1.3 ▲	TR	Turn right onto unmarked, formed trail, directly under power lines. Zero trip meter.
▼ 0.1	TR	Turn right and pass under I-10.
1.2 ▲	TL	Pass under I-10 and turn left at T-intersection onto graded dirt road.
		GPS: N33°30.85' W113°01.64'
▼ 0.2	SO	Exit under freeway; track on right parallels freeway.
1.1 ▲	SO	Track on left; pass under I-10.
▼ 0.4	BL	Track on right.
0.9 ▲	SO	Track on left.
▼ 0.5	SO	Tracks on left and right.
0.8 ▲	SO	Tracks on left and right.
▼ 0.8	SO	Two tracks on left.
0.5 ▲	BL	Two tracks on right.
▼ 1.3		Trail ends at intersection with wide, graded gravel Indian School Road. Turn left and travel 4.8 miles to Tonopah and I-10.
0.0 ▲		Trail starts near Tonopah. To reach the trailhead from I-10, exit 94 (Tonopah), proceed south, and turn west on Indian School Road immediately south of the gas station. Zero trip meter at the intersection. The turn is sign-posted to El Dorado Hot Springs. Proceed west along the paved road, passing the hot springs on the left. The road turns to dirt. The start of the trail is 4.8 miles from Tonopah and is immediately before the road starts to wind up a small hill. At the intersection, zero trip meter and proceed northwest on small, formed dirt trail. The turn is unmarked.
		GPS: N33°29.88' W113°01.29'

CENTRAL REGION TRAIL #14

Saddle Mountain Trail

Starting Point:	**Courthouse Road, near Tonopah**
Finishing Point:	**Saddle Mountain**
Total Mileage:	**2.6 miles**
Unpaved Mileage:	**2.6 miles**
Driving Time:	**45 minutes**
Elevation Range:	**1,300–1600 feet**
Usually Open:	**Year-round**
Best Time to Travel:	**October to May**
Difficulty Rating:	**3**
Scenic Rating:	**8**
Remoteness Rating:	**+0**

Special Attractions

- Excellent rockhounding for chalcedony and fire agate.
- Views and access to Saddle Mountain.

Description

This short trail is part of a loop that encircles Saddle Mountain. In mid-2000, a major washout rendered the complete loop impassable, but we hope it will be repaired, making the loop complete once again.

The major appeal of this trail is the excellent rockhounding opportunities on the northern side of Saddle Mountain. There are numerous desert roses (pieces of chalcedony) that can be picked up from the desert pavement almost everywhere on the north side. It is rarely necessary to hunt; just step out of your vehicle and start looking. The lighter-colored chalcedony stands out against the darker surface. There is plenty of fire agate to be found as well, but spotting shards of this rock requires a little more patience. Also to be found are quartz crystals.

The trail also offers good views of imposing Saddle Mountain and some pleasant backcountry camping opportunities on the bajadas of Saddle Mountain. The trail is narrow and rough in places and has some ditchy gullies. However, the entire trail is suitable for high-clearance 4WDs.

Saddle Mountain

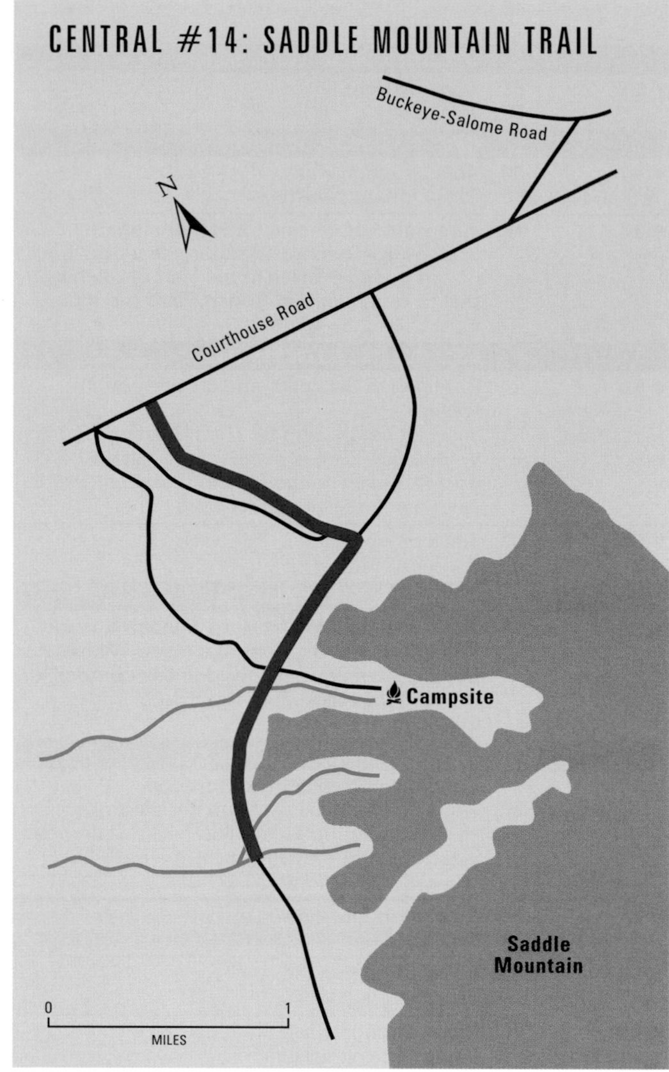

Current Road Information

Bureau of Land Management
Phoenix Field Office
2015 West Deer Valley Rd.
Phoenix, AZ 85027
(623) 580-5500

Map References

BLM Little Horn Mts.
USGS 1:24,000 Saddle Mt.
1:100,000 Little Horn Mts.
Maptech CD-ROM: Southwest Arizona/Yuma
Arizona Atlas & Gazetteer, p. 56

Route Directions

▼ **0.0**	From I-10 at exit 94 (Tonopah), zero trip meter on south side of freeway and continue south for 2.5 miles to T-intersection. Turn right onto

paved Buckeye-Salome Road and proceed west for 4.9 miles, following the signs for Harquahala Valley. Turn south on paved Courthouse Road and proceed 2.1 miles. Turn south on unmarked dirt trail and zero trip meter. There are several smaller trails before this turnoff. This trail is the better used of the possibilities.

GPS: N33°27.88' W113°03.69'

▼ 0.7	BL	Track on right.
		GPS: N33°27.37' W113°03.40'
▼ 0.8	BL	Faint track on right.
▼ 0.9	TL	Join well-used small trail.
		GPS: N33°27.14' W113°03.25'
▼ 1.1	TR	T-intersection. Turn onto well-used trail, heading toward a gap in Saddle Mountain. Zero trip meter.
		GPS: N33°27.06' W113°03.10'
▼ 0.0		Continue toward gap.
▼ 0.1	SO	Cross through wash.
▼ 0.6	TL	Bear right; then turn left through fence line. Track on right before fence and track on left after fence. Go 0.6 miles to small campsite at the mouth of the canyon.
		GPS: N33°26.81' W113°03.72'
▼ 0.7	SO	Cross through two washes.
▼ 0.8	SO	Cross through wash.
▼ 1.1	SO	Cross through wash.
▼ 1.4	SO	Cross through deep wash with loose entrance.
▼ 1.5		Trail is washed out at deep wash. Sign says road is blocked and impassable 6.4 miles ahead, but crossing is impassable to all but extreme 4WDs from here.
		GPS: N33°26.21' W113°04.14'

CENTRAL REGION TRAIL #15

Agua Caliente Road

Starting Point:	Old Highway 80
Finishing Point:	Old Agua Caliente Road
Total Mileage:	45.9 miles
Unpaved Mileage:	42.1 miles
Driving Time:	3 hours
Elevation Range:	600–1,500 feet
Usually Open:	Year-round
Best Time to Travel:	Fall to spring
Difficulty Rating:	1
Scenic Rating:	8
Remoteness Rating:	+1

Special Attractions

- Remote, lightly traveled, easy trail through the Gila Bend Mountains.
- Ghost town of Sundad.
- Agua Caliente Pioneer Cemetery.
- Rockhounding for agate near Fourth of July Butte.

Railroad crossing with Saddle Mountain in the background

History

The hot springs at Agua Caliente (Spanish for "hot water") have been visited constantly since the first Indian travelers in the region. The earliest recorded visit by Spanish missionary Father Jacobo Sedelmayr notes that local Indians used the hot mud and waters for healing purposes. The Spaniard seems to have been the first to name the Indian rancheria Santa Maria del Agua Caliente. King Woolsey later enjoyed the hot waters and established a health resort there, which by the late 1860s was enticing travelers along this part of the Southern Overland Trail. The gold rush also brought many clients to Agua Caliente. In addition to the resort, Agua Caliente also boasted a well-established ranch by the 1870s, which used the overflow from the hot springs. Woolsey sold his resort but continued to hold on to the water rights and part of the land. Apparently, the water rights passed to his heirs upon his death. Some of the earlier resort ruins can be seen close to the currently unused buildings. With the coming of the nearby Southern Pacific Railroad, Arizona 85, and eventually I-8, Agua Caliente was bypassed and the resort faded. It is not operating now, and the springs are diverted to the ranch. There are no soaking opportunities currently available.

"Fourth of July" was the name suggested for the prominent butte and wash after an enjoyable camping expedition by a small group of people to this area on Independence Day during the 1890s.

Not much is known about the ghost town of Sundad. Although originally a mining settlement, the site was once touted as being a suitable location for the state sanatorium. The idea never got off the ground and Sundad faded into obscurity. Today it can be reached by traveling 1 mile down a spur trail off the main Agua Caliente Road. Little is left except for some small foundations, mine shafts, a tank, and the old bottle dump.

Description

This wide graded road allows passenger vehicles to travel through some spectacular desert scenery on a seldom-used trail. The road passes across a wide plain toward the Gila Bend Mountains. It winds within the mountain range, passing the prominent Fourth of July Butte and Yellow Medicine Butte. There are a few old mines located along the trail. One of the

The trail approaching the Gila Bend Mountains and Fourth of July Butte

closest, the remains of the Dixie Mine, is only 0.1 miles north of the graded road. Little is left except some deep shafts, concrete foundations, and tailings piles. For rock hounds, some nice specimens of pale banded agate can be found scattered in the region of Fourth of July Butte.

The section of the trail that winds through the jagged larval peaks of the Gila Bend Mountains is the most spectacular. There are some very pleasant, although a bit exposed, backcountry camping spots and distant views north to the Eagletail Mountains Wilderness Area.

The trail leaves the mountains and cuts across the sloping bajadas of Sacaton Flats, passing the turnoff to Sundad. The short spur trail is suitable for high-clearance vehicles; passenger vehicles would have a hard time on the rougher surface. Some interesting stonework marks the turn. Light-colored rocks have been laid out to spell the name Sundad and to depict an arrow and other symbols.

The trail finishes at the turn to the old settlement of Agua Caliente. The Pioneer Cemetery can be found 0.6 miles down the dirt road on the left, and the remains of the hot springs are another 0.4 miles up the trail. Although suitable for passenger vehicles in dry weather, this trail is very lightly traveled. All vehicles should be equipped for desert travel and should have a full-size spare.

Current Road Information

Bureau of Land Management
Phoenix Field Office
2015 West Deer Valley Rd.
Phoenix, AZ 85027
(623) 580-5500

Map References

BLM Phoenix South, Little Horn Mts., Dateland
USGS 1:24,000 Arlington, Spring Mt., Gillespie, Fourth of July Butte, Cortez Peak, Yellow Medicine Butte, Hyder NE, Hyder SE, Agua Caliente
1:100,000 Phoenix South, Little Horn Mts., Dateland
Maptech CD-ROM: Phoenix/Superstition Mountains; Southwest Arizona/Yuma
Arizona Atlas & Gazetteer, pp. 56, 55
Arizona Road & Recreation Atlas, pp. 45, 46 & pp. 79, 80
Recreational Map of Arizona

Route Directions

▼ 0.0			From Old Highway 80, 2.9 miles north of the breached Gillespie Dam, turn west at the sign for Agua Caliente Road and zero trip meter at cattle guard. Road is paved at the start.
	2.9 ▲		Trail ends at Old Highway 80, 2.9 miles north of the breached Gillespie Dam. Turn left for Phoenix; turn right for Gila Bend.
			GPS: N33°15.61′ W112°47.81′
▼ 0.6		TR	Turn onto graded dirt road at the sign for Agua Caliente.
	2.3 ▲	TL	Turn left onto paved road.
			GPS: N33°15.44′ W112°48.50′
▼ 0.8		SO	Track on left.
	2.1 ▲	SO	Track on right.
▼ 0.9		SO	Cross through wash.
	2.0 ▲	SO	Cross through wash.
▼ 2.5		SO	Track on left and track on right along petroleum pipeline.
	0.4 ▲	SO	Track on left and track on right along petroleum pipeline.
▼ 2.7		SO	Pass under power lines. Small tracks on left and right along power lines.
	0.2 ▲	SO	Pass under power lines. Small tracks on left and right along power lines.
▼ 2.9		BR	Track on left. Zero trip meter.
	0.0 ▲		Continue along Agua Caliente Road.
			GPS: N33°15.72′ W112°50.93′
▼ 0.0			Continue along Agua Caliente Road.
	6.5 ▲	SO	Track on right. Zero trip meter.
▼ 0.2		SO	Cross through wash.
	6.3 ▲	SO	Cross through wash.
▼ 2.1		SO	Cattle guard.
	4.4 ▲	SO	Cattle guard.
▼ 2.3		BR	Track on left. Remain on main graded road.
	4.2 ▲	BL	Track on right. Remain on main graded road.
			GPS: N33°15.30′ W112°53.28′
▼ 3.6		SO	Cross through wash.
	2.9 ▲	SO	Cross through wash.
▼ 4.0		SO	Cross through wash.
	2.5 ▲	SO	Cross through wash.
▼ 4.2		SO	Track on right.
	2.3 ▲	SO	Track on left.
▼ 5.0		SO	Cross through wash; then track on left.
	1.5 ▲	SO	Track on right; then cross through wash.
			GPS: N33°16.94′ W112°54.82′
▼ 5.8		SO	Track on right; then track on left.
	0.7 ▲	SO	Track on right; then track on left.
▼ 6.5		SO	Track on left; then cattle guard. Cross over railroad track; then tracks on right and left along rail line. Zero trip meter at rail line.
	0.0 ▲		Continue toward Old Highway 80; cattle guard and track on right.
			GPS: N33°17.17′ W112°56.19′
▼ 0.0			Continue toward Agua Caliente, crossing cattle guard and second track on right. Pass under power lines.
	7.3 ▲	SO	Pass under power lines; track on left; then cattle guard. Tracks on right and left along rail line; then cross over railroad track. Zero trip meter at rail line.
▼ 0.1		SO	Cross through wash.
	7.2 ▲	SO	Cross through wash.
▼ 0.3		SO	Cross through wash.
	7.0 ▲	SO	Cross through wash.

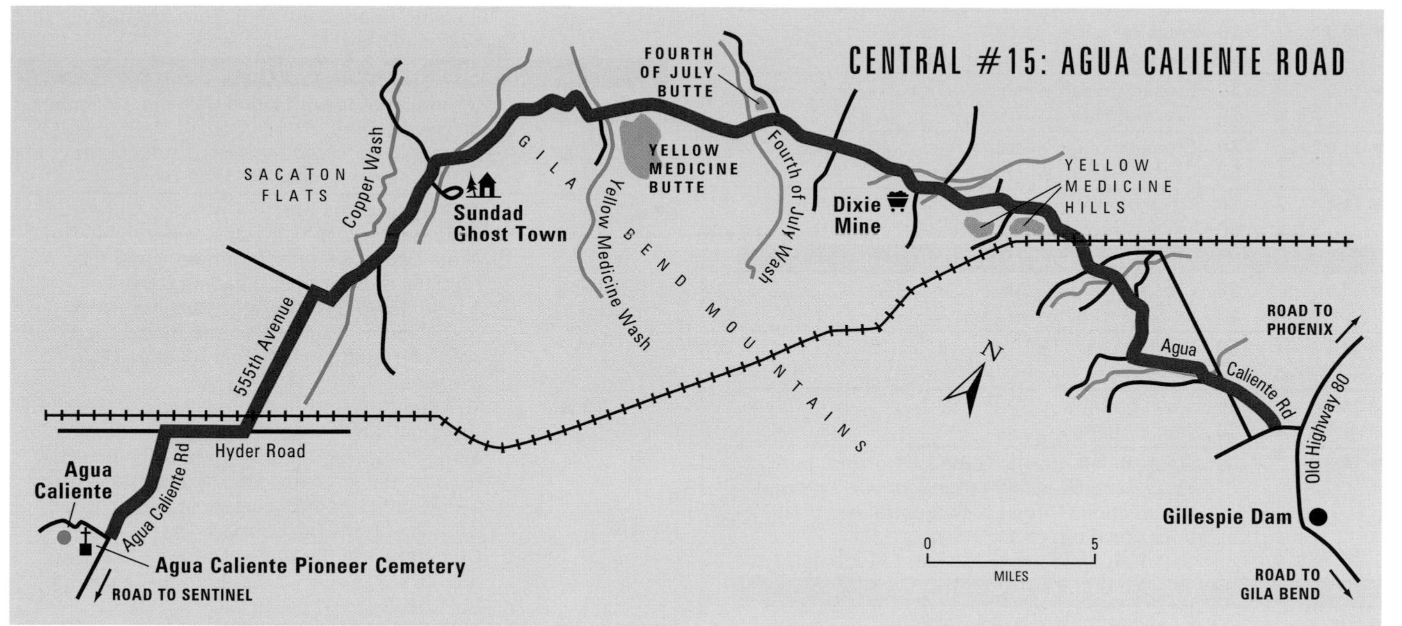

▼ 0.9	SO	Track on right and Yellow Medicine Hills on left.
6.4 ▲	SO	Track on left and Yellow Medicine Hills on right.
▼ 1.9	SO	Track on left.
5.4 ▲	SO	Track on right.
▼ 2.2	SO	Track on left.
5.1 ▲	SO	Track on right.
▼ 3.0	SO	Cross through wash; then faint track on right.
4.3 ▲	SO	Faint track on left; then cross through wash.
▼ 4.3	SO	Track on left.
3.0 ▲	SO	Track on right.
▼ 4.4	SO	Track on right.
2.9 ▲	SO	Track on left.
▼ 4.6	SO	Track on left; cross through wash; then track on right.
2.7 ▲	SO	Track on left; cross through wash; then track on right.
		GPS: N33°16.84′ W113°00.75′
▼ 5.4	SO	Faint track on left.
1.9 ▲	SO	Faint track on right.
▼ 5.5	SO	Track on left goes to the remains of the Dixie Mine—some deep square shafts and concrete foundations; then cross through wash.
1.8 ▲	SO	Cross through wash; then track on right goes to the remains of the Dixie Mine—some deep square shafts and concrete foundations.
		GPS: N33°16.54′ W113°01.58′
▼ 6.1	SO	Cross through wash.
1.2 ▲	SO	Cross through wash.
▼ 6.9	SO	Track on right.
0.4 ▲	SO	Track on left.
▼ 7.3	SO	Graded track on right and faint track on left before cattle guard. Zero trip meter.
0.0 ▲		Continue along Agua Caliente Road.
		GPS: N33°16.67′ W113°03.36′
▼ 0.0		Continue toward Fourth of July Butte, the conical butte directly ahead.
14.8 ▲	SO	Cattle guard; then graded track on left and faint track on right. Zero trip meter.

▼ 0.8	SO	Track on left.
14.0 ▲	SO	Track on right.
▼ 0.9	SO	Track on right.
13.9 ▲	SO	Track on left.
▼ 2.5	SO	Track on right.
12.3 ▲	SO	Track on left.
▼ 2.7	SO	Track on right.
12.1 ▲	SO	Track on left.
▼ 3.1	SO	Fourth of July Butte immediately on the right.
11.7 ▲	SO	Fourth of July Butte immediately on the left.
		GPS: N33°16.31′ W113°06.63′
▼ 3.5	SO	Cross through wide Fourth of July Wash.
11.3 ▲	SO	Cross through wide Fourth of July Wash.
▼ 4.3	SO	Cross through wash.
10.5 ▲	SO	Cross through wash.
▼ 4.6	SO	Cross through wash.
10.2 ▲	SO	Cross through wash.
▼ 6.3	SO	Cross through wash.
8.5 ▲	SO	Cross through wash.
▼ 7.0	SO	Track on left.
7.8 ▲	SO	Track on right.
▼ 7.6	SO	Track on left.
7.2 ▲	SO	Second entrance to track on right.
▼ 7.7	SO	Second entrance to track on left.
7.1 ▲	SO	Track on right.
▼ 7.8	SO	Cross through wash.
7.0 ▲	SO	Cross through wash.
▼ 8.0	SO	Cross through wash.
6.8 ▲	SO	Cross through wash.
▼ 8.1	SO	Track on left.
6.7 ▲	SO	Track on right.
		GPS: N33°14.45′ W113°10.99′
▼ 8.2	SO	Cross over Yellow Medicine Wash; then track on left.
6.6 ▲	SO	Track on right; then cross over Yellow Medicine Wash.
▼ 8.4	SO	Track on left.
6.4 ▲	SO	Track on right.
▼ 10.8	SO	Cross through wash.
4.0 ▲	SO	Cross through wash.

▼ 10.9		SO	Track on left.
	3.9 ▲	SO	Track on right.
▼ 11.3		SO	Cross through wash.
	3.5 ▲	SO	Cross through wash.
▼ 11.4		SO	Cross through wash.
	3.4 ▲	SO	Cross through wash.
▼ 11.6		SO	Track on left goes to well.
	3.2 ▲	SO	Track on right goes to well.
			GPS: N33°13.52′ W113°13.51′
▼ 14.0		SO	Cross through wash.
	0.8 ▲	SO	Cross through wash.
▼ 14.1		SO	Faint track on left.
	0.7 ▲	SO	Faint track on right.
▼ 14.4		SO	Track on right.
	0.4 ▲	SO	Track on left.
▼ 14.8		SO	Track on left goes to Sundad. No sign, but rocks have been laid out in pathways around the junction. There are two entrances to the track. Zero trip meter.
	0.0 ▲		Continue toward the Gila Bend Mountains.
			GPS: N33°10.84 W113°14.74′
▼ 0.0			Continue toward Agua Caliente.
	4.9 ▲	SO	Track on right goes to Sundad. No sign, but rocks have been laid out in pathways around the junction. There are two entrances to the track. Zero trip meter.
▼ 2.1		SO	Track on left.
	2.8 ▲	SO	Track on right.
▼ 2.2		SO	Track on left.
	2.7 ▲	SO	Track on right.
▼ 3.4		SO	Cross through Copper Wash.
	1.5 ▲	SO	Cross through Copper Wash.
			GPS: N33°07.92′ W113°15.34′
▼ 4.2		SO	Cross through wash.
	0.7 ▲	SO	Cross through wash.
▼ 4.5		BR	Cattle guard. Faint track on left along boundary fence.
	0.4 ▲	BL	Cattle guard. Faint track continues ahead along boundary fence.
▼ 4.9		TL	Turn left at 555th Avenue at the sign and zero trip meter.
	0.0 ▲		Continue to the east.
			GPS: N33°07.01′ W113°16.27′
▼ 0.0			Continue to the south.
	4.2 ▲	TR	Turn right onto the graded Agua Caliente Road at the T-intersection and zero trip meter.
▼ 0.9		SO	Road on right and road on left.
	3.3 ▲	SO	Road on right and road on left.
▼ 2.8		SO	Road on right.
	1.4 ▲	SO	Road on left.
			GPS: N33°04.44′ W113°16.27′
▼ 4.0		SO	Pass under power lines.
	0.2 ▲	SO	Pass under power lines.
▼ 4.2		TR	Faint tracks on right and left alongside rail line; then cross over rail line and turn onto graded Hyder Road. The junction is signed. Zero trip meter.
	0.0 ▲		Continue away from rail line.
			GPS: N33°03.19′ W113°16.28′
▼ 0.0			Continue along rail line to the southwest.
	2.1 ▲	TL	Turn left onto the graded 555th Avenue at sign. Zero trip meter and cross over rail line; faint tracks on right and left alongside rail line.
▼ 2.1		TL	Turn left at stop sign onto paved Agua Caliente Road at the sign. Zero trip meter.
	0.0 ▲		Continue on graded dirt road.
			GPS: N33°02.19′ W113°18.34′
▼ 0.0			Continue on toward Agua Caliente, remaining on paved road.
	3.2 ▲	TR	Turn right onto wide graded dirt road immediately before railroad. Zero trip meter.
▼ 3.2			Trail ends at the junction with the Old Agua Caliente Road, which leads to the right. The Agua Caliente Pioneer Cemetery and the remains of the hot springs are 0.6 miles and 1 mile down the Old Agua Caliente Road, respectively. Continue on the paved road south for 10.6 miles to join I-8 at exit 87 (Sentinel).
	0.0 ▲		To reach the start of the trail, take I-8 to exit 87 (Sentinel) and proceed north for 10.6 miles along the paved road to Agua Caliente. A dirt road on the left is the Old Agua Caliente Road. Zero trip meter at the signpost and proceed north along the paved road. The Pioneer Cemetery and the remains of the hot springs are 0.6 miles and 1 mile along the Old Agua Caliente Road, respectively.
			GPS: N32°59.19′ W113°18.32′

CENTRAL REGION TRAIL #16

Robbins Butte Wildlife Area Trail

Starting Point:	**Arizona 85, 0.1 miles south of mile marker 147**
Finishing Point:	**Old Highway 80, 1.8 miles south of Gillespie Dam**
Total Mileage:	**15.2 miles**
Unpaved Mileage:	**15.2 miles**
Driving Time:	**1 hour**
Elevation Range:	**800–1,000 feet**
Usually Open:	**Year-round**
Best Time to Travel:	**Fall to spring**
Difficulty Rating:	**2**
Scenic Rating:	**7**
Remoteness Rating:	**+0**

Special Attractions

- Robbins Butte Wildlife Area.
- Easy trail located close to Phoenix.
- Gillespie Dam.

Description

This trail, within easy reach of Phoenix, is a pleasant way to spend a couple of hours. It passes through the two wildlife areas of Robbins Butte and Powers Butte. Leaving Arizona 85, it immediately enters into the wildlife area along a roughly graded dirt road. Initially, the trail passes along the northern edge

Saguaros line the trail as it skirts the Buckeye Hills

of the Buckeye Hills, winding along the edge of the reserve toward Robbins Butte, an isolated conical outcropping. Many smaller tracks lead into the reserve. During the hunting season, these roads are heavily used, but you are unlikely to meet anyone at other times. Hunting for quail is permitted during the season with the appropriate license. To the right of the boundary fence is an area reserved for nonfirearm hunting.

The scenery becomes prettier the farther you go, and after 7.8 miles, at some disused farm buildings, the trail makes a sharp left along the fence line and drops slightly in standard. From here to the end of the trail, it is rougher and in places slightly washed out. A short section, only 100 yards long, immediately before the junction with the Gila Bend Canal, is the roughest.

The trail follows along the levee of the Gila Bend Canal for a short distance before exiting onto Old Highway 80, just south of the Gillespie Dam. The breached dam can be seen north of the road bridge.

No camping is permitted in the reserve. For those wishing to camp, some backcountry sites can be found along the nearby North Maricopa Mountains Trail.

Current Road Information

Bureau of Land Management
Phoenix Field Office
2015 West Deer Valley Rd.
Phoenix, AZ 85027
(623) 580-5500

Map References

BLM Phoenix South
USGS 1:24,000 Buckeye, Hassayampa, Arlington, Spring Mt., Cotton Center NW
1:100,000 Phoenix South
Maptech CD-ROM: Phoenix/Superstition Mountains
Arizona Atlas & Gazetteer, p. 56
Arizona Road & Recreation Atlas, p. 46 & p. 80

Route Directions

▼ 0.0			From Arizona 85, 0.1 miles south of mile marker 147, turn west on graded dirt road, cross through a fence line, and zero trip meter. There is a sign for Robbins Butte, Black Butte Wildlife Area.
	3.1 ▲		Trail ends on Arizona 85. Turn right for Gila Bend; turn left for Phoenix.
			GPS: N33°19.12' W112°37.40'
▼ 0.1		SO	Well on left.
	3.0 ▲	SO	Well on right.
▼ 0.3		BL	Parking area; then track on right is for authorized vehicles only.
	2.8 ▲	SO	Track on left is for authorized vehicles only; then parking area.
			GPS: N33°19.05' W112°37.77'
▼ 0.6		SO	Track on left.
	2.5 ▲	SO	Track on right.
▼ 0.7		BR	Cattle guard; then faint track on left.
	2.4 ▲	BL	Faint track on right; then cattle guard.
▼ 0.8		SO	Track on left.
	2.3 ▲	SO	Track on right.
▼ 1.3		SO	Track on left.
	1.8 ▲	SO	Track on right.
▼ 1.9		SO	Faint tracks on left; then cross through wash.
	1.2 ▲	SO	Cross through wash; then faint tracks on right.
▼ 2.0		SO	Cross through wash; then track on left.
	1.1 ▲	SO	Track on right; then cross through wash.
			GPS: N33°18.70' W112°39.34'
▼ 2.4		SO	Faint track on left.
	0.7 ▲	SO	Faint track on right.
▼ 2.6		SO	Cross through wash.
	0.5 ▲	SO	Cross through wash.
▼ 2.8		SO	Track on left. Robbins Butte directly ahead.
	0.3 ▲	BL	Track on right.
▼ 2.9		SO	Cross through wash; then track on right.
	0.2 ▲	SO	Track on left; then cross through wash.
			GPS: N33°18.88' W112°40.16'
▼ 3.1		BL	Two tracks on right; remain on main graded dirt road. Junction is at the base of Robbins Butte.
	0.0 ▲		Continue along main graded trail.
			GPS: N33°18.95' W112°40.30'
▼ 0.0		SO	Continue to the west.
	4.7 ▲	BR	Two tracks on left; remain on main graded dirt road. Junction is at the base of Robbins Butte. Zero trip meter.
▼ 0.2		SO	Track on right.
	4.5 ▲	SO	Track on left.
▼ 0.4		SO	Cross through wash.
	4.3 ▲	SO	Cross through wash.
▼ 0.5		SO	Track on left and tank on left; then cross through wash.
	4.2 ▲	SO	Cross through wash; then tank on right and track on right.
			GPS: N33°18.86' W112°40.86'
▼ 0.6		BL	Stockyard on right; then track on right.
	4.1 ▲	SO	Track on left; then stockyard on left.
▼ 0.8		SO	Private house on right; track on left.
	3.9 ▲	SO	Track on right; private house on left.
▼ 1.5		SO	Cross through wash; tracks on right and left up and down wash.
	3.2 ▲	SO	Cross through wash; tracks on right and left up and down wash.
▼ 1.8		SO	Small track on left.
	2.9 ▲	SO	Small track on right.
▼ 2.4		SO	Track on left. Powers Butte is ahead. Trail is running along the outside edge of the Gila River Wash.

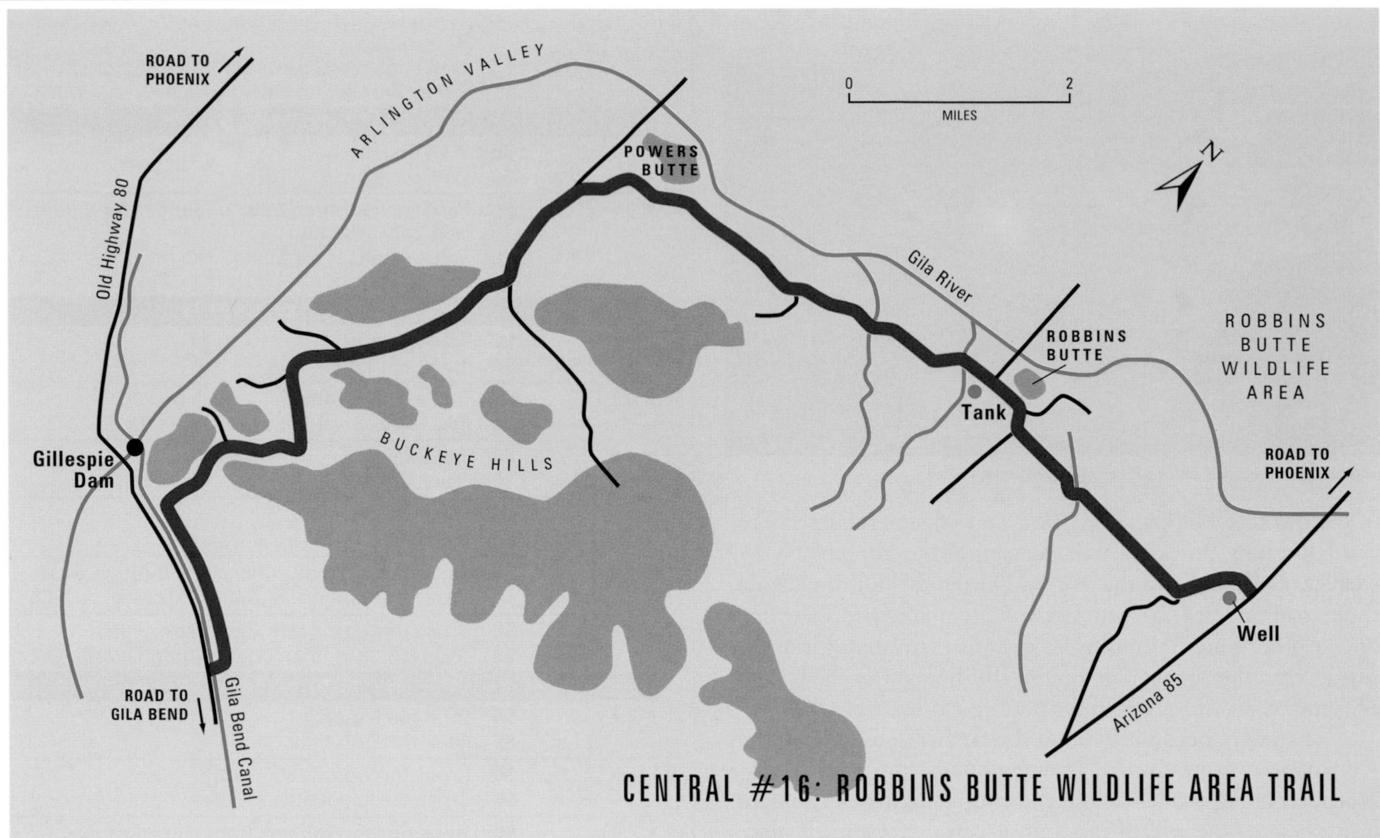

▼	▲		
	2.3 ▲	SO	Track on right. Trail is running along the outside edge of the Gila River Wash.
▼ 2.6		SO	Track on left.
	2.1 ▲	SO	Track on right.
▼ 3.5		SO	Track on left.
	1.2 ▲	SO	Track on right.
▼ 3.6		SO	Cross through old fence line at the foot of Powers Butte.
	1.1 ▲	SO	Cross through old fence line at the foot of Powers Butte.
			GPS: N33°18.27' W112°43.89'
▼ 3.8		SO	Cross through wash.
	0.9 ▲	SO	Cross through wash.
▼ 4.7		TL	Pass through gate and turn left in front of farm buildings. Track straight on. Zero trip meter.
	0.0 ▲		Continue away from farm buildings.
			GPS: N33°17.78' W112°44.73'
▼ 0.0			Continue along fence line to the south.
	5.7 ▲	TR	Turn right and pass through fence line. Farm buildings on left and track on left. Zero trip meter.
▼ 0.6		SO	Track on right.
	5.1 ▲	SO	Track on left.
▼ 0.7		SO	Track on right to corral.
	5.0 ▲	SO	Track on left to corral.
▼ 1.1		SO	Track on left; then cattle guard. Leaving Powers Butte Game Reserve.
	4.6 ▲	SO	Cattle guard; then track on right. Entering Powers Butte Game Reserve.
			GPS: N33°16.77' W112°44.67'
▼ 1.2		SO	Track on left.
	4.5 ▲	SO	Track on right.
▼ 1.6		SO	Track on right; then cross through wash. Vehicles travel to the right down the wash.
	4.1 ▲	SO	Cross through wash; vehicles travel to the left down wash. Track on left.
▼ 1.8		SO	Track on left; then cross through wash.
	3.9 ▲	SO	Cross through wash; then track on right.
▼ 2.3		SO	Track on left under power lines.
	3.4 ▲	SO	Track on right under power lines.
▼ 2.4		SO	Cross through wash.
	3.3 ▲	SO	Cross through wash.
▼ 2.7		BL	Major graded road on right. Views to the right into Arlington Valley.
	3.0 ▲	SO	Major graded road on left. Views to the left into Arlington Valley.
			GPS: N33°15.49' W112°45.24'
▼ 3.1		SO	Track on left.
	2.6 ▲	BR	Track on right.
▼ 3.3		SO	Track on right through fence line.
	2.4 ▲	SO	Track on left through fence line.
			GPS: N33°14.97' W112°45.48'
▼ 3.8		SO	Cross through wash.
	1.9 ▲	SO	Cross through wash.
▼ 4.1		SO	Track on left; then cross through wash.
	1.6 ▲	SO	Cross through wash; then track on right.
▼ 4.7		SO	Well-used track on right.
	1.0 ▲	BR	Well-used track on left.
			GPS: N33°14.29' W112°45.43'
▼ 5.1		SO	Track on left.
	0.6 ▲	BL	Track on right.
▼ 5.5		BR	Track on left; bear right past gas pipeline valve.
	0.2 ▲	SO	Track on right.
▼ 5.6		SO	Track on left.
	0.1 ▲	BL	Track on right; bear left, passing to the left of the gas pipeline valve.

▼ 5.7		TL	T-intersection with graded trail along Gila Bend Canal. Zero trip meter. Road on right dead-ends at Gillespie Dam. There is a footbridge across to the dam but no vehicle exit.
	0.0 ▲		Continue away from canal.
			GPS: N33°13.54' W112°45.66'
▼ 0.0			Continue alongside canal.
	1.7 ▲	TR	Turn away from canal and head for gas pipeline valve. Road straight ahead dead-ends at Gillespie Dam. There is a footbridge across to the dam but no vehicle exit.
▼ 1.6		BL	Bear left off canal bank and immediately turn right through gap in canal.
	0.1 ▲	SO	Continue northwest along canal levee.
▼ 1.7			Trail finishes at junction with Old Highway 80. Turn right for Phoenix; turn left for Gila Bend.
	0.0 ▲		Trail commences on Old Highway 80, 0.8 miles south of mile marker 21, 1.8 miles south of the eastern edge of the Gillespie Dam on the Gila River. Turn northeast through gap in Gila Bend Canal and immediately turn left and ascend to the canal bank.
			GPS: N33°12.99' W112°44.08'

CENTRAL REGION TRAIL #17

Margie's Peak Trail

Starting Point:	**Arizona 85, 0.5 miles north of mile marker 134**
Finishing Point:	**Arizona 85, 0.4 miles south of mile marker 141**
Total Mileage:	**14.9 miles**
Unpaved Mileage:	**14.9 miles**
Driving Time:	**1.5 hours**
Elevation Range:	**880–1,400 feet**
Usually Open:	**Year-round**
Best Time to Travel:	**Fall to spring**
Difficulty Rating:	**2**
Scenic Rating:	**7**
Remoteness Rating:	**+0**

Special Attractions

- Seldom-used, easy trail close to Phoenix.
- Hiking access to North Maricopa Mountains Wilderness Area.
- Sonoran desert wildlife-viewing.

Description

From Arizona 85, the unsigned trail turns off 0.5 miles north of mile marker 134. If you come to two abandoned houses on the east side of the highway, with a trail running alongside them, you are 0.3 miles too far to the north. The trail entrance is easier to spot when traveling from north to south, as it turns east from the highway and immediately swings south, alongside the road to dip down and cross through a wash. It then

The remains of Mountain Well and tank

turns east again and passes through a gate alongside a couple corrals and Hedges Well.

The trail is easygoing as it heads toward the Maricopa Mountains. The wilderness area is on the south side as the trail enters a gap in the range, traveling along a wash. To the north, Margie's Peak rears up to nearly 2,500 feet. The mostly formed trail surface is smooth, and although there are a couple of soft sections in the wash, the naturally gravelly surface makes for easy driving.

The scenery along the trail is spectacular, providing distant vistas on either side of the range. The rocky ridges and peaks of Margie's Peak are to the north and Sheep Mountain is to the south as the trail travels through the gap in the Maricopa Range. It is possible to see a wide variety of wildlife—the elusive desert bighorn sheep, javelinas, desert mule deer, coyotes, and a wide variety of snakes and lizards. The best time for viewing is early in the morning or just around dusk.

After 3.6 miles a vehicle corridor leads into the wilderness area for 1.2 miles, traveling down Margie's Cove to Margie's West Hiking Trailhead. The hike (approximately 9 miles) that begins here is a lovely day's outing. It is unmarked and travels mainly along washes and vehicle trails. There is a basic BLM camping area at the trailhead (no water).

The main trail continues in the wash, passing through the gap and out toward Little Rainbow Valley. The scenery opens out as the trail gradually descends to join the graded road running along the pipeline in the valley. From here, it is 5.3 miles to Arizona 85.

Current Road Information

Bureau of Land Management
Phoenix Field Office
2015 West Deer Valley Rd.
Phoenix, AZ 85027
(623) 580-5500

Map References

BLM Phoenix South
USGS 1:24,000 Cotton Center NW, Margie's Peak
1:100,000 Phoenix South
Maptech CD-ROM: Phoenix/Superstition Mountains
Arizona Atlas & Gazetteer, p. 56
Arizona Road & Recreation Atlas, p. 46 & p. 80

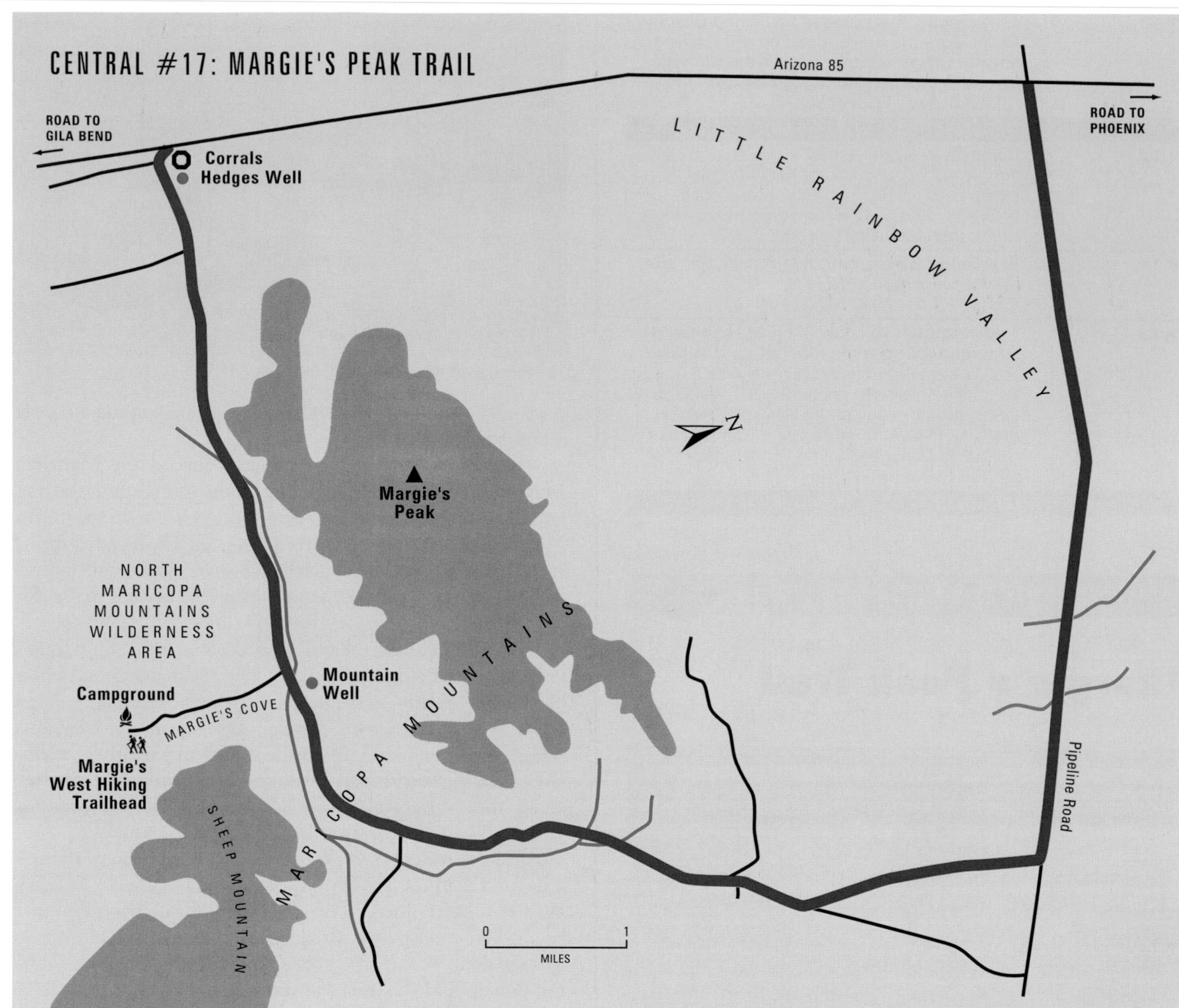

Route Directions

▼ 0.0			From Arizona 85, 0.5 miles north of mile marker 134, turn east off the road and immediately swing south to cross a wash and then east again to pass through a gate alongside a couple of corrals. Zero trip meter at the gate. Track on right at end of corrals.
	3.6 ▲		Track on left before corrals; then trail ends back at Arizona 85, 0.5 miles north of mile marker 134. Turn right for Phoenix; turn left for Gila Bend.
			GPS: N33°08.38' W112°38.96'
▼ 0.6		SO	Track on right before BLM sign.
	3.0 ▲	SO	Track on left after BLM sign.
▼ 0.8		SO	Track on left and track on right under power lines.
	2.8 ▲	SO	Track on left and track on right under power lines.
			GPS: N33°08.44' W112°38.04'
▼ 1.0		SO	Faint track on left.
	2.6 ▲	SO	Faint track on right.
▼ 1.1		SO	Well-used track on left.
	2.5 ▲	BL	Well-used track on right.
			GPS: N33°08.39' W112°37.71'
▼ 1.7		SO	North Maricopa Mountains Wilderness Area begins on right.
	1.9 ▲	SO	End of North Maricopa Mountains Wilderness Area on left. BLM land is now on both sides of the trail.
▼ 1.9		SO	Enter wash. Trail is following in or alongside wash.
	1.7 ▲	SO	Exit wash.
▼ 2.2		SO	Exit wash.
	1.4 ▲	SO	Enter wash.
▼ 2.5		SO	Cross through wash.
	1.1 ▲	SO	Cross through wash.
▼ 2.6		SO	Cross through wash.
	1.0 ▲	SO	Cross through wash.
▼ 2.8		SO	Cross through wash.
	0.8 ▲	SO	Cross through wash.
			GPS: N33°08.59' W112°35.95'
▼ 2.9		BL	Track on right. Bear left over wash. Many faint

		turnouts on right and left; remain on main trail.
0.7 ▲	BR	Track on left. Bear right over wash.
		GPS: N33°08.59' W112°35.90'
▼ 3.0	SO	Pass through wire gate.
0.6 ▲	SO	Pass through wire gate. Many faint turnouts on right and left; remain on main trail.
		GPS: N33°08.62' W112°35.80'
▼ 3.2	SO	Cross through wash.
0.4 ▲	SO	Cross through wash.
▼ 3.3	SO	Cross through wash.
0.3 ▲	SO	Cross through wash.
▼ 3.5	SO	Cross through wash.
0.1 ▲	SO	Cross through wash.
▼ 3.6	SO	Cross through wash; then wider track on right travels a wilderness corridor for 1.2 miles to Margie's West Hiking Trailhead. BLM sign at junction. Zero trip meter.
0.0 ▲		Continue west and cross through wash.
		GPS: N33°08.63' W112°35.11'
▼ 0.0		Continue to the east.
4.1 ▲	SO	Wider track on left travels a wilderness corridor for 1.2 miles to Margie's West Hiking Trailhead. BLM sign at junction. Zero trip meter.
▼ 0.1	SO	Track on right; then cross through wide wash; tracks on right and left lead up and down wash.
4.0 ▲	SO	Cross through wide wash; tracks on right and left lead up and down wash, followed by track on left.
▼ 0.2	SO	Mountain Well on left (dry). Part of the windmill and tank remain.
3.9 ▲	SO	Mountain Well on right (dry). Part of the windmill and tank remain.
		GPS: N33°08.67' W112°34.91'
▼ 0.3	SO	Cross through wash.
3.8 ▲	SO	Cross through wash.
▼ 1.4	BL	Well-used track on right.
2.7 ▲	BR	Well-used track on left.
		GPS: N33°09.16' W112°33.86'
▼ 1.6	SO	Cross through wash. Tracks on right and left up and down wash.
2.5 ▲	SO	Cross through wash. Tracks on right and left up and down wash.
▼ 1.7	SO	Cross through wash.
2.4 ▲	SO	Cross through wash.
▼ 1.9	SO	Cross through wash. Tracks on left and right up and down wash.
2.2 ▲	SO	Cross through wash. Tracks on left and right up and down wash.
▼ 2.1	SO	Cross through wash.
2.0 ▲	SO	Cross through wash.
▼ 2.3	SO	Cross through wash.
1.8 ▲	SO	Cross through wash.
▼ 2.5	SO	Cross through wash; then track on left.
1.6 ▲	SO	Track on right; then cross through wash.
▼ 2.8	SO	Cross through wash.
1.3 ▲	SO	Cross through wash.
▼ 3.1	SO	Track on right.
1.0 ▲	SO	Track on left.
		GPS: N33°10.60' W112°33.47'
▼ 3.3	SO	Cross through wash.
0.8 ▲	SO	Cross through wash.
▼ 3.5	SO	Cross through wash.
0.6 ▲	SO	Cross through wash.
▼ 3.8	SO	Two tracks on left.
0.3 ▲	BL	Two tracks on right.
▼ 3.9	SO	Track on right.
0.2 ▲	SO	Track on left.
		GPS: N33°11.20' W112°33.14'
▼ 4.0	SO	Cross through wash; then track on right.
0.1 ▲	BR	Track on left; then cross through wash.
▼ 4.1	BL	Fork in trail: two equally used tracks. Take left-hand track and zero trip meter. Narrow and brushy track on right goes 1.9 miles to pipeline road.
0.0 ▲		Continue to the south.
		GPS: N33°11.27' W112°33.09'
▼ 0.0		Continue to the north. Views down into Little Rainbow Valley.
1.9 ▲	SO	Narrow and brushy, equally used track on left goes 1.9 miles back to pipeline road. Zero trip meter.
▼ 0.1	SO	Track on right.
1.8 ▲	BR	Track on left.
▼ 0.5	TR	Cross through fence line; then track on left.
1.4 ▲	TL	Track on right; then turn and cross through fence line.
		GPS: N33°11.80' W112°33.08'
▼ 1.1	SO	Cross through wash.
0.8 ▲	SO	Cross through wash.
▼ 1.4	SO	Cross through wash.
0.5 ▲	SO	Cross through wash.
▼ 1.9	TL	T-intersection with larger pipeline road. Cattle guard immediately on the right. Zero trip meter.
0.0 ▲		Continue on smaller trail.
		GPS: N33°13.00' W112°32.83'
▼ 0.0		Continue west along the gas pipeline.
5.3 ▲	TR	Turn right onto smaller unmarked trail immediately before a cattle guard and a left-hand turn. Zero trip meter.
▼ 1.2	SO	Cross through wash.
4.1 ▲	SO	Cross through wash.
▼ 1.7	SO	Cross through wash.
3.6 ▲	SO	Cross through wash.
▼ 1.9	SO	Cattle guard.
3.4 ▲	SO	Cattle guard.
		GPS: N33°13.47' W112°34.86'
▼ 3.9	SO	Small track on left under power lines.
1.4 ▲	SO	Small track on right under power lines.
▼ 4.4	SO	Cattle guard; then small track on left.

The trail rising and falling as it negotiates the firm sand ridges

	0.9 ▲	SO	Small track on right; then cattle guard.
▼ 4.8		SO	Cross through fence line. Trail follows the fence line of the southwest regional landfill.
	0.5 ▲	SO	Cross through fence line.
▼ 5.3			Trail ends at the junction with Arizona 85. Turn right for Phoenix; turn left for Gila Bend.
	0.0 ▲		Trail commences from Arizona 85, 0.4 miles south of mile marker 141. Turn through a fence line onto the wide, graded pipeline road. The trail leaves immediately south of the large power lines, north of the southwest regional landfill; there is no sign at the turn. Initially, the trail runs along the northern fence line of the landfill.
			GPS: N33°13.64′ W112°38.48′

CENTRAL REGION TRAIL #18

Butterfield Pass Trail

Starting Point:	**Maricopa Road, 0.6 miles east of mile marker 10**
Finishing Point:	**Maricopa Road at Estrella**
Total Mileage:	**11.8 miles**
Unpaved Mileage:	**11.8 miles**
Driving Time:	**1 hour**
Elevation Range:	**1,200–1,800 feet**
Usually Open:	**Year-round**
Best Time to Travel:	**Fall to spring**
Difficulty Rating:	**3**
Scenic Rating:	**8**
Remoteness Rating:	**+0**

Special Attractions

- Part of the historic Butterfield Stage Route.
- Access to the North Maricopa Mountains Wilderness Area.
- Rugged Sonoran desert scenery.

The trail crossing a gap in the Maricopa Mountains

History

This route, which follows an earlier emigrant trail, was laid out in the 1850s as part of the Stockton–Los Angeles Road. It was used by the Butterfield Overland Mail stagecoaches between St. Louis and San Francisco from 1858 to 1861. This was the first overland mail route to operate on a regular schedule. The journey was difficult and dangerous. Attacks and looting by the Apache were common; the western side of Butterfield Pass was a notorious spot for stages to be ambushed. Happy Camp Cistern, located on the trail, was the only source of water along the arid stretch between Maricopa Wells and Gila Bend. The water to fill the tank was shipped in from Gila Ranch Station.

Description

The short section of this trail that crosses Butterfield Pass has been adopted and maintained by the Boy Scouts of America as a community project. Their work includes signage and information boards along the route.

The trail starts from the paved Maricopa Road, which leaves Arizona 85 immediately north of Gila Bend, 0.2 miles northeast from where Arizona 85 passes under I-8. Turn east onto Maricopa Road and proceed 10 miles to the start of the trail. Initially, the trail crosses through the flat at the southern end of the Maricopa Mountains to Gap Well. From here, it joins the Butterfield Stage Route as it winds its way through the desert, following the path of a wash. The surface is generally smooth. The roughest section (the one that merits the trail's 3 rating) comes on the climb to Butterfield Pass, where a few wheels may spin on the loose surface.

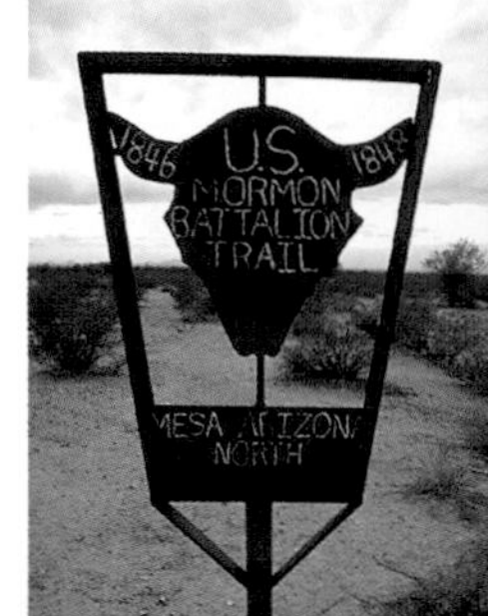

A marker for the Mormon Battalion Trail

In the reverse direction, the trail starts at Estrella on the Maricopa Road. Estrella is shown on many maps, but it is a place in name only.

Current Road Information

Bureau of Land Management
Phoenix Field Office
2015 West Deer Valley Rd.
Phoenix, AZ 85027
(623) 580-5500

Map References

BLM Gila Bend, Phoenix South
USGS 1:24,000 Bosque, Cotton Center SE, Butterfield Pass
1:100,000 Gila Bend, Phoenix South
Maptech CD-ROM: Phoenix/Superstition Mountains
Arizona Atlas & Gazetteer, pp. 56, 57
Arizona Road & Recreation Atlas, p. 46 & p. 80

Route Directions

▼ 0.0	From Maricopa Road, 10 miles east of Gila Bend, 0.6 miles east of mile marker 10, turn north on formed dirt trail at a wooden sign for Butterfield Trail. Zero trip meter.

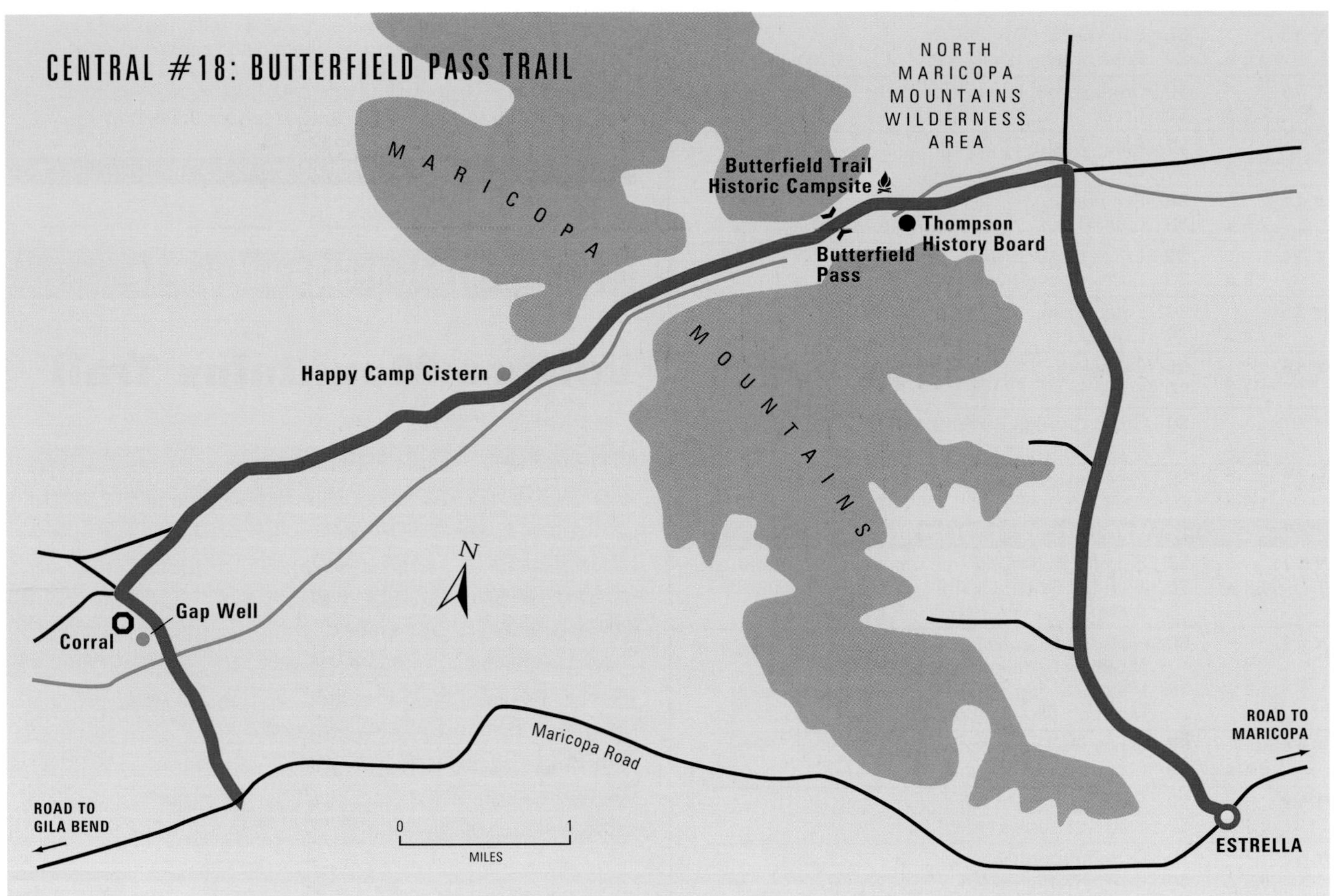

1.3 ▲		Trail ends on paved Maricopa Road. Turn right for Gila Bend; turn left for Maricopa.
		GPS: N32°59.57′ W112°31.31′
▼ 0.1	SO	Track on left.
1.2 ▲	SO	Track on right.
▼ 0.2	SO	Track on left.
1.1 ▲	SO	Track on right.
▼ 0.5	SO	Cross through wash.
0.8 ▲	SO	Cross through wash.
▼ 0.6	SO	Track on right; then cross through wash.
0.7 ▲	SO	Cross through wash; then track on left.
▼ 0.7	SO	Track on left.
0.6 ▲	SO	Track on right.
▼ 0.9	SO	Cross through wash; then track on left.
0.4 ▲	SO	Track on right; then cross through wash.
▼ 1.1	BL	Gap Well. Pass through fence line with corral on left. Wooden marker post for Butterfield Stage Trail by fence line. Track on right after fence line.
0.2 ▲	BR	Gap Well. Corral on right; track on left. Bear right and pass through fence line.
		GPS: N33°00.43′ W112°31.92′
▼ 1.3	TR	Turn onto well-used trail at sign for Butterfield Stage Route Trail. Zero trip meter.
0.0 ▲		Continue toward Maricopa Road.
		GPS: N33°00.56′ W112°32.19′
▼ 0.0		Continue along the historic stage route.
6.3 ▲	TL	Turn onto formed dirt trail at sign for Butterfield Stage Route Trail (facing the other way). Zero trip meter.

▼ 0.4	SO	Track on left, followed by numerous tracks on left for next 0.2 miles.
5.9 ▲	SO	Track on right.
▼ 0.6	SO	Track on left.
5.7 ▲	SO	Track on right, followed by numerous tracks on right for next 0.2 miles.
▼ 0.8	SO	Well-used track on left. North Maricopa Mountains Wilderness Area begins on left.
5.5 ▲	SO	North Maricopa Mountains Wilderness Area ends on right. Well-used track on right.
		GPS: N33°01.10′ W112°31.64′
▼ 1.0	SO	Track on right goes to corral.
5.3 ▲	BR	Track on left goes to corral.
▼ 1.6	SO	Cross through wash.
4.7 ▲	SO	Cross through wash.
▼ 1.8	SO	Cross through wash.
4.5 ▲	SO	Cross through wash.
▼ 2.5	SO	Cross through wash.
3.8 ▲	SO	Cross through wash.
▼ 2.6	SO	Happy Camp Cistern—stone water tank on left and information board on right.
3.7 ▲	SO	Happy Camp Cistern—stone water tank on right and information board on left.
		GPS: N33°01.83′ W112°29.97′
▼ 3.1	SO	Cross through wash.
3.2 ▲	SO	Cross through wash.
▼ 3.3	SO	Game water tank on left.
3.0 ▲	SO	Game water tank on right.
▼ 3.4	BL	Enter line of the wash.
2.9 ▲	BR	Exit line of the wash.

▼ 3.8 BL Exit wash.
2.5 ▲ SO Enter wash.

▼ 3.9 SO Cross through wash.
2.4 ▲ SO Cross through wash.

▼ 4.1 SO Enter wash.
2.2 ▲ SO Exit wash.

▼ 4.2 SO Exit wash.
2.1 ▲ SO Enter wash.

▼ 4.4 SO Cross through wash.
1.9 ▲ SO Cross through wash.

▼ 4.5 SO Enter wash.
1.8 ▲ SO Exit wash.

▼ 4.6 SO Exit wash.
1.7 ▲ SO Enter wash.

▼ 4.7 SO Cross through wash.
1.6 ▲ SO Cross through wash.

▼ 4.8 SO Pass through gate. Butterfield Pass.
1.5 ▲ SO Pass through gate. Butterfield Pass.

GPS: N33°02.84' W112°28.09'

▼ 5.1 SO Sign for Butterfield Trail Campsite on left of trail.
1.2 ▲ SO Sign for Butterfield Trail Campsite on right of trail.

▼ 5.2 SO History of James Lewis Thompson, of the Mormon Battalion, posted on right of trail.
1.1 ▲ SO History of James Lewis Thompson, of the Mormon Battalion, posted on left of trail.

▼ 5.4 SO Cross through wash.
0.9 ▲ SO Cross through wash.

▼ 5.9 SO Cross through wash.
0.4 ▲ SO Cross through wash.

▼ 6.2 SO Cross through wash.
0.1 ▲ SO Cross through wash.

▼ 6.3 TR Information board on right. Track on left and track ahead. Zero trip meter.
0.0 ▲ Continue toward Butterfield Pass.

GPS: N33°03.28' W112°26.70'

▼ 0.0 Continue toward Maricopa Road.
4.2 ▲ TL Turn left at sign for the Butterfield Trail; pass information board on left. Track on right and track ahead. Zero trip meter.

▼ 1.5 SO Cross through wash.
2.7 ▲ SO Cross through wash.

▼ 1.8 SO Track on right.
2.4 ▲ BR Track on left.

GPS: N33°01.71' W112°26.29'

▼ 2.0 SO Track on right.
2.2 ▲ BR Track on left.

▼ 2.4 SO Cross through wash.
1.8 ▲ SO Cross through wash.

▼ 2.7 SO Cross through wash.
1.5 ▲ SO Cross through wash.

▼ 2.9 SO Track on right at large pile of rocks.
1.3 ▲ BR Track on left at large pile of rocks.

GPS: N33°00.84' W112°26.29'

▼ 3.0 SO Cross through wash; then many small pull-in areas on right. Numerous small tracks on right and left for the next mile; remain on the main trail.
1.2 ▲ SO Many small pull-in areas on left; then cross through wash.

▼ 4.2 Trail ends at the junction with the paved Maricopa Road at Estrella. Turn right for Gila Bend; turn left for Maricopa.
0.0 ▲ From the Maricopa Road, 0.1 miles northeast of mile marker 17 at Estrella, turn west on ungraded sandy trail and zero trip meter. There is a sign for the Mormon Battalion Trail at the junction. There are numerous faint tracks on right and left for the first mile; remain on main trail.

GPS: N33°00.06' W112°25.28'

CENTRAL REGION TRAIL #19

Vulture Mountains Trail

Starting Point:	**US 60 in Morristown**
Finishing Point:	**Vulture Mine Road, 3.3 miles southwest of US 60**
Total Mileage:	**13.3 miles**
Unpaved Mileage:	**13.1 miles**
Driving Time:	**2.5 hours**
Elevation Range:	**1,800–2,800 feet**
Usually Open:	**Year-round**
Best Time to Travel:	**October to April**
Difficulty Rating:	**3**
Scenic Rating:	**8**
Remoteness Rating:	**+0**

Special Attractions

- Rugged Vulture Mountains and Sonoran desert vegetation.
- Remains of the Mammoth Spar and the Big Spar Mines.
- Many side trails to explore.

History

Morristown was named after George Morris, the first inhabitant of the settlement, who also discovered the Mack Morris Mine in Gila County. Originally Morristown was known as Vulture Siding because of the influence of the Vulture Mine to the west. By the late 1890s the name had been changed to Hot Springs Junction because the Vulture Mine had dwindled and the town had become the jump-off point for the stage route northwest to Castle Hot Springs. Wells Fargo established a stage station there in 1903.

Hassayampa is an Indian word that means "place of big rocks and water." Judging by some of the rumors that the miners passed along, it could possibly mean "tall tales" as well. Many an unbelievable story of newfound and fabulous riches circulated up and down the Hassayampa River. A common ragging description of the bearer of these tales was, "Been drinking Hassayampa water again," which implied the narrator was a deluded soul.

The Vulture Mountains seem to have gained their name from the discovery of the Vulture Mine. The association of these buzzards with the day of discovery comes in two tales. Either the discoverer, Henry Wickenburg, was out shooting and found worthwhile ore bedside one of the fallen birds or he looked up to see the creatures circling when he accidentally

Crossing through the site of the Mammoth Spar Mine—beware of shafts close to the trail

found his first worthwhile outcropping. Either way, the name stuck, and an extremely prosperous mine began. Wickenburg, who gained little from the mines overall and finished his days as a farmer, shot himself in later life.

Description

This trail is one of many through an area riddled with 4WD trails that are mainly old mining roads. For those with more time, it is possible to spend anywhere from an additional couple of hours to a few days exploring these side roads, many of which lead to other mines.

The trail leaves Morristown and travels along the graded dirt road until it reaches a crossing of the Hassayampa River. This wide, sandy riverbed crossing should not be attempted when the river is flowing. After the river, the trail becomes narrower and roughly graded and starts to climb into the Vulture Mountains. There are many turns along its length; however, most of the route follows the major trail. There are a couple of potentially confusing turns—one near the Mammoth Spar Mine is easy to mistake, as it is the smaller turn out of the wash opposite a well.

For the most part, the trail is small but well maintained. The scenery is diverse with some good views across the red Vulture Mountains. There are some pleasant backcountry campsites scattered along the trail and very prolific desert vegetation.

The trail passes by the remains of the Big Spar Mine before eventually coming to an end on Vulture Mine Road.

Current Road Information

Bureau of Land Management
Phoenix Field Office
2015 West Deer Valley Rd.
Phoenix, AZ 85027
(623) 580-5500

Map References

BLM Phoenix North
USGS 1:24,000 Wittmann, Wickenburg SW, Wickenburg, Vulture Peak
1:100,000 Phoenix North
Maptech CD-ROM: Phoenix/Superstition Mountains
Arizona Atlas & Gazetteer, p. 48

Route Directions

▼ 0.0			From US 60 in Morristown, turn southwest off the highway onto the paved Gates Road at the sign and zero trip meter. Proceed southwest and cross over the railroad.
	2.1 ▲		Trail ends at the intersection with US 60 in Morristown. Turn right for Phoenix; turn left for Wickenburg.
			GPS: N33°51.18' W112°37.30'
▼ 0.1		BR	Cross railroad and bear right, remaining on paved road.
	2.0 ▲	BL	Cross railroad and bear left toward US 60.
▼ 0.2		SO	Graded road on right and left; remain on major road, which turns to graded gravel.
	1.9 ▲	SO	Graded road on right and left; remain on major road, which is now paved.
▼ 0.5		SO	Track on right.
	1.6 ▲	SO	Track on left.
▼ 1.4		SO	Two roads on left.
	0.7 ▲	SO	Two roads on right.
			GPS: N33°50.88' W112°38.37'
▼ 1.5		SO	Small track on left.
	0.6 ▲	SO	Small track on right.
▼ 2.1		TL	Smaller track on left back along wash; then turn left and cross wash at a right angle. Turn is opposite Little San Domingo Wash. Zero trip meter.
	0.0 ▲		Continue along the graded road.
			GPS: N33°51.13' W112°39.49'
▼ 0.0			Continue on and cross the very wide, sandy, open Hassayampa River wash. Do not attempt if river is flowing.
	4.1 ▲	TR	Exit wash. Track on right on far side. Turn right and join graded dirt road. Zero trip meter at far side.
▼ 0.2		SO	Exit wash; track on right and left on west side of wash; cross through wire gate.
	3.9 ▲	SO	Cross through wire gate; then start to cross the very wide, sandy, open Hassayampa River wash. Do not attempt if river is flowing.
▼ 0.3		SO	Track on left.
	3.8 ▲	BL	Track on right.
▼ 0.4		BL	Well-used track on right; remain on larger trail.
	3.7 ▲	BR	Well-used track on left; remain on larger trail.
			GPS: N33°51.14' W112°39.93'
▼ 0.5		BR	Track on left, followed by second track to water tank. Bear right and remain on larger trail.
	3.6 ▲	BL	Track on right to water tank, followed by second track on right. Bear left at second track, remaining on larger trail.
			GPS: N33°51.04' W112°40.08'
▼ 0.6		SO	Second track on left to water tank.
	3.5 ▲	SO	Track on right to water tank.
▼ 0.8		SO	Track on right.
	3.3 ▲	SO	Track on left.
▼ 1.7		SO	Track on left and track on right.
	2.4 ▲	SO	Track on left and track on right.
			GPS: N33°51.40' W112°41.21'
▼ 1.9		SO	Well-used track on right.
	2.2 ▲	SO	Well-used track on left.
▼ 2.0		BR	Well-used track on left.
	2.1 ▲	SO	Well-used track on right.
			GPS: N33°51.43' W112°41.49'
▼ 2.5		SO	Track on left.
	1.6 ▲	SO	Track on right.
▼ 2.7		BR	Cross through wash; then track on left.

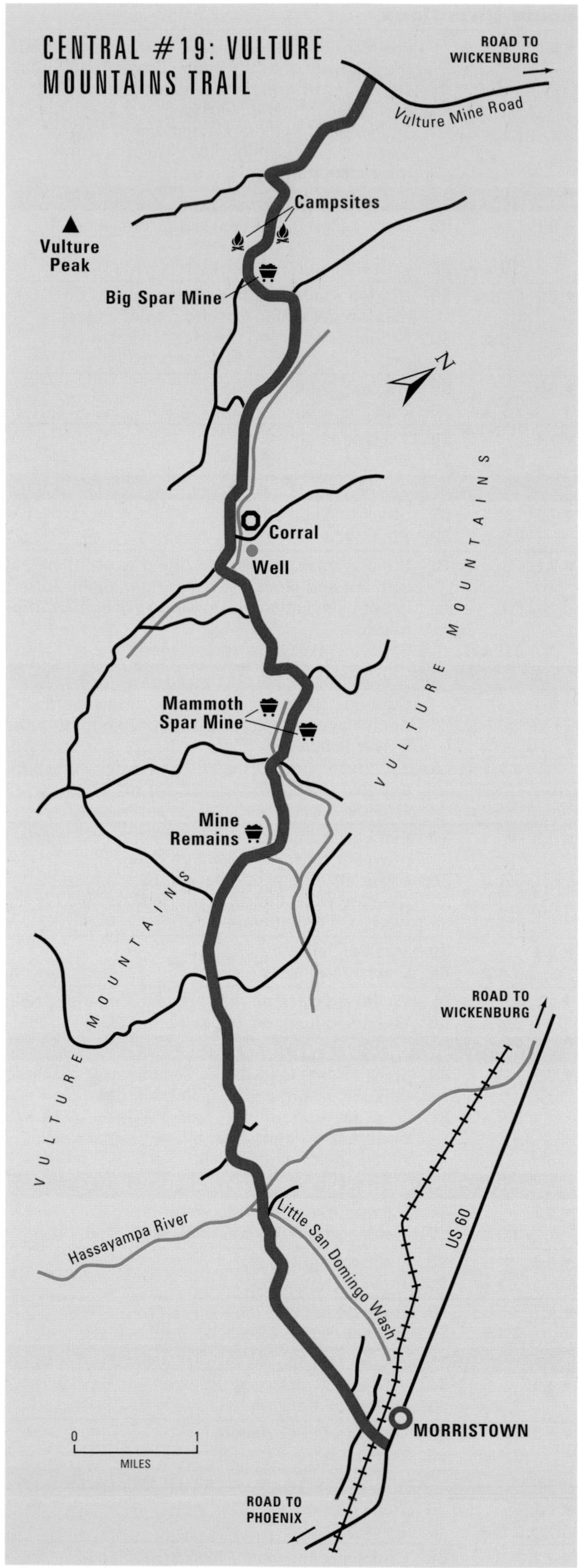

	1.4 ▲	BL	Track on right; then cross through wash.
▼ 2.8		SO	Cross through two washes.
	1.3 ▲	SO	Cross through two washes.
▼ 2.9		SO	Cross through wash.
	1.2 ▲	SO	Cross through wash.
▼ 3.2		SO	Fenced mine shaft on left and diggings on right; then cross through two washes.
	0.9 ▲	SO	Cross through two washes; then fenced mine shaft on right and diggings on left.
			GPS: N33°52.15' W112°42.26'
▼ 3.3		SO	Cross through wash.
	0.8 ▲	SO	Cross through wash.
▼ 3.4		SO	Enter wash.
	0.7 ▲	SO	Exit wash.
▼ 3.5		SO	Exit wash.
	0.6 ▲	SO	Enter wash.
▼ 3.6		SO	Enter wash.
	0.5 ▲	SO	Exit wash.
▼ 3.9		BR	Exit wash; then bear right; track on left.
	0.2 ▲	SO	Track on right; then enter wash.
			GPS: N33°52.46' W112°42.80'
▼ 4.1		TL	T-intersection with a wash. Track on right up wash. Turn left up wash and zero trip meter.
	0.0 ▲		Continue south out of the wash.
			GPS: N33°52.55' W112°42.86'
▼ 0.0			Continue in wash.
	2.4 ▲	TR	Leave wash to the right. Track continues down wash ahead. Zero trip meter.
▼ 0.2		BR	Bear right up smaller wash and then immediately bear left out of wash onto a well-formed trail.
	2.2 ▲	BL	Drop down into small wash; track on left up wash; then immediately bear left down larger wash; track on right up larger wash.
			GPS: N33°52.68' W112°43.03'
▼ 0.3		BR	In front of concrete footings, bear right and drop back toward the small wash. Then immediately bear left, following the formed vehicle trail that climbs up the ridge.
	2.1 ▲	BR	Descend to small wash and then bear right away from the wash up a small hump. At the top, there are concrete footings on the right; swing sharp left. Many diggings now on both sides of the trail.
▼ 0.4		SO	Shafts, tailings, and diggings on right and left of trail: Mammoth Spar Mine.
	2.0 ▲	SO	Shafts, tailings, and diggings on left and right of trail: Mammoth Spar Mine.
			GPS: N33°52.79' W112°43.15'
▼ 0.5		SO	Track on left.
	1.9 ▲	SO	Track on right.
▼ 0.6		SO	Track on left and shaft on right.
	1.8 ▲	SO	Track on right and shaft on left.
▼ 0.7		BL	Small digging; then small track on right, followed by fork in trail. Well-used track goes to the right; bear left.
	1.7 ▲	BR	Well-used track on left; bear right. Then small track on left before small digging.
			GPS: N33°52.94' W112°43.42'
▼ 0.9		SO	Pass through wire gate.
	1.5 ▲	SO	Pass through wire gate.
▼ 1.0		SO	Cross through wash.
	1.4 ▲	SO	Cross through wash.
▼ 1.1		SO	Cross through wash.
	1.3 ▲	SO	Cross through wash.
▼ 1.4		SO	Saddle.
	1.0 ▲	SO	Saddle.

			GPS: N33°52.83′ W112°43.85′
▼ 1.5		SO	Cross through wash.
	0.9 ▲	SO	Cross through wash.
▼ 1.6		BR	Track on left.
	0.8 ▲	BL	Track on right.
			GPS: N33°52.81′ W112°44.11′
▼ 1.8		SO	Track on right.
	0.6 ▲	SO	Track on left.
▼ 2.0		SO	Cross through wash.
	0.4 ▲	SO	Cross through wash.
▼ 2.2		TR	Trail drops down to enter wash. Track on left up wash; turn right into wash.
	0.2 ▲	TL	Turn sharp left and exit wash.
			GPS: N33°52.72′ W112°44.56′
▼ 2.3		SO	Track on right; remain in main wash. Then second small track on right.
	0.1 ▲	SO	Small track on left; then second track on left. Remain in main wash.
▼ 2.4		TL	Well and corral on right. Turn left immediately opposite corral up smaller wash, leaving main wash. Zero trip meter.
	0.0 ▲		Continue to the southeast.
			GPS: N33°52.85′ W112°44.66′
▼ 0.0			Continue to the west. Trail runs in or alongside the wash for the next 1.1 miles.
	2.1 ▲	TR	Turn right down larger wash; corral and well straight ahead. Zero trip meter. Track on left up wash.
▼ 1.1		BL	Exit wash on left, immediately followed by track on left.
	1.0 ▲	SO	Track on right; then enter wash and continue down wash. Trail runs in or alongside the wash for the next 1.1 miles.
			GPS: N33°53.37′ W112°45.59′
▼ 1.2		SO	Enter wash; track on right in wash. Trail runs in or alongside wash for next 0.9 miles.
	0.9 ▲	BR	Track on left in wash; bear right and exit wash.
			GPS: N33°53.82′ W112°45.97′
▼ 2.1		TL	T-intersection. Turn left onto well-used, roughly graded trail. Zero trip meter.
	0.0 ▲		Continue to the southeast.
			GPS: N33°53.98′ W112°46.39′
▼ 0.0			Continue to the southwest.
	2.6 ▲	TR	Turn right and enter the wash course. Trail runs in or alongside wash for next 0.9 miles. Zero trip meter.
▼ 0.2		BR	Track on right.
	2.4 ▲	SO	Track on left.
▼ 0.3		SO	Track on right; then tank on right and concrete footings of the Big Spar Mine.
	2.3 ▲	SO	Tank and concrete footings of the Big Spar Mine on left; then track on left.
			GPS: N33°53.78′ W112°46.64′
▼ 0.4		BR	Bear right, joining large graded road.
	2.2 ▲	TL	Turn left onto smaller graded trail. Old water tank is visible just after turn on left—turn is on right-hand bend.
			GPS: N33°53.75′ W112°46.67′
▼ 0.8		SO	Track on left.
	1.8 ▲	SO	Track on right.
▼ 0.9		SO	Track on right.
	1.7 ▲	SO	Track on left.
▼ 1.0		SO	Faint track on right.
	1.6 ▲	SO	Faint track on left.
▼ 1.1		SO	Track on left; then cattle guard.
	1.5 ▲	SO	Cattle guard; then track on right.
▼ 1.3		BR	Track on left.
	1.3 ▲	BL	Track on right.
			GPS: N33°54.22′ W112°47.38′
▼ 1.6		SO	Track on left and camping area on left.
	1.0 ▲	SO	Track on right and camping area on right.
▼ 2.0		SO	Camping area on right.
	0.6 ▲	SO	Camping area on left.
▼ 2.5		SO	Small track on right.
	0.1 ▲	SO	Small track on left.
▼ 2.6			Trail ends at junction with paved Vulture Mine Road. Turn right for Wickenburg.
	0.0 ▲		Trail commences on the paved Vulture Mine Road, 3.3 miles southwest of US 60. Zero trip meter and turn southeast on wide graded Vulture Peak Road. There is a road sign at the junction.
			GPS: N33°55.15′ W112°47.79′

CENTRAL REGION TRAIL #20

Buckhorn Creek Trail

Starting Point:	**US 60 in Wickenburg**
Finishing Point:	**Morristown–Castle Hot Springs Road**
Total Mileage:	**24.7 miles**
Unpaved Mileage:	**22.6 miles**
Driving Time:	**2 hours**
Elevation Range:	**2,200–4,200**
Usually Open:	**Year-round**
Best Time to Travel:	**October to May**
Difficulty Rating:	**2**
Scenic Rating:	**8**
Remoteness Rating:	**+0**

Special Attractions

- Easy trail passing through varied desert scenery.
- Close to the site of Constellation and the Copperopolis and Abe Lincoln Mines.
- Views of the Wickenburg Mountains.

History

The town of Constellation was formed around the Monte Cristo Mine, a mine that was promoted for longer than it operated. Ezra W. Thayer, a hardware merchant from Phoenix, actively tried to attract investors for the mine between 1912 and 1920; but he never actually operated the mine. The Monte Cristo went through various owners, none of whom succeeded in doing much with it.

Constellation had a post office as early as 1901, but it was not until the 1920s that the mine went into production and a small camp of approximately 250 people settled around it. There was a two-story saloon, gambling den, stores, and a dance hall. Other mines worked by those who settled in Constellation were the Oro Grande, Black Rock, and Gold Bar Mines.

Another mine close to this trail was the Copperopolis Mine to the north. It was active in the 1880s and had a small post office for a while. According to one source, the mine was named because "it was a copper metropolis that didn't metrop."

Description

This scenic, easy trail travels in a loop through the Wickenburg Mountains, mainly in the gravelly wash of Buckhorn Creek. It leaves the center of Wickenburg and goes up the graded dirt Constellation Road before turning east on the smaller graded Buckhorn Creek Trail. Continuing ahead up the Constellation Road leads to the remains of the Monte Cristo Mine and the site of Constellation. The remains of the Gold Bar Mine are farther north.

The trail is roughly graded as it winds through many small blocks of private property and crosses King Solomon Gulch. Wickenburg and the mountains beyond can be seen back to the south.

Once you are in the gravelly wash, the views are good; the wash is wide, often with spectacular cliff walls on either side. The surface is generally solid; this wash does not have the loose, deep gravel that makes travel in other washes slow. The wide trail is devoid of the close brush that can scratch a vehicle. The remains of the original trail, which had been washed out badly in the past, can be seen suspended as high as eight feet over the wash. Exercise care after storms as the trail can rearrange itself after every flood. High clearance is needed to negotiate uneven sections, but in normal conditions 4WD is not required.

Descending to Buckhorn Creek in the Wickenburg Mountains

Campers should note that much of this trail crosses private land and is posted, although some sections are not. Be sure you are on public land before making camp. Once the trail has turned off Constellation Road, campsites are scarce to none.

The trail finishes at the intersection with the Morristown–Castle Hot Springs Road.

Current Road Information

Bureau of Land Management
Phoenix Field Office
2015 West Deer Valley Rd.
Phoenix, AZ 85027
(623) 580-5500

Map References

BLM Phoenix North, Bradshaw Mts.
USGS 1:24,000 Wickenburg, Sam Powell Peak, Morgan Butte, Copperopolis
1:100,000 Phoenix North, Bradshaw Mts.

CENTRAL #20: BUCKHORN CREEK TRAIL

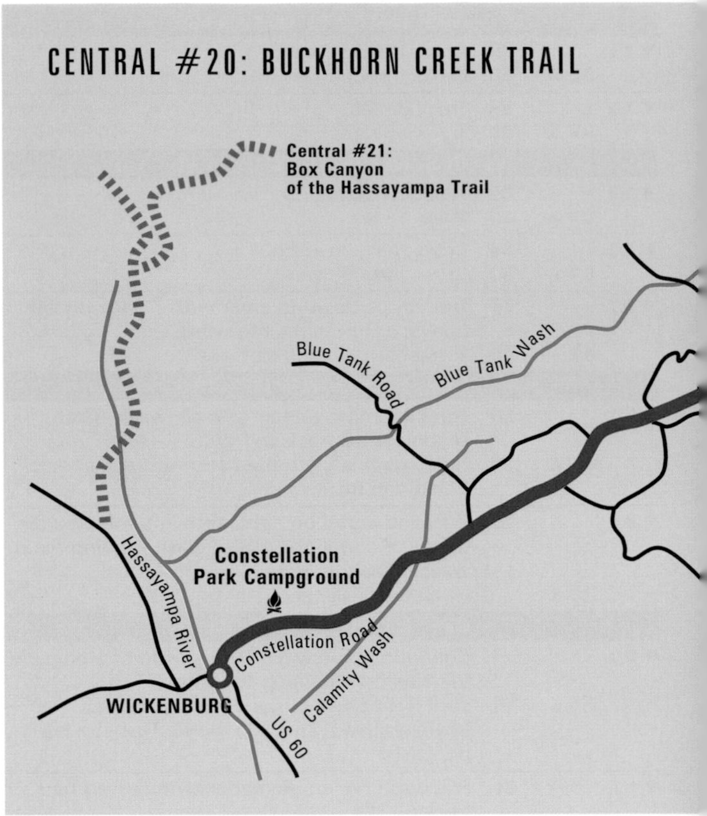

Maptech CD-ROM: Phoenix/Superstition Mountains; Flagstaff/Sedona/Prescott
Arizona Atlas & Gazetteer, pp. 48, 49
Arizona Road & Recreation Atlas, p. 40 & p. 74 (incomplete)
Recreational Map of Arizona (incomplete)

Route Directions

▼ 0.0			From US 60 in Wickenburg, east of the Hassayampa River, turn northwest on paved El Recreo Drive and zero trip meter.
	2.1 ▲		Trail ends at the intersection with US 60 in Wickenburg, east of the Hassayampa River.
			GPS: N33°58.35' W112°43.40'
▼ 0.2		SO	Road is now called Constellation Road. Remain on this road.
	1.9 ▲	SO	Road is now called El Recreo Drive. Remain on this road.
▼ 0.9		SO	Constellation Park on left—city-run campground (small fee charged). Rodeo grounds on the right.
	1.2 ▲	SO	Constellation Park on right—city-run campground (small fee charged). Rodeo grounds on the left.
▼ 2.1		SO	Road turns to graded dirt at county line—entering Yavapai County. Zero trip meter.
	0.0 ▲		Continue toward Wickenburg.
			GPS: N33°59.28' W112°41.54'
▼ 0.0			Continue to the northeast.
	6.0 ▲	SO	Road is now paved at county line—entering Maricopa County. Zero trip meter.
▼ 0.1		SO	Two tracks on left.
	5.9 ▲	SO	Two tracks on right.
▼ 0.2		SO	Cross through Calamity Wash.
	5.8 ▲	SO	Cross through Calamity Wash.
▼ 0.8		BR	Graded road on left is Blue Tank Road.
	5.2 ▲	SO	Graded road on right is Blue Tank Road.

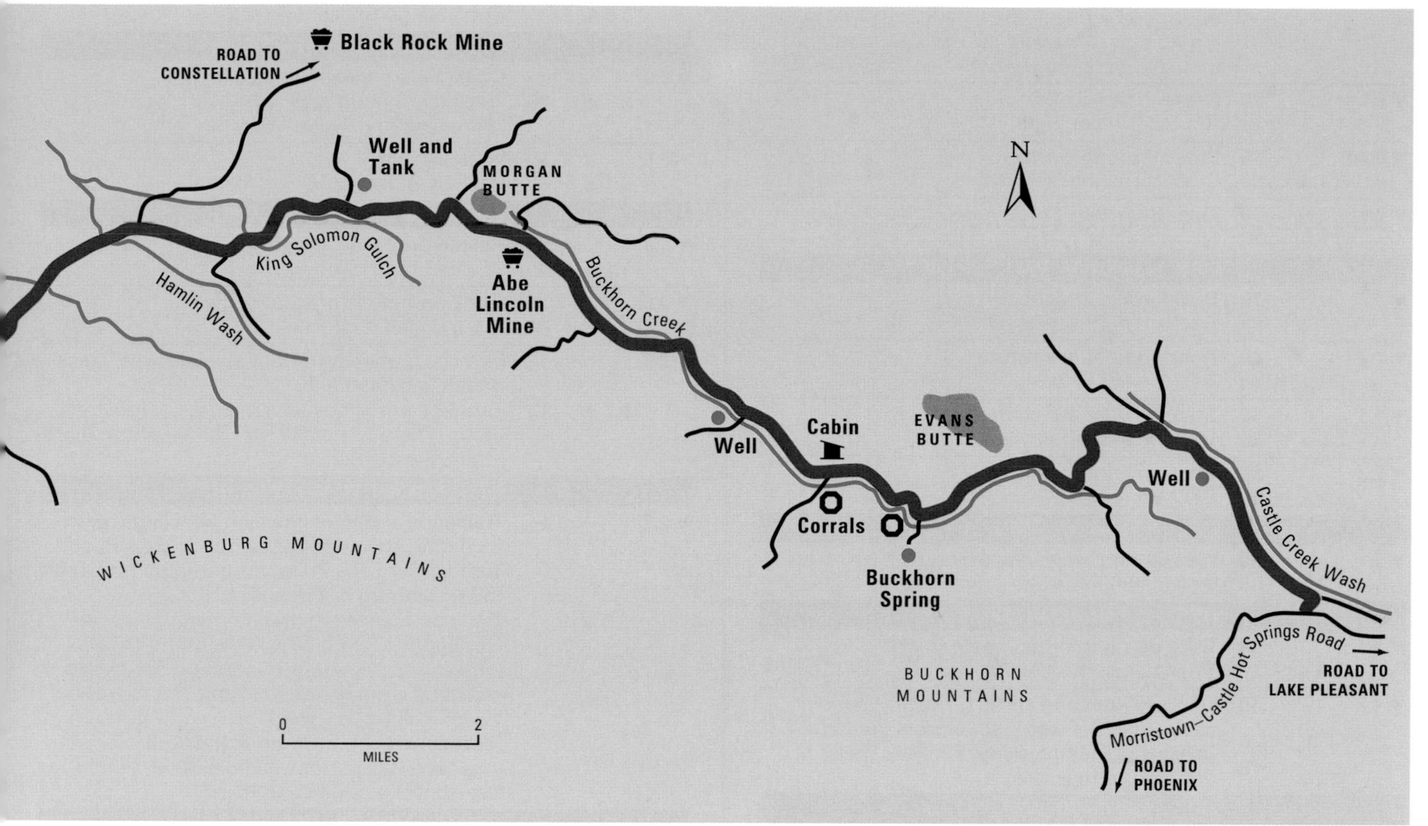

		GPS: N33°59.64′ W112°40.87′
▼ 1.8	SO	Track on right.
4.2 ▲	SO	Track on left.
▼ 2.4	SO	Track on left.
3.6 ▲	SO	Track on right.
▼ 3.0	SO	Track on right; then track on left.
3.0 ▲	SO	Track on right; then track on left.
		GPS: N34°00.74′ W112°39.00′
▼ 3.5	SO	Track on right.
2.5 ▲	SO	Track on left.
▼ 3.6	SO	Track on left; then cattle guard; then track on right.
2.4 ▲	SO	Track on left; then cattle guard; then track on right.
		GPS: N34°00.98′ W112°38.45′
▼ 4.1	SO	Track on left.
1.9 ▲	SO	Track on right.
▼ 4.7	SO	Track on right is private.
1.3 ▲	SO	Track on left is private.
▼ 4.9	SO	Cross through Blue Tank Wash.
1.1 ▲	SO	Cross through Blue Tank Wash.
▼ 5.3	SO	Track on right.
0.7 ▲	SO	Track on left.
▼ 5.6	SO	Cross through Hamlin Wash.
0.4 ▲	SO	Cross through Hamlin Wash.
▼ 6.0	TR	Turn right onto graded road at the sign for Owl Springs Ranch. Zero trip meter. Continuing straight on for 3.1 miles takes you to the site of Constellation.
0.0 ▲		Continue to the southwest.
		GPS: N34°02.53′ W112°36.72′
▼ 0.0		Continue to the east.
4.9 ▲	TL	Turn left onto graded road at the T-intersection. Proceeding right here for 3.1 miles takes you to the site of Constellation. Zero trip meter.
▼ 0.9	BL	Graded road on right.
4.0 ▲	BR	Graded road on left.
		GPS: N34°02.39′ W112°35.82′
▼ 1.3	SO	Cross through wash.
3.6 ▲	SO	Cross through wash.
▼ 2.1	SO	Cross through wash; then track on left.
2.8 ▲	SO	Track on right; then cross through wash.
		GPS: N34°02.81′ W112°34.95′
▼ 2.2	SO	Start to follow line of wash in King Solomon Gulch.
2.7 ▲	SO	Exit wash.
▼ 2.6	SO	Track on left; then well and tank set back from track on left.
2.3 ▲	SO	Well and tank set back from track on right; then track on right.
▼ 2.7	SO	Exit away from wash.
2.2 ▲	SO	Start to follow line of wash in King Solomon Gulch.
▼ 3.8	SO	Track on right.
1.1 ▲	SO	Track on left.
▼ 4.1	SO	Track on left. Morgan Butte on left.
0.8 ▲	SO	Track on right. Morgan Butte on right.
		GPS: N34°02.92′ W112°33.37′
▼ 4.3	SO	Cattle guard.
0.6 ▲	SO	Cattle guard.
▼ 4.9	SO	Track on right goes to the Abe Lincoln Mine, tailings, and concrete footings; then mine adit on left on far side of wash (slightly obscured by trees). Zero trip meter.
0.0 ▲		Continue to the west.
		GPS: N34°02.77′ W112°32.67′
▼ 0.0		Continue to the east.
4.3 ▲	SO	Mine adit on right on far side of wash (slightly

obscured by trees); then track on left goes to the Abe Lincoln Mine, tailings, and concrete footings. Zero trip meter.

▼ 0.1 SO Graded road on left.
4.2 ▲ SO Graded road on right.

▼ 0.7 SO Cross through wash.
3.6 ▲ SO Cross through wash.

▼ 0.8 SO Enter Buckhorn Creek wash.
3.5 ▲ SO Exit wash and climb up ridge.

GPS: N34°02.46' W112°32.04'

▼ 1.2 SO Track on left in wash.
3.1 ▲ BL Track on right in wash.

▼ 1.6 SO Track on right in wash.
2.7 ▲ BR Track on left in wash.

▼ 1.8 SO Track on right out of wash.
2.5 ▲ SO Track on left out of wash.

▼ 2.3 SO Track on left in wash.
2.0 ▲ BL Track on right in wash.

GPS: N34°01.91' W112°30.72'

▼ 3.1 SO Well on right in private property.
1.2 ▲ SO Well on left in private property.

GPS: N34°01.46' W112°30.20'

▼ 3.4 SO Track on right through gate.
0.9 ▲ SO Track on left through gate.

▼ 4.3 SO Track on right and corral on right; then old cabin on left of wash, set back in the trees. Cabin is private property. Zero trip meter.
0.0 ▲ Continue to the west.

GPS: N34°00.80' W112°29.10'

▼ 0.0 Continue to the east.
4.7 ▲ SO Old cabin on right of wash, set back in the trees. Cabin is private property. Track on left and corral on left. Zero trip meter.

▼ 0.8 SO Track on left.
3.9 ▲ SO Track on right.

▼ 1.1 SO Old corral on right; then track on right to Buckhorn Spring.
3.6 ▲ SO Track on left to Buckhorn Spring; then old corral on left.

GPS: N34°00.54' W112°28.03'

▼ 1.8 SO Track on left.
2.9 ▲ SO Track on right.

▼ 2.2 SO Track on right; then old mine dredge on right.
2.5 ▲ SO Old mine dredge on left; then track on left.

GPS: N34°00.97' W112°27.02'

▼ 2.4 SO Track on right up wash and old road on left.
2.3 ▲ BR Track on left up wash and old road on right.

▼ 2.7 SO Cattle guard.
2.0 ▲ SO Cattle guard.

▼ 3.2 BL Bear left out of wash; track continues straight on in wash to well.
1.5 ▲ SO Drop down and enter Buckhorn Wash. Track on left in wash goes to well.

GPS: N34°00.90' W112°26.23'

▼ 3.9 SO Cross through wash.
0.8 ▲ SO Cross through wash.

▼ 4.5 SO Cattle guard.
0.2 ▲ SO Cattle guard.

▼ 4.6 TR Drop down and turn right down Castle Creek Wash. Track on left up wash.
0.1 ▲ TL Turn left and exit wash up ridge. Track continues straight on up Castle Creek Wash.

GPS: N34°01.55' W112°25.58'

▼ 4.7 SO Track on left up side wash with county "Primitive Road" sign. Zero trip meter.
0.0 ▲ Continue northwest up wash.

GPS: N34°01.50' W112°25.55'

▼ 0.0 Continue southeast down wash.
2.7 ▲ SO Track on right up side wash with county "Primitive Road" sign. Zero trip meter.

▼ 0.6 SO Well on right.
2.1 ▲ SO Well on left.

GPS: N34°01.26' W112°25.01'

▼ 1.3 SO Private property on right.
1.4 ▲ SO Private property on left.

▼ 2.0 SO Track on right is private.
0.7 ▲ BR Track on left is private.

▼ 2.5 TR Exit wash; then turn right at mailboxes. Track on left is a dead end.
0.2 ▲ TL Turn left at mailboxes and enter Castle Creek Wash. There is a small sign for Buckhorn Road at the intersection.

GPS: N34°00.17' W112°23.67'

▼ 2.7 Trail ends at the intersection with large, graded dirt Morristown–Castle Hot Springs Road. Turn left for Lake Pleasant; turn right for US 60 to Wickenburg or Phoenix.
0.0 ▲ Trail commences on the Morristown–Castle Hot Springs Road, 20 miles north of US 60. Zero trip meter and turn north on graded dirt road at the unmarked junction. The turn is on top of a slight rise and if coming from Morristown you bear left at the Y-junction. If you get to a sign for Champie Road, you have overshot the turn by 0.8 miles.

GPS: N34°00.04' W112°23.74'

CENTRAL REGION TRAIL #21

Box Canyon of the Hassayampa Trail

Starting Point:	**US 93, 1.6 miles northwest of Wickenburg, at intersection with Rincon Road**
Finishing Point:	**Rincon Road at the Hassayampa River crossing**
Total Mileage:	**12.7 miles**
Unpaved Mileage:	**10.6 miles**
Driving Time:	**1.5 hours**
Elevation Range:	**2,200–2,700 feet**
Usually Open:	**Year-round**
Best Time to Travel:	**Year-round**
Difficulty Rating:	**4**
Scenic Rating:	**9**
Remoteness Rating:	**+0**

Special Attractions

- Box Canyon of the Hassayampa River.
- Sandy trail running up the Hassayampa River.
- Panoramic vistas over the Hassayampa River and the Wickenburg Mountains.

The trail follows the wash through the narrows in Hassayampa River Canyon

Description

This trail, close to Wickenburg, is popular with locals and visitors for its stunning, varied scenery and a rare chance to dip your toes in a desert river. The trail leaves US 93 up the well-marked Rincon Road, 1.6 miles northwest of Wickenburg. After 2.7 miles, the trail turns off the road and follows a path up the wash of the Hassayampa River. Although the river flows year-round, for much of the time it flows underground, leaving a wide, sandy, dry wash on the surface. Most of the year, the first part of the trail is deep sand with no water. Because the sand is deep, you will probably need to lower tire pressures. There are many vehicle tracks to follow—they all go the same way, so pick the best-looking route up the wash.

After a mile or so, as the canyon starts to narrow, you are likely to encounter water. The river is shallow and sandy, usually only a few inches deep as it meanders through the red-walled canyon. Again, pick the best line through the sand and water. One potential hazard is quicksand, but if you follow existing tire tracks you should be able to see if previous drivers ran into trouble; if so, avoid those spots. The main difficulties of the trail are the deep sand and, in places, the soft riverbed of the Hassayampa.

Two miles up the wash, the trail enters The Box, a narrow section of canyon with high red walls. This section is definitely the highlight of the river portion of the route. There are a couple of campsites tucked up to one side out of the wash, but it is not a good place to choose if there is any chance of flash flooding. One particularly pleasant, shady spot is beside the ruins of an old homestead located up a short section of narrows in a side canyon.

There are two possible ways to complete the loop—your choice will likely depend on the water level farther up the canyon. A trail leads up to join the loop road a short distance past The Box, and if the water is getting deeper and the riverbed softer, then this is the one to take. Much of the time, though, you can continue up the riverbed before swinging up a sandy rise to join the graded loop road at the top.

Once on the graded road, the trail returns to Wickenburg via a section of ridge road, which offers panoramic views back down over the Hassayampa River, the Wickenburg Mountains, and Wickenburg itself with prominent Vulture Peak behind it.

The loop finishes back on Rincon Road at the Hassayampa River crossing. In addition to a couple of campsites in The Box, there are other campsites with great views down the river on the first exit from the canyon and on other side trails off the graded dirt road.

Current Road Information

Bureau of Land Management
Phoenix Field Office
2015 West Deer Valley Rd.
Phoenix, AZ 85027
(623) 580-5500

Map References

BLM Phoenix North, Bradshaw Mts.
USGS 1:24,000 Wickenburg, Sam Powell Peak, Flores
1:100,000 Phoenix North, Bradshaw Mts.
Maptech CD-ROM: Phoenix/Superstition Mountains; Flagstaff/Sedona/Prescott
Arizona Atlas & Gazetteer, p. 48
Arizona Road & Recreation Atlas, p. 40 & p. 74 (incomplete)
Recreational Map of Arizona (incomplete)

Route Directions

▼ 0.0		From US 93, 1.6 miles northwest of Wickenburg, turn northeast on Rincon Road at the road sign and zero trip meter. Road is paved and the turn is well signed.
		GPS: N33°59.43' W112°44.69'
▼ 0.5	SO	Road is graded dirt.
▼ 0.6	SO	Cross through Martinez Wash.
▼ 0.7	BR	Graded road to guest ranch on left; then start to cross Hassayampa riverbed.
▼ 1.1	BL	Exit river wash; road is paved. Paved road on right.
▼ 1.5	SO	Blue Tank Road on right.
▼ 2.4	SO	Wagon Box Ranch Road on right.
▼ 2.7	TR	Turn right and follow tire marks up Hassayampa riverbed. Zero trip meter.
		GPS: N34°01.72' W112°44.56'
▼ 0.0		Continue northeast up riverbed in deep, soft sand.
▼ 2.0	SO	Track on right along smaller canyon.
		GPS: N34°02.75' W112°43.54'
▼ 2.1	SO	Second track on right. Remain in riverbed. Entering The Box.
▼ 2.2	SO	Campsite under trees and short section of canyon narrows on left. Old homestead site on left. The Mistake Mine is on right up the ridge.
		GPS: N34°02.94' W112°43.39'
▼ 2.5	SO	Canyon opens out again.
▼ 2.6	SO	Track on left out of canyon is shorter loop that exits the canyon and can be taken if the water is too deep farther up. Trail continues in canyon. Zero trip meter.
		GPS: N34°02.86' W112°43.01'

Shorter Loop Exiting River

▼ 0.0		Continue up sandy track away from river. Other entrance comes in on right immediately.
		GPS: N34°02.86' W112°43.01'
▼ 0.2	SO	Campsite and track on left.
▼ 0.3	SO	Campsites on right and left with small tracks leading off the main trail on right and left.

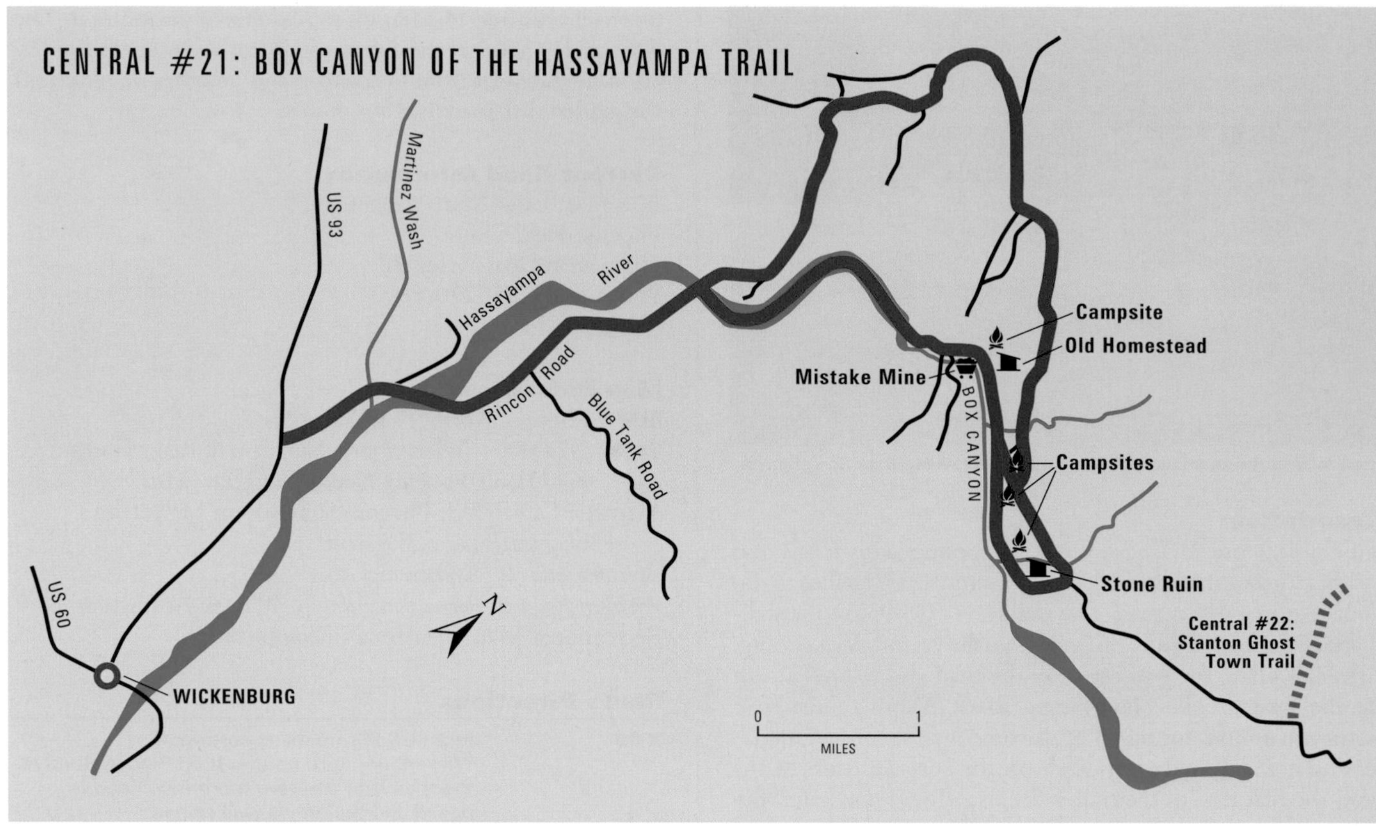

▼ 0.4	TL	Trail rejoins main loop; turn left to return to Wickenburg.
		GPS: N34°02.83′ W112°42.63′

Continuation of Main Trail

▼ 0.0	SO	Continue in riverbed up the canyon.
		GPS: N34°02.86′ W112°43.01′
▼ 0.7	SO	Track on left goes to elevated campsites above riverbed.
		GPS: N34°02.60′ W112°42.28′
▼ 0.8	TL	Turn left out of riverbed; vehicles can continue in the wash, depending on water levels. Bear right up embankment; there are a few tracks in all directions; proceed northeast on main trail.
		GPS: N34°02.58′ W112°42.19′
▼ 0.9	SO	Top of ridge; tracks on left down off ridge.
▼ 1.0	SO	Small stone ruin on left.
		GPS: N34°02.68′ W112°42.01′
▼ 1.2	SO	Pass through wire gate.
▼ 1.3	BL	Track on right.
▼ 1.4	TL	Join graded dirt road and turn left to continue around the loop. Turn right for Central #22: Stanton Ghost Town Trail. Zero trip meter.
		GPS: N34°02.88′ W112°41.94′
▼ 0.0		Continue west on graded gravel road.
▼ 0.1	SO	Cross through wash; then cattle guard.
▼ 0.2	SO	Track on right; then track on left.
▼ 0.5	SO	Track on left.
▼ 0.6	SO	Two tracks on left—second, more-used one is the end of the shorter loop and goes 0.4 miles back to the Hassayampa River. Zero trip meter.
		GPS: N34°02.83′ W112°42.63′
▼ 0.0		Continue to the west.
▼ 0.2	SO	Track on left is second entrance to shorter loop.

▼ 0.3	SO	Cross through wash; then track on left and track on right.
▼ 0.4	SO	Track on left.
▼ 0.6	SO	Track on left is private.
▼ 0.7	SO	Track on left.
▼ 0.9	SO	Cross through wash.
▼ 1.6	SO	Track on left.
▼ 1.7	SO	Track on left.
▼ 1.9	SO	Cattle guard.
		GPS: N34°03.47′ W112°44.42′
▼ 2.3	SO	Cross through wash; two entrances to track on right up wash.
▼ 2.8	SO	Two tracks on right; then cattle guard.
▼ 3.0	TL	Turn left onto smaller, roughly graded trail. The junction is unmarked, but there is a stop sign at the intersection. Zero trip meter.
		GPS: N34°03.31′ W112°45.27′
▼ 0.0		Continue to the east; immediately track on right.
▼ 0.1	SO	Track on left and track on right.
▼ 0.3	SO	Track on left; then overlook on left over Hassayampa River.
		GPS: N34°03.10′ W112°45.05′
▼ 0.7	TL	Intersection. Graded road on right; track straight ahead; turn left onto graded road.
		GPS: N34°02.77′ W112°45.28′
▼ 1.6	SO	Cattle guard; then track on left.
▼ 1.8	SO	Track on left.
▼ 1.9	TR	Track on left at old mine site.
		GPS: N34°02.06′ W112°44.38′
▼ 2.1	SO	Track on left.
▼ 2.3	SO	Start to cross wide, sandy wash of Hassayampa River.
▼ 2.4		Trail ends back at the start of the loop where it enters the riverbed. Continue straight ahead on Rincon Road to return to Wickenburg.
		GPS: N34°01.72′ W112°44.56′

CENTRAL REGION TRAIL #22

Stanton Ghost Town Trail

Starting Point:	**Rincon Road, 1.6 miles east of Central #21: Box Canyon of the Hassayampa Trail**
Finishing Point:	**Arizona 89, 0.8 miles north of mile marker 269**
Total Mileage:	**14.5 miles**
Unpaved Mileage:	**14.5 miles**
Driving Time:	**2 hours**
Elevation Range:	**2,400–3,600 feet**
Usually Open:	**Year-round**
Best Time to Travel:	**October to May**
Difficulty Rating:	**2**
Scenic Rating:	**8**
Remoteness Rating:	**+0**

Special Attractions

- Ghost town of Stanton and historic Octave Mine.
- Old cemeteries at Octave and Weaver.
- Easy, quiet trail through spectacular desert scenery close to Wickenburg.

History

In 1863 a party lead by Pauline Weaver, a famous explorer of the Southwest, stopped for the night along Antelope Creek. A Mexican man in the group named Alvaro climbed the rocky hill beside the creek and stumbled across a rich field of gold nuggets. This lucky find formed the basis of three mining communities—Stanton, Weaver, and Octave.

The first of the three to flourish was Stanton, then called Antelope Station. The hill was appropriately named Rich Hill; soon the area was being prospected by a small community of miners. Rich Hill was a very profitable region, and the lucky earliest miners were able to pick up thousands of dollars' worth of gold nuggets using nothing more than their pocketknives.

Stanton is indelibly associated with Charles P. Stanton, a conniving and ruthless man who almost single-handedly managed to cause tremendous upset and violence in the settlement. The town boasted stores and a stage station. The stage station was run by an Englishman named William Partridge, and the general store was run by G. H. "Yaqui" Wilson. Enmity between the two men began when Wilson's pigs escaped and ran into Partridge's garden. This trivial incident started a long-running feud that would eventually come to a tragic end.

Stanton, who was from Ireland, came to the gold camps in central Arizona from Nevada. Previously the assayer at the Vulture Mine near Wickenburg, he entered the picture when he arrived in town in the early 1870s. From the start he was almost universally disliked and was mockingly known as the "Irish Lord." By unfair means, he had acquired a half-interest in the Leviathan Mine near Rich Hill, built a cabin, and opened a small store. Envious of the patronage of Wilson's general store and the trade attached to Partridge's stage station, he plotted to destroy the competition. Stanton played upon the mutual dislike between the two men, inciting them into a gunfight during which Partridge killed Wilson. Partridge was found guilty of murder and sent to Yuma Territorial Prison, where he said he was haunted every night by Wilson's ghost.

The old Stanton stage station now used as a saloon

Stanton didn't succeed in getting his hands on the two businesses immediately. A silent partner named Timmerman claimed Wilson's store, and Partridge's creditors claimed the stage station and sold it to Barney Martin. Stanton was not discouraged. He hired a band of outlaws led by Francisco Vega to do his dirty work. Vega killed Timmerman, ambushing him as he returned from Phoenix with $700 of gold and setting his body ablaze. No one was surprised when Stanton produced a will, purportedly made by Timmerman, which named Stanton as the heir. He was free to take on the position of postmaster, which he did, changing the name of the settlement to Stanton.

The only person of importance left in the town apart from Stanton was Barney Martin. However Martin and his family quickly departed for Phoenix. They never arrived and some weeks later their bodies and a burned wagon were found a few miles from Stanton. No one was ever charged with the murders, but the gossip around town pointed to Stanton. There were many murders in the town at this time, and it seemed that each time only Stanton profited. He always loudly protested his innocence, and as he was well spoken and wordy, the territorial newspapers always

The remains of the Weaver post office

took up his cause, proclaiming him an upstanding citizen.

Happily, Stanton didn't live long enough to profit from his deeds. Later that same year he was gunned down in his office by a man in Vega's gang, whose sister he had insulted. The town of Stanton closed down a few years later when the mines were exhausted. The post office closed finally in 1905.

In 1950, the *Saturday Evening Post* bought the town site and gave it to the winner of a jingle competition. Today, Stanton is owned by the Lost Dutchman Mining Association, which has restored the original buildings. Partridge's stage station, now called the Hotel Stanton, still stands as well. Another building still around is the store in which Charles Stanton was murdered.

The second site along the trail is Weaver, named for explorer and scout Pauline Weaver. Initially, a tent city during the first rush of prospectors to the region, Weaver gradually acquired more permanent buildings. Weaver had a wilder crowd than Stanton, and murders and shootings were commonplace. Many of the thugs hired by Charles Stanton found refuge in Weaver. After the murder of William Segna, a storekeeper, a newspaper article called for Weaver to be closed. Many of the decent folk relocated to nearby Octave.

One of the more unusual incidents associated with Weaver concerned the local Indians. In December 1863, three Mexicans who made their living cutting grama grass strayed farther than normal from the town. While working, they were surrounded by Indians who first demanded their firearms, then their guns, then their burros, and finally their clothes. The Indians departed, leaving the naked Mexicans to slink back home to Weaver.

The gold eventually played out, and by 1899 the remaining people of Weaver had moved to Octave.

The third township of the trio, Octave, was also the last to get going. Although claims were staked as early as 1864, the town was not developed until the late 1890s when it was purchased by a group of eight men—hence the name Octave. The post office at Weaver (the remains are near the Weaver Cemetery) was transferred to Octave a year later. Octave eventually developed a stage stop, school, and general store. The mine netted $50,000 a month for a while, and it persisted until 1942 when it was shut down. It is now privately owned and there is no access to the town site itself, but mining remains and buildings can be seen clearly from the public road.

Description

This trail, suitable for a high-clearance vehicle in dry weather, is without the steep grades and low-traction surfaces that make 4WD a necessity. However, it is a rugged, single-track trail that passes many points of interest. To reach the trail, continue east along the graded dirt road that forms the return portion of the loop of Central #21: Box Canyon of the Hassayampa Trail. After 1.6 miles, the trail turns off onto a well-used, formed, single-track trail and runs along a ridge with deep washes that drain into the Hassayampa River on both sides. The views are tremendous as the trail continues toward the Octave Mine.

At Decision Corner, a 5-way intersection, which is the old town site of Octave, there is a choice of trails from which you can see the various historic sights. If you turn sharp right (immediately back on yourself), it is 0.3 miles to the old Octave Cemetery. Restored by various 4WD clubs, the cemetery has many boulder-marked graves set among the cacti. Back at Decision Corner, a right turn will take you to a vista (0.3 miles) overlooking the historic Octave Mine. There are a large number of workings and a few timber buildings. The area is privately owned so views are restricted to what you can see from the gate.

Saguaros growing among the boulders on Rich Hill

If you continue straight ahead at Decision Corner, in 0.8 miles you arrive at the overgrown Weaver Cemetery, set near the workings of the Myers Mine along Weaver Creek. The old Weaver Post Office is nearby.

Retrace your steps to Decision Corner and then continue along the graded road toward Stanton. There are a couple of the original old wooden buildings remaining at Stanton. The site is now owned by the Lost Dutchman Mining Association, but visitors are permitted between 9 A.M. and 5 P.M. when the gate is open. The Hotel Stanton is still standing as well as two other buildings. From Stanton the trail follows an easy graded road to Arizona 89.

Current Road Information

Bureau of Land Management
Phoenix Field Office
2015 West Deer Valley Rd.
Phoenix, AZ 85027
(623) 580-5500

Map References

BLM Bradshaw Mts.
USGS 1:24,000 Sam Powell Peak, Yarnell, Congress
1:100,000 Bradshaw Mts.
Maptech CD-ROM: Flagstaff/Sedona/Prescott
Arizona Atlas & Gazetteer, p. 48
Arizona Road & Recreation Atlas, p. 40 & p. 74 (incomplete)
Recreational Map of Arizona (incomplete)

Route Directions

▼ 0.0	From the farthest point along the loop of Central #21: Box Canyon of the Hassayampa Trail, turn east and continue along graded road for 1.6 miles. Turn northwest on formed dirt trail; this is the start of Stanton Ghost Town Trail. The start of the trail is 8.1 miles northeast along Rincon Road from where Rincon Road crosses the Hassayampa River wash. If the road does a sharp right turn and descends down to cross a wash, you have overshot the turn.

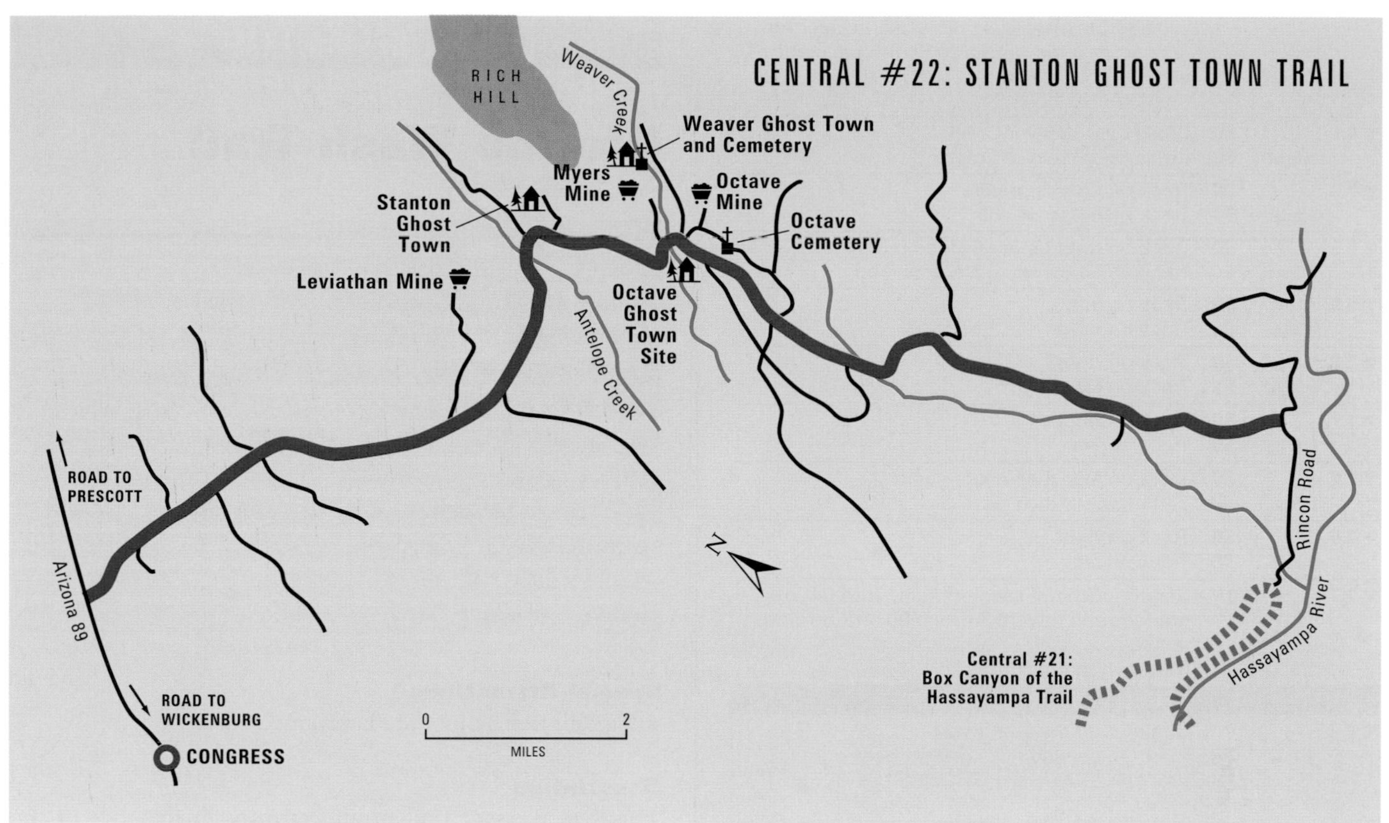

Mileage		Direction	Description
	3.7 ▲		Trail ends at the intersection with Rincon Road. Turn right to continue 1.6 miles to Central #21: Box Canyon of the Hassayampa Trail to Wickenburg.
			GPS: N34°03.62′ W112°40.55′
▼ 1.3		SO	Gate.
	2.4 ▲	SO	Gate.
			GPS: N34°04.51′ W112°41.39′
▼ 1.4		SO	Track on left.
	2.3 ▲	SO	Track on right.
▼ 1.8		SO	Well-used track on left crosses wash.
	1.9 ▲	SO	Well-used track on right crosses wash.
			GPS: N34°04.86′ W112°41.52′
▼ 2.6		SO	Gate.
	1.1 ▲	SO	Gate.
▼ 2.8		SO	Well-used track on left.
	0.9 ▲	SO	Second well-used track on right.
			GPS: N34°05.73′ W112°41.87′
▼ 2.9		SO	Second track on left.
	0.8 ▲	SO	Track on right.
▼ 3.7		BL	Well-used track on right; sign for Angel's Ranch on right. Zero trip meter.
	0.0 ▲		Continue to the southwest.
			GPS: N34°06.42′ W112°42.04′
▼ 0.0			Continue to the northwest.
	3.0 ▲	BR	Well-used track on left; sign for Angel's Ranch on left. Zero trip meter.
▼ 0.2		SO	Track on right.
	2.8 ▲	SO	Track on left.
▼ 0.5		SO	Cattle guard.
	2.5 ▲	SO	Cattle guard.
▼ 0.9		SO	Cross through wash.
	2.1 ▲	SO	Cross through wash.
▼ 1.0		SO	Track on left and track on right.
	2.0 ▲	SO	Track on left and track on right.
			GPS: N34°06.91′ W112°42.81′
▼ 1.3		SO	Track on left.
	1.7 ▲	SO	Track on right.
▼ 1.4		SO	Track on left.
	1.6 ▲	BL	Track on right.
▼ 1.8		SO	Track on right and track on left.
	1.2 ▲	SO	Track on right and track on left.
▼ 2.7		SO	Well-used track on left.
	0.3 ▲	BL	Well-used track on right.
			GPS: N34°08.40′ W112°42.85′
▼ 3.0		TL	5-way intersection at Decision Corner. Track on right goes to the Octave Mine (0.3 miles). Track straight on goes to the Weaver Cemetery and town site (0.8 miles). Turning immediately right just before the junction, heading back on yourself, goes to Octave Cemetery (0.3 miles)—look for fence line. When finished viewing the historic sites, return to this junction; zero trip meter and continue west on the graded road to Stanton.
	0.0 ▲		Continue to the southwest on main trail.
			Coordinates at Decision Corner—
			GPS: N34°08.64′ W112°42.82′
			Coordinates at Octave Cemetery—
			GPS: N34°08.35′ W112°42.77′
			Coordinates at Weaver Cemetery—
			GPS: N34°09.22′ W112°42.39′
▼ 0.0			Continue west on graded road toward Stanton.
	1.7 ▲	TR	5-way intersection at Decision Corner. Track straight on goes to the Octave Mine (0.3 miles). Track on left goes to the Weaver Cemetery and town site (0.8 miles). The main trail turns right, and immediately there is a track on the left that goes to Octave Cemetery (0.3 miles)—look for fence line. When finished

			viewing the historic sites, return to Decision Corner, zero trip meter, and continue southwest on the formed trail toward the Hassayampa River.
▼ 0.1		SO	Cross over Weaver Creek.
	1.6 ▲	SO	Cross over Weaver Creek.
▼ 0.2		SO	Track on right is private.
	1.5 ▲	SO	Track on left is private.
▼ 0.5		SO	Track on right to small stone building.
	1.2 ▲	SO	Track on left to small stone building.
▼ 0.9		SO	Track on left.
	0.8 ▲	SO	Track on right.
▼ 1.0		SO	Track on right.
	0.7 ▲	SO	Track on left.
▼ 1.1		SO	Track on right.
	0.6 ▲	SO	Track on left.
▼ 1.2		SO	Track on left; then cattle guard.
	0.5 ▲	SO	Cattle guard; then track on right.
▼ 1.5		SO	Track on right.
	0.2 ▲	SO	Track on left.
▼ 1.7		TL	Stanton. Graded road on right. Turn left on graded road toward Arizona 89 and zero trip meter.
	0.0 ▲		Continue to the southeast.
			GPS: N34°09.76' W112°43.74'
▼ 0.0			Continue to the southwest.
	6.1 ▲	BR	Stanton. Graded road on left. Bear right on graded road toward Octave and zero trip meter.
▼ 0.1		SO	Lost Dutchman Mining Association property on right.
	6.0 ▲	SO	Lost Dutchman Mining Association property on left.
▼ 0.2		SO	Cross over Antelope Creek.
	5.9 ▲	SO	Cross over Antelope Creek.
▼ 0.3		SO	Buzzard Road on right.
	5.8 ▲	SO	Buzzard Road on left.
▼ 0.6		SO	Cattle yard on left.
	5.5 ▲	SO	Cattle yard on right.
▼ 1.6		SO	Graded dirt road on left.
	4.5 ▲	SO	Graded dirt road on right.
▼ 2.3		SO	Track on right.
	3.8 ▲	SO	Track on left.
▼ 2.8		SO	Track on left.
	3.3 ▲	SO	Track on right.
▼ 3.6		SO	Track on right.
	2.5 ▲	SO	Track on left.
▼ 4.1		SO	Graded dirt road on right and track on left.
	2.0 ▲	SO	Graded dirt road on left and track on right.
			GPS: N34°10.47' W112°47.25'
▼ 4.6		SO	Track on left.
	1.5 ▲	SO	Track on right.
▼ 5.1		SO	Track on right and track on left.
	1.0 ▲	SO	Track on right and track on left.
▼ 5.5		SO	Track on left.
	0.6 ▲	SO	Track on right.
▼ 6.1			Cattle guard; then trail ends at Arizona 89. Turn left for Wickenburg; turn right for Prescott.
	0.0 ▲		Trail commences on Arizona 89, 11.8 miles north of US 93. Zero trip meter and turn east on Yavapai County Road 109 signed to Stanton. The intersection is 0.8 miles north of mile marker 269.
			GPS: N34°10.96' W112°49.45'

CENTRAL REGION TRAIL #23

Orofino Wash Trail

Starting Point:	**CR 60 (Wagoner Road), 6 miles southeast of Kirkland Junction**
Finishing Point:	**Arizona 89, east of Wilhoit**
Total Mileage:	**9.1 miles**
Unpaved Mileage:	**9.1 miles**
Driving Time:	**1 hour**
Elevation Range:	**4,000–5,100 feet**
Usually Open:	**Year-round**
Best Time to Travel:	**Year-round in dry weather**
Difficulty Rating:	**2**
Scenic Rating:	**8**
Remoteness Rating:	**+0**

Special Attractions

- Pleasant trail along the Hassayampa River.

Description

This very pleasant trail meanders through the edge of the Prescott National Forest, following the Hassayampa River for much of the way. It leaves from Wagoner Road and undulates over a few ridges before descending sharply to the Hassayampa River channel, which in spring and summer appears as a bright green ribbon on the duller green landscape.

There are many wells along the trail—the area is used for cattle grazing. The trail leaves the path of the Hassayampa River to travel up Orofino Wash. Here the surface becomes sandy and loose, but it is still suitable for high-clearance vehicles in dry weather. In wet weather, the trail is impassable.

The trail ends on Arizona 89 immediately east of the small settlement of Wilhoit.

The trail approaching the lush vegetation along the Hassayampa River

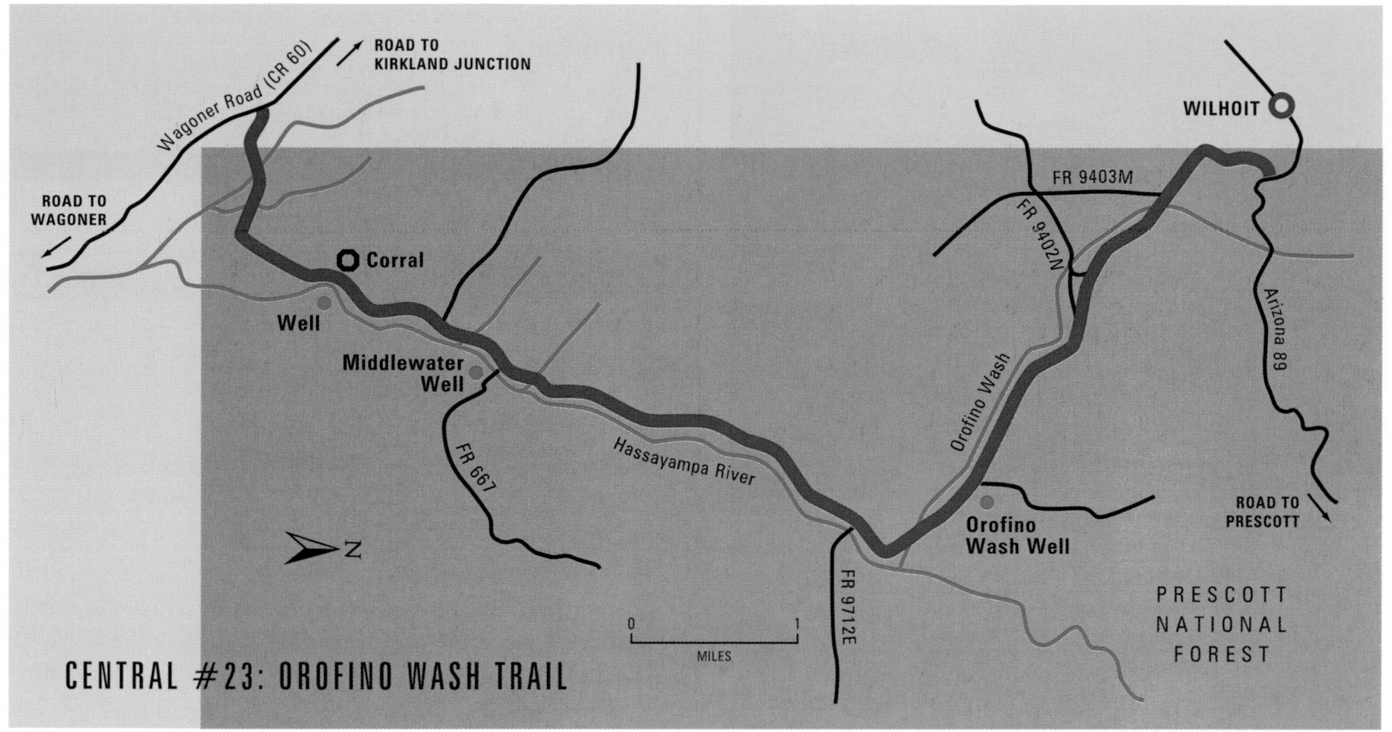

Current Road Information
Prescott National Forest
Crown King Work Station
(520) 632-7740

Map References
BLM Bradshaw Mts.
USFS Prescott National Forest: Bradshaw Ranger District
USGS 1:24,000 Walnut Grove, Wilhoit
1:100,000 Bradshaw Mts.
Maptech CD-ROM: Flagstaff/Sedona/Prescott
Arizona Atlas & Gazetteer, p. 48
Arizona Road & Recreation Atlas, p. 40 & p. 74

Route Directions

▼ 0.0			From CR 60 (Wagoner Road), 6 miles southeast of Kirkland Junction, zero trip meter and turn northeast on formed dirt road. The road is sign-posted from the county road as FR 72.
	2.8 ▲		Trail ends at the T-intersection with paved CR 60. Turn left for Wagoner; turn right for Kirkland Junction.
			GPS: N34°20.25′ W112°35.20′
▼ 0.2		SO	Cattle guard. Entering Prescott National Forest; then track on right.
	2.6 ▲	SO	Track on left; then cattle guard. Leaving Prescott National Forest.
			GPS: N34°20.17′ W112°35.00′
▼ 0.5		SO	Cross through wash.
	2.3 ▲	SO	Cross through wash.
▼ 0.7		SO	Cross through wash.
	2.1 ▲	SO	Cross through wash.
▼ 1.0		SO	Cross through wash.
	1.8 ▲	SO	Cross through wash.
▼ 1.4		SO	Track on right.
	1.4 ▲	SO	Track on left.
▼ 1.6		SO	Track on left; then well on right and corral on left.
	1.2 ▲	SO	Well on left and corral on right; then track on right.
			GPS: N34°20.69′ W112°34.08′
▼ 2.1		SO	Track on right.
	0.7 ▲	SO	Track on left.
▼ 2.2		SO	Track on left.
	0.6 ▲	SO	Track on right.
▼ 2.3		SO	Track on left.
	0.5 ▲	SO	Track on right.
▼ 2.4		SO	Cross through wash.
	0.4 ▲	SO	Cross through wash.
			GPS: N34°21.28′ W112°33.74′
▼ 2.6		SO	Middlewater Well on right; then cattle guard.
	0.2 ▲	SO	Cattle guard; then Middlewater Well on left.
▼ 2.8		SO	Track on right is FR 667; forest marker at the intersection. Zero trip meter.
	0.0 ▲		Continue to the southwest.
			GPS: N34°21.55′ W112°33.54′
▼ 0.0			Continue to the northeast.
	2.7 ▲	SO	Track on left is FR 667; forest marker at the intersection. Zero trip meter.
▼ 0.3		SO	Cross through wash.
	2.4 ▲	SO	Cross through wash.
▼ 0.5		SO	Cross through wash.
	2.2 ▲	SO	Cross through wash.
▼ 0.8		SO	Track on right.
	1.9 ▲	SO	Track on left.
▼ 0.9		SO	Cattle guard.
	1.8 ▲	SO	Cattle guard.
▼ 1.0		SO	Track on left.
	1.7 ▲	SO	Track on right.
			GPS: N34°22.39′ W112°33.24′
▼ 1.7		SO	Cross through wash.
	1.0 ▲	SO	Cross through wash.
▼ 1.8		SO	Track on right.

The trail beside the Hassayampa River wash

	0.9 ▲	SO	Track on left.
▼ 2.0		SO	Cross through wash.
	0.7 ▲	SO	Cross through wash.
▼ 2.1		SO	Cross through wash.
	0.6 ▲	SO	Cross through wash.
▼ 2.2		SO	Track on right.
	0.5 ▲	SO	Track on left.
			GPS: N34°23.34' W112°32.63'
▼ 2.7		SO	Well-used track on right through wire gate is FR 9712E. Zero trip meter.
	0.0 ▲		Continue to the southeast, following alongside the Hassayampa River wash.
			GPS: N34°23.50' W112°32.37'
▼ 0.0			Continue to the northwest, leaving the Hassayampa River wash and follow alongside Orofino Wash.
	3.6 ▲	SO	Well-used track on left through wire gate is FR 9712E. Zero trip meter.
▼ 0.5		SO	Cross through wash.
	3.1 ▲	SO	Cross through wash.
▼ 0.7		SO	Track on right to well; then cattle guard.
	2.9 ▲	SO	Cattle guard; then track on left to well.
			GPS: N34°23.94' W112°32.81'
▼ 1.5		SO	Track on left; then cross through wash.
	2.1 ▲	SO	Cross through wash; then track on right.
▼ 1.7		SO	Track on left.
	1.9 ▲	SO	Track on right.
▼ 1.8		SO	Track on left; trail leaves path of Orofino Wash.
	1.8 ▲	SO	Track on right; trail follows along path of Orofino Wash.
▼ 2.1		SO	Track on left is FR 9402N.
	1.5 ▲	SO	Track on right is FR 9402N.
			GPS: N34°24.53' W112°34.12'
▼ 2.2		SO	Cross through wash.
	1.4 ▲	SO	Cross through wash.
▼ 2.6		SO	Cross through wash.
	1.0 ▲	SO	Cross through wash.
▼ 2.8		SO	Cattle guard; then track on left is FR 9403M.
	0.8 ▲	SO	Track on right is FR 9403M; then cattle guard.
			GPS: N34°24.97' W112°34.63'
▼ 3.3		SO	Cattle guard.
	0.3 ▲	SO	Cattle guard.
▼ 3.6			Trail ends at the T-intersection with paved Arizona 89, immediately east of Wilhoit. Turn right for Prescott; turn left for Wilhoit.
	0.0 ▲		Trail commences on Arizona 89, immediately east of Wilhoit. Zero trip meter and turn southwest onto roughly graded road. The road is marked FR 72 immediately past the intersection.
			GPS: N34°25.46' W112°34.73'

CENTRAL REGION TRAIL #24

Senator Highway

Starting Point:	**East Gurley Street in Prescott**
Finishing Point:	**Crown King**
Total Mileage:	**36.3 miles**
Unpaved Mileage:	**29.6 miles**
Driving Time:	**4.5 hours**
Elevation Range:	**5,300–7,200 feet**
Usually Open:	**Year-round**
Best Time to Travel:	**Dry weather**
Difficulty Rating:	**2**
Scenic Rating:	**8**
Remoteness Rating:	**+0**

Special Attractions

- Long, historic route through the Prescott National Forest.
- Historic Palace Stage Station.
- The interesting small settlement of Crown King.

History

This old pioneer route takes its name from the Senator Mine and the community of the same name, which was active in the late 1800s. The route was unnamed for many years before S. O. Fredericks named it after his Senator Mine. The mine was later owned by Phelps Dodge and was worked on and off as late as the 1930s. The road was constructed slowly as the mining camps along it developed. Initially the road only went from Prescott as far as the Senator Mine, but in 1877 a wagon road pushed through as far as Crooks Canyon and the Peck Mine. In 1900 a new road opened along a better route. The road linked the mines and communities of Bueno, Meesville, Goodwin, and Tip Top, before connecting with Black Canyon Road to Phoenix. At one time the road out of Prescott was a toll road; the charge was $1.50 per wagon.

The remains of a steel mining building below the trail near Groom Creek

Groom Creek, established in 1901, was first known as Oak-dale, but the name was changed to Groom Creek after R. W. (Bob) Groom, a territorial legislator who also became very rich from his interests in the Sterling Mine near Prescott.

Palace Station is a stagecoach station that dates back to 1875. It was built by Alfred B. Spence, originally from Missouri, and his wife, Matilde. They briefly settled in Groom Creek and operated a sawmill before moving to the site of Palace Station, where they built the cabin that still stands today. They chose the location because it was halfway between Prescott and the Peck Mine, which at the time was an important mine. The original cabin, two rooms and a loft, was expanded a few years later. The Spences provided meals for travelers and feed for horses en route to the Peck Mine. Palace Station has been owned by the Prescott National Forest since 1963.

Another site along the route is that of Bradshaw City, founded in 1863 by William D. Bradshaw. Its fortunes were tied to those of the Tiger Mine, found a short distance along Central #26: Crown King Backroad. For a long time, Bradshaw had many saloons and dance halls, but no churches. Its peak population was approximately 5,000 people. It was accessed by a wagon train from Prescott—a journey that took two and a half days.

Many of the mine managers and owners from the Bradshaw Mining District built ornate houses in Prescott. Some of those houses, which have been carefully restored, can be seen along Mt. Vernon Street at the start of this trail.

The trail finishes at Crown King. (For information on Crown King, refer to Central #26: Crown King Backroad.)

Description

Considering that this trail is a major route through the Prescott National Forest, it is suprisingly quiet. Even on weekends, the only sounds are the chirping birds, the breeze in the pine, and the persistent buzz of insects. Shady pines, prolific bird life, and the long meandering trail make it a pleasure to travel.

The route begins at the center of Prescott, and for the first few miles it follows a well-used paved road that leads through housing areas, past hiking trailheads (including the handicapped accessible Lions Creek Nature Trail), and Goldwater Lake Park.

The trail gradually becomes smaller and less used until it becomes a rough, single-track road that winds through the mature forest vegetation of the Prescott National Forest. For the most part it travels under the forest canopy—spruces, pines, oaks, and a scattering of aspens. There are many good campsites along the way as well as developed national forest campgrounds close by. Many old mine workings dot the area, most of which are within the Bradshaw Mining District.

The old Palace Stage Station building is maintained by the forest service for the use of its personnel. The building can be admired from behind the fence, but it is not open to the public and is considered a private residence. There are no facilities or conveniences at the site. Past Palace Station, the road follows Turkey Creek for part of the way as it winds its way down to join the western end of Central #25: Mayer-Goodwin Road. There are a couple of good campsites along the creek. The site of Goodwin, the old supply point for the Bradshaw Mining District, is immediately north of this intersection; however, nothing remains of the town.

Turkey Creek cuts through rocky outcrops

The southern half of the trail travels along a series of ridge tops with great views to the east and west over the remote Bradshaw Mountains. This lower end is narrow and has a couple of rocky places. The road forks at Hooper Saddle, with FR 362 continuing south to Wagoner. Senator Highway swings around to the east, passing below Towers Mountain where there is a fire lookout that was erected in 1933. There has been a lookout at this site since about 1902. This section of the trail, a wide shelf road with great views to the south, passes the site of Bradshaw City, although little remains except for the forest service information sign. Central #26: Crown King Backroad—a very rough 4WD trail—leaves to the south before the main trail swings up to enter the settlement of Crown King. Crown King has a few year-round residents and is positively bustling in the summer. It is a popular destination for all kinds of outdoor enthusiasts. There is a general store, saloon, and a restaurant. Hours for these businesses vary, so check ahead. Limited lodging and gas are available at the general store. From Crown King, if you have sufficient time, you can backtrack to take Central #26: Crown King Backroad to Lake Pleasant or take the shorter route to I-17 via Cleator and the old railroad grade.

Current Road Information

Prescott National Forest
Crown King Work Station
(520) 632-7740

Map References

BLM Prescott, Bradshaw Mts.
USFS Prescott National Forest: Bradshaw Ranger District
USGS 1:24,000 Prescott, Groom Creek, Battleship Butte, Battle Flat, Minniehaha, Crown King
1:100,000 Prescott, Bradshaw Mts.
Maptech CD-ROM: Flagstaff/Sedona/Prescott
Arizona Atlas & Gazetteer, p. 49
Arizona Road & Recreation Atlas, p. 40 & p. 74
Recreational Map of Arizona

Route Directions

▼ 0.0	From the center of Prescott at the intersection of East Gurley Street and Mt. Vernon Avenue, turn south on Mt. Vernon Avenue and zero trip meter. Remain on Mt. Vernon Avenue.
6.8 ▲	Trail ends in the center of Prescott at the intersection of East Gurley Street and Mt. Vernon Avenue.

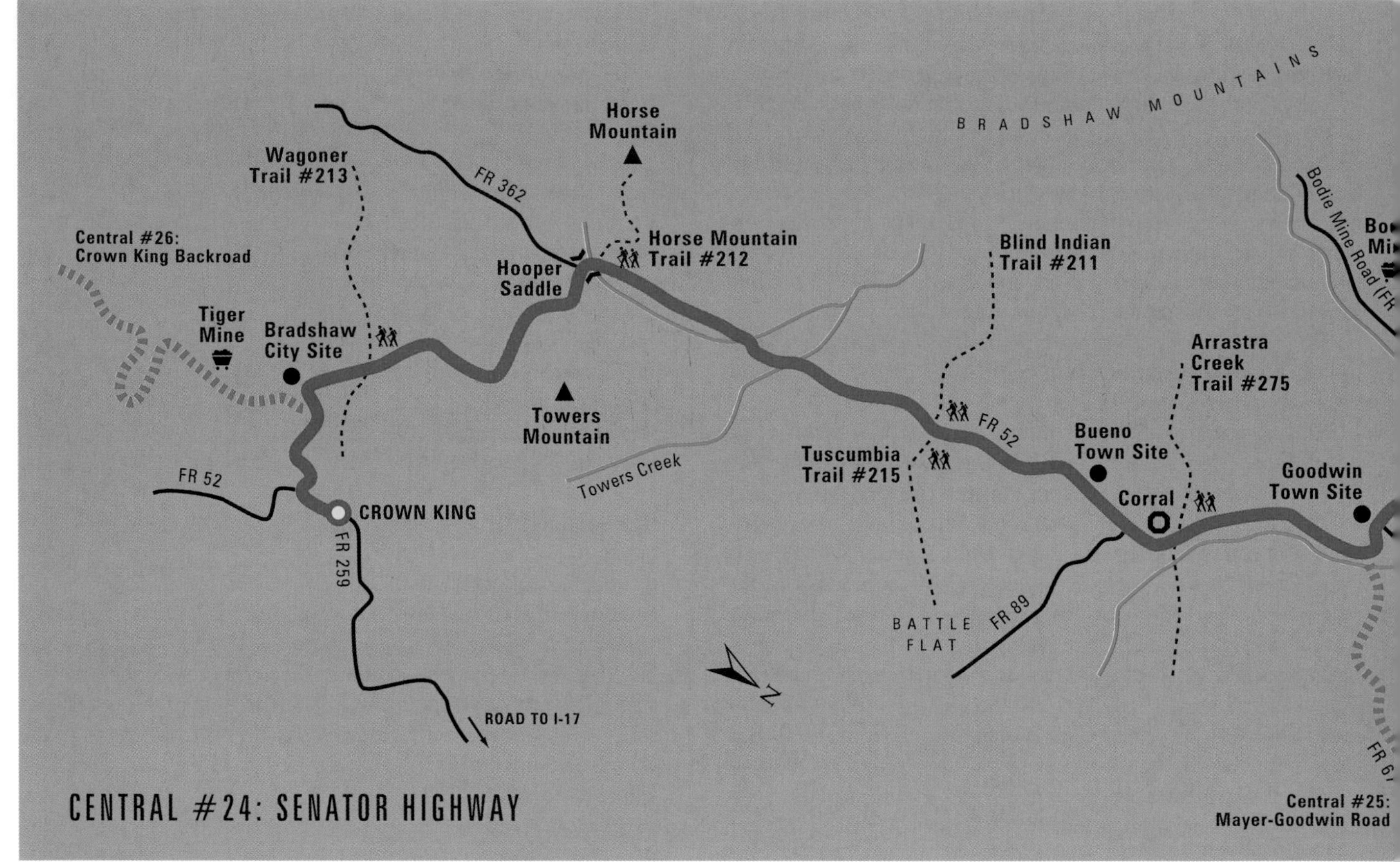

GPS: N34°32.50′ W112°27.76′

▼ 3.0 SO Entering Prescott National Forest.
3.8 ▲ SO Leaving Prescott National Forest.

GPS: N34°30.33′ W112°26.77′

▼ 3.2 SO Goldwater Lake Park on right.
3.6 ▲ SO Goldwater Lake Park on left.

GPS: N34°30.15′ W112°26.60′

▼ 3.9 SO Graded road on right is School House Gulch Road.
2.9 ▲ SO Graded road on left is School House Gulch Road.

GPS: N34°29.66′ W112°26.32′

▼ 4.3 SO Private road on right.
2.5 ▲ SO Private road on left.

▼ 4.7 SO Track on left; then paved road on right is Marapai Road. Many private roads and driveways on left and right.
2.1 ▲ SO Paved road on left is Marapai Road; then track on right.

GPS: N34°29.06′ W112°25.95′

▼ 4.9 SO Track on right.
1.9 ▲ SO Track on left.

▼ 5.2 SO Cross over creek on bridge.
1.6 ▲ SO Cross over creek on bridge.

▼ 5.3 SO Old Miner Road on left.
1.5 ▲ SO Old Miner Road on right.

GPS: N34°28.52′ W112°25.83′

▼ 5.4 SO Paved road on right is FR 64A, immediately followed by the Groom Creek Ranger Station on right; then track on left is FR 62677X.
1.4 ▲ SO Track on right is FR 62677X; then Groom Creek Ranger Station on left; then paved road on left is FR 64A. Many private roads and driveways on left and right.

GPS: N34°28.44′ W112°25.87′

▼ 5.7 SO Lions Creek Nature Trail on left.
1.1 ▲ SO Lions Creek Nature Trail on right.

▼ 5.9 SO Track on right is FR 9403W.
0.9 ▲ SO Track on left is FR 9403W.

GPS: N34°28.12′ W112°26.28′

▼ 6.2 SO Groom Creek Trailhead on left, TR 307, for hikers, horses, and mountain bikes.
0.6 ▲ SO Groom Creek Trailhead on right, TR 307, for hikers, horses, and mountain bikes.

GPS: N34°27.88′ W112°26.44′

▼ 6.7 SO Road is now graded dirt.
0.1 ▲ SO Road is now paved.

▼ 6.8 BL Graded road on right goes to Arizona 89 and to Upper and Lower Wolf Creek Campgrounds. Zero trip meter.
0.0 ▲ Continue to the west.

GPS: N34°27.41′ W112°26.54′

▼ 0.0 Continue to the east.
3.4 ▲ BR Graded road on left goes to Arizona 89 and to Upper and Lower Wolf Creek Campgrounds. Zero trip meter.

▼ 0.2 BL Graded road on right is FR 79 to Whispering Pines Camp.
3.2 ▲ SO Graded road on left is FR 79 to Whispering Pines Camp.

GPS: N34°27.31′ W112°26.52′

▼ 0.8 BL Track on right is FR 80; then track on left is FR 79. End of winter maintenance.
2.6 ▲ SO Track on right is FR 79; then track on left is FR

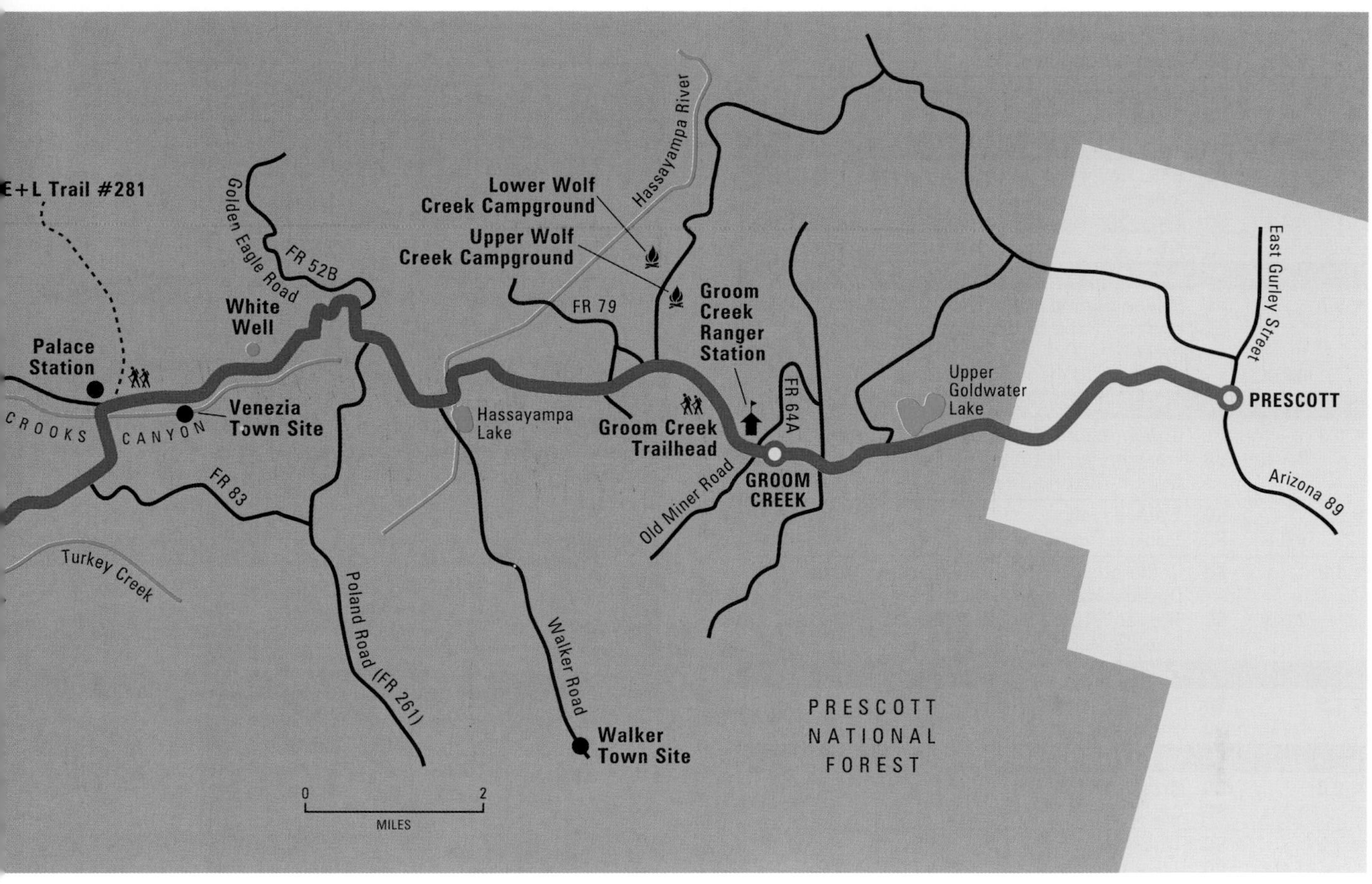

			80. Road is maintained in winter past this point.
			GPS: N34°26.99' W112°26.19'
▼ 1.3		SO	Adit on left.
	2.1 ▲	SO	Adit on right.
▼ 3.1		SO	Cross over Hassayampa River wash.
	0.3 ▲	SO	Cross over Hassayampa River wash.
			GPS: N34°25.71' W112°25.66'
▼ 3.4		SO	Graded road on left is Walker Road. Zero trip meter.
	0.0 ▲		Continue to the northwest and cross over creek.
			GPS: N34°25.54' W112°25.48'
▼ 0.0			Continue to the southeast.
	5.7 ▲	BL	Cross over creek; then bear left, remaining on Senator Highway. Graded road on right is Walker Road.
▼ 0.2		BR	Graded road on left is Wiggler Road; then private road on right.
	5.5 ▲	SO	Private road on left; then graded road on right is Wiggler Road.
▼ 0.3		SO	Track on left is private.
	5.4 ▲	SO	Track on right is private.
▼ 0.6		BR	Bear right, remaining on main trail. Track on left.
	5.1 ▲	BL	Bear left, remaining on main trail. Track on right.
			GPS: N34°25.15' W112°25.78'
▼ 0.9		SO	Old mine on left; then track on left.
	4.8 ▲	SO	Track on right; then old mine on right.
▼ 1.4		BR	Track on left is FR 261, Poland Road. Bear right over cattle guard, following the sign for Senator Highway to Crown King. Immediately followed by track on left, FR 9403E, and mine shaft on right.
	4.3 ▲	SO	Track on right is FR 9403E and mine shaft on left. Cattle guard; then track on right is FR 261, Poland Road. Continue straight on, following the sign for Senator Highway to Prescott.
			GPS: N34°24.84' W112°25.99'
▼ 1.8		BL	Track on right is FR 52B, Golden Eagle Road; then cross through creek.
	3.9 ▲	SO	Cross through creek; then track on left is FR 52B, Golden Eagle Road.
▼ 3.0		SO	Track on right.
	2.7 ▲	SO	Track on left.
▼ 3.4		SO	Track on right; then track on left to old mining area.
	2.3 ▲	SO	Track on right to old mining area; then track on left.
			GPS: N34°24.19' W112°25.54'
▼ 3.5		SO	Track on left.
	2.2 ▲	SO	Track on right.
▼ 3.7		SO	Cross through creek; then track on left is FR 9403G. Trail is entering Crooks Canyon.
	2.0 ▲	SO	Track on right is FR 9403G; then cross through creek.
			GPS: N34°23.96' W112°25.33'
▼ 3.8		SO	White Well on right; then cross through creek.
	1.9 ▲	SO	Cross through creek; then White Well on left.
▼ 4.0		SO	Track on right.
	1.7 ▲	SO	Track on left.
▼ 4.3		SO	Cross through creek; then track on left; then cross through creek.
	1.4 ▲	SO	Cross through creek; then track on right; then cross through creek.
▼ 4.4		SO	Cross through creek.
	1.3 ▲	SO	Cross through creek.

▼ 4.8 SO Cross through creek.
0.9 ▲ SO Cross through creek.

▼ 5.0 SO Cross over creek on bridge.
0.7 ▲ SO Cross over creek on bridge.

GPS: N34°23.13′ W112°24.80′

▼ 5.5 SO E+L Trail #281 on right; then cross through creek.
0.2 ▲ SO Cross through creek; then E+L Trail #281 on left.

GPS: N34°22.73′ W112°24.66′

▼ 5.7 BL Palace Station Historic Site on right. Track on right is FR 82, Bodie Mine Road. Zero trip meter.
0.0 ▲ Continue to the northwest.

GPS: N34°22.60′ W112°24.55′

▼ 0.0 Continue to the east.
3.6 ▲ BR Track on left is FR 82, Bodie Mine Road. Palace Station Historic Site on left. Zero trip meter.

▼ 0.6 SO Track on left.
3.0 ▲ SO Track on right.

▼ 1.0 SO Cattle guard; FR 83 on left is also Yankee Doodle Trail #284. Trail on right.
2.6 ▲ SO Trail on left. FR 83 on right is also Yankee Doodle Trail #284; then cattle guard.

GPS: N34°22.67′ W112°23.74′

▼ 1.5 SO Track on left is FR 85.
2.1 ▲ SO Track on right is FR 85.

GPS: N34°22.36′ W112°23.45′

▼ 2.0 SO Cross through creek.
1.6 ▲ SO Cross through creek.

▼ 2.2 SO Track on left.
1.4 ▲ SO Track on right.

▼ 2.6 SO Cross through creek twice.
1.0 ▲ SO Cross through creek twice.

▼ 2.9 SO Cross through creek.
0.7 ▲ SO Cross through creek.

▼ 3.0 SO Cattle guard; then track on left through gate is FR 84.
0.6 ▲ SO Track on right through gate is FR 84; then cattle guard.

GPS: N34°21.46′ W112°22.91′

▼ 3.2 SO Cross through creek.
0.4 ▲ SO Cross through creek.

▼ 3.3 SO Cross through creek. This is the site of Goodwin.
0.3 ▲ SO Cross through creek. This is the site of Goodwin.

▼ 3.5 SO Track on left.
0.1 ▲ SO Track on right.

▼ 3.6 SO Track on left is Central #25: Mayer-Goodwin Road, FR 67. Zero trip meter.
0.0 ▲ Proceed to the northwest on FR 52, following the sign to Prescott.

GPS: N34°21.40′ W112°22.43′

▼ 0.0 Proceed to the southeast on FR 52, following the sign to Crown King.
2.9 ▲ SO Track on right is Central #25: Mayer-Goodwin Road, FR 67. Zero trip meter.

▼ 0.1 SO Cattle guard; then two tracks on left.
2.8 ▲ SO Two tracks on right; then cattle guard.

▼ 0.5 SO Track on left to campsites along Turkey Creek.
2.4 ▲ SO Track on right to campsites along Turkey Creek.

▼ 0.9 SO Track on right and track on left; then cross through wash.
2.0 ▲ SO Cross through wash; then track on right and track on left.

▼ 1.0 SO Small track on right.
1.9 ▲ SO Small track on left.

▼ 1.1 SO Track on left.
1.8 ▲ SO Track on right.

▼ 1.3 SO Cross through wash; then track on right; then track on left.
1.6 ▲ SO Track on right; then track on left; then cross through wash.

GPS: N34°20.36′ W112°22.49′

▼ 1.7 SO Track on right is FR 9268U.
1.2 ▲ SO Track on left is FR 9268U.

GPS: N34°20.01′ W112°22.42′

▼ 2.1 SO Arrastra Creek Trail #275 crosses road; corral on right; then cross through wash. Trail now leaves Turkey Creek.
0.8 ▲ SO Cross through wash; trail is now following Turkey Creek. Corral on left; then Arrastra Creek Trail #275 crosses road.

GPS: N34°19.69′ W112°22.21′

▼ 2.3 BR Bear right, following the sign to Crown King. Track on left.
0.6 ▲ SO Bear left, following the sign to Prescott. Track on right.

GPS: N34°19.70′ W112°22.06′

▼ 2.6 SO Cross through wash.
0.3 ▲ SO Cross through wash.

▼ 2.9 SO Track on left is FR 89 to Battle Flat. Zero trip meter.
0.0 ▲ Continue to the north.

GPS: N34°19.21′ W112°22.05′

▼ 0.0 Continue to the south.
4.1 ▲ SO Track on right is FR 89 to Battle Flat. Zero trip meter.

▼ 0.6 BR Track on left on right-hand bend is Bradshaw Trail #216.
3.5 ▲ BL Track on right on left-hand bend is Bradshaw Trail #216.

GPS: N34°18.81′ W112°22.31′

▼ 1.9 SO Cattle guard.
2.2 ▲ SO Cattle guard.

▼ 2.7 BR Tuscumbia Trail #215 on left for hikers, horses, mountain bikes, and motorbikes only. Cross over wash. Blind Indian Trail #211 on right.
1.4 ▲ BL Blind Indian Trail #211 on left; then cross over wash. Tuscumbia Trail #215 on right for hikers, horses, mountain bikes, and motorbikes only.

GPS: N34°17.37′ W112°22.57′

▼ 3.5 SO Track on right.
0.6 ▲ SO Track on left.

▼ 4.1 SO Track on left joins the Bradshaw Trail in 1 mile; track on right. Zero trip meter at sign.
0.0 ▲ Continue to the northeast on FR 52.

GPS: N34°16.66′ W112°22.77′

▼ 0.0 Continue to the southeast on FR 52.
3.7 ▲ SO Track on right joins the Bradshaw Trail in 1 mile; track on left. Zero trip meter at sign.

▼ 0.2 SO Cross over creek.
3.5 ▲ SO Cross over creek.

▼ 0.9 SO Cross over creek.
2.8 ▲ SO Cross over creek.

▼ 1.2 SO Cross through Towers Creek. Trail follows alongside Towers Creek.

2.5 ▲	SO	Cross through Towers Creek. Trail leaves Towers Creek.
▼ 1.5	SO	Trail leaves Towers Creek.
2.2 ▲	SO	Trail follows alongside Towers Creek.
▼ 2.0	SO	Track on right; then cross through North Pine Creek.
1.7 ▲	SO	Cross through North Pine Creek; then track on left.
		GPS: N34°15.45' W112°23.00'
▼ 2.1	SO	Cross through two washes; then tank on left.
1.6 ▲	SO	Tank on right; then cross through two washes.
▼ 2.2	SO	Corral on left; track on left is FR 9259A.
1.5 ▲	SO	Track on right is FR 9259A; corral on right.
		GPS: N34°15.28' W112°23.04'
▼ 2.7	SO	Cross over wash.
1.0 ▲	SO	Cross over wash.
▼ 3.6	SO	Horse Mountain Trail #212 on right.
0.1 ▲	SO	Horse Mountain Trail #212 on left.
▼ 3.7	BL	Cattle guard; then turn left on Hooper Saddle, remaining on FR 52. Track on right is FR 362 to Wagoner. Zero trip meter.
0.0 ▲		Continue to the north, following the sign to Prescott.
		GPS: N34°14.07' W112°23.37'
▼ 0.0		Continue to the southeast, following the sign to Crown King.
2.2 ▲	SO	Track on left at Hooper Saddle is FR 362 to Wagoner. Keep straight on FR 52 and cross cattle guard. Zero trip meter.
▼ 0.7	SO	Towers Mountain Trail #131 on left for hikers, horses, and mountain bikes only.
1.5 ▲	SO	Towers Mountain Trail #131 on right for hikers, horses, and mountain bikes only.
		GPS: N34°13.83' W112°22.82'
▼ 2.2	SO	Track on left is FR 52C to Towers Lookout; track on right. Zero trip meter.
0.0 ▲		Continue to the north on Senator Highway.
		GPS: N34°13.34' W112°21.99'
▼ 0.0		Continue to the south on Senator Highway and cross through wash.
2.3 ▲	SO	Cross through wash; then track on right is FR 52C to Towers Lookout. Also track on left. Zero trip meter.
▼ 0.1	SO	Track on left.
2.2 ▲	SO	Track on right.
▼ 0.4	SO	Track on left.
1.9 ▲	SO	Track on right.
▼ 0.6	SO	Two tracks on right to tank below road.
1.7 ▲	SO	Two tracks on left to tank below road.
▼ 0.8	BL	Major track on right.
1.5 ▲	SO	Major track on left.
		GPS: N34°12.68' W112°21.98'
▼ 0.9	SO	Two tracks on right.
1.4 ▲	SO	Two tracks on left.
▼ 1.0	SO	Track on left; then track on right.
1.3 ▲	SO	Track on left; then track on right.
▼ 1.1	SO	Track on left is FR 9273G.
1.2 ▲	SO	Track on right is FR 9273G.
		GPS: N34°12.49' W112°21.80'
▼ 1.2	SO	Wagoner Trail #213 on left and track on right.
1.1 ▲	SO	Wagoner Trail #213 on right and track on left.
		GPS: N34°12.41' W112°21.81'
▼ 2.2	SO	Information board on right at site of Bradshaw City; then cross over creek.
0.1 ▲	SO	Cross over creek; then information board on left at site of Bradshaw City.
		GPS: N34°11.79' W112°21.28'
▼ 2.3	SO	Track on right is Central #26: Crown King Backroad, FR 192. Track on left to campsite. Zero trip meter.
0.0 ▲		Continue to the southwest on FR 52.
		GPS: N34°11.89' W112°21.15'
▼ 0.0		Continue to the northeast on FR 52.
1.1 ▲	SO	Track on left is Central #26: Crown King Backroad, FR 192. Track on right to campsite. Zero trip meter.
▼ 0.4	SO	Track on right.
0.7 ▲	SO	Track on left.
▼ 0.8	SO	Track on left is FR 9235B to USFS Heliport.
0.3 ▲	SO	Track on right is FR 9235B to USFS Heliport.
		GPS: N34°11.83' W112°20.58'
▼ 1.1	TL	Graded road on right is FR 52 to Horsethief Basin. Turn left onto FR 259 to Crown King. Zero trip meter.
0.0 ▲		Continue to the west.
		GPS: N34°11.94' W112°20.35'
▼ 0.0		Continue to the north.
0.5 ▲	TR	Graded road straight on is FR 52 to Horsethief Basin. Turn right onto FR 52 to Prescott and Goodwin.
▼ 0.5		Trail ends in Crown King. Continue straight to exit to I-17.
0.0 ▲		Trail commences in Crown King with the turn to the general store on right and the turn to Mill Restaurant and Lodge on the left. Zero trip meter and continue south on FR 259 past the Yavapai County Sign. Road not maintained past this point.
		GPS: N34°12.33' W112°20.21'

CENTRAL REGION TRAIL #25

Mayer-Goodwin Road

Starting Point:	Central Avenue in Mayer
Finishing Point:	Central #24: Senator Highway, 20 miles south of Prescott
Total Mileage:	11 miles
Unpaved Mileage:	10.3 miles
Driving Time:	45 minutes
Elevation Range:	4,500–5,800 feet
Usually Open:	Year-round
Best Time to Travel:	Dry weather
Difficulty Rating:	2
Scenic Rating:	8
Remoteness Rating:	+0

Special Attractions

- Historic site of Goodwin.
- Winding road through the edge of the Bradshaw Mountains.
- Can be combined with part of Central #24: Senator Highway to form a loop trail.

A corral at the start of the Arrastra Creek hiking trail

History

Mayer is named after Joe Mayer, who established a store, saloon, and stage station at the location in 1882. The small town was soon a hub for the surrounding agricultural community. Nearby mining increased the town's importance and in 1884, Joe Mayer added a two-story hotel.

Mayer gained in importance again when the Prescott & Eastern Railroad, the brainchild of Frank Murphy, reached the town in 1898. However, the railroad did not stop there. Frank Murphy had the wild idea of connecting Mayer to the rich mining district at Crown King. People scoffed at the idea, calling the scheme "Murphy's Impossible Railroad." Crown King was 2,000 feet higher in elevation than Mayer, and the proposed route through the mountains was steep and tortuous. Murphy was not discouraged and advertised in newspapers in the East for workers to lay the grade, offering double the going rate at the time—a dollar a day. In 1901 construction started. First to be finished was a short spur from Poland Junction (to the north of Mayer) to the mines near Poland. Construction was delayed on this leg in 1902 when a dynamite blast revealed a significant gold deposit. Many of the construction workers were tempted and immediately turned to prospecting, abandoning the railroad construction. It was some time before a new crew could be found.

Mature pine trees near Wolf Creek

The more difficult construction to Crown King was completed in 1904. The route used many high wooden trestles, a tunnel, 10 twisting switchbacks, and a steeper grade than is normally associated with railroads. The railroad ran for many years until the mines were quiet. The tracks were removed in 1927, and the grade now serves as a vehicle route to Crown King.

Goodwin was named after John N. Goodwin, the first governor to serve the Arizona Territory. The town operated as a supply center for mines in the Bradshaw Mountains from 1882 and had a stage station, a hotel, and a general store.

Description

This roughly graded road travels from the interesting small town of Mayer west to intersect with Central #24: Senator Highway, the major north-south road through the Bradshaw Mountains. The winding trail travels over open hills covered with low vegetation. Two major creeks along the route, Wolf Creek and Turkey Creek, often have running water and offer shady camping and picnic sites under ponderosa pines.

The trail is suitable for high-clearance 2WD vehicles, as there are a few rough sections that could catch the undercarriage of low-slung passenger vehicles. It is best traveled in dry weather.

The trail finishes at the intersection Central #24: Senator Highway. The site of Goodwin is along Senator Highway 0.3 miles to the north. Nothing remains of the former town.

Current Road Information

Prescott National Forest
Crown King Work Station
(520) 632-7740

Map References

BLM Bradshaw Mts.
USFS Prescott National Forest: Bradshaw Ranger District
USGS 1:24,000 Mayer, Poland Junction, Battle Flat
1:100,000 Bradshaw Mts.
Maptech CD-ROM: Flagstaff/Sedona/Prescott
Arizona Atlas & Gazetteer, p. 49
Arizona Road & Recreation Atlas, p. 40 & p. 74
Recreational Map of Arizona

Route Directions

▼ 0.0			From Arizona 69, exit onto Central Avenue in Mayer. At the 4-way stop sign, zero trip meter and turn southwest on Oak Street; then immediately turn left on Main Street.
	2.0 ▲		Turn right onto Oak Street. Trail ends at the 4-way stop sign on Central Avenue in Mayer. Turning right and then left will bring you out to Arizona 69.
			GPS: N34°23.98' W112°14.27'
▼ 0.1		TR	Turn onto First Street, following the sign to Goodwin and the Prescott National Forest.
	1.9 ▲	TL	Turn left onto Main Street.
			GPS: N34°23.92' W112°14.20'
▼ 0.2		TL	Turn left onto Fair Mist Avenue (which turns into Jefferson Street). Remain on major paved street, ignoring turns to left and right.
	1.8 ▲	TR	Follow Jefferson Street around to the left (which turns into Fair Mist Avenue). Then turn right onto First Street.
▼ 0.7		SO	Road turns to graded dirt.
	1.3 ▲	SO	Road turns to paved.
▼ 1.3		SO	Cattle guard.
	0.7 ▲	SO	Cattle guard.
▼ 1.5		SO	Mayer Cemetery on right and left.
	0.5 ▲	SO	Mayer Cemetery on right and left.
			GPS: N34°22.98' W112°14.92'

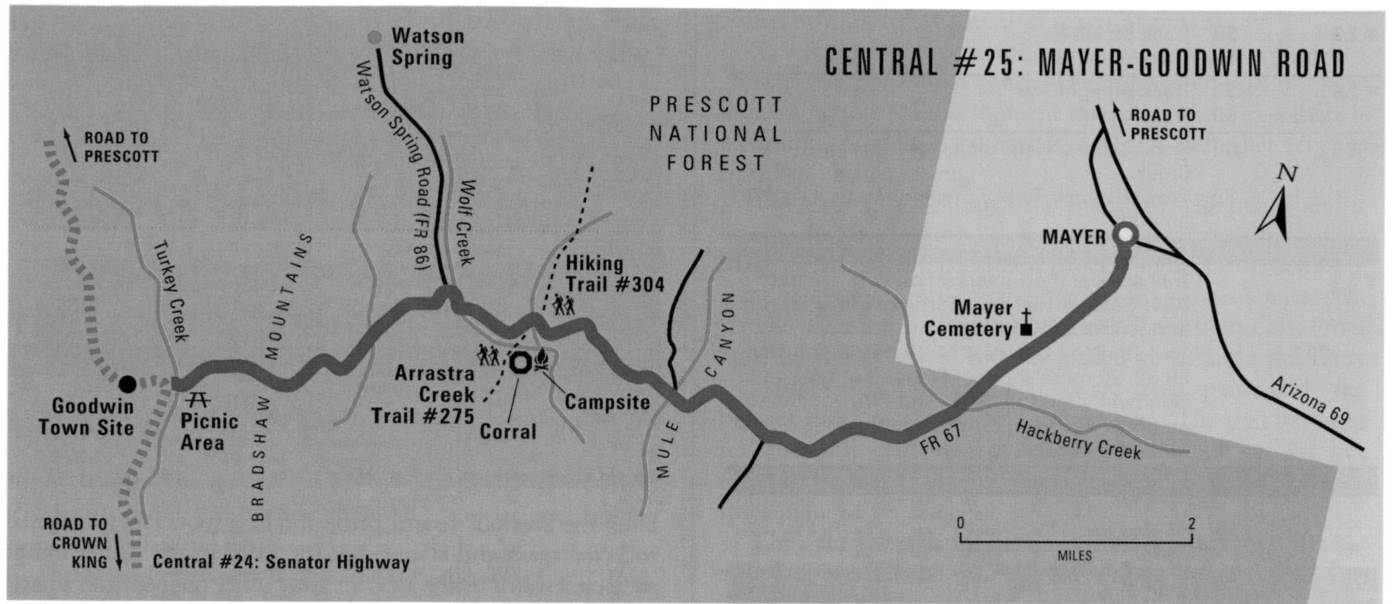

▼ 1.9	SO	Cattle guard.
0.1 ▲	SO	Cattle guard.
▼ 2.0	SO	Track on right; entering Prescott National Forest at sign. Road is now designated FR 67. Zero trip meter.
0.0 ▲		Continue to the northeast.
		GPS: N34°22.62′ W112°15.32′
▼ 0.0		Continue to the southwest.
4.8 ▲	SO	Leaving Prescott National Forest at sign; track on left. Zero trip meter.
▼ 0.1	SO	Cross through Hackberry Creek; then track on left.
4.7 ▲	SO	Track on right; then cross through Hackberry Creek.
▼ 0.7	SO	Track on left is blocked around the corner.
4.1 ▲	SO	Track on right is blocked around the corner.
▼ 1.1	SO	Two tracks on right.
3.7 ▲	SO	Two tracks on left.
▼ 1.5	SO	Cattle guard.
3.3 ▲	SO	Cattle guard.
▼ 2.0	SO	Track on left.
2.8 ▲	SO	Track on right.
▼ 2.4	SO	Track on left.
2.4 ▲	SO	Track on right.
▼ 2.9	SO	Track on left; then cattle guard.
1.9 ▲	SO	Cattle guard; then track on right.
		GPS: N34°22.05′ W112°17.82′
▼ 3.2	SO	Track on right; then cross through Mule Canyon wash.
1.6 ▲	SO	Cross through Mule Canyon wash; then track on left.
▼ 3.6	SO	Cattle guard.
1.2 ▲	SO	Cattle guard.
▼ 4.0	SO	Cross through wash.
0.8 ▲	SO	Cross through wash.
▼ 4.2	SO	Track on right.
0.6 ▲	SO	Track on left.
▼ 4.8	SO	Track on left to campsite; then hiking trail #304 on right. Zero trip meter at sign.
0.0 ▲		Continue to the east.
		GPS: N34°22.51′ W112°19.32′
▼ 0.0		Continue to the south and cross through Little Wolf Creek.
1.1 ▲	SO	Cross through Little Wolf Creek; then hiking trail #304 on left. Then track on right to campsite. Zero trip meter.
▼ 0.1	SO	Cattle guard.
1.0 ▲	SO	Cattle guard.
▼ 0.3	SO	Arrastra Creek Trail #275 on left through gate. Corral at gate.
0.8 ▲	SO	Arrastra Creek Trail #275 on right through gate. Corral at gate.
		GPS: N34°22.30′ W112°19.50′
▼ 0.8	SO	Cross through Wolf Creek.
0.3 ▲	SO	Cross through Wolf Creek.
▼ 0.9	SO	Track on right.
0.2 ▲	SO	Track on left.
▼ 1.1	TL	Track on right is FR 86, Watson Spring Road. Zero trip meter. Turn sharp left and climb up hill.
0.0 ▲		Continue to the southeast.
		GPS: N34°22.54′ W112°20.14′
▼ 0.0		Continue to the southwest.
3.1 ▲	TR	Track on left at bottom of hill is FR 86, Watson Spring Road. Zero trip meter.
▼ 0.7	SO	Cattle guard.
2.4 ▲	SO	Cattle guard.
		GPS: N34°22.23′ W112°20.64′
▼ 0.9	SO	Track on left; then cross through wash.
2.2 ▲	SO	Cross through wash; then track on right.
▼ 1.1	SO	Track on left; then entering private land. Remain on main graded road, ignoring private tracks on right and left.
2.0 ▲	SO	Leaving private land; then track on right.
▼ 1.8	SO	Cross through wash.
1.3 ▲	SO	Cross through wash.
▼ 2.0	SO	Re-entering Prescott National Forest. Track on right is FR 289 for ATVs, motorbikes, mountain bikes, horses, and hiking use only—no 4WD vehicles. Cross through wash.
1.1 ▲	SO	Cross through wash; then enter private land; remain on main graded road, ignoring private tracks on right and left. Track on left is FR 289 for ATVs, motorbikes, mountain bikes, horses, and hiking use only—no 4WD vehicles.
		GPS: N34°21.60′ W112°21.45′

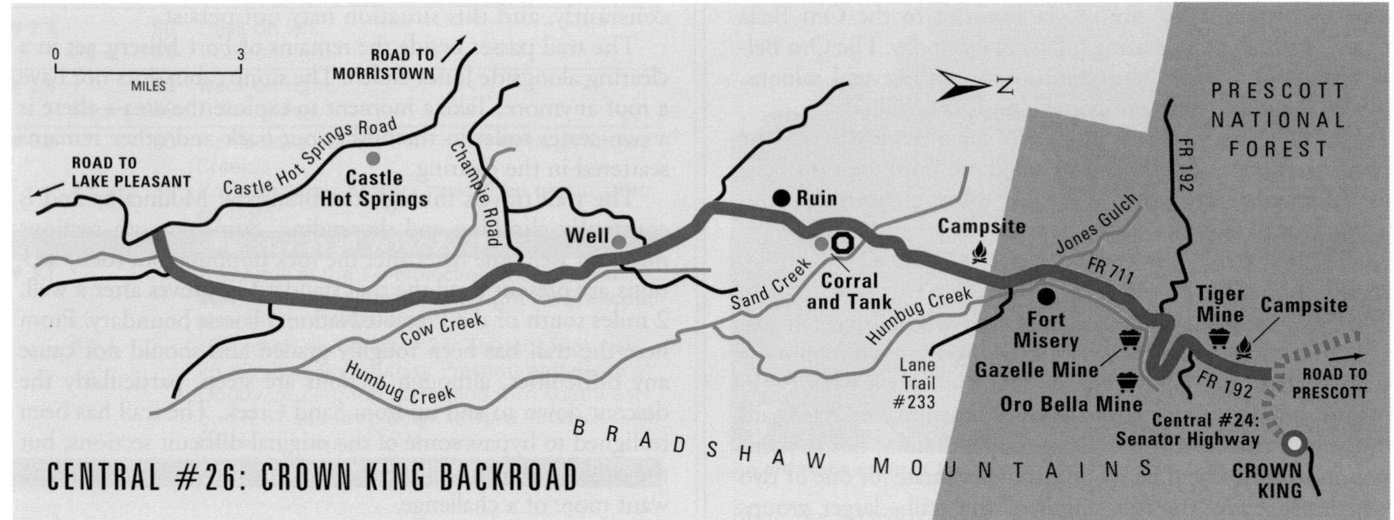

CENTRAL #26: CROWN KING BACKROAD

Mileage		Dir.	Description
			GPS: N34°10.96′ W112°21.22′
▼ 1.7		BR	Track on left climbs up the hill. Continue to ascend. Old mine building is visible down in gully on right. Remain on FR 192.
	2.2 ▲	SO	Track on right climbs up the hill. Continue to descend. Old mine building is visible down in gully on left.
			GPS: N34°10.77′ W112°21.33′
▼ 1.9		SO	Track on right.
	2.0 ▲	BR	Track on left.
			GPS: N34°10.64′ W112°21.34′
▼ 3.0		SO	Remains of the Oro Bella Mine on left.
	0.9 ▲	SO	Remains of the Oro Bella Mine on right.
			GPS: N34°10.26′ W112°20.81′
▼ 3.3		SO	Cross through creek.
	0.6 ▲	SO	Cross through creek.
			GPS: N34°10.25′ W112°21.04′
▼ 3.4		SO	Cross through creek.
	0.5 ▲	SO	Cross through creek.
▼ 3.5		SO	Track on left; then cross through creek.
	0.4 ▲	SO	Cross through creek; then track on right.
▼ 3.7		SO	Cattle guard.
	0.2 ▲	SO	Cattle guard.
▼ 3.9		TL	Turn left onto FR 711. FR 192 continues ahead. Zero trip meter. Most traffic turns left.
	0.0 ▲		Continue to the east.
			GPS: N34°10.35′ W112°21.62′
▼ 0.0			Continue to the south.
	3.8 ▲	TR	Turn right onto FR 192, which also continues to the left. Zero trip meter. Most traffic turns right.
▼ 0.2		SO	Cross through creek.
	3.6 ▲	SO	Cross through creek.
▼ 0.3		SO	Cross through Humbug Creek; then Gazelle Mine on left.
	3.5 ▲	SO	Gazelle Mine on right; then cross through Humbug Creek.
			GPS: N34°10.07′ W112°21.50′
▼ 0.5		SO	Cross through creek.
	3.3 ▲	SO	Cross through creek.
▼ 0.6		SO	Cross through creek.
	3.2 ▲	SO	Cross through creek.
▼ 0.7		SO	Mine on left below road with deep shaft.
	3.1 ▲	SO	Mine on right below road with deep shaft.
			GPS: N34°09.79′ W112°21.67′
▼ 1.0		SO	Cross through creek.
	2.8 ▲	SO	Cross through creek.
▼ 1.1		SO	Cross through creek twice.
	2.7 ▲	SO	Cross through creek twice.
▼ 1.2		SO	Track on left.
	2.6 ▲	SO	Track on right.
			GPS: N34°09.54′ W112°21.76′
▼ 1.6		SO	Track on left.
	2.2 ▲	BL	Track on right.
▼ 1.8		SO	Campsite on left.
	2.0 ▲	SO	Campsite on right.
▼ 2.7		BR	Faint track on right up Jones Gulch; then second track on right. Remain on main trail.
	1.1 ▲	BR	Track on left; then faint track on left up Jones Gulch. Remain on main trail.
			GPS: N34°08.51′ W112°22.08′
▼ 2.8		SO	Cross through wash; then Fort Misery (remains of stone cabin) on left of trail. Trail forks around cabin and immediately rejoins.
	1.0 ▲	SO	Fort Misery (remains of stone cabin) on right of trail. Trail forks around cabin and immediately rejoins. Cross through wash.
			GPS: N34°08.43′ W112°22.00′
▼ 3.3		SO	Cross through creek.
	0.5 ▲	SO	Cross through creek.
▼ 3.4		SO	Cross through creek.
	0.4 ▲	SO	Cross through creek.
▼ 3.5		SO	Lane Trail #233 on left.
	0.3 ▲	SO	Lane Trail #233 on right.
			GPS: N34°07.94′ W112°21.60′
▼ 3.7		SO	Tracks left and right into camping area.
	0.1 ▲	SO	Tracks left and right into camping area.
			GPS: N34°07.80′ W112°21.64′
▼ 3.8		SO	Track on right; then cattle guard; leaving Prescott National Forest. Entering cattle ranching area—Eagle Rock Ranch. Zero trip meter.
	0.0 ▲		Continue to the north.
			GPS: N34°07.74′ W112°21.63′
▼ 0.0			Continue to the south.
	5.7 ▲	SO	Cattle guard; then track on left; entering Prescott National Forest (no sign). Zero trip meter at cattle guard.
▼ 0.1		SO	Cross through creek; then rocky tight pinch before campsite on right.

5.6 ▲ SO Campsite on left; then rocky tight pinch; then cross through creek.

▼ 0.7 SO Two tracks on right.
5.0 ▲ SO Two tracks on left.

GPS: N34°07.15' W112°21.75'

▼ 0.8 SO Cross through wash.
4.9 ▲ SO Cross through wash.

▼ 1.0 SO Cross through wash.
4.7 ▲ SO Cross through wash.

▼ 1.2 SO Cross through wash.
4.5 ▲ SO Cross through wash.

▼ 1.6 SO Major track on left to well. Intersection is unmarked.
4.1 ▲ SO Major track on right to well. Intersection is unmarked.

GPS: N34°06.46' W112°21.83'

▼ 2.0 SO Views to the left over Lake Pleasant.
3.7 ▲ SO Views to the right over Lake Pleasant.

▼ 2.2 SO Track splits three ways and rejoins almost immediately. The three forks are different levels of difficulty. Steep descent to creek.
3.5 ▲ SO Track splits three ways and rejoins almost immediately. The three forks are different levels of difficulty. Steep ascent from creek.

▼ 2.4 SO Cross through Sand Creek.
3.3 ▲ SO Cross through Sand Creek.

GPS: N34°05.90' W112°21.97'

▼ 2.9 SO Corral and tank on left.
2.8 ▲ SO Corral and tank on right.

▼ 3.4 SO Stock tank on right.
2.3 ▲ SO Stock tank on left.

▼ 3.8 SO Track on left.
1.9 ▲ SO Track on right.

▼ 4.0 SO Cross through creek.
1.7 ▲ SO Cross through creek.

▼ 4.4 SO Ruins on right.
1.3 ▲ SO Ruins on left.

GPS: N34°04.62' W112°21.98'

▼ 5.1 BR Track on left.
0.6 ▲ SO Track on right.

GPS: N34°04.16' W112°21.92'

▼ 5.7 TL Turn left onto graded road and zero trip meter.
0.0 ▲ Continue to the northwest.

GPS: N34°03.64' W112°21.89'

▼ 0.0 Continue to the northeast.
3.8 ▲ TR Turn right onto formed trail. An old sign points to Crown King and there is a yellow Yavapai County sign saying the road is unmaintained. Zero trip meter.

▼ 0.7 SO Cattle guard.
3.1 ▲ SO Cattle guard.

▼ 0.8 SO Cross through wash.
3.0 ▲ SO Cross through wash.

▼ 1.2 SO Cross through wash.
2.6 ▲ SO Cross through wash.

▼ 1.4 SO Cross through wash.
2.4 ▲ SO Cross through wash.

▼ 1.5 SO Faint track on right.
2.3 ▲ SO Faint track on left.

▼ 1.7 SO Cattle guard.
2.1 ▲ SO Cattle guard.

▼ 1.8 SO Well on right.
2.0 ▲ SO Well on left.

GPS: N34°02.68' W112°20.70'

▼ 2.0 SO Track on left; then cattle guard.
1.8 ▲ BL Cattle guard; then track on right.

▼ 2.3 SO Track on right.
1.5 ▲ BR Track on left.

▼ 2.5 SO Two tracks on left.
1.3 ▲ SO Two tracks on right.

▼ 2.6 SO Track on left.
1.2 ▲ SO Track on right.

▼ 2.8 SO Track on right.
1.0 ▲ SO Track on left.

▼ 2.9 SO Cross through wash.
0.9 ▲ SO Cross through wash.

▼ 3.1 SO Cross through wash.
0.7 ▲ SO Cross through wash.

▼ 3.8 SO Graded road on right is Champie Road. Zero trip meter.
0.0 ▲ Continue to the northwest on Cow Creek Road toward Crown King.

GPS: N34°01.18' W112°20.21'

▼ 0.0 Continue to the southeast on Cow Creek Road toward Lake Pleasant.
4.4 ▲ SO Graded road on left is Champie Road. Zero trip meter.

▼ 0.4 SO Cross through wash.
4.0 ▲ SO Cross through wash.

▼ 0.6 SO Track on left.
3.8 ▲ SO Track on right.

▼ 0.9 SO Enter Cow Creek.
3.5 ▲ SO Exit creek.

GPS: N34°00.62' W112°19.52'

▼ 1.2 SO Exit creek.
3.2 ▲ SO Enter Cow Creek.

▼ 1.5 SO Track on left.
2.9 ▲ SO Track on right.

▼ 2.0 SO Cattle guard.
2.4 ▲ SO Cattle guard.

▼ 4.4 TR Graded road on left to Humbug Creek. Zero trip meter.
0.0 ▲ Continue to the north, following sign to Crown King.

GPS: N33°57.93' W112°18.70'

▼ 0.0 Continue to the west.
2.5 ▲ BL Graded road on right to Humbug Creek. Zero trip meter.

▼ 1.3 SO Private road on right.
1.2 ▲ SO Private road on left.

▼ 1.6 SO Track on left.
0.9 ▲ SO Track on right.

▼ 1.8 SO Track on left.
0.7 ▲ SO Track on right.

▼ 2.1 SO Cross through wash on concrete ford.
0.4 ▲ SO Cross through wash on concrete ford.

GPS: N33°56.34' W112°19.09'

▼ 2.2 SO Cross through wash.
0.3 ▲ SO Cross through wash.

▼ 2.5 Trail ends at the intersection with Castle Hot Springs Road. Turn right for Morristown; turn left for Lake Pleasant.
0.0 ▲ Trail commences on Castle Hot Springs Road, 2.8 miles west of the Lake Pleasant Regional Park. Zero trip meter and turn northeast on graded dirt road, Cow Creek Road, sign-posted to Crown King, 35 miles.

GPS: N33°56.17' W112°19.43'

▼ 1.0	SO	Cross through wash.
3.5 ▲	SO	Cross through wash.
▼ 1.1	SO	Cattle guard.
3.4 ▲	SO	Cattle guard.
▼ 1.7	SO	Cross through wash.
2.8 ▲	SO	Cross through wash.
▼ 2.1	SO	Cattle guard.
2.4 ▲	SO	Cattle guard.
▼ 2.5	SO	Cross over creek.
2.0 ▲	SO	Cross over creek.
▼ 3.0	SO	Cattle guard.
1.5 ▲	SO	Cattle guard.
▼ 3.4	SO	Campsite on right, next to Roundtree Creek.
1.1 ▲	SO	Campsite on left, next to Roundtree Creek.
		GPS: N34°08.77′ W111°50.11′
▼ 4.5		Trail ends in Bloody Basin at the intersection with Central #30: Bloody Basin Road (FR 269). Turn left to exit to I-17.
0.0 ▲		Trail commences at the intersection of Central #30: Bloody Basin Road (FR 269) and Cave Creek Road, at the eastern end of the Bloody Basin Road, 24.7 miles east of I-17. Zero trip meter and turn south on FR 24, following the sign to Camp Creek.
		GPS: N34°09.34′ W111°49.27′

CENTRAL REGION TRAIL #28

Big Maggie May Trail

Starting Point:	**Central #27: Camp Creek Road**
Finishing Point:	**Viewpoint over Grays Gulch; old cabin on the north side of Cramm Mountain**
Total Mileage:	**9 miles (round-trip)**
Unpaved Mileage:	**9 miles**
Driving Time:	**1.5 hours**
Elevation Range:	**3,600–4,200 feet**
Usually Open:	**Year-round**
Best Time to Travel:	**October to May**
Difficulty Rating:	**4**
Scenic Rating:	**8**
Remoteness Rating:	**+0**

Special Attractions

- Winding trail with many moderately steep hill climbs and descents.
- Views of Grays Gulch and New River Mesa.
- Interesting stone and timber cabin.

Description

This spectacular winding trail offers many moderately steep hill climbs and descents as it winds along the ridge tops within the Tonto National Forest. The trail leaves the Camp Creek Road and is marked as FR 468. After 0.8 miles the trail drops in standard to become a small, well-used, formed trail and it follows alongside Big Maggie May Creek, climbing to the ridge tops above it. There are views back to Cramm Mountain and down into the wash.

An old cabin above the wash that incorporates two trees into its structure

After 1.6 miles, the main FR 468 turns left. The trail ahead, FR 1940, continues for 0.9 miles to a mine adit. This entertaining drive climbs and descends several moderately steep hills. The road has a good surface and offers reasonable traction. Past the adit is the loosest descent of the spur. The trail continues for only another 0.4 miles past the adit before petering out. The mine adit is the best place to turn back. There are panoramic views into Grays Gulch and over to New River Mesa from this section of the trail.

Back on FR 468, the trail descends to a creek and winds along on a small loose-surfaced trail. An old stone and timber cabin, constructed around two trees, is reached at 1.6 miles. The cabin sits above the creek and is a pleasant place to camp; it is the suggested turnaround for this leg. Beyond the cabin the trail continues for another mile to a stock tank—beyond that, it is rarely used.

Although marked with forest route numbers, this trail does not appear on the Tonto National Forest Map or the BLM Map.

Current Road Information

Tonto National Forest
Cave Creek Ranger District
40202 North Cave Creek Rd.
Scottsdale, AZ 85262
(480) 595-3300

Map References

BLM Theodore Roosevelt Lake (incomplete)
USFS Tonto National Forest: Cave Creek Ranger District (incomplete)
USGS 1:24,000 Humboldt Mt., New River Mesa
1:100,000 Theodore Roosevelt Lake (incomplete)
Maptech CD-ROM: Phoenix/Superstition Mountains
Arizona Atlas & Gazetteer, p. 49

Route Directions

▼ 0.0		From Central #27: Camp Creek Road, 0.6 miles north of the Cave Creek Group Campsite, zero trip meter and turn northwest

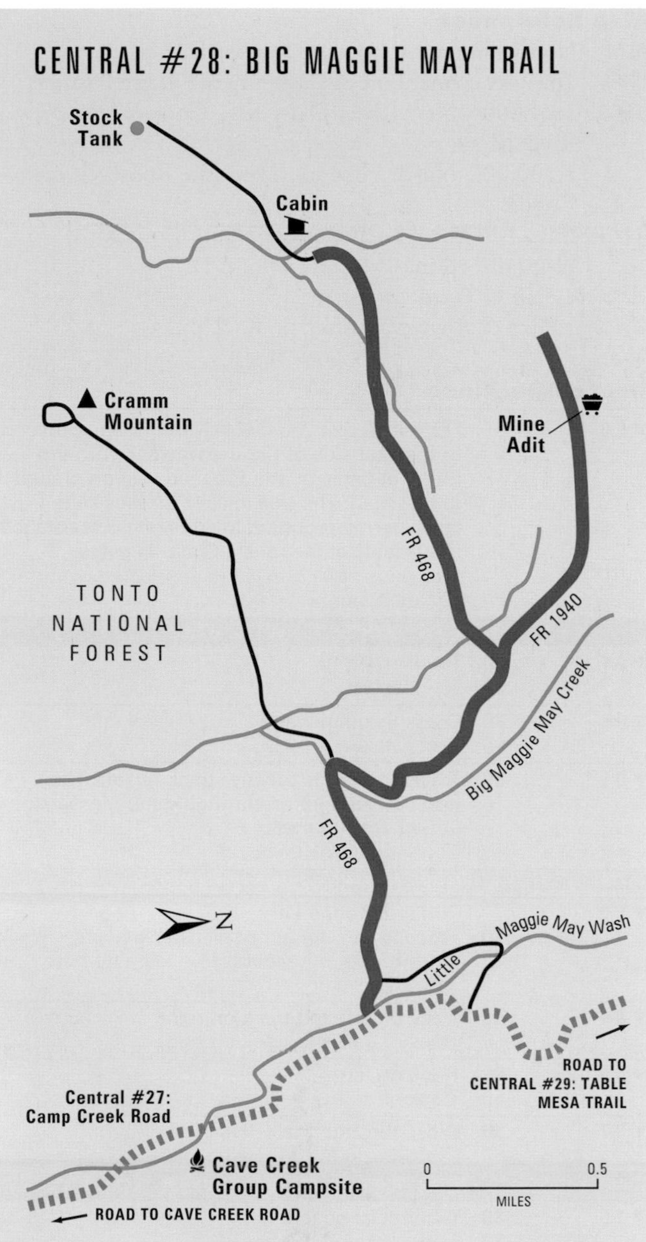

		onto small, roughly graded trail and immediately cross through Little Maggie May Wash. The trail is marked FR 468.
		GPS: N33°58.93' W111°52.31'
▼ 0.1	BL	Track on right.
▼ 0.4	SO	Track on left.
▼ 0.8	TR	Track on left is FR 472 and is closed immediately ahead. Turn right, remaining on FR 468 and cross through Big Maggie May Creek.
		GPS: N33°58.90' W111°53.11'
▼ 1.6	SO	Well-used track on left is FR 468. Trail ahead is FR 1940. From here there are two spurs. Zero trip meter.
		GPS: N33°59.35' W111°53.37'

Spur Trail to Mine Adit, FR 1940

▼ 0.0		Continue to the west.
▼ 0.1	SO	Track on left is alternative way around the next steep descent.
▼ 0.2	SO	Track on left rejoins.
▼ 0.6	SO	Views ahead over Grays Gulch to New River Mesa and Black Mesa.
▼ 0.8	SO	Track on left.
		GPS: N33°59.56' W111°54.06'
▼ 0.9	SO	Adit on right; track on left. This is the best point to turn around.
▼ 1.3	UT	Trail peters out and is not used past this point.
		GPS: N33°59.48' W111°54.39'

Spur Trail to Cabin, FR 468

▼ 0.0	TL	Continue southwest on FR 468.
		GPS: N33°59.35' W111°53.37'
▼ 0.2	SO	Cross through wash.
▼ 0.5	SO	Faint track on left at saddle; views ahead over Grays Gulch and New River Mesa.
▼ 0.9	TR	4-way intersection. Track on left is FR 172; track ahead is unmarked. Turn right, remaining on FR 468.
		GPS: N33°59.08' W111°54.11'
▼ 1.0	SO	Cross through wash.
▼ 1.2	SO	Faint track on right to tank; then well-used track on left at wash crossing.
		GPS: N33°59.07' W111°54.37'
▼ 1.3	SO	Track on right.
		GPS: N33°59.05' W111°54.47'
▼ 1.5	SO	Track on right and track on left.
		GPS: N33°58.97' W111°54.68'
▼ 1.6		Old stone and timber cabin on right; also a pleasant campsite on a rise above the wash. The trail continues past this point for 1 mile to a stock tank, after which it is hardly used.
		GPS: N33°58.93' W111°54.67'

CENTRAL REGION TRAIL #29

Table Mesa Trail

Starting Point:	**I-17 at exit 236**
Finishing Point:	**Central #27: Camp Creek Road, 3.1 miles north of Seven Springs Recreation Site**
Total Mileage:	**18.2 miles**
Unpaved Mileage:	**18.2 miles**
Driving Time:	**3.5 hours**
Elevation Range:	**2,200–4,200 feet**
Usually Open:	**Year-round**
Best Time to Travel:	**October to May**
Difficulty Rating:	**5**
Scenic Rating:	**9**
Remoteness Rating:	**+0**

Special Attractions

- Extremely pretty, moderately rated trail through classic desert scenery.
- Views of New River Mesa and the New River.
- Interesting old line cabin.

Granite boulders stand out against the quiet Sonoran desert landscape

Description

This moderate trail crosses from I-17 north of New River to join Central #27: Camp Creek Road to the north of Carefree. The western section of the trail crosses through a mixture of private property and state trust land. Access across the private property is granted under the Sportsman-Landowner Respect Program. Please respect the landowners' property; access can be revoked at any time. To travel this trail, a state land permit is also required.

After 4 miles the trail enters the Tonto National Forest and travels along a rough, formed road around the side of the New River Mountains toward West Point. The surface is loose and lumpy, with a mixture of embedded rocks and rubble. Off-road tires are a big advantage, both for traction on the unstable surface and to reduce the risk of a flat from the sharp stones. The trail climbs a narrow shelf road to a saddle near West Point. This climb is probably the most challenging part of the trail, but a high-clearance 4WD and a careful driver should have no difficulty. As you climb, you can see the small town of New River back to the west.

From the saddle, the trail undulates its way to the east toward New River Canyon through some extremely scenic Sonoran desert scenery. Some of the short climbs can be steep, but generally the trail is consistent in its standard. Travel is slow for the most part, but the spectacular and varied vegetation—giant saguaros, ocotillos, prickly pears, creosote bushes, chollas, and barrel cacti—scattered over the rugged canyon terrain makes it pure pleasure to drive slowly. There are also very photogenic groupings of large granite rocks and boulders.

Midway along the trail is an old cabin constructed of stone, timber, and corrugated iron. It is very likely that the structure was used as a line cabin for cowboys during cattle roundups.

Shortly after the cabin, the trail standard improves to a roughly graded dirt road as it runs along the ridge top to join Central #27: Camp Creek Road.

Current Road Information

Tonto National Forest
Cave Creek Ranger District
40202 North Cave Creek Rd.
Scottsdale, AZ 85262
(480) 595-3300

Map References

BLM North Phoenix, Theodore Roosevelt Lake, Payson
USFS Tonto National Forest: Cave Creek Ranger District
USGS 1:24,000 New River, Daisy Mt., Cooks Mesa, New River Mesa
1:100,000 North Phoenix, Theodore Roosevelt Lake, Payson
Maptech CD-ROM: Phoenix/Superstition Mountains; Flagstaff/Sedona/Prescott
Arizona Atlas & Gazetteer, p. 49
Arizona Road & Recreation Atlas, p. 40 & p. 74

Route Directions

▼ 0.0		From I-17, exit 236 (Table Mesa Road), proceed to the east side of the freeway and zero trip meter at cattle guard. Proceed east on graded gravel road. The trail initially crosses state trust land; permit required. In addition no assistance is available at the ranch. Close all gates.
0.9 ▲		Trail ends at I-17, exit 236, immediately north of New River.
		GPS: N33°58.11' W112°07.56'
▼ 0.1	SO	Track on right.
0.8 ▲	SO	Track on left.
▼ 0.5	SO	Cross through wash.
0.4 ▲	SO	Cross through wash.
▼ 0.9	SO	Track on right is private; track on left. Then proceed straight on through gate; please close gate. Zero trip meter.
0.0 ▲		Continue to the west.
		GPS: N33°58.42' W112°06.65'
▼ 0.0		Continue to the east.
3.1 ▲	SO	Proceed through gate; please close gate. Track on right and private track on left after gate. Zero trip meter.
▼ 0.4	SO	Track on left and track on right.
2.7 ▲	SO	Track on left and track on right.
▼ 0.5	SO	Track on left.
2.6 ▲	SO	Track on right.
▼ 0.7	SO	Cross through New River.
2.4 ▲	SO	Cross through New River.
		GPS: N33°58.43' W112°05.92'
▼ 1.0	SO	Two tracks on left.
2.1 ▲	SO	Two tracks on right.
▼ 1.6	BL	Cross through wash; then bear left with the quarry on your right. Trail drops in standard to become a formed trail.
1.5 ▲	BR	Trail standard is now a roughly graded road. Bear right with the quarry on your left and cross through wash.
		GPS: N33°58.39' W112°05.02'
▼ 1.7	SO	Track on right.
1.4 ▲	SO	Track on left.
▼ 1.8	SO	Track on left.
1.3 ▲	SO	Track on right.
▼ 1.9	SO	Two tracks on left.
1.2 ▲	SO	Two tracks on right.
▼ 2.1	SO	Track on left.
1.0 ▲	SO	Track on right.
▼ 2.4	SO	Cross through wash.
0.7 ▲	SO	Cross through wash.
▼ 2.9	SO	Cross through wash.
0.2 ▲	SO	Cross through wash.
▼ 3.1	SO	Cattle guard; corral on right. Entering Tonto

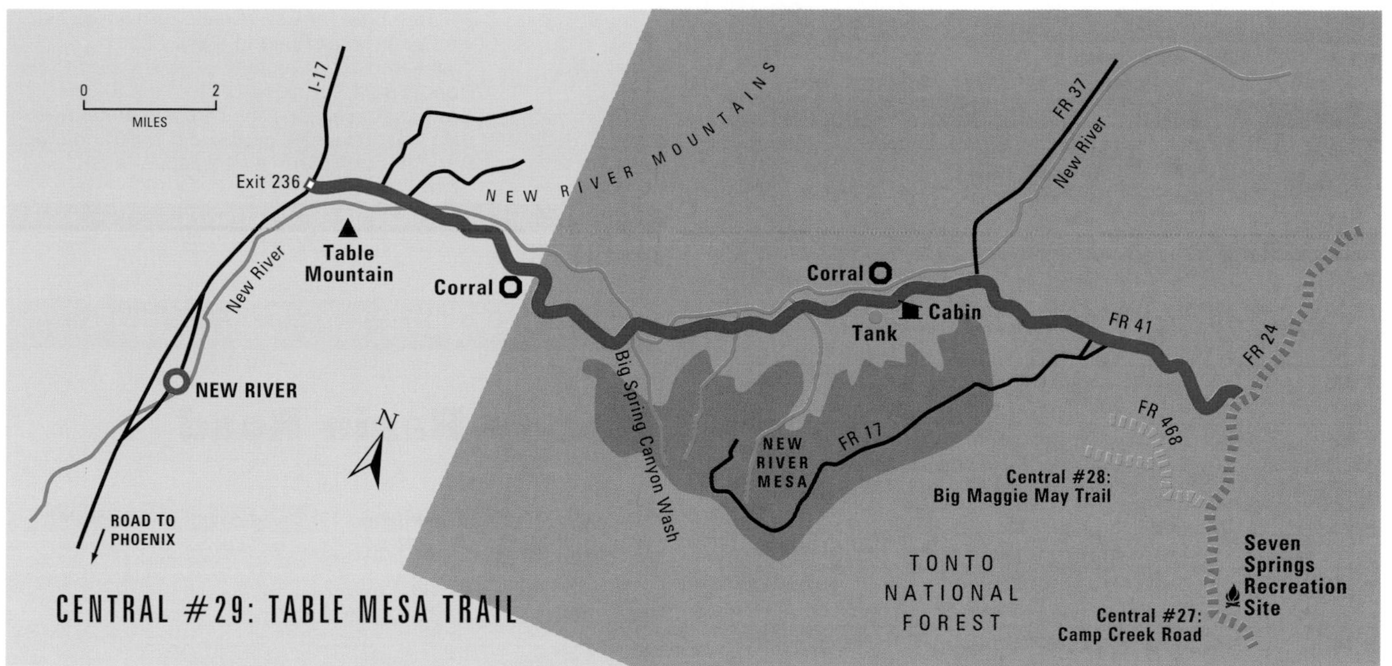

			National Forest. Zero trip meter. Road is now marked FR 41.
	0.0 ▲		Continue to the west.
			GPS: N33°58.29' W112°03.86'
▼ 0.0			Continue to the east; track on right.
	7.1 ▲	SO	Track on left; leaving Tonto National Forest over cattle guard. Corral on left. Zero trip meter.
▼ 0.1		BR	Cross through wash; then bear right, remaining on FR 41. Track on left is FR 1484; then second track on left.
	7.0 ▲	BL	Bear left, remaining on FR 41. Two tracks on right, second of which is FR 1484.
			GPS: N33°58.33' W112°03.72'
▼ 0.8		SO	Track on right. Trail starts to climb to saddle.
	6.3 ▲	SO	Track on left; end of descent from saddle.
▼ 1.2		SO	Saddle; top of climb.
	5.9 ▲	SO	Saddle; top of climb.
			GPS: N33°57.87' W112°03.24'
▼ 1.8		SO	Cattle guard.
	5.3 ▲	SO	Cattle guard.
▼ 2.1		SO	Track on right at saddle.
	5.0 ▲	SO	Track on left at saddle.
			GPS: N33°57.84' W112°02.35'
▼ 2.8		SO	Cross through Big Spring Canyon wash.
	4.3 ▲	SO	Cross through Big Spring Canyon wash.
			GPS: N33°58.13' W112°02.03'
▼ 3.0		SO	Cross through New River wash.
	4.1 ▲	SO	Cross through New River wash.
			GPS: N33°58.15' W112°01.79'
▼ 3.1		SO	Cross through wash.
	4.0 ▲	SO	Cross through wash.
▼ 3.4		SO	Cross through New River wash.
	3.7 ▲	SO	Cross through New River wash.
▼ 3.6		SO	Track forks and rejoins almost immediately.
	3.5 ▲	SO	Track forks and rejoins almost immediately.
			GPS: N33°58.26' W112°01.39'
▼ 3.8		SO	Small track on left.
	3.3 ▲	SO	Small track on right.
▼ 4.4		SO	Cross through wash.
	2.7 ▲	SO	Cross through wash.
▼ 4.7		SO	Cross through wash.
	2.4 ▲	SO	Cross through wash.
			GPS: N33°58.72' W112°00.43'
▼ 5.0		SO	Track on left.
	2.1 ▲	SO	Track on right.
▼ 5.2		BR	Cross through wash; then trail forks; right-hand fork is easier.
	1.9 ▲	SO	Fork rejoins.
▼ 5.3		SO	Fork rejoins in front of large pile of balanced rocks.
	1.8 ▲	BL	Trail forks by large pile of balanced rocks; left-hand fork is easier.
▼ 5.8		SO	Cross through wash.
	1.3 ▲	SO	Cross through wash.
			GPS: N33°59.35' W111°59.77'
▼ 6.3		SO	Small track on left.
	0.8 ▲	SO	Small track on right.
▼ 6.5		SO	Cross through wash.
	0.6 ▲	SO	Cross through wash.
▼ 6.6		SO	Pass through wire gate.
	0.5 ▲	SO	Pass through wire gate.

This old cabin stands beside the trail near Robbers Roost Spring

			GPS: N33°59.57′ W111°59.13′
▼ 6.7		SO	Track on left.
	0.4 ▲	BL	Track on right; bear left away from wash.
			GPS: N33°59.61′ W111°59.06′
▼ 7.1		SO	Tank on right; corral on left; pass through wire gate and zero trip meter.
	0.0 ▲		Continue to the southwest and pass corral on right and tank on left.
			GPS: N33°59.72′ W111°59.66′
▼ 0.0			Continue to the northeast and pass cabin on right.
	1.8 ▲	SO	Cabin on left; then pass through wire gate and zero trip meter.
▼ 0.1		SO	Cross through two washes.
	1.7 ▲	SO	Cross through two washes.
▼ 0.4		SO	Pass through wire gate; then corral on right.
	1.4 ▲	SO	Corral on left; then pass through wire gate.
			GPS: N33°59.91′ W111°58.34′
▼ 0.6		SO	Cross through wash.
	1.2 ▲	SO	Cross through wash.
▼ 1.0		SO	Cross through wash.
	0.8 ▲	SO	Cross through wash.
▼ 1.7		SO	Cross through wash.
	0.1 ▲	SO	Cross through wash.
▼ 1.8		TR	T-intersection. Track on left is FR 37. Turn right, remaining on FR 41. Zero trip meter.
	0.0 ▲		Continue to the south. Trail is now a formed trail.
			GPS: N34°00.57′ W111°57.23′
▼ 0.0			Continue to the east. Trail is now a roughly graded single track.
	2.5 ▲	TL	Turn left, remaining on FR 41. Track ahead becomes FR 37. Zero trip meter.
▼ 1.5		SO	Cross through wash.
	1.0 ▲	SO	Cross through wash.
▼ 2.1		SO	Viewpoint on left at saddle.
	0.4 ▲	SO	Viewpoint on right at saddle.
▼ 2.3		SO	Track on left is FR 374; then cattle guard.
	0.2 ▲	SO	Cattle guard; then track on right is FR 374.
			GPS: N34°00.43′ W111°55.32′
▼ 2.5		SO	Track on right is FR 17. Zero trip meter.
	0.0 ▲		Continue to the west.
			GPS: N34°00.42′ W111°55.07′
▼ 0.0			Continue to the east.
	2.8 ▲	SO	Track on left is second entrance to FR 17. Zero trip meter.
▼ 0.1		BL	Track on right is second entrance to FR 17. Continue on FR 41.
	2.7 ▲	BR	Track on left is FR 17. Continue on FR 41.
			GPS: N34°00.43′ W111°54.92′
▼ 0.7		SO	Track on right is FR 321.
	2.1 ▲	SO	Track on left is FR 321.
			GPS: N34°00.48′ W111°54.43′
▼ 1.5		SO	Track on right.
	1.3 ▲	SO	Track on left.
▼ 2.4		BL	Track on right is FR 1115.
	0.4 ▲	BR	Track on left is FR 1115.
			GPS: N34°00.29′ W111°52.93′
▼ 2.6		SO	Track on left.
	0.2 ▲	SO	Track on right.
▼ 2.7		SO	Cross through two washes.
	0.1 ▲	SO	Cross through two washes.
▼ 2.8			Cross through wash. Trail ends at the intersection with Central #27: Camp Creek Road, FR 24. Turn right for Cave Creek; turn left to exit via Camp Creek Road to Bloody Basin.
	0.0 ▲		Trail commences on Central #27: Camp Creek Road, FR 24, 3.1 miles north of the Seven Springs Recreation Site. Zero trip meter and turn west on small, graded dirt road and cross through creek. Turn is marked FR 41 to New River Canyon.
			GPS: N34°00.55′ W111°52.75′

CENTRAL REGION TRAIL #30

Bloody Basin Road

Starting Point:	**Central #27: Camp Creek Road (FR 24)**
Finishing Point:	**I-17, exit 259**
Total Mileage:	**24.7 miles**
Unpaved Mileage:	**24.6 miles**
Driving Time:	**2 hours**
Elevation Range:	**3,000–5,000 feet**
Usually Open:	**Year-round**
Best Time to Travel:	**October to May**
Difficulty Rating:	**2**
Scenic Rating:	**9**
Remoteness Rating:	**+0**

Special Attractions

- Agua Fria National Monument and Agua Fria River.
- Panoramic views of Bloody Basin and the surrounding mountains.

Description

This easygoing trail passes through some spectacular, remote scenery east of the Agua Fria River as well as in the Agua Fria National Monument. In dry weather it is suitable for high-clearance vehicles, but in wet weather it becomes impassable, as signs at the start and finish of the trail warn. In addition the

Prickly pears, mesquites, and ocotillos stand out against the red ridges in Bloody Basin

Agua Fria River, a lush oasis in this dry landscape

ford through the Agua Fria River near the western end of the trail can be temporarily impassable after heavy rain.

The roughly graded trail leaves Bloody Basin to climb up a high ridge. From the top there are broad views back into Bloody Basin and over a rugged group of hills to the south in Tonto National Forest. North of the ridge is the Hutch Gulch drainage; to the south is Mud Spring Creek. The red soil of the road, the distant mountains, and the contrasting green vegetation—prickly pears, mesquites, ocotillos, and yuccas—make the views from this section some of the best along the trail. Many people have become lost in this rough region, including a family whose members were lost in Bloody Basin in 1949 and nearly froze to death before being found.

Bloody Basin supposedly gained its name from the number of Indian fights in it. There are Indian ruins scattered over the area, many of which are now incorporated into the Agua Fria National Monument, designated by President Clinton in 1999. Within the national monument the standard of the road improves and has a light gravelly surface. This section is suitable for passenger vehicles in dry weather. Within the monument the scenery is gentler and the vegetation is sparser as you descend. Sagebrush replaces the more varied vegetation on the ridge tops. The road swoops down to cross through the deep gorge containing the Agua Fria River—Spanish for "cold water." There is no bridge, but under normal conditions the river just trickles over the concrete ford. Do not enter the crossing if the water level is high.

Rock hounds can sometimes find specimens of peacock scattered around the old copper workings throughout the national forest.

Current Road Information

Tonto National Forest
Cave Creek Ranger District
40202 North Cave Creek Rd.
Scottsdale, AZ 85262
(480) 595-3300

Map References

BLM Payson, Bradshaw Mts.
USFS Tonto National Forest: Cave Creek Ranger District
USGS 1:24,000 Bloody Basin, Brooklyn Peak, Joes Hill, Cordes Junction
1:100,000 Payson, Bradshaw Mts.
Maptech CD-ROM: Flagstaff/Sedona/Prescott
Arizona Atlas & Gazetteer, p. 49
Arizona Road & Recreation Atlas, pp. 41, 40 & pp. 75, 74
Recreational Map of Arizona

Route Directions

Mileage			Directions
▼ 0.0			From the intersection of Central #27: Camp Creek Road (FR 24) and Bloody Basin Road (FR 269) at Bloody Basin, zero trip meter and turn west on FR 269, following the sign to I-17.
	8.1 ▲		Trail ends at the intersection with Central #27: Camp Creek Road (FR 24). Turn right to continue along this trail to Cave Creek; continue straight to visit Sheep Bridge.
			GPS: N34°09.34' W111°49.27'
▼ 0.2		SO	Track on right.
	7.9 ▲	SO	Track on left.
▼ 0.5		SO	Cross through wash.
	7.6 ▲	SO	Cross through wash.
▼ 0.6		SO	Track on left is FR 552.
	7.5 ▲	SO	Track on right is FR 552.
▼ 0.7		SO	Cross through wash.
	7.4 ▲	SO	Cross through wash.
			GPS: N34°09.73' W111°49.83'
▼ 2.2		SO	Track on left.
	5.9 ▲	SO	Track on right.
▼ 2.3		SO	Track on right.
	5.8 ▲	SO	Track on left.
▼ 2.7		SO	Cross through wash.
	5.4 ▲	SO	Cross through wash.
▼ 3.4		SO	Cattle guard.
	4.7 ▲	SO	Cattle guard.
▼ 3.9		SO	Track on right is FR 578.
	4.2 ▲	SO	Track on left is FR 578.
			GPS: N34°11.10' W111°51.45'
▼ 6.5		SO	Track on right is FR 399.
	1.6 ▲	SO	Track on left is FR 399.
			GPS: N34°12.25' W111°53.07'
▼ 7.5		SO	Top of saddle. Rugged Mesa on right. Views back into Bloody Basin.
	0.6 ▲	SO	Top of saddle. Rugged Mesa on left. Views ahead into Bloody Basin.
			GPS: N34°12.71' W111°53.32'
▼ 8.0		SO	Track on right.
	0.1 ▲	SO	Track on left.
			GPS: N34°12.75' W111°53.81'
▼ 8.1		SO	Well-used track on left is FR 58, which goes 0.6 miles to Wood Camp Cabin. Cabin destroyed by fire in late 1990s. Zero trip meter.
	0.0 ▲		Continue to the east.
			GPS: N34°12.73' W111°53.91'
▼ 0.0			Continue to the west and cross through wash. Track on right after wash is FR 44.
	5.8 ▲	SO	Track on left is FR 44; then cross through wash. Then well-used track on right is FR 58, which goes 0.6 miles to Wood Camp Cabin. Cabin destroyed by fire in late 1990s. Zero trip meter.
▼ 0.1		SO	Cattle guard.
	5.7 ▲	SO	Cattle guard.
▼ 0.2		SO	Cross through wash.
	5.6 ▲	SO	Cross through wash.
▼ 0.6		SO	Track on left to stock tank.
	5.2 ▲	SO	Track on right to stock tank.

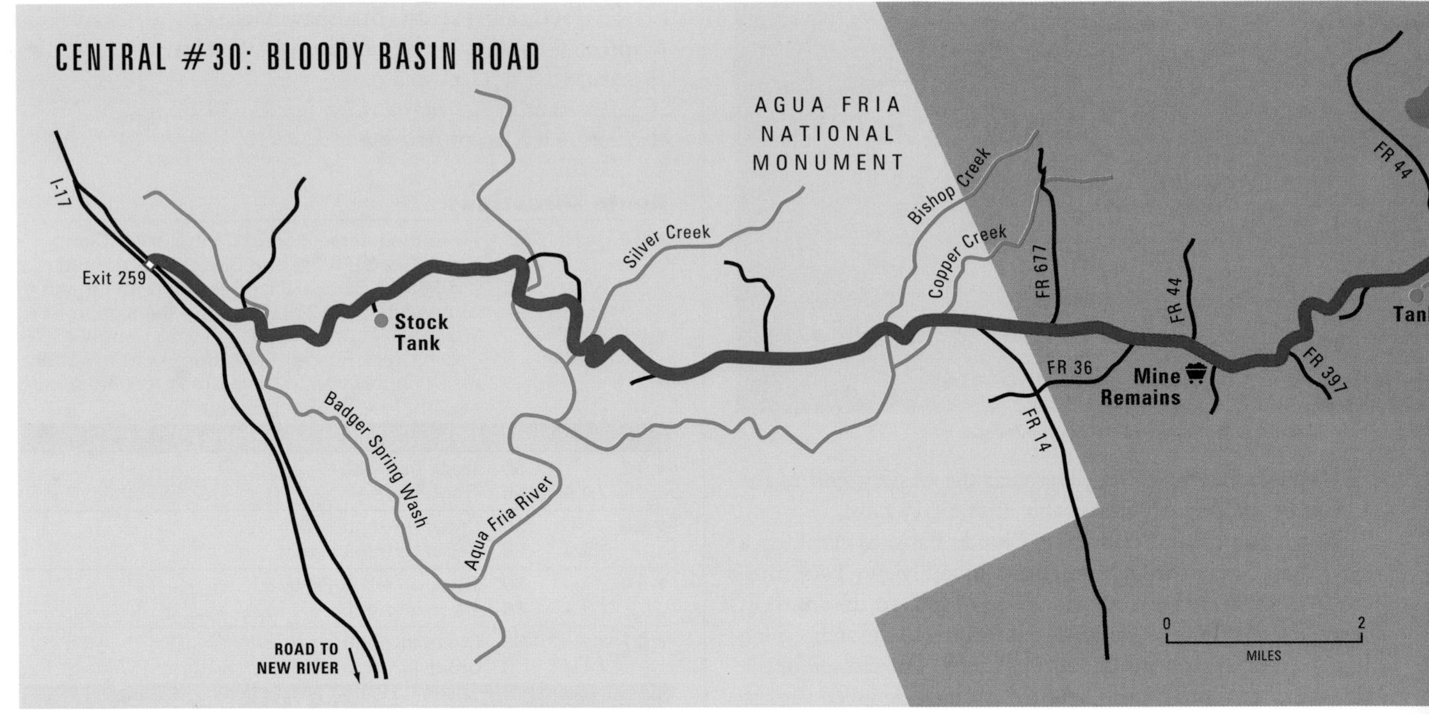

▼ 0.9 SO Track on right; then track on left on top of ridge. Trail now descends toward the Agua Fria River.
4.9 ▲ SO Track on right; then track on left on top of ridge. Trail now descends toward Bloody Basin.

GPS: N34°12.69' W111°54.80'

▼ 1.2 SO Track on right.
4.6 ▲ SO Track on left.

▼ 2.6 SO Track on left is FR 397; then cross through wash.
3.2 ▲ SO Cross through wash; then track on right is FR 397.

▼ 3.0 SO Cattle guard.
2.8 ▲ SO Cattle guard.

▼ 3.1 SO Track on left.
2.7 ▲ SO Track on right.

GPS: N34°12.36' W111°56.69'

▼ 3.3 SO Track on left to diggings. Mine tailings visible on hill on left.
2.5 ▲ SO Track on right to diggings. Mine tailings visible on hill on right.

▼ 3.4 SO Track on left.
2.4 ▲ SO Track on right.

▼ 3.6 SO Track on right is FR 44.
2.2 ▲ SO Track on left is FR 44.

GPS: N34°12.67' W111°56.99'

▼ 4.7 SO Track on left is FR 36.
1.1 ▲ SO Track on right is FR 36.

GPS: N34°13.03' W111°58.07'

▼ 4.9 SO Cross through wash.
0.9 ▲ SO Cross through wash.

▼ 5.5 SO Track on right is FR 677, also part of the Great Western Trail.
0.3 ▲ SO Track on left is FR 677, also part of the Great Western Trail.

GPS: N34°13.36' W111°58.80'

▼ 5.8 SO Entering the Agua Fria National Monument over cattle guard. Zero trip meter.
0.0 ▲ Continue to the east.

GPS: N34°13.50' W111°59.10

▼ 0.0 Continue to the west toward the Agua Fria River.
5.4 ▲ SO Entering Tonto National Forest over cattle guard. Zero trip meter.

▼ 0.3 SO Two tracks on right to stock tank.
5.1 ▲ SO Two tracks on left to stock tank.

▼ 0.4 SO Track on left is FR 14.
5.0 ▲ SO Track on right is FR 14.

GPS: N34°13.68' W111°59.47'

▼ 0.7 SO Cross through Copper Creek on paved ford.
4.7 ▲ SO Cross through Copper Creek on paved ford.

GPS: N34°13.82' W111°59.82'

▼ 0.9 SO Track on left.
4.5 ▲ SO Track on right.

▼ 1.3 SO Track on right; then cross through Bishop Creek.
4.1 ▲ SO Cross through Bishop Creek; then track on left.

GPS: N34°13.91' W112°00.37'

▼ 2.7 SO Track on right; then cattle guard.
2.7 ▲ SO Cattle guard; then track on left.

▼ 2.9 SO Track on right.
2.5 ▲ SO Track on left.

▼ 3.7 SO Track on left.
1.7 ▲ SO Track on right.

▼ 4.2 SO Cattle guard.
1.2 ▲ SO Cattle guard.

▼ 4.9 SO Track on left; then cross through Silver Creek.
0.5 ▲ SO Cross through Silver Creek; then track on right.

GPS: N34°14.82' W112°03.42'

▼ 5.0 SO Track on right.
0.4 ▲ SO Track on left.

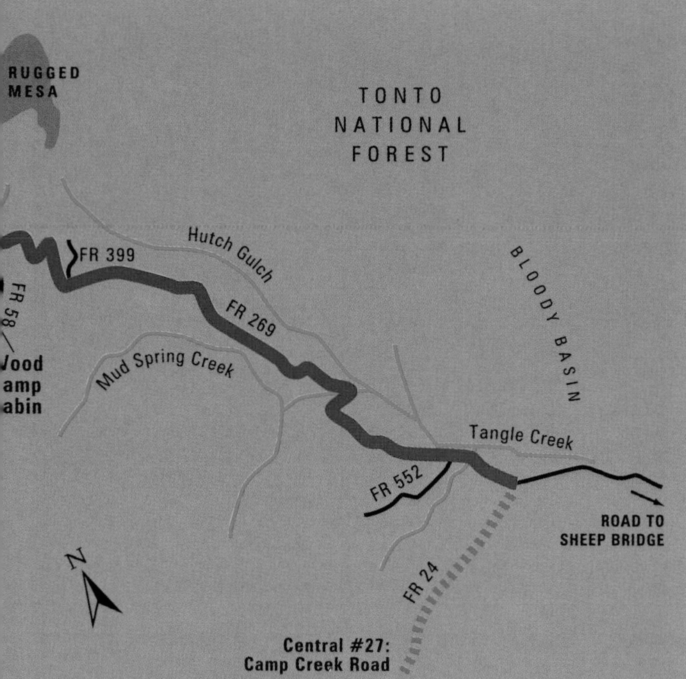

Mileage		Description
▼ 5.4	BL	Graded road on right goes into private property. Bear left, remaining on FR 269. Zero trip meter.
0.0 ▲		Continue to the south.
		GPS: N34°15.18′ W112°03.26′
▼ 0.0		Continue to the northwest toward I-17.
5.4 ▲	SO	Graded road on left goes into private property. Bear right, remaining on FR 269, following the sign for Bloody Basin. Zero trip meter.
▼ 0.2	SO	Cattle guard.
5.2 ▲	SO	Cattle guard.
▼ 0.6	SO	Cross through Agua Fria River on concrete ford.
4.8 ▲	SO	Cross through Agua Fria River on concrete ford.
		GPS: N34°15.43′ W112°03.79′
▼ 0.8	SO	Graded road on right is private.
4.6 ▲	SO	Graded road on left is private.
		GPS: N34°15.59′ W112°03.68′
▼ 2.6	SO	Two tracks on left to stock tank.
2.8 ▲	SO	Two tracks on right to stock tank.
▼ 3.0	SO	Cattle guard.
2.4 ▲	SO	Cattle guard; passing through Horseshoe Ranch.
		GPS: N34°15.99′ W112°05.56′
▼ 4.0	SO	Cross through wash.
1.4 ▲	SO	Cross through wash.
▼ 4.1	SO	Cross through Badger Spring Wash.
1.3 ▲	SO	Cross through Badger Spring Wash.
▼ 4.8	SO	Track on right is emergency use only.
0.6 ▲	SO	Track on left is emergency use only.
▼ 5.3	SO	Cattle guard; road turns to paved.
0.1 ▲	SO	Cattle guard; road turns to graded dirt.
▼ 5.4		Trail ends at the intersection of I-17 at exit 259.
0.0 ▲		Trail commences from I-17 at exit 259. Exit the freeway and proceed to the east side. Zero trip meter and continue southeast on paved road, signed Bloody Basin Road.
		GPS: N34°17.07′ W112°07.17′

CENTRAL REGION TRAIL #31

Indian Spring Wash Trail

Starting Point:	**Bartlett Dam Road, 9 miles east of intersection with Central #27: Camp Creek Road**
Finishing Point:	**Verde River**
Total Mileage:	**5.6 miles**
Unpaved Mileage:	**5.6 miles**
Driving Time:	**45 minutes (one-way)**
Elevation Range:	**1,800–3,300 feet**
Usually Open:	**Year-round**
Best Time to Travel:	**October to May**
Difficulty Rating:	**3**
Scenic Rating:	**8**
Remoteness Rating:	**+0**

Special Attractions

- Access to the Verde River.
- Easy, scenic trail along Indian Spring Wash.

Description

This delightful trail takes a meandering route of 5.6 miles to reach an open section of the Verde River. The trail is easygoing and smooth for its length as it drops steadily down along Indian Spring Wash. There are a few uneven, moguled sections that give the trail its 3-rating; these will stretch your suspension.

The trail follows along Indian Spring Wash before turning to run along the ridge tops, passing between St. Clair Peak and Indian Butte. The canyon is fairly wide and there are good views down to the Verde River Valley and the Mazatzal Mountains on the far side.

The trail is single-vehicle width only and fairly densely vegetated; however, it is well used and not especially brushy. Be careful of fast-moving, oncoming vehicles. The twists and turns of the trail make it hard to see other vehicles.

The gradual sandy descent of Indian Spring Wash

The Verde River at the end of the trail

The trail finishes at the Verde River, a cool, welcome spot for a break. There are a couple of campsites at the end of the trail. The river usually has enough water in it for a good splash.

Current Road Information

Tonto National Forest
Cave Creek Ranger District
40202 North Cave Creek Rd.
Scottsdale, AZ 85262
(480) 595-3300

Map References

BLM Theodore Roosevelt Lake
USFS Tonto National Forest: Cave Creek Ranger District
USGS 1:24,000 Bartlett Dam, Horseshoe Dam
1:100,000 Theodore Roosevelt Lake
Maptech CD-ROM: Phoenix/Superstition Mountains
Arizona Atlas & Gazetteer, p. 50
Arizona Road & Recreation Atlas, p. 41 & p. 75

Route Directions

▼ 0.0		From Bartlett Dam Road, 9 miles east of the intersection with Central #27: Camp Creek Road, zero trip meter and turn north on graded dirt road marked FR 532 at the sign for Indian Spring Wash.
		GPS: N33°51.57' W111°42.21'
▼ 0.7	SO	Track on left.
▼ 0.9	SO	Track on right through campsite. Remain on FR 532.
		GPS: N33°52.29' W111°42.14'
▼ 1.4	BL	Trail forks; track on right.
		GPS: N33°52.70' W111°42.24'
▼ 1.7	SO	Track on right. Trail climbs up ridge—there is a choice of ways to climb up.
		GPS: N33°53°06' W111°42.36'
▼ 1.9	SO	Track on left.
▼ 2.1	BL	Track on right toward Indian Butte.
		GPS: N33°53.25' W111°42.46'
▼ 2.2	TR	Track straight on is FR 1104. Turn right and start to descend. Zero trip meter.
		GPS: N33°53.27' W111°42.60'

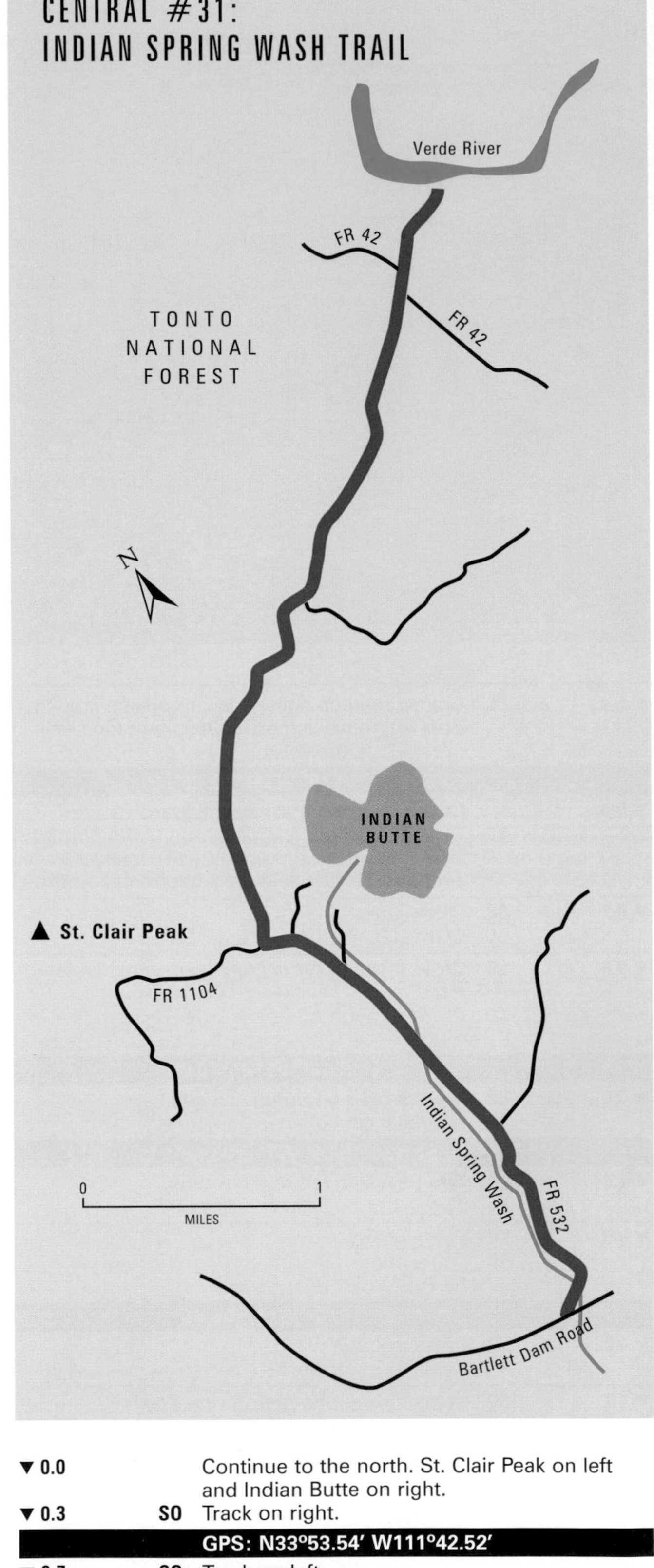

▼ 0.0		Continue to the north. St. Clair Peak on left and Indian Butte on right.
▼ 0.3	SO	Track on right.
		GPS: N33°53.54' W111°42.52'
▼ 0.7	SO	Track on left.
▼ 1.6	SO	Track on right.
		GPS: N33°54.30' W111°41.76'
▼ 1.9	SO	Track on left.
		GPS: N33°54.51' W112°41.49'

▼ 2.9	SO	Well-used track on right is FR 42.
		GPS: N33°55.07′ W111°40.71′
▼ 3.1	SO	Well-used track on left is also FR 42. Zero trip meter.
		GPS: N33°55.23′ W111°40.56′
▼ 0.0		Continue to the northeast.
▼ 0.2	SO	Track on right.
		GPS: N33°55.34′ W111°40.37′
▼ 0.3		Trail ends at the Verde River. Tracks on right and left to small campsites.
		GPS: N33°55.38′ W111°40.30′

CENTRAL REGION TRAIL #32

Control Road

Starting Point:	**Arizona 260, 14.5 miles northeast of Payson**
Finishing Point:	**Arizona 87, 3 miles south of Pine**
Total Mileage:	**22.1 miles**
Unpaved Mileage:	**21.2 miles**
Driving Time:	**1.25 hours**
Elevation Range:	**5,200–6,000 feet**
Usually Open:	**Year-round**
Best Time to Travel:	**Year-round**
Difficulty Rating:	**1**
Scenic Rating:	**7**
Remoteness Rating:	**+0**

Special Attractions

- Views of the scarp face of the Mogollon Rim.
- Access to many small trails and shady backcountry campsites.
- The East Verde River.

Bray Creek crossing

Description

Control Road follows a loop along the base of the Mogollon (pronounced "muggy-own") Rim. Most of the trail runs through tall ponderosa pines, which provide shade over a number of campsites. Many small trails crisscross the main trail, giving access to the base of the Mogollon Rim and into the pine forest on the south of the trail. Other side trails lead to hiking trails.

The trail is wide, smooth, graded dirt along its length. Those driving passenger vehicles should have no problems in dry weather. Tonto Village has a small cafe, bar, and general store, but otherwise there are no services along the trail. The village is home to many holiday communities and some more-permanent settlers.

The steep face of the Mogollon Rim in the distance

The trail passes close to the site of one of the worst forest fires in Arizona history. In June 1990 the Dude Fire, started by a lightning strike, burned more than 24,000 acres of forest. Six lives were lost and 50 homes were destroyed. The historic Zane Grey Cabin was also lost in the blaze.

For rock hounds, samples of very clear quartz crystals can be found in the creek bed along the Diamond Point Road (FR 65).

Current Road Information

Tonto National Forest
Payson Ranger District
1009 East Highway 260
Payson, AZ 85541
(520) 474-7900

Map References

BLM Payson
USFS Tonto National Forest: Payson Ranger District
USGS 1:24,000 Promontory Butte, Diamond Point, Dane Canyon, Kehl Ridge, Payson North, Buckhead Mesa
1:100,000 Payson
Maptech CD-ROM: Flagstaff/Sedona/Prescott
Arizona Atlas & Gazetteer, p. 50
Arizona Road & Recreation Atlas, p. 41 & p. 75
Recreational Map of Arizona

Route Directions

▼ 0.0			From Arizona 260, 14.5 miles northeast of Payson at mile marker 267, zero trip meter and turn northwest on paved FR 64, which is signposted for Control Road and Tonto Village. Cross cattle guard; then track on right at message board.
	0.9 ▲		Track on left at message board; then cattle guard. Then trail ends at intersection with Arizona 260. Turn right for Payson; turn left for Heber.
			GPS: N34°19.01′ W111°06.91′
▼ 0.2		SO	Track on right.
	0.7 ▲	SO	Track on left.
▼ 0.4		SO	Track on right along power lines.
	0.5 ▲	SO	Track on left along power lines.
▼ 0.5		SO	Track on left.
	0.4 ▲	SO	Track on right.
▼ 0.7		SO	Track on left.
	0.2 ▲	SO	Track on right.
▼ 0.9		BL	Bear left and cross through wash on concrete ford; road is now graded dirt. Paved road on right goes into Tonto Village. Small track on left. Zero trip meter.

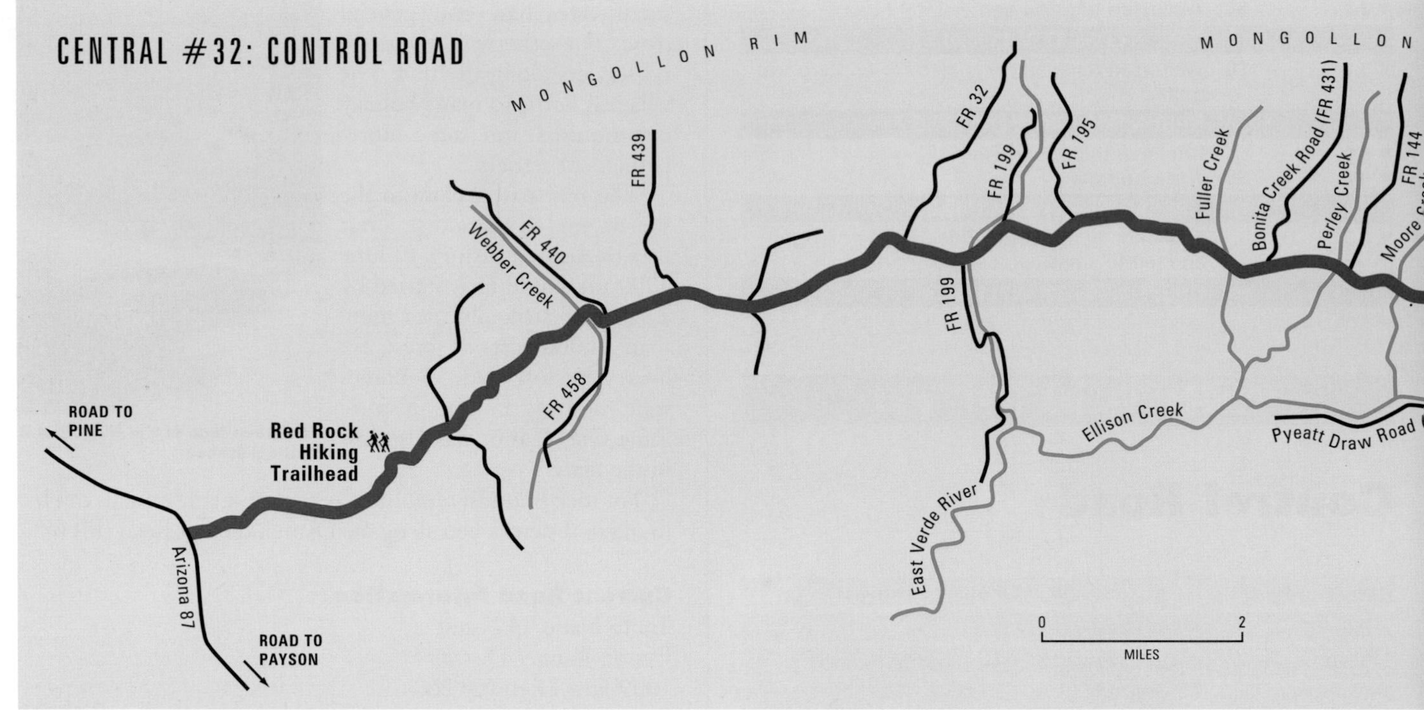

▼	▲		
	0.0 ▲		Continue to the east.
			GPS: N34°18.97′ W111°07.88′
▼ 0.0			Continue to the west.
	3.0 ▲	SO	Cross through wash on concrete ford; road is now paved. Paved road on left goes into Tonto Village. Small track on right. Zero trip meter.
▼ 0.5		SO	Graded road on right.
	2.5 ▲	SO	Graded road on left.
▼ 0.6		SO	Track on left.
	2.4 ▲	SO	Track on right.
▼ 0.8		SO	Track on left.
	2.2 ▲	SO	Track on right.
▼ 1.0		SO	Track on right.
	2.0 ▲	SO	Track on left.
▼ 1.4		SO	Track on left.
	1.6 ▲	SO	Track on right.
▼ 1.5		SO	Track on right.
	1.5 ▲	SO	Track on left.
▼ 1.7		SO	Track on left.
	1.3 ▲	SO	Track on right.
▼ 2.4		SO	Track on left.
	0.6 ▲	SO	Track on right.
▼ 2.6		SO	Cross over Jim Roberts Draw on bridge. Large camping area on left after bridge.
	0.4 ▲	SO	Large camping area on right; then cross over Jim Roberts Draw on bridge.
			GPS: N34°19.74′ W111°10.35′
▼ 2.7		SO	Track on right.
	0.3 ▲	SO	Track on left.
▼ 3.0		SO	Graded road on right is FR 29, Mead Ranch Road, to Tonto Creek. Zero trip meter.
	0.0 ▲		Continue toward Tonto Village.
			GPS: N34°19.75′ W111°10.82′
▼ 0.0			Continue to the west.
	5.0 ▲	SO	Graded road on left is FR 29, Mead Ranch Road, to Tonto Creek. Zero trip meter.
▼ 0.1		SO	Graded road on left is FR 65 to Diamond Point Lookout.
	4.9 ▲	SO	Graded road on right is FR 65 to Diamond Point Lookout.
			GPS: N34°19.83′ W111°10.92′
▼ 0.5		SO	Cattle guard.
	4.5 ▲	SO	Cattle guard.
▼ 0.6		SO	Track on right.
	4.4 ▲	SO	Track on left.
▼ 1.0		SO	Two tracks on left.
	4.0 ▲	SO	Two tracks on right.
▼ 1.3		SO	Track on left is FR 198, Pyeatt Draw Road.
	3.7 ▲	SO	Track on right is FR 198, Pyeatt Draw Road.
			GPS: N34°20.47′ W111°11.53′
▼ 1.6		SO	Cross over creek; then track on right.
	3.4 ▲	SO	Track on left; then cross over creek.
▼ 1.7		SO	Cross over Ellison Creek on bridge; then track on left is FR 149 to summer homes.
	3.3 ▲	SO	Track on right is FR 149 to summer homes; then cross over Ellison Creek on bridge.
▼ 1.8		SO	Track on right.
	3.2 ▲	SO	Track on left.
▼ 2.1		BL	Graded road on right is Pyle Ranch Road, FR 430, to summer homes.
	2.9 ▲	SO	Graded road on left is Pyle Ranch Road, FR 430, to summer homes.
			GPS: N34°21.06′ W111°11.44′
▼ 2.3		SO	Track on right; then cross over Lewis Creek on bridge.
	2.7 ▲	SO	Cross over Lewis Creek on bridge; then track on left.
▼ 2.6		SO	Track on right is FR 31.
	2.4 ▲	SO	Track on left is FR 31.
			GPS: N34°21.42′ W111°11.67′
▼ 2.9		SO	Track on left.
	2.1 ▲	SO	Track on right.
▼ 3.4		SO	Track on right.
	1.6 ▲	SO	Track on left.

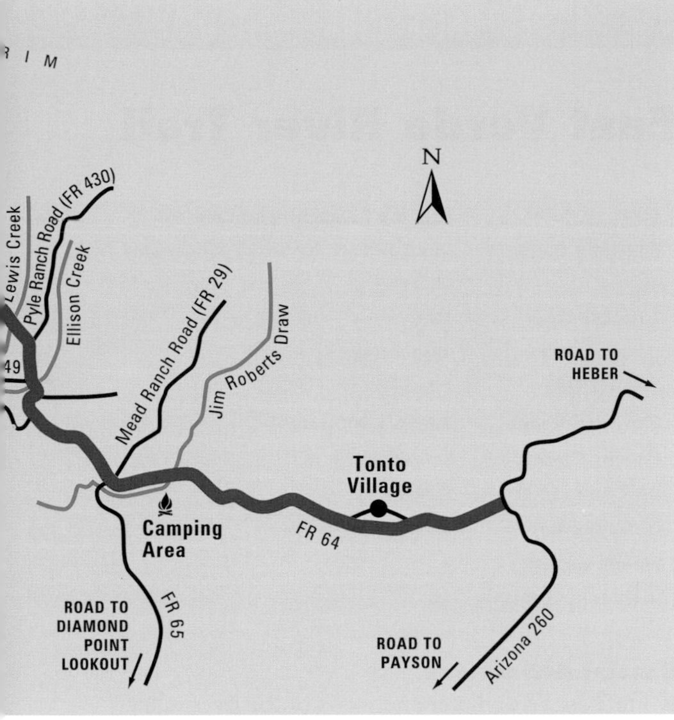

▼	▲		
▼ 3.6		SO	Track on right.
	1.4 ▲	SO	Track on left.
▼ 3.7		SO	Cross over Moore Creek on bridge.
	1.3 ▲	SO	Cross over Moore Creek on bridge.
▼ 3.8		SO	Cattle guard.
	1.2 ▲	SO	Cattle guard.
▼ 4.1		SO	Track on right is FR 144; also track on left.
	0.9 ▲	SO	Track on left is FR 144; also track on right.
			GPS: N34°21.90' W111°12.99'
▼ 4.3		SO	Cross over Perley Creek on bridge.
	0.7 ▲	SO	Cross over Perley Creek on bridge.
▼ 4.4		SO	Track on right.
	0.6 ▲	SO	Track on left.
▼ 4.9		SO	Track on left.
	0.1 ▲	SO	Track on right.
▼ 5.0		SO	Graded road on right is Bonita Creek Road, FR 431. Zero trip meter.
	0.0 ▲		Continue to the east on FR 64.
			GPS: N34°22.14' W111°13.85'
▼ 0.0			Continue to the west on FR 64 and cross over Bonita Creek on bridge.
	3.7 ▲	SO	Cross over Bonita Creek on bridge; then graded road on left is Bonita Creek Road, FR 431. Zero trip meter.
▼ 0.2		SO	Cattle guard.
	3.5 ▲	SO	Cattle guard.
▼ 0.4		SO	Cross through Walk Moore Canyon.
	3.3 ▲	SO	Cross through Walk Moore Canyon.
▼ 0.6		SO	Cross through Fuller Creek.
	3.1 ▲	SO	Cross through Fuller Creek.
▼ 0.8		SO	Track on right.
	2.9 ▲	SO	Track on left.
▼ 0.9		SO	Two tracks on left.
	2.8 ▲	SO	Two tracks on right.
▼ 1.2		SO	Cross over Brody Creek.
	2.5 ▲	SO	Cross over Brody Creek.
▼ 1.5		SO	Track on left.
	2.2 ▲	SO	Track on right.
▼ 1.6		SO	Track on right.
	2.1 ▲	SO	Track on left.
▼ 1.7		SO	Cattle guard.
	2.0 ▲	SO	Cattle guard.
▼ 1.9		SO	Track on right.
	1.8 ▲	SO	Track on left.
▼ 2.0		SO	Track on right.
	1.7 ▲	SO	Track on left.
▼ 2.2		SO	Track on right; then large track on right is FR 195.
	1.5 ▲	SO	Large track on left is FR 195; then track on left.
			GPS: N34°22.87' W111°15.73'
▼ 3.2		SO	Graded road on right is FR 1990 (shown as FR 199 on map).
	0.5 ▲	SO	Graded road on left is FR 1990.
			GPS: N34°22.93' W111°16.64'
▼ 3.6		SO	Graded road on left is Neal Drive; then cross over East Verde River on bridge.
	0.1 ▲	SO	Cross over East Verde River on bridge; then graded road on right is Neal Drive.
▼ 3.7		BR	Graded road on left is FR 199 to Whispering Pines Residential Area. FR 199 continues to join Arizona 87. Zero trip meter.
	0.0 ▲		Continue to the east, following sign for Arizona 260.
			GPS: N34°22.70' W111°17.03'
▼ 0.0			Continue to the northwest, following sign for Arizona 87.
	3.9 ▲	BL	Graded road on right is FR 199 to Whispering Pines Residential Area. FR 199 continues to join Arizona 87. Zero trip meter.
▼ 0.1		SO	Cattle guard.
	3.8 ▲	SO	Cattle guard.
▼ 0.4		SO	Track on left.
	3.5 ▲	SO	Track on right.
▼ 0.6		SO	Graded road on right is FR 32 to Washington Park Trailhead. Then track on left; then track on right.
	3.3 ▲	SO	Track on left; then track on right. Then graded road on left is FR 32 to Washington Park Trailhead.
			GPS: N34°22.96' W111°17.61'
▼ 0.8		SO	Track on right.
	3.1 ▲	SO	Track on left.
▼ 1.2		SO	Track on left.
	2.7 ▲	SO	Track on right.
▼ 1.3		SO	Track on left.
	2.6 ▲	SO	Track on right.
▼ 1.5		SO	Track on left.
	2.4 ▲	SO	Track on right.
▼ 1.6		SO	Track on left.
	2.3 ▲	SO	Track on right.
▼ 1.8		SO	Track on left and track on right.
	2.1 ▲	SO	Track on left and track on right.
			GPS: N34°22.64' W111°18.84'
▼ 2.3		SO	Track on left and track on right.
	1.6 ▲	SO	Track on left and track on right.
▼ 3.1		SO	Track on right is FR 439.
	0.8 ▲	SO	Track on left is FR 439.
			GPS: N34°22.90' W111°20.05'
▼ 3.2		SO	Track on left; then cattle guard.
	0.7 ▲	SO	Cattle guard; then track on right.
▼ 3.5		SO	Cross through Bray Creek on concrete ford.
	0.4 ▲	SO	Cross through Bray Creek on concrete ford.
			GPS: N34°22.79' W111°20.40'

▼	▲		
▼ 3.7		SO	Track on right.
	0.2 ▲	SO	Track on left.
▼ 3.9		SO	Graded road on right is FR 440 to Camp Geronimo; graded road on left is FR 458 to summer houses. Zero trip meter.
	0.0 ▲		Continue to the southeast on Control Road.
			GPS: N34°22.71' W111°20.83'
▼ 0.0			Continue to the northwest on Control Road and cross over Webber Creek on bridge.
	5.6 ▲	SO	Cross over Webber Creek on bridge; graded road on left is FR 440 to Camp Geronimo, and graded road on right is FR 458 to summer houses.
▼ 0.3		SO	Two tracks on right and track on left.
	5.3 ▲	SO	Two tracks on left and track on right.
▼ 0.5		SO	Track on right; then track on left.
	5.1 ▲	SO	Track on right; then track on left.
▼ 0.7		SO	Cross over creek.
	4.9 ▲	SO	Cross over creek.
▼ 1.0		SO	Track on right is FR 3054.
	4.6 ▲	SO	Track on left is FR 3054.
▼ 1.1		SO	Track on left.
	4.5 ▲	SO	Track on right.
▼ 1.3		SO	Track on left; then track on right.
	4.3 ▲	SO	Track on left; then track on right.
			GPS: N34°22.43' W111°21.84'
▼ 1.9		SO	Track on right.
	3.7 ▲	SO	Track on left.
▼ 2.3		SO	Track on right; then track on left.
	3.3 ▲	SO	Track on right; then track on left.
▼ 2.4		SO	Track on left is marked with primitive road sign.
	3.2 ▲	SO	Track on right is marked with primitive road sign.
			GPS: N34°22.09' W111°22.67'
▼ 2.9		SO	Cattle guard; then track on left.
	2.7 ▲	SO	Track on right; then cattle guard.
▼ 3.2		SO	Red Rock hiking trailhead and parking area on right.
	2.4 ▲	SO	Red Rock hiking trailhead and parking area on left.
			GPS: N34°21.89' W111°23.29'
▼ 3.5		SO	Track on right.
	2.2 ▲	SO	Track on left.
▼ 4.0		SO	Track on left.
	1.6 ▲	SO	Track on right.
▼ 4.7		SO	Track on right.
	0.9 ▲	SO	Track on left.
▼ 4.8		SO	Track on left.
	0.8 ▲	SO	Track on right.
▼ 5.0		SO	Track on left.
	0.6 ▲	SO	Track on right.
▼ 5.1		SO	Track on left.
	0.5 ▲	SO	Track on right.
▼ 5.2		SO	Track on right.
	0.4 ▲	SO	Track on left.
▼ 5.4		SO	Three tracks on left.
	0.2 ▲	SO	Three tracks on right.
▼ 5.6			Trail ends at the intersection with Arizona 87. Turn left for Payson; turn right for Pine.
	0.0 ▲		Trail starts on Arizona 87, 0.1 miles north of mile marker 265, 3 miles south of Pine. Zero trip meter and turn east on graded dirt road over cattle guard. Turn is unmarked.
			GPS: N34°21.61' W111°25.43'

CENTRAL REGION TRAIL #33

East Verde River Trail

Starting Point:	**Arizona 87 at mile marker 256**
Finishing Point:	**Central #34: Mazatzal Wilderness Trail, FR 406**
Total Mileage:	**13.5 miles**
Unpaved Mileage:	**13.5 miles**
Driving Time:	**2 hours**
Elevation Range:	**3,600–4,900 feet**
Usually Open:	**Year-round**
Best Time to Travel:	**Year-round**
Difficulty Rating:	**4**
Scenic Rating:	**9**
Remoteness Rating:	**+0**

Special Attractions

- The East Verde River and views of the river valley.
- Remains of the Crackerjack Mine.
- Varied vegetation and scenery.
- Views of the Mazatzal Mountains.

Description

This extremely scenic, moderately rated trail can be driven as a loop by combining it with Central #34: Mazatzal Wilderness Trail. The trail is fairly challenging, having several narrow sections as well as some loose surfaces on some of the climbs. However, the surface is generally good and the trail should be within the reach of all SUVs.

The dirt trail, which leaves Arizona 87 north of Payson at mile marker 256, is well used. It runs along and often crosses Ash Creek, which usually has water in it. The easy crossings can often have a few inches to splash through. Along this part of the trail, there are some beautiful rock formations that add interest and color to the route.

The trail descends to the East Verde River and crosses it on a narrow concrete bridge. The river normally has water, and although there may not be enough for a swim, you can probably enjoy a cooling splash; the boulders along the river make for sunny spots to dry off. If you are traveling in summer, do not attempt the crossing if the river is in flood, and be aware that the trail can be extremely muddy after rain and may be impassable.

After the crossing, the trail climbs above the river valley to wind around the base of Connally and Crackerjack

A shot of the trail near Ash Creek

Mesas, two red rock mesas that rise up to the north. The East Verde River Valley is to the south of the trail, and there are views over the valley to the Mazatzal Mountains. The Crackerjack Mine is on the left—two long adits, a concrete pad, and some sheets of corrugated iron are all that remain.

The entrance to Crackerjack Mine

The trail surface becomes rougher and looser at this point, and there are a couple of climbs on which vehicles may lose traction. After a saddle the trail starts the long descent to rejoin the East Verde River. This road is shown on the Tonto National Forest Map as FR 209A but is marked along the trail as FR 406.

The descent to the East Verde River is gradual and easy until the final section. This is the steepest and loosest section along the trail, although it is still consistent with the trail's overall difficulty rating of 4. The river crossing normally has some shallow rivulets of water; again, do not attempt to cross if the river is in flood. The trail finishes 0.3 miles from the end of Central #34: Mazatzal Wilderness Trail.

There are several places for camping and picnicking along this trail. The best sites are within the first couple of miles along Ash Creek and close to both crossings of the East Verde River.

Current Road Information

Tonto National Forest
Payson Ranger District
1009 East Highway 260
Payson, AZ 85541
(520) 474-7900

Map References

BLM Payson
USFS Tonto National Forest: Payson Ranger District
USGS 1:24,000 Payson North, Buckhead Mesa, North Peak
1:100,000 Payson
Maptech CD-ROM: Flagstaff/Sedona/Prescott
Arizona Atlas & Gazetteer, p. 50
Arizona Road & Recreation Atlas, p. 41 & p. 75

Route Directions

▼ 0.0			From Arizona 87 at mile marker 256, south of the East Verde River, turn west on formed dirt road (FR 209) and immediately cross cattle guard and zero trip meter. Turn is unmarked, but there is a forest service limited-use road sign after the cattle guard.
	2.9 ▲		Cross cattle guard. Trail ends at the intersection with Arizona 87. Turn right for Payson; turn left for Pine.
			GPS: N34°17.06' W111°20.01'
▼ 0.1		SO	Cross through Ash Creek twice; trail follows path of creek.
	2.8 ▲	SO	Cross through Ash Creek twice.
▼ 0.5		SO	Track on left.
	2.4 ▲	SO	Track on right.
▼ 0.6		SO	Large camping area on left.
	2.3 ▲	SO	Large camping area on right.
▼ 0.7		SO	Track on left; then second track on left.
	2.2 ▲	SO	Track on right; then second track on right.
			GPS: N34°17.03' W111°20.65'
▼ 0.9		SO	Cross through Ash Creek; there are many crossings of Ash Creek for the next 0.7 miles.
	2.0 ▲	SO	Cross through Ash Creek.
▼ 1.6		SO	Cross through Ash Creek.
	1.3 ▲	SO	Cross through Ash Creek; there are many crossings of Ash Creek for the next 0.7 miles.
▼ 1.8		SO	Cross through creek.
	1.1 ▲	SO	Cross through creek.
▼ 2.0		SO	Track on left; then cross through creek.
	0.9 ▲	SO	Cross through creek; then track on right.
			GPS: N34°17.12' W111°21.88'
▼ 2.3		SO	Track on left.
	0.6 ▲	SO	Track on right.
▼ 2.5		SO	Track on right into private property.
	0.4 ▲	SO	Track on right into private property.
			GPS: N34°17.33' W111°22.15'
▼ 2.8		SO	Camping area on right; then trail runs along the East Verde River.
	0.1 ▲	SO	Camping area on left.
▼ 2.9		SO	Cross over the East Verde River on small concrete bridge. Trail becomes smaller. Zero trip meter.
	0.0 ▲		Continue to the north toward Arizona 87.
			GPS: N34°17.24' W111°22.44'
▼ 0.0			Continue to the southwest.
	4.5 ▲	SO	Cross over the East Verde River on small concrete bridge. Trail becomes slightly larger. Zero trip meter.
▼ 0.5		SO	Track on left.
	4.0 ▲	SO	Track on right.

Crossing the East Verde River on a small concrete bridge

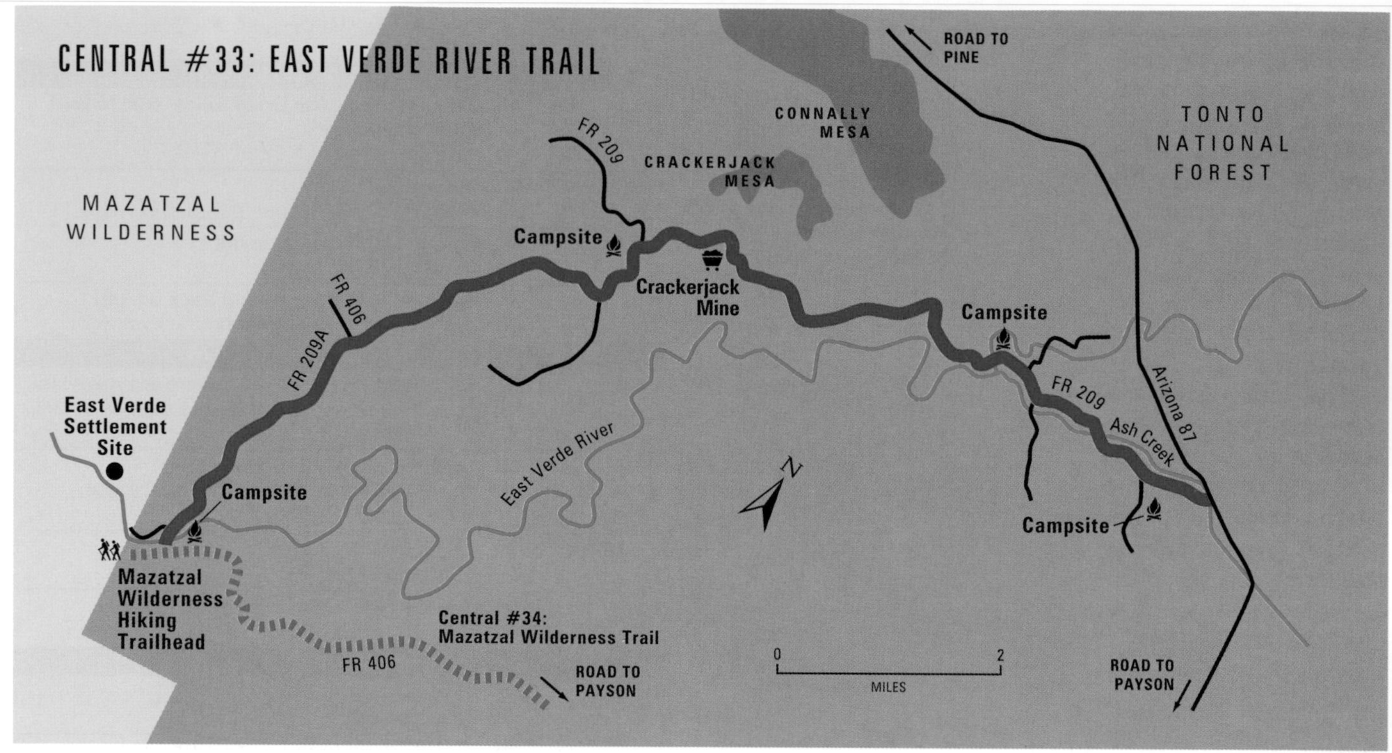

▼ 0.8 SO Track on left; continue straight on through wire gate; then second track on left.

3.7 ▲ SO Track on right; continue straight on through wire gate; then second track on right.

GPS: N34°17.25' W111°23.07'

▼ 1.1 SO Track on right.

3.4 ▲ SO Track on left.

▼ 1.2 SO Cattle guard.

3.3 ▲ SO Cattle guard.

▼ 3.4 BR Two adits and remains of the Crackerjack Mine on the left. Trail bears right and drops in standard.

1.1 ▲ BL Two adits and remains of the Crackerjack Mine on the right. Trail standard improves.

GPS: N34°17.08' W111°25.14'

▼ 3.5 SO Cattle guard.

1.0 SO Cattle guard.

▼ 3.6 BR Track on left; take upper trail.

0.9 SO Track on right.

▼ 3.7 SO Track on left to two mine shafts and track on right at saddle.

0.8 SO Track on right to two mine shafts and track on left at saddle.

GPS: N34°17.09' W111°25.27'

▼ 4.5 TL Small track on left; then T-intersection. Turn left at T-intersection onto FR 406, following the sign to Lower East Verde. (Note that FR 406 is shown as FR 209A on the Tonto National Forest Map.) The well-used track on the right is FR 209, which returns to Arizona 87. Zero trip meter.

0.0 ▲ Continue to the northeast.

GPS: N34°16.82' W111°25.88'

▼ 0.0 Continue to the south.

6.1 ▲ TR Turn right at intersection onto FR 209. Well-used track on left is also FR 209, which goes to Arizona 87. Zero trip meter. In this direction the intersection is unmarked, but after you have completed the turn, there is a sign for travelers in the opposite direction, marking the trails.

▼ 0.1 SO Campsite on right.

6.0 ▲ SO Campsite on left.

▼ 0.7 SO Well-used track on left.

5.4 ▲ SO Well-used track on right.

GPS: N34°16.32' W111°26.02'

▼ 3.0 SO Pass through wire gate.

3.1 ▲ SO Pass through wire gate.

GPS: N34°15.35' W111°27.75'

▼ 5.0 SO Pass through wire gate.

1.1 ▲ SO Pass through wire gate.

GPS: N34°13.72' W111°28.43'

▼ 5.9 SO Enter East Verde River wash. Track on left and track on right. Then cross through main river channel and small track on right.

0.2 ▲ SO Small track on left; then cross through main river channel. Track on left and track on right; then exit East Verde River wash.

GPS: N34°13.11' W111°28.67'

▼ 6.0 SO Track on left down wash and nice picnicking and camping spot under large cottonwood on right.

0.1 ▲ SO Track on right down wash and nice picnicking and camping spot under large cottonwood on left.

▼ 6.1 SO Large open camping area on left; then trail ends at T-intersection with Central #34: Mazatzal Wilderness Trail. Turn left over cattle guard for Payson; turn right for hiking trailhead into Mazatzal Wilderness.

0.0 ▲ Trail commences on Central #34: Mazatzal Wilderness Trail, FR 406, immediately before the end of the trail. The turn is immediately after a cattle guard. Immediately after the turn is a sign for the East Verde River. Zero trip meter and continue north past the open camping area on the right toward the East Verde River wash.

GPS: N34°13.00' W111°28.60'

CENTRAL REGION TRAIL #34

Mazatzal Wilderness Trail

Starting Point:	**Arizona 87 in Payson**
Finishing Point:	**Mazatzal Wilderness Trailhead**
Total Mileage:	**10.7 miles**
Unpaved Mileage:	**8.9 miles**
Driving Time:	**45 minutes**
Elevation Range:	**3,500–5,000 feet**
Usually Open:	**Year-round**
Best Time to Travel:	**October to May**
Difficulty Rating:	**2**
Scenic Rating:	**7**
Remoteness Rating:	**+0**

Special Attractions

- Hiking access to the Mazatzal Wilderness.
- Views of the Mazatzal Mountains.
- Backcountry camping near the East Verde River.
- Can be driven as a loop from Payson with the more difficult Central #33: East Verde River Trail.

History

The Mazatzal Wilderness has been more or less continuously used by Native Americans for the past 5,000 years. Since the 1500s the Yavapai Indians have used the area for hunting, food, and resources. Tonto Apaches used the area from approximately 1700 to the late 1880s when Native Americans were confined to reservations by the U.S. government. There are two possible explanations for the name Mazatzal (which is locally mispronounced as "madda-zell" but is more correctly pronounced "mah'zat-zall"). To the Aztecs, the word meant "place of deer." Although deer certainly live in the Mazatzal Wilderness, there is no record of the Aztecs ever occupying the area. An alternative explanation is that the word means "empty space between" to the Paiute Indians.

The start of the Mazatzal Wilderness Trailhead

In the late 1800s settlers came to the area bringing horses, sheep, and cattle. There were a couple of small mining camps and a Mormon settlement known as East Verde Settlement, which was just east of the present wilderness boundary. Another Mormon settlement, Mazatzal City, was established in 1878 near the present-day location of Doll Baby Ranch. There were orchards, a sawmill, and a dairy; but the settlement was abandoned, possibly due to harassment by Indians. The settlers moved on to the Strawberry-Pine area.

The Mazatzal Primitive Area was established in May 1938 by the national forest service and it was declared a wilderness area in June 1940. In 1984 the wilderness area was expanded to its present size.

A view of the trail as it descends toward the Mazatzal Wilderness

Description

The main purpose of this trail is to provide access to the hiking trailhead for the Mazatzal Wilderness. However, it also gives access to a few other backcountry trails, including Central #33: East Verde River Trail. The road leaves from the center of Payson. Once it leaves the edge of town, it quickly deteriorates to a roughly graded road. It winds along through open shrubland, giving excellent views of the Mazatzal Mountains, in particular North Peak (7,449 feet).

As the trail nears the end, there are a couple of rough descents that require a high-clearance vehicle. The trail passes the City Creek hiking and pack trailhead before crossing through City Creek. It runs beside the intriguingly named Doll Baby Ranch and then passes the southern end of Central #33: East Verde River Trail. There are some shady backcountry campsites at the start of this trail along the East Verde River, but be wary of camping within the river wash. The main trail finishes at the boundary of the Mazatzal Wilderness at the start of the Bull Spring Hiking Trail. There is a pleasant camping area at the trailhead on a flat, grassy area close to the East Verde River. There is a private road extending into the wilderness that is used, under special permit, by a rancher—no other vehicles are permitted.

Current Road Information

Tonto National Forest
Payson Ranger District
1009 East Highway 260
Payson, AZ 85541
(520) 474-7900

Map References

BLM Payson
USFS Tonto National Forest: Payson Ranger District
USGS 1:24,000 Payson South, North Peak
1:100,000 Payson
Maptech CD-ROM: Flagstaff/Sedona/Prescott

Arizona Atlas & Gazetteer, p. 50
Arizona Road & Recreation Atlas, p. 41 & p. 75
Recreational Map of Arizona

Route Directions

▼	▲		
▼ 0.0			Trail commences on Arizona 87 in the center of Payson. At the light, turn west on West Main Street and zero trip meter. Remain on West Main Street, ignoring roads on right and left. West Main Street turns into West Country Club Drive.
	4.9 ▲		Trail finishes at the light on West Main Street and Arizona 87 in the center of Payson.
			GPS: N34°13.84′ W111°19.49′
▼ 1.7		SO	Road on right is South Vista Road; continue straight on West Country Club Drive, which turns into Doll Baby Ranch Road.
	3.2 ▲	SO	Road on left is South Vista Road. Continue straight on West Country Club Drive. Many roads on right and left; remain on main road, which turns into West Main Street.
▼ 1.8		SO	Road turns to graded dirt. Continue following FR 406 toward the East Verde River.
	3.1 ▲	SO	Road turns to paved.
			GPS: N34°13.91′ W111°21.45′
▼ 2.2		BL	Track on right into ranch.
	2.7 ▲	SO	Track on left into ranch.
▼ 2.3		SO	Cross through creek.
	2.6 ▲	SO	Cross through creek.
▼ 2.5		SO	Cattle guard.
	2.4 ▲	SO	Cattle guard.
▼ 2.7		SO	Cross through American Gulch.
	2.2 ▲	SO	Cross through American Gulch.
▼ 3.6		SO	Track on right.
	1.3 ▲	SO	Track on left.
▼ 4.1		SO	Track on left is FR 441 to Peach Orchard Spring and Arizona 87.
	0.8 ▲	SO	Track on right is FR 441 to Peach Orchard Spring and Arizona 87.
			GPS: N34°13.08′ W111°23.12′
▼ 4.3		SO	Track on left.
	0.6 ▲	SO	Track on right.
▼ 4.7		SO	Cattle guard.
	0.2 ▲	SO	Cattle guard.
▼ 4.9		SO	Track on left is FR 414 to Cypress Thicket. Zero trip meter.
	0.0 ▲		Continue to the east.
			GPS: N34°13.05′ W111°23.81′
▼ 0.0			Continue to the west.
	5.5 ▲	SO	Track on right is FR 414 to Cypress Thicket. Zero trip meter.
▼ 0.7		SO	Track on right is FR 67; also track on left.
	4.8 ▲	SO	Track on left is FR 67; also track on right.
			GPS: N34°13.23′ W111°24.39′
▼ 1.4		SO	Cattle guard; then track on right through gate.
	4.1 ▲	SO	Track on left through gate; then cattle guard.
			GPS: N34°13.40′ W111°25.15′
▼ 2.0		SO	Track on right to tank.
	3.5 ▲	SO	Track on left to tank.
▼ 3.5		SO	Cross through wash.
	2.0 ▲	SO	Cross through wash.
			GPS: N34°12.96′ W111°27.08′
▼ 3.6		SO	Cattle guard.
	1.9 ▲	SO	Cattle guard.
▼ 4.0		SO	Cross through creek.
	1.5 ▲	SO	Cross through creek.
▼ 4.2		SO	Track on right; then cattle guard.
	1.3 ▲	SO	Cattle guard; then track on left.
▼ 4.3		SO	Track on left.
	1.2 ▲	SO	Track on right rejoins.
▼ 4.4		SO	Track on left rejoins.
	1.1 ▲	SO	Track on right.
▼ 4.5		SO	Track on left.
	1.0 ▲	SO	Track on right.
▼ 4.6		SO	City Creek Trail #23 on left; then parking area for the trail on right.
	0.9 ▲	SO	Parking area for City Creek Trail #23 on left; then City Creek Trail #23 on right.
			GPS: N34°13.02′ W111°27.89′
▼ 4.8		SO	Cross through City Creek. Then cattle guard and well on right.
	0.7 ▲	SO	Well on left; then cross cattle guard. Then cross through City Creek.
▼ 5.0		SO	Entrance to Doll Baby Ranch on right.
	0.5 ▲	SO	Entrance to Doll Baby Ranch on left.

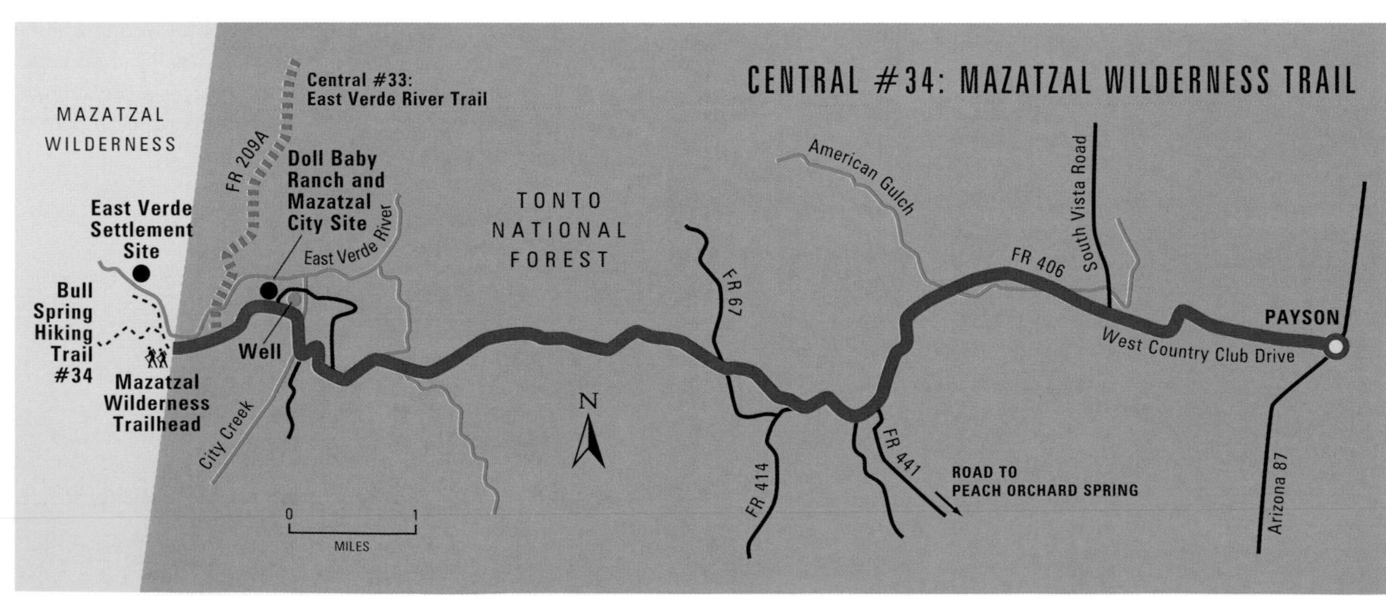

▼ 5.5	SO	Cattle guard; then track on right is Central #33: East Verde River Trail. Zero trip meter.
0.0 ▲		Continue to the northeast and cross cattle guard.
		GPS: N34°13.00' W111°28.60'
▼ 0.0		Continue to the west.
▼ 0.1	SO	Track on right.
▼ 0.3		Trail ends at Mazatzal Wilderness hiking trailhead at the start of Bull Spring Hiking Trail #34 on the boundary of the Mazatzal Wilderness. There is flat, grassy camping area at the trailhead.
		GPS: N34°12.86' W111°28.84'

CENTRAL REGION TRAIL #35

Mount Ord Trail

Starting Point:	**Arizona 87 (Beeline Highway), 5.5 miles north of Sunflower**
Finishing Point:	**Mount Ord**
Total Mileage:	**7.6 miles**
Unpaved Mileage:	**7.6 miles**
Driving Time:	**45 minutes (one-way)**
Elevation Range:	**4,200–7,000 feet**
Usually Open:	**Year-round**
Best Time to Travel:	**Year-round**
Difficulty Rating:	**2**
Scenic Rating:	**9**
Remoteness Rating:	**+0**

Special Attractions

- Long, easy shelf road.
- Spectacular views of the Mazatzal Mountains.
- Mount Ord Lookout Tower.

Description

Mount Ord in the Mazatzal Mountains has a fire lookout tower as well as several communications towers. The road that accesses them is a very pleasant, short drive to the summit of Mount Ord. The lower end of the road leaves Arizona 87, the Beeline Highway, at a marked turnoff. When we mapped this trail, a second stretch of Arizona 87, to the east of the original one, was under construction. It is not known how this new section will change access to the trail. Access will be retained, but it is still unclear if the trail will only be accessed from the easternmost lanes.

Once away from the highway, the trail climbs steadily as a roughly graded road and follows a wide, smooth shelf road with Joe Canyon on the right. Initially, the vegetation is open, with small oaks and desert agave, but as the trail climbs it enters a forest of pines, alligator junipers, and manzanitas around 5,500 feet.

The trail narrows to single-vehicle width, but there are plenty of passing places. The Mogollon Rim can be seen to the north as you climb around the north side of Mount Ord.

A section of narrow shelf road climbing Mount Ord

Near the top is the gate to the fire tower, which is closed daily at 6 P.M. and reopens at 9 A.M. when the tower is manned. If the tower is not manned, the trail finishes here. When the tower is manned, you are normally welcome to climb up to see the view.

Current Road Information

Tonto National Forest
Mesa Ranger District
26 North MacDonald
Mesa, AZ 85211
(480) 610-3300

Tonto National Forest
Tonto Basin Ranger District
Highway 88
HC 02 Box 4800
Roosevelt, AZ 85545
(520) 467-3200

Map References

BLM Theodore Roosevelt Lake
USFS Tonto National Forest: Mesa and Tonto Basin Ranger Districts
USGS 1:24,000 Reno Pass
1:100,000 Theodore Roosevelt Lake
Maptech CD-ROM: Phoenix/Superstition Mountains
Arizona Atlas & Gazetteer, p. 50
Arizona Road & Recreation Atlas, p. 41 & p. 75

Route Directions

▼ 0.0		From Arizona 87, the Beeline Highway, 5.5 miles north of Sunflower, zero trip meter and turn southeast on wide graded dirt road, FR 626, signed to Mount Ord.
		GPS: N33°55.87' W111°27.82'
▼ 0.2	SO	Track on right.
▼ 0.7	SO	Pass under power lines.
▼ 1.2	SO	Trail crosses new freeway construction. Zero trip meter.

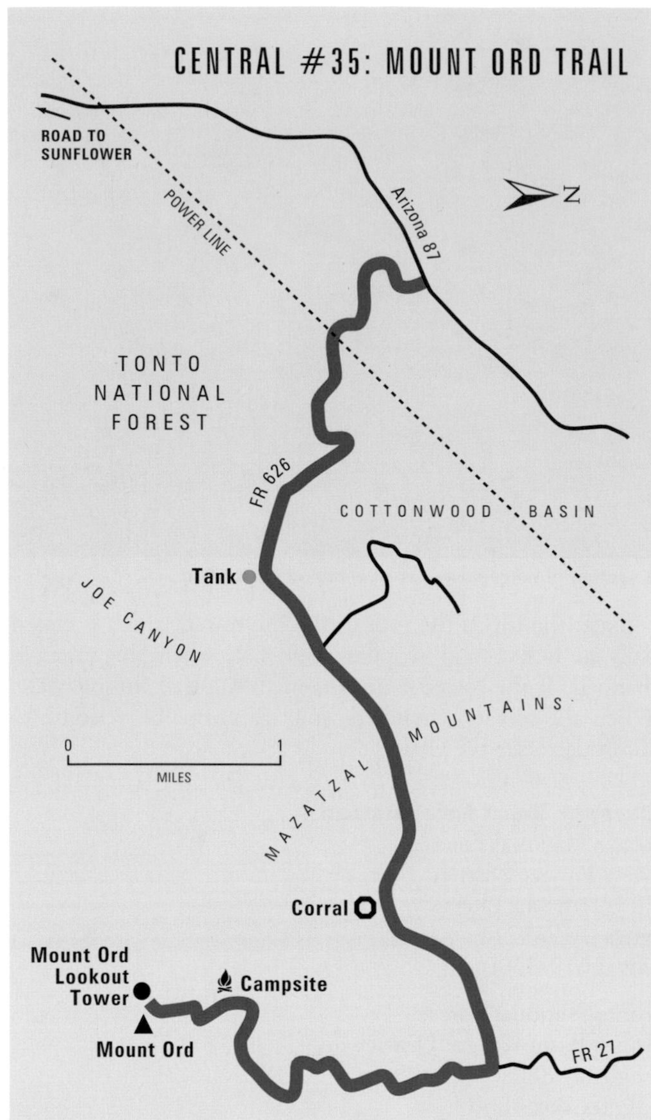

		GPS: N33°55.29' W111°27.27'
▼ 0.0		Continue to the east.
▼ 0.4	SO	Cattle guard.
▼ 1.0	SO	Concrete tank on right.
▼ 1.5	SO	Track on left.
▼ 1.6	SO	Cattle guard; then track on right.
▼ 2.7	SO	Track on right at corral; then cattle guard.
		GPS: N33°55.32' W111°24.83'
▼ 4.0	BR	Well-used track on left is FR 27, which takes a steeper route to Arizona 87. Zero trip meter.
		GPS: N33°55.60' W111°23.93'
▼ 0.0		Continue to the south.
▼ 1.2	SO	Cattle guard.
		GPS: N33°54.84' W111°23.98'
▼ 1.7	SO	Two tracks on right.
		GPS: N33°54.71' W111°24.36'
▼ 1.8	SO	Mount Ord Lookout site gate. Gate is closed from 6 P.M. to 9 A.M. Campsite at gate.
		GPS: N33°54.67' W111°24.47'
▼ 2.4		Trail ends at the Mount Ord Lookout Tower.
		GPS: N33°54.30' W111°24.52'

CENTRAL REGION TRAIL #36

El Oso Road

Starting Point:	**Arizona 87, 4.6 miles north of the intersection with the Bush Highway**
Finishing Point:	**Arizona 188**
Total Mileage:	**26.3 miles**
Unpaved Mileage:	**26.3 miles**
Driving Time:	**3 hours**
Elevation Range:	**2,200–6,000 feet**
Usually Open:	**Year-round**
Best Time to Travel:	**October to May**
Difficulty Rating:	**3**
Scenic Rating:	**9**
Remoteness Rating:	**+0**

Special Attractions

- Panoramic views of the Tonto Basin and the Four Peaks Wilderness Area.
- Saguaro Lake near the start of the trail and Theodore Roosevelt Lake near the end of the trail.
- Many hiking trails into the Four Peaks Wilderness.
- Easy trail that makes a good day trip from Phoenix.

History

In April 1996 this region was burned by the Lone Pine Fire, the largest wildfire in the history of Tonto National Forest, which was the result of an unattended campfire near the Lone Pine Trailhead. It lasted for six days and burned 60,000 acres of desert chaparral and forest. In an extensive operation to contain the fire, fire engines, airplanes, helicopters, and ground crews with beaters worked around the clock.

Only a 3-square-mile lush area in a drainage region on the western slope of Mount Oso escaped being burned. This green patch, which was visible on satellite imagery right after the fire, became a haven for a population of black bears. A study by the Arizona Game and Fish Department showed that between 20 and 28 bears took refuge in this tiny area. The bears' behavior astounded the researchers who expected the bears to fight each other. Although it appeared that all the adult bears survived, no cubs did. It is not clear if the cubs perished in the fire or if the adult bears killed them. The bear population continued to thrive in the close quarters, and by 2000, they were slowly returning to the fire-scarred region.

Saguaros are prominent along the lower section of this trail

The Four Peaks region was

the site of a few battles between the U.S. Army and Indians between 1867 and 1874.

Description

For the most part, this long trail is suitable for passenger vehicles in dry weather. However, there is one section, a 0.5-mile-long stretch immediately east of the Mud Springs Trailhead, for which high-clearance vehicles, preferably 4WDs, are required. The day the trail was surveyed there was a VW Beetle abandoned on this stretch of trail. The unfortunate vehicle suffered major damage to its undercarriage and was hopelessly stuck on the embedded rocks. The driver was lucky enough to catch a ride with a passing vehicle, but only after he had spent the night along the trail.

Four Peaks Mountain looming ahead of the trail

Drivers of passenger vehicles can access either end of the trail but should not attempt to drive the full trail. For those who have high-clearance vehicles, the trail is a delight to drive, offering a cool escape from Phoenix in spring and fall and possibly a light sprinkle of snow in winter.

The trail leaves the Beeline Highway north of Fountain Hills. The highway is divided at this point, but there is a crossing point from the southbound lane. The wide, graded dirt road passes the turnoff to popular Saguaro Lake. Some challenging 4WD trails lead to Saguaro Lake, but these are very heavily used at all times of the year. Many of these side trails are popular with owners of ATVs.

The main trail starts a gradual climb to wrap along the north side of the Four Peaks Wilderness. The mainly open desert vegetation is attractive but provides no shade. Central #37: Edwards Park Trail leads off from the saddle before the road descends down Theodore Roosevelt Lake, which can be seen below. This section of the trail is shown on maps as El Oso Road (which means "bear road" in Spanish), but the trail is known by its popular name: Four Peaks Road.

Current Road Information

Tonto National Forest
Mesa Ranger District
26 North MacDonald
Mesa, AZ 85211
(480) 610-3300

Tonto National Forest
Tonto Basin Ranger District
Highway 88
HC 02 Box 4800
Roosevelt, AZ 85545
(520) 467-3200

Map References

BLM Theodore Roosevelt Lake
USFS Tonto National Forest: Mesa and Tonto Basin Ranger Districts
USGS 1:24,000 Adams Mesa, Mine Mt., Four Peaks, Tonto Basin
1:100,000 Theodore Roosevelt Lake
Maptech CD-ROM: Phoenix/Superstition Mountains
Arizona Atlas & Gazetteer, pp. 58, 50
Arizona Road & Recreation Atlas, p. 41 & p. 75
Recreational Map of Arizona

Route Directions

▼ 0.0		From Arizona 87, 4.6 miles north of the intersection with the Bush Highway, 0.9 miles north of mile marker 203, zero trip meter and turn east across cattle guard onto the graded El Oso Road (FR 143) at the sign for Four Peaks.
2.0 ▲		Trail ends at the intersection with Arizona 87. Turn right for Payson; turn left for Phoenix.
		GPS: N33°40.69′ W111°30.12′
▼ 0.7	SO	Parking area on right; then track on right is FR 1863.
1.3 ▲	SO	Track on left is FR 1863; then parking area on left.
		GPS: N33°40.17′ W111°29.68′
▼ 1.4	SO	Track on right is FR 1832.
0.6 ▲	SO	Track on left is FR 1832.
		GPS: N33°40.15′ W111°29.02′
▼ 2.0	BL	Track on right is FR 401 to Cottonwood Camp. Zero trip meter.
0.0 ▲		Continue to the west, remaining on FR 143.
		GPS: N33°40.01′ W111°28.39
▼ 0.0		Continue to the northeast, remaining on FR 143.
8.4 ▲	BR	Track on left is FR 401 to Cottonwood Camp. Zero trip meter.
▼ 0.4	SO	Cross through wash.
8.0 ▲	SO	Cross through wash.
▼ 0.5	SO	Track on left.
7.9 ▲	SO	Track on right.
▼ 1.1	SO	Cattle guard.
7.3 ▲	SO	Cattle guard.
▼ 1.2	BR	Track on left is TR 11, part of the Great Western Trail.
7.2 ▲	BL	Track on right is TR 11, part of the Great Western Trail.
		GPS: N33°40.90′ W111°27.97′
▼ 1.6	SO	Track on left; then cross through wash.
6.8 ▲	SO	Cross through wash; then track on right.
▼ 1.7	SO	Track on right.
6.7 ▲	SO	Track on left.
▼ 1.9	BL	Track on right.
6.5 ▲	BR	Track on left.
▼ 2.0	SO	Cross through Mesquite Wash.
6.4 ▲	SO	Cross through Mesquite Wash.
▼ 2.3	SO	Cross through wash.
6.1 ▲	SO	Cross through wash.
▼ 2.5	SO	Track on left to viewpoint.
5.9 ▲	SO	Track on right to viewpoint.
		GPS: N33°41.57′ W111°27.39′
▼ 2.9	SO	Cross through wash.
5.5 ▲	SO	Cross through wash.
▼ 3.1	SO	Cross through wash; then track on right.
5.3 ▲	SO	Track on left; then cross through wash.
▼ 3.4	SO	Track on left.
5.0 ▲	SO	Track on right.
▼ 3.9	SO	Cross through wash; then track on right and track on left.

Description

Scenic Edwards Park Trail (FR 422) follows the Mazatzal Divide, the ridgeline that runs north of Four Peaks to Edwards Park—a distance of just over 10 miles. There are, however, a few good turnaround points. This trail is rated as a 6, mostly because of a few steep rocky sections. On the north end of the trail there are areas with close brush. As the trail follows the ridgeline, it offers expansive views to the east over the Tonto Basin and Roosevelt Lake, to the west into the valley, to the south to the Superstition Mountains, and to the north toward Mount Ord and the Mogollon Rim. Along the way there is an optional detour past the remains of the El Oso Mine and the Jolene Mine, but this detour is 7-rated and should be treated with caution. These trails are entirely above 5,000 feet, affording some relief from summer heat.

Sections of the trail are loose, steep, and rocky

The road continues through chaparral forests. The southern part of this trail passes through an area that was burned in the 1996 Lone Pine Fire. The fire burned more than 60,000 acres in the Four Peaks area. The remaining forest of black, leafless trees initially resembles something out of a horror film. A closer look reveals that the forest is beginning to regenerate. The chaparral gives way to pine forest at Little Pine Flat, which offers shade and good camping areas. Farther north, there is a short hill climb just off the main trail that affords excellent views in all directions. This is a good turnaround point for a day trip. The main trail continues several more miles to Edwards Park, a flat area composed of forest and meadows. There are some good places to camp here as well. At the end, two hiking trails, TR 66 and TR 68, lead toward Reno Pass.

Two miles from the start of the main trail there is an interesting detour along FR 463 to the east that leads to the remains of two mines. This trail links up with the main trail—FR 422—after about 3 miles. This optional detour is 7-rated and not recommended for longer vehicles. A field of large sharp-edged rocks must be negotiated while making a sharp right turn. A spotter is recommended, as well as skid plates. FR 463 then descends a narrow trail to the remains of the El Oso Mine. Farther down the trail are the remains of the Jolene Mine. At a fork in the road, a right takes you a short distance to the mine. The left turn goes up a steep hill, climbing about 500 feet in half a mile, toward FR 422.

Theodore Roosevelt Lake, seen in the distance from the trail

The Edwards Park Trail can be accessed from either Arizona 87 or Arizona 188 along Central #36: El Oso Road. The shorter way to the start of the trail is from Arizona 188; in addition to being shorter, this trail is in better condition than the western approach.

One unusual aspect of this trail is that cell phone coverage is often available for most of its length—probably because of line-of-site coverage to antennas either east or west of the mountain range.

Current Road Information

Tonto National Forest
Tonto Basin Ranger District
Highway 88
HC 02 Box 4800
Roosevelt, AZ 85545
(520) 467-3200

Map References

BLM Theodore Roosevelt Lake
USFS Tonto National Forest: Tonto Basin Ranger District
USGS 1:24,000 Four Peaks, Mine Mt., Boulder Mt., Tonto Basin
1:100,000 Theodore Roosevelt Lake
Maptech CD-ROM: Phoenix/Superstition Mountains
Arizona Atlas & Gazetteer, pp. 50, 58
Arizona Road & Recreation Atlas, p. 41 & p. 75

Route Directions

▼ 0.0		On Central #36: El Oso Road, at the intersection of FR 422 and FR 143, 8.5 miles west of Arizona 188, zero trip meter and turn northwest over cattle guard onto FR 422.
		GPS: N33°43.82' W111°20.82'
▼ 0.3	SO	Track on left.
▼ 1.8	BL	Track on right is Jolene Mine detour trail, FR 463; bear left remaining on FR 422. Zero trip meter.
		GPS: N33°44.74' W111°22.18'

Detour Trail to Jolene Mine (FR 463)

▼ 0.0	TR	Turn onto the Jolene Mine detour trail. Zero trip meter.
		GPS: N33°44.74' W111°22.18'
▼ 0.5	TL	Track on right leads to Big Pine Flat.
		GPS: N33°45.20' W111°22.24'
▼ 0.9	SO	Look in this area for the remains of the El Oso Mine.
		GPS: N33°45.24' W111°22.53'
▼ 2.8	BL	At the Y, left goes up a steep hill to FR 422. Go right a short distance to find the remains of the Jolene Mine; then return to this point and turn right to FR 422.
		GPS: N33°46.34' W111°22.82'

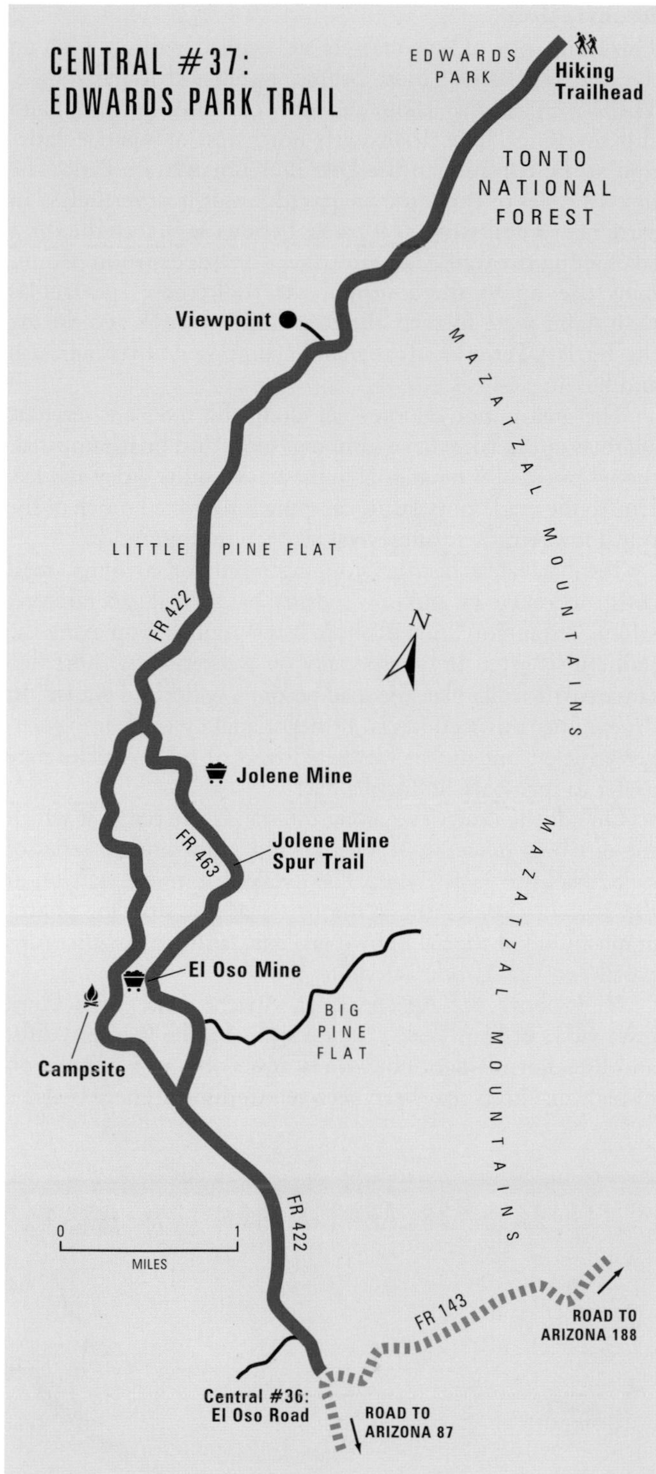

▼ 3.3	TR	Back at FR 422. Zero trip meter.
		GPS: N33°46.43'W111°23.18'

Continuation of Main Trail

▼ 0.0		Continue to the northwest.
		GPS: N33°44.74' W111°22.18'
▼ 0.4	SO	Entering an area that was burned by the Lone Pine Fire of 1996.
		GPS: N33°44.96' W111°22.47'
▼ 0.8	SO	Steep and rocky section.
		GPS: N33°44.98' W111°22.80'
▼ 1.2	BR	Wide, flat area. Some camping sites nearby.
		GPS: N33°45.29' W111°22.81'
▼ 1.5	SO	Road comes in from behind on the left. Be sure to bear left on return.
		GPS: N33°45.55' W111°22.82'
▼ 3.1	SO	The Jolene Mine detour trail, FR 463, rejoins on the right. Zero trip meter.
		GPS: N33°46.43' W111°23.18'
▼ 0.0		Continue to the northwest.
▼ 1.2	SO	Start of Little Pine Flat.
		GPS: N33°47.27' W111°23.23'
▼ 2.9	BR	Turn left up the hill for good views; then return. This is a good turnaround point for a day trip. Bear right to continue to Edwards Park.
		GPS: N33°48.53' W111°23.05'
▼ 5.7		Trail ends at the wide, flat, grassy area of Edwards Park.
		GPS: N33°50.35' W111°22.46'

CENTRAL REGION TRAIL #38

Apache Trail

Starting Point:	**Arizona 88, 5 miles northeast of Apache Junction, at Lost Dutchman State Park**
Finishing Point:	**Arizona 188, near Theodore Roosevelt Dam**
Total Mileage:	**38.5 miles**
Unpaved Mileage:	**20.1 miles**
Driving Time:	**3.5 hours**
Elevation Range:	**1,500–3,000 feet**
Usually Open:	**Year-round**
Best Time to Travel:	**October to May**
Difficulty Rating:	**1**
Scenic Rating:	**9**
Remoteness Rating:	**+0**

Special Attractions

- Boating, swimming, picnicking, and camping at three lakes along the Salt River.
- Indian ruins at Tonto National Monument.
- Popular tourist trail that follows Arizona's first historic and scenic highway.

History

The first people to travel along part of the route now known as the Apache Trail were early Indians, most likely the Salado Indians, who traveled between the mountains and the Salt River Valley along the Tonto, or Yavapai, Trail. In the 1600s, the Spanish explored the Superstition Mountains, which they called Sierra de la Espuma, or "Mountains of Foam," in their quest for gold. Supposedly, many Jesuit priests had acquired large caches of gold, and unwilling to pay a share to the king

Salado Indian cliff dwellings in Tonto National Monument

of Spain as was the custom, they hid the gold in several locations throughout the Southwest before they were recalled to Spain. The Superstition Mountains are reputed to be one of those hiding places.

During the 1880s the Salt River was suggested as a possible water storage and dam to supply Phoenix and Mesa. Construction of a road, following the path of the Salt River and the original Yavapai Trail, was started in 1903. Using mainly Indian labor, two crews started from each end of the trail. Both crews were needed to work on the section of road that descends to Fish Creek Canyon—the most demanding section of construction with its long grades that average 10 percent.

The trail running beside Salt River

Tortilla Flat was a freight station and camp along the new route. The road reached Tortilla Flat in November 1904 and people started coming out from Phoenix to see how the new road was going. Mail service along the road started in 1904, although initially an 8-mile stretch in the middle still relied on horses and mules. In the 1920s the road, now officially called the Apache Trail, was promoted as being a tourist attraction. The Apache Trail was designated as Arizona's first historic and scenic highway in 1988.

Roosevelt Dam, originally known as Tonto Dam, was completed February 5, 1911, after nearly eight years of construction. Local stone and timber from the Sierra Anchas were used in the construction of the dam, which originally measured 280 feet high and 723 feet long. During construction, workers used 350,000 cubic yards of stone with some blocks weighing as much as 10 tons each. Theodore Roosevelt dedicated the dam on March 18, 1911. Canyon Lake was formed in 1925 by the Mormon Flat Dam; and the deepest of the three lakes, Apache Lake, was created by the Horse Mesa Dam in 1927.

Description

This trail—one of Arizona's classic scenic drives—is high on the must-do lists of most people, locals and tourists alike. The drive passes by lakes, canyons, old mining towns, and cliff dwellings. The drive starts northwest of Apache Junction at the entrance to the Lost Dutchman State Park. The first 18 miles of the route are paved, but it is nevertheless an extremely scenic drive as it passes beside the first of the three lakes along the trail, Canyon Lake. The Superstition Mountains rise up to the south of the trail; these spectacular mountains were formed about 29 million years ago during the Tertiary Period and are mainly composed of volcanic ash and basalt.

The area is not remote—all along the road are services. Marinas at the lakes have camping, food, and boat ramps, although most of the national forest areas require a day-use fee. Due to the road's popularity, camping is restricted much of the way. However, there are several lakeside campgrounds.

Tortilla Flat, a historic stopping point for cowboys, road construction crews, and now tourists, has a small general store, saloon, restaurant, and gift shop. It is a popular stop along the trail and is often busy, especially on weekends. A short distance past Tortilla Flat, the road becomes wider and graded. In dry weather this section can be negotiated by those in passenger vehicles, but in wet weather drivers of such vehicles may prefer to turn back at Tortilla Flat.

One of the best views along the trail is the point at which the dirt road descends 1,500 feet in 3 miles along a series of switchbacks to Fish Creek. The overlook into the canyon at the start of the descent is the best place to stop for photographs. One of the 20 known geologic faults in Arizona runs parallel to Fish Creek Canyon.

High above the Apache Lake, Apache Lake Vista Point gives views of Four Peaks, Goat Mountain, the Painted Cliffs, and Buckhorn Ridge. The area is now home to a population of bighorn sheep that have been reintroduced. There is also a

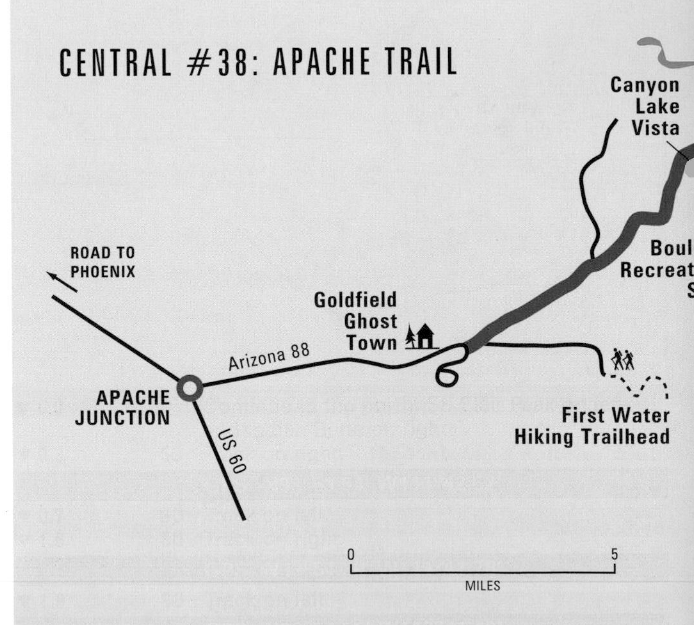

marina at Apache Lake with a restaurant, camping sites, and fishing and boating facilities.

The final section of the trail runs alongside wide Salt River to Roosevelt Dam before finishing at the intersection with Arizona 188. The designated Apache Trail continues along the paved highway to Globe.

One final point of interest to be found immediately south of Roosevelt Dam is Tonto National Monument, which consists of a substantial Salado cliff dwelling.

Current Road Information

Tonto National Forest
Mesa Ranger District
26 North MacDonald
Mesa, AZ 85211
(480) 610-3300

Tonto National Forest
Tonto Basin Ranger District
Highway 88
HC 02 Box 4800
Roosevelt, AZ 85545
(520) 467-3200

Map References

BLM Mesa, Theodore Roosevelt Lake
USFS Tonto National Forest: Mesa and Tonto Basin Ranger Districts
USGS 1:24,000 Goldfield, Mormon Flat Dam, Horse Mesa Dam, Pinyon Mt., Theodore Roosevelt Dam
1:100,000 Mesa, Theodore Roosevelt Lake
Maptech CD-ROM: Phoenix/Superstition Mountains; East Central Arizona/White Mountains
Arizona Atlas & Gazetteer, p. 58
Arizona Road & Recreation Atlas, pp. 47, 41 & pp. 81, 75
Recreational Map of Arizona

Route Directions

▼ 0.0		From Apache Junction, proceed northeast, following the signs for Arizona 88. Shortly after passing Goldfield ghost town on the left, at the turn to Lost Dutchman State Park and the sign for the start of the Apache Trail, zero trip meter and continue northeast on the paved Apache Trail.
6.8 ▲		Trail ends at the Lost Dutchman State Park, approximately 5 miles northeast of Apache Junction. Continue along Arizona 88 for Apache Junction and Phoenix.
		GPS: N33°27.85′ W111°28.90′
▼ 0.2	SO	Entering Tonto National Forest; graded road on left. Many tracks on right and left for the next 2.3 miles.
6.6 ▲	SO	Graded road on right; leaving Tonto National Forest.
▼ 0.3	SO	Road on right goes to First Water Hiking Trailhead.
6.5 ▲	SO	Road on left goes to First Water Hiking Trailhead.
▼ 2.5	SO	Paved road on right to Needle Vista Viewpoint.
4.3 ▲	SO	Paved road on left to Needle Vista Viewpoint. Many tracks on right and left for next 2.3 miles.
		GPS: N33°30.00′ W111°27.68′
▼ 2.8	SO	Track on left.
4.0 ▲	SO	Track on right.
▼ 6.7	SO	Track on left at corral.
0.1 ▲	SO	Track on right at corral.
		GPS: N33°32.47′ W111°27.00′
▼ 6.8	SO	Canyon Lake Vista on right. Zero trip meter.
0.0 ▲		Continue to the north.
		GPS: N33°32.46′ W111°26.90′
▼ 0.0		Continue to the south.
4.7 ▲	SO	Canyon Lake Vista on left. Zero trip meter.
▼ 0.2	SO	Graded road on left.
4.5 ▲	SO	Graded road on right.
▼ 1.0	SO	Cross over Canyon Lake on bridge.
3.7 ▲	SO	Cross over Canyon Lake on bridge.

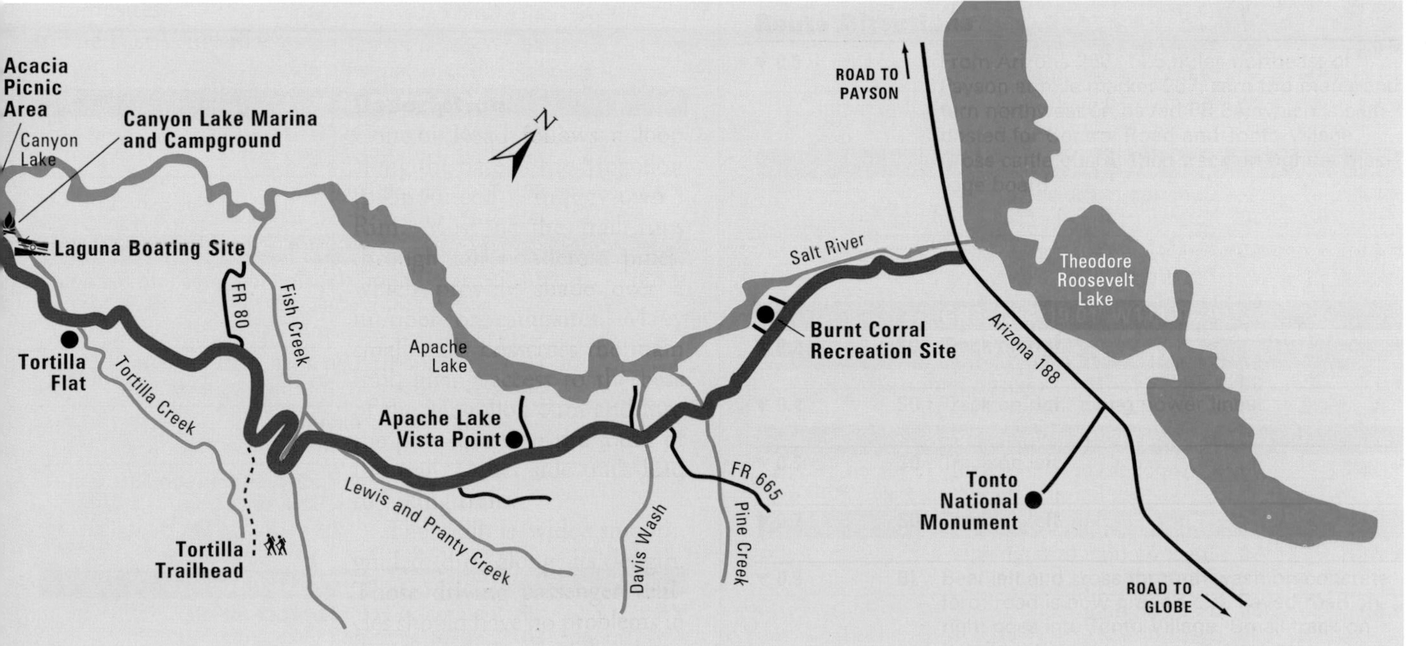

▼ 1.8 SO Acacia Picnic Area on left.
2.9 ▲ SO Acacia Picnic Area on right.

GPS: N33°32.15′ W111°25.88′

▼ 2.1 SO Palo Verde Boating Site on left.
2.6 ▲ SO Palo Verde Boating Site on right.

▼ 2.3 SO Boulder Recreation Site on right.
2.4 ▲ SO Boulder Recreation Site on left.

GPS: N33°31.95′ W111°25.55′

▼ 2.4 SO Cross over Boulder Creek on bridge.
2.3 ▲ SO Exit bridge.

▼ 2.5 SO Exit bridge. Then Boulder Canyon Hiking Trail #103 on right; Canyon Lake Marina and Campground on left.
2.2 ▲ SO Boulder Canyon Hiking Trail #103 on left; Canyon Lake Marina and Campground on right. Then cross over Boulder Creek on bridge.

GPS: N33°32.04′ W111°25.32′

▼ 2.8 SO Laguna Boating Site on left.
1.9 ▲ SO Laguna Boating Site on right.

GPS: N33°32.00′ W111°25.02′

▼ 4.7 SO Paved road on left goes to Tortilla Campground, closed May 1 to September 1; then enter Tortilla Flat. Zero trip meter.
0.0 ▲ Continue to the west.

GPS: N33°31.58′ W111°23.35′

▼ 0.0 Continue to the northeast and cross over Tortilla Creek.
6.3 ▲ SO Cross over Tortilla Creek; then enter Tortilla Flat. Paved road on right goes to Tortilla Campground. Zero trip meter.

▼ 0.6 SO Track on left.
5.7 ▲ SO Track on right.

▼ 1.0 SO Track on left and track on right.
5.3 ▲ SO Track on left and track on right.

▼ 1.2 SO Track on left.
5.1 ▲ SO Track on right.

▼ 4.2 SO Track on left is FR 80; also track on right.
2.1 ▲ SO Track on right is FR 80; also track on left.

GPS: N33°32.66′ W111°20.22′

▼ 5.4 SO Road turns to graded dirt.
0.9 ▲ SO Road is now paved.

GPS: N33°32.27′ W111°19.48′

▼ 5.9 SO Track on left; corral on left.
0.4 ▲ SO Track on right; corral on right.

▼ 6.3 SO Tortilla Trailhead on right. Zero trip meter.
0.0 ▲ Continue to the west.

GPS: N33°31.57′ W111°19.10′

▼ 0.0 Continue to the east.
8.0 ▲ SO Tortilla Trailhead on left. Zero trip meter.

▼ 0.9 SO Parking, picnic area, and overlook on left at Fish Creek Hill.
7.1 ▲ SO Parking, picnic area, and overlook on right at Fish Creek Hill.

GPS: N33°31.99′ W111°18.77′

▼ 2.4 SO Cross over Fish Creek on bridge.
5.6 ▲ SO Cross over Fish Creek on bridge.

GPS: N33°31.52′ W111°18.28′

▼ 3.6 SO Cross over Lewis and Pranty Creek on bridge.
4.4 ▲ SO Cross over Lewis and Pranty Creek on bridge.

GPS: N33°32.23′ W111°17.77′

▼ 6.0 SO Track on right through gate.
2.0 ▲ SO Track on left through gate.

▼ 6.1 SO Track on right.
1.9 ▲ SO Track on left.

▼ 6.3 SO Track on right goes to Reavis Trailhead.
1.7 ▲ SO Track on left goes to Reavis Trailhead.

GPS: N33°32.80′ W111°15.42′

▼ 8.0 SO Graded road on left goes to Apache Lake Resort. Apache Lake Vista Point immediately before turn. Zero trip meter.
0.0 ▲ Continue to the south.

GPS: N33°33.83′ W111°14.38′

▼ 0.0 Continue to the north.
6.7 ▲ SO Graded road on right goes to Apache Lake Resort. Apache Lake Vista Point immediately after the turn. Zero trip meter.

▼ 2.1 SO Graded road on left; track on right.
4.6 ▲ SO Graded road on right; track on left.

GPS: N33°34.95′ W111°12.96′

▼ 2.4 SO Cross over Davis Wash on bridge; then track on right.
4.3 ▲ SO Track on left; then cross over Davis Wash on bridge.

▼ 3.0 SO Track on left is FR 1081; then cattle guard.
3.7 ▲ SO Cattle guard; then track on right is FR 1081.

GPS: N33°35.26′ W111°12.62′

▼ 3.1 SO Track on right is FR 665.
3.6 ▲ SO Track on left is FR 665.

▼ 4.2 SO Cross over Pine Creek on bridge.
2.5 ▲ SO Cross over Pine Creek on bridge.

GPS: N33°35.93′ W111°12.11′

▼ 5.5 SO Cattle guard.
1.2 ▲ SO Cattle guard.

▼ 6.0 SO Small track on right.
0.7 ▲ SO Small track on left.

▼ 6.7 SO Paved road on left is FR 183, which goes to Burnt Corral Recreation Site, campground, and boat ramp. Zero trip meter.
0.0 ▲ Continue to the south.

GPS: N33°37.42′ W111°11.69′

▼ 0.0 Continue to the north.
6.0 ▲ SO Paved road on right is FR 183, which goes to Burnt Corral Recreation Site, campground, and boat ramp. Zero trip meter.

▼ 0.1 SO Cattle guard.
5.9 ▲ SO Cattle guard.

▼ 0.3 SO Track on right is FR 49.
5.7 ▲ SO Track on left is FR 49.

GPS: N33°37.68′ W111°11.69′

▼ 0.5 SO Track on right is FR 51.
5.5 ▲ SO Track on left is FR 51.

▼ 0.7 SO Track on left is FR 52.
5.2 ▲ SO Track on right is FR 52.

GPS: N33°38.02′ W111°11.77′

▼ 2.8 SO Track on right; track on left goes into fee area.
3.2 ▲ SO Track on right goes into fee area; track on left.

▼ 3.7 SO Cattle guard; then small track on left.
2.2 ▲ SO Small track on right; then cattle guard.

▼ 4.5 SO Road turns to paved.
1.4 ▲ SO Road turns to graded dirt.

▼ 4.9 SO Parking area for Roosevelt Dam on left. Trail passes alongside Roosevelt Dam.
1.1 ▲ SO Trail passes alongside Roosevelt Dam. Parking area for Roosevelt Dam on right.

GPS: N33°40.09′ W111°09.65′

▼ 5.5 SO Inspiration Point Lookout on left.
0.5 ▲ SO Inspiration Point Lookout on right.

▼ 6.0		Trail ends at the intersection with Arizona 88 and Arizona 188. Turn right for Globe; turn left for Payson.
	0.0 ▲	Trail commences at the intersection of Arizona 88 and Arizona 188. Zero trip meter and turn southwest onto Arizona 88, following the sign to Apache Junction.
		GPS: N33°40.34' W111°09.13'

CENTRAL REGION TRAIL #39

Montana Mountain Trail

Starting Point:	**US 60, 2 miles east of Florence Junction**
Finishing Point:	**US 60, 1.1 miles west of Superior**
Total Mileage:	**33.4 miles**
Unpaved Mileage:	**31.2 miles**
Driving Time:	**4 hours**
Elevation Range:	**2,000–5,400 feet**
Usually Open:	**Year-round**
Best Time to Travel:	**Year-round**
Difficulty Rating:	**4**
Scenic Rating:	**9**
Remoteness Rating:	**+0**

Special Attractions

- Beautiful trail skirting the southern edge of the Superstition Mountains.
- Panoramic views south from Montana Mountain.
- Moderately challenging trail with shelf road and interesting climbs.

Description

The Montana Mountain Trail is a loop trail off US 60 that starts near Florence Junction and finishes close to Superior. The majority of the trail is 4-rated, but the initial section of the trail has been upgraded to provide easier access to the Rogers Trough and Woodbury Trailheads. Passenger vehicles can travel as far as the Woodbury Trailhead turnoff with ease; past this point, a high-clearance 4WD is required.

The trail following the course of Happy Camp Canyon

A view of one of the switchbacks descending toward Superior

The trail passes through varied landscapes. The lower elevations are classic Sonoran desert landscape with prolific vegetation. Saguaros, chollas, prickly pears, and ocotillos stud the rugged, red hillsides of Byous Butte and Roblas Butte, the latter of which was named after a Mexican who ranched on the eastern slope of the butte. The trail travels up Hewitt Canyon, gradually climbing toward the Superstition Mountains. Past the Woodbury Trailhead turnoff, the trail becomes rougher and climbs steeply toward the Rogers Trough Trailhead and the start of FR 650, which winds around the south face of Montana Mountain.

This road is much tamer than it was a few years ago, but it is still a challenging and exciting drive. Moguls and a sprinkling of large boulders will have you watching your wheel placement; some sections have a loose surface, and the long sections of shelf road along the face of the mountain are narrow enough that the driver can't afford to spend too much time admiring the panoramic view. Once you reach the shelf road, the granitic road surface is smooth. There are many viewpoints and opportunities to pull over and admire the view to the south over Reavis Canyon, Superior, and the uneven bulk of Picketpost Mountain. Campers have a wide choice of sites—there are lower elevation sites among the saguaros, and higher sites with great views and cooler evenings. The trail can usually be driven at any time of year, but the lower elevations may be uncomfortably hot in summer and the higher elevations may have light snow in winter.

The trail descends abruptly to the desert floor via a series of switchbacks. Although this section is steep and slightly loose in places, it is unlikely to give you trouble. Those driving longer vehicles may need to back up to make a couple of the tighter turns.

Once down from the mountain, the narrow trail winds alongside or through Wood Camp Canyon, Whitford Canyon, and then Happy Camp Canyon. Just off the trail, an old stone cabin with a tin roof can be found. The cabin is well constructed and has mining adits behind. The coordinates of the cabin are GPS: N33°22.76' W111°06.80'.

There are several rocky sections along this leg of the trail, particularly on a short stretch in Happy Camp Wash. After passing a corral, the trail is roughly graded and faster going as it heads to rejoin US 60 near Superior.

Current Road Information

Tonto National Forest
Globe Ranger District
Route 1 Box 33
Globe, AZ 85501
(520) 402-6200

Map References

BLM Mesa
USFS Tonto National Forest: Mesa and Globe Ranger Districts
USGS 1:24,000 Florence Junction, Picketpost Mt., Iron Mt., Haunted Canyon, Superior
1:100,000 Mesa
Maptech CD-ROM: Phoenix/Superstition Mountains
Arizona Atlas & Gazetteer, p. 58
Arizona Road & Recreation Atlas, p. 47 & p. 81

Route Directions

▼ 0.0		From US 60, 2 miles east of Florence Junction and 0.7 miles west of mile marker 215, zero trip meter and turn northeast on paved Queen Valley Road, which is sign-posted to Queen Valley Resort.
4.6 ▲		Trail finishes at the intersection with US 60. Turn right for Florence Junction and Phoenix; turn left to return to Superior.
		GPS: N33°15.49' W111°18.05'
▼ 1.7	BR	Bear right onto wide, graded gravel road signed as Hewitt Station Road, FR 357. Road follows railroad.
2.9 ▲	BL	Bear left onto paved Queen Valley Road.
		GPS: N33°16.51' W111°16.85'
▼ 2.0	SO	Cross over railroad; then track on right.
2.6 ▲	SO	Track on left; then cross over railroad.
▼ 2.1	SO	Cross through wash.
2.5 ▲	SO	Cross through wash.
▼ 2.3	SO	Cattle guard; then track on right.
2.3 ▲	SO	Track on left; then cattle guard.
		GPS: N33°16.75' W111°16.17'
▼ 2.4	SO	Cross through wash.
2.2 ▲	SO	Cross through wash.
▼ 2.5	SO	Cattle guard; then two tracks on right.
2.1 ▲	SO	Two tracks on left; then cattle guard.
▼ 3.1	SO	Track on right; then cross over railroad.
1.5 ▲	SO	Cross over railroad; then track on left.
▼ 3.3	SO	Two tracks on right.
1.3 ▲	SO	Two tracks on left.
▼ 3.5	SO	Cross through wash.
1.1 ▲	SO	Cross through wash.
▼ 3.6	SO	Track on left is FR 3493; then track on left and track on right.
1.0 ▲	SO	Track on left and track on right; then second track on right is FR 3493.
		GPS: N33°17.69' W111°15.49'
▼ 3.8	SO	Track on right.
0.8 ▲	SO	Track on left.
▼ 4.0	SO	Cross through wash.
0.6 ▲	SO	Cross through wash.
▼ 4.2	SO	Track on left to corral and well.
0.4 ▲	SO	Track on right to corral and well.
▼ 4.4	SO	Two tracks on right.
0.2 ▲	SO	Two tracks on left.
▼ 4.6	TL	Turn left over cattle guard at the sign for Rogers Trough and Woodbury Trailheads. Zero trip meter.
0.0 ▲		Continue to the southwest on FR 357.
		GPS: N33°18.04' W111°14.63'
▼ 0.0		Continue to the northwest and immediately cross through wide Queen Creek wash. Road is marked FR 172.
1.6 ▲	TR	Cross through wide Queen Creek wash; then turn right after the cattle guard onto wide graded road, FR 357, at the T-intersection.
▼ 0.5	BR	Cross through wash; then cattle guard; then bear right, remaining on FR 172. Track on left is FR 1900.
1.1 ▲	BL	Track on right is FR 1900. Bear left, remaining on FR 172 and cross cattle guard; then cross through wash.
		GPS: N33°18.51' W111°14.75'
▼ 0.7	SO	Track on right under power lines.
0.9 ▲	SO	Track on left under power lines.
▼ 1.0	SO	Cross through wash.
0.6 ▲	SO	Cross through wash.
▼ 1.6	SO	Track on right and track on left are both FR 252. Zero trip meter.
0.0 ▲		Continue to the south.
		GPS: N33°19.19' W111°14.32'
▼ 0.0		Continue to the north.
5.4 ▲	SO	Track on right and track on left are both FR 252. Zero trip meter.
▼ 0.1	SO	Cross through wash.
5.3 ▲	SO	Cross through wash.
▼ 0.3	SO	Cross through wash.
5.1 ▲	SO	Cross through wash.
▼ 0.8	SO	Cross through wash, passing under Roblas Butte on the right.
4.6 ▲	SO	Cross through wash, passing under Roblas Butte on the left.
		GPS: N33°19.83' W111°13.86'
▼ 1.0	SO	Cross through wash.
4.4 ▲	SO	Cross through wash.
▼ 1.1	SO	Cross through wash; then track on left.
4.3 ▲	SO	Track on right; then cross through wash.
▼ 1.3	SO	Cross through wash.
4.1 ▲	SO	Cross through wash.
▼ 1.8	SO	Cross through wash; tracks on right and left up and down the wash.
3.6 ▲	SO	Cross through wash; tracks on right and left up and down the wash.
		GPS: N33°20.45' W111°13.39'
▼ 1.9	SO	Cattle guard; then cross through wash.
3.5 ▲	SO	Cross through wash; then cattle guard.
▼ 2.0	SO	Cross through wash; track on right up wash. Trail forks and immediately rejoins.
3.4 ▲	SO	Trail forks and immediately rejoins. Cross through wash; track on left up wash.
▼ 2.5	SO	Cross through wash.
2.9 ▲	SO	Cross through wash.

▼ 2.7		SO	Cross through wash.
	2.7 ▲	SO	Cross through wash.
▼ 2.8		SO	Cross through wash; then track on right.
	2.6 ▲	SO	Track on left; then cross through wash.
▼ 2.9		SO	Cross through wash; then track on right.
	2.5 ▲	SO	Track on left; then cross through wash.
▼ 3.0		SO	Track on left.
	2.4 ▲	SO	Track on right.
▼ 3.1		SO	Track on left.
	2.3 ▲	SO	Track on right.
▼ 3.2		SO	Cross through wash.
	2.2 ▲	SO	Cross through wash.
▼ 3.4		SO	Cross through wash.
	2.0 ▲	SO	Cross through wash.
			GPS: N33°21.43′ W111°12.51′
▼ 4.1		SO	Cross through wash.
	1.3 ▲	SO	Cross through wash.
▼ 4.4		SO	Cross through wash.
	1.0 ▲	SO	Cross through wash.
▼ 4.9		SO	Cross through wash.
	0.5 ▲	SO	Cross through wash.
▼ 5.0		SO	Cross through wash.
	0.4 ▲	SO	Cross through wash.
▼ 5.3		SO	Cross through wash.
	0.1 ▲	SO	Cross through wash.
▼ 5.4		SO	Track on left to well and corral. Zero trip meter.
	0.0 ▲		Continue to the south.
			GPS: N33°22.71′ W111°11.49′
▼ 0.0			Continue to the north.
	1.8 ▲	SO	Track on right to well and corral. Zero trip meter.
▼ 0.4		SO	Cross through wash; then track on left.
	1.4 ▲	SO	Track on right; then cross through wash.
▼ 0.8		SO	Cross through wash twice.
	1.0 ▲	SO	Cross through wash twice.
▼ 0.9		SO	Cross through wash.
	0.9 ▲	SO	Cross through wash.
▼ 1.0		SO	Cross through wash.
	0.8 ▲	SO	Cross through wash.
			GPS: N33°23.52′ W111°11.72′
▼ 1.6		SO	Track on left.
	0.2 ▲	SO	Track on right.
▼ 1.7		SO	Track on right.
	0.1 ▲	SO	Track on left.
▼ 1.8		BR	Track on left goes to Woodbury Trailhead. Bear right onto FR 172A, following the sign to Rogers Trough Trailhead. Zero trip meter.
	0.0 ▲		Continue to the south on FR 172.
			GPS: N33°23.91′ W111°11.79′
▼ 0.0			Continue to the northeast on FR 172A.
	3.4 ▲	SO	Track on right goes to Woodbury Trailhead. Continue straight on; trail is now FR 172. Zero trip meter.
▼ 0.2		SO	Cross through wash.
	3.2 ▲	SO	Cross through wash.
▼ 0.3		SO	Cross through wash.
	3.1 ▲	SO	Cross through wash.

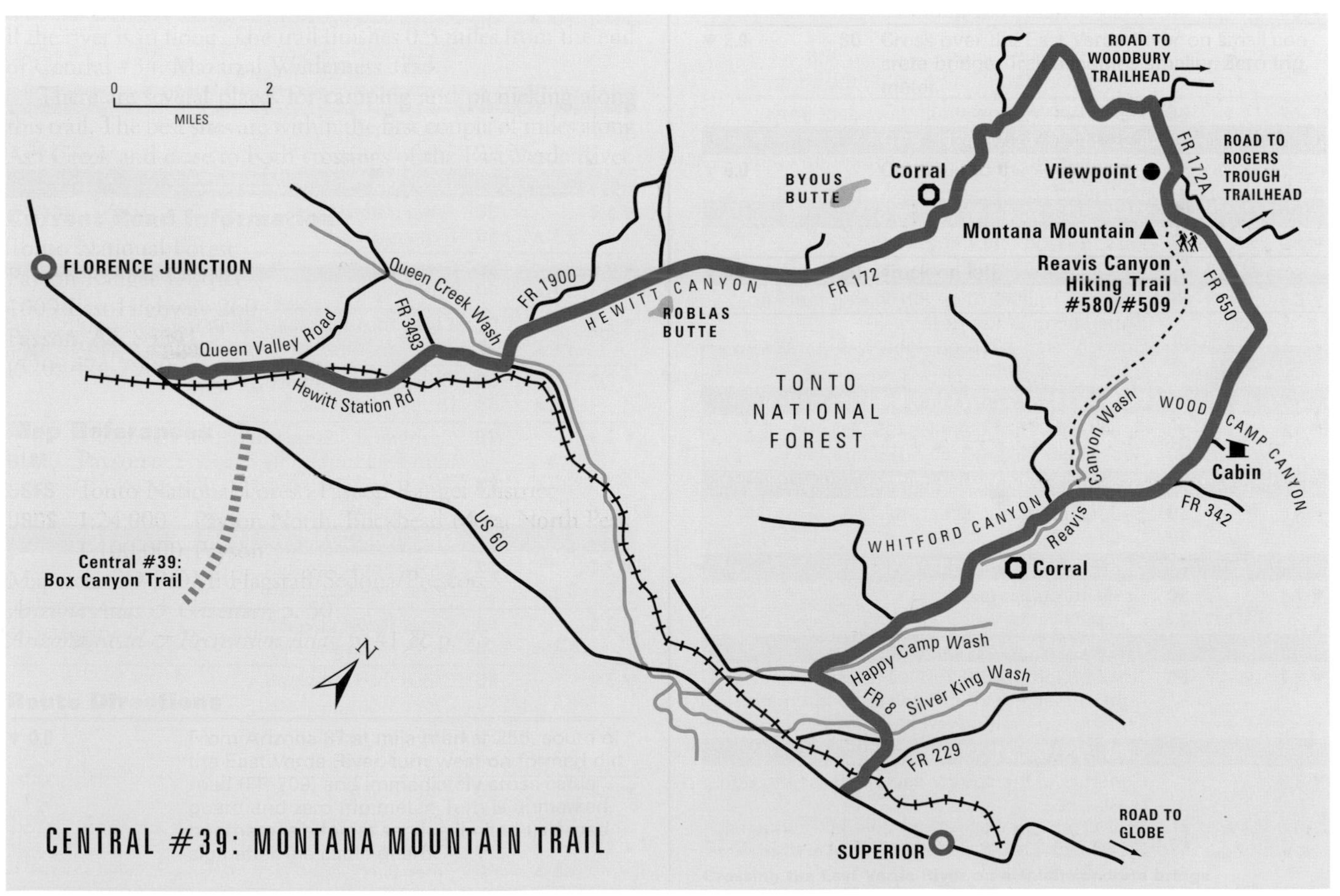

▼	▲		
▼ 1.0		SO	Cross through wash.
	2.4 ▲	SO	Cross through wash.
▼ 1.2		SO	Track on right.
	2.2 ▲	SO	Track on left.
			GPS: N33°24.35' W111°11.27'
▼ 1.7		BR	Cattle guard.
	1.7 ▲	BL	Cattle guard.
▼ 3.4		BR	Bear right onto FR 650 and zero trip meter. FR 172A continues straight ahead to Rogers Trough Trailhead.
	0.0 ▲		Continue to the southwest.
			GPS: N33°25.03' W111°10.42'
▼ 0.0			Continue to the east; trail is well used and marked for the Arizona Trail.
	7.7 ▲	BL	Bear left onto FR 172A and zero trip meter. FR 172A also goes to the right to Rogers Trough Trailhead.
▼ 0.6		SO	Cross through wash.
	7.1 ▲	SO	Cross through wash.
▼ 1.1		SO	Track on left.
	6.6 ▲	SO	Track on right.
▼ 1.2		BR	Wire gate; bear right; track on left.
	6.5 ▲	BL	Track on right; bear left through wire gate.
			GPS: N33°24.73' W111°09.61'
▼ 1.4		SO	Viewpoint on right.
	6.3 ▲	SO	Viewpoint on left.
▼ 1.9		SO	Reavis Canyon Hiking Trail #580/#509 on right.
	5.8 ▲	SO	Reavis Canyon Hiking Trail #580/#509 on left.
			GPS: N33°24.33' W111°09.35'
▼ 2.3		SO	Track on left; view of Superior and Picketpost Mountain on right to the south.
	5.4 ▲	SO	Track on right; view of Superior and Picketpost Mountain on left to the south.
▼ 2.7		SO	Pass through fence line. View right down Reavis Canyon.
	5.0 ▲	SO	Pass through fence line. View left down Reavis Canyon.
			GPS: N33°24.44' W111°08.67'
▼ 2.8		SO	Pass through fence line.
	4.9 ▲	SO	Pass through fence line.
▼ 2.9		BR	Spencer Trail #275 on left; hiking trail into Superstition Wilderness.
	4.8 ▲	BL	Spencer Trail #275 on right; hiking trail into Superstition Wilderness.
			GPS: N33°24.37' W111°08.44'
▼ 4.8		SO	Rock Creek Hiking Trail #195 on left.
	2.9 ▲	SO	Rock Creek Hiking Trail #195 on right.
			GPS: N33°24.00' W111°07.38'
▼ 5.5		SO	Saddle; start of descent.
	2.2 ▲	SO	Saddle; end of climb.
			GPS: N33°23.61' W111°07.31'
▼ 7.6		SO	Cross through wash.
	0.1 ▲	SO	Cross through wash.
			GPS: N33°22.77' W111°07.02'
▼ 7.7		BR	Track on left goes 0.2 miles to cabin. Bear right, remaining on FR 650. Zero trip meter.
	0.0 ▲		Continue to the northwest.
			GPS: N33°22.71' W111°06.99'
▼ 0.0			Continue to the southwest and cross through wash.
	0.7 ▲	BL	Cross through wash; then bear left, remaining on FR 650. Zero trip meter. Track on right goes 0.2 miles to cabin.
▼ 0.4		SO	Cross through wash.
	0.3 ▲	SO	Cross through wash.
▼ 0.5		SO	Cross through wash.
	0.2 ▲	SO	Cross through wash.
▼ 0.6		SO	Cross through wash.
	0.1 ▲	SO	Cross through wash.
▼ 0.7		SO	Track on left is FR 342. Continue straight, remaining on FR 650. Zero trip meter.
	0.0 ▲		Continue to the northwest.
			GPS: N33°22.13' W111°07.00'
▼ 0.0			Continue to the south.
	5.8 ▲	BL	Track on right is FR 342; bear left, remaining on FR 650. Zero trip meter.
▼ 0.4		SO	Cross through wash.
	5.4 ▲	SO	Cross through wash.
			GPS: N33°21.83' W111°07.06'
▼ 0.6		SO	Cross through wash.
	5.2 ▲	SO	Cross through wash.
▼ 0.7		SO	Track on right.
	5.1 ▲	SO	Track on left.
▼ 0.8		SO	Cross through wash.
	5.0 ▲	SO	Cross through wash.
▼ 1.0		SO	Track on left; then cross through wash.
	4.8 ▲	SO	Cross through wash; then track on right.
▼ 1.2		SO	Two tracks on left.
	4.6 ▲	SO	Two tracks on right.
▼ 1.4		SO	Cross through wash.
	4.4 ▲	SO	Cross through wash.
▼ 1.6		SO	Track on right is Reavis Canyon Trail #509, part of the Arizona Trail; then cross through Reavis Canyon Wash.
	4.2 ▲	BR	Cross through Reavis Canyon Wash; then track on left is Reavis Canyon Trail #509, part of the Arizona Trail.
			GPS: N33°21.14' W111°07.87'
▼ 1.7		SO	Track on right.
	4.1 ▲	SO	Track on left.
			GPS: N33°20.99' W111°07.85'
▼ 1.9		SO	Enter wash.
	3.9 ▲	SO	Exit wash.
▼ 2.0		SO	Exit wash.
	3.8 ▲	SO	Enter wash.
▼ 2.1		SO	Cross through wash; then track on right.
	3.7 ▲	SO	Track on left; then cross through wash.
▼ 2.2		SO	Cross through wash.
	3.6 ▲	SO	Cross through wash.
▼ 2.3		SO	Corral and shed on left. Trail standard improves to roughly graded road.
	3.5 ▲	SO	Corral and shed on right. Trail is now a rough, formed trail.
			GPS: N33°20.50' W111°07.95'
▼ 2.4		SO	Cross through wash.
	3.4 ▲	SO	Cross through wash.
▼ 2.6		SO	Cross through wash.
	3.2 ▲	SO	Cross through wash.
▼ 3.0		SO	Cross through wash.
	2.8 ▲	SO	Cross through wash.
▼ 3.1		SO	Track on right up wash.
	2.7 ▲	SO	Track on left up wash.
▼ 3.6		SO	Enter wash.
	2.2 ▲	SO	Exit wash.
▼ 4.0		SO	Exit wash.
	1.8 ▲	SO	Enter wash.

▼ 4.1		SO	Track on right.
	1.7 ▲	SO	Track on left.
▼ 4.3		SO	Cross through wash; then track on right.
	1.5 ▲	SO	Track on left; then cross through wash.
▼ 4.8		SO	Track on right.
	1.0 ▲	SO	Track on left.
▼ 4.9		SO	Cross through wash; then cattle guard.
	0.9 ▲	SO	Cattle guard; then cross through wash.
▼ 5.0		SO	Enter wash.
	0.8 ▲	SO	Exit wash.
▼ 5.1		SO	Exit wash.
	0.7 ▲	SO	Enter wash.
▼ 5.2		SO	Cross through wash twice.
	0.6 ▲	SO	Cross through wash twice.
▼ 5.3		SO	Cross through wash.
	0.5 ▲	SO	Cross through wash.
▼ 5.5		SO	Cross through wash; then track on right.
	0.3 ▲	SO	Track on left; then cross through wash.
▼ 5.6		SO	Enter wash.
	0.2 ▲	SO	Exit wash.
▼ 5.8		TL	Exit wash; then T-intersection. Turn left onto FR 8. Zero trip meter.
	0.0 ▲		Continue to the northwest and enter wash.
			GPS: N33°17.75' W111°08.86'
▼ 0.0			Continue to the northeast.
	1.7 ▲	TR	Turn right onto FR 650, narrow graded road. There is a marker post at the intersection. Zero trip meter.
▼ 0.8		SO	Track on right.
	0.9 ▲	SO	Track on left.
▼ 1.0		SO	Track on right.
	0.7 ▲	SO	Track on left.
▼ 1.2		SO	Cross through Silver King Wash.
	0.5 ▲	SO	Cross through Silver King Wash.
▼ 1.3		SO	Two tracks on right; track on left.
	0.4 ▲	SO	Two tracks on left; track on right.
			GPS: N33°17.82' W111°07.52'
▼ 1.4		SO	Cross through wash.
	0.3 ▲	SO	Cross through wash.
▼ 1.6		SO	Cross through wash.
	0.1 ▲	SO	Cross through wash.
▼ 1.7		BR	Bear right, remaining on FR 8. Graded road on left is FR 229. Zero trip meter
	0.0 ▲		Continue to the northwest.
			GPS: N33°17.53' W111°07.38'
▼ 0.0			Continue to the south.
	0.7 ▲	BL	Bear left, remaining on FR 8. Graded road ahead is FR 229. Zero trip meter.
▼ 0.1		SO	Cross through wash.
	0.6 ▲	SO	Cross through wash.
▼ 0.3		SO	Cross over disused railroad; then tracks on left and right into works area.
	0.4 ▲	SO	Tracks on left and right into works area; then cross over disused railroad.
▼ 0.5		SO	Cattle guard; road is paved.
	0.2 ▲	SO	Cattle guard; road turns to graded dirt.
▼ 0.7			Trail ends at intersection with US 60 on the western edge of Superior.
	0.0 ▲		Trail commences on US 60 on the western edge of Superior, immediately west of the "Welcome to Superior" sign, 0.1 miles east of mile marker 225. Zero trip meter and turn northeast up paved Silver King Road.
			GPS: N33°17.08' W111°07.54'

CENTRAL REGION TRAIL #40

Telegraph Canyon Trail

Starting Point:	**US 60, on the western edge of Superior**
Finishing Point:	**Central #41: Box Canyon Trail, 6.7 miles from US 60**
Total Mileage:	**12.2 miles**
Unpaved Mileage:	**10.6 miles**
Driving Time:	**2.5 hours**
Elevation Range:	**2,600–3,800 feet**
Usually Open:	**Year-round**
Best Time to Travel:	**October to May**
Difficulty Rating:	**5**
Scenic Rating:	**9**
Remoteness Rating:	**+0**

Special Attractions

- Moderately challenging rocky trail in scenic Telegraph Canyon.
- Remains of Orphan Boy and Ajax Mines.
- Trail passes through a wide variety of desert scenery.
- Views of Picketpost Mountain, Superior, and the Superstition Mountains.

Description

This interesting and challenging trail can be combined with many other trails in the region to make a full day's travel. The trail's main challenges come, first, from the rocky sections at the start of the trail as it proceeds toward Telegraph Canyon and, second, from a narrow pathway between the edge of the shelf road and some deep washouts. In between these sections, the trail is interesting driving, but of a more moderate standard.

The trail leaves from Superior and travels along a well-used forest road (FR 4) as it skirts the edge of a quarry and rises over a ridge. From here, there are panoramic views back over Superior, far down in the valley, and toward the immense bulk of

The trail in Telegraph Canyon with Picketpost Mountain looming in the background

The Ajax Mine shaft and foundations

Picketpost Mountain. The Superstition Mountains behind Superior can be seen, and on a clear day, Weavers Needle can be seen to the northwest. The narrow canyon of Arnett Creek can also be seen from the trail. All at once, the trail becomes rough and winding with an uneven surface, small rock ledges, and a loose, moguled surface.

The trail drops down, enters Telegraph Canyon, and proceeds north, traveling above the wash as it slowly rises to exit from the head of the canyon. The canyon is fairly wide, surrounded by jagged peaks, and has excellent views in all directions—better than you would normally expect for a trail contained within a canyon.

Once you emerge from Telegraph Canyon, the trail is smoother although there are still a few steep sections and moguls. It intersects with the Arizona Trail, a cross-Arizona foot and pack trail, although vehicles are permitted on this section. As the trail winds around the head of the canyon, climbing its way up to the ridge, the views get better and better. The section of trail before the Ajax Mine has some fairly deep washouts that have left a narrow pathway, which is just wide enough to get a full-size vehicle through; but both sets of wheels will be very close to the edge.

The trail becomes easy on the final section down to join Central #41: Box Canyon Trail to Florence.

Current Road Information

Tonto National Forest
Globe Ranger District
Route 1 Box 33
Globe, AZ 85501
(520) 402-6200

Map References

BLM Mesa
USFS Tonto National Forest: Globe Ranger District
USGS 1:24,000 Superior, Picketpost Mt., Mineral Mt.
1:100,000 Mesa
Maptech CD-ROM: Phoenix/Superstition Mountains
Arizona Atlas & Gazetteer, p. 58
Arizona Road & Recreation Atlas, p. 47 & p. 81

Route Directions

▼ 0.0			From US 60 on the western edge of Superior, turn south on Mary Drive and zero trip meter.
	1.6 ▲		Trail ends at the intersection with US 60 on the western edge of Superior.
			GPS: N33°17.14' W111°06.99'
▼ 0.1		SO	Cross through wash on concrete ford. Remain on main paved Mary Drive.
	1.5 ▲	SO	Cross through wash on concrete ford.
▼ 0.5		TR	Turn right onto paved road—no street sign at intersection but the cemetery is opposite turn.
	1.1 ▲	TL	Turn left onto paved Mary Drive. The cemetery is opposite the turn.
▼ 0.6		SO	Cattle guard.
	1.0 ▲	SO	Cattle guard.
▼ 1.6		SO	Paved road on left; track on right. Continue straight on; road turns to dirt. Zero trip meter.
	0.0 ▲		Continue to the north toward Superior.
			GPS: N33°15.79' W111°06.98'
▼ 0.0			Continue to the south.
	5.7 ▲	SO	Paved road on right; track on left. Continue straight on; road is now paved. Zero trip meter.
▼ 0.1		SO	Track on left.
	5.6 ▲	SO	Track on right.
▼ 0.2		BR	Major graded road continues on left; bear second right onto smaller formed trail, FR 4, marked by forestry marker post. FR 230 is straight on; unmarked road on right.
	5.5 ▲	SO	Track on right is FR 230; unmarked track on left; continue straight on toward Superior on larger graded road.
			GPS: N33°15.63' W111°07.10'
▼ 0.3		SO	Track on left and track on right. Picketpost Mountain is ahead.
	5.4 ▲	SO	Track on right and track on left.
▼ 0.4		SO	Track on left; then cross through Arnett Creek.

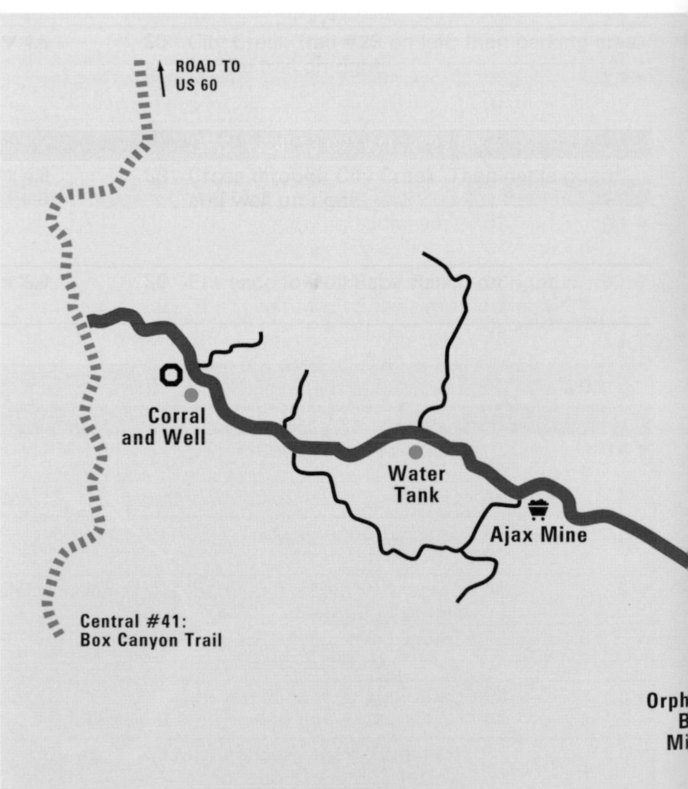

CENTRAL #40: TELEGRAPH CANYON TRAIL

	5.3 ▲	SO	Cross through Arnett Creek; then track on right.
			GPS: N33°15.57' W111°07.33'
▼ 0.5		TL	Pass through quarry; then turn left after quarry. Track continues straight ahead.
	5.2 ▲	TR	Track on left; turn right through quarry; then left across wash.
			GPS: N33°15.61' W111°07.39'
▼ 0.7		SO	Cattle guard.
	5.0 ▲	SO	Cattle guard.
			GPS: N33°15.59' W111°07.54'
▼ 0.8		SO	Cross through wash; track on left down wash. Keep out of wash, heading up ridge.
	4.9 ▲	SO	Cross through wash; track on right down wash.
▼ 0.9		BR	Trail forks and rejoins almost immediately; track on left leads off from left-hand fork.
	4.8 ▲	BL	Trail forks and rejoins almost immediately; track on right leads off from right-hand fork.
▼ 1.2		SO	Faint track on right.
	4.5 ▲	SO	Faint track on left.
▼ 1.4		BL	Faint track on right; then cattle guard.
	4.3 ▲	BR	Cattle guard; then faint track on left. Views ahead to Superior and Queen Canyon.
▼ 2.0		SO	Track on left.
	3.7 ▲	SO	Track on right.
▼ 2.1		SO	Enter wash.
	3.6 ▲	SO	Exit wash.
			GPS: N33°15.10' W111°08.60'
▼ 2.2		SO	Exit wash and follow alongside wash in Telegraph Canyon.
	3.5 ▲	SO	Enter wash.
▼ 2.4		SO	Cross through Telegraph Canyon Wash.
	3.3 ▲	SO	Cross through Telegraph Canyon Wash; trail leaves wash path.
▼ 2.5		SO	Cross through wash.
	3.2 ▲	SO	Cross through wash.
▼ 2.7		SO	Cross through wash.
	3.0 ▲	SO	Cross through wash.
▼ 3.6		SO	Track on left.
	2.1 ▲	SO	Track on right.
			GPS: N33°14.11' W111°08.60'
▼ 3.8		SO	Cross through wash.
	1.9 ▲	SO	Cross through wash.
▼ 4.0		SO	Cross through two washes.
	1.7 ▲	SO	Cross through two washes.
▼ 4.1		SO	Cross through wash.
	1.6 ▲	SO	Cross through wash.
▼ 4.4		SO	Cross through wash.
	1.3 ▲	SO	Cross through wash.
			GPS: N33°13.53' W111°08.72'
▼ 4.9		SO	Cross through wash; then track on right.
	0.8 ▲	SO	Track on left; then cross through wash.
			GPS: N33°13.07' W111°08.85'
▼ 5.2		SO	Cross through three washes.
	0.5 ▲	SO	Cross through three washes.
▼ 5.7		BR	Track on left is part of the Arizona Trail and goes 0.1 miles to a mine with tin shed and timber structures. Zero trip meter at Arizona Trail marker post.

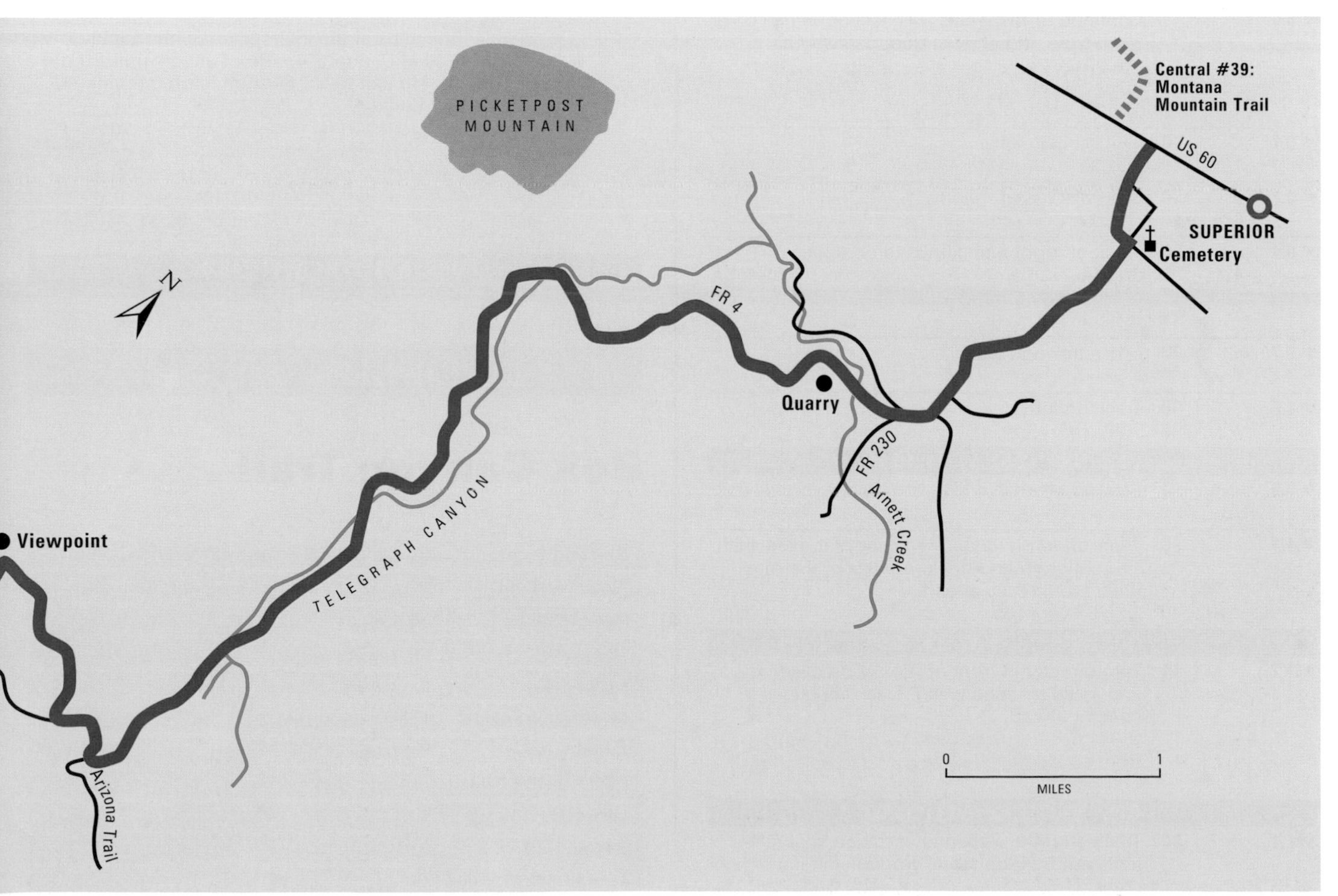

	0.0 ▲		Continue on to the northeast and enter the upper reaches of Telegraph Canyon, leaving the Arizona Trail.
			GPS: N33°12.41′ W111°08.97′
▼ 0.0			Continue to the north; trail is leaving Telegraph Canyon and now follows the Arizona Trail.
	1.5 ▲	SO	Track on right is part of the Arizona Trail and goes 0.1 miles to a mine with tin shed and timber structures. Zero trip meter at marker post.
▼ 0.1		SO	Cross through wash.
	1.4 ▲	SO	Cross through wash.
▼ 0.4		SO	Track on left goes 0.1 miles to the Orphan Boy Mine and great views to the north and south.
	1.1 ▲	SO	Track on right goes 0.1 miles to the Orphan Boy Mine and great views to the north and south.
			GPS: N33°12.45′ W111°09.22′
▼ 0.9		SO	Cattle guard.
	0.6 ▲	SO	Cattle guard.
			GPS: N33°12.64′ W111°09.51′
▼ 1.4		SO	Viewpoint on right; the Ajax Mine is visible farther along the trail. Then track on right goes back to viewpoint and is part of the Arizona Trail, marked by wooden posts.
	0.1 ▲	SO	Track on left goes to viewpoint and is part of the Arizona Trail, marked by wooden posts. Then viewpoint on left.
			GPS: N33°12.75′ W111°09.94′
▼ 1.5		TR	Well-used track on left in front of small hillock goes to the Orphan Boy Mine. Zero trip meter.
	0.0 ▲		Continue to the north.
			GPS: N33°12.66′ W111°09.93′
▼ 0.0			Continue to the west. This section of trail can be narrow and uneven due to washouts.
	2.8 ▲	TL	Well-used track continues straight on past small hillock and goes to the Orphan Boy Mine. Zero trip meter.
▼ 0.1		SO	Old track on left.
	2.7 ▲	SO	Old track on right rejoins.
▼ 0.2		SO	Old track on left rejoins.
	2.6 ▲	SO	Old track on right.
▼ 0.4		SO	Track on right and campsite on right.
	2.4 ▲	SO	Track on left and campsite on left. This section of trail can be narrow and uneven due to washouts.
▼ 0.7		SO	Cross through wash.
	2.1 ▲	SO	Cross through wash.
▼ 0.8		SO	Track on left.
	2.0 ▲	SO	Track on right.
			GPS: N33°12.52′ W111°10.76′
▼ 0.9		SO	Blocked-off shaft on left immediately beside trail.
	1.9 ▲	SO	Blocked-off shaft on right immediately beside trail.
▼ 1.1		SO	Track on left to concrete bases and mine shaft. The concrete and brick remains of the Ajax Mine are directly ahead.
	1.7 ▲	SO	Track on right to concrete bases and mine shaft.
			GPS: N33°12.48′ W111°10.97′
▼ 1.2		TR	Turn directly in front of Ajax Mine buildings and cross through wash. Track continues straight ahead.
	1.6 ▲	TL	Cross through wash and turn left directly in front of the buildings of the Ajax Mine. Track on right.
			GPS: N33°12.42′ W111°11.00′
▼ 1.3		SO	Track on right. Sections of the original mine trail with built-up stone work on left (far side of creek).
	1.5 ▲	SO	Track on left. Sections of the original mine trail with built-up stone work on right (far side of creek).
▼ 1.7		BL	Track on right; then tank on left.
	1.1 ▲	SO	Tank on right; then track on left.
			GPS: N33°12.36′ W111°11.51′
▼ 1.9		SO	Cross through wash.
	0.9 ▲	SO	Cross through wash.
▼ 2.0		SO	Cross through wash.
	0.8 ▲	SO	Cross through wash.
▼ 2.3		SO	Track on left; then track on right.
	0.5 ▲	SO	Track on left; then track on right.
▼ 2.5		SO	Two tracks on right.
	0.3 ▲	SO	Two tracks on left.
▼ 2.6		SO	Track on left.
	0.2 ▲	SO	Track on right.
▼ 2.7		SO	Cross through wash.
	0.1 ▲	SO	Cross through wash.
▼ 2.8		SO	Cross through wash; then well and corral on left; track on right. Zero trip meter.
	0.0 ▲		Continue to the east and cross through wash.
			GPS: N33°11.98′ W111°12.48′
▼ 0.0			Continue to the west and cross through wash.
	0.6 ▲	SO	Well and corral on right; track on left; then cross through wash. Zero trip meter.
▼ 0.1		SO	Cross through wash.
	0.5 ▲	SO	Cross through wash.
▼ 0.4		SO	Cross through wash.
	0.2 ▲	SO	Cross through wash.
▼ 0.5		SO	Cross through wash; then track on right.
	0.1 ▲	SO	Track on left; then cross through wash.
▼ 0.6			Trail ends at the intersection with roughly graded Central #41: Box Canyon Trail. Turn right to exit to US 60; turn left to continue to Box Canyon.
	0.0 ▲		Trail starts on Central #41: Box Canyon Trail, 6.7 miles from the north end of the trail. The intersection is unmarked but is on a slight right-hand bend immediately before a wash crossing. Zero trip meter and turn northeast on well-used, formed trail.
			GPS: N33°11.84′ W111°13.02′

CENTRAL REGION TRAIL #41

Box Canyon Trail

Starting Point:	**US 60, 3.6 miles east of Florence Junction**
Finishing Point:	**Arizona 79, 2 miles north of Florence**
Total Mileage:	**25.4 miles**
Unpaved Mileage:	**25.4 miles**
Driving Time:	**2.5 hours**
Elevation Range:	**1,500–2,900 feet**
Usually Open:	**Year-round**
Best Time to Travel:	**October to May**
Difficulty Rating:	**5**
Scenic Rating:	**8**
Remoteness Rating:	**+0**

An old adobe building in Box Canyon with ocotillo fence

Special Attractions

- Extremely narrow, deep Box Canyon.
- Moderate rock crawling section within the canyon.
- Varied desert views.

Description

Although this trail is rated 5 for difficulty, only 1.3 miles in the narrow section of Box Canyon merit this rating. The remainder of the trail is rated 2. However, given that this section is in the middle of the trail and there is no alternate way around it, the trail has been rated 5.

The trail leaves US 60 and enters a military firing range. A notice board at the junction gives dates of live firing practice. In addition, a red flag is flown from the flagpole at the start of the trail when live firing is in progress. Most of this trail is on state land, and a valid permit is required.

The northern section of the trail is wide and roughly graded as it wanders through prolific Sonoran desert vegetation. There are many tracks to the right and left, and a great number of them lead to popular camping areas, which are often used as base camps by ATV owners and horseback riders.

Other trails are longer and worth exploring as there are many old mines in the region. Two of them are detailed in this book: Central #40: Telegraph Canyon Trail and Central #42: Martinez Mine Trail (which leads to Central #43: Cochran Coke Ovens Trail). Farther along, the trail rises to give excellent views of Dromedary Peak and Weavers Needle to the north, and of North Butte to the south.

The trail passing through a very narrow section in Box Canyon

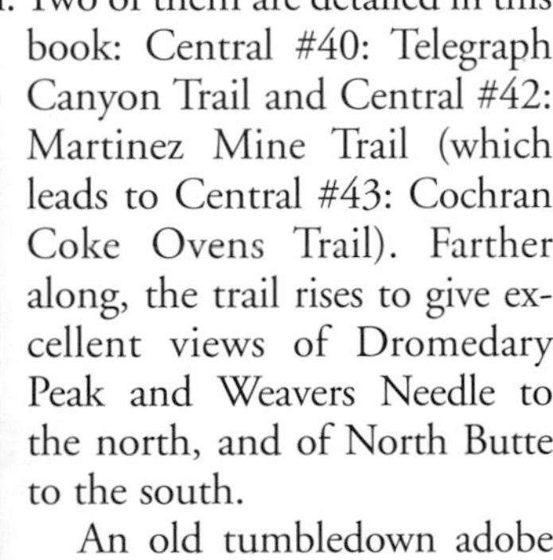

An old tumbledown adobe casita is passed in Box Canyon. It is interesting to speculate on who might have lived here. Of particular interest is the fence, which was constructed from the branches of ocotillos. These have sprouted, creating a living fence line.

Immediately past the turnoff for Central #42: Martinez Mine Trail, the main trail enters the narrows of Box Canyon and the start of the 5-rated section. The trail is very twisty and narrow, and there are large boulders and rocks that must be negotiated. Vehicles with side steps, low-hanging brush bars, or low-clearance will be at a definite disadvantage. This trail is not recommended for such vehicles because of the likelihood of damage. Even though this section is better suited for smaller vehicles, we have seen a full-size pickup drive through successfully, although the driver needed to back up to avoid some obstacles. In several spots the driving line is extremely tight between the rocks, and depending on your wheelbase, you must be prepared to ride extremely large boulders. Drivers have stacked rocks to ease the driving line. The high, steep red walls inside the canyon are dramatic. The wash is rearranged after every storm and may not be passable after heavy flooding.

Once out of Box Canyon, the trail reverts to a 2-standard, graded dirt road that runs over flatter ground to join Price Road. It then follows the railroad and joins Arizona 79, 2 miles north of Florence.

Current Road Information

Bureau of Land Management
Phoenix Field Office
2015 West Deer Valley Rd.
Phoenix, AZ 85027
(623) 580-5500

Map References

BLM Mesa
USGS 1:24,000 Florence Junction, Florence NE, Mineral Mt., North Butte, Florence SE, Florence
1:100,000 Mesa
Maptech CD-ROM: Phoenix/Superstition Mountains
Arizona Atlas & Gazetteer, p. 58
Arizona Road & Recreation Atlas, p. 47 & p. 81
Recreational Map of Arizona (incomplete)

Route Directions

▼ 0.0			From US 60, 3.6 miles east of Florence Junction, zero trip meter and turn south over cattle guard on unmarked, well-used dirt road. You are entering the military firing range. This is Mineral Mountain Road, but it is not marked.
	6.0 ▲		Cattle guard; then trail ends on US 60. Turn right for Superior; turn left for Phoenix via Florence Junction.
			GPS: N33°15.80' W111°16.47'
▼ 0.3		SO	Track on right.
	5.7 ▲	SO	Track on left.
▼ 0.5		SO	Track on left and track on right follow path of gas pipeline. Corral on left.
	5.5 ▲	SO	Track on left and track on right follow path of gas pipeline. Corral on right.
▼ 0.8		SO	Track on left and track on right.
	5.2 ▲	SO	Track on left and track on right.
▼ 1.1		SO	Track on left.
	4.9 ▲	SO	Track on right.
			GPS: N33°14.75' W111°16.29'
▼ 1.2		SO	Track on right.
	4.8 ▲	SO	Track on left.

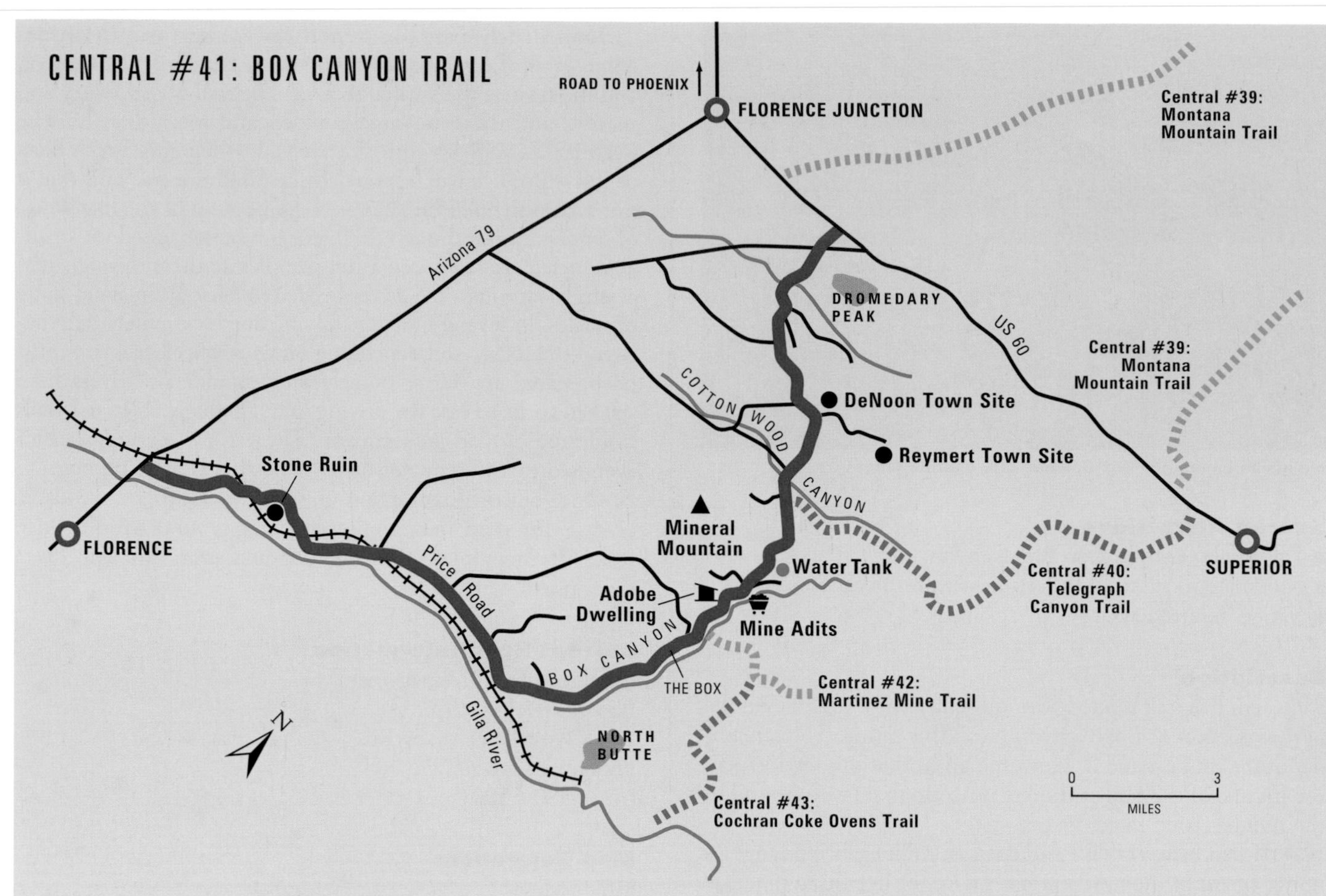

▼	▲		
▼ 1.3		SO	Cross through wash.
	4.7 ▲	SO	Cross through wash.
▼ 1.4		SO	Track on right.
	4.6 ▲	SO	Track on left.
▼ 1.9		SO	Cross through wash; then track on left.
	4.1 ▲	SO	Track on right; then cross through wash.
▼ 2.1		SO	Track on left.
	3.9 ▲	SO	Track on right.
▼ 2.3		SO	Cross through two washes.
	3.7 ▲	SO	Cross through two washes.
▼ 2.5		SO	Track on right.
	3.5 ▲	SO	Track on left.
▼ 2.7		SO	Track on right.
	3.3 ▲	SO	Track on left.
▼ 3.6		SO	Track on left.
	2.4 ▲	SO	Track on right.
▼ 4.0		SO	Track on right and track on left.
	2.0 ▲	SO	Track on right and track on left.
▼ 4.2		SO	Track on right.
	1.8 ▲	BR	Track on left.
			GPS: N33°13.12' W111°14.20'
▼ 4.5		SO	Cross through fence line.
	1.5 ▲	SO	Cross through fence line.
▼ 4.6		SO	Track on left.
	1.4 ▲	SO	Track on right.
			GPS: N33°13.22' W111°13.89'
▼ 4.7		SO	Track on left.
	1.3 ▲	SO	Track on right.
▼ 6.0		SO	Track on right goes to Arizona 79. Zero trip meter.
	0.0 ▲		Continue to the north.
			GPS: N33°12.17' W111°13.45'
▼ 0.0			Continue to the south.
	0.7 ▲	SO	Track on left goes to Arizona 79. Zero trip meter.
▼ 0.1		BL	Cross through wash; entering Cottonwood Canyon. Trail follows alongside wash, crossing it often for next 0.5 miles.
	0.6 ▲	BR	Cross through wash; then bear right, leaving Cottonwood Canyon.
▼ 0.2		SO	Track on left.
	0.5 ▲	SO	Track on right.
▼ 0.6		SO	Exit wash.
	0.1 ▲	SO	Enter wash; trail follows alongside wash, crossing it often for next 0.5 miles.
▼ 0.7		BR	Track on left is Central #40: Telegraph Canyon Trail. Zero trip meter.
	0.0 ▲		Continue to the northwest.
			GPS: N33°11.84' W111°13.02'
▼ 0.0			Continue to the east and cross through wash.
	4.1 ▲	BL	Cross through wash; then track on right is Central #40: Telegraph Canyon Trail. Zero trip meter.
▼ 0.1		SO	Track on right and well-used track on left. Continue straight on and cross through wash.
	4.0 ▲	SO	Cross through wash; then track on left and well-used track on right.
			GPS: N33°11.83' W111°12.99'
▼ 0.2		SO	Cross through wash.
	3.9 ▲	SO	Cross through wash.

▼ 0.5		SO	Track on right.
	3.6 ▲	SO	Track on left.
▼ 0.6		SO	Track on left.
	3.5 ▲	SO	Track on right.
▼ 1.1		SO	Saddle with views in all directions.
	3.0 ▲	SO	Saddle with views in all directions.
			GPS: N33°11.21' W111°12.32'
▼ 1.2		SO	Two tracks on right.
	2.9 ▲	SO	Two tracks on left.
▼ 1.4		SO	Track on right.
	2.7 ▲	SO	Track on left.
▼ 1.6		SO	Track on left at water tank goes to mine.
	2.5 ▲	SO	Track on right at water tank goes to mine.
			GPS: N33°10.88' W111°12.19'
▼ 1.7		SO	Track on right; enter wash. Start to enter side canyon.
	2.4 ▲	SO	Exit side canyon. Track on left; exit wash.
▼ 2.0		SO	Track on right.
	2.1 ▲	SO	Track on left.
▼ 2.3		SO	Adits on left.
	1.8 ▲	SO	Adits on right.
			GPS: N33°10.27' W111°12.20'
▼ 2.4		SO	Track on right and corral on right.
	1.7 ▲	SO	Track on left and corral on left.
▼ 2.5		SO	Track on left.
	1.6 ▲	SO	Track on right.
▼ 2.6		SO	Track on left. Main trail now joins Box Canyon; then track on right.
	1.5 ▲	SO	Track on left; then track on right. Main trail now leaves Box Canyon up a side wash.
			GPS: N33°10.08' W111°12.04'
▼ 2.9		SO	Track on left.
	1.2 ▲	SO	Track on right.
▼ 3.0		SO	Track on left.
	1.1 ▲	SO	Track on right.
▼ 3.1		SO	Track on right goes to old adobe dwelling alongside main trail in canyon.
	1.0 ▲	SO	Track on left goes to old adobe dwelling alongside main trail in canyon.
			GPS: N33°09.71' W111°12.10'
▼ 3.6		SO	Two tracks on right.
	0.5 ▲	SO	Two tracks on left.
▼ 4.1		SO	Well-used track on left is start of Central #42: Martinez Mine Trail. There is a yellow road direction arrow at the junction. Zero trip meter.
	0.0 ▲		Continue to the northwest.
			GPS: N33°08.98' W111°12.05'
▼ 0.0			Continue to the south.
	5.7 ▲	BL	Well used track on right is start of Central #42: Martinez Mine Trail. There is a yellow road direction arrow at the junction. Zero trip meter.
▼ 0.2		SO	Track on right; then cattle guard. Enter the narrow section of Box Canyon.
	5.5 ▲	SO	Exit the narrow section of Box Canyon. Cattle guard; then track on left.
▼ 0.5		SO	Tight clearance between boulders requires you to ride large rocks.
	5.2 ▲	SO	Tight clearance between boulders requires you to ride large rocks.
▼ 0.8		SO	Large boulder in center of wash; drivers have stacked rocks to create a driving line.
	4.9 ▲	SO	Large boulder in center of wash; drivers have stacked rocks to create a driving line.
▼ 1.5		SO	Exit tight section of Box Canyon.
	4.2 ▲	SO	Enter the narrow section of Box Canyon.

▼ 1.8		BL	Bear left out of wash, following roughly graded trail.
	3.9 ▲	SO	Re-enter wash.
▼ 2.2		SO	Re-enter wash.
	3.5 ▲	SO	Exit wash.
▼ 2.4		SO	Bear left out of wash.
	3.3 ▲	SO	Enter wash.
▼ 2.6		SO	Track on left.
	3.1 ▲	SO	Track on right.
▼ 3.2		SO	Enter wash; trail runs in or alongside it for next 0.5 miles.
	2.5 ▲	SO	Exit wash.
▼ 3.7		SO	Exit wash.
	2.0 ▲	SO	Enter wash; trail runs in or alongside wash for next 0.5 miles.
▼ 3.9		SO	Track on right.
	1.8 ▲	SO	Track on left.
▼ 4.0		SO	Track on left.
	1.7 ▲	SO	Track on right.
▼ 4.1		SO	Track on right; then cattle guard; then track on left.
	1.6 ▲	SO	Track on right; then cattle guard; then track on left.
			GPS: N33°06.23' W111°13.48'
▼ 4.9		SO	Track on left.
	0.8 ▲	SO	Track on right.
▼ 5.1		SO	Railroad comes in from the left; track on right.
	0.6 ▲	SO	Railroad exits to the right; track on left.
			GPS: N33°05.81' W111°14.15'
▼ 5.7		SO	Track on left crosses rail line into private property. Zero trip meter.
	0.0 ▲		Continue to the east alongside rail line.
			GPS: N33°06.06' W111°14.71'
▼ 0.0			Continue to the west alongside rail line.
	3.3 ▲	SO	Track on right crosses rail line into private property. Zero trip meter.
▼ 0.1		SO	Cross through wash; then cattle guard.
	3.2 ▲	SO	Cattle guard; then cross through wash.
▼ 0.3		SO	Track on right.
	3.0 ▲	SO	Track on left.
▼ 0.5		SO	Cross through wash. Trail leaves rail line; track on left.
	2.8 ▲	SO	Trail follows along rail line; track on right. Cross through wash.
▼ 1.5		SO	Track on left.
	1.8 ▲	SO	Track on right.
▼ 1.6		SO	Track on right.
	1.7 ▲	SO	Track on left.
▼ 2.5		SO	Track on left.
	0.8 ▲	SO	Track on right.
▼ 3.2		SO	Track on right through gate into artillery range. Rail line is on the left.
	0.1 ▲	SO	Track on left through gate into artillery range. Rail line is on the right.
			GPS: N33°05.79' W111°17.95'
▼ 3.3		SO	Track on right; then cross over rail line. Zero trip meter
	0.0 ▲		Continue to the east.
			GPS: N33°05.70' W111°18.01'
▼ 0.0			Continue to the west.
	5.6 ▲	SO	Cross over rail line; then track on left. Zero trip meter at crossing.
▼ 0.3		SO	Enter wash.
	5.3 ▲	SO	Exit wash.

▼ 0.9		SO	Exit wash; then cattle guard.
	4.7 ▲	SO	Cattle guard; then enter wash.
▼ 1.5		SO	Cross over rail line.
	4.1 ▲	SO	Cross over rail line.
			GPS: N33°04.84' W111°19.17'
▼ 2.6		SO	Stone ruin on left.
	3.0 ▲	SO	Stone ruin on right.
▼ 3.2		SO	Cross over rail line; tracks on right and left along rail line after the crossing. Many tracks on right and left into fields.
	2.4 ▲	SO	Tracks on right and left along rail line; then cross over rail line.
			GPS: N33°04.79' W111°20.74'
▼ 3.3		SO	Cross through wash.
	2.3 ▲	SO	Cross through wash.
▼ 3.8		SO	Road on left; then cross through wash.
	1.8 ▲	SO	Cross through wash; then road on right.
▼ 4.6		SO	Cross through wash.
	1.0 ▲	SO	Cross through wash.
▼ 5.6			Trail ends at junction with Arizona 79. Turn left for Florence; turn right for Phoenix.
	0.0 ▲		From the intersection of Arizona 79 and Arizona 287 in Florence, proceed north on Arizona 79 for 2 miles to the railroad crossing. Zero trip meter and turn northeast on wide, graded dirt road immediately south of the crossing. The intersection is not marked. The first 2.4 miles have many tracks on right and left into fields.
			GPS: N33°03.62' W111°22.70'

CENTRAL REGION TRAIL #42

Martinez Mine Trail

Starting Point:	**Central #41: Box Canyon Trail, 10.8 miles south of US 60**
Finishing Point:	**Martinez Mine**
Total Mileage:	**3.4 miles**
Unpaved Mileage:	**3.4 miles**
Driving Time:	**45 minutes (one-way)**
Elevation Range:	**2,200–2,700 feet**
Usually Open:	**Year-round**
Best Time to Travel:	**October to May**
Difficulty Rating:	**4**
Scenic Rating:	**8**
Remoteness Rating:	**+0**

Special Attractions

- Wooden and adobe cabins at the Martinez Mine.
- Tight, red-walled Martinez Canyon.
- Wide-ranging desert views and prolific desert vegetation.

Description

Initially, this short trail travels along an easy, smooth road that undulates through the craggy peaks of the region. There are fantastic views as the trail crests a saddle and starts to drop down toward Martinez Canyon. After 2 miles, Central #43: Cochran Coke Ovens Trail leads off to the right. The main trail runs alongside Martinez Wash before dropping down farther to enter the red walls of Martinez Canyon. The trail in the canyon is narrow and lumpy, with several tight corners and boulders to negotiate, but the standard is moderate throughout.

Rock formations like these are a feature of the trail

The remains of the old Martinez Mine are under several cottonwoods, which provide shade for a pleasant break. There is a timber cabin, built in 1947, and a white painted rock and adobe casita. The area is private, but access is currently permitted.

The trail ends here for most vehicles, but it is possible to drive or hike farther up the wash to view the remains of the Martinez Mill. The drive is difficult and body damage can be expected. It is approximately 0.4 miles from the mine cabins to the mill site, a rewarding hike through the spectacular canyon.

Current Road Information

Bureau of Land Management
Phoenix Field Office
2015 West Deer Valley Road
Phoenix, AZ 85027
(623) 580-5500

Map References

BLM Mesa
USGS 1:24,000 Mineral Mt.
1:100,000 Mesa
Maptech CD-ROM: Phoenix/Superstition Mountains
Arizona Atlas & Gazetteer, p. 58

Route Directions

▼ 0.0		From Central #41: Box Canyon Trail, zero trip meter and proceed northeast up the wash. There is a track immediately on the right. The intersection is 10.8 miles from the north end of Box Canyon Trail and is at a fork in the wash. There is a yellow directional arrow at the junction, but this may be removed in future.
	2.0 ▲	Trail ends at the intersection with Central #41: Box Canyon Trail. Turn sharp right to exit to

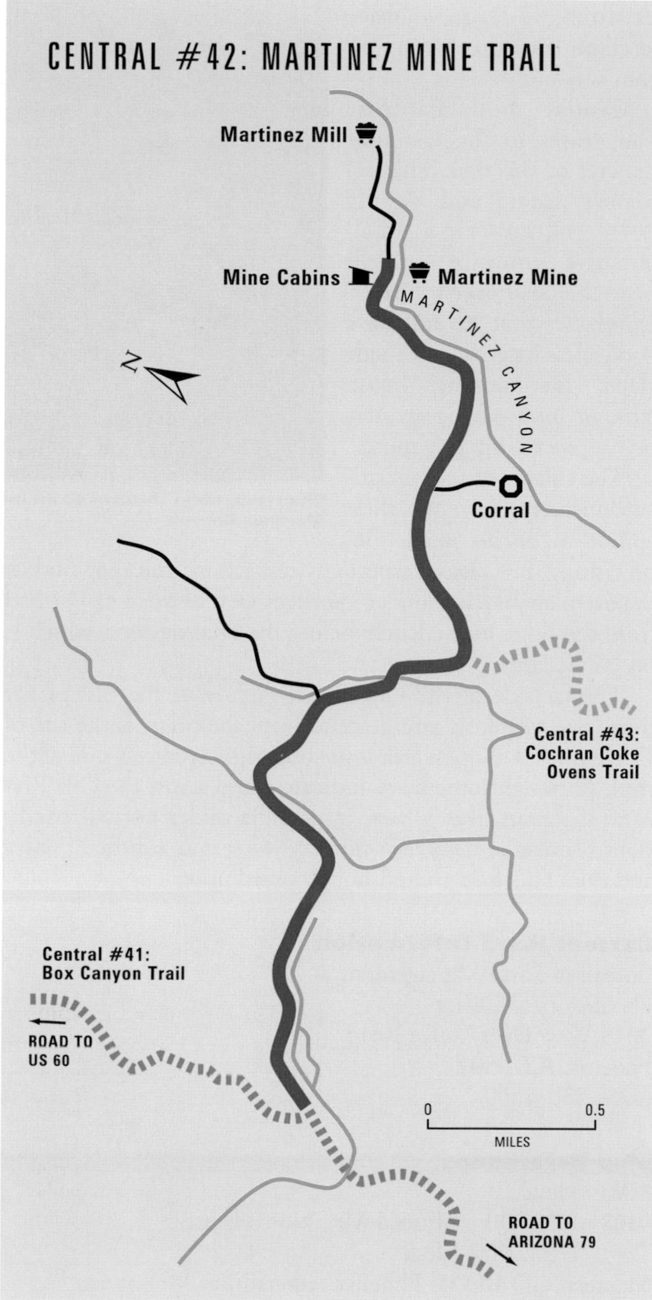

US 60; turn left to travel through the Box Canyon to Florence.

GPS: N33°08.98' W111°12.05'

▼ 0.2	SO	Track on left.
1.8 ▲	SO	Track on right.
▼ 0.3	SO	Well and water tank on left. Then track on right and track on left; remain on main trail.
1.7 ▲	SO	Track on right and track on left; remain on main trail. Then well and water tank on right.
		GPS: N33°09.17' W111°11.91'
▼ 0.4	SO	Track on left.
1.6 ▲	SO	Track on right.
▼ 0.5	SO	Exit wash.
1.5 ▲	SO	Enter wash.
▼ 0.7	SO	Cattle guard at saddle.
1.3 ▲	SO	Cattle guard at saddle.
▼ 0.9	SO	Track on right. Enter wash.
1.1 ▲	SO	Exit wash. Track on left.
▼ 1.1	SO	Track on left; then second track on left to well.
0.9 ▲	SO	Track on right to well; then second track on right.
		GPS: N33°09.49' W111°11.22'
▼ 1.3	SO	Exit wash.
0.7 ▲	SO	Enter wash.
▼ 1.5	SO	Track on left.
0.5 ▲	SO	Track on right.
		GPS: N33°09.45' W111°10.91'
▼ 1.7	SO	Cross through wash.
0.3 ▲	SO	Cross through wash.
▼ 2.0	TL	Cross through wash; then track on right is Central #43: Cochran Coke Ovens Trail. Zero trip meter.
0.0 ▲		Continue to the northwest.
		GPS: N33°09.22' W111°10.61'
▼ 0.0		Continue to the northeast on final section of trail.
1.4 ▲	TR	Track straight on is Central #43: Cochran Coke Ovens Trail. Zero trip meter. Turn right and cross through wash.
▼ 0.2	SO	Cross through wash.
▼ 0.5	BL	Track on right goes to corral (0.2 miles).
		GPS: N33°09.49' W111°10.18'
▼ 0.6	SO	Enter wash.
▼ 1.3	SO	Large shaft on right.
		GPS: N33°09.84' W111°09.74'
▼ 1.4	SO	Old mining buildings of Martinez Mine. These are private property, but you can walk around the buildings. Please respect the old buildings.
		GPS: N33°09.85' W111°09.63'

CENTRAL REGION TRAIL #43

Cochran Coke Ovens Trail

Starting Point:	**Central #42: Martinez Mine Trail, 2 miles from west end**
Finishing Point:	**Cochran Coke Ovens**
Total Mileage:	**4.9 miles**
Unpaved Mileage:	**4.9 miles**
Driving Time:	**2 hours**
Elevation Range:	**1,800–2,600 feet**
Usually Open:	**Year-round**
Best Time to Travel:	**October to May**
Difficulty Rating:	**7**
Scenic Rating:	**9**
Remoteness Rating:	**+1**

Special Attractions

- Challenging trail within the capability of most stock vehicles.
- Well-preserved, historic Cochran Coke Ovens.
- Panoramic scenery over Martinez Canyon and the Gila River.

History

Cochran, the small settlement that used to sit on the south side of the Gila River opposite the coke ovens, was a mining camp and a stop on the Santa Fe, Prescott & Phoenix Railroad. Named for John S. Cochran, the postmaster, the town once supported a population of about 100, a general store, boardinghouse, and other businesses.

Cochran's post office was set up in January 1905 but closed 10 years later. Today there is little to be seen of Cochran itself, except the famous and much photographed row of five charcoal kilns, or coke ovens, that sits at the end of this trail on the north side of the river. It is not known exactly when they were built—around 1882 is the best guess. It is likely they were built by the Pinal Consolidated Mining Company and used to turn mesquite into charcoal in order to smelt the ore from the mines that supported Cochran.

In the 1980s the owner of the ovens modified them with the idea of using them as guest cottages. Windows were added in the back, the roofs leak-proofed, and concrete poured for the floors. One of the ovens has even had a mezzanine level added. They are currently abandoned.

Description

This difficult trail will provide an exciting challenge to an experienced driver with a good stock vehicle. Although the trail is short, you should allow two hours to complete it.

After leaving the intersection with Central #42: Martinez Mine Trail, the trail immediately reveals its challenges. A large boulder, 0.4 miles from the start of the trail, has to be negotiated. This obstacle is easier to overcome than it first appears. Most vehicles will climb over it with little trouble—just watch long overhangs. The entire trail is rocky and lumpy, and there are a couple of steep ascents and descents, made harder by the very loose surface and rock ledges.

There are excellent views over North Butte and down into Martinez Canyon as the trail travels along a ridge before descending steeply into the canyon. This is possibly the roughest descent along the trail, and you will need to place your wheels carefully to avoid scraping the undercarriage. Unless you plan on exiting by the easier but longer Central #44: Battleaxe Trail to Arizona 177, you will have to climb back up this hill on your way out.

The coke ovens with South Butte in the background

Central #44: Battleaxe Trail leaves to the east near the end of the trail. This extremely scenic and slightly easier trail can serve as an alternative entrance or exit from the coke ovens. Drivers of vehicles that do not have good clearance or have side steps, low-hanging brush bars, or long overhangs may be happier taking this route.

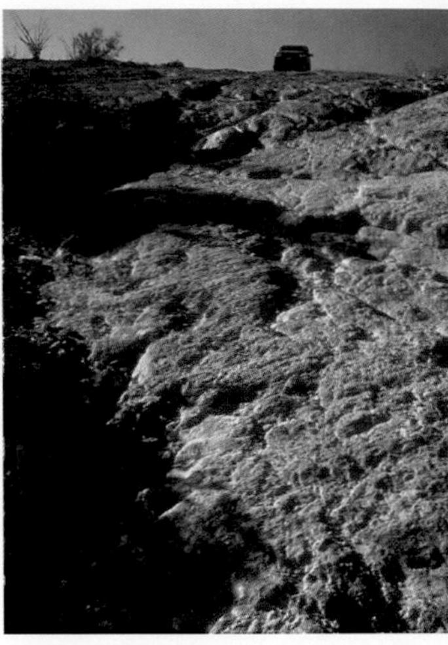

The steep, rocky descent down into Martinez Canyon

The coke ovens sit on private property. Currently, there appear to be no restrictions on visiting, but please respect any restrictions you may find. If the ovens are blocked off, an excellent view of them can be had from the ridge immediately before the final descent, which is on public land.

The far side of the Gila River, slightly to the east of the ovens and visible as you descend from the ridge, is the site of Cochran. A flat, open area is the only sign from this side of the river. Although some maps indicate a ford across the Gila River to Cochran, this is near impossible under normal conditions because of deep, fast-flowing water and a difficult entry and exit. This ford should not be relied upon.

Current Road Information

Bureau of Land Management
Phoenix Field Office
2015 West Deer Valley Road
Phoenix, AZ 85027
(623) 580-5500

Map References

BLM Mesa
USGS 1:24,000 Mineral Mt., North Butte
1:100,000 Mesa
Maptech CD-ROM: Phoenix/Superstition Mountains
Arizona Atlas & Gazetteer, p. 58

Route Directions

▼ 0.0		From Central #42: Martinez Mine Trail, 2 miles from the west end, zero trip meter and turn southeast on formed, rough trail. Turn is immediately after a wash crossing and is well used.
2.5 ▲		Trail finishes at the intersection with Central #42: Martinez Mine Trail. Continue straight on to visit the Martinez Mine; turn left to exit to Central #41: Box Canyon Trail to Florence.
		GPS: N33°09.22' W111°10.61'
▼ 0.1	SO	Track on right to campsite.
2.4 ▲	SO	Track on left to campsite.
▼ 0.3	SO	Small dam on right; then track on right.
2.2 ▲	SO	Track on left; then small dam on left.
		GPS: N33°09.01' W111°10.47'

▼ 0.4 SO First large boulder to climb over.
2.1 ▲ SO Final large boulder to climb over.

GPS: N33°08.92' W111°10.41'

▼ 1.1 SO Faint track on right; then steep, rocky descent toward Martinez Canyon.
1.4 ▲ SO End of climb out of Martinez Canyon; then faint track on left.

▼ 1.3 BL Trail forks and rejoins almost immediately; left fork is easier.
1.2 ▲ BR Trail forks and rejoins almost immediately; right fork is easier.

GPS: N33°08.28' W111°10.37'

▼ 1.4 SO Cross through Martinez Canyon wash; then faint track on left. Trail now climbs out of Martinez Canyon—this climb is easier than the descent.
1.1 ▲ SO Faint track on right; then cross through Martinez Canyon wash. Start of steep, difficult climb out of canyon.

GPS: N33°08.22' W111°10.35'

▼ 2.5 SO Cross through wash; then track on right. There is a campsite at the junction. Zero trip meter.
0.0 ▲ Continue to the west.

GPS: N33°07.52' W111°10.21'

▼ 0.0 Continue to the east and climb loose, rubbly slope.
1.4 ▲ SO Campsite on left and track on left; zero trip meter and cross through wash. Trail climbs out of wash.

▼ 0.1 SO Cross through two washes.
1.3 ▲ SO Cross through two washes.

▼ 0.3 SO Top of climb; track on right.
1.1 ▲ BR Track on left; trail descends to cross wash.

GPS: N33°07.39' W111°09.91'

▼ 0.6 BR Track on left.
0.8 ▲ SO Track on right.

▼ 0.8 SO Track on left.
0.6 ▲ BL Track on right.

GPS: N33°07.45' W111°09.46'

▼ 1.1 SO Track on left.
0.3 ▲ BL Track on right.

GPS: N33°07.22' W111°09.49'

▼ 1.4 BR Fork in trail. Track on left is Central #44: Battleaxe Trail. Zero trip meter.
0.0 ▲ Continue to the north.

GPS: N33°06.89' W111°09.51'

▼ 0.0 Continue to the south.
1.0 ▲ SO Track on right is Central #44: Battleaxe Trail.

▼ 0.5 BL Fork in trail. Both ways go to the coke ovens, but the left fork is much easier. The right fork has several large ledges to descend. Excellent view over the coke ovens from right-hand fork.
0.5 ▲ SO Fork rejoins.

GPS: N33°06.50' W111°09.75'

▼ 0.7 SO Gate.
0.3 ▲ SO Gate.

▼ 0.8 SO Track on right rejoins; then two tracks on left.
0.2 ▲ SO Two tracks on right; then track on left rejoins trail in 0.3 miles and is a harder exit that climbs several large ledges. There is an excellent view of the coke ovens from the top.

GPS: N33°06.24' W111°09.77'

▼ 0.9 SO Abandoned house on right; then track on right.
0.1 ▲ SO Track on left; then abandoned house on left.

▼ 1.0 Trail ends at the coke ovens. Exit either by retracing your steps or via Central #44: Battleaxe Road to Arizona 177.
0.0 ▲ Trail commences at the coke ovens. Zero trip meter and proceed southeast toward the abandoned house.

GPS: N33°06.26' W111°09.85'

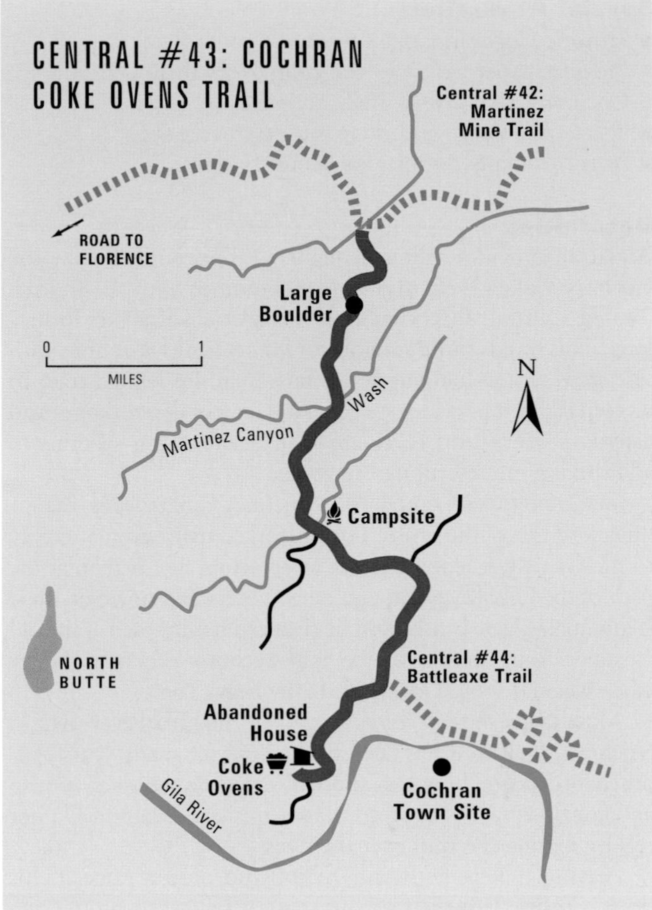

CENTRAL REGION TRAIL #44

Battleaxe Trail

Starting Point:	**Central #43: Cochran Coke Ovens Trail, 1 mile before the coke ovens**
Finishing Point:	**Arizona 177**
Total Mileage:	**12.2 miles**
Unpaved Mileage:	**12.2 miles**
Driving Time:	**3 hours**
Elevation Range:	**1,800–3,000 feet**
Usually Open:	**Year-round**
Best Time to Travel:	**October to May**
Difficulty Rating:	**5**
Scenic Rating:	**9**
Remoteness Rating:	**+1**

Special Attractions

- Historic Cochran Coke Ovens.
- Provides easier access to the coke ovens than Central #43: Cochran Coke Ovens Trail.
- Spectacular gorge and ridge top desert scenery.
- Access to many popular backcountry trails.

Description

This trail provides a longer, slightly easier route to view the Cochran Coke Ovens and can be combined with the shorter, 7-rated Central #43: Cochran Coke Ovens Trail to form a loop. This trail is more suitable for longer vehicles or ones with side steps or low-hanging brush bars than the 7-rated trail. In its own right, it provides spectacular views of desert ranges and canyon scenery, and there are many challenging sections to add driving interest along the way.

The trail leaves Central #43: Cochran Coke Ovens Trail, 1 mile northeast of the ovens. The unmarked trail descends steeply to the Gila River along a loose, low-traction hill. It follows the path of the Gila River through dense vegetation; however, there is minimal vehicle brushing. The river can be glimpsed at the old crossings. This section of the trail becomes extremely boggy when wet and should be avoided after heavy rain.

Most maps show a ford crossing of the Gila River over to Cochran. That ford has been washed out for many years. Another ford exists; however, most of the time the river is deep and fast flowing and the ford has a very steep entrance. Do not rely on exiting the trail over the river.

Leaving the river, the trail climbs up onto a ridge. (This slope is easier than the previous one.) It follows along the side of the range, offering views down to the Gila River. The surface is fairly smooth; there are some eroded sections, but it is generally a lot easier than the difficult Cochran Coke Ovens Trail.

After passing through a cove of mountains known as The Rincon (Spanish for "the corner"), the trail climbs a short but steep section of shelf road. This narrow section has only a few passing places and the surface is loose shale, which may cause traction problems. One tricky point along the shelf road offers two choices: Keep tight against the hill and ride a large boulder in the middle of the trail—an off-camber option that will tilt your vehicle toward the drop; the second option is to squeeze past between the boulder and the drop, which is more nerve-racking but keeps the vehicle more level.

Scenic buttes and saguaros are typical along this trail

View from the trail looking down at the Gila River

At the saddle, the trail descends again toward the large tilted mesas of the White Canyon Wilderness. This section provides spectacular scenery as the trail enters the canyon and then follows along Walnut Canyon Wash. The trail joins a graded road underneath Copper Butte, and from there it is an easy ride out to join Arizona 177. Some maps show this trail as Battleaxe Road.

Current Road Information

Bureau of Land Management
Phoenix Field Office
2015 West Deer Valley Rd.
Phoenix, AZ 85027
(623) 580-5500

Map References

BLM Mesa
USGS 1:24,000 North Butte, Grayback, Teapot Mt.
1:100,000 Mesa
Maptech CD-ROM: Phoenix/Superstition Mountains
Arizona Atlas & Gazetteer, pp. 58, 59

Route Directions

▼ 0.0		From Central #43: Cochran Coke Ovens Trail, 1 mile northeast of the coke ovens, 3.9 miles from the start of the trail, zero trip meter and turn southeast on unmarked, formed trail. Trail immediately starts to drop steeply on narrow shelf road.
2.2 ▲		Trail ends at the junction with Central #43: Cochran Coke Ovens Trail. Turn left to visit the coke ovens; turn right to exit via the 7-rated Cochran Coke Ovens Trail.
		GPS: N33°06.89' W111°09.51'
▼ 0.2	BL	Fork in trail; track on right.
2.0 ▲	SO	Track on left.
		GPS: N33°06.83' W111°09.32'
▼ 0.3	SO	Track on right is fork rejoining.
1.9 ▲	BR	Fork in trail; track on left.
▼ 0.4	SO	Bottom of descent; cross through wash.
1.8 ▲	SO	Cross through wash; trail climbs up toward the coke ovens.
▼ 0.6	SO	Disused well and tank on left.
1.6 ▲	SO	Disused well and tank on right.

		GPS: N33°06.71' W111°08.99'
▼ 0.8	SO	Track on left; then track on right fords Gila River.
1.4 ▲	SO	Track on left fords Gila River; then track on right.
		GPS: N33°06.74' W111°08.79'
▼ 0.9	BL	Track on right through fence line is old ford over Gila River—now washed out. Cross through wash; track on right at wash; then continue to ascend ridge.
1.3 ▲	BR	Bottom of descent; track on left; then cross through wash. Bear right in clearing, track on left is old ford over Gila River—now washed out.
		GPS: N33°06.72' W111°08.69'
▼ 1.7	SO	Cross through wash; then track on left.
0.5 ▲	BL	Track on right; then cross through wash.
		GPS: N33°06.95' W111°08.27'
▼ 2.2	SO	Well-used track on right. Zero trip meter.
0.0 ▲		Continue to the southwest.
		GPS: N33°06.87' W111°07.92'
▼ 0.0		Continue to the northeast; second track on right.
3.1 ▲	SO	Small track on left followed by well-used track on left. Zero trip meter.
▼ 0.2	SO	Two small tracks on right go to mine workings.
2.9 ▲	SO	Two small tracks on left go to mine workings.
▼ 0.6	SO	Cross through wash.
2.5 ▲	SO	Cross through wash.
▼ 0.9	SO	Small track on left.
2.2 ▲	SO	Small track on right.
▼ 1.1	SO	Track on left.
2.0 ▲	SO	Track on right.
		GPS: N33°07.23' W111°07.10'
▼ 1.3	SO	Cross through wash.
1.8 ▲	SO	Cross through wash.
▼ 1.4	SO	Cross through two washes.
1.7 ▲	SO	Cross through two washes.
▼ 1.5	SO	Track on right.
1.6 ▲	SO	Track on left.
▼ 1.6	SO	Track on left.
1.5 ▲	SO	Track on right.
		GPS: N33°07.40' W111°06.78'
▼ 1.8	SO	Faint track on left.
1.3 ▲	SO	Faint track on right.
		GPS: N33°07.47' W111°06.47'
▼ 2.1	BR	Cross through wash; then bear right and cross through wide wash.
1.0 ▲	BL	Cross through wide wash; then bear left and cross through second wash.
▼ 2.2	SO	Well on left.
0.9 ▲	SO	Well on right.
		GPS: N33°07.54' W111°06.21'
▼ 2.4	BR	Small track on left.
0.7 ▲	BL	Small track on right.
		GPS: N33°07.78' W111°06.14'
▼ 2.6	SO	Track on right.
0.5 ▲	SO	Track on left.
▼ 2.7	SO	Cross through wash.
0.4 ▲	SO	Cross through wash.
▼ 3.0	SO	Cross through wash.
0.1 ▲	SO	Cross through wash.
		GPS: N33°07.87' W111°05.79'
▼ 3.1	TL	Small track on left; small track on right; then T-intersection. Turn left at T-intersection and zero trip meter.

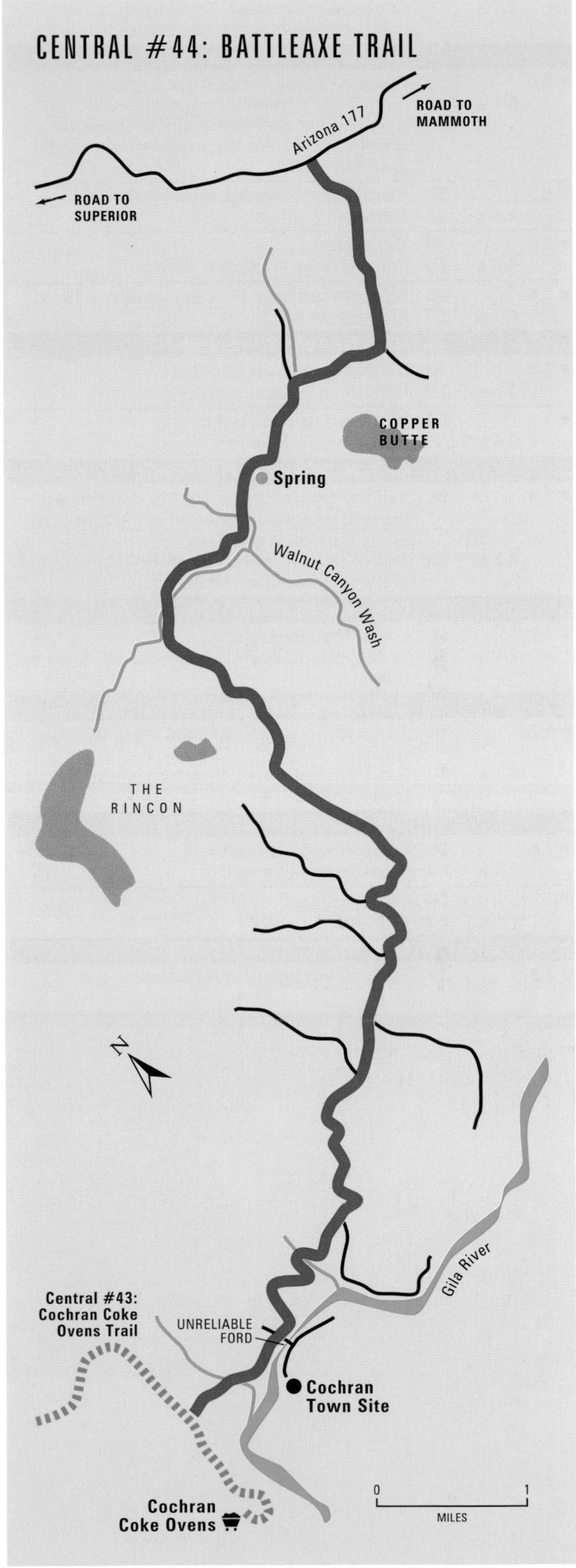

▼	▲		
	0.0 ▲		Continue to the west. The cove of buttes called The Rincon is straight ahead.
			GPS: N33°07.90′ W111°05.77′
▼ 0.0			Continue to the north; track on right.
	5.1 ▲	TR	Track on left; then turn right onto well-used trail; another well-used trail continues ahead. Small track on left; then small track on right. Zero trip meter.
▼ 0.3		SO	Start to cross through wide wash.
	4.8 ▲	SO	Exit wash.
▼ 0.5		SO	Exit wash.
	4.6 ▲	SO	Start to cross through wide wash.
▼ 1.0		SO	Start of shelf road climbing up side of butte.
	4.1 ▲	SO	End of shelf road.
			GPS: N33°08.68′ W111°05.74′
▼ 1.3		SO	Difficult crawl over boulder.
	3.8 ▲	SO	Difficult crawl over boulder.
▼ 1.7		SO	Well-used track on right.
	3.4 ▲	SO	Well-used track on left.
			GPS: N33°08.89′ W111°05.55′
▼ 1.9		BL	Saddle; track on right. Start to descend with the wilderness boundary on left. Views over White Canyon Wilderness.
	3.2 ▲	BR	End of climb at saddle. Track on left; bear right and start to descend shelf road.
			GPS: N33°09.17′ W111°05.53′
▼ 2.5		SO	Cross through wash.
	2.6 ▲	SO	Cross through wash; wilderness boundary on right.
			GPS: N33°09.63′ W111°05.47′
▼ 2.7		TR	T-intersection; turn right and cross through wash.
	2.4 ▲	TL	Cross through wash; then turn left; track continues ahead.
			GPS: N33°09.68′ W111°05.28′
▼ 2.8		SO	Cross through fence line.
	2.3 ▲	SO	Cross through fence line.
▼ 3.2		SO	Enter wash.
	1.9 ▲	SO	Exit wash.
			GPS: N33°09.47′ W111°04.77′
▼ 3.3		SO	Track on right goes to artisan well.
	1.8 ▲	BR	Track on left goes to artisan well.
▼ 3.7		SO	Spring on right.
	1.4 ▲	SO	Spring on left.
			GPS: N33°09.68′ W111°04.39′
▼ 4.5		SO	Exit wash. Tracks on left up wash; then track on left.
	0.6 ▲	SO	Track on right; then enter wash. Tracks on right up wash.
			GPS: N33°09.88′ W111°03.75′
▼ 4.8		SO	Track on left.
	0.3 ▲	SO	Track on right.
			GPS: N33°09.66′ W111°03.54′
▼ 4.9		SO	Faint track on right.
	0.2 ▲	SO	Faint track on left.
▼ 5.1		TL	T-intersection. Turn left onto graded road. Copper Butte is to the right. Zero trip meter.
	0.0 ▲		Continue to the west.
			GPS: N33°09.51′ W111°03.30′
▼ 0.0			Continue to the northeast.
	1.8 ▲	TR	Turn right onto roughly graded trail; Copper Butte is directly ahead. Trail continues ahead. Zero trip meter.
▼ 0.2		SO	Corral on right; then track on right.
	1.6 ▲	SO	Track on left; then corral on left.
▼ 0.5		SO	Track on left.
	1.3 ▲	SO	Track on right.
▼ 0.8		SO	Track on right to dam.
	1.0 ▲	SO	Track on left to dam.
▼ 1.7		SO	Track on right.
	0.1 ▲	BR	Track on left.
			GPS: N33°10.65′ W111°02.37′
▼ 1.8			Trail ends at intersection with paved Arizona 177. Turn left for Superior; turn right for Mammoth.
	0.0 ▲		Trail commences on Arizona 177, 0.1 miles north of mile marker 158, 2.3 miles north of the visitor viewpoint over the open-pit mine at Ray. Zero trip meter and turn south on graded dirt road over cattle guard. Turn is unmarked but is on a slight rise in road.
			GPS: N33°10.78′ W111°02.32′

The South Region

Trails in the South Region

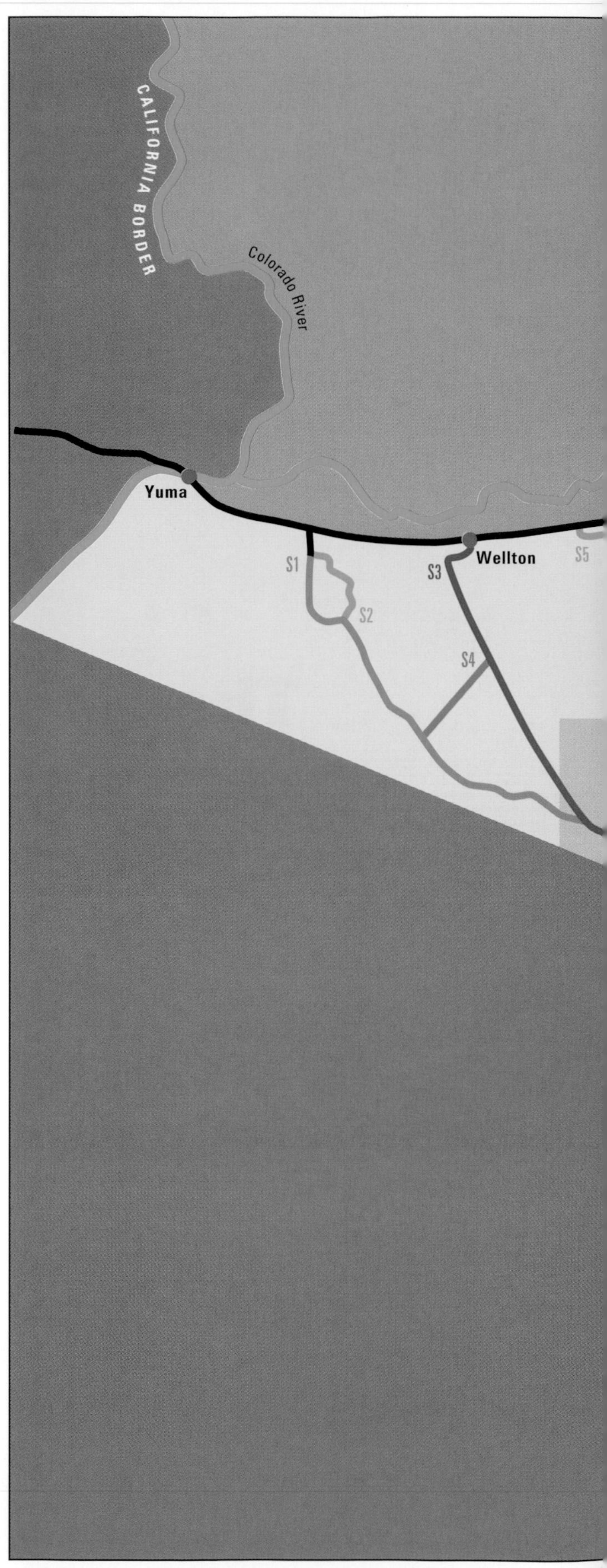

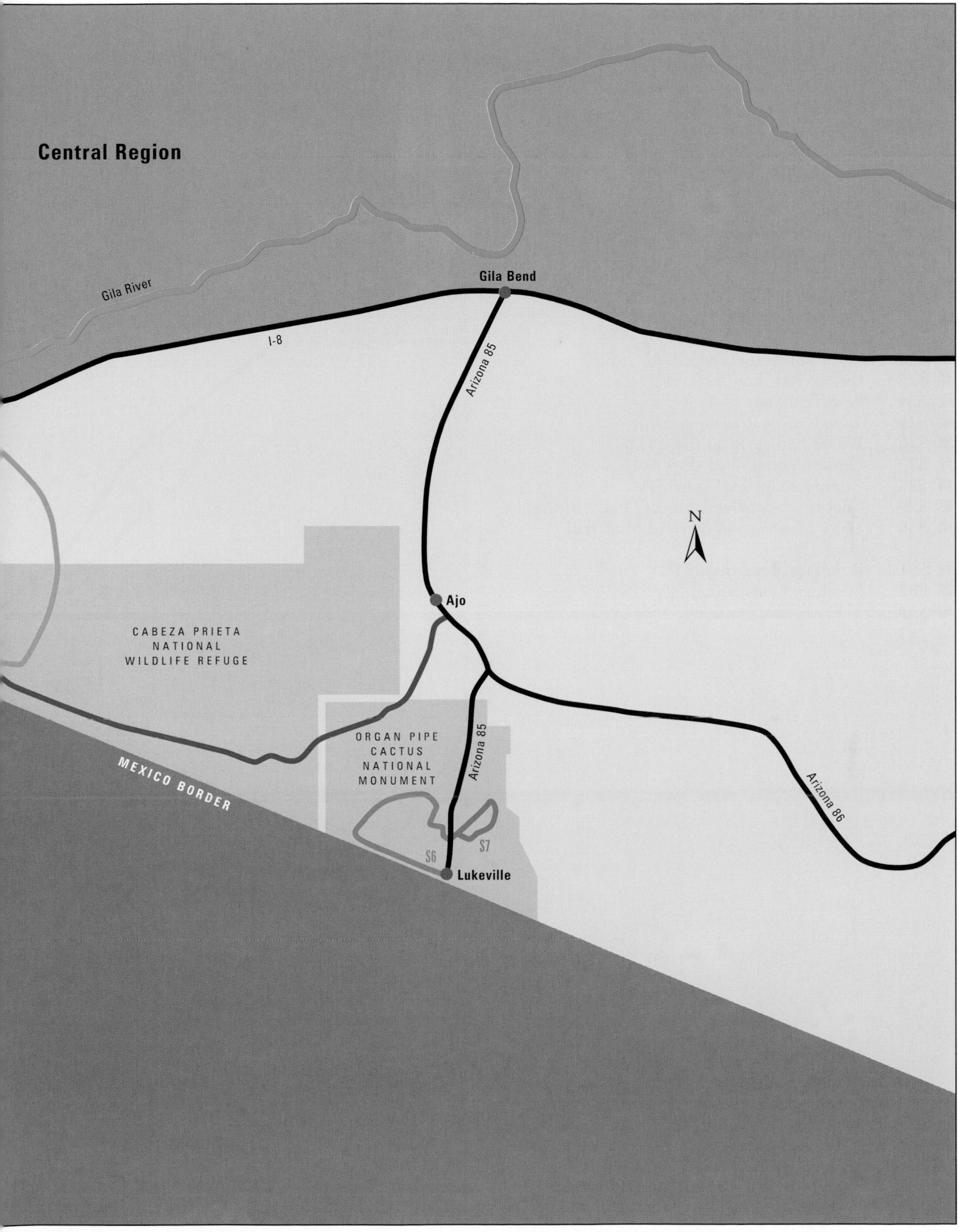

Central Region

Gila River

Gila Bend

I-8

Arizona 85

N

Ajo

CABEZA PRIETA
NATIONAL
WILDLIFE REFUGE

ORGAN PIPE
CACTUS
NATIONAL
MONUMENT

Arizona 85

MEXICO BORDER

S6

S7

Lukeville

Arizona 86

MAP CONTINUES ON PAGE 464

Trails in the South Region

MAP CONTINUES ON PAGE 463

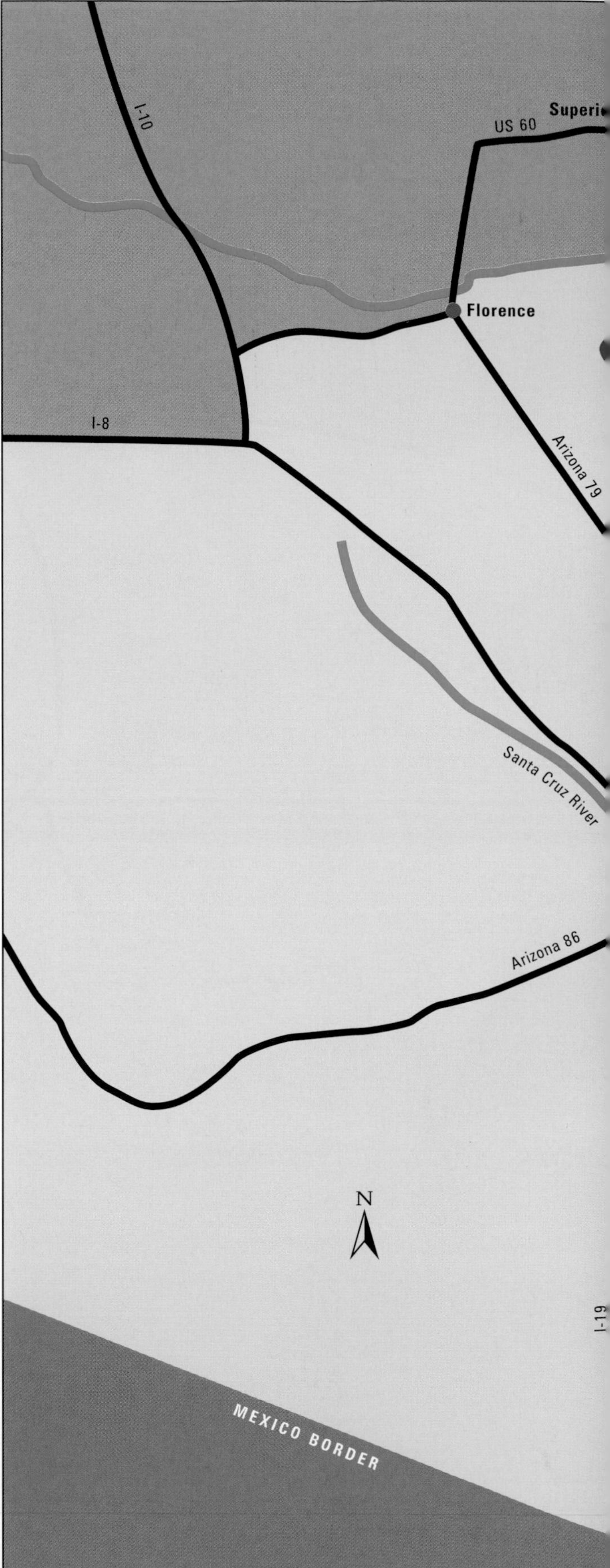

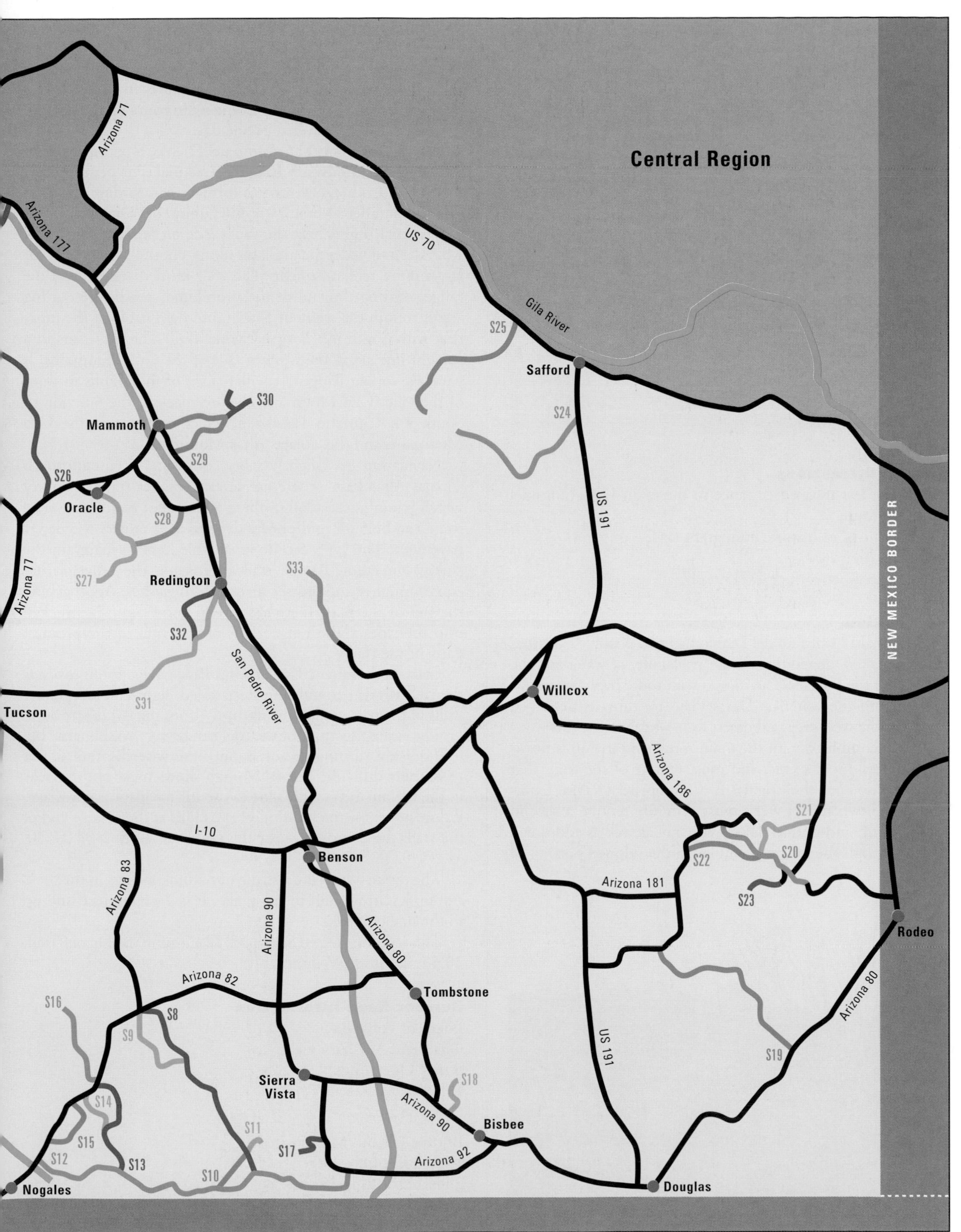
Central Region
Arizona 77
Arizona 177
US 70
Gila River
S25
Safford
S24
S30
Mammoth
S29
S26
Oracle
S28
US 191
S27
Redington
S33
Arizona 77
S32
San Pedro River
NEW MEXICO BORDER
Willcox
S31
Tucson
Arizona 186
S21
I-10
Benson
S22
S20
Arizona 181
S23
Arizona 83
Arizona 90
Arizona 80
Rodeo
Arizona 82
Tombstone
Arizona 80
S16
S8
S9
US 191
S19
Sierra Vista
S18
S14
Arizona 90
Bisbee
S11
S15
S17
Arizona 92
S12
S13
S10
Nogales
Douglas

SOUTH REGION TRAIL #1

Tinajas Altas Pass Trail

Starting Point:	**Foothills Boulevard**
Finishing Point:	**South #3: El Camino del Diablo, 30.4 miles south of Wellton**
Total Mileage:	**35 miles**
Unpaved Mileage:	**35 miles**
Driving Time:	**2 hours**
Elevation Range:	**400–1,200 feet**
Usually Open:	**Year-round**
Best Time to Travel:	**November to March**
Difficulty Rating:	**3**
Scenic Rating:	**9**
Remoteness Rating:	**+2**

Special Attractions

- Remote, less-traveled entrance to the main El Camino del Diablo route.
- Western end of historic immigrant trail.
- Tinajas Altas Pass.
- Access to a network of 4WD trails.

Description

The original El Camino del Diablo had two possible exits that could be taken, depending on the availability of water and the stamina of the traveler. The rugged west route over Tinajas Altas Pass and the waterless Davis Plain to Yuma is described here. For the well-prepared desert four-wheel driver, this western route combined with the main route over to Ajo is possibly the best, most scenic, and most remote of the trails that follow sections of the original El Camino del Diablo. Combining the two routes will almost certainly require a second night's camp and a third day on the trail as well as additional fuel. Although the length is similar to the skipped portion of the main route, the rougher and sandier trail surface is slower going and will use more fuel.

The trail with an ocotillo in the foreground and the Gila Mountains in the background

An option for those with less time who still want to sample the remote grandeur of this historic trail is to combine this west route with the faster leg of the main route up to Wellton. This route can be traveled in one day.

As with the main El Camino del Diablo, a permit to enter the Barry M. Goldwater Range is essential. For permit information and other necessary information regarding travel in this region, refer to South #3: El Camino del Diablo Trail.

The trail begins near the south side of Yuma at exit 14 on I-8. Fuel and water are available along Foothills Boulevard for last-minute replenishment. The trail immediately enters the range, skirting the end of the prohibited area before cutting across to join the route of El Camino del Diablo at the junction with South #2: Fortuna Mine Trail. The trail runs in a straight line along the western face of the Gila Mountains. It parallels Vopoki Ridge, a smaller ridge of mountains in front of the taller Gila Mountains, before meeting the junction of South #4: Cipriano Pass Trail, which is between the Gila Mountains and the Tinajas Altas Mountains.

Navigation gets slightly more confusing as you approach Tinajas Altas Pass—there are several smaller trails, many of which rejoin later, so often there is not one "main" trail. The route can be faint and poorly defined as it crosses the desert pavement. The GPS can be invaluable here to maintain the correct direction. As the trail approaches the range, it becomes rougher and crosses several deep washes. Approaching the gap of the pass, there are several good campsites tucked into the side of the range. This area is one of the prettiest parts of the trail.

Once in the gap of Tinajas Altas Pass, navigation is easier as the trail winds through the steep-sided, light-colored granite walls of the pass, which rise abruptly from the flat desert floor.

The earliest sections of the trail can be very washboardy before quickly turning to soft sand; otherwise the trail is not technically difficult. The BLM map shows most of the tracks in the region and is sufficient to use for navigation. However, it does not show the location of the tanks at the eastern end of the trail: the coordinates for the tanks are GPS: N32°18.70' W114°03.00'

The tanks, which are a string of natural pockets in the rock, run up a narrow cleft in the range. It is a strenuous climb up to the higher tanks.

The trail finishes on South #3: El Camino del Diablo Trail, 30.4 miles from Wellton.

Current Road Information

Luke Air Force Base
Gila Bend Auxiliary Field
Range Operations
Gila Bend, AZ 85337
(520) 683-6272

Bureau of Land Management
Yuma Field Office
2555 Gilda Ridge Road
Yuma, AZ 85365
(520) 317-3200

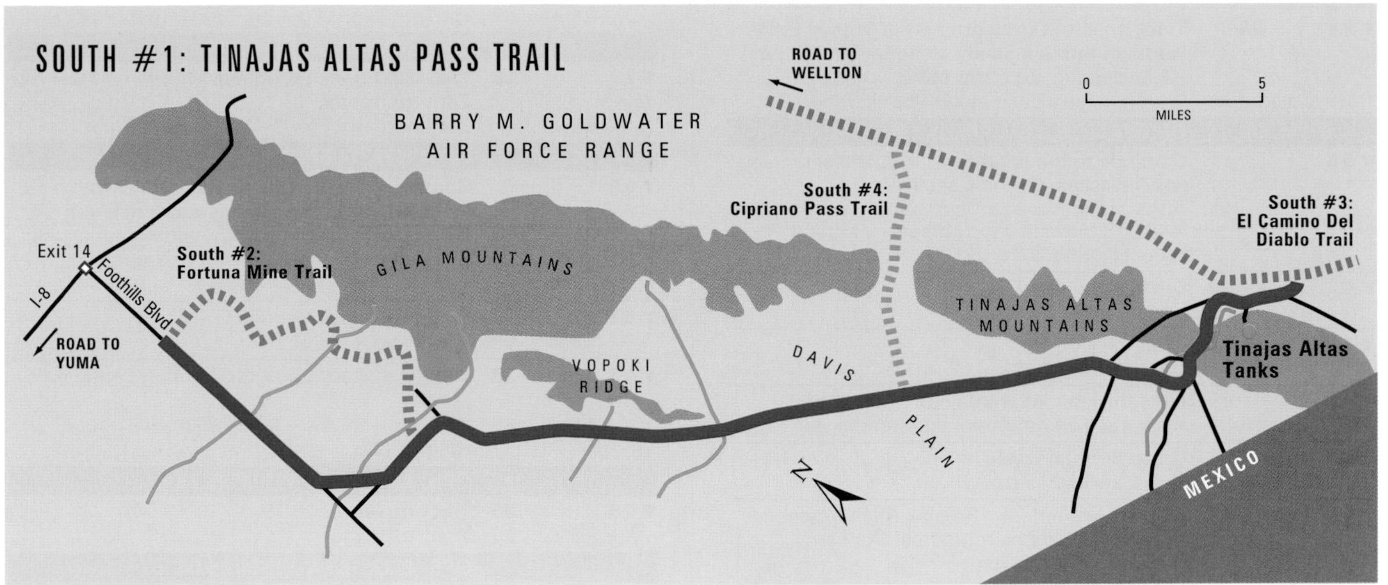

Map References

BLM Yuma, Tinajas Altas Mts.
USGS 1:24,000 Fortuna, Fortuna SW, Vopoki Ridge, Cipriano Pass, Butler Mts., Tinajas Altas Mts.
1:100,000 Yuma, Tinajas Altas Mts.
Maptech CD-ROM: Southwest Arizona/Yuma
Arizona Atlas & Gazetteer, p. 62

Route Directions

Mileage		Directions
▼ 0.0		From exit 14 on I-8, turn onto Foothills Boulevard and proceed south for 1.8 miles. At the crossroads where the paved road turns left, continue straight on into the Barry M. Goldwater Range and zero trip meter. A valid range permit is essential beyond this point. Proceed south on the wide, graded dirt road. Road on left is South #2: Fortuna Mine Trail.
3.8 ▲		Trail ends at the south end of Foothills Boulevard on the edge of Yuma. Continue north for 1.8 miles to reach exit 14 on I-8. Road on right is South #2: Fortuna Mine Trail.
		GPS: N32°37.60' W114°24.55'
▼ 0.1	SO	Track on left, trail is following alongside telegraph lines.
3.7 ▲	SO	Track on right.
▼ 2.9	SO	Cross through wash.
0.9 ▲	SO	Cross through wash.
▼ 3.0	SO	Cross through wash.
0.8 ▲	SO	Cross through wash.
▼ 3.8	BL	Equally used track on right. Zero trip meter.
0.0 ▲		Continue north toward Yuma following alongside telegraph lines.
		GPS: N32°34.06' W114°24.51'
▼ 0.0		Continue to the southeast.
3.2 ▲	SO	Equally used track on left. Zero trip meter.
▼ 1.1	SO	Track on left and track on right.
2.1 ▲	SO	Track on left and track on right.
▼ 2.5	SO	Cross through wash.
0.7 ▲	SO	Cross through wash.
▼ 3.2	TL	Turn left at T-intersection along the edge of the prohibited area.
0.0 ▲		Continue northwest toward Yuma.
		GPS: N32°31.43' W114°22.94'
▼ 0.0		Continue east toward the Gila Mountains.
1.2 ▲	TR	Turn right at unmarked junction onto well-used sandy trail. Zero trip meter.
▼ 1.2	BR	Track on left is South #2: Fortuna Mine Trail. Junction is marked by marker post A3 and a sign for El Camino del Diablo. Zero trip meter.
0.0 ▲		Continue to the west.
		GPS: N32°31.51' W114°21.61'
▼ 0.0		Continue to the east.
8.4 ▲	BL	Track on right is South #2: Fortuna Mine Trail. Junction is marked by marker post A3 and a sign for El Camino del Diablo. Zero trip meter.
▼ 0.7	BR	Track on left joins South #2: Fortuna Mine Trail. Bear right to the south following along the edge of the prohibited area (on right).
7.7 ▲	BL	Track on right joins South #2: Fortuna Mine Trail. Bear left following along the edge of the prohibited area (on left).
		GPS: N32°31.41' W114°20.82'
▼ 1.5	SO	Cross through wash.
6.9 ▲	SO	Cross through wash.
▼ 1.9	SO	Track on left.
6.5 ▲	SO	Track on right.
		GPS: N32°30.38' W114°20.43'
▼ 2.1	SO	Cross through wash.
6.3 ▲	SO	Cross through wash.
▼ 2.8	SO	Cross through wash.
5.6 ▲	SO	Cross through wash.
▼ 3.3	SO	Faint track on left.
5.1 ▲	SO	Faint track on right.
▼ 4.9	SO	Cross through wash; then small track on left. Vopoki Ridge is to the left.
3.5 ▲	SO	Small track on right; then cross through wash.
		GPS: N32°28.44' W114°18.20'
▼ 6.9	SO	Passing directly beside the southern end of Vopoki Ridge.
1.5 ▲	SO	Trail starts to angle away from Vopoki Ridge.
		GPS: N32°27.11' W114°16.87'
▼ 8.3	SO	Two well-used tracks on right enter prohibited area.
0.1 ▲	BR	Two well-used tracks on left enter prohibited area.
		GPS: N32°26.32' W114°15.73'

▼ 8.4 BR/BL Track on left at southern end of Vopoki Ridge leads off through sandy clearing. Marker post A4 in clearing. Zero trip meter.
0.0 ▲ Continue northwest along Vopoki Ridge.

GPS: N32°26.22' W114°15.53'

▼ 0.0 Continue to the southeast. Trail crosses many small washes over this section.
4.9 ▲ BL Track on right at southern end of Vopoki Ridge leads off through sandy clearing. Marker Post A4 in clearing. Zero trip meter.

▼ 0.1 SO Cross through wash.
4.8 ▲ SO Cross through wash.

▼ 0.2 SO Faint track on left.
4.7 ▲ SO Faint track on right.

▼ 0.5 SO Faint track on left, remain on main trail.
4.4 ▲ SO Faint track on right, remain on main trail.

▼ 0.7 SO Cross through wash.
4.2 ▲ SO Cross through wash.

▼ 4.3 SO Sign on left, entering Tinajas Altas Mountains Area of Critical Environmental Concern. Survey marker on left.
0.6 ▲ SO Sign on right, leaving Tinajas Altas Mountains Area of Critical Environmental Concern. Survey marker on right.

GPS: N32°23.98' W114°11.56'

▼ 4.9 SO Track on left is South #4: Cipriano Pass Trail. Turn is well-used but unmarked apart from wooden marker post A5 immediately after the turn. Zero trip meter at marker post.
0.0 ▲ Continue to the northwest.

GPS: N32°23.61' W114°11.23'

▼ 0.0 Continue to the southeast. Tinajas Altas Mountains are now on the left.
5.7 ▲ SO Track on right is South #4: Cipriano Pass Trail. Turn is well-used but unmarked apart from wooden marker post A5 immediately before the turn. Zero trip meter at marker post.

▼ 5.7 SO Track on left is the northern pass through the Tinajas Altas Mountains. Wooden marker post A6 at the junction. Zero trip meter.
0.0 ▲ Continue to the northwest along the west face of the range.

GPS: N32°20.33' W114°06.67'

▼ 0.0 Continue to the south. Trail is faint and poorly defined in places.
2.7 ▲ SO Track on right is the northern pass through the Tinajas Altas Mountains. Wooden marker post A6 at the junction. Zero trip meter.

▼ 0.1 SO Track on right and faint track on left.
2.6 ▲ SO Track on left and faint track on right.

GPS: N32°20.18' W114°06.75'

▼ 0.2 BR Track on left at wooden post.
2.5 ▲ SO Track on right at wooden post.

GPS: N32°20.15' W114°06.74'

▼ 1.4 BR Faint track on left followed by a fork, bear right at fork.
1.3 ▲ BL Track on right, keep left followed by second faint track on right.

GPS: N32°19.48' W114°06.24'

▼ 1.5 SO Faint track on right. Many tire tracks, remain on main, most-used trail.
1.2 ▲ SO Faint track on left. Many tire tracks, remain on main, most-used trail.

▼ 2.2 SO Track on right.
0.5 ▲ BR Track on left.

GPS: N32°18.85' W114°05.84'

▼ 2.6 SO Track on right.
0.1 ▲ BR Track on left.

GPS: N32°18.64' W114°05.52'

▼ 2.7 SO Well-used track on right at wooden marker A8. Zero trip meter.
0.0 ▲ Continue away from Tinajas Altas Pass.

GPS: N32°18.67' W114°05.46'

▼ 0.0 Continue toward Tinajas Altas Pass. Trail now leads into the range and is more defined.
5.1 ▲ SO Well-used track on left at wooden marker A8. Zero trip meter. Trail is faint and poorly defined in places.

▼ 0.1 SO Well-used track on right.
5.0 ▲ BR Well-used track on left.

▼ 0.3 SO Well-used track on right. Entering gap in range.
4.8 ▲ BR Well-used track on left. Trail leaves gap in range.

GPS: N32°18.76' W114°05.23'

▼ 0.6 SO Track on left.
4.5 ▲ SO Track on right.

GPS: N32°18.94' W114°05.04'

▼ 0.7 SO Cross through wash in pass.
4.4 ▲ SO Cross through wash in pass.

▼ 0.8 SO Cristate saguaro on right of trail (fan-shaped mutation).
4.3 ▲ SO Cristate saguaro on left of trail (fan-shaped mutation).

GPS: N32°18.95' W114°04.77'

▼ 1.1 SO Cross through wash.
4.0 ▲ SO Cross through wash.

▼ 1.2 BL Bear left up wash.
3.9 ▲ BR Bear right out of wash.

GPS: N32°18.87' W114°04.38'

▼ 1.3 SO Exit wash.
3.8 ▲ SO Enter wash.

▼ 1.4 SO Cross through wash.
3.7 ▲ SO Cross through wash.

▼ 1.5 SO Faint track on right.
3.6 ▲ SO Faint track on left.

▼ 1.6 SO Start to cross wide wash.
3.5 ▲ SO Exit wash crossing.

▼ 1.7 SO Exit wash crossing. Many small tracks on right and left are dead-ends, some lead to pleasant campsites.
3.4 ▲ SO Start to cross wide wash.

▼ 1.9 SO Cross through wash.
3.2 ▲ SO Cross through wash.

▼ 2.2 SO Cross through wash then well-used track on left exits to El Camino del Diablo further to the north. Exiting gap in range, looking ahead across the Lechuguilla Desert to the Cabeza Prieta Mountains.
2.9 ▲ SO Well-used track on right returns to El Camino del Diablo; then cross through wash. Many small tracks on right and left are dead-ends, some lead to pleasant campsites.

GPS: N32°19.37' W114°03.48'

▼ 2.6 SO Track on left.
2.5 ▲ SO Track on right.

▼ 2.7 SO Track on left.
2.4 ▲ BL Track on right.

GPS: N32°19.32' W114°03.02'

▼ 3.0 BR Cross through wash; then bear right along better-used trail, staying close to the range.
2.1 ▲ SO Track on right; then cross through wash.

▼ 3.1		SO	Well-used track on left. Keep right along range.
	2.0 ▲	BL	Well-used track on right. Keep left along range.
▼ 3.3		SO	Track on right goes to Tinajas Altas Tanks, then cross through wash.
	1.8 ▲	SO	Cross through wash, then track on left goes to Tinajas Altas Tanks.
			GPS: N32°18.81' W114°02.84'
▼ 3.6		SO	Cross through wash; then faint track on right. Main trail is heading away from range.
	1.5 ▲	SO	Faint track on left; then cross through wash. Remain on main trail as it runs close to the range.
▼ 3.8		TR	Closed trails ahead and on left.
	1.3 ▲	TL	Closed trails ahead and on right.
			GPS: N32°18.64' W114°02.44'
▼ 4.2		SO	Track on right.
	0.9 ▲	SO	Track on left.
▼ 5.1			Trail ends at South #3: El Camino del Diablo Trail. Turn left to exit to Wellton.
	0.0 ▲		Trail commences on South #3: El Camino del Diablo Trail, 30.4 miles south of Wellton. Turn at the BLM sign for Tinajas Altas and proceed west along formed, sandy trail. The trail starts at the southernmost sign for Tinajas Altas. If approaching from Wellton, note that you will have passed two previous signs for Tinajas Altas.
			GPS: N32°18.13' W114°01.17'

SOUTH REGION TRAIL #2

Fortuna Mine Trail

Starting Point:	**South #1: Tinajas Altas Pass Trail**
Finishing Point:	**Foothills Boulevard**
Total Mileage:	**12 miles**
Unpaved Mileage:	**11 miles**
Driving Time:	**1.5 hours**
Elevation Range:	**400–600 feet**
Usually Open:	**Year-round**
Best Time to Travel:	**November to March**
Difficulty Rating:	**3**
Scenic Rating:	**8**
Remoteness Rating:	**+0**

Special Attractions

- Old Fortuna Mine.
- Varied trail winding in the Gila Mountains.
- Panoramic views over the Barry M. Goldwater Air Force Range.

History

The rich outcrop that became the site of the Fortuna Mine was first discovered by Charles W. Thomas, William H. Holbert, and Laurent Albert in 1894. Two years later the mine was sold to Charles D. Lane, an experienced miner from Angel's Camp, California who paid $150,000 for the claim. Lane set about organizing La Fortuna Gold Mining

The trail heading up a ridge toward Red Top Mountain

and Milling Company, which built a twenty-stamp mill and employed 80 to 100 Mexican and American miners. The main problem the fledgling company had to overcome was the lack of water at the site. A 100-horsepower pump on the Gila River and more than twelve miles of pipeline to bring the water to the mine solved the problem.

The mining camp that sprang up around the mine was by all accounts a rowdy one. Known as Fortuna, it had a hotel, many saloons, and a stage line that linked it with Blaisdell on the Southern Pacific Railroad. Prostitutes and gamblers regularly made the trip down from Yuma, and fights were common. The saloon did a roaring trade, supposedly because the water tasted so bad the miners turned to the stronger stuff.

The mine was a rich and productive one, with an average yield per month of $80,000. In 1899 a cyanide treatment plant was constructed to treat the accumulated tailings, yielding a further $5 per ton. A potential problem with the mine was that the vein was erratic and the ore was contained around an intersection of two short veins. In 1900 the productive vein was lost on a fault line, and only a small segment was found with further exploration. However, between 1896 and 1904, more than $2,500,000 in bullion was sent from the Fortuna Mine to the Selby smelter in California's San Francisco Bay area. The major life of the camp was over in 1904.

The Fortuna Mine reopened briefly a couple of times after 1904, producing a further $25,000 worth of gold. In 1954 the mine was included in the Barry M. Goldwater Air Force Range.

Description

The trail commences 8.2 miles from the north end of South #1: Tinajas Altas Pass Trail and wraps back up along the face of the Gila Mountains to the outskirts of Yuma. It is a well-traveled, popular, short day trip from Yuma. The trail crosses along a desert pavement ridge top before dropping down to enter a wash. The wash is stony, rubbly, and slow going. The trail meanders in and around the wash up to the historic Fortuna Mine, which sits in a cove in the range. Red Top Mountain set to the north of the mine is distinguished by its sandy reddish-colored top, which stands out from the other darker gray rocks of the Gila Range.

Two main tracks run into the mine area, and several smaller tracks run all around the mine to the various remains of

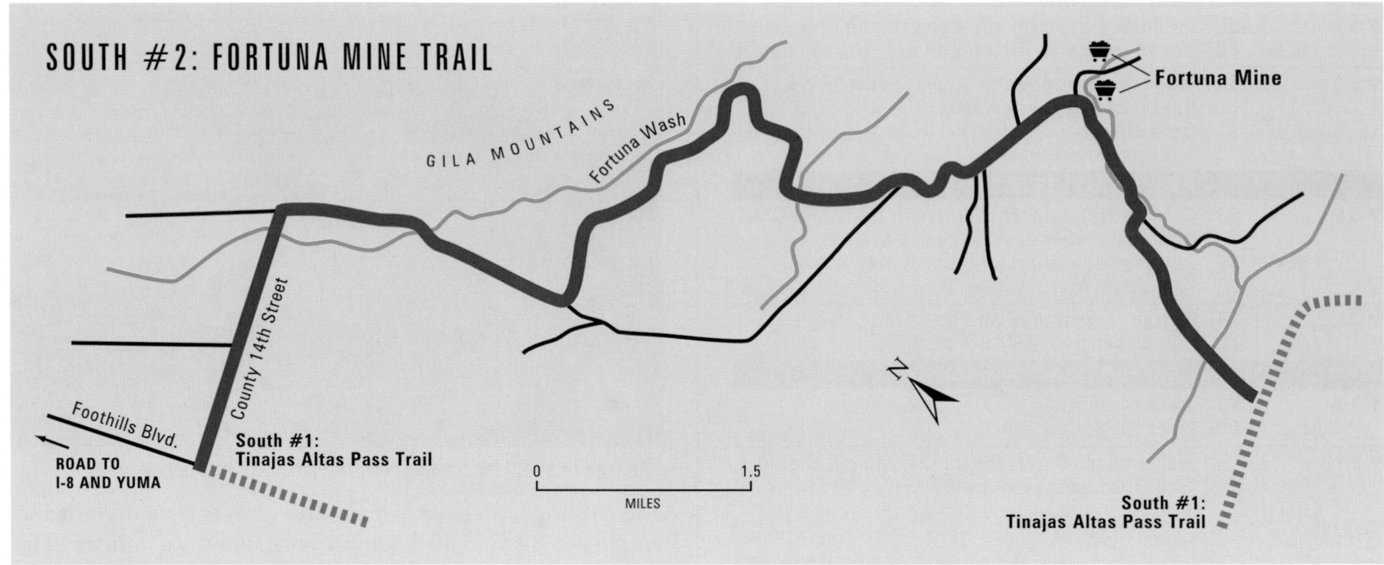

buildings and mine workings. The mill site is easily recognizable by the large embankment walls slightly elevated directly to the east.

From the Fortuna Mine, the trail crosses the bajada on the western slope of the Gila Mountains. The route this trail takes runs close to the range, running for a couple of miles along a ridge top with a steep drop down to the wide Fortuna Wash. It crosses the desert pavement, traveling as a well-defined two-track. There are panoramic views to the west over the Barry M. Goldwater Air Force Range.

The trail joins a well-used trail that travels north toward Yuma. In the reverse direction, this junction is easy to miss as it is unmarked and there are no distinguishing features to mark the turn. The trail finishes on the outskirts of Yuma, along County 14 Street. Continuing west along this street leads to Foothills Boulevard, immediately south of exit 14 on I-8.

A permit to enter the Barry M. Goldwater Air Force Range is essential in order to travel this trail. For permit information and other necessary information regarding travel in this region, refer to South #3: El Camino del Diablo Trail.

Current Road Information

Luke Air Force Base
Gila Bend Auxiliary Field
Range Operations
Gila Bend, AZ 85337
(520) 683-6272

Bureau of Land Management
Yuma Field Office
2555 Gilda Ridge Road
Yuma, AZ 85365
(520) 317-3200

Map References

BLM Yuma
USGS 1:24,000 Fortuna Mine, Fortuna SW, Fortuna
1:100,000 Yuma
Maptech CD-ROM: Southwest Arizona/Yuma
Arizona Atlas & Gazetteer, p. 62

Route Directions

Mileage		Direction
▼ 0.0		From South #1: Tinajas Altas Pass Trail, 8.2 miles from the north end of the trail, turn northeast at marker post A3 and zero trip meter.
2.6 ▲		Trail ends at the intersection with South #1: Tinajas Altas Pass Trail. Turn right to exit to Yuma, turn left to continue along to Tinajas Altas Pass.
		GPS: N32°31.51' W114°21.61'
▼ 0.4	SO	Cross through wide wash.
2.2 ▲	SO	Exit wide wash crossing.
▼ 0.5	SO	Exit wide wash crossing.
2.1 ▲	SO	Cross through wide wash.
		GPS: N32°31.90' W114°21.41'
▼ 0.7	SO	Cross through wash.
1.9 ▲	SO	Cross through wash.
▼ 1.0	SO	Cross through wash.
1.6 ▲	SO	Cross through wash.
▼ 1.1	SO	Cross through wash, then trail runs up small ridge. Red Top Mountain ahead.
1.5 ▲	SO	Cross through wash.
▼ 1.5	BR	Bear right and swing down off ridge.
1.1 ▲	BL	Climb up ridge then bear left along ridge top.
		GPS: N32°32.62' W114°20.74'
▼ 1.6	BL	Track on right.
1.0 ▲	BR	Track on left.
		GPS: N32°32.58' W114°20.64'
▼ 1.7	SO	Cross through wash. Trail now follows the line of the wash, crossing it often for next 0.5 miles.
0.9 ▲	SO	Exit line of wash.
▼ 2.2	SO	Exit wash.
0.4 ▲	SO	Enter wash, trail now follows the line of the wash, crossing it often for the next 0.5 miles.
		GPS: N32°32.91' W114°20.18'
▼ 2.3	SO	Small track on left, diggings on right. Start of the diggings of the Fortuna Mine.
0.3 ▲	SO	Small track on right, diggings on left. Leaving the Fortuna Mine.
▼ 2.4	SO	Cross through wash.

	0.2 ▲	SO	Cross through wash.
▼ 2.5		SO	Cross through wash.
	0.1 ▲	SO	Cross through wash.
▼ 2.6		BL	Two tracks on right lead into main area of Fortuna Mine. Zero trip meter.
	0.0 ▲		Continue to the south.
			GPS: N32°33.19' W114°20.01'
▼ 0.0			Continue to the northwest.
	5.5 ▲	BR	Two tracks on left lead into main area of Fortuna Mine. Zero trip meter.
▼ 0.1		SO	Cross through wash. Small stone ruins dotted nearby.
	5.4 ▲	SO	Cross through wash. Small stone ruins dotted nearby.
▼ 0.4		SO	Cross through wide wash.
	5.1 ▲	SO	Cross through wide wash.
▼ 0.5		SO	Climb up out of wash. Track on right.
	5.0 ▲	SO	Track on left, descend to cross through wide wash.
			GPS: N32°33.44' W114°20.42'
▼ 0.6		SO	Track on right.
	4.9 ▲	SO	Track on left.
▼ 0.7		SO	Cross through wash; then faint track on left. Remain on main trail.
	4.8 ▲	SO	Faint track on right; then cross through wash. Remain on main trail.
▼ 0.8		SO	Two faint tracks on left.
	4.7 ▲	SO	Two faint tracks on right.
▼ 1.3		SO	Cross through wide wash.
	4.2 ▲	SO	Cross through wide wash.
			GPS: N32°33.80' W114°21.00'
▼ 1.6		SO	Cross through wash.
	3.9 ▲	SO	Cross through wash.
▼ 1.7		BR	Track on left. Bear right to the north following the slightly less-used trail that runs closer to the hills. Track looks fainter at the start, but is well defined immediately over the ridge.
	3.8 ▲	SO	Track on right is equally used. Continue to the southeast.
▼ 1.8		SO	Cross through small wash.
	3.7 ▲	SO	Cross through small wash.
▼ 2.0		SO	Cross through wash.
	3.5 ▲	SO	Cross through wash.
▼ 2.1		BL	Faint track on right, remain on main trail.
	3.4 ▲	SO	Faint track on left, remain on main trail.
▼ 2.3		SO	Start to cross wide Fortuna Wash.
	3.2 ▲	SO	Exit wash.
▼ 2.4		BR	Exit wash and bear right.
	3.1 ▲	BL	Bear left and start to cross wide Fortuna Wash.
			GPS: N32°34.66' W114°21.38'
▼ 2.8		SO	Cross through wide wash.
	2.7 ▲	SO	Cross through wide wash.
			GPS: N32°34.76' W114°20.98'
▼ 2.9		SO	Track on right.
	2.6 ▲	BR	Track on left.
			GPS: N32°34.81' W114°20.98'
▼ 3.4		BL	Smaller track continues straight on. Bear left and continue along ridge.
	2.1 ▲	BR	Smaller track on left.
			GPS: N32°35.15' W114°20.75'
▼ 4.1		BL	Smaller track on right drops down into wash.
	1.4 ▲	SO	Smaller track on left drops down into wash.
			GPS: N32°35.44' W114°21.37'
▼ 4.7		SO	Track on left.
	0.8 ▲	SO	Track on right.
▼ 4.8		BL	Faint track continues straight on.
	0.7 ▲	BR	Bear right up ridge top, faint track on left. Beware—abrupt turn with drop straight ahead!
			GPS: N32°35.75' W114°21.94'
▼ 5.0		SO	Cross through wash.
	0.5 ▲	SO	Cross through wash.
▼ 5.2		SO	Track on left goes up rise.
	0.3 ▲	BL	Track on right goes up rise.
			GPS: N32°35.74' W114°22.39'
▼ 5.5		TR	T-intersection with well-used trail. Turn right and zero trip meter. The junction is unmarked with no noticeable features to mark it.
	0.0 ▲		Continue to the east.
			GPS: N32°35.75' W114°22.64'
▼ 0.0			Continue to the north toward Yuma and cross through wash.
	3.9 ▲	TL	Cross through wash; then turn left onto well-used trail. The junction is unmarked with no noticeable features to mark it. Zero trip meter.
▼ 0.8		SO	Cross through wash.
	3.1 ▲	SO	Cross through wash.
			GPS: N32°36.46' W114°22.51'
▼ 0.9		SO	Small track on left.
	3.0 ▲	SO	Small track on right.
▼ 1.1		SO	Cross through wide wash; then track on right.
	2.8 ▲	BR	Track on left; then cross through wide wash.
			GPS: N32°36.80' W114°22.39'
▼ 1.3		BL	Faint track on right.
	2.6 ▲	SO	Faint track on left.
▼ 1.4		SO	Track on left.
	2.5 ▲	BL	Track on right.
			GPS: N32°37.04' W114°22.46'
▼ 1.6		BR	Track on left.
	2.3 ▲	SO	Track on right.
▼ 1.8		SO	Leaving Barry M. Goldwater Air Force Range, many small tracks on right and left around boundary, remain on main trail.
	2.1 ▲	SO	Entering Barry M. Goldwater Air Force Range, valid permit required beyond this point. Many small tracks on right and left around boundary, remain on main trail.
			GPS: N32°37.39' W114°22.48'
▼ 2.0		BL	Track on right.
	1.9 ▲	SO	Track on left.
▼ 2.1		TL	Turn left onto wide graded dirt road opposite small reservoir.
	1.8 ▲	TR	Turn right onto ungraded dirt trail opposite small reservoir. Trail is past the end of the golf course.
			GPS: N32°37.60' W114°22.58'
▼ 2.9		SO	Road is paved. Road on right is 14E Street. Now traveling on County 14th Street.
	1.0 ▲	SO	Road turns to dirt. Road on left is 14E Street.
▼ 3.9			Trail ends at the intersection with Foothills Boulevard. Turn right to exit to I-8. Trail on left is the start of South #1: Tinajas Altas Pass Trail.
	0.0 ▲		Trail starts at the intersection of Foothills Boulevard and County 14th Street. Zero trip meter and turn east on County 14th Street. Dirt trail to the south at this point is South #1: Tinajas Altas Pass Trail.
			GPS: N32°37.60' W114°24.55'

SOUTH REGION TRAIL #3

El Camino del Diablo Trail

Starting Point:	**I-8, exit 30 at Wellton**
Finishing Point:	**Arizona 85, 2.2 miles south of Ajo**
Total Mileage:	**114.1 miles**
Unpaved Mileage:	**110 miles**
Driving Time:	**2 days**
Elevation Range:	**200–2,000 feet**
Usually Open:	**Year-round**
Best Time to Travel:	**November to April**
Difficulty Rating:	**4**
Scenic Rating:	**9**
Remoteness Rating:	**+2**

Special Attractions

- Extremely long, remote 4WD adventure.
- Historic route used by Indians, Spanish, and gold rush travelers.
- Wide range of spectacular desert scenery.
- Bates Well homestead and site.
- Organ Pipe Cactus National Monument.

History

El Camino del Diablo (Spanish for "The Road of the Devil," although the popular translation is "The Devil's Highway") has long been used by many people crossing the dry Sonoran deserts. The region was first used by Indians to transport salt and shells back from the Sea of Cortez. These early inhabitants, Pinacatenos and Arenenos, both clans of the Tohono O'odham, eked out an existence in the arid landscape.

The first person known to pioneer a trail across the region was Captain Melchior Diaz, a member of Coronado's expedition who led a party through the desert en route to California in 1540.

It was another Spaniard who first provided some real information on the area and traveled it extensively himself. Between 1698 and 1702, the Jesuit missionary, Padre Eusebio Francisco Kino repeatedly traveled El Camino del Diablo as he carried out his missionary work while pioneering a route to California. Known as "The Padre on Horseback," Kino explored extensively, making the first maps of the region which, most importantly, included many of the major water holes.

An adobe casita at Tule Well

Throughout the 1700s, El Camino del Diablo saw a lot of use, mainly by Spanish priests who used it as a shorter route to the missions in California. Although it was a hard route, it was considerably shorter than the alternative land route via Tucson and Gila Bend, which looped to the north, or the long sea route, which passed to the south of Baja California. There was also less risk of being attacked by Apaches. Well-known names who traveled the route in the 1700s include Juan Bautista de Anza (1774–1776) as he searched for the Lost Seven Cities of Gold, Fray Francisco Garcés (1779–1781), and Pedro Fages (1781–1782).

Today, this section of El Camino del Diablo does not strictly follow the old paths, as such there were, which meandered south down into Mexico. Different travelers took different routes, and at times the faint trails were obliterated by wind and shifting sand.

In 1781, the Yuma Indian uprising at the Colorado River crossing meant that fewer travelers were willing to brave the route and it reverted to a seldom-used trail. It was not until 1849 and the onset of the California Gold Rush that El Camino del Diablo once again saw travelers. It was during this time that El Camino acquired its well-deserved reputation as the most deadly of immigrant roads. "Locally, it is known as El Camino del Diablo, and few names are more appropriate," said Capt. D. D. Gaillard in 1896.

The number of deaths that have occurred along this so-called road may never be known. Men trying to connect the vague trail of waterholes along the way had their work cut out for them. Shifting sands meant any real trace of a trail was lost and many died of hunger, thirst, and sheer fatigue. It is thought that between 400 and 2,000 people died of thirst along the road and were buried in often unmarked, unremembered graves. There are approximately 50 known graves along the trail, but only a handful are marked in any way.

One of the most obvious graves is that of Dave O'Neill, who is buried on the pass through the hills that bear his name. A prospector near the turn of the twentieth century, he died of exposure and dehydration. His burros made their way into Papago Well without him, prompting a search, and he was buried where his body was found in the pass.

Early travelers had a few options when they reached the natural tanks of Tinajas Altas. Called Agua Escondido, "hidden water" by Padre Kino, the string of nine natural water tanks running up a cleft in the Tinajas Altas Range were one of the major water points along the trail. When full, these tinajas could hold 20,000 gallons, but more often than not, the lower tanks were drained dry. The climb up to the higher tanks is a difficult one by anyone's standards. Many people died as they were too weak to make the steep climb up to the higher tanks.

If the tanks were dry, travelers had little choice but to swing to the north following the east side of the Tinajas Altas Mountains to the water and shade along the Gila River. This route

An old tank standing guard beside the trail

was later known as "The Smugglers Trail" after it was resurrected by liquor smugglers during prohibition days. If the tanks had water, stronger and more daring travelers were able to cross through the Tinajas Altas Range and proceed more directly to Yuma Crossing.

Other people who passed this way include a wave of Mexican and American boundary surveyors who were formalizing the boundaries of the land acquired by the United States in the 1853–54 Gadsden Purchase. Miners in the 1860s were also rushing to the Colorado River to mine the placer gold discovered there.

The railroad reached Yuma in 1870 and El Camino del Diablo waned. Few were willing to risk their lives crossing the trail when there was the safer option of the railroad available. El Camino was quiet until more recent times, when scientists began to study the desert in depth, and even more recently, the road gained popularity as an exciting and beautiful route for backcountry adventurers.

Other current users of the trail are a steady stream of undocumented aliens and drug smugglers who take advantage of the extremely remote, unpopulated area to gain access into the United States. The border patrol is active in the region, and there are signs along the Mexican border warning potential border crossers of the dangers of the area they are entering. In spite of this, every year people die of thirst and heat exhaustion as they try to cross the deserts to civilization.

Through the years, travelers have named the features they found along El Camino. Many are named after early travelers; others reflect the physical characteristics of the features they saw. Others are less obvious—Raven Butte, a very dark-colored butte near the eastern end of Cipriano Pass, is not named for its color, but because the ravens in the region were surprisingly trusting and tame.

The Gila Mountains were formerly known as the Sierra de la Gila, when in 1854 Lt. N. Michler reported that they extended north of the Gila River. For a while they were the Gila City Mountains, after the nearby booming settlement of Gila City.

The agave plant, which is plentiful in this desert is called *lechuguilla* in Spanish, meaning frill or ruff, a name that reflects the lower shape of the plant. Hence, the Lechuguilla Desert became an obvious name for this region.

The Cabeza Prieta (Spanish for "dark head") is a reflection of the mountain's structure. They were considered to be part of the Tule Mountains to the southeast until the early 1920s when it was thought the gap at Tule Well where El Camino del Diablo passed through was significant enough to divide the range.

Early emigrants learned fast by necessity that in the desert they would find tule plants growing near water and so the name Tule Well developed though no such plant can be found here today. The name Tule is also given to the nearby mountains to the south, which cross the border into Mexico. These mountains were formerly known as the badlands in Spanish—Mesa de Malpais.

At the eastern end of the trail is Bates Well, a former small settlement now contained within Organ Pipe Cactus National Monument. A well was dug here in the 1890s by a man called Bates. Henry Gray was the last rancher at Bates Well before it came under the full control of the national monument. Henry continued ranching after the monument's founding in 1937. When he died in 1976, ranching ceased, and only the decaying cabins, corrals, and well remain.

The trail ends in Ajo, a historic mining town. The name Ajo seems to derive from the Papago Indians' use of the ores there that produced their red face paint (*au'auho* was their word for paint). Another possible explanation is that the town was named after a lily that grows there, whose root resembles in looks and taste a spring onion. *Ajo* means "garlic" in Spanish.

Though Captain Peter Brady was one of the first to lead mining ventures in the Ajo area after scouting the region for the route of the thirty-second parallel railroad in 1853, his ventures soon ran dry as the copper ore was too costly to process. Basic farming was the main activity of the few folks who remained in old Ajo. The abundant rich ores remained in the ground until the 1910s when leaching processes were developed that allowed the New Cornelia Mine (named by Colonel Greenway) to prosper to boom levels. Several thousand people moved to this growing region. The mine grew so large that the old Ajo town was engulfed by the spreading mine. Phelps Dodge is still the current owner of the mine, which is classed as an active mine due to a few people being employed mainly for security/safety reasons. No serious mining has occurred since the price of copper dropped in the 1980s, resulting in the town developing an almost ghost town atmosphere compared to its former frantic activity. Now at the turn of the twenty-first century it is becoming an attractive winter retirement setting for many folks, although its growth is restricted by the military land, the Indian reservation, and the federal lands that surround it.

Today, El Camino del Diablo crosses through three distinct land management boundaries. The Barry M. Goldwater Air Force Range occupies most of the western section. The middle section is contained within the Cabeza Prieta National Wildlife Area, and the Organ Pipe Cactus National Monument occupies the eastern end of the trail.

The Barry M. Goldwater Air Force Range is currently public land, which is leased to the military. It was established in 1941 to train World War II pilots and continues in use to this day by the U.S. Air Force and U.S. Marine Corps. It is used for air-to-ground and air-to-air training missions. Ground-based marines also use the 2 million-acre range for ground maneuvers and ground-to-air training exercises.

Although it has been accessible to the public for many years under a permit system, the military uses always take precedence, so from time to time the range is closed to the public. Parts of the range are not accessible at anytime.

The Cabeza Prieta National Wildlife Refuge is also overflown by the military, but the area is now designated as wilderness, with vehicle access permitted on designated corridors only.

El Camino del Diablo was placed on the National Register of Historic Places in 1978.

Today, nearly three hundred years after El Camino acquired its fearsome reputation, people still speak of the trail with awe, wonder, and more than a little trepidation. In many respects, little has changed, and many of the earliest travelers would have little difficulty in recognizing their landmarks today. If you take this historic trail, it is an experience that will remain with you long after the sand, dust, and scratches have been cleaned from your vehicle.

Description

For the well-prepared adventurer, this route is a two-day excursion through some of the most remote territory in Arizona. Although becoming more well known and increasingly traveled, the trail should not be treated lightly. Advance preparation is required, as a permit to travel the Barry M. Goldwater Air Force Range and the Cabeza Prieta National Wildlife Refuge is essential (see permit information below).

However, once you are ready to go, two unforgettable days of traveling through some of the most spectacular desert scenery in Arizona awaits. You will need a minimum of two days for the trail, longer if you intend to explore some of the other trails in the region.

Ocotillos and saguaros beside the trail and the Tinajas Altas Mountains in the distance

The trail commences in Wellton, along I-8, 25 miles east of Yuma. Top off the fuel tank and proceed south and briefly west along the Mohawk Canal before swinging south to enter the Barry M. Goldwater Air Force Range. The trail within the range is easygoing, being a wide, graded road for the most part, as it runs down a broad, flat-bottomed valley, with the Gila Mountains to the west and the lower Wellton Hills to the east. The Gila Mountains are composed of light-colored granite and are bare of vegetation on their slopes. As you get closer to them, you can appreciate the weathering of the pockmarked granite. The southern range is called the Tinajas Altas; the Spanish means "high tanks" and refers to the natural water pockets where the sparse rainfall can collect. Two other 4WD trails lead across the range—South #4: Cipriano Pass Trail is the northernmost trail and South #1: Tinajas Altas Pass Trail crosses at the southern end of the range.

Along the wide valley the trail is normally straight and wide enough that two vehicles can pass without pulling over. Remember you are in a military reserve and can expect to see some signs of its presence. There are some sections, however, where the trail twists and is narrower. It may be slightly brushy for wider vehicles and you need to watch for oncoming, fast-moving vehicles. There are many small tracks to the left and right within the range but only the marked or most noticeable ones have been given in the route directions.

After 31 miles the trail leaves the Barry M. Goldwater Air Force Range and enters the Cabeza Prieta National Wildlife Refuge. From here some of the most interesting, scenic, and difficult parts of the route commence.

The area is also rich in wildlife. Some twenty-four species of snake, including six types of rattlesnake, make the refuge their home, as well as the desert tortoise, horned lizard, bighorn sheep, coyote, kit fox, kangaroo rat, and eleven species of bat. Many species of migrating birds pass through the refuge. The best times of year to view them are February to May and August to November. Bird watchers may see warblers, phoebes, flycatchers, and swallows. Year-round there are red-tailed hawks and Gambel's quails. The refuge is also habitat for the rare and elusive Sonoran pronghorn antelope, an endangered species.

The trail is a narrow single track as it winds its way through the Cabeza Prieta Mountains. The sand can be deep and lower tire pressures may be necessary. This deep sand is where you will start to chew through the fuel. There are also some rocky sections. The trail is a lot narrower and can be brushy along this section, although with a little care it is possible to avoid the worst of it. The scenery within the Cabeza Prieta Mountains is wonderful. The very light-colored granite mountains, winding trail, saguaros, and ocotillos with their brilliant flags of flowers make for interest and photographic opportunities all the way. There are virtually no public access side trails within the Cabeza Prieta, as it travels along a wilderness corridor. Most old vehicle trails are now designated for management vehicles only. Most of them are given to assist the route directions, but smaller, fainter, and overgrown side trails have been omitted.

It is possible to camp anywhere within the range or the Cabeza Prieta as long as you stay within 50 feet of the trail. There are some pleasant sites for one or two vehicles within the Cabeza Prieta Mountains, but larger groups are probably better off selecting the sites at Tule Well or Papago Well. At Tule Well there are four sites, each with a picnic table and BBQ, as well as additional space for more vehicles. However, there is limited shade at these sites. At Tule Well, there is a small adobe casita, built by the National Wildlife Refuge workers in 1941. Also at Tule Well is the tank itself—dry on our visit. Next to the adobe casita is the junction with South #5: Christmas Pass Trail, which provides access to I-8.

From Tule Well, the trail runs only a couple of miles from the international border with Mexico. A major highway runs along the border on the Mexican side, Mexican Highway 2, which can often provide the only sign of civilization in two days; it is possible to catch glimpses of trucks on the highway.

As you cross over a gap in the hills, a keen eye will spot one of the many graves along the route. The location of most graves is unknown, and the elements, animals, and people often disturb the markers, making them hard to find.

Fourteen miles after Tule Well, the trail starts to cross the Pinacate Lava Flow. The lava flow originated in Mexico in the region now contained within the Pinacate Natural Reserve. There are approximately 70 volcanic peaks and a large, barren region covered by black cinders. The region is named for the desert stink beetle, or darkling beetle—a beetle that stands on its head and emits a foul odor when threatened; it is commonly found in Mexico. The Aztecs called this beetle *pinacatl* in their Nahuatl language.

The five miles that cross the Pinacate Lava Flow are some of the roughest of the entire trail. They are not difficult, just extremely lumpy and rough. Take it slowly and enjoy the dramatically different scenery.

The Pinta Sands are an area of soft sand dunes on either side of the Pinacate Lava Flow. On the east side of the Pinta Sands are Las Playas ("the beaches"), a deceptive area of deep, fine sand, often referred to as "bulldust." The trail here has worn down so that it is below the level of the surrounding area. In wet weather, it becomes totally impassable, as the powder-fine sand turns to deep goo. The BLM requests that you do not attempt to cross in wet weather or cut new tracks attempting to pass. This section is also the most brushy part of the trail, and minor scratches are inevitable for all vehicles. The worst section is between the Pinacate Lava Flow and the O'Neill Hills.

There is a second suggested area for group camping at Papago Well. There are cleared areas in the creosote bushes, and four picnic tables and BBQs. The border patrol maintains an active presence around here as it is so close to the international border, and you are likely to be awakened at night by their low-flying, unlit helicopters. Another option for groups needing more space is a pleasant area approximately 1.5 miles east of Papago Well, where there is a smooth, flat, relatively open area set among large saguaros on the western edge of Papago Mountain.

After passing through the well-named Cholla Pass, the trail enters the Organ Pipe Cactus National Monument. The old vehicle trail via Pozo Well to join South #6: Puerto Blanco Drive joins on the right, but has been closed to the public since 1998.

A popular spot for lunch is the old homestead and well at Bates Well. There are the old buildings, cabins, and corrals to explore and even a bit of shade. Past Bates Well, the trail is roughly graded and suitable for 2WD vehicles and it is an easy run into Ajo, passing the huge New Cornelia copper mine as you do.

Ajo has limited supplies and a couple of motels and eating places, as well as fuel.

Permit Information

In recent years the permit system has been streamlined, so that one permit now covers access into the Barry M. Goldwater Air Force Range, the Cabeza Prieta National Wildlife Refuge, and Organ Pipe Cactus National Monument. It is essential that you obtain a permit before you go. The permit allows you to cross Organ Pipe Cactus National Monument on the Bates Well Road only. To visit any other areas of the monument, you need to pay a separate park fee.

A separate permit is required for each person traveling over the age of 18 years. Children under 18 do not need a separate permit if accompanied by a permitted adult. Be prepared to provide details of yourself and your vehicle. You will also have to sign a "Hold Harmless" agreement, which informs you of the many dangers you are likely to encounter and absolves the military of any responsibility.

Permits can be obtained in person or via mail. Faxed applications are no longer accepted due to the requirement of an original signature on the permit application. The application takes about 20 minutes in person. You can also telephone to have an application mailed to you, but allow ample time before your proposed trip if applying via mail. There is no charge for the permit, and it is valid from July 1 to June 30 for multiple trips into the area.

Range permits may be obtained from the following places:

Luke Air Force Base
Gila Bend Auxiliary Field
Range Operations
Gila Bend, AZ 85337
(520) 683-6272

Range Management Department
Box 99160
Marine Corps Air Station
Yuma, AZ 85369-9160
(520) 341-3402

Bureau of Land Management
Yuma Field Office
2555 Gilda Ridge Road
Yuma, AZ 85365
(520) 317-3200

Bureau of Land Management
Phoenix Field Office
2015 West Deer Valley Road
Phoenix, AZ 85027
(602) 580-5500

Cabeza Prieta National Wildlife Refuge
1611 North 2nd Avenue
Ajo, AZ 85321
(520) 387-5226

Note that these offices all keep limited hours and are not open on weekends.

In addition, before each visit you MUST call 1-877-CAMP-010. This free call is answered 24 hours a day, 7 days a week. Be prepared to give permit numbers for all travelers, vehicle details, proposed route, and dates of entry and exit to the range. This number cannot answer any questions regarding permits, routes, or general inquiries.

Be aware, too, that authorized routes within the range are subject to change, either permanently or temporarily due to military exercises. It is your responsibility to be aware of any changes or restrictions that apply each time you enter the range. A map showing authorized travel routes is available when you get your permit.

Management of the range is currently handled mainly by the Bureau of Land Management. In July 2002, the military is scheduled to take over management of the range, which may mean changes in access or permit availability.

Special Considerations

Special considerations for El Camino del Diablo and trails within the Barry M. Goldwater Air Force Range:

The exceptional remoteness of this trail carries with it additional responsibilities for the traveler. As there are no facilities and no water available, you should be totally self-sufficient. The trail is very lightly traveled, so you cannot rely on a passing driver to help you out. It is especially important to carry ample water over and above your anticipated requirements. Parts of the trail cross areas that are impassable when wet—if you have to sit and wait out a wet spell you don't want to be hungry and thirsty.

Consider traveling as part of a group. This reduces the risk of being stranded and enables you to share essential equipment and vehicle spares. Thirsty vehicles may require additional fuel.

You must have a street-registered four-wheel drive vehicle to enter the Cabeza Prieta NWR. ATVs and 2WD vehicles are not permitted on the refuge.

The proximity of the international border with Mexico carries with it additional hazards. The area is a high-traffic area for undocumented aliens crossing from Mexico into the United States. It is likely that you will encounter these people. Refer to the section on the international border for more details. Nine times out of ten, you will just be asked for water and food and then left alone. If you feel uneasy or uncomfortable with this situation, consider traveling as part of a larger group. Lone vehicles and small groups are far more likely to be approached for assistance.

It is also highly recommended that you top up your fuel tank at Wellton.

Current Road Information

Luke Air Force Base
Gila Bend Auxiliary Field
Range Operations
Gila Bend, AZ 85337
(520) 683-6272

Bureau of Land Management
Yuma Field Office
2555 Gilda Ridge Road
Yuma, AZ 85365
(520) 317-3200

Cabeza Prieta National Wildlife Refuge
1611 North 2nd Avenue
Ajo, AZ 85321
(520) 387-5226

Map References

BLM Yuma, Tinajas Altas Mts., Cabeza Prieta Mts., Ajo
USGS 1:24,000 Wellton, Wellton Hills, Raven Butte, Tinajas Altas, Coyote Water, Tule Mts., Sierra Arida, Paradise Canyon, Monument Bluff, Las Playas, O'Neill Hills, Agua Dulce Mts., North of Agua Dulce Mts., Palo Verde Camp, Bates Well, Ajo South
1:100,000 Yuma, Tinajas Altas Mts., Cabeza Prieta Mts., Ajo
Maptech CD-ROM: Southwest Arizona/Yuma
Arizona Atlas & Gazetteer, pp. 62, 63, 64, 71, 70
Arizona Road & Recreation Atlas, pp. 44, 50, 51 & pp. 78, 84, 85
Recreational Map of Arizona (incomplete)

Route Directions

▼ 0.0		From I-8, exit 30 at Wellton, zero trip meter immediately on the south side of the freeway at the eastbound freeway entrance/exit. Exit ramp and proceed south on the paved road. Immediately cross over the Wellton Canal.
5.1 ▲		Trail ends at exit 30 on I-8 at the settlement of Wellton.
		GPS: N32°39.56' W114°08.49'
▼ 1.3	TR	Turn right onto graded dirt road, immediately before the Mohave Canal and levee.
3.8 ▲	TL	Turn left onto paved road.
▼ 5.1	TL	Zero trip meter and turn left and cross over Mohawk Canal on bridge, then immediately turn left again.
0.0 ▲		Continue along the north bank of the canal.
		GPS: N32°38.13' W114°12.60'
▼ 0.0		Continue toward Barry M. Goldwater Air Force Range.
13.3 ▲	TR	Turn right and cross over Mohawk Canal on bridge, then immediately turn right alongside canal. Zero trip meter.
▼ 0.1	SO	Cross over levee bank, tracks on right and left along the top.
13.2 ▲	SO	Cross over levee bank, tracks on right and left along the top.
▼ 1.2	SO	Crossroads, edge of the Barry M. Goldwater Air Force Range. Valid permit essential from this point. Graded road on right and left along the boundary.
12.1 ▲	SO	Crossroads, leaving the Barry M. Goldwater Air Force Range. Graded road on right and left along the boundary.
		GPS: N32°37.20' W114°12.57'
▼ 1.5	SO	Cross through fence line.
11.8 ▲	SO	Cross through fence line.
▼ 1.9	SO	Track on right.
11.4 ▲	SO	Track on left.
▼ 2.2	SO	Several tracks on right, remain on main graded trail.
11.1 ▲	SO	Several tracks on left, remain on main graded trail.
▼ 6.3	SO	Track on left and right under small power lines.

	7.0 ▲	SO	Track on right and left under small power lines.
			GPS: N32°33.36' W114°09.92'
▼ 8.3		SO	Track on right to old military tank.
	5.0 ▲	SO	Track on left to old military tank.
▼ 8.4		SO	Track on right to old military tank, second track on right.
	4.9 ▲	SO	Track on left, then second track on left to old military tank.
			GPS: N32°31.74' W114°08.77'
▼ 9.1		SO	Track on right is marked S23.
	4.2 ▲	SO	Track on left is marked S23.
			GPS: N32°31.12' W114°08.38'
▼ 9.5		SO	Track on right is marked B3.
	3.8 ▲	SO	Track on left is marked B3.
▼ 10.4		SO	Track on right and left is marked B4.
	2.9 ▲	SO	Track on left and right is marked B4.
			GPS: N32°30.18' W114°07.71'
▼ 10.5		SO	Track on right is marked S24.
	2.8 ▲	SO	Track on left is marked S24.
▼ 11.8		SO	Track on right.
	1.5 ▲	SO	Track on left.
▼ 11.9		SO	Track on right is marked S57; then second track on right.
	1.4 ▲	SO	Track on left, then second track on left is marked S57.
			GPS: N32°29.00' W114°06.84'
▼ 12.0		SO	Track on right.
	1.3 ▲	SO	Track on left.
▼ 13.3		SO	Tracks on left and right are marked B5. The track on right is South #4: Cipriano Pass Trail. Zero trip meter.
	0.0 ▲		Continue to the northwest.
			GPS: N32°27.87' W114°06.27'
▼ 0.0			Continue to southeast. Raven Butte is visible to the south in front of the Tinajas Altas Mountains.
	2.8 ▲	SO	Tracks on left and right are marked B5. The track on left is South #4: Cipriano Pass Trail. Zero trip meter.
▼ 0.6		SO	Track on right.
	2.2 ▲	SO	Track on left.
▼ 2.5		SO	Track on right is marked B5.
	0.3 ▲	SO	Track on left is marked B5.
			GPS: N32°25.80' W114°05.18'
▼ 2.7		SO	Track on right is marked S32.
	0.1 ▲	SO	Track on left is marked S32.
▼ 2.8		SO	El Camino del Diablo information board on right. Zero trip meter.
	0.0 ▲		Continue to the northwest.
			GPS: N32°25.50' W114°05.01'
▼ 0.0			Continue to the southeast.
	6.6 ▲	SO	El Camino del Diablo information board on left. Zero trip meter.
▼ 0.6		SO	Tracks on right and left are marked S33.
	6.0 ▲	SO	Tracks on right and left are marked S33.
			GPS: N32°25.00' W114°04.74'
▼ 0.7		SO	Faint track on right.
	5.9 ▲	SO	Faint track on left.
▼ 2.6		SO	Track on right and sign for the Tinajas Altas Mountains, Area of Critical Environmental Concern.
	4.0 ▲	SO	Track on left and sign for the Tinajas Altas Mountains, Area of Critical Environmental Concern.
			GPS: N32°23.33' W114°03.95'
▼ 5.4		SO	Track on right.
	1.2 ▲	SO	Track on left.
▼ 5.8		SO	Well-used track on right.
	0.8 ▲	BR	Well-used track on left.
			GPS: N32°20.51' W114°02.94'
▼ 6.6		BL	Track on right is signed to Tinajas Altas. This joins South #1: Tinajas Altas Pass Trail via a maze of small trails. Zero trip meter at sign.
	0.0 ▲		Continue on El Camino del Diablo.
			GPS: N32°19.83' W114°02.94'
▼ 0.0			Continue on El Camino del Diablo.
	2.6 ▲	SO	Track on left is signed to Tinajas Altas. This joins South #1: Tinajas Altas Pass Trail via a maze of small trails. Zero trip meter at sign.
▼ 0.4		TL	T-intersection, track on right.
	2.2 ▲	BR	Turn right following better-used graded trail. Track continues straight on.
			GPS: N32°19.50' W114°02.81'
▼ 0.6		SO	Track on left is marked S34.
	2.0 ▲	SO	Track on right is marked S34.
▼ 2.1		SO	Track on left is marked S35.
	0.5 ▲	SO	Track on right is marked S35.
			GPS: N32°18.48' W114°01.51'
▼ 2.6		SO	Track on right through the bare area is South #1: Tinajas Altas Pass Trail (west route of El Camino del Diablo). Leaving the Area of Critical Environmental Concern. Zero trip meter.
	0.0 ▲		Continue toward Wellton.
			GPS: N32°18.13' W114°01.17'
▼ 0.0			Continue east, toward Tordillo Mountain.
	3.5 ▲	SO	Track on left through the bare area is South #1: Tinajas Altas Pass Trail (west route of El Camino del Diablo). Entering the Area of Critical Environmental Concern. Zero trip meter.
▼ 1.6		SO	Faint track on right.
	1.9 ▲	SO	Faint track on left.
▼ 3.5		SO	Exiting the military area and entering the Cabeza Prieta National Wildlife Refuge; permit required. Zero trip meter at boundary.
	0.0 ▲		Continue into the Barry M. Goldwater Air Force Range.
			GPS: N32°16.92' W113°57.64'
▼ 0.0			Continue into the Cabeza Prieta NWR.
	13.1 ▲	SO	Exiting the Cabeza Prieta National Wildlife Refuge and entering the Barry M. Goldwater Air Force Range; permit required. Zero trip meter at boundary.
▼ 4.3		SO	Management vehicle tracks on right and left. Tordillo Mountain is on left.
	8.8 ▲	SO	Management vehicle tracks on right and left. Tordillo Mountain is on right.
			GPS: N32°15.39' W113°53.32'
▼ 4.6		SO	Cross through wash and ascend short ridge.
	8.5 ▲	SO	Descend short ridge and cross through wash.
			GPS: N32°15.30' W113°52.97'
▼ 7.0		SO	Track on left is numbered 54.
	6.1 ▲	SO	Track on right is numbered 54.
			GPS: N32°14.77' W113°50.66'
▼ 8.2		SO	Cross through wash.
	4.9 ▲	SO	Cross through wash.
▼ 9.9		SO	Track on right and track on left is for management vehicles only.
	3.2 ▲	SO	Track on right and track on left is for management vehicles only.
			GPS: N32°13.22' W113°48.17'
▼ 10.0		SO	Old trail on left is for management vehicles only.

3.1 ▲	SO	Old trail on right is for management vehicles only.
▼ 10.1	SO	Cross through wash.
3.0 ▲	SO	Cross through wash.
▼ 11.0	SO	Cross through wash.
2.1 ▲	SO	Cross through wash.
▼ 11.3	SO	Track on left is for management vehicles only.
1.8 ▲	SO	Track on right is for management vehicles only.
▼ 11.4	SO	Cross through wash.
1.7 ▲	SO	Cross through wash.
▼ 12.6	SO	Cross through wash.
0.5 ▲	SO	Cross through wash.
▼ 12.9	SO	Cross through wash.
0.2 ▲	SO	Cross through wash.
▼ 13.1	BR	Tule Well camping area. Major track to the left is South #5: Christmas Pass Trail to I-8. There is a small adobe casita at the junction. The hillock behind the casita has a stone plaque recording the dedication of the Cabeza Prieta Refuge in 1941. Zero trip meter.
0.0 ▲		Continue toward the Barry M. Goldwater Air Force Range.
		GPS: N32°13.56' W113°44.92'
▼ 0.0		Continue along El Camino del Diablo.
24.1 ▲	BL	Tule Well camping area. Major track on right is South #5: Christmas Pass Trail to I-8. There is a small adobe casita at the junction. The hillock behind the casita has a stone plaque recording the dedication of the Cabeza Prieta Refuge in 1941. Zero trip meter.
▼ 0.1	SO	Cross through wash.
24.0 ▲	SO	Cross through wash.
▼ 0.3	SO	Cross through wash.
23.8 ▲	SO	Cross through wash.
▼ 0.7	SO	Cross through wash.
23.4 ▲	SO	Cross through wash.
▼ 0.9	SO	Cross through wash.
23.2 ▲	SO	Cross through wash.
▼ 1.0	SO	Track on right, #18, is for management vehicles only.
23.1 ▲	SO	Track on left, #18, is for management vehicles only.
▼ 2.1	BL	Route marker for Papago Well and Ajo on left. Track on right and track on left are for management vehicles only.
22.0 ▲	BR	Track on right and track on left are for management vehicles only.
▼ 3.1	SO	Cross through wash.
21.0 ▲	SO	Cross through wash.
▼ 3.2	SO	Cross through wash.
20.9 ▲	SO	Cross through wash.
▼ 3.3	SO	Grave on left, just after the wash crossing.
20.8 ▲	SO	Grave on right, just before wash crossing.
		GPS: N32°11.34' W113°42.60'
▼ 3.7	SO	Grave on left, little remains to mark the spot except some white stones.
20.4 ▲	SO	Grave on right, little remains to mark the spot except some white stones.
		GPS: N32°11.12' W113°42.45'
▼ 4.0	SO	Cross through wash.
20.1 ▲	SO	Cross through wash.
▼ 4.3	SO	Cross through wash.
19.8 ▲	SO	Cross through wash.
▼ 5.0	SO	Cross through wash.
19.1 ▲	SO	Cross through wash.

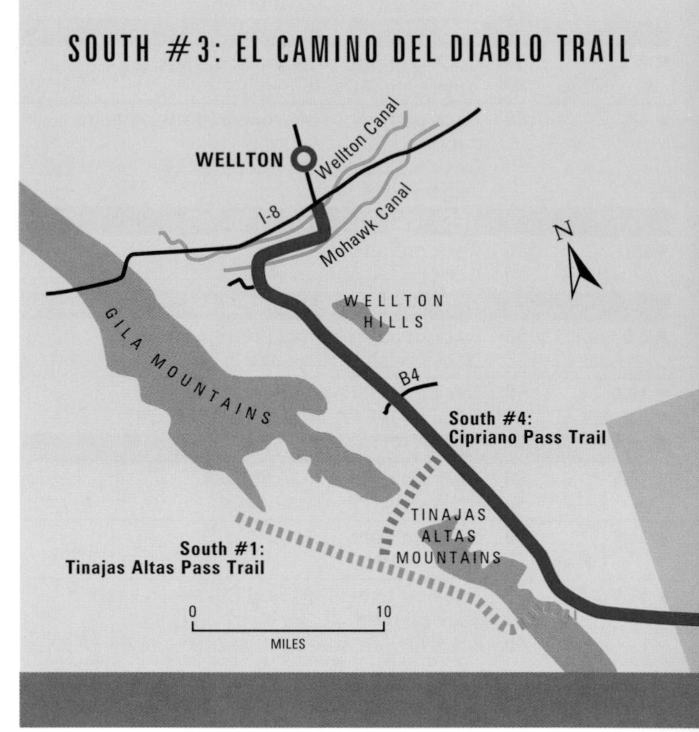

▼ 5.1	SO	Cross through wash.
19.0 ▲	SO	Cross through wash.
▼ 6.4	SO	Cross through wash. Leaving the Cabeza Prieta Mountains and starting to cross the Tule Desert.
17.7 ▲	SO	Cross through wash. Leaving the Tule Desert and entering the Cabeza Prieta Mountains.
▼ 7.2	SO	Cross through wash.
16.9 ▲	SO	Cross through wash.
▼ 7.6	SO	Cross through wash.
16.5 ▲	SO	Cross through wash.
▼ 8.8	SO	Cross through wash.
15.3 ▲	SO	Cross through wash.
▼ 14.0	SO	Starting to cross the Pinacate Lava Flow.
10.1 ▲	SO	Leaving the lava flow to cross the Pinta sands.
▼ 16.8	SO	Turnout on right and cairn on hillock.
7.3 ▲	SO	Turnout on left and cairn on hillock.
		GPS: N32°06.56' W113°30.12'
▼ 19.3	SO	Leaving the Pinacate Lava Flow, re-entering the Pinta Sands.
4.8 ▲	SO	Leaving the Pinta Sands to cross the Pinacate Lava Flow.
▼ 22.7	SO	Tracks on right and left.
1.4 ▲	SO	Tracks on right and left.
		GPS: N32°05.48' W113°24.20'
▼ 24.1	SO	Route marker pointing back for Tule Well, Tule Tank, and Tinajas Altas. Zero trip meter.
0.0 ▲		Continue toward the Pinacate Lava Flow.
		GPS: N32°05.27' W113°22.83'
▼ 0.0		Continue toward the O'Neill Hills.
5.6 ▲	SO	Route marker for Tule Well, Tule Tank, and Tinajas Altas. Zero trip meter.
▼ 1.6	SO	Grave of Dave O'Neill on left of the trail, marked by a cross and a pile of stones. Trail is passing through O'Neill Pass.
4.0 ▲	SO	Grave of Dave O'Neill on right of the trail, marked by a cross and a pile of stones. Trail is passing through O'Neill Pass.

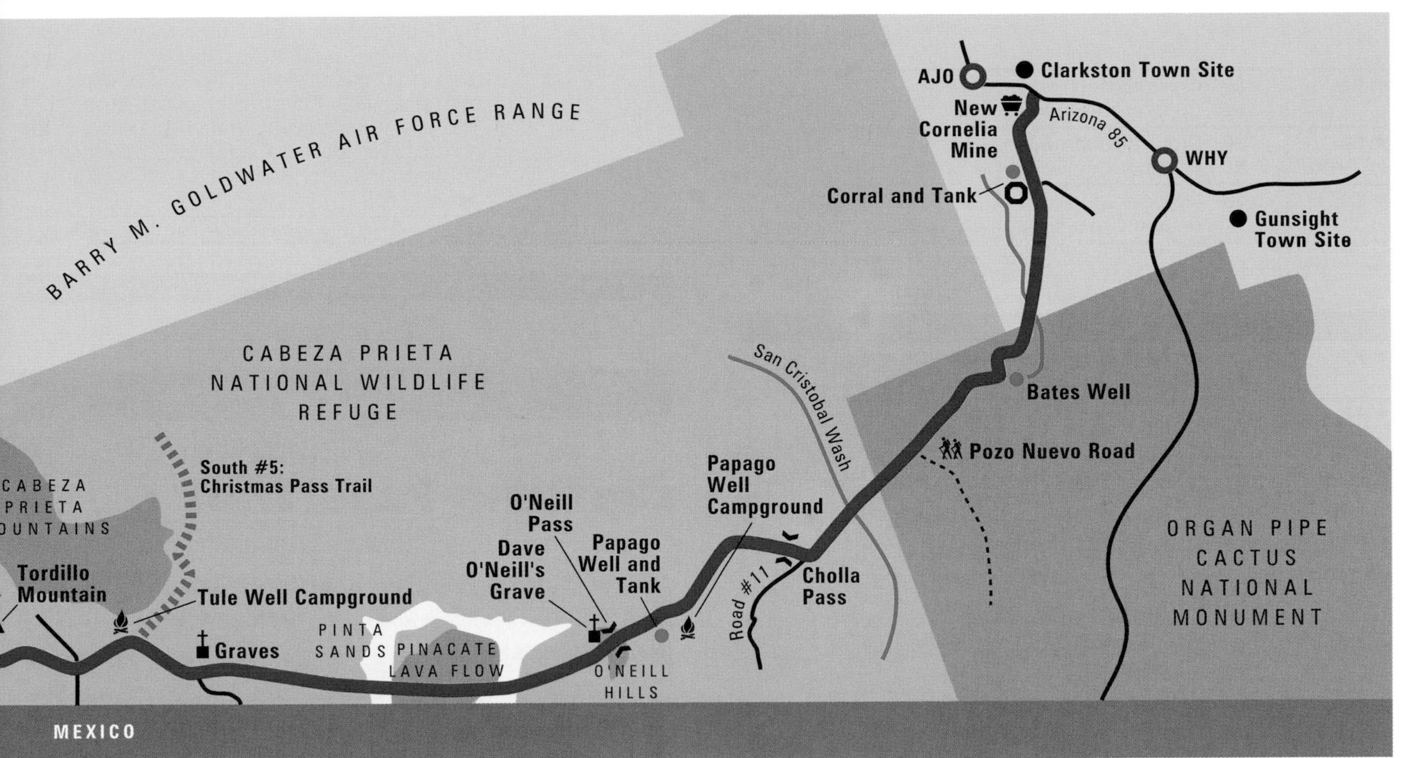

		GPS: N32°05.83′ W113°21.23′
▼ 4.8	SO	Cross through wash.
0.8 ▲	SO	Cross through wash.
▼ 5.5	SO	Route marker pointing back for Tule Well, Tule Tank, and Tinajas Altas.
0.1 ▲	SO	Route marker for Tule Well, Tule Tank, and Tinajas Altas.
▼ 5.6	SO	Papago Well and tank on right. Zero trip meter.
0.0 ▲		Continue toward the O'Neill Hills.
		GPS: N32°05.95′ W113°17.16′
▼ 0.0		Continue toward the Organ Pipe Cactus National Monument.
8.4 ▲	SO	Papago Well and tank on left. Zero trip meter.
▼ 0.1	SO	Papago Well Camp on right.
8.3 ▲	SO	Papago Well Camp on left.
		GPS: N32°05.98′ W113°16.99′
▼ 8.4	SO	Well-used track, #11, on right is for management vehicles only. Zero trip meter.
0.0 ▲		Continue toward Papago Well.
		GPS: N32°06.17′ W113°09.95′
▼ 0.0		Continue toward the Organ Pipe Cactus National Monument following the sign to Ajo.
4.9 ▲	BR	Well-used track, #11, on the left is for management vehicles only. Zero trip meter.
▼ 4.9	SO	Track on right is for management vehicles only; then cattle guard. Leaving Cabeza Prieta NWR and entering Organ Pipe Cactus National Monument. Track on left after cattle guard. Zero trip meter.
0.0 ▲		Continue into the Cabeza Prieta National Wildlife Refuge.
		GPS: N32°07.83′ W113°05.09′
▼ 0.0		Continue straight on into the Organ Pipe Cactus NM.
8.4 ▲	SO	Track on right; then exit Organ Pipe Cactus National Monument over cattle guard and enter the Cabeza Prieta NWR. Track on left is for management vehicles. A valid range permit is essential beyond this point. Zero trip meter.
▼ 2.5	SO	Track on right is the Pozo Nuevo Road, which is closed to vehicles.
5.9 ▲	SO	Track on left is the Pozo Nuevo Road, which is closed to vehicles.
		GPS: N32°08.73′ W113°02.58′
▼ 7.2	SO	Cross through wash.
1.2 ▲	SO	Cross through wash.
▼ 8.1	SO	Cattle guard.
0.3 ▲	SO	Cattle guard.
▼ 8.4	SO	Bates Well on right. Zero trip meter.
0.0 ▲		Continue through the Organ Pipe Cactus National Monument. The route is now a formed trail.
		GPS: N32°10.20′ W112°57.05′
▼ 0.0		Continue on toward Ajo. The road is now roughly graded.
3.8 ▲	SO	Bates Well on left. Zero trip meter.
▼ 1.6	SO	Track on left is closed to vehicles and goes a short distance to two mines.
2.2 ▲	SO	Track on right is closed to vehicles and goes a short distance to two mines.
▼ 3.8	SO	Exiting Organ Pipe Cactus National Monument over cattle guard. Track on right before cattle guard and track on left after cattle guard. Zero trip meter.
0.0 ▲		Continue into the Organ Pipe Cactus National Monument.
		GPS: N32°12.02′ W112°54.28′
▼ 0.0		Continue toward Ajo.
11.9 ▲	SO	Track on right; then enter Organ Pipe Cactus National Monument over cattle guard; then track on left. Zero trip meter.
▼ 0.2	SO	Two entrances to track on left.
11.7 ▲	SO	Two entrances to track on right.
▼ 0.7	SO	Track on left; then cross through wash; then track on right.

11.2 ▲	SO	Track on left; then cross through wash; then track on right.
▼ 1.2	SO	Cross through wash.
10.7 ▲	SO	Cross through wash.
▼ 1.6	SO	Cross through wash.
10.3 ▲	SO	Cross through wash.
▼ 3.0	SO	Major graded road on left; continue straight on and cross through wash; then small tracks on left and right.
8.9 ▲	BL	Small tracks on left and right, then cross through wash; then major graded road to the right.
		GPS: N32°14.42' W112°52.83'
▼ 3.7	SO	Cross through wash, then faint track on right.
8.2 ▲	SO	Faint track on left, then cross through wash.
▼ 3.8	SO	Smaller track on right.
8.1 ▲	BR	Smaller track on left; remain on main graded road.
▼ 5.1	SO	Cross through wash.
6.8 ▲	SO	Cross through wash.
▼ 5.2	SO	Track on right.
6.7 ▲	SO	Track on left.
▼ 5.3	SO	Track on right.
6.6 ▲	SO	Track on left.
▼ 5.6	SO	Track on right.
6.3 ▲	SO	Track on left.
▼ 5.8	SO	Two tracks on right.
6.1 ▲	SO	Two tracks on left.
▼ 6.4	SO	Cross through wash; then track on right.
5.5 ▲	SO	Track on left; then cross through wash.
▼ 7.0	SO	Track on right; then tank and corral on right.
4.9 ▲	SO	Tank and corral on left; then track on left.
		GPS: N32°17.81' W112°51.52'
▼ 7.3	SO	Cross through wash.
4.6 ▲	SO	Cross through wash.
▼ 7.5	SO	Tracks on right and left.
4.4 ▲	SO	Tracks on right and left.
▼ 7.6	SO	Track on left.
4.3 ▲	SO	Track on right.
▼ 8.0	SO	Cross through wash.
3.9 ▲	SO	Cross through wash.
▼ 8.2	SO	Cross through wash.
3.7 ▲	SO	Cross through wash.
▼ 9.1	SO	Track on left.
2.8 ▲	SO	Track on right.
▼ 9.6	SO	Cross through wash.
2.3 ▲	SO	Cross through wash.
▼ 9.7	SO	Track on right; Black Mountain is on the right. The New Cornelia Mine is directly ahead.
2.2 ▲	SO	Track on left; Black Mountain is on the left.
▼ 9.8	SO	Track on right is private.
2.1 ▲	SO	Track on left is private.
▼ 10.0	SO	Cross through wash.
1.9 ▲	SO	Cross through wash.
▼ 10.1	SO	Graded road on left and right is Scenic Loop Road. Continue straight on remaining on Bates Well Road. Street signs mark both junctions. Many smaller roads on right and left, remain on main graded road.
1.8 ▲	SO	Graded road on left and right is Scenic Loop Road. Continue straight on remaining on Bates Well Road. Street signs mark both junctions.
		GPS: N32°20.37' W112°50.93'
▼ 11.9		Trail ends at the junction with Arizona 85, Ajo Highway. Turn left for Ajo, turn right for Lukeville and Why.
0.0 ▲		Trail commences at the junction with Arizona 85, 2.2 miles south of Ajo. Turn southwest on the wide graded Darby Well Road running past the south side of the tailings of the New Cornelia Mine. Zero trip meter and cross cattle guard. Many smaller roads to the right and left for the next 1.8 miles, remain on the main graded road.
		Note: It is highly recommended that you top your tank at Ajo.
		GPS: N32°21.34' W112°49.59'

SOUTH REGION TRAIL #4

Cipriano Pass Trail

Starting Point:	**South #3: El Camino del Diablo Trail, 18.4 miles south of Wellton**
Finishing Point:	**South #1: Tinajas Altas Pass Trail, 21.5 miles south of Yuma**
Total Mileage:	**7.0 miles**
Unpaved Mileage:	**7.0 miles**
Driving Time:	**1 hour**
Elevation Range:	**800–1,200 feet**
Usually Open:	**Year-round**
Best Time to Travel:	**November to March**
Difficulty Rating:	**2**
Scenic Rating:	**8**
Remoteness Rating:	**+1**

Special Attractions

- Alternative crossing through the spectacular Tinajas Altas Mountains.
- Remote, lightly traveled trail.
- Enables a shorter loop route between the east and west routes of El Camino del Diablo for those with less time.

Description

This trail, although a scenic trail in its own right, provides an easy cut across the Tinajas Altas Mountains that is further to the north than the more popular Tinajas Altas Pass. By combining the earlier parts of El Camino del Diablo's east and west route with Cipriano Pass, those people who prefer not to camp, or who have less time available, can still sample parts of the historic route.

The trail cuts through the gap in the ranges passing between the Tinajas Altas Mountains to the south and the Gila Mountains to the north. On the east side, it passes close to the dark lava-capped Raven Butte, similar in appearance to the Cabeza Prieta Peak that gives the wildlife refuge its name. It follows close to the actual Cipriano Pass, which is slightly to the south of this trail and does not have a vehicle route along its entire length. The trail is well defined, but can be confusing as there are numerous small tracks to the right and left along its length.

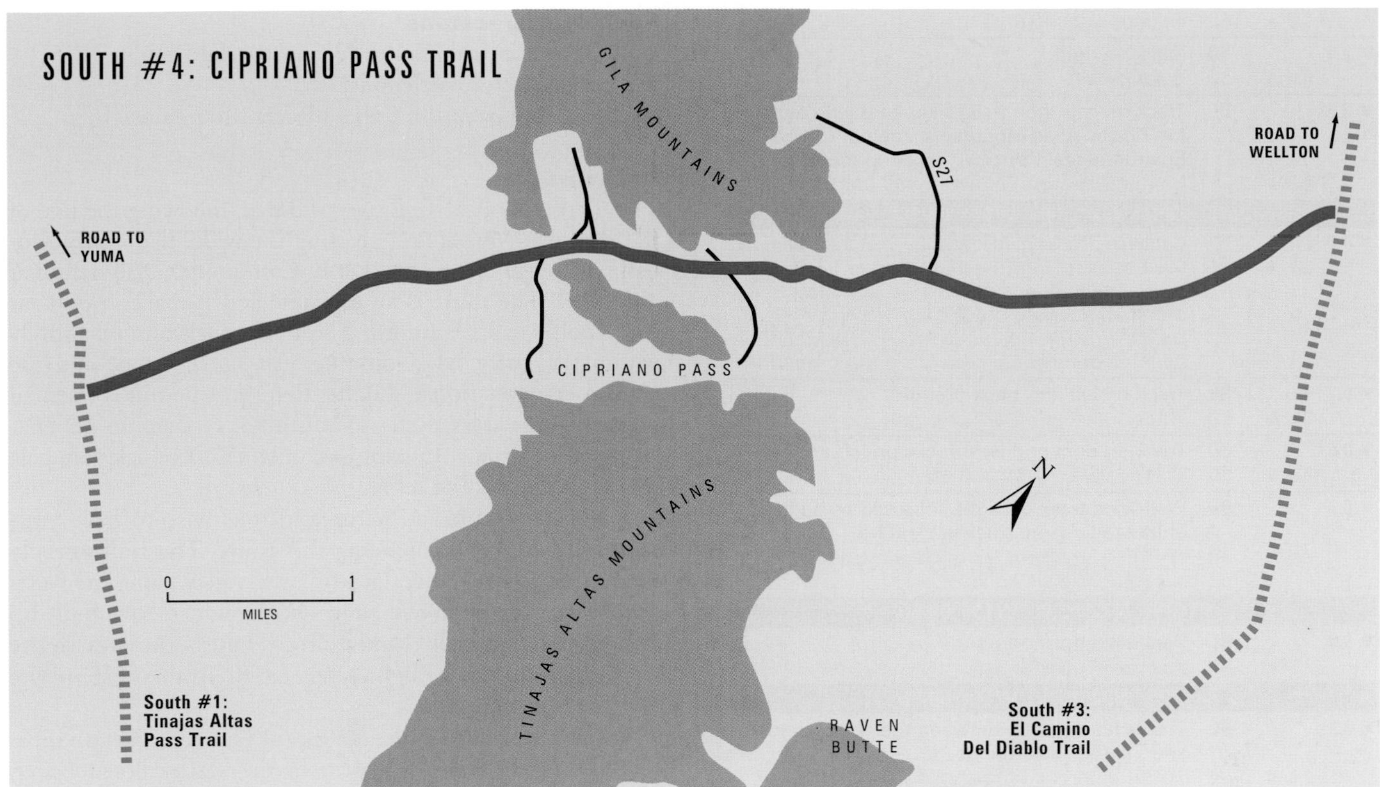

Only the larger, more noticeable trails are mentioned in the route directions. If in doubt remain on the most-used trail.

The trail is smooth and well-used for the most part; where it enters the gap it is somewhat narrower. There are some pleasant backcountry campsites scattered around in the gap and around the base of the mountains on both sides of the pass. The trail is particularly attractive in spring, when the green of the vegetation contrasts well with the pale-colored granite range. The trail finishes on South #1: Tinajas Altas Pass Trail (the west route of El Camino del Diablo), 21.5 miles south of Foothills Boulevard on the edge of Yuma.

The trail is wholly contained within the air force range. You must have a valid permit to enter the Barry M. Goldwater Air Force Range to travel this trail. For permit information and special considerations regarding this area, refer to South #3: El Camino del Diablo Trail.

The trail heading across Lechuguilla Desert

Current Road Information

Luke Air Force Base
Gila Bend Auxiliary Field
Range Operations
Gila Bend, AZ 85337
(520) 683-6272

Bureau of Land Management
Yuma Field Office
2555 Gilda Ridge Road
Yuma, AZ 85365
(520) 317-3200

Map References

BLM Tinajas Altas Mts.
USGS 1:24,000 Raven Butte, Cipriano Pass
1:100,000 Tinajas Altas Mts.
Arizona Atlas & Gazetteer, p. 62

Route Directions

▼ 0.0		Trail starts 18.4 miles south of Wellton on South #3: El Camino del Diablo Trail. Turn south on well-used, graded sandy trail and zero trip meter. There is a wooden marker post B5 at the junction, but no sign.
3.5 ▲		Trail finishes on South #3: El Camino del Diablo Trail, 18.4 miles south of Wellton at marker post B5. Turn left for Wellton and I-8, turn right to continue along El Camino del Diablo.
		GPS: N32°27.88' W114°06.27'
▼ 2.3	SO	Track on right is marked S27.
1.2 ▲	SO	Track on left is marked S27.
		GPS: N32°26.42' W114°07.88'
▼ 2.5	SO	Faint track on right.

	1.0 ▲	SO	Faint track on left.
▼ 2.9		SO	Track on right.
	0.6 ▲	SO	Track on left.
▼ 3.5		BL	Track on left; then trail forks; bear left past sign for Tinajas Altas Mountains, Area of Critical Environmental Concern. Zero trip meter.
	0.0 ▲		Continue toward El Camino del Diablo.
			GPS: N32°25.89' W114°08.80'
▼ 0.0			Continue past sign, followed by faint track on right.
	3.5 ▲	BL	Faint track on left; then larger track leading back to the left at sign for Tinajas Altas Mountains (facing other way), leaving Area of Critical Environmental Concern. Pass sign then bear left at fork after sign. Zero trip meter.
▼ 0.3		SO	Track on left and track on right.
	3.2 ▲	SO	Track on left and track on right.
▼ 0.6		SO	Track on right and two tracks on left.
	2.9 ▲	SO	Two tracks on right and track on left.
▼ 0.7		BL	Well-used track on right, followed by second entrance to same track in clearing.
	2.8 ▲	SO	Well-used track on left in clearing, followed by second entrance on left.
			GPS: N32°25.60' W114°09.50'
▼ 0.8		BL	Well-used track on right.
	2.7 ▲	BR	Well-used track on left.
			GPS: N32°25.55' W114°09.56'
▼ 0.9		SO	Trail is leaving gap between the Gila Range and Tinajas Altas Range.
	2.6 ▲	SO	Trail is entering gap between the Gila Range and Tinajas Altas Range.
▼ 1.0		BR	Trail forks at small hillock.
	2.5 ▲	SO	Track on right at small hillock.
▼ 3.5			Trail ends at the junction South #1: Tinajas Altas Pass Trail, at marker post A5. Turn right for Yuma, turn left to continue southeast on South #1: Tinajas Altas Pass Trail.
	0.0 ▲		Trail commences on South #1: Tinajas Altas Pass Trail, 21.5 miles from the north end. Turn northeast on formed trail, which leaves through a bare area at marker post A5 and zero trip meter.
			GPS: N32°23.61' W114°11.22'

SOUTH REGION TRAIL #5

Christmas Pass Trail

Starting Point:	**I-8, exit 42 (Tacna)**
Finishing Point:	**South #3: El Camino del Diablo Trail near Tule Well**
Total Mileage:	**44.1 miles**
Unpaved Mileage:	**44.1 miles**
Driving Time:	**3.5 hours**
Elevation Range:	**300–1,200 feet**
Usually Open:	**Year-round**
Best Time to Travel:	**November to March**
Difficulty Rating:	**3**
Scenic Rating:	**8**
Remoteness Rating:	**+2**

Special Attractions

- Alternative entry point to El Camino del Diablo.
- Remote desert experience.
- Rugged and beautiful Cabeza Prieta Mountains.

Description

The Christmas Pass Trail sweeps down, following the line of the Mohawk Mountains, crossing the wide, flat, sandy Mohawk Valley to join South #3: El Camino del Diablo Trail at Tule Well. The route is an easy one and it makes a popular entry point to El Camino. The trail travels almost entirely within the Barry M. Goldwater Air Force Range and the Cabeza Prieta National Wildlife Refuge. A permit is essential for both these areas. Refer to South #3: El Camino del Diablo Trail for details. In addition, only 4WD vehicles are permitted in the wildlife refuge.

Fuel is available in Tacna, and it is wise to have your tank full before commencing this route. The trail initially follows along the wide, flat Mohawk Valley along the western edge of the Mohawk Sand Dunes, which have built up against the Mohawk Mountains. These structures, more ridge than dunes, are lightly vegetated. To the west are the Copper Mountains.

As you continue south, the gap of Cipriano Pass is visible to the west immediately north of the black-colored Raven Butte. The trail passes the Point of the Pintas, the northern end of the Sierra Pinta, or "Painted Range," before entering the Cabeza Prieta National Wildlife Refuge. The trail becomes narrower, sandy, and less-used. It follows the channel of the Mohawk Wash, and the dense vegetation along the channel makes the trail narrow and brushy in places. Watch for oncoming vehicles that may be moving fast in the soft sand.

A bird's nest craddled in a saguaro cactus

Christmas Pass camp area is reached as the trail starts to enter the Cabeza Prieta Mountains. This is one of the suggested group camping areas for El Camino del Diablo. There are no facilities, but it is a pleasant, flat granitic area tucked into the north side of the Drift Hills. Christmas Pass itself is a narrow shelf caught between the hillside and a wash. Some rough concrete has been poured to stop the trail from washing out, but this section is still the roughest part. It is also the prettiest as it winds through the small peaks and ridges of the Cabeza Prieta Mountains.

The trail ends at Tule Well on South #3: El Camino del Diablo Trail. There is a small adobe casita built at Tule Well and a camping area with picnic tables and BBQs tucked into the creosote bushes. From here, the quickest way out of El Camino is to turn right and exit via Wellton along the smoother trail through the Barry M. Goldwater Air Force Range.

Current Road Information

Luke Air Force Base
Gila Bend Auxiliary Field
Range Operations
Gila Bend, AZ 85337
(520) 683-6272

Bureau of Land Management
Yuma Field Office
2555 Gilda Ridge Road
Yuma, AZ 85365
(520) 317-3200

Cabeza Prieta National Wildlife Refuge
1611 North 2nd Avenue
Ajo, AZ 85321
(520) 387-5226

Map References

BLM Dateland, Cabeza Prieta Mts.
USGS 1:24,000 Tacna, Mohawk, Mohawk SE, Mohawk Mts. SW, Point of the Pintas, Christmas Pass, Sierra Arida
1:100,000 Dateland, Cabeza Prieta Mts.
Maptech CD-ROM: Southwest Arizona/Yuma
Arizona Atlas & Gazetteer, pp. 62-63
Arizona Road & Recreation Atlas, pp. 45, 51 & pp. 79, 85

Route Directions

▼ 0.0 From exit 42 (Tacna) on I-8, proceed to the south side of the freeway and turn east. Turn is immediately south of the eastbound freeway entrance onto a wide graded dirt road that runs alongside the freeway. Zero trip meter.
5.7 ▲ Trail ends on the southside of I-8 at exit 42 (Tacna).

GPS: N32°41.48' W113°57.15'

▼ 0.5 **SO** Track on right.
5.2 ▲ SO Track on left.

▼ 0.6 **SO** Track on right.
5.1 ▲ SO Track on left.

▼ 0.7 **SO** Track on right.
5.0 ▲ SO Track on left.

▼ 1.0 **SO** Track on right.
4.7 ▲ SO Track on left.

▼ 2.0 **SO** Graded road on left and graded road on right.
3.7 ▲ SO Graded road on left and graded road on right.

▼ 3.4 **SO** Cross through wash.
2.3 ▲ SO Cross through wash.

▼ 3.5 **SO** Graded road on left goes into private property.
2.2 ▲ SO Graded road on right goes into private property.

▼ 3.7 **SO** Cross the abandoned runway of Colfred Airfield.
2.0 ▲ SO Cross second runway.

GPS: N32°41.63' W113°53.15'

▼ 4.1 **SO** Cross second runway.
1.6 ▲ SO Cross the abandoned runway of Colfred Airfield.

▼ 5.7 **TR** Intersection. Turn right and enter the Barry M. Goldwater Air Force Range past the sign on smaller graded dirt road. Marker post F1 at junction. Zero trip meter.
0.0 ▲ Continue west toward Tacna.

GPS: N32°41.62' W113°50.95'

▼ 0.0 Continue to the south into the permit area.

Crossing the Cabeza Prieta Mountains

16.7 ▲ TL Intersection at marker post F1. Turn left exiting the Barry M. Goldwater Air Force Range onto wide, graded dirt road. Zero trip meter.

▼ 16.7 **SO** Crossroads at marker post F3. Zero trip meter.
0.0 ▲ Continue to the north.

GPS: N32°29.53' W113°40.81'

▼ 0.0 Continue south toward the Cabeza Prieta NWR.
5.1 ▲ SO Crossroads at marker post F3. Zero trip meter.

▼ 4.8 **SO** Track on left at wooden marker post F4. Small mine shaft on the small hillock opposite and a flat area suitable for camping. Point of the Pintas is on the left.
0.3 ▲ SO Track on right at wooden marker post F4. Small mine shaft on the small hillock opposite and a flat area suitable for camping. Point of the Pintas is on the right.

GPS: N32°25.39' W113°40.07'

▼ 5.1 **SO** Enter the Cabeza Prieta National Wildlife Refuge. Only 4WD vehicles are permitted past this point. Zero trip meter at sign.
0.0 ▲ Continue into the Barry M. Goldwater Air Force Range.

GPS: N32°25.09' W113°40.17'

▼ 0.0 Continue into the Cabeza Prieta NWR.
8.2 ▲ SO Enter the Barry M. Goldwater Air Force Range.

▼ 2.0 **SO** Bean Pass visible to the left.
6.2 ▲ SO Bean Pass visible to the right.

▼ 3.9 **SO** Management track on left. Trail is following the line of Mohawk Wash.
4.3 ▲ SO Management track on right.

GPS: N32°21.52' W113°39.91'

▼ 5.5 **SO** Cross through wash.
2.7 ▲ SO Cross through wash.

GPS: N32°20.06' W113°39.62'

▼ 8.1 **SO** Management track on left.
0.1 ▲ SO Management track on right.

▼ 8.2 **BL** Bear left out of the main channel. Vehicle marks continue on ahead, but the trail dead-ends in approximately 100 yards. This turn is easy to miss. Zero trip meter.
0.0 ▲ Continue to the north.

GPS: N32°17.65' W113°40.02'

▼ 0.0 Continue toward Tule Well.
2.0 ▲ SO Enter the wash channel. Vehicle marks go to the left but the trail dead-ends in approximately 100 yards. Zero trip meter.

▼ 1.9 **SO** Faint tracks on left at base of Drift Hills. Entering the gap in the range.
0.1 ▲ BL Keep left and remain on main trail, exiting the gap in the range.

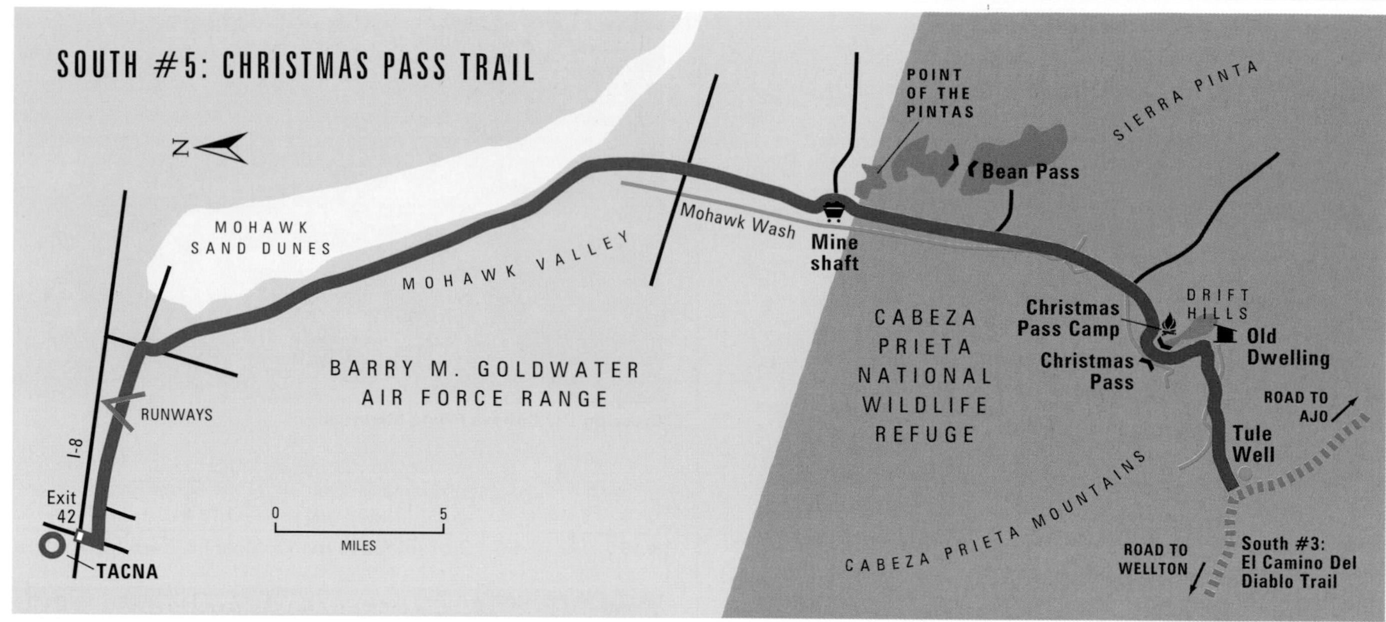

▼ 2.0	SO	Christmas Pass Camp on left marked by a sign. Zero trip meter at sign.
0.0 ▲		Continue through the NWR.
		GPS: N32°16.65' W113°41.53'
▼ 0.0		Continue toward Tule Well.
6.4 ▲	SO	Christmas Pass Camp on right marked by a sign. Zero trip meter.
▼ 0.1	BL	Trail swings left in front of wash and crosses Christmas Pass.
6.3 ▲	BR	Trail follows down alongside wash and swings right to cross Christmas Pass.
		GPS: N32°16.64' W113°41.60'
▼ 1.1	SO	Cross through small wash.
5.3 ▲	SO	Cross through small wash.
▼ 1.6	SO	Cross through wash.
4.8 ▲	SO	Cross through wash.
▼ 1.8	SO	Remains of old dwelling on left, then cross through small wash.
4.6 ▲	SO	Cross through small wash, remains of old dwelling on right.
		GPS: N32°15.34' W113°40.94'
▼ 1.9	SO	Cross through wash.
4.5 ▲	SO	Cross through wash.
▼ 2.0	BR	Management track on left.
4.4 ▲	BL	Management track on right.
▼ 2.6	SO	Cross through wash.
3.8 ▲	SO	Cross through wash.
▼ 2.8	SO	Cross through wash.
3.6 ▲	SO	Cross through wash.
▼ 3.2	SO	Cross through wash.
3.2 ▲	SO	Cross through wash.
▼ 3.3	SO	Cross through wash.
3.1 ▲	SO	Cross through wash.
▼ 3.9	SO	Cross through wash.
2.5 ▲	SO	Cross through wash.
▼ 4.3	SO	Cross through wash.
2.1 ▲	SO	Cross through wash.
▼ 5.4	SO	Cross through wash.
1.0 ▲	SO	Cross through wash.
▼ 6.1	SO	Cross through wide wash.
0.3 ▲	SO	Cross through wide wash.
		GPS: N32°13.76' W113°44.70'
▼ 6.4		Trail ends at Tule Well at the junction with South #3: El Camino del Diablo Trail. Turn left to travel El Camino to Ajo, turn right for the quicker exit out via Wellton.
0.0 ▲		Trail commences at Tule Well on South #3: El Camino del Diablo Trail. Turn northeast past the small adobe building onto well-used, formed trail and zero trip meter.
		GPS: N32°13.56' W113°44.92'

SOUTH REGION TRAIL #6

Puerto Blanco Drive

Starting Point:	**Arizona 85, at the Organ Pipe Cactus National Monument Visitor Center**
Finishing Point:	**Arizona 85, near Lukeville**
Total Mileage:	**35.6 miles**
Unpaved Mileage:	**35.4 miles**
Driving Time:	**3 hours**
Elevation Range:	**1,100–2,000 feet**
Usually Open:	**Year-round**
Best Time to Travel:	**Fall to spring**
Difficulty Rating:	**1**
Scenic Rating:	**8**
Remoteness Rating:	**+1**

Special Attractions

- Easy drive wholly contained within the Organ Pipe Cactus National Monument.
- The green oasis of Quitobaquito Springs.
- Access to backcountry hiking trails and picnic areas.

History

The region of the Organ Pipe Cactus National Monument has human history stretching back to archaic times over 9,000 years ago when the Hohokam Indians used the warm waters of Quitobaquito Springs. There is evidence of a foot trail running north from the springs up through the Bates Mountains and south to the Gulf of Mexico (called the Gulf of California on American maps).

In 1699 a Jesuit missionary, Padre Eusebio Francisco Kino crossed the Tohono O'odham lands to the east and passed through what is now the monument, continuing on to cross El Camino del Diablo.

Later inhabitants included many miners, who have left their mark and their mines in the hillsides. One mine that can easily be seen beside the trail is the Golden Bell Mine, which include the diggings of Charlie Bell who mined there in the 1930s. He did find some gold and silver, but it was low-grade ore. Other mines, such as the Dripping Springs Mine and the Milton Mine, can be reached by backcountry hiking. The oldest and most productive mine in the monument is the Victoria Mine, which operated for nearly 100 years, having a total production of $125,000. However, compared to the staggering figures produced by mines in other regions of Arizona, the Victoria Mine's overall yield is relatively poor.

The Puerto Blanco Range was also referred to as the Dripping Springs Range after the springs close to the northern end of the range. The later name of Puerto Blanco (Spanish for "white port") comes from two white rocks used as a marker for a pass through this rugged region.

Chainfruit cholla, ocotillos, and organ pipe cacti with the Little Continental Divide in the background

The Quitobaquito Hills and Quitobaquito Springs have been a savior to many travelers, including the earliest of the Spanish expeditions. In 1540 Melchior Diaz, a member of Coronado's expedition, passed by the springs on his expedition to find a route to the Colorado River mouth. Padre Kino was known to have visited many villages in Sonora and would have appreciated these springs in his travels around El Camino del Diablo.

The Papago Indians referred to the springs as Alivaipai. The name Quitobaquito appears to be a corruption of the Papago term *ko to bac,* meaning a watering place. Another suggestion is that they are named after an old Mexican town called Quito Bac.

Today, these springs are still providing water for other travelers on dangerous trails: The region is heavily trafficked by undocumented aliens attempting to enter the United States.

Description

This is the longer of the two backcountry drives entirely within Organ Pipe Cactus National Monument. It is a good graded, gravel road that winds around the Puerto Blanco Mountains before running along the international border with

Flowering ocotillos with Pinkley Peak in the background

Mexico to finish in Lukeville. Although the loop is fairly well traveled in the cooler months, it is still a remote area, and you should take proper precautions for desert travel, including carrying plenty of water.

If you intend to drive the entire length of the trail, you must travel counterclockwise starting at the visitor center. The majority of the trail is one-way with the two-way section stretching from Lukeville to the junction of the Pozo Nuevo Road. Although shown on park maps as a vehicle trail, the Pozo Nuevo Road, which connects Puerto Blanco Drive to El Camino del Diablo, has been closed to vehicle travel since 1998. Increasing use by undocumented aliens traveling at night, mainly in 2WD vehicles, had the National Park Service concerned about resource damage along the rough trail. There are currently no plans to reopen the trail for public vehicle access.

The first part of the trail is beautiful as it winds to the north of the Puerto Blanco Mountains and to the south of the Bates Mountains. The volcanic Pinkley Peak is a dominant feature on the early part of the drive; the peak rises to 3,145 feet and was named for Frank Pinkley, the earliest superintendent of Casa Grande National Monument.

Views further around the loop stretch down the Valley of the Ajo, a broad flat valley running between the Bates Mountains and the Ajo Mountains. The most prominent peak in the Bates Mountains is Kino Peak, which is named for Padre Eusebio Francisco Kino.

One unexpected feature along the Puerto Blanco Drive is the desert oasis of Quitobaquito Springs. These warm springs are surrounded by a small marshland oasis with mature trees. It attracts many species of birds and is home to a rare species of freshwater fish, the Quitobaquito Springs Pupfish. Quitobaquito Springs are located 0.4 miles down a spur trail from the main drive, followed by a short walk to the spring-fed ponds. There is a parking lot and a pit toilet directly adjacent to the international border with Mexico. Note that the wire fence immediately south of the parking lot is the international boundary, although it is not well marked. The border is patrolled, and it is illegal to cross into Mexico, even briefly, at any point other than at an authorized border crossing point. The National Park Service recommends that you do not leave your vehicle unattended here or at any other point along the border due to numerous break-ins.

From Quitobaquito Springs, the trail follows mainly along the international border. The major Mexican Highway 2 is on the far side of the border, and there are many side trails that

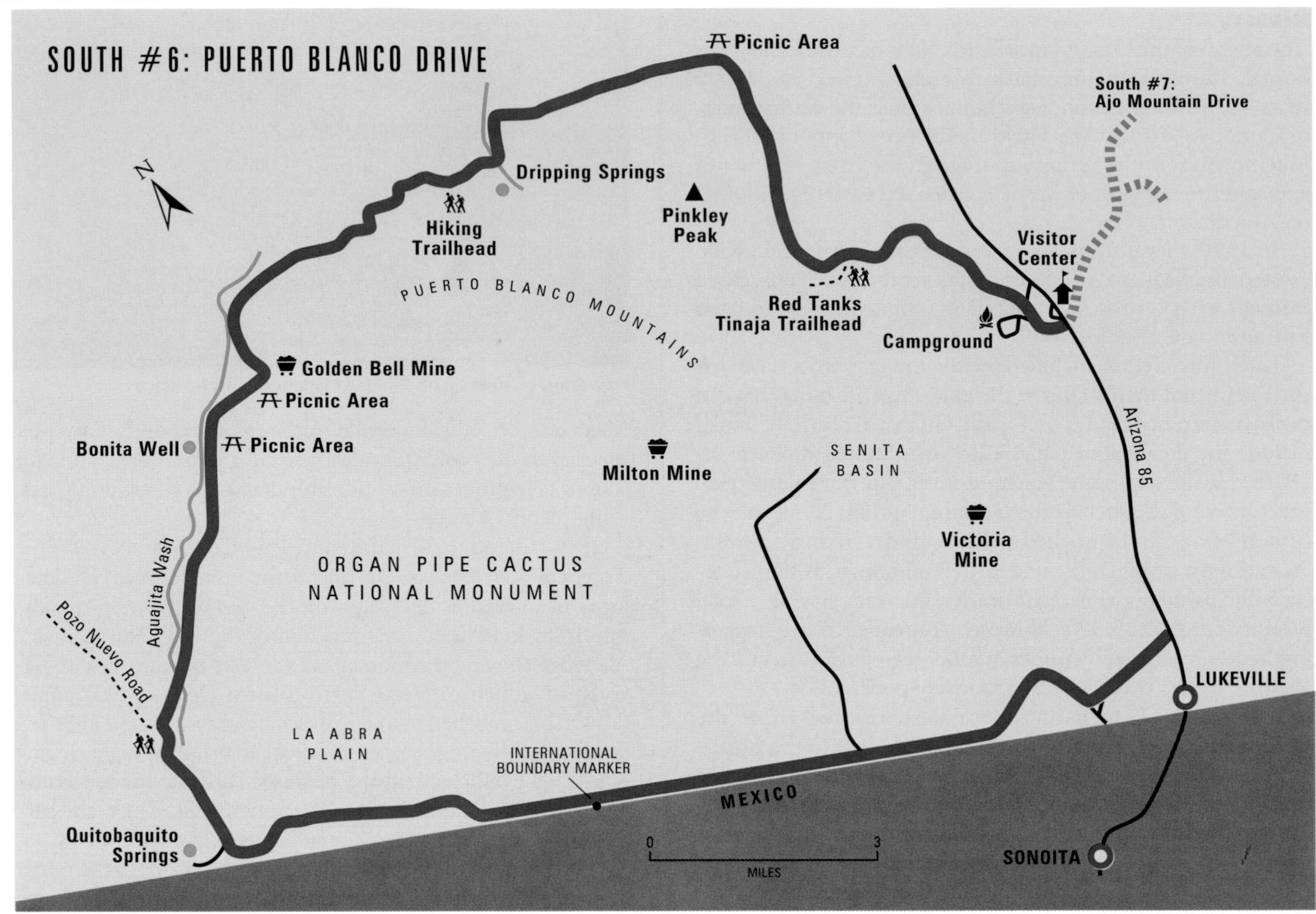

lead south to the border, which are used by illegal border crossers in both directions. These trails are not authorized trails within the monument.

A second major side trail leads 4 miles to Senita Basin where you can see the senita cacti and the elephant tree, two species found mainly in Mexico.

The trail ends just north of Lukeville, named after Charles Luke, and the border crossing point into Mexico.

Note that no dogs or bicycles are allowed on the hiking trails and vehicle camping is not permitted along the drive. The route directions only detail major wash crossings; there are many smaller ones along the drive.

Current Road Information

Organ Pipe Cactus National Monument
Route 1 Box 100
Ajo, AZ 85321
(520) 387-6849

Map References

BLM Lukeville, Ajo
USGS 1:24,000 Lukeville, Tillotson Peak, Kino Peak, West of Lukeville, Quitobaquito Springs
1:100,000 Lukeville, Ajo
Maptech CD-ROM: Southwest Arizona/Yuma
Trails Illustrated, Organ Pipe Cactus National Monument
Arizona Atlas & Gazetteer, p. 70
Arizona Road & Recreation Atlas, pp. 51, 52 & pp. 85, 86
Recreational Map of Arizona
Other: Organ Pipe Cactus Park Map (free leaflet handed out by park service)

Route Directions

▼ 0.0		From the visitor center at Organ Pipe Cactus National Monument, continue south through the parking lot, then turn west on the paved road at the sign for Puerto Blanco Drive and zero trip meter.
		GPS: N31°57.27' W112°48.02'
▼ 0.1	BR	Paved road on left goes to campground. Follow signs for North Puerto Blanco Drive.
▼ 0.2	SO	Paved road on left is for authorized vehicles only. Information board on the left. Road is now graded dirt.
▼ 0.5	SO	Service road on right.
▼ 1.5	SO	Cross through wash.
▼ 2.5	SO	Cross through wash.
▼ 3.4	SO	Cross through wash.
▼ 3.7	SO	Red Tanks Tinaja primitive hiking trail leads off to the left.
		GPS: N31°59.09' W112°50.23'
▼ 3.8	SO	Parking area for hiking trailhead on left.
▼ 4.1	SO	Cross through wash.
▼ 4.4	SO	Cross through wash.
▼ 6.9	SO	Cross through wash.

			GPS: N32°01.67' W112°50.09'
▼ 7.1		SO	Picnic table in shade of ironwood on right at marker post #6. Zero trip meter.
			GPS: N32°01.72' W112°50.27'
▼ 0.0			Continue around loop and cross through wash.
▼ 0.9		SO	Cross through wash.
▼ 1.2		SO	Cross through wash.
▼ 1.4		SO	Cross through wash.
▼ 1.8		SO	Cross through wash.
▼ 3.2		SO	Cross through wash.
			GPS: N32°02.15' W112°53.23'
▼ 4.0		SO	Little Continental Divide. All arroyos to the north drain into the Gila River, those to the south drain to the Rio Sonoyta in Mexico.
			GPS: N32°01.85' W112°53.80'
▼ 4.3		SO	Dripping Springs Mine primitive hiking trail and parking area on left. Zero trip meter.
			GPS: N32°01.86' W112°54.15'
▼ 0.0			Continue around the loop.
▼ 0.2		SO	Cross through wash.
▼ 0.7		SO	Cross through wash. Views to the right over the plain and wash area to the Bates Mountains and Kino Peak.
▼ 1.5		SO	Cross through wash.
▼ 4.0		SO	Cross through wash.
▼ 4.4		SO	Cross through wash.
▼ 4.8		SO	Golden Bell Mine on left. Picnic tables with limited shade under a palo verde.
			GPS: N32°00.98' W112°57.34'
▼ 5.5		SO	Cross through wash.
▼ 6.1		SO	Bonita Well and corral on right. Pit toilets on right, picnic tables, shade ramada, and old hut on left. Zero trip meter.
			GPS: N32°00.56' W112°58.45'
▼ 0.0			Continue around loop.
▼ 0.2		SO	Cross through wash.
▼ 0.4		SO	Short trail on right leads to cristate saguaro—abnormal fan-shaped growth.
			GPS: N32°00.20' W112°58.67'
▼ 3.0		SO	Cross through Aguajita Wash.
▼ 3.6		TL	Track on right is the Pozo Nuevo Road, closed to vehicles. Start of two-way section. Zero trip meter.
			GPS: N31°58.04' W113°00.70'
▼ 0.0			Continue south along two-way road.
	1.7 ▲	UT	Track straight on is the Pozo Nuevo Road, closed to vehicles. The road to the right is no-entry for vehicles traveling in this direction. Turn around and retrace your steps to Lukeville.
▼ 0.3		SO	Cross through wash.
	1.4 ▲	SO	Cross through wash.
▼ 1.5		SO	Cross through wash.
	0.2 ▲	SO	Cross through wash.
▼ 1.7		TL	Track straight on goes 0.4 miles to Quitobaquito Springs. Zero trip meter.
	0.0 ▲		Continue away from the international border.
			GPS: N31°56.53' W113°00.66'
▼ 0.0			Continue along the international border.
	8.1 ▲	TR	Track on left goes 0.4 miles to Quitobaquito Springs. Zero trip meter.
▼ 0.9		SO	Cross through wash.
	7.2 ▲	SO	Cross through wash.
▼ 1.0		SO	Cross through wash.
	7.1 ▲	SO	Cross through wash.
▼ 2.0		SO	Cross through wash.
	6.1 ▲	SO	Cross through wash.
▼ 2.3		SO	Cross through wash.
	5.8 ▲	SO	Cross through wash.
▼ 3.6		SO	Cross through wash.
	4.5 ▲	SO	Cross through wash.
▼ 3.7		SO	Cross through wash, the trail is now running alongside the international border.
	4.4 ▲	SO	Cross through wash, the trail now leaves the international border.
▼ 4.9		SO	International boundary marker on right of trail.
	3.2 ▲	SO	International boundary marker on left of trail.
			GPS: N31°55.01' W112°56.20'
▼ 6.1		SO	Cross through wash.
	2.0 ▲	SO	Cross through wash.
▼ 6.2		SO	Cross through wash.
	1.9 ▲	SO	Cross through wash.
▼ 8.1		SO	Track on left leads 4 miles to Senita Basin. Zero trip meter.
	0.0 ▲		Continue toward Quitobaquito Springs.
			GPS: N31°54.03' W112°52.99'
▼ 0.0			Continue toward Lukeville.
	4.7 ▲	SO	Track on right leads 4 miles to Senita Basin. Zero trip meter.
▼ 3.4		SO	Track on right is for authorized vehicles only.
	1.3 ▲	SO	Track on left is for authorized vehicles only.
▼ 3.5		SO	Track on right is for authorized vehicles only.
	1.2 ▲	BR	Track on left is for authorized vehicles only.
▼ 4.3		SO	Information board on left.
	0.4 ▲	SO	Information board on right.
			GPS: N31°53.52' W112°49.15'
▼ 4.7			Trail ends at the junction with the Arizona 85, 1 mile north of Lukeville. Turn right for Lukeville, turn left for Ajo.
	0.0 ▲		Trail starts on Arizona 85, 1 mile north of Lukeville and 4 miles south of the park visitor center. Turn west on graded dirt road at the sign for Puerto Blanco Drive South and zero trip meter. The first section of the trail follows mainly along the international border with Mexico.
			GPS: N31°53.62' W112°48.72'

SOUTH REGION TRAIL #7

Ajo Mountain Drive

Starting Point:	**Arizona 85, at Organ Pipe Cactus National Monument Visitor Center**
Finishing Point:	**Arizona 85, at Organ Pipe Cactus National Monument Visitor Center**
Total Mileage:	**18.9 miles**
Unpaved Mileage:	**17.2 miles**
Driving Time:	**1.5 hours**
Elevation Range:	**1,700–2,800 feet**
Usually Open:	**Year-round**
Best Time to Travel:	**Fall to Spring**
Difficulty Rating:	**1**
Scenic Rating:	**9**
Remoteness Rating:	**+0**

Some wonderful organ pipe cacti along the trail

Special Attractions

- Organ pipe cactus and varied Sonoran desert scenery and vegetation.
- Easy drive contained within the Organ Pipe Cactus National Monument.
- Access to hiking trails within the monument.
- Large natural arch at Arch Canyon.
- Quiet picnic sites.

History

The Organ Pipe Cactus National Monument region has a long history of human habitation from Indians to miners to today's tourists. Spanish explorers and missionaries were some of the most frequent travelers who named many of the features you see today.

On the return section of the trail, as you head south on the eastern side of the Diablo Mountains, you are looking southwest at Diaz Spire and Diaz Peak. These are named in remembrance of Melchior Diaz who, as a member of Coronado's expedition, found a route west to the mouth of the Colorado River. On his return journey Diaz died after fending off a hound that was threatening their sheep. Apparently his own long lance caught in the ground as he charged the hound. The lance pierced Diaz in the kidney resulting in his death shortly after, despite efforts by his men to save him.

The view from the Diablo Canyon picnic area

Description

This graded gravel road is one of only two backcountry roads within Organ Pipe Cactus National Monument. It is a loop that travels through prolific and varied Sonoran desert vegetation before climbing around the face of the Diablo Mountains on the edge of the Ajo Range. The drive is a one-way loop that commences 1.9 miles from the start of the trail.

As the trail drops out of the range, there are wide ranging views over the Sonoyta Valley down into Mexico. The vegetation is as spectacular as the rugged Ajo Range: There are giant saguaros and ocotillos, creosote bush, palo verde, ironwood, mesquite, jojoba, and Mexican jumping bean. The Ajo Range was formed approximately 2 million years ago as volcanoes dumped thick layers of lava and ash over the landscape. Faulting and erosion continued to shape the landscape into the jagged peaks and deep canyons characteristic of the region.

The trail passes several picnic areas that make great places to stop for a while and soak up the desert scenery. All of them have a picnic table and a couple have shade ramadas. Several hiking trails leave from along the drive. One of the best leaves the picnic area and travels up Arch Canyon. There are two arches that can be seen from the trail. The lower larger one measures approximately 120 by 30 feet. The other is a smaller 10 by 6 feet. No dogs or bicycles are allowed on the hiking trails.

It is necessary to pay the national monument entrance fee before driving on any of the backcountry roads within the monument. The road is graded gravel for its entire length and is suitable for passenger vehicles. Short sections are paved, typically some of the wash crossings and a longer section as the trail climbs into the Ajo Range.

In the summer months, keep an eye on the weather; thunderstorms can move in quickly. Do not attempt to enter a flooded, fast-moving wash bed; wait for the water to subside before attempting to cross.

Current Road Information

Organ Pipe Cactus National Monument
Route 1 Box 100
Ajo, AZ 85321
(520) 387-6849

Map References

BLM Lukeville, Ajo
USGS 1:24,000 Lukeville, Diaz Peak, Mt. Ajo
1:100,000 Lukeville, Ajo
Maptech CD-ROM: Southwest Arizona/Yuma
Trails Illustrated, Organ Pipe Cactus National Monument
Arizona Atlas & Gazetteer, p. 70
Arizona Road & Recreation Atlas, p. 52 & p. 86
Recreational Map of Arizona
Other: Organ Pipe Cactus Park Map (free leaflet handed out by park service)

Route Directions

▼ 0.0	From Arizona 85, turn east on graded gravel road at sign for Ajo Mountain Drive. The turn is opposite the exit from the visitor center. Zero trip meter.

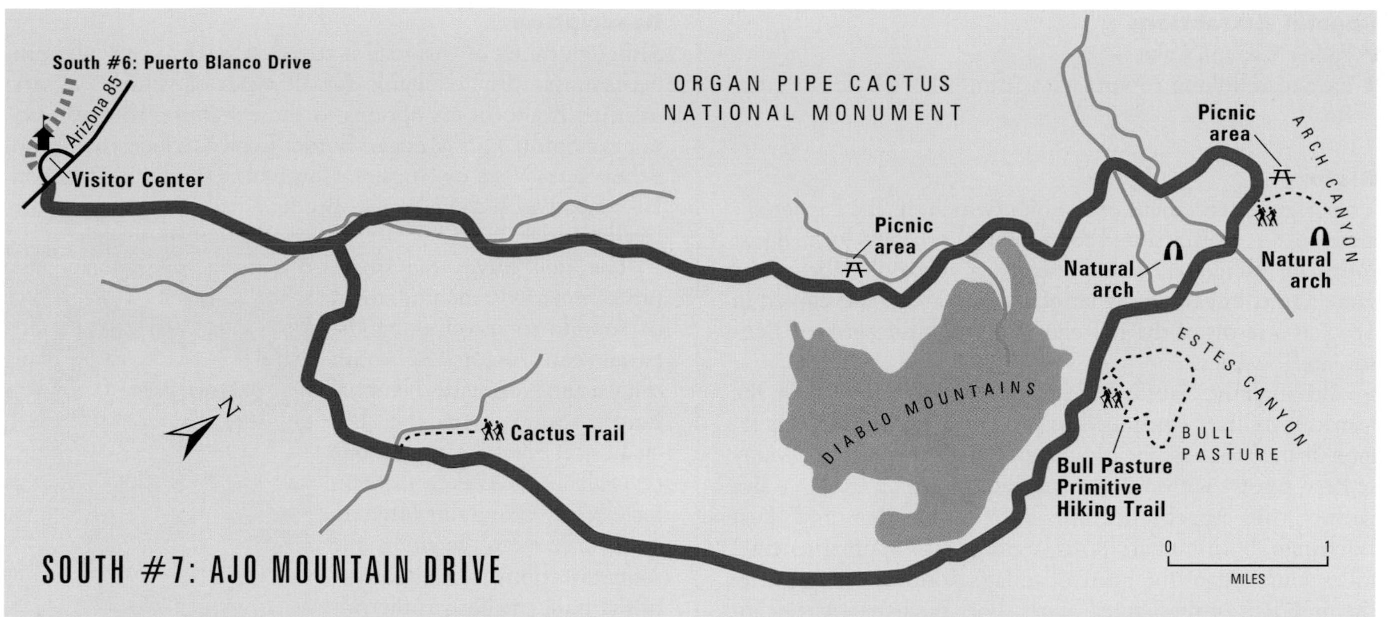

GPS: N31°57.22′ W112°47.94′		
▼ 0.3	SO	Information board on right.
▼ 0.9	SO	Cross through wash on concrete ford.
▼ 1.8	SO	Cross through wash on concrete ford.
▼ 1.9	SO	Graded road on right is the end of the one-way loop. Zero trip meter.
GPS: N31°58.24′ W112°46.44′		
▼ 0.0		Continue around the start of the loop.
▼ 0.2	SO	Cross through wash on concrete ford.
▼ 0.9	SO	Cross through wash.
▼ 3.4	SO	Diablo Canyon picnic area on left. Picnic table and shade ramada. Zero trip meter.
GPS: N32°00.36′ W112°43.99′		
▼ 0.0		Continue around the loop.
▼ 0.1	SO	Road is paved as it starts to climb into the Ajo Range.
▼ 0.4	SO	Birdseye Point on left. Picnic table.
GPS: N32°00.63′ W112°43.87′		
▼ 0.6	SO	Cross through wash on concrete ford.
▼ 1.4	SO	Road turns back to graded dirt.
GPS: N32°01.17′ W112°43.41′		
▼ 1.5	SO	Road returns to paved; then cross through wash.
▼ 1.7	SO	Road turns back to graded dirt.
▼ 2.0	SO	Cross through wash on concrete ford.
▼ 2.4	SO	Cross through wash on paved ford.
▼ 2.8	SO	Cross through wash on concrete ford. First glimpse of natural arch high up to the right.
GPS: N32°02.21′ W112°43.24′		
▼ 3.2	BR	Picnic table on left and parking area and hiking trail up Arch Canyon. The natural arch can clearly be seen high on the cliff.
▼ 3.6	SO	Cross through paved ford.
▼ 3.9	SO	Small arch on rise to the right.
GPS: N32°01.68′ W112°42.79′		
▼ 4.5	SO	Road is paved.
▼ 4.7	SO	Road returns to dirt.
▼ 4.9	SO	Estes Canyon picnic area and pit toilets on right. Two picnic tables and shade ramada. Zero trip meter. Estes Canyon Bull Pasture Primitive Hiking Trail leaves to the left, a 4-mile round trip.
GPS: N32°00.97′ W112°42.67′		
▼ 0.0		Continue around loop and cross through wash.
▼ 0.5	SO	Cross through wash.
▼ 1.7	SO	Turn out on the left overlooks Diaz Spire, the leftmost of the two rocky peaks.
GPS: N31°59.63′ W112°42.42′		
▼ 5.1	SO	The Cactus Trail—a short hiking trail leads off to the right. Cross through wash on concrete ford.
GPS: N31°57.78′ W112°45.20′		
▼ 5.6	SO	Teddy Bear Pass Trail leads off to the left at marker post 21. Zero trip meter.
GPS: N31°57.68′ W112°45.66′		
▼ 0.0		Continue around the loop.
▼ 0.7	SO	Cross through wash on concrete ford.
▼ 1.2	TL	End of loop. Turn left and retrace your steps for 1.9 miles back to Arizona 85.
GPS: N31°58.24′ W112°46.44′		

SOUTH REGION TRAIL #8

Parker Canyon Lake Road

Starting Point:	**Arizona 82 in Sonoita**
Finishing Point:	**South #12: Mexican Border Road**
Total Mileage:	**31.6 miles**
Unpaved Mileage:	**8.7 miles**
Driving Time:	**2 hours**
Elevation Range:	**4,800–5,800 feet**
Usually Open:	**Year-round**
Best Time to Travel:	**Year-round**
Difficulty Rating:	**1**
Scenic Rating:	**7**
Remoteness Rating:	**+0**

Special Attractions

- Parker Canyon Lake.
- Easy road linking Sonoita with South #12: Mexican Border Road.

History

The original settlement of Sonoita (which, in the Papago dialect, means a place suited for growing corn) was located just south of Patagonia. The present-day town that bears the same name, but is somewhat north of that site, developed in 1882 as a result of the railroad that was built between Benson and Nogales.

Although the Gadsden Treaty came into effect in 1854, the Mexican military continued to protect the settlers in this region against the Apache as best they could until 1856. Many settlers, uneasy with the constant raids, gave up trying to live within this Apache region. Fort Crittenden and Fort Buchanan, both military posts, were located approximately 2 miles southeast of the heart of today's Sonoita. Named after the president of the United States, Fort Buchanan was established in 1857 by the First United States Dragoons in an attempt to protect the settlers.

By the 1860s a few people were gaining the confidence to settle. Then in 1861, the stand-off between Lt. Bascom and the Apache Chief Cochise at Apache Pass resulted in about six deaths on both sides. In retaliation, Cochise started what was to be ten years of warfare. Worse still, with the outbreak of the Civil War, Fort Buchanan was abandoned and nearby settlers were left to fend for themselves. Many fought to survive as the Apache raided their crops and cattle, and many gave in, moving to more peaceful territories. When troops were available after the Civil War, Fort Crittenden was built in 1867 just a half mile closer to today's Sonoita. The earlier Fort Buchanan adobe buildings were in ruins, having been burnt under orders before being abandoned. Settlers returned, and mining gained importance with many new prospects being worked. Fort Crittenden, which was also referred to as Camp Crittenden, was short lived and abandoned in the early 1870s.

Parker Canyon, which runs from the Huachuca Mountains southwest into Mexico, is named after a family that relocated from Phoenix to escape over-crowding.

Parker Canyon Lake

Description

Although much of this road is paved, it is still a very pleasant backcountry drive, suitable for all types of vehicles in dry weather. It also offers options to those wanting to drive sections of South #12: Mexican Border Road as a loop road from either Sierra Vista or Nogales. Combining the Parker Canyon Lake Road with the Mexican Border Road allows for a more leisurely drive.

A ridge and off-camber section that requires care to avoid scratching your vehicle

The trail leaves the small, predominantly ranching town of Sonoita to travel along the paved road, Arizona 82, south toward the Coronado National Forest. Sonoita is the last chance to purchase fuel. None is available at Parker Canyon Lake. Only the major intersections have been given in the route directions for this section of the trail; smaller mainly private entrances have been omitted from the directions.

The trail passes both ends of South #9: Canelo Hills Trail, a very pretty, more rugged alternative to the paved section of this trail. Just off the trail is the Black Oak Cemetery, first used by pioneer families in 1900 and still in use today.

Parker Canyon Lake, constructed in 1966 by the Arizona Game and Fish Department, offers fishing for trout. However, over the years people have illegally introduced northern pike and other species into the lake. The pike are having a particularly detrimental effect as they feed almost exclusively on other fish, upsetting the ecological balance and potentially having an adverse effect on the quality of trout fishing.

Parker Canyon Lake has a national forest campground—Lakeview Campground—along the shore of the lake. A second area is suitable for RVs. A fee is required for camping. A small store, bait shop, and boat launching facilities are the only other amenities.

Past the lake, the road starts to climb away, following a graded gravel road. The entrances to South #10: Blacktail Ridge Trail and South #11: Sunnyside Trail are passed, and then the trail winds down through open landscape to finish at the intersection with South #12: Mexican Border Road.

Current Road Information

Coronado National Forest
Sierra Vista Ranger District
5990 South Hwy 92
Hereford, AZ 85615
(520) 378-0311

Map References

BLM Fort Huachuca, Nogales
USFS Coronado National Forest: Nogales and Sierra Vista Ranger Districts

USGS 1:24,000 Sonoita, Elgin, O'Donnell Canyon, Pyeatt Ranch, Huachuca Peak
1:100,000 Fort Huachuca, Nogales
Maptech CD-ROM: Southeastern Arizona/Tucson
Arizona Atlas & Gazetteer, p. 73
Arizona Road & Recreation Atlas, p. 54 & p. 88
Recreational Map of Arizona

Route Directions

▼ 0.0		From Arizona 82 in Sonoita, zero trip meter and turn south on the paved Arizona 83 at the sign for Parker Canyon Lake and zero trip meter.
4.0 ▲		Trail ends at the intersection with Arizona 82 in Sonoita.
		GPS: N31°40.74' W110°39.31'
▼ 0.4	BL	South #9: Canelo Hills Trail is straight ahead. Bear left, remaining on the main paved road.
3.6 ▲	BR	South #9: Canelo Hills Trail is on the left. Bear right, remaining on major paved road to Sonoita.
		GPS: N31°40.40' W110°39.31'
▼ 2.8	BR	Bear right remaining on Arizona 83. Lower Elgin Road is on the left.
1.2 ▲	BL	Bear left remaining on Arizona 83. Lower Elgin Road is on the right.
		GPS: N31°40.41' W110°36.65'
▼ 4.0	SO	Paved road on left is Elgin Road. Graded dirt road on right is Wagon Wheel Road. Zero trip meter.
0.0 ▲		Continue to the north.
		GPS: N31°39.54' W110°36.26'
▼ 0.0		Continue to the south.
6.6 ▲	SO	Paved road on right is Elgin Road. Graded dirt road on left is Wagon Wheel Road. Zero trip meter.
▼ 3.5	BL	Graded road straight on and to the right. Remain on paved road following sign for Parker Canyon Lake.
3.1 ▲	BR	Graded road straight on and to the left. Remain on paved road.
		GPS: N31°36.51' W110°35.18'
▼ 4.0	BR	Graded road on left, remain on paved road.
2.6 ▲	BL	Graded road on right, remain on paved road.
▼ 4.4	BL	Graded road ahead, remain on paved road.
2.2 ▲	BR	Graded road on left, remain on paved road.
		GPS: N31°36.05' W110°34.68'
▼ 5.4	SO	Cross through Vaughn Canyon Wash on concrete ford.
1.2 ▲	SO	Cross through Vaughn Canyon Wash on concrete ford.
▼ 5.6	BR	Graded road on left, remain on paved road.
1.0 ▲	BL	Graded road ahead, remain on paved road.
▼ 6.6	SO	Graded road on right is South #9: Canelo Hills Trail, sign-posted as Vaughn Loop Road. Zero trip meter.
0.0 ▲		Continue to the northeast.
		GPS: N31°35.14' W110°33.74'
▼ 0.0		Continue to the southeast.
2.6 ▲	SO	Graded road on left is South #9: Canelo Hills Trail, sign-posted as Vaughn Loop Road. Zero trip meter.
▼ 1.3	SO	Entering Coronado National Forest. There is no sign at the boundary.
1.3 ▲	SO	Leaving Coronado National Forest. There is no sign at the boundary.
▼ 1.5	SO	Track on left is FR 4620 and track on right.
1.1 ▲	SO	Track on right is FR 4620 and track on left.
▼ 2.1	SO	Track on left is FR 4619A, track on right is FR 4619B.
0.5 ▲	SO	Track on right is FR 4619A, track on left is FR 4619B.
		GPS: N31°33.57' W110°33.18'
▼ 2.3	SO	Cattle guard.
0.3 ▲	SO	Cattle guard.
▼ 2.6	SO	Track on right and left is FR 4622. Sign for Black Oak Cemetery on left. Left goes 0.2 to cemetery. Zero trip meter.
0.0 ▲		Continue to the northwest.
		GPS: N31°33.21' W110°32.95'
▼ 0.0		Continue to the southeast.

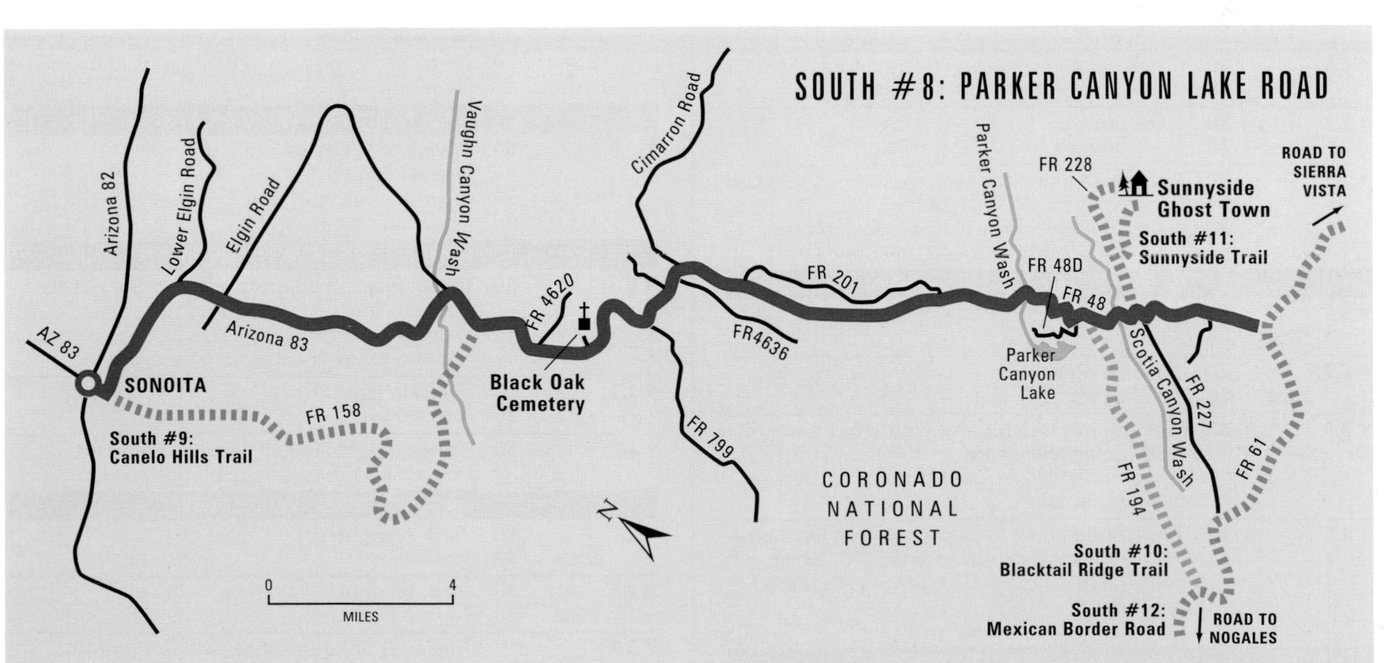

	3.5 ▲	SO	Track on right and left is FR 4622. Sign for Black Oak Cemetery on right. Right goes 0.2 miles to cemetery. Zero trip meter.
▼ 0.4		SO	Track on left is FR 5630; then track on right.
	3.1 ▲	SO	Track on left; then track on right is FR 5630.
▼ 1.3		SO	Ranch road on left; then track on right.
	2.2 ▲	SO	Track on left; then ranch road on right.
▼ 2.1		TL	Remain on paved Arizona 83. Graded dirt road FR 799 continues ahead. Follow sign to Parker Canyon Lake.
	1.4 ▲	TR	Remain on paved Arizona 83. Graded dirt road FR 799 on left.
			GPS: N31°32.57′ W110°31.74′
▼ 2.7		SO	Track on right is FR 4892.
	0.8 ▲	SO	Track on left is FR 4892.
▼ 3.0		SO	Graded road on left is Membrillo Lane.
	0.5 ▲	SO	Graded road on right is Membrillo Lane.
			GPS: N31°32.54′ W110°30.87′
▼ 3.2		SO	Graded road on right is FR 4636.
	0.3 ▲	SO	Graded road on left is FR 4636.
▼ 3.5		SO	Paved road on left is Cimarron Road to Fort Huachuca. Zero trip meter.
	0.0 ▲		Continue to the southwest.
			GPS: N31°32.61′ W110°30.38′
▼ 0.0			Continue to the southeast.
	9.8 ▲	SO	Paved road on right is Cimarron Road to Fort Huachuca. Zero trip meter.
▼ 1.4		SO	Graded road on left and right.
	8.4 ▲	SO	Graded road on left and right.
▼ 3.4		SO	Track on right.
	6.4 ▲	SO	Track on left.
▼ 6.2		SO	Cattle guard, road turns to graded gravel.
	3.6 ▲	SO	Cattle guard, road turns to paved.
			GPS: N31°27.97′ W110°27.77′
▼ 6.3		SO	FR 201 on left opposite mile marker 7.
	3.5 ▲	SO	FR 201 on right opposite mile marker 7.
▼ 6.4		SO	Entering Cochise County.
	3.4 ▲	SO	Entering Santa Cruz County.
▼ 6.6		SO	Track on left and track on right.
	3.2 ▲	SO	Track on right and track on left.
▼ 6.8		SO	Track on right.
	3.0 ▲	SO	Track on left.
▼ 6.9		SO	Cross through wash on concrete ford.
	2.9 ▲	SO	Cross through wash on concrete ford.
▼ 7.2		SO	Track on left.
	2.6 ▲	SO	Track on right.
▼ 7.9		SO	Two tracks on right; then cross through Parker Canyon Wash on concrete ford.
	1.9 ▲	SO	Cross through Parker Canyon Wash on concrete ford; then two tracks on left.
			GPS: N31°26.68′ W110°26.76′
▼ 8.6		SO	Track on left.
	1.2 ▲	SO	Track on right.
▼ 8.7		SO	Track on right.
	1.1 ▲	SO	Track on left.
▼ 9.3		SO	Entering private property, then cross through wash on concrete ford.
	0.5 ▲	SO	Cross through wash on concrete ford, leaving private property.
▼ 9.8		TL	Turn left on FR 48 following the sign for Sierra Vista and Nogales. Ahead is FR 48D, which goes 0.5 miles to Parker Canyon Lake. Zero trip meter.
	0.0 ▲		Continue to the northeast.
			GPS: N31°25.74′ W110°26.40′
▼ 0.0			Continue to the southeast.
	0.6 ▲	TR	Turn right at T-intersection following sign for Sonoita and Tucson. Road on left is FR 48D, which goes 0.5 miles to Parker Canyon Lake. Zero trip meter.
▼ 0.1		SO	Road into houses on right.
	0.5 ▲	SO	Road into houses on left.
▼ 0.6		SO	South #10: Blacktail Ridge Trail, FR 194, graded gravel road, marked South Lake Road on right; then cattle guard. Zero trip meter.
	0.0 ▲		Continue to the north.
			GPS: N31°25.48′ W110°26.15′
▼ 0.0			Continue to the south.
	1.5 ▲	SO	Cattle guard; then South #10: Blacktail Ridge Trail, FR 194, graded gravel road, marked South Lake Road on left. Zero trip meter.
▼ 0.1		SO	Track on right.
	1.4 ▲	SO	Track on left.
▼ 0.2		SO	Track on left.
	1.3 ▲	SO	Track on right.
▼ 0.6		SO	Track on right; then cross through wash.
	0.9 ▲	SO	Cross through wash; then track on left.
▼ 0.7		SO	Track on left and track on right.
	0.8 ▲	SO	Track on left and track on right.
▼ 0.8		SO	Cross through Scotia Canyon Wash; then track on left.
	0.7 ▲	SO	Track on right; then cross through Scotia Canyon Wash.
			GPS: N31°25.12′ W110°25.72′
▼ 1.3		SO	Cattle guard.
	0.2 ▲	SO	Cattle guard.
▼ 1.5		SO	Graded road on left is South #11: Sunnyside Trail, FR 228. Zero trip meter at signpost. Track on right.
	0.0 ▲		Continue to the northwest toward Sonoita.
			GPS: N31°24.83′ W110°25.52′
▼ 0.0			Continue to the southeast to Coronado National Memorial.
	3.0 ▲	SO	Graded road on right is South #11: Sunnyside Trail, FR 228. Zero trip meter at signpost. Track on left.
▼ 0.1		SO	Graded road on right is FR 227 to Lochiel and Nogales.
	2.9 ▲	SO	Graded road on left is FR 227 to Lochiel and Nogales.
			GPS: N31°24.68′ W110°25.45′
▼ 0.5		SO	Private property on right, grave at intersection.
	2.5 ▲	SO	Private property on left, grave at intersection.
			GPS: N31°24.48′ W110°25.25′
▼ 0.6		SO	Cattle guard; then cross through Sunnyside Canyon. Track on left up wash.
	2.4 ▲	SO	Cross through Sunnyside Canyon. Track on right up wash; then cattle guard.
▼ 1.3		SO	Track on left.
	1.7 ▲	SO	Track on right.
▼ 1.9		SO	Track on right and left; then cattle guard.
	1.1 ▲	SO	Cattle guard; then track on right and left.
			GPS: N31°23.62′ W110°24.69′
▼ 2.1		SO	Track on right.
	0.9 ▲	SO	Track on left.
▼ 2.8		SO	Track on right.
	0.2 ▲	SO	Track on left.
▼ 3.0			Trail ends at intersection with South #12: Mexican Border Road, FR 61. Continue straight

		on for Sierra Vista and Coronado National Memorial, turn right for Nogales.
0.0 ▲		Trail starts on South #12: Mexican Border Road, FR 61, 8.4 miles west of Montezuma Pass. Zero trip meter and turn northwest on graded dirt road, FR 48, signposted to Sonoita and Parker Canyon Lake.
		GPS: N31°22.79′ W110°24.13′

SOUTH REGION TRAIL #9

Canelo Hills Trail

Starting Point:	**Arizona 83 in Sonoita**
Finishing Point:	**South #8: Parker Canyon Lake Road, 0.7 miles south of mile marker 21**
Total Mileage:	**14.7 miles**
Unpaved Mileage:	**12.7 miles**
Driving Time:	**2.5 hours**
Elevation Range:	**4,900–5,600 feet**
Usually Open:	**Year-round**
Best Time to Travel:	**October to June**
Difficulty Rating:	**4**
Scenic Rating:	**7**
Remoteness Rating:	**+0**

Special Attractions

- Small winding trail through the Canelo Hills.
- Views of the Santa Rita and Whetstone Mountains.
- Many pleasant backcountry campsites.
- Trail is popular with horse riders and mountain bikers.

Description

This short winding trail passes through the northern edge of the Canelo Hills (Spanish for "cinnamon-colored") in the Coronado National Forest south of Sonoita. Private property has altered the route of the trail from that shown on the various maps of the region. The trail detailed here is longer and harder to navigate than the straight trail depicted on the forest map.

Looking across the trail to the Santa Rita Mountains

It leaves from the edge of Sonoita, initially traveling along a paved and then a graded road into the forest. It undulates through grasslands dotted with low shrubs, giving views to the Whetstone Mountains and the Santa Rita Mountains. After 4.2 miles, the graded road ends at private property, and the route turns onto a small formed trail. This section is eroded in places, with many moguls as it climbs in and out of O'Leary Creek. It is muddy when wet as the remaining ruts testify.

The section that travels within O'Leary Canyon is the roughest along the trail with a couple of short rocky sections. It is also moderately brushy for wider vehicles.

The final section of the trail is again graded dirt road as it leads through open national forest to rejoin South #8: Parker Canyon Lake Road.

Current Road Information

Coronado National Forest
Sierra Vista Ranger District
5990 South Hwy 92
Hereford, AZ 85615
(520) 378-0311

Map References

BLM Fort Huachuca
USFS Coronado National Forest: Nogales and Sierra Vista Ranger Districts
USGS 1:24,000 Sonoita, Mt. Hughes, O'Donnell Canyon
1:100,000 Fort Huachuca
Maptech CD-ROM: Southeast Arizona/Tucson
Arizona Atlas & Gazetteer, p. 73
Arizona Road & Recreation Atlas, p. 54 & p. 88
Recreational Map of Arizona

Route Directions

▼ 0.0		From Sonoita, turn south on Arizona 83 at the sign for Parker Canyon Lake. Proceed 0.4 miles to where South #8: Parker Canyon Lake Road (Arizona 83) bears left to Parker Canyon Lake and continue straight ahead on Papago Spring Road. Zero trip meter at intersection. Remain on paved twisty road, ignoring turns to right and left.
3.2 ▲		Trail ends at the intersection of Papago Spring Road and South #8: Parker Canyon Lake Road (Arizona 83). Continue straight on to Sonoita, turn right to travel to Parker Canyon Lake.
		GPS: N31°40.40′ W110°39.31′
▼ 2.0	SO	Road turns to gravel at primitive road sign.
1.2 ▲	SO	Road is now paved.
▼ 2.6	SO	Cattle guard.
0.6 ▲	SO	Cattle guard.
▼ 3.2	BL	Bear left remaining on the major graded road, FR 158. Track on right is FR 636 to Papago Spring. Many pleasant campsites along that trail. Zero trip meter.
0.0 ▲		Continue to the northwest.
		GPS: N31°37.68′ W110°37.86′

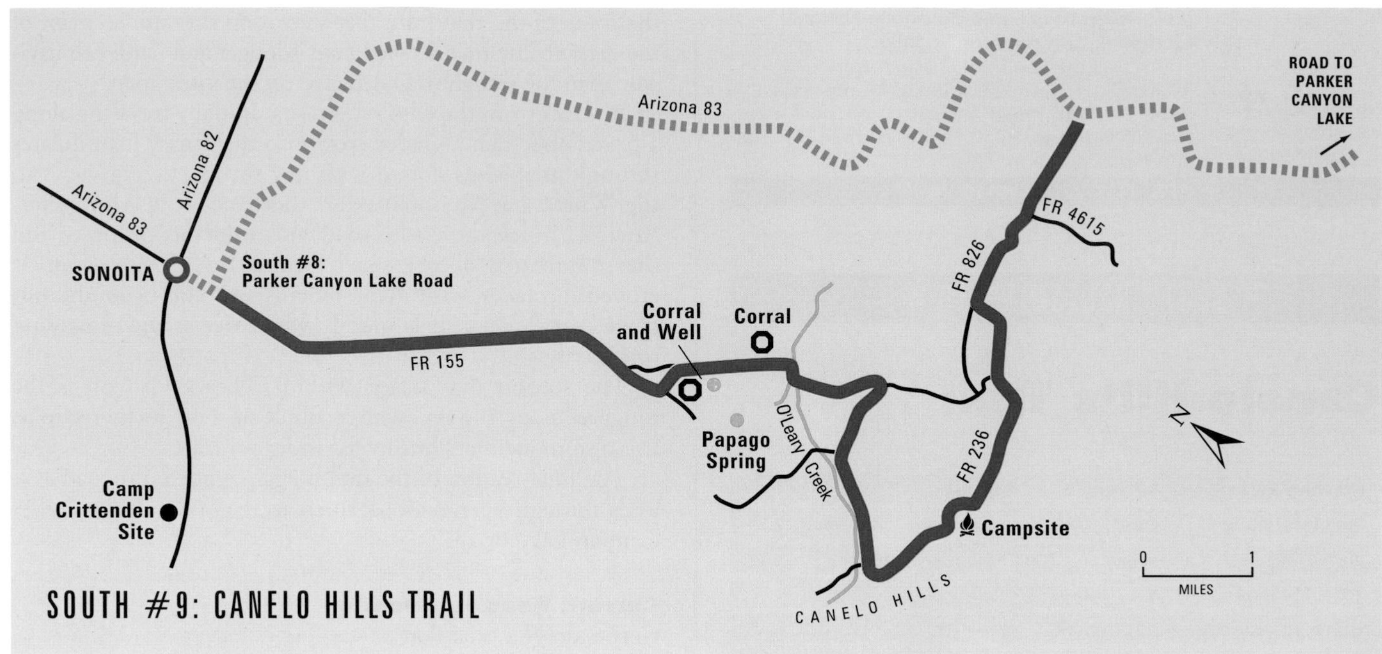

Mileage	Reverse	Dir.	Directions
▼ 0.0			Continue to the southeast and cross cattle guard.
	1.0 ▲	SO	Cattle guard; then track on left is FR 636 to Papago Spring. Many pleasant campsites along that trail. Zero trip meter.
▼ 0.1		SO	Track on right.
	0.9 ▲	SO	Track on left.
▼ 0.9		SO	Cross through wash.
	0.1 ▲	SO	Cross through wash.
▼ 1.0		TR	Turn right onto small, formed trail at marker for FR 158. Graded road continues into private property. Zero trip meter.
	0.0 ▲		Continue to the west.
			GPS: N31°37.26' W110°38.02'
▼ 0.0			Continue to the south.
	2.8 ▲	TL	Join larger graded road and turn left. Private property on the right. Zero trip meter.
▼ 0.3		SO	Track on right.
	2.5 ▲	SO	Track on left.
▼ 0.4		TL	Track straight on.
	2.4 ▲	TR	Track on left.
			GPS: N31°36.90' W110°38.01'
▼ 0.5		SO	Pass through fence line, corral on right, then pass through second fence line.
	2.3 ▲	SO	Pass through fence line, corral on left, then pass through second fence line.
▼ 0.7		SO	Track on left goes into private property.
	2.1 ▲	SO	Track on right goes into private property.
▼ 0.9		SO	Track on left and well on right; then cross through wash.
	1.9 ▲	SO	Cross through wash; then track on right and well on left.
			GPS: N31°36.72' W110°37.57'
▼ 1.0		SO	Cross through wash.
	1.8 ▲	SO	Cross through wash.
▼ 1.1		SO	Cross through wide wash.
	1.7 ▲	SO	Cross through wide wash.
▼ 1.2		SO	Cross through wash.
	1.6 ▲	SO	Cross through wash.
			GPS: N31°36.47' W110°37.45'.
▼ 1.5		SO	Faint track on left at corral.
	1.3 ▲	SO	Faint track on right at corral.
			GPS: N31°36.33' W110°37.28'
▼ 1.6		SO	Pass through wire gate.
	1.2 ▲	SO	Pass through wire gate.
▼ 1.8		SO	Cross through wash.
	1.0 ▲	SO	Cross through wash.
▼ 1.9		SO	Cross through two washes.
	0.9 ▲	SO	Cross through two washes.
▼ 2.2		SO	Off-camber section around a fallen tree will test the side tilt angle of your vehicle.
	0.6 ▲	SO	Off-camber section around a fallen tree will test the side tilt angle of your vehicle.
▼ 2.8		TR	Pass through wire gate, then turn right onto small unmarked track. Zero trip meter. Ahead goes to private property.
	0.0 ▲		Continue to the northeast.
			GPS: N31°35.40' W110°36.84'
▼ 0.0			Continue to the west.
	0.9 ▲	TL	T-intersection. Turn left and pass through wire gate. Zero trip meter. Track on right goes to private property.
▼ 0.3		SO	Cross through wash.
	0.6 ▲	SO	Cross through wash.
▼ 0.7		SO	Pass through wire gate.
	0.2 ▲	SO	Pass through wire gate.
			GPS: N31°35.46' W110°37.55'
▼ 0.9		TL	Turn left onto small trail and zero trip meter. Trail goes into the trees and can be a little hard to spot as it goes slightly back on itself.
	0.0 ▲		Continue to the southeast.
			GPS: N31°35.53' W110°37.65'
▼ 0.0			Continue to the southwest.
	3.9 ▲	TR	Turn right at T-intersection and zero trip meter.
▼ 0.3		SO	Cross through wash.
	3.6 ▲	SO	Cross through wash.
▼ 0.4		SO	Cross through rocky wash.
	3.5 ▲	SO	Cross through rocky wash.
▼ 0.6		SO	Cross through wash.

3.3 ▲	SO	Cross through wash.
▼ 0.9	SO	Dam on right.
3.0 ▲	SO	Dam on left.
		GPS: N31°34.88' W110°38.17'
▼ 1.1	SO	Cross through wash.
2.8 ▲	SO	Cross through wash.
▼ 1.2	TL	T-intersection, small track on right.
2.7 ▲	TR	Track on left.
		GPS: N31°34.79' W110°38.36'
▼ 1.5	SO	Track on right.
2.4 ▲	SO	Track on left.
▼ 1.8	SO	Cross through wash.
2.1 ▲	SO	Cross through wash.
▼ 1.9	SO	Old dam on left.
2.0 ▲	SO	Old dam on right.
▼ 2.2	SO	Gate.
1.7 ▲	SO	Gate.
▼ 2.4	SO	Track on left, campsite on right.
1.5 ▲	SO	Track on right, campsite on left.
		GPS: N31°34.40' W110°37.52'
▼ 2.7	BL	Track on right to tanks.
1.2 ▲	BR	Track on left to tanks.
▼ 3.1	SO	Track on right to campsite.
0.8 ▲	BR	Track on left to campsite.
▼ 3.6	SO	Track on right to campsite.
0.3 ▲	SO	Track on left to campsite.
▼ 3.7	SO	Pass through wire gate at primitive road sign.
0.2 ▲	SO	Pass through wire gate at primitive road sign.
		GPS: N31°34.49' W110°36.27'
▼ 3.9	SO	Join graded dirt road at marker for FR 236. Zero trip meter.
0.0 ▲		Continue to the south.
		GPS: N31°34.65' W110°36.24'
▼ 0.0		Continue to the north.
2.9 ▲	TL	On right-hand bend, turn left onto FR 236, formed dirt trail and zero trip meter. There is a sign for FR 236.
▼ 0.3	SO	Track on right is private.
2.6 ▲	SO	Track on left is private.
▼ 0.9	TR	Turn right onto FR 826 at sign. FR 826 also continues straight ahead.
2.0 ▲	TL	Turn left at T-intersection onto graded FR 158 at sign. FR 826 is on the right.
		GPS: N31°35.13' W110°35.70'
▼ 1.5	SO	Cattle guard.
1.4 ▲	SO	Cattle guard.
▼ 1.6	SO	Cross through wash.
1.3 ▲	SO	Cross through wash.
▼ 1.9	SO	FR 4615 on right. Exiting Coronado National Forest.
1.0 ▲	SO	FR 4615 on left. Entering Coronado National Forest.
▼ 2.1	SO	Cattle guard.
0.8 ▲	SO	Cattle guard.
▼ 2.9		Trail ends at the T-intersection with the paved South #8: Parker Canyon Lake Road. Turn right for Parker Lake, turn left for Sonoita.
0.0 ▲		From South #8: Parker Canyon Lake Road, 0.7 miles south of mile marker 21, turn west on the graded dirt Vaughn Loop Road, FR 826. Zero trip meter and cross cattle guard.
		GPS: N31°35.14' W110°33.74'

SOUTH REGION TRAIL #10

Blacktail Ridge Trail

Starting Point:	South #12: Mexican Border Road, 7.4 miles west of the intersection with South #8: Parker Canyon Lake Road
Finishing Point:	South #8: Parker Canyon Lake Road, 0.6 miles south of Parker Canyon Lake turnoff
Total Mileage:	6.4 miles
Unpaved Mileage:	6.4 miles
Driving Time:	45 minutes
Elevation Range:	5,000–5,700 feet
Usually Open:	Year-round
Best Time to Travel:	October to May
Difficulty Rating:	2
Scenic Rating:	7
Remoteness Rating:	+0

Special Attractions

- Easy trail running over grasslands.
- Panoramic views of the Huachuca Mountains and down into Mexico.
- Alternative access to Parker Canyon Lake.

Description

This easy, formed trail runs in a straight line along a wide ridge connecting South #12: Mexican Border Road with South #8: Parker Canyon Lake Road. It follows FR 4016 and FR 194, shown on the Coronado National Forest Map. (FR 4016 is shown on the map but not labeled.)

The trail is open and offers good views down into Bodie Canyon on the east. Further up, the trail follows alongside Jones Canyon on the west.

The whole trail is very exposed with little shade. For those wishing to camp, the north end, near the junction of the Arizona Trail, is the best option. However, nicer spots can be found along the Parker Canyon Lake Road and in the nation-

Crossing the grassland toward Mexico

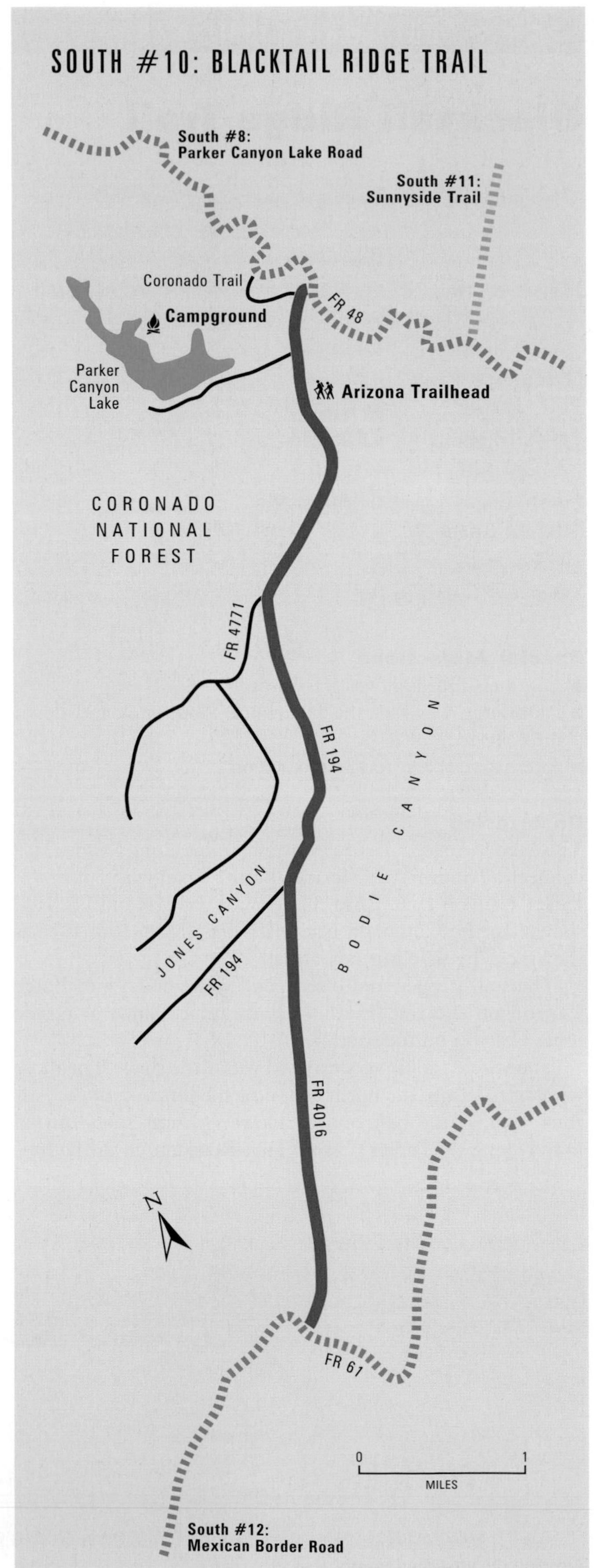

al forest campground at Parker Canyon Lake.

The open views make it easy to spot many raptors. In addition, javelina and desert pronghorn antelope may be seen in the grasslands.

Current Road Information

Coronado National Forest
Sierra Vista Ranger District
5990 South Hwy 92
Hereford, AZ 85615
(520) 378-0311

Map References

BLM Nogales
USFS Coronado National Forest: Nogales and Sierra Vista Ranger Districts
USGS 1:24,000 Campini Mesa, Huachuca Peak
1:100,000 Nogales
Maptech CD-ROM: Southeast Arizona/Tucson
Arizona Atlas & Gazetteer, p. 73
Arizona Road & Recreation Atlas, p. 54 & p. 88
Recreational Map of Arizona

Route Directions

▼ 0.0			From South #12: Mexican Border Road, 7.4 miles west of the intersection with South #8: Parker Canyon Lake Road, zero trip meter and turn east on small formed trail, FR 4016. Initally the trail crosses grasslands.
	2.7 ▲		Trail ends at the T-intersection with South #12: Mexican Border Road. Turn right to continue to Lochiel, turn left to continue toward Sierra Vista.
			GPS: N31°20.91' W110°29.67'
▼ 0.2		SO	Track on left.
	2.5 ▲	SO	Track on right.
▼ 0.7		SO	Track on right and track on left.
	2.0 ▲	SO	Track on right and track on left.
▼ 0.9		SO	Cattle guard.
	1.8 ▲	SO	Cattle guard.
▼ 1.8		SO	Track on left; then track on right.
	0.9 ▲	SO	Track on left; then track on right.
▼ 2.0		BL	Track on right.
	0.7 ▲	SO	Track on left.
			GPS: N31°22.54' W110°28.57'
▼ 2.3		SO	Track on right. Several tracks on left and right, remain on main trail.
	0.4 ▲	SO	Track on left. Several tracks on left and right, remain on main trail.
▼ 2.7		SO	Track on left is FR 194. Continue straight ahead also on FR 194. Zero trip meter.
	0.0 ▲		Continue to the southwest.
			GPS: N31°22.98' W110°28.16'
▼ 0.0			Continue to the northeast.
	3.2 ▲	BL	Track on right is the continuation of FR 194. Bear left onto FR 4016 and zero trip meter.
▼ 0.1		SO	Cattle guard.
	3.1 ▲	SO	Cattle guard.
▼ 1.7		BR	Track on left is FR 4771. Bear right and cross cattle guard, then track on left.
	1.5 ▲	BL	Track on right, cattle guard, then track on right is FR 4771. Bear left remaining on unmarked FR 194.
			GPS: N31°24.26' W110°27.42'

▼ 2.4		SO	Track on right through fence line.
	0.8 ▲	SO	Track on left through fence line.
▼ 2.9		SO	Campsite on left, no shade but views of Parker Canyon Lake.
	0.3 ▲	SO	Campsite on right, no shade but views of Parker Canyon Lake.
▼ 3.1		SO	Track on left, then Arizona Trail parking on left and right. The Arizona Trail on the left and right is for horses and hikers only.
	0.1 ▲	SO	The Arizona Trail on the left and right is for horses and hikers only. Trailhead parking on left and right, then track on right.
			GPS: N31°25.16' W110°26.47'
▼ 3.2		SO	Cattle guard. Zero trip meter.
	0.0 ▲		Continue to the southwest.
			GPS: N31°25.20' W110°26.44'
▼ 0.0			Continue to the northeast.
	0.5 ▲	SO	Cattle guard. Zero trip meter.
▼ 0.1		SO	Service road on left.
	0.4 ▲	SO	Service road on right.
▼ 0.2		SO	Cattle guard.
	0.3 ▲	SO	Cattle guard.
▼ 0.4		SO	Graded road on left called Coronado Trail.
	0.1 ▲	SO	Graded road on right called Coronado Trail.
▼ 0.5			Trail ends at the intersection with South #8: Parker Canyon Lake Road. Turn left for Parker Canyon Lake, turn right to return to South #12: Mexican Border Road.
	0.0 ▲		0.6 miles south of Parker Canyon Lake turn west from South #8: Parker Canyon Lake Road immediately before a cattle guard. Zero trip meter and continue west on South Lake Road, FR 194.
			GPS: N31°25.48' W110°26.15'

SOUTH REGION TRAIL #11

Sunnyside Trail

Starting Point:	**South #8: Parker Canyon Lake Road, 2.1 miles south of Parker Canyon Lake**
Finishing Point:	**Sunnyside**
Total Mileage:	**8.4 miles (round-trip)**
Unpaved Mileage:	**8.4 miles (round-trip)**
Driving Time:	**45 minutes (one-way)**
Elevation Range:	**5,700–6,000**
Usually Open:	**Year-round**
Best Time to Travel:	**October to May**
Difficulty Rating:	**2**
Scenic Rating:	**8**
Remoteness Rating:	**+0**

Special Attractions

- Remains of Sunnyside ghost town.
- Sunnyside Cemetery.
- Hiking trail access to Miller Peak Wilderness and the Copper Glance Mine.
- Views into Sunnyside Canyon and the Huachuca Mountains.

Some of the buildings still located at Sunnyside

History

Sunnyside, now a ghost town, was established in the 1890s as a religious community led by Samuel Donnelly, an ex-alcoholic, originally from Scotland. Donnelly, who was a former boxer and sailor, found salvation and sobriety at a Salvation Army meeting in San Francisco. The community of 50 families was a sort of socialist cooperative, with members working at whatever their talents allowed and pooling their money. The members spent their time singing hymns, reading the Bible, and mining the nearby Copper Glance Mine. Other income for the hard-working community came from cutting hay for the military post of Fort Huachuca, running a sawmill, and working on the railroad. There were no stores in Sunnyside. None were needed as the residents pooled everything and cooked and ate in communal areas. The women cooked together and did the laundry in large tubs. Slackers were not tolerated. Anyone who wouldn't work was asked to leave.

Sunnyside Cemetery

Communal living seemed to work very well for the settlement. Visitors would often remark how happy everyone appeared to be, and there was none of the violence, hard drinking, or prostitution often associated with mining camps of the era. Indeed, the community practiced what it preached and often gave food, supplies, and money to people in need.

Samuel Donnelly died in 1901, but the Donnelites, as they were known, remained on. The little town, which was the only settlement in Arizona known to be wholly religious, got a post office on July 16, 1914. It finally closed after 20

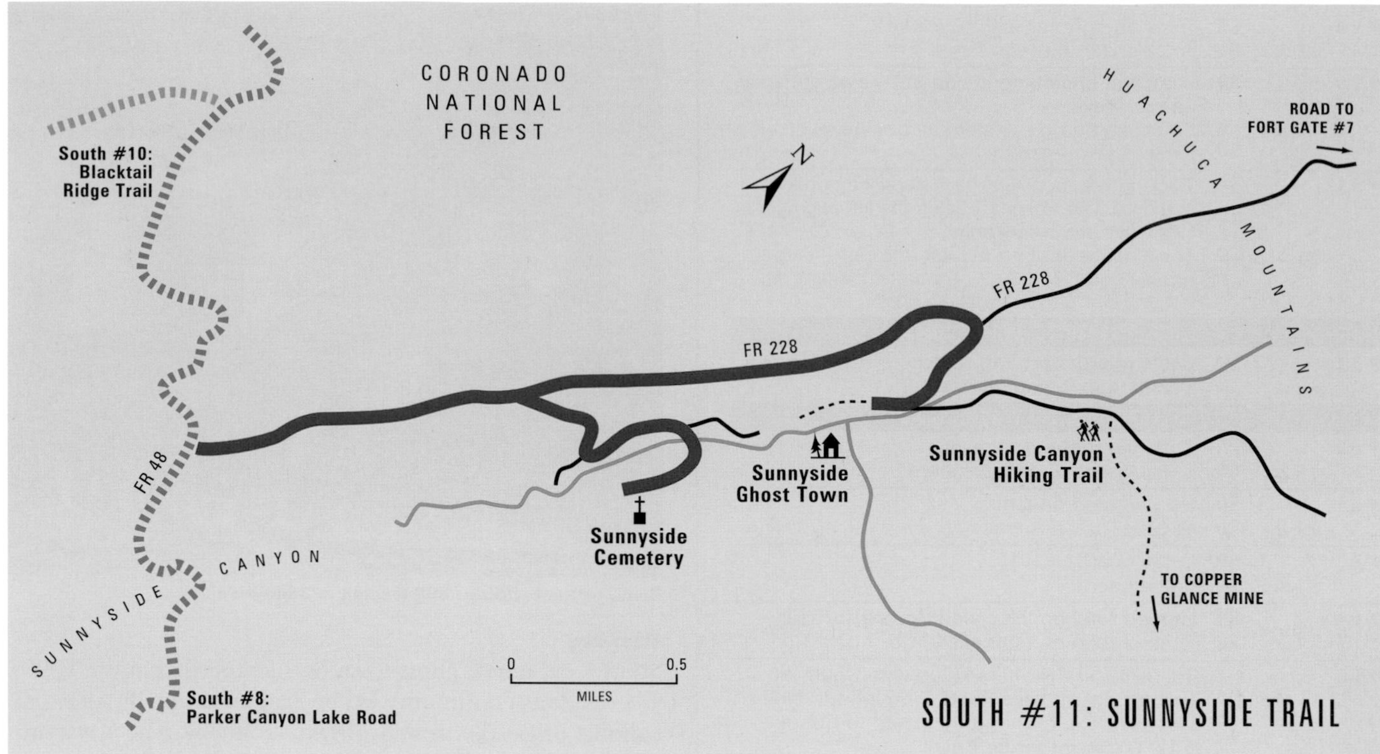

years when the mines were exhausted. The Donnelites dispersed after giving the mine to their creditors.

To the north of Sunnyside is Fort Huachuca, a cavalry post founded in 1877 that played a prominent role in subduing the last significant Indian group ranging outside of reservations in the United States. The group, the Chiricahua Apache, were led by Geronimo and ranged across into Mexico pursued by the cavalry. The post was also the headquarters of the "Buffalo Soldiers," the name given by Native Americans to black soldiers. The post was the headquarters for the army's four all-black regiments: 9th and 10th Cavalry Regiments, and the 24th and 25th Infantry Regiments. The fort survives today as an active military installation.

Description

This short trail follows alongside Sunnyside Canyon, traveling on a roughly graded dirt road. The trail gradually climbs, giving excellent views over the Huachuca Mountains. At a T-intersection, the trail makes the loop around to the Sunnyside town site. A sign-posted track on the left leads to the wilderness boundary, and the start of a hiking trail that leads to the remains of the Copper Glance Mine, which was worked successfully by the Donnelites for many years. Sunnyside is a short distance past the mine. The town site is now privately owned and posted. However, it is possible to get a good view of the remains of the two substantial wooden houses that remain, some smaller buildings, and water tanks. The original schoolhouse collapsed a few years ago, and most of the remaining buildings are in a precarious state.

After viewing the wooden buildings, retrace your steps nearly to the start of the trail and visit the Sunnyside Cemetery. The trail to the cemetery is small with many turns and it is easy to get confused. The most reliable way of finding it is to enter the coordinates for the spur to the cemetery into your GPS and use the GoTo feature to help you navigate.

The cemetery has undergone restoration work over the years but looks a little dilapidated these days. The small plot is enclosed by a sagging wire fence. Most of the graves are marked with plaques. The trail peters out immediately after the cemetery.

Current Road Information

Coronado National Forest
Sierra Vista Ranger District
5990 South Hwy 92
Hereford, AZ 85615
(520) 378-0311

Map References

BLM Nogales
USFS Coronado National Forest: Nogales and Sierra Vista Ranger Districts
USGS 1:24,000 Huachuca Peak
1:100,000 Nogales
Maptech CD-ROM: Southeast Arizona/Tucson
Arizona Atlas & Gazetteer, p. 73
Arizona Road & Recreation Atlas, p. 54 & p. 88
Recreational Map of Arizona

Route Directions

▼ 0.0	From South #8: Parker Canyon Lake Road, 2.1 miles south of Parker Canyon Lake, zero trip

meter and turn northeast on graded dirt road, sign-posted to Sunnyside Canyon, FR 228.

GPS: N31°24.83' W110°25.52'

▼ 0.1 SO Cattle guard.
▼ 0.5 SO Large camping area on right.
▼ 0.9 BL Track on right is the start of spur trail to Sunnyside Cemetery. Zero trip meter.

GPS: N31°25.48' W110°24.98'

Spur to Sunnyside Cemetery

▼ 0.0 BR At the fork in the trail pointing toward Sunnyside, take the right fork (northeast) and zero trip meter.

GPS: N31°25.48' W110°24.98'

▼ 0.3 SO Track on right.
▼ 0.5 SO Track on right.

GPS: N31°25.54' W110°24.69'

▼ 0.6 SO Gate; then track on right.

GPS: N31°25.63' W110°24.65'

▼ 0.8 BR Bear right, track on left, then cross through wash and bear right again, track on left.

GPS: N31°25.77' W110°24.53'

▼ 0.85 TR Turn right at top of bank in open area.

GPS: N31°25.75' W110°24.47'

▼ 0.9 BL Turn left, well-used track on right.

GPS: N31°25.67' W110°24.46'

▼ 1.0 BR Enter trees, well-used track on left, bear right. Then small track on right.

GPS: N31°25.64' W110°24.45'

▼ 1.2 UT Sunnyside Cemetery on left, enclosed by wire fence. Retrace your steps to the start of the spur trail.

GPS: N31°25.53' W110°24.53'

Continuation of Trail

▼ 0.0 Zero trip meter and continue to the north.
▼ 0.8 SO Track on left.
▼ 1.2 SO Cattle guard.

GPS: N31°26.41' W110°24.29'

▼ 1.5 SO Cross through wash.
▼ 1.6 TR T-intersection. FR 228 to Fort Gate #7 on left, FR 204 to Sunnyside Canyon and Copper Glance on right.

GPS: N31°26.50' W110°24.13'

▼ 1.8 SO At sign for Sunnyside Canyon and Copper Glance, continue straight on. Left goes 0.7 miles to the boundary of the Miller Peak Wilderness and the start of Sunnyside Canyon hiking trail which goes approximately 3.5 miles to the Copper Glance Mine. Zero trip meter.

GPS: N31°26.28' W110°24.12'

▼ 0.0 Continue to the south.
▼ 0.2 Cross through creek, then trail ends at a gate. Sunnyside ghost town is just beyond the gate. No camping is permitted. The town site is on private property, hike for 0.1 miles down the wash to view the buildings from public land.

GPS: N31°26.13' W110°24.19'

SOUTH REGION TRAIL #12

Mexican Border Road

Starting Point:	**Arizona 92, 0.8 miles past mile marker 334**
Finishing Point:	**Arizona 82, 4.1 miles north of Nogales**
Total Mileage:	**50.4 miles**
Unpaved Mileage:	**43.6 miles**
Driving Time:	**5 hours**
Elevation Range:	**3,600–6,600 feet**
Usually Open:	**Year-round**
Best Time to Travel:	**November to June**
Difficulty Rating:	**1**
Scenic Rating:	**10**
Remoteness Rating:	**+0**

Special Attractions

- Old border crossing town of Lochiel.
- Washington Camp and Duquesne ghost towns.
- Montezuma Pass and the Coronado National Monument.
- Sweeping views of mountains and grasslands in the United States and Mexico.

History

The Spanish padres criss-crossed the route of this trail on many of their missions. Two of the best known of these early European travelers were Padre Eusebio Francisco Kino and Fray Marcos de Niza (who is believed to be the earliest European to pass this way back in 1539). The development of this route started at the western end and over time forged its way to the east.

Further Spanish exploration in the 1760s extended the trail east. In the 1860s miners forged a trail through to Washington Camp as they pressed onward searching for the next lucky strike. The trail then lengthened again, pushing farther east to more mines at Luttrell, later known as Lochiel, and on to Sunnyside, which was a timber supply point for the mines at Washington Camp and Duquesne. The final section of the trail was cut through by the Civilian Conservation Corps in

Ore-loading hopper at the Kansas Mine

1933 and went east over Montezuma Pass. Early travelers reported abundant wildlife throughout this region including Mexican wolves, bears, wild horses, and panthers.

Thomas Shane and his associate Mr. Capen brought life back to Washington Camp with the discovery of the Bonanza Mine in the early 1880s. Claims changed hands often, until the Duquesne Company took hold of many of the mining claims in the late 1880s, and the boom was on. The Duquesne and Washington Camps were less than a mile apart with over 70 mines active and nearly 2,000 residents between the two. Washington Camp built a smelter for use by both camps and was the site of the school. The towns flourished and survived into the early 1900s but by 1920, the lights of the towns all but went out. A brief mining resurgence in the early 1940s brought a momentary flicker back to the virtual ghost town. A number of houses have remained occupied over the years as nature has reclaimed the dozens of mine shafts.

Duquesne's most famous resident was probably George Westinghouse of household appliance fame. He amazed his neighbors by having hot and cold running water in his bathroom long before it was commonplace. At the turn of the twenty-first century the camps took on a new boom in the form of real estate. Many of the mining remains of the two camps were bulldozed and the landscape was "tamed." Though Duquesne and Washington Camps may rise again as residential settlements, it appears their days as mining camps are over.

Lochiel, situated right on the Mexican border, was named after the first settlers' village back in Scotland. The Camerons were partners in securing the nearby San Rafael de la Zanja Land Grant in 1888 from its original owner, Manuel Bustello, who purchased it from the Mexican government in 1825. Records are confused, but Lochiel appears to be the same place as two other settlements known as Luttrell and La Noria. Luttrell housed the Holland Company Smelter and associated workers' cottages. In the 1890s the U.S.-Mexican border was resurveyed as the earlier survey was deemed inaccurate. The new border split the settlement down the middle, and neighbors suddenly found themselves living in different countries.

The green pastures of the San Rafael de la Zanja Land Grant, which refers to "the ditch," or water basin, of the Santa Cruz River, have been good grazing lands over the centuries. The cattle attracted the Apache Indians who came to kill them and Texan rustlers who would rustle them and escape with guns blazing into Mexico. The rustlers at least were deterred when settlers rounded up some of the offenders and publicly hung them in Tombstone. Other cattle rustlers came north from Mexico. One notorious name was Francisco Pancho Villa, seen as somewhat of a Mexican freedom fighter and rebel. Much of his funds were gained by rounding up the community's cattle and returning south to sell off the bootie. More recently, these same rolling pastures were featured in the making of various movies, *Tom Horn, Monte Wash,* and *Oklahoma.*

An old house in Duquesne ghost town

An abandoned mine along the trail

Lochiel finally controlled its "visitors" with the construction of an official U.S. Customs House. But in time this was seen as an unnecessary expense in a remote region and the border crossing performed its last passport stamp in 1986. The border fence has also faded with time, with massive cottonwoods falling across it and sections of the fence gaping open.

The Coronado National Memorial commemorates Francisco Vasquez de Coronado and his 1549 expedition in search of the fabled Cíbola and the Seven Cities of Gold. From Compostela, located 750 miles south on Mexico's western coast, Coronado led an ambitious expedition up through Arizona into New Mexico. With a contingent of 339 soldiers, 4 Franciscan priests, 1,100 Indians and 1,500 livestock, the expedition made slow progress.

The original suggestion put forward was for an international memorial for Coronado, but the Mexican government declined to participate. Their reasons were fair: The Spanish conquistadors were often regarded as looters, taking what they wanted by force when trading was not an option. So the monument remains on the U.S. side.

Description

This long and greatly varied trail travels through some spectacular scenery in southern Arizona, at times running less than a mile north of the border with Mexico. Although the trail can be completed in five hours, it is best to allow a full day to appreciate the many things of interest along the way.

The trail leaves from Arizona 92 south of Sierra Vista and immediately travels through ranchland as a paved road. It enters the Coronado National Memorial where there are picnic areas, an informative visitor center, and the start of several hiking trails within the memorial.

From the visitor center, the trail switchbacks up Montezuma Canyon to Montezuma Pass at the southern end of the Huachuca Mountains and one of the best views along the trail. From here there are broad, panoramic views west into the San Rafael Valley, the Sierra Madre Mountains in Sonora, Mexico, the Patagonia Mountains to the northwest, and the Huachuca Mountains immediately to the north. A short trail leads out from the parking area to the shade ramada at the edge of Coronado Peak, south of the pass. Other trails lead north into the Huachuca Mountains.

From the pass, the trail switchbacks down the south side of the Huachuca Mountains along a wide shelf road, before running parallel to the Mexican border for several miles through a mixture of open grassland and ranchland. You are likely to encounter the U.S. Border Patrol in their distinctive white and green vehicles patrolling the border fence, as well as possibly surprising groups of undocumented aliens from Mexico. (Refer to the Border Patrol section, p. 12 for information on safety and how to handle unexpected encounters.) Many small tracks lead south from the main trail toward the border, these are mainly pushed through by border crossers (in both directions) and when one is closed, another one opens. The route directions have tried to account for the majority of better-used tracks to aid in navigation, but due to constantly changing situations, some may not be accurate. However, the main graded trail is easy to follow and there is little chance of becoming lost.

These sweeping grasslands are home to a wide variety of wildlife: Pronghorn antelopes, javelinas, mule deer, and coyotes are the animals most often sighted. Cattle also graze in the area.

The trail passes the southern end of South #8: Parker Canyon Lake Road and South #10: Blacktail Ridge Trail, before continuing through an open landscape toward the small settlement of Lochiel. A handful of people still call Lochiel home, but the customs house and border crossing are no longer active. This is one place where you cannot just pop around to the neighbor's house to borrow a cup of sugar; it is illegal to cross the international border other than at a recognized crossing point. The township is worth the short detour to see the customs house.

The next point of interest along the trail is the old mining camp of Duquesne. The route directions detour from the main graded road at this point to loop past the original settlement of Duquesne, which stands on privately owned land. Currently, Duquesne is in the process of being converted into a residential subdivision, so the future of the remaining houses from the original settlement is uncertain. Currently there are two substantial, old timber and stone houses that would have been considered opulent in their day; the ruins of two adobe houses and various other timber buildings remain as well. The ruins are posted as private property, but are easily viewed from the road. The trail rejoins the main FR 61 at Washington Camp, once a thriving mining camp, now a community of year-round houses and holiday homes. Little remains of the original mining camp.

The trail then climbs toward an unnamed pass in the Patagonia Mountains, passing the wooden hopper of the Kansas Mine still clinging to the side of the hillside immediately west of the southern end of South #13: Harshaw Road. Below the trail in Washington Gulch are the remains of the Pride Mine.

From the pass, the trail descends along a wide shelf road through the Patagonia Mountains, one of the prettiest sections of this long trail. This final section through Sycamore Canyon and the surrounding low hills of the Patagonia Mountains has the best campsites along the trail, even though they are well used.

The trail ends on Arizona 82, a few miles north of Nogales.

Current Road Information

Coronado National Forest
Sierra Vista Ranger District
5990 South Hwy 92
Hereford, AZ 85615
(520) 378-0311

Map References

BLM Nogales
USFS Coronado National Forest: Nogales and Sierra Vista Ranger Districts
USGS 1:24,000 Nicksville, Bob Thompson Peak, Montezuma Pass, Miller Peak, Huachuca Peak, Campini Mesa, Lochiel, Duquesne, Harshaw, Cumero Canyon, Kino Springs
1:100,000 Nogales
Maptech CD-ROM: Southeast Arizona/Tucson
Arizona Atlas & Gazetteer, pp. 74, 73
Arizona Road & Recreation Atlas, p. 54 & p. 88
Recreational Map of Arizona

Route Directions

▼ 0.0		From Arizona 92, 13 miles south of Sierra Vista, 0.8 miles south of mile marker 334, zero trip meter and turn south on paved road signposted to Coronado National Memorial. The road is marked as S. Coronado Memorial Drive. There is a forest sign after the turn, giving distances along the route. The road is also called FR 61. Remain on the paved road.
4.6 ▲		Trail ends at the T-intersection with Arizona 92. Turn left for Sierra Vista, turn right for Bisbee.
		GPS: N31°22.78' W110°12.39'
▼ 2.9	SO	Cattle guard, entering Coronado National Memorial.
1.7 ▲	SO	Cattle guard, leaving Coronado National Memorial.
		GPS: N31°20.91' W110°13.44'
▼ 4.6	SO	Coronado National Memorial Visitor Center on right, zero trip meter.
0.0 ▲		Continue to the northeast.
		GPS: N31°20.76' W110°15.16'
▼ 0.0		Continue to the southwest.
3.2 ▲	SO	Coronado National Memorial Visitor Center on left, zero trip meter.
▼ 0.1	SO	Picnic area and start of Joe's Canyon hiking trail on left.
3.1 ▲	SO	Picnic area and start of Joe's Canyon hiking trail on right.
		GPS: N31°20.73' W110°15.22'
▼ 0.2	SO	Road turns to dirt.
3.0 ▲	SO	Road turns to paved.
▼ 1.6	SO	Cross through wash on concrete ford.
1.6 ▲	SO	Cross through wash on concrete ford.
▼ 3.2	SO	Cattle guard, then Montezuma Pass. Parking area on left and short hiking trail to the ramada. Crest hiking trail on right after cattle guard. Zero trip meter.

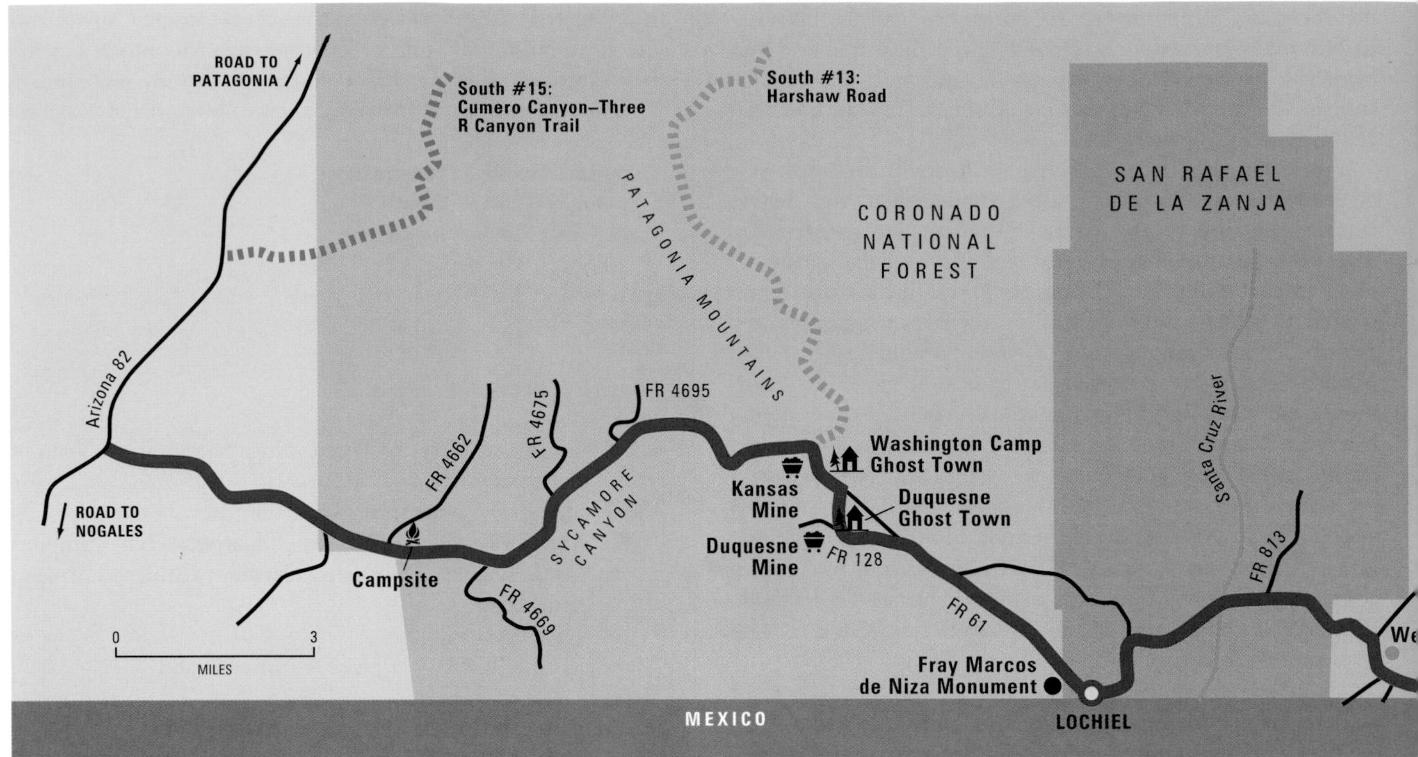

0.0 ▲ Continue down from the saddle to the northeast.

GPS: N31°21.05' W110°17.09'

▼ 0.0 Continue down from the saddle to the northwest.
3.5 ▲ SO Montezuma Pass. Parking area on right and short hiking trail to the ramada. Crest hiking trail on left, then cross cattle guard. Zero trip meter.

▼ 1.3 SO Track on right up Copper Canyon and track on left; then cross through Copper Canyon Wash.
2.2 ▲ SO Cross through Copper Canyon Wash; then track on left up Copper Canyon and track on right.

GPS: N31°21.74' W110°17.97'

▼ 1.8 SO Cattle guard, end of descent from pass.
1.7 ▲ SO Cattle guard, trail starts to climb toward Montezuma Pass.

▼ 2.1 SO Track on left.
1.4 ▲ SO Track on right.

▼ 2.3 SO Track on left.
1.2 ▲ SO Track on right.

▼ 3.5 SO Track on right is FR 771 to Huachuca Mountain Trailhead. Zero trip meter.
0.0 ▲ Continue to the northeast.

GPS: N31°22.31' W110°19.91'

▼ 0.0 Continue to the southwest.
4.9 ▲ SO Track on left is FR 771 to Huachuca Mountain Trailhead. Zero trip meter.

▼ 0.3 SO Track on right.
4.6 ▲ SO Track on left.

▼ 0.6 SO Cattle guard; then track on left.
4.3 ▲ SO Track on right; then cattle guard.

▼ 0.9 SO Track on left.
4.0 ▲ SO Track on right.

▼ 1.0 SO Track on right, then cross over Cave Canyon Creek on bridge.
3.9 ▲ SO Cross over Cave Canyon Creek on bridge, then track on left.

GPS: N31°22.36' W110°20.72'

▼ 1.1 SO Track on left.
3.8 ▲ SO Track on right.

▼ 1.7 SO Track on right and track on left; then cattle guard.
3.2 ▲ SO Cattle guard; then track on right and track on left.

▼ 2.0 SO Track on left.
2.9 ▲ SO Track on right.

▼ 2.3 SO Cross over Bear Creek on bridge.
2.6 ▲ SO Cross over Bear Creek on bridge.

GPS: N31°22.80' W110°21.76'

▼ 2.4 SO Well-used track on right.
2.5 ▲ SO Well-used track on left.

▼ 2.6 SO Track on left.
2.3 ▲ SO Track on right.

▼ 3.0 SO Cross over creek.
1.9 ▲ SO Cross over creek.

▼ 3.1 SO Track on left.
1.8 ▲ SO Track on right.

▼ 3.2 SO Cattle guard.
1.7 ▲ SO Cattle guard.

▼ 3.4 SO Cross through wash; then track on right.
1.5 ▲ SO Track on left, then cross through wash.

▼ 3.7 SO Track on left.
1.2 ▲ SO Track on right.

▼ 4.0 SO Cross over wash; then track on right.
0.9 ▲ SO Track on left; then cross over wash.

▼ 4.1 SO Track on left; then cross through Sycamore Canyon Wash.
0.8 ▲ SO Cross through Sycamore Canyon Wash; then track on right.

GPS: N31°22.63' W110°23.45'

▼ 4.3 SO Cross through Joaquin Canyon Wash, track on

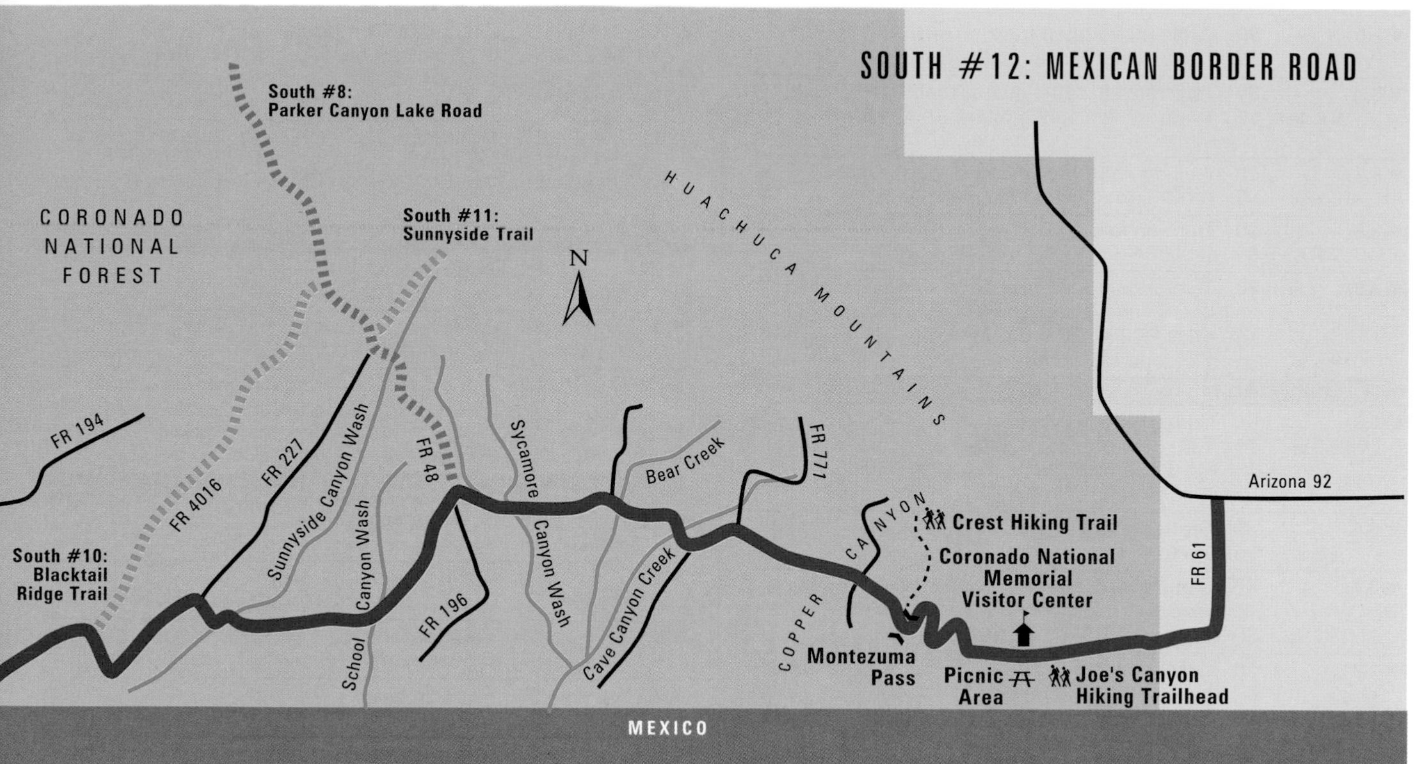

		right; then cattle guard.
0.6 ▲	SO	Cattle guard, track on left; then cross through Joaquin Canyon Wash.
▼ 4.9	TL	Graded road straight on is South #8: Parker Canyon Lake Road, FR 48. Zero trip meter.
0.0 ▲		Continue southeast following the sign for Sierra Vista.
		GPS: N31°22.79' W110°24.13'
▼ 0.0		Continue south following the sign to Nogales.
5.1 ▲	TR	Graded road on left is South #8: Parker Canyon Lake Road, FR 48. Zero trip meter.
▼ 0.1	SO	FR 196 on left goes to ranch.
5.0 ▲	SO	FR 196 on right goes to ranch.
▼ 2.2	SO	Track on left; then cattle guard, crossing through School Canyon.
2.9 ▲	SO	Cattle guard; then track on right, crossing through School Canyon.
▼ 2.3	SO	Track on right; then cross through School Canyon Wash; then track on left.
2.8 ▲	SO	Track on right; then cross through School Canyon Wash; then track on left.
		GPS: N31°21.15' W110°25.47'
▼ 2.6	SO	Track on left.
2.5 ▲	SO	Track on right.
▼ 2.8	SO	Track on right.
2.3	SO	Track on left.
▼ 3.3	SO	Track on left and track on right along fence line.
1.8 ▲	SO	Track on left and track on right along fence line.
▼ 3.8	SO	Cattle guard.
1.3 ▲	SO	Cattle guard.
▼ 4.5	SO	Cattle guard, entering Santa Cruz County.
0.6 ▲	SO	Cattle guard, entering Cochise County.
		GPS: N31°21.23' W110°27.56'
▼ 4.6	SO	Cross through Sunnyside Canyon Wash.
0.5 ▲	SO	Cross through Sunnyside Canyon Wash.
▼ 4.7	SO	Track on left.
0.4 ▲	SO	Track on right.
▼ 5.1	BL	Graded road on right is FR 227 to Parker Canyon Lake. Zero trip meter at sign and continue following the sign to Nogales.
0.0 ▲		Continue toward the Coronado National Memorial.
		GPS: N31°21.43' W110°28.04'
▼ 0.0		Continue toward Lochiel.
2.3 ▲	BR	Graded road on left is FR 227 to Parker Canyon Lake. Zero trip meter and continue following the sign to Sierra Vista.
▼ 0.1	SO	Cattle guard.
2.2 ▲	SO	Cattle guard.
▼ 0.2	SO	Track on left.
2.1 ▲	SO	Track on right.
▼ 0.5	SO	Track on right.
1.8 ▲	SO	Track on left.
▼ 1.8	SO	Cross through Bodie Canyon Wash.
0.5 ▲	SO	Cross through Bodie Canyon Wash.
		GPS: N31°20.46' W110°29.42'
▼ 2.2	SO	Track on left.
0.1 ▲	SO	Track on right.
▼ 2.3	SO	Track on right is South #10: Blacktail Ridge Trail, FR 4016. Zero trip meter.
0.0 ▲		Continue to the south.
		GPS: N31°20.91' W110°29.67'
▼ 0.0		Continue to the north.
3.9 ▲	SO	Track on left is South #10: Blacktail Ridge Trail, FR 4016. Zero trip meter.
▼ 0.6	SO	Track on right.
3.3 ▲	SO	Track on left.
▼ 1.7	SO	Track on left.
2.2 ▲	SO	Track on right.
▼ 1.9	SO	Cross through wash.
2.0 ▲	SO	Cross through wash.

▼ 2.0		SO	Cattle guard; then track on left.
	1.9 ▲	SO	Track on right; then cattle guard.
▼ 3.3		SO	Track on left, cattle guard, then track on left.
	0.6 ▲	SO	Track on right, cattle guard, then track on right.
▼ 3.7		SO	Well on right; then cross through wash.
	0.2 ▲	SO	Cross through wash; then well on left.
▼ 3.8		SO	Track on left.
	0.1 ▲	SO	Track on right.
▼ 3.9		TL	Turn onto graded road following the sign to Lochiel and Patagonia. Graded road straight on is FR 194. Zero trip meter.
	0.0 ▲		Continue to the south.
			GPS: N31°20.79′ W110°33.02′
▼ 0.0			Continue to the west.
	5.3 ▲	TR	Turn onto graded road following the sign to Parker Canyon Lake and Sierra Vista. Graded road on left is FR 194. Zero trip meter.
▼ 0.4		SO	Track on right.
	4.9 ▲	SO	Track on left.
▼ 0.7		SO	Cattle guard. Entering private land, remain on road.
	4.6 ▲	SO	Cattle guard, entering national forest.
▼ 1.8		SO	Graded road on right is FR 813, track on left is for authorized vehicles only.
	3.5 ▲	SO	Graded road on left is FR 813, track on right is for authorized vehicles only.
			GPS: N31°21.28′ W110°34.72′
▼ 2.1		SO	Cattle guard.
	3.2 ▲	SO	Cattle guard.
▼ 2.4		SO	Cross over the Santa Cruz River on bridge. Then cattle guard and track on right.
	2.9 ▲	SO	Track on left and cattle guard. Then cross over the Santa Cruz River on bridge.
			GPS: N31°21.35′ W110°35.34′
▼ 2.8		SO	Track on left is for authorized vehicles only.
	2.5 ▲	SO	Track on right is for authorized vehicles only.
▼ 3.0		SO	Cross through wash.
	2.3 ▲	SO	Cross through wash.
▼ 3.2		SO	Track on left is for authorized vehicles only.
	2.1 ▲	SO	Track on right is for authorized vehicles only.
▼ 4.0		TL	Graded road straight ahead is for authorized vehicles only. Turn left following signs for Lochiel and Nogales.
	1.3 ▲	TR	T-intersection. Graded road on left is for authorized vehicles only.
			GPS: N31°20.86′ W110°36.71′
▼ 4.3		SO	Track on left is for authorized vehicles only, then cattle guard.
	1.0 ▲	SO	Cattle guard, then track on right is for authorized vehicles only.
▼ 4.6		SO	Cattle guard.
	0.7 ▲	SO	Cattle guard.
▼ 4.7		SO	Track on left.
	0.6 ▲	SO	Track on right.
▼ 4.8		SO	Track on right.
	0.5 ▲	SO	Track on left.
▼ 5.2		SO	Cattle guard.
	0.1 ▲	SO	Cattle guard.
▼ 5.3		BR	Graded road on left is Lochiel Road, which goes 0.2 miles to Lochiel, the old customs house and border crossing. Zero trip meter.
	0.0 ▲		Continue to the east on FR 61.
			GPS: N31°20.14′ W110°37.40′
▼ 0.0			Continue to the northwest on FR 61.
	3.4 ▲	BL	Graded road on right is Lochiel Road, which goes 0.2 miles to Lochiel, the old customs house, and border crossing. Zero trip meter.
▼ 0.1		SO	Monument to Fray Marcos de Niza on left of road.
	3.3 ▲	SO	Monument to Fray Marcos de Niza on right of road.
			GPS: N31°20.35′ W110°37.60′
▼ 0.4		SO	Track on left.
	3.0 ▲	SO	Track on right.
▼ 0.6		SO	Cattle guard, entering San Antonio Ranch.
	2.8 ▲	SO	Cattle guard, leaving San Antonio Ranch.
▼ 1.6		SO	Cattle guard, entering Coronado National Forest. FR 4911 on left after cattle guard.
	1.8 ▲	SO	FR 4911 on right; then cattle guard, entering San Antonio Ranch.
			GPS: N31°21.20′ W110°38.61′
▼ 2.5		SO	Private road on right.
	0.9 ▲	SO	Private road on left.
▼ 2.9		SO	Cattle guard.
	0.5 ▲	SO	Cattle guard.
▼ 3.1		SO	Track on left.
	0.3 ▲	SO	Track on right.
▼ 3.3		SO	Track on left.
	0.1 ▲	SO	Track on right.
▼ 3.4		TL	Turn onto smaller graded road, FR 128, signed to Duquesne. Zero trip meter.
	0.0 ▲		Continue toward Lochiel.
			GPS: N31°22.06′ W110°40.13′
▼ 0.0			Continue toward Duquesne.
	1.8 ▲	TR	Turn right and rejoin FR 61.
▼ 0.1		SO	Track on left.
	1.7 ▲	SO	Track on right.
▼ 0.2		SO	Track on left and campsite on left.
	1.6 ▲	SO	Track on right and campsite on right.
▼ 0.3		SO	Cross through Washington Gulch.
	1.5 ▲	SO	Cross through Washington Gulch.
			GPS: N31°22.13′ W110°40.45′
▼ 0.8		SO	Cross through wash.
	1.0 ▲	SO	Cross through wash.
▼ 1.0		BR	Graded road on left is FR 7015, which goes past Duquesne Mine.
	0.8 ▲	BL	Graded road on right is FR 7015, which goes past Duquesne Mine.
			GPS: N31°22.19′ W110°41.07′
▼ 1.1		SO	Duquesne. Old timber houses on left and right.
	0.7 ▲	SO	Duquesne. Old timber houses on left and right.
▼ 1.2		SO	Mine on left.
	0.6 ▲	SO	Mine on right.
▼ 1.3		SO	Track on right.
	0.5 ▲	SO	Track on left.
▼ 1.8		TL	Turn left and rejoin FR 61. Zero trip meter.
	0.0 ▲		Continue toward Duquesne.
			GPS: N31°22.74′ W110°41.18′
▼ 0.0			Continue to the west.
	0.7 ▲	TR	Turn right onto graded road, FR 128, signed to Duquesne. Zero trip meter.
▼ 0.1		SO	Trail enters Washington Camp.
	0.6 ▲	SO	Leave Washington Camp.
▼ 0.4		SO	Track on left. Leave Washington Camp.
	0.3 ▲	SO	Track on right. Trail enters Washington Camp.

▼ Miles	▲ Miles	Dir	Description
▼ 0.7		BL	Graded road on right is South #13: Harshaw Road to Patagonia and Harshaw. Zero trip meter.
	0.0 ▲	SO	Continue to the southeast toward Duquesne.
			GPS: N31°23.19′ W110°41.47′
▼ 0.0			Continue to the northwest toward Nogales.
	7.7 ▲	SO	Graded road on left is South #13: Harshaw Road to Patagonia and Harshaw. Zero trip meter.
▼ 0.3		SO	Loading hopper of the Kansas Mine on left of trail, mine remains on right, below trail.
	7.4 ▲	SO	Loading hopper of the Kansas Mine on right of trail, mine remains on left, below trail.
			GPS: N31°23.22′ W110°41.80′
▼ 0.4		SO	Track on left.
	7.3 ▲	SO	Track on right.
▼ 0.5		SO	FR 4704 on right.
	7.2 ▲	SO	FR 4704 on left.
			GPS: N31°23.31′ W110°41.95′
▼ 1.3		SO	Cross through wash.
	6.4 ▲	SO	Cross through wash.
▼ 1.5		SO	Cattle guard on saddle.
	6.2 ▲	SO	Cattle guard on saddle.
			GPS: N31°23.17′ W110°42.83′
▼ 3.4		SO	FR 4695 on right.
	4.3 ▲	SO	FR 4695 on left.
			GPS: N31°23.39′ W110°44.32′
▼ 3.8		SO	FR 4677 on right.
	3.9 ▲	SO	FR 4677 on left.
			GPS: N31°23.19′ W110°44.69′
▼ 4.0		SO	Track on left, enter Sycamore Canyon.
	3.7 ▲	SO	Track on right, leave Sycamore Canyon.
▼ 4.4		SO	Cattle guard; then track on left.
	3.3 ▲	SO	Track on right; then cattle guard.
▼ 4.7		SO	FR 4675 on right.
	3.0 ▲	SO	FR 4675 on left.
			GPS: N31°22.64′ W110°45.42′
▼ 5.1		SO	Track on left is FR 4763.
	2.6 ▲	SO	Track on right is FR 4763.
▼ 5.5		SO	Cross through Sycamore Wash.
	2.2 ▲	SO	Cross through Sycamore Wash.
▼ 5.6		SO	FR 4671 on left.
	2.1 ▲	SO	FR 4671 on right.
▼ 6.1		SO	Track on left to corral, cattle guard; then FR 4668 on left. Leaving Sycamore Canyon.
	1.6 ▲	SO	Track on right is FR 4668, cattle guard; then track on right to corral. Entering Sycamore Canyon.
▼ 6.3		SO	Track on right is FR 4669.
	1.4 ▲	SO	Track on left is FR 4669.
			GPS: N31°21.82′ W110°46.52′
▼ 7.3		SO	Two tracks on left are FR 4902 followed by FR 4667.
	0.4 ▲	SO	Two tracks on right are FR 4667 followed by FR 4902.
			GPS: N31°21.85′ W110°47.51′
▼ 7.5		SO	Cattle guard; then large camping area on right.
	0.2 ▲	SO	Large camping area on left; then cattle guard.
			GPS: N31°21.92′ W110°47.80′
▼ 7.6		SO	Track on left and FR 4662 on right.
	0.1 ▲	SO	Track on right and FR 4662 on left.
			GPS: N31°21.97′ W110°47.90′
▼ 7.7		SO	Exiting the Sierra Vista Ranger District at sign. Zero trip meter.
	0.0 ▲		Continue to the east.
			GPS: N31°22.00′ W110°48.00′
▼ 0.0			Continue to the west.
	4.0 ▲	SO	Entering the Sierra Vista Ranger District at sign. Zero trip meter.
▼ 0.4		SO	Graded road on left.
	3.6 ▲	SO	Graded road on right.
▼ 1.3		SO	FR 4516 on left, leaving Coronado National Forest at sign.
	2.7 ▲	SO	Entering Coronado National Forest, then FR 4516 on right.
			GPS: N31°22.47′ W110°49.29′
▼ 1.5		SO	Cattle guard.
	2.5 ▲	SO	Cattle guard.
▼ 2.5		SO	Cross through wash.
	1.5 ▲	SO	Cross through wash.
▼ 2.6		SO	Cross through wash.
	1.4 ▲	SO	Cross through wash.
▼ 3.0		SO	Track on right, road is now paved.
	1.0 ▲	SO	Road turns to graded dirt. Track on left.
▼ 4.0			Trail ends at intersection with Arizona 82. Turn left for Nogales, turn right for Patagonia.
	0.0 ▲		Trail commences on Arizona 82 at Bayerville, 4.1 miles northeast of Nogales. Zero trip meter and turn southeast on paved road, signed Duquesne Road. Turn is next to the school, 0.1 miles south of mile marker 6 and 0.1 miles north of the Santa Cruz River Bridge.
			GPS: N31°23.30′ W110°52.29′

SOUTH REGION TRAIL #13

Harshaw Road

Starting Point:	**Arizona 82 in Patagonia**
Finishing Point:	**South #12: Mexican Border Road at Washington Camp, 12.3 miles from the eastern end of the trail**
Total Mileage:	**15.6 miles**
Unpaved Mileage:	**9.9 miles**
Driving Time:	**1 hour**
Elevation Range:	**4,100–5,600 feet**
Usually Open:	**Year-round**
Best Time to Travel:	**October to May**
Difficulty Rating:	**1**
Scenic Rating:	**7**
Remoteness Rating:	**+0**

Special Attractions

- Harshaw town site and cemetery.
- Views to the south over the grasslands toward Mexico.
- Trail can be combined with either South #14: Flux Canyon Trail or South #12: Mexican Border Road for an interesting day's drive.

Adobe ruin at Harshaw ghost town

History

Harshaw sprang up in 1877 principally because of the Hermosa Mine, discovered by a rancher, David Tecumseh Harshaw. Harshaw used to graze cattle on Apache land and was asked to relocate. He moved his herd to the valley around what is now Harshaw. While tending his cattle, David discovered the rich silver vein that became the Hermosa Mine. Soon after operations began, 150 men and a 20-stamp mill were employed. The town at one time had 30 buildings ranging from hotels and saloons to stores, blacksmith shops, and corrals. Flooding, a major fire, and the closing of the Hermosa Mine in 1881 quieted Harshaw for a while, but it persisted until the early 1900s.

The surrounding area was rich in silver and lead. One of the most famous mines in the region was the Patagonia, which dated back to Spanish times. Army Lt. Sylvester Mowry, known for his flamboyance, left the military and bought the mine in 1859, changing the name to the Mowry Mine. Under Mowry's leadership in the early 1860s, it was one of the richest mines in the nation, producing $1.5 million of silver and lead and employing more than 100 workers. Mowry was arrested as a Confederate sympathizer during the Civil War and jailed in Fort Yuma. Meanwhile, his mine was pillaged, and Mowry spent the rest of his life trying to raise capital in the East and Europe to refurbish and reopen the looted mine. Apache wars closed most mining in the area in the late 1860s, but Harshaw and other mining camps and towns in the area, including Washington Camp and Duquesne thrived again in the last years of the nineteenth century before finally petering out in the early 1900s.

A graded section of the trail in the Patagonia Mountains

Description

This road is wide, graded, and easygoing; in dry weather, passenger vehicles can enjoy the varied scenery found along its length. The trail commences in the picturesque small town of Patagonia, where you can top up with fuel, enjoy a meal at one of several cafes, or purchase food for a picnic. The information center housed in the old railroad station is worth a visit.

The road initially is paved as it leaves Patagonia and enters the forest, running alongside Harshaw Creek, which is lined with sycamores and cottonwoods. This route is well traveled and you are likely to see many people enjoying a shady picnic alongside the creek. The town site of Harshaw is encountered after 7.5 miles. There are the remains of an adobe building on the corner, and opposite by a large parking area is the cemetery. There are many interesting stories pertaining to the lives of the pioneers of the region on the grave markers.

From Harshaw, the road continues south through the forest, passing many trails that invite exploration, including South #14: Flux Canyon Trail, and a turn to the old mine at Mowry, before descending slowly down to join South #12: Mexican Border Road at Washington Camp. From here the exit to the highway is via the Mexican Border Road. The shortest way out is to turn right to Nogales.

Current Road Information

Coronado National Forest
Sierra Vista Ranger District
5990 South Hwy 92
Hereford, AZ 85615
(520) 378-0311

Map References

BLM Fort Huachuca, Nogales
USFS Coronado National Forest: Nogales and Sierra Vista Ranger Districts
USGS 1:24,000 Patagonia, Mt. Hughes, Harshaw
1:100,000 Fort Huachuca, Nogales
Maptech CD-ROM: Southeast Arizona/Tucson
Arizona Atlas & Gazetteer, p. 73
Arizona Road & Recreation Atlas, p. 54 & p. 88
Recreational Map of Arizona

Route Directions

▼ 0.0		In Patagonia on Arizona 82 at the old Patagonia Railroad Station, zero trip meter and turn southeast on 3rd Avenue and then immediately left on McKeown Avenue.
3.0 ▲		Turn right onto 3rd Avenue in Patagonia, then the trail ends at the intersection with Arizona 82 in the center of town. Turn right for Sonoita, turn left for Nogales.
		GPS: N31°32.44′ W110°45.15′
▼ 0.2	SO	Road becomes Harshaw Avenue and swings east.
2.8 ▲	SO	Road becomes McKeown Avenue.
▼ 1.2	SO	Cross over creek on bridge, then Red Rock Drive on left.

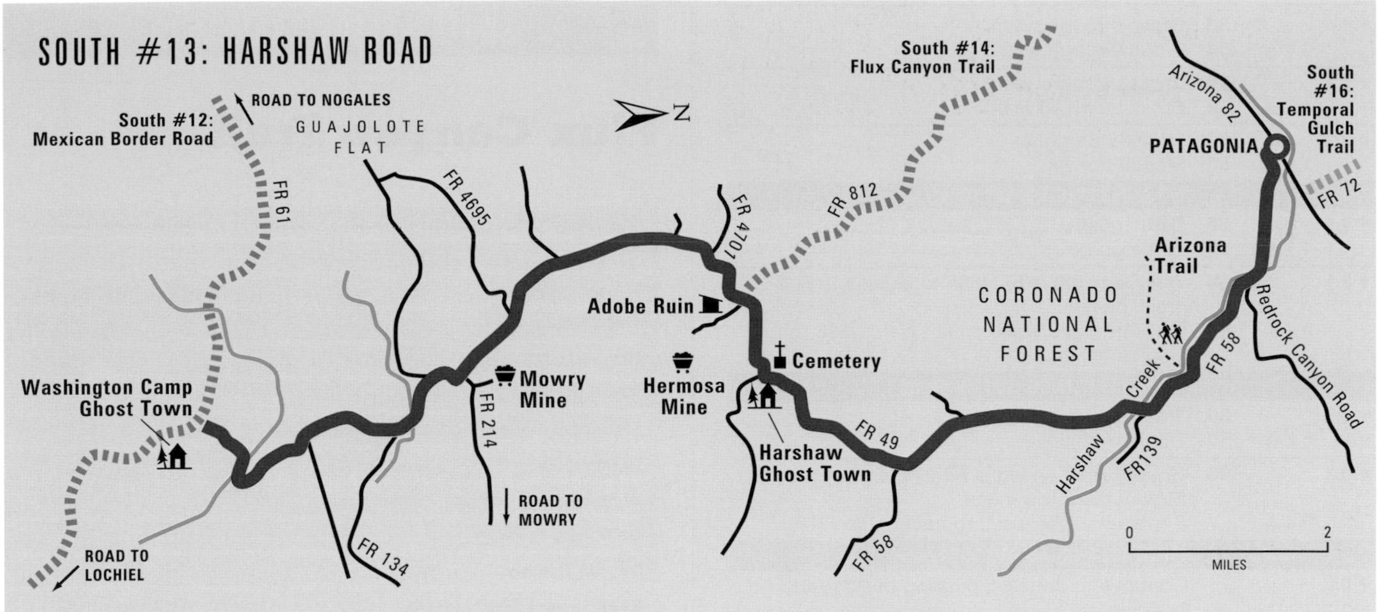

1.8 ▲ SO Red Rock Drive on right; then cross over creek on bridge.

▼ 1.3 SO Redrock Canyon Road on left.
1.7 ▲ SO Redrock Canyon Road on right.

▼ 1.8 SO Cattle guard; then graded road on left.
1.2 ▲ SO Graded road on right; then cattle guard.

▼ 2.6 SO Cattle guard.
0.4 ▲ SO Cattle guard.

▼ 2.7 SO Entering the Coronado National Forest. Track on right is trailhead and parking area for the Arizona Trail.
0.3 ▲ SO Track on left is trailhead and parking area for the Arizona Trail. Leaving the Coronado National Forest.

GPS: N31°31.62' W110°42.65'

▼ 2.8 SO Cattle guard.
0.2 ▲ SO Cattle guard.

▼ 3.0 BR Graded road on left is FR 139. Bear right, remaining on paved road. Zero trip meter.
0.0 ▲ Continue to the northwest.

GPS: N31°31.52' W110°42.43'

▼ 0.0 Continue to the southeast and cross over Harshaw Creek on bridge.
2.7 ▲ SO Cross over Harshaw Creek on bridge, then graded road on right is FR 139. Bear left, remaining on paved road. Zero trip meter.

▼ 0.2 SO Cattle guard.
2.5 ▲ SO Cattle guard.

▼ 1.5 SO Well on right; then cattle guard. Road is now FR 58.
1.2 ▲ SO Cattle guard; then well on left.

▼ 1.7 SO Track on right.
1.0 ▲ SO Track on left.

▼ 2.7 TR Road turns to graded dirt, then turn right onto large graded dirt road FR 49, sign-posted to Harshaw and Lochiel. Zero trip meter. FR 58 continues ahead. Entering private land.
0.0 ▲ Continue to the northwest. Road becomes paved.

GPS: N31°29.32' W110° 41.52'

▼ 0.0 Continue to the southwest and cross over wash.
2.5 ▲ TL Cross over wash; then T-intersection, turn left onto large graded dirt road FR 58, to Patagonia. Road immediately becomes paved. Re-entering the national forest. Zero trip meter.

▼ 0.5 SO Cattle guard.
2.0 ▲ SO Cattle guard.

▼ 0.6 SO Cross through wash.
1.9 ▲ SO Cross through wash.

▼ 1.1 SO Cattle guard.
1.4 ▲ SO Cattle guard.

▼ 1.8 SO Track on left. The old site of Harshaw is at the intersection, marked by an adobe ruin. Harshaw Cemetery is on the right off the large parking area.
0.7 ▲ SO Track on right. The old site of Harshaw is at the intersection, marked by an adobe ruin. Harshaw Cemetery is on the left off the large parking area.

GPS: N31°28.07' W110°42.44'

▼ 2.5 SO Cattle guard, then track on right is South #14: Flux Canyon Road (FR 812). Zero trip meter at sign.
0.0 ▲ Continue to the northeast toward Patagonia on FR 49.

GPS: N31°27.90' W110°43.13'

▼ 0.0 Continue to the southwest toward Lochiel on FR 49.
3.8 ▲ SO Track on left is South #14: Flux Canyon Road (FR 812), then cattle guard. Zero trip meter at sign.

▼ 0.1 SO Adobe ruin on left; then track on left.
3.7 ▲ SO Track on right; then adobe ruin on right.

▼ 0.3 SO Cross through wash.
3.5 ▲ SO Cross through wash.

▼ 0.5 SO Cattle guard.
3.3 ▲ SO Cattle guard.

▼ 0.6 SO Cross through wash.
3.2 ▲ SO Cross through wash.

▼ 0.7 SO Track on right is FR 4701.
3.1 ▲ SO Track on left is FR 4701.

▼ 0.9 SO Cross through wash.
2.9 ▲ SO Cross through wash.

▼ 1.1 SO Track on right.
2.7 ▲ SO Track on left.

▼ 1.4		SO	Cross through wash.
	2.4 ▲	SO	Cross through wash.
▼ 2.2		SO	Cross through wash.
	1.6 ▲	SO	Cross through wash.
▼ 2.3		SO	FR 4698 on right.
	1.5 ▲	SO	FR 4698 on left.
			GPS: N31°26.19' W110°43.42'
▼ 2.5		SO	Cattle guard.
	1.3 ▲	SO	Cattle guard.
▼ 3.1		SO	Track on right is FR 4695 to Guajolote Flat. Track on left.
	0.7 ▲	SO	Track on right. Track on left is FR 4695 to Guajolote Flat.
			GPS: N31°25.86' W110°42.86'
▼ 3.6		SO	Track on left.
	0.2 ▲	SO	Track on right.
▼ 3.8		SO	Graded road on left is FR 214, sign-posted to Mowry. Zero trip meter.
	0.0 ▲		Continue to the west, remaining on FR 49.
			GPS: N31°25.46' W110°42.27'
▼ 0.0			Continue to the east, passing beside ranch buildings.
	3.6 ▲	SO	Pass beside ranch buildings, then graded road on right is FR 214, sign-posted to Mowry. Zero trip meter.
▼ 0.4		BL	FR 4695A on right through gate.
	3.2 ▲	BR	FR 4695A on left through gate.
			GPS: N31°25.16' W110°42.16'
▼ 0.8		SO	Cross through wash.
	2.8 ▲	SO	Cross through wash.
▼ 0.9		SO	Track on left.
	2.7 ▲	SO	Track on right.
▼ 1.0		SO	FR 134 on left.
	2.6 ▲	SO	FR 134 on right.
			GPS: N31°24.89' W110°41.58'
▼ 1.7		SO	Cattle guard; then FR 5589 on right and track on left.
	1.9 ▲	SO	FR 5589 on left and track on right; then cattle guard.
			GPS: N31°24.37' W110°41.67'
▼ 2.0		SO	Track on right.
	1.6 ▲	SO	Track on left.
▼ 2.1		SO	Track on left.
	1.5 ▲	SO	Track on right.
▼ 2.2		SO	Track on left through gate.
	1.4 ▲	SO	Track on right through gate.
▼ 2.3		SO	Track on left.
	1.3 ▲	SO	Track on right.
▼ 2.9		SO	Track on left; then cross through wash.
	0.7 ▲	SO	Cross through wash; then track on right.
▼ 3.0		SO	Track on right.
	0.6 ▲	SO	Track on left.
▼ 3.5		SO	Cattle guard.
	0.1 ▲	SO	Cattle guard.
▼ 3.6			Trail ends at the intersection with South #12: Mexican Border Road, FR 61, immediately west of Washington Camp. Turn right for Nogales, turn left for Lochiel.
	0.0 ▲		Trail starts on South #12: Mexican Border Road, FR 61, on the west side of Washington Camp, 12.3 miles from the eastern end of the trail. Zero trip meter and turn north on graded dirt road at the sign for Patagonia. The road is marked as Harshaw Road and FR 61.
			GPS: N31°23.18' W110°41.47'

SOUTH REGION TRAIL #14

Flux Canyon Trail

Starting Point:	**South #13: Harshaw Road, 8.2 miles from Patagonia**
Finishing Point:	**Arizona 82, 2.0 miles south of Patagonia**
Total Mileage:	**6.9 miles**
Unpaved Mileage:	**6.9 miles**
Driving Time:	**1 hour**
Elevation Range:	**4,000–7,000 feet**
Usually Open:	**Year-round**
Best Time to Travel:	**Year-round**
Difficulty Rating:	**4**
Scenic Rating:	**8**
Remoteness Rating:	**+0**

Special Attractions

- Views down Alum Gulch.
- Many mining remains.
- Easy trail that winds through the Patagonia Mountains.

History

The mines along this trail were mainly associated with Harshaw. One of them, the World's Fair Mine, was a big operation, but probably due to the steep terrain had no permanent settlement. Instead, the mine workers lived in nearby settlements.

Legendary Jesuit missionary, Padre Eusebio Francisco Kino was active throughout this area, first visiting local Indian villages in 1692. However, the locale was the scene of much strife between the Apache and Pima Indians, with the Pima eventually being forced farther west toward Tucson. Two or three

Near the beginning of the route bordered by private property

miles southwest of Patagonia was the site of the Indian village of Sonoita, not to be confused with the present-day town. Sonoita is a Papago word meaning "place where corn will grow." In 1701 the Jesuits established the mission of San Gabriel de Guevavi near Sonoita. Under Chief Coro, the Sobaipuri Indians had moved there after abandoning villages a few miles away at Quiburi and Santa Cruz for fear of retaliation by the Apache, whom they had earlier defeated.

One of early Arizona's most colorful characters, Irishman James "Paddy" Graydon, operated a saloon, the U.S. Boundary Hotel, about 10 miles north of Patagonia in the 1850s, near Fort Buchanan. Graydon, a former U.S. cavalryman, immigrated to America from Ireland in 1853 and wound up in the Sonoita area after a stint with the cavalry in New Mexico Territory. At his hotel, Graydon provided enlisted men with everything from prostitutes to sardines and was a self-appointed regulator of law and order in times of strife. He was part of a hunting party that chased down a band of Indians who were led by Cochise and accused of stealing a Mexican boy from the ranch of another Irishman, John Ward. After much bloodshed, it turned out that Cochise's band was not guilty. The boy had grown up among the Pinal Indians and was one of General Crook's foremost "Apache" scouts during the Geronimo campaign of the 1880s. There is a historical marker on Arizona 82 to mark the event. When the Civil War broke out, Fort Buchanan was abandoned and Graydon rejoined the U.S. Army as captain of an independent spy unit that operated behind Confederate lines. However, he never returned to his hotel. He died in a gunfight at Fort Stanton, New Mexico, a few months after the Civil War battle of Valverde.

Description

This trail passes through the Harshaw mining district, alongside many of the mines associated with the town of Harshaw. In addition, the trail travels in or above the deep canyons of Flux Canyon and Alum Gulch. The trail climbs up from South #13: Harshaw Road along Alum Gulch, past rugged, red mountain scenery. The first section of the trail passes through private property, before re-entering Coronado National Forest as it climbs toward the saddle separating Alum Gulch from Flux Canyon. This first section of the trail is easygoing, roughly graded road as it winds past the tailings piles and adits of the Blue Eagle and World's Fair Mines, both large producers in their time.

Part of the trail around Alum Gulch and Flux Canyon follows an easy shelf road with ample width for one vehicle and plenty of passing places. As the trail descends toward Arizona 82, it starts to merit its 4-difficulty rating. The trail is steep and the surface is loose enough that 4WD is required for traction.

The trail finishes by running alongside Alum Gulch again, passing through a few houses before exiting onto the highway, a couple of miles south of Patagonia.

Current Road Information

Coronado National Forest
Sierra Vista Ranger District
5990 South Hwy 92
Hereford, AZ 85615
(520) 378-0311

The trail becomes more difficult as it climbs out of Alum Gulch

Map References

BLM Nogales, Fort Huachuca
USFS Coronado National Forest: Nogales and Sierra Vista Ranger Districts
USGS 1:24,000 Harshaw, Cumero Canyon, Patagonia
1:100,000 Nogales, Fort Huachuca
Maptech CD-ROM: Southeast Arizona/Tucson
Arizona Atlas & Gazetteer, p. 73
Arizona Road & Recreation Atlas, p. 54 & p. 88

Route Directions

▼ 0.0			From South #13: Harshaw Road, 0.7 miles south of Harshaw town site and 8.2 miles south of Patagonia, zero trip meter and turn northwest on the roughly graded trail, FR 812 at the sign for Flux Canyon.
	3.2 ▲		Trail ends at the intersection with South #13: Harshaw Road, 0.7 miles south of Harshaw town site. Turn left for Patagonia, turn right for Washington Camp and South #12: Mexican Border Road.
			GPS: N31°27.90' W110°43.13'
▼ 1.1		SO	Cattle guard.
	2.1 ▲	SO	Cattle guard.
			GPS: N31°28.16' W110°43.66'
▼ 1.2		BL	Cross through wash; then track on right.
	2.0 ▲	BR	Track on left; then cross through wash.
▼ 1.3		SO	Track on right.
	1.9 ▲	BR	Track on left.
▼ 1.5		BR	FR 4685 on left.
	1.7 ▲	SO	FR 4685 on right.
			GPS: N31°28.41' W110°43.96'
▼ 2.1		BL	Track on right to World's Fair Mine—concrete foundations and tailings.
	1.1 ▲	SO	Track on left to World's Fair Mine—concrete foundations and tailings.
			GPS: N31°28.78' W110°44.19'
▼ 3.1		SO	Adit on left.
	0.1 ▲	SO	Adit on right.
▼ 3.2		BR	FR 215 on left. Zero trip meter.
	0.0 ▲		Continue to the northeast.
			GPS: N31°29.19' W110°44.78'
▼ 0.0			Continue to the west.
	2.4 ▲	BL	FR 215 on right. Zero trip meter.
▼ 0.1		BR	Track on left is gated. Cross saddle and start to run down the side of Flux Canyon.

	2.3 ▲	SO	Cross saddle and start to run alongside Alum Gulch.
▼ 0.7		SO	Track on left goes to the Flux Mine.
	1.7 ▲	BL	Track on right goes to the Flux Mine.
			GPS: N31°29.38' W110°45.29'
▼ 0.8		SO	Track on right.
	1.6 ▲	BR	Track on left.
▼ 1.1		SO	Mine shaft below track on right is part of the Blue Eagle Mine.
	1.3 ▲	SO	Mine shaft below track on left is part of the Blue Eagle Mine.
			GPS: N31°29.70' W110°45.48'
▼ 1.4		SO	Cattle guard. Exiting national forest.
	1.0 ▲	SO	Sign for FR 812. Entering national forest.
▼ 1.9		SO	Cattle guard.
	0.5 ▲	SO	Cattle guard.
▼ 2.3		SO	Cattle guard.
	0.1 ▲	SO	Cattle guard.
▼ 2.4		SO	Join larger graded dirt road. Zero trip meter
	0.0 ▲		Continue to the east.
			GPS: N31°30.24' W110°46.12'
▼ 0.0			Continue to the west.
	1.3 ▲	BR	Bear right onto smaller roughly graded dirt road and zero trip meter. Intersection is unmarked.
▼ 0.1		SO	Graded road on right. Trail follows along the lower end of Alum Gulch.
	1.2 ▲	SO	Graded road on left.
▼ 0.7		SO	Cross through two washes.
	0.6 ▲	SO	Cross through two washes.
▼ 0.9		SO	Cross through wash.
	0.4 ▲	SO	Cross through wash.
▼ 1.0		SO	Cross through wash.
	0.3 ▲	SO	Cross through wash.
			GPS: N31°30.65' W110°47.00'
▼ 1.3			Cattle guard, then trail ends at intersection with Arizona 82. Turn right for Patagonia, left for Nogales.
	0.0 ▲		Trail commences on Arizona 82, 2.0 miles south of Patagonia, 0.1 miles south of mile marker 17. Zero trip meter and turn south on graded dirt road marked Flux Canyon Road and cross cattle guard. Initially the trail crosses private property.
			GPS: N31°30.94' W110°47.04'

SOUTH REGION TRAIL #15

Cumero Canyon—Three R Canyon Trail

Starting Point:	**Arizona 82, 7.5 miles northeast of Nogales**
Finishing Point:	**Arizona 82, 4.2 miles south of Patagonia**
Total Mileage:	**9 miles**
Unpaved Mileage:	**9 miles**
Driving Time:	**1.5 hours**
Elevation Range:	**3,900–4,600 feet**
Usually Open:	**Year-round**
Best Time to Travel:	**September to June**
Difficulty Rating:	**3**
Scenic Rating:	**7**
Remoteness Rating:	**+0**

Special Attractions

- Tres de Mayo Mine.
- Winding trail along the western edge of the Patagonia Mountains.

Description

This pleasant trail winds along the western side of the Patagonia Mountains and offers beautiful views of the mountains as well as good backcountry camping opportunities.

Both ends of the trail cross private land; access is granted under the Sportsman Landowners respect program. Please stay on the trail and leave gates as you find them. Continued access to the trail depends on responsible trail behavior.

Once in the Coronado National Forest, the standard drops slightly and the small, well-formed trail is rougher as it undulates through open vegetation, mainly grasslands and scattered mesquite; it is not brushy to the sides of a vehicle. The trail then travels up a ridge alongside Cumero Canyon before crossing over to descend down Maggies Canyon, Cox Gulch,

Shrine of the Telles family near the northern end of the trail

and finally, the well-used Three R Canyon. Navigation is easy as the major tracks have national forest route markers on them. The trail is marked on the Coronado Forest Map as FR 235 and FR 215, but the section that connects Maggies Canyon with Cox Gulch is not shown.

Approximately halfway along the trail the Tres de Mayo Mine can be reached up a short, 4-rated spur to the west. There are some stone foundations at the mine, a well, and a very deep shaft.

The historic site of Johnny Ward's Ranch is located 1.5 miles north of the northern end of the trail along Arizona 82. This early ranching pioneer had a ranch here from 1858 to 1903. A plaque sits below the family shrine of the Telles family. Started in 1941 in exchange for the safety of their sons in war, the shrine is maintained to this day.

Current Road Information

Coronado National Forest
Sierra Vista Ranger District
5990 South Hwy 92
Hereford, AZ 85615
(520) 378-0311

Map References

BLM Nogales
USFS Coronado National Forest: Nogales and Sierra Vista Ranger Districts
USGS 1:24,000 Cumero Canyon
1:100,000 Nogales
Maptech CD-ROM: Southeast Arizona/Tucson
Arizona Atlas & Gazetteer, p. 73
Arizona Road & Recreation Atlas, p. 54 & p. 88

Route Directions

▼	▲		
▼ 0.0			From Arizona 82, 7.5 miles northeast of Nogales, 0.2 miles north of mile marker 9, zero trip meter and turn northeast on unmarked, formed, red dirt road, marked FR 235, and cross cattle guard. Immediately the trail forks, bear left, passing designated access sign. Trail is crossing private property.
	1.5 ▲		Trail ends on Arizona 82. Turn left for Nogales, turn right for Patagonia.
			GPS: N31°25.65' W110°50.55'
▼ 1.1		SO	Cattle guard, entering Coronado National Forest.
	0.4 ▲	SO	Cattle guard, trail crosses into private property.
			GPS: N31°25.72' W110°49.48'
▼ 1.5		BL	Track on right is marked Paloma Road, FR 4659. Zero trip meter.
	0.0 ▲		Continue to the west.
			GPS: N31°25.76' W110°49.03'
▼ 0.0			Continue to the east.
	2.5 ▲	SO	Track on left is marked Paloma Road, FR 4659. Zero trip meter.
▼ 0.7		BR	Track on left is FR 4658; then corral on right.
	1.8 ▲	BL	Corral on left; then track on right is FR 4658.
			GPS: N31°25.96' W110°48.37'
▼ 0.8		SO	Track on right.
	1.7 ▲	SO	Track on left.
▼ 1.2		BL	Cross through wash, bear left following sign for Three R Canyon, remaining on FR 235. Track on right is FR 4680.
	1.3 ▲	BR	Track on left is FR 4680, bear right and cross through wash.
			GPS: N31°26.14' W110°47.81'
▼ 1.7		BL	Campsite on right, bear left and cross through Cumero Canyon Wash.
	0.8 ▲	BR	Cross through Cumero Canyon Wash, bear right upon exit, campsite on left.
			GPS: N31°26.35' W110°47.50'
▼ 1.9		BL	Track on right.
	0.6 ▲	BR	Track on left.
▼ 2.1		SO	Cross through wash.
	0.4 ▲	SO	Cross through wash.
▼ 2.4		SO	Cross through wash.
	0.1 ▲	SO	Cross through wash.
▼ 2.5		BR	Track on left is FR 4658 which goes 0.4 miles to Tres de Mayo well and mine. Trail continues past the mine. Zero trip meter.
	0.0 ▲		Continue to the southeast.
			GPS: N31°26.85' W110°47.67'
▼ 0.0			Continue to the east.
	2.3 ▲	BL	Track on right is FR 4658 which goes 0.4 miles to Tres de Mayo well and mine. Trail continues past the mine. Zero trip meter.
▼ 0.5		SO	Cross through wash.
	1.8 ▲	SO	Cross through wash.
▼ 0.9		SO	Cross through wash.
	1.4 ▲	SO	Cross through wash.

Crossing the Three R Canyon Wash

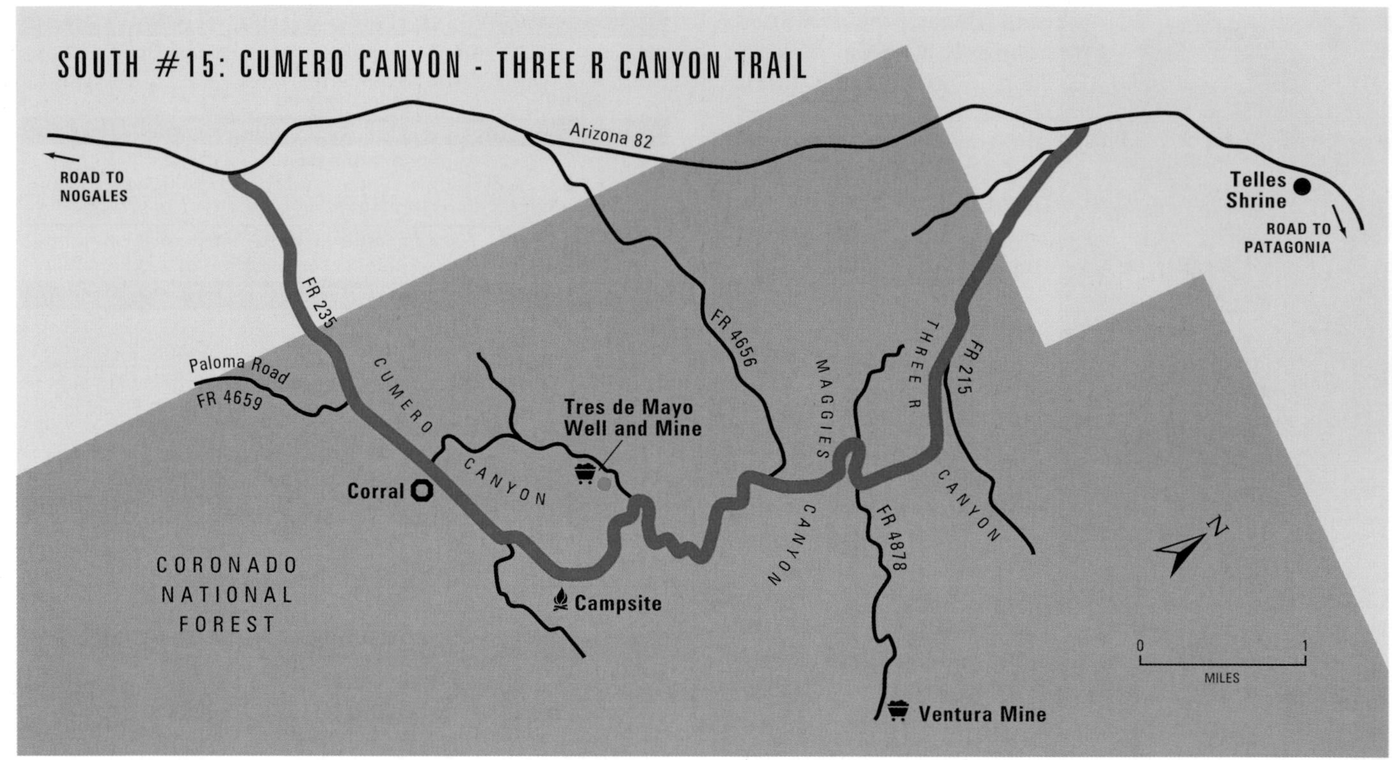

GPS: N31°27.27' W110°47.45'

▼ 1.0 SO Track on right to campsite.
1.3 ▲ SO Track on left to campsite.

▼ 1.4 SO Small track on left is FR 4656.
0.9 ▲ SO Small track on right is FR 4656.

GPS: N31°27.54' W110°47.44'

▼ 1.5 SO Gate. Entering into the top end of Maggies Canyon.
0.8 ▲ SO Gate. Leaving Maggies Canyon.

▼ 1.8 SO Cross through wash.
0.5 ▲ SO Cross through wash.

▼ 1.9 SO Cross through wash.
0.4 ▲ SO Cross through wash.

▼ 2.1 BR Closed track on left.
0.2 ▲ BL Closed track on right.

GPS: N31°28.02' W110°47.41'

▼ 2.3 TL T-intersection. Track on right is FR 4878, which goes up Cox Gulch toward Ventura Mine. Zero trip meter.
0.0 ▲ Continue to the west.

GPS: N31°27.95' W110°47.18'

▼ 0.0 Continue to the north.
2.7 ▲ TR Turn right remaining on main trail. Track straight on is FR 4878, which goes up Cox Gulch toward Ventura Mine. Zero trip meter.

▼ 0.8 SO Cross through Three R Canyon Wash.
1.9 ▲ SO Cross through Three R Canyon Wash.

GPS: N31°28.51' W110°47.46'

▼ 1.1 SO Cross through wash. Trail is following alongside wash in Three R Canyon.
1.6 ▲ SO Cross through wash.

▼ 1.2 TL Turn left and cross through wash. Track on right is FR 215, which travels up Three R Canyon. Small track ahead.
1.5 ▲ TR Cross through wash and turn right at sign onto FR 235, sign-posted to Palomas Mesa. FR 215 continues ahead to Three R Canyon. Small track on left.

GPS: 31°28.69' W110°47.72'

▼ 1.4 SO Cross through wash. Track on right up wash is closed, track on left is FR 4653.
1.3 ▲ SO Cross through wash. Track on left up wash is closed, track on right is FR 4653.

GPS: N31°28.83' W110°47.91'

▼ 1.5 SO Cross through wash.
1.2 ▲ SO Cross through wash.

▼ 1.6 SO Track on left to concrete foundations; then cross through wash.
1.1 ▲ SO Cross through wash; then track on right to concrete foundations.

▼ 1.8 SO Cross through wash.
0.9 ▲ SO Cross through wash.

▼ 1.9 SO Cattle guard, leaving Coronado National Forest, then cross through wash. Road is now graded dirt as it crosses private land.
0.8 ▲ SO Cross through wash then cattle guard, entering Coronado National Forest. Trail is marked FR 215. Road is now formed trail.

GPS: N31°29.11' W110°48.16'

▼ 2.3 SO Cross through wash.
0.4 ▲ SO Cross through wash.

▼ 2.6 SO Track on left; then cross through wash.
0.1 ▲ SO Cross through wash; then track on right. Trail is following alongside wash in Three R Canyon.

▼ 2.7 Trail ends at junction with Arizona 82. Turn left for Nogales, turn right for Patagonia.
0.0 ▲ Trail commences on Arizona 82, 4.2 miles south of Patagonia, 0.3 miles south of mile marker 15. Zero trip meter and turn southeast across cattle guard on graded dirt road. Trail initially crosses private property and is marked FR 215.

GPS: N31°29.80' W110°48.62'

SOUTH REGION TRAIL #16

Temporal Gulch Trail

Starting Point:	**Arizona 82 in Patagonia**
Finishing Point:	**Walker Basin**
Total Mileage:	**11.7 miles**
Unpaved Mileage:	**11.2 miles**
Driving Time:	**1.5 hours (one-way)**
Elevation Range:	**4,100–5,800 feet**
Usually Open:	**Year-round**
Best Time to Travel:	**Year-round**
Difficulty Rating:	**5**
Scenic Rating:	**9**
Remoteness Rating:	**+0**

Special Attractions

- Extremely scenic Temporal Gulch.
- Prolific bird life.
- Trail travels along a section of the Arizona Trail.
- Views over Temporal Gulch, the Patagonia Mountains, and Mt. Wrightson.

Description

This spur trail travels through one of the most scenic and varied canyons in the Santa Rita Mountains. The fantastic views and moderately challenging trail, coupled with excellent backcountry camping and birding opportunities, combine to make this trail a favorite among many.

The trail departs the picturesque town of Patagonia, and for the first 6.1 miles is well-graded dirt, as it travels through the open grasslands alongside Gringo Gulch and into Coronado National Forest.

The trail travels along a section of the Arizona Trail; at the parking area and information boards for the hiking trail, the vehicle trail drops in standard to become a lumpy, formed trail.

The scenery is spectacular as you climb up Temporal Gulch, which offers views of the extremely pretty canyon as well as more far-reaching views to Mt. Wrightson. There are rough spots on the trail at this stage as it winds along the canyon. Campers should note that there are excellent shady campsites under large cottonwoods in the first mile past the hiking trailhead. These are the best sites along the trail. Further up they become fewer and farther between.

The trail crosses back and forth through the wash in Temporal Gulch

Natural rock tanks above the dam at the end of the trail in Walker Basin

After 3.7 miles, the trail leaves Temporal Gulch and climbs up along a steep shelf road toward Walker Basin. On the return trip, this section gives excellent views back over the gulch to the Patagonia Mountains. Bird watchers may see the vermilion flycatcher and Strickland's woodpecker, among others.

After crossing a small saddle, the trail descends along the side of the wooded Walker Canyon. It descends steeply along a well-formed trail to finish in Walker Basin. There is a series of natural tanks in the creek at the end of the trail, just above a small concrete dam. The trail continues for 0.2 miles to the wilderness boundary where all vehicle travel must stop. The final 0.2 miles are extremely steep and are beyond the scope of this book.

The major difficulties of the trail are the steep low-traction climbs out of Temporal Gulch into Walker Basin and back out again. In spring and summer, Temporal Gulch can have water in it; 12 inches is not uncommon after summer rains. Although the latter part of the trail passes through woodland, the trail is wide and is not brushy for any vehicle. This trail is also popular with mountain bikers.

Current Road Information

Coronado National Forest
Nogales Ranger District
303 Old Tucson Road
Nogales, AZ 85621
(520) 281-2296

Map References

BLM Fort Huachuca
USFS Coronado National Forest: Nogales and Sierra Vista Ranger Districts
USGS 1:24,000 Mt. Hughes, Patagonia, Mt. Wrightson
1:100,000 Fort Huachuca
Maptech CD-ROM: Southeast Arizona/Tucson
Arizona Atlas & Gazetteer, p. 73
Arizona Road & Recreation Atlas, p. 54 & p. 88
Recreational Map of Arizona

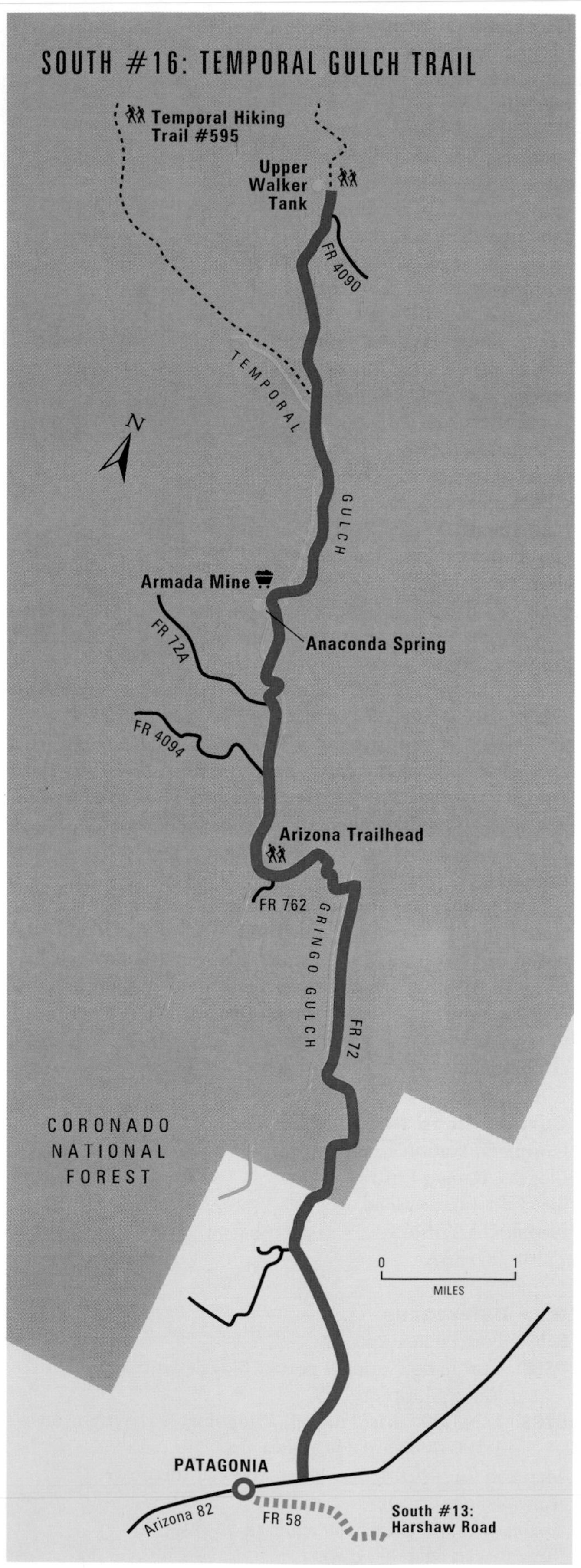

Route Directions

▼ 0.0		From Arizona 82 in Patagonia, zero trip meter and turn northwest on 1st Avenue, 0.2 miles north of the town center. Road is paved and leads off south of the high school. Remain on 1st Avenue, ignoring turns to the right and left.
		GPS: N31°32.64' W110°44.85'
▼ 0.5	SO	Cattle guard. Road is now graded dirt.
▼ 0.8	SO	Cross through wash.
▼ 1.0	SO	Cattle guard.
▼ 1.9	BR	Graded road on left.
		GPS: N31°33.99' W110°45.67'
▼ 2.2	SO	Two tracks on right.
▼ 2.3	SO	Entering Coronado National Forest over cattle guard. Zero trip meter. Road is now marked as FR 72.
		GPS: N31°34.35' W110°45.67'
▼ 0.0		Continue to the north.
▼ 0.9	SO	Track on right.
▼ 1.3	SO	Cattle guard; then track on right.
▼ 2.2	SO	Track on right.
▼ 2.7	SO	Cross through wash, climb out of Gringo Gulch.
▼ 2.9	SO	Cattle guard.
		GPS: N31°36.21' W110°46.57'
▼ 3.6	SO	FR 762 on left. FR 72 continues straight ahead.
		GPS: N31°36.12' W110°47.05'
▼ 3.8	BL	Cattle guard; then Arizona trailhead parking on right. Information boards. Zero trip meter.
		GPS: N31°36.17' W110°47.20'
▼ 0.0		Continue to the northwest. Trail drops in standard and becomes a formed trail.
▼ 0.1	SO	Cross through wash.
▼ 0.3	SO	Cross through wash.
▼ 0.5	SO	Cross through wash; then track on left is FR 4094; then cross through wash again.
▼ 0.6	SO	Cross through wash.
▼ 0.8	SO	Cattle guard.
▼ 0.9	SO	Cross through wash, track on left to campsite, then second track on left is FR 72A. Route marker at junction. Zero trip meter.
		GPS: N31°36.92' W110°47.46'
▼ 0.0		Continue to the north and cross through wash.
▼ 0.1	SO	Two tracks on right to private property; then well on left.
		GPS: N31°37.05' W110°47.51'
▼ 0.3	SO	Adit on right of trail.
▼ 0.4	SO	Cross through wash.
▼ 0.5	SO	Cross through wash.
		GPS: N31°37.27' W110°47.72'
▼ 0.6	SO	Cross through wash.
▼ 1.0	SO	Cross through wash. Anaconda Spring on left, then the Armada Mine on left.
		GPS: N31°37.65' W110°47.93'
▼ 1.2	SO	Cross through wash; then mine on left.
		GPS: N31°37.78' W110°47.96'
▼ 1.3	SO	Cross through wash.
▼ 1.4	SO	Faint track on right. Canyon becomes wider.
▼ 1.5	SO	Cross through wash.
▼ 1.6	SO	Cross through wash.
▼ 1.7	SO	Track on left.
		GPS: N31°38.18' W110°47.90'
▼ 2.2	SO	Cross through wash.
▼ 2.3	SO	Cross through wash.
▼ 2.4	SO	Cross through two washes.
▼ 2.6	SO	Cross through two washes; then track on left to campsite.

▼ 2.7	SO	Cross through wash. Sign on left for Temporal hiking trail #595 to Mt. Wrightson, 9.4 miles. The Arizona Trail continues along the main trail and climbs out of Temporal Gulch along shelf road.
		GPS: N31°38.92' W110°48.31'
▼ 2.9	SO	Pass through wire gate.
▼ 3.1	SO	Saddle. Track on left to small campsite with great view. Trail descends.
		GPS: N31°39.18' W110°48.52'
▼ 3.6	SO	Track on right. End of shelf road.
		GPS: N31°39.51' W110°48.67'
▼ 3.8	SO	Trail crosses saddle leaving the Temporal Gulch drainage and starts to descend to Walker Basin. Walker Canyon on right.
▼ 4.2	BR	Track on left.
		GPS: N31°39.97' W110°48.90'
▼ 4.3	SO	Cross through two small washes.
▼ 4.4	TL	Track on right is FR 4090.
		GPS: N31°40.11' W110°48.88'
▼ 4.7		Trail ends at Upper Walker Tank where there is a small concrete dam in the wash. A sign points the way to the Walker Basin Trail and Mt. Wrightson.
		GPS: N31°40.30' W110°48.95'

SOUTH REGION TRAIL #17

Carr Canyon Trail

Starting Point:	**Arizona 92, 0.5 miles south of the national forest ranger station**
Finishing Point:	**Carr Peak Hiking Trailhead**
Total Mileage:	**7.4 miles**
Unpaved Mileage:	**6.3 miles**
Driving Time:	**45 minutes (one-way)**
Elevation Range:	**4,800–7,400 feet**
Usually Open:	**April to November**
Best Time to Travel:	**April to November**
Difficulty Rating:	**2**
Scenic Rating:	**8**
Remoteness Rating:	**+0**

Special Attractions

- Panoramic views over the Sierra Vista Valley and mountains to the east.
- Access to hiking trails and national forest campgrounds.
- Reef town site.

History

Reef town site was a mining settlement that was active from 1893, when the first gold and silver mines were discovered, all the way through to 1926. Over 100 people lived at Reef, which had a post office, a spring for water, and a phone line to Tombstone down in the valley. Reef gained a mill for processing gold in 1899. The mill, when built, was the most advanced of its kind, but it was used for only six weeks before technical problems forced its closure. In 1903 the mill was dismantled and moved down the mountain.

The shelf road affords some great views

In World War I, Reef turned to mining tungsten, and a tungsten-processing mill was constructed on the site of the original mill. Later still, the site mined quartz; the light-colored piles of quartz left behind can be seen from the hiking trailhead opposite the Reef Town Site Campground.

Description

The higher elevations of the Huachuca Mountains near Sierra Vista provide many people the opportunity for some cooler hiking and camping in the summer months. This graded road accesses the Miller Peak Wilderness Area as well as two shady and pleasant national forest campgrounds.

The trail is graded and climbs steadily up Carr Canyon toward Carr Peak. The trail runs along a high shelf road, wide enough for two vehicles to pass with care. Rough and lumpy sections, particularly on the tight switchbacks, mean the trail is better suited to high-clearance vehicles.

As you climb, there are panoramic views east over the San Pedro Valley. The Mule Mountains are visible, as are the Dragoon Mountains and Sierra Vista down at the base of the range.

There are two national forest campgrounds near the top of the trail—Reef town site and Ramsey Vista. Both have pleasant, shady campsites, and Ramsey Vista also has good views and a public-use horse corral. A fee is required at both sites.

The hiking trailheads to Carr Peak are at the end of the trail.

Current Road Information

Coronado National Forest
Sierra Vista Ranger District
5990 South Hwy 92
Hereford, AZ 85615
(520) 378-0311

Map References

BLM Nogales
USFS Coronado National Forest: Nogales and Sierra Vista Ranger Districts

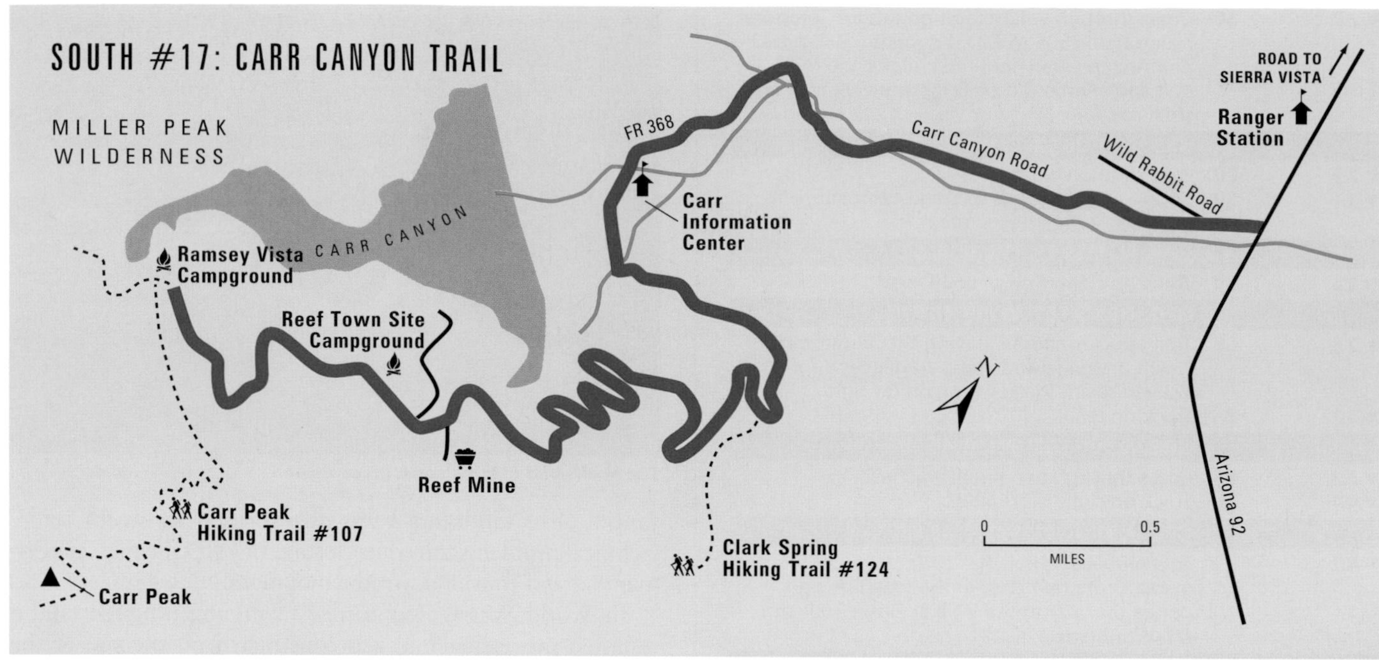

USGS 1:24,000 Miller Peak
1:100,000 Nogales
Maptech CD-ROM: Southeast Arizona/Tucson
Arizona Atlas & Gazetteer, p. 74
Arizona Road & Recreation Atlas, p. 54 & p. 88
Recreational Map of Arizona

Route Directions

▼ 0.0 From Arizona 92, 0.5 miles south of the national forest ranger station south of Sierra Vista, zero trip meter and turn southwest onto the paved Carr Canyon Road at the road sign for Carr Canyon.

GPS: N31°27.22' W110°15.43'

▼ 0.1 SO Wild Rabbit Road on right.
▼ 1.1 SO Pavement ends. Cross through wash, road is now graded dirt.
▼ 1.4 SO Cattle guard, entering Coronado National Forest. Road is now marked as FR 368. Zero trip meter.

GPS: N31°26.91' W110°16.82'

▼ 0.0 Continue to the northwest and cross through wash.
▼ 0.2 SO Parking area on right and left.
▼ 0.7 SO Cross through wash on concrete ford, then Carr Information Center on left.

GPS: N31°26.50' W110°17.18'

▼ 1.0 SO Closure gate, cross over creek on bridge.

GPS: N31°26.29' W110°17.08'

▼ 1.9 SO Clark Spring hiking trail #124 on left to Miller Canyon Road.

GPS: N31°26.16' W110°16.43'

▼ 4.1 SO Track on left to campsite.

GPS: N31°25.79' W110°16.96'

▼ 4.5 SO Information board on left. End of switchbacks and shelf.
▼ 4.6 SO Track on left goes 0.1 miles to flat area at the quartz heaps of the Reef Mine.

GPS: N31°25.66' W110°17.30'

▼ 4.8 SO Reef Town Site Campground on right and track on right to trailhead parking for Old Sawmill hiking trail to Carr Peak and Miller Peak. Zero trip meter.

GPS: N31°25.67' W110°17.40'

▼ 0.0 Continue to the northwest.
▼ 0.1 SO Group campground on right. Reservations required.
▼ 1.1 BR One-way section.
▼ 1.2 SO Trail ends at the trailhead parking to Carr Peak hiking trail #107, which goes to Carr Peak, and Comfort Springs hiking trail, #109. Ramsey Vista Campground is straight ahead, fee area.

GPS: N31°25.68' W110°18.16'

SOUTH REGION TRAIL #18

Mule Mountains Trail

Starting Point:	**Arizona 80, immediately north of the tunnel north of Bisbee**
Finishing Point:	**Gate before communications tower**
Total Mileage:	**3.6 miles**
Unpaved Mileage:	**3.2 miles**
Driving Time:	**30 minutes (one-way)**
Elevation Range:	**5,800–7,000 feet**
Usually Open:	**Year-round**
Best Time to Travel:	**Year-round**
Difficulty Rating:	**2**
Scenic Rating:	**8**
Remoteness Rating:	**+0**

A view across to Escabrosa Ridge

Special Attractions

- Short trail that climbs into the Mule Mountains.
- Views of Bisbee.

Description

This short trail is a perfect accompaniment to a trip to Bisbee, giving a bird's-eye view over the town as well as over the lightly vegetated Mule Mountains. The trail leaves from the top of the Mule Tunnel, following along the line of the old road to Mule Pass. At the top of the pass there is a marker to the road constructed by prison labor in 1913. From the divide, the road climbs steeply up into the Mule Mountains. The standard is good. There are a few houses up the road, so although it is steep, it is well constructed and roughly graded. As the road climbs, Bisbee appears nestled in Tombstone Canyon. The Escabrosa Ridge is seen off to the west.

Rough spots along the road and steep grades make a high-clearance vehicle preferable as the trail switchbacks steeply up to the ridge in the Mule Mountains. The trail ends at the gate to the radio towers near the top of the mountain.

Current Road Information

Bureau of Land Management
Tucson Field Office
12661 East Broadway Blvd.
Tucson, AZ 85748
(520) 722-4289

Map References

BLM Douglas
USGS 1:24,000 Bisbee
1:100,000 Douglas
Maptech CD-ROM: Southeast Arizona/Tucson
Arizona Atlas & Gazetteer, p. 74

Route Directions

▼ 0.0		From Arizona 80, north of the Mule Tunnel, turn east on unmarked paved road and zero trip meter.
		GPS: N31°27.78′ W109°56.87′
▼ 0.4	TL	Top of old road over Mule Pass at saddle, turn sharp left onto graded dirt primitive road. Road immediately climbs steeply.
		GPS: N31°27.50′ W109°56.53′
▼ 1.4	BL	Track on right is private road.
▼ 1.9	SO	Track on left.
▼ 2.4	SO	Track on left to communications towers.
		GPS: N31°28.35′ W109°57.10′
▼ 2.5	SO	Main track on left to communications towers. Zero trip meter.
		GPS: N31°28.42′ W109°57.18′
▼ 0.0		Continue to the northwest.
▼ 0.1	SO	Track on left.
▼ 0.3	SO	Track on left.
▼ 0.6	SO	Two tracks on left.
		GPS: N31°28.74′ W109°57.65′
▼ 1.0	SO	Track on left is 4-rated and goes 0.2 miles via a couple of campsites to a viewpoint over Soto Canyon.
		GPS: N31°28.96′ W109°57.54′
▼ 1.1		Trail ends at gate to communications towers.

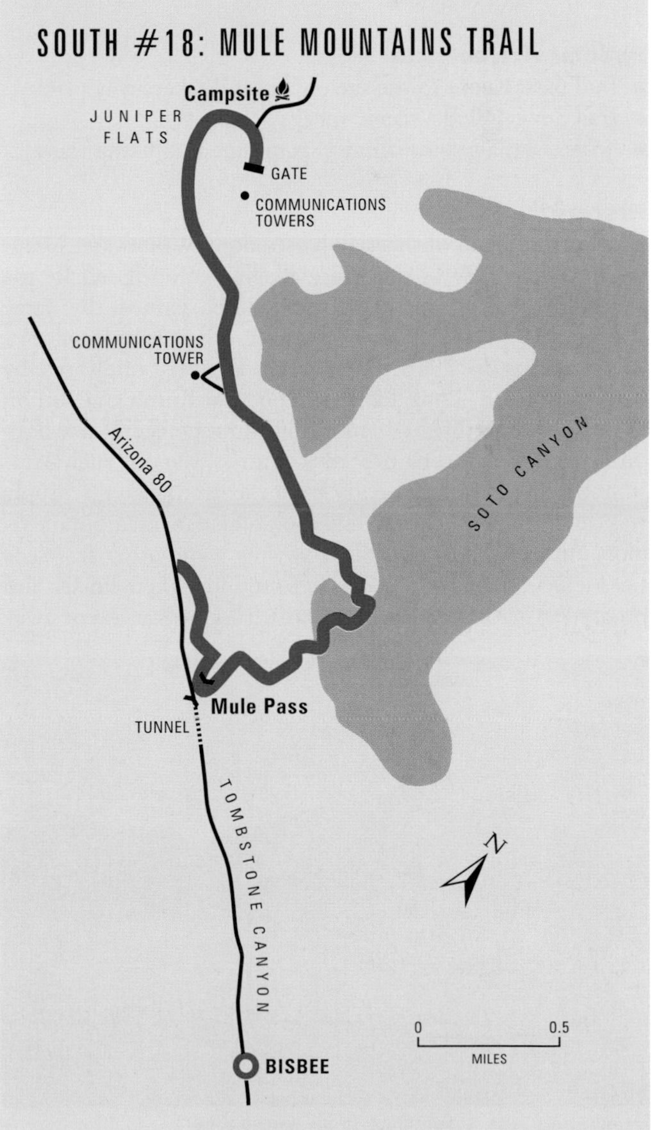

SOUTH REGION TRAIL #19

Tex Canyon Trail

Starting Point:	**Kuykendall Cutoff Road, 7.3 miles south of the intersection of Arizona 181**
Finishing Point:	**Arizona 80, 0.3 miles northeast of mile marker 396**
Total Mileage:	**26.3 miles**
Unpaved Mileage:	**26.3 miles**
Driving Time:	**2.5 hours**
Elevation Range:	**4,700–6,000 feet**
Usually Open:	**Year-round**
Best Time to Travel:	**Year-round**
Difficulty Rating:	**1**
Scenic Rating:	**9**
Remoteness Rating:	**+0**

Special Attractions

- Trail passes close to the site of Camp Rucker army post.
- Trail down a wide, scenic valley.
- Access to many backcountry campsites and hiking trails.

History

The northern end of this trail passes along Whitewater Draw, so-named because of the white alkaline coloring left by the water. A nearby ranch and post office gained the same Whitewater name, though the post office lasted only 11 years, closing in 1918. Whitewater Draw is amply fed by Rucker Canyon, Long John Canyon, and Bruno Canyon on the western side of the Chiricahua Mountains and has been prone to flash flooding over the centuries. On one such occasion in 1878, a military party from the nearby Camp Supply was caught in a downpour and took refuge in a temporary saloon until the rains abated. Following some other travelers, Lt. Henley and Lt. John Rucker mounted their horses and proceeded across the swelling wash. Henley was swept away first with Rucker following in an attempt to save his friend. Both men drowned despite the efforts of fellow travelers and the accompanying Apache scouts who risked their own lives trying to save the officers. After this, the name of Camp Supply was changed to Camp Rucker and the canyon became known as Rucker Canyon.

Velvet mesquite with Sunset Peak in the background

Camp Rucker, originally built to protect the settlers of the region, was an important base for the military in its efforts to subdue the warring Chiricahua Apache following the wrongful killing of Cochise's tribe members at Fort Bowie in 1861. Cochise, who formerly had only fought with the Mexicans, killed his hostages and declared revenge on the settlers. The warfare lasted for many years.

One incident at Camp Rucker helped precipitate the famous "Gunfight at the O.K. Corral" in the notoriously rowdy town of Tombstone. In July 1880, some mules were stolen from the Camp Rucker stables by the McLaury brothers of Tombstone. The military camp enlisted the aid of U.S. Deputy Marshall Virgil Earp to find the mules. They eventually turned up with the brands altered on the McLaury ranch.

Camp Rucker had developed into a small settlement by the late 1880s, gaining its own post office with the temporary name of Powers before reverting to the name Rucker Canyon in 1929, by which time most of the settlers had moved on to greener pastures.

Tex Canyon gained its name from Tex Whaley who settled there in the late 1880s. He assisted in the military's efforts to convince Geronimo to bring about peace with the Apache.

The southern end of the trail terminates in the San Bernardino Valley at the site of Chiricahua, a small community that flourished between the years of 1907 and the early 1920s. For many years it was a cattle-loading station on the railroad to Douglas. The valley takes it name from the San Bernardino Land Grant of the 1820s, which after the Gadsden Purchase of 1853–54, straddled the international border between Mexico and the United States. The grant had been purchased by Lieutenant Ignacio Perez from the Mexican government for $90, springs included. He ran cattle on his ranch until the Apache raids of the 1830s became too much of a risk and he was forced to abandon his cattle for good.

In the mid-1880s the Slaughter family operated a cattle ranch on the American portion of the San Bernardino Land Grant, approximately 23,500 acres of the original 70,000. The Slaughters waged war on the cattle rustlers of this region and were so good at delivering their message that their cattle, marked with the famous "Z" brand, were left untouched by most rustlers.

To the north of Rucker Canyon, in Turkey Creek Canyon, is the grave of cattle rustler and Tombstone gunfighter Johnny Ringo. Ringo's death was shrouded in mystery. His body was found propped against an oak tree with a single bullet wound to the head. He was buried a few yards from the tree. Although the coroner's verdict said suicide, many believe that he was murdered, and there is an impressive and famous list of suspects to choose from. Wyatt Earp and Lou Cooley are both likely to have killed him, but most of the evidence points to a small-time gambler called Johnny-behind-the-deuce, a.k.a. John O'Rourke.

Lichen-covered rocks beside a typical section of trail

Description

This smooth road passes along two canyons within the Coronado National Forest: Rucker Canyon and Tex Canyon. Initially the graded gravel road crosses ranchland as it follows alongside the low Swisshelm Mountains. Within the national forest, the standard of the road falls slightly and it becomes narrower, but is still suitable for passenger vehicles in dry weather. It can be washboardy in sections.

A major road on the left goes to the site of Camp Rucker, 11.4 miles from the northern end of the trail. The site is now a national forest campground. This road continues on past other developed campgrounds to Rucker Lake. From the intersection, the main trail follows alongside shady Cottonwood Creek through open forest and grassland. The trail then travels along wide Tex Canyon. The vegetation is scattered: alligator juniper, oaks, yuccas, agave, and small pines. There are many excellent backcountry campsites along this section as well as many short side trails to explore. Most only go a couple of miles to the wilderness boundary, but give access to some very pretty hiking trails.

The trail exits the forest to travel across open ranchland in the San Bernadino Valley. It finishes on Arizona 80 at the site of the old settlement of Chiricahua. Nothing remains of the settlement now except the name on the map.

Current Road Information

Coronado National Forest
Douglas Ranger District
381 North Leslie Canyon Rd.
Douglas, AZ 85607
(520) 364-3468

Map References

BLM Chiricahua Peak
USFS Coronado National Forest: Chiricahua-Peloncillo Mts. Ranger District
USGS 1:24,000 Square Top Hills East, Swisshelm Mt., Bruno Peak, Stanford Canyon, Chiricahua Peak, Swede Peak, Pedregosa Mts. East, Paramore Crater
1:100,000 Chiricahua Peak

Maptech CD-ROM: Southeast Arizona/Tucson
Arizona Atlas & Gazetteer, p. 75
Arizona Road & Recreation Atlas, p. 55 & p. 89
Recreational Map of Arizona

Route Directions

▼ 0.0			On the Kuykendall Cutoff Road, 7.3 miles south of Arizona 181, zero trip meter and turn east on the wide graded gravel Rucker Road signed to Rucker. Intersection is also 9 miles from Arizona 191 to the west.
	5.0 ▲		Trail ends at the intersection of Rucker Road and the Kuykendall Cutoff Road. Turn left to exit to Arizona 191, turn right to exit to Arizona 181.
			GPS: N31°47.07' W109°32.34'
▼ 0.3		SO	Cattle guard; then track on left.
	4.7 ▲	SO	Track on right; then cattle guard.
▼ 1.7		SO	Cattle guard.
	3.3 ▲	SO	Cattle guard.
▼ 2.6		BL	Cross Whitewater Draw on concrete ford; then bear left on the far side. Track on right after crossing.
	2.4 ▲	BR	Track on left; then cross Whitewater Draw on concrete ford.
			GPS: N31°45.18' W109°30.79'
▼ 2.8		SO	Two cattle guards.
	2.2 ▲	SO	Two cattle guards.
▼ 2.9		SO	Cattle guard.
	2.1 ▲	SO	Cattle guard.
▼ 4.0		SO	Cattle guard.
	1.0 ▲	SO	Cattle guard.
▼ 5.0		TL	T-intersection. Turn left following sign to Rucker. Zero trip meter.
	0.0 ▲		Continue to the northwest.
			GPS: N31°44.22' W109°28.59'
▼ 0.0			Continue to the northeast.
	3.4 ▲	TR	Turn right onto wide gravel road. Zero trip meter. Intersection is unmarked in this direction.
▼ 0.7		SO	Cross through Whitewater Draw.
	2.7 ▲	SO	Cross through Whitewater Draw.
▼ 0.9		SO	Cross over Whitewater Draw on bridge.
	2.5 ▲	SO	Cross over Whitewater Draw on bridge.
▼ 1.7		SO	Track on right.
	1.7 ▲	SO	Track on left.
▼ 2.0		SO	Cattle guard.
	1.4 ▲	SO	Cattle guard.
▼ 2.5		SO	Cattle guard.
	0.9 ▲	SO	Cattle guard.
▼ 2.7		SO	Cross through wash.
	0.7 ▲	SO	Cross through wash.
▼ 3.4		BR	Graded road on left is private. Zero trip meter and bear right following sign to Rucker Recreation Area.
	0.0 ▲		Continue to the west.
			GPS: N31°45.30' W109°25.27'
▼ 0.0			Continue to the east.
	3.0 ▲	SO	Graded road on right is private. Zero trip meter.
▼ 0.2		SO	Cattle guard; then cross through wash on concrete ford.
	2.8 ▲	SO	Cross through wash on concrete ford; then cattle guard.

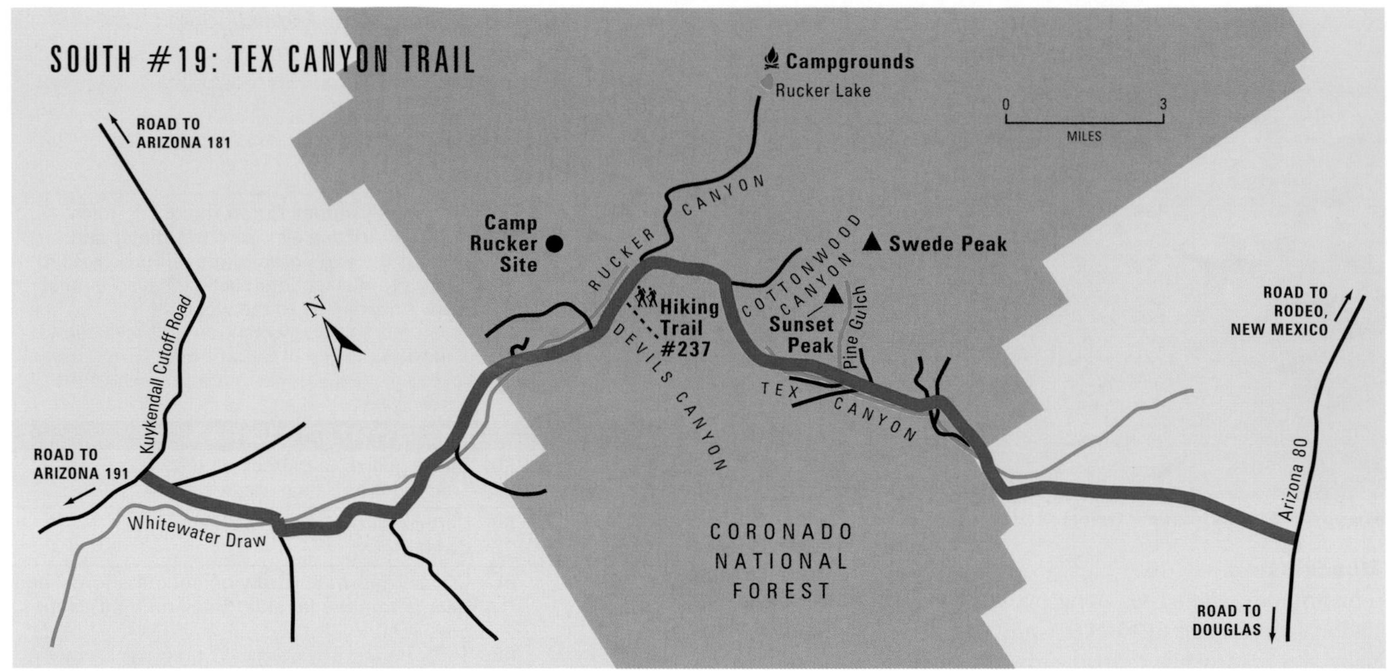

▼ 1.6		SO	Track on left is designated access route.
	1.4 ▲	SO	Track on right is designated access route.
			GPS: N31°44.98' W109°23.56'
▼ 2.4		SO	Hiking trail #237 on right to Devils Canyon, marked as a forest trail.
	0.6 ▲	SO	Hiking trail #237 on left to Devils Canyon, marked as a forest trail.
			GPS: N31°45.20' W109°22.85'
▼ 3.0		SO	Cattle guard, then graded road on left goes to Rucker, Rucker Lake, and NFS campgrounds. Zero trip meter and carry on following sign to Douglas and Arizona 80. (Douglas is sign-posted in both directions at this point.)
	0.0 ▲		Continue to the southwest.
			GPS: N31°45.39' W109°22.18'
▼ 0.0			Continue to the northeast.
	5.9 ▲	SO	Graded road on right goes to Rucker, Rucker Lake, and NFS campgrounds. Zero trip meter and continue following sign to Douglas. (Douglas is sign-posted in both directions at this point.)
▼ 0.5		SO	Cattle guard.
	5.4 ▲	SO	Cattle guard.
▼ 0.6		SO	Track on left to corral.
	5.3 ▲	SO	Track on right to corral.
▼ 0.7		SO	Track on left through gate—hiking access only.
	5.2 ▲	SO	Track on right through gate—hiking access only.
▼ 1.1		SO	Cross through wash; then tracks on left and right.
	4.8 ▲	SO	Tracks on left and right; then cross through wash.
▼ 1.2		SO	Track on left.
	4.7 ▲	SO	Track on right.
▼ 1.4		SO	Track on left continues alongside Cottonwood Canyon.
	4.5 ▲	SO	Track on right continues alongside Cottonwood Canyon.
			GPS: N31°44.72' W109°21.08'
▼ 1.9		SO	Track on right.
	4.0 ▲	SO	Track on left.
▼ 2.5		SO	Cattle guard at saddle; then track on right.
	3.4 ▲	SO	Track on left; then cattle guard at saddle.
			GPS: N31°43.86' W109°21.18'
▼ 3.4		SO	Track on right.
	2.5 ▲	SO	Track on left.
▼ 3.8		SO	Track on left.
	2.1 ▲	SO	Track on right.
			GPS: N31°42.89' W109°21.05'
▼ 4.0		SO	Cross over creek on bridge.
	1.9 ▲	SO	Cross over creek on bridge.
▼ 4.2		SO	Track on right. Sunset Peak is on the left.
	1.7 ▲	SO	Track on left. Sunset Peak is on the right.
▼ 4.3		SO	Track on right.
	1.6 ▲	SO	Track on left.
▼ 4.6		SO	Track on left.
	1.3 ▲	SO	Track on right.
▼ 4.7		SO	Cattle guard.
	1.2 ▲	SO	Cattle guard.
▼ 5.3		SO	Track on right is private.
	0.6 ▲	SO	Track on left is private.
▼ 5.7		SO	Track on right.
	0.2 ▲	SO	Track on left.
▼ 5.9		SO	Track on left goes to Pine Gulch, Sunset Peak, and Swede Peak. Zero trip meter at sign.
	0.0 ▲		Continue to the northwest.
			GPS: N31°41.61' W109°19.72'
▼ 0.0			Continue to the southeast.
	2.6 ▲	SO	Track on right goes to Pine Gulch, Sunset Peak, and Swede Peak. Zero trip meter at sign.
▼ 0.7		SO	Track on right.
	1.9 ▲	SO	Track on left.
▼ 0.8		SO	Track on left.
	1.8 ▲	SO	Track on right.
			GPS: N31°41.03' W109°19.18'
▼ 1.0		SO	Track on right; then cattle guard.
	1.6 ▲	SO	Cattle guard; then track on left.
▼ 1.1		SO	Track on left.
	1.5 ▲	SO	Track on right.
▼ 1.2		SO	Cross over creek.
	1.4 ▲	SO	Cross over creek.
▼ 1.3		SO	Track on right and track on left.

	1.3 ▲	SO	Track on right and track on left.
▼ 2.1		SO	Cattle guard; then track on left.
	0.5 ▲	SO	Track on right; then cattle guard.
▼ 2.2		SO	Cross through wash.
	0.4 ▲	SO	Cross through wash.
▼ 2.6		SO	Track on right; then cattle guard. Leaving Coronado National Forest into private land. Zero trip meter at cattle guard.
	0.0 ▲		Continue to the north.
			GPS: N31°39.68' W109°18.64'
▼ 0.0			Continue to the south.
	6.4 ▲	SO	Cattle guard, entering Coronado National Forest; then track on left. Zero trip meter at cattle guard.
▼ 0.2		SO	Cross through wash.
	6.2 ▲	SO	Cross through wash.
▼ 0.7		SO	Cattle guard.
	5.7 ▲	SO	Cattle guard.
▼ 1.4		SO	Cattle guard.
	5.0 ▲	SO	Cattle guard.
▼ 6.4		SO	Cattle guard. Then trail ends on Arizona 80 in the San Bernadino Valley. Turn right for Douglas, turn left for Rodeo, NM.
	0.0 ▲		Trail commences on Arizona 80, approximately 28 miles northeast of Douglas, 0.3 miles northeast of mile marker 396. Zero trip meter and turn northwest over a cattle guard onto the graded dirt road at the sign for Rucker Canyon. Road is called Krentz Ranch Road.
			GPS: N31°35.63' W109°14.34'

SOUTH REGION TRAIL #20

Pinery Canyon Trail

Starting Point:	**Southwestern Research Station, 5.1 miles from Portal**
Finishing Point:	**Arizona 181, 2.8 miles east from Arizona 186, immediately before the entrance to Chiricahua National Monument**
Total Mileage:	**18 miles**
Unpaved Mileage:	**17.9 miles**
Driving Time:	**1.5 hours**
Elevation Range:	**5,200–7,600 feet**
Usually Open:	**April to December**
Best Time to Travel:	**April to December**
Difficulty Rating:	**1**
Scenic Rating:	**8**
Remoteness Rating:	**+0**

Special Attractions

- One of the prime bird-watching areas in southeastern Arizona.
- Easy, graded trail through spectacular, sky island scenery.
- Many backcountry campsites and developed campgrounds.
- Chiricahua National Monument at the western end of the trail.

History

A view of the trail as it climbs toward Onion Saddle

Portal, the settlement near the start of this trail, is descriptively named after the town's location at the mouth of Cave Creek Canyon and is thought to have been founded by the Duffener brothers, who came from Paradise, just about the turn of the twentieth century. Their mining activities drew them toward what became known as Portal. The tiny post office was opened in 1905 and still operates today.

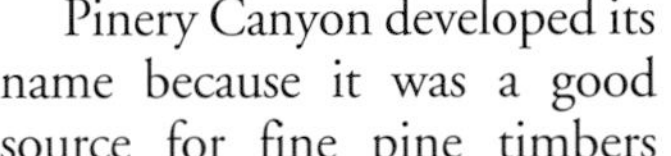

Pinery Canyon developed its name because it was a good source for fine pine timbers used in 1862 for the construction of Fort Bowie near Apache Pass. The fort was an important stronghold in the continued conflict and warfare with the Chiricahua Apaches.

The trail runs up alongside Cave Creek on the eastern side of the range. Cave Creek got its name not only from the many caves along its striking bluffs but also from an impressive underground cavern named Crystal Cavern, which is upstream from where the trail enters the creek line. Around 1878, one of the earliest pioneers in the region, a man named Reed, sold out to the Hands brothers. The brothers are credited with the development of the original trail that traverses this part of the Chiricahua Mountains from Pinery Canyon up, over, and down to the Portal region.

Onion Saddle is also a descriptive name as the original trail passed by a creek that was noted for its wild onions.

As you enter the mouth of Pinery Canyon, you pass close to Riggs Spring, named after one of the earliest pioneer families in the area. Ed and Lilian Riggs were active in the creation of the Chiricahua National Monument in 1924, and Ed is credited with being one of the first Americans to discover many of the eerie, towering, rhyolite rock shapes now within the monument. Ed's father-in-law, Neil Erickson, had accidentally entered this magnificent wonderland in the late 1880s while tracking an Apache who had stolen one of the military's horses. Though it was many months before the horse was found, the real find was the region's unique, rocky terrain. The Chiricahua Apache who Erickson had trailed was known as Massai and was one of the last of the Chiricahua Indians to be relocated to Florida. Ed Riggs later suggested the name of Massai Point for the high point within the national monument.

Description

The Chiricahua Mountains are one of the "sky islands" of Arizona's southeast mountain ranges where the altitude of the range creates mini-climate zones of flora and fauna typically found much further to the north. These islands stand out as cool oases in the summer heat, refuges where outdoor enthusiasts can hike, 4WD, and camp in relative coolness.

In winter, these sky islands can often receive several inches of snow; consequently many of these high altitude trails can be closed to vehicles in winter months. Some are open to snowmobiles; others are limited to skis and snowshoes.

The Pinery Canyon Trail is one of only two graded roads that cross the range from east to west. The drive is suitable for passenger vehicles in dry weather, and there are some smaller, more difficult trails that lead off from the main trail. The trail passes many primitive campsites as well as five developed national forest campgrounds along or near the trail; three of them along the paved road to Portal at the eastern end of the trail. These can be extremely popular in summer.

The Chiricahuas are a prime destination for bird watchers from around the world. Over 330 species of birds can be seen in the mountains, including 14 different types of hummingbirds and 10 species of owls. The rare and elegant trogon nests in the Chiricahuas, one of its few nesting sites in the United States. A popular time for birders to visit is during the spring migration in late April to early May, when many thousands of colorful songbirds make their annual move northward. Hummingbirds and other tropical species are best seen between April and September. The Southwestern Research Station at the western end of this trail is a research station of the American Museum of Natural History, which opened in 1955.

Basin Hiking Trail leads off on the western side of the range

Other wildlife that can be seen are mule deer, javelina, bobcats, coyotes, and black bears. Like all the sky islands, the Chiricahuas support a flourishing population of black bears, which can be active around the campgrounds in summer. Take due precautions with food, and of course, never ever feed a bear!

From Portal, the graded road winds alongside Cave Creek. A major graded road leads back to Paradise, a small settlement within the Chiricahuas, which at one time had thirteen saloons. The original jail there was in the open air; prisoners were shackled to a chain running between two trees. The mines closed in 1907 but the town still has a few residents.

The main trail climbs up to Onion Saddle at 7,600 feet before descending along Pinery Canyon through cool stands of pine, oak, and alligator juniper to finish on Arizona 181 at the entrance to Chiricahua National Monument.

To reach the start of the trail, proceed south from Portal on the main paved road, passing the ranger station on the right. Continue for 3.1 miles, then swing right remaining on the paved road. Continue for another 2.0 miles, then at the junction of FR 42A to the left, zero trip meter. The start of the trail is immediately past the cluster of buildings on the left that is the Southwestern Research Station.

The graves of Frank and Grace Hands, who are connected with Hilltop, are near the beginning of the trail over Hands Pass. For more information about the Hands family, see South #21: Hands Pass Trail.

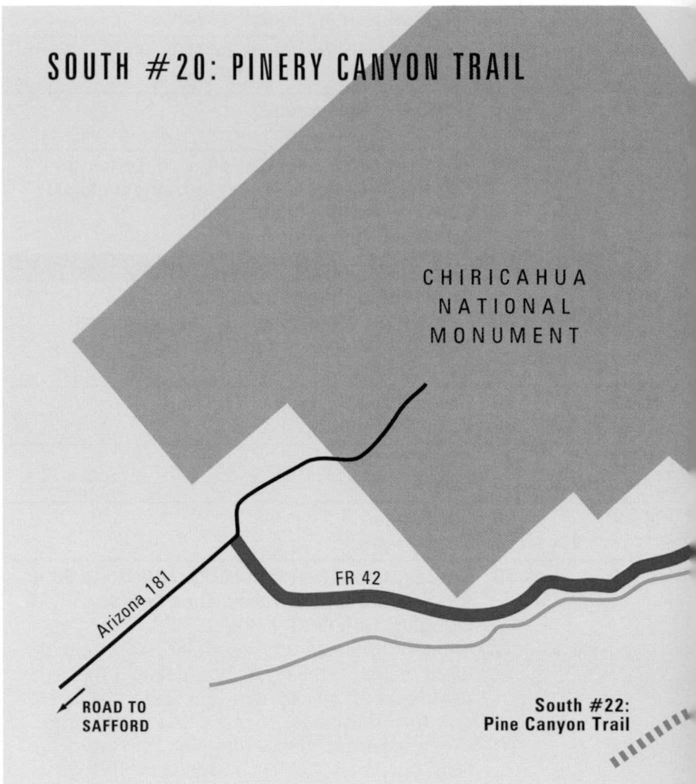

This road is not maintained for winter travel and may be impassable in winter months. Call ahead for information. However, it may be open for longer than the dates given above.

Current Road Information

Coronado National Forest
Douglas Ranger District
381 North Leslie Canyon Rd.
Douglas, AZ 85607
(520) 364-3468

Map References

BLM Willcox, Chiricahua Peak
USFS Coronado National Forest: Chiricahua-Peloncillo Mts. Ranger Districts
USGS 1:24,000 Portal, Rustler Park, Fife Peak, Bowie Mountain South
1:100,000 Willcox, Chiricahua Peak
Maptech CD-ROM: Southeast Arizona/Tucson
Arizona Atlas & Gazetteer, p. 75
Arizona Road & Recreation Atlas, p. 55 & p. 89
Recreational Map of Arizona

Route Directions

▼ 0.0	At the intersection of FR 42 and FR 42A, at the Southwestern Research Station, zero trip meter and continue northwest on the paved FR 42, following the signs for Rustler Park and Arizona 181.
3.7 ▲	Trail ends at the intersection of FR 42 and FR 42A at the Southwestern Research Station. Continue along the road and follow the signs for 5.1 miles to Portal.

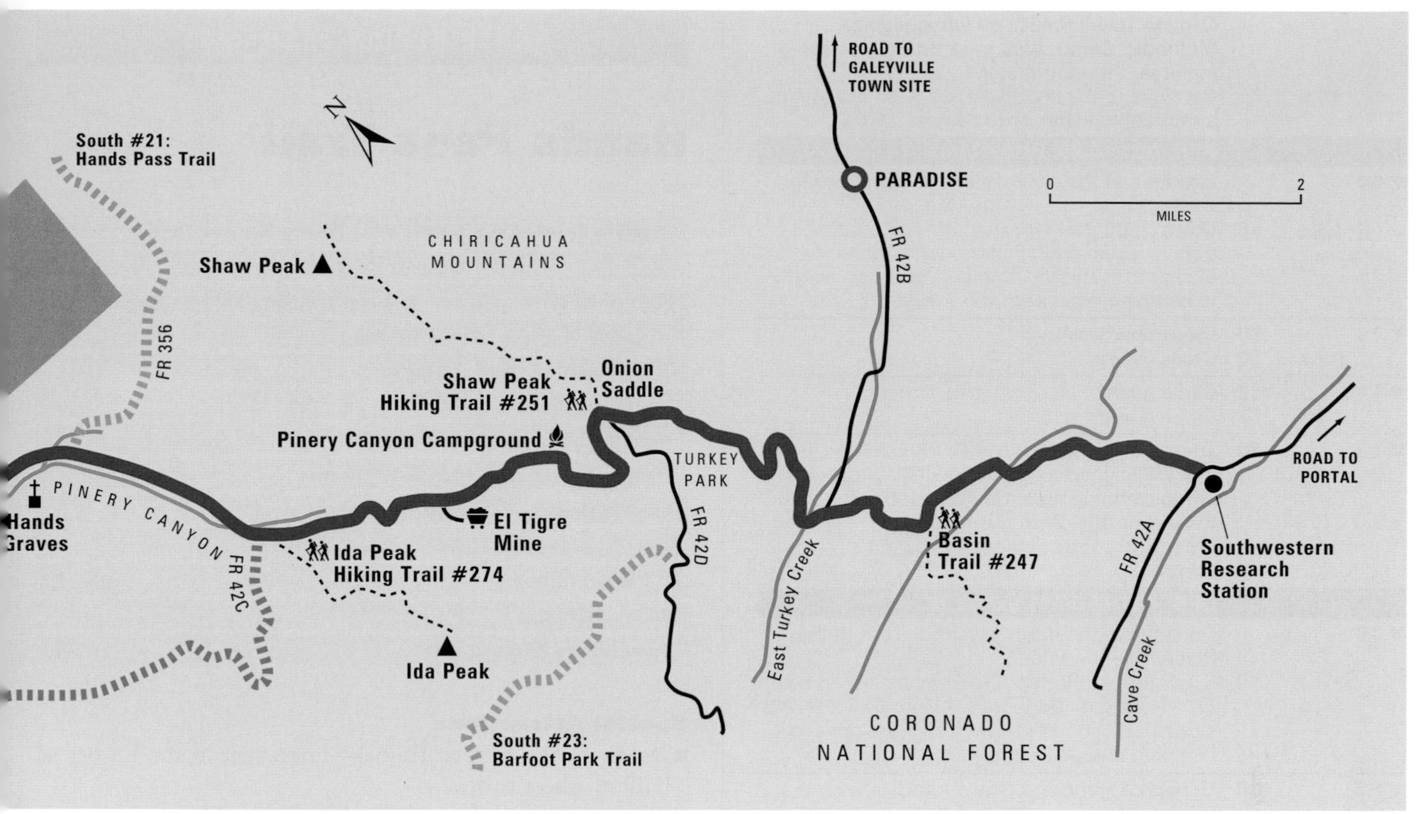

		GPS: N31°53.07′ W109°12.34′
▼ 0.1	SO	Road turns to graded dirt. Dispersed camping now permitted. Entering Coronado National Forest.
3.6 ▲	SO	Camping in designated campgrounds only. Road is crossing private land.
▼ 1.1	SO	Track on right.
2.6 ▲	SO	Track on left.
▼ 1.7	SO	Cross over creek.
2.0 ▲	SO	Cross over creek.
▼ 2.0	SO	Track on left.
1.7 ▲	SO	Track on right.
▼ 2.2	SO	Track on right.
1.5 ▲	SO	Track on left.
▼ 2.6	SO	Basin Trail #247 on left goes to Herb Martyr Dam—hiking and pack trail.
1.1 ▲	SO	Basin Trail #247 on right goes to Herb Martyr Dam—hiking and pack trail.
		GPS: N31°53.98′ W109°14.28′
▼ 2.8	SO	Track on left.
0.9 ▲	SO	Track on right.
▼ 3.1	SO	Cattle guard; then loop of old road on right.
0.6 ▲	SO	Loop of old road on left; then cattle guard.
▼ 3.7	SO	Graded road on right is FR 42B to Paradise. Zero trip meter.
0.0 ▲		Continue to the east toward Portal.
		GPS: N31°54.52′ W109°15.03′
▼ 0.0		Continue to the west and cross over East Turkey Creek; then track on left.
3.1 ▲	SO	Track on right; then cross over East Turkey Creek. Then graded road on left is FR 42B to Paradise. Zero trip meter.
▼ 3.1	SO	Onion Saddle. Track on right is also start of Shaw Peak hiking trail #251, graded road on left is FR 42D to Rustler Park and South #23: Barfoot Park Trail. Continue straight on, following the sign for Arizona 181. Zero trip meter at saddle.
0.0 ▲		Continue to the southeast.
		GPS: N31°55.99′ W109°15.78′
▼ 0.0		Continue on to the northwest and cross cattle guard.
4.5 ▲	SO	Cattle guard; then Onion Saddle. Track on left is also start of Shaw Peak hiking trail #251, graded road on right is FR 42D to Rustler Park and South #23: Barfoot Park Trail. Continue straight on, following the sign for Portal. Zero trip meter at saddle.
▼ 1.7	SO	Pinery Canyon Campground on right.
2.8 ▲	SO	Pinery Canyon Campground on left.
		GPS: N31°55.97′ W109°16.30′
▼ 2.8	SO	Track on left goes 0.2 miles to El Tigre Mine and continues past it. There is a large timber-framed adit and two smaller ones.
1.7 ▲	BL	Track on right goes 0.2 miles to El Tigre Mine and continues past it. There is a large timber-framed adit and two smaller ones.
		GPS: N31°56.31′ W109°17.22′
▼ 3.2	SO	Track on right.
1.3 ▲	SO	Track on left.
▼ 3.3	SO	Cross over creek on bridge.
1.2 ▲	SO	Cross over creek on bridge.
		GPS: N31°56.41′ W109°17.55′
▼ 4.0	SO	Cross over creek on bridge.
0.5 ▲	SO	Cross over creek on bridge.
		GPS: N31°56.63′ W109°18.01′
▼ 4.4	SO	Ida Peak hiking trail #274 on left.
0.1 ▲	SO	Ida Peak hiking trail #274 on right.
		GPS: N31°56.82′ W109°18.36′
▼ 4.5	SO	Track on right to concrete footings and large camping area followed by South #22: Pine

			Canyon Trail (FR 42C) on left at sign to Methodist Camp. Also track on right to camping area. Zero trip meter.
	0.0 ▲		Continue to the southeast, track on left to concrete footings and large camping area.
			GPS: N31°56.89′ W109°18.43′
▼ 0.0			Continue to the northwest and cross through wash.
	1.6 ▲	SO	Cross through wash; then graded road on right is South #22: Pine Canyon Trail (FR 42C) at sign to Methodist Camp. Also track on left to camping area. Zero trip meter.
▼ 0.9		SO	Cross over wash.
	0.7 ▲	SO	Cross over wash.
▼ 1.4		SO	Cattle guard.
	0.2 ▲	SO	Cattle guard.
▼ 1.6		SO	Track on right is South #21: Hands Pass Trail (FR 356) signed to North Fork. Also track on left to camping area. Continue following sign to Arizona 181. Zero trip meter.
	0.0 ▲		Continue to the southeast following sign for Portal.
			GPS: N31°58.16′ W109°19.20′
▼ 0.0			Continue to the northwest and cross through Pinery Creek wash.
	1.4 ▲	SO	Cross through Pinery Creek wash; then track on left is South #21: Hands Pass Trail (FR 356) signed to North Fork. Track on right goes to camping area. Zero trip meter.
▼ 0.3		SO	Graves of Frank and Grace Hands are on the left surrounded by a wire fence.
	1.1 ▲	SO	Graves of Frank and Grace Hands are on the right surrounded by a wire fence.
			GPS: N31°58.25′ W109°19.54′
▼ 1.0		SO	Cattle guard.
	0.4 ▲	SO	Cattle guard.
▼ 1.4		SO	Leaving Coronado National Forest at sign. Zero trip meter.
	0.0 ▲		Continue to the east.
			GPS: N31°58.29′ W109°20.69′
▼ 0.0			Continue to the west.
	3.7 ▲	SO	Entering Coronado National Forest at sign. Zero trip meter.
▼ 0.1		SO	Cattle guard.
	3.6 ▲	SO	Cattle guard.
▼ 0.2		SO	Cross over creek.
	3.5 ▲	SO	Cross over creek. Trail is running alongside Pinery Creek.
▼ 0.4		SO	Cross over creek.
	3.3 ▲	SO	Cross over creek.
▼ 1.6		SO	Two cattle guards.
	2.1 ▲	SO	Two cattle guards.
			GPS: N31°58.89′ W109°22.21′
▼ 3.6		SO	Cattle guard, road is now paved.
	0.1 ▲	SO	Cattle guard, road turns to graded gravel.
▼ 3.7			Trail ends at the intersection of Arizona 181 and Pinery Canyon road, immediately before the entrance into the Chiricahua National Monument. Turn right to visit the national monument, turn left to exit to Safford.
	0.0 ▲		At the junction of Arizona 181 and Pinery Canyon road, immediately before the entrance into the Chiricahua National Monument, zero trip meter and turn east on the paved Pinery Canyon road at the sign.
			GPS: N32°00.41′ W109°23.34′

SOUTH REGION TRAIL #21

Hands Pass Trail

Starting Point:	**South #20: Pinery Canyon Trail, 5.1 miles from the western end**
Finishing Point:	**San Simon–Paradise Road, 5 miles north of Paradise**
Total Mileage:	**12 miles**
Unpaved Mileage:	**12 miles**
Driving Time:	**3.5 hours**
Elevation Range:	**4,600–6,700 feet**
Usually Open:	**Year-round**
Best Time to Travel:	**April to October**
Difficulty Rating:	**6**
Scenic Rating:	**8**
Remoteness Rating:	**+0**

Special Attractions

- Access to the Kasper Tunnel—important in the history of Hilltop ghost town.
- Picturesque trail through the Chiricahua Mountains.
- Backcountry camping.
- Hands Pass and views of Cochise Head.

History

Originally from England, Frank, John, and Alfred Hands were partly responsible for opening up this region to mining in the 1890s. They were also behind the early construction of trails that linked the mining settlements in this region; Hands Pass, named after them, is one such trail. They acquired the Hilltop Mine, formerly known as Ayers Camp, from its founder, Jack Dunn, who struck upon it some ten years earlier. The mine developed further into Hilltop Town when the brothers sold their interests to a St. Louis investor in 1913. Frank Hands and his wife, Grace, are buried very close to the southern end of Hands Pass. The site is noted on South #20: Pinery Canyon Trail.

Hilltop had developed on both sides of Shaw Peak by the late 1910s, with the small Kasper Tunnel serving as the link. The later-developing east side of the town grew even more than the original west side. No buildings remain on the western slopes except for several concrete footings and the outlet of the Kasper Tunnel. In its prime, Hilltop hosted a dance hall, restaurant, pool hall, an impressive manager's house, bunkhouses, and more. By the 1930s mining activities were greatly reduced and the town was losing its residents. Various small groups attempted to continue mining through to the late 1940s but the closure of the post office in 1945 marked the final years of Hilltop. A few remnants of the town on the eastern side of the Kasper Tunnel survive on private land; permission is required to visit these.

Harris Mountain, at the eastern end of the trail, is named after a family who unwisely tried to take a short cut through the Chiricahua Mountains in 1873 and died at the hands of the Chiricahua Apache. Traveling by themselves from the San Simon Wash up Hunt Canyon toward Hands Pass, the parents and their two youngest children were killed and their 15-year-old daughter was abducted. Their disappearance remained a mystery until the daughter retold the tragic events when she was found in Mexico by the military many years later. She was able to lead a party to the Hunt Canyon site and to the bones of her family.

Jhus Canyon is a reminder of one of the leading Chiricahua Apache. Jhus was instrumental in encouraging the Apache to leave the San Carlos Reservation and to attempt to reclaim lands they considered stolen.

Five miles south of the end of the trail is the small settlement of Paradise. Supposedly it was named by a young couple, George and Reed Walker, who were so happy with their chosen home site that they felt they lived in paradise. In 1901 a mine developed near Paradise, which altered the solitude of this remote settlement completely. The mine attracted some of the more colorful and wild characters from Tombstone and forever altered the peaceful existence of the settlers. The saloons were busy and the jail tree (later the jailhouse) was well-used. The mines were considered economically unsound by the 1910s and the miners departed, yet the settlement of Paradise lingered. By the early 1940s, Paradise was all but deserted and the post office closed its doors. Perhaps there is something contagious in the name or the peaceful mountainside location as a few lights have managed to linger on in this tiny settlement as it enters into the twenty-first century.

Description

This challenging trail skirts below Chiricahua National Monument, traveling over Hands Pass and heading steeply down to join East Whitetail Creek. Although it is an exciting drive, most carefully driven, high-clearance SUVs with good tires can safely navigate the trail. Those driving vehicles with side steps, long overhangs, or low-hanging brush or towbars should think twice. There are several places along the trail where these are a distinct disadvantage and there is a risk of damage.

The trail commences on South #20: Pinery Canyon Trail, very close to the graves of Frank and Grace Hands. The intersection is sign-posted to North Fork, FR 356, and leads off alongside the creek, passing some good campsites along the way.

The western entrance to Kasper Tunnel

After 1.9 miles, a spur trail leads off to the southwest end of the Kasper Tunnel, a long tunnel dug through the hillside, which allowed for the relocation of Hilltop to its current location. The spur trail is rated a 5, mainly because of its eroded nature and sections of narrow shelf road. It ends at the Kasper Tunnel, which appears now as a small hole dug in the solid rock. The turnout for vehicles is on a huge pile of excavated rock that came out of the tunnel. An idea of the length of the tunnel can be gained by studying the enormous amount of material that came out of such a small hole. The hiking trail to Shaw Peak also starts here.

A narrow section along East Whitehall Creek

From the main trail, you start to climb in earnest up to Hands Pass. The shelf road is a comfortable width for a single vehicle and there are adequate passing places. The surface on the north side of the pass is loose and there are a couple of small rock ledges, but this side of the pass is the easier of the two. In wet weather, or after a sprinkle of snow, the red soil can become very greasy. There are views of the Kasper Tunnel and its workings to the east, Shaw Peak to the southeast, and as you crest the top of Hands Pass, Cochise Head can be seen directly ahead. The oddly shaped mountain resembles a face looking upwards with the top of the head pointing east. The rock formations make the nose, eyebrows, and lips. It is so named because the famous Chiricahua Apache chief eluded capture for many years in this region.

Once over the crest of Hands Pass the difficult descent down the south side begins. The trail here is rocky and very stony, and traction is low. The most challenging section is 0.7 miles south of the pass. There the trail is badly eroded on one side, leaving a trail too narrow for most SUVs to traverse. ATVs and possibly the smallest subcompacts may fit, but check carefully before you attempt this route, as it is very off-camber with a deep gully at the end. Most vehicles will need to bridge the eroded section, putting the passenger-side wheels up tight to the bank where there is a narrow edge for tires to grab. This section needs a driver with good nerve and tires with good tread; otherwise there is a risk that the vehicle will slip down into the gully, risking possible body damage. A spotter is a big advantage. The trail is informally and actively maintained; however, previous drivers have placed rocks to build up an edge for tires to grab and in other strategic places to try to control further trail erosion.

The trail continues 6-rated for 0.3 miles as it travels along

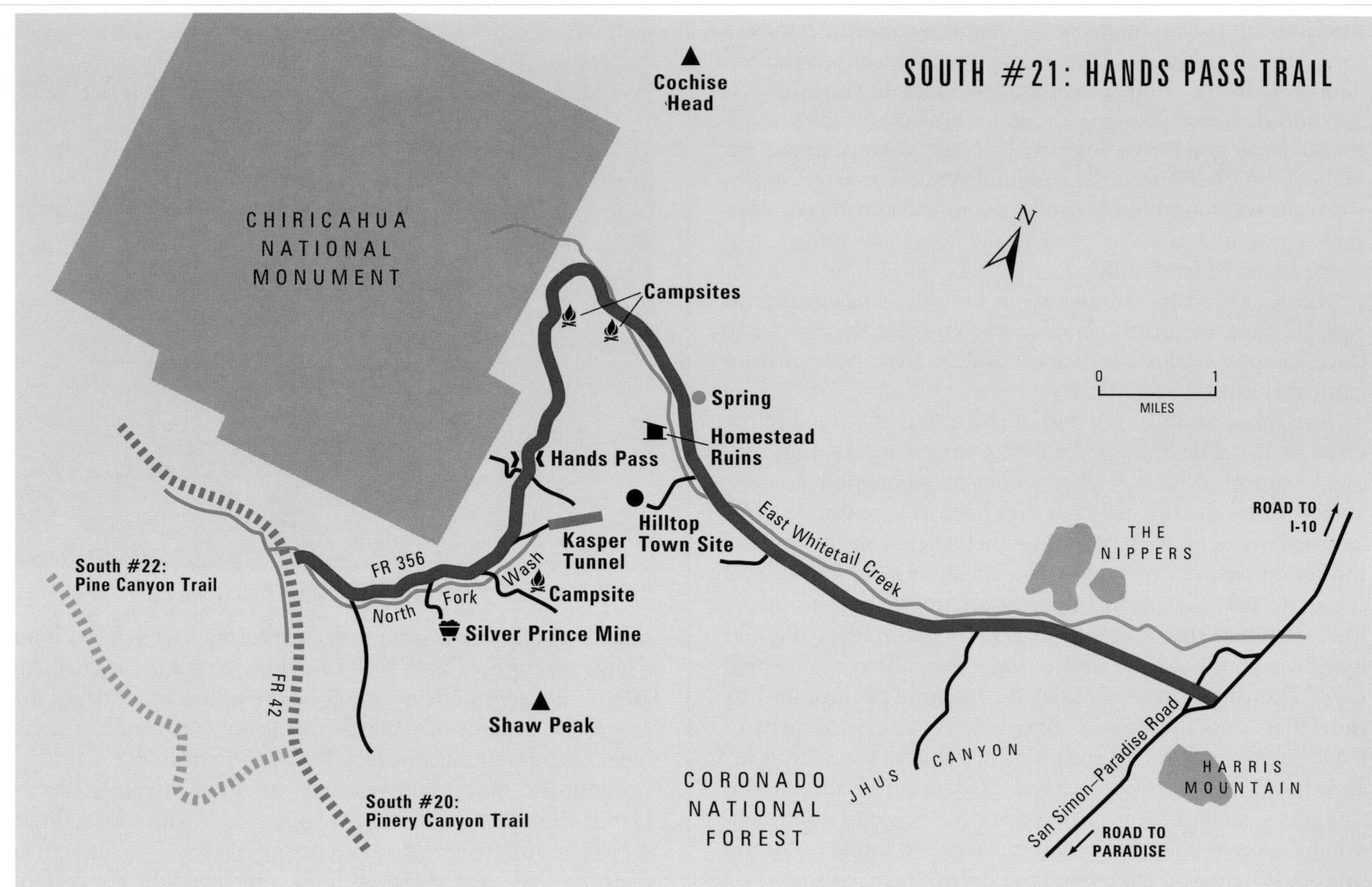

a narrow channel strewn with large boulders. You will need to watch your wheel placement carefully. A farther 0.3 miles along the trail, there is a very deep, ditchy wash crossing. Be extremely careful with front and rear overhangs. If you are driving this trail in the reverse direction and you don't like the look of this wash, then turn back at this point.

After the wash, the major difficulties are past. The trail now follows alongside or in the bed of East Whitetail Creek. There are still some slow-going sections as the trail crawls over large river-rock boulders. This end of the trail passes through private property. The boundaries are clearly marked, and the property owners request that you fill in your vehicle details in order to pass through. Please comply with their reasonable request and treat the access through the property as a privilege not a right. It can be rescinded at any time. Considerate use of the trail will help ensure access for future users.

The site of Hilltop is just off the main trail. It too stands on private property, and vehicle access is by permission only. The final section of the trail travels past private property, open forest, and ranchland to end at the intersection with the San Simon–Paradise Road, 5 miles north of Paradise.

Current Road Information

Coronado National Forest
Douglas Ranger District
381 North Leslie Canyon Rd.
Douglas, AZ 85607
(520) 364-3468

Map References

BLM Chiricahua Peak, Willcox
USFS Coronado National Forest: Chiricahua-Peloncillo Mts. Ranger Districts
USGS 1:24,000 Rustler Park, Cochise Head, Portal, Blue Mt.
1:100,000 Chiricahua Peak, Willcox
Maptech CD-ROM: Southeast Arizona/Tucson
Arizona Atlas & Gazetteer, p. 75
Arizona Road & Recreation Atlas, p. 55 & p. 89
Recreational Map of Arizona (incomplete)

Route Directions

▼ 0.0		From South #20: Pinery Canyon Trail, 1.4 miles east of Coronado National Forest boundary, zero trip meter and turn east onto small formed trail at the marker for FR 356, signed to North Fork. Small track on right at intersection goes to camping area.
1.9 ▲		Trail ends at the junction with South #20: Pinery Canyon Trail. Turn right for Arizona 181, turn left to follow the Pinery Canyon Trail to Portal. Small track straight on goes to camping area.
		GPS: N31°58.16′ W109°19.20′
▼ 0.1	SO	Cattle guard.
1.8 ▲	SO	Cattle guard.
▼ 0.2	SO	Cross through North Fork Wash.
1.7 ▲	SO	Cross through North Fork Wash.
▼ 0.4	SO	Track on right; then cross through North Fork Wash.
1.5 ▲	SO	Cross through North Fork Wash; then track on left.

		GPS: N31°58.08′ W109°18.78′
▼ 0.6	BL	Corral, cabin, and well on left followed by track on right. Bear left and cross through wash.
1.3 ▲	SO	Cross through wash; then track on left. Corral, cabin, and well on right.
		GPS: N31°56.06′ W109°18.57′
▼ 0.7	SO	Track on left underneath power lines. Trail is following alongside North Fork Wash.
1.2 ▲	SO	Track on right underneath power lines.
▼ 0.9	SO	Enter North Fork Wash.
1.0 ▲	BR	Exit wash to the right.
▼ 1.0	BL	Bear left on trail out of wash, tracks continue in wash.
0.9 ▲	SO	Enter North Fork Wash, vehicle tracks go up the wash to the left.
▼ 1.1	SO	Cross through wash.
0.8 ▲	SO	Cross through wash.
▼ 1.3	SO	Well-used track on right goes 0.4 miles to Silver Prince Mine and private cabin. Nothing remains of mine. Continue to the northeast along wash course. Trail immediately forks and rejoins again.
0.6 ▲	SO	Trails rejoin, then well-used track on left goes 0.4 miles to Silver Prince Mine and private cabin. Nothing remains of mine.
		GPS: N31°58.40′ W109°18.08′
▼ 1.4	SO	Trails rejoin.
0.5 ▲	SO	Trail immediately forks and rejoins again.
▼ 1.5	SO	Pass through fence line; then track on right at well.
0.4 ▲	SO	Track on left at well; then pass through fence line.
		GPS: N31°58.52′ W109°17.89′
▼ 1.6	SO	Cross through two washes.
0.3 ▲	SO	Cross through two washes.
▼ 1.7	SO	Track on right at concrete pad.
0.2 ▲	SO	Track on left at concrete pad.
▼ 1.8	BL	Cross through wash; then bear left and climb away from the creek. Track on right goes to campsite.
0.1 ▲	SO	Track now follows alongside North Fork Wash. Track on left at bottom of hill goes to campsite.
		GPS: N31°58.63′ W109°17.66′
▼ 1.9	SO	Track on right goes 0.7 miles to the southwest end of the Kasper Tunnel. Zero trip meter. Coordinates at Kasper Tunnel—GPS: N31°59.14′ W109°17.39′
0.0 ▲		Continue to the southwest.
		GPS: N31°58.72′ W109°17.61′
▼ 0.0		Continue to the north.
5.5 ▲	SO	Track on left goes 0.7 miles to the southwest end of the Kasper Tunnel. Zero trip meter. Coordinates at Kasper Tunnel—GPS: N31°59.14′ W109°17.39′
▼ 0.1	SO	Second entrance to spur trail to Kasper Tunnel on right.
5.4 ▲	SO	Track on left joins spur trail to Kasper Tunnel.
		GPS: N31°58.79′ W109°17.61′
▼ 0.5	SO	View to the right of workings of Kasper Tunnel.
5.0 ▲	SO	View to the left of workings of the Kasper Tunnel.
▼ 1.0	SO	Hands Pass. Pass through gate; then track on right and left. Views ahead to Cochise Head. Trail descends the north side of Hands Pass.
4.5 ▲	SO	Track on right and left at top of Hands Pass. Pass through gate. Trail descends the south side of Hands Pass.
		GPS: N31°59.45′ W109°17.71′
▼ 1.7	SO	Difficult rutted section.
3.8 ▲	SO	Difficult rutted section.
		GPS: N32°00.05′ W109°17.73′
▼ 1.8	SO	Cross through wash.
3.7 ▲	SO	Cross through wash.
▼ 2.0	SO	End of difficult section.
3.5 ▲	SO	Start of difficult section.
		GPS: N32°00.26′ W109°17.94′
▼ 2.3	SO	Cross through deep, ditchy wash. Watch overhangs and fuel tanks.
3.2 ▲	SO	Cross through deep, ditchy wash. If you don't like the look of this wash, then go no further.
		GPS: N32°00.43′ W109°18.10′
▼ 2.5	SO	Campsite at small saddle.
3.0 ▲	SO	Campsite at small saddle.
▼ 3.0	SO	Cross through wash.
2.5 ▲	SO	Cross through wash.
		GPS: N32°00.94′ W109°18.15′
▼ 3.1	SO	Cross through two washes.
2.4 ▲	SO	Cross through two washes.
▼ 3.2	SO	Cross through wash.
2.3 ▲	SO	Cross through wash.
▼ 3.3	TR	Track on left crosses wash. Turn right and follow alongside East Whitetail Creek, trail enters or runs alongside it.
2.2 ▲	TL	Exit creek. Turn left before wash crossing and start to climb toward saddle, leaving East Whitetail Creek. Track on right crosses wash.
		GPS: N32°01.07′ W109°18.00′
▼ 3.5	SO	Exit creek wash and follow alongside above creek.
2.0 ▲	SO	Enter creek wash.
		GPS: N32°00.93′ W109°17.86′
▼ 3.7	SO	Campsite on far side of creek.
1.8 ▲	SO	Campsite on far side of creek.
▼ 3.8	SO	Gate, entering private land. Please remain on trail, then cross through wash. Please keep gate closed. Please respect the landowners' conditions of entry that are posted at the gate.
1.7 ▲	SO	Entering Coronado National Forest.
		GPS: N32°00.83′ W109°17.54′
▼ 3.9	SO	Cross through two washes.
1.6 ▲	SO	Cross through two washes.
▼ 4.0	SO	Cross through wash.
1.5 ▲	SO	Cross through wash.
▼ 4.2	SO	Track on left through gate is private. Trail standard improves.
1.3 ▲	BL	Bear left following sign for trailhead parking. Re-enter wash course. Trail standard becomes more difficult. Track on right through gate is private.
		GPS: N32°00.69′ W109°17.20′
▼ 4.7	SO	Exit wash, spring on left.
0.8 ▲	SO	Spring on right, enter wash.
		GPS: N32°00.42′ W109°16.78′
▼ 4.8	SO	Gate, exiting private property into national forest. Please keep gate closed. Track on left.
0.7 ▲	SO	Track on right. Entering private property through gate. Please keep gate closed and respect landowners' conditions of entry that are posted at the gate.
		GPS: N32°00.39′ W109°16.77′

Mileage		Directions
▼ 4.9	SO	Track on right crosses creek to small ruin of adobe homestead in paddock; then faint track on left.
0.6 ▲	SO	Faint track on right; then track on left crosses creek to small ruin of adobe homestead in paddock.
		GPS: N32°00.28' W109°16.66'
▼ 5.3	SO	Entering private property.
0.2 ▲	SO	Exiting private property.
▼ 5.4	SO	Gate, leaving private property. Remain on trail.
0.1 ▲	SO	Gate, trail passes through private property, remain on trail.
		GPS: N32°00.01' W109°16.32'
▼ 5.5	TL	Cross through East Whitetail Creek, then turn left in front of house. Zero trip meter. Track on right goes to Hilltop. Vehicle access to Hilltop by permission only.
0.0 ▲		Continue to the northwest.
		GPS: N31°59.97' W109°16.25'
▼ 0.0		Continue to the east.
4.6 ▲	TR	Track straight on goes to Hilltop. Turn right in front of house and cross through East Whitetail Creek. Zero trip meter. Vehicle access to Hilltop by permission only.
▼ 0.1	SO	Cattle guard, crossing private property.
4.5 ▲	SO	Cattle guard.
▼ 0.3	SO	Property boundary. Track on right.
4.3 ▲	SO	Crossing private property. Track on left.
▼ 0.6	SO	Track on left; then track on right.
4.0 ▲	SO	Track on left; then track on right.
▼ 0.8	SO	Track on right.
3.8 ▲	SO	Track on left.
▼ 1.7	SO	Cattle guard; then track on left.
2.9 ▲	SO	Track on right; then cattle guard.
▼ 2.4	SO	Cattle guard.
2.2 ▲	SO	Cattle guard.
▼ 2.6	SO	Track on right.
2.0 ▲	SO	Track on left.
▼ 3.0	SO	Track on right; then cattle guard.
1.6 ▲	SO	Cattle guard; then track on left.
		GPS: N32°00.14' W109°13.19'
▼ 3.4	SO	Cattle guard.
1.2 ▲	SO	Cattle guard.
▼ 3.7	SO	Cattle guard.
0.9 ▲	SO	Cattle guard.
▼ 4.3	SO	Cross through wash.
0.3 ▲	SO	Cross through wash.
▼ 4.4	SO	Cattle guard; then track on left.
0.2 ▲	SO	Track on right; then cattle guard.
▼ 4.5	SO	Track on right joins Paradise Road.
0.1 ▲	SO	Track on left joins Paradise Road.
▼ 4.6		Trail ends at junction with San Simon–Paradise Road. Harris Mountain is ahead; to the left are The Nippers. Turn right for Paradise, turn left for I-10.
0.0 ▲		Trail commences on the San Simon–Paradise Road, 5 miles north of Paradise, 18 miles south of San Simon. Zero trip meter at the sign and turn southwest on the well-graded, dirt road following the sign for East Whitetail Canyon. Harris Mountain is on the west side of the San Simon–Paradise Road and The Nippers are on the right.
		GPS: N32°00.21' W109°11.44'

SOUTH REGION TRAIL #22

Pine Canyon Trail

Starting Point:	**South #20: Pinery Canyon Trail, 6.7 miles west of Arizona 181**
Finishing Point:	**Oak Ranch on Arizona 181, 0.1 miles north of mile marker 56**
Total Mileage:	**12.1 miles**
Unpaved Mileage:	**12.1 miles**
Driving Time:	**2 hours**
Elevation Range:	**4,900–6,400 feet**
Usually Open:	**Year-round**
Best Time to Travel:	**Year-round**
Difficulty Rating:	**3**
Scenic Rating:	**8**
Remoteness Rating:	**+0**

Special Attractions

- Views of the jagged rock formations that form Pine Canyon.
- Shady trail that crosses Pine Creek numerous times.
- Access to hiking trails into the Chiricahua Wilderness.
- Many pleasant backcountry camping sites.

History

This trail approaches the Chiricahua Mountains from the eastern flats and offers a good view of Fife Peak before heading up Fife Canyon. Both features were named in remembrance of Mrs. Fife, one of two wives of a Mormon polygamist who ranched locally. She was approached by one of her Mexican employees for food, and though she offered the food, the employee shot and killed her. He was captured soon after near Fort Bowie, was identified, and hung.

Description

Pine Canyon Trail is a rough, rocky single track that travels through two canyons—Pine Canyon and the wider Fife

One of the many crossings of Pine Creek

A view of the rock crags that form the walls of Pine Canyon

Canyon. Initially the trail follows a roughly graded, single-lane dirt road as it travels across Downing Pass, past some spectacular, jagged red rock formations. At one point there is a view ahead looking down into narrow Pine Canyon.

The trail then turns onto a small, formed track that winds alongside Pine Creek, crossing it often. All the crossings have firm, stony bottoms. Normally the creek has a few inches of water, but in spring and after summer storms, depths of 18 inches or more are not uncommon and the difficulty of the trail increases accordingly. The canyon is tight and passes below the red rock formations glimpsed earlier from Downings Pass. The vegetation is predominantly oak, pine, and alligator juniper, and the entire trail is moderately brushy for most vehicles, the lower section of Pine Canyon being the worst. The lower section of Pine Canyon is also the slowest going as the trail crawls over small but lumpy river rocks.

The trail opens out as it exits Pine Canyon. It is wider and travels through manzanita, alligator juniper, and low shrubs. It crosses into the wider, lower Fife Canyon and becomes smoother as it follows alongside Fife and Fivemile Creeks.

The lower end of the trail spills out into open grasslands and runs along the national forest boundary before crossing private property for the final two miles. Access through the private property is granted under the Sportsman-Landowners Respect Program. The designated route passes through the ranch yards and right past the ranch house. Access is not permitted after dark. Please respect this restriction to avoid disturbing the owners, and drive slowly to avoid making unnecessary dust.

There are several good campsites along this trail; the best ones are at the north end of Pine Creek where there are several good sites along the creek, underneath mature trees, and farther down alongside Fivemile Creek where there are several more open ones.

Current Road Information

Coronado National Forest
Douglas Ranger District
381 North Leslie Canyon Rd.
Douglas, AZ 85607
(520) 364-3468

Map References

BLM Chiricahua Peak
USFS Coronado National Forest: Chiricahua-Peloncillo Mts. Ranger Districts
USGS 1:24,000 Rustler Park, Fife Peak
1:100,000 Chiricahua Peak
Maptech CD-ROM: Southeast Arizona/Tucson
Arizona Atlas & Gazetteer, p. 75
Arizona Road & Recreation Atlas, p. 55 & p. 89

Route Directions

Mileage		Direction	Description
▼ 0.0			From South #20: Pinery Canyon Trail, 6.7 miles from western end, turn southwest on graded dirt road FR 42C at sign for the Methodist Camp and zero trip meter.
	1.4 ▲		Trail finishes at the intersection with South #20: Pinery Canyon Trail. Turn left to exit to Arizona 181, turn right to follow along Pinery Canyon to Portal.
			GPS: N31°56.89' W109°18.43'
▼ 0.1		SO	Cross through wash.
	1.3 ▲	SO	Cross through wash.
▼ 0.8		SO	Track on left.
	0.6 ▲	SO	Track on right.
▼ 0.9		SO	Saddle at Downings Pass.
	0.5 ▲	SO	Saddle at Downings Pass.
			GPS: N31°56.44' W109°18.88'
▼ 1.4		TR	At sign for Pine Canyon, turn right onto small formed trail. Zero trip meter.
	0.0 ▲		Continue to the northeast.
			GPS: N31°56.11' W109°19.15'
▼ 0.0			Continue to the northwest.
	2.5 ▲	TL	T-intersection, turn left onto larger graded trail, following sign for Pinery Road. Zero trip meter.
▼ 0.2		SO	Track on right to campsite; then cross through Pine Creek.
	2.3 ▲	SO	Cross through Pine Creek; then track on left to campsite.
▼ 0.6		SO	Cross through creek.
	1.9 ▲	SO	Cross through creek.
▼ 0.7		SO	Cross through creek.
	1.8 ▲	SO	Cross through creek.
▼ 0.9		SO	Gate.
	1.6 ▲	SO	Gate.
			GPS: N31°56.61' W109°19.69'
▼ 1.2		SO	Cross through creek.
	1.3 ▲	SO	Cross through creek.
▼ 1.3		SO	Cross through creek.
	1.2 ▲	SO	Cross through creek.
▼ 1.8		SO	Cross through creek.
	0.7 ▲	SO	Cross through creek.
▼ 2.2		SO	Cross through creek.
	0.3 ▲	SO	Cross through creek.
▼ 2.3		SO	Track on left goes to Hoovey Canyon hiking trailhead.
	0.2 ▲	SO	Track on right goes to Hoovey Canyon hiking trailhead.
			GPS: N31°57.13' W109°20.89'
▼ 2.5		BR	Track on left goes to Green Canyon. Bear right following sign to Fife Canyon and zero trip meter.
	0.0 ▲		Continue to the southeast.
			GPS: N31°57.24' W109°21.12'
▼ 0.0			Continue to the north; and cross through creek.
	2.6 ▲	BL	Cross through creek, then track on right goes to Green Canyon. Bear left; there is a sign at the junction for Green and Fife Canyons. Zero trip meter.
▼ 0.3		SO	Track on left to campsite.
	2.3 ▲	SO	Track on right to campsite.
▼ 0.6		SO	Cross through creek.

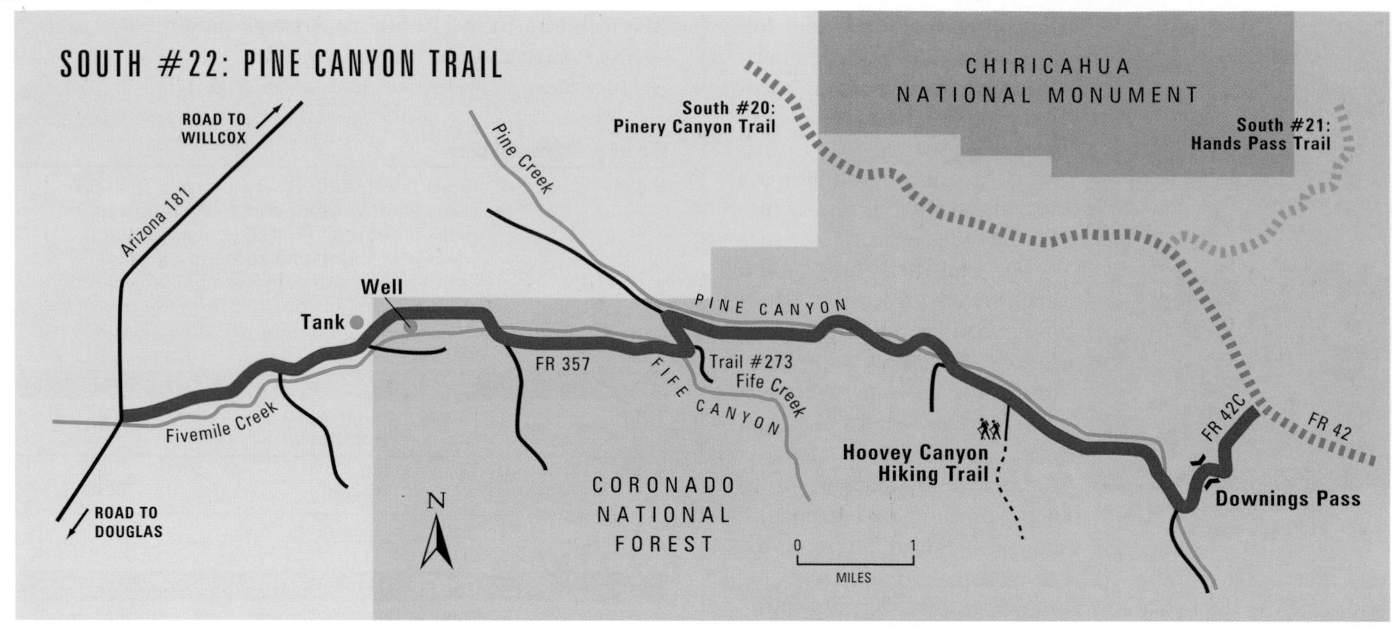

▼	▲		
	2.0 ▲	SO	Cross through creek.
▼ 0.8		SO	Cross through creek.
	1.8 ▲	SO	Cross through creek.
			GPS: N31°57.54' W109°21.85'
▼ 1.0		SO	Enter creek.
	1.6 ▲	SO	Exit creek.
▼ 1.1		SO	Exit creek.
	1.5 ▲	SO	Enter creek.
▼ 1.3		SO	Cross through creek.
	1.3 ▲	SO	Cross through creek.
▼ 1.6		SO	Clearing on left.
	1.0 ▲	SO	Clearing on right.
▼ 1.8		SO	Cross through Pine Creek.
	0.8 ▲	SO	Cross through Pine Creek.
▼ 2.6		TL	Turn left, following the NFS sign for Fife Canyon, FR 357. Faint track on right and track ahead to campsite. Intersection is in small clearing. Zero trip meter.
	0.0 ▲		Continue to the northeast.
			GPS: N31°57.70' W109°23.64'
▼ 0.0			Continue to the southeast, leaving Pine Canyon.
	3.4 ▲	TR	Turn right in clearing. Track on left goes to campsite, faint track straight on. There is a NFS sign pointing to Fife Canyon (the direction you have come). Zero trip meter. There is an old fallen down sign for Green Canyon and Rustler Park FR 357. Trail now enters Pine Canyon.
▼ 0.2		SO	Gate. Entering Fife Canyon.
	3.2 ▲	SO	Leaving Fife Canyon. Gate.
			GPS: N31°57.54' W109°23.48'
▼ 0.3		TR	Track on left is Trail #273 into Fife Canyon. It is used by vehicles at the lower end and then enters wilderness. Turn right, following the sign to Oak Ranch.
	3.1 ▲	TL	Turn left following the sign for Pine Canyon. Ahead is Trail #273 into Fife Canyon. It is used by vehicles at the lower end and then enters wilderness.
			GPS: N31°57.46' W109°23.47'
▼ 0.5		SO	Cross through Fife Creek.
	2.9 ▲	SO	Cross through Fife Creek.

▼	▲		
			GPS: N31°57.48' W109°23.66'
▼ 0.8		SO	Cross through wash.
	2.6 ▲	SO	Cross through wash.
▼ 1.8		SO	Faint track on right.
	1.6 ▲	SO	Faint track on left.
▼ 2.0		SO	Track on left is Trail #258.
	1.4 ▲	SO	Track on right is Trail #258.
			GPS: N31°57.63' W109°25.19'
▼ 2.1		SO	Cross through Fivemile Creek; then track on left.
	1.3 ▲	SO	Track on right; then cross through Fivemile Creek.
▼ 2.2		BL	Track on right, bear left along fence line—the national forest boundary.
	1.2 ▲	BR	Track on left, bear right toward Fivemile Creek.
			GPS: N31°57.76' W109°25.22'
▼ 2.7		SO	Track on left to campsite.
	0.7 ▲	SO	Track on right to campsite.
▼ 2.9		SO	Well on left.
	0.5 ▲	SO	Well on right.
			GPS: N31°57.77' W109°25.89'
▼ 3.4		SO	Tank on right; then track on left across Fivemile Creek. Continue straight on through gate into private property. Access is granted under the Sportsman-Landowners Respect Program. Please close gate. There is no access to the private property after dark. Zero trip meter.
	0.0 ▲		Continue to the north. Track on right along Fivemile Creek; then tank on left. Continue straight on.
			GPS: N31°57.58' W109°26.38'
▼ 0.0			Continue to the south and pass through second gate and track on right.
	2.2 ▲	SO	Track on left; then pass through gate. Then pass through second gate, leaving private property into the national forest. Zero trip meter at second gate. Please close gates.
▼ 0.2		SO	Well on left.
	2.0 ▲	SO	Well on right.
▼ 0.8		SO	Track on left.
	1.4 ▲	SO	Track on right.
▼ 1.0		SO	Cattle guard; then gate.
	1.2 ▲	SO	Gate; then cattle guard.

▼ 1.9		SO	Track on left through gate.
	0.3 ▲	SO	Track on right through gate.
▼ 2.0		BL	Track on right, bear left and cross cattle guard and pass through ranch yard, keeping residences on right. Please go very slowly to avoid dust or disturbing the owners.
	0.2 ▲	BR	Pass through ranch yard, keeping residences on the left; then cross cattle guard and bear right, track on left.
			GPS: N31°57.08' W109°28.39'
▼ 2.1		SO	Track on right; then cattle guard.
	0.1 ▲	SO	Cattle guard; then track on left.
▼ 2.2			Trail ends at junction of paved Arizona 181. Turn right for Willcox, turn left for Douglas.
	0.0 ▲		Trail commences on Arizona 181, 0.1 miles north of mile marker 56. Turn east through the gate of Oak Ranch and zero trip meter. Access is granted under the Sportsman-Landowners Respect Program. The trail initially passes through the ranch yard past the houses, so please drive very slowly to avoid dust or disturbing the owners. Access through the private property is not permitted after dark.
			GPS: N31°57.11' W109°28.61'

SOUTH REGION TRAIL #23

Barfoot Park Trail

Starting Point:	**Intersection of FR 357 and FR 42D, 2 miles south of Onion Saddle**
Finishing Point:	**Pine Creek**
Total Mileage:	**3.1 miles**
Unpaved Mileage:	**3.1 miles**
Driving Time:	**45 minutes (one-way)**
Elevation Range:	**7,000–8,400 feet**
Usually Open:	**April to December**
Best Time to Travel:	**April to December**
Difficulty Rating:	**4**
Scenic Rating:	**7**
Remoteness Rating:	**+0**

Special Attractions

- Cool woodland trail that offers excellent birding.
- Remote backcountry camping at Barfoot Park.
- Barfoot Lookout.

Description

This short trail is part of a through route that connects Barfoot Park to South #22: Pine Canyon Trail near the Methodist Camp lower down in Pine Canyon. However, Pine Creek heavily washed out a few years ago and a short section is considered impassable to most vehicles, most unmodified 4WDs included.

The trail starts from the Rustlers Park Road, FR 42D, 2 miles south of Onion Saddle. In the 1870s and 1880s, rustling cattle from Mexico for resale in Arizona was a common activity. Rustler Park was a favorite stopover point for the rustlers, who had time to re-brand, rest up, and feed the cattle on the park's higher-altitude green pastures.

The narrow trail as it descends through the woods alongside Pine Creek

A hiking trail near the start of the trail goes a short but steep distance to the old lookout and a great view. Barfoot Park is a small, pretty meadow, which in late spring is studded with wild iris. A spring trickles across the meadow and at one end there are the remains of an old national forest campground. The concrete picnic tables and benches remain, and there is plenty of shade and many spots in which to camp under the pines. An unmarked hiking trail climbs back up to the Barfoot Lookout on Buena Vista Peak. Barfoot Peak can be seen to the north. Birders will enjoy searching for some of the high elevation species, such as Mexican chickadees, red crossbills, and red-faced warblers.

The trail standard gets tougher as it becomes a small well-formed narrow trail and starts to descend toward Pine Canyon on a shelf road. Views are limited as it travels within the woodland canopy. Three miles from the start, as the trail enters Pine Creek, there is a white Road Closed sign, which marks the start of the extremely challenging section. The forest service placed the sign there to warn most road users that the road is impassable ahead. However, it is not currently an official road closure (which would be denoted by a national forest closed trail sign), and experienced drivers in modified rigs may wish to continue along the forest road, which exits through the Methodist Camp near the start of South #22: Pine Canyon Trail. This section of the trail is beyond the scope of this book and is not mapped.

For drivers without the modified equipment necessary to treat the trail as a through road, it is possible to drive in from the south end through the Methodist Camp to access some pleasant shady campsites along Pine Creek and the hiking trail to Rattlesnake Peak.

Current Road Information

Coronado National Forest
Douglas Ranger District
381 North Leslie Canyon Rd.
Douglas, AZ 85607
(520) 364-3468

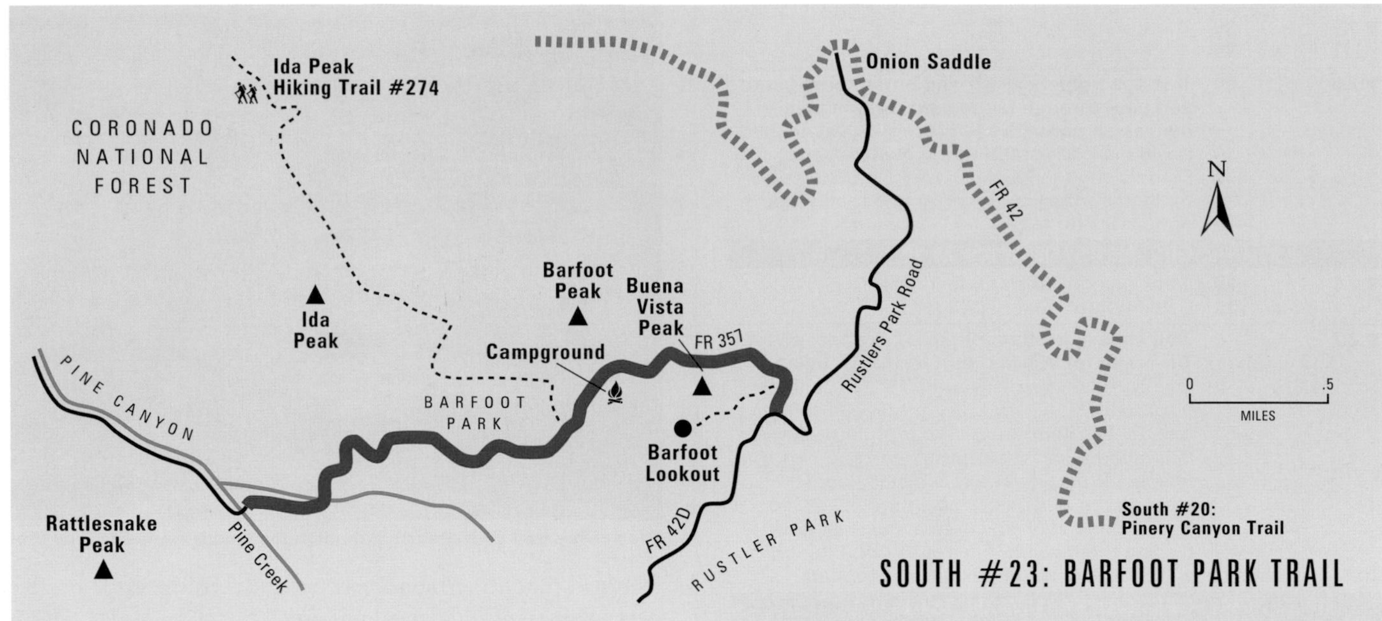

Map References

BLM Chiricahua Peak
USFS Coronado National Forest: Chiricahua-Peloncillo Mts. Ranger Districts
USGS 1:24,000 Rustler Park
1:100,000 Chiricahua Peak
Maptech CD-ROM: Southeast Arizona/Tucson
Arizona Atlas & Gazetteer, p. 75
Arizona Road & Recreation Atlas, p. 55 & p. 89

Route Directions

▼ 0.0		From FR 42D, 2 miles south of Onion Saddle, zero trip meter and turn north on FR 357, following the sign for Barfoot Park. The road is roughly graded at this point. Second small track on right at junction.
		GPS: N31°54.88' W109°16.08'
▼ 0.1	SO	Hiking trail at sign on left to Barfoot Lookout.
		GPS: N31°55.01' W109°16.05'
▼ 0.5	SO	Cattle guard on saddle.
▼ 0.9	BR	Barfoot Park. Barfoot Peak is directly to the north. Concrete footings on right, then track on left to campsite. Hiking trail to Barfoot Lookout on left is unsigned, but is edged with rocks at the start.
		GPS: N31°55.03' W109°16.75'
▼ 1.0	BL	Track on right.
▼ 1.1	SO	Track on left; then track on right goes 0.2 miles to Barfoot Helispot and Ida Peak hiking trail #274 to South #20: Pinery Canyon Trail. Old corral and picnic tables at junction.
▼ 1.9	BL	Track on right goes 0.1 miles to campsite.
		GPS: N31°54.92' W109°17.55'
▼ 2.1	SO	Track on left.
		GPS: N31°54.82' W109°17.62'
▼ 2.5	SO	Cross through the head of Pine Creek.
		GPS: N31°54.74' W109°17.80'
▼ 3.1		Trail ends at Road Closed sign where trail meets Pine Creek. Past this point the trail is suitable for modified 4WDs only.
		GPS: N31°54.70' W109°18.10'

SOUTH REGION TRAIL #24

Swift Trail

Starting Point:	US 191 at Swift Trail Junction
Finishing Point:	Clark Peak Hiking Trailhead #301
Total Mileage:	32.4 miles
Unpaved Mileage:	11.8 miles
Driving Time:	2.5 hours (one-way)
Elevation Range:	3,200–9,500 feet
Usually Open:	April 15 to November 15
Best Time to Travel:	April 15 to November 15
Difficulty Rating:	1
Scenic Rating:	8
Remoteness Rating:	+0

Special Attractions

- Easy trail traveling through many life zones, ultimately climbing to 9,531 feet.
- Cool summer camping opportunities.
- Summer wildflower viewing.
- Trout fishing in Riggs Flat Lake.

History

The towns of Safford and Thatcher were first settled in 1872 and quickly became substantial agricultural communities, utilizing water from the Gila River to irrigate the surrounding countryside. Residents sought a refuge from the blistering summer heat of the valley and looked to Mt. Graham to provide the escape. The Swift Trail was constructed initially as a timber road for the pioneers, but later the settlers used it as their route up the mountain for their annual summer migration.

View across Sulphur Springs Valley toward Galiuro Mountains

The road was later upgraded by the forest service and the Civilian Conservation Corps (CCC), which had many camps in the region.

There are many historical points of interest along the Swift Trail: the first comes at the boundary of the Coronado National Forest. A historical plaque commemorates P. J. and George Jacobson who constructed a sawmill further up the canyon. The mill commenced operations in 1895 and provided the lumber for many of the buildings in the region. A second plaque commemorates Theodore T. Swift, who was supervisor of the Crook National Forest, now called the Coronado National Forest, from 1908 to 1923. Swift was the major force behind the upgrade of the original logging trail, and today the trail bears his name.

The first picnic ground to be reached, Noon Creek, is named as it was the mid-day rest stop for the early pioneers on their way up the mountains for the summer. The major CCC camp of the region was located near the picnic ground. Two hundred workers were housed in eight barracks in the complex. The summer camp was at Columbine; the winter camp was at Noon Creek. Some of the work completed by the CCC included fire lookouts and improvements to the Swift Trail. The Noon Creek Camp housed German prisoners of war after its closure.

Twenty miles from the start of the trail is Heliograph Peak, so called because the army used it as a signaling point in the Apache War. Signals were flashed across southern Arizona by using mirrors to reflect the bright sunlight.

Shortly after Heliograph Peak, a side trail leads to Treasure Park, which has one of the most exciting stories of the trail. Supposedly, Mexican bandits buried nineteen bags of gold and silver here before the Gadsden Purchase. The gold has never been recovered. This is also the site of the first CCC camp in Arizona.

Hospital Flat, a short distance farther, gets its name from its use as a hospital in the summer by the soldiers from Fort Grant at the base of the north side of the mountain. Fort Grant was constructed as a military post in 1872 and housed soldiers who were active in the Indian Wars. It is now a state prison.

The University of Arizona's Steward Observatory houses three world-class telescopes and is a world-ranking astrophysical research organization. As well as housing its own equipment, the observatory also houses the Vatican Advanced Technology Telescope and Germany's Max Planck Submillimeter Telescope. A fourth telescope is under construction.

The next two sites along the trail commemorate early settlers. Peters Flat is named after Scottish-born Peter McBride, an early Gila Valley settler. While working as a logger on the mountain, McBride, as any good Scot would, planted potatoes. He stored them in long, earthen trenches before carrying them down the mountain to Safford for sale.

The second plaque is at Chesley Flat, which is named after the Chesley family, which had a cabin here in the 1890s. The family grazed cattle. Sarah Jane Chesley made and sold cheese from the milk.

The 11-acre Riggs Flat Lake was put in by the Arizona Game and Fish Department in 1957. The lake is named after Lew Riggs, who used the area as summer pasture for his cattle in the late 1870s and early 1880s.

Description

This easy trail is paved for two-thirds of its length and the remainder is a well-graded gravel road, making it a pleasant trail for those in passenger vehicles or anyone wanting to experience some cooler mountain temperatures and spectacular scenery. The trail commences on US 191, seven miles south of Safford at a well-marked intersection. Almost immediately the paved road starts to climb, switchbacking its way up into the Pinaleño Mountains. The creosote bush, mesquite, and cactus desert plains are quickly left behind, as the road passes through the pinyon pine, alligator juniper, and desert oak of the slightly higher elevations.

As the trail continues to climb into the national forest, there are many cool and shady picnic areas. Noon Creek is at the lowest elevation. Although shown on the forest maps as a campground, Noon Creek is now for picnicking only. A short distance farther along is the start of the Round-the-Mountain pack trail. There are horse corrals and a couple of pleasant picnic sites at the start. A historical plaque commemorates the work done by the CCC camps located in the Pinaleño Mountains.

Most of the side trails leading off the main Swift Trail are either very short, only a mile or two in length, or are inaccessible to the public by vehicle. The higher elevations have been designated as a refuge for the endangered Mt. Graham red squirrel since 1988. The forest service is currently considering

Riggs Flat Lake

whether to permit foot access into the area. Check with the national forest office in Safford for details.

Another road leads to the site of the University of Arizona Astrophysical Site. No public access is permitted to the observatory site.

There are many camping opportunities along this trail at any of several developed national forest service campgrounds or at undeveloped sites that can be found along many of the short spur trails. In addition, there are undeveloped sites along the main trail, particularly around the turnoff to Riggs Flat Lake.

Riggs Flat Lake is an 11-acre lake developed by the Arizona Game and Fish Department in 1957. The lake is stocked with trout. The popular campground surrounding it is one of the most pleasant along the trail. Campers should be aware that black bears abound in the Pinaleño Mountains and can be troublesome around the campgrounds. Normal and sensible precautions should be taken, and of course no food should be left outside at night unless it is in a bear-proof container. All trash containers at the picnic and camping ground are bear-proof.

The vehicle trail ends shortly after the turn to Riggs Flat Lake at the hiking trailhead for Taylor Pass.

The closure gate at the end of the paved road is locked each year from November 15 to April 15 due to snow. Snowmobiles can use the road during these months.

Current Road Information

Coronado National Forest
Safford Ranger District
504 5th Ave., 3rd Floor
Safford, AZ 85546
(520) 428-4150

Map References

BLM Safford
USFS Coronado National Forest: Safford and Santa Catalina Ranger Districts
USGS 1:24,000 Artesia, Mt. Graham, Stockton Pass, Webb Peak
1:100,000 Safford
Maptech CD-ROM: East Central Arizona/White Mountains
Arizona Atlas & Gazetteer, pp. 68-69
Arizona Road & Recreation Atlas, pp. 48, 49 & pp. 82, 83
Recreational Map of Arizona

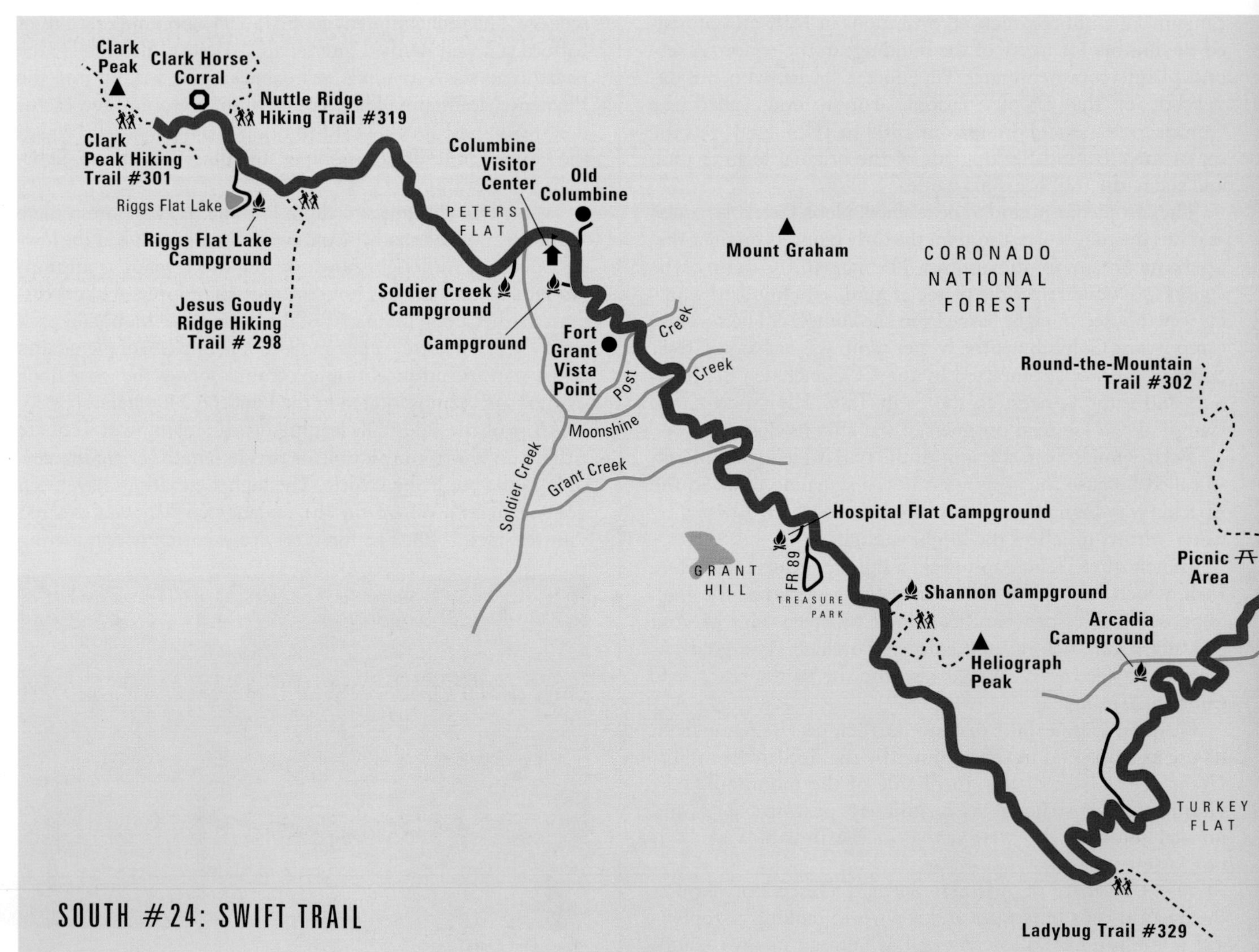

SOUTH #24: SWIFT TRAIL

Route Directions

▼ 0.0 From US 191, 7 miles south of Safford and 0.3 miles south of mile marker 114, zero trip meter and turn southwest on paved road sign-posted for the Swift Trail (AZ 366).

GPS: N32°43.82' W109°42.85'

▼ 1.3 SO Cattle guard.
▼ 1.7 SO Graded road on left; then cattle guard.
▼ 3.1 SO Track on right.

GPS: N32°41.58' W109°45.03'

▼ 3.7 SO Cattle guard, road starts to climb and switch-back.
▼ 4.5 SO Entering Coronado National Forest. Two historical plaques on right before the sign commemorate P. J. and George Jacobson and Theodore T. Swift.

GPS: N32°41.14' W109°45.95'

▼ 5.5 SO FR 861 on right goes to Jacobson Overlook and a view of the Gila Valley.

GPS: N32°40.55' W109°46.65'

▼ 6.2 SO FR 667 on left.

GPS: N32°40.20' W109°47.19'

▼ 6.7 SO Noon Creek Picnic Ground on right. Zero trip meter.

GPS: N32°40.08' W109°47.65'

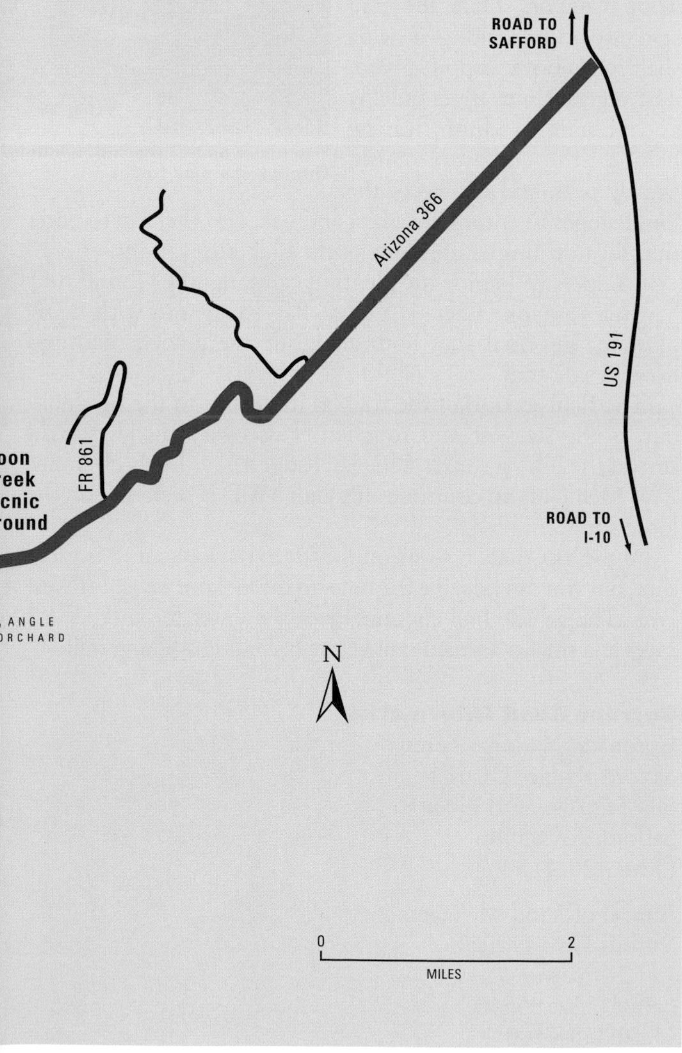

▼ 0.0 Continue along paved road up the mountain.
▼ 0.3 SO T 329 Road on left goes to Angle Orchard and Ladybug Trail.

GPS: N32°39.92' W109°47.75'

▼ 0.4 SO Picnic area on right. Round-the-Mountain Trail #302 to Marijalda Creek (3.5 miles) and Frye Canyon Trail #36 lead off through picnic ground.
▼ 2.3 BL Picnic area on right. Bear left and cross over creek. Closure gate.

GPS: N32°39.07' W109°48.75'

▼ 4.0 SO Arcadia Campground on right. Fee area on right. Zero trip meter.

GPS: N32°38.95' W109°49.07'

▼ 0.0 Continue to climb up mountain followed by road on left.
▼ 0.1 SO Track on right to Upper Arcadia Group Area.
▼ 0.6 SO Track on left before closure gate.

GPS: N32°38.66' W109°49.01'

▼ 2.3 SO Track on left and track on right. Turkey Flat hiking trail #330 and Ladybug Trail #329 on left. Start of Turkey Flat summer home area, many tracks on left and right to private cabins.

GPS: N32°37.94' W109°48.93'

▼ 2.7 SO Track on right before closure gate.
▼ 5.1 SO Hiking trailhead #329, Ladybug Trail on left, then closure gate. Ladybug Saddle.

GPS: N32°37.34' W109°49.38'

▼ 6.3 SO Road starts to level off. Views to south over Sulphur Springs Valley.
▼ 8.9 SO Snow Flat Road on left marked by a sign. Zero trip meter.

GPS: N32°38.94' W109°51.71'

▼ 0.0 Continue along paved road.
▼ 0.6 SO Graded road on right goes to Heliograph Peak. The road is closed to vehicles but you can hike up. Second track on right leads to Shannon Campground.

GPS: N32°39.38' W109°51.58'

▼ 1.0 SO Track on right is closed road to High Peak, road turns to graded dirt. Closure gate, road is closed past this point from Nov 15 to April 15. Zero trip meter.

GPS: N32°39.58' W109°51.87'

▼ 0.0 Continue on graded dirt road.
▼ 0.7 SO Track on left is FR 89, a short loop to Treasure Park.

GPS: N32°39.88' W109°52.36'

▼ 0.9 SO Track on right to group campsite; then track on left to Hospital Flat Campground and nature trail.
▼ 1.6 SO Track on right and track on left. Track on left is closed to vehicles after a short distance, parking for Grant Hill loop trail #322 for mountain bikes and hiking.

GPS: N32°40.11' W109°52.78'

▼ 2.7 SO Cross over Grant Creek.
▼ 3.1 SO Two tracks on left.
▼ 3.2 SO Cunningham Loop hiking trail #316 which goes to Grant Hill on right, for mountain bikes and hiking.

GPS: N32°40.80' W109°53.56'

▼ 3.3 SO Track on left to Cunningham Campground and corrals. Crane Creek hiking trailhead #305 leads off through campground.
▼ 3.9 SO Cross over Moonshine Creek and track on left.
▼ 4.7 SO Cross over Post Creek.
▼ 5.0 SO Fort Grant Vista Point, elevation 9,356 feet.

		Views to Fort Grant at the foot of the mountain.
		GPS: N32°41.54' W109°54.24'
▼ 5.6	SO	Graded road on right leads to observatory site.
▼ 5.9	SO	Track on left to campsites.
		GPS: N32°41.88' W109°54.56'
▼ 6.3	SO	Track on right goes to Old Columbine. Zero trip meter and continue following the sign to Riggs Flat Lake. Columbine Work Center on the left at the intersection.
		GPS: N32°42.23' W109°54.71'
▼ 0.0		Continue to the northwest.
▼ 0.1	SO	Columbine Visitor Center on left, track on right to Ash Creek trailhead and public corral.
▼ 0.4	SO	Track on left; then track on right.
▼ 0.5	SO	Soldier Creek Campground on left.
		GPS: N32°42.13' W109°55.15'
▼ 0.9	SO	Track on right.
▼ 1.4	SO	Historical marker on left for Peters Flat.
▼ 2.4	SO	Chesley Flat. Historical marker on right.
		GPS: N32°42.96' W109°56.35'
▼ 3.0	SO	Track on right.
▼ 3.6	SO	Track on right and campsite on right.
▼ 3.7	SO	Jesus Goudy Ridge hiking trail #298 on left.
▼ 3.8	SO	Riggs Flat Lake is glimpsed through the trees on the left.
▼ 4.4	SO	Track on left is FR 287, which goes 0.4 miles to Riggs Flat Lake and campground.
		GPS: N32°42.83' W109°57.82'
▼ 4.5	SO	Track on left.
▼ 4.7	SO	Nuttle Ridge hiking trail #319 on right, several campsites. Then tracks on left and right.
▼ 4.9	SO	Clark Horse Corral and two campsites with picnic tables and fire rings on right.
		GPS: N32°43.17' W109°58.15'
▼ 5.5		Trail ends at a small turnaround, with a view to the northwest. A small vehicle trail does a short loop back to the road. Carter Nuttle #315 and Clark Peak #301 hiking trailheads commence here and travel 7 miles to West Peak Lookout and 4 miles to Taylor Pass.
		GPS: N32°43.04' W109°58.60'

SOUTH REGION TRAIL #25

Tripp Canyon Road

Starting Point:	**US 70, immediately west of Pima**
Finishing Point:	**Blue Jay Peak**
Total Mileage:	**26.4 miles**
Unpaved Mileage:	**25.7 miles**
Driving Time:	**2 hours (one-way)**
Elevation Range:	**2,900–8,600**
Usually Open:	**April to November**
Best Time to Travel:	**April to November**
Difficulty Rating:	**3**
Scenic Rating:	**8**
Remoteness Rating:	**+0**

Special Attractions

- Fire lookout tower.
- Popular backcountry camping at the sawmill.
- Access to many hiking trails.

Description

This is one of two roads that access the top of the Pinaleño Mountains; other roads access the side canyons but do not climb to the top. The Tripp Canyon Road is the quieter and shorter of the two, climbing high along the side of Tripp Canyon, winding its way to the fire lookout at the top.

The trail leaves just west of Pima on US 70 at the sign for Tripp Canyon Road. The first few miles are graded dirt road as it sweeps around the bajada on the west side of the Pinaleño Mountains. The road can be extremely washboardy depending on when it last saw the grader. There are some pleasant views to the north and over eroded washes to Bear Springs Flat.

The upper end of the trail winding through the pine forest

After 14.5 miles it enters the Coronado National Forest and starts to follow alongside wide Tripp Canyon. Here the trail starts to climb along a wide shelf road above Tripp Canyon. The vegetation changes quickly as you start to climb, leaving behind the creosote bush, prickly pear, and chollas of the lower slopes to enter manzanita and oak, and then on to enter the alligator juniper and pine of the higher elevations.

Campers will enjoy the plentiful camping to be found near Sawmill Canyon. There is a large, flat, shady area with many pleasant, informal sites both alongside the graded road and down a side trail.

The final section of the trail, as it ascends to the fire lookout, is the steepest and roughest. Passenger vehicles should stop at the hiking trail to Blue Jay Ridge #314. High-clearance 2WD vehicles can continue although 4WD is preferred on the loose surface.

At the top, there is a trail on the left to the lookout. It is gated shut, but you can hike the 0.2 miles to the lookout tower on West Peak. The vehicle trail continues past the tower for another 1.7 miles as a smaller formed trail before becoming a hiking trail.

Current Road Information

Coronado National Forest
Safford Ranger District
504 5th Ave., 3rd Floor
Safford, AZ 85546
(520) 428-4150

Bureau of Land Management
Safford Field Office
711 14th Ave.
Safford, AZ 85546
(520) 348-4400

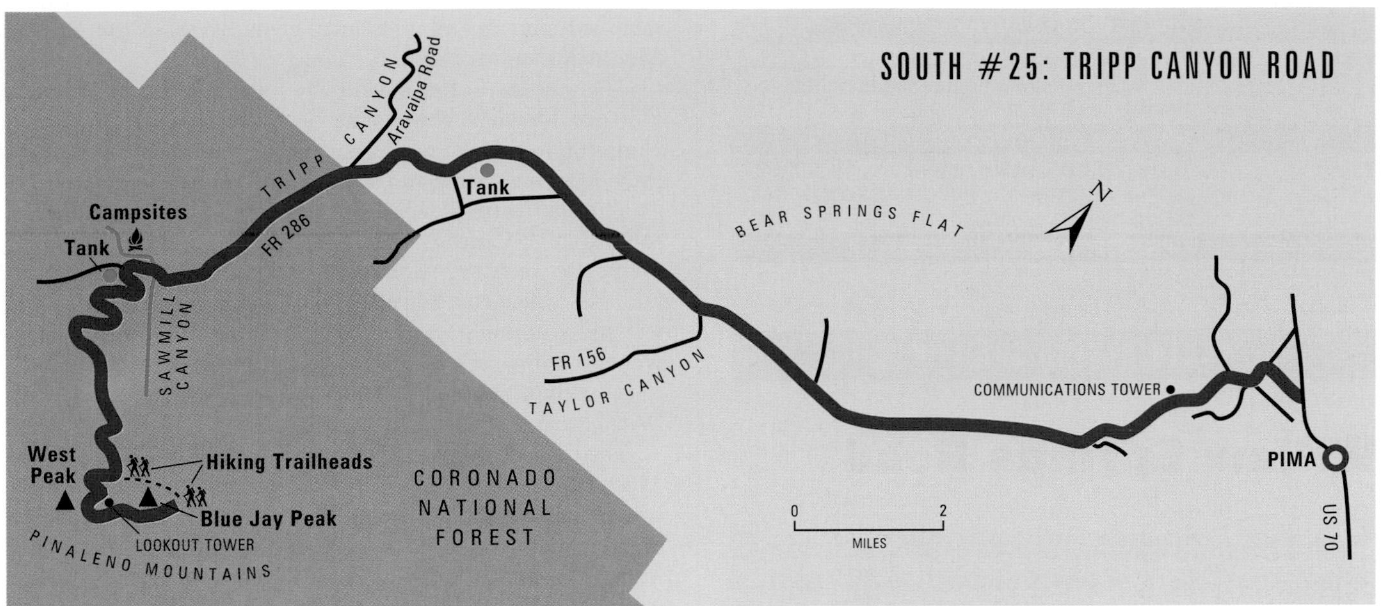

Map References

BLM Safford
USFS Coronado National Forest: Safford and Santa Catalina Ranger Districts
USGS 1:24,000 Pima, Thatcher, Shingle Mill Mt., Tripp Canyon
1:100,000 Safford
Maptech CD-ROM: East Central Arizona/White Mountains
Arizona Atlas & Gazetteer, p. 68
Arizona Road & Recreation Atlas, pp. 49, 48 & pp. 83, 82
Recreational Map of Arizona

Route Directions

▼ 0.0		From US 70, immediately west of Pima, zero trip meter and turn west on the paved Tripp Canyon Road. Immediately cross railroad.
		GPS: N32°54.00' W109°50.40'
▼ 0.7	TL	T-intersection. Turn left onto graded dirt road.
		GPS: N32°54.01' W109°51.08'
▼ 0.9	TR	Crossroads, turn right, ahead is a dead end.
		GPS: N32°53.80' W109°51.10'
▼ 1.2	BL	Cattle guard; then bear left, remaining on main graded road. Two tracks on right.
▼ 1.8	SO	Track on left.
▼ 2.1	SO	Communications tower on right.
		GPS: N32°53.05' W109°51.80'
▼ 2.8	SO	Track on left; then cattle guard.
▼ 3.4	SO	Track on left.
▼ 4.3	SO	Communications tower on left; then cattle guard.
▼ 6.0	SO	Graded road on left and track on right.
		GPS: N32°50.76' W109°54.64'
▼ 7.1	SO	Well-used track on right.
		GPS: N32°50.51' W109°55.74'
▼ 8.1	SO	Track on right.
▼ 8.9	BR	Cattle guard, then bear right, following sign to Tripp Canyon, FR 286. Track on left is FR 156 to Taylor Canyon. Zero trip meter.
		GPS: N32°50.36' W109°57.57'
▼ 0.0		Continue to the west.
▼ 0.4	SO	Track on right.
▼ 1.1	SO	Track on left.
		GPS: N32°50.35' W109°58.78'
▼ 1.8	SO	Track on left is private.
▼ 2.0	SO	Track on left.
▼ 2.1	SO	Cattle guard.
▼ 2.4	SO	Track on left.
▼ 3.5	SO	Tank on left.
		GPS: N32°50.19' W110°01.25'
▼ 4.1	SO	Track on left.
▼ 5.4	SO	Cattle guard.
▼ 5.6	SO	Track on right is Aravaipa Road, then cattle guard. Entering Coronado National Forest. Zero trip meter.
		GPS: N32°48.95' W110°02.58'
▼ 0.0		Continue to the southwest.
▼ 0.9	SO	Corral on right.
▼ 3.2	SO	Cross over wash; then cattle guard. Entering Sawmill Canyon.
		GPS: N32°46.64' W110°03.80'
▼ 3.3	SO	Corral and two tracks on right (both to campsites).
		GPS: N32°46.65' W110°03.87'
▼ 3.4	SO	Concrete and stone footings on right. Large camping area.
		GPS: N32°46.58' W110°03.96'
▼ 3.5	SO	Two tracks on right at mile marker 7. Zero trip meter.
		GPS: N32°46.56' W110°04.00'
▼ 0.0		Continue to the south.
▼ 0.1	SO	Concrete tank on right.
▼ 0.3	SO	Small track on left.
▼ 1.2	SO	Faint track on right.
▼ 3.9	SO	Track on left at mile marker 3 goes to shady campsites and dry lake. Zero trip meter.
		GPS: N32°45.26' W110°03.20'
▼ 0.0		Continue to the south.
▼ 1.5	SO	Hiking trail on left is Blue Jay Ridge hiking trail #314.
		GPS: N32°44.65' W110°02.35'
▼ 2.8	SO	Track on left is gated and goes to the lookout tower. It is 0.2 miles to the tower, which is manned during the wildfire season.

		GPS: N32°44.15′ W110°02.40′
▼ 3.9	SO	Hiking trail straight on is Blue Jay Ridge hiking trail #314; small hiking trail out to right at this point.
		GPS: N32°44.45′ W110°01.46′
▼ 4.5		Trail ends for vehicles at turn around at base of Blue Jay Peak. It continues as a single-track, hiking trail.
		GPS: N32°44.83′ W110°01.56′

SOUTH REGION TRAIL #26

Willow Springs Road

Starting Point:	**Arizona 177 at Kelvin**
Finishing Point:	**Arizona 77, 5.8 miles southwest of Oracle**
Total Mileage:	**49.8 miles**
Unpaved Mileage:	**48.2 miles**
Driving Time:	**1.5 hours**
Elevation Range:	**1,800–3,200 feet**
Usually Open:	**Year-round**
Best Time to Travel:	**October to June**
Difficulty Rating:	**2**
Scenic Rating:	**7**
Remoteness Rating:	**+0**

Special Attractions

- Long, easy trail through scenic ranchland.
- Site of the old settlement of Barkerville.
- Sweeping vistas and grasslands.

Description

A glance at the maps of the region gives an indication of what some of the earliest travelers and settlers thought of this area. Suffering Wash, Bloodsucker Wash, Rattlesnake Tank, and Hot Boy Mine tell their own tales. This trail runs through an arid region of southern Arizona, passing through some old, established ranches and grasslands, giving views of the Tortilla Mountains and the Santa Catalinas.

A view across the trail to a corral and Black Mountain beyond

The trail leaves Kelvin, initially following the well-graded Florence–Kelvin Highway. The views are sweeping as the trail climbs up to the plateau. Jumbled rocks and cacti combine to provide an interesting and scenic landscape.

The trail turns down alongside Box O Wash and heads toward small Cottonwood Hill, which is the site of Barkerville. Between 1924 and 1933 Barkerville had a small store and post office run by the Barker family. At the time there was still a motor stage between Florence and Tucson. There was also a small school serving the children of the surrounding ranches. Nowadays the children attend school in Winkelman and Superior.

The trail is easygoing and roughly graded its entire length. Much of it passes through private ranchland, only some of which is posted. If you take any side trails or make camp, make certain that you are on public lands. Part of the trail runs through state land and a valid permit is required.

The final part of the trail passes through Willow Springs Ranch and eventually joins with Arizona 77 near Oracle. There are excellent views of the Santa Catalinas from this section of the trail.

Current Road Information

Bureau of Land Management
Tucson Field Office
12661 East Broadway Blvd.
Tucson, AZ 85748
(520) 722-4289

Map References

BLM Globe, Mesa, Casa Grande, Mammoth
USGS 1:24,000 Kearny, Grayback, Ninetysix Hills NE, Ninetysix Hills SE, Black Mt., Fortified Peak, North of Oracle, Oracle
1:100,000 Globe, Mesa, Casa Grande, Mammoth
Maptech CD-ROM: East Central Arizona/White Mountains; Phoenix/Superstition Mountains
Arizona Atlas & Gazetteer, pp. 59, 67
Arizona Road & Recreation Atlas, p. 48 & p. 82
Recreational Map of Arizona

Route Directions

▼ 0.0		From Arizona 177, at the turn for Kelvin, turn southwest immediately north of the railroad crossing and zero trip meter. Road is paved and is known as the Florence–Kelvin Highway. Cross cattle guard, and follow along the north side of the railroad, remaining on paved road.
12.4 ▲		Trail ends at the intersection with Arizona 177 at Kelvin. Turn left for Superior, turn right for Winkelman.
		GPS: N33°07.28′ W110°58.49′
▼ 1.2	SO	Cross railroad; then cross over Gila River on bridge.
11.2 ▲	SO	Cross over Gila River on bridge; then cross railroad.
▼ 1.3	SO	Road on left is Riverside Road. Continue straight ahead on paved Florence–Kelvin Highway.

11.1 ▲	SO	Road on right is Riverside Road. Continue straight ahead to Kelvin.
		GPS: N33°06.14' W110°58.43'
▼ 1.6	SO	Road turns to graded dirt.
10.8 ▲	SO	Road is now paved.
▼ 1.8	SO	Cattle guard.
10.6 ▲	SO	Cattle guard.
▼ 3.7	SO	Cross through Ripsey Wash, track on left up wash.
8.7 ▲	SO	Cross through Ripsey Wash, track on right up wash.
		GPS: N33°05.81' W111°00.39'
▼ 4.0	BL	Ranch road on right.
8.4 ▲	BR	Ranch road on left.
		GPS: N33°05.85' W111°00.62'
▼ 5.6	SO	Cross through Zelleweger Wash, tracks on right and left down wash.
6.8 ▲	SO	Cross through Zelleweger Wash, tracks on right and left down wash.
▼ 7.1	SO	Cross through wash.
5.3 ▲	SO	Cross through wash.
▼ 7.3	SO	Track on left.
5.1 ▲	SO	Track on right.
▼ 7.8	SO	Track on left.
4.6 ▲	SO	Track on right.
▼ 8.2	BL	Graded road on right goes to radio tower.
4.2 ▲	BR	Graded road on left goes to radio tower.
		GPS: N33°02.73' W111°02.78'
▼ 9.8	SO	Track on left.
2.6 ▲	SO	Track on right.
▼ 10.1	SO	Track on left.
2.3 ▲	SO	Track on right.
▼ 10.8	SO	Track on right.
1.6 ▲	SO	Track on left.
▼ 11.1	SO	Track on right; then cattle guard.
1.3 ▲	SO	Cattle guard; then track on left.
▼ 11.2	SO	Cross through wash.
1.2 ▲	SO	Cross through wash.
▼ 11.3	SO	Cross through wash.
1.1 ▲	SO	Cross through wash.
▼ 11.5	SO	Cross through wash.
0.9 ▲	SO	Cross through wash.
▼ 11.7	SO	Track on right to Teacup Ranch.
0.7 ▲	SO	Track on left to Teacup Ranch.
▼ 12.4	SO	Track on left through gate onto well-used, formed track. Zero trip meter.
0.0 ▲		Continue to the northeast.
		GPS: N33°00.04' W111°03.84'
▼ 0.0		Continue to the southwest.
4.1 ▲	SO	Track on right through gate onto well-used formed track. Zero trip meter.
▼ 0.1	SO	Cattle guard; then private access road on left.
4.0 ▲	SO	Private access road on right; then cattle guard.
▼ 2.0	SO	Track on right.
2.1 ▲	SO	Track on left.
▼ 2.2	SO	Cross through wide Donnelly Wash.
1.9 ▲	SO	Cross through wide Donnelly Wash.
▼ 2.8	SO	Track on right to rock formations.
1.3 ▲	SO	Track on left to rock formations.
▼ 3.1	BL	Graded road on right is Cochran Road, leads out to an area of tumbled boulders.
1.0 ▲	BR	Graded road on left is Cochran Road, leads out to area of tumbled boulders.
		GPS: N32°59.23' W111°06.84'
▼ 3.5	SO	Track on right.
0.6 ▲	SO	Track on left.
▼ 4.1	TL	At crossing of Box O Wash, turn left onto graded road alongside wash, signed Barkerville Road. Zero trip meter.
0.0 ▲		Continue to the northeast.
		GPS: N32°58.49' W111°07.47'
▼ 0.0		Continue to the south.
13.9 ▲	TR	Turn right onto wide, graded dirt road, signed Florence–Kelvin Highway. Zero trip meter.
▼ 0.1	SO	Cattle guard, road swings away from wash.
13.8 ▲	SO	Cattle guard, road runs alongside Box O Wash.
▼ 0.4	SO	Track on right.
13.5 ▲	SO	Track on left.
▼ 1.3	SO	Track on right; then track on left.
12.6 ▲	SO	Track on right; then track on left.
▼ 1.6	SO	Track on left.
12.3 ▲	SO	Track on right.
▼ 1.7	SO	Track on left.
12.2 ▲	SO	Track on right.
▼ 2.4	BL	Track on right.
11.5 ▲	BR	Second entrance to track on left.
		GPS: N32°56.79' W111°06.05'
▼ 2.5	SO	Second entrance to track on right, then track left.
11.4 ▲	SO	Track on right; then track on left.
▼ 5.3	SO	Cattle guard.
8.6 ▲	SO	Cattle guard.
▼ 5.6	SO	Cross through wash.
8.3 ▲	SO	Cross through wash.
▼ 6.0	SO	Track on left; then cross through wash.
7.9 ▲	SO	Cross through wash; then track on right.
▼ 6.3	SO	Cross through wash; then track on right.
7.6 ▲	SO	Track on left; then cross through wash.
		GPS: N32°54.20' W111°03.39'
▼ 7.3	SO	Track on left.
6.6 ▲	SO	Track on right.
▼ 8.8	SO	Track on right.
5.1 ▲	SO	Track on left.
		GPS: N32°52.82' W111°01.44'
▼ 9.9	SO	Track on left.
4.0 ▲	SO	Track on right.
		GPS: N32°52.49' W111°00.34'
▼ 11.1	SO	Cattle guard, well on left, then track on left past well. Second track left and track on right.
2.8 ▲	SO	Track on left, track on right, then second track on right at well, then cattle guard.
		GPS: N32°51.82' W110°59.27'
▼ 11.3	SO	Cross gas pipeline, tracks on right and left along pipeline.
2.6 ▲	SO	Cross gas pipeline, tracks on right and left along pipeline.
▼ 11.7	SO	Cattle guard, track on left along fence line.
2.2 ▲	SO	Cattle guard, track on right along fence line.
▼ 12.2	SO	Track on right.
1.7 ▲	SO	Track on left.
▼ 12.6	SO	Track on left.
1.3 ▲	SO	Track on right.
▼ 12.9	SO	Cross through wash.
1.0 ▲	SO	Cross through wash.
▼ 13.6	SO	Track on left.
0.3 ▲	SO	Track on right.
▼ 13.8	SO	Cross through Brady Wash, track on right up wash. Traveling through Haystack Valley, Cottonwood Hill is on left.

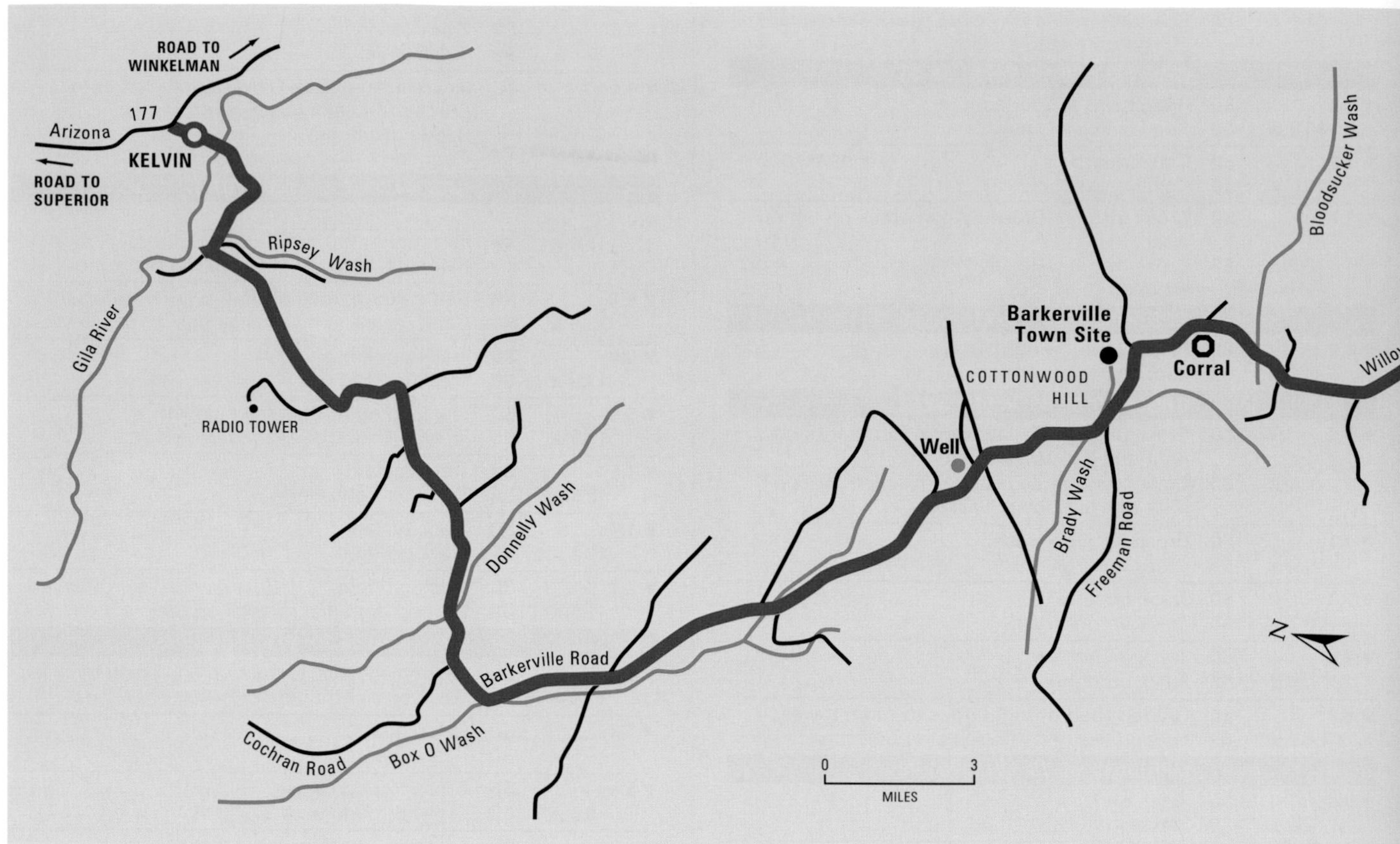

	0.1 ▲	SO	Cross through Brady Wash, track on left up wash. Traveling through Haystack Valley, Cottonwood Hill is on the right.
			GPS: N32°50.13′ W110°57.66′
▼ 13.9		BL	Graded road on right is Freeman Road. Zero trip meter.
	0.0 ▲		Continue to the northwest on Barkerville Road.
			GPS: N32°50.03′ W110°57.53′
▼ 0.0			Join Freeman Road and continue to the east.
	1.5 ▲	BR	Graded road on left is Freeman Road. Zero trip meter.
▼ 0.1		SO	Track on right, then cross through Haystack Valley Wash.
	1.4 ▲	SO	Cross through Haystack Valley Wash, then track on left.
▼ 0.3		SO	Two tracks on right to corral.
	1.2 ▲	SO	Two tracks on left to corral.
▼ 0.4		SO	Cross through wash.
	1.1 ▲	SO	Cross through wash.
▼ 0.6		SO	Cattle guard.
	0.9 ▲	SO	Cattle guard.
▼ 0.7		SO	Track on left. Barkerville town site.
	0.8 ▲	SO	Track on right. Barkerville town site.
▼ 1.1		SO	Cattle guard.
	0.4 ▲	SO	Cattle guard.
▼ 1.2		SO	Track on right.
	0.3 ▲	SO	Track on left.
▼ 1.5		TR	Turn onto graded dirt Willow Springs Road. Zero trip meter.
	0.0 ▲		Continue southwest on Freeman Road.
			GPS: N32°50.08′ W110°55.93′
▼ 0.0			Continue south on Willow Springs Road.
	9.7 ▲	TL	Turn left onto graded dirt Freeman Road. Zero trip meter.
▼ 0.5		SO	Track on right.
	9.2 ▲	SO	Track on left.
▼ 1.5		SO	Several tracks on left, corral on right and track on right.
	8.2 ▲	SO	Several tracks on right, corral on left and track on left.
			GPS: N32°49.07′ W110°54.94′
▼ 1.6		SO	Cattle guard.
	8.1 ▲	SO	Cattle guard.
▼ 1.9		SO	Track on left.
	7.8 ▲	SO	Track on right.
▼ 2.1		SO	Cross through wash; then track on right.
	7.6 ▲	SO	Track on left; then cross through wash.
▼ 2.6		SO	Cattle guard.
	7.1 ▲	SO	Cattle guard.
▼ 3.1		SO	Track on right; then track on left.
	6.6 ▲	SO	Track on right; then track on left.
▼ 3.7		SO	Track on right.
	6.0 ▲	SO	Track on left.
			GPS: N32°47.43′ W110°55.52′
▼ 3.8		SO	Track on left; then cattle guard.
	5.9 ▲	SO	Cattle guard; then track on right.
▼ 4.3		SO	Track on right.
	5.4 ▲	SO	Track on left.
▼ 4.8		SO	Cattle guard.
	4.9 ▲	SO	Cattle guard.
▼ 5.4		SO	Track on right.
	4.3 ▲	SO	Track on left.
			GPS: N32°45.98′ W110°55.12′
▼ 5.8		SO	Cattle guard.
	3.9 ▲	SO	Cattle guard.

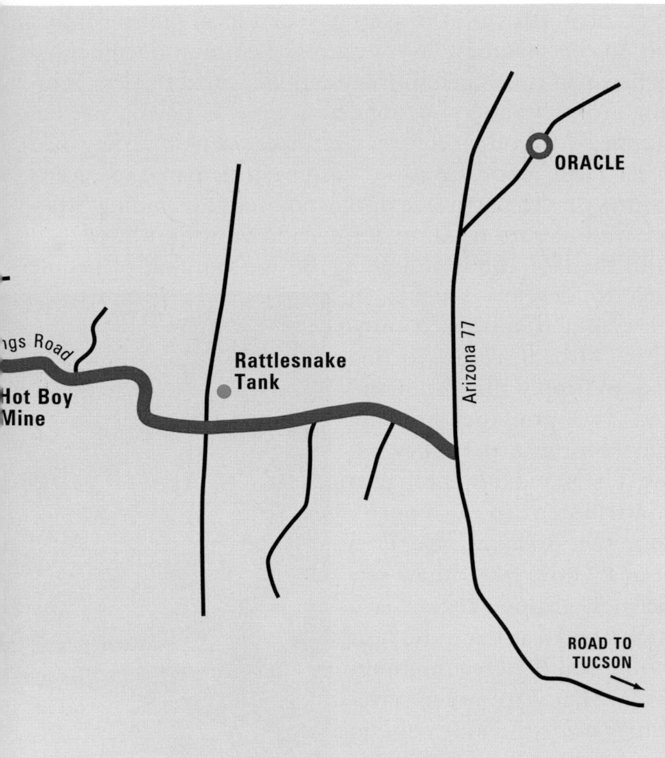

SOUTH #26: WILLOW SPRINGS ROAD

▼ 6.5		SO	Track on left.
	3.2 ▲	SO	Track on right.
			GPS: N32°45.29' W110°54.17'
▼ 6.8		SO	Track on right.
	2.9 ▲	SO	Track on left.
▼ 7.2		SO	Track on left.
	2.5 ▲	SO	Track on right.
▼ 7.5		SO	Remains of Hot Boy Mine on right.
	2.2 ▲	SO	Remains of Hot Boy Mine on left.
			GPS: N32°44.50' W110°53.77'
▼ 8.1		SO	Cross through wash, tracks on right and left up and down wash.
	1.6 ▲	SO	Cross through wash, tracks on left and right up and down wash.
▼ 8.3		SO	Track on right.
	1.4 ▲	SO	Track on left.
▼ 8.7		SO	Track on left; then cattle guard.
	1.0 ▲	SO	Cattle guard; then track on right.
▼ 9.0		SO	Cross through wash.
	0.7 ▲	SO	Cross through wash.
▼ 9.7		SO	Major graded road on left goes into Willow Springs Ranch. Zero trip meter.
	0.0 ▲		Continue to the north.
			GPS: N32°42.80' W110°53.61'
▼ 0.0			Continue to the south.
	8.8 ▲	SO	Major graded road on right goes into Willow Springs Ranch. Zero trip meter.
▼ 0.1		SO	Track on right.
	8.7 ▲	SO	Track on left.
▼ 0.5		SO	Track on right follows gas pipeline.
	8.3 ▲	SO	Track on left follows gas pipeline.
▼ 1.6		SO	Cross through wash.
	7.2 ▲	SO	Cross through wash.
▼ 2.7		SO	Track on right.
	6.1 ▲	SO	Track on left.
▼ 2.8		SO	Exit Willow Springs Ranch.
	6.0 ▲	SO	Enter Willow Springs Ranch under archway.
			GPS: N32°41.20' W110°53.83'
▼ 3.8		SO	Track on left and track on right along pipeline.
	5.0 ▲	SO	Track on left and track on right along pipeline.
▼ 4.5		SO	Track on left.
	4.3 ▲	SO	Track on right.
▼ 4.6		SO	Track on left.
	4.2 ▲	SO	Track on right.
▼ 4.9		SO	Track on left.
	3.9 ▲	SO	Track on right.
▼ 5.1		SO	Track on left; then cross through wash.
	3.7 ▲	SO	Cross through wash; then track on right.
▼ 6.0		SO	Track on right, cattle guard; then track on right.
	2.8 ▲	SO	Track on left, cattle guard; then track on left.
▼ 7.5		SO	Track on right.
	1.3 ▲	SO	Track on left.
▼ 7.6		SO	Track on right underneath power lines; then cattle guard.
	1.2 ▲	SO	Cattle guard; then track on left underneath power lines.
▼ 8.0		SO	Track on right; then cross through wash.
	0.8 ▲	SO	Cross through wash; then track on left.
▼ 8.5		SO	Track on right.
	0.3 ▲	SO	Track on left.
▼ 8.8			Trail ends at the intersection with Arizona 77, turn left for Oracle, turn right for Tucson.
	0.0 ▲		Trail commences on Arizona 77, just south of mile marker 96, at sign for Willow Springs Road. Zero trip meter and turn north over cattle guard on graded dirt road.
			GPS: N32°36.03' W110°52.26'

SOUTH REGION TRAIL #27

Oracle Control Road

Starting Point:	**Catalina Highway at Summerhaven**
Finishing Point:	**American Avenue in Oracle**
Total Mileage:	**26.9 miles**
Unpaved Mileage:	**23.7 miles**
Driving Time:	**2.5 hours**
Elevation Range:	**4,500–7,900 feet**
Usually Open:	**Year-round**
Best Time to Travel:	**Year-round**
Difficulty Rating:	**2**
Scenic Rating:	**8**
Remoteness Rating:	**+0**

Special Attractions

- Less-traveled dirt road that accesses Summerhaven at the top of Mt. Lemmon.
- Historic site of American Flag.

History

The Santa Catalina Mountains have been a magnet for many people over the years because of their cool, lofty heights that offer a respite from summer heat. Some of the earliest people to visit the mountains were the Hohokam Indians and later the Apache, who reaped food and made clothing and medicine from the various plants in this magnificent range. The Tohono O'odham tribe to the south thought the mountain range was shaped like an enormous frog and named it Babad Do'ag (Frog Mountain in their tongue).

One of the early mining pioneers in this region, Albert Weldon, had traveled west around Cape Horn in the *The Oracle.* When he finally settled in a likely spot in the early 1880s, he gave the name Oracle to the region around his small adobe homestead where he prospected on a small scale. Later the Apache Mine started producing bigger returns. Another early mine was the American Flag just south of Oracle. It was founded and developed by Isaac Lorraine in the late 1870s. He worked it until he was bought out by the Richardson Mining Company in the East. Lorraine developed a ranch with the proceeds. The mine had played out by the mid-1880s and the small community of American Flag dwindled.

Nevertheless, Oracle continued to slowly evolve and by 1895 a successful rancher, Bill Neal, and his wife had built the comfortable Mountain View Hotel, which soon attracted many travelers en route to Tucson. Bill had spent time riding with Buffalo Bill Cody in his earlier years, so one of their regular guests was Buffalo Bill himself, who took an interest in the local mines until his death in 1917.

The most famous peak in the Santa Catalina Mountains is undoubtedly Mt. Lemmon. It was named after botanist John Lemmon who, along with his new bride, came from California in 1881 to study the plant life in the Santa Catalinas. Having unsuccessfully attempted to reach the peak from the southern side, they completed their ascent from the north with the assistance of a local pioneer miner and rancher named Oliver Stratton. Lemmon documented six new plants on their journey and identified the less-common Arizona variety of ponderosa pine as having needles clumped in groups of five; the more regular variety had three. Their guide, Stratton, has given his name to several features on the north side of the mountain, including Stratton Wash, Stratton Camp Spring, and Stratton Mine.

An old corral at the start of the Arizona Trail

In the late 1880s and early 1890s a number of people tried to develop ranches in the Santa Catalina Mountains. Others came to log trees to supply the mines and feed the growing housing construction in the valley below. The name Summerhaven is attributed to a reporter from the *Arizona Star*, Fred Kimball, who like others saw the high altitude region as a summer retreat from the heat and named the area Summerhaven. Early summer vacationers made the long haul up this southern approach from Oracle by mule and horse to be rewarded with the cooler climate. The first inn was constructed on the mountain in the 1920s and was located in what is now Summerhaven.

A large alligator juniper beside the trail

The original route was a lot narrower and more twisty than it is today. The switchbacks near the top were so tight that vehicles had to back up several times to make the turn. The road was only wide enough for a single vehicle; as the area gained popularity traffic jams were not uncommon. A novel solution to the problem was adopted. A timber arch at the bottom and top marked the start of a controlled section of the road where travelers were required to drive in a set direction for a specified time interval. For a certain number of hours a day only uphill travel was permitted. Then the direction was reversed for the next few hours. Fines were imposed on anyone who broke the honor system. This unique system of traffic flow led to the name in use today: the Oracle Control Road.

By the early 1930s, Summerhaven residents and merchants craved a speedier road to their summer retreat, and an alternative route from Tucson was sought. Under the suggestion of Frank Hitchcock, the general postmaster at the time, discussions took place regarding the use of prison labor to construct a new route from the south at a reduced cost. President Hoover authorized the use of thousands of non-violent inmates to build the Hitchcock Highway, also known as the Catalina Highway. Construction of the new southerly approach began in 1933 and was completed in 1950.

The original Oracle Control Road remained as an emergency escape route from wildfire on the mountain, as well as a scenic drive for recreationalists. Many have complained of its condition over the decades, yet it remains a peaceful northerly approach to the Santa Catalina Mountains.

Description

The Oracle Control Road provides alternative access to the paved Catalina Highway, which climbs up Mt. Lemmon from Tucson. The graded dirt road travels the north side of the mountain and gives access to other 4WD trails, campsites, and hiking trails. At the highest elevations of the trail, on Mt. Lemmon, travelers pass through oak and pine forests. The trail gradually descends, giving great views of Marble Peak and further down the San Pedro River Valley with the San Manuel Copper Mine visible in front of the Galiuro Mountains. The trail surface is rough enough that a high-clearance vehicle is preferred as the trail follows a shelf road down toward Oracle. The shelf road is wide enough for a single vehicle with plenty of passing places.

As the trail gradually descends, it leaves behind the pine trees of the higher elevations and passes through scrubby oak, mesquite, and grassland. The vegetation is more open and the views more wide-ranging. The trail winds around the east side of Oracle Ridge, passing Rice Peak (7,575 feet). Tracks lead off in both directions from this section and there are many campsites with excellent views, although little shade.

The national forest campground at Peppersauce Wash is passed opposite the start of the Rice Peak Trail, a challenging trail that climbs to the top of Rice Peak. The campground can get full very quickly on weekends. A fee is required. Peppersauce Wash was named by a group of hot sauce-loving cowboys who used to stash their bottle of peppersauce in a hollow tree near where they traditionally camped.

After the campground, the trail standard improves to a wide, graded road. Passenger vehicles will have no difficulty traveling from Oracle to Peppersauce Campground.

The lower end of the trail passes by the remains of American Flag. A historical marker is affixed to the major surviving building, the old post office, which is still in use today as a private cabin.

The trail can be open year-round, but snowfall may close the trail briefly some winters. Call ahead if in doubt.

Current Road Information

Coronado National Forest
Santa Catalina Ranger District
5700 North Sabino Canyon Rd.
Tucson, AZ 85750
(520) 749-8700

Map References

BLM Tucson, Mammoth
USFS Coronado National Forest: Safford and Santa Catalina Ranger Districts
USGS 1:24,000 Mt. Lemmon, Mt. Bigelow, Campo Bonito, Oracle
1:100,000 Tucson, Mammoth
Maptech CD-ROM: Southeast Arizona/Tucson; Phoenix/Superstition Mountains
Arizona Atlas & Gazetteer, p. 67
Arizona Road & Recreation Atlas, p. 48 & p. 82
Recreational Map of Arizona

Route Directions

Mileage		Directions
▼ 0.0		From Summerhaven, at the end of the Catalina Highway from Tucson, zero trip meter and turn north on the paved Oracle Control Road signposted to Peppersauce Campground and Oracle. The intersection is north of mile marker 21.
6.3 ▲		Trail ends at Summerhaven, on the Catalina Highway from Tucson. Turn right for Summerhaven, turn left for Tucson.
		GPS: N32°26.88' W110°45.24'
▼ 0.1	SO	Pass through fire stations and closure gate. Road turns to graded dirt.
6.2 ▲	SO	Road is now paved. Pass through closure gate and fire stations.
▼ 0.2	SO	Oracle Ridge hiking trail #1 on left and parking area, then cattle guard.
6.1 ▲	SO	Cattle guard, then Oracle Ridge hiking trail #1 on right and parking area.
		GPS: N32°27.09' W110°45.21'
▼ 1.5	SO	Track on left to campsites.
4.8 ▲	SO	Track on right to campsites.
▼ 2.3	SO	Track on right to campsite.
4.0 ▲	SO	Track on left to campsite.
▼ 2.7	SO	Closure gate; then track on left.
3.6 ▲	SO	Track on right; then closure gate.
▼ 2.8	SO	Track on left; then Crystal Spring hiking trail #17 on right.
3.5 ▲	SO	Crystal Spring hiking trail #17 on left; then track on right.
		GPS: N32°26.95' W110°44.20'
▼ 5.0	SO	Track on left.
1.3 ▲	SO	Track on right.
		GPS: N32°27.82' W110°44.13'
▼ 5.4	SO	Track on right; then cattle guard, then second well-used track on right.
0.9 ▲	SO	Well-used track on left; then cattle guard, then second track on left.
		GPS: N32°27.82' W110°43.89'
▼ 6.3	TR	Well-used track on left is private road to Oracle Ridge Mine. Zero trip meter.
0.0 ▲		Continue to climb toward Summerhaven.
		GPS: N32°28.42' W110°43.55'
▼ 0.0		Continue to descend toward Oracle, then small track on right.
2.4 ▲	TL	Small track on left; then well-used track straight ahead is private road to Oracle Ridge Mine. Zero trip meter.
▼ 0.4	SO	Pipeline on left and right.
2.0 ▲	SO	Pipeline on left and right.
▼ 1.0	SO	Cross over wash.
1.4 ▲	SO	Cross over wash.
▼ 1.4	SO	Campsite on right with good views.
1.0 ▲	SO	Campsite on left with good views.
▼ 1.6	SO	Track on right.
0.8 ▲	SO	Track on left.
▼ 2.4	SO	Graded road on right through gate. Zero trip meter
0.0 ▲		Continue to the southwest on FR 38.
		GPS: N32°28.70' W110°42.50'
▼ 0.0		Continue to the northeast.
4.5 ▲	SO	Graded road on left through gate, continue straight on remaining on FR 38. Zero trip meter.
▼ 0.2	SO	Cross through wash.
4.3 ▲	SO	Cross through wash.

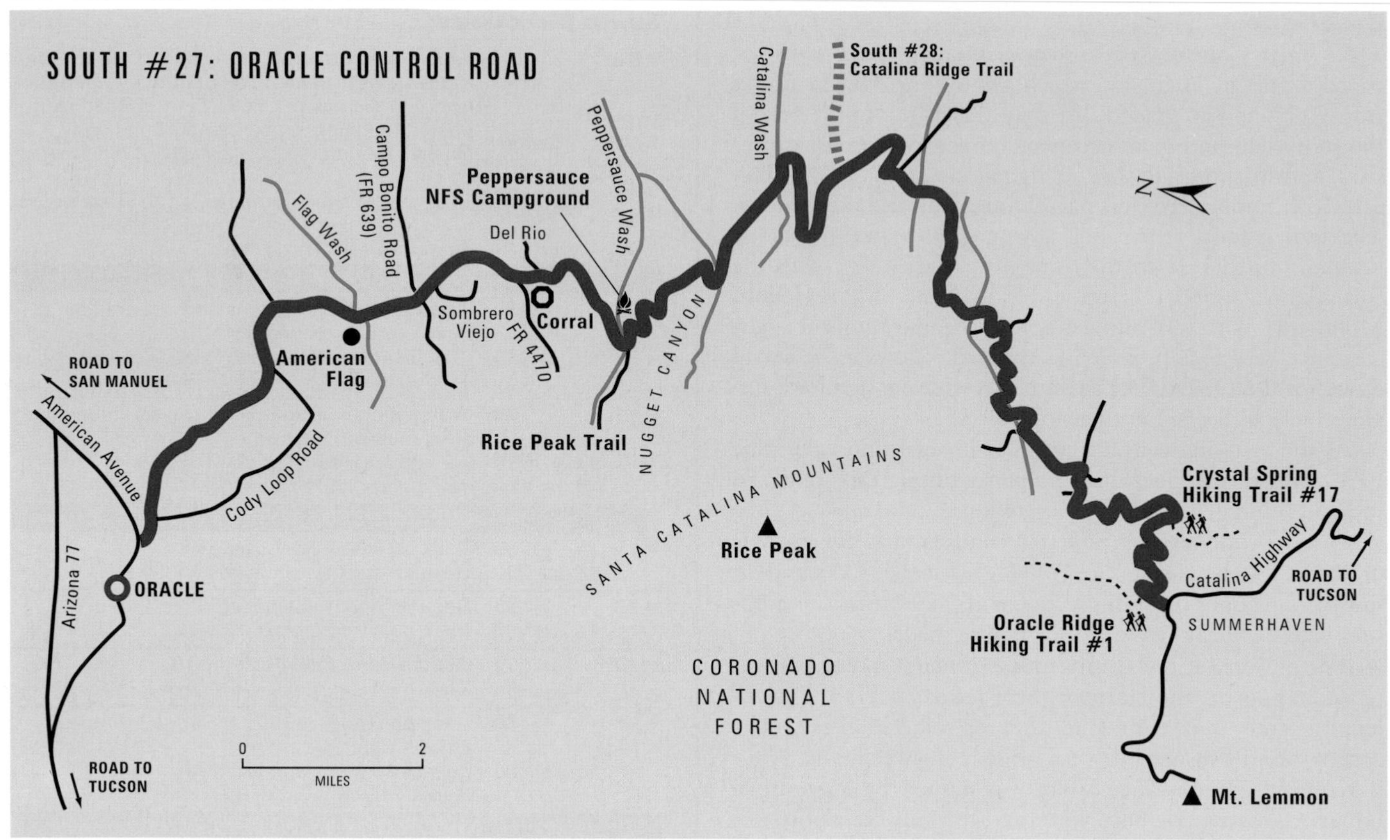

▼ 0.5		SO	Track on left.
	4.0 ▲	SO	Track on right.
▼ 0.7		SO	Cross over Gibb Wash on bridge.
	3.8 ▲	SO	Cross over Gibb Wash on bridge.
▼ 1.0		SO	Track on right.
	3.5 ▲	SO	Track on left.
▼ 1.8		SO	Cattle guard.
	2.7 ▲	SO	Cattle guard.
			GPS: N32°29.35' W110°41.71'
▼ 2.1		SO	Cross over wash.
	2.4 ▲	SO	Cross over wash.
▼ 2.9		SO	Cross over wash on bridge.
	1.6 ▲	SO	Cross over wash on bridge.
			GPS: N32°29.66' W110°41.05'
▼ 3.0		SO	Private drive on left; then cattle guard.
	1.5 ▲	SO	Cattle guard; then private drive on right.
▼ 3.1		SO	Cross through wash.
	1.4 ▲	SO	Cross through wash.
▼ 3.3		SO	Track on right is private.
	1.2 ▲	SO	Track on left is private.
▼ 3.5		SO	Cross through wash.
	1.0 ▲	SO	Cross through wash.
			GPS: N32°30.04' W110°40.89'
▼ 4.2		SO	Track on right.
	0.3 ▲	SO	Track on left.
▼ 4.4		SO	Track on right.
	0.1 ▲	SO	Track on left.
▼ 4.5		SO	Track on right is South #28: Catalina Ridge Trail. Zero trip meter.
	0.0 ▲		Continue to the southeast.
			GPS: N32°30.33' W110°40.88'
▼ 0.0			Continue to the northwest.
	5.7 ▲	SO	Track on left is South #28: Catalina Ridge Trail. Zero trip meter. Intersection is unmarked.
▼ 0.5		SO	Cattle guard.
	5.2 ▲	SO	Cattle guard.
▼ 1.5		SO	Cattle guard.
	4.2 ▲	SO	Cattle guard.
			GPS: N32°30.82' W110°41.01'
▼ 1.8		SO	Track on right.
	3.9 ▲	SO	Track on left.
▼ 2.2		SO	Cross through Catalina Wash.
	3.5 ▲	SO	Cross through Catalina Wash.
			GPS: N32°30.98' W110°41.15'
▼ 3.3		SO	Track on right.
	2.4 ▲	BR	Track on left.
			GPS: N32°31.42' W110°41.92'
▼ 3.4		SO	Track on right and track on left.
	2.3 ▲	SO	Track on right and track on left.
			GPS: N32°31.39' W110°42.03'
▼ 3.7		SO	Track on right; then cross over Nugget Canyon on bridge.
	2.0 ▲	SO	Cross over Nugget Canyon on bridge; then track on left.
▼ 4.3		SO	Cross through wash.
	1.4 ▲	SO	Cross through wash.
▼ 4.4		SO	Track on left and track on right.
	1.3 ▲	SO	Track on left and track on right.
▼ 4.7		SO	Track on right.
	1.0 ▲	SO	Track on left.
▼ 5.5		SO	Cross over wash on bridge.
	0.2 ▲	SO	Cross over wash on bridge.
▼ 5.7		SO	Peppersauce NFS Campground on right, track on left is Rice Peak Trail. Zero trip meter.
	0.0 ▲		Continue to the southeast.
			GPS: N32°32.26' W110°43.05'

▼ 0.0			Continue to the northwest and cross through Peppersauce Wash.
	3.3 ▲	SO	Cross through Peppersauce Wash; then Peppersauce NFS Campground on left. Track on right is Rice Peak Trail. Zero trip meter.
▼ 0.5		SO	Track on right.
	2.8 ▲	SO	Track on left.
▼ 1.0		SO	Cattle guard.
	2.3 ▲	SO	Cattle guard.
▼ 1.5		SO	Track on left.
	1.8 ▲	SO	Track on right.
▼ 1.7		SO	Road on right is Del Rio, corral on left.
	1.6 ▲	SO	Road on left is Del Rio, corral on right.
			GPS: N32°33.13' W110°42.46'
▼ 2.0		SO	Track on left is FR 4470.
	1.3 ▲	SO	Track on right is FR 4470.
			GPS: N32°33.35' W110°42.51'
▼ 2.4		SO	Private road on left, cross through wash.
	0.9 ▲	SO	Cross through wash, private road on right.
▼ 2.7		SO	Private road on left, two tracks on right.
	0.6 ▲	SO	Private road on right, two tracks on left.
▼ 3.0		SO	Road on left is Sombrero Viejo.
	0.3 ▲	SO	Road on right is Sombrero Viejo.
▼ 3.3		SO	Large graded road on left and right is Campo Bonito Road, FR 639. Road is now Mt. Lemmon Road. Zero trip meter.
	0.0 ▲		Continue to the southeast toward Peppersauce Campground.
			GPS: N32°34.23' W110°42.88'
▼ 0.0			Continue to the northwest toward Oracle.
	4.7 ▲	BL	Large graded road on left and right is Campo Bonito Road, FR 639. Zero trip meter.
▼ 0.2		SO	Track on left.
	4.5 ▲	SO	Track on right.
▼ 0.7		SO	Track on left; then cross through Flag Wash. Arizona Trail trailhead #9 on left beside corral and on right. This section is for hikers only. This is the site of American Flag.
	4.0 ▲	SO	Arizona Trail trailhead #9 on right beside corral and on left. This section is for hikers only. Cross through Flag Wash; then track on right. This is the site of American Flag.
			GPS: N32°34.85' W110°43.18'
▼ 0.8		SO	Track on left.
	3.9 ▲	SO	Track on right.
▼ 1.1		SO	Cattle guard.
	3.6 ▲	SO	Cattle guard.
▼ 1.6		SO	Paved road joins on right. Road is now paved.
	3.1 ▲	BR	Bear right onto graded dirt road, following the sign for the YMCA Ranch Camp.
			GPS: N32°35.59' W110°43.16'
▼ 2.2		SO	Track on right and track on left; then Cody Loop Road on left.
	2.5 ▲	SO	Cody Loop Road on right; then track on right and track on left.
▼ 3.0		SO	Leaving Coronado National Forest.
	1.7 ▲	SO	Entering Coronado National Forest.
			GPS: N32°35.97' W110°44.41'
▼ 3.6		SO	Cross through wash, Oracle State Park, Center for Environmental Education on right. Many roads on right and left, remain on main road.
	1.1 ▲	SO	Oracle State Park, Center for Environmental Education on left, then cross through wash.
			GPS: N32°36.35' W110°44.83'
▼ 4.7			Trail ends at the T-intersection with American Avenue in Oracle. Turn right for San Manuel, turn left for Tucson.
	0.0 ▲		Trail commences on American Avenue on the east side of Oracle. Zero trip meter and turn east on the paved Mt. Lemmon Road signposted for Mt. Lemmon. Many roads on right and left for first 1.1 miles, remain on main road. American Avenue is the main street running through Oracle. Oracle is bypassed by Arizona 77. The turn is immediately south of the post office.
			GPS: N32°36.60' W110°45.89'

SOUTH REGION TRAIL #28

Catalina Ridge Trail

Starting Point:	**South #27: Oracle Control Road, 5.7 miles southeast of Peppersauce Campground**
Finishing Point:	**Arizona 76, 2.7 miles south of San Manuel**
Total Mileage:	**10.1 miles**
Unpaved Mileage:	**10.1 miles**
Driving Time:	**2 hours**
Elevation Range:	**3,000–4,600 feet**
Usually Open:	**Year-round**
Best Time to Travel:	**October to June**
Difficulty Rating:	**2**
Scenic Rating:	**7**
Remoteness Rating:	**+0**

Special Attractions

- Gently sloping trail offers views of the San Pedro River Valley and Galiuro Mountains.
- Alternative access to the trails on the east side of the Santa Catalina Mountains.

Description

This 2-rated trail travels down a long, gently sloping ridge between Stratton Wash and Catalina Wash. Although a very small, formed trail, it is easygoing and suitable for

Cattle at a tank along the trail

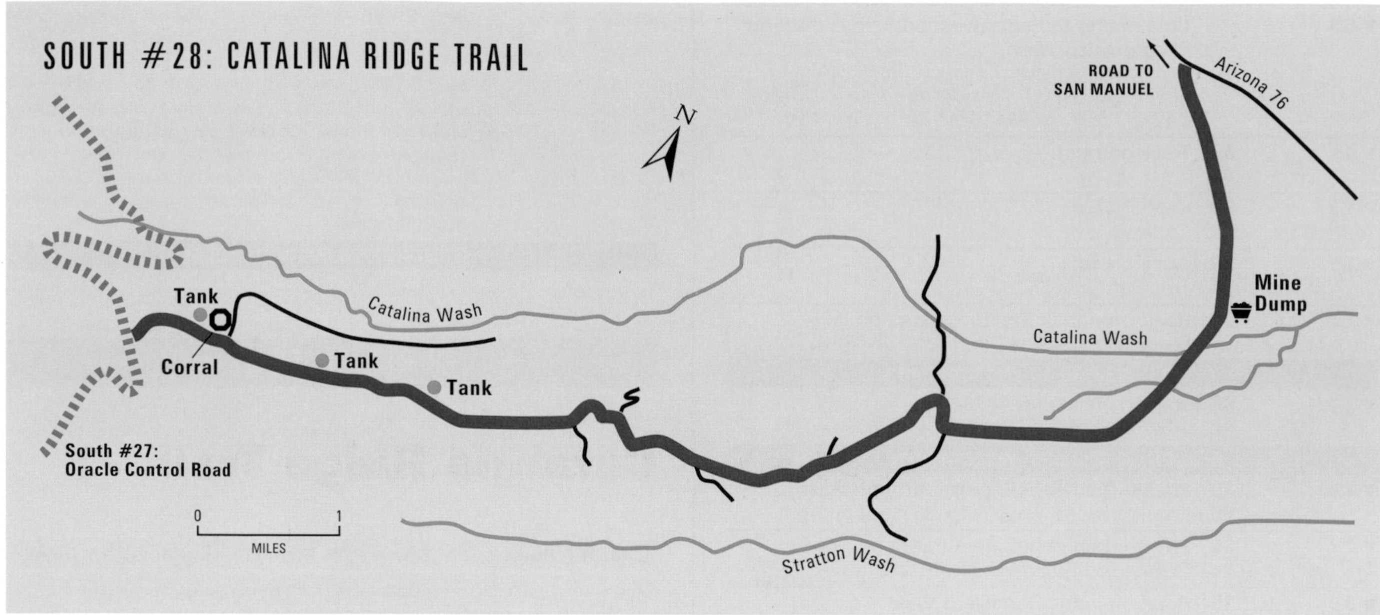

high-clearance 2WD vehicles. It is entirely contained within state land, and a valid state land use permit is required.

The trail leaves South #27: Oracle Control Road (also called the Mt. Lemmon Back Trail) south of Peppersauce Campground. Although small, the trail is well defined as it heads toward a large water tank, which is easily visible farther along the trail. The trail heads directly east, giving striking views of the San Pedro River Valley and the Galiuro Mountains on the far side. Travelers in the opposite direction will have equally panoramic views of the Santa Catalina Mountains.

The state lands are grazed by cattle and horses, and the many tanks and dams are for their use. Much of the lower portion of the trail does not appear on BLM or topographic maps. The trail joins the graded dirt road that leads past closed mine workings before ending at the intersection with Arizona 76, south of the BHP mining town of San Manuel. The copper mine closed in July 1999, but most facilities are available in San Manuel.

Current Road Information

Coronado National Forest
Santa Catalina Ranger District
5700 North Sabino Canyon Rd.
Tucson, AZ 85750
(520) 749-8700

Map References

BLM Mammoth
USFS Coronado National Forest: Safford and Santa Catalina Ranger Districts
USGS 1:24,000 Campo Bonito, Peppersauce Wash
1:100,000 Mammoth
Maptech CD-ROM: Phoenix/Superstition Mountains
Arizona Atlas & Gazetteer, p. 67
Arizona Road & Recreation Atlas, p. 48 & p. 82

Route Directions

Mileage		Direction
▼ 0.0		From South #27: Oracle Control Road, 5.7 miles southeast of Peppersauce Campground, zero trip meter and turn northeast on unmarked, formed trail. There is a large iron tank visible further down the trail that acts as a marker.
4.1 ▲		Trail ends at the intersection with the South #27: Oracle Control Road. Turn left for Mt. Lemmon, turn right for Oracle.
		GPS: N32°30.34' W110°40.89'
▼ 0.2	BR	Trail follows fence line heading for iron tank.
3.9 ▲	BL	Trail swings away from fence line.
		GPS: N32°30.53' W110°40.72'
▼ 0.6	SO	Large iron tank on left.
3.5 ▲	SO	Large iron tank on right.
		GPS: N32°30.54' W110°40.42'
▼ 0.7	SO	Small dam on left; then corral on left. Pass through gate continuing in a northeasterly direction.
3.4 ▲	SO	Pass through gate, continuing in a southwesterly direction. Corral on right; then small dam on right.
		GPS: N32°30.54' W110°40.25'
▼ 0.8	SO	Track on left.
3.3 ▲	SO	Track on right.
▼ 1.4	SO	Concrete tank on left.
2.7 ▲	SO	Concrete tank on right.
▼ 2.2	SO	Concrete tank and dam on left.
1.9 ▲	SO	Concrete tank and dam on right.
		GPS: N32°30.70' W110°38.66'
▼ 3.0	SO	Small dam on right; then track on right.
1.1 ▲	SO	Track on left; then small dam on left.
		GPS: N32°30.92' W110°37.85'
▼ 3.3	BR	Concrete tank on left.
0.8 ▲	BL	Concrete tank on right.
▼ 3.5	SO	Track on left.
0.6 ▲	SO	Track on right.
		GPS: N32°31.06' W110°37.44'
▼ 3.9	SO	Small dam on right.
0.2 ▲	SO	Small dam on left.

▼ 4.1		BL	Fork in trail, well-used track on right goes 0.3 to a tank. Zero trip meter.
	0.0 ▲		Proceed to the southwest.
			GPS: N32°31.02' W110°36.84'
▼ 0.0			Proceed to the northeast.
	1.9 ▲	SO	Well-used track on left goes 0.3 miles to a tank. Zero trip meter.
▼ 1.0		SO	Track on left.
	0.9 ▲	SO	Track on right.
			GPS: N32°31.35' W110°35.94'
▼ 1.3		BL	Fork in trail, track on right.
	0.6 ▲	SO	Track on left.
			GPS: N32°31.59' W110°35.70'
▼ 1.4		SO	Cross gas pipeline, tracks on left and right follow pipeline.
	0.5 ▲	SO	Cross gas pipeline, tracks on left and right follow pipeline.
			GPS: N32°31.67' W110°35.69'
▼ 1.7		BL	Track on right through gate into well.
	0.2 ▲	SO	Track on left through gate into well.
			GPS: N32°31.92' W110°35.52'
▼ 1.9		TR	T-intersection. Zero trip meter
	0.0 ▲		Continue to the west.
			GPS: N32°31.94' W110°35.37'
▼ 0.0			Continue to the southeast.
	1.3 ▲	TL	Turn left toward well, which is visible over the creosote bushes. Zero trip meter.
▼ 0.1		SO	Cross through wash.
	1.2 ▲	SO	Cross through wash.
▼ 0.2		TL	Two tracks on right.
	1.7 ▲	TR	Turn right, track on left and track straight on.
			GPS: N32°31.82' W110°35.28'
▼ 1.3		TL	Turn onto wide graded road. There is a small track opposite. Zero trip meter.
	0.0 ▲		Continue to the southwest.
			GPS: N32°32.19' W110°34.17'
▼ 0.0			Continue to the north.
	2.8 ▲	TR	Turn right onto unmarked, well-used, formed trail at the top of slight rise; there is a small track opposite. Zero trip meter.
▼ 0.4		SO	Cattle guard; then cross through wash.
	2.4 ▲	SO	Cross through wash; then cattle guard.
			GPS: N32°32.56' W110°34.02'
▼ 0.6		SO	Track on right.
	2.2 ▲	SO	Track on left.
▼ 0.7		SO	Cross through Catalina Wash.
	2.1 ▲	SO	Cross through Catalina Wash.
			GPS: N32°32.84' W110°33.93'
▼ 1.0		BL	Small track on left, cattle guard, then bear left with mine dump on right.
	1.8 ▲	BR	Bear right past mine dump, then cattle guard, small track on right.
			GPS: N32°33.11' W110°33.84'
▼ 2.5		SO	Track on left.
	0.3 ▲	SO	Track on right.
▼ 2.8			Small track on left, cattle guard, then trail ends at junction with Arizona 76. Turn left for San Manuel.
	0.0 ▲		Trail commences on Arizona 76 at mile marker 47, 2.7 miles south of San Manuel. On a left-hand bend, turn right into paved entrance and then immediately right again in front of the old closed road. There is a small sign for Oracle Ridge Mine. Cross cattle guard and proceed southwest along wide, graded gravel road.
			GPS: N32°34.42' W110°34.86'

SOUTH REGION TRAIL #29

Copper Creek Mining District Trail

Starting Point:	**Main Street in Mammoth**
Finishing Point:	**San Pedro River Road**
Total Mileage:	**21.2 miles**
Unpaved Mileage:	**20.7 miles**
Driving Time:	**2 hours**
Elevation Range:	**2,400–4,500 feet**
Usually Open:	**Year-round**
Best Time to Travel:	**October to May**
Difficulty Rating:	**2**
Scenic Rating:	**8**
Remoteness Rating:	**+0**

Special Attractions

- Rugged cliffs of Sombrero Butte.
- Historic Copper Creek Mining District.
- Remains of the Bunker Hill and other mines.

History

Copper Creek Mining District was very active and was composed of many mines. Founded in 1880, by 1910 it was at its zenith, with three mining companies active in the area. As you would expect from the name, copper was the dominant mineral, but silver and lead were also present. The town had about 500 people, 50 buildings, a physician, post office, stage line, and mansion. Because it was located within a deep canyon, the town was built in tiers.

The mines operated until 1917 and reopened again in 1933 when the Arizona Molybdenum Corporation took an interest in Copper Creek. However, they closed again in 1942, at which time the post office also closed after more than 35 years of service.

Copper Creek is closely associated with Roy Sibley and the

Bridge and loading chute at the Childs and Atwilkle Mine

Timbers in the entrance to Bunker Hill Mine

Sibley Mansion. Refer to South #30: Sibley Mansion and Bluebird MineTrail.

At the start of the trail sits the town of Mammoth, named in the 1870s for the Old Mammoth Mine above town, where gold ore deposits were so rich they were said to be mammoth in proportion. The town had a mill, where ore was shuttled in tramway buckets from the mine above the town. The ore buckets were then filled with drinking water for the return journey to the thirsty miners.

The Galiuro Mountains form the backdrop to Copper Creek, and this remote range too has its share of history and intrigue. In 1918 it was the location of a shootout between a posse and brothers Tom and John Power. The Power brothers were charged with evading the draft and four lawmen were dispatched to bring them in. For reasons that remain a mystery, after the posse surrounded the Powers' cabin, Jeff Power, Tom and John's father, lay dead. In the gunfight that followed, three of the four lawmen were killed.

What followed was one of Arizona's greatest manhunts. The two Power brothers and a family friend, Tom Sisson, were captured by the U.S. Cavalry just below the Mexican border. Local newspapers had already convicted the Power boys, public opinion was against them, and the trial was a formality. Given life sentences, they were sent to state prison in Florence. They always maintained their innocence, saying the posse had shot and killed their father without identifying itself and that they reacted in self-defense.

Despite fervent pleadings from the men's relatives at hearings, parole boards refused to release the three men. Sisson died in 1956. Five years after Sisson's death, the Power brothers were released after serving 42 years, having endured the longest sentences in Arizona history at the time. The brothers spent most of their remaining years in the Galiuro Mountains area.

The nearby San Pedro River runs through Mammoth before joining the Gila at Winkelman. Back in the 1820s, in the heyday of beaver hats when pelts were known as "hairy bank notes" and the fur trade was one of the nation's greatest economic engines, beavers were in such abundance in the San Pedro River that it was renamed, at least temporarily, Beaver River.

Description

This roughly graded road leads the traveler past many mining remains of the historic Copper Creek Mining District situated on the west side of the rocky Galiuro Mountains. The trail, which starts in Mammoth, climbs gradually up the gently sloping bajada to the edge of the range. As you climb, there are panoramic views back to the west over the San Pedro River Valley to the Santa Catalina Mountains. The large open pit mine at San Manuel (closed in July 1999) can also be seen.

The trail is lumpy in spots as it climbs up a ridge between the drainages of Well Canyon to the north and Copper Creek to the south. Ahead, the Galiuro Mountains rear up with the red-topped Sombrero Butte prominent to the southeast.

There is a short section of wide shelf road as you descend toward Copper Creek, with ample room for two vehicles to pass. Copper Creek normally has water in it for approximately six months of the year, and is lined with large cottonwoods. There are a couple of pleasant picnic spots near the creek.

The trail continues as a shelf road over Copper Creek. This section is wide enough for a single vehicle, and there are limited passing places. In the mining district there are many remnants of the mining activity that made this district famous. The area is still worked actively and some areas may not be accessible to the public; please respect any restrictions placed on the private property and mining claims.

A section of shelf road above Copper Creek Mining District

At the old Copper Creek sign, which is embedded in a rock wall, the trail leading off to the north along Copper Creek is the difficult South #30: Sibley Mansion and Bluebird Mine Trail. There is a pleasant picnic or camping spot underneath the cottonwoods at the start of the trail that can be seen from the sign.

The second half of the trail passes through the Bunker Hill Mining District and past the remains of the Bunker Hill Mine. There are excellent views of Sombrero Butte and the jagged escarpment of the Galiuro Mountains. The trail is smooth as it descends the bajada, following the path of Mulberry Wash to rejoin the San Pedro River Road, 3 miles south of the starting point.

The trail crosses a combination of state, private, and BLM land. A valid state land use permit is required.

Current Road Information

Bureau of Land Management
Tucson Field Office
12661 East Broadway Blvd.
Tucson, AZ 85748
(520) 722-4289

Coronado National Forest
Santa Catalina Ranger District
5700 North Sabino Canyon Rd.
Tucson, AZ 85750
(520) 749-8700

Map References
BLM Mammoth
USGS 1:24,000 Mammoth, Clark Ranch, Holy Joe Peak, Rhodes Peak, Oak Grove Canyon
1:100,000 Mammoth
Maptech CD-ROM: Phoenix/Superstition Mountains
Arizona Atlas & Gazetteer, p. 67
Arizona Road & Recreation Atlas, p. 48 & p. 82

Route Directions

▼ 0.0		In Mammoth, from Arizona 77, turn east on Main Street into the business district of Mammoth. Proceed for 0.7 miles, then turn east on Bluebird Street. Zero trip meter at intersection and proceed east on Bluebird Street, graded dirt road.
0.7 ▲		Trail ends at the intersection of Bluebird Street and Main Street in the center of Mammoth. Turn left to exit to Arizona 77.
		GPS: N32°43.25' W110°38.31'
▼ 0.2	SO	Cross through San Pedro River wash. Road becomes paved.
0.5 ▲	SO	Cross through San Pedro River wash. Road is now graded dirt.
▼ 0.3	SO	Track on right.
0.4 ▲	SO	Track on left.
▼ 0.7	SO	Paved San Pedro River Road on left and right, continue straight onto small, roughly graded dirt road and zero trip meter.
0.0 ▲		Continue toward Mammoth on paved road.
		GPS: N32°43.39' W110°37.59'
▼ 0.0		Continue to the northeast on dirt road that follows the wash.
6.8 ▲	SO	Paved San Pedro River Road on right and left, continue straight onto unmarked paved road and zero trip meter.
▼ 0.1	SO	Pass underneath power lines.
6.7 ▲	SO	Pass underneath power lines.
▼ 0.7	SO	Exit wash.
6.1 ▲	SO	Enter wash.
▼ 1.5	SO	Track on left.
5.3 ▲	SO	Track on right.
▼ 2.0	SO	Track on right.
4.8 ▲	SO	Track on left.
▼ 2.3	SO	Track on left.
4.5 ▲	SO	Track on right.
		GPS: N32°44.14' W110°35.43'
▼ 2.4	SO	Track on left and track on right.
4.4 ▲	SO	Track on left and track on right.
		GPS: N32°44.15' W110°35.27'
▼ 2.5	SO	Cross through wash.
4.3 ▲	SO	Cross through wash.
▼ 2.6	SO	Corral and tanks on left.
4.2 ▲	SO	Corral and tanks on right.
		GPS: N32°44.22' W110°35.07'
▼ 4.1	SO	Cattle guard.
2.7 ▲	SO	Cattle guard.
		GPS: N32°44.39' W110°33.63'
▼ 4.8	SO	Track on left to tank.
2.0 ▲	SO	Track on right to tank.
		GPS: N32°44.50' W110°33.03'
▼ 5.0	SO	Track on right.
1.8 ▲	SO	Track on left.
▼ 5.8	SO	Tank on left.
1.0 ▲	SO	Tank on right.
▼ 6.1	SO	Track on left.
0.7 ▲	SO	Track on right.
▼ 6.3	SO	Cattle guard, entering private property, please remain on road.
0.5 ▲	SO	Cattle guard, entering public land.
		GPS: N32°44.82' W110°31.50'

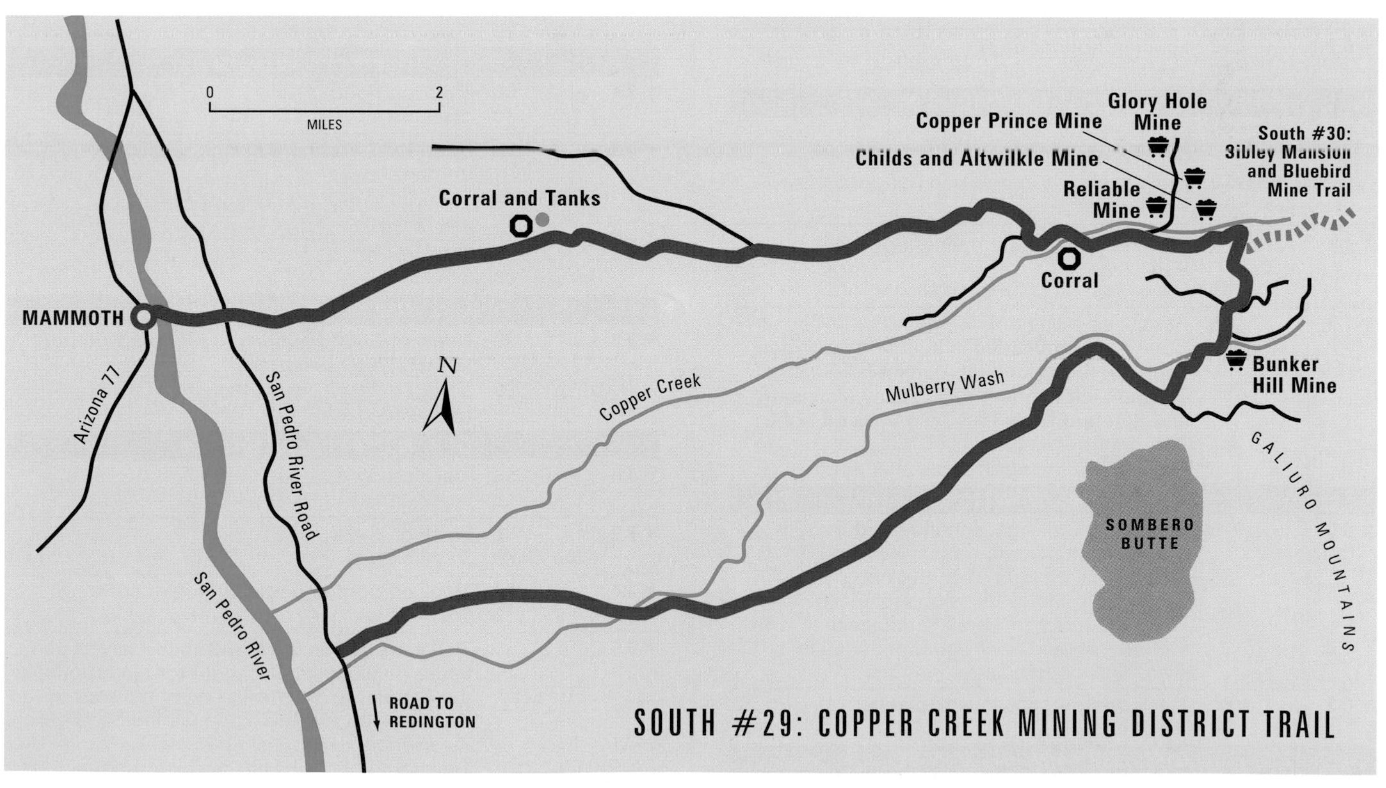

▼ 6.8		SO	Well-used track on left leads off saddle. Zero trip meter.
	0.0 ▲		Continue to the southwest.
			GPS: N32°45.03' W110°31.04'
▼ 0.0			Continue on around the loop to the northeast.
	1.7 ▲	SO	Well-used track on right leads off saddle. Zero trip meter.
▼ 0.7		SO	Track on right.
	1.0 ▲	SO	Track on left.
			GPS: N32°44.90' W110°30.46'
▼ 0.8		SO	Track on right, then trail follows shelf road over Copper Creek.
	0.9 ▲	SO	Track on left, end of shelf road.
▼ 1.1		SO	Tailings pile above trail on left.
	0.6 ▲	SO	Tailings pile above trail on right.
▼ 1.3		SO	Old corral on right then track on right. Remain on main trail. End of shelf road.
	0.4 ▲	SO	Track on left then old corral on left. Remain on main trail. Start of shelf road.
			GPS: N32°44.91' W110°30.05'
▼ 1.4		SO	Cross through Copper Creek.
	0.3 ▲	SO	Cross through Copper Creek.
			GPS: N32°44.89' W110°29.98'
▼ 1.7		BR	Fork in trail before fenced settling ponds. The left fork drops down and crosses through Copper Creek. The sites of Reliable Mine, Copper Prince Mine, and Glory Hole Mine are up this trail. Zero trip meter.
	0.0 ▲		Continue down alongside Copper Creek.
			GPS: N32°45.01' W110°29.66'
▼ 0.0			Continue past settling ponds.
	1.3 ▲	SO	Track on right immediately past settling ponds drops down and crosses through Copper Creek. The sites of Reliable Mine, Copper Prince Mine, and Glory Hole Mine are up this trail. Zero trip meter.
▼ 0.5		SO	Tailings pile on right.
	0.8 ▲	SO	Tailings pile on left.
▼ 0.7		SO	Loading hopper on left.
	0.6 ▲	SO	Loading hopper on right.
			GPS: N32°45.10' W110°28.94'
▼ 0.8		SO	Iron walkway across creek; then small waterfall in creek on left.
	0.5 ▲	SO	Small waterfall in creek on right; then iron walkway across creek.
▼ 1.0		SO	Concrete footings and timbers on right above trail.
	0.3 ▲	SO	Concrete footings and timbers on left above trail.
▼ 1.3		BR	At tank on hill and rock wall with old Copper Creek sign embedded in it, bear right to continue the loop along the Bunker Hill Road. Track on left is South #30: Sibley Mansion and Bluebird Mine Trail. Also track on right. Zero trip meter.
	0.0 ▲		Continue to the north along shelf road.
			GPS: N32°45.07' W110°28.62'
▼ 0.0			From rock wall sign, continue to the south along the shelf road.
	2.2 ▲	SO	Tank on hill on right, then track on right is South #30: Sibley Mansion and Bluebird Mine Trail. There is a rock wall at the junction with the old Copper Creek sign embedded in it. Also track on left. Zero trip meter.
▼ 0.3		BL	Track on right, continue to climb.
	1.9 ▲	SO	Track on left.
			GPS: N32°44.88' W110°28.61'
▼ 0.5		SO	Track on left.
	1.7 ▲	BL	Track on right.
▼ 0.9		SO	Saddle, track on left. Sombrero Butte is directly ahead.
	1.3 ▲	SO	Saddle, track on right.
			GPS: N32°44.57' W110°28.58'
▼ 1.0		SO	Track on right.
	1.2 ▲	SO	Track on left.
▼ 1.2		SO	Cross through wash, well-used track on left at wash.
	1.0 ▲	SO	Cross through wash, well-used track on right at wash.
			GPS: N32°44.38' W110°28.64'
▼ 1.5		SO	Timber-framed adit on left, track on left, then concrete footings of the Bunker Hill Mine on left.
	0.7 ▲	SO	Concrete footings of the Bunker Hill Mine on right, then track on right and timber-framed adit on right.
			GPS: N32°44.22' W110°28.72'
▼ 2.2		TR	T-intersection with well-used dirt track. Zero trip meter.
	0.0 ▲		Continue to the northwest.
			GPS: N32°43.80' W110°29.05'
▼ 0.0			Continue to the southwest.
	8.5 ▲	TL	Turn left on well-used dirt track, well-used track continues ahead. Zero trip meter.
▼ 0.4		SO	Cross through Mulberry Wash.
	8.1 ▲	BR	Cross through Mulberry Wash.
▼ 1.4		SO	Cattle guard. Trail is running alongside Mulberry Wash.
	7.1 ▲	SO	Cattle guard. Trail is running alongside Mulberry Wash.
			GPS: N32°43.80' W110°30.07'
▼ 1.8		SO	Turnout on left, viewpoint for Sombrero Butte.
	6.7 ▲	SO	Turnout on right, viewpoint for Sombrero Butte.
▼ 2.4		SO	Cattle guard; then track on right.
	6.1 ▲	SO	Track on left; then cattle guard.
			GPS: N32°43.23' W110°30.72'
▼ 2.8		SO	Track on right.
	5.7 ▲	SO	Track on left.
▼ 2.9		SO	Road forks around tank and rejoins immediately.
	5.6 ▲	SO	Road forks around tank and rejoins immediately.
▼ 4.9		BR	Track on left.
	3.6 ▲	SO	Track on right.
			GPS: N32°41.74' W110°32.69'
▼ 5.8		SO	Cross through Mulberry Wash, track on right to corral after wash.
	2.7 ▲	SO	Track on left to corral, then cross through Mulberry Wash.
			GPS: N32°41.62' W110°33.56'
▼ 6.0		SO	Track on right.
	2.5 ▲	SO	Track on left.
▼ 6.2		SO	Track on right.
	2.3 ▲	SO	Track on left.
▼ 8.0		SO	Track on right underneath power lines.
	0.5 ▲	SO	Track on left underneath power lines.
▼ 8.5			Trail ends at the junction with the paved San Pedro River Road. Turn right for Mammoth via the San Pedro River crossing at the start of the trail, turn left for Redington via the San Pedro River Road.
	0.0 ▲		Trail commences on the San Pedro River

Road, 3 miles south of the intersection with the road that crosses the Gila River to Mammoth. Zero trip meter and turn east up wide graded dirt road. The intersection is unmarked, but is immediately north of a wash crossing, where the road turns to dirt.

GPS: N32°40.97′ W110°36.20′

SOUTH REGION TRAIL #30

Sibley Mansion and Bluebird Mine Trail

Starting Point:	**South #29: Copper Creek Mining District Trail at Copper Creek sign**
Finishing Point:	**Sibley Mansion/Bluebird Mine**
Total Mileage:	**8 miles (round-trip, both spurs)**
Unpaved Mileage:	**8 miles**
Driving Time:	**3 hours**
Elevation Range:	**3,900–4,700 feet**
Usually Open:	**Year-round**
Best Time to Travel:	**October to May**
Difficulty Rating:	**7 (Sibley Mansion); 4 (Bluebird Mine)**
Scenic Rating:	**8**
Remoteness Rating:	**+1**

Special Attractions

- Extremely challenging, rough, rocky trail.
- Ruins of the 20-room Sibley Mansion.
- Remains of the Bluebird Mine.

History

The history of the Sibley Mansion, as it came to be known, is closely intertwined with that of the Copper Creek Mining District. Roy Sibley was the manager of the Minnesota Mining Company, one of the three companies active in Copper Creek around the turn of the century. The Minnesota Mining Company eventually bought out the majority of the Copper Creek claims, and Sibley took on the role of promoting the district to potential investors. In 1908 construction (supposedly using Indian labor) began on a fabulous 20-room mansion. The extravagant estate was located a short distance up Copper Creek from the main town site. Altogether, the mansion had 20 rooms, including 2 towers, one at each end that were 3-stories high. There were polished wooden floors, fruit trees growing on the front patio, and a wooden verandah that ran around the second story and gave inhabitants views of the sycamore grove and the hills behind. Large windows to catch the breezes and opulent furnishings completed the picture. The Sibleys wanted to present a picture of refined opulence, and potential investors were invited to stay at the mansion.

The Sibleys moved out of their home in 1910 and the majority of the flooring and other furnishings of the mansion were stripped and moved elsewhere shortly afterward.

Original access to the mansion was from Klondyke, on the east side of the Galiuro Mountains. Klondyke was established in the early 1900s and was named after the famous gold rush in Alaska (which incidentally is spelled Klondike). The town once had a population of about 500 but now supports only a dozen residents. Silver and lead mines nearby were the reason for the town's existence.

A rock section of the trail

Nowadays the Sibley Mansion is crumbling slowly back to earth. The outside walls remain, as do the 3-story towers. The surrounding vegetation is encroaching on the mansion, but you can still clearly see the size and grandeur of the original building.

Description

These two short spur trails lead off from South #29: Copper Creek Mining District Trail. The moderately rated spur to the Bluebird Mine is a scenic shelf road that leads to two old cabins and the remains of the mine. The Sibley Mansion spur travels an extremely difficult and rocky trail along Copper Creek to the remains of the 20-room Sibley Mansion.

The start of the Sibley Mansion spur starts off innocuously enough, but quickly becomes difficult. It follows the path of Copper Creek, crossing it often. The difficulty rating of the trail comes from the very large, loose boulders that have to be negotiated. High-clearance is essential and side steps and low-hanging brush bars risk being damaged. This trail is not suited to a novice driver. Possibly the hardest section is alongside a small pool, where there is an off-camber rock pile to be climbed.

The mansion is set slightly back from the creek. In front of it is an idyllic picnic or camping area under large sycamore trees. The mansion has two, square three-story towers still standing, as well as the remains of the outer and inner walls. Opposite, on the far side of the creek, are the remains of a stone building that housed offices and a store house.

Sibley Mansion remains

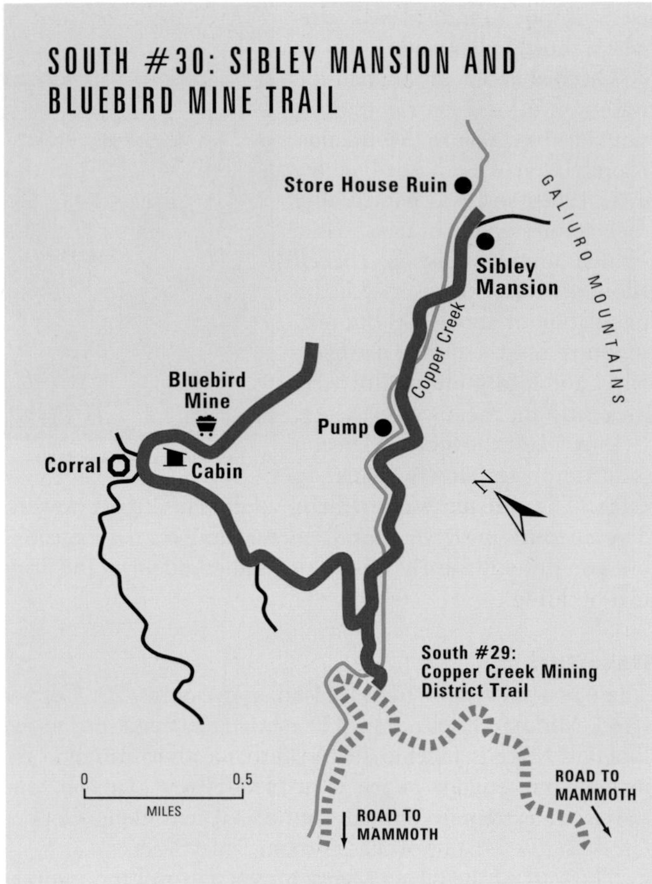

Sibley Mansion stands on private property, but at the time of writing it is not posted and is freely visited by 4-wheelers, hikers, and horse riders. Please treat the property with respect, so that it may continue to remain open.

The second spur to the Bluebird Mine is not as challenging as the trail to Sibley Mansion. It follows a shelf road all the way, climbing high above Copper Creek. There are panoramic views over the San Pedro River Valley to the Santa Catalinas and closer views over the Copper Creek drainage and the Galiuro Mountains.

Immediately before the mine, two cabins are passed—one adobe and one timber. The mine has concrete foundations and a large tailings pile remaining. On the hill above the mine are many stone walls constructed around the hillside. Opposite is a deep crevasse in the hill, where it looks like the miners followed a vein of ore.

Current Road Information

Bureau of Land Management
Tucson Field Office
12661 East Broadway Blvd.
Tucson, AZ 85748
(520) 722-4289

Coronado National Forest
Santa Catalina Ranger District
5700 North Sabino Canyon Rd.
Tucson, AZ 85750
(520) 749-8700

Map References

BLM Mammoth
USGS 1:24,000 Oak Grove Canyon
1:100,000 Mammoth
Maptech CD-ROM: Phoenix/Superstition Mountains
Arizona Atlas & Gazetteer, p. 67

Route Directions

▼ 0.0		From the old Copper Creek sign embedded in the rock wall, 10.5 miles from the start of South #29: Copper Creek Mining District Trail, zero trip meter and turn northeast on the trail that descends toward Copper Creek.
		GPS: N32°45.07' W110°28.62'
▼ 0.1	BR	Ford Copper Creek, then switchback to the right up creek. Track on left at switchback.
		GPS: N32°45.10' W110°28.56'
▼ 0.3	SO	Track on right crosses wash.
		GPS: N32°45.16' W110°28.39'
▼ 0.4	BL	Trail forks at large cottonwoods. To the right is the spur to the Sibley Mansion. To the left is the spur to the Bluebird Mine. Left climbs up ridge away from Copper Creek and continues to the Bluebird Mine. Zero trip meter.
		GPS: N32°45.18' W110°28.34'

Bluebird Mine Spur

▼ 0.0		At the intersection, bear left away from Copper Creek and start to climb ridge.
		GPS: N32°45.18' W110°28.34'
▼ 0.1	SO	Track on left.
▼ 0.7	BR	Track on left on right-hand switchback.
		GPS: N32°45.48' W110°28.46'
▼ 1.2	BR	Track on left. Bear right and pass corral on left.
		GPS: N32°45.85' W110°28.42'
▼ 1.3	SO	Track on left after corral, then remains of rock and adobe cabin on right.
▼ 1.4	SO	Timber cabin on right.
		GPS: N32°45.89' W110°28.32'
▼ 1.5	SO	Bluebird Mine.
		GPS: N32°45.77' W110°28.24'
▼ 1.8	SO	Track on right goes 0.1 miles to campsite.
▼ 2.1	UT	Trail reaches campsite, the old road past this point is seldom-used. Turn around and retrace your steps to the intersection where you last zeroed your trip meter.
		GPS: N32°45.67' W110°27.73'

Sibley Mansion Spur

▼ 0.0	BR	At the intersection where the trail forks, bear right and continue up Copper Creek.
		GPS: N32°45.18' W110°28.34'
▼ 0.1	BL	Track on right, bear left and exit wash.
		GPS: N32°45.20' W110°28.20'
▼ 0.2	SO	Re-enter wash.
▼ 0.3	SO	Cross rock fall; then cross through Copper Creek, start of difficult section.
		GPS: N32°45.27' W110°28.08'
▼ 0.4	SO	Cross through creek.
▼ 0.5	SO	Cross through creek.
▼ 0.6	SO	Old pump on left of trail; then cross through creek.
		GPS: N32°45.29' W110°27.87'

▼ 0.7	SO	Cross through creek.
▼ 0.9	SO	Cross through creek.
		GPS: N32°45.37′ W110°27.86′
▼ 1.0	SO	Cross through creek.
		GPS: N32°45.40′ W110°27.61′
▼ 1.1	SO	Cross through creek.
		GPS: N32°45.42′ W110°27.54′
▼ 1.2	SO	Cross through creek.
		GPS: N32°45.47′ W110°27.50′
▼ 1.3	SO	Difficult off-camber climb up loose rock pile with pool on right; then small stone ruin on left.
		GPS: N32°45.46′ W110°47.39′
▼ 1.4	SO	Enter picnic area under sycamores alongside Copper Creek. Sibley Mansion is on the right of the trail.
		GPS: N32°45.46′ W110°27.24′
▼ 1.5	UT	Track on right climbs difficult; moguled hill and loops around to rejoin the trail near the start of the spur to Bluebird Mine. Bear left and cross the creek to the store house ruin. Spur trail ends. Turn around and retrace your steps to South #29: Copper Creek Mining District Trail.
		GPS: N32°45.50′ W110°27.13′

SOUTH REGION TRAIL #31

Redington Road

Starting Point:	**San Pedro River Road at Redington**
Finishing Point:	**Tucson**
Total Mileage:	**23.3 miles**
Unpaved Mileage:	**23.3 miles**
Driving Time:	**2 hours**
Elevation Range:	**2,800–4,400 feet**
Usually Open:	**Year-round**
Best Time to Travel:	**October to May**
Difficulty Rating:	**2**
Scenic Rating:	**8**
Remoteness Rating:	**+0**

Special Attractions

- Easy trail winding through the Coronado National Forest and state lands close to Tucson.
- Access to many 4WD trails and backcountry campsites.
- Panoramic views of the San Pedro River Valley, Galiuro Mountains, and Rincon Mountains.
- Many hiking trails, including a short trail to Tanque Verde Falls.

History

Today Redington is a small ranching settlement, but there are some hair-raising tales associated with its past. The area was settled in 1875 by the Redfield brothers, Henry and Lem, who established a post office on their ranch, some six miles south

Corral along the trail

of where the present-day settlement is located. They wanted to call the site Redfield, but this was denied by the post office, so they decided upon Redington.

Over the next several years, the area around Redington attracted many outlaws who hid in the hills. In 1883 outlaws robbed a stage and murdered a man just north of the Riverside stage station. The bandits were tracked to the Redfield Ranch, and Joe Tuttle, Frank Carpenter, and Lem Redfield were caught with the money. They were taken to the prison at Florence, where Tuttle confessed, saying that Lem Redfield was to be given a share of the profits for providing the hideout, an accusation that Lem denied.

Meanwhile Henry Redfield rounded up seven of his friends and a deputy marshall and went to Florence to try to free his brother. Incensed by what they perceived as a bypassing of justice, the citizens of Florence lynched both Lem Redfield and Joe Tuttle. To this day, no one knows for sure if Lem was guilty; in fact much of the available evidence points to his innocence.

The Redington post office was closed in December 1940.

Tanque Verde Canyon, which is near the western end of the trail, is named after water holes in the canyon that contain green algae. The name dates back to the 1860s.

Description

Redington Road is a popular exit from Tucson for backcountry travelers. Not only does the trail provide a scenic and peaceful alternative to I-10 for eastbound travelers, but it is a beautiful drive in its own right. Its proximity to Tucson means it is popular for weekend camping, four-wheeling, and hiking.

The trail travels across grasslands, dotted with mesquite and abundant prickly pear, on the edge of the Santa Catalina Mountains. The Rincon Mountains are to the south and to the east are the Galiuro Mountains and the San Pedro River Valley.

The initial part of the trail crosses a mixture of state land and private ranchlands, following alongside the wash in Youtcy Canyon for a short distance before continuing to climb toward the boundary of the Coronado National Forest. There is a good chance of seeing wildlife within the national forest. Mule deer, Gambel's quail, javelina, many birds of prey, and reptiles live in the rocky hills. It is fairly easy to find a pleasant, peaceful campsite as well. There are some spots directly on the graded road and other quieter spots down the many side trails.

The final portion of the trail runs around a wide shelf road, with views down into Tanque Verde Canyon, before ending on the outskirts of Tucson.

The trail could be traversed by a passenger vehicle with care. It is regularly graded, but is still more suited to a high-clearance vehicle because of the lumps and rough sections.

Current Road Information

Coronado National Forest
Santa Catalina Ranger District
5700 North Sabino Canyon Rd.
Tucson, AZ 85750
(520) 749-8700

Map References

BLM Tucson
USFS Coronado National Forest: Safford and Santa Catalina Ranger Districts
USGS 1:24,000 Redington, Buehman Canyon, Piety Hill, Agua Caliente Hills
1:100,000 Tucson
Maptech CD-ROM: Southeast Arizona/Tucson
Arizona Atlas & Gazetteer, p. 67
Arizona Road & Recreation Atlas, p. 54 & p. 88
Recreational Map of Arizona

Route Directions

▼ 0.0			From San Pedro River Road, 13 miles south of San Manuel at a fork in the graded road, zero trip meter and turn southwest on graded dirt road marked Redington Road.
	1.2 ▲		Trail ends at junction with San Pedro River Road. Turn left for Mammoth, turn right for Benson.
			GPS: N32°27.09' W110°29.22'
▼ 0.4		SO	Graded road on right.
	0.8 ▲	SO	Graded road on left.
▼ 0.5		SO	Cross through Edgar Canyon wash; then cattle guard. Track on left after cattle guard.
	0.7 ▲	SO	Track on right, cattle guard; then cross through Edgar Canyon wash.
▼ 0.6		SO	Two tracks on right along pipeline.
	0.6 ▲	SO	Two tracks on left along pipeline.
▼ 1.0		SO	Track on left.
	0.2 ▲	SO	Track on right.
▼ 1.1		SO	Track on right.
	0.1 ▲	SO	Track on left.
▼ 1.2		SO	South #32: Buehman Canyon Trail is on the right. Zero trip meter.
	0.0 ▲		Continue to the north.
			GPS: N32°26.21' W110°29.80'
▼ 0.0			Continue to the south.
	7.9 ▲	SO	South #32: Buehman Canyon Trail is on the left. Zero trip meter.
▼ 0.6		SO	Cross through wide wash.
	7.3 ▲	SO	Cross through wide wash.
▼ 0.7		SO	Private road on left, track on right.
	7.2 ▲	SO	Private road on right, track on left.

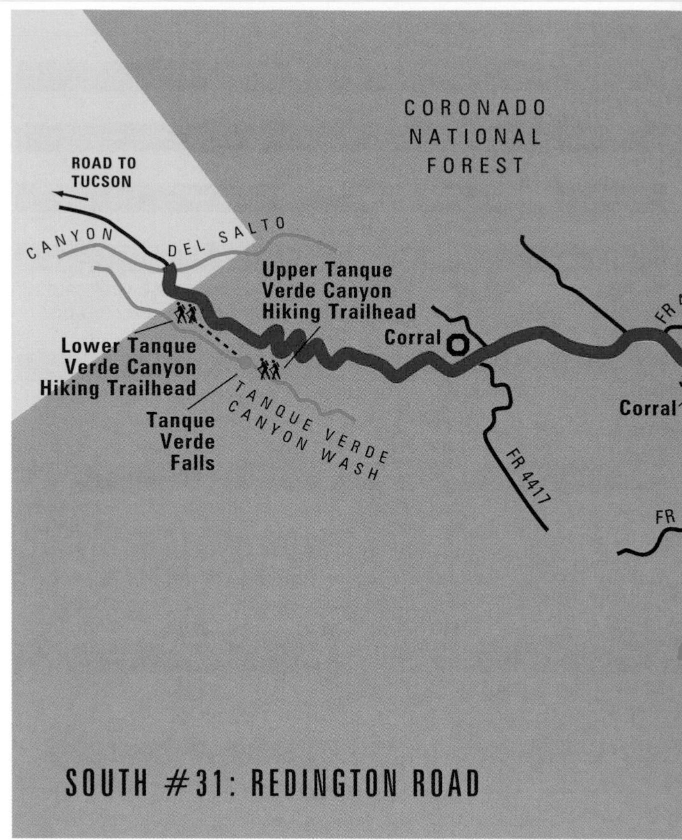

			GPS: N32°25.57' W110°29.96'
▼ 1.4		SO	Track on left.
	6.5 ▲	SO	Track on right.
▼ 1.6		SO	Track on right.
	6.3 ▲	SO	Track on left.
▼ 2.0		SO	Track on right.
	5.9 ▲	SO	Track on left.
▼ 2.1		SO	Cattle guard.
	5.8 ▲	SO	Cattle guard.
▼ 2.5		SO	Track on right.
	5.4 ▲	SO	Track on left.
▼ 3.4		SO	Track on right.
	4.5 ▲	SO	Track on left.
▼ 4.0		SO	Track on left.
	3.9 ▲	SO	Track on right.
▼ 4.2		SO	Track on left.
	3.7 ▲	SO	Track on right.
▼ 4.5		SO	Track on right.
	3.4 ▲	SO	Track on left.
			GPS: N32°22.91' W110°31.14'
▼ 4.9		SO	Track on left.
	3.0 ▲	SO	Track on right.
▼ 6.2		SO	Track on left and track on right.
	1.7 ▲	SO	Track on right and track on left.
▼ 6.4		BR	Track on left followed by graded ranch road on left.
	1.5 ▲	BL	Graded ranch road on right; then track on right.
			GPS: N32°21.31' W110°31.08'
▼ 6.7		SO	Cross through wash.
	1.2 ▲	SO	Cross through wash.
▼ 7.0		SO	Track on right.

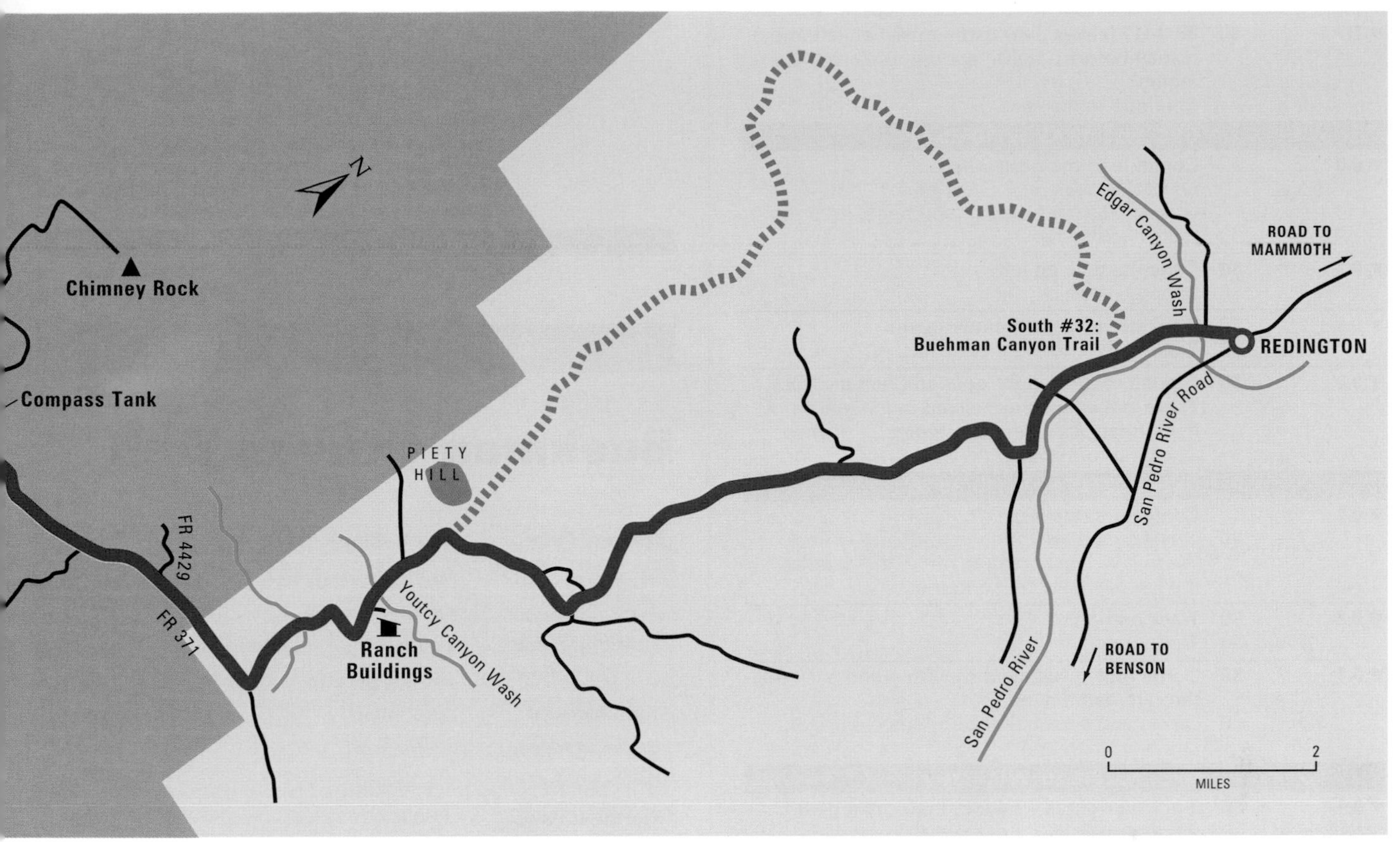

	0.9 ▲	SO	Track on left.
▼ 7.5		SO	Track on right and track on left.
	0.4 ▲	SO	Track on left and track on right.
▼ 7.8		SO	Cattle guard.
	0.1 ▲	SO	Cattle guard.
▼ 7.9		SO	Track on right on saddle at left-hand bend is south end of South #32: Buehman Canyon Trail. There is a campsite on the junction and an old white sign warning, "Travel at own risk." Piety Hill is to the northwest. Zero trip meter.
	0.0 ▲		Continue to the northeast.
			GPS: N32°20.89' W110°32.40'
▼ 0.0			Continue to the south.
	3.6 ▲		Track on left on saddle at right-hand bend is south end of South #32: Buehman Canyon Trail. There is a campsite at the intersection and an old white sign warning, "Travel at own risk." Zero trip meter. Piety Hill is to the northwest.
▼ 0.5		SO	Cross through wash; then track on right.
	3.1 ▲	SO	Track on left; then cross through wash.
			GPS: N32°20.45' W110°32.41'
▼ 0.7		SO	Cross through wash, then cattle guard.
	2.9 ▲	SO	Cattle guard, then cross through wash.
▼ 0.9		SO	Cross through Youtcy Canyon wash, ranch buildings and well on left, then cattle guard.
	2.7 ▲	SO	Cattle guard, ranch buildings and well on right, then cross through Youtcy Canyon wash.
			GPS: N32°20.07' W110°32.35'
▼ 1.0		SO	Track on left to ranch.
	2.6 ▲	SO	Track on right to ranch.
▼ 1.4		SO	Track on left.
	2.2 ▲	SO	Track on right.
▼ 2.0		SO	Cross through wash.
	1.6 ▲	SO	Cross through wash.
▼ 2.1		SO	Track on right.
	1.5 ▲	SO	Track on left.
▼ 2.9		BR	Well-used track on left.
	0.7 ▲	BL	Well-used track on right.
			GPS: N32°18.80' W110°32.46'
▼ 3.4		SO	Cross through wash.
	0.2 ▲	SO	Cross through wash.
▼ 3.6		SO	Entering Coronado National Forest over cattle guard. Road is now designated FR 371. No forest boundary sign, just the route marker. Zero trip meter at cattle guard.
	0.0 ▲		Continue into ranch lands.
			GPS: N32°18.77' W110°33.14'
▼ 0.0			Continue into the Coronado National Forest.
	2.7 ▲	SO	Leaving Coronado National Forest over cattle guard. Zero trip meter.
▼ 0.5		SO	Track on right is FR 4429.
	2.2 ▲	SO	Track on left is FR 4429.
			GPS: N32°18.74' W110°33.71'
▼ 0.6		SO	Track on left.
	2.1 ▲	SO	Track on right.
▼ 1.3		SO	Track on left.
	1.4 ▲	SO	Track on right.
▼ 1.4		SO	Track on right.
	1.3 ▲	SO	Track on left.
			GPS: N32°18.38' W110°34.53'
▼ 1.6		SO	Two tracks on left.
	1.1 ▲	SO	Two tracks on right.
			GPS: N32°18.30' W110°34.72'
▼ 2.1		SO	Campsite on left.
	0.6 ▲	SO	Campsite on right.

Mileage			Directions
▼ 2.7		SO	FR 4417 leaves over cattle guard on left immediately before a right-hand bend. Zero trip meter.
	0.0 ▲		Continue to the east.
			GPS: N32°18.13′ W110°35.78′
▼ 0.0			Continue to the northwest.
	0.8 ▲		FR 4417 leaves over cattle guard on right immediately after a left-hand bend. Zero trip meter.
▼ 0.1		SO	Concrete tank on left.
	0.7 ▲	SO	Concrete tank on right.
▼ 0.4		SO	Track on right, then cattle guard.
	0.4 ▲	SO	Cattle guard, then track on left.
▼ 0.8		SO	Graded road on right goes to Chimney Rock. There is a small grass island in the middle of the intersection. Zero trip meter.
	0.0 ▲		Continue to the east.
			GPS: N32°18.41′ W110°36.26′
▼ 0.0			Continue to the west.
	2.7 ▲	SO	Graded road on left goes to Chimney Rock. There is a small grass island in the middle of the intersection. Zero trip meter.
▼ 0.2		SO	Track on right.
	2.5 ▲	SO	Track on left.
▼ 0.4		SO	Corral on left followed by hiking and pack trail through gate on left.
	2.3 ▲	SO	Hiking and pack trail through gate on right; then corral on right.
			GPS: N32°18.20′ W110°36.71′
▼ 0.9		SO	Track on right is FR 4435, then cattle guard.
	1.8 ▲	SO	Cattle guard, then track on left is FR 4435.
			GPS: N32°18.18′ W110°37.07′
▼ 1.2		SO	Track on right.
	1.5 ▲	SO	Track on left.
▼ 2.3		SO	Track on right.
	0.4 ▲	SO	Track on left.
▼ 2.7		SO	FR 4417 on left across cattle guard. Track on right alongside corral. Zero trip meter.
	0.0 ▲		Continue to the north.
			GPS: N32°16.90′ W110°37.96′
▼ 0.0			Continue to the south.
	4.4 ▲	SO	Corral, then track on left alongside corral, FR 4417 on right. Zero trip meter.
▼ 0.2		SO	Cattle guard.
	4.2 ▲	SO	Cattle guard.
▼ 3.0		SO	Upper Tanque Verde Canyon hiking trail on left. Small parking areas on left and right.
	1.4 ▲	SO	Upper Tanque Verde Canyon hiking trail on right. Small parking areas on left and right.
			GPS: N32°15.48′ W110°39.29′
▼ 3.6		SO	Lower Tanque Verde Canyon hiking trail on left, goes 0.5 miles to Tanque Verde Falls. Parking area on right.
	0.8 ▲	SO	Lower Tanque Verde Canyon hiking trail on right, goes 0.5 miles to Tanque Verde Falls. Parking area on left.
			GPS: N32°15.22′ W110°39.90′
▼ 3.9		SO	Leaving Coronado National Forest over cattle guard.
	0.5 ▲	SO	Entering Coronado National Forest over cattle guard.
			GPS: N32°15.20′ W110°40.10′
▼ 4.4			Trail ends at the start of the paved road on the outskirts of Tucson, at the crossing of Canyon del Salto. Continue straight on along Redington Road for Tucson.
	0.0 ▲		To reach the trailhead, from the intersection of Houghton Road and Tanque Verde Road in southeast Tucson, proceed east on Tanque Verde Road for 5.5 miles. The road changes to Redington Road. The trail starts at the intersection of Redington View Road and Redington Road, immediately after the road crosses over Canyon del Salto. The road turns from paved to gravel at this point.
			GPS: N32°15.23′ W110°40.38′

SOUTH REGION TRAIL #32

Buehman Canyon Trail

Starting Point:	**South #31: Redington Road, 1.2 miles from the north end, 0.1 miles north of mile marker 26**
Finishing Point:	**South #31: Redington Road, 0.2 miles southwest of mile marker 18**
Total Mileage:	**11.6 miles**
Unpaved Mileage:	**11.6 miles**
Driving Time:	**2.5 hours**
Elevation Range:	**3,000–4,200 feet**
Usually Open:	**Year-round**
Best Time to Travel:	**October to May**
Difficulty Rating:	**4**
Scenic Rating:	**8**
Remoteness Rating:	**+0**

Special Attractions

- Pleasant, easy trail traversing a variety of scenery.
- Lush and shady Buehman Canyon.
- Steep climb out of Buehman Canyon.

Description

Buehman Canyon is one of the deep canyons that drains the east side of the Santa Catalina Mountains. The Buehman Canyon Trail leaves South #31: Redington Road and climbs up the open grassy ridge away from the San Pedro River. Initially the trail crosses private property; access is granted under the Sportsman-Landowners Respect Program. The trail is easygoing as it winds along a gravelly surface, passing stands of saguaro, prickly pear, palo verde, and the ubiquitous creosote bush. Farther along, the vegetation is open grassland studded with palmillas (soaptree yucca) and mesquite.

Sycamores line the trail in Buehman Canyon

The trail drops gradually down toward the deep gash of Buehman Canyon, passing a large cristate

Looking down on the trail as it exits Buehman Canyon

saguaro near the bottom of the descent. Within the canyon the terrain is lush and shady. Large cottonwoods and sycamores provide shade, and there is water in the creek approximately six months of the year. As this is private property, access to the creek itself is restricted.

The 200 yards of bumpy river rock immediately before leaving Buehman Canyon are the lumpiest part of the trail. It then swings around and starts to climb steeply out of the canyon back toward South #31: Redington Road. The trail is steep and powdery as it climbs. Vehicles with less aggressive tires may spin wheels. It climbs quickly up a ridge giving excellent views over Buehman Canyon and the Santa Catalinas before continuing to undulate along a ridge with steep drops on either side. The trail then rejoins South #31: Redington Road near Piety Hill.

The trail is not shown in its entirety on the BLM map, but it is shown on the National Forest Service map, where it is marked as FR 654 and FR 801.

Current Road Information

Coronado National Forest
Santa Catalina Ranger District
5700 North Sabino Canyon Rd.
Tucson, AZ 85750
(520) 749-8700

Map References

BLM Tucson
USFS Coronado National Forest: Safford and Santa Catalina Ranger Districts
USGS 1:24,000 Redington, Buehman Canyon, Piety Hill
1:100,000 Tucson
Maptech CD-ROM: Southeast Arizona/Tucson
Arizona Atlas & Gazetteer, p. 67

Route Directions

▼ 0.0		Trail commences 1.2 miles from the north end of South #31: Redington Road. Zero trip meter and turn west on unmarked, well-used, formed trail. Immediately pass through a gate onto private property.
5.3 ▲		Trail ends on South #31: Redington Road, 1.2 miles from the north end of the trail. Turn left for San Manuel, turn right for Tucson via Redington Road.
		GPS: N32°26.21′ W110°29.80′
▼ 0.2	SO	Track on left.

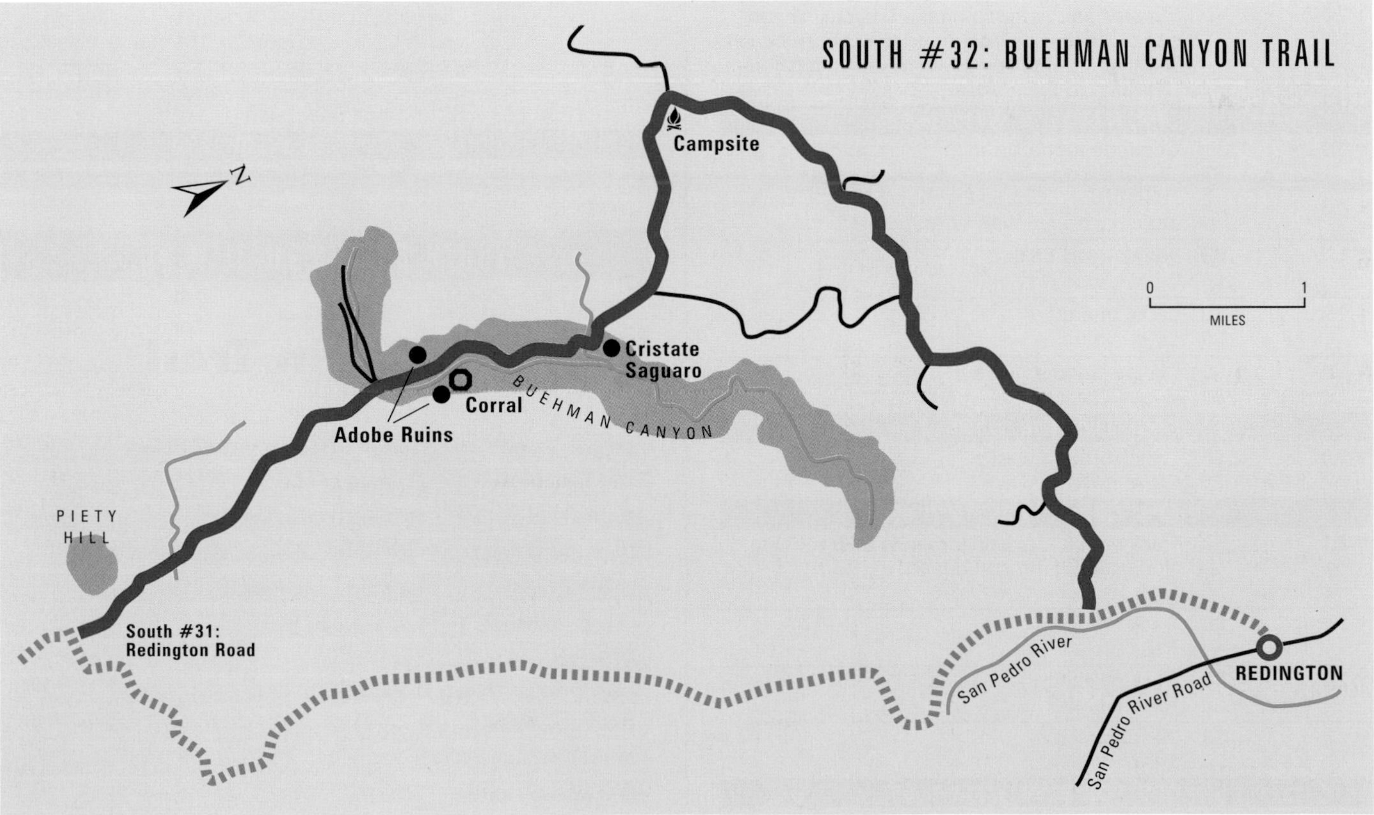

SOUTH #32: BUEHMAN CANYON TRAIL

Campsite
Cristate Saguaro
Corral
Adobe Ruins
BUEHMAN CANYON
PIETY HILL
South #31: Redington Road
San Pedro River
San Pedro River Road
REDINGTON
0 1 MILES
N

	5.1 ▲	SO	Track on right.
▼ 0.5		SO	Track on right.
	4.8 ▲	SO	Track on left.
▼ 1.0		BR	Small track on left and small track ahead. Bear right, remaining on main trail.
	4.3 ▲	BL	Small track on right and small track ahead. Bear left, remaining on main trail.
			GPS: N32°26.23' W110°30.63'
▼ 1.2		SO	Cross through wash.
	4.1 ▲	SO	Cross through wash.
▼ 1.3		SO	Track on right; then gate, entering state land. Permit required.
	4.0 ▲	SO	Gate, entering private land; then track on left.
			GPS: N32°26.42' W110°30.84'
▼ 1.7		SO	Cross through wash. Trail follows wash course, crossing it often for next 0.4 miles.
	3.6 ▲	SO	Cross through wash.
▼ 2.1		SO	Leave wash course.
	3.2 ▲	SO	Cross through wash. Trail follows wash course, crossing it often for the next 0.4 miles.
▼ 2.6		SO	Track on left.
	2.7 ▲	SO	Track on right.
▼ 2.7		SO	Track on left.
	2.6 ▲	SO	Track on right.
▼ 3.0		SO	Private road on left. Continue straight on, remaining on designated access route.
	2.3 ▲	SO	Private road on right. Continue straight on, remaining on designated access route.
▼ 4.0		SO	Track on right.
	1.3 ▲	SO	Track on left.
▼ 4.6		SO	Cattle guard. Entering private property on designated access route. Remain on main trail.
	0.7 ▲	SO	Cattle guard. Entering state land.
			GPS: N32°25.64' W110°33.62'
▼ 5.3		BL	Well-used track on right. Zero trip meter. Intersection is unmarked but there is a camping area just before it on the left. Trail ahead can be seen running around the hill on the left. Track on right drops down toward the canyon.
	0.0 ▲		Continue to the north.
			GPS: N32°25.16' W110°34.02'
▼ 0.0			Continue to the south.
	3.5 ▲	BR	Well-used track on left. Zero trip meter. Intersection is unmarked but there is a camping area immediately after it on the right.
▼ 1.4		SO	Private road on left.
	2.1 ▲	SO	Private road on right.
▼ 1.7		SO	Cattle guard.
	1.8 ▲	SO	Cattle guard.
▼ 1.9		SO	Cristate saguaro on left.
	1.6 ▲	SO	Cristate saguaro on right.
			GPS: N32°24.18' W110°32.76'
▼ 2.0		SO	Cross through wash.
	1.5 ▲	SO	Cross through wash.
			GPS: N32°24.19' W110°32.95'
▼ 2.1		SO	Track on left is private. Road is now running alongside Buehman Canyon.
	1.4 ▲	SO	Track on right is private.
▼ 2.6		SO	Track on right.
	0.9 ▲	SO	Track on left.
▼ 2.8		SO	Track on right.
	0.7 ▲	SO	Track on left.
▼ 2.9		SO	Corral on left.
	0.6 ▲	SO	Corral on right.
			GPS: N32°23.38' W110°33.05'
▼ 3.0		SO	Corner of adobe ruin on left; then pass through gate. Old well on left. Second adobe ruin on right just off trail.
	0.5 ▲	SO	Adobe ruin on left, pass through gate, well on right, followed by corner of adobe ruin on right.
			GPS: N32°23.37' W110°32.99'
▼ 3.1		SO	Cross through wash; then track on right is foot access only.
	0.4 ▲	SO	Track on left is foot access only; then cross through wash.
▼ 3.5		TL	Pass a small, square tank on the left, then turn sharp left past the tank onto trail leading steeply out of Buehman Canyon. There is a large tank in the trees at the intersection and a well-used track straight on and to the right. Zero trip meter.
	0.0 ▲		Continue to the northeast.
			GPS: N32°22.99' W110°33.08'
▼ 0.0			Continue to the south.
	2.8 ▲	TR	Enter Buehman Canyon, continue straight on and pass a small, square tank on the right, then turn right down the wash. Zero trip meter. There is a large tank in the trees at the intersection and a track on the left and a track straight on.
▼ 0.8		SO	Top of climb.
	2.0 ▲	SO	Start to descend toward Buehman Canyon.
			GPS: N32°22.49' W110°32.98'
▼ 1.3		SO	Gate.
	1.5 ▲	SO	Gate.
▼ 2.0		SO	Cross through wash.
	0.8 ▲	SO	Cross through wash.
▼ 2.8			Trail ends at the junction of the graded dirt South #31: Redington Road. Turn left for Redington, turn right for Tucson.
	0.0 ▲		Trail commences on the graded dirt South #31: Redington Road. Turn north on unmarked, well-used, formed trail. There is a campsite at the start and an old white sign warns, "Not a thru road." The turn is 0.2 miles southwest of mile marker 18. The track is not shown on the BLM map, but is shown as FR 801 on the forest map.
			GPS: N32°20.89' W110°32.40'

SOUTH REGION TRAIL #33

Jackson Cabin Trail

Starting Point:	**Muleshoe Ranch Visitor Center**
Finishing Point:	**Jackson Cabin**
Total Mileage:	**13.4 miles (one-way)**
Unpaved Mileage:	**13.4 miles (one-way)**
Driving Time:	**3.5 hours (one-way)**
Elevation Range:	**4,200–4,800 feet**
Usually Open:	**Year-round**
Best Time to Travel:	**September to May**
Difficulty Rating:	**4**
Scenic Rating:	**9**
Remoteness Rating:	**+0**

Special Attractions

- Historic cabins at Pride Ranch and Jackson Cabin.
- Panoramic views of the Galiuro Mountains.
- Wildlife viewing and bird watching.

History

The Muleshoe Ranch was not always the serene and peaceful desert oasis you see today. In its past were ruptured friendships, disagreements over ownership, and bloodshed.

The first owner of the ranch was supposedly Dr. Glendy King, who owned the hot springs (now known as Hooker Hot Springs) and the area immediately surrounding them. His nearest neighbors to the north were Melvin Jones and Ed Drew who ranched in the Bass Canyon area. Jones and Drew believed they were the legitimate owners of part of King's holdings. King, on the other hand, believed that Jones and Drew had simply annexed part of his ranch. In August 1884 the neighbors settled their dispute with gunfire, and Dr. King was killed.

In 1885, King's Ranch (minus the disputed section) was bought at auction by Colonel Hooker and added to his substantial Sierra Bonita holdings. Hooker was host to many visitors from the East, including Augustus Thomas, a famous American playwright, who subsequently based his leading characters of the stage play *Arizona* on Colonel Hooker and his daughter-in-law Forrestine. *Arizona* appeared on Broadway in 1889 and went on to become a novel and finally was the basis of the John Wayne movie *'Neath Arizona Skies* in 1934.

In the meantime, Ed Drew continued to ranch in Bass Canyon. His holdings were in his name alone now, because he had dissolved the partnership with Melvin Jones, feeling Jones was not living up to his side of the deal. Jones established his own ranch nearby. Ed Drew, originally from Montana, moved to Arizona in 1873 with his parents, three brothers, and his sister, Cora, who happened to be an exceptional horsewoman. Cora's prowess later led her to be offered a place in Buffalo Bill Cody's Wild West Show, an offer her mother made her turn down, fearing it was not a suitable place for a girl of only sixteen. The Drews were active in the local area. Besides running the ranch, the youngest brother, David, ran a butcher shop in Willcox, selling meat from the family ranch. Ed was also a champion rodeo rider in Arizona for many years.

Life was hard and a little too exciting at times for the settlers of Muleshoe Ranch. Apaches were still active in the area, and they raided the settlers' cattle, on one occasion butchering them in sight of the house, and in 1886 attacking Melvin Jones's ranch close by.

Jackson Cabin

The trail drops down into Sycamore Canyon

In 1898 Sam and Johnny Boyett purchased the Drew Ranch and Ed Drew became the foreman of the Sierra Bonita. Later, he was elected sheriff of Graham County. He died in 1911 in a saloon gunfight.

Johnny Boyett took over as foreman of the Hot Springs Ranch in 1899, and in 1900, on an Independence Day gathering in a Willcox saloon, he killed Warren Earp in a gunfight. Warren was one of the infamous Earp brothers, best known for their association with the rowdy town of Tombstone.

By 1930, the original Drew Ranch in Bass Canyon had been added to Colonel Hooker's ranch and the new expanded ranch was renamed the Muleshoe Ranch. In 1935 it was purchased by Mrs. Jessica MacMurray, who wanted the solitude that ranch life offered. She lived there with her longtime companion, Mrs. Patterson, for many years. One summer, Mrs. MacMurray toured Italy, giving her friend permission to build a small cottage on the grounds of the ranch. On her return she was horrified to find a massive stone lodge of ten rooms, a swimming pool, and private hot tubs. Mrs. Patterson was immediately ordered off the property, but to compensate for the building, she was given the deeds to the original Drew Ranch. The building still stands adjacent to the conservancy headquarters.

The Nature Conservancy now owns all the holdings of Muleshoe Ranch and the Drew Ranch. Encompassing 49,120 acres of land, the Muleshoe Ranch Cooperative Management Area is jointly owned by the Nature Conservancy, the U.S. Forest Service, and the Bureau of Land Management. Within the area are important riparian conservation areas, including seven permanently flowing streams.

Description

The historic Jackson Cabin is reached by 26 miles of graded dirt road, followed by a 14-mile, rough 4WD trail. The

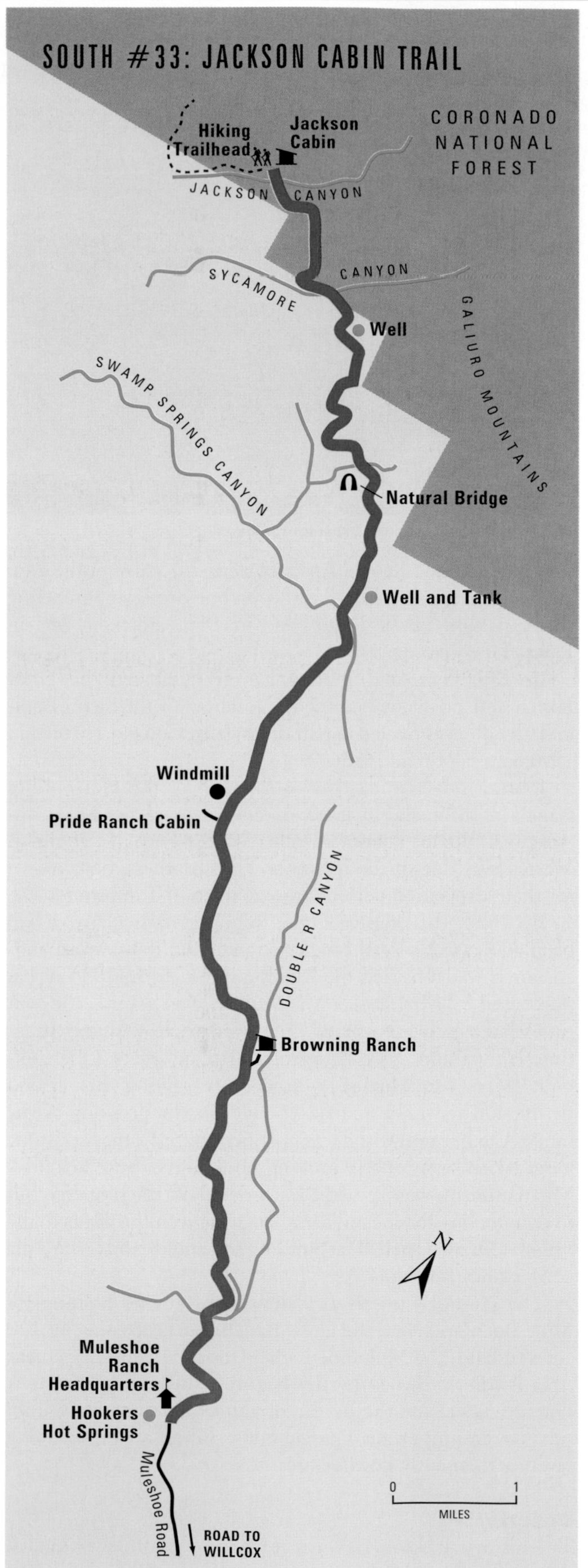

scenery around the beautiful Galiuro Mountains, combined with the lush riparian habitat, abundance of birds and wildlife, and many hiking trails, make the area well worth visiting. The trail crosses Muleshoe Ranch, now owned by the Arizona Nature Conservancy as well as the BLM and the National Forest Service. It commences outside the gate of the Muleshoe Ranch Visitor Center. The visitor center is normally open from 9 to 5 daily and is well worth a visit to learn about the plants, birds, and wildlife of the area. There are also small casitas that can be rented by the night. Contact Muleshoe Ranch for prices and bookings. The Hooker Hot Springs are available for use as well.

At the start of the trail is a trail log. All users are required to sign in and out. The trail leaves along a wash before climbing up onto a ridge. It undulates as a well-used, formed trail, with a loose, uneven surface. However, both the grades and the surface should be no trouble to any 4WD, SUV, or truck.

The section along the ridge top has one of the best views along the trail. The west face of the Galiuro Mountains rises abruptly from the valley floor. A short spur leads down to the remains of the Browning Ranch, set beside the Double R Canyon creek. A corral and a small adobe ruin remain. There are also two informal campsites with fire rings beside the creek. Other campsites, mainly for single vehicles, exist along the trail. There are other good camping places in Sycamore Canyon as well.

The Pride Ranch Cabin, which belongs to the Nature Conservancy, is a small brick, three-room cabin, with few facilities. It can be rented in advance for a nominal fee, but be aware that it is extremely primitive with very limited furniture and extremely basic facilities.

The latter part of the trail drops down into Sycamore Canyon and passes through a gap in the high, red walls before climbing out again and heading over a saddle for the final descent down to Jackson Cabin. The final part of the trail travels along a narrow, rough shelf road as it descends; this is possibly the trickiest part of the trail. The final 0.2 miles are slightly brushy as the trail runs along in the wash. But apart from this section there is little close brush along the trail.

The trail ends at the small stone and timber three-room Jackson Cabin sitting in a clearing in Jackson Canyon. Return to Muleshoe Ranch headquarters along the same road. Don't forget to sign back out.

To reach Muleshoe Ranch from Willcox, get off I-10 at exit 340 and proceed to the south side of the highway. Immediately turn right (south) at the stop light on Bisbee Avenue and continue for 0.7 miles. Turn right (west) onto Airport Road. Continue straight on, the pavement runs out and the road is now the graded dirt Cascabel Road. Proceed for 14.1 miles and then bear right onto Muleshoe Road following the sign for Mule Shoe. Continue for 13.1 miles to the entrance to Muleshoe Ranch and then another 0.4 miles to the visitor center. The Hooker Hot Springs are for use by casita guests only. There are five casitas available for overnight stays. Pride Ranch Cabin is also available for overnight stays.

Current Road Information

Coronado National Forest
Santa Catalina Ranger District
5700 North Sabino Canyon Rd.
Tucson, AZ 85750
(520) 749-8700

Map References

BLM Tucson
USFS Coronado National Forest: Safford and Santa Catalina Ranger Districts
USGS 1:24,000 Hooker Hot Springs, Soza Mesa, Cherry Spring Peak
1:100,000 Tucson
Maptech CD-ROM: Southeast/Tucson
Arizona Atlas & Gazetteer, p. 68
Arizona Road & Recreation Atlas, p. 54 & p. 88

Route Directions

▼ 0.0		At the entrance to the Muleshoe Ranch HQ, zero trip meter and proceed north on formed trail, following the sign to Jackson Cabin. Immediately on the left is an information board and trail register. You must sign in and out of the area. Trail initially crosses private property.
		GPS: N32°20.26′ W110°14.20′
▼ 0.5	SO	Cross gas pipeline, foot access permitted on left along pipeline; then track on right.
▼ 0.8	SO	Pass through fence line.
▼ 1.0	SO	Cross through wash.
▼ 1.2	SO	Pass through fence line.
▼ 1.4	SO	Cross through wash, a tributary of Double R Canyon, then enter public land.
		GPS: N32°21.35′ W110°14.28′
▼ 2.4	SO	Cross through small wash.
▼ 2.9	SO	Pass through fence line.
		GPS: N32°22.11′ W110°15.00′
▼ 3.6	SO	Track on right goes 0.2 miles to the remains of the Browning Ranch.
		GPS: N32°22.74′ W110°15.09′
▼ 3.9	SO	Entering private land.
		GPS: N32°22.98′ W110°15.19′
▼ 5.4	SO	Pass through fence line.
▼ 5.8	SO	Track on right to well, track on left to Pride Ranch Cabin. Zero trip meter.
		GPS: N32°24.16′ W110°16.21′
▼ 0.0		Continue to the north.
▼ 0.1	SO	Second track on left to Pride Ranch Cabin.
▼ 0.2	SO	Pass through fence line; then second cabin and windmill on left.
		GPS: N32°24.30′ W110°16.27′
▼ 0.5	SO	Entering public land.
		GPS: N32°24.52′ W110°16.20′
▼ 0.7	SO	Pass through fence line.
▼ 1.9	SO	Cross through Swamp Springs Canyon wash, follow alongside wash.
		GPS: N32°25.62′ W110°15.99′
▼ 2.0	SO	Cross through wash.
▼ 2.3	SO	Cross through wash, then climb away from wash.
▼ 2.4	SO	Well and stone tank on right. Zero trip meter opposite well.
		GPS: N32°26.00′ W110°16.16′
▼ 0.0		Continue to the northeast.
▼ 1.0	SO	Natural bridge on left of trail, then pass through fence line.
		GPS: N32°26.72′ W110°16.46′
▼ 1.3	SO	Cross through wash.
		GPS: N32°26.84′ W110°16.69′
▼ 1.8	SO	Cross through wash and follow alongside it for next 0.2 miles.
▼ 2.6	SO	Cross through wash.
▼ 3.0	SO	Well on right; then cross through wash.
		GPS: N32°27.53′ W110°17.29′
▼ 3.2	SO	Cross through wash.
▼ 3.6	SO	Entering Sycamore Canyon. Many campsites under the trees alongside the wash.
▼ 3.7	SO	Cross through wash.
▼ 3.9	SO	Cross through wash, then pass through fence line. Fence line is NFS boundary. Start to climb up to saddle.
		GPS: N32°27.81′ W110°17.79′
▼ 4.5	SO	Saddle. Jackson Cabin can be seen ahead down in Jackson Canyon. Trail descends shelf road down canyon.
		GPS: N32°28.23′ W110°17.94′
▼ 5.1	SO	End of shelf. Cross through wash; then hiking trails on left are West Divide Trail #289 and Powers Garden Trail #96.
		GPS: N32°28.33′ W110°18.41′
▼ 5.2		Trail ends at Jackson Cabin. There is also a second stone shed and corrals on the left. There are some semi-shaded campsites at the end of the trail around the cabin.
		GPS: N32°28.38′ W110°18.42′

Selected Further Reading

Massey, Peter, and Jeanne Wilson. *4WD Adventures: Colorado.* Castle Rock, Colo.: Swagman Publishing, Inc., 1999.

—. *4WD Adventures: Utah.* Castle Rock, Colo.: Swagman Publishing, Inc., 2000.

50 Common Reptiles and Amphibians of the Southwest. Tucson, Ariz.: Southwest Parks and Monuments Association, 1989.

100 Desert Flowers of the Southwest. Tucson, Ariz.: Southwest Parks and Monuments Association, 1989.

100 Roadside Wildflowers of the Southwest. Tucson, Ariz.: Southwest Parks and Monuments Association, 1989.

Ahnert, Gerald T. *Retracing the Butterfield Overland Trail Through Arizona: A Guide to the Route of 1857–1861.* N.p.: Westernlore Press, 1973.

Alden, Peter, and Peter Friederici. *National Audubon Society: Field Guide to the Southwestern States.* New York: Alfred A. Knopf, 1999.

Anderson, Dorothy Daniels. *Arizona Legends and Lore.* Phoenix: Golden West Publishers, 1991.

Annerino, John. *Adventuring in Arizona: The Sierra Club Travel Guide to the Grand Canyon State.* San Francisco: Sierra Club Books, 1991.

Arizona: A State Guide. New York: Hastings House, 1940.

Arizona Highways 34, no. 11 (November 1958).

Arizona Highways 61, no. 10 (October 1965).

Arizona: The Grand Canyon State. Vol. 1. N.p.: Western States Historical Publishers, Inc., 1975.

Arizona: The Grand Canyon State. Vol. 2. N.p.: Western States Historical Publishers, Inc., 1975.

Ayer, Eleanor H. *Birds of Arizona.* Phoenix: Renaissance House Publishers, 1988.

Bahti, Tom, and Mark Bahti. *Southwestern Indian Tribes.* Las Vegas: KC Publications, 1997.

Bailowitz, Richard, and Douglas Danforth. *70 Common Butterflies of the Southwest.* Tucson, Ariz.: Southwest Parks and Monuments Association, 1997.

Barker, Scott. *Arizona off the Beaten Path.* Old Saybrook, Conn.: The Globe Pequot Press, 1996.

Barnes, Will C. *Arizona Place Names.* Tucson, Ariz.: The University of Arizona Press, 1988.

Beale Wagon Road Historic Trail. U.S. Government Printing Office: Kaibab National Forest, 1990.

Billingsley, George H., Spamer, Earle E., and Menkes, Don. *Quest for the Pillar of Gold: The Mines and Miners of the Grand Canyon.* N.p.: Grand Canyon Association, 1997.

Bischoff, Mike. *Touring Arizona Hot Springs.* Helena, Mont.: Falcon Publishing, Inc., 1999.

Black, Harry G. *The Lost Dutchman Mine: A Short Story of Tall Tales.* Boston: Branden Press, 1975.

Bowers, Janice Emily. *100 Desert Wildflowers of the Southwest.* Tucson, Ariz.: Southwest Parks and Monuments Association, 1989.

Brandes, Ray. *Fontier Military Posts of Arizona.* Globe, Ariz.: Dale Stuart King, 1960.

Brant, Keith L. Jr. *History of the Atchison, Topeka and Santa Fe Railway.* London: University of Nebraska Press, 1974.

Burrill, Larry C., Steven A. Dewey, David W. Cudney, B. E. Nelson, Richard D. Lee, Robert Parker. *Weeds of the West.* 5th Edition. Edited by Tom D. Whitson. Jackson, Wyo.: The Western Society of Weed Science; Western United States Land Grand Universities Cooperative Extension Services, 1999.

Burke, Larry. *Arizona Boonies: The Arizona Even the Zonies Don't Know About.* Phoenix: Niche Publishing, 1998.

Canyon De Chelly National Monument: Motoring Guide to the South and North Rims. N.p.: Southwest Parks and Monument Association, 1999.

Canyon De Chelly Official Map and Guide. N.p.: U.S. Department of the Interior, n.d.

Canyon Overlook: A Visitor's Guide to Canyon de Chelly National Monument. N.p.: N.p., n.d.

Casebier, Dennis G., *Camp Eldorado Arizona Territory.* N.p.: Arizona Historical Foundation, 1970.

Chronic, Halka. *Roadside Geology of Arizona.* Missoula, Mont.: Mountain Press Publishing Company, 1983.

Conner, Daniel Ellis. *Joseph Reddeford Walker and the Arizona Adventure.* London: University of Oklahoma Press, 1956.

Cook, James E., Sam Negri, and Marshall Trimble. *Travel Arizona: The Back Roads.* 3rd ed. Edited by Dean Smith and Wesley Holden. Phoenix: Book Division of Arizona Highways Magazine, 1994.

Cowgill, Pete. *Back Roads and Beyond.* 2nd ed. Tucson, Ariz.: Broken Toe Press, 1997.

Cross, Jack L., Elizabeth H. Shaw, and Kathleen Scheifele, eds. *Arizona: Its People and Resources.* Tucson, Ariz.: the University of Arizona Press, 1960.

Crutchfield, James A. *It Happened in Arizona.* Helena, Mont.: Falcon Press Publishing Co., 1994.

Dale, Edward Everett. *The Indians of the Southwest.* London: University of Oklahoma Press, 1949.

Dunning, Charles H. *Rocks to Riches.* N.p.: Southwest Publishing Company, Inc., 1959.

Earle, W. Hubert *Cacti of the Southwest.* Phoenix: Arizona Cactus and Native Flora Society, Inc., 1963.

Eastep, Alan, and Ron Locke. *Bradshaw Mountains Back Roads.* Litchfield Park, Ariz.: Back Road Press, 1996.

Elmore, Francis H. *Shrubs and Trees of the Southwest Uplands.* Tucson, Ariz.: Southwest Parks and Monuments Association, 1976.

Epple, Anne Orth. *A Field Guide to the Plants of Arizona.* Helena, Mont.: Falcon, 1995.

Etter, Patricia A. *To California on the Southern Route 1849: A History and Annotated Bibliography.* Spokane, Wash.: The Arthur H. Clark Company, 1998.

Fagan, Damian. *Canyon Country Wildflowers.* Helena, Mont.: Falcon Publishing Co., Inc., 1998.

Farrell, Robert J., and Bob Albano, eds. *Wild West Collections.* 4 vols. Phoenix: Book Division of Arizona Highways Magazine, 1997–99.

Faulk, Odie B. *Destiny Road: The Gila Trail and the Opening of the Southwest.* New York: Oxford University Press, 1973.

Fireman, Bert M. *Arizona: Historic Land.* New York: Alfred A. Knof, 1982.

Flint, Timothy. *The Personal Narrative of James Ohio Pattie of Kentucky.* Cincinnati: John H. Wood, 1831. [Reprinted in paperback edition, New York: Lippincott, 1962]

Florin, Lambert. *Ghost Towns of the West.* New York: Promontory Press, 1993.

Gray, Mary Taylor. *Watchable Birds of the Southwest.* Missoula, Mont.: Mountain Press Publishing Company, 1995.

Granger, Byrd Howell, *Arizona's Names: X Marks the Place.* N.p.: Falconer Publishing Company, 1983.

Grubbs, Bruce. *Camping Arizona.* Helena, Mont.: Falcon Publishing, Inc., 1999.

Hait, Pam. *Shifra Stein's Day Trips from Phoenix, Tucson, and Flagstaff.* Old Saybrook, Conn.: The Globe Pequot Press, 1986.

Heatwole, Thelma. *Arizona off the Beaten Path!.* Phoenix: Golden West Publishers, 1982.

—. *Ghost Towns and Historical Haunts in Arizona.* Phoenix: Golden West Publishers, 1981.

Hernandez, Luis F. Aztlan: *The Southwest and Its Peoples.* Rochelle Park, N.J.: Hayden Book Company, Inc., 1975.

Hinton, Richard J. *The Handbook to Arizona: Its Resources, History, Towns, Mines, Ruins and Scenery.* Tucson, Ariz.: Arizona Silhouettes, 1954.

Hirschfelder, Arlene. *Native Americans: A History in Pictures.* New York: Dorling Kindersley Publishing, Inc., 2000.

Hoff, David and Nearing, Richard. *Arizona Military Installations: 1752–1922.* Tempe, Ariz.: Gem Publishing, 1995.

Hoxie, Frederick E., ed. *Encyclopedia of North American Indians.* Boston: Houghton Mifflin Company, 1996.

Jaeger, Edmund C. *Desert Wildlife.* Stanford, Calif.: Stanford University Press, 1950.

Johnston, Charles H. L. *Famous Scouts.* N.p.: The Colonial Press, 1910.

Kaufman, LynnHassler. *Birds of the American Southwest.* Tucson, Ariz.: Rio Nuevo Publishers, 2000.

Kosik, Fran. *Native Roads.* Tucson, Ariz.: Treasure Chest Books, 1996.

Lamb, Edgar, and Brian Lamb. *Pocket Encyclopedia of Cacti in Colour.* Revised ed. London: Blandford, 1969.

Leland, Hanchett L., Jr. *Catch the Stage to Phoenix.* Phoenix: Pine Rim Publishing, 1998.

Lingenfelter, Richard E. *Steamboats on the Colorado River, 1852–1916.* Tucson, Ariz.: The University of Arizona Press, 1978.

Lockwood, Frank C. *Pioneer Days in Arizona.* New York: The Macmillan Company, 1932.

—. *Thumbnail Sketches of Famous Arizona Desert Riders 1538–1946.* Tucson, Ariz.: University of Arizona, 1946.

Lombardi, L. L. *Tortilla Flat Arizona: the Real Story.* Tortilla Flat, Ariz.: Sunshower Corporation, 1996.

Love, Frank. *Mining Camps and Ghost Towns.* N.p.: Westernlore Press, 1974.

Malach, Roman. *White Hills.* N.p.: Mohave Board of Supervisors, 1982.

Maurer, Stephen G. *Visitors Guide: Mogollon Rim.* Albuquerque, N.Mex.: Southwest Natural and Cultural Heritage Association, 1991.

—. *Visitors Guide: Coconino National Forest.* Albuquerque, N.Mex: Southwest Natural and Cultural Heritage Association, 1990.

Marks, Paula Mitchell. *And Die in the West.* New York: Simon and Schuster Inc., 1989.

Martin, Douglas D. *Tombstone's "Epitaph".* London: University of Oklahoma Press, 1958.

McCarty, Kieran, ed. *A Frontier Documentary: Sonora and Tucson, 1821–1848.* Tucson, Ariz.: The University of Arizona Press, 1997.

McGavin, George C. *Insects Spiders and Other Terrestrial Anthropods.* New York: Dorling Kindersley Publishing, Inc., 2000.

Messersmith, Dan W. *The History of Mohave County to 1912.* N.p.: Mohave County Historical Society, 1991.

Milne, Lorus J., and Rayfield, Susan. *National Audubon Society Pocket Guide Insects and Spiders.* New York: Alfred A. Knopf, Inc., 1988.

—. *National Audubon Society Field Guide to North American Insects and Spiders.* New York: Alfred A. Knopf, 1980.

Miller, Donald C. *Ghost Towns of the Southwest.* Boulder, Colo.: Pruett Publishing Company.

Mitchell, James R. *Gem Trails of Arizona.* Baldwin Park, Calif.: Gem Guides Book Co., 1995.

Mitchell, John D. *Lost Mines of the Great Southwest.* Glorieta, N. Mex.: The Rio Grande Press, Inc., 1933.

Morris, Eleanor, and Steve Cohen. *Adventure Guide to Arizona.* Edison, N. Jer.: Hunter Publishing, 1996.

Murbarger, Nell. *Ghost of the Adobe.* Tucson, Ariz.: Treasure Chest Publications, Inc., 1964.

Nash, Robert. *Encyclopedia of Western Lawmen and Outlaws.* New York: Da Capo Press, 1989.

Nearing, Richard, and David Hoff. *Arizona Military Installations: 1752–1922.* Tempe, Ariz.: Gem Publishing, 1995.

Noble, David Grant. *Ancient Ruins of the Southwest.* Flagstaff, Ariz.: Northland Publishing, 1991.

Officer, James E. *Hispanic Arizona, 1536–1856.* Tucson, Ariz.: The University of Arizona Press, 1987.

O'Neal, Bill. *Encyclopedia of Western Gunfighters.* Norman, Okla.: University of Oklahoma Press, 1979.

Overland Road Historic Trail. U.S. Government Printing Office: Kaibab National Forest, 1990.

Paher, Stanley W. *Western Arizona Ghost Towns.* Las Vegas: Nevada Publications, 1990.

Palatki Red Cliffs. N.p.: U.S. Forest Service, n.d.

Palatki Red Cliffs Tour Guide. N.p.: The Friends of the Forest, n.d.

Penfield, Thomas. *Dig Here!* San Antonio, Tex.: The Naylor Company, 1962.

Pry, Mark E. *The Town on the Hassayampa: The History of Wickenburg, Arizona.* Wickenburg, Ariz.: Desert Caballeros Western Museum, 1997.

Quinn, Meg. *Wildflowers of the Desert Southwest.* Tucson, Ariz.: Rio Nuevo Publishers, 2000.

Recreation Sites in Southwestern National Forests and Grasslands. N.p.: United States Department of Agriculture, n.d.

Ruland-Thorne, Kate. *Experience Sedona Legends and Legacies.* Sacramento, Calif.: Thorne Enterprises Publications, Inc., 1999.

Schuler, Stanley, ed. *Simon and Schuster's guide to Cacti and Succulents.* New York: Simon and Schuster Inc., 1985.

Searchy, Paula. *Travel Arizona: The Scenic Byways.* Edited by Bob Albano, Evelyn Howell, and Laura A. Lawrie. Phoenix: Book Division of Arizona Highways Magazine, 1997.

Sheffer, Henry H., III, and Sharyn R. Sheffer. *The Legend of the Lost Dutchman.* N.p.: Norseman Publications, 1998.

Sheridan, Thomas E. *Arizona: A History.* London: The University of Arizona Press, 1995.

Sherman, James E., and Barbara H. Sherman. *Ghost Towns of Arizona.* Norman, Okla.: University of Oklahoma Press, 1969.

Snyder, Ernest E. *Prehistoric Arizona.* Phoenix: Golden West Publishers, 1987.

Spellenberg, Richard. *National Audubon Society Field Guide to North American Wildflowers: Western Region.* New York: Alfred A. Knopf, 1979.

Stebbins, Robert C., *A Field Guide to Western Reptiles and Amphibians.* 2nd ed. Boston: Houghton Mifflin Company, 1985.

Stephenson, Patricia, and Alex Jay Kimmelman. *Tom Marshall's Tucson.* Tucson, Ariz.: N.p., 1996.

Stoops, Erik D., and Jeffrey L. Martin. *Scorpions and Venomous Insects of the Southwest.* Phoenix: Golden West Publishers, 1997.

Stoops, Erik D., and Annette Wright. *Snakes and Other Reptiles of the Southwest.* 5th ed. Phoenix: Golden West Publishers, 1993.

Taylor, Colin F. *The Native Americans: The Indigenous People of North America.* London: Thunder Bay Press, 1991.

Tefertiller, Casey. *Wyatt Earp: The Life Behind the Legend.* New York: John Wiley and Sons, Inc., 1997.

Thompson, Gerald. *Edward F. Beale and the American West.* Albuquerque, N. Mex.: University of New Mexico Press, 1983.

Thrapp, Dan L. *Al Sieber, Chief of Scouts.* London: University of Oklahoma Press, 1964.

—. *Encyclopedia of Frontier Biography.* 3 vols. London: University of Nebraska Press, 1988.

Trimble, Marshall. *Arizona Adventure!.* Phoenix: Golden West Publishers, 1982.

Trimble, Marshall. *Arizona: A Cavalcade of History.* Tucson, Ariz.: Treasure Chest Publications, 1989.

Trimble, Marshall. *Roadside History of Arizona.* Missoula, Mont.: Mountain Press Publishing Company, 1986.

Tweit, Susan J. *The Great Southwest Nature Factbook.* Anchorage: Alaska Northwest Books, 1992.

Udvardy, Miklos D. F. *National Audubon Society: Field Guide to North American Birds: Western Region.* New York: Alfred A. Knopf, 1994.

Varney, Philip. *Arizona Ghost Towns and Mining Camps.* Phoenix: Book Division of Arizona Highways Magazine, 1994.

—. *Arizona's Best Ghost Town.* Flagstaff, Ariz.: Northland Press, 1980.

Walker, Henry P., and Don Bufkin. *Historical Atlas of Arizona.* 2nd ed. London: University of Oklahoma Press, 1979.

Wagoner, Jay J. *Early Arizona: Prehistory to Civil War.* Tucson, Ariz.: The University of Arizona Press, 1975.

Wagoner, Jay J. *Arizona's Heritage.* Salt Lake City: Peregrine Smith, Inc., 1977.

Wahmann, Russell. *Auto Road Log.* Cottonwood, Ariz.: Starlight Publishing, 1982.

Waldman, Carl. *Atlas of the North American Indian.* New York: Checkmark Books, 2000.

—. *Encyclopedia of Native American Tribes.* New York: Facts on File, 1988.

Ward, Geoffrey C. *The West: an Illustrated History.* Boston: Little, Brown and Company, 1996.

Warren, Scott S. *Exploring Arizona's Wild Areas.* Seattle: Mountaineers Books, 1996.

Weight, Harold O. *Lost Mines of Old Arizona.* Ridgecrest, Calif.: Hubbard Printing, 1959.

Werner, Floyd, and Carl Olson. *Learning about and Living with Insects of the Southwest.* Tucson, Ariz.: Fisher Books, 1994.

Wilderness and Primitive Areas in Southwestern National Forests. N.p.: United States Department of Agriculture, n.d.

Wilson, Bruce M. *Crown King and the Southern Bradshaws: A Complete History.* Chandler, Ariz.: Crown King Press, 1990.

Wolle, Muriel Sibell. *The Bonanza Trail: Ghost Towns and Mining Camps of the West.* Chicago: The Swallow Press Incorporated, 1953.

Zauner, Phyllis. *Those Legendary Men of the Wild West.* Sacramento, Calif.: Zanel Publications, 1991.

http://ag.arizona.edu/bta

http://my.ispchannel.com/~mives/locale.html

http://redrock.sedona.net/heritage

http://seamonkey.ed.asu.edu/~storslee/flagstaff.html

http://yumachamber.org

http://www.americanwest.com/pages/docholid.htm

http://www.azcentral.com/travel/destinations/arizona/river/yuma.shtml

http://www.crown-king.com/history.html

http://www.desertusa.com/Cities/az/flagstaff.html

http://www.visityuma.com

http://www.techline.com/~nicks/earp.htm

http://www.purcellstudios.com

http://www.ghosttowns.com

http://www.flagstaff.az.us/

http://www.experiencesedona.com

http://www.sedonaretreats.com

http://www.superior-arizona.com

http://www.tucsonchamber.org

25 Favorite Trails

	Trail Name	Difficulty rating (Hardest = 10)	Scenic Rating (Best = 10)	Length (miles)
1	South #3: El Camino del Diablo Trail	4	9	114.1
2	Central #26: Crown King Backroad	6	9	24.1
3	Northeast #45: Canyon de Chelly Trail	5	10	46.6
4	Central #44: Battleaxe Trail	5	9	12.2
5	Northeast #47: Lukachukai Mountains Trail	3	10	11.2
6	South #33: Jackson Cabin Trail	4	9	13.4
7	South #12: Mexican Border Road	1	10	50.4
8	South #16: Temporal Gulch Trail	5	9	11.7
9	Northeast #25: Broken Arrow Trail	7	9	4.5
10	Central #6: Engesser Pass Trail	4	8	42.4
11	Central #43: Cochran Coke Ovens Trail	7	9	4.9
12	Northwest #19: Flag Mine Trail	5	9	34.0
13	Central #30: Bloody Basin Road	2	9	24.7
14	South #31: Redington Road	2	8	23.3
15	Northeast #36: The Mogollon Rim Road	1	9	41.3
16	South #1: Tinajas Altas Pass Trail	3	9	35.0
17	Central #39: Montana Mountain Trail	4	9	33.4
18	Northeast #24: Schnebly Hill Road	2	9	11.4
19	Northeast #12: Sycamore Point Trail	2	10	7.5
20	Northwest #26: Portland Mine Road	4	9	31.8
21	Northeast #5: O'Leary Basin Trail	3	10	13.6
22	Central #29: Table Mesa Trail	5	9	18.2
23	Central #5: Big Eye Wash Trail	3	9	14.5
24	Northwest #8: Red Mountain Trail	6	8	3.8
25	Central #33: East Verde River Trail	4	9	13.5

25 Longest Trails

	Trail Name	Length (Miles)	Difficulty Rating (Hardest = 10)	Scenic Rating (Best = 10)
1	South #3: El Camino del Diablo Trail	114.1	4	9
2	Northwest #15: Alamo Lake Road	53.9	1	8
3	South #12: Mexican Border Road	50.4	1	10
4	South #26: Willow Springs Road	49.8	2	7
5	Northeast #45: Canyon de Chelly Trail	46.6	5	10
6	Central #15: Agua Caliente Road	45.9	1	8
7	South #5: Christmas Pass Trail	44.1	3	8
8	Central #6: Engesser Pass Trail	42.4	4	8
9	Northeast #36: The Mogollon Rim Road	41.3	1	9
10	Central #38: Apache Trail	38.5	1	9
11	Central #24: Senator Highway	36.3	2	8
12	South #6: Puerto Blanco Drive	35.6	1	8
13	Northwest #31: Santa Maria Mountains Loop	35.3	2	8
14	South #1: Tinajas Altas Pass Trail	35.0	3	9
15	Northwest #19: Flag Mine Trail	34.0	5	9
16	Central #39: Montana Mountain Trail	33.4	4	9
17	South #24: Swift Trail	32.4	1	8
18	Northeast #40: Defiance Plateau Trail	32.3	2	7
19	Northwest #26: Portland Mine Road	31.8	4	9
20	South #8: Parker Canyon Lake Road	31.6	1	7
21	Northeast #44: Fluted Rock Road	31.1	2	9
22	Northwest #22: Oatman Warm Springs Trail	29.9	3	8
23	Northeast #13: Perkinsville Road	29.8	1	8
24	Central #27: Camp Creek Road	28.5	1	7
25	Northeast #11: White Horse Lake Loop Trail	28.0	2	8

25 Shortest Trails

	Trail Name	Length (Miles)	Difficulty Rating (Hardest=10)	Scenic Rating (Best=10)
1	Northwest #23: Moss Mine Trail	2.0	3	8
2	Northwest #5: Glory Hole Mine Trail	2.1	5	8
3	Northwest #27: Powerline Road	2.2	6	8
4	Northeast #23: Soldier Pass Road	2.5	5	8
5	Central #14: Saddle Mountain Trail	2.6	4	8
6	Northeast #25: Broken Arrow Trail	3.1	7	9
7	South #23: Barfoot Park Trail	3.1	4	7
8	Central #42: Martinez Mine Trail	3.4	4	8
9	Northwest #9: Gray Eagle Mine Trail	3.6	4	8
10	South #18: Mule Mountains Trail	3.6	2	8
11	Northeast #21: Sugarloaf Mountain Trail	3.7	3	8
12	Northwest #8: Red Mountain Trail	3.8	6	8
13	Northwest #13: Swansea Pumping Plant Trail	3.8	4	9
14	Northeast #29: Apache Maid Fire Lookout Trail	4.0	2	9
15	Northwest #11: Railroad Canyon Trail	4.1	3	7
16	Northwest #10: Nellie Mine Road	4.1	1	7
17	Northeast #22: Dry Creek Road	4.2	2	9
18	Northeast #26: Rattlesnake Canyon Trail	4.4	5	8
19	Northwest #16: McCracken Peak Trail	4.7	5	8
20	Central #43: Cochran Coke Ovens Trail	4.9	7	9
21	Northwest #24: Mossback Wash	5.6	4	8
22	Central #31: Indian Spring Wash Trail	5.6	3	8
23	South #10: Blacktail Ridge Trail	6.4	2	7
24	Northwest #2: Plomosa Range Trail	6.4	3	8
25	Northeast #8: Freidlein Prairie Trail	6.4	3	8

25 Hardest Trails

	Trail Name	Difficulty rating (Hardest = 10)	Scenic Rating (Best = 10)	Length (miles)
1	South #30: Sibley Mansion and Bluebird Mine Trail	7	8	8.0
2	Central #43: Cochran Coke Ovens Trail	7	9	4.9
3	Northeast #25: Broken Arrow Trail	7	9	3.1
4	Central #26: Crown King Backroad	6	9	24.1
5	Northwest #8: Red Mountain Trail	6	8	3.8
6	South #21: Hands Pass Trail	6	8	12.0
7	Northwest #27: Powerline Road	6	8	2.2
8	Central #37: Edwards Park Trail	6	8	10.8
9	Central #29: Table Mesa Trail	5	9	18.2
10	Central #44: Battleaxe Trail	5	9	12.2
11	Northwest #16: McCracken Peak Trail	5	8	4.7
12	Northeast #18: Mingus Mountain Road	5	9	16.6
13	Northeast #26: Rattlesnake Canyon Trail	5	8	4.4
14	Central #41: Box Canyon Trail	5	8	25.4
15	Central #8: Bighorn Pass Trail	5	8	17.6
16	Northwest #14: Rawhide Mountains Trail	5	9	16.3
17	South #16: Temporal Gulch Trail	5	9	11.7
18	Central #40: Telegraph Canyon Trail	5	9	12.2
19	Northeast #45: Canyon de Chelly Trail	5	10	46.6
20	Northwest #25: Thumb Butte Trail	5	8	14.5
21	Northwest #5: Glory Hole Mine Trail	5	8	2.1
22	Northwest #19: Flag Mine Trail	5	9	34.0
23	Central #12: Harquahala Mountain Trail	5	9	10.3
24	Northwest #7: Mineral Wash-Bill Williams River Trail	5	9	16.2
25	Northeast #23: Soldier Pass Road	5	8	2.5

25 Easiest Trails

	Trail Name	Difficulty rating (Hardest = 10)	Scenic Rating (Best = 10)	Length (miles)
1	South #7: Ajo Mountain Drive	1	9	18.9
2	Northwest #15: Alamo Lake Road	1	8	53.9
3	Central #38: Apache Trail	1	9	38.5
4	Northeast #9: Bill Williams Mountain Loop Trail	1	8	17.4
5	Northeast #39: Black Canyon Trail	1	9	16.8
6	Northeast #41: Black Creek Trail	1	8	11.6
7	Northeast #38: Chevelon Crossing Road	1	8	24.0
8	Central #32: Control Road	1	7	22.1
9	Central #11: Harquahala Mine Trail	1	7	12.1
10	South #13: Harshaw Road	1	7	15.6
11	Central #10: Hovatter Road	1	7	21.4
12	Central #3: King Valley Road	1	7	22.7
13	Northeast #34: Long Lake Road	1	7	16.2
14	Northwest #10: Nellie Mine Road	1	7	4.2
15	Central #1: Palm Canyon Road	1	7	6.7
16	South #8: Parker Canyon Lake Road	1	7	31.6
17	Northeast #13: Perkinsville Road	1	8	29.8
18	South #20: Pinery Canyon Trail	1	8	18.0
19	South #6: Puerto Blanco Drive	1	8	35.6
20	Northwest #17: Signal Road	1	7	17.9
21	Northwest #6: Swansea Road	1	9	24.6
22	South #24: Swift Trail	1	8	32.4
23	South #19: Tex Canyon Trail	1	9	26.3
24	Northeast #36: The Mogollon Rim Road	1	9	41.3
25	South #12: Mexican Border Road	1	10	50.4

25 Scenic Trails

	Trail Name	Scenic rating (Best = 10)	Difficulty Rating (Hardest = 10)	Length (miles)
1	Northeast #45: Canyon de Chelly Trail	10	5	46.6
2	Northeast #47: Lukachukai Mountains Trail	10	3	11.2
3	South #12: Mexican Border Road	10	1	50.4
4	Northeast #5: O'Leary Basin Trail	10	3	13.6
5	Northeast #4: O'Leary Peak Trail	10	2	8.7
6	Northeast #12: Sycamore Point Trail	10	2	7.5
7	South #7: Ajo Mountain Drive	9	1	18.9
8	Northeast #29: Apache Maid Fire Lookout Trail	9	2	4.0
9	Central #38: Apache Trail	9	1	38.5
10	Central #44: Battleaxe Trail	9	5	12.2
11	Central #5: Big Eye Wash Trail	9	3	14.5
12	Northeast #39: Black Canyon Trail	9	1	16.8
13	Central #30: Bloody Basin Road	9	2	24.7
14	Central #21: Box Canyon of the Hassayampa Trail	9	4	12.7
15	Northeast #20: Boynton Pass Trail	9	2	10.5
16	Northeast #25: Broken Arrow Trail	9	7	3.1
17	Northeast #27: Cedar Flat Road	9	1	10.8
18	Northeast #6: Cinder Hills Loop	9	3	18.9
19	Central #43: Cochran Coke Ovens Trail	9	7	4.9
20	Central #26: Crown King Backroad	9	6	24.1
21	Northeast #22: Dry Creek Road	9	2	4.2
22	Central #33: East Verde River Trail	9	4	13.5
23	South #3: El Camino del Diablo Trail	9	4	114.1
24	Central #36: El Oso Road	9	3	26.3
25	Northwest #19: Flag Mine Trail	9	5	34.0

About the Authors

Peter Massey grew up in the outback of Australia, where he acquired a life-long love of the backcountry. After retiring from a career in investment banking in 1986 at the age of thirty-five, he served as a director of a number of companies in the United States, the United Kingdom, and Australia. He moved to Colorado in 1993.

Jeanne Wilson was born and grew up in Maryland. After moving to New York City in 1980, she worked in advertising and public relations before moving to Colorado in 1993.

After traveling extensively in Australia, Europe, Asia, and Africa, the authors covered more than 80,000 miles touring the United States and the Australian outback between 1993 and 1997. Since then they have traveled more than 25,000 miles doing research for their two guidebook series: *Backcountry Adventures* and *4WD Trails*.

Photograph Credits

Unless otherwise indicated in the following list of acknowledgments (which is organized by section and page number), all color photographs were taken by Peter Massey and are copyrighted by Swagman Publishing Inc., or by Peter Massey.

Abbreviations: Arizona State Library, Archives & Public Records, Phoenix (ASL); Sharlot Hall Museum, Prescott, Arizona (Sharlot Hall); Northern Arizona University, Cline Library, Flagstaff (Cline Library); Arizona Historical Society, Tucson (AHS); Denver Public Library Western History Collection (Denver Public Library); Corel Stock Photo Library (Corel).

23 ASL #97-1000; **24** ASL #97-0615a; **25** Sharlot Hall; **27** ASL #96-2357; **28** ASL #97-1143; **30** ASL #98-0722; **31** Cline Library; **32** Bushducks; **33** (left) Cline Library; (right) AHS, Tucson; **34** (left) ASL #97-7361; (right) Cline Library; **35** ASL (upper) #96-3204, (lower) #95-2831; **36** ASL (upper left) #97-6799, (lower left) #97-7561, (right) #96-4333; **37** ASL #95-9074; **38** ASL #96-3566; **40** ASL #97-1452; **41** ASL #96-1936; **43** (upper) AHS; (lower right) ASL #98-0704; **44** ASL #98-3807; **45** (left) Cline Library; (right) AHS; **46** (left) AHS; (right) ASL #96-1591; **47** ASL (left) #97-4041, (right) #98-6458; **48** ASL (left) #98-0738, (right) #97-1230; **49** Cline Library; **50** (left) Cline Library; (right) Bushducks; **51** (upper) AHS; (lower) Bushducks; **52** ASL #97-2843; **53** (upper) AHS; (lower) ASL #97-2856; **54** ASL #97-9676; **55** (left) ASL #95-9089; (right) Sharlot Hall; **56** ASL #95-9812; **57** ASL #96-2125; **58** ASL #97-1958; **63** Denver Public Library; **64** Denver Public Library; **65** ASL (left) #97-1445, (right) #98-0729; **66** (left) ASL #97-2856; (right) Denver Public Library; **68** ASL #97-7027; **71** (upper right) Utah State Historical Society; (lower right) AHS; **72** (left) Utah State Historical Society; (right) AHS; **73** (upper) Huntington Library; (lower) ASL #97-9491; **74** AHS; **75** ASL #97-2651; **76** Denver Public Library; **78** ASL #96-1391; **79** ASL #97-7064; **80** ASL #97-4666; **81** (left) ASL #97-8329; **82** AHS; **83** (left) ASL #95-2822; (right) AHS; **84** AHS; **85** (upper) AHS; (lower) ASL #97-8574; **87** (left) AHS; (right) ASL #97-7957; **89** Bushducks; **90** (left) ASL #97-4566; (right) Denver Public Library; **91** ASL Denver Public Library; (lower) #98-5992; **92** Utah State Historical Society; **93** ASL #97-6680; **94** (left) Utah State Historical Society; (right) ASL #97-1364; **95** ASL (upper) #99-0107a, (lower left) #98-6000; **97** (upper) Utah State Historical Society; (lower) ASL #97-7723; **99** AHS; **100** (upper) Cline Library; (lower) ASL #97-1057; **101** ASL #97-0750; **102** Bushducks; **103** AHS; **104** ASL (upper left) #98-0388, (lower left) #97-1446, (right) #97-1474; **107** (left) Corel Photo Library; (upper right) Paul Berquist; (middle & lower right) Corel; **108-109** Corel; **110** (upper & middle left) Corel (lower right) Earle Robinson; (right) Paul Berquist; **111** Corel; **112** (upper left) Corel; (lower left) Paul Berquist; (upper right) Corel; (lower right) Bushducks; **113** (left) Corel; (upper right) Paul Berquist; (middle right) Doug Von Gausig; (lower right) Arizona-Sonora Desert Museum; **114** (upper left) Doug Von Gausig; (lower left & upper right) Corel; (lower right) Lauren Livo & Steve Wilcox; **115** (left) Corel; (upper right) Corel; (lower right) Bushducks; **116** (upper left) Doug Von Gausig; (middle & lower left) Corel; (right-all) Corel; **117** (upper left) Earle Robinson; (middle left) Bushducks; (lower left) Corel; (upper right) Arizona-Sonora Desert Museum; (middle right) Corel; (lower right) Doug Von Gausig; **118** (left) Corel; (upper right) Doug Von Gausig; (lower right) Corel; **119** (upper left) James C. Cokendolpher; (lower left) Corel; (upper right) Earle Robinson; (lower right) Doug Von Gausig; **120** (upper left) Lauren Livo & Steve Wilcox; (middle & lower left) James C. Cokendolpher; (upper & middle right) Corel; (lower right) Earle Robinson; **121** (upper left) Earle Robinson; (all others) Corel; **122** (upper left) Earle Robinson; (lower left & upper right) Corel; (middle & lower right) Earle Robinson; **123** (left) Corel; (upper & middle right) PhotoDisc; (lower right) Don Baccus Photography; **124** (left) Earle Robinson; (upper right) Corel; (middle right) Don Baccus Photography; (lower right) Earle Robinson; **125** (upper left) Corel; (lower left & upper right) Denver Botanical Gardens; (middle right) Doug Von Gausig; (lower right) Denver Botanical Gardens; **126** (upper & middle left) Denver Botanical Gardens; (lower left) Bushducks; (upper & lower right) Tucson Botanical Gardens; (middle right) Doug Von Gausig; **127** (upper left) Tucson Botanical Gardens; (middle left) Doug Von Gausig; (lower left & upper right) Denver Botanical Gardens; (middle & lower left) Doug Von Gausig; **128** (upper left) Doug Von Gausig; (middle & lower left) Tucson Botanical Gardens; (upper right) Denver Botanical Gardens; (middle right) Tucson Botanical Gardens; (middle & lower right) Doug Von Gausig; **129** (upper left) Bushducks; (middle left) Doug Von Gausig; (upper right) Tucson Botanical Gardens; (middle right) Doug Von Gausig; (lower middle right) Bushducks; (lower right) Tucson Botanical Gardens; **130** (upper left) Tucson Botanical Gardens; (upper right) Doug Von Gausig; (middle & lower right) Bushducks; **131** (middle & lower left) Bushducks; (upper right) Bushducks; **132** (middle left) Lauren Livo & Steve Wilcox; (lower left & upper right) Denver Botanical Gardens; (middle right) Bushducks; (lower right) Tucson Botanical Gardens; **133** (left) Bushducks; (right) Corel; **134** (upper & lower left) Corel; (middle left) Bushducks; (right) Corel; **138-559** (all) Bushducks

Front cover photography: Bushducks

Rear cover photography: (Saguaro flowers) Corel Photo Library; (NE #44) Bushducks; (NE #45) Bushducks; (Ringtail) Paul Berquist; (Geronimo on horseback) Arizona State Library, Phoenix

Index

ABOUT THE SERIES OF

swagman guides

71 TRAILS
232 PAGES
209 PHOTOGRAPHS
PRICE $29.95
ISBN: 0-9665675-5-2

The Adventures series of backcountry guidebooks are the ultimate for both adventurous four-wheelers and scenic sightseers. Each volume in the Adventures series covers an entire state or a distinct region. In addition to meticulously detailed route directions and trail maps, these full-color guides include extensive information on the history of towns, ghost towns, and regions passed along the way, as well as a history of the American Indian tribes who lived in the area prior to Euro-American settlement. The guides also provide wildlife information and photographs to help readers identify the great variety of native birds, plants, and animals they are likely to see. All you need is your SUV and your Adventures book to confidently explore all the best sites in each state's backcountry.

4WD Adventures: Colorado gets you safely to the banks of the beautiful Crystal River or over America's highest pass road, Mosquito Pass. This book guides you to the numerous lost ghost towns that speckle Colorado's mountains. In addition to the enormously detailed trail information, there are hundreds of photos of historic mining operations, old railroad routes, wildflowers, and native animals. Trail history is brought to life through the accounts of sheriffs and gunslingers like Bat Masterson and Doc Holliday; millionaires like Horace Tabor and Thomas Walsh; and American Indian warriors like Chiefs Ouray and Antero.

175 TRAILS
544 PAGES
532 PHOTOGRAPHS
PRICE $34.95
ISBN: 1-930193-12-2

Backcountry Adventures: Utah navigates you along 3,721 miles through the spectacular Canyonlands region of Utah, to the top of the Uinta Range, across vast salt flats, and along trails unchanged since the late 19th century when riders of the Pony Express sped from station to station and daring young outlaws wreaked havoc on newly established stage lines, railroads, and frontier towns. In addition to enormously detailed trail information, there are hundreds of photos of frontier towns, historic mining operations, old rail-

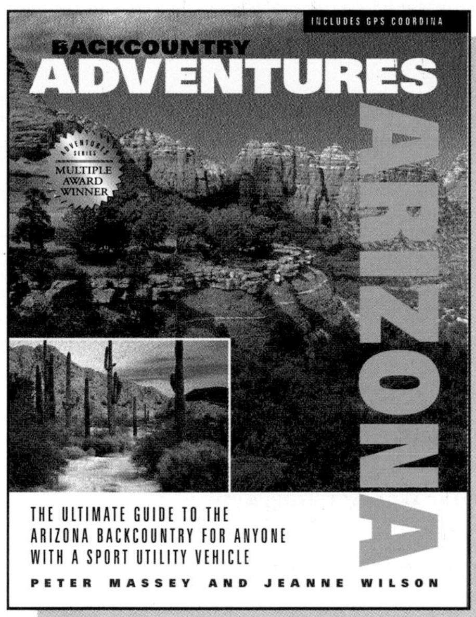

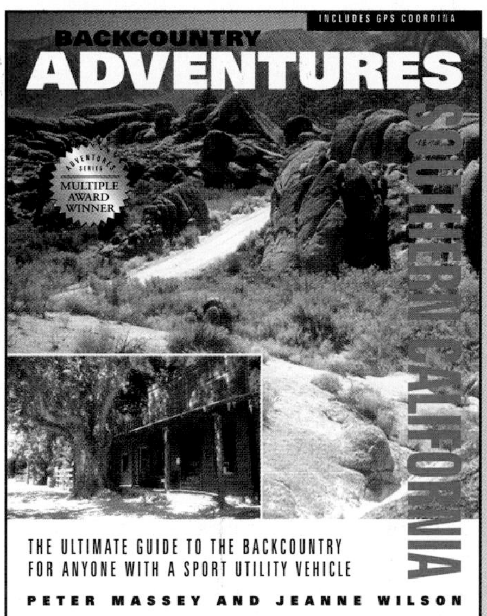

153 TRAILS
640 PAGES
645 PHOTOGRAPHS
PRICE $34.95
ISBN: 1-930193-04-1

157 TRAILS
576 PAGES
524 PHOTOGRAPHS
PRICE $34.95
ISBN: 0-9665675-0-1

road routes, wildflowers, and native animals. Trail history is brought to life through the accounts of outlaws like Butch Cassidy and his Wild Bunch; explorers and mountain men like Jim Bridger; and early Mormon settlers led by Brigham Young.

Backcountry Adventures: Arizona guides you along the back roads of the state's most remote and scenic regions, from the lowlands of the Yuma Desert to the high plains of the Kaibab Plateau. In addition to the enormously detailed trail information, there are hundreds of photos of frontier towns, historic mining operations, old railroad routes, wildflowers, and native animals. Trail history is brought to life through the accounts of Indian warriors like Cochise and Geronimo; trailblazers like Edward F. Beale; and the famous lawman Wyatt Earp, a survivor of the Shoot-out at the O.K. Corral in Tombstone.

Backcountry Adventures: Southern California takes you from the beautiful mountain regions of Big Sur, through the arid Mojave Desert, and straight into the heart of the aptly named Death Valley. In addition to the enormously detailed trail information, there are hundreds of photos of frontier towns, historic mining operations, old railroad routes, wildflowers, and native animals. Trail history is brought to life through the accounts of Spanish missionaries who first settled the coastal regions of Southern California; eager prospectors looking to cash in during California's gold rush; and legends of lost mines still hidden in the state's expansive backcountry.

Additional titles in the series will cover other states with four-wheel driving opportunities. Northern California is scheduled for release during 2002. Information on all upcoming books, including special pre-publication discount offers, can be found on the Internet at www.4WDbooks.com.

backcountry adventures series

WINNER OF FOUR PRESTIGIOUS BOOK AWARDS

"The 540-page tome is an incredible resource for getting to, and returning from, almost anywhere in Utah. Concise maps, backed with GPS, make getting lost something you'd have to do on purpose...To borrow a line from a well-known company: Don't leave home without it."

— Truck Trend

"Based on our initial experience, we expect our review copy of *Backcountry Adventures: Arizona* to be well used in the coming months... To say we'd strongly recommend this book is an understatement."

— Auto Week

"*4WD Adventures*...serves as a regional travel guide, complete with glossaries and color photos of wildflowers, animals, famous towns, and natural wonders."

— Four Wheeler Magazine

"Tired of being cooped up in your house because of the weather? This book, designed for owners of SUVs will get you out of the suburbs, off the highways, out of the cities, and into the backcountry..."

— Salt Lake Magazine

"The authors have compiled information that every SUV owner will find handy...Whether you want to know more about four-wheel driving techniques or if you are a snowmobiler or SUV owner looking for places to explore, *4WD Adventures* is the ultimate book...[They] bring the history of these trails to life through their accounts of the pioneers who built them to open up the territory to mining, ranching, and commerce in the 1800s."

— The Denver Post

"[The book]...is a massive undertaking, a textbook-size guide that seems well worth its price. Using this book, SUV owners should be able to explore areas they never knew existed, plus identify plants, animals, ghost towns and Indian history they'll see along the way."

— The Arizona Republic

"Similar to any good history book, once you get started, it's hard to put it down. Not only will it help flesh out your adventures off road, it will also broaden your appreciation of this beautiful country...The wealth of information is second to none, and the presentation makes it a pleasure to read."

— 4 Wheel Drive & Sport Utility Magazine

"This comprehensive book provides over 500 pages of photographs, maps, and detailed information about the trails and sights that make for fun 'wheeling in the Beehive State."

— Peterson's 4Wheel & Off-Road Magazine

"This book is a 10. It contains, in one volume, every kind of information I would want on a 4WD excursion."

— Awards Judge